REFORMED
DOGMATICS

Herman Bavinck (1854–1921)
Graphite Sketch by Erik G. Lubbers

REFORMED DOGMATICS

VOLUME 4: HOLY SPIRIT, CHURCH,
AND NEW CREATION

HERMAN BAVINCK

JOHN BOLT, GENERAL EDITOR
JOHN VRIEND, TRANSLATOR

Baker Academic
a division of Baker Publishing Group
Grand Rapids, Michigan

© 2008 by the Dutch Reformed Translation Society
PO Box 7083, Grand Rapids, MI 49510

Published by Baker Academic
a division of Baker Publishing Group
PO Box 6287, Grand Rapids, MI 49516-6287
www.bakeracademic.com

Second printing, December 2008

Printed in the United States of America

Library of Congress Cataloging-in-Publication Data

Bavinck, Herman, 1854–1921.
    [Gereformeerde dogmatiek. English]
    Reformed dogmatics / Herman Bavinck ; John Bolt, general editor ; John Vriend, translator.
      p. cm.
    Contents: v. 1. Prolegomena ; v. 2. God and creation ; v. 3. Sin and salvation in Christ ; v. 4. Holy Spirit, church, and new creation
    Includes bibliographical references and indexes.
    ISBN 978-0-8010-2632-4 (cloth : v. 1)
    ISBN 978-0-8010-2655-3 (cloth : v. 2)
    ISBN 978-0-8010-2656-0 (cloth : v. 3)
    ISBN 978-0-8010-2657-7 (cloth : v. 4)
    1. Christelijke Gereformeerde Kerk (Netherlands)—Doctrines. 2. Reformed Church—Doctrines. 3. Theology, Doctrinal. I. Bolt, John, 1947– II. Vriend, John, d. 2002. III. Title.
    BX9474.3.B38 2003
    230′.42—dc21
                                                   2003001037

To the memory of
Robert G. den Dulk
1937–2007

CONTENTS

7

Dutch Reformed Translation Society

11

Dr. Richard A. Muller
    P. J. Zondervan Professor of Histori-
      cal Theology
    Calvin Theological Seminary
    Grand Rapids, Michigan

Dr. Adriaan Neele
    Jonathan Edwards Center
    Yale University
    New Haven, Connecticut

Dr. Carl Schroeder
    Calling Pastor for Senior Citizens
    Central Reformed Church
    Grand Rapids, Michigan

Mr. Gise Van Baren
    Businessman
    Crete, Illinois

Mr. Henry I. Witte
    President, Witte Travel
    Consul of the Government of the
      Netherlands
    Grand Rapids, Michigan

PREFACE

The Dutch Reformed Translation Society (DRTS) was formed in 1994 by a group of businesspersons and professionals, pastors, and seminary professors, representing five different Reformed denominations, to sponsor the translation and facilitate the publication in English of classic Reformed theological and religious literature published in the Dutch language. The society is incorporated as a nonprofit corporation in the State of Michigan and governed by a board of directors.

Believing that the Dutch Reformed tradition has many valuable works that deserve wider distribution than the limited accessibility the Dutch language allows, society members seek to spread and strengthen the Reformed faith. The first project of the DRTS is the definitive translation of Herman Bavinck's complete four-volume *Gereformeerde Dogmatiek* (*Reformed Dogmatics*). The society invites those who share its commitment to, and vision for, spreading the Reformed faith to write for additional information.

Acknowledgments

It is with gratitude to God, a deep sense of relief, and a measure of satisfaction that I as editor set aside the task that has occupied more than a decade of my life. I take a degree of pride in the quality of the final four-volume product, believing as I do that Bavinck's *Reformed Dogmatics* is a work for the ages and that we have presented its best face forward. I also fear that with my name featured so prominently on the cover I may receive more credit than I am rightly due for the completion of this work. This has been a communal effort; my debt to those who contributed to the project is enormous. Without my colleagues on the Dutch Reformed Translation Society board of directors, whose vision and courage to forge ahead with this work when we had only a hope and not a penny in our treasury, who provided wise counsel, raised money, patiently dealt with my pace, regularly provided encouragement and prayers—without them I could not have sustained my efforts. For this remarkably ecumenical and dedicated Reformed group of men who have become good friends, I am profoundly grateful to our covenant God. Our number was reduced by two who have gone to be with the Lord: translator John Vriend and board member Eugene Osterhaven, both of whom played significant roles and are missed. We are grateful that their memory and legacy are enhanced by these volumes.

This is also the place to acknowledge with gratitude the many faithful members of the body of Christ who contributed considerable financial resources to make the translation, editing, and publication possible. Special thanks to Baker Publishing Group and then-president Rich Baker for his willingness to take on the admittedly risky venture of providing a quality version of a one-hundred-year-old theological work in an environment that is decidedly antihistorical and preoccupied with the pragmatic present. The professional editorial staff at Baker, beginning with Allan Fisher in the early years and followed by Jim Kinney and project editor Wells Turner of Baker Academic, have been not only competent and patiently helpful but also a joy to work with. In addition to the names of the

Calvin Theological Seminary students listed in the footnote to the bibliography, I must name several others. As editor, I was immensely helped by the competent and careful checking of the English translation by the De Moor sisters, Tanya (Vander Veen) and Renée (Van Keulen), who read the Dutch text of the four volumes to each other for profit, fun, and sororal fellowship. During the last year, while I was completing work on the fourth volume, Calvin Seminary student David Sytsma provided more help to me than I can describe. Without his computer savvy, keen theological mind, editorial sensitivity, and solid work ethic, the job might still not be complete. From the beginning, Becky Knapp has been the project's faithful and supercompetent typist. Not only did she put John Vriend's lengthy handwritten translation manuscripts into usable electronic and hardcopy text, complete with Hebrew and Greek script, but she also patiently suffered through the editor's several revisions and corrections with willing, efficient service and good cheer. And finally, to my wife and best friend, Ruth, who I know shares all the satisfaction, gratitude, and joy and, I suspect, some of my relief at the project's completion—who you are and what you so faithfully do daily is indispensable to whatever wholeness I enjoy and to our family's well-being. I could not have done this without you. To all of you, thanks, from deep within my heart.

John Bolt
Canadian Thanksgiving Day, 2006

On August 2, 2007, while this volume was in its finishing stages of production, our colleague and brother in Christ, Robert G. den Dulk, went to be with his Lord and ours. The Dutch Reformed Translation Society mourns the loss of our fellow board member and generous benefactor. As the former president of Westminster Theological Seminary (Escondido, California), Bob increased the broad institutional representation on our board and generously used the resources of the Den Dulk Foundation to make affordable copies of Bavinck's *Reformed Dogmatics* available to many students at the various American Reformed theological schools. We thank God for Bob's life and service to Christ's church, especially in the arena of theological education and publication. We shall miss him deeply and in gratitude dedicate this volume to his memory.

EDITOR'S
INTRODUCTION

This, the fourth and final full volume of Herman Bavinck's *Reformed Dogmatics* in English translation prepared by the Dutch Reformed Translation Society, represents the culmination of a twelve-year project. Prior to the first full volume on prolegomena, published by Baker Academic in 2003,[1] the second on God and creation in 2004,[2] and the third on sin and salvation in Christ in 2006,[3] two half-volume works—one on the eschatology section of volume 4[4] and the other on the creation section of volume 2[5]—were published. The present volume includes the chapters published in the single volume on eschatology (appearing here as chs. 12–18) as well as material on the Holy Spirit and Spirit-led renewal, the church and sacraments, and the new creation—material never before available in the English language. This volume thus provides additional insight into the genius of Bavinck's theology. We will briefly consider these new dimensions and their contemporary relevance later in this introduction, but first, a few words about the author of *Reformed Dogmatics*. Who was Herman Bavinck, and why is this work of theology so important?

Herman Bavinck's *Gereformeerde Dogmatiek,*[6] first published one hundred years ago, represents the concluding high point of some four centuries of remarkably

1. Herman Bavinck, *Reformed Dogmatics,* vol. 1, *Prolegomena,* ed. John Bolt, trans. John Vriend (Grand Rapids: Baker Academic, 2003).

2. Herman Bavinck, *Reformed Dogmatics,* vol. 2, *God and Creation,* ed. John Bolt, trans. John Vriend (Grand Rapids: Baker Academic, 2004).

3. Herman Bavinck, *Reformed Dogmatics,* vol. 3, *Sin and Salvation in Christ,* ed. John Bolt, trans. John Vriend (Grand Rapids: Baker Academic, 2006).

4. Herman Bavinck, *The Last Things: Hope for This World and the Next,* ed. John Bolt, trans. John Vriend (Grand Rapids: Baker, 1996). This volume presents the second half of volume 4 of the *Gereformeerde Dogmatiek.*

5. Herman Bavinck, *In the Beginning: Foundations of Creation Theology,* ed. John Bolt, trans. John Vriend (Grand Rapids: Baker, 1999). This volume presents the second half of volume 2 of the *Gereformeerde Dogmatiek.*

6. Kampen: Bos, 1895–1901.

productive Dutch Reformed theological reflection. From Bavinck's numerous citations of key Dutch Reformed theologians such as Voetius, De Moor, Vitringa, van Mastricht, Witsius, and Walaeus (as well as the important Leiden *Synopsis purioris theologiae*),[7] it is clear that he knew that tradition well and claimed it as his own. At the same time it also needs to be noted that Bavinck was not simply a chronicler of his own church's past teaching. He seriously engaged other theological traditions, notably the Roman Catholic and the modern liberal Protestant ones, effectively mined the church fathers and great medieval thinkers, and placed his own distinct neo-Calvinist stamp on the *Reformed Dogmatics*.

KAMPEN AND LEIDEN

To understand the distinct Bavinck flavor, a brief historical orientation is necessary. Herman Bavinck was born on December 13, 1854. His father was an influential minister in the Dutch Christian Reformed Church (Christelijke Gereformeerde Kerk) that had seceded from the National Reformed Church in the Netherlands twenty years earlier.[8] The secession of 1834 was in the first place a protest against the state control of the Dutch Reformed Church; it also tapped into a long and rich tradition of ecclesiastical dissent on matters of doctrine, liturgy, and spirituality as well as polity. In particular, mention needs to be made here of the Dutch equivalent to English Puritanism, the so-called Second Reformation (*Nadere Reformatie*),[9] the influential seventeenth- and early-eighteenth-century movement of experiential Reformed theology and spirituality,[10] as well as an early-nineteenth-century international, aristocratic, evangelical revival movement known as the *Réveil*.[11] Bavinck's church, his family, and his own spirituality were thus definitively shaped by strong patterns of deep pietistic Reformed spirituality. It

7. The Leiden *Synopsis,* first published in 1625, is a large manual of Reformed doctrine as it was defined by the Synod of Dort. Well into the twentieth century it served as a standard reference textbook for the study of Reformed theology. (It is even cited by Karl Barth in his *Church Dogmatics.*) As an original-source reference work of classic Dutch Reformed theology, it is comparable to Heinrich Heppe's nineteenth-century, more broadly continental anthology *Reformed Dogmatics: Set Out and Illustrated from the Sources,* rev. and ed. Ernst Bizer, trans. G. T. Thomson (London: Allen & Unwin, 1950; reprinted, Grand Rapids: Baker Academic, 1978). While serving as the minister of a Christian Reformed church in Franeker, Friesland, Bavinck edited the sixth and final edition of this handbook, which was published in 1881.

8. For a brief description of the background and character of the Secession Church, see James D. Bratt, *Dutch Calvinism in Modern America* (Grand Rapids: Eerdmans, 1984), ch. 1: "Secession and Its Tangents."

9. See Joel R. Beeke, "The Dutch Second Reformation (*Nadere Reformatie*)," *Calvin Theological Journal* 28 (1993): 298–327.

10. The crowning theological achievement of the *Nadere Reformatie* is the devout and theologically rich work of Wilhelmus à Brakel, *Redelijke godsdienst,* first published in 1700 and frequently thereafter (including twenty Dutch editions in the eighteenth century alone!). This work is now available in English translation (ET): *The Christian's Reasonable Service,* trans. B. Elshout, 4 vols. (Ligonier, PA: Soli Deo Gloria, 1992–95).

11. The standard work on the *Réveil* is M. Elisabeth Kluit, *Het Protestantse Réveil in Nederland en daarbuiten, 1815–1865* (Amsterdam and Paris, 1970). Bratt also gives a brief summary in *Dutch Calvinism in Modern America,* 10–13.

is also important to note that though the earlier phases of Dutch pietism affirmed orthodox Reformed theology and were also nonseparatist in their ecclesiology, by the mid-nineteenth century the Seceder group had become significantly separatist and sectarian in outlook.[12]

The second major influence on Bavinck's thought comes from the period of his theological training at the University of Leiden. The Christian Reformed Church had its own theological seminary, the Kampen Theological School, established in 1854. Bavinck, after studying at Kampen for one year (1873–74), indicated his desire to study with the University of Leiden's theological faculty, a faculty renowned for its aggressively modernist, "scientific" approach to theology.[13] His church community, including his parents, was stunned by this decision, which Bavinck explained as a desire "to become acquainted with the modern theology firsthand" and to receive "a more scientific training than the Theological School is presently able to provide."[14] The Leiden experience gave rise to what Bavinck perceived as the tension in his life between his commitment to orthodox theology and spirituality and his desire to understand and appreciate what he could about the modern world, including its worldview and culture. A telling and poignant entry in his personal journal at the beginning of his study period at Leiden (September 23, 1874) indicates his concern about being faithful to the faith he had publicly professed in the Christian Reformed Church of Zwolle in March of that same year: "Will I remain standing [in the faith]? God grant it."[15] Upon completion of his doctoral work at Leiden in 1880, Bavinck candidly acknowledged the spiritual impoverishment that Leiden had cost him: "Leiden has benefited me in many ways: I hope always to acknowledge that gratefully. But it has also greatly impoverished me, robbed me, not only of much ballast (for which I am happy), but also of much that I recently, especially when I preach, recognize as vital for my own spiritual life."[16]

It is thus not unfair to characterize Bavinck as a man between two worlds. One of his contemporaries once described Bavinck as "a Secession preacher and a rep-

12. Bavinck himself called attention to this in his Kampen rectoral oration of 1888, when he complained that the Seceder emigration to America was a spiritual withdrawal and abandonment of "the Fatherland as lost to unbelief" ("The Catholicity of Christianity and the Church," trans. John Bolt, *Calvin Theological Journal* 27 [1992]: 246). Recent historical scholarship, however, suggests that this note of separatism and cultural alienation must not be exaggerated. Though clearly a marginalized community in the Netherlands, the Seceders were not indifferent to educational, social, and political responsibilities. See John Bolt, "Nineteenth- and Twentieth-Century Dutch Reformed Church and Theology: A Review Article," *Calvin Theological Journal* 28 (1993): 434–42.

13. For an overview of the major schools of Dutch Reformed theology in the nineteenth century, see James Hutton MacKay, *Religious Thought in Holland during the Nineteenth Century* (London: Hodder & Stoughton, 1911). For more detailed discussion of the "modernist" school, see K. H. Roessingh, *De moderne theologie in Nederland: Hare voorbereiding en eerste periode* (Groningen: Van der Kamp, 1915); Eldred C. Vanderlaan, *Protestant Modernism in Holland* (London and New York: Oxford University Press, 1924).

14. R. H. Bremmer, *Herman Bavinck en zijn tijdgenoten* (Kampen: Kok, 1966), 20; cf. V. Hepp, *Dr. Herman Bavinck* (Amsterdam: W. Ten Have, 1921), 30.

15. Bremmer, *Herman Bavinck en zijn tijdgenoten,* 19.

16. Hepp, *Dr. Herman Bavinck,* 84.

resentative of modern culture," concluding: "That was a striking characteristic. In that duality is found Bavinck's significance. That duality is also a reflection of the tension—at times crisis—in Bavinck's life. In many respects it is a simple matter to be a preacher in the Secession Church, and, in a certain sense, it is also not that difficult to be a modern person. But in no way is it a simple matter to be the one as well as the other."[17] However, it is not necessary to rely only on the testimony of others. Bavinck summarizes this tension in his own thought clearly in an essay on the great nineteenth-century liberal Protestant theologian Albrecht Ritschl:

> Therefore, whereas salvation in Christ was formerly considered primarily a means to separate man from sin and the world, to prepare him for heavenly blessedness and to cause him to enjoy undisturbed fellowship with God there, Ritschl posits the very opposite relationship: the purpose of salvation is precisely to enable a person, once he is freed from the oppressive feeling of sin and lives in the awareness of being a child of God, to exercise his earthly vocation and fulfill his moral purpose in this world. The antithesis, therefore, is fairly sharp: on the one side, a Christian life that considers the highest goal, now and hereafter, to be the contemplation of God and fellowship with him, and for that reason (always being more or less hostile to the riches of an earthly life) is in danger of falling into monasticism and asceticism, pietism and mysticism; but on the side of Ritschl, a Christian life that considers its highest goal to be the kingdom of God, that is, the moral obligation of mankind, and for that reason (always being more or less adverse to the withdrawal into solitude and quiet communion with God), is in danger of degenerating into a cold Pelagianism and an unfeeling moralism. *Personally, I do not yet see any way of combining the two points of view, but I do know that there is much that is excellent in both, and that both contain undeniable truth.*[18]

A certain tension in Bavinck's thought—between the claims of modernity, particularly its this-worldly, scientific orientation, and Reformed pietist orthodoxy's tendency to stand aloof from modern culture—continues to play a role even in his mature theology expressed in the *Reformed Dogmatics*. In his eschatology Bavinck in a highly nuanced way still continues to speak favorably of certain emphases in a Ritschlian this-worldly perspective.[19]

17. Cited by Jan Veenhof, *Revelatie en Inspiratie* (Amsterdam: Buijten & Schipperheijn, 1968), 108. The contemporary cited is the Reformed jurist A. Anema, who was a colleague of Bavinck at the Free University of Amsterdam. A similar assessment of Bavinck as a man between two poles is given by F. H. von Meyenfeldt, "Prof. Dr. Herman Bavinck: 1854–1954, 'Christus en de Cultuur,'" *Polemios* 9 (October 15, 1954); and G. W. Brillenburg-Wurth, "Bavincks Levensstrijd," *Gereformeerde Weekblad* 10.25 (December 17, 1954).

18. Herman Bavinck, "De Theologie van Albrecht Ritschl," *Theologische Studiën* 6 (1888): 397; cited by Veenhof, *Revelatie en Inspiratie,* 346–47, emphasis added by Veenhof. Kenneth Kirk contends that this tension, which he characterizes as one between "rigorism" and "humanism," is a fundamental conflict in the history of Christian ethics from the outset. See K. Kirk, *The Vision of God* (London: Longmans, Green, 1931), 7–8.

19. See below, 721 (#578; = *Last Things*, 161). According to Bavinck, Ritschl's this-worldliness "stands for an important truth" over against what he calls the "abstract supernaturalism of the Greek Orthodox and Roman Catholic Church."

In the section on the doctrine of creation in volume 2 (chs. 8–14), we see the tension repeatedly in Bavinck's relentless efforts to understand and, where he finds appropriate, either to affirm, correct, or repudiate modern scientific claims in light of scriptural and Christian teaching.[20] Bavinck takes modern philosophy (Kant, Schelling, Hegel), Darwin, and the claims of geological and biological science seriously but never uncritically. His willingness as a theologian to engage modern thought and science seriously is a hallmark of his exemplary work. It goes without saying that though Bavinck's theological framework remains a valuable guide for contemporary readers, many of the specific scientific issues he addresses in this volume are dated by his own late nineteenth-century context. As Bavinck's own work illustrates so well, today's Reformed theologians and scientists learn from his example not by repristination but by fresh address to new and contemporary challenges.

GRACE AND NATURE

It is therefore too simple merely to characterize Bavinck as a man trapped between two apparently incommensurate tugs at his soul, that of otherworldly pietism and this-worldly modernism. His heart and mind sought a trinitarian synthesis of Christianity and culture, a Christian worldview that incorporated what was best and true in both pietism and modernism, while above all honoring the theological and confessional richness of the Reformed tradition dating from Calvin. After commenting on the breakdown of the great medieval synthesis and the need for contemporary Christians to acquiesce in that breakdown, Bavinck expressed his hope for a new and better synthesis: "In this situation, the hope is not unfounded that a synthesis is possible between Christianity and culture, however antagonistic they may presently stand over against each other. If God has truly come to us in Christ, and is, in this age too, the Preserver and Ruler of all things, such a synthesis is not only possible but also necessary and shall surely be effected in its own time."[21] Bavinck found the vehicle for such an attempted synthesis in the trinitarian worldview of Dutch neo-Calvinism and became, along with neo-Calvinism's visionary pioneer Abraham Kuyper,[22] one of its chief and most respected spokesmen as well as its premier theologian.

Unlike Bavinck, Abraham Kuyper grew up in the National Reformed Church of the Netherlands in a congenially moderate-modernist context. Kuyper's student years, also at Leiden, confirmed him in his modernist orientation until a series of experiences, especially during his years as a parish minister, brought about a dramatic conversion to Reformed, Calvinist orthodoxy.[23] From that time

---

20. Bavinck, *In the Beginning,* passim (= *Reformed Dogmatics,* II, 407–619 [##250–306]).

21. Herman Bavinck, *Het Christendom,* Groote Godsdiensten 2.7 (Baarn: Hollandia, 1912), 60.

22. For a brief overview, see J. Bratt, *Dutch Calvinism in Modern America,* ch. 2: "Abraham Kuyper and Neo-Calvinism."

23. Kuyper chronicles these experiences in a revealing autobiographical work titled *Confidentie* (Amsterdam: Höveker, 1873). A rich portrait of the young Abraham Kuyper is given by G. Puchinger, *Abraham Kuyper: De*

Kuyper became a vigorous opponent of the modern spirit in church and society[24]—which he characterized by the siren call of the French Revolution, "Ni Dieu! Ni maitre!"[25]—seeking every avenue to oppose it with an alternative worldview, or as he called it, the "life-system" of Calvinism:

> From the first, therefore, I have always said to myself, "If the battle is to be fought with honor and with a hope of victory, then principle must be arrayed against principle; then it must be felt that in Modernism the vast energy of an all-embracing life-system assails us, then also it must be understood that we have to take our stand in a life-system of equally comprehensive and far-reaching power.... When thus taken, I found and confessed and I still hold, that this manifestation of the Christian principle is given us in Calvinism. In Calvinism my heart has found rest. From Calvinism have I drawn the inspiration firmly and resolutely to take my stand in the thick of this great conflict of principles."[26]

Kuyper's aggressive this-worldly form of Calvinism was rooted in a trinitarian theological vision. The "dominating principle" of Calvinism, he contended, "was not soteriologically, justification by faith, but in the widest sense cosmologically, the Sovereignty of the Triune God over the whole Cosmos, in all its spheres and kingdoms, visible and invisible."[27]

For Kuyper, this fundamental principle of divine sovereignty led to four important derivatory and related doctrines or principles: common grace, antithesis, sphere sovereignty, and the distinction between the church as institution and the church as organism. The doctrine of common grace[28] is based on the conviction that prior to and, to a certain extent, independent of the particular sovereignty of divine grace in

---

Jonge Kuyper (1837–1867) (Franeker: T. Wever, 1987). See also the somewhat hagiographic biography by Frank Vandenberg, *Abraham Kuyper* (Grand Rapids: Eerdmans, 1960); and the more theologically and historically substantive one by Louis Praamsma, *Let Christ Be King: Reflection on the Times and Life of Abraham Kuyper* (Jordan Station, ON: Paideia, 1985). Brief accounts can also be found in Benjamin B. Warfield's introduction to Abraham Kuyper, *Encyclopedia of Sacred Theology: Its Principles,* trans. J. H. De Vries (New York: Charles Scribner's, 1898); and in the translator's biographical note in Abraham Kuyper, *To Be Near to God,* trans. J. H. De Vries (Grand Rapids: Eerdmans, 1925).

24. See especially his famous address *Het modernisme, een Fata Morgana op Christelijke gebied* (Amsterdam: De Hoogh, 1871). On page 52 of this work he acknowledges that he, too, once dreamed the dreams of modernism. This important essay is now available in J. Bratt, ed., *Abraham Kuyper: A Centennial Reader* (Grand Rapids: Eerdmans, 1998), 87–124.

25. Abraham Kuyper, *Lectures on Calvinism* (Grand Rapids: Eerdmans, 1931), 10.

26. Ibid., 11–12.

27. Ibid., 79.

28. Kuyper's own position is developed in his *De gemeene gratie,* 3 vols. (Amsterdam and Pretoria: Höveker & Wormser, 1902). A thorough examination of Kuyper's views can be found in S. U. Zuidema, "Common Grace and Christian Action in Abraham Kuyper," in *Communication and Confrontation* (Toronto: Wedge, 1971), 52–105. Cf. J. Ridderbos, *De theologische cultuurbeschouwing van Abraham Kuyper* (Kampen: Kok, 1947). The doctrine of common grace has been much debated among conservative Dutch Reformed folk in the Netherlands and the United States, tragically leading to church divisions. For an overview of the doctrine in the Reformed tradition, see H. Kuiper, *Calvin on Common Grace* (Goes: Oostebaan & Le Cointre, 1928).

redemption, there is a universal divine sovereignty in creation and providence, restraining the effects of sin and bestowing general gifts on all people, thus making human society and culture possible even among the unredeemed. Cultural life is rooted in creation and common grace and thus has a life of its own apart from the church.

This same insight is expressed more directly via the notion of sphere sovereignty. Kuyper was opposed to all Anabaptist and ascetic Christian versions of world flight but was also equally opposed to the medieval Roman Catholic synthesis of culture and church. The various spheres of human activity—family, education, business, science, art—do not derive their raison d'être and the shape of their life from redemption or from the church, but from the law of God the Creator. They are thus relatively autonomous—also from the interference of the state—and are directly responsible to God.[29] In this regard Kuyper clearly distinguished two different understandings of the church: the church as institution gathered around the Word and sacraments, and the church as organism diversely spread out in the manifold vocations of life. It is not explicitly as members of the institutional church but as members of the body of Christ, organized in Christian communal activity (schools, political parties, labor unions, institutions of mercy) that believers live out their earthly vocations. Though aggressively this-worldly, Kuyper was an avowed and articulate opponent of the *volkskerk* tradition, which tended to merge national sociocultural identity with that of a theocratic church ideal.[30]

To state this differently: Kuyper's emphasis on common grace, used polemically to motivate pious, orthodox Dutch Reformed Christians to Christian social, political, and cultural activity, must never be seen in isolation from his equally strong emphasis on the spiritual antithesis. The regenerating work of the Holy Spirit breaks humanity in two and creates, according to Kuyper, "two kinds of consciousness, that of the regenerate and the unregenerate; and these two cannot be identical." Furthermore, these "two kinds of people" will develop "two kinds of science." The conflict in the scientific enterprise is not between science and faith but between "two scientific systems, . . . each having its own faith."[31]

It is here in this trinitarian, world-affirming, but nonetheless resolutely antithetical Calvinism that Bavinck found the resources to bring some unity to his thought.[32] "The thoughtful person," he notes, "places the doctrine of the Trinity

---

29. "In this independent character a special *higher authority* is of necessity involved and this highest authority we intentionally call *sovereignty in the individual social sphere,* in order that it may be sharply and decidedly expressed that these different developments of social life have *nothing above themselves but God,* and that the state cannot intrude here, and has nothing to command in their domain" (*Lectures on Calvinism*, 91).

30. On Kuyper's ecclesiology, see H. Zwaanstra, "Abraham Kuyper's Conception of the Church," *Calvin Theological Journal* 9 (1974): 149–81; on his attitude toward the *volkskerk* tradition, see H. J. Langman, *Kuyper en de volkskerk* (Kampen: Kok, 1950).

31. Kuyper, *Lectures on Calvinism,* 133; cf. *Encyclopedia of Sacred Theology,* 150–82. A helpful discussion of Kuyper's view of science is given by Del Ratzsch, "Abraham Kuyper's Philosophy of Science," *Calvin Theological Journal* 27 (1992): 277–303.

32. The relation between Bavinck and Kuyper, including differences as well as commonalities, is discussed in greater detail in John Bolt, "The Imitation of Christ Theme in the Cultural-Ethical Ideal of Herman Bavinck"

in the very center of the full-orbed life of nature and mankind. . . . The mind of the Christian is not satisfied until every form of existence has been referred to the triune God and until the confession of the Trinity has received the place of prominence in all our life and thought."[33] Repeatedly in his writings Bavinck defines the essence of the Christian religion in a trinitarian, creation-affirming way. A typical formulation: "The essence of the Christian religion consists in this, that the creation of the Father, devastated by sin, is restored in the death of the Son of God, and re-created by the Holy Spirit into a kingdom of God."[34] Put more simply, the fundamental theme that shapes Bavinck's entire theology is the trinitarian idea that grace restores nature.[35]

The evidence for "grace restores nature" being the fundamental defining and shaping theme of Bavinck's theology is not hard to find. In an important address on common grace given in 1888 at the Kampen Theological School, Bavinck sought to impress on his Christian Reformed audience the importance of Christian sociocultural activity. He appealed to the doctrine of creation, insisting that its diversity is not removed by redemption but cleansed. "Grace does not remain outside or above or beside nature but rather permeates and wholly renews it. And thus nature, reborn by grace, will be brought to its highest revelation. That situation will again return in which we serve God freely and happily, without compulsion or fear, simply out of love, and in harmony with our true nature. That is the genuine religio naturalis." In other words: "Christianity does not introduce a single substantial foreign element into the creation. It creates no new cosmos but rather makes the cosmos new. It restores what was corrupted by sin. It atones the guilty and cures what is sick; the wounded it heals."[36]

THE HOLY SPIRIT AND RENEWAL

The title of this volume is *Holy Spirit, Church, and New Creation*, and its divisions point to the Spirit's work in the renewal of the Christian person, the community of the church, and finally the renewal of all things. The title reflects the importance of noting the pneumatological cast of Bavinck's strong emphasis on creation, a not-always-recognized significant feature of Reformed thought more generally. In the creation section of volume 2 (chs. 8–14) we see how Bavinck's

(PhD diss., University of St. Michael's College, Toronto, 1982), especially ch. 3: "Herman Bavinck as a Neo-Calvinist Thinker."

33. Herman Bavinck, *The Doctrine of God*, trans. W. Hendriksen (Grand Rapids: Eerdmans, 1951), 329 (= *Reformed Dogmatics*, II, 329–34 [#231]).

34. Bavinck, *Reformed Dogmatics*, I, 112 (#35).

35. This is the conclusion of Veenhof, *Revelatie en Inspiratie*, 346; and Eugene Heideman, *The Relation of Revelation and Reason in E. Brunner and H. Bavinck* (Assen: Van Gorcum, 1959), 191, 195. See below, 697n5 (#572; = *Last Things*, 200n4).

36. Herman Bavinck, "Common Grace," trans. Raymond Van Leeuwen, *Calvin Theological Journal* 24 (1989): 59–60, 61.

doctrine of creation served as a key starting place for his theology.[37] It does this because Bavinck is convinced that the doctrine of creation is the starting point and distinguishing characteristic of true religion. Creation is the formulation of human dependence on a God who is distinct from the creature but who nonetheless in a loving, fatherly way preserves it. Creation is a distinct emphasis of the Reformed tradition according to Bavinck, a way of affirming that God's will is its origin and God's glory its goal. Creation thus is the presupposition of all religion and morality, especially Christian teaching about the image of God in all human beings.

Yet, of course, the truth of the Christian religion cannot be known through creation. A special revelation of God's grace is essential for knowing what our dilemma is and what our misery consists of as human beings (our sin), and how we are to be delivered from it (salvation). As we see in volume 3, *Sin and Salvation in Christ*, so too in this volume Bavinck's theology is a profoundly biblical theology. Bavinck once again reveals himself to be a careful student of Holy Scripture, one whose very thought patterns are shaped by those of the Bible. However, as he often does, Bavinck surprises us with the wide range of his knowledge by linking the Holy Spirit's application of Christ's work to the larger context of the Triune God's purposes in creation.

Now, the same attention to the doctrine of creation characterizes this final volume in Bavinck's theological system. The final goal of God's redemptive work in Jesus Christ is the new creation, the new heaven and the new earth. Yet he also avoids the latent universalism of contemporary emphases on salvation as renewal of creation by maintaining a clear antithesis between life in the service of sin that leads to eternal punishment and life lived before the gracious face of God. There is a wonderful scriptural reserve evident in Bavinck; he is open to a wide embrace of God's mercy (see #579) but always insists that we must bow to Scripture's testimony and be silent on matters not directly addressed, such as the thorny pastoral issues of salvation of pagans and children who die in infancy. Committed to neo-Calvinism's program of cultural engagement, he was nonetheless cautious about triumphalism and keenly attuned to the prospect of apostasy and cultural decline in the West. While strong in his affirmation of the earthly, life-affirming, bodily character of Christian hope, he is also true to his pietist roots when he insists that a this-worldly hope alone is inadequate. The goal of all Christian longing is eternal fellowship with God.

Not only does the renewing work of the Holy Spirit undergird the cosmic vision of the new heaven and the new earth; Bavinck's theological structure also affirms the same about the new birth in Christ. Consider the opening sentence of this volume: "God produces both creation and new creation by his Word and Spirit." The Protestant emphasis on the proclaimed Word is not enough; genuine rebirth by means of the Holy Spirit must take place. Furthermore, spiritual

---

37. See "Editor's Introduction," in Bavinck, *Reformed Dogmatics,* II, 19–21.

rebirth is like natural life in that it must be nourished in order to grow (#449). And, in true Calvinian fashion, Bavinck insists that forensic justification imputed to us as a benefit of Christ's obedience, while foundational and essential, is not enough. Salvation is to make us holy; the Holy Spirit who unites us with Christ in his death also raises us to newness of life. That Holy Spirit is the guarantee and pledge of our full deliverance, our glorious destiny when we his children will see God face to face.

Bavinck's *Reformed Dogmatics* is biblically and confessionally faithful, pastorally sensitive, challenging, and still relevant. Bavinck's life and thought reflect a serious effort to be pious, orthodox, and thoroughly contemporary. To pietists fearful of the modern world on the one hand and to critics of orthodoxy skeptical about its continuing relevance on the other, Bavinck's example suggests a model answer: an engaging trinitarian vision of Christian discipleship in God's world.

In conclusion, I add a few words about the editing decisions that govern this translated volume, which is based on the second, expanded edition of the *Gereformeerde Dogmatiek*.[38] The eighteen chapters of this volume correspond to thirteen in the original. The three major divisions of the eschatology section (part 3) were originally three chapters in the Dutch; from that material we have created seven distinct chapters. In addition, all subdivisions and headings are new. The latter along with the chapter synopses, which are also not in the original, have been supplied by the editor. Bavinck's original footnotes have all been retained and brought up to contemporary bibliographic standards. Additional notes added by the editor are clearly marked. Works from the nineteenth century to the present are noted, usually with full bibliographic information given on first occurrence in each chapter and with subsequent references abbreviated. Classic works produced prior to the nineteenth century (the church fathers, Aquinas's *Summa*, Calvin's *Institutes*, post-Reformation Protestant and Catholic works), for which there are often numerous editions, are cited only by author, title, and standard notation of sections. More complete information for the originals, or accessible editions, is given in the bibliography appearing at the end of this volume. Where English translations (ET) of foreign titles were available and could be consulted, they have been used rather than the originals. Unless indicated in the note by direct reference to a specific translation, renderings of Latin, Greek, German, and French material are those of the translator working from Bavinck's original text. References in the notes and bibliography that are incomplete or unconfirmed are marked with an asterisk (*). To facilitate comparison with the Dutch original, this English edition retains the subparagraph numbers (##433–580 in square brackets in the text) used in the Dutch edition. Cross-references cite the page numbers of the translated volumes of *Reformed Dogmatics*, but include the

---

38. The four volumes of the first edition of *Gereformeerde Dogmatiek* were published in the years 1895 through 1901. The second revised and expanded edition appeared between 1906 and 1911; the third edition, unaltered from the second, in 1918; the fourth, unaltered except for different pagination, in 1928.

subparagraph numbers (marked with #) of *Gereformeerde Dogmatiek* to facilitate cross-reference to any of the Dutch editions. When no volume number is given, the cross-reference can be assumed to be to the present volume. The notes appearing in *The Last Things* have been updated and corrected in chapters 12–18 of this volume, as has the bibliography.

PART I

THE SPIRIT GIVES
NEW LIFE TO BELIEVERS

1

CALLING AND REGENERATION

The Triune God produces all things in creation and new creation by his Word and Spirit. All things thus speak to us of God. God's call as law comes to all people in nature, in history, and in a variety of experiences. While insufficient unto salvation, this call upholds human existence in society and culture, despite the ubiquity of sin. Though the restricted call unto salvation comes through the word of the gospel, it may not be separated from nature and history. The Logos who became incarnate is the same as he by whom all things were made. Grace does not abolish nature but restores it. Still, the special call of the gospel does not proceed from law and invite us to obedience, but it flows forth from grace and invites us to faith.

The call to faith must be universally preached; this is Christ's command. The outcome must be left in God's hands; we are simply to obey. The gospel is to be preached to human beings, not as elect or reprobate, but as sinners, all of whom need redemption. Of course, not to each individual person can it be said, "Christ died in your place." But neither do those who preach a hypothetical universalism do that since they only believe in the possibility of universal salvation, conditional upon human acceptance. And this no one knows for sure. God's offer is sincere in that he only tells us what we must do—believe. Since it is clear from history that the outcome of God's call does not universally lead to faith, we cannot avoid the intellectual problem. It is not solved through weakening the call by expanding it for the purpose of greater inclusiveness. Acknowledging in humility the mystery of God's will, we recognize that God's own glory is its final purpose and believe that his Word never returns to him empty.

The call of law also prepares the way for the gospel, not in the Arminian sense of an evolution from preparatory grace to saving grace through human willing, but as the created natural foundation for salvation. God does link his work of grace to our natural lives; creation, redemption, and sanctification are the work of the Triune God in the divine economy of Father, Son, and Holy Spirit. God is sovereign and his grace is rich and varied. Following Augustine, Reformed theology distinguishes an external or revealed call from the savingly efficacious internal call of the Holy Spirit. This distinction honors the universality of sin, the need to have the word of proclamation take root in a sinner's heart by a special

29

work of God, and ascribes all of our salvation to God's mercy and activity. This change is so dramatic that it is properly called "rebirth" or "regeneration."

The notion of rebirth is found in other religions of the Ancient East, notably in mystery religions such as Mithraism. Attempts to explain the Christian understanding of regeneration by means of the dying and rising gods of the mystery religions are not very persuasive. Even considering the paucity of our knowledge about the mystery religions, their ideas and practices come from a different religious environment and worldview. The New Testament here rather builds on the Old Testament, where the whole people of Israel as well as individual persons are told that they need new hearts, a new birth only God can accomplish (Ps. 51:1–3). From the baptism of John through the preaching of Jesus and into the apostolic proclamation, the one consistent message is the need for μετανοια, for a radical turnabout, if one wishes to enter the kingdom of heaven. One must be "born from above" (John 3:6–8). By faith, Christ or his Spirit is the author and origin of a new life in those who are called (Gal. 3:2; 4:6) so that they are now a "new creation" (2 Cor. 5:17). While there is a difference between the Old Testament and New Testament in language and manner of presentation, the basic truth is the same. Whether rebirth is called "circumcision of the heart," the giving of a new heart and a new spirit, a drawing from the Father, or a birth from God, it is always in the strict sense a work of God by which a person is inwardly changed and renewed. This change is signified and sealed in baptism.

In the missionary context of the early church, the rebirth signified by baptism was a momentous and life-changing event for the believer. Moving beyond this context, as the church began baptizing infants and children, the connection between baptism and regeneration had to be modified. In Western Catholicism, regeneration was increasingly understood in terms of the infusion of sacramental grace at the time of baptism. In the Eastern church, a similar result was achieved but thought of in terms of implanting a new seed of immortality. A new quality was infused into the soul, and baptism itself became essential for salvation. Remaining in the state of grace depends on the mediation of the church and its sacraments.

It is this sacramental system that the Reformation protested, restoring a direct relationship between God and the soul through the Holy Spirit. The Word of Scripture took priority over church and sacrament. This brought its own difficulties as the Anabaptists rejected church and sacraments as means of grace and made personal faith and confession the condition for baptism. In response, Lutherans again made regeneration dependent on baptism and, by implication, on the church, thus creating a dualism between primary regeneration, which precedes faith, and subsequent secondary renewal, which arises from faith. Reformed theologians wrestled mightily with this issue but found no solution satisfactory to everyone when it came to grounds for baptizing the children of believers. The attempt to ground it in a notion of prebaptismal regeneration satisfied some but ran aground on the reality that some who are baptized do not come to full faith as adults. Maintaining the continuity of the spiritual life proved difficult, and due to the Enlightenment, the notion of rebirth fell into disfavor and was replaced by humanistic notions of moral development, improvement, and nurture.

It was Schleiermacher who restored the idea of regeneration to theology, making it the center of his understanding of the Christian faith. For him, regeneration is the new consciousness of God's grace and human dependence on God gained by sharing in the consciousness of Christ. In the Mediating Theology, sin played a more significant role, but at bottom the new life in Christ was a participation in a new personality; there was no objective atonement for sin or justification, only a subjective appropriation of new consciousness. Faith's content is here reduced to mystical experience.

This locus of theology, namely, soteriology, is as beset with difficulties as are the doctrines of the Trinity and of the two natures of Christ. While it is understandable that missionary proclamation begins with repentance and faith and only after that speaks of regeneration, upon reflection on Scripture and experience we come to realize that, properly speaking, regeneration must precede faith. If salvation rests in God's will and not in the human will, that order is inviolable. Augustine must be chosen over Pelagius. However, there are ethical/ practical considerations too. Could overemphasis on regeneration lead some to feel uncertain about their regeneration and thus be paralyzed in their response to the gospel call—waiting for God to regenerate them? Similarly, what about children of believers? Does the church baptize children of believers on the ground of presumed regeneration? Or, as in Roman Catholicism and Lutheranism, does baptism somehow impart a seed of regeneration? The Reformed tradition distinguishes regeneration and faith, baptizes infants on the basis of covenant promises, but also acknowledges that the Holy Spirit could work sovereignly in the hearts of children apart from the preaching of the Word.

Because notions of rebirth are found outside of Scripture in the world's religions, it is important to be clear about the distinguishing features of the biblical view. Unlike Buddhism or Hinduism, rebirth does not mean reincarnation. While rebirth does apply to the Christian understanding of conversion, it is not sufficient to compare the biblical view with initiation into Greek mystery religions or even with Jewish proselytism. It is more than a change of consciousness, an enlightenment of the mind, or even a reformation of conduct, though it includes all of these. Nor should we be satisfied with the gnostic notion of redemption as the deliverance of the inner self from the "flesh" or matter. Neither rationalism nor mysticism provides us with a correct view of regeneration.

It is helpful to recognize a broader and more narrow use of the term "regeneration." In the broadest and fullest sense, regeneration refers to the total transformation of a person; in the restricted sense, it has in view the implantation of new life that then leads to conversion and further sanctification. The active word of God here—calling—must also be differentiated from the passive reception or fruit of God's initiating work. God's call has both an external and internal component. The external proclaimed Word addresses human consciousness persuasively; human response requires an inner work of the Holy Spirit. In Reformed thought, God's inner call logically precedes the outward call, though Word and Spirit must never be separated. The Reformed tradition also acknowledges the reality of the faith community's involvement in the external call upon its own children as a gracious work of God the Holy Spirit.

This operation of the Holy Spirit is both immediate *and* irresistible*. The point made by Reformed theology here against the Pelagians, Arminians, and theologians of Saumur is that God's operation on the human person is independent of the will as well as the intellect. There is no room here to speak of cooperation or of God merely enlightening the mind, which then informs and changes the will. Though the term "irresistible" was used by opponents of the Reformed faith and does not sufficiently capture the Reformed view, its meaning is clear: When God freely chooses to renew a person's will, no one can withstand God. God's inner call is efficacious.*

While the Augustinian and Reformed view can and does make room for human beings as created, rational, moral agents, the Pelagian and Remonstrant view cannot account for Scripture's teaching about the radical need for grace. If grace is resistible, God is deprived of his sovereignty; if the human will is capable on its own of assenting to God, then regeneration is unnecessary; and if, as the Pelagian and Remonstrant position teaches, some prevenient grace is necessary to prompt human willing, then the notion of an indifferent will remains a fiction. The only gain here is an apparent but not real one, as becomes apparent with the case of children who die in infancy. Either they are saved by sovereign grace alone without any choosing on their part, or such grace is insufficient and all infants who die before choosing are lost. The Pelagian and Arminian position is not at all merciful.

The purpose of regeneration is to make us spiritual people, those who live and walk by the Spirit. This life is a life of intimate communion with God in Christ. Though believers are made new creatures in Christ, this does not mean that their created nature is qualitatively transformed. Believers remain fully human, fully created image-bearers of God as in the beginning. As in creation itself, no new substance enters into the world with redemption; the creature is liberated from sin's futility and bondage. Sin is not of the essence of creation but its deformity; Christ is not a second Creator but creation's Redeemer. Salvation is the restoration of creation and the reformation of life. Redemption is not coercive; it delivers people from the compulsion and power of sin. The new life comes from God and is born in his love.

THE CALL OF GOD

[433] God produces both creation and new creation by his Word and Spirit. By his speech he calls all things into being out of nothing (Gen. 1; Ps. 33:6; John 1:3; Heb. 1:3; 11:3); by the word of his almighty power he again raises up the fallen world. He personally calls Adam (Gen. 3:9), Abram (Gen. 12:1; Isa. 51:2), Israel (Isa. 41:9; 42:6; 43:1; 45:4; 49:1; Jer. 31:3; Ezek. 16:6; Hos. 11:1); and by his servants he issues the invitation to repentance and life (Deut. 30; 2 Kings 17:13; Isa. 1:16ff.; Jer. 3; Ezek. 18; 33; etc.; Rom. 8:28–29; 2 Cor. 5:20; 1 Thess. 2:12; 5:24; 2 Thess. 2:14; 1 Pet. 2:9; 5:10; etc.). Inasmuch as this call of God comes to people in and through the Son and Christ is the one who obtains our salvation, it is also especially credited to him. Just as the Father created all things through him and he is himself also the creator of all things, so he is also himself the one who calls (Matt. 11:28; Mark 1:15; 2:17; Luke 5:32; 19:10), who sends laborers into his vineyard (Matt. 20:1–7), invites guests to the wedding feast (22:2), gathers children as a hen gathers her chicks (23:37), appoints apostles and teachers (Matt. 10; 28:19; Luke 10; Eph. 4:11), whose voice has gone out to all the earth (Rom. 10:18). So, though the calling essentially originates with God or Christ, in this connection he nevertheless employs people, not only in the narrow sense of prophets and apostles, pastors and teachers, but also including parents and relatives, schoolteachers and friends generally. There is even a voice speaking to us from all the works of God's hands, from the movements of history, and from the leadings and experiences of our life. All things speak to the believer of God. Although the call in a restricted sense comes to us also through the word of the gospel, the latter may not be separated from what comes to us through nature and history. The covenant of grace is sustained by the cosmic covenant of nature. Christ, the mediator of the covenant of grace, is the same as he who as Logos created all things, who as light shines into the darkness, and who enlightens every human coming into the world. He leaves no one without a witness but does good from heaven and fills also the hearts of Gentiles with food and good cheer (Ps. 19:2–4; Matt. 5:45; John 1:5, 9–10; Acts 14:16–17; 17:27; Rom. 1:19–21; 2:14–15).

EXTERNAL CALL

Accordingly, we must first of all distinguish a real call (*vocatio realis*), which comes to humans not so much in clear language as in things (*res*), through nature, history, environment, various leadings, and experiences. The medium of this calling is not the gospel but the law, and by it, as it comes to expression in the family, society, and state, in religion and morality, in heart and conscience, it calls human beings to obedience and obligates them to do good.[1] This call is admittedly insufficient for salvation, because it knows nothing of Christ and his grace and therefore cannot lead anyone to the Father (John 14:6; Acts 4:12; Rom. 1:16). Even with this call, the world in its folly and darkness did not know God (John 1:5, 10; Rom. 1:21ff.; 1 Cor. 1:21; Eph. 2:12). Still, it is a rich form of God's involvement with his creatures, a witness of the Logos, a working of the Spirit of God of great significance for humankind. We owe it to this call that, despite the reality of sin, humankind continued to exist; that it organized itself into families, societies, and states; that there remained in it a sense of religion and morality; and that it did not disappear into a sinkhole of bestiality. All things hold together in Christ, who upholds all things by the word of his power (Col. 1:16; Heb. 1:3). This call also specifically serves, both in the life of peoples and in that of particular persons, to pave the way for the higher and better calling of the gospel. As Logos, by various ways and means, Christ lays the groundwork for his own work of grace. He himself first appeared publicly only in the fullness of time. When the world by its wisdom did not know God, it pleased God through the folly of preaching to save those who believe (1 Cor. 1:21). The gospel does not come to all peoples at the same time, but over many centuries continues its progress through the world. Also, in the case of special persons it comes at the moment that God himself has providentially prepared and planned.

Now, however important this real vocation is, of a higher kind is the verbal call (*vocatio verbalis*), which comes to people not only via the revealed law but specifically through the gospel. This call, while it does not cancel out the calling that comes through nature and history, incorporates it into itself, confirms it, and indeed transcends it by far. It is, after all, a call that proceeds not from the Logos but specifically from Christ. As its real means, it does not so much employ the law as the gospel. It invites us not to obedience to divine law but to faith in God's grace. Further, it is always accompanied by a certain working and witness of the Spirit, whom Christ poured out as his Spirit upon the church (John 16:8–11; Matt. 12:31; Acts 5:3; 7:51; Heb. 6:4). This call is not universal in the sense held by the old Lutherans who, on the basis of Matt. 28:10; John 3:16; Rom. 10:18; Col. 1:23; and 1 Tim. 2:4, claimed that at the time of Adam, Noah, and Christ, the gospel had in fact been known to all peoples and had again been lost through their own fault,[2] but may and must nevertheless be brought to all people without

1. *Synopsis purioris theologiae*, disp. 30, 2, 3; P. van Mastricht, *Theoretico-practica theologia* (Utrecht: Appels, 1714), VI, 2, 15; H. Witsius, *The Oeconomy of the Covenants between God and Man*, 3 vols. (New York: Lee & Stokes, 1798), III, 5, 7–15; J. Marck, *Compendium theologiae christianae didactico-elencticum* (Groningen: Fossema, 1686), 17, 10; B. de Moor, *Commentarius . . . theologiae*, 6 vols. (Leiden: J. Hasebroek, 1761–71), III, 386–87.

2. Formula of Concord in *The Book of Concord: The Confessions of the Evangelical Lutheran Church*, ed. R. Kolb and T. J. Wengert (Minneapolis: Fortress, 2000), 481–660. Ed. note: A careful check of the passages cited here by Bavinck in the Scripture index of *The Book of Concord* (= Kolb and Wengert below) failed to locate this

distinction. Scripture expressly commands this (Matt. 28:19) and further states that many who do not come are nevertheless called (Matt. 22:14; Luke 14:16–18). They reject the gospel (John 3:36; Acts 13:46; 2 Thess. 1:8) and are therefore guilty of the appalling sin of unbelief (Matt. 10:15; 11:22, 24; John 3:36; 16:8–9; 2 Thess. 1:8; 1 John 5:10).

UNIVERSAL PROCLAMATION OF THE GOSPEL

But universalists advance against the Reformed that the latter, on their position, cannot accept such a universal call through the gospel. According to their position, after all, Christ did not die for all, but only for the elect. Their message cannot be, "Christ has made satisfaction for you; your sins have been atoned; only believe." For the unconverted the message can only consist in the demand of the law. If they maintain the universal offer of grace, it cannot be sincerely meant on the part of God and is, furthermore, useless and ineffective.[3]

These objections are undoubtedly weighty and have evoked a variety of responses from the camp of the Reformed. Some got to the point where they only preached the law to the unconverted and offered the gospel only to those who had already learned to know themselves as sinners and felt the need for redemption. Others, maintaining the universal offer of grace, justified this offer by saying that Christ's sacrifice was sufficient for all, or that Christ had also acquired numerous and varied blessings for those who would not believe in him, or that the gospel was only offered to them on condition of faith and repentance. Still others, taking a position close to universalism, taught that, on the basis of an initial universal decree of God, Christ had made satisfaction for all, or had acquired for all the legal possibility of being saved, and had brought everyone into a "salvable state," or even that the acquisition of salvation was universal and that its application was particular.[4] However much it might seem that the confession of election and limited atonement might require something else, the Reformed as a rule maintained the universal offer of grace.

specific reference. Joseph T. Müller, *Die symbolischen Bücher der evangelisch-lutherischen Kirche*, 8th ed. (Gütersloh: Bertelsmann, 1898), 709; ed. note: This specific reference is to Formula of Concord, "Solid Declaration," art. 11, pars. 24–28 (Kolb and Wengert, 644–45); J. Gerhard, *Loci theologici*, ed. E. Preuss, 9 vols. (Berlin: G. Schlawitz, 1863–75), VII, ch. 7; J. A. Quenstedt, *Theologia*, III, 465–76; cf. also the Remonstrants and others in C. Vitringa, *Doctrina christiana religionis*, 8 vols. (Leiden: Joannis le Mair, 1761–86), III, 167.

3. See also J. Arminius, *Opera theologica* (Leiden: Godefridum Basson, 1629), 661ff.; *The Confession or Declaration of the Ministers or Pastors Which in the United Provinces Are Called Remonstrants concerning the Chief Points of Christian Religion* (1622; repr., London: Francis Smith, 1676), c. 7; ed. note: This is available via Early English Books Online and will henceforth be cited as Remonstrant Confession. S. Episcopius, *Apologia pro confessione sive declaratione sententiae eroum, qui in Foederato Belgio vocantur Remonstrantes, super praecipuis articulis religionis Christianae: Contra censuram quatuor professorum Leidensium* (1629). Ed. note: The *Apologia* can be found in S. Episcopius, *Opera*, III, 88–89, 187–205; idem, *Antidotum*, ch. 9, in *Opera theologica*, 2 vols. (Amsterdam: Johan Blaeu, 1650–65), II, 2, 38; P. van Limborch, *Theologia christiana* (Amsterdam: Arnhold, 1735), IV, 3, 12–18.

4. Cf. H. Bavinck, *Reformed Dogmatics* III, 460 (#405).

[434] And this is absolutely correct for the following reasons:

1. Scripture leaves no doubt that the gospel may and must be preached to all creatures. Whether we can square this with a particular outcome is another question. In any case, the command of Christ is the end of all contradiction. The rule for our conduct is only the revealed will of God. The result of that preaching is certain not only according to those who confess predestination but also on the position of those who only recognize divine foreknowledge. God cannot be self-deceived; for him the result of world history cannot be a disappointment. And with all due respect, it is not our task but God's responsibility to square this outcome with the universal offer of salvation. We only know that the outcome, in accordance with God's decree, is bound to and acquired by all the ways and means that have been laid down for us. And among them is the preaching of the gospel to all creatures. In that connection, we have nothing to do with the decree of election and reprobation. The gospel is preached to humans not as elect or reprobate but as sinners, all of whom need redemption. Administered by people who do not know the hidden counsel of God, the gospel can only be universal in its offer. Just as a net cast into the sea catches both good and bad fish, just as the sun shines simultaneously on wheat and on weeds, just as the seed of the sower falls not only on good soil but also on stony and dry places, so also the gospel, in its being administered, comes to all people without distinction.

2. The message of that gospel is not to all people individually: "Christ has died in your place; all your sins have been atoned for and forgiven." For even though universalists imagine they can say this to every human being without any further qualification, upon a little reflection it is clear that also for the universalist position this is by no means the case. After all, according to them, Christ has secured only the possibility of forgiveness and salvation, for that forgiveness and salvation become real only if people believe and continue to believe that message. Accordingly, they too can only preach, as the content of the gospel, the message: "Believe in the Lord Jesus and you will receive the forgiveness of sins and eternal life."

Now Reformed preachers say the same thing. They too offer the gospel to all humans and can, may, and must do this. Though the forgiveness of sins and eternal salvation are there, they become ours only by means of faith. Yet there is in this connection an important difference between the universalists and the Reformed, a difference that is totally to the advantage of the Reformed. In the view of the former, Christ secured only the possibility of salvation. Whether salvation actually becomes a reality for a person depends on that person herself or himself. Faith is a condition, a work, which alone turns a possible salvation into an actual salvation, and so leaves a person forever in doubt, at least till death. But, in the view of the Reformed, Christ secured full, real, and total salvation. Faith, accordingly, is not a work, a condition, an intellectual assent to the statement "Christ died for you" but an act of reliance on Christ himself, of trusting in his sacrifice alone. It is a living faith that is much simpler than it can be with the universalist view, one that much more certainly brings salvation with it than universalists consistent with their position can ever promise. The error here is solely that humans are always inclined to reverse the God-appointed order. They want to be sure of the outcome before using the means and in order to be exempt from using the means. But it is the will of God that we shall take the way of faith, and then he unfailingly assures us of complete salvation in Christ.

3. The offer of salvation on the part of God, therefore, is seriously and sincerely meant. For in that offer he does not say what he himself will do—whether or not he will bestow that faith. He has kept that to himself. He only tells us what he wants us to do: that we humble ourselves and seek our salvation in Christ alone. If it be objected that God nevertheless offers salvation to those to whom he has decided not to grant faith and salvation, then this is an objection equally applicable to the position of our opponents. For in that case, God also offers salvation to those whom he infallibly knows will not believe. It is the case after all, not only according to the Reformed but also according to all Christ-confessors, that the outcome of world history is eternally and unchangeably certain.[5] The only difference is that the Reformed have had the courage to say that that outcome corresponds to God's will and purpose. Although it is beyond our comprehension, God must have been able to will all that is and takes place, subject to all his virtues and perfections, or else God would no longer be God. History cannot and may not be a sparring partner for God.

4. The preaching of the gospel is neither ineffective nor useless. Indeed, if either from ignorance or incapacity God really aimed, through the universal offer of the gospel, at the salvation of all, it would be useless and vain. For how small the number is in whom this purpose is realized! In that case, it would itself harbor a contradiction, which, for the purpose of resolving it, would tempt us toward ever-greater departure from Scripture. For, if the will and purpose of God, if the atonement of Christ, is strictly universal, then the offer of salvation must also be unqualifiedly universal. And since that is evidently not the case, people gradually arrive at a variety of "solutions." Either, like the old Lutherans, they flatly contradict history and claim that the apostles already preached the gospel to all peoples, or, like many modern theologians, they assume there will be gospel preaching also on the other side of the grave;[6] or worse, along with rationalists and mystics, they believe that "the law of nature" or "the inner light" is sufficient for salvation. The farther one thus, in defiance of history, expands the call, the weaker, the more bland and insipid it becomes. In quality and intensity one loses what one has seemingly gained in quantity and scope. The contrast between God's intent and the outcome of it becomes increasingly more pronounced.

5. Although through this call salvation becomes the possession of only a few, as everyone must admit, it nevertheless retains its great value and significance

---

5. Cf. H. Bavinck, *Reformed Dogmatics* II, 377 (#242).

6. W. Schmidt, "Die Universalität des göttlichen Heilswillens und die Particularität der Berufung," *Theologische Studien und Kritiken* 60/1 (1887): 1–44.

also for those who reject it. For everyone without distinction, it is proof of God's infinite love and seals the saying that he has no pleasure in the death of sinners but rather that they should turn and live (Ezek. 18:23, 32). It proclaims to all that Christ's sacrifice is sufficient for the expiation of all sins, that no one is lost because the call is insufficiently rich and powerful, that no demand of the law, no power of sin, no rule of Satan can block its application, for the free gift is not like the trespass (Rom. 5:15). Frequently, even for those who harden themselves in their unbelief, it is a source of various blessings. The enlightenment of the mind, a taste of the heavenly gift, partaking of the Holy Spirit, enjoyment of the Word of God, the experience of the powers of the age to come—these have sometimes even come to those who later fell away and held the Son of God in contempt (Heb. 6:4–6).

6. And this is not all. For the external call by law and gospel also reaches the goal God has in view. What God does is never futile. His word never returns to him empty; it accomplishes everything he purposes and prospers in the thing for which he sends it (Isa. 55:11). But this purpose is not only, and not in the first place, the eternal salvation of human beings, but the glory of his name. In this calling by law and gospel God continues to press his claim on his human creatures. The sinner assumes that by sinning he or she becomes free from God and his service. But it is not so. God's claim on humans, also the most degraded ones, is inalienable and inviolable. Human beings, resigning from the service of God, can become profoundly wretched, but they remain creatures and are therefore dependent. Sin does not make them less dependent but even more so. They cease to be children and become servants, slaves, powerless instruments used by God according to his will. God never releases his grip on us and never abandons his claims on us, on our service, and on our complete consecration. And for that reason, by nature and history, heart and conscience, blessings and judgments, law and gospel, he summons us to return to him. The call, in its broadest sense, is the preaching of God's claims upon his fallen creatures.

7. As such it maintains in each person and in the whole human race the religious and moral awareness of dependence, awe, respect, duty, and responsibility, without which humanity cannot exist. Religion, morality, law, art, science, family, society, the state—they all have their root and foundation in the call that comes from God to all people. Take it away, and what we get is a war of all against all, each person becoming a wolf against one's neighbor. The call, by law and gospel, restrains sin, diminishes guilt, and stems the corruption and misery of humankind. It is "repressive grace." It is proof that God is God, that he is indifferent toward nothing, and that not only the world beyond but also this world has value to him. Accordingly, however much people may be inclined to hide behind their powerlessness, or with Pelagius and Kant to deduce their power from their duty, also in

that way they acknowledge that God's claims and our duty remain undiminished and they themselves are inexcusable.[7]

8. Finally, this call is not only a repressive but also a preparatory grace. Christ came into the world for judgment (κρίσις), for a fall but also for a rising of many (Mark 4:12; Luke 2:34; 8:10; John 9:39; 15:22; 2 Cor. 2:16; 1 Pet. 2:7–8). This call by law and gospel is also intended, through what it gives and brings about both in humanity as a whole and in individual persons, to pave the way for the coming of Christ. Reformed theologians[8] have definitely rejected such a preparatory grace in an Arminian sense.[9] The spiritual life that is implanted in regeneration differs essentially from the natural and moral life that precedes it. It is brought about, not by human activity or evolution, but by a creative act of God. Some theologians, accordingly, preferred to call the activities that precede regeneration "antecedent actions" rather than "preparatory actions." Still one can speak of "preparatory grace" in a sound sense. The expression is even eminently valuable against all Methodist trends that ignore the natural life. For the confession of preparatory grace does not imply that, by doing what they can on their own—regularly going to church, listening attentively to the Word of God, acknowledging their sins, and yearning for salvation, and so on—people can earn or make themselves receptive to the grace of regeneration on the basis of a merit of congruity. On the contrary, it implies that God is the creator, sustainer, and ruler of all things and that, even generations before they are born, he orders the life of those on whom he will in due time bestow the gift of faith. Humans did not originate on the sixth day by evolving from lower creatures, but are created by the hand of God. Still, his creation may be considered prepared by the antecedent acts of God. Though Christ himself came down from above, yet his coming had been prepared for centuries. Although nature and grace are distinct and may not be confused or mingled, God does link the two. Creation, redemption, and sanctification are, in an "economic"

---

7. On the nature and fruits of external calling, cf. the literature on common grace: H. Bavinck, *Reformed Dogmatics*, I, 301ff. (##85ff.); III, 216ff. (##347ff.); W. Twisse, *Guilielmi Twissi opera theologica polemico anti-Arminiana* (Amsterdam, 1699), I, 660ff.; J. Trigland, *Opuscula* (Amsterdam: Marten Jansz. Brandt, 1639–40), I, 430ff.; II, 809ff.; F. Gomarus, *Opera theologica omnia* (Amsterdam: J. Jansson, 1664), I, 97ff.; *Synopsis purioris theologiae*, disp. 30, 40–46; G. Voetius, *Selectae disputationes theologicae*, 5 vols. (Utrecht, 1648–69), II, 256; P. van Mastricht, *Theologia*, VI, 2, 16; F. Turretin, *Institutes of Elenctic Theology*, trans. G. M. Giger, ed. J. T. Dennison, 3 vols. (Phillipsburg, NJ: Presbyterian & Reformed, 1992), XV, qu. 2, and also XIV, 14, 51; H. Witsius, *The Oeconomy of Covenants between God and Man*, II, 9, 4; III, 5, 20; J. H. Heidegger, *Corpus theologiae*, 2 vols. (Zurich: J. H. Bodmer, 1700), XXI, 9–11; J. Alting, *Opera omnia theologica*, 5 vols. (Amsterdam: Borst, 1687), 187; B. de Moor, *Comm. theol.*, III, 1071; C. Hodge, *Systematic Theology*, 3 vols. (New York: Charles Scribner's Sons, 1888), II, 641ff.; W. G. T. Shedd, *Dogmatic Theology*, 3rd ed., 3 vols. (New York: Scribner, 1888–94), I, 451; II, 482ff.; R. S. Candlish, *The Atonement: Its Reality, Completeness, and Extent* (London: T. Nelson & Sons, 1861), 169ff.; A. Robertson, *History of the Atonement Controversy in Connection with the Secession Church* (Edinburgh: Oliphant, 1846).

8. Canons of Dort, I, 4; J. Trigland, *Antapologia* (Amsterdam: Joannam Janssonium et al., 1664), ch. 25ff.; J. Maccovius, *Loci communes* (Amsterdam: n.p., 1658), 699ff.; P. van Mastricht, *Theologia*, VI, 3, 19–28; H. Witsius, *The Oeconomy of Covenants between God and Man*, III, 6, 9.

9. Remonstrant Confession and *Apologia pro confessione*, XI, 4.

sense, attributed to the Father, Son, and Spirit, but these three constitute the one true God, and together they accomplish the whole work of redemption. No one can come to Christ unless the Father draws him or her; and no one receives the Holy Spirit except those to whom the Son sends him.

For that reason we can properly speak of a preparatory grace. God himself, in many different ways, prepares for his gracious work in human hearts. He aroused in Zacchaeus the desire to see Jesus (Luke 19:3), produced distress in the crowd that listened to Peter (Acts 2:37), caused Paul to fall to the ground (9:4), disconcerted the jailer at Philippi (16:27), and so directs the lives of all his children even before and up to the hour of their rebirth. Even if on their part they have not yet received the benefits of reconciliation and justification and have not yet been born again and given faith, yet they are already the objects of his eternal love, and he himself already leads them by his grace to the Spirit, who alone can regenerate and comfort them. All things, accordingly, are connected by divine prearrangement to their subsequent "enlistment" and calling in the church. Conception and birth, family and lineage and people and land, upbringing and education, development of heart and mind, preservation from hideous sins, above all from blaspheming the Holy Spirit, or perhaps abandonment to all sorts of wickedness, disasters and judgment, blessings and benefits, the preaching of law and gospel, distress about sin and fear of judgment, development of conscience and the felt need for salvation: all of this is grace preparing people for rebirth by the Holy Spirit and for the role that they as believers will later play in the church. True: there is only one way to heaven, but many are the leadings of God both before and on that journey, and the grace of the Holy Spirit is abundant and free. Jeremiah, John the Baptist, and Timothy were brought into the kingdom differently from either Manasseh or Paul, and each performed a different task in the service of God. Pietism and Methodism tend to ignore these leadings, limit God's grace, and want to convert and mold everyone according to a single model. But Reformed theology respects the free sovereignty of God and marvels at the riches of his grace.[10]

---

10. Preparatory grace is treated in W. Musculus, *Loci communes theologiae sacrae* (Basel: Heruagiana, 1567), 24; P. Martyr Vermigli, *Loci communes*, ed. R. Massonius (London, 1576), 312; Z. Ursinus, *The Commentary of Dr. Zacharius Ursinus on the Heidelberg Catechism,* trans. G. W. Williard (Grand Rapids: Eerdmans, 1954), qu. 88–90; H. Heppe, *Dogmatik des deutschen Protestantismus im sechzehnten Jahrhundert,* 3 vols. (Gotha: F. A. Perthes, 1857), II, 372; W. Perkins, *The Workes of That Famous and Worthy Minister of Christ,* 3 vols. (London: John Legatt, 1612–18), III, 127ff.; W. Ames, *Conscience with the Power and Cases Thereof* (London: Rothwell, Slater & Blacklock, 1643), II, 4; H. Visscher, *Guilielmus Amesius: Zijn leven en werken* (Haarlem: J. M. Stap, 1894), 125; A. Kuyper Jr., *Johannes Maccovius* (Leiden: D. Donner, 1899), 57, 339ff.; 352ff.; the British theologians at the Synod of Dordt on the third and fourth articles; *Synopsis purioris theologiae,* disp. 32, 6; H. Witsius, *The Oeconomy of Covenants between God and Man,* III, 6, 11–15; G. Voetius, *Select. disp.,* II, 402–24; B. de Moor, *Comm. theol.,* IV, 482; C. Vitringa, *Korte schets van de christelyke zeden-leere, ofte van het geestelyk leven ende deselfs eigenschappen* (Amsterdam: Antoni Schoonenburg, 1724), ch. 4 (ed. note: Bavinck cites a 1739 edition). W. van Eenhorn, *Euzoia, ofte, welleven* (Amsterdam: Adriaan Wor, 1746–53), I, 220; G. Van Aalst, *Geestelyke mengelstoffen: Ofte godvrugtige bedenkingen over eenige gewigtige waarheden* (1754; repr., Ermelo: Sneek, 2000), 298, 369; A. Comrie, *Stellige en praktikale verklaring van den Heidelbergschen Catechismus* (Minnertsga: J. Bloemsma, 1844), qu. 20–23; J. Owen, *De rechtvaardiging uit het geloof door de toerekening van*

THE PARTICULAR CALL OF GRACE

[435] Scripture and experience testify, however, that all these workings of external calling do not always and in every case lead people to a sincere faith and salvation. Hence the question arises: What is the ultimate cause of this diverse outcome? In the Christian church, in the main, a threefold answer was given to that question. Some said that this diverse outcome was due to the human will, whether that will had received the power to accept or reject the gospel from its natural self, or from the grace of the Logos, or from the grace of baptism, or from that of the calling. According to this view, there is no distinction between external and internal, or between efficient and efficacious calling. Inwardly and essentially the calling is always and in every case the same. It is only called efficacious in terms of the outcome when a person responds to the call. After everything we have said previously about Pelagianism,[11] this answer does not call for a lengthy refutation. It clearly offers no solution. In practice one can indeed confine oneself to the proximate cause and attribute unbelief specifically to the human will. In that case, one is speaking truthfully (Deut. 30:19; Josh. 24:15; Isa. 65:12; Matt. 22:2–3; 23:37; John 7:17; Rom. 9:32; etc.): the sinful will of humans is responsible for their unbelief. But even in practice all believers at all times and in all schools of thought have attributed their faith and salvation to God's grace alone.[12] There is nothing that distinguishes them other than that gift of grace (1 Cor. 4:7). Ultimately, therefore, this difference cannot lie in the human will. If one nevertheless insists on considering will the final cause, one is instantly faced with all the psychological, ethical, historical, and theological objections that have at all times been raised against Pelagianism. It introduces incalculable caprice and weakens sin; the decision about the outcome of world history is put in the hands of humans, the governance over all things is taken away from God; his grace is canceled out. Even if one ascribes the power to choose for or against the gospel to the restoration of grace, this does not help matters. In that case one introduces a grace that consists solely in the restoration of volitional choice, one that is nowhere mentioned in Scripture, that actually presupposes regeneration and yet has to bring it about only after the right choice has been made.[13] On this position one also gets stuck with all the millions of people who have never heard of the gospel or died as infants and for that reason were never in a position to ac-

---

Christus gerechtigheid, trans. M. van Werkhoven (Amsterdam: Martinus de Bruyn, 1779), ch. 1, 83ff.; ed. note: original English: *The Doctrine of Justification by Faith* (Glasgow: John Bryce, 1760); A. Kuyper, *Het werk van den Heiligen Geest,* 3 vols. in 1 (Amsterdam: Wormser, 1888–89), II, 111; ed. note: ET: *The Work of the Holy Spirit,* trans. Henri de Vries, 3 vols. (New York: Funk & Wagnalls, 1900); H. Bavinck, *Roeping en wedergeboorte* (Kampen: Zalsman, 1903), 137ff.

11. H. Bavinck, *Reformed Dogmatics,* II, 374ff. (##241ff.); III, 506–12 (##414–15), 564–69 (#427b).

12. Ibid., II, 377–79 (#242).

13. F. H. R. Frank, *System der Christlichen Wahrheit,* 2nd ed., 4 vols. in 2 (Erlangen: A. Deichert, 1884), II, 325.

cept or reject Christ. Accordingly, the free will of humans cannot be the ultimate cause of faith and unbelief.

Another answer to the above question was therefore devised by Bellarmine. He rejected both the doctrine of Pelagius and that of Augustine, sought a path somewhere between them, and said that the efficacy of the call depended on whether it came to a person at an opportune time when the will was inclined to follow it (*congruitas*).[14] Agreeing with this congruism are the views of Pajon, Kleman, as well as Shedd, who considers salvation "in the highest degree probable" for everyone who makes serious and diligent use of the means of grace.[15] But this answer, too, is unsatisfactory. In this congruity theory there is indeed an important truth that, while ignored by Methodism, comes into its own in the Reformed doctrine of preparatory grace. But it is completely unable to explain the efficacy of the call. The reason is that it is inherently nothing other than moral suasion, which in the nature of the case is powerless to create the spiritual life that, according to Scripture, is the result of regeneration. Further, it presupposes that a human being is fit one moment and unfit the next to accept grace, thus locating sin in circumstances and weakening it in humans. In addition, it makes the ultimate decision dependent on the human will and thereby again provokes all the objections mentioned above and lodged by Bellarmine himself against Pelagianism. Finally, it links calling and conversion by a thread of congruity, which, being moral in nature, can at all times be broken by the will and hence cannot guarantee the efficacy of the call.

Augustinians, Thomists, and Reformed theologians, therefore, located the reason why in one person the calling bore fruit and in another it did not in the nature of the calling itself. The first group said that when the call was efficacious, a "triumphant delight" (*delectatio victrix*) was present, which granted not only the capacity to act (*posse*) but also the will to act (*velle*). The Thomists spoke of a "natural predetermination" or "natural action of God" that prompted the capacity to act (*posse agere*), conferred by "sufficient calling," to pass into action.[16] The Reformed, however, objecting to the use of these terms, took exception especially to the description of an act of God in conversion as "natural" and preferred to speak of an "external" and an "internal" call. This distinction already occurs in Augustine,[17] was taken over from him by Calvin,[18] and was further adopted in Reformed theology. Earlier this twofold calling was referred to by other terms as well, such as the "material and formal," the "revealed" call and the call of "God's good pleasure," the common and the personal, the universal and the special call,[19]

14. Cf. H. Bavinck, *Reformed Dogmatics*, III, 515 (#416).

15. W. G. T. Shedd, *Dogm. Theol.*, II, 511–28.

16. On Augustinians and Thomists, see H. Bavinck, *Reformed Dogmatics*, III, 514 (#416).

17. Augustine, *On the Predestination of the Saints*, ch. 8.

18. Calvin, on Rom. 10:16; idem, "Acta Synodi Tridentinae cum antidoto" (1547), sess. 6, in *Calvini opera*, VII (CR, XXXV), 480; idem, *Institutes of the Christian Religion*, III.xxiv.8.

19. A. Polanus, *Syntragma theologiae christianae*, 5th ed. (Hanover: Aubry, 1624), VI, ch. 32; C. Vitringa, *Doctr. christ.*, III, 156.

but the terms "external" and "internal" call gained the upper hand and gradually pushed out the others.

Now although this distinction does not occur in so many words in Scripture, it is based on Scripture.

1. It is already implied in the fact that all humans are the same by nature, worthy of condemnation before God (Rom. 3:9–19; 5:12; 9:21; 11:32), dead in sins and trespasses (Eph. 2:2–3), darkened in their understanding (1 Cor. 2:14; Eph. 4:18; 5:8). They cannot see the kingdom of God (John 3:3), are the slaves of sin (8:34; Rom. 6:20), enemies of God (8:7; Col. 1:21), do not and cannot submit to God's law (Rom. 8:7), are unable to think or do anything good from within themselves (John 15:5; 2 Cor. 3:5); though the gospel is for the benefit of humans, they are hostile toward it and despise it as an offense or folly (1 Cor. 1:23; 2:14). Hence the difference that occurs among people after the calling is inexplicable in terms of human capacities. God and his grace alone make the difference (1 Cor. 4:7).

2. Simply the preaching of the Word by itself is not sufficient (Isa. 6:9–10; 53:1; Matt. 13:13ff.; Mark 4:12; John 12:38–40; etc.). Hence in the Old Testament already we learn of the promised Spirit who would teach everyone and grant them all a new heart (Isa. 32:15; Jer. 31:33; 32:39; Ezek. 11:19; 36:26; Joel 2:28). To that end he was poured out on the day of Pentecost to witness to Christ along with and through the apostles (John 15:26–27), to convict the world of sin and righteousness and judgment (John 16:8–11), to regenerate people (John 3:5ff.; 6:63; 16:13), and to lead them to confess Jesus as Lord (1 Cor. 12:3).

3. The work of redemption, therefore, is ascribed completely, both subjectively and objectively, to God. This is not just meant in a general sense, the way we say that God works all things by his providence, but definitely in the restricted sense that by a special divine power he works regeneration and conversions. So it depends not on human will or exertion, but on God who shows mercy (Rom. 9:16). The calling is the implementation of divine election (8:28; 11:29). It is God who renews the human heart and inscribes his law on it (Ps. 51:12; Jer. 31:33; Ezek. 36:26), who enlightens the eyes of the heart (Ps. 119:18; Eph. 1:18; Col. 1:9–11), opens the heart (Acts 16:14), makes his own recognize his Son as the Christ (Matt. 11:25; 16:17; Gal. 1:16), and draws people to him with spiritual power (John 6:44; Col. 1:12–13). He causes the gospel to be preached, not only in words but also in demonstration of the spirit and power (1 Cor. 2:4; 1 Thess. 1:5–6), and himself gives wisdom (1 Cor. 2:6–9). He, in short, is at work in us, enabling us both to will and to work according to his good pleasure (Phil. 2:13) and to that end uses a power like the power by which he raised Christ from the dead and made him sit at his right hand (Eph. 1:18–20).

4. The very act by which God accomplishes this change in humans is often called "rebirth" (John 1:13; 3:3ff.; Titus 3:5; etc.), and the fruit of it is called a new heart (Jer. 31:33), a new creation (2 Cor. 5:17), his workmanship created in Christ Jesus (Eph. 2:10), the work of God (Rom. 14:20), and his building (1 Cor. 3:9; Eph. 2:21; etc.). This is to say that what is brought about in humans by the grace of God is much too rich and great for it to be explained in terms of the "moral suasion" of the preaching of the Word.

5. Finally, Scripture itself speaks of calling in a dual sense. Repeatedly it refers to a calling and invitation to which there was no positive response (Isa. 65:12; Matt. 22:3, 14; 23:37; Mark 16:15–16; etc.). In that case it could say that while God did everything on his part (Isa. 5:4), people in their obstinacy refused to believe and resisted God's counsel, the Holy Spirit, and calling (Matt. 11:20ff.; 23:37; Luke 7:30; Acts 7:51). But Scripture also knows a calling from God—a realization of election—that is always efficacious. This is especially true in Paul (Rom. 4:17; 8:30; 9:11, 24; 1 Cor. 1:9; 7:15ff.; Gal. 1:6, 15; 5:8; Eph. 4:1, 4; 1 Thess. 2:12; 2 Tim. 1:9; also cf. 1 Pet. 1:15; 2:9; 5:10; 2 Pet. 1:3). Believers are therefore repeatedly described simply as "those who are called" (Rom. 1:7; 1 Cor. 1:2, 24), and "those who are called in Christ" or "in the Lord" (1 Cor. 7:22); that is, those who are called by God belong to Christ and live in communion with him. In addition, Paul also knows of a preaching of the gospel to those who reject it. To them the gospel is foolishness (1 Cor. 1:18, 23), a fragrance from death to death (2 Cor. 2:15–16). They do not understand it (1 Cor. 2:14). As a power of God (1 Cor. 1:18, 24), it proves itself to those who are called by God according to his purpose (Rom. 8:28; 9:11; 11:28; Eph. 1:4–5).

REBIRTH IN OTHER RELIGIONS

[436] Inasmuch as the efficacious call, as Paul speaks of it, incorporates within itself the external verbal call (*vocatio verbalis externa*) and even the real calling (*vocatio realis*), we must in this connection call to mind all the work of God accomplished on his part by Word and Spirit externally and internally, mediately and immediately, suasively and efficaciously—to bring to birth in unspiritual human beings a spiritual person who from the very first moment receives life from him, in communion with Christ and by the power of the Holy Spirit. This call, accordingly, is irrevocably connected with and automatically leads to that other benefit of the covenant of grace that is usually called regeneration or rebirth. The Greek word παλινγενεσια or παλιγγενεσια does not occur for the first time in the New Testament but also elsewhere in literature and had several meanings. In Stoic philosophy, it was used for the cosmic renewal that was to begin after the conclusion of the present dispensation. *Palingenesis* was the term for what is otherwise called ἀποκαταστασις των παντων (universal restoration [Acts 3:21]), and it was thought to occur not just once but repeatedly. The Stoic school believed

in a "periodic rebirth of all things." The school of Pythagoras, however, used the word to denote the rebirth of souls from death. Following departure from this life comes the return to life, or rebirth, in other words, the transmigration of the soul or reincarnation. Aside from these two eschatological meanings, the word acquired a variety of metaphorical senses as well. Philo, for example, calls Noah and his family, who were spared in the flood, "the leaders of the rebirth and founders of the second period." Josephus speaks of the return of the Jews from Babylonia to Palestine as a "rebirth of the fatherland." Cicero, being restored after his exile to a position of dignity and honor, called it a rebirth; and Olympiodorus writes: "The memory is the rebirth of understanding."[20]

The idea of rebirth gradually began to play a large role in the mystery cults that, coming from the East, in the early centuries of the Christian calendar penetrated the West and greatly expanded there. Common to all of them is the idea that a god or goddess dies and again awakens to a new life. In the Eleusinian mysteries, for example, Kore (Persephone) was first kidnapped by Pluto, taken to the underworld, and later returned to her mother. The same idea underlies the Phrygian, Phoenician, and Egyptian mysteries. But that idea was not developed and argued didactically but rather enacted visually and dramatically before an audience of initiates. In the words of Rohde, the mysteries were religious pantomimes combined with sacred songs and solemn sayings.[21] Only by participation in a series of ceremonies, submitting to various ablutions, and eating and drinking the food and drink offered by priests could the initiates—who were usually further divided into classes—penetrate the mysteries and appropriate the divine life forces made available in these cults. This came to expression especially in Mithraism, which, rooted in Persia, passed through Phrygia to Rome and reached its acme there in the third century after Christ. At the core of the Mithraic liturgy was the killing of a bull by Mithra, represented as a youthful god. The initiate received a blood bath by letting the blood of the bull drip down on his head, lips, eyes, ears, and cheeks. He even drank the blood and then presented himself to the crowd for veneration. For, having been baptized with blood and cleansed, he was like the deity, born again forever. These mysteries, naturally, made a very diverse impression on participants and spectators. Some viewed them as little more than nature myths that visually represented the death and rebirth of the life force. Others, construing them more spiritually, saw them as the process of dying and resurrection that every human, all of humanity, and the whole world had to undergo to obtain immortality, eternal life, and divinity.[22]

20. H. Cremer, *Biblico-Theological Lexicon of New Testament Greek,* trans. D. W. Simon and W. Urwick (Edinburgh: T&T Clark; New York: Charles Scribners Sons, 1895); s.v. παλιγγενεσια; P. Gennrich, *Die Lehre von der Wiedergeburt* (Leipzig: Deichert, 1907), 3, 4; Bartlett, "Regeneration," in *DB,* IV, 214.

21. E. Rohde, *Psyche: Seelenkult und Unsterblichkeitsglaube der Griechen*, 2nd ed. (Freiburg: J. C. B. Mohr, 1898).

22. F. V. M. Cumont, *Die orientalischen Religionen im römischen Heidentum,* trans. Georg Gehrich (Leipzig: Teubner, 1910), 80–82; W. Staerk, *Neutestamentliche Zeitgeschichte,* 2 vols. (Berlin: G. J. Göschen, 1907), I,

In recent years it is being said by proponents of the history-of-religions method that Christianity is a syncretistic religion that underwent the influence of these pagan mysteries not only in the later formation of its dogmas but already in its early period of doctrinal development. We cannot, of course, treat this weighty question here,[23] but at least with respect to the idea of rebirth this assertion is not well grounded. In the first place, it is noteworthy that the word for rebirth (παλιγγενεσια) occurs only twice in the New Testament (Matt. 19:28; Titus 3:5); and with regard to Matt. 19:28, we must remember that we do not know how Jesus expressed in Aramaic the idea that the evangelist translated by the Greek (παλιγγενεσια). Furthermore, in the mysteries the idea of rebirth was always connected with ceremonial and even sacramental actions, but in Scripture it repeatedly occurs by itself apart from any such connection (John 3:5; James 1:18; 1 Pet. 1:3, 23). Even in Titus 3:5 the link with or allusion to baptism is uncertain. Moreover, the explanation of many practices followed in the mysteries, such as the killing of the bull in Mithraism, is still very problematic. For one thing our knowledge of the mysteries is largely based on witnesses dating from the second to the fourth century AD, when it flourished in the Roman Empire. It is therefore possible that Christianity on its part exerted influence on the interpretation of these mysteries. In any case, if early Christianity had originally been shaped under the influence of the mysteries, this must have started already in Palestine, with Paul, John, and the entire church of that time. But proof for this assumption is totally lacking. The faith of the early Christian church was centered in the person of Christ and from the beginning took an antithetic position to all pagan religions. Finally, the New Testament as a rule employs the same words that were current in the common Greek of that time. How else could the gospel have found a hearing and acceptance? But it often attributes to those words another, deeper sense and gradually makes that meaning the content of human consciousness. That is the case with words such as σωτηρια (salvation), ζωη (life), ἀπολυτρωσις (redemption) as well as with the idea of rebirth, which in Scripture is only twice rendered by παλιγγενεσια and for the rest by many other terms.

REGENERATION: SCRIPTURAL TEACHING

[437] The idea of rebirth has its roots in the Old Testament. The word παλιγγενεσια does not occur in the Septuagint except that Job says (14:14): ὑπομενω ἑως ἀν παλιν γενωμαι ("I would wait until my release should come"). But materially the idea of rebirth clearly occurs already in Israelite religion. Entirely in keeping with the Old Testament dispensation, it is first of all a matter for the people as a whole. At the time of the giving of the law and later in prophecy the word is first of all addressed to all the people God has included in his covenant,

---

99ff.; J. Felten, *Neutestamentliche Zeitgeschichte*, 2 vols. (Regensburg: Manz, 1910), II, 542–53; P. Gennrich, *Wiedergeburt*, 39–41.

    23. Cf. H. Bavinck, *Reformed Dogmatics*, III, 270–74 (#361).

and on the basis of that covenant the people are confronted with the demand that they serve the Lord with all their heart and soul (Deut. 11:13; Josh. 22:5). But as apostasy, unfaithfulness, and the hardness of people's hearts became more and more evident in history, the prophets stressed with increasing forcefulness that an inner change had to come, not only among the people as a whole, but also in the heart of every member of that people in particular. And in that respect human beings of themselves are unable to bring it about (Gen. 6:5; 8:21; Job 14:4; 15:16; Ps. 51:5). No more than an Ethiopian can change his skin or the leopard his spots can Israel do good, for it has learned to do evil (Jer. 13:23). The heart is deceitful above all things and lethally corrupt (17:9). A stupid man will no more get understanding than the colt of a wild ass is born human (Job 11:12). But what human beings cannot bring about in themselves or others God will do in the future. He alone can create a clean heart (Ps. 51:10–12). He will take away their stony heart and give them a heart of flesh, circumcise the foreskin of their heart, put a new spirit within them, inscribe the law in their heart, and cause them to walk in his statutes. Then Israel will be his people, a shoot of his planting, a work of his hands, that he may be glorified (Deut. 10:16; 30:1–6; Isa. 54:13; 60:21; Jer. 24:7; 31:18, 31ff.; 32:8ff.; Ezek. 11:19; 36:25ff.).

Initially John the Baptist and then Jesus required such an internal change from all who want to enter the kingdom of heaven. The people of Israel, despite all its external privileges, was nevertheless corrupt through and through. Despite its circumcision, it needed baptism, the baptism of repentance for the forgiveness of sins, in which a person is totally immersed in order to rise again as another person to a new life (Matt. 3:2ff.). To obtain the benefits of the kingdom, a radical turnaround, a μετανοια, is needed. Those who want to enter the kingdom must break with their entire previous life, lose their life (Matt. 10:37–39; 16:25; Luke 14:26), leave behind everything (14:33), take up their cross and follow Jesus (Matt. 10:38), become a child (18:3), return to the Father with a confession of sin (Luke 15:18), and go through the narrow gate and walk down the narrow path (Matt. 7:14). Those who really do this are enabled to do so by God himself. For human beings are by nature evil (7:11). Out of their hearts come nothing but wickedness (15:19). Like a bad tree, they cannot produce good fruit (7:17ff.). Accordingly, if there is to be good fruit, the tree must be made good first, something only God can do (19:26). Children of God and citizens of his kingdom are those who have been planted by the heavenly Father (15:13), to whom the Son has revealed the Father and the Father the Son (11:25–27; 13:11; 16:17). Whereas they were spiritually dead before, they have a true life now and await eternal life (8:22; Luke 15:24; 18:30). In all Christ's teaching as we find it in the first three Gospels, though the word "rebirth" does not occur, the matter itself is clearly presented. So when in his conversation with Nicodemus Jesus says that no one can see the kingdom of God unless he or she is born anew (from above) of water and the Spirit (John 3:3–8), he is not contradicting his teaching in the other Gospels but briefly and pointedly summing up for the teacher Nicodemus what he has explained elsewhere at greater length and in more popular form. Nicodemus, we must know, was a distinguished man, a teacher in Israel, a member of the supreme council. He had heard of Jesus's miracles and on that basis regarded him a teacher sent by God. But being still in doubt whether Jesus was the Messiah, he went to Jesus by night for fear of the Jews in order to achieve certainty through a confidential interview with him. Nicodemus, accordingly, began the conversation with the admission that he viewed Jesus as a teacher sent by God and endowed by God with the capacity to do his works, and evidently wanted to go on to ask what one must do to enter the kingdom of God. Jesus, not giving him the time to pose that question, immediately answered: "Truly, truly, I say to you, unless one is born anew, he cannot see the kingdom of God" [John 3:3 RSV]. And with that answer, he abruptly cut off all human self-effort, all Pharisaic law observance, as the way to the kingdom.

Also, for that reason, Jesus does not speak of being born a second time, literally *anew*, but of being born *from above*. He stresses, not that entry into the kingdom requires a second birth (although regeneration can of course be called that), but wants especially to bring out for Nicodemus that only a birth from above (v. 3), of water and the Spirit (v. 5), of the Spirit (v. 8), admits a person to the kingdom. This birth occurs in contrast to that of the flesh, for what is born of the flesh is flesh (v. 6). It is not of blood, nor of the will of the flesh, nor of the will of humans, but of God (John 1:13). For that reason it is as equally incomprehensible in origin and direction as the wind, but nevertheless possible, for it is a birth of the Spirit (3:8). After first having said in general that it is a birth from water and spirit (both without the article, v. 5), he specifically speaks in verses 6 and 8 of *the* Spirit (with the article) and that this Spirit, as the Spirit of God, can bring about this great work of regeneration from above. Hence, in speaking of water in verse 5, Jesus is not speaking of baptism, but describes by this term the nature of birth from above. It is a birth that has the character of a renewal, a purification, of which water is a symbol (Ezek. 36:25; cf. the combination of Spirit and fire, Matt. 3:11), and confers the existence of a new spiritual life. And that is something this birth from above can bring about, for it is a birth from *the* Spirit, who is God himself (John 3:6–8).

[438] The apostles, too, frequently speak of regeneration but describe it in varied terms, sometimes viewing it in a broad, and then again in a narrow sense. James (1:18) says that God of his own will brought us forth (ἀπεκυησεν; cf. the same word in v. 15: "Sin when it is full-grown brings forth death" [RSV]), that we should be a kind of firstfruits of his creatures. This ἀποκυεῖν arises from the will of God, from whom all good and perfect gifts descend, and who offers us the greatest proof of his fatherly love in that he has brought us forth as his people. This came about by means of the word of truth (or just the truth [3:14; 5:19], or the perfect law, the law of liberty, the royal law [1:25; 2:8, 12]), which did not stop outside of or over against us so that we can only hear it, but was planted in us, is written on the tables of our hearts, according to Heb. 8:10; 10:16, and can therefore save our souls (James 1:21). And the

goal of this regenerative process is that Christians should be the firstfruits of God's creation, as the true Israel, the special possession of God, like the people of Israel who existed in the days of the Old Testament (Exod. 19:5; Deut. 7:6; 14:2; 26:18; Ps. 135:4; Isa. 43:21; Mal. 3:17; cf. 1 Pet. 1:23; 2:9) and as such the firstfruits of the kingdom that God will establish throughout his creation (cf. Rom. 8:19–23; Heb. 12:23). Peter uses the word ἀναγενναν, which was not customary in ordinary Greek (though Philo sometimes alternates παλιγγενεσις with ἀναγεννησις, and Porphyry once used the adjective ἀναγεννητικος) and which literally means "to bring forth anew." Also, Peter attributes this rebirth to God and to his mercy (1 Pet. 1:3) and has it come about by the living and enduring word of God, which is identical with the word of the gospel preached among his readers (vv. 23, 25). But Peter differs from James in that, on the one hand, he links that rebirth to the resurrection of Christ and on the other, to the living hope. The resurrection of Christ, certainly, is the intermediate cause by which God regenerated them to a living hope (1:3). The resurrection and glorification of Christ above all took place so that their faith and hope should be in God (1:21). Believers, as living stones, are built upon him as the cornerstone (2:2–4) and live in communion with him (5:14). They learned of this resurrection of Christ from the word of the gospel, which had been preached among them in the power of the Holy Spirit, who had been sent from heaven (1:12, 23, 25). As such a word from God, it is living and enduring (1:23).

Whether this living and enduring word of God is identical with the imperishable seed or distinct from it is hard to decide. The use of different prepositions (ἐκ σπορας and δια λογου) is not a decisive argument against the first view, for it can be adequately explained by noting that Peter first expresses the matter in figurative language and then without it. Neither does a comparison with 1 John 3:9 prove the distinction, for Peter uses the word σπορα and John σπερμα. Nor is John by any means speaking of the manner in which, or the means by which, birth from God takes place, but, as the context shows, wants to assert that being born of God and sinning are absolutely mutually exclusive. Those who are born of God do not sin and cannot even sin, because the "seed" of God, which is undoubtedly the new life principle implanted by God in their hearts, remains in them. Peter, on the other hand, aims to show that those who are born again by the living and enduring word of God are called and enabled to purify themselves by obedience to the truth and practicing sincere brotherly love among themselves (1 Pet. 1:22). That which can and must manifest itself so vigorously in life must have its origin in something living and enduring. And that is the imperishable seed of the word of God. The context therefore suggests that "seed" and "word" refer to the same thing, and this hunch is reinforced by the fact that in verses 24 and 25 there is no longer any mention of the seed, and that the flesh, which like grass is perishable, is contrasted only to the word. Now inasmuch as this rebirth is to be attributed to God, who brought it about by the resurrection of Christ and by the living word, it is a rebirth to a living hope. In Peter this train of thought is as it were a single concept. The content of the new life is hope. The life of believers is totally sustained and guided by hope. Hope characterizes their whole lifestyle. In any case it is not a static possession but living, active, and strong. It reaches out and binds believers to the heavenly inheritance (1:4–13). It also enables them to live a holy life in accordance with Christ's example (1:14ff.). Rebirth-to-a-living-hope is simultaneously a rebirth to a new and holy life.

In the writings of Paul, rebirth is already implicit in the call of which he consistently speaks in an efficacious sense. For that reason the word occurs only once in his writings, in Titus 3:5, where he says that God saved us, not by our own good deeds, but by virtue of his own mercy "through the washing of regeneration and renewal by the Holy Spirit," that is, by means of the washing of the rebirth and renewal effected by the Holy Spirit. Some find here an allusion or direct reference to baptism. Others believe that the apostle represents rebirth and renewal by the Holy Spirit in the image of a bath. The matter itself is not affected by the question, but the first idea is undoubtedly Pauline. Romans 6 is proof of this. When those who are preordained by God are called in time—efficaciously, as Paul himself had experienced it on the way to Damascus—when they, as the apostle puts it elsewhere (Phil. 3:12), have been taken hold of by Jesus Christ himself, then at that very moment they obtain faith and by that faith they receive justification and the adoption as children (Rom. 3:22, 24; 4:5; 5:1; Gal. 3:26; 4:5; etc.), with the assurance of sonship by the witness of the Holy Spirit (Rom. 8:15–16; Gal. 4:6; 2 Cor. 1:22; Eph. 1:13; 4:30). But this is not the only change that occurs with them. Those who are efficaciously called are also immediately, by faith, included in fellowship with Christ. They are buried, raised (Rom. 6:3ff.) and made alive with him (Eph. 2:1, 5), and conformed to his image (Rom. 8:29–30; 1 Cor. 4:15–16; 2 Cor. 3:18; Gal. 4:19). Christ lives in them and they live in Christ (Gal. 2:20). But since by his resurrection Christ was made a life-giving Spirit (1 Cor. 15:45; 2 Cor. 3:17), one can also say that they received the Spirit of Christ (Rom. 5:5; 8:15; 1 Cor. 2:12; 2 Cor. 11:4; Gal. 3:2; 4:6; 5:18), that the Spirit lives in them (Rom. 8:11), and that they live in the Spirit and walk according to the Spirit (Rom. 8:2, 4–5, 9; etc.). By faith Christ or his Spirit is the author and origin of a new life in those who are called (Gal. 3:2; 4:6) so that now they are very different, new, and spiritual people. The old has gone; all things have become new (2 Cor. 5:17). They have passed from death into life (Eph. 2:5; 5:14; Col. 3:1). They have been crucified to the flesh and to the world (Gal. 5:24; 6:14). They themselves no longer live, but Christ lives in them (Gal. 2:20). They are new creations (2 Cor. 5:17), God's workmanship (Eph. 2:10). They walk in newness of life, are now temples of the Holy Spirit, and are led by the Holy Spirit (Rom. 6:4; 8:14; 1 Cor. 6:19; Gal. 5:25; etc.). And this entire transformation takes concrete form for them in baptism. For them this is now the great turning point in their lives, the break with all their previous conduct, complete surrender to Christ and his service. But from God's side, baptism is also the seal showing that they are taken up into communion with Christ and participate in all his benefits (Rom. 6:3ff.; Gal. 6:17). So, although the word "rebirth" may occur only once in the works of Paul, materially it is implied there in the efficacious calling by which Christ unites with himself in his death and resurrection those who have been foreknown (Rom. 6:5).

Even more than in Paul, rebirth or regeneration occupies a central place in John. For what is born of flesh is flesh (3:6) and hostile to God. Those who are born only of natural descent (1:13) are of the world (8:23; 15:19) and belong to the world (14:17, 19, 22; etc.), are from below (8:23) and from the devil (8:44), do not comprehend the light of the Logos (1:5), do not receive him (1:11), love the darkness more than the light (3:19–20), do not hear what God says (8:47), do not know God (8:19; 15:21), do not see the kingdom of God (3:3), walk in darkness (12:35), hate the light (3:20), and are the slaves of sin (8:34). Neither *can* they see the kingdom of God (3:3), believe (5:44; 12:39), hear the Word of God (8:43), come to Christ (6:44), or receive the Holy Spirit (14:17). What is needed, therefore, is rebirth or regeneration. Such an event is a γεννηθῆναι ἄνωθεν ("being born from above": 3:3; cf. 3:31; 8:23; 19:11; of God: 1:13; 1 John 3:9; etc.) of water and Spirit (John 3:5), that is, of the Spirit (3:6, 8), whose cleansing activity is symbolized by water (cf. Ezek. 36:25–27; Matt. 3:11). It is mysterious and marvelous, so that no one knows its origin or essence (John 3:8). In John this event of rebirth, therefore, is not as directly connected with the call as it is in Paul, but viewed rather as a work of the Father, who gave his own to Christ beforehand and leads them to Christ in time. Even before his incarnation, after all, Christ worked in the world as Logos (1:1–13). As light he shone in the world, but the world did not recognize him (1:5, 9–10). He came to his own, to Israel, but his own did not receive him (1:11). But even then his coming was not totally fruitless, for as many as received him already received power to become children of God. And they were such as were born of God (1:12–13; cf. 1 John 5:1). Before people came to Christ and believed in him, they were already of God (John 8:47), of the truth (18:37). They were given to the Son by the Father (6:37, 39; 17:2, 9). He drew them to Christ (6:44), and all those who thus come to Christ, far from being rejected or lost, are preserved by him for eternal life (6:39; 10:28; 17:12). Christ came to bring into the fold those who were already his sheep given him by the Father (10:27), to impel them to hear his voice and follow him, and to gather them into one flock (10:16; 11:52). He came to give those who in a sense were already the children of God (11:52), the ἐξουσια, the right and authority, to become such children [1:12], with a view toward manifesting themselves as such, as people born of God, as τεκνα του θεου, and to show this particularly in brotherly love, in love for those who are similarly born of God (1 John 5:1).

Some scholars mistakenly trace this Johannine teaching to a gnostic dualism.[24] But this dualism is not intrinsic in creation, for all things were originally created by the Logos (John 1:3). The world in general is the object of God's love (3:16). God gave his Son, not to condemn the world, but to save it (3:17; 12:47). By

---

24. J. H. Scholten, *Het Evangelie naar Johannes* (Leiden: Engels, 1864), 89ff.; H. J. Holtzmann, *Lehrbuch der neutestamentlichen Theologie* (Freiburg i.B. and Leipzig: Mohr, 1897), II, 468ff.

nature all people belong to the world, which hates the light because its works are evil (3:19–20). So then it depends on faith whether a person receives eternal life (3:15–16, 36). That faith is a "work" (ἐργον, 6:29), a coming (5:40; 6:35, 37, 44; 7:37), an act of receiving (1:11–12; 3:11ff.; 5:43), thirsting and drinking, hungering and eating (4:13–15; 6:35, 50ff.; 7:37). It does not bypass the intellect and will; in fact, only those who want to do the Father's will can know whether Jesus's teaching is from God or whether he speaks on his own authority (7:17). Unbelief, therefore, is also attributed to the stubborn will of people (5:40; 8:44). A person remains responsible for it (3:19; 9:41; 12:43; 15:22, 24). God sent his Son into the world, so that whoever believes in him should not perish but have eternal life (3:16, 36; 6:47; 20:31). By faith, therefore, one receives eternal life, passes from death into life (1 John 3:14), has overcome the evil one and the world (2:14; 5:4), and possesses the anointing of the Holy One (2:20, 27). Perdition is no longer an issue, for Christ preserves his own (John 10:28–29) and the seed of God remains in them (1 John 3:9). Yet believers are still admonished to remain in Christ and in his word (John 15:4–10; 1 John 2:24), that they may manifest the new life that is given to them in doing right (2:29), in self-purification (3:3), in self-preservation (5:18), and in love for God and one's fellow believers, for God is love (4:7–8; 5:1). For sin continues to cling to believers throughout their lives (1:8). Perfect godlikeness will be their lot only in the future (3:2).

Accordingly, in the Scriptures of the Old and New Testaments, while there is a difference between them in language and manner of presentation, there is essentially complete agreement. Whether rebirth is called the "circumcision of the heart," the giving of a new heart and a new spirit, "efficacious calling," a drawing by the Father, or birth from God, it is always in the strict sense a work of God by which a person is inwardly changed and renewed. It has its deepest cause in God's mercy; it is based on the resurrection of Christ and is brought about in communion with Christ, to whom the Word bears witness, and manifests itself in a holy life. Sometimes, as in John, the words stress that it is the principle of the new life whose consequence is the faithful hearing and reception of Jesus's words. Sometimes the other side comes more clearly to the fore. Then it is the unfolding and development of that new life that stands out. The two are most intimately intertwined, however, and belong inseparably to the one concept of regeneration. There is one verse, however, in which the word "rebirth" is given a much broader meaning. In Matt. 19:28 Jesus says that at the "renewal of all things," when the Son of Man sits on his glorious throne, the twelve disciples who had left everything behind and followed him would also sit on twelve thrones, judging the twelve tribes of Israel. The absence of all further detail is proof that the word that Jesus used in the Aramaic must have referred to something that was well known. And that was in fact the case. Old Testament prophecy, focusing on the end time, already expected a renewal of heaven and earth (Isa. 11:1–9; 65:17–25; 66:22; etc.). This expectation carried over into apocryphal literature and into the faith of the entire Jewish people.[25] The messianic kingdom would also bring with it a metamorphosis in nature and all earthly relations. Jesus confirms this expectation, as also the apostles do later (2 Pet. 3:10–13; Rev. 21:1, 5), and describes the change as a "rebirth." If we link this meaning with the above, it turns out that Scripture speaks of rebirth mainly in three ways: (1) as the principle of the new life planted by the Spirit of God in humans before they believe, (2) as the moral renewal of humans manifesting itself in a holy walk of life, and finally (3) as the restoration of the whole world to its original completeness. Thus rebirth encompasses the entire scope of re-creation from its very first beginning in the heart of people to its ultimate completion in the new heaven and new earth.

THE DOCTRINE OF REGENERATION IN CHURCH HISTORY

[439] In the first period of the church, the conversion that was triggered by the preaching of the gospel in the world brought with it a huge external change in the life of everyone who accepted that gospel. It was accompanied by, and revealed its seriousness and truth in, a complete break with either Judaism or paganism and [involved] the act of joining a poor and unsophisticated church of Christ. Baptism cut a deep trench between the past and the present. Hence many people testified again and again to the great turnabout that took place in their lives. They rejoiced in the redemption from their earlier empty walk of life and the freedom of their being children of God, in which they had now been put by Christ. Christians felt themselves to be a unique, chosen people, a new kind of people, new creatures, who in Christ had obtained communion with God and a new and authentic life.[26] Rebirth was an event that they had lived through in their own lives and souls, but the moment they began to think and write about it, the explanation was inadequate. As a rule people confined themselves in their theoretical reflections to the demands of the gospel, faith, and repentance, but did not push through to the inner, hidden workings of the Spirit that lay behind them. Over against the fatalism of paganism, they highlighted the independence and freedom of humans and downplayed their corruption. The work of salvation was confined on God's part to his calling, and when people on their part listened to that call, repented, and believed, they received in baptism the forgiveness of all their past sins. From the very beginning that baptism was central. No distinction was made between the sign and the thing signified. There was little reflection on, and theorizing about, the connection between the two. It was enough for them that the cleansing of the body was at the same time a cleansing of the heart from a bad conscience. Baptism was the great turning point, the radical change, the

---

25. F. W. Weber, *System der altsynagogalen palästinischen Theologie* (Leipzig: Dörffling & Franke, 1880), 380ff.

26. See, e.g., *Barnabas* 6, 11; Ignatius, *To the Ephesians* 19–20; idem, *To the Magnesians* 1, 9; idem, *To the Smyrneans* 4; *1 Clement* 29, 58.

decisive passage from a sinful past into the holy present. In some sense it was the rebirth itself.[27]

When, having gradually stopped being a missionary church, the church gained its members more from its own children than from among Jews and pagans and for that reason universally introduced infant baptism, people continued to maintain this close connection between baptism and regeneration but had to modify it in important ways. In the case of persons who converted to Christianity as adults, the church could maintain the requirement of preceding repentance and faith, but in the case of children born of Christian parents, this was impossible. They were therefore baptized on the basis, not of their personal faith, but of the faith of the church in whose fellowship they were born. Further, when baptism was administered to adults upon confession of faith, it was a mighty turning point on their life journey, a mortification of the old and a rising to a new and spiritual life. In the case of children, this striking significance of baptism naturally receded into the background, and the regeneration that took place in it was more or less detached from the past and the future. It was no longer a break with the old and the principle of a new life but an infusion of supernatural power that, as the children grew up, could be used for good or for ill. Finally, in looking at regeneration one could more readily focus on the negative than on the positive side of it. For since the infants were not guilty of actual sins, forgiveness, which occurs in baptism and only applies to past sins, could not bear on these either but only on original sin. However, to the extent this original sin was also viewed as guilt, or only as pollution, or even—more tenuously still—exclusively as a deficiency, the meaning of forgiveness in infant baptism shifted its focus to an infusion of a new supernatural power.

In the East, accordingly, baptismal regeneration was especially associated with the implantation of a seed of immortality.[28] In the West, though original sin was first viewed more seriously by Tertullian, Cyprian, and Augustine (et al.), it gradually assumed a negative character as a result of the doctrine of the superadded gift. Hence regeneration lost its real meaning and changed into justification. The doctrine of regeneration in Catholicism, consequently, took the following form. To adults after the seven preparations, and to children of believers without any preparation (excepting the negative one of not posing an obstacle), the church, in the sacrament of baptism administered by the priest, imparts infused grace, both justifying and sanctifying grace. This grace delivers the baptized person from guilt and eternal punishment insofar as they rest on him or her on account of past sins, and mortifies the original pollution insofar as it restrains lust and only allows it to

---

27. *Barnabas* 11; *2 Clement* 6; Shepherd of Hermas, *Mandate* 4.3. By restricting the matter of forgiveness given in baptism to past sins, it became very difficult to learn what to do with sins committed after baptism. This issue will be dealt with later. For now, cf. K. Lake, "Zonde en Doop," *Theologisch Tijdschrift* 43 (1909): 538–44.

28. P. Gennrich, *Wiedergeburt*, 95; R. H. Hofmann, *Symboliek of stelselmatige uiteenzetting van het onderscheidene Christelijke kerkgenootschappen en voornaamste sekten* (Utrecht: Kemink en Zoon, 1861), 187.

continue as a stimulus to sin. Concretely, it consists in a divine quality inhering in the soul, a quality that is materially identical with the superadded gift that has been lost. Hence, it fashions a person into conformity to God, incorporates one into the church as the body of Christ and hence into Christ himself, and enables him or her to perform supernaturally good works and to merit eternal life. Aside from a number of extraordinary cases, this infused grace can only be obtained through the sacrament of the church. Baptism is therefore strictly necessary for salvation and people, consequently, are absolutely dependent on the church and its priest. This is true not only at the beginning but throughout life. For not only do they need the sacrament of penance for venial sins committed later, but they can also again lose the grace received in baptism as a result of mortal sins and regain it only through the mediation of the church. Regeneration is not an enduring good but is continually dependent on human effort, both for its existence and development.[29]

[440] By asserting the principle that humans are justified by grace through faith alone, the Reformation pushed the church aside as mediatrix of salvation and restored the direct connection between the soul and God, subject only to the mediation of Christ and his Word. Consequently, it gave Scripture priority over the church, and the Word priority over the sacrament. But this principle brought with it special dangers and difficulties. For the Anabaptists extended this principle to the point where they completely rejected the church and the sacraments as means of grace, made regeneration as new life dependent on an active faith and repentance, and therefore admitted people to baptism only on the basis of a personal confession. Luther then backtracked halfway, and Lutherans later unanimously taught that the sacrament indeed presupposes faith and repentance but that, since in the case of children this cannot be expected, baptism operating through the power of the Spirit, which unites itself with the water of baptism, confers on them in advance the grace that the sacrament actually demands and presupposes. Hence, in their polemic against Anabaptists, they turned the argument around. Instead of deciding that infants, inasmuch as they cannot as yet exercise faith and repentance, had to remain unbaptized, they reasoned that they in fact had to be baptized *in order* to obtain faith and salvation. "Therefore they must be baptized in order that faith and salvation may follow."[30] According to Titus 3:5, after all, baptism is the washing of regeneration, which is especially for children because as a means of grace the Word cannot yet be effective.[31] The grace granted in baptism consists in the gift of faith, the forgiveness of sins, and eternal life, and

29. The Council of Trent, sess. VI, 4ff.; Roman Catechism, II, ch. 2, qu. 25ff. Ed. note: The post–Vatican II edition titled *The Roman Catechism* (trans. Robert I. Bradley, SJ, and Eugene Kevane [Boston: Daughters of St. Paul, 1985]) drops the enumeration of the introduction so that ch. 1 begins the section on baptism. In this annotation, the proper reference would be II, ch. 3, qu. 26ff.; H. Bavinck, *Reformed Dogmatics*, III, 514–17 (#416).

30. J. Gerhard, *Loci theol.*, 1.XX, 195.

31. Ibid., 1.XX, 186.

it is entirely adequate for children who die in infancy. But in the case of children who grow up to the years of discretion, that grace is tested. For when a person does not appropriate this grace by acts of faith and repentance, it is lost. And even when, through faith and repentance, that person experiences rebirth in the sense of renewal, this new life, along with all the grace received, remains amissible to the end. Thus also for children as a rule (exceptions were made for extraordinary cases),[32] Lutherans on their part made regeneration dependent on baptism and, by implication, on the church. They, too, break up the continuity of the spiritual life by consistently making rebirth amissible and by positing a distinction and a dualism between the primary regeneration, which precedes faith and repentance, and the subsequent secondary regeneration (renewal). In so doing, they ran the danger of reducing the former to a power that enabled people to believe but that left it in doubt whether they would ever in fact believe.[33]

The theologians of the Reformed persuasion naturally faced the same difficulty and, in addition, found no solution that was satisfactory to everyone. Like the gospel when it was preached in the beginning, and every religious movement that later surfaced within the boundaries of Christianity, the Reformation also had to turn first to adults and hence make the preaching of faith and repentance a priority. By that faith one received regeneration: the new spiritual life. "Our regeneration by faith" is the title of the third chapter of book III of Calvin's *Institutes*. But by taking this route, one got into difficulties with the children of believers and their baptism. To escape them, theologians adopted a variety of approaches. They grounded the baptism of the children of the church in the faith of the parents or of the church, in the faith children would exercise in the future, or in a largely undefined covenant of grace in which children were included with their parents. Another approach, illustrated by the examples of John and Jesus, held that the Holy Spirit can work in the hearts of children before they become self-conscious and before their birth. Others based it on the reality, assumed to exist by faith in the promise of the covenant of grace, that the Holy Spirit had wrought in their hearts an established disposition of faith and hence of rebirth (in the narrow sense, as the very first life principle).[34] In the works of theologians, Calvin among them,[35] several of these lines of argument occur side by side, and not one of them is made dominant.

32. Ibid., 1.XX, 236.

33. H. F. F. Schmid, *Die Dogmatik der evangelisch-lutherischen Kirche*, 7th ed. (Gütersloh: Bertelsmann, 1893), 54.

34. In this connection compare the history-of-dogma study of G. Kramer, a doctoral student in theology at the Free University, on the connection between baptism and regeneration, *Het verband van doop en wedergeboorte*, introduced by A. Kuyper (Breukelen: De Vecht, 1897). This study, though very important, is overly controlled by the attempt to turn Reformed theologians as much as possible into proponents of a prebaptismal regeneration. Admittedly this view is cautiously expressed from time to time by some Reformed theologians, but it is certainly not shared by all.

35. Occasionally Calvin says that the children of believers are already made holy by a supernatural grace before baptism (*Institutes*, IV.xvi.31), that the seed of faith and repentance is present in them by a hidden

The last-mentioned opinion of a prebaptismal regeneration receives additional support from the thought that the moment faith and repentance are considered in connection with the deep corruption of human nature, one has to go back to a secret internal operation of the Holy Spirit from which they could arise and in light of which they could be explained. In that connection regeneration and repentance had to be distinguished, at least logically, and the former placed before the latter. But theologians had scarcely expressed the opinion that in the case of infants regeneration precedes baptism before still other objections arose. No one dared to say that this was always and without exception the case; theologians therefore confined themselves to saying that this was usually how it happened. Moreover, one could still with some ground say this of children of the covenant who died in infancy, but the confession of election already made many people speak with caution concerning these children. And with respect to children who stayed alive and grew up, reality frequently offered a different picture from what their baptism would lead one to expect. Theologians, in any case, were forced to adopt the restriction that only elect children were as a rule regenerated before their baptism. And in view of the fact that many baptized persons only come to faith and repentance at a much later age and after years of living in bondage to sin, even this last opinion was too bold for many people. They therefore confined themselves to the general statement that regeneration could take place before, during, or at some time after, baptism.[36]

---

operation of the Holy Spirit (ibid., IV.xvi.20), that the grace of regeneration comes to them by virtue of the promise, and that baptism follows by way of a seal (G. Kramer, *Het verband van doop en wedergeboorte*, 145). But it cannot be said with certainty precisely what the force of these expressions is. Caution is needed, for Calvin also says that his own baptism was of no benefit to him so long as he neglected the promise offered to him in baptism (*Institutes*, IV.xv.17); that though God is not dependent on external means, he ordinarily binds us to them (ibid., IV.i.5, 16, 19); that for those who hear the gospel, the word of God is the "only seed of spiritual regeneration" (ibid., IV.xvi.18); that infant baptism requires no greater force than that it confirms the covenant of grace and that the further meaning of the sacrament follows later (ibid., IV.xvi.21); that for adults God's word is the incorruptible seed of rebirth, but "when we are not old enough to be taught, God keeps his own timetable of regeneration" (ibid., IV.xvi.31). Also see P. J. Kromsigt, "Iets over Calvijns doopsbeschouwing," *Troffel en Zwaard* 8 (1905): 102–6.

36. Reformed theologians unanimously agreed on the following points: (1) that the benefits of the covenant of grace were usually distributed by God in connection with the means of grace; hence regeneration is in connection with the Word; (2) that God, however, is not bound to these means, and hence he could also take an unusual route and regenerate and save especially young children without the Word; (3) that he, as a rule, worked that way in the case of children of believers who were taken by death before reaching the age of discretion; (4) that the baptized children of believers who were part of the life of the congregation had to be considered elect and regenerate until the contrary was evident from what they said and did; and (5) that this, however, was a judgment of charity, which must indeed be the rule for our attitude toward these children but cannot claim to be infallible. On the other hand, from the very beginning there was disagreement over whether the children of believers, to the extent that they were elect, were regenerated already before, or in, or only after baptism. Some—like Martyr, à Lasco, Dathenus, Alting, Witsius, Voetius, Mastricht—tended to favor the first view. But the majority—Calvin, Beza, Musculus, Ursinus, de Brès, Acronius, Cloppenburg, Walaeus, Maccovius, Bucanus, Turretin, Heidegger, and others—left the question undecided. See also the work of G. Kramer, *Het verband van doop en wedergeboorte*. There is disagreement about the position in the liturgical form for baptism

But beyond this, if regeneration occurred in infancy before or after baptism, in what did it consist? Most Reformed theologians maintained the continuity of the spiritual life. Rebirth in infancy, they said, planted that vital principle in the heart that was continually kept alive by God, later manifested itself in deeds of faith and repentance, and then continued in sanctification. But a fairly large group of Anglican theologians gradually began to make a distinction between "baptismal regeneration" and the later renewal that followed upon faith and repentance. By the former they meant the infusion of spiritual power that in later years enabled the baptized to believe and repent and was therefore dependent on faith and repentance for its continuation.[37] And when the church increasingly fell into decline and conformity to the world, many sought to rescue themselves by making a sharp distinction between an "internal" and an "external" covenant of grace and by reducing the sacraments to signs and seals of the latter. Baptism neither secured nor presupposed regeneration but only included children in the covenant of grace to the extent that they received through it an assurance of God's universal love and goodwill and were invited and obligated to accept the gospel and to turn to God in repentance.[38] In that way, just as in Methodism, Pietism, and rationalism, the relationship between regeneration and faith was again reversed. Human

[of the Dutch Reformed Church]; see G. Oorthuys, "Het gebed vóór den doop in ons doopsformulier," *Troffel en Zwaard* 10 (1907): 351–74.

37. According to G. Voetius, *Select. disp.*, II, 409, certain British theologians (Davenant, Ward, et al.) taught that baptism conferred grace on all children because they were not able to pose an obstacle to it. But children received this grace, consisting in the forgiveness of sins and regeneration, according to their ability to receive it as little children, not in accordance with adult rationality. Accordingly, it did not lead them with infallible certainty to salvation, but obligated and empowered them to believe and repent at a later age. Hence these theologians made a specific distinction between sacramental regeneration and spiritual regeneration. In Tractarianism, this view was revived by Gosham, Denison, Pusey, Newman, and others. Cf. J. C. Ryle, *Knots Untied,* 11th ed. (London: William Hunt, 1886), 132–96; J. Buchanan, *The Office and Work of the Holy Spirit* (1842; repr., Edinburgh: Banner of Truth Trust, 1984), 230ff.; R. Buddensieg, "Traktarianismus," in *PRE*[3], XX, 46–47.

38. In the early years, the "internal" and "external" covenants of grace were not yet very clearly distinguished— in any case, not in these words. Hoping to be able to unite the covenant of grace with election, theologians regarded the fact of children being born within the circle of the covenant of grace as presumptive proof of their election and held to the judgment of charity. But materially the distinction was present from the beginning, in fact already in Calvin (cf. G. Kramer, *Het verband van doop en wedergeboorte*, 119). Among the grounds for infant baptism, the following were also important: that the children of believers belong to the covenant; that they are holy, separated from the world; that they are baptized on the basis of the faith of the parents or of the church; and that belonging to the covenant of grace is sufficient ground for baptism (ibid.). Added to this is that the benefits the children of believers receive were viewed and described in very different ways. It was said that the children belonged to the covenant of grace, to the church, to the body of Christ; that they were holy in an objective or also a subjective sense; that they were offered or granted grace, or the promise, or the adoption, or the right to grace; and that they had or could have the Holy Spirit, the Spirit of regeneration, the seed of regeneration, the disposition for the faith, the seed of faith and repentance (G. Kramer, *Het verband van doop en wedergeboorte*, 143, 161, 166, 169, 171, 172, 204, 223, 237, 255, 259, 319, 333). When in the conflict over predestination the distinction between the internal and external covenant of grace was formalized, many authors soon made use of it in their defense of infant baptism (see Donteclock, Damman, Trigland, Gomarus, Maccovius, Voetius, H. Alting; in G. Kramer, *Het verband van doop en wedergeboorte*, 250, 265, 267, 268, 270, 274, 279, 281, 324, 325, 330). In the eighteenth century some theologians took another step in this direction

beings were obligated, and, according to the increasingly prevailing view, also still possessed the moral strength to believe and repent. The "you must" ("du sollst") presupposed and demanded the "you can" ("du kannst"). By that faith a person was then regenerated and amended his or her life. In the Enlightenment, finally, people got to the point where they preferred to avoid the term "rebirth" altogether. "Enlightenment," "culture," "development," "moral nurture," and "amendment of life," it was said, were greatly superior terms and also materially much more apt.

MODERN REINTERPRETATIONS OF REGENERATION

[441] But after the Enlightenment had exchanged the term "rebirth" for that of moral amendment, it was picked up again by idealistic philosophy. Just as this philosophy sought to disentangle itself everywhere from the rule of the intellect and with the aid of speculative reason to track down the deeper meaning in nature and history, so it also strove to bring out the hidden idea inherent in Christian dogmas. Accordingly, words like "Trinity," "incarnation," "atonement," "redemption," and similarly the word "regeneration" or "rebirth" returned in the vocabulary of Kant and Fichte, Schelling and Hegel, and later also in that of Schopenhauer and von Hartmann.[39] Of course, they filled these terms with a meaning that was far removed from the view of the church. Yet this tie-in with Christian truths remains very remarkable. With respect to the term "rebirth," what came out in it was the conviction that the moral corruption of humans was much more deep-rooted than in the intellect alone. There is in human beings "a bent toward evil," and therefore no enlightenment and development was sufficient for their restoration; what was needed was nothing less than a radical reformation, a revolution of their minds, a total reversal in the maxims of their lives and conduct. Kant and Fichte (in his first period) considered such a revolution possible by a free intelligible act of the will. But later, when idealistic philosophy developed in a pantheistic direction, such a rebirth of humans was viewed simultaneously as their own deed and a work of God: it was a "divine transmutation."[40]

Similar thoughts also occur in later philosophers[41] and have in recent years been developed especially by Rudolf Eucken. According to this philosopher, the

---

and viewed baptism exclusively as a sacrament of the external covenant (cf. ch. 10, below, "The Spirit's Means of Grace: Baptism").

39. The doctrine of redemption held by all these philosophers has already been briefly described in H. Bavinck, *Reformed Dogmatics*, III, 540–55 (##423–26).

40. F. W. Schelling, *Ausgewählte Werke*, 4 vols. (Darmstadt: Wissenschaftliche Buchgesellschaft, 1968), IV, 332; idem, "Philosophische Untersuchungen über das Wesen der menschlichen Freiheit und die damit zusammenhängenden Gegenstände" (*Werke*, I/7, 388). Profound also is Goethe's saying in the poem "A Holy Longing": "And as long as you do not possess it / this: die and be reborn / You are only a troubled guest on the dark earth" (translation of Henry Hatfield, *Goethe, a Critical Introduction* [Cambridge: Harvard University Press, 1963], 118).

41. Cf. H. Lotze, *Mikrokosmos*, 3 vols. (Leipzig: S. Hirzel, 1872–78), III, 361ff.; ed. note: ET: *Microcosmus*, trans. E. Hamilton and E. E. Constance Jones (New York: Scribner & Welford, 1886); M. Carrière, *De*

spiritual life in humans nevertheless plays a unique role. It manifests itself in the ideals of the true, the good, and the beautiful, which it shapes; in the norms in conformity to which it seeks to develop; and in the profuse cultural labors on which it puts its stamp. All these manifestations prove the independence, unity, and freedom of the life of the spirit vis-à-vis the mechanism of nature but at the same time demonstrate the rights of religion. For religion is not a means to happiness but the "self-preservation" and "self-assertion" of the life of the spirit in the power of God. "Religion rests on the presence of a Divine Life in man; it unfolds itself through the seizure of this Life as one's own nature. Religion, too, subsists in the fact that man in the inmost foundation of his own being is raised into the Divine Life, and participates in the Divine Nature."[42]

When Christianity acts as a religion of redemption, it by implication assumes the existence of a sharp contrast between what humans are and what they ought to be. It expresses their inability to reach the summit by gradual self-improvement, and proclaims a transformation and elevation by an immediate intervention of the divine. And this is confirmed by the general experience of the spiritual life. For it shows "how the Spiritual Life is unable to find its necessary self-reliance in the world of ordinary experience; we have seen a breach between genuine spirituality and the world taking place; and we have seen how the effects of all this carry a new world within themselves. In spiritual things every pathway of man leads to a Yea through a Nay, and all toil is in vain without an inner elevation through the energy of an Absolute Life."[43]

In theology the concept of regeneration was again restored by Schleiermacher. In his thought the concept even became the center of the redemptive order for religion. Specifically, Christianity was not a revealed doctrine, nor a moral code that enjoins activity upon us, but life, personal life in communion with God. In keeping with this, redemption consisted objectively in the impartation of the holiness and blessedness of Christ's God-consciousness, to which regeneration then corresponds subjectively, with the assumption of humans into living fellowship with Christ. When Christ encounters us and vigorously exerts his influence in us, the previously feeble and oppressed God-consciousness is raised up, reinforced, and brought to dominion in us. Within us there then arises a new religious personality who breaks with the old state, starts a new life, and develops and completes it in sanctification. Regeneration, accordingly, is "the turning point at which the earlier life as it were breaks off and the new begins." Schleiermacher's virtue is that he again included regeneration in dogmatics, understood by it a religious-ethical process of change, and also related it to the person of Christ. But in the process he was not able to disentangle himself completely from the influence of pantheistic philosophy. This

zedelijke wereldorde, trans. P. C. van Oosterzee (Utrecht: Kemink, 1880), 328; I. de Bussy, *Ethische Idealisme* (Amsterdam: J. H. de Bussy, 1875), 39ff.

42. R. Eucken, *The Truth of Religion,* trans. W. T. Jones (New York: G. P. Putnam's Sons, 1911), 206.

43. Ibid., 240; cf. also, idem, *Hauptprobleme der Religionsphilosophie der Gegenwart,* 2nd ed. (Berlin: Reuther & Reichard, 1907), 83ff.; 95ff.

is apparent, in the first place, in the fact that, in connection with his view of sin as sensuousness and of Christ's appearance as the rebirth of the human race, he views the rebirth of the individual as a moment, be it a very significant moment, in the process in which the human spirit, in fellowship with God, elevates itself above and frees itself from the dominion of the sensuous nature. On the other hand, this again carries within itself the consequence that justification is made dependent on repentance. The assumption into a fellowship of life with Christ, which is regeneration, has two dimensions. On the one hand, it brings about a change in one's relationship to God, which is justification; on the other hand it consists in a change of life and is called conversion (further differentiated into repentance and faith). The moment a person is reborn, repenting and believing, one no longer as in the past faces God as the Holy and Righteous One but experiences his love and grace and loses the consciousness of guilt and doom by which one was burdened in the past. Regeneration includes a change of consciousness and in that respect is called justification. But in Schleiermacher's doctrine, there is no room for an objective justification that precedes conversion, is based on the righteousness of Christ, and is accepted and enjoyed by faith alone.[44]

It was "Mediating Theology" (*Vermittelungstheologie*)[45] that sought to make provision for the first void by taking sin more seriously (Julius Müller) and by doing more justice to the totally unique divine nature of Christ (I. A. Dorner). But it remained nevertheless true to Schleiermacher's basic idea that Christianity had primarily introduced a new life. It worked this out by saying that what Christ's coming did for the human race, regeneration does for the individual. Christ as Logos was already the life and light of human beings and by his incarnation and further by his resurrection made this life the possession of all humanity. As the central individual he became the head of a new humanity. But this life must also be transplanted from him into the individual human being, which is what happens in regeneration. After Christ by his resurrection and ascension has himself been perfected, he by his Spirit successively guides the individual, humanity, and the entire cosmos into communion with his divine-human life. He expands his individual life to the dimensions of a universal divine-human life. Regeneration, accordingly, though it does not constitute a transubstantiation, is nevertheless a representation of the divine human personality of Christ in us. By it the personal life of human beings is transformed into a divine-human life—life in its loftiest and fullest reality. And when God looks thus at a person in Christ, incorporated into his fellowship and a participant in his life, he pronounces him or her righ-

---

44. F. Schleiermacher, *The Christian Faith,* ed. H. R. MacIntosh and J. S. Steward (Edinburgh: T&T Clark, 1928), 106–9; J. H. T. Weerts, "Schleiermachers Lehre von der Wiedergeburt in ihrem Verhältnis zu Kants Begriff des intelligibelen Charakters," *Neue kirchliche Zeitschrift* 20 (1909): 400–415.

45. Ed. note: Mediating theology, inspired by Schleiermacher, proceeded from the subjectivity of faith and attempted to join Christian faith with the modern scientific worldview of its "cultured despisers." Cf. H. Bavinck, *Reformed Dogmatics,* I, 49 (#9), 127 (#39), 166 (#51), 519–20 (#135), 522–24 (#136).

teous.[46] In this connection some thinkers even took a theosophical direction and attributed to regeneration a substantial effect on the whole person. Luther had already stated that the real enjoyment of the flesh and blood of Christ in the Lord's Supper also renews the body, and that the water of baptism prepares the body for eternal life. Originally these expressions could indeed be given a good sense, but in the circles of Pietism, particularly by Bengel and his pupil Fr. Chr. Oetinger, they were later construed very realistically. By his suffering and death, Christ—it was said—was elevated to become the prince of life, a high priest according to the law of an incorruptible life, and as such possesses the power, by his blood (which he took to heaven with him and with which he sprinkles his own), to impart spirit, life, and glory to a fallen, carnal, and unspiritual nature. Regeneration, accordingly, consists in a process in which an unspiritual, carnal, sin-corrupted, and worldly person, is totally spiritualized, divinized, and glorified in spirit, soul, and body. Serving as a means to that end is the Word, but especially the sacrament, for in the sacrament Christ himself, with his flesh and blood, is present and creates in us an entirely new person, not only spiritually but also physically. Even now already there is being formed in us "a highly refined spiritual body" that will one day manifest itself in its full glory, for corporeality is the end of God's ways and works.[47]

These ideas, which lived on in pietistic circles, again came to the fore in the theosophical speculations of Schelling, von Baader, Hamberger, and also registered with a number of meditation theologians. In Rothe, regeneration begins with conversion, which is a work of divine grace but also a free human act. In conversion, human beings align themselves with God, lose their consciousness of guilt, and are not only justified but also gain a new life. Regeneration consists in a person's becoming spirit: achieving an absolute union between thought and existence, idea and nature. It starts at a certain central point in one's personality but continues, especially under the influence of the sacraments, in a process of spiritualization until a person's entire organism is spiritualized, and Christ or the Spirit completely indwells him or her.[48] According to Franz Delitzsch, regeneration consists in a work of Christ by which he, who by his resurrection became a life-giving spirit, transforms the antidivine being of human persons into divine being and not only

---

46. Cf. H. Martensen, *Christian Dogmatics,* trans. W. Urwick (Edinburgh: T&T Clark, 1871), 360ff.; F. A. Lange, *Geschichte des Materialismus und Kritik seiner Bedeutung in der Gegenwart,* 8th ed. (Leipzig: Baedekker, 1908), II, 921ff., 945ff.; L. Schöberlein, *Prinzip und System der Dogmatik* (Heidelberg: C. Winter, 1881), 652, 811. In that case, the emphasis lies, as it did in ancient times in Greek theology, more on the person than on the work of Christ, more on his incarnation than on his atoning death, more on what he is than on what he does. The same idea controls many Anglican theologians. Cf. Ch. Gore, *The Incarnation of the Son of God* (London: Murray, 1909); Cf. H. Bavinck, *Reformed Dogmatics,* III, 380–85 (#387).

47. J. A. Bengel, *Gnomon of the New Testament,* 5 vols. (Edinburgh: T&T Clark, 1877), on Hebrews 12:24; F. C. Oetinger, *Die Theologie aus der Idee des Lebens abgeleitet und auf sechs Hauptstücke zurückgeführt* (Stuttgart: J. F. Steinkopf, 1852), 284ff.; Cf. A. Ritschl, *Geschichte des Pietismus in der reformierten Kirche* (Bonn: A. Marcus, 1880), III, 79ff.; P. Gennrich, *Wiedergeburt,* 186ff.

48. R. Rothe, *Theologische Ethik,* 2nd rev. ed., 5 vols. (Wittenberg: Zimmermann, 1867–71), 742–76.

changes our consciousness by faith but also imparts to us his spirit, soul, and flesh, so that around our believing ego a new human-in-process-of-becoming is formed who participates in the divine nature. Regeneration, therefore, is simultaneously an ethical and a substantial restoration of human beings.[49] In this view, which as such already strikes one as strange, the Reformation doctrine of justification by faith is not given its due and is even switched onto a Roman Catholic track.

Given this defect of the Mediating Theology, which took its cue from Schleiermacher, Ritschl tried to compensate for it when he again put justification into the limelight, conceived it as a synthetic judgment, and regarded it as a possession of the church.[50] Among the objections that in time were raised against his system, however, was that the individual subjects, in other words, regeneration and mysticism, did not come into their own. Justification, after all, at least the justification that is once for all pronounced on the church in the gospel of Jesus, becomes a person's own possession when—usually in the way of a Christian upbringing—one joins the church, lets go of all distrust toward God by trusting in the person of Jesus, and in one's moral calling makes the ultimate goal of God (the kingdom of God) one's own life task. That's really all that can be said about it, for a penitential struggle (German: *Busskampf*) is far from being necessary for everyone and remains an exception, and the story of how a person comes to the faith is too individual for it to be closely examined and objectively described. It should be sufficient, therefore, to say that those who join the church are justified and born again. The two are essentially identical.[51]

Herrmann similarly equates regeneration with the experience of justification in the faith. In his book *Der Verkehr des Christen mit Gott*,[52] he aims to eliminate all mysticism from religion. A Christian's communion with God, he argues, in no way consists in any stirrings and impressions of the emotions. If that were the case, such feelings would have to be sought out and cultivated, and the rest of life, such as one's work and occupation, would be slighted as being inferior. Furthermore, religion itself would be robbed of its content, for all mysticism is in the nature of the case monotonous. Communion with God is objectively available to us in the person of Christ. In him, and in him alone, God is present to us, comes to us, makes himself known as a God of grace who forgives sins,

---

49. F. Delitzsch, *A System of Biblical Psychology*, trans. R. E. Wallis, 2nd ed. (Edinburgh: T&T Clark, 1875), 381–417. Related ideas on rebirth also occur, in varying degrees, in J. T. Beck, *Vorlesungen über christliche Glaubenslehre*, 2 vols. (Gütersloh: Bertelsmann, 1896–97), I, 250ff.; *Rocholl, "Spiritualismus und Realismus," *Neue kirchliche Zeitschrift* 9 (1898); *Rocholl, "Umkehr zum Idealismus," *Neue kirchliche Zeitschrift* 15 (1904): 622ff.; K. Lechler, *Die biblische Lehre vom heiligen Geiste*, 3 vols. (Gütersloh: Bertelsmann, 1899–1904), I, 79ff.; II, 360ff.

50. Cf. H. Bavinck, *Reformed Dogmatics*, III, 590 (#432).

51. A. Ritschl, *The Christian Doctrine of Justification and Reconciliation*, trans. H. R. Mackintosh and A. B. Macaulay (Clifton, NJ: Reference Book Publishers, 1966), III, 170ff., 590ff.; idem, *Unterricht in der christlichen Religion,* 3rd ed. (Bonn: A. Marcus, 1886), 36ff., 46ff.; cf. also P. Conrad, "Begriff und Bedeutung der Gemeinde in Ritschls Theologie," *Theologische Studien und Kritiken* 84/2 (1911): 230–92.

52. W. Herrmann, *Der Verkehr des Christen mit Gott*, 6th ed. (Stuttgart: Cotta, 1908), 276ff., 280ff.

enters into communion with us, and effects our moral deliverance. Another kind of communion with God, apart from the historical Christ, does not exist, nor is it needed. If we let the image of Jesus have its impact on our inner lives, if in his person we experience God's forgiving love by faith, we at that very moment and as a result of it become totally new people. We are freed from feelings of guilt, fear, and dread, are assured of God's love, and calmly and courageously proceed to do our moral work. Herrmann, accordingly, does not deny that a transformation has to occur in the "natural man." On the contrary, he emphasizes personal experience and one's personal religious life as strongly as he can. But this transformation is brought about in us by looking up to Jesus, by faith in the love of God revealed in him. A different rebirth, distinct from the one just described and concurrent to it, consisting for example in our infusion of real power in baptism, does not exist. Faith naturally carries with it rebirth, a new mind-set, and new courage. Regeneration, in fact, is nothing other than faith.[53]

For this reason Kaftan removes regeneration as well as justification from the discussion of the order of salvation and restores it to the work of Christ. He thus considers regeneration as a benefit objectively prepared for the church in Christ's resurrection. It is only by faith in the resurrection that the individual person gains regeneration.

REGENERATION: VARIOUS VIEWS

[442] The relation to justification, though very important, is definitely not the only issue that presents itself in connection with regeneration. Those who expect the problems that occur in this locus and the solutions offered for them to be significantly less numerous than those occurring in connection with the dogmas of the Trinity, the incarnation, atonement, and so forth are in for severe disappointment. The diversity of opinions is so immense that it is hard to gain a clear overview of it. In the first period, when Christianity made its debut in the world, people held to a simple sequence: faith and repentance opened the way to the benefits of the forgiveness of sins and eternal life. In this connection, they simply aligned themselves with the preaching of John the Baptist, Jesus, and the apostles. And even now that is still the way the public proclamation of the gospel of Christ proceeds both in the church and on the mission field. It cannot come with the demand of regeneration, but can only call adults to faith and repentance. Every new religious movement, such as the Reformation and later Methodism, therefore begins with the same invitation: as soon and as long as the gospel has to do with adults, faith and repentance are in the foreground. Calvin even made that his starting point and in the order of redemption placed regeneration after faith. Numerous theologians, in all modalities and every period, refrained from following that pattern in the order of redemption. After treating the calling, they proceed to deal with the loci of faith and repentance.

53. J. Kaftan, *Dogmatik* (Tübingen: Mohr, 1901), 54–55.

But as soon as the church has gained an enduring place in the world and awakens to the need for reflection, two objections to this order present themselves. The first derives from the position of the children of believers, who cannot be counted as Gentiles, yet in their infancy cannot in fact believe and repent either. If they all remained alive, the difficulty could be somewhat relieved by the consideration that they would later have the opportunity to repent and believe. But this is not the case: thousands upon thousands of infants die before, during, or shortly after birth.[54] And not only Christian sentiment, but also the scriptural doctrine of the covenant of grace in which not only believers themselves but also their children are included, resists the idea that these children are all lost. Now if no one can enter the kingdom of heaven except by faith and repentance, one is compelled to make a distinction between faith as capacity and faith as act, between conversion in a passive and an active sense—in other words, between regeneration and repentance (faith), and in the order of redemption to have the former precede the latter.

Added to this, there was still another consideration that drove people in the same direction. As long as the church lives by the simple preaching of the gospel and remains a missionary church, it can acquiesce in the calling to faith and repentance. In that situation it confines itself to perceptible phenomena and feels no need to penetrate the underlying reasons for these phenomena. But that cannot last long. Reflection, specifically religious reflection and not just curiosity, inevitably awakens. The Christian church, after all, was convinced from the outset that the salvation it had received was a gift of God. The moment it began to try to account for this fact and to examine Scripture more deeply on this point, it could no longer simply consider faith and repentance as human acts but had to answer the question of what lay behind these acts, whether they originated in the human will or in the grace of God. It was all the harder pressed to answer it because, both inside and outside the church, it saw so many people grow up who never came to faith and repentance. At that point there was a parting of the ways. Some people—all the followers of Pelagius of earlier and later date—maintained that after the call from God the way of salvation started with human beings, with *their* acts of faith and repentance, and that these acts therefore ultimately originated in their free will. But Augustine and his followers felt compelled by the witness of Scripture and their own experience to trace the acts of faith and repentance to a prior, internal, and efficacious grace of God, in other words, to regeneration. Thus, not only in the case of infants but equally in the case of adults, regeneration came to be placed prior to faith and repentance.

---

54. Although in recent decades mortality rates are regularly going down for all age groups and in all civilized countries, in the Netherlands the rate in 1908 for infants less than one year old was still 12.48 per 100 born alive, and for children 1–4 it was 15.4 per thousand. See a study on infant mortality made by H. W. Methorst, "Eenige cijfers betreffende de sterfte van kinderen beneden hat jaar in Nederland," *Economist* 58 (Sept. 1909): 665, as well as the article "Sterblichkeit," in *Meyers kleines Konversations-Lexicon*, 3 vols. (Leipzig: Bibliographisches Institut, 1892–93).

In reality, however, this separation was far more complex than the contrasting principles would lead one to expect. Many theologians were intent on mediation and moved in this direction by an ethical interest. For if regeneration were totally detached from faith and repentance, it apparently could only consist in a magical infusion of spiritual energy completely independent of the human consciousness and will. For this reason, numerous theologians still today, as many did in the past, place regeneration *after* faith and repentance and make it more or less dependent on them. In that case one naturally faces the question of how salvation can be said to be a work of God from start to finish if faith and repentance at the same time have to be free acts of human beings. One may try to resolve the difficulty by pointing out that the unconverted can still attend church, listen to the Word of God, and examine the Scriptures. They then can do their best ("do what is in them to do"), for they still possess the ability to apply themselves to grace or the possibility of refraining from active resistance. Finally, in the call or in baptism, they then receive the power to believe if they want to. Alternatively, one could say that there is no opposition or even distinction between the divine and the human activity, since the two are one and the same thing viewed from two perspectives. It hardly needs saying, however, that all these proposed attempts at reconciliation are futile. If God and human beings are distinct though not separate, one always has to face the question: at the end of all the interactions, who makes the final decision? Who ultimately settles the issue? If it is the human person, then Pelagius is fundamentally correct and the decision concerning what is most important in human history—namely, eternal salvation—rests in human hands. If, however, the last word rests with God and his omnipotent grace, one sides with Augustine and accepts a preceding rebirth (internal grace) in which the human person is passive. In other words, by placing regeneration after faith and repentance, one does not escape the problem but wraps oneself in an insoluble contradiction.

The same thing is true if in the case of the children of believers one wants to hold on to regeneration's dependence on faith and repentance. Of course, in that case it will not do to assume a rebirth in the heart of those children accomplished by the Holy Spirit apart from all means. Neither can one say that the Holy Spirit employs the Word in moving young covenant children to faith and repentance, those who have not yet reached the age of discretion, for "this cannot be accomplished verbally with infants but only with adults who have reached the age of discretion."[55] On this point, accordingly, all Catholics, Lutherans, Anabaptists, and others are agreed. The last group remains consistent even to the point of rejecting infant baptism, though as a rule it assumes the salvation of children who die in infancy and in so doing weakens the doctrine of original sin. But Catholics and Lutherans looked for a solution precisely in infant baptism. While this baptism presupposes nothing, at least nothing more than external privileges (such as being born of Christian parents), it produces much: incorporation into Christ and his

---

55. J. Gerhard, *Loci theol.*, 1.XX, 186.

body. However, by taking this position they have in a questionable way changed the character of the sacrament. For while the sacrament was instituted as a *sign* and *seal* of the covenant of grace and of participation in its benefits, baptism serves here to introduce children into that covenant and to gain for them the benefits of that covenant. In this process, baptism acquired a power that it cannot possess of itself but that is conferred on it by the Word and Spirit that mysteriously united themselves with the water of baptism. This scenario bears a much more magical character than that which the creators of it sought to escape on ethical grounds. Given this view, it is hard to see why baptism, if it really bestows grace, could not be administered to the children of unbelievers. But this is further than people were prepared to go. Of the original rule that faith and repentance need to precede baptism, Rome has even kept a memory in the doctrine that at least no obstacle is to be posed to the reception of supernatural grace.

Lutherans meanwhile maintained that while the young children of believers do not bring faith to their baptism and were not baptized on the basis of their parents' faith, the Holy Spirit nevertheless worked that faith in their heart by baptism in union with the Word so that they accepted Christ and obtained the forgiveness of sins and eternal life. Inasmuch as they accorded logical priority to faith and made regeneration second, they insisted that faith, produced in the heart of children by the Holy Spirit, was an active faith and not an inactive, bare disposition. Naturally they did not deny that in the life of children faith operates differently than in adults. The children's faith was active not with respect to its external activities but to internal activities and the qualities of faith. As such, it was still a faith that put on Christ (Gal. 3:27), received the kingdom of heaven (Mark 10:15), and participated in regeneration and salvation (John 3:5), and so forth.[56] We may not be able to picture this activity of faith in children, any more than that of adults when the latter are in an unconscious state. Still, this is not a sufficient reason to deny an active faith to children. This attempt on the part of Lutherans thus to remain faithful to the old order of redemption also in connection with infant baptism was, however, gradually abandoned. It proved psychologically difficult to maintain [belief in] an active faith in the case of young children. And since the regeneration granted in baptism still always remained amissible and was frequently lost as a result of unbelief when the children grew older,[57] regeneration actually came down to a combination of the powers of believing.[58]

56. Ibid., 1.XX, 227.
57. Quenstedt, *Theologia*, III, 146; D. Hollaz, *Examen theologicum acroamaticum* (Rostock and Leipzig: Russworm, 1718), 883.
58. H. F. F. Schmid, *Dogmatik der evangelisch-lutheranischen Kirche*, 340, 342; C. Vitringa, *Doctr. christ.*, III, 222ff.; Right into our own times, Lutherans have been divided over the nature and role of regeneration. Luther himself sometimes had regeneration follow upon faith, in the sense that faith itself was the rebirth, and at other times had it precede faith, inasmuch as regeneration in paedobaptism coincided with the gift of faith. In the Augsburg Confession, we are sometimes told (art. 20) that we receive the Holy Spirit by faith, hence that regeneration follows faith, and then again (art. 5) that the Holy Spirit works faith and, hence, that regeneration precedes it. No agreement was achieved. In the orthodoxy and pietism of the seventeenth and eighteenth

For all these reasons Reformed theologians gradually came to make a distinction between regeneration and faith (conversion). In the early period [of the Reformation] they also occasionally based the baptism of infants on the faith of the parents or the church, or on their future faith (Calvin, Beza). But soon they pulled back from this position and arrived at the unanimous confession that the children of believers were as much included in the covenant of grace as their believing parents—not only by means of or after, but already before baptism. Thus the Holy Spirit could grant them the grace of regeneration equally well as adults, for regeneration also occurs among adults apart from their will and before faith. There was disagreement over the time at which this regeneration took place in the children of believers. But they agreed that the Holy Spirit could also work in the hearts of children aside from the calling through the Word, and that he did this consistently in the children of believers who died in childhood. They also agreed that the Holy Spirit also frequently did this in the case of children who were born in the church, grew up in it, and later joined it by a personal confession. Therefore, in general the children of believers should, in accordance with the judgment of charity, be regarded as elect and regenerate until from their "talk" or their "walk" the contrary was evident. Hence both in the case of adults and children, regeneration in the restricted sense preceded—if not temporally than certainly always logically— faith and repentance.

---

centuries, the two views came to be opposed to each other. And this opposition continued into the nineteenth and twentieth centuries. Ritschl stressed justification, Schleiermacher regeneration. In the works of some, the focus is on personal faith (conversion, moral change), which can only be exercised consciously, and baptism is reduced to a sacrament of calling, approximately in the same way later Reformed folk saw in it only a sign and a seal of the external covenant of grace. Thus Ritschl, Herrmann, Kaftan, Kirn, Häring, Cremer, Althaus, Kähler, and others. In this connection, some, like Dieckmann, Wendt, and Schmidt, vigorously defended free will. Schmidt, for example, states that for "those who do not want to be saved, there is nothing that can help them, not even the Holy Spirit"; W. Schmidt, *Christliche Dogmatik,* 4 vols. (Bonn: E. Weber, 1895–98), II, 431. Others, by contrast, brought regeneration into the foreground and had it take place in baptism. Thus Martensen, Beck, Rocholl, Hofmann, Thomasius, Frank, Lütgert, Hardeland, von Oettingen, et al. In this connection, one again encounters a difference in that some construe baptismal regeneration as being so weak as to necessitate a later personal rebirth (Thomasius, Martensen), while others see subsequent conversion as no more than the appropriation of an antecedent regeneration in baptism (Kahnis, von Oettingen, Frank). Lütgert (*Gottes Sohn und Gottes Geist: Vorträge zur Christologie und zur Lehre vom Geiste Gottes* [Leipzig: A. Deichert (G. Böhme), 1905]) defines the contrast as follows: "One is not regenerated by faith but becomes believing as a result of regeneration." In Ebrard, a free personal conversion precedes regeneration as the subjective condition, for in it the two are distinguished thus: conversion denotes the change in one's *conscious* spiritual life, but regeneration denotes nothing less than a mysterious, mystical impartation of the substance of Christ to the substantial center of the human being (J. H. A. Ebrard, *Christliche Dogmatik,* 2nd ed., 2 vols. [Königsberg: A. W. Unser, 1862–63], II, 308, 314). In this way, Ebrard attempts to maintain the mystical character of regeneration and at the same time to eliminate all magical components from it (Ebrard, *Chr. Dogm.,* II, 323ff., 332ff.). The physical view of regeneration proposed here by Ebrard, an event by which the nature of humans is changed, is rooted in theosophy and, despite its rejection in the Formula of Concord, "Solid Declaration," II, 81 (Kolb and Wengert, 559–60; Joseph T. Müller, *Die symbolischen Bücher,* 607), occurs in many neo-Lutherans such as Delitzsch, Martensen, Thomasius, Höfling, Luthardt, et al. Cf. above, 62–63 (#441).

THE NATURE AND EXTENT OF REGENERATION

[443] Even greater than the differences over the order and time is the disagreement existing in dogmatics over the nature of rebirth or regeneration. As stated above,[59] the word "rebirth" is also used outside of Scripture and in very different senses. Sometimes it was used to denote the doctrine of metempsychosis (reincarnation), which, coming perhaps from India, penetrated Greece and found ardent advocates in Pythagoras and his school. When, from the end of the eighteenth century onward, the literature of India became known in Europe, Oriental wisdom began to exert strong influence on Western thought. Buddhism and theosophy penetrated Christianity, and along with them the doctrine of metempsychosis was welcomed by many, under the name "rebirth," as noble divine wisdom.[60] But this Indian rebirth has nothing in common, other than the name, with the Christian doctrine of rebirth. Whereas Scripture means by rebirth an internal, spiritual, and moral transformation that only indirectly influences the body, Buddhism construes it as a countlessly repeated incorporation of souls in a series of different bodies without it effecting any change in the soul itself. And to Buddhists, this repeated reincarnation is not an object of hope and eager expectation but, on the contrary, an object of fear and dread from which they seek to free themselves by the suppression of their consciousness and will.[61] This doctrine of metempsychosis, accordingly, does not belong in this section but will be treated later, in the doctrine of the last things.[62] That is also the case with the meaning of the word "rebirth" (παλιγγενεσια), which occurs, among other places, in Matthew 19:28. The world renewal referred to there can most certainly be described with the word "rebirth" and is also closely associated with the internal, spiritual rebirth of believers, but is nevertheless distinct from it. It is no longer implied in the word "rebirth" as it is ordinarily used today and will be discussed later in the locus of eschatology.[63]

The Greeks, furthermore, spoke of initiates in the mysteries as the "born-again," and the Jews similarly described proselytes. This usage seems also to have been followed by Christian authors when they repeatedly applied the word "rebirth" to the act of converting to Christianity and specifically to baptism, the rite in which this passage became visible to all.[64] In this connection one cannot tell either whether, and to what extent, the meaning of the word included an inner renewal of the heart. In the early years of the church the sign and the thing signified always went hand in hand and were not so clearly differentiated as was the case later. In any

59. See above, 44–46 (#436).

60. Sometimes its proponents try to represent reincarnation also as a Christian doctrine that Jesus himself taught; cf. C. Andresen, *Die Lehre von der Wiedergeburt auf theistischer Grundlage,* 2nd ed. (Hamburg: Gräfe & Sillem, 1899).

61. P. Gennrich, *Wiedergeburt,* 275–355; J. S. Speyer, *De Indische Theosophie en hare Beteekenis voor Ons* (Leiden: Van Doesburgh, 1910), 86–93.

62. Ed. note: See below, 705 (#575; = *Last Things,* 146).

63. Ed. note: See below, ch. 18 (= *Last Things,* ch. 7).

64. J. C. Suicerus, *Thesaurus ecclesiasticus* (Amsterdam: J. H. Wetsten, 1682), s.v. ἀναγεννησις.

case, the internal change also automatically implied an external, visible turnabout, the abandonment of Judaism or paganism, and the act of joining the Christian church by baptism. Even today such an objective sense is occasionally attached to "rebirth." Bishop Waterland, for example, said that regeneration is not "a change of mind" but "a change of stand," so that even Simon Magus, though he remained in "the gall of bitterness," could be called "regenerate."[65] Ritschl, too, spoke of a "state" or "stand" of rebirth ["Stand der Wiedergeburt"].[66]

Akin to this is the view of regeneration held by those who regard the human will as not at all corrupted, or merely weakened, by sin. In that case, as in the thinking of Pelagius, no internal grace is needed or, as in the case of the semi-Pelagians, only an ancillary, cooperating kind of grace. And regeneration, accordingly, need not consist in a renewal of the faculties of intellect and will, in an infusion of new dispositions, but only concerns the operations of those faculties. This was the view of regeneration presented by Socinians, Remonstrants, and rationalists. They were even more or less averse to the word, emphasizing, when they continued to use it, that it was a "figurative way of speaking, whose elements are not to be pressed, unless we want to fall into many absurdities."[67] Rebirth is a figurative expression for the "reformation of life as previously lived, according to the teaching of our Lord Jesus"; it only relates to the habits and actions of life. Actually regeneration and conversion are one and the same thing, viewed in the former case from God's perspective and in the latter from the human perspective.[68]

According to others, regeneration consists in a renewal of the human consciousness. But here again we must distinguish two distinct tendencies. Reformed theologians, like their Catholic and Lutheran counterparts, taught that regeneration not only brought about a change in the actions but especially also in the faculties of a person. As a result of the psychological view that the will always and automatically follows the latest pronouncement of the practical intelligence and with a view toward maintaining the moral nature of humans also in conversion, John Cameron [1580–1625], who for a short while was a professor at Montauban, adopted the view that in regeneration the enlightenment of the mind was sufficient since in consequence the will would automatically be guided in the right direction.[69] The Reformed in the Netherlands almost unanimously opposed this view and stuck with the pronouncement of the Synod of Dort that in regeneration the Holy Spirit not only enlightens the mind but also infuses new qualities into the

65. C. Hodge, *Systematic Theology*, III, 597, 529.

66. A. Ritschl, *Justification and Reconciliation*, III, 590.

67. Thus the Remonstrants at the Hague Conference, according to C. Vitringa, *Doctr. christ.*, III, 227.

68. See the various quotations from Socinian and Remonstrant writings in ibid., III, 225–29; B. de Moor, *Comm. theol.*, IV, 782–84; Cf. Canons of Dort, III–IV, 3. Also, cf. the views, akin to those of the Remonstrants, of the theologians of the New Divinity School in America, Emmons, Finney, and Taylor, in C. Hodge, *Systematic Theology*, III, 7–15.

69. Cf. H. Bavinck, *Roeping en wedergeboorte*, 70ff.

will.[70] Still, Cameron exerted great influence on the school of Saumur (Amyraut, Cappellus, Pajon) and by his ideas laid the groundwork for the later rationalism.[71] Here, accordingly, regeneration is equated with the illumination that precedes faith. It is also possible, however, to equate regeneration with the renewal of the consciousness that arises from faith or coincides with it. Luther, for example, saw regeneration one moment as the gift of faith and another as the change effected in the consciousness by faith and consisting in comfort, joy, peace, and so forth. "Where the forgiveness of sin is, there is life and blessedness."[72] This terminology is also followed in the Lutheran confessions: one moment regeneration is a benefit distinct from justification and then again the two are equated.[73] Ritschl and his disciples appealed to the latter meaning of the word "regeneration" when they accepted no other rebirth than that which originates by faith. In the Christian, a new life begins with the birth of faith. This faith brings with it a fundamental transformation of the mind, a life in the power of God in place of the incapacity that prevailed till then.[74] And not only the Göttingen school promoted this doctrine but others as well, especially H. Cremer, E. Cremer, and Althaus, who, having adopted it, defended it with vigor.[75]

70. Canons of Dort, III–IV, art. 12, "Rejection of Errors IV." In this connection one can again differentiate between the faculties that are transformed in regeneration or conversion. Depending on whether sin is located more in the intellect, the emotions, or the will, and, accordingly, viewed more as darkness, passion, or aversion from and hostility to God, the emphasis in re-creation is on the enlightenment of the mind, the regulation of the emotions, or the renewal of the will. The picture also differs depending on the way conversion itself is experienced, in keeping with one's personal sinful state. Even one's psychology exerts its influence. Melanchthon, for example, in the early period spoke only of the mind and heart (affections) and barely mentioned the will. It was included in and subject to the emotions. As a result, conversion consisted mainly in the infusion of new emotions. Later, when he spent more time with Aristotle and adopted his psychology, he distinguished the will from the emotions, placed the will outside of and above them, gave it a measure of power to regulate and guide them, and even came to the point where he gave it the power, in conversion, to cooperate with God's grace (synergism). Cf. E. F. Fischer, *Melanchthons Lehre von der Bekehrung* (Tübingen: Mohr, 1905), 19ff., 47ff., 97ff.

71. A. Schweizer, *Die protestantischen Centraldogmen in ihrer Entwicklung innerhalb der reformirten Kirche*, 2 vols. (Zurich: Orell, Fuessli, 1854–56), II, 235ff.

72. Cf. F. Loofs, *Leitfaden zum Studium der Dogmengeschichte*, 4th ed. (Halle a.S.: M. Niemeyer, 1906), 754ff., 766, 782.

73. Joseph T. Müller, *Die symbolischen Bücher*, 98, 108, 109, 115, 528, 613, 615; ed. note: These specific references are to the following Lutheran documents: Apology of the Augsburg Confession, art. 4, pars. 61–67 (Kolb and Wengert, 130–31); ibid., art. 4, pars. 111–28 (Kolb and Wengert, 139–40); ibid., art. 4, pars. 156–61 (Kolb and Wengert, 145); Formula of Concord, "Epitome," art. 3 (Kolb and Wengert, 495–96); ibid., "Solid Declaration," art. 3, pars. 16–28 (Kolb and Wengert, 564–66).

74. W. Herrmann, *Der Verkehr des Christen mit Gott*, 267; O. Kirn, "Wiedergeburt," in *PRE*[3], XXI, 246–56, esp. 255.

75. H. Cremer, *Taufe, Wiedergeburt, und Kindertaufe*, 2nd ed. (Gütersloh: Bertelsmann, 1901); E. Cremer, *Rechtfertigung und Wiedergeburt* (Gütersloh: Evangelischer Verlag der Rufer, 1907); P. Althaus, *Die Heilsbedeutung der Taufe im Neuen Testament* (Gütersloh: Bertelsmann, 1897); *R. Steinmetz, "Zusammenhang von Taufe und Wiedergeburt," *Neue kirchliche Zeitschrift* 13 (1902); E. Wacker, *Wiedergeburt und Bekehrung in ihrem gegenseitigen Verhältnis nach der Heiligen Schrift* (Gütersloh: Bertelsmann, 1893); Cf. P. Rutz, "Taufe und Wiedergeburt mit besonderer Berücksichtigung der Kindertaufe," *Neue kirchliche Zeitschrift* 12 (1901):

Overlooked here, however, is the fact that Luther and his followers often speak of regeneration in a different sense and distinguish it from justification. When they do, it is not just an elevation and renewal of the consciousness resulting from the exercise of faith but specifically an infusion of spiritual energies preceding faith. Catholics in this connection spoke of "infused grace."[76] Lutheran theologians spoke of "the gift of spiritual life," "a generous bestowal of the powers of believing and of saving faith," or "the illumination of our mind and the arousal in our heart of trust,"[77] and the Reformed express themselves along similar lines. But they stressed even more vigorously that not just the actions and not even the faculties alone but also the whole person with all one's capacities, soul and body, heart, intellect, and will, is the subject of regeneration. Regeneration, therefore, consists in dying to the "old man" that must not only be suppressed but also killed and in the rising of a totally new person created in the likeness of God in true righteousness and holiness.[78]

But it struck many that not even this concept of regeneration is deep enough. According to Gnosticism, true redemption consists in the deliverance of the inner self from the bonds of matter. On account of its corruptibility, the body is not susceptible to redemption, and also the soul, which is most intimately bound up with the body, cannot be purged of its many defects. Redemption, therefore, has a bearing only on the spirit (πνευμα) and is obtained by humans, first of all, through knowledge, but second, also by means of the mysteries, among them particularly a threefold baptism with water, fire, and spirit. These mysteries free the spirit, protect it from evil angels, impart to it heavenly and divine powers, and make it a partaker of the divine nature. Rebirth, accordingly, is at the center of doctrine and cultic worship but is at the same time, as it is in the pagan mysteries, transmuted into a physical process.[79] Similarly, in Neoplatonism people sought a most intimate union with the deity by way of purification, illumination, and contemplation; the soul (or the spirit), we are told, is by nature divine but is oppressed by the external world (matter, observation, conceptual imagery, and so forth) and hindered from becoming one with the deity. But when it frees itself from all earthly ties, suppresses all its conceptual images, kills consciousness and will, and turns inward to its own deepest being, it finds God himself there and enters into full communion with him. On this sublime level there is no longer any barrier between God and the soul. The soul has become pure luminosity,

585–620; O. Scheel, *Die dogmatische Behandlung der Tauflehre in der modernen positiven Theologie* (Tübingen: Mohr, 1906).

76. Cf. H. Bavinck, *Reformed Dogmatics*, III, 514–17 (#416 and the literature cited there).

77. H. F. F. Schmid, *Dogmatik der evangelisch-lutherische Kirche*, 340–42.

78. J. Calvin, *Institutes*, III.iii.5; A. Polanus, *Synt. theol.*, 466ff.; G. Voetius, *Select. disp.*, II, 432ff.; J. Macovius, *Loci comm.*, 750ff.; P. van Mastricht, *Theologia*, VI, 3, 6–18; *Synopsis purioris theologiae*, disp. 32, 13, 18–19; H. Witsius, *The Oeconomy of the Covenants between God and Man*, III, 6, 4; B. de Moor, *Comm. theol.*, IV, 781; Cf. also, Canons of Dort, III–IV, 11.

79. G. Krüger, "Gnosis, Gnosticismus," in *PRE*³, VI, 733–34; P. Gennrich, *Wiedergeburt*, 92ff.

spiritualized and divinized. All distinction and separation is gone: God and the soul are one.[80]

These ideas, which are essentially characteristic of all mysticism, also penetrated the Christian church, primarily through the writings of Pseudo-Dionysius. In part they were taken over and standardized by Rome in the doctrine of the superadded gift, of habitual grace, and of the vision of God in terms of being (*per essentiam*); and they return in all mystics in Protestantism as well as in Catholicism. Of course, by that time they have all been given a Christian coloring, elaborated by some in a more theistic direction, by others in a more pantheistic direction. But in all cases, they insist on claiming a higher knowledge of God and a more intimate fellowship with God than those that are attainable by the ordinary believer. According to this position, regeneration becomes an essential participation in the divine nature, a substantial union of the soul with the deity. This reality is expressed in various ways: God voices his eternal word in the soul; he brings forth his Son in us; Christ himself is born in us, just as he was once conceived in Mary; he is born and brought forth in us just as the Son was eternally born of the Father; God so accomplishes the creation of the new creature that he gives up Adam's flesh and blood into death and offers a new heavenly flesh and blood in its place; Christ changes us, not by reparation but by annihilation; he does not bestow another set of qualities but another nature and another being; and to be born again is to become truly Spirit.[81]

When regeneration is thus traced back from the actions to the faculties, and from the faculties to the soul itself, and from the soul to its essence and substance, it naturally and necessarily has to take place in the unconscious. Now in the past, in psychology and hence also in the locus on regeneration, little notice was taken of the unconscious. Factually it was assumed, for the benefit of regeneration was also granted to small children before they became self-conscious. The Holy Spirit,

---

80. Cf. H. Bavinck, *Reformed Dogmatics*, III, 528–31 (#420).

81. See quotes from Eckhart, Tauler, et al. in P. Gennrich, *Wiedergeburt*, 112–20; from Weigel, *De fratres roseae crucis*, Barclay, Deurhof, Pontiaan van Hattem in C. Vitringa, *Doctr. christ.*, III, 229–31, as well as the works of Erbkam, Goebel, H. Heppe (*Geschichte des Pietismus und der Mystik in der Reformirten Kirche* [Leiden: Brill, 1879]), and Ritschl. Related ideas occur in the Christian theosophists (cf. above, 66–73 [##442–43]) and in the proponents of conditional immortality. According to Edward White (*Life in Christ*, 3rd rev. ed. [London: Elliott, Stock, 1878], 117): "The very object of redemption is to change our nature, not only from sin to holiness, but from mortality to immortality, from a constitution whose present structure is perishable in all its parts to one which is eternal, so that those, who are partakers of the blessing, pass from death to life, from a corruptible nature into one which is incorruptible in all its parts, physical and spiritual." Flacius, on the other hand, cannot be put in this category. He did indeed call original sin "the substance of humans" (H. Bavinck, *Reformed Dogmatics*, III, 106–10 [#324]), and if he had meant what this expression implies, he would have had to define also regeneration as an infusion of substance. But over against Strigel, who called sin an "accident," he wanted to bring out sharply that before God our fallen "substance" and "nature" is a "sin, i.e., something on account of which God is angry with me." This does not yet make the expression defensible, but his opponents certainly made too much of it. Cf. Formula of Concord, esp. "Epitome, I, Negative Theses" (Kolb and Wengert, 89–91); G. Kawerau, "Flacius," in *PRE³*, VI, 82–92, esp. 88. Many Lutherans, also in the Netherlands, therefore, sided with Flacius. Cf. Dr. J. W. Pont, *De Luthersche kerken in Nederland* (Baarn: Hollandia, 1908), 14, 22.

it was said, could also work in their hearts apart from the Word preached. And "although our children do not understand these things, we may not therefore exclude them from baptism, since they are without their knowledge partakers of the condemnation in Adam, and so again are received unto grace in Christ."[82] Moreover, against the Anabaptists it was stated that believers did not have to know, and could not always know, the time of their regeneration.[83] Rebirth as such, it was said, was not a matter of experience but of faith. "This birth is neither seen nor apprehended but only believed."[84] But ever since Leibniz "the unconscious" has become of great significance both in philosophy and in psychology. The term, however, is unclear and can be taken to mean very different things. If we leave out of account, as being irrelevant here, those workings of our biological, physiological, and negative functions that occur completely outside of our consciousness and can be known only by intentional scientific research, there still remain essentially two areas that may be treated under the heading of the unconscious.

In the first place, one can list under this heading all those impressions, ideas, passions, desires, and so forth, that at any given moment are not present in our consciousness but that, surrounding it on all sides or more or less dimly hidden beneath the threshold of it, may return to it on some occasion or other by recollection, association, and so forth. Belonging to this storehouse are all those impressions we have accumulated since our early childhood, as well as all those skills and abilities we have acquired by long practice and training. In the second place, the unconscious may also be associated with all those intuitions that strike the consciousness like lightning, have such weighty significance in the lives of geniuses, heroes, prophets, and seers, and also assert themselves in clairvoyance, somnambulism, telepathy, and a wide range of occult phenomena. In the opinion of many people, these phenomena point back to mysterious forces hidden in the human mind or to another spiritual world with which humans are, or can be, in touch.

Depending on whether the unconscious was viewed in the former or the latter sense, modern psychologists of religion presented a different version of regeneration or conversion. In the first case, regeneration was said to occur when concepts, impressions, experiences, and so forth sometimes dating back to one's earliest years, gradually or suddenly returned to one's consciousness as a result of some shocking event, drove out the up-until-then-dominant conceptions and desires, and brought into existence a whole new world of thoughts and ideals. In that case regeneration essentially meant a transformation of one's consciousness. But others found this explanation unsatisfactory, not because it was contradicted by the facts, but because it would deprive *religious* phenomena of all their validity

---

82. Ed. note: The language Bavinck cites here is taken from the traditional Dutch Reformed liturgy for administering infant baptism. See *Psalter Hymnal* of the Christian Reformed Church in North America (Grand Rapids: CRC Publications, 1987), "Liturgical Forms and Resources," p. 957.

83. J. Calvin, *Institutes*, III.iii.2.

84. Luther in W. Herrmann, *Der Verkehr des Christen mit Gott*, 278.

and value. Hence they assumed the presence in these phenomena, specifically in conversion, of the operation of an objective supernatural factor that guarantees not indeed the form but the content of these phenomena. All people, after all, interpret the experiences they have in their own way, in their own language and concepts. But the experience itself arises from contact, from a connection, with the supreme reality we call God. And from that connection there comes to people new energy, a new, broader, and richer life. They feel united with that Being, who works throughout the universe and saves both themselves and all the world.

Both explanations of regeneration (conversion) appear to be new and original but are reminiscent of those that have been given to it throughout the centuries, by rationalism on the one hand and mysticism on the other. The former is more deistic, the latter more pantheistic. The former explains everything in terms of the working of the word; the latter goes back behind the word and speaks of the spirit. In the former, regeneration has a purely moral character; in the latter, it is the revelation of a supernatural power. Both interpretations, however, bring out the serious weaknesses inherent in the psychology of religion. If, in accordance with its original intent, this science seeks to be totally unbiased and does not wish to be guided by any a priori conviction, it can, at least to some extent, observe and describe the religious phenomena in question, but it cannot penetrate their inner nature, nor, in the absence of any norm, pronounce itself on their validity and value. It remains embarrassed and powerless as it faces the question of truth. It may perhaps clarify a good many things psychologically, but it has no answer based on logic. Inasmuch as it cannot be content with such a negative outcome— since every science after all is in pursuit of truth—in pursuing its investigations it very soon comes into conflict with the impartiality it initially adopted, views the phenomena in light of certain religious or philosophical convictions, and attempts to offer an explanation that is composed on the basis of these rather free, subjective, and arbitrary premises. Consequently, and by way of example, conversion then becomes a phenomenon that is on a level with various other alterations of human consciousness, or, equally arbitrarily, is explained in terms of the unconscious inward operation of some supernatural factor. But what conversion really is and, similarly, what faith, prayer, justification, religion, and so forth really are, neither the psychology nor the philosophy of religion can tell us. Only Scripture can.[85]

REGENERATION: AN ATTEMPT AT DEFINITION

[444] When we note the many related concepts (calling, illumination, conversion, renewal, purification, sanctification, and so forth), in the midst of which regeneration plays its role in holy Scripture, and observe the many divergent views concerning it occurring in theology, it seems a precarious undertaking to want

85. Many objections against the empirical psychology of religion have been developed in detail in the work of Dr. J. G. Geelkerken, *De empirische godsdienstpyschologie* (Amsterdam: Scheltema & Holkema, 1909), 273ff.

to furnish a definition of it that can claim general approval. Yet such an attempt does not seem to be impossible.

The theosophical and the eschatological view of regeneration can at once be set aside, since the former does not belong in Christianity and the latter will automatically, based as it is on Matt. 19:28, be considered in the doctrine of the last things.[86] This leaves us actually with only three remaining meanings of the word.

In the first place, one can use it to describe the transformation that begins in the human consciousness as a result of the believing acceptance of the gospel, by which it is relieved of all feeling of guilt and fear and filled with comfort, peace, and joy. This is indeed a great and wonderful transformation and regeneration of human consciousness. Not only Luther and the Lutheran confessions sometimes speak of regeneration in those terms; this terminology also occurs occasionally among Reformed theologians. Polanus, for example, says that regeneration consists in "mortification" and "vivification," and that the latter again has two parts: the "gladdening of the conscience" and "spiritual governance."[87] Yet it is not advisable to describe this change in consciousness with the term "regeneration." For (1) this is, at least nowadays, an uncommon use of the word; (2) the thing expressed by it will automatically come up in connection with justification; and (3) one can easily foster by it the misunderstanding that regeneration actually coincides with justification and ought not to be distinguished from it.

If for these reasons we also reject this meaning of the word "regeneration," one can still construe this term in a broad as well as a more restricted sense. In the early years of the Reformation, theologians commonly used the word in the broad sense.[88] In that case, regeneration included the total renewal of a person as the renewal was brought about by and out of faith and coincided with repentance (*resipiscentia*, μετανοια, not penitence in the medieval sense). The result was that one moment "regeneration" and another time "conversion" was described as existing in two parts, the mortification of the "old man" and the rising of the "new."[89] But various causes, already summed up earlier,[90] converged to prompt theologians to view regeneration in a restricted sense and to have it precede faith and repentance. The progress of regeneration after and by faith was then usually given another name (repentance, renewal, sanctification). This terminology gradually spread to the point where today almost nobody identifies regeneration with sanctification. The restricted sense of the word became established, and this makes sense: the word does not include the growth and development of the new life but suggests the genesis or origin of that life. Accordingly, when dogmatics restricts the term to the implantation of the spiritual life, it is giving it a more restricted sense than that in which Scripture usually speaks of "regeneration" (or

---

86. Ed. note: See below, 705 (#575; = *Last Things*, 146).
87. A. Polanus, *Synt. theol.*, 468.
88. Cf. H. Bavinck, *Reformed Dogmatics*, III, 579–84 (#430).
89. Cf. A. Polanus, *Synt. theol.*, 468; and the Heidelberg Catechism, Q 88.
90. Cf. H. Bavinck, *Reformed Dogmatics*, III, 579–84 (#430); see above, 55–59 (#440).

"birth from above" or "birth from God") and must therefore be on its guard not to cite it by its sound alone. This is no objection, however, since the dogmatician uses the language of confession in reference to every doctrine and must base his use of it, not on the sound of words, but on divine revelation.

Regeneration in the restricted sense further requires a distinction between the activity of God by which he regenerates, and the fruit of that activity in the person who is being regenerated; in other words, between active and passive regeneration. In reality both things are closely interconnected and are frequently summed up in the one word "regeneration." But differentiation is indispensable for a correct understanding here. Regeneration in the active sense, the regenerative activity of God, is only another name for the call: the efficacious call of God. And the connection between the calling in this sense (active regeneration) and regeneration in the passive sense is the same as that between the Father's speaking and our learning from him (John 6:45), between the Father's drawing and our following (6:44), between the Father's granting and our accepting (6:65), between the efficacious offer and our passive acceptance of salvation, between the sowing and what is sown.[91] So in regeneration we must first focus our attention on the activity of God (a subject already discussed in part above in connection with "calling" and to which the following now needs to be added).

Just as "calling" is partly external and partly internal, so the action of God in regeneration includes both a moral and a "hyperphysical" (a provisional term to be explained later) operation.[92] The first-mentioned operation occurs by the agency of the Word, is aimed at the human consciousness (not only theoretical but above all practical reason with the conscience) and through it at the human will. In the preaching of the gospel to adults, especially on the mission field, the external call is therefore anterior to regeneration, although it may coincide with it in time. Now Pelagians of all stripes recognize no activity of God in regeneration other than this moral suasion. They deem it sufficient for adults because, in their view, the human will is either not at all affected or only weakened by sin, and therefore can, if it wants to, obey this moral suasion. In addition, insofar as it concerns children, this moral suasion is unnecessary because original sin is either totally denied or considered a nonculpable defect.[93]

Among the proponents of this view are indeed those who speak not only of the word of the gospel, the image of Jesus in the Gospels,[94] and so forth but also

91. W. Ames, *Marrow of Theology*, trans. and ed. J. D. Eusden (1968; repr., Grand Rapids: Baker Academic, 1997), I.26.7ff. (pp. 157–60); G. Voetius, *Select. disp.*, II, 452, 463ff.; J. H. Heidegger, *Corpus theologiae*, XXI, 61.

92. G. Voetius, *Select. disp.*, II, 449; Cf. H. Bavinck, *Roeping en wedergeboorte*, 88.

93. P. van Limborch (*Theol. christ.*, IV, 12, 2), accordingly, equates the external with the internal calling: "The internal call is not the power of the Spirit operating apart from the Word but by the Word and is always present in the Word, so that the calling is in truth one and the same thing but may be called external and internal depending on the viewpoint."

94. Thus, esp. W. Herrmann, *Der Verkehr des Christen mit Gott*, 45ff. On p. 147 he says, "We must therefore totally reject the idea that God can draw near to the individual soul by letting himself be found in Christ." On

of the Spirit and his activity and even in a sense have the latter precede the Word. But when speaking of the "Spirit," they have in mind the holy spirit of community that indwells believers as a body,[95] or the objective divine power (*Potenz*) in which God imparts himself,[96] or the life orientation and life force that emanated from Jesus's person and work—as it did from other great men—and continues on in history;[97] but they no longer believe in the Holy Spirit as he participates with the Father and the Son in the same divine being, yet as a person is distinct from them,[98] and therefore they no longer have any room left for a special divine activity in regeneration. The Christian church, however, has consistently—and all the more vigorously as it gained more insight into the personality and deity of the Holy Spirit—assumed a special divine activity in regeneration. Just as, to the extent it became more firmly persuaded of the necessity of internal grace, it confessed all the more decisively and joyfully the personality and deity of the Holy Spirit.[99] The one thing is inseparably connected with the other. If God is triune, then in addition to a work of the Father in creation and a work of the Son in redemption, there has to be a special divine work of the Holy Spirit in sanctification. The Christian church, based as it is on the foundation of the trinitarian dogma, therefore unanimously confessed an "infused" grace. However, whereas Roman Catholics and Lutherans in the case of infants linked this infusion of grace (regeneration) to baptism, the Reformed learned to see by the light of Scripture that the children of believers are included in the covenant of grace, not *by* but even *before* baptism, not *on account of* their parents by virtue of their natural birth, but *with* their parents by virtue of divine compassion. In their case, accordingly, regeneration could take place and, in their view, often did take place without the external calling by the Word. External and internal calling, Word and Spirit, the moral and the "hyperphysical" activity of God in regeneration, therefore, in reality frequently diverged rather widely.

It is remarkable, nevertheless, that the Reformed, in their polemics with the Anabaptists, consistently tried to maintain the connectedness of the two and in their confessions, catechisms, and dogmatic manuals, remained steadfastly faithful to the order of calling and regeneration. Even Maccovius, who locates active justification before regeneration and has faith and passive justification follow it, nevertheless deals—under the heading of the royal office of Christ—with the external means by which he exercises his government, and has active justification

---

this basis, there is no need for an operation of God's Spirit in a person. Cf. K. F. Nösgen, *Das Wesen und Wirken des Heiligen Geistes,* 2 vols. (Berlin: Trowitzsch, 1905–7), 189–94.

95. F. Schleiermacher, *Christian Faith,* 123ff., 170ff.

96. F. A. B. Nitzsch, *Lehrbuch der evangelischen Dogmatik* (Freiburg i.B.: J. C. B. Mohr, 1892), 439.

97. M. W. T. Reischle, *Leitsätze für eine akademische Vorlesung über die christliche Glaubenslehre* (Halle a.S.: Niemeyer, 1899), 105ff.; O. Kirn, *Grundriss der evangelischen Dogmatik* (Leipzig: Deichert, 1905), 105; H. Schultz, *Grundriss der evangelischen Dogmatik* (Göttingen: Vandenhoeck & Ruprecht, 1892), 91, 103.

98. Reischle (*Leitsätze für eine akademische Vorlesung,* 54), for example, speaks of Father, Son, and Spirit as of three sides or operational modes of God.

99. Cf. H. Bavinck, *Reformed Dogmatics,* II, 311ff. (#227).

take place in the gospel (Gen. 3:15) that is made known to us by the Word.[100] And they [Reformed theologians] had good grounds for maintaining this order.

1. When the children of believers are regenerated in infancy, before they are able to hear the word of the gospel, this is always true only for the children of believers; that is, for such children who from their conception and birth are included in the covenant of grace. This covenant of grace, accordingly, precedes their regeneration. It is objectively made ready for them as a gracious ordinance of God. It consists, independently of them, in the gospel and the sacraments; and they are passively incorporated in it and baptized at this time as members of that covenant. The sacrament of baptism would not be a sacrament if it were not attached as a sign and seal to the Word. The internal calling by which the children are regenerated therefore remains closely tied in with the Word, even though the children themselves do not yet have any glimmering of it.

2. When in dogmatics the person and work of Christ (soteriology) has been treated, one cannot immediately begin in soteriology with regeneration, but must first in some fashion deal (in the doctrine of the Holy Spirit: the covenant of grace, the church, the means of grace, the external rule of Christ, the calling, and so forth) with the way in which and the means by which the objective salvation in Christ is made known in the world and passed down from generation to generation. For if regeneration were objectively detached from the Word, one would not only no longer be able to make any judgments about the presence and activity of the Holy Spirit,[101] but might also draw the obvious conclusion that actually Christ's person and work are not necessary to salvation, and that God may equally well regenerate the sinner aside from Christ by the Holy Spirit alone. At most Christ then remains necessary only to reveal God's name and glory in the world of human consciousness.

3. It is not correct to say without qualification that regeneration is effected by the word of God, that is, by God's power. For although the expression "word of God" not infrequently has that meaning,[102] in 1 Pet. 1:23–25 the apostle obviously has in mind the word of the Lord that had been proclaimed among his readers, and the word by which regeneration is effected—even if one links it only with internal calling—is not after all the word of God in general, not his word in creation and providence, but his word in re-creation, that is, the word that in Christ he speaks in our hearts by his Spirit. In other words, the Spirit who works regeneration is specifically the Spirit of Christ, who has been acquired by Christ and, after

---

100. J. Maccovius, *Loci comm.*, 647ff., 676.

101. Cf. Formula of Concord, "Solid Declaration," art. II, ##48–73 (Kolb and Wengert, 553–58); Joseph T. Müller, *Die symbolischen Bücher*, 602.

102. Cf. H. Bavinck, *Reformed Dogmatics*, I, 401–2 (#108).

Christ himself had completed his work on earth and ascended into heaven, was sent into the church and now lives and works in it and takes everything from him. This bond is only retained if in one way or another one remains faithful to the order of calling and regeneration, for otherwise the work of Christ and the work of the Spirit end up on two separate parallel tracks.

4. In addition to these arguments, there are still a number of other considerations that, though secondary, are not without significance. When some Reformed theologians preferred to place regeneration *before* or *during* baptism, not only in the case of children who die in infancy but also of covenant children who remain alive, this was not a dogma fixed somewhere by the church, but a judgment of charity according to which the church had to view and treat its young children until the contrary was evident from their lives. Complete certainty was and is not obtainable here. In reference to the external call, it must be remembered, furthermore, that it certainly does not occur only as a consequence of public preaching or even by reading and studying Holy Scripture, but also takes place in the simple words spoken in the home by father and mother and heard by the child, and no one can say when and how this word can begin to influence the mind of the children. One must further consider that, though the internal calling or regeneration in order undoubtedly always precedes the *saving* hearing of the Word of God, as Maccovius[103] correctly asserted, but certainly not always the external hearing, nor the moral influence exerted by the Word on the heart and the mind. God can open human hearts before but also during the hearing of his Word (Acts 16:14). He can make Ezekiel prophesy over dead bones that they shall live (Ezek. 37:14ff.); make Lazarus, upon hearing the voice of Jesus calling him, come out of his grave (John 11:43–44); and call into existence the things that do not exist (Rom. 4:17). And, finally, one should keep in mind that the purpose of calling in general is absolutely not only to bring to faith and repentance those who are born again but also has meaning for all people. There is a universal, a general, and a special call. But this beautiful confession cannot come into its own if the calling is placed after regeneration and is associated only with the regenerate.

IMMEDIATE AND IRRESISTIBLE

[445] For all these reasons the Reformed unanimously held on to the linkage between external and internal calling and hence also to the order of calling and regeneration.[104] They opposed the notion that the division of the call into an

---

103. J. Maccovius, *Loci comm.*, 710–24.

104. J. Calvin, *Institutes*, III.xxiv; A. Polanus, *Synt. theol.*, 448ff.; *Synopsis purioris theologiae*, disp. 30; J. H. Heidegger, *Corpus theologiae*, II, 205ff.; F. Turretin, *Institutes of Elenctic Theology*, XV; B. de Moor, *Comm. theol.*, IV, 463–65, 469; C. Vitringa, *Doctr. christ.*, III, 169, 170–232; cf. also Kleyn, *De zoon Gods onder de wet en het leven van Christus onder de wet* (Sneek, 1901), 57. One must remember, however, that

external and an internal one was a "division into two separate species" and viewed it as a "division of the whole into its parts and members."[105] Just as, by taking this position, they turned against the Anabaptists on the one hand, so against Pelagians of all sorts they took the position that the external call and moral suasion by the Word is insufficient for salvation and has to be followed by a special operation of the Holy Spirit in the human heart.[106]

This operation of the Spirit was, first of all, called an *immediate* one. With this term they did not, however, intend to negate what they had earlier said about the connection between the external and internal call, but rather to define their position against two alternative currents. First of all, against the Remonstrants, who held the working of God's Spirit to be a purely moral one, a working whose fruit was dependent on human assent and compliance. Posted between God's activity and its effect in the human heart (which is regeneration) is thus the free human will. Over against that position the Reformed said that the operation of God's Spirit in regeneration is *immediate*; in other words, that God's Spirit itself directly enters the human heart and with infallible certainty brings about regeneration without in any way being dependent on the human will. Second, by adopting the term "immediate," they sided against Cameron and the theologians of Saumur, who deemed the "enlightenment of the intellect" to be sufficient in regeneration and believed that this enlightened intellect then so impacts the will that, by virtue of its character, it must necessarily follow the intellect. Accordingly, what we have here is an immediate operation of God's Spirit in the human intellect but not in the human will. Over against this Saumurian position the Reformed generally claimed that the Holy Spirit not only impacted the human will *through* the intellect, but also that it penetrated the will directly and there instilled new habits immediately.[107]

In the second place, if the operation of God's Spirit in regeneration is absolutely independent of the human will, it may be called "irresistible." Augustine already stated: "Aid must be given to the weakness of the human will in order that divine grace may be inexorably and invincibly effective."[108] Materially the Augustinians and Thomists among Catholic theologians, such as the Jansenists, also agreed with this position, for they assume an essential distinction between "sufficient" and "efficacious" grace, seeing the former as conferring the capacity and the latter as conferring the actual willing and accomplishing, and hence taught an infallible

---

though Reformed theologians regarded this order as the usual one, they nevertheless always also left room for an extraordinary calling: *Synopsis purioris theologiae*, disp. 30, 15, 33; F. Turretin, *Institutes of Elenctic Theology*, XI, 1, 10.

105. C. Vitringa, *Doctr. christ.*, III, 157.

106. Cf. above, 41–44 (#435).

107. Cf. H. Bavinck, *Roeping en wedergeboorte*, 68–74.

108. Augustine, *On Admonition and Grace* XII, 30; cf. J. Pohle, *Lehrbuch der Dogmatik*, II, 457ff.; J. B. Heinrich and K. Gutberlet, *Dogmatische Theologie*, 2nd ed., 10 vols. (Mainz: Kircheim, 1881–1900), VIII, 438ff.; C. Pesch, *Praelectiones dogmaticae*, 9 vols. (Freiburg: Herder, 1902–10), V, 154ff.

activity of efficacious grace.[109] But Rome firmly rejected this doctrine. At Trent it stated that when the human heart has been touched by the illumination of the Holy Spirit, "neither is man himself utterly without doing anything while he receives that inspiration, forasmuch as *he is also able to reject it*; yet he is not able, by his own free will, without the grace of God, to move himself unto justice in his sight."[110] And to remove all doubt and uncertainty concerning the sense of this pronouncement, it declared at the [First] Vatican Council: "Faith in itself is a gift of God, even if it does not work through love; and an act of faith is a work pertaining to salvation. Through this act man freely renders obedience to God Himself by consenting to and by cooperating with His grace, *when he could resist it*."[111] By that decree the infallible operation of grace is factually denied and the decision about whether a person will be saved or not is made a matter of the human will. From ancient times, that was the teaching of Pelagians and semi-Pelagians, which in the Molinistic and Congruistic systems of the Jesuits won out over Augustine and Thomas and found acceptance also among the Anabaptists, Socinians, the later Lutherans (et al.),[112] and in the Netherlands by the Remonstrants.[113]

The term "irresistible grace" is not really of Reformed origin but was used by Jesuits and Remonstrants to characterize the doctrine of the efficacy of grace as it was advocated by Augustine and those who believed as he did. The Reformed in fact had some objections to the term because it was absolutely not their intent to deny that grace is often and indeed always resisted by the unregenerate person and therefore could be resisted. They therefore preferred to speak of the efficacy or of the insuperability of grace, or interpreted the term "irresistible" in the sense that grace is ultimately irresistible. The point of the disagreement, accordingly, was not whether humans continually resisted and could resist God's grace, but whether they could ultimately—at the specific moment in which God wanted to regenerate them and work with his efficacious grace in their heart—still reject that grace. The answer to this question, as is clearly evident from the five articles of the Remonstrants, is most intimately tied in with the doctrine of the corruption of human nature; with election (based or not based on foreseen faith); the universality and particularity of Christ's atonement; the identification of, or the distinction between, the sufficient call (external) and the efficacious call (internal); and the correctness of the distinction between the will of God's good pleasure and the revealed will in the divine being. Whereas the Remonstrants appealed to Isa. 5:1–8; 65:2–3; Ezek. 12:2; Matt. 11:21–23; 23:37; Luke 7:30; John 5:34; and Acts 7:51, and to all the exhortations to faith and repentance occurring in Scripture, the Reformed theologians took their cue from the picture Scripture

---

109. Cf. H. Bavinck, *Reformed Dogmatics*, III, 514–17 (#416).

110. Decree of the Council of Trent, VI, 5.

111. Documents of the Vatican Council I, III, 3.

112. Cf. C. Vitringa, *Doctr. christ.*, III, 171–217.

113. Remonstrant Confession, art. 17; S. Episcopius, *Apologia pro confessione*, art. 17; idem, *Op. theol.*, III, 88–89, 187–205; P. van Limborch, *Theol. christ.*, IV, c. 13–14.

offers of fallen humanity as blind, powerless, natural, dead in sins and trespasses (Jer. 13:23; Matt. 6:23; 7:18; John 8:34; Rom. 6:17; 8:7; 1 Cor. 2:14; 2 Cor. 3:5; Eph. 2:1; etc.), and from all the forceful words and images with which the work of grace in the human soul is described (Deut. 30:6; Jer. 31:31; Ezek. 36:26; John 3:3, 5; 6:44; Eph. 2:1, 6; Phil. 2:13; 1 Pet. 1:3; etc.). So they spoke of the efficacy and invincibility of God's grace in regeneration and articulated this truth in a confession at the Synod of Dort.[114]

Third, the activity of God in regeneration was also described as a "physical operation." But there was much controversy over the correctness of this description. People were agreed that the adjective "moral" or "ethical" was too weak and wide open to misunderstanding as well. Just as on the point of human incapacity people had objected to calling it "moral incapacity,"[115] although this incapacity was in no way rooted in the substance of human nature, so in connection with the work of God's Spirit in the human heart, people could not confine themselves to the term "moral." This word, after all, had been used by the Remonstrants to indicate that the operation of grace was dependent on human consent and compliance and therefore resulted only externally in a change of the actions of the will, a reformation of life. And people could be even less content with the word "moral" when later, in the Reformed churches themselves, Cameron and his pupils Amyraut, Testard, Daillé, and Blondel described "particular" or "subjective" grace (which they distinguished from "universal" or "objective" grace) as an "ethical" or "moral" grace and in so doing paved the way for the congruist doctrine of Pajon and Placaeus.[116] But then exactly what was the correct description was hard to say. The Synod of Dort stated that "regeneration, the new creation, the raising from the dead and the making alive . . . is an entirely supernatural work, one that is at the same time most powerful and most pleasing, a marvelous, hidden, and inexpressible work, which is not lesser than or inferior in power to that of creation or of raising the dead, as Scripture (inspired by the author of this work) teaches."[117] And theologians speak of a "physical" or "hyperphysical," a "real" or "effective," a "persuasive" or "effective," a "supernatural" or "divine" working of the Holy Spirit.[118] But whatever word was used, the intent was clear: the working of grace in regeneration is not "simply natural" because it has to do with a rational, moral

114. Canons of Dort, III–IV; cf. *Acta Synodi nationalis: In nomine Domini nostri Jesu Christi* (Dortrechti: Isaaci Joannidis Canini, 1620), 218–24, and the judgments on the third and fourth article of the Remonstrants (pp. 53–219). In addition, see, F. Gomarus, "De gratia conversionis," *Op.*, I, 85–126; J. Trigland, *Antapologia*, c. 27ff., 365ff.; F. Spanheim, *Dubia evangelica* (Geneva: Petri Chovet, 1655–58), III, 1182ff.; P. van Mastricht, *Theologia*, VI, 3, 20; F. Turretin, *Institutes of Elenctic Theology*, XV, qu. 4–6; B. de Moor, *Comm. theol.*, IV, 496–534; C. Vitringa, *Doctr. christ.*, III, 171–217.

115. Cf. H. Bavinck, *Reformed Dogmatics*, III, 119–25 (#327).

116. C. Vitringa, *Doctr. christ.*, III, 175–80.

117. Canons of Dort, III–IV, 12.

118. J. Maccovius, *Loci comm.*, 696; F. Spanheim, *Opera*, 3 vols. (Lyon: Cornelium Boutestein, 1701–3), III, 1183; P. van Mastricht, *Theologia*, VI, 3, 9, 26; H. Witsius, *The Oeconomy of the Covenants between God and Man*, III, 6, 4; F. Turretin, *Institutes of Elenctic Theology*, XV, 4, 18; B. de Moor, *Comm. theol.*, IV, 496ff.

being, who, however corrupted by sin, nevertheless remains a human being and therefore has to be restored in keeping with that human nature. Neither is this working "simply ethical," for it is not dependent on the consent of humans but, with divine power, penetrates their inmost being and re-creates them, in principle, according to the image of God. It is therefore in a class of its own, simultaneously ethical and natural (supernatural), powerful and most pleasing.

THE REMONSTRANT OBJECTION

[446] Against this confession of God's omnipotent and infallibly effective grace in regeneration, the Remonstrants cite a series of Scripture verses that contain all sorts of admonitions and threats and are addressed to the heart and conscience, the mind and the will, of humans. But against this Scripture "proof," the Reformed are nevertheless consistently in a more favorable position than their opponents. For if one proceeds from the free will and wants to maintain it before all else as the most precious good, one cannot possibly do justice to all those texts that unmistakably teach God's efficacious and insuperable grace. On the other hand, if one proceeds along theological lines and seeks above all to secure the rights of God, one will still always have room left for the content of the Scripture verses that consistently address and treat humans as rational, moral beings. This is how humans were created by God, this is how they are upheld by his providence, and this is how they are renewed and saved in re-creation. But this is precisely what is denied by the Remonstrants. Their primary objection is always that the doctrine of efficacious and insuperable grace introduces a "natural" coercion into the spiritual life, militates against the nature of rational beings, renders humans totally passive, and undermines moral freedom and responsibility. Pelagianism, accordingly, is always out to maintain the resistibility of the calling and to let regeneration, conversion, sanctification, preservation, and so forth, depend on a decision of the will. Regenerated and justified are only those persons who voluntarily and antecedently meet some condition—believes, repents, is disposed to keep God's commandments, and so forth.

In so doing, Pelagianism immediately wraps itself up in countless insoluble difficulties. If humans are by nature capable of meeting those conditions, they are in fact so good that there is no need whatever for regeneration in a scriptural sense. In that case, a moral upbringing and self-improvement are more than sufficient. If humans have to receive the power to accept or reject the gospel in advance by the prevenient grace conferred in baptism or calling, then here too a kind of irresistible grace precedes believing, for preparatory grace is granted to all without their knowledge or consent. Then regeneration actually does occur before the decision of the human will, for "functioning follows being" (*operari sequitur esse*). The act follows the ability to act. The will enabling persons to accept the gospel, according to the Gospel of John, is a renewed and regenerate will existing prior to the act of acceptance. In that case, however, it is impossible to understand how, after all this, a "free" act of volition is still possible. The will, after all, thanks to the good power conferred on it without its consent, has already been determined for good, and is so determined precisely in the same measure as it received the power to make a good choice. The more one construes the will as being weakened by sin, the more power one accords to it in prevenient grace, the more, and to the same degree, its indifferent freedom ceases to exist. In addition, it is unfathomable why such an act of free will is still necessary. For if God has to renew human beings beforehand and irresistibly to the extent that they can choose for the gospel, what purpose does the maintenance of the indifferent freedom of the will still serve other than again to frustrate God's grace, to render his covenant of grace as shaky and unstable as the covenant of works was before the fall, and to picture Christ as being even more powerless and loveless than Adam? For he has accomplished and acquired everything, but when he wants to apply it, his power and his love bounce off the human will, a will, mind you, that has even been endowed with new energies! Merely to rescue a pseudofreedom attributed to humans, God is deprived of his sovereignty, the covenant of grace of its firmness, and Christ of his royal power.

This would be somewhat understandable if something were gained by it, but in reality one loses everything. Not only is the indifferent freedom of the will saved only in appearance, but in the case of infants this whole doctrine proves inadequate and even merciless. We have to make a choice here: *either* the grace granted to children is sufficient for salvation and, if they die in infancy, opens the gates of heaven—and in that case they are saved without any contribution of their own and without having made a choice of their own—*or* it is not sufficient, but in that case all infants who die before they can make a choice are lost, and of the children who grow to maturity, thousands upon thousands apostatize by their own freewill choices.

Pelagianism in its various forms seems to be merciful, but in essence this attitude is nothing other than the mercy of the Pharisee, who does not trouble himself about publicans. In order to save freedom of the will in the case of a few thousand adults—and then only in appearance—it is prepared, proportionately speaking, to abandon millions of infants to damnation. In the final analysis, it remains a riddle what Pelagianism can have against God glorifying his efficacious grace in the lives of sinners.

If it raised the question why God would only grant his grace to many and not to all, it would find a well-disposed response everywhere. Who has not felt that question rising in his or her own mind and has not been profoundly moved by it? But that question comes back in either case and is answered neither by Pelagius nor by Augustine. All without distinction must rest in the good pleasure of God. Those who confess God's sovereignty are by no means in a less favorable position than the defenders of free will. For, as was shown above, external grace, in the Reformed view, grants to all who live under the gospel at least as much grace as, in the Pelagian view, is granted to them in so-called "sufficient grace," and is judged sufficient by them for making a free choice for or against the gospel. The doctrine of the internal calling does not deprive the external calling of any blessing or benefit that according to Pelagianism or semi-Pelagianism, Roman Catholics, Lutherans, or Remonstrants is bestowed in it by God. According to the Reformed view, all those who are externally called remain objectively in the same condition as that in which they are according to other confessions. The Reformed only claim that all that abundant grace for and in humans, if it is not specifically the grace of regeneration, is insufficient to move people to a free and decisive acceptance of the gospel. What is needed to believe in Christ, according to the clear teaching of the Gospel of John, is nothing less than a rebirth, a working of God's power on a par with raising Christ from the dead (Eph. 1:19–20). All lesser grace, however rich and wonderful it may be, is insufficient. A grace that does not regenerate people yet restores their will to the point where they can opt *for* the gospel is nowhere taught in Scripture and is also a psychological absurdity. Even if their response were wrong (hence a "no"), it would produce absolutely no detrimental change in the condition of those who, according to the confessions of all Christians, will finally perish on account of their unbelief.

In any case the Reformed have the edge over the proponents of free will. The advantage is that God's counsel will stand, that his covenant of grace will not waver, that Christ is the true and perfect Savior, that goodness will one day triumph infallibly over evil. What serious objections could possibly be raised against that position? If, without our knowledge, we can share in Adam's condemnation—a fact that nobody can deny—why could we not much more, without our knowledge, be received into God's favor in Christ? Certainly this grace is not one that involves force. To speak for a moment in strong language: if this grace did not by virtue of its very nature exclude force and God actually used force, who would in the end have the right or even the desire to complain if by this action he or she were snatched out of eternal perdition and transferred into eternal life? Who would agree with the man who complained that someone had rescued him from mortal danger without respecting his freedom of choice? But it is not so: in the internal calling and regeneration, there is no coercion on the part of God. Not a single godly person, even if one had been snatched like a piece of kindling from the fire, has ever spoken of coercion in connection with the work of grace. It would likely have been their wish that God had more forcefully broken sin in them and made them partakers of salvation and blessedness without their having to travel such a long road of struggle and grief. But that is not how God acts in the work of grace: all coercion is alien to its essence. There is no more reason to speak of coercion here than in connection with a person's birth. It is indisputably the case that the differences among people—in gender, class, privileges, physical strength, gifts of intellect and heart (and so forth)—are not first of all caused by their conduct but come along with their conception and birth. Who has a right to complain if he or she has been apportioned less than others? Who can boast if he or she has been entrusted, not with one or two, but with five or ten talents?

Who are so foolish as to throw away the gifts bestowed on them over others, the inheritance that their parents have left them, the treasures of culture available to them at birth because they received them apart from their consent and knowledge, out of pure grace?

If one should wish to call this unequal apportionment in the natural or spiritual domain a kind of physical coercion or dare to charge it with being unjust, one must adopt the theory of Origen and of present-day theosophists that originally all souls were the same and that all diversity is due to the varying behaviors and actions of people. In that perspective only the law of karma prevails in the world, the law of reward based on performance, as it was also set forth and elaborated by nomistic Judaism. But the Christian religion is diametrically opposed to this view. Jesus did not pronounce blessed the self-righteous but the poor in spirit and the meek. He came not to call the righteous but publicans and sinners to repentance, to seek and to save what is lost. The grace of God in Christ, grace that is full, abundant, free, omnipotent, and insuperable, is the heart of the gospel.

BECOMING SPIRITUAL PERSONS

[447] Earlier we made a distinction between active and passive regeneration. Up until now we dealt with the former; now the latter is the focus of discussion. What, in the human soul, is regeneration as such? What is it that is effected and brought forth by the regenerative activity of God in the human heart? Scripture describes this product of the re-creating grace of God with various words and images. It describes it as a circumcised heart (Deut. 30:6; Rom. 2:29), a pure heart and a firm spirit (Ps. 51:17), a heart of flesh instead of a heart of stone (Jer. 31:33ff.; Ezek. 11:19; 36:25), a new creation (2 Cor. 5:17), God's workmanship (Rom. 14:20; Eph. 2:10), a new self (Eph. 4:24; Col. 3:10 NRSV), a new life (Rom. 6:11; Eph. 2:5; Col. 3:3), and so forth. Noteworthy also is that Scripture pictures regeneration as transforming a human into a spiritual person. What is born of flesh is flesh and what is born of the Spirit is spirit (John 3:6). By regeneration a "natural" human becomes a "spiritual" human (1 Cor. 4:1; Gal. 6:1). Believers are together built up into a spiritual house, a holy priesthood, to offer spiritual sacrifices (1 Pet. 2:5). They have spiritual understanding (Col. 1:9) and as spiritual people they discern all things without being subject to anyone else's scrutiny (1 Cor. 2:15). They sing spiritual songs (Col. 3:16) and no longer bear the image of the first man, who was from the earth, a man of dust, and became a living soul; but bear the image of the second who became a life-giving spirit and is the Lord from heaven (1 Cor. 15:45–49). They will therefore one day receive a spiritual body (1 Cor. 15:44) that will be like the glorious body of Christ (Phil. 3:21). They love the law that is spiritual (Rom. 7:14) and serve in the new life of the Spirit, not under the old written code (Rom. 7:6; cf. 2 Cor. 3:6). All this cannot mean that humans by nature possess only a soul and a body and by regeneration acquire a spirit (πνευμα) as a new component of their being, for

also the natural human possesses a spirit (πνευμα) in a psychological sense (Gen. 41:8; 45:27; Zech. 12:1; Luke 23:46; John 11:33; Acts 7:59; 17:16; 1 Cor. 2:11; 5:3; 7:34; 2 Cor. 7:1; 1 Thess. 5:23; Heb. 4:12; 12:9, 23; etc.). "Spirit" and "soul" are used interchangeably in Scripture. In one place a human is defined as a body and soul, in another as a body and spirit. Sometimes psychological activities and feelings are attributed to the spirit and at other times to the soul. The act of dying is sometimes described as a giving up of the soul, at other times as a giving up of the spirit.[119] But although humans possess a *pneuma* in a psychological sense, before regeneration they are still "natural" humans who possess no other life than that which they received by way of conception and birth from their parents and which is animated and controlled by sin. To lose this life and to acquire a spiritual life, they must deny themselves, take up their cross, and follow Jesus, leaving everything behind to be Jesus's disciples—in a word, to be born again of water and the Spirit (John 3:3, 5).

This Spirit is the Spirit of God, for like humans, God also has a Spirit (1 Cor. 2:11). By that Spirit God created and upholds the world (Gen. 1:2; Pss. 33:6; 104:30), distributes gifts and powers (Exod. 31:3; Judg. 6:34; 14:6), sends and anoints the prophets (Isa. 48:16; 59:21; Ezek. 37:1) and renews and sanctifies his people (Pss. 51:10; 143:10; Isa. 11:2; 28:6; 32:15ff.; Ezek. 36:27; 39:29; Zech. 12:10). Christ was conceived by that Spirit, and with that Spirit he was abundantly anointed. By that Spirit he accomplished all his work. Consequently he so completely acquired that Spirit that he himself can be called the Spirit, the life-giving Spirit (2 Cor. 3:17; 1 Cor. 15:45), that henceforth the Spirit of God is the Spirit of his Father, the Spirit of the Son, the Spirit of Christ, the Spirit of the Lord Jesus (Matt. 10:20; Rom. 8:2, 9; 2 Cor. 3:17–18; Gal. 3:2; 4:6; Phil. 1:19; 1 Pet. 1:11; Rev. 3:13), and that he can be fully imparted by Christ to his church (John 15:26; 16:7; Acts 2:4, 33, etc.).

In that early period [of the church] this Spirit, whom all believers receive either in baptism (Acts 2:38) or by the laying on of hands before (9:17) or after baptism (8:17; 19:6), was primarily the author of a wide array of extraordinary gifts and powers, such as glossolalia, prophecy, manifestations, revelations, and miraculous healings, which frequently filled bystanders with fear and amazement (2:7, 37, 43; 3:10; 4:13; 5:5; etc.). But from the very beginning he was, and was gradually recognized—especially by Paul—as being the author of the new Christian life in its totality, of all the benefits that Christ had acquired and were imparted to his church. Jesus himself already stated that the Spirit was the author of regeneration, of the conviction of sin, and of consolation (John 3:3, 5; 15:26; 16:7–11). Immediately after being poured out on the day of Pentecost, he became the giver of boldness in public speech (Acts 4:8, 31), of the power of faith (6:5; 11:24), of consolation and joy (9:31; 13:52). And later, when the extraordinary gifts decreased, his presence and working were especially perceived in that he brought

---

119. Cf. H. Bavinck, *Reformed Dogmatics*, II, 555 (#291).

people to confess Jesus as Lord (1 Cor. 12:3), assured believers of their status as children of God, guided all believers (Rom. 8:14–16; Gal. 4:6), poured the love of God into their hearts (Rom. 5:5), and renewed and sanctified them (1 Cor. 6:11; Titus 3:5; 1 Pet. 1:2). He caused them to bear spiritual fruits (Gal. 5:22–23), faith, hope, and above all love (1 Cor. 13). He sealed them for the day of promise (Rom. 8:23; 2 Cor. 1:22; 5:5; Eph. 1:13; 4:30), indwelled their bodies so that the parts of their bodies became instruments of righteousness (Rom. 6:13; 1 Cor. 3:16; 6:19) and therefore also made their bodies share in the life that was already granted to them by Christ in the present and would one day be fully manifested in the resurrection (Rom. 8:11; Col. 3:4; 1 Cor. 15:42ff.).

Accordingly, having received that Spirit, believers have become very different. They have become new, spiritual people. They are, and live, in the Spirit (Rom. 8:9; Gal. 5:25), walk according to the Spirit (Rom. 8:4), set their minds on the things of the Spirit (8:5), pray in the Spirit (8:26), rejoice in the Spirit (14:17), live under the law of the Spirit (8:2), are led by the Spirit (8:14; Gal. 5:18), and are assured by him of their adoption as children, of the love of God, of peace with God, and of their future glory. Their full adoption as children and the perfect revelation of the new life still awaits them at Christ's appearing (Rom. 8:23; Col. 3:4). But even now already they have received the spirit of adoption as children (Rom. 8:15; Gal. 4:5) and are partakers in that new spiritual and eternal life that flows in upon them from the resurrection of Christ (Rom. 6:4–11; 8:10; 2 Cor. 4:10). By that Spirit they are in fact most closely united with Christ. To be in the Spirit is the same as being in Christ, and the idea that the Spirit indwells someone can also be expressed by saying that Christ is in someone, for Christ only dwells in our hearts by his Spirit (Eph. 3:16–17; 6:10), and those who do not have the Spirit of Christ do not belong to him (Rom. 8:9). The new life is the life of the Spirit but just as much the life of Christ in us (Rom. 6:8, 23; Gal. 2:20; Col. 3:4; Phil. 1:21). Believers have been crucified, have died, been buried and raised, set at God's right hand, and glorified with Christ (Rom. 6:4ff.; Gal. 2:20; 6:14; Eph. 2:6; Col. 2:12, 20; 3:3; etc.). They have put on Christ, have been formed in his likeness, reveal in their bodies the suffering as well as the life of Christ, and are perfected in him. In a word, "Christ is all and in all" (Rom. 13:14; 2 Cor. 13:11; Gal. 4:19; Col. 1:24; 2:10; 3:11), and they are "one spirit with him" (1 Cor. 6:17). In Christ, by the Spirit, God himself dwells in them (1 Cor. 3:16–17; 6:19).

The life that originates in rebirth can, from the human perspective, be called a life of faith (Gal. 2:20), but objectively it is the life of the Spirit, the life of Christ, the life of God in the believer, and therefore supernatural and miraculous in its origin and essence. Just as the wind blows where it chooses, without letting any human prescribe its course, and just as its sound is heard, but no one can tell where it comes from or where it is headed, so it is with everyone who is born of the Spirit (John 3:8). The working of the Spirit in regeneration is free, superior to any human attempt at defining its limits, untraceable by and unfathomable to human knowledge. In Christ and by the Spirit, God himself is the origin of the new life (John 1:13; 5:21, 25; Eph. 1:17–19). Just as at the creation the light flashed on only at God's word of power, so it is he who shines in our hearts in order to make known his glory in the face of Christ (2 Cor. 4:6). Equally marvelous is the spiritual life in its essence and functioning, for as long as Christ who is the origin and content of it is in heaven with God, so long also the life of believers will remain hidden with Christ in God (Col. 3:3)—hidden, that is, from the world and still hidden to some extent from believers themselves. Their life is—and on earth cannot be other than—a life of faith. So Christians in their spiritual existence, are a work, a creation, something fashioned by God (Rom. 14:20; 2 Cor. 5:17; Gal. 6:15; Eph. 2:10), born, not of the world but from above, from God, a marvel to others, a miracle above all to themselves.

Finally, we must add that, though the life of the Spirit is most certainly a gift to each believer in particular, at the same time it is from the very beginning a life of intimate communion. The calling proceeds from God (Rom. 8:30). It is the Father who reveals his Son in our hearts (Matt. 11:25; 16:17; Gal. 1:16) and by his Spirit bestows conversion, faith, and regeneration (John 3:3, 5; 16:8–11; 1 Cor. 12:3; 2 Cor. 3:3; 1 Thess. 1:6; Titus 3:5; cf. Rom. 12:3; Eph. 2:8; and Phil. 1:29, where, however, no mention is made of the Spirit). But to those who believe, God now further grants the Spirit of consolation, the Spirit of adoption as children, of sanctification (John 14:16–17; Gal. 3:14), just as the Spirit has also been poured out upon the whole church, specifically on the day of Pentecost (Acts 2).

Now this Spirit, whom all believers receive as a permanent possession, is a Spirit of communion—not a community spirit, as Schleiermacher believed, which could equally well be the product as the principle of community—for the Holy Spirit who dwells in the church is the Spirit of God or of Christ and comes from above, is poured out, sent, bestowed, given (John 14:16; 15:26; 16:7; Acts 2:33; Rom. 5:5; 2 Cor. 1:22; 5:5; Gal. 3:5; 4:6; 1 Thess. 4:8; 1 John 3:24; 4:13) and received by believers (Rom. 8:15; 1 Cor. 2:12; 2 Cor. 11:4; Gal. 3:2, 14; 1 John 2:27). At the same time, however, he is a Spirit of community who not only brings believers individually into communion with Christ and with God but also incorporates and confirms them mutually in that communion. They are all baptized into one body by one Spirit (1 Cor. 12:13), all have access to the Father by one Spirit (Eph. 2:18), are together one body and one Spirit (Eph. 4:4), are built together on one foundation into a spiritual house, a dwelling place of God in the Spirit (1 Cor. 3:9; Eph. 2:22; 1 Pet. 2:5), and enjoy the same fellowship of the Spirit (2 Cor. 13:13; Phil. 2:1). It is the Spirit of Christ who by his Word speaks continually to the churches (Rev. 2:7ff.) and who, along with the bride of Christ, prayerfully looks forward to his return (22:17).[120]

120. Cf. ibid., II, 272–79 (##216–17); and III, 495–508 (##411–14) and the literature cited there. Add to this also M. Kähler, "Das schriftmässige Bekenntnis zum Geiste Christi," in *Dogmatische Zeitfragen: Alte und neue Ausführungen zur Wissenschaft der christlichen Lehre*, 2nd ed., 3 vols. (Leipzig: Deichert, 1907–13), 193–233.

[448] Surveying this work of the Spirit from Gen. 1 to Rev. 22 and specifically focusing on his regenerative activity, we need not refute the opinion that regeneration is totally or in part a human achievement and exists solely in the moral improvement of one's life and conduct. Scripture speaks of this salvific benefit in language that is much too strong for us to interpret it purely as an internal change or even as a modification in the focus of one's will and the goal of one's life. If life were no more than an adaptation of internal to external relations ([Herbert] Spencer), or if, in keeping with the assumption of modern psychology, the soul did not exist and there were only psychic phenomena as the product or concomitant of physiological changes, there would be no room for regeneration, or the word would serve to denote only a reconstruction of relations or ideas. The revival of vitalism proves that mechanical theory does not explain life, and while modern psychology may confine itself to the study of psychic phenomena, it is never able to stop there and always returns to a bearer (substrate, subject, or whatever one may call it) of those phenomena, either materialistically to matter, or pantheistically to a substance underlying both thought and extension, or theistically to a principle of life that is distinct from mechanical and chemical forces and has from ancient times as a rule been designated with the word "soul." Life is sui generis, which in the nature of the case we cannot look at from the inside but exists and makes itself known to us in certain specific phenomena (self-movement, self-nourishment, self-propagation). This is also how Scripture speaks of life; but it also refers to another kind of life, the life that is characteristic of the life of creatures, specifically of humans by virtue of their conception and birth. It is a life that can only be obtained and enjoyed in communion with God; includes peace, joy, and salvation; and transcends sin, corruption, and death. It is life that is real and true, blessed and eternal, a life that alone is worthy of the name and can be lived in time and impermanence. But like all life, so a fortiori this highest form of life is not a chemical article, a product of human labor, a fruit of slow and long evolution, but a product only of a creative act of God, a special supernatural operation of God's Spirit.

Thus speaking of the new life, Scripture remains faithful to itself and to its teaching concerning the originally created and fallen humanity. Humans, who originally were the image of God, lived and experienced blessedness in communion with God, lost that life, and were subject in soul and body to corruption. Sin began with an act but penetrated the very nature of humans and corrupted them totally. It may not be a substance, but it is not merely an act either. It is an inner moral corruption of the whole person, not only of one's thoughts, words, and deeds but also of one's intellect and will; and again not only of these faculties but also of the human heart, from which all iniquities flow, of the central inner core, the root of one's existence, the human self. And for that reason, according to Scripture, regeneration consists and can exist in nothing less than the total renewal and re-creation of human beings. If humans are radically evil, then, for their redemption, a rebirth of their entire being is indispensable. A tree must first be made good if it is ever to bear good fruit, for "functioning follows being."

RE-FORMATION, NOT RE-CREATION

At the same time, according to Scripture, regeneration does not exist either in a totally new second creation. In not a single respect does it introduce any new substance into the existing creation. The re-creation does not do this, if we take it in an objective sense and think in that connection of the person of Christ and the work of salvation accomplished by him. For Christ, though conceived by the Holy Spirit, assumed his entire, complete human nature from the flesh and blood of Mary and did not bring it with him from heaven. But neither does re-creation do this in a subjective sense in regeneration, for the people in question are and remain the same persons who were once darkness (Eph. 5:8); dead in trespasses and sins (Eph. 2:1); robbers, misers, and so forth (1 Cor. 6:11); and are now washed, sanctified, and justified. The continuity of the self, their entire human nature with all its capacities and powers, is maintained. Finally also the re-creation that will take place in the renewal of heaven and earth (Matt. 19:28) is not the destruction of this world and the subsequent creation out of nothing of another world but the liberation of the creature that is now subject to futility. Nor can it be otherwise, for God's honor as Savior hinges precisely on his reconquest from the power of Satan of *this* human race and *this* world. Christ, accordingly, is not a second Creator, but the Redeemer and Savior of this fallen creation, the Reformer of all things that have been ruined and corrupted by sin. Neither, for that matter, is sin a substance, but consists in lawlessness (ἀνομία); it is an actualized privation (*privatio actuosa*) that has indeed violated the form (*forma*) of the entire created world but did not and could not destroy its substance or essence. Hence, when the re-creation removes sin from creation, it does not deprive it of anything essential, nothing that was essentially and originally characteristic of it (though it was "by nature") and belonged to its essence. For sin is not part of the essence of creation; it pushed its way in later, as something unnatural and contrary to nature. Sin is deformity. When re-creation removes sin, it does not violate and suppress nature, but restores it.

Similarly, it does not introduce a new "substance" into a human nature. Regeneration does not consist in an infusion of a new heavenly substance, nor in a communication of the divine human life of Jesus or of the divine life itself such that our spiritual life would be made substantially or essentially homogeneous with it and in a real sense divinized or eternalized. Neither does it consist in a physiological change of our body effected by the implantation of the germ of our spiritual resurrection body. All this is excluded in Scripture by the fact that communion with God and with Christ is always effected and remains in effect by the Spirit: not in a magical or "natural" fashion but in a spiritual and personal way. Those who view the Holy Spirit purely as a supernatural force that descends upon humans, controlling and impelling them as it were from without, run the danger of regarding regeneration as a pantheistic or theosophical change. But the confession of the Trinity protects us from such a view. It knows of no other union than a union of persons, even if such a union is as close as that between a vine and a branch, between the head and the parts of a body, between a husband and a wife. Regeneration, in a word, does not remove anything from us other than what, if all were well, we should do without, and it restores to us what we, in keeping with the design of our being, should have but lost as a result of sin. In principle it restores us to the likeness and image of God.

But if, on the one hand, regeneration is not merely a reformation of life and conduct and, on the other, not an infusion of some new substance, then what is it concretely? Here, too, as with any other dogma, it is easier to reject an error than constructively to unfold the truth, for in all that God reveals, we finally encounter an impenetrable mystery at the point where the eternal touches the temporal, the infinite the finite, the Creator the creature. That is how it is in the realm of nature but even more so in the realm of grace. No personal experience, no mystical contemplation, no study of the life of godliness, no psychology of religion, pushes aside the curtain of phenomena and situates humans face to face with the Eternal One. On earth that which lies behind the phenomena remains, for others and for ourselves, an object of faith; the spiritual life is hidden with Christ in God (Col. 3:3). But if we let ourselves be guided by the testimonies of Scripture, we can nevertheless say, with an appropriate degree of modesty, that the whole person is the subject of regeneration. Not only are their deeds and conduct, their life's purpose and direction, their ideas and activities changed, but also humans themselves are transformed and renewed in the core of their being. To describe this process Scripture refers to the heart "from which flow the springs of life" (Prov. 4:23), in one's consciousness as well as in the emotions and will. If, as Jesus says (Matt. 15:19), it is from the heart that all evil and incomprehension flows, then that is the center where the change called regeneration must occur. Involved in it are all the constituents, capacities, and powers of human beings, each in accordance with its own nature, not only the lower and not only the higher functions, not only the intellect and will, not only the soul or the spirit, but also the whole person, soul and spirit, intellect, will and emotions, consciousness and feeling share in the blessing of regeneration. Not even the body is excluded from it. Granted, theosophy was on a wrong track when it associated regeneration with an infusion of heavenly powers and an implantation of the germ of the future pneumatic resurrection body, but this should not keep us from extending regeneration also to the body. Paul expressly states that the Holy Spirit also dwells in the body as his temple (1 Cor. 6:19), that the resurrection of the body has to follow because of the Spirit who dwells in it (Rom. 8:11), that spiritual persons make the different body parts into instruments of righteousness (6:13), that the life of Jesus also becomes visible in our mortal flesh (2 Cor. 4:11), and that glorification is closely tied in with calling and justification (Rom. 8:29–30;

2 Cor. 3:18). But just as the body is not the seat of sin, but its instrument, so it shares—indirectly—in regeneration and serves as organ of the soul. "The body is regenerated through the medium of the rational soul, for regeneration does not occur in something inanimate."[121]

Now if regeneration is neither an actual creation (an infusion of substance) nor a merely external moral amendment of life, it can only consist in a spiritual renewal of those inner dispositions of humans that from ancient times were called "habits" or "qualities."[122] These new "habits" are distinguished, on the one hand, from the Holy Spirit, who effects them but does not coincide with them; they serve, on the other hand, as intermediaries between the essence (or substance) of the human soul and body and the activities that, as people mature and receive the enlightenment of Scripture and the guidance of the Spirit, spring from those "habits" in the intellect, the emotions, and the will. Hence, though these are new qualities that regeneration implants in a person, they are nevertheless no other than those that belong to human nature, just as health is the normal state of the body. They are "habits," dispositions, or inclinations that were originally included in the image of God and agreed with the law of God and whose restoration liberates the fallen, sinful human nature from its darkness and slavery, its misery and death. They cannot be described in more beautiful language than what is used in the confession of Dort: "When God carries out his good pleasure in his chosen ones, he, by the effective operation of the same regenerating Spirit, also penetrates into the inmost being of man, opens the closed heart, softens the hard heart, and circumcises the heart that is uncircumcised. He infuses new qualities into the will, making the dead will alive, the evil one good, the unwilling one willing, and the stubborn one compliant; he activates and strengthens the will so that, like a good tree, it may be enabled to produce the fruits of good deeds."[123]

Regeneration, accordingly, works so little with coercion that it is truer to say that it liberates people from the compulsion and power of sin: it "is at the same time most powerful and most pleasing." In addition, the Holy Spirit confers on these infused qualities a lasting character: though they are not inherently inamissible and do not owe their permanence to the will of humans, they derive their stability from the communion of the Holy Spirit, who created them, continually preserves and confirms them, and elevates the life that was infused in regeneration to a level above sin, corruption, and death. From its earliest beginnings the spiritual life is eternal life, and the seed that remains in the regenerate is imperishable.

This has been denied by all who make the regeneration that is granted to the children of believers in their youth dependent for its continuity on a decision of the will that they must make later and leads to the distinction between a first

121. J. Maccovius, *Collegia theologica,* 3rd ed. (Franeker: Joannis Fabiani Deuring, 1641), 410.
122. J. Edwards, *Religious Affections* (1746; repr., New Haven: Yale University Press, 1959), 206 (part III, 1), spoke of "principles of nature," but added "for want of a word of more determinate signification"; cf. J. Laidlaw, *The Bible Doctrine of Man* (Edinburgh: T&T Clark, 1895), 258ff.
123. Canons of Dort, III–IV, art. 12.

and a second regeneration, between baptismal regeneration and a later spiritual renewal that again depends on the persons themselves. One cannot even stop here but must, in the interest of consistency, proceed to the acceptance of a series of rebirths, all of which can be lost and regained. Hollaz, for example, tried to argue that regeneration can be nullified three, four, or more times and yet regained.[124] By taking that position, we are absolutely misjudging the love of God, the grace of the Son, and the communion of the Spirit, as well as the nature of the spiritual life. For this life is essentially distinct from all natural life. It is born of God, flows down to us from the resurrection of Christ, and is from the beginning effected, maintained, and confirmed in the fellowship of the Holy Spirit. For that reason it cannot sin or die, but lives, works, and grows, and in due time manifests itself in deeds of faith and conversion.

124. D. Hollaz, *Examen theologicum acroamaticum*, 883; M. Schneckenburger and E. Güder, *Vergleichende Darstellung des lutherischen und reformirten Lehrbegriffs*, 2 vols. (Stuttgart: J. B. Metzler, 1855), I, 233ff., 285–439.

2

Faith and Conversion

The new life in Christ, just like all natural life, must be nourished and strengthened. This is possible only in communion with Christ in the Holy Spirit and through the word of Scripture. Enlightened by the Spirit, believers gain a new knowledge of faith. The gospel is the food of faith and must be known to be nourishment. Salvation that is not known and enjoyed is no salvation. God saves by causing himself to be known and enjoyed in Christ.

Biblically speaking, faith is trust-filled surrender to God and his word of promise. In the New Testament, this trust involves acceptance of the apostolic witness concerning Christ and personal trust in Christ as Savior and risen, exalted Lord. In church history, however, as in the case of Rome, faith was often reduced to intellectual assent. Personal assurance was decidedly secondary and often lost altogether. For Calvin, faith was personal confidence in God's benevolence toward us "revealed to our minds and sealed on our hearts" by the Holy Spirit.

The Reformation, however, did make it clear that knowledge was not to be set aside. Knowledge and trust, intellect and will, were both included in the understanding of faith. In spite of this, Reformation Christians also struggled with the problem of assurance. The churches were often torn between those who emphasized the mind and those who sought assurance in the mysticism of the heart or in the good works of practical Christianity.

We can make headway here only when we acknowledge that reconciliation as well as expiation, or atonement, is objective. Reconciliation, forgiveness, and holiness have been completely secured by Christ and are fully ours in communion with him. To underscore the surety of the divine initiative, Reformed theology came to consider the strict sense of regeneration, as the implanting of new life, to be the logically first step in the order of salvation. Reformed churches do not baptize children of believers on the basis of a presumed regeneration but do hold a judgment of charity with respect to them, not considering them as pagans the way Anabaptists and Methodists, for example, do.

Since there is no active faith apart from the Word of God, there must be a connection between knowledge (assent) and faith. Though the relationship between knowledge and faith is complex and varies from person to person, logically speaking historical knowledge precedes faith though it can never on its own produce faith. Saving faith is a sure knowledge that produces assurance and certainty. Knowledge and trust go together; faith is the assurance of things hoped for and the conviction of things unseen (Heb. 11:1).

The new life implanted in regeneration yields, in relation to the intellect, faith and knowledge and wisdom; in relation to the will, conversion and repentance. This includes but may not be reduced to psychological categories such as a "personality change." It is rather deeply rooted in the heart and includes turning away from sin and positively toward God and his law. Not superficial regret but godly sorrow that leads to salvation is called for. Worldly sorrow, based on short-term regret, only leads to death.

In some cases, we do need to speak of the conversion of believers when they fall into gross sin and for a period of time. This fact has caused much consternation in the church. At times perfectionist movements, such as those of Montanus and Novatian, attempted to impose a hard line of rigorous moralism on church members by refusing those who lapse into sin their return to the church. Over time excessive rigor was replaced by a more humane system of penance, an approach that led to the corrupt practice of indulgence. This practice, along with the elaborate casuistry brought about by the distinction between contrition and attrition (imperfect contrition) in the Roman Catholic sacramental system, tended in popular piety to create the impression of being saved by doing good deeds of penance.

By contrast, the Reformation rejected the complicated Roman sacramental system and understood conversion to be a twofold action of dying to self and rising to Christ in a life of obedience. All of this was a gift of grace, the application of Christ's finished work to the believer. Renewed by the regenerating grace of God, the believer is called to make turning from sin, dying to self, and striving to greater holiness a daily as well as a once-for-all matter. True conversion is a religious-ethical matter that involves the whole person in a turn from sin and to God.

Conversion as a lifelong turning to God takes form in different people in a variety of ways. It is a mistake to prescribe only one normative pattern. Some may experience a serious religious crisis; others find themselves more gradually and quietly growing in grace and knowledge. Some from earliest moments of self-consciousness know that they are a child of God; others go through deathbed conversions. It is a mistake to force people into a single mode or to hurry the work of the Spirit in a person's life. The Bible only requires that sorrow for sin be genuine and that a person wholeheartedly seek God's favor. One does not need to know the exact hour of one's conversion; one must seek genuine amendment of life.

Absolution is a free gift of grace based on the meritorious work of Christ.
It is not the prerogative of the church or of a priest; only God can forgive sins.
Similarly, though Christians do sin after their baptism and in this world
experience tribulation, the suffering of believers must never be reckoned as
punishment. Christ has accomplished it all; the church can only announce this
good news. Its "power of the keys" consists in its administering the Word of God.

THE KNOWLEDGE OF FAITH

[449] The spiritual life implanted in regeneration is similar to the natural life in that it must be nourished and strengthened for it to expand and grow. In other ways there is a great difference between them, of course, inasmuch as the spiritual life originates in God as Savior, is acquired by the resurrection of Christ, and is eternal life that can neither sin nor die. Nevertheless regenerate persons continually need to be "strengthened in their inner being with power through God's Spirit" (cf. Eph. 3:16). This strengthening of the spiritual life, like its beginning, originates with God and the riches of his grace. The life of spiritual persons, also after its origination, cannot for a moment be separated from God and his fellowship; in the same strict and particular sense in which this life is from God, it also is through and for him. It is he who nourishes and maintains it, never abandons it, prompts it to engage in certain activities, and not only bestows the capacity but also the willing and the working according to his good pleasure (Phil. 2:13; 2 Cor. 3:5). It is a life in communion with Christ. In baptism, believers are united with Christ, both in his death and in his resurrection (Rom. 6:5). They are in Christ, and Christ lives in them (2 Cor. 13:5; Gal. 2:20). They cannot do anything if they do not remain in him as branches in the vine (John 15:4–5). They can only become strong in the Lord and in the strength of his might (Eph. 6:10) by the Spirit of Christ and in communion with him (Rom. 8:13, 26; 2 Cor. 13:13; Eph. 3:16). But in the case of the regenerate, that Spirit works from the center of their being to the circumference. This is both possible and proper since the "new person" is not immediately perfected in "degrees" but in "parts." In regeneration the whole person is, in principle, re-created. A person's self dies and lives again in and by the power of Christ (Gal. 2:20). From the very start it is a new human (καινος ἀνθρωπος, *kainos anthrōpos*) who is created in Christ (Eph. 4:24; Col. 3:10), a creation that, though small and delicate, is nevertheless complete in all its parts. The Holy Spirit, accordingly, works at various aspects to make the new person grow evenly and proportionately in all one's parts. He works as the Spirit of wisdom, holiness, and glory, and adorns believers with an array of powers and gifts and virtues (Rom. 15:13; 1 Cor. 12:3ff.; Gal. 6:22–23).

In terms of the intellect, the Spirit specifically develops the virtues of faith, knowledge, and wisdom (and so forth). The spiritual life, though mysteriously and untraceably implanted in humans by the Spirit (John 3:8), is nevertheless from the beginning—the moment it becomes conscious of itself—bound to the

Word of God. After all it originated, even in the case of children, in the circle of the covenant of grace and in the gospel dispensation. In the internal calling, this spiritual life was called into being by an all-powerful word of God, a word, however, that he spoke in and through Christ. And it is born of that Spirit, who in the new life immediately implants the power to believe, writes the new law in one's heart, and internalizes the word of God (cf. "the implanted word" of James 1:21; 1 Pet. 1:23). When the spiritual life grows, it grows up in rapport with that word, which in various forms of instruction and admonition comes to a child in the home and, by virtue of its own nature, feels bound to that word that now comes through to the ear and the heart in intelligible sounds. The inexpressible word that was written in the human heart learns to know itself by the word that Christ speaks in Scripture. There is here a natural congeniality inasmuch as the Spirit testifies that the Spirit is truth. Just as a plant is bound up with the soil in which it is rooted and from which it draws its nourishment, so also the spiritual life is by virtue of its very nature bound up with Scripture. The external and the internal calling belong together and share the same word. But just as the external calling is not by itself sufficient to bring about the birth of the spiritual life, so also in bringing about increase and growth it is not sufficient by itself. The internal calling, accordingly, does not happen just once and stop when it has called the new life into being, but it continues indefinitely. Just as at the beginning God first created all things by the word and then upholds all things by the same word, so also the internal calling is active in the maintenance and development of the spiritual life. Believers are those who are called (Rom. 1:6), those who share in the heavenly calling (Heb. 3:1), who are perpetually called by God to his kingdom until they have in fact inherited it (1 Thess. 2:12; 5:24).

Now in Scripture the act by which the Holy Spirit causes us to understand the word of Christ in its spiritual sense and content and opens our consciousness to the truth is called by the particular term "enlightenment." Since sin has darkened the mind (Rom. 1:21; 1 Cor. 1:21; 2:14; Eph. 4:18; 5:8), what is needed is a renewal of the mind (Rom. 12:2; Eph. 4:23). This renewal is accomplished by God, who by revelation takes away from a person the hindrance that up until that time blocked the true understanding of things (Matt. 11:25; 16:17; Gal. 1:16). He does this by bestowing the Holy Spirit, who is a spirit of wisdom and revelation (Eph. 1:17), leads in all truth (John 16:13), teaches all things (14:26; 1 John 2:20), and enables us to understand the things of God (1 Cor. 2:10–16). Just as at the creation God, by his word of power, caused light to shine out of darkness, so by his Son (Matt. 11:27) and by the Spirit he shone in the hearts of people (2 Cor. 4:6) and enlightened the eyes of the heart (Eph. 1:18). Consequently they know the things granted them by God in the gospel (1 Cor. 2:12) and possess a knowledge (a deeply personal and penetrating knowledge) of the Father (Matt. 11:27; 2 Cor. 4:6; Eph. 1:17), of Christ (Matt. 16:17), and of the things of the Spirit of God (1 Cor. 2:14; etc.). As a result they are children of light (Luke 16:8; Eph. 5:8; 1 Thess. 5:5), citizens of the kingdom of light (Col. 2:12; 1 Pet. 2:9), and they walk in the light (Eph. 5:8; 1 John 1:7; 2:9–11). As recipients of the enlightenment of the Holy Spirit, they gain a totally new understanding of all things, of God, Christ, sin, grace, Scripture, church, world, death, judgment, and so forth. In God's light they now see light (Ps. 36:9).[1]

This knowledge is further defined in Scripture as the knowledge of faith. It is completely in accord with Scripture to say that the knowledge of God in the face of Jesus Christ saves, justifies, and bestows on us the forgiveness of sins and eternal life (1 Kings 8:43; 1 Chron. 28:9; Ps. 89:15; Isa. 1:3; 11:9; 53:11; Jer. 4:22; 31:34; Hos. 2:19; 4:1, 6; Matt. 11:27; Luke 1:77; John 8:32; 10:4, 14; 17:3; Rom. 10:3; 2 Cor. 2:14; Gal. 4:9; Eph. 4:13; Heb. 8:11; 2 Pet. 1:2; 3:18; 1 John 5:20). But because by virtue of its origin, essence, and object it bears a uniquely special character, it is called the knowledge of faith. Although it is thus qualified, this term by no means implies that this "knowledge of faith" is something that is alien to human nature and is added to it as a "superadded gift" (*donum superadditum*). Darkness, error, lies, and so forth are unnatural, the characteristics of a fallen nature, but the light of knowledge belongs to the image of God, which originally was integral to human nature. Furthermore, the knowledge of faith is not a supernatural addition to human nature. Believing in general is something every person does, always and in all areas of life, especially also in the area of scientific knowledge. There is no knowledge without some belief. The dualism between faith and science is both theoretically and practically impossible. Even in dogmatics theologians also speak of historical and miraculous faith in addition to saving faith. Though the latter two kinds of faith are essentially distinct from the first and occur also in the case of the unregenerate, they bear so much resemblance to it that they can have the same name: faith. But not even faith in the restricted sense, "justifying" or "saving" faith, is a superadded gift in the Catholic sense. Faith is indeed a gift of God (Acts 5:31; Eph. 2:8; Phil. 1:29), the product of his power (1 Cor. 2:4–5; Eph. 1:19; 1 Thess. 2:13) and specifically bestowed by the Holy Spirit (1 Cor. 12:3; 2 Cor. 4:13).

FAITH AS A UNIVERSAL CREATED CAPACITY

Still faith is a gift that is not necessary in an absolute sense, but only incidentally, on account of sin. Re-creation, we must remember, never introduces a new substance into the world or humankind, Also, in the case of faith, it does not bestow on humans a new capacity, function, or activity that human nature created in God's image did not originally possess. On the contrary, the Reformed correctly asserted against the Remonstrants[2] that before the fall Adam possessed the natural capacity to believe in Christ, even though he did not of course know Christ and

---

1. Cf. H. Bavinck, *Reformed Dogmatics*, I, 347–48 (#96); II, 191 (#200); C. Vitringa, *Doctrina christiana religionis*, 8 vols. (Leiden: Joannis le Mair, 1761–86), III, 224; R. Seeberg, "Erleuchtung," in *PRE*[3], V, 457–59.

2. J. Arminius, *Opera theologica* (Leiden: Godefridum Basson, 1629), 160.

at the time did not need him as Savior.[3] And against the Roman Catholics, they similarly maintained that as a human being on earth Christ had lived by faith.[4] Now since regeneration is basically the re-creation of the whole person in the image of him who created humans, the capacity to believe (potential, seminal, or "habitual" faith, the seed or root of faith) is automatically implied. Just as babies are rational creatures before they possess the actual power to reason, so if they are children of the covenant, they are also believers before they can actually believe. With reference to children, the Lutheran theologians would rather not speak of regeneration, because in the case of adults they had regeneration follow upon and proceed from faith, and wanted to remain faithful to this order also in the case of children. They therefore preferred to speak of the "kindling," "inception," or "bestowal" of faith or of "the conferring of the powers of believing."[5] Gradually, however, this view led to a distinction between two kinds of regeneration: one that in baptism bestowed the powers of believing and another that occurred later and consisted in the renewal that is contingent upon the right use of the power of faith granted in baptism. In that way, the blessing granted to children in baptism was increasingly weakened and the continuity of the spiritual life broken. In addition, it was overlooked that in regeneration the seeds of hope and love (and so forth) are always implanted as well, that in principle the whole person is renewed by it. Aside from this, however, it is perfectly true that in regeneration, along with all human capacities and powers, the capacity to believe is also restored. To the regenerate person, believing in God or in Christ as such is just as natural as it is for everyone to believe in the world of the senses. Admittedly, just as every potentiality results in actions only when it receives a kind of stimulus from without, and a grain of wheat only germinates in the warm shelter of the soil, so also the capacity to believe implanted by regeneration only becomes an act of faith in response to the ongoing internal calling. But in regeneration, God nevertheless restores the vital rapport that originally existed between him and humanity. Created in God's image, humans are again related to God himself and to all that is his: to his Christ, to the things of the Spirit, to his Word, to his church, to his heaven, to the things that are above. Crucified to the world and to sin, the regenerate live to God. And

---

3. F. Gomarus, *Opera theologica omnia* (Amsterdam, 1644), I, 63; B. de Moor, *Commentarius... theologiae*, 6 vols. (Leiden: J. Hasebroek, 1761–71), IV, 461; W. G. T. Shedd, *Dogmatic Theology*, 3rd ed., 3 vols. (New York: Scribner, 1891–94), I, 454; II, 482ff.

4. Cf. H. Bavinck, *Reformed Dogmatics*, III, 311–16 (#372). Proof for the thesis that Jesus also exercised faith would become even much stronger if J. Haussleiter (*Der Glaube Jesu Christi und der christlichen Glaube* [Erlangen and Leipzig: A. Deichert (G. Böhme), 1891]), and G. Kittel ("Πίστις Ἰησου Χριστου bei Paulus," *Theologische Studien und Kritiken* 79 [1906]: 419–36) are correct in saying that the genitive in this expression ("the faith of Jesus Christ") is a subjective genitive. That would then mean that Christ, the righteous one (Rom. 1:17), lived by faith, and by faith (trust in God, obedience even to death) became an expiation by his blood (Rom. 3:25). But this exegesis is rightly rejected by many scholars: H. J. Holtzmann, *Lehrbuch der neutestamentlichen Theologie*, 2 vols. (Freiburg and Leipzig: Mohr, 1897), II, 122.

5. C. Vitringa, *Doctr. christ.*, III, 82, 222.

thus, having been enlightened by the Holy Spirit, they also know God and are saved through that knowledge (John 17:3).

But this must not be understood in the sense that the regenerate draw this knowledge of God in Christ from their own hearts, from the internal instruction of the Holy Spirit. Mysticism has always pitted Word and Spirit against each other, despised the letter, highlighted the internal word at the expense of the external word, and even appealed for this position to Holy Scripture (Isa. 54:13; Jer. 31:34; Matt. 11:25, 27; 16:17; John 6:45; 1 Cor. 2:10; 2 Cor. 3:6; Heb. 8:10; 1 John 2:20, 27).

Against this we want to advance the following:

1. It is altogether certain that all knowledge, both in the domain of nature and that of the spirit, presupposes a relationship or kinship between the object and the subject. For us to see, we need eyes, and both object and subject must be illumined by the same light. For us to know, we need an intellect, and it is the same Logos who created the object known and the knowing subject for each other. So also in the spiritual realm, for us to know God in the face of Christ, the Spirit has to be added to the Word, the internal calling to the external calling, and illumination to revelation.

2. Scripture states this truth firmly and clearly in the above and other verses. In God's light alone we see light. But it nowhere tells us that the regenerate can or must draw the material content of this knowledge from within themselves. In 1 John 2:20–27, the apostle very closely links the anointing of the Spirit—which believers received from the Holy One, meaning Christ—with the truth they have heard from the beginning (vv. 21–24). If they remain in it, they will also remain in the Son and in the Father and need no other instruction. Scripture everywhere refers believers away from themselves and to the revelation of God in nature, the law, and the gospel (Deut. 4:1; Isa. 8:20; John 5:39; Rom. 1:20; 15:4; 2 Tim. 3:15; 1 Pet. 1:25; 2 Pet. 1:19; etc.).

3. In the natural world, it is the case that—though humans bring with them consciousness, intellect, and reason—they must nevertheless obtain the entire content of their knowledge from without.[6] This is even much more the case in matters spiritual. For though all believers are also taught by the Lord, they do still live in the flesh and remain prone to error. Over and over thoughts occur to them that they must "take captive to obey Christ" (2 Cor. 10:5). Left to themselves, they would immediately lapse into error and lies. Needed here, accordingly, is an objective revelation serving as a rule for doctrine and life.

4. Add to this, that it is not visible but invisible, spiritual, and eternal things that constitute the object of this religious knowledge. What no eye has seen

---

6. Cf. H. Bavinck, *Reformed Dogmatics*, I, 78–81 (#20); 217–19 (#65); II, 68–70 (#170).

nor ear heard nor the human heart conceived, *that* God has prepared in the gospel for those who love him (1 Cor. 2:9). How shall we know these things, firmly and surely, unless they are presented to us in a faithful image, pure and unalloyed? We do not walk here by sight; so then we must behold the glory of the Lord in a mirror that we may be changed into his likeness (cf. 2 Cor. 3:18).

5. Finally, just as in the natural world every creature seeks the food that suits it, so the new life in the believer is always drawn toward the gospel, the word of Christ, the Scriptures, as the basis of its support, as the food by which it is strengthened. Scripture becomes not more but increasingly less dispensable and more glorious to those who are growing in the faith. The witness of the Holy Spirit in their hearts binds them to Scripture to the same degree and with the same force as to the person of Christ himself.[7]

From all this it is now also becoming clear why religious knowledge in Scripture is described as "the knowledge of faith" and why, in the subjective work of salvation, faith is so prominently featured. Properly speaking, it is not faith or knowledge that saves us but God in Christ by the Holy Spirit.[8] He saves us by bestowing the benefits of the covenant, by giving Christ and himself to us sinners. But how would that salvation benefit us if we did not know about it? In that case it would not even be real. To the Buddhist, "unconscious" salvation may be the pinnacle of being, and many people today prefer nonbeing to being, but to the Christian the highest state of being is to know God and by that knowledge to have eternal life. Knowledge, therefore, is not an accidental and externally added component of salvation but integral to it. Salvation that is not known and enjoyed is no salvation. Of what benefit would the forgiveness of sins, regeneration, and complete renewal by the Holy Spirit, the glories of heaven, be to us if we did not know about them? They could not exist. They presuppose and require consciousness, knowledge, enjoyment, and in these confer salvation. God saves by causing himself to be known and enjoyed in Christ. But since on earth the benefits of the covenant of grace are only granted to us in part; since communion with God, regeneration, and sanctification are still incomplete; and since our knowledge is imperfect, has invisible things for its object, and is bound to Scripture, our knowledge of God on earth is "a knowledge of faith." Faith is the only way it can be appropriated, the only form in which it can take shape. Indeed, all benefits (forgiveness, regeneration, sanctification, perseverance, the blessedness of heaven) exist for us only by faith. We enjoy them only by faith. We are saved only through hope (cf. Rom. 8:24).

7. Cf. ibid., I, 592–93 (#153).

8. B. B. Warfield, "Faith," in *DB*, I, 837: "The saving power of faith resides thus not in itself, but in the Almighty Saviour, on whom it rests."

FAITH KNOWLEDGE IN SCRIPTURE

[450] In the Old Testament there is as yet no technical term for what in the Christian religion is now called "faith." The thing itself, however, occurs frequently, for from the beginning, salvation appeared in the form of a promise that can only be accepted by faith, and it assumed the form of a covenant that rests in the electing love of God and, on the part of humans, demands voluntary consent (Gen. 3:15; 6:22; 7:5; 8:22; 12:4; 15:6; 17:21ff.; 22:2; Exod. 20:2; Deut. 7:8; 14:1; etc.). Stories of the deeds and activities of faith are therefore told to us on virtually every page of the Old Testament (Heb. 11). But the religious relationship of human beings to God is usually expressed by other words such as fearing, serving, loving, adhering to, trusting God, relying on him, leaning on him, hoping and waiting for him, and so forth.[9]

Most closely related to our word "believing" in the Old Testament is the verb הֶאֱמִין, the hiph. of אָמַן. In qal, this verb means: to care for, to bring up (Esther 2:7, 20); active participle: nurse, caretaker, "upbringer," foster father (Num. 11:12; Ruth 4:6; 2 Sam. 4:4; 2 Kings 10:1, 5; Isa. 49:23); passive participle: "those who are brought up" (Lam. 4:5). In the niphal, the verb means "to be carried" (Isa. 60:4; 66:12) and further "to be established" (2 Sam. 7:16), "to be verified" (Gen. 42:20; Isa. 7:9), "to be reliable" (of God, his Word, his law, people; Pss. 19:7; 93:5; etc.). In the hiphil, it means "to make firm, to attach oneself to something, lean on, trust," and is sometimes used absolutely (Isa. 7:9; 28:16) but mostly with the preposition בְּ or לְ of the person or thing on which a person trusts (Gen. 16:5; 45:26; etc.) or with an infinitive following (Job 15:22; Ps. 27:13) or with a noun clause (Exod. 4:5; Job 9:16). Most important for the religious meaning of the word are Gen. 15:6; Isa. 7:9; and Hab. 2:4. In Gen. 15:6 we read of Abraham that he believed the Lord and this faith "was reckoned to him as righteousness." Meant here is not only that Abraham took note of the promise concerning his descendants without questioning it but very clearly that he did this because, hoping against hope, he trusted God unconditionally. The same is true in the two other verses. In Isa. 7:9 we read that Ahaz, seeking help from Assyria and relying on it, will not be established unless he backs off and trusts in God alone. In Hab. 2:4 it is said, over against the Chaldees who make their military power into their god and whose soul is inflated with arrogance, that the righteous shall live by faith in God and his promise. Faith and trust go hand in hand. Psalm 78:22 says that God's wrath was kindled against his people because they did not believe in him and did not trust his saving power. God is the faithful one (Deut. 7:9; Pss. 33:4; 89:37; Isa. 49:7; 65:16), and those who—despite all the conflict and opposition—continue to believe in him are the faithful in the land (2 Sam. 20:19; Pss. 12:1; 31:23; 101:6).[10]

---

9. Cf. H. Bavinck, *Reformed Dogmatics*, III, 491–95 (#410).

10. Cf. regarding the Hebrew word for believing, inter alia, also A. von Schlatter, *Der Glaube im Neuen Testament*, 3rd ed. (Stuttgart: Vereinsbuchhandlung, 1905), 555–65; L. Bach, *Der Glaube nach der Anschauung des Alten Testamentes* (Gütersloh: C. Bertelsmann, 1900).

This trust-filled surrender to God and his word that includes the Old Testament concept of faith was often greatly valued by the Jews as well. They strayed from the right track, however, when they took this faith to be an extraordinarily good work that could claim to be highly meritorious.[11]

Also Philo repeatedly speaks most beautifully about the faith that, looking away from all that is earthly, focuses on God alone. However, in his thought, faith has usually lost its soteriological content and clings more firmly to God as the invisible and eternal One than to the God of grace and salvation.[12] On the other hand, the word πιστις (faith) in the New Testament is given its full religious significance. John the Baptist already proclaimed that all the self-righteousness of the Jews is valueless in the sight of God, and that conversion (μετανοια) and baptism are a prerequisite for everyone to enter the kingdom of heaven. Jesus took up this message but added that this kingdom had made its initial appearance in him, the Son of Man. Of this kingdom he brought the good news, and so he made his public debut with the demand: "Repent and believe the gospel." When Jesus does this, he opens no other avenue to salvation than the one that, though less clearly, had already been pictured and presented in the Old Testament, for Abraham and all the heroes of faith of the old covenant are examples to us (Rom. 4:3ff.; Gal. 3:6; Heb. 11). Believers of the New Testament share in this faith of Abraham, are his children (Rom. 4:16) and walk in his footsteps (4:12). They are saved in the same way as the faithful of the Old Testament (John 5:45; Acts 10:43; 15:11). Then and now the truth is that the righteous will live by faith (Hab. 2:4; Rom. 1:17; Gal. 3:11; Heb. 10:38).[13] By saying this, however, we are not nullifying the difference between the dispensations of the same covenant of grace. On the contrary, just as, objectively, the promise became fulfillment, so also subjective religion assumed another form. Then the eyes of the faithful were hopefully and expectantly focused on the coming Messiah; now the life of the church aligns itself with the Christ who appeared in the person of Jesus. Then hope was central; now faith is.

That this is so is evident simply from the fact that the noun for faith (πιστις) and the verb "to believe" (πιστευειν) each occur approximately 240 times in the New Testament. The verb is lacking only in Colossians, Philemon, 2 Peter, 2 and 3 John, and the Apocalypse, and the noun is missing only in the Gospel of John and in 2 and 3 John; both verb and noun are lacking only in 2 and 3 John. In addition, the two words almost always have a religious significance; they are used only a few times in a more general sense (e.g., Matt. 24:23; John 9:18; Acts 9:26; 1 Cor. 11:18; etc.). Even more significant is the fact that the two words soon

---

11. F. W. Weber, *System der altsynagogalen palästinischen Theologie* (Leipzig: Dörffling & Franke, 1880), 292, 295ff.

12. A. F. Dähne, *Geschichtliche darstellung der jüdisch-alexandrinischen Religions-Philosophie*, 2 vols. (Halle: Waisenhauses, 1834), I, 392; B. B. Warfield, "Faith," in *DB*, I, 828; A. von Schlatter, *Der Glaube im Neuen Testament*, 578ff.

13. Cf. H. Bavinck, *Reformed Dogmatics*, III, 219–24 (#348).

acquired a technical meaning: to believe is to become a Christian (Acts 2:44; 4:4; 13:48; etc.); "believers" is another word for Christians (10:43; 1 Tim. 4:3, 12). Furthermore, "faith" is frequently synonymous with the Christian religion, which has now become an objective power in the church (Acts 6:7; Gal. 3:23, 25; 6:10; etc.).[14]

The Greek word πίστις only gradually, of course, acquired this rich meaning. In the Synoptics it refers directly to God as its object (Mark 11:22) and to Jesus insofar as people trusted him and were convinced that God spoke and performed miracles through him (Matt. 8:10; 9:2, 28–29; 15:28; 17:20; 21:21–22; etc.). But by these actions Jesus nevertheless bound people to himself and led them to a deeper insight into their own spiritual needs and their need of him in a sense other than only as the healer of their body. His miraculous power was a revelation and proof of his all-around redemptive power so that he could not just heal diseases but also forgive their sins (Matt. 9:2). Salvation is bound to faith (Luke 7:50; Mark 5:34). Even where there is no express mention of faith, it is nevertheless tacitly assumed. To leave all things for his and the gospel's sake and then to take up one's cross and follow him (Matt. 10:22f.; 16:24ff.) is only possible by faith in his person. Accordingly, as soon as Jesus arose from the dead, ascended into heaven, and sent the Holy Spirit, they began to proclaim him as the one whom God had made both Lord and Messiah (Acts 2:36) that he might give repentance to Israel and forgiveness of sins (2:38; 5:31). And before long a church originated that was marked by the fact that it believed in the Lord (5:14; 9:42; 11:17; 14:23).

From the very beginning this faith included two elements: (1) acceptance of the apostolic message concerning the Christ and (2) personal trust in that Christ as now living in heaven and mighty to forgive sins and to bestow complete salvation. Although both dimensions occur side by side in the writings of the apostles, John especially emphasizes the first components, πιστευειν with the accusative or a noun clause or with the dative of the thing (John 2:22; 4:50; 5:47; 6:69; 8:24; 11:42; 13:19; 17:8, 21; 1 John 5:1, 5). Paul, on the other hand, stresses the second, and speaks of πιστις with the genitive of Jesus (Rom. 3:22; Gal. 2:16, 20; 3:22; Eph. 3:12; Phil. 3:9), of the truth (2 Thess. 2:13), of the gospel (Phil. 1:27), προς θεον (1 Thess. 1:8); Χριστον (Col. 2:5; Philem. 5); ἐν Χριστῳ (Gal. 3:26; Eph. 1:15; 2 Tim. 3:15), and of πιστευειν τινι (Rom. 4:3; Gal. 3:6; 2 Tim. 1:12; Titus 3:8), ἐπι τινα (Rom. 4:5, 24); ἐπι τινι (Rom. 9:33; 10:11; 1 Tim. 1:16) and especially εἰς τινα (Col. 2:5; Phil. 1:29; etc.). But the contrast is not absolute, for John often speaks of πιστευειν εἰς τινα (2:11; 3:16, 18, 36; 4:39; 6:29; etc.), εἰς το ὄνομα (1:12; 2:23; 1 John 5:13) and also τινι (3:15; 5:24, 38, 46; 6:30) and τῳ ὀνοματι (1 John 3:23); and Paul also construes πιστευειν with τι and ὁτι (Rom. 10:9; 1 Cor. 13:7; cf. 15:14, 17; 1 Thess. 4:14). It is especially wrong to equate the later distinction

14. B. B. Warfield, "Faith," in *DB*, I, 828–31; also in 1 Tim. 1:19; 3:9; 4:1; etc.; the verb πιστευειν [or the noun πιστις], in his view, does not refer to the doctrine of the faith but to "subjective faith conceived of objectively as a power" (831).

between believing God and believing in God, or that between a historical and a saving faith with the above-mentioned one. For frequently the construction of πιστευειν with ότι (for example, that Jesus is the Christ) definitely includes saving faith (John 6:69; 8:24; 11:27; 17:8; 1 John 5:5; Rom. 10:9); and πιστευειν τινι or εἰς τινα is often no more than a historical faith (John 7:31, 38ff.; 8:30ff.; 10:42; 11:45, 48; 12:11, 42). In 1 John 5:10 we even read of πιστευειν εἰς την μαρτυριαν ("believing in the testimony").

In the description of faith, moreover, the apostles' individuality comes out. Each one looks at it from his own perspective. James, opposing a one-sided intellectualistic view of faith, shows that genuine faith in Jesus Christ (2:1), which gives access to God in prayer (1:6; 5:15) and is the principle of virtues (1:3), must prove itself as a living faith in the performance of good works (2:17ff.). Peter, the apostle of hope, relates faith—which also in his thinking makes us partakers in the righteousness of Christ (2 Pet. 1:1) and is the principle of good works (1 Pet. 1:7, 21; 5:9)—especially to obtaining the outcome of faith, which is salvation, for which believers are kept by the power of God (1 Pet. 1:5, 9; 2:6). In speaking of faith, Paul focuses especially on its object, Jesus Christ, whom God made our wisdom, righteousness, sanctification, and redemption (1 Cor. 1:30), and in whose person and benefits we can participate only by faith apart from the works of the law (Rom. 3:21–28). In the next breath, however, he stresses with equal vigor that faith—inasmuch as it does not only trust in Christ but also incorporates us in him and in his fellowship and makes us partakers of his Spirit—is the source and guarantee of a new life (Rom. 6ff.). The author of the Letter to the Hebrews, on the other hand, though recognizing that Jesus Christ is the object (3:14; 10:22; 13:7–8) as well as "the pioneer and perfecter of our faith" (12:2), looks at faith much more from its subjective than from its objective side. His readers, after all, were in danger of relapsing and shrinking back, to their own destruction (4:1; 6:1; 10:39). For that reason, he points out that faith consists in the assurance of things unseen, eternal, and still coming (11:1); that it must prove its genuineness by clinging to God's faithfulness (11:11), power (11:18–19), and promises (4:1–2; 6:12; 10:36; 11:6, 9, 26); and that its virtues consist mainly in boldness (3:6; 4:16; 10:19, 35), firmness (3:14; 11:1), endurance (10:36; 12:1), and hope (3:6; 6:11, 18; 10:23). Finally, John mainly presents faith to us from the perspective of not just its future but also its present reality, not to the Gnostic but to everyone who truly believes that Jesus Christ came in the flesh (1 John 4:2) and grants us eternal life (John 3:16; 5:24; 6:47, 54; 20:31; 1 John 3:14–15; 5:11); for that life appeared to us in Christ as in no other (John 1:4; 1 John 1:1–2; 5:11). He who has the Son has life (1 John 5:12).

Nevertheless, in all this colorful diversity, the unity remains perfectly intact. Believing always includes acceptance of the witness God has given of his Son through the apostles as well as unlimited trust in the person of Christ. The two are inseparable. Those who truly accept the apostolic witness trust in Christ alone for their salvation; and those who put their trust in Christ as the Son of God also freely and readily accept the apostolic witness concerning that Christ. The two together, subjectively speaking, constitute the essence of Christianity. If Christ were only a historical person who by his doctrine and life had left us an example, historical belief in the witness handed down to us would be sufficient. However, in that case Christianity would never mature into true religion, that is, into true communion with God, and Deism would be right. Conversely, if Christ, in keeping with the pantheistic view, were not the historical but solely the ideal Christ, belief in an apostolic witness would be totally superfluous, and Christ would be nothing other than the life of God in us, but then there could not be true communion between God and us either, for such communion presupposes an essential distinction between the two.

But now Christ is both: a historical person, the Christ of the Scriptures, and at the same time the glorified Lord in heaven who still lives and reigns as the head of his church. He secured salvation in the past but personally applies it in the present. And the benefits of the covenant secured by him encompass the re-creation of existence and human consciousness. They consist in justification and renewal, in light and life, in truth and in grace. They transform human beings in their thought world; free them from lies, error, and darkness; make known to them God as the gracious One who forgives sins; put them in the right relationship to God and all things; set their minds on the things that are above; and in the faith give them a firm basis for things hoped for and proof for things not seen. And they also transform humans in their very being, free them from the pollution of sin; cause them, in the hiddenness of their heart, to live in communion with God through Christ in the Holy Spirit; make them citizens of the kingdom of heaven; regenerate them from above; and re-create them to be conformed to the image of his Son that he may be the firstborn among many brothers.

And these two, Christ and his "brothers," are inseparable. For the Christ who descended is he who also ascended far above all the heavens that he might fill all things (Eph. 4:10). The Holy Spirit who regenerates is he who also witnesses to Christ in us. Scripture guides us to Christ, who is above, seated at the right hand of God; and Christ, who lives in our heart by the Spirit, guides us back to Scripture. For a person believes with the heart and so is justified, and confesses with the mouth, and so is saved (Rom. 10:10). Faith as Scripture speaks of it excludes both: a faith of the heart that does not confess and a confession that is not rooted in the faith of the heart. It is simultaneously mystical and noetic, an unlimited and unwavering trust in Christ as he who, as Scripture says, has accomplished everything for me and on that basis is now and forever my Lord and my God.

ROME AND THE REFORMATION ON FAITH

[451] In theology this multifaceted scriptural doctrine of faith did not come into its own because theologians proceeded from the ordinary everyday

meaning of the word and lost sight of the religious sense it had acquired in Scripture.[15]

In the case of Rome, this gradually led to the following view:

1. Believing is always and everywhere, also in the Christian religion, an act of the intellect—regardless of whether it is more an act of the theoretical or of the practical intellect—consisting in a sort of thinking with assent. In religion, it is "a firm and assured assent to the things that God enjoins us to believe" (*assensus firmus ac certus ad ea omnia, quae Deus credenda proponit*).

2. Thus considered, faith as uninformed faith (*fides informis*) is indeed a good and precious virtue, even a gift of God.[16] For the will that, in keeping with the rule "no one believes except by wanting to" (*nemo credit nisi volens*), always precedes believing, has been moved to this by the grace of God. Granted, the demons also have this uninformed faith, but they do not receive it as a gift of God but believe because in their intellect they cannot contradict the truth. But human beings, moved by the grace of God, have voluntarily assented to the revelation of God and thereby performed a meritorious act that can claim a reward, an act that as one of the seven requisite preparations prepares them for justification. Yet faith as such, as uninformed faith, is not sufficient to save people and make them righteous.

3. Faith as such needs the addition of love: uninformed faith must become an informed faith (*fides formata*). The answers to the question how that happens vary. Some say that uninformed faith and informed faith are two distinct dispositions, so that when the latter appears, the former vanishes. Others assert that the two continue to exist concomitantly. Still others are convinced that the two, viewed intellectually, are one and the same disposition and only bear different names in view of the fact that "informed faith," as love, has its seat in the will.[17] Only this informed faith justifies and saves; but also those who possess only "uninformed faith" must be regarded as believers, Christians, as true, though incomplete, members of the church.

4. The object of faith is not, as the Reformers say, the special grace of God in Christ, but everything that God has revealed. Of course, it is not possible and therefore not required that all believers, even the most simple, know and differentiate between all the articles of faith. They believe many things

15. Cf. H. Bavinck, *Reformed Dogmatics*, I, 571 (#148).

16. Ed. note: Uninformed faith (*fides informis*) does not mean "ignorant faith" or "faith without knowledge" as the term suggests in ordinary English usage. Rather, it is contrasted in medieval scholastic theology with *fides caritate formata* ("faith informed by love"), which is "faith that is animated and instructed by love (*caritas*) and is therefore active in producing good works.... This conception of faith is denied by the Reformers and the Protestant orthodox insofar as it implies the necessity of works for justification" (Richard A. Muller, *Dictionary of Latin and Greek Theological Terms* [Grand Rapids: Baker Academic, 1985], s.v. *fides caritate formata; fides informis*).

17. T. Aquinas, *Summa theol.*, II, 2, qu. 4, art. 4.

that they do not know and possess a "faith veiled in mystery."[18] Certainly they should possess some knowledge and have an explicit faith with respect to the dogmas that God exists and is one who rewards people, and that he is triune and in Christ became flesh, but for the rest they can limit themselves to an implicit faith and thereby embrace "all that mother church believes to be sacrosanct." On the one hand, therefore, faith is not trust in God's mercy in Christ, as Luther said, nor knowledge or cognition, as Calvin taught, but a simple assent more readily defined by not knowing than by knowing.[19]

5. [For Rome], faith definitely does not consist in the confidence that Christ is *my* Lord and *my* Savior, and that *my* sins are forgiven *me*. For in the first place, faith is a matter of the intellect and trust a matter of the will, and one and the same virtue cannot simultaneously have its seat in two faculties. In the second place, trust is not itself faith but a consequence or fruit of faith. If I firmly believe something, I trust in it. "Faith comes first; faith generates trust." Third, the confidence that my sins have been forgiven me does not coincide with the faith by which I reach out to Christ in order to receive the forgiveness of sin by and from him. Fourth, if faith in the sense of trust justified a person, that would topple the thesis that we are justified by faith alone, for trust also contains hope and love.[20] For all these reasons the confidence that my sins have been forgiven cannot be faith itself but follows it and flows from it.

6. Finally [for Rome], this confidence can never be absolute unless this is communicated by special revelation. It is and remains a moral and conjectural certitude that does not exclude the possibility of error and loss of grace.[21]

Knowledge and Trust

Since the Reformation was born out of the personal experience that humans are not justified by the works of the law but only by faith, it soon opposed Rome with a totally different view of the object and essence of faith. Initially, indeed, Luther still aligned himself with the old definition—derived from Heb. 11:1—that faith is the substance of things hoped for and not seen, but he soon arrived at the insight that it is trust, a matter of confiding in God alone, "trust in a compassion promised on Christ's account." And this became the view of the entire Lutheran Church and theology. Though faith was considered as a kind of knowledge (*notitia; credere Deum* = to believe [in the existence] of God; not yet saving faith) and intellectual assent (*assensus in intellectu; credere Deo* = to believe God; that is, accept his Word; not saving faith), it was above all a willing trust (*fiducia in voluntate; credere in Deum* = a personal trust and love of God that is saving). This

18. P. Lombard, *Sent.*, III, 25.

19. R. Bellarmine, "De justif.," in *Controversiis*, I, c. 7.

20. Ibid., I, c. 10.

21. T. Aquinas, *Summa theol.*, II, 1, qu. 112, art. 5; R. Bellarmine, "De justif.," in *Controversiis*, I, c. 2ff.; Council of Trent, VI, c. 9, can. 13–15; cf. H. Bavinck, *Reformed Dogmatics*, I, 571 (#148); III, 514–17 (#416).

was not a general belief that God exists and that forgiveness and salvation are present in Christ, but a special confidence that forgiveness and salvation have also been granted to me personally. Thus faith was not merely a historical knowledge, but a faith that also believes in the effect of history, specifically the article of the remission of sins, since through Christ we obviously have grace, righteousness, and the remission of sins. Faith was therefore a willingness even to accept the offered promise of the remission of sins and of justification.[22] Calvin indeed pictured the matter somewhat differently and before all else stressed that faith is a "firm and certain knowledge of God's benevolence toward us." He therefore describes it as "cognition" (*cognitio*) and not as "trust" (*fiducia*), and accents the "full and constant certainty" more than "comprehension" (*apprehensio*) in faith.[23] Elsewhere he writes that in Eph. 3:12 the apostle "deduces confidence from faith."[24]

But this is not a real difference between them. Also for Calvin saving faith is not "a knowledge of history" any more than an implicit assent, for without any knowledge faith is inconceivable.[25] Just as in Luther, so for Calvin the special object of this faith is the promise of God in Christ or Christ himself in the garment of Scripture.[26] In Calvin the "assent" of faith too is more of the heart than of the brain, more affect than understanding.[27] Elsewhere Calvin describes faith as "firm and effective confidence"[28] (*firma et efficax fiducia*), and of "the knowledge of divine benevolence toward us" he states that it is "both revealed to our minds and *sealed upon our hearts* through the Holy Spirit."[29]

The difference between the Roman Catholic and the Reformational understanding of faith, accordingly, is this:

1. In the teaching of Rome, faith does not yet include a personal relationship with God but consists in a free and meritorious assent of the intellect—made possible by the grace of God—to all the truths ("mysteries") that God has

22. J. Köstlin, *The Theology of Luther in Its Historical Development and Inner Harmony*, trans. C. E. Hay, 2 vols. (Philadelphia: Lutheran Publication Society, 1897), I, 96ff., 155ff., 507ff.; II, 425ff. Ed. note: Bavinck's own annotation for Köstlin's first German edition is I, 72ff.; III, 130, 134; II, 434ff.; P. Melanchthon, *Corpus doctrinae christianae* (Leipzig: Ernesti Voegelini Constantiensis, 1560), 418ff.; E. F. K. Müller, *Die Bekenntnisschriften der reformierten Kirche* (Leipzig: Deichert, 1903), 46, 95; H. Heppe, *Dogmatik des deutschen Protestantismus im sechzehnten Jahrhundert*, 3 vols. (Gotha: F. A. Perthes, 1857), II, 283ff.; H. F. F. Schmid, *The Doctrinal Theology of the Evangelical Lutheran Church*, trans. C. A. Hay and H. Jacobs, 5th ed. (Philadelphia: United Lutheran Publication House, 1899), 412ff.

23. J. Calvin, *Institutes*, II.ii.7, 14.

24. Ibid., III.ii.15; cf. Piscator, according to H. Heppe, *Dogmatik des deutschen Protestantismus*, 387; G. Voetius, *Selectae disputationes theologicae*, 5 vols. (Utrecht, 1648–69), V, 288–300; A. Ritschl, *The Christian Doctrine of Justification and Reconciliation*, trans. H. R. Mackintosh and A. B. Macaulay (Clifton, NJ: Reference Book Publishers, 1966), 98–99.

25. J. Calvin, *Institutes*, III.ii.2–5.

26. Ibid., II.vi.4; III.ii.7.

27. Ibid., III.ii.8.

28. J. Calvin, *Commentary on Romans*, 10:10.

29. J. Calvin, *Institutes*, III.ii.7.

revealed and the church believes. A personal relationship with God comes into being only by love that is added to faith. But in the thought of the Reformers, faith—though it presupposes some "knowledge of history," in other words, a "general belief"—is in essence and from the start a personal relationship with God, hence of a religious nature through and through.

2. As "special faith," accordingly, it also has a special object, not, as in Rome, all revealed truths, but specifically the divine benevolence in Christ and even more specifically the forgiveness of sins. And this forgiveness, like all of Christ's benefits as well as his person, is not the product of faith nor in any way generated by faith, but totally and completely available in Christ. Hence, it precedes faith and is only accepted and received by that faith.

3. Faith in the case of the Reformers, therefore, whether it is described as knowledge (*cognitio*) or as confident trust (*fiducia*), is always a *certain* knowledge, a *firm* confidence. By its very nature it is the opposite of doubt and includes the certainty of personal salvation. Admittedly, there always remain in believers various kinds of uncertainty, but faith as such is always certainty.[30]

[452] Upon reflection, however, the view of faith presented by the Reformation prompted a variety of questions. At the very outset, there was the relationship between "knowing" and "trusting," general and special faith. The Heidelberg Catechism simply put the two side by side, connecting them only by "not only but also." Simply from a psychological perspective alone, this juxtaposition was problematic, for how could one and the same virtue be simultaneously rooted in two faculties? The usual reply to this question was that the intellect and the will did not differ in reality but only in reason, and that, even if they did differ in reality, there are qualities—such as philosophy, original sin, the image of God—that are rooted in more than one faculty.[31] This reply can hardly be considered satisfactory, for in its first part it proves too much and would erase all distinction between the intellectual and the ethical virtues. In the second part, it makes comparisons that do not hold water, since original sin is not an isolated quality or disposition but the sum total of sinful corruption in human nature as a whole. Many theologians, therefore, continued to feel the difficulty and tried to propose another solution. Some of them, aligning themselves with Calvin, described faith only by the word "knowledge" or "cognition." By this they meant not the knowledge (*scientia*) that is acquired by logical demonstration and not even a purely theoretical knowledge but rather a knowledge of the practical human intellect that has been effected by the Holy Spirit and consists in the conviction ("being persuaded") that Christ is one's Savior.[32]

30. Ibid., III.ii.17ff.

31. J. Maccovius, *Loci communes theologici* (Amsterdam: n.p., 1658), 762; F. Turretin, *Institutes of Elenctic Theology*, trans. G. M. Giger, ed. J. T. Dennison, 3 vols. (Phillipsburg, NJ: Presbyterian & Reformed, 1992), XV, 8, 13.

32. J. Zanchi, *De operum theologicorum*, 8 vols. (Geneva: Samuelis Crispini, 1617), VIII, 712ff.; J. Piscator (and J. Calvin), *Aphorismi doctrinae Christianae, maximam partem ex Institutione Calvini excerpti*, 5th ed.

But this description seemed to others to be much too intellectual and not clearly enough distinguished from the Roman Catholic view. They therefore took a very different direction, indeed accepting that knowledge (*notitia* or *cognitio*) is a prerequisite for faith, but insisting that saving faith consists in trust and is rooted in the will.[33] By far the majority, however, took the middle road, regarding faith not as one, simple disposition but as a composite created by aggregation, which cannot be described by one single act but includes numerous acts belonging to different faculties.[34] But this position also failed to bring satisfaction, for if faith embraces several distinct acts, the question at once arises: What are they and how many are there? In the early period theologians usually spoke of two: knowing and trusting. But Melanchthon had already listed three: knowledge (*notitia*), assent (*assensus*), and trust (*fiducia*),[35] and though many stopped there, others went further and listed many more. Turretin, for example, speaks of seven acts of faith: knowledge, theoretical assent, fiducial and practical assent, taking refuge in Christ, reception of Christ or adhesion to him, reflexive act, consolation and confidence.[36] Witsius even has nine: knowledge, assent, love, hunger and thirst for Christ, reception of Christ, resting on Christ, surrender to Christ, reflexive act, and trust.[37] These various acts of faith are then again reduced to a number of classes, mainly three: the preceding acts (knowledge, theoretical assent, the humbling and denial of the self, and so forth); concomitant acts (practical assent, the yearning for Christ, taking refuge in Christ, apprehension of Christ, and so forth); and subsequent acts (vivifying, soothing, confirming, and fructifying grace).[38]

(Herborn: Chr. Corvinus, 1600), 57: "This faith, therefore, is the certain and firm knowledge of the grace of God, reconciled to us by the merit of the death of Christ, and attested by the word of promise, by which everyone of the faithful individually applies it to himself, holding certain that it pertains to him no less than to the rest of the faithful." Cf. also F. Gomarus, J. van Lodensteyn, J. Patius, *Disputationes theologicarum repetitarum* (Leiden: Ioannis Patii, 1600), XXIII, 12, 22–23; G. Voetius, *Select. disp.*, II, 499ff.; V, 288–300; A. Schweizer, *Die protestantischen Centraldogmen in ihrer Entwicklung innerhalb der reformirten Kirche*, 2 vols. (Zurich: Orell Fussli, 1854–56), II, 239ff.

33. Thus especially "the practicians" (*practici*) in England; cf. P. van Mastricht, *Theoretico-practica theologia* (Utrecht: Appels, 1714), I, 1, 22; B. Keckermann, *Systema s.s. theologiae* (Hanover: Guilielmum Antonium, 1602), 427ff.: "Justifying or saving faith presupposes some knowledge, but in a formal sense it is a [volitional or spiritual] reaching out (*affectus*) toward the promise of grace," and it consists therefore "in the [volitional or spiritual] outreach (*affectus*) applying the promise of grace to the individual (*ad individuum*), not only to humanity in general (*ad speciem tantum*)." Ed. note: Bavinck cites the title as *Syst. theol.* Cf. C. Vitringa, *Doctr. christ.*, III, 51.

34. F. Turretin, *Institutes of Elenctic Theology*, XV, 8, 13.

35. P. Melanchthon, *Loci communes* (Berlin: G. Schlawitz, 1856); O. Kirn, "Glaube," in *PRE*[3], VI, 678.

36. F. Turretin, *Institutes of Elenctic Theology*, XV, qu. 8.

37. H. Witsius, *The Oeconomy of the Covenants between God and Man*, 3 vols. (New York: Lee & Stokes, 1798), II, c. 7; Cf. C. Vitringa, *Doctr. christ.*, III, 49.

38. G. Voetius, *Select. disp.*, II, 499ff.; J. H. Heidegger, *Corpus theologiae* (Zurich: J. H. Bodmer, 1700), XXI, 97ff.; Cf. P. van Mastricht, *Theologia*, I, 1, 21: this faith resides "originatively (*radicaliter*) in the intellect, formally (*formaliter*) in the will, and operatively in the remaining faculties of the soul."

Faith as Disposition (Habit)

Of all these acts specifically the reception or apprehension of Christ was usually considered the formal act of faith, yet it is remarkable that among all these acts love was also listed. Wittichius even listed it between assent and trust as the second act of faith, while others similarly saw a connection between love and faith.[39] In this way it became difficult—against Roman Catholics, Socinians, and generally speaking, against nomists of all kinds—to retain faith as the appropriating organ in justification. This danger moved Comrie and his followers, in defining faith, to work back from the act to the disposition (*habitus*). In this connection the older Reformed usually made a distinction between an active and a passive side to faith and confined themselves to saying that in justification faith only serves as a receptive organ or instrument, while in sanctification it functions as a work and as the principle of good works. Against this view, the Remonstrants asserted that faith, precisely as an instrument, is an act that we are obligated to perform and by which we accept Christ.[40] Comrie's position actually agreed with that of the Remonstrants: if we are justified by faith as an act, then justification is based on works. It is for this reason that in justification faith is not at all considered as act but solely as disposition (*habitus*).[41] No act gives to faith its peculiar form or essence but faith, worked by God in the heart as disposition, immediately possesses its content and form completely within itself. Knowledge, assent, and trust are integral to it and all belong to it equally and essentially.[42] But these elements do not, as acts, justify us; on the contrary, there must be something in the inner nature of faith by which it is truly distinguished from all works, whatever they are called.[43] This is the reason Comrie distinguishes the ingrafting into Christ by faith as disposition from the acts of faith and accords it precedence over these acts by which we on our part accept Christ and so forth. This is also why in his exposition of Q&A 21 of the Heidelberg Catechism he proceeds from the answer to question 20.[44] However astutely Comrie unfolds all this, one cannot suppress the question whether this interpretation does justice to the words of answer 21 and to the position of the Reformers. Can the disposition of faith (seed, root, faculty or principle of faith) really be formally called faith? Was Voetius not right when he wrote concerning faith as root, faculty, and so forth? "This [principle]

39. Cf. B. de Moor, *Comm. theol.*, IV, 358ff.; C. Vitringa, *Doctr. christ.*, III, 70; T. van der Groe and H. P. Scholte (*Het zaligmakende geloof*, new ed. [Amsterdam: H. Höveker, 1838], 56) consider a righteous love for and honoring of Christ as part of the essence of faith.

40. Apologia pro Confessione, c. 10; S. Episcopius, *Opera theologica*, 2 vols. (Amsterdam, 1650–55), II, 165; J. Trigland, *Antapologia* (Amsterdam: Joannam Janssonium et al., 1664), 318ff.

41. A. Comrie, *Stellige en praktikale verklaring van den Heidelbergschen Catechismus* (Minnertsga: J. Bloemsma, 1856), 386.

42. Ibid., 412.

43. Ibid., XXVI.

44. Ibid., 373ff.; cf. N. Holtius, *Godgeleerde verhandeling over het oprecht geloof* (Leiden, 1747), in this edition (Bolsward, 1851) published at the back of his *Verhandeling over de Rechtvaerdigmaking door het geloof*, 215–62.

cannot be called faith except by analogy and improperly by metonymy of the cause or of the principle: formally this is no more faith than a seed is a tree, or an egg a chicken, or a bulb a flower."[45]

[453] No less serious were the problems that arose when theologians reflected on the nature of trust or confidence (*fiducia*), which was regarded by so many of them as the true formal act of faith. Bellarmine had already objected that my confidence that all my sins have been forgiven me cannot possibly be identical to the faith by which I accept Christ unto the forgiveness of my sins but can only be a consequence and fruit of it. This criticism made a deep impression. Gomarus substantially accepted it as valid when he made a distinction between the faith through which we are justified (*fides, per quam justificamur*) and the faith by which we believe that through Christ our sins have been forgiven (*fides, qua credimus nobis per Christum remissa esse peccata*). The former precedes justification, the latter follows it. The former is enjoined on all by Scripture; the latter follows from Scripture, from the witness of our own conscience, and is as it were the conclusion of a syllogism.[46] This distinction was intended more in a logical than in a temporal sense, was accepted by all the theologians,[47] and would not yet by itself have had such important consequences had it not been reinforced by two considerations. The first was of a theoretical nature and was derived from the doctrine of limited, or particular, atonement. According to the Reformed confession, Christ did not obtain salvation for all humans individually but only for the elect. In Scripture, however, these elect are not mentioned by name, and the gospel is preached to all without distinction and all are called and obligated to believe. No one, accordingly, can and may start by believing that Christ has made satisfaction for oneself and that one's sins are forgiven. But inasmuch as the gospel says that all who believe receive forgiveness and life, he may only, if he believes, conclude from his faith that he has received the forgiveness of his sins. Thus, between the direct act of faith by which I, in my lost condition, take

---

45. G. Voetius, *Select. disp.*, II, 499; V, 288. Ed. note: in the Heidelberg Catechism, Q&A 20–21 read as follows:

> Q 20: Are all saved through Christ just as all were lost in Adam?
> A: No, only those who by true faith are grafted into Christ and accept his blessings.
> Q 21: What is true faith?
> A: True faith is not only a knowledge and conviction that everything God reveals in his Word is true. It is also a deep-rooted assurance, created in me by the Holy Spirit through the gospel, that, out of sheer grace, earned for us by Christ, not only others, but I too have had my sins forgiven, have been made forever right with God, and have been granted salvation.

46. F. Gomarus, in an appendix to his commentary on the Epistle to the Hebrews, *Op.*, I, 654ff.

47. W. Ames, *The Marrow of Theology*, trans. J. D. Eusden (1968; repr., Grand Rapids: Baker Academic, 1997), I.27.16 (p. 162); J. Maccovius, *Loci comm.*, 765; P. van Mastricht, *Theologia*, I, 1, 25; G. Voetius, *Select. disp.*, II, 502; F. Turretin, *Institutes of Elenctic Theology*, XV, qu. 8, 7, 11; qu. 10, 3; qu. 12, 6; A. Comrie, *Catechismus*, 447; W. à Brakel, *The Christian's Reasonable Service*, trans. Bartel Elshout, 4 vols. (Ligonier, PA: Soli Deo Gloria, 1992–95), III, 357ff. (Dutch: XXXIV, 27). Cf. also, Westminster Confession, c. 18, 3; Rev. D. Beaton, "'The Marrow of Modern Divinity' and the Marrow Controversy," *Princeton Theological Review* 4 (July 1906): 327–31.

refuge in Christ—in order to receive from him forgiveness and salvation—and the reflexive act of faith by which I return to myself in the consciousness that I truly possess forgiveness and salvation, a serious question intervened: Do I truly believe in Christ, is my faith genuine, and does it bear the stamp of truth? Could it be only a temporal or historical faith?

The Problem of Certainty

And this split between the outgoing and the returning act of faith is fostered by that other consideration that is grounded in the practice of life. The Reformers did not yet make that distinction in the faith, because they walked in the full assurance of faith. They believed and therefore spoke. Their mouths ran over with what filled their heart. But this period of strong faith and the clear consciousness of faith soon passed. Another generation appeared that had no longer personally experienced this internal spiritual reformation. In their confession church members might say that faith consisted in a deep-rooted assurance "that I too have had my sins forgiven," but reality conveyed a very different message. Assured Christians were rare. Most of the members of the church were indifferent, content with their orthodoxy, or seekers and doubters who could not find peace of mind and heart. Though the doctrine had been purified, life left very much to be desired. Under the influence of English and Scottish practicians, a series of men arose who lamented the decay of the church and the doctrine of morals, announced the judgments of God and saw them coming in the form of disasters of various kinds and wars and only expected salvation from a reformation of human hearts and lives.[48] They summoned governments and church ministers to do their duty and urged everyone to practice serious and painstaking self-examination. Orthodoxy, church membership, being born of believing parents, baptism, confession of faith, communion—all of these were insufficient. He who has no more than that "takes the shell of truth he has just confessed to be the truth itself."[49] Others even more

---

48. Great influence was exerted mainly by W. Teellinck, Witsius, and Lodenstein: W. Teellinck, *Noodwendigh vertoogh, aengaende den tegen woordigen bedroef den staet van Gods volck* (Middelburg: Hans vander Hellen, 1627); idem, *De Toetsteen des geloofs, waerin de gelegentheijt des waren saligmakende geloofs nader ontdekt wordt, soo dat een ijder sich selven daer an kann toetsen of hij oock het ware saligmakende geloove heft*, published after his death in 1662; H. Witsius, *Twist des Heeren met zijn wijngaard* (1699; 5th ed., Utrecht: Jacob van Poolsum, 1719); J. van Lodensteyn, *Beschouwinge van Zion* (Utrecht: Willem Clerck, 1674).

49. Lodensteyn in W. Schortinghuis, **Zedig antwoord op het historisch verhaal van den Hoogerw. en Z. Gel. Heere Daniel Gerdes enz.* (Groningen, 1740), 99:

> The husk of the truth
>   you just confessed [in church],
> you take for truth itself.
> You poor erring creature—
> Truth is the being
>   that shines from above,
>   into our reason. (editor's translation)

Ed. note: Schortinghuis's treatise appears to be a response to critique of his *Het innige Christendom*, 2nd ed. (Groningen: Jurjen Spandaw; 's Gravenhage: Ottho and Pieter van Thol, 1740) by the theological faculty

vigorously took up arms against mere knowledge of the letter and groaned: "O Lord, save us from the letter that has killed thousands, and put the stamp of your Spirit upon it!" They fought fervently for a practical, kindhearted, and experiential Christianity.[50] But also those who avoided this extreme in practice virtually abandoned the doctrine of regeneration before baptism; had little confidence in a so-called "evangelical conversion"; insisted on the contrition of the heart, conviction of sin, and a sense of misery as conditions for obtaining Christ and his benefits; and in the order of salvation accorded a place to justification and rebirth *after* faith.[51]

Viewing this dejected and indecisive state of people's spiritual life, still others sought to take a safer route and again included the certainty of salvation in the essence of faith. But in so doing, they usually erred as far to the left as their adversaries erred to the right and regarded deep-seated confidence not just as an essential component but as the full substance, the formal act (*actus formalis*), of the faith.[52] This in turn led very easily to the antinomian view that faith

of the University of Groningen, *Historisch verhaal aengaande de akademische approbatie van de hoog eerw. theol. faculteit van de Universiteit van Stad en Lande over een zeker boek* (Groningen: Hajo Spandaw, 1740).

50. So especially J. Eswijler, *Ziels-eenzame meditatiën* (Rotterdam: H. van Pelt, 1739); ed. note: Bavinck cites the 1685 edition. J. Verschuir, *Waarheid in het binnenste, of bevindelyke Godtgeleer theit*, 5th ed. ('s Gravenhage: J. Thierry, 1776); ed. note: Bavinck cites the 1841 edition. W. Schortinghuis, *Het innige Christendom*, 2nd ed. (1740); ed. note: Bavinck cites 1710 edition. Dr. J. C. Kromsigt, *Wilhelmus Schortinghuis* (Groningen: J. B. Wolters, 1904), 141ff.

51. Cf. Jac. Koelman, *De natuur en gronden des geloofs*, 4th ed. (Utrecht: Willem David Gromme, 1700); ed. note: Bavinck cites the 5th ed. (Rotterdam, 1768). T. van der Groe, *Toetssteen der waare en valsche genade*, 8th ed., 2 vols. (Rotterdam: H. van Pelt & A. Douci Pietersz, 1752–53), I, 151, 251; II, 743ff., 951ff.; Van der Groe nevertheless maintained that though assurance is not the entire substance of faith (as van Hattem believed), it is an essential ingredient in it. On this point he was vehemently attacked by Jacob Groenewegen, Adriaan van der Willegen, and Theodorus van der Groe, *Beschrijvinge van het oprecht en zielzaligend geloove* (Rotterdam: R. C. Huge, 1742). According to Lampe, faith precedes regeneration (F. A. Lampe, *De verborgenheit van het genaade-verbondt*, 4 vols. [Amsterdam: Antony Schoonenburg, 1726–39], 254–69, 287); ed. note: Bavinck cites the 1718 edition. Lampe divides believers into the "weak" and the "strong." In the case of the former, there is first a desire, a hungering and thirsting for Christ, then a going, coming, seeking, taking refuge in, and an unashamed adhesion to Christ; in the case of the latter, there is first of all a boldness to appropriate Christ, to mine, kiss, eat, and drink him, then a full assurance, a reliance on, a resting, and a delighting in Christ. A. Driessen, professor in Groningen, in his polemic against van Thuynen, also initially took the same position. According to him, the essence of faith consists in hungering and thirsting for the righteousness of Christ, that is, in a refuge-taking trust. Deep-rooted trust, on the other hand, can only arise if by self-examination one has become persuaded of the genuineness of one's faith. Later he became more moderate and acknowledged that the hungering and thirsting to some extent implied the eating and being satisfied. Those who truly seek Jesus enjoy him as well; those who seek have found. Deep-rooted assurance, accordingly, does not arise from refuge-taking trust as the root grows from the seed. The latter is itself a kind of implicit trust. Cf. J. C. Kromsigt, *Wilhelmus Schortinghuis*, 82ff.; 96ff.

52. Jac. Schuts (*Beschrijving van het Zaligmahend Geloof* [Rotterdam: R. van Doesburgh, 1692]) says that all the acts of faith—knowing, assenting, trusting, and so forth—already presuppose faith, and that faith essentially consists in holding as true God's witness concerning Christ (20, 34), hence in assent. Especially Theod. van Thuynen (*Korte uitlegginge van het gereformeerde geloof* [Leeuwarden: Henrick Halma, 1722]) sought to demonstrate that though hungering and thirsting, taking refuge in Christ, and so forth, precede faith and

consists in the intellectual acceptance of the sentence "Your sins are forgiven," a sentence not first uttered in the gospel by God himself but contained from all eternity in the decree of election, and finally only revealed by the person and work of Christ.[53]

Rationalism and Moralism

[454] In this manner the ground was prepared for the rationalistic and moralistic approach to the order of redemption followed by nearly all theologians in the eighteenth century. Abandoning Reformed principles, this school of thought aligned itself with Socinians[54] and Arminians[55] and taught that faith—conceived only as assent or to some extent also as trust (*fiducia*)—could itself justify a person only insofar as it contained within itself the new obedience and was a source of virtue.[56] Against this one-sided position Schleiermacher had a valid point when he said that religion was neither a matter of knowledge nor of action but had its seat in the heart, and that the Christian religion differs from all other religions by the fact that everything in it is related to the redemption brought about by Jesus of Nazareth. But this position in turn led theologians, when speaking of faith, to put all the emphasis on the mysticism of the heart. Faith did not consist in some doctrine but in "the appropriation of the perfection and blessedness of Christ,"[57] "the secret point of union between Christ and the individual,"[58] personal communion with Christ, a moral power, a sanctifying principle, a new life.[59] Ritschl therefore presented a view of faith that diverged

---

lead to it, faith itself essentially consists in the deep-rooted confidence that we are reconciled to God and have received the forgiveness of sins. In his opinion, the precisionists, whom he combats, turn the order around. They think that God is reconcilable and that he is only reconciled by their faith (religious experience, good works). They—like Roman Catholics and Remonstrants—have justification follow faith, whereas, according to the Reformed confession, it precedes it. Joining van Thuynen in this position were (inter al.) Ph. Themmen, H. Stegnerus, and C. Vrolikhert (*Godgeleerde oeffeningen* [Middelburg: P. Gillisfen, 1732]) in his two-theological treatises on the covenant of works, the imputation of Christ's active obedience, and the nature and essence of faith. Cf. A. Ritschl, *Geschichte des Pietismus in der reformierten Kirche* (Bonn: A. Marcus, 1880), 321ff.; J. C. Kromsigt, *Wilhelmus Schortinghuis*, 74ff.

53. Cf. on Van Hattem, Verschoor, Leenhof, and others, H. Bavinck, *Reformed Dogmatics*, III, 528–31 (#420), 564–69 (#427b); C. Vitringa, *Doctr. christ.*, III, 100, 108; B. de Moor, *Comm. theol.*, IV, 419–23, 833; J. C. Kromsigt, *Wilhelmus Schortinghuis*, 7, 8.

54. O. Fock, *Der Socinianismus* (Kiel: C. Schröder, 1847), 673; C. Vitringa, *Doctr. christ.*, III, 73.

55. *The Confession of the Remonstrants* (London, 1676), ch. 11; P. van Limborch, *Theologia christiana* (Amsterdam: Arnhold, 1735), V, 9, 24ff.; Cf. C. Vitringa, *Doctr. christ.*, III, 75.

56. K. G. Bretschneider, *Handbuch der Dogmatik der evangelisch-lutherischen Kirche*, 4th ed., 2 vols. (Leipzig: J. A. Barth, 1838), II, 319; G. C. Knapp, *Vorlesungen über die christliche Glaubenslehre*, 2 vols., ed. Carl Thilo (Halle: Waisenhauses, 1827), II, 324–25; J. A. L. Wegscheider, *Institutiones theologiae christianae dogmaticae*, 3rd ed. (Halle: Gebauer, 1819), 159; cf. on neonomism, H. Bavinck, *Reformed Dogmatics*, III, 531–35 (#421).

57. F. Schleiermacher, *The Christian Faith*, ed. H. R. MacIntosh and J. S. Steward (Edinburgh: T&T Clark, 1928), 108; cf. H. Bavinck, *Reformed Dogmatics*, III, 550–54 (#425).

58. H. L. Martensen, *Christian Dogmatics*, trans. William Urwick (Edinburgh: T&T Clark, 1871), 368.

59. H. Bavinck, *De theologie van Prof. Dr. Daniel Chantepie de la Saussaye*, 2nd ed. (Leiden: D. Donner, 1903), 62ff.

from that of Mediating Theology (*Vermittelungstheologie*)[60] in three ways. In the first place, he went back from the exalted Christ to the "historical" Jesus as depicted specifically in the Synoptic Gospels. Second, in his thinking the person of Christ receded behind the gospel he preached and the work he accomplished. Third, faith did not consist in a mystical union with the glorified Christ but in the heart's trust in the revelation of God in the historical Jesus and, more specifically, in the revelation that God out of his grace forgave sin and wishes to establish a spiritual kingdom in humankind.[61] In distinction from this theology of Schleiermacher and Ritschl, the characteristic features of Positive Theology[62] are that it makes the whole Christ as he is portrayed to us in Scripture—specifically including his expiatory suffering and death—the object of faith. Furthermore, it also views this faith, though not exclusively, as assent[63] and binds believers to the word of God in Scripture. Finally, it gives to conversion, in the sense of sorrow over sin, and, in that connection, to the preaching of the law a larger place in the formation of the Christian life than usually happens in other schools of theological thought.[64]

60. Ed note: On "Mediating Theology" (*Vermittelungstheologie*), see H. Bavinck, *Reformed Dogmatics*, I, 49n49 (#9).

61. A. Ritschl, *Justification and Reconciliation*, 98ff., 568ff., 582ff.; J. Kaftan, *Dogmatik* (Tübingen: Mohr, 1901), 3, 69; W. Herrmann, *Der Verkehr des Christen mit Gott*, 4th ed. (Stuttgart: Cotta, 1908), 170ff.; ed. note: Bavinck cites the 1903 edition. J. Gottschick, *Die Kirchlichkeit der soganannte kirchliche Theologie* (Freiburg i.B.: Mohr, 1890), 11–53; cf. also H. Bavinck, *Reformed Dogmatics*, III, 550–54 (#425).

62. I. A. Dorner, *A System of Christian Doctrine*, trans. Alfred Cave and J. S. Banks, rev. ed., 4 vols. (Edinburgh: T&T Clark, 1888), I, 19ff.; II, 152ff.; F. A. Philippi, *Kirchliche Glaubenslehre*, 3rd ed., 7 vols. (Gütersloh: Bertelsmann, 1883–1902), V, 1, 41ff.; C. E. Luthardt, *Compendium der Dogmatik* (Leipzig: Dörffling & Francke, 1865), 63; F. H. R. Frank, *System der Christlichen Wahrheit*, 2nd ed., 4 vols. in 2 (Erlangen: A. Deichert, 1884), II, 333ff.; A. von Oettingen, *Lutherische Dogmatik*, 2 vols. (Munich: C. H. Beck, 1897), I, 316ff.; III, 542ff.; G. Runze, *Katechismus der Dogmatik* (Leipzig: J. J. Weber, 1898), 263ff.; R. B. Kübel, *Ueber der Unterschied zwischen der positiven und der liberalen Richtung in der modernen Theologie*, 2nd ed. (Munich: C. H. Beck, 1893), 26ff.

63. This happens most vigorously in E. König, "Glaubensgewissheit und Schriftzeugniss," *Neue kirchliche Zeitschrift* 1 (1890): 439–63, 515–30; idem, *Der Glaubensact des Christen nach Begriff und Fundament untersucht* (Erlangen: Deichert, 1891); idem, "Der biblisch-reformatorische Glaubensbegriff und seine neueste Bekämpfung," *Neue kirchliche Zeitschrift* 19 (1908): 628–60; W. Herrmann, "Lage und Aufgabe der evangelische Dogmatik," *Zeitschrift für Theologie und Kirche* 17 (1907): 1–33. According to König, there is no difference between Rome and the Reformation concerning "general faith," for faith is always and everywhere the acceptance of a truth on the basis of a witness, hence intellectual knowledge and assent. However, since this "general faith" relates in a religious sense to a specific content, i.e., to the salvific promises of God in Christ, it becomes a "special faith" and results in "the strongest resonance in the world of feeling and the most powerful impact on the will." Although König makes very weighty comments against viewing faith as "experience" (*Erlebnis*), he leaves general faith and special faith standing unresolved side by side and makes saving faith depend on the doubtful results of historical research.

64. All the above-mentioned proponents of a Positive Theology consider so-called penitence an essential element in conversion, whether they assign to it a place *before* or *in* the faith, but specify nothing about the degree, time, or duration of it. By contrast, such further specifications occur frequently in Methodist circles, also in the so-called modern fellowship movement. Cf. M. Schian, *Die moderne Gemeinschaftsbewegung* (Stuttgart: Greiner & Pfeiffer, 1909), 9ff.

Despite this and other points of difference, however, the new views of faith also have important features in common. Peculiar to them, in the first place, is an attempt to transcend the ancient opposition between Pelagianism and Augustinianism, and to let faith arise by way of the psychological, pedagogical, and historical path God follows with almost all human beings. In this path divine and human activities constantly interact with each other,[65] or else are one and the same activity considered either from the divine or the human perspective.[66] Second, all agree that the essence of saving faith consists in trust, that is, in a personal relationship with God as he has revealed himself as a God of grace and salvation in Christ. Some, out of reaction against orthodoxy, have gone so far in this connection as to remove knowledge and assent entirely from faith and locate it exclusively in trust. This is how the split ended, which in the beginning had been made by Ritschl and his school between ontological and value judgments and in the Parisian school of Symbolo-fideism between faith and beliefs.[67] But this dichotomy soon proved untenable. If faith, however inwardly conceived, is to remain Christian and hence bound to the revelation of God in the person of Christ, it will always presuppose or include a certain "knowledge" and "assent."[68] When Ménégoz was attacked from all directions over his formula "salvation by faith independently of beliefs," he explained himself further by saying that he had no desire to deny the pedagogical importance of beliefs, nor to sever the connection between "beliefs" and "faith," but only wanted to warn against confusing and equating the two. Beliefs are so indispensable to faith that "belief even engenders faith and there is no faith without belief."[69] Faith is independent of beliefs only in the sense that "our beliefs, whatever they are—true or false—do not account for anything in the judgment God brings down upon us. God does not look at our beliefs—only at our hearts. Whoever gives his heart to him, that is, whoever has true faith, is pleasing to him, whatever his doctrinal errors may be; and whoever does not give his heart to him, that is, whoever is an unbeliever, will be condemned, however orthodox he has been. We are saved by faith *alone*—sola fide—independently of our beliefs."[70] Conversely, Positive Theology emphasizes as strongly as possible

65. Cf. A. Ritschl, *Justification and Reconciliation*, 568, 588; J. Kaftan, *Dogmatik*, 624ff.; W. Herrmann, *Der Verkehr des Christen mit Gott*, 82ff., 171ff., 183; H. Bavinck, *Reformed Dogmatics*, II, 371 (#239); III, 550–54 (#425).

66. Cf. von Hartmann in H. Bavinck, *Reformed Dogmatics*, III, 540–45 (#423).

67. Cf. H. Bavinck, *Reformed Dogmatics*, I, 195 (#58), 550 (#144), 557 (#146), 571 (#148); H. Haldimann, *Le Fidéisme* (Paris: Fischbacher, 1907).

68. W. Herrmann, *Der Verkehr des Christen mit Gott*, 180: "The Christian faith is not, first of all, concerned generally about doctrine, but rather about an encounter that firmly impacts the life of people who are called to faith. Nonetheless, knowledge is indeed a precondition of faith." Cf. ibid., 45ff.; idem, "Der geschichtliche Christus, der Grund unseres Glaubens," *Zeitschrift für Theologie und Kirche* 2 (1892): 232ff.; M. Reischle, *Der Streit über die Begründung des Glaubens auf den geschichtlichen Jesus Christus* (Freiburg i.B.: J. C. B. Mohr, 1897), 171ff.; J. Gottschick, *Die Kirchlichkeit der sogenannte kirchlichen Theologie*, 6, 8; J. Kaftan, *Dogmatik*, 25ff.

69. E. Ménégoz, *Publications diverses sur le Fidéisme* (Paris: Fischbacher, 1900), 251.

70. Ibid., 262.

that "general faith," however indispensable, is insufficient, and that "particular faith" consists in the confidence of the heart. The only remaining difference—a difference that is not unimportant—concerns the question whether "general faith" precedes or flows from a "particular faith."

Finally, the newer descriptions of faith further show great convergence in that, in addition to its religious nature, they powerfully underscore the ethical nature of faith. Inasmuch as Ritschl regarded justification as a possession of the church and viewed it more as a presupposition than as the content of faith, mysticism did not come into its own in his thinking, and he ran the danger of collapsing religion into morality. Faith, after all, consists especially in working for the kingdom of God and essentially coincides with love.[71] Over against this view, others rightly maintain the religious nature of faith and regard justification and the mystical union as benefits that are also granted to every individual believer, but they too do their best to hold on to the inner connectedness between faith and love, between justification and sanctification, and to bring to the fore the morally renewing powers of the Christian religion.[72]

FAITH AND REGENERATION: WHICH IS PRIOR?

[455] The descriptions that have been given of faith since the Reformation are so numerous and divergent as to make a person almost despair of the possibility of correctly and clearly defining the nature of faith. Roman Catholic theology has the advantage of a very simple and understandable definition when it describes faith solely as assent. But in so doing it puts saving faith on a level with all other historical faith, denies its religious nature, must therefore later complement it with love, and thus makes the forgiveness of sins and the eternal blessed life depend on our good works. In Scripture, however, faith is not merely an intellectual act of accepting the witness of the apostles concerning Christ, but also a personal relation, a spiritual bond, with Christ who is now seated at the right hand of the power of God. There it occupies such a central place that it can be called "the work of God" par excellence (John 6:29). It is the principle of the Christian life as a whole, the means by which we obtain Christ and all his benefits, the subjective source of all salvation and blessing. While through Scripture it binds us to the historical Christ, it at the same time lifts us up to the invisible world and causes us to live in communion with the Lord from heaven. Wherever faith may be rooted

---

71. A. Ritschl, *Justification and Reconciliation*, 584: "The belief in Christ and God falls under the scope of ... the concept of love. It is the continuous direction of the will to God and Christ, which is part of the content of faith itself." Ibid., 100ff.

72. W. Herrmann, *Der Verkehr*, 241ff.; J. Kaftan, *Dogmatik*, 22; T. Häring, *The Christian Faith*, trans. John Dickie and George Ferries, 2 vols. (London: Hodder & Stoughton, 1913), II, 691ff.; F. H. R. Frank, *System der christlichen Wahrheit*, II, 354ff.; A. von Oettingen, *Lutherische Dogmatik*, III, 542, 572; W. Schmidt, *Christliche Dogmatik*, 4 vols. (Bonn: E. Weber, 1895–98), II, 3ff.; M. Kähler, *Dogmatische Zeitfragen: Alte und neue Ausführungen zur Wissenschaft der christlichen Lehre*, 2nd ed., 3 vols. (Leipzig: Deichert, 1907–13), 467ff. Kähler incorporates ethics in his dogmatics under the heading "The Corroboration of Faith in Justification."

in human beings, it affects all our capacities and powers, gives us direction and guidance; controls our intellect and heart, our thinking and activity, our life and conduct. Christians are believers (πιστοι). Faith is mystical and noetic, receptive and spontaneous, passive and active, the opposite of all works and itself the work of God par excellence, the means of justification and the principle of sanctification, accompanying us throughout our lives and changing into sight only at death. It is only natural that theology has to struggle to give a somewhat correct definition of it. But even if it succeeded in doing this, it would never be able to control human life and prevent all its one-sidednesses and aberrations in practice. Still, it should not be impossible, in the order of redemption, to give faith the place and the significance that is due to it according to Scripture.

To that end it needs to be in the foreground of our consciousness that all the benefits of salvation are secured by Christ and present in him and that he himself, as the Lord from heaven, is by his Spirit the one who distributes and applies them. Neither faith nor conversion is the condition that in any way acquires salvation for us. They are only the way in which the benefits of the covenant enter into the subjective possession of those for whom they were acquired. To that extent it is completely correct to say that justification, like the other benefits of the covenant, precedes faith. In "the pact of salvation" (*pactum salutis*) the Son already acted as the Guarantor and Mediator of his own. According to 2 Cor. 5:19, God reconciles the world to himself in Christ, not counting its trespasses against it, and Rom. 4:25 clearly states that Christ, who was handed over to death on account of our sins, was raised for our justification; that is, to acquire this justification by his death and to communicate it to us by his resurrection. Reconciliation (καταλλαγη) is not distinguished from expiation (ἱλασμος) by the fact that while the latter is objective the former is subjective. The former is also objective. The content of the gospel message is this: God *has been* reconciled, accept this reconciliation, and believe the gospel. Reconciliation, forgiveness, sanctification, and so forth, are not effected by our faith or our conversion but have been completely secured by Christ, who distributes them at his pleasure.

This needs to be remembered all the more since there is no participation in the benefits of Christ except by communion with his person. The benefits of the covenant are not material goods that can be owned and enjoyed apart from the mediator of that covenant. They are included in him and never exist independently of him. When it is said that Christ secured them, this means that God grants these benefits out of grace without violating his righteousness and can grant them in communion with Christ. Among the benefits Christ has secured, there is, specifically, also the gift of the Holy Spirit. He himself became Spirit. By his suffering and death he made the Spirit of the Father and the Son also *his* Spirit, the Spirit of Christ, and therefore distributes that Spirit at his pleasure while the Spirit himself takes all things from him. The gift of the Spirit, accordingly, presupposes that God has already imparted and granted his Christ, and that Christ has given himself. Also, the very first benefit of salvation is a benefit of the covenant that presupposes the objective mystical union. Not only is there no resurrection, but neither is there a crucifixion and a burial, no mortification of the old self, except in communion with Christ. This imputation and donation of Christ and his benefits already took place, ideally, in the decree and from all eternity. It was objectively realized in Christ as head and mediator when he became human, died, and was raised. Materially it is also the content of the word of the gospel. It is individually applied and distributed only in the internal calling and passively accepted on the human side in regeneration. Whether it takes place in childhood, youth, or later, before or during the hearing of the Word, logically it always precedes the act of really believing. "For no one can hear the word of God salvifically unless he is regenerate."[73] No one can come to Christ unless the Father draws him (John 6:44; also cf. Rom. 8:7; 1 Cor. 2:14; 12:3; etc.).

But regeneration in a restricted sense, as the infusion of the principle of the new life, may also temporally precede faith. In their polemic with Anabaptists, the Reformed gradually arrived at the insight that the faculty, seed, or disposition of faith, in other words, regeneration in a restricted sense, could already occur in infancy before the awakening of consciousness, in or before baptism, or even before birth. They appealed to the examples of Jeremiah (1:5), John the Baptist (Luke 1:15), Paul (Gal. 1:15), and Jesus himself (Luke 1:35); and beyond these examples, to the teaching of Scripture concerning circumcision and baptism, church and the covenant of grace; in other words, they appealed to all those proofs that were advanced in support of pedobaptism that will be discussed later. If regeneration did not occur in infancy, either [the doctrine of] original sin would be weakened, or one would have to despair of the salvation of children who die in their infancy. However, since the grace of God is pure grace and hence absolutely independent of any human condition, and since, especially in the New Testament dispensation of it, it is abundant (Rom. 5:15) and extended to all races and peoples, there need not be either any weakening of [the doctrine of] original sin or any denial of salvation for all those who die in their infancy. For God no door is locked, no creature unapproachable, no heart inaccessible. With his Spirit he can enter the innermost being of every human, with or without the Word, by way of or apart from all consciousness, in old age or from the moment of conception. Christ's own conception by the Holy Spirit in Mary's womb is proof that the Holy Spirit can, from that moment on and continually, be active in a human being with his sanctifying presence.

The objection raised against this view always comes down to the fact that in this way the freedom and independence of a person is abandoned and a decision is made concerning people's salvation entirely apart from them. But, in the first place, this objection applies in the same degree with respect to the regeneration that occurs at a later age. For, unless one wants to take the Pelagian route and make regeneration dependent on a person's free religious choice, regeneration in this

---

73. J. Maccovius, *Loci communes*, 710.

case precedes faith and takes place *in* a person *without* input from that person. Second, it is an undeniable fact that all children have been conceived and born in sin and are therefore subject to all manner of misery, even to condemnation itself. Against this background, it is a most comforting thought that as children they are similarly received without their knowledge unto grace in Christ. And, third, this confession finds support in the manner in which God, in creation and providence, goes to work in the distribution of his gifts. No one can say to him: What are You doing? For no one makes us different but God. What have we that we did not receive? And if we received it, why do we boast as if it were not a gift? (cf. 1 Cor. 4:7).

The doctrine of regeneration in a restrictive sense, therefore, is a precious part of our Reformed confession. Godly parents derive from it the consolation that they need not doubt the election and salvation of their children whom God takes from this life in their infancy, even though in their case the spiritual life could not yet manifest itself in acts of faith and repentance. Here, too, lies the possibility for us to hold on to the continuity of the spiritual life from its very earliest beginnings to its highest point of development and perfection. For regeneration in the restricted sense, according to our Reformed ancestors, does not merely consist in the gift of the power to believe, in the restoration of free will in a baptismal regeneration that differs from regeneration as a renewal of life and is dependent for its permanence on subsequent acts of personal assent and acceptance. On the contrary, it is immediately a regeneration in the full sense of the word, encompassing in principle the whole person, initially renewing all of one's capacities and powers, and later manifesting and confirming itself in all directions, in faith and repentance, in sanctification and good works. It is one and the same life that is infused in regeneration, is continually strengthened in the process of growing up, and will be completed in the eternal blessed life of the hereafter.

The confession of regeneration as the implantation of the new life principle, accordingly, further holds within it an excellent pedagogical value. It is not an incontrovertible dogma, of course, that *all* covenant children or even all *elect* covenant children have already been regenerated in their infancy before or in baptism. Reformed theologians have never held this view in this rigorous sense. But they firmly maintained that such a rebirth in early childhood before the years of discretion *could* take place, since the Spirit of Christ is not bound to the consciousness and will of human beings. They confessed that such a rebirth in early life in fact often *did* take place, especially in the case of children whom God took from this life in their infancy. Finally, they held firmly to the rule that we must regard and treat all covenant children born and baptized in the fellowship of the church not as pagan children, but in accordance with the judgment of charity, as true children of the covenant, until from their "talk" and "walk" the contrary is evident. At this point we cannot set forth in detail the great power and value inherent in this view for Christian nurture, the nurture that occurs in the family as well as that which takes place in the school and the church.[74] But it characterizes Reformed education and upbringing in distinction from that of Anabaptists and Methodists; maintains the bond between nature and grace; proceeds from the reality of the covenant of grace and baptism; believes in the unity and organic development of the spiritual life; and fully recognizes that God does not always work faith and repentance in the human heart suddenly, but often—indeed as a rule—causes them to proceed and develop from the implanted life gradually, by a psychological and pedagogical process.

This view is absolutely not inconsistent with the fact that in Scripture faith is consistently described as a gift of God (Matt. 11:25–27; 16:17; John 1:12–13; 6:44; 1 Cor. 12:3; Gal. 1:16; Eph. 1:11; 2:8; Phil. 1:29; 2:13), just as it is also always eagerly and gratefully recognized as such by all true believers. For the way in which God carries out his counsel in no way detracts from the reality and power of that counsel and is in fact itself included and defined in that counsel. God can bring the person whom he regenerated according to his will to faith and repentance either suddenly or gradually, but always remains the same gracious omnipotent God, who works both the willing and the working according to his good pleasure. After all, just as in creation, after calling forth all things out of nothing, he did not withdraw from the world and leave it to its own devices, so also in re-creation he does not abandon the work he began in regeneration. By his Spirit he indwells the entire created world, and by that same Spirit, as the Spirit of Christ, he is present in the entire church and in each of its members. He does not have to break in from without or come down from above, but by his Spirit, who dwells in Christ and in the church as his body, he penetrates the innermost parts of human beings, opens what is closed, softens the hardened heart, makes his home there, and never again leaves it. He continually strengthens the new life from within (Eph. 3:16) and feeds it from without by the proclamation of his Word. The internal and external calling go hand in hand. Just as God causes the seed in the field to swell and break open from within, causes it to sink its roots downward and to germinate and sprout upward and in this process uses the nutrients and juices present in the soil, rain, and sunshine as his means, so also he strengthens and nourishes the spiritual life [of his children] from moment to moment by the power of his grace and the blessing of his Word. He is at work, not just for a moment, but continually enabling us both to will and to work according to his good pleasure. He indeed grants us the capacity to believe and the power of faith but also the will to believe and faith itself, not mechanically or magically, but inwardly, spiritually, organically, in connection with the word that he brings to people in various ways. These include the reading of Scripture, the advice and admonition of parents, the instruction of teachers, and public preaching. The moment faith awakens out of the seedbed of the new life, it links up with that word, and the moment it has heard that word, it in turn finds resonance in that

---

74. H. Bavinck, *Paedegogischen beginselen* (Kampen: Kok, 1904), 90–92.

new life. Just as a human being, becoming conscious, automatically and without coercion recognizes the world outside oneself, so the soul, which lives from out of God's communion, in childlike faith accepts the word of Christ, gratefully and with joy. Faith and the Word of God belong together. Faith comes from what is heard, and what is heard comes through the word of Christ (Rom. 10:17).

FAITH AS KNOWLEDGE AND TRUST

[456] If there is no active faith apart from the word of God, there has to be some connection between knowledge (*notitia* and *assensus*) and faith (*fides*). This simply follows from the fact that religious (salvific) faith could not bear the same name as historical, temporary, and miraculous faith and as the faith of which we speak regularly in our daily lives, if they did not have one or more features in common. And Scripture would not have been able to describe a person's relationship to God with the Hebrew word הֶאֱמִין and the Greek word πιστευειν—words with which it is also familiar and which it also uses aside from the religious sense—if there were no correspondence whatever between the religious and the common meaning of those words. And in fact there is really no one who, upon reflection, can completely break or actually breaks the connection between knowledge (*notitia*) and faith (*fides*). Out of reaction to intellectualism, people may for a time put all emphasis on the element of feeling and trust that is present in saving faith, but all exaggeration hurts and triggers an opposite reaction. The history of value judgments in the school of Ritschl and of "salvation by faith independently of beliefs" in the Parisian school makes this very clear. Not a single school that regards religion as something more than a purely psychological phenomenon and clings to its truth and value can separate religion totally from the past and from its surroundings and remove from faith all knowledge and assent. In this connection a modernist and an orthodox person have no reason to reproach each other for anything, since *formally* they do precisely the same thing. The former also has to trust in a witness that comes to oneself from God in nature, history, conscience, or the heart and that one must, accordingly, know and accept.

It is supremely important, however, to construe correctly the relationship between faith as knowledge (*notitia* and *assensus*) and faith as trust (*fiducia*). Experience teaches us a number of different facts: there are many who from their earliest childhood have been deeply receptive to religious truth and have from the beginning received and accepted it with a saving faith, and never merely with a historical faith. There are others who have been raised from childhood in a certain milieu of religious ideas and have adopted them with a historical faith, and who, either never or much later, arrive at a personal and independent religious life. There are also those who in their early lives were never confronted with any specifically religious ideas or never even accepted them with a historical faith, but who at a given time are particularly struck by some kind of message (such as about sin and judgment, about God's love and grace, and so forth) and on that basis are led to accept other and related truths. Put in more concrete terms, one could say: there are those who are brought to Christ by the Scriptures and also those who are brought to the Scriptures by Christ.[75]

No fixed rule can be obtained from these experiences, taken directly from the observation of life. Things change, however, when we examine the logical connection between knowledge (*notitia*) and faith (*fides*). For then we discover that historical faith (*notitia* and often also *assensus*, but both taken in a purely historical sense here) indeed often precedes saving faith but never does or can produce saving faith from within itself. Between the two, though, there is no difference in measure or degree; there is a difference in principle and essence. When someone who was brought up in historical faith later obtains a saving faith, then the knowledge of the truth that one obtained through a historical faith may indeed be very useful to oneself (for truth remains truth), whether it is accepted solely with the intellect or also with the heart, but in that case the *notitia* and *assensus* change totally in character and essence. They do not remain a knowledge and assent that is merely historical, accepted as true like other historical facts, but they become a personal knowledge that is related to the salvation of the soul, a "firm and certain knowledge."[76] The content of the knowledge remains the same but is now processed differently. The truth does not change but it is viewed by the believer in another light. It is now accepted and embraced as a divine truth that is more or less directly related to a person's eternal interests.

That is the truth that Pietism with its experiential knowledge defended against a merely formal knowledge. However, it erred when it extended the difference in the way in which the truth is processed by historical and saving faith to the content and began to speak of a different, higher, spiritual truth or of a truth behind the truth. It was completely on target, however, in asserting that the believer understands and processes that same truth in a totally different way than the person who lacks this personal spiritual life. The Reformation, for that matter, had from the beginning said the same thing. When Calvin described faith as "a firm and certain knowledge," he was thinking, not of historical faith, but most definitely of saving faith, for the object of this knowledge was "God's benevolence toward us." Calvin located this knowledge more in the heart than in the intellect.[77]

Moreover, says Calvin, a person obtains religious certainty only by the witness of the Holy Spirit, that is, by the witness of the same Spirit who leads all believers into all truth, assures them of their status as God's children, and guarantees to them their heavenly inheritance.[78] According to the unanimous confession of all Reformed theologians, therefore, no one can hear the word of God salvifically unless one is regenerated. In saying this, they were basing themselves on the witness of Scripture, which over and over states clearly that the "natural" human

75. Cf. H. Bavinck, *Reformed Dogmatics*, I, 569–70 (#148).
76. Cf. Calvin above, 110–12 (#451).
77. J. Calvin, *Institutes*, II.vi.7–8.
78. Cf. H. Bavinck, *Reformed Dogmatics*, I, 583–85 (#151), 593–98 (#154).

does not understand the things of the Spirit, and that only the regenerate see the kingdom of heaven. While historical faith, therefore, may often precede saving faith in time and as such have undeniable pedagogical value, the "firm and certain knowledge" of God's grace in Christ plus all the truths of salvation are the fruit, or rather the content, of true saving faith. The knowledge and assent inherent in historical faith, which were sometimes a person's intellectual property at an earlier stage, are later grafted onto saving faith as onto a new root and as a result draw different and better nourishment from them.

When the knowledge of saving faith is understood in this sense and is essentially distinguished from a purely historical knowledge and assent (*notitia* and *assensus*), the description of saving faith as the "firm and certain knowledge of God's benevolence toward us," as Calvin put and meant it, can be considered correct as well as complete. For not only does Scripture repeatedly alternate "believing" with "knowing" (John 6:69; 7:3–4; 1 Cor. 1:21; 2 Cor. 4:6; etc.), but also in Calvin's definition *general* faith (*fides generalis*; here meant not as historical faith but as the saving acceptance of the truths of redemption grouped around the central promise of salvation in Christ, such as, for example, the apostolic witness as a divine witness, Scripture as the Word of God) and *special* faith (*fides specialis*, faith whose object is the central promise of salvation, God's benevolence toward us) are organically interrelated. A saving faith as knowledge accepts, in a single act as it were, Christ as Savior and Scripture as the Word of God. It knows and accepts Christ in the garment of Scripture, "clothed with his gospel,"[79] and so avoids both an arid rationalism and a false mysticism. Actually, no more beautiful definition is conceivable than that faith is a firm and certain knowledge of the mercy that God has shown us in Christ. Essentially what else is Christian faith but the assurance—based on God's witness and worked in our heart by the Holy Spirit—that "the eternal Faith of our Lord Jesus Christ, who out of nothing created heaven and earth and still upholds and governs them by his eternal counsel and providence, is our God and Father because of Christ his Son" (Heidelberg Catechism, answer 26)?

Yet theology, having accepted Calvin's definition, did not stop there, for in practice it proved inadequate. In the first place, there was the obvious danger of confusing the "knowledge" (*cognitio*) of saving faith with the "knowledge" (*notitia*) and "assent" (*assensus*) of historical faith (though the two are essentially different) and thus of returning to the Roman Catholic view of faith.[80] This danger became all the more acute when in Protestant churches first of all dead orthodoxy and then rationalism gained the upper hand. In the second place, it therefore became

---

79. J. Calvin, *Institutes*, III.ii.6.

80. Roman Catholics expressly reject the distinction between historical faith and saving faith, as does R. Bellarmine ("De justif.," in *Controversiis*, I, ch. 4), but sharply separate faith and love (ibid., ch. 15). The Remonstrants, on the other hand, deny the distinction between temporary and saving faith and include obedience in faith, and so forth. Remonstrant Confession of Faith, X; Apologia pro confessione, XVIII; cf. C. Vitringa, *Doctr. christ.*, III, 72, 93, 96–98.

necessary to make a clear distinction between the knowledge (*cognitio*) of saving faith and the knowledge (*notitia*) of historical faith. But the moment this was attempted, theologians saw themselves compelled to describe the knowledge of saving faith more as a matter of the heart than of the intellect—in the same way Calvin had. In so doing, however, they at the same time shifted the center of gravity of saving faith from knowing to trusting, and laid the groundwork for the somewhat polarized idea that true faith is not only knowledge (*cognitio*) but also (and hence especially) assurance (*fiducia*). Assurance (*fiducia*), accordingly, forced knowledge (*cognitio*) (the Heidelberg Catechism, answer 21, speaks only of *notitia*) into the background as being of less value. In the third place, the description of true faith as assurance (*fiducia*) proved uniquely problematic, both theoretically and practically. It required the further distinction between merely taking refuge and an assured confidence, between the direct act and the reflex act, the "being" and the "well-being" of faith, between the act with which the believer reaches out to Christ and accepts him as Savior and the act by which he returns to himself and assures himself of his communion with Christ and all its concomitant benefits.

Although making these distinctions was not wrong as such, it soon led people to view these two acts of faith as temporally consecutive, to insert the practice of self-examination between taking refuge and an assured confidence, to view the different activities of faith as so many stages in believing. In keeping with these stages [there came a tendency] to divide believers into groups, each of which—in the application of sermons and in devotional literature—was then addressed separately. In short, the Reformation's restoration of the religious nature of faith; the discovery that faith is something quite different from holding as true a number of religious beliefs, the profound insight that true faith is a special faith with a special object, namely, the person of Christ (God's grace in Christ, God's benevolence toward us)—all this made progressively more clear that in looking at faith one had to deal not with one simple thing but with a vastly complex phenomenon. It was not a matter of the intellect alone, but also of the will; it was not just rooted in one faculty but in two faculties.[81] It was knowledge in the intellect, agreement in the will, love, desire, joy.[82] It includes countless properties.[83] Any number of activities converge in it, even if people limit them in the main to knowing, assenting, and trusting, or even if one accords the central place to the reception of Christ.[84] Saving faith is not "one simple disposition but a composite one, one that cannot be comprehended under a single heading."[85]

81. J. Maccovius, *Loci communes*, 762.
82. P. van Mastricht, *Theologia*, II, 1, 8–10.
83. See especially A. Comrie, *Verhandeling van eenige eigenschappen des zaligmakenden geloofs*, 2nd ed. (Leiden: Johannes Haesbroek; Amsterdam: Nicolaas Byl, 1744).
84. P. van Mastricht, *Theologia*, II, 1, 11; A. Comrie, *The ABC of Faith*, trans. J. Marcus Banfield (Ossett: Zoar, 1978).
85. F. Turretin, *Institutes of Elenctic Theology*, XV, 8, 13.

Comrie, accordingly, returned from all the acts and activities to the habit or disposition of faith (*habitus fidei*) by which we are incorporated into Christ, just as in modern times Frank located the essence of Christian faith in the experience of rebirth, Herrmann in the personal experience [*Erlebnis*] of Jesus's moral grandeur, and Ménégoz in the faith (*foi*) that underlies all beliefs (*croyances*). In the history of the Reformation, which aligned itself on this point with the teaching of Scripture, faith increasingly became the name for that new, normative, spiritual, and comprehensive relationship in which God first of all (in regeneration or habitual faith) directs us to himself, and we, with all our capacities and powers (in actual faith), direct ourselves to God. Actually, it coincides with subjective religion (considered from a certain point of view), for this subjective religion may and must bear the name "faith." The reason is that in the here and now on earth it always relates, in all its attributes and activities, to the eternal, omnipotent, gracious, and merciful God, whom we have not seen but whom we nevertheless believe, trust, love, thank, and serve, based on Christ's witness to him, until one day this faith becomes sight and we will see God face to face.

[457] Now if this is the nature of saving faith, it does not much matter whether one describes it as knowledge or trust or as both in conjunction. For the knowledge (*cognitio*) as Calvin views it includes trust (*fiducia*), and trust in turn is not possible without knowledge. The two do not just stand in juxtaposition, nor are they merely linked by the words "not only but also," but they are organically interconnected. In both of them what counts is the reception of Christ, a personal acceptance, not of a doctrine but of the person of Christ, as he is presented to us in the gospel. True faith, in short, is the great benefit of the covenant of grace by which we are incorporated into Christ and accept him with all his benefits. Just as the offer of the grace of God in Christ must be preached to all, so it may also be accepted by all with a childlike faith. This faith, after all, does not come with conditions that a person must first meet in order to be allowed to believe. Nor does anyone need special assurance or a special revelation before one may believe. The freedom to believe and the assurance of faith are abundantly present for everyone—in Scripture, in God's unfeigned call, and in his solemn promise to grant soul rest and eternal life to all who come to him and believe.[86] Nor is sorrow over sin a condition, since as penitence (*poenitentia*) it may be called preparatory grace (*gratia praeparans*) exclusively in the sense described earlier, and as repentance (*resipiscentia*) it is the fruit and proof of faith. Neither is faith a condition for receiving the other benefits (justification, sanctification), at least not in the sense that these benefits are in any way effected or acquired by it but at most only in the sense that faith is subjectively necessary for obtaining the benefits already available in Christ. Faith, accordingly, is by its very nature nothing other than the subjective, personal (passive in habitual faith, active in actual faith) acceptance of Christ along with all his benefits.

86. Canons of Dort, III–IV, art. 8.

This faith, finally, carries its own certainty with it. Just as in knowing the consciousness of knowing is included, so also faith by its very nature includes complete certainty. It is the opposite of anxiety (Matt. 6:31; 8:26; 10:31), of fear (Mark 4:40; 5:36), of doubt (Matt. 14:31; 21:21; Rom. 4:20; James 1:6), and of being troubled (John 14:1). It is unlimited confidence (Matt. 17:20), the assurance (ὑπόστασις) and conviction (ἔλεγχος) of unseen things (Heb. 11:1). Out of that assurance of faith the godly people of the Old and New Testaments spoke and gave glory to God (Gen. 49:18; Pss. 16:8–10; 23:4–6; 31:1; 56:4, 9–10; 57:3; etc.; Rom. 4:18, 21; 8:38; 2 Tim. 4:7–8; Heb. 11; etc.). And when Rome rejected this certainty,[87] the Reformation, especially Calvin,[88] again asserted it in keeping with the Scriptures. "Faith is never ignorant of itself."[89] The mistake of antinomianism, therefore, was not that it included assurance in faith but that it equated faith with assurance, denied all the other activities of faith, and accordingly could only understand faith as the intellectual acceptance of the sentence "Your sins have been forgiven you."

Nomistic Pietism, on the other hand, erred when it shifted the assurance of salvation from the "being" (wezen) to the "well-being" (welwezen) of faith and considered it attainable—aside from extraordinary revelations—only in the way of continual introspection and prolonged and anxious self-examination. Instead of leading one's spiritual life by this method to the mountaintop, it gradually deprived that life of all certainty and robbed it of all spontaneity. "Nothing more certainly inhibits a feeling than continual meticulous examination of the question [of] whether one has it. Rarely does this preoccupation produce anything other than a lament over one's own 'deadness.' And even more than spontaneous feeling, it is spontaneous action that is inhibited by this continual introspection. The good seed cannot flourish when it is repeatedly dug up for the purpose of examining its growth. This preoccupation with religious experiences paralyzes the will. People become too occupied with themselves to attain to vigorous action."[90]

In keeping with Reformation principles and against both forms of one-sidedness, therefore, we must maintain that faith and the life of faith is much too rich to be reduced to "naked assent" (nudus assensus) to the article concerning the forgiveness of sins; it also essentially includes certainty. This certainty, which relates both to the objective grace of God in Christ and to the believer's subjective participation in it, is not an external additive to faith but is in principle integral to it from the start. It is not obtained by looking at ourselves but by looking away from ourselves to Christ. It is grounded in the promises of God, not in changing experiences or imperfect good works. Doubts and fears do certainly arise from time to time in the believer's heart (Matt. 8:25; 14:30; Mark 9:24), and believers

---

87. Council of Trent, VI, c. 9, can. 13–15.

88. J. Calvin, *Institutes*, III.ii.14ff.

89. G. Sohn, *Opera sacrae theologiae*, 2 vols. (Herborn: C. Corvin, 1598), I, 976.

90. J. C. Kromsigt, *Wilhelmus Schortinghuis*, 333. Cf. H. Bavinck, *The Certainty of Faith*, trans. H. der Nederlanden (St. Catharines, ON: Paideia, 1980).

must certainly fight against them throughout their lives. However, they can only wage that struggle and only prevail in that struggle by the power of the faith that holds on to God's promise, rests in the completed work of Christ, and is thus by nature certain.[91] Therefore, the various acts of faith, such as knowing, assenting, trusting, and so forth,[92] acts that in turn must be distinguished from the fruits of faith or good works, are not the steps or stages of faith that succeed each other in time but activities that themselves, and in connection with each other, can be either weak or strong. There are children and youths, men and fathers in Christ. But those who embrace the gospel with a true faith are, in proportion to the vigor with which they do this, also certain of their own salvation, and vice versa. The one thing is most closely connected with the other and rises and falls with it. So then faith is and remains by its very nature an unlimited and unconditional trust of the heart in the riches of God's grace in Christ. Today it is essentially still the same as what it was in the days of the Old and New Testaments, a believing against hope (Rom. 4:18), the assurance of things hoped for and the conviction of things unseen (Heb. 11:1), a deep-seated confidence that with God all things are possible (Mark 10:27; 11:23–24), that he who raised Christ from the dead (Rom. 4:24; 10:9) still raises the dead, still saves sinners, and forever calls into existence the things that do not exist (4:17).

FAITH AND RENEWAL OF THE WILL (CONVERSION)

[458] Just as the spiritual life implanted in regeneration develops, in relation to the intellect, under the influence of God's Word and Spirit into faith, knowledge, and wisdom, so in relation to the will, it manifests itself under that same illumination and guidance in conversion. If one takes this word (conversion) in its broadest sense and designates as such every religious change by which a human breaks with one's sinful past and enters upon the path of virtue, one can also speak of conversion in the case of many who have never heard of Christianity or have only undergone an external and superficial effect of it.[93] God, after all, has not left himself without a witness to any person, but through nature and history, heart and conscience, effects a "real" [mediated through things] call that keeps alive religious and moral consciousness among all peoples. All humans have a more or less acute consciousness of sin, guilt, and punishment and at the same time also of the moral law and of the good they are obligated to do. Although the Gentiles do not know the law of Moses, they do by nature what the law requires and thereby show that what the law requires is written on their hearts, while their consciences

---

91. J. Calvin, *Institutes*, III.ii.17ff.; J. Zanchi, *Op. theol.*, VIII, 712ff.

92. G. Voetius, *Select. disp.*, II, 409–512; H. Witsius, *The Oeconomy of Covenants between God and Man*, III, ch. 7; F. Turretin, *Institutes of Elenctic Theology*, XIV, qu. 8; A. von Comrie, *The ABC of Faith*.

93. T. Pfanner, *Systema theologiae gentilis purioris* (Basel: Joh. Hermann Widerhold, 1679), c. 13; and others named by J. A. Fabricius in his *Bibliographia antiquaria* (Hamburg and Leipzig: Christian Liebezeit, 1713); C. Vitringa, *Doctr. christ.*, III, 116.

also bear witness, and the thoughts and reasonings that they exchange with each other are the clearest proof of this, for they are all either of an accusatory or an exculpatory nature (Rom. 2:14–15). The insight that Gentiles have into the human soul is often profound. [Their thinkers and dramatists] had a clear sense of the repentance, regret, and remorse that follows a sinful deed and personified these feelings in the Furies, which are so graphically depicted especially by Aeschylus. "It is their own evil deed, their own terror that torments them more than anything else; each of them is harassed and driven to madness by his own crime; his own evil thoughts and the stings of conscience terrify him."[94] But people also knew that the main obstacle to conversion from a sinful to a virtuous life is a lack of self-knowledge. Most people do not know themselves. They forget their own defects and see only the defects of others, and when they cannot deny them, they blame others, circumstances, the gods, or fate. Self-knowledge, therefore, along with remorse and confession, is the first step on the road to self-improvement. "Penitence [personified] is a saving deity." "The person who profoundly regrets having sinned is almost innocent; desperation is often the cause of hope." It is difficult indeed to change one's mind. But everyone has the power and the option to do it. Virtue is a person's own work. At the crossroads of life a person can either take one direction or another, and it is never too late to choose the path of virtue. "Penitence is never too late."[95]

History, accordingly, also attests to many such conversions in the non-Christian world. From Greek antiquity, for example, there is the well-known story of Polemo, the son of a wealthy Athenian, who in his youth led a wild life but was converted to a rigorously moral life by the serious personality and impressive speeches of Xenocrates.[96] Tradition tells us that Buddha, born of a distinguished family, first lived a carefree and pleasurable life and had no notion of this world's misery. But one day, when he encountered and saw in succession a worn-out old man, a sick man, a corpse, and a monk, he was so distraught that he left his palace and spent six years in ascetic self-affliction. At the end of this period he experienced spiritual enlightenment and began to preach the Indian gospel of salvation.[97] Similarly the founder of the Jain sect, Vardhamana, pursued a worldly lifestyle in his youth, but when he was thirty years old, he was so struck by the seriousness of life that he left his wife and family and traveled through the country as an ascetic. After spending twelve years in heavy asceticism and deep meditation, he too became enlightened, attained the rank of a saint, and won many adherents by

94. M. T. Cicero, *Pro sexto Rosico Amerino*, in *The Speeches*, trans. John Henry Freese (London: W. Heinemann; New York: G. P. Putnam's Sons, 1930), c. 24; F. F. K. Fischer, *De deo Aeschyleo* (Amsterdam: J. A. Wormser, 1892), 62ff.; R. Mulder, *De conscientiae notione* (Leiden: Brill, 1908).

95. For a great many similar statements [from antiquity], see R. Schneider, *Christliche Klänge* (Leipzig: Siegismund & Volkening, 1877), 272ff.

96. E. Zeller, *Die Philosophie der Griechen*, 4th ed., 3 vols. (Leipzig: O. R. Reisland, 1879), II, 99.

97. P. D. Chantepie de la Saussaye, *Lehrbuch der Religionsgeschichte*, 2 vols. (Freiburg i.B.: Mohr [Siebeck], 1887–89), I, 82ff.

his preaching.[98] Muhammad was already forty years old when he first received a revelation, but from that moment onward he felt called to be a prophet and moved many people to the [Islamic] faith by his preaching of approaching judgment and the sensual delights of paradise. All religions and systems gain influence by the conversions they bring about, the changes they produce in the ideas, dispositions, and actions of people. Some conversions are more religious, others more ethical, still others more intellectual or aesthetic, but all agree in that the lives of people are organized around a new center of ideas, and that their soul begins to take an interest in things they did not know before, neglected, or despised. Such a change marked the life of Thomas Carlyle, who in a weighty moment of his life shook off all fear of death and the devil and acquired the courage of conviction by which his later life was governed. In that hour, as he himself said, his "Spiritual new birth" took place.[99] Also John Stuart Mill experienced such a crisis when in the fall of the year 1826 he was rescued from the depressed and indifferent state of mind in which he had been for months by reading Marmontel's memoirs and the poems of Wordsworth and was cheered up into a happier life.[100]

These examples could easily be augmented with many others, and this is even much more the case when the term "conversion" is taken so broadly as to be applicable to all sorts of changes that may occur in the convictions, dispositions, and actions of people. The psychology of religion not infrequently made this error when it not only used all "personality changes" to psychologically illustrate conversion in a Christian sense but also equated it with them. As an antidote against this leveling of all differences, however, one needs to consider that conversion does have a specific meaning and belongs in the sphere of religion, and that psychological illustration is something very different from scientific explanation. The psychology of religion is in the nature of the case powerless to penetrate to the essential nature of conversion, and by virtue of its arbitrarily adopted starting point of "presuppositionlessness" lacks the criterion by which it can discern and distinguish the psychological phenomena that it categorizes as conversion. Furthermore, Scripture provides us with a very specific and clear concept of conversion.[101]

To discover this concept one must of course start with the words that have been translated in our own language as "repentance" or "conversion," but we cannot stop there. For what we describe as conversion is not just expressed by Scripture in words but also described in other ways and pictured to us in instructive examples. The most frequent words used in the Old Testament are נָחַם (nāḥam) and שׁוּב (šûb).

The first (נָחַם) means to be sorry, to suffer grief, to repent and is construed with עַל ('al, on, over), אֶל ('el, toward), or כִּי (kî, for, concerning) for the thing one is sorry over. It is used with reference to persons (Judg. 21:6, 15; Job 42:6;

98. Ibid., I, 69.
99. G. Jackson, *The Fact of Conversion* (New York and Chicago: Fleming H. Revell, 1908), 138ff.
100. Ibid., 140.
101. Cf. H. Bavinck, *Reformed Dogmatics*, III, 584–88 (#431).

Jer. 8:6; 31:19) but especially of God (Gen. 6:6–7; Exod. 32:12, 14; Deut. 32:36; Judg. 2:18; etc.) even though all repentance is denied him elsewhere (Num. 23:19; 1 Sam. 15:29). The substantive נֹחַם (*nōḥam*) occurs only once (in Hos. 13:14).

The other word (שׁוּב) first of all means to turn, to turn around, to turn back, and more or less metaphorically, to turn away from some activity, to cease doing something, for example, to turn from sin (1 Kings 8:35), from iniquity (Job 36:10), from transgression (Isa. 59:20), from wickedness (Ezek. 3:19), and from wicked works (Neh. 9:35; etc.). The direction to which a person then turns is indicated by the preposition אֶל (*ʾel*, toward), for example, to the Lord (Ps. 51:13; Isa. 10:21; Jer. 4:1; Hos. 14:2; Amos 4:8; Mal. 3:7; etc.).

But this word שׁוּב is not, any more than נֹחַם, always used for what we in dogmatics call repentance or conversion. For it is not only applied to God to express that he is turning away from something, say, from his wrath (Exod. 32:12), or from his intent to punish (Jer. 4:28), but also in the case of people it sometimes means that they turn away from the Lord and toward idols (Josh. 22:16, 18, 23; Judg. 2:19). The noun תְּשׁוּבָה (*těšûbâ*) never even occurs in a religious-ethical sense in the Old Testament but as a rule retains its literal meaning of return (1 Sam. 7:17; 2 Sam. 11:1; etc.) and sometimes takes on the meaning of answer (retorts) (Job 21:34; 34:36). In Hosea 11:7 it [the noun מְשׁוּבָה] even expresses a turning away or apostasy from the Lord. In prophecy, however, the word שׁוּב increasingly acquired a religious-ethical meaning. History, after all, shows us all too clearly that the people of Israel did not continue to walk in the ways of the Lord but allowed themselves to be seduced into serving other gods. And when the measure of their iniquities was full, the messengers of the Lord announced the punishment of the exile, but also planted hope of a return to the land of Canaan. That return, however, would not and could not be something merely local and temporal but had to and would be accompanied by, and as it were coincide with, a conversion in a religious-ethical sense, a change of heart and life. In the prophets it is sometimes hard to tell whether the word שׁוּב denotes the first meaning or the second (Isa. 10:21; Jer. 31:21; 46:27; Hos. 6:1; 14:7; Zech. 9:12). This much is certain: a total, not just an external but also an internal, change is needed for the people. The sacrifices that are well pleasing to the Lord consist in a broken and contrite heart (Ps. 51:17); true circumcision is a circumcision of the heart (Deut. 10:16; Jer. 4:4); true fasting and mourning consists in rending one's heart and not one's garments (Joel 2:13). The Lord demands a conversion of the whole heart (2:12). He not only demands this, however, but also promises it and will some day grant it in the days of the new covenant (Jer. 31:31ff.; Ezek. 36:25ff.; Zech. 13:1; Mal. 4:6).

The nomistic trend that arose after the exile abandoned this prophetic line of thought, however, and increasingly viewed conversion as a work that had to compensate for the sins committed earlier. It consisted in a shorter or longer period of repentance, a shallower or deeper form of repentance, the confession of sins, and also in self-imposed punishment, such as fasting, abstinence, and self-affliction.

This penitence had the power to atone for the sin committed and to redress the past. The תְּשׁוּבָה (tĕšûbâ, return, renewal) consisted in a תקנתא (tqnt ')—a comprehensive restitution, a restoration to the class of the righteous—or a תפואה (tpw 'h), a healing. And when this restoration had been obtained by penitence, then by the observance of the law a person could again accumulate merits that gave them a claim to reward here or in the hereafter.[102]

REPENTANCE

[459] Against this externalization of conversion, John the Baptist and Jesus came and demanded μετανοια (*metanoia*, repentance). This Greek word is not as such a religious term but simply denotes any change in a person's opinion, a change of mind. Yet, even in ordinary Greek, the verb μετανοειν already acquired the sense of being sorry, if not about one's entire sinful past, then about certain sinful acts. Even the noun μετανοια already denoted, especially in Plutarch, the moral change by which a person breaks with one's previous life and turns to a better life. In the Septuagint, the word μετανοειν (*metanoein*) served as the translation, sometimes of שׁוּב (*šûb*) but usually of נָחַם (*nāḥam*), which was also translated a number of times by ἐπιμελεισθαι (*epimeleisthai*). Usually, however, שׁוּב was translated by ἐπιστρεφειν (*epistrephein*), which also occurs already in ordinary Greek in a (metaphorical) moral sense and was also repeatedly used in that sense by New Testament writers. A few times it has transitive significance here, "to convert others" (Luke 1:16–17; Acts 26:18; James 5:19–20), but as a rule it is used intransitively in the sense of repenting (converting) oneself. Sometimes when this verb is used, both the negative aspect (turning away) and the positive aspect (turning toward) is expressed, as in Acts 14:15 (turning from vain things to the living God); 15:19 (turning from the Gentiles to God); 26:18 (turning from darkness to light); and 1 Thess. 1:9 (turning from idols to God). In other verses, only the negative (Acts 3:26 [ἀποστρεφω]; James 5:19–20) or only the positive aspect (Luke 1:16–17; Acts 9:35; 11:21; 2 Cor. 3:16; 1 Pet. 2:25) or neither of the two (Matt. 13:15; Luke 22:32; John 12:40 [στρεφω]; Acts 3:19; 28:27) is mentioned. In Luke 17:4; Acts 3:19; and 26:20 the words "repent" (μετανοειν) and "turn again" (ἐπιστρεφειν) occur side by side. In Mark 1:15, the word "believe" (πιστευειν, *pisteuein*) occurs separately alongside of "repent" (μετανοειν) and in Luke 22:32 and Acts 11:21 it [or a cognate noun] occurs alongside of "turning" (ἐπιστρεφειν). Also compare Acts 2:38, where "repent" is augmented with "be baptized every one of you in the name of Jesus Christ." Alongside of these two words, also the verb μεταμελεσθαι (*metamelesthai*, to repent) occurs a few times in the New Testament (Matt. 21:29, 32; 27:3; 2 Cor. 7:8; Heb. 7:21). Since in Matt. 27:3 this word is used with reference to Judas's repentance, some interpreters believe that μετανοια always refers to an evangelical and saving conversion, while

---

102. Cf. ibid., III, 495–99 (#411).

μεταμελεια (*metameleia*) always refers to a "worldly sorrow," but that seems to be incorrect.[103] For in Matt. 21:32 the verb μεταμελεσθαι is used with reference to the good kind of repentance that leads to faith (in this case, in John the Baptist); and in Heb. 12:17, according to the exegesis of some, μετανοια is used with reference to the repentance that Esau displayed after the loss of his birthright, but which did not consist in true repentance.[104] Between μετανοια and ἐπιστροφη there is indeed a distinction: the first word accentuates the internal change of mind that moves a person to turn away from one's sinful past, while the second focuses more on the new relation in which, as a result of that change of mind, that person manifests him or herself outwardly.

However, these biblical terms for what we call repentance or conversion are not defined logically or dogmatically but are used variously in a broader or more restricted sense. One only need recall that the Hebrew words נִחַם and שׁוּב are sometimes applied even to God; that the words μετανοια and ἐπιστροφη (*epistrophē*) sometimes include πιστις (*pistis*, faith), at other times occur alongside of it, and are also frequently implied in it. The doctrine of conversion, accordingly, is certainly not based exclusively on those texts in which the word occurs, but is rooted in everything Scripture portrays to us with respect to the natural state of humankind and the necessity, character, manner, and fruit of the religious and moral turnabout of humans. Jesus, for example, in preaching μετανοια, sometimes refers to it alone (Matt. 4:17), elsewhere connects it with πιστις (faith) to the gospel (Mark 1:15), and speaks to Nicodemus only of rebirth (John 3:3, 5, 8). In addition, he illustrates the repentance required for entry into the kingdom in numerous different ways. He does this when in the Sermon on the Mount he assigns the kingdom of God to the poor in spirit, those who mourn, those who hunger and thirst after righteousness, and so forth (Matt. 5:3ff.); when he says that one can enter eternal life only by passing through the small gate and by taking the narrow road (7:14); when he calls not the righteous but publicans and sinners to repentance and invites to himself the weary and the burdened (9:13; 11:28); when he enjoins his disciples to change and become like a child (18:3); when he tells them they must leave everything behind, deny themselves, lose their life, and take up their cross to be worthy of him (Matt. 10:37ff., 16:24ff.); when in the parable of the prodigal son—to mention only one example—he depicts for us how this young man, prompted by hunger and misery, came to his senses, arose, and returned to his Father with a confession of sin. In the writings of Paul, as well, there are relatively few references to repentance (Rom. 2:4; 2 Cor. 7:9–10; 1 Thess. 1:9; 2 Tim. 2:25), but it is implied in dying; in being crucified, buried, and, above all,

---

103. H. Witsius, *The Oeconomy of the Covenants between God and Man*, III, 12, 130–36.

104. It is perhaps better to read the last word in this verse, αὐτην, as referring back to εὐλογια, not to μετανοια, as follows: Esau still wanted to inherit the blessing, but though he later sought it with tears, he was rejected because he found no place (opportunity) for repentance, for a true conversion. Whether μετανοιειν in Matthew 11:21 and 12:41 has to be interpreted as referring to a merely external or also to a true internal repentance is in question.

resurrected to a new life in Christ (Rom. 6:3ff.; Gal. 2:19–20); in putting off the old self and putting on the new (Eph. 4:22–24; Col. 3:9–10); in putting to death one's earthly nature (Col. 3:5); in crucifying one's sinful nature (Gal. 5:24); in resisting the subtle temptations of the devil (Eph. 5:11) and walking by the Spirit (Rom. 8:4); in being alive to God in Christ Jesus (6:11); and in offering the parts of our body to God as instruments of righteousness (6:13; etc.).

In addition, Scripture not only speaks of conversion using various terms but also describes and pictures it in the life story of various persons. In this connection one must note that Scripture distinguishes between varying kinds of repentance. In 2 Cor. 7:10 Paul refers to a godly sorrow that brings repentance leading to salvation and leaves no regrets, and a worldly sorrow that produces death. This latter sorrow is not godly, is not in keeping with God's will, and does not flow from the knowledge of God and his law, but rather is worldly and occurs also among the children of this world. It pertains not to sin as sin, inasmuch as it evokes the wrath of God, but to a specific sinful act and its consequences. For instance, when a man has committed a crime and does not obtain what he expected from it, but loses his money, goods, honor, name, and position and knows he has covered himself with shame and disgrace, he not infrequently awakens to his situation, considers his wretched state, and feels himself assailed by remorse, regret, and self-indictment for having committed this wretched act. Sometimes this remorse can become so intense that it turns into all-consuming despair and renders him unable to see any way out other than suicide. Of this kind, Scripture furnishes us the appalling examples of Cain, Esau, Ahithophel, and especially of Judas. It may also happen that a person is temporarily brought to a halt in one's sinful career, that by a special event in one's life (a death, a disaster, adversity, and so forth) one is momentarily brought to one's senses, that he is deeply impacted by the preaching of the law or the gospel (Matt. 13:20–21), and plans to amend his life, joins the church, and even tastes the heavenly gift and the powers of the coming age (Heb. 6:4–5). Yet later, despite all this, he will still be offended and fall away when oppression or persecution makes itself felt. Scripture shows us examples of this in Ahab (1 Kings 21:27) and in the mass conversions that sometimes occurred under Moses, Joshua, the judges, and the pious kings of Israel, in which, though not everything was chaff, yet, as in all religious movements, there was much chaff amid the wheat. Compare Jon. 3:5ff., and consider Simon the sorcerer (Acts 8:9ff.); Demas, who again fell in love with the present world (2 Tim. 4:10); Hymenaeus and Alexander, who made shipwreck of their faith (1 Tim. 1:19–20; 2 Tim. 2:17); and the many who, even in the apostolic period, "went out from us because they were not of us" (1 John 2:19) and denied the Master, who had bought them (2 Pet. 2:1).

All of these fall short of being true conversions. According to 2 Cor. 7:10, true conversion arises from godly sorrow, that is, from a sorrow in keeping with God's will, one that, therefore, is not merely ethical but bears a religious character, pertains to God, his will and his word, and to sin as sin even aside from its consequences. It is demanded by God but also God-given as a free gift. This is the sorrow that produces repentance leading infallibly to salvation (whereas worldly sorrow results in death and destruction). That sorrow-unto-salvation, therefore, is without regrets. It never causes any regret and cannot do this because its principle is godly sorrow and its goal and destiny is salvation.

Of such genuine repentance Scripture also offers many examples and testimonies. Just think of Naaman the Syrian (2 Kings 5:15); Manasseh (2 Chron. 33:12–13); the crowds that came to John and had themselves baptized by him, confessing their sins (Matt. 3:6); Nathanael (John 1:46ff.); Levi (Matt. 9:9 [Mark 2:14]); Zacchaeus (Luke 19:8); the man born blind (John 9:38); the Samaritan woman (John 4:29, 39); the murderer on the cross (Luke 23:42); the three thousand souls added on the feast of Pentecost (Acts 2:37ff.); the Ethiopian (8:37); Paul (9:6ff.); Cornelius (10:44ff.); Lydia (16:14); the jailer at Philippi (16:30ff.); and so forth.

There is a great deal of commonality in all these stories. Conversion always consists in an internal change of mind that prompts persons to look at their sinful past in the light of God's face; leads to sorrow, regret, humiliation, and confession of sin; and is, both inwardly and outwardly, the beginning of a new religious-moral life. But for all the similarity in the stories, there is also much diversity in the circumstances under which, the time and manner in which, and the occasion in terms of which the conversion takes place. Sometimes a miracle (Acts 5:14; 9:35; 13:12; 19:17), then again a lengthy demonstration from Scripture (8:35; 17:3; 18:28), or a simple message concerning faith in Christ (16:31) served as the means by which God worked conversion in the heart of a person. Of greater importance is the difference between Jews and Gentiles in the matter of their conversion. The Jews knew the one true God, and many of those who later believed in Christ had long before that time been born again and converted. But sometimes they doubted for a long time whether the historical person of Jesus was the Messiah who had been promised to the fathers. A few people saw and believed it immediately, like Simeon, who had received a revelation (Luke 2:26), and Anna, who was a prophetess (Luke 2:36), but others doubted or were, like John the Baptist (Matt. 11:2ff.), shaken in their faith. Paul in particular was offended by the cross and neither could nor would believe that he who was hanged on the cross and cursed by God and humans was the only-begotten Son of the Father and the Savior of the world. Their conversion, therefore, consisted not in learning to know and serve another God but in recognizing Jesus as the Messiah, seeing in him the fulfillment of law and prophecy, and drawing from this the conclusions that flowed from it with respect to the entire Old Testament dispensation of the covenant of grace.

By contrast, the change that occurred in the conversion of the Gentiles bore a very different character. These Gentiles, after all, were not participants in the covenant of grace before that time but "walked in their own ways" (Acts 14:16). At that time they were "without Christ, alienated from the commonwealth of Israel, and strangers to the covenants of promise, having no hope and without

God in the world" (Eph. 2:12 RSV) and guilty of an array of horrifying sins: idolatry, fornication, immorality, drunkenness, and so forth (1 Cor. 6:10–11). Hence in the case of the Gentiles, conversion did not just consist in the recognition of Jesus as the Christ but was at the same time a turning away from vain things to the living God (Acts 14:15; 15:19; 26:20; 1 Thess. 1:9) and implied a total break with their whole previous religious and moral lives. Scripture indeed tells us of many conversions that occurred at a later age and at times suddenly, but it also knows of such persons as Samuel (1 Sam. 2:26), Jeremiah (Jer. 1:5), John (Luke 1:80), and Timothy (2 Tim. 3:15), who were instructed in the Scriptures and walked in the fear of God from their childhood onward. It is even said of the children of the covenant that theirs is the kingdom of heaven (Matt. 19:14) and that theirs is the promise along with their parents (Acts 2:39), that they must obey their parents in the Lord, that is, in fellowship with Christ, and be brought up by them in the discipline and instruction of the Lord (Eph. 6:1, 4). Of the baptized, accordingly, it is never said in the New Testament that they were later converted. Conversion always applies to those who, having been raised as Jews or Gentiles, joined the church and were incorporated into it by baptism as the sign and seal of that conversion. The New Testament does not contain the history of the established church but tells the story of the founding of the church in the then-known world.

CONVERSION OF BELIEVERS?

Finally, it still needs to be said that in a few cases Scripture nevertheless also speaks of conversion in the case of believers. Believers, as we know, do not attain perfection here on earth. In many things they still stumble (James 3:2), and when they say that they have no sin, they deceive themselves (1 John 1:8). They must therefore continue the struggle against sin till the day they die and bring forth fruit that is worthy of and corresponds to that conversion (Matt. 3:8; Luke 3:8; Acts 26:20). The first and fundamental conversion, therefore, must be continued in an ongoing conversion that embraces the whole of life and never stops until life on earth is over. And this is not all. Believers may err, fall into gross sin, and even remain in it for a long period; and then, as it were, a second conversion is needed. In the Old Testament, David is an example of this (2 Sam. 12:13), as is Peter in the New (Matt. 26:75). Jesus had warned Peter in advance (Luke 22:32) and, through John, Jesus similarly exhorts the—in many ways aberrant—churches in Asia Minor to repent and do their first works (Rev. 2:5, 16, 21–22; 3:3, 19). This second conversion, too, is God's work. Peter owed his restitution to Christ, to his faithfulness and intercession (Luke 22:32), even though Christ used means (Ps. 19:7; James 5:19–20). And so it is with conversion from beginning to end: it is the work of God (Jer. 31:18; Lam. 5:21) and his gift (Acts 5:31; 11:18), but it is realized through a person's own intellect and will. When God converts someone, that person is converted (Lam. 5:21), and that person then converts him- or herself

(2 Kings 23:25; 2 Chron. 15:4; Pss. 22:27; 51:13; Isa. 19:22; Matt. 11:21; Luke 15:7, 10; Acts 9:35; 11:21; etc.).

[460] The preaching of the gospel found acceptance not only with some Jews but especially among the Gentiles, and in many circles brought about a striking change in doctrine and life. Even those who remained unbelieving could not shut their eyes to this fact and sometimes, despite themselves, gave powerful witness to the new godly and moral life found in the churches. The Apostolic Fathers, accordingly, following the example of the New Testament letters, insisted with all the seriousness they could muster on the adornment of the Christian confession with a holy life.

> It is a splendid ideal of life that all the writings of the postapostolic era prescribe as a religious requirement with whose fulfillment salvation is connected. The main features of this ideal are love within the church, gentleness and patience toward those who are without, faithfulness and confession, purity and sanctification over against all the moral pollution prevailing in the world, truth and trustworthiness in social relations, keeping marriage and the life of the family undefiled, and the faithful fulfillment of one's vocation.[105]

Soon after the church had been established, the catechumenate also made its debut. Gentiles who wanted to join the church were not immediately admitted to baptism but first received instruction in the Christian faith and had to commit themselves to conduct their lives in accordance with it. In that early period careful supervision and rigorous discipline were maintained over the members of the church.

Soon, however, difficulties occurred in this connection. It was generally believed that baptism, as the sign and seal of the first conversion, only forgave the sins committed before that time and had no bearing on those committed later. For that reason many people postponed baptism as long as possible. However, when the church was established and propagated itself more from within its own membership than by additions from without and in that connection generally administered child baptism, this postponement naturally became impossible and increasingly became the exception rather than the rule.

As for the sins that believers committed after they had been baptized, it could not of course be expected that they would completely stop. The apostles had too clearly made the point that in many things we all continue to make mistakes, and that those who say they have no sin deceive themselves (James 3:2; 1 John 1:8). Still, people cherished the hope that believers would abstain from gross sins and continually exercise themselves in the ways of holiness.[106] This necessitated a distinction between minor and major sins, which in many cases was hard to prove

---

105. R. Knopf, *Das nachapostolische Zeitalter* (Tübingen: Mohr, 1905), 421–22.

106. Cf. Kirsopp Lake, "Zonde en doop," *Theologische Tijdschrift* 43 (1909): 538–54. See H. Windisch, *Taufe und Sünde im ältesten Christentum bis auf Origenes* (Tübingen: J. C. B. Mohr, 1908); concerning which, one

but was gradually worked out in practice. With reference to the former category, people thought of all sorts of daily transgressions (speaking falsehood, spite, envy, quarrels, deceptions, slander, minor dishonesties in business), and with reference to the latter they thought of rare, public, and very offensive crimes (murder, robbery, deception on a grand scale, adultery, infanticide, poisoning, apostasy, idolatry, sorcery, and so forth). People were also disappointed in thinking that Christians would never commit such major offenses. In fact, such cases gradually became more numerous also in the church. A party of hard-liners wanted to simply remove such offensive people from membership in the church by a ban and never again give them a chance to return and rejoin the church. About the middle of the second century Montanus and Novatian attempted to restore this practice. But from the beginning, there were others who judged the offenders more gently and in such cases considered at least one more conversion possible.[107] It was their theory that gradually gained the upper hand and prevailed also in practice.

Penance

For, in the first place, the rigorous practice could not be maintained when major sins increased in the church and the number of the fallen (*lapsi*), especially in the days of the Decian persecution, mounted alarmingly. And in the second place, everyone took a different position with regard to the minor sins, which, after all, are sins too. Concerning these sins, it was the general belief—partly as a result of Jewish influence and in any case completely in agreement with it[108]—that they could be expiated and made good by the believers themselves. While these lesser sins are inevitable, the believer, in contrast to the unbeliever, has the advantage of being a member of the church and can wipe out these sins by patiently bearing the punishment set for them, by private or public conversion or by the doing of good works (fasting, alms, prayer). And since the boundary between minor and major sins was often arbitrary and fluid, various sins assigned to the latter category could easily pass into the former. Gradually counted among the major sins were, in the main, only murder, fornication, and apostasy, sins that gave public offense and brought shame upon the church. For those who were guilty of such a major sin and had been removed from the fellowship of the church, restoration was possible in that early period only when they submitted to the penalty stipulated (in varying degrees) by the bishop and, upon having paid this penalty, publicly confessed it in the midst of the church. In that way there arose, in addition to the penance of the catechumens in baptism and the ongoing penance of the faithful consisting in alms, prayers, and fasting, a third penalty, the penance of the fallen, which could again effect reconciliation by doing penance and making a public confession. Yet

---

should consult the review by J. Kunze, *Theologisches Literaturblatt* 21 (21 May 1909): 244–50; and especially the review by P. Wernle, *Theologische Literaturzeitung* 34 (1909): 586–90.

107. Shepherd of Hermas, *Visions* II.2; *Mandates* III; *Similitudes* VIII.11; but elsewhere he expresses himself less generously. R. Knopf, *Das nachapostolische Zeitalter*, 432ff.

108. H. Bavinck, *Reformed Dogmatics*, III, 170–73 (#338).

also this severe disciplinary process was gradually relaxed. In many cases no formal excommunication took place because "the peace and tranquillity of the church" made gentler methods necessary. Depending on whether a sin was more or less public and offensive, a complete or only a semicomplete public confession was required, and sometimes the church was even content with a private confession. Thus public penance increasingly became a rarity that had almost completely lost the character of church discipline and served only as a means of public justice.

In addition, to the degree that the penance of the fallen was either not imposed at all or only rarely and the world penetrated the church, the penance of the faithful was stressed all the more by serious men—by monks like Cassian and popes like Gregory. This penance consisted occasionally, and for a long time even exclusively, in making a confession of guilt before God in solitude. But from ancient times, there was the idea that, for his venial sins, the believer had to pay the penalty, bear the punishment, or perform the good works and could obtain forgiveness only by this method. The translation of the Greek words μετανοια and μετανοειν by "penitence" and "doing penance" favored this opinion, for "penitence" included the idea of *poena* (punishment), and the term "doing penance" promoted the idea of *doing*. To this must be added that in the penance of the fallen, the church (that is, the bishop) imposed the penalty and pronounced the reconciliation, that the monks in the monasteries were frequently obligated to confess their transgressions before the superior in charge, and that the Irish-Scotch church recommended voluntary confession before the priest. Consequently, since the Carolingian period in the Frankish church, the practice of voluntary confession before a priest was increasingly followed and viewed as a mark of piety, especially during the time of fasting and before celebrating the Lord's Supper. Hence, the moment believers had confessed their sins before a priest, they received absolution, forgiveness absolving them of the guilt of their sins for Christ's sake. But they remained obligated to perform the penance or penalty that the priest simultaneously imposed on them. This in turn necessitated the distinction between the liability to guilt (*reatus culpae*) and the liability to punishment (*reatus poenae*).[109] Immediately after the confession of sins, the priest pronounced forgiveness, but he still had to impose a penance proportionate to the severity of the sins confessed (prayers or other good works) in order that the confessants would thereby make themselves inwardly free from the power of sin. Inasmuch as this penance as a rule could not be completely carried out in this life, the deficit had to be made up in the hereafter by suffering in purgatory.

Indulgences

[461] There was, however, another and much easier way to be relieved in part or in whole from this penance. For from ancient times already, the time of penance could be shortened and the penance itself decreased or alleviated for the

109. Ibid., III, 495–99 (#411).

fallen who displayed sincere and deep repentance. According to Cyprian, such a mitigation of punishment for the repentant fallen could be effected by the intercession and merits of the confessors. From this evolved the later custom in which the bishops remitted part of the punishment or changed a severe penalty into a lighter one for those who proved themselves zealous in their penitential practice or could not perform it on account of illness. All this, however, concerned an individual act that the bishop or priest had to arrange in each individual case. Especially since the eleventh century, however, this commutation or relaxation of penance (also called the remission of sins) assumed a more general character. It now assumed the form that everyone who met a certain condition (such as taking part in a war against infidels, in a crusade, or sponsoring someone else for this at the sponsor's expense, and so forth) could obtain partial or full remission (indulgence) from the penalty imposed. From that time on, with the cooperation of the papacy, indulgences so increased in number that finally they developed into a complete business. The conditions under which they could be obtained were gradually relaxed and robbed of all seriousness. While Johann Tetzel still required repentance for a personal indulgence, he considered this unnecessary in the case of an indulgence for the deceased.

It was his opinion—later also defended by others and not firmly rejected by the pope—that "as soon as the coin in the coffer rings, the soul from purgatory springs." In that period, for a small sum of money, letters of indulgence were issued that could be submitted to the father confessor, whereupon he could grant full absolution after repentance. Whoever contributed something to the building of a church, a hospital, a bridge, or any other work of common interest received a reduction in temporal punishments that he still had to endure for his sins. For Rome, the indulgence trade was a bountiful source of revenues and yielded even more profits when, from the thirteenth century onward, the effect of indulgences was extended also to the poor souls in purgatory, be it only "in the manner of suffrage." Alexander Hales especially was the theologian who defended this entire indulgence practice with the theory that the church was in possession of a treasury of superfluous merits secured by Christ and the saints and can distribute from this resource to those who fall short in their penitence. At Trent, the Roman Catholic Church indeed condemned the abuses that had crept into the sale of indulgences but firmly maintained the use of indulgences as being "most salutary for Christian people."[110] "There is basically no objection," says a Roman Catholic scholar, "against this custom of granting indulgences to the promoters of works of common utility and in this way to link the giving of money with indulgences."[111]

---

110. Council of Trent, sess. 25 cont., "Decretum de indulgentiis."

111. N. Paulus in M. Buchberger, *Kirchliches Handlexikon*, 2 vols. (Freiburg i.B.: Herder, 1907–12), I, 21. The origin of indulgences, for that matter, has not yet been fully clarified. Some look for it more in the earlier penitential system; others more in the propaganda of popes on behalf of holy wars against Saracens, Vikings, Moors, and on behalf of crusades to Palestine. Cf. N. Paulus, *Johann Tetzel, der Ablassprediger* (Mainz: Kirchheim, 1899). A. Kurz, *Die katholische Lehre vom Ablass vor und nach dem Auftreten Luthers* (Paderborn: F. Schöningh,

In all fairness, with respect to this Roman Catholic sacrament of penance, one must bear in mind that the "work of satisfaction" (*satisfactio operis*) and similarly indulgences is not meant to obtain the forgiveness of guilt (in other words, absolution from eternal punishment) for the believer who committed a serious sin. This has already been secured by Christ and is granted the penitent after "the contrition of the heart" (*contritio cordis*) and "confession of the mouth" (*confessio oris*). The "work of satisfaction" consists only in bearing the temporal punishment the penitent has merited by his sin and for which he can obtain a reduction or abbreviation by means of an indulgence.[112] But the fine distinctions in which Catholic dogmatics and ethics abound frequently fail to penetrate the consciousness of the common people and are much too subtle to govern life. The practice of penance and the availability of indulgences tend to foster the notion that grace only serves to enable people, by bearing their punishment and doing good works, to secure their eternal salvation. The distinction between perfect and imperfect contrition, or in other words between contrition and attrition, tends in the same direction. It came up in the period of Scholasticism, found support especially in Thomas,[113] and became standard church doctrine at Trent.[114]

Contrition and Absolution

Contrition is the sorrow over sins that arises solely from love toward God, hence from perfect love. Actually it already carries the forgiveness of sins with it before the believer has confessed and received absolution from the priest. This does not render the sacrament of penance superfluous, however, for Christ has subjected all grave sins to the church's power of the keys exercised in the sacrament, and contrition as such includes the "promise of the sacrament" (*votum sacramentum*). But in reality, such perfectly pure contrition occurs only rarely. Accordingly, besides contrition, there is also a kind of attrition: a sorrow over sin that arises from a consideration of the ugliness of sin or from the fear of hell and punishments, and, further, excludes the will to sin and includes the hope of forgiveness. This

---

1900). F. Beringer, *Die Ablässe, ihr Wesen und Gebrauch* (Paderborn: F. Schöningh, 1900). A. Gottlob, *Kreuzablass und Almosenablass* (Stuttgart: F. Enke, 1906). Th. Brieger, "Indulgenzen," in *PRE³*, IX, 76–94; H. Boehmer, *Luther im Lichte der neueren Forschung*, 2nd ed. (Leipzig: Teubner, 1910), 67ff.; M. A. Gooszen, "Jubeljaar en Jubelaflaat," *Theologische Tijdschrift* (1903): 97–110; C. Vitringa, *Doctr. christ.*, III, 140–52.

112. The definition of an indulgence, accordingly, is usually the following: "Indulgence is the remission, in the divine court (*in foro Dei*), of the temporal penalty owed for sin, as validated by application [of merit] from the treasury of the church." Cf. J. H. Oswald, *Die dogmatische Lehre von den heiligen Sakramenten der katholischen Kirche*, 2nd ed., 2 vols. in 1 (Münster: Aschendorff, 1864), II, 201.

113. Thomas clarifies the terms "contrition" and "attrition" as follows: "In corporeal matters, those things are said to be attrite, which in some way are diminished, but not perfectly; whereas contrition is identified, when all parts are removed at the same time by division to the least; and for that reason attrition in spiritual matters signifies some dissatisfaction with sins committed, but not perfectly, but contrition perfectly [signifies dissatisfaction]." F. A. Loofs, *Leitfaden zum Studium der Dogmengeschichte*, 4th ed. (Halle a.S.: M. Niemeyer, 1906), 586; cf. also, J. H. Oswald, *Die dogmatische Lehre*, II, 72ff.; C. Stuckert, *Die katholische Lehre von der Reue* (Freiburg: J. C. B. Mohr, 1896).

114. Council of Trent, sess. XIV, c. 4.

attrition, moreover, does not make people into hypocrites and greater sinners, but is a supernatural gift of God, an operation of the Holy Spirit, who, though not as indwelling but as heart-moving Spirit, prepares persons and makes them fit for the reception of the sacrament. While on account of its imperfection attrition does not carry the forgiveness of sins with it, in connection with sacramental absolution it does justify persons and absolves them from eternal punishment.

In connection with this whole development, absolution also acquired a different meaning. Formerly, the priest was viewed as only a witness to the confession and an assistant in the reconciliation, who prayed for God's forgiveness of the sins of the penitent or noted the fact of forgiveness, which the penitent had already received by contrition; now the priest became the authorized dispenser of the benefits of forgiveness acquired by Christ. Hence, after the twelfth century, the earlier intercessory formula (still maintained in the Greek Orthodox Church) became declaratory: "I absolve you."[115] In Roman Catholicism, therefore, the absolution pronounced in the sacrament of penance is absolute. This, however, is more appearance than reality. For, in the first place, the father confessor cannot judge the human heart and can only pronounce the absolution on the assumption that the penitent is sincere in one's repentance and confession. In the second place, the statement "I absolve you" is always—as theologians put it—a "mixed judgment." On the one hand, it is a release (*solutio*) from sin (its guilt and eternal punishment), but on the other a binding (*ligatio*) with temporal punishment. Actually the priest only absolves the penitent on the assumption of "the temporal satisfaction that must still be made." The penitent will only be truly free "when he or she has paid the stipulated penalty as satisfaction."[116] For that reason the "work of satisfaction" does not belong to the essence of the sacrament but to its wholeness. It is an integrating part of the sacrament.

The Roman Catholic penitential system culminated when penance was included among the seven sacraments, first by theologians such as Hugo of St. Victor and Lombard and subsequently by the Council of Florence (1439). The holy sacrament of penance (this is how Rome formulates it, not speaking, as it does in the case of baptism and the Eucharist, of "holy penance") is a second baptism but, with a view toward the work of satisfaction, a "laborious baptism," a "second plank after a shipwreck," the only and absolutely necessary remedy for those who by a mortal sin have lost the sanctifying grace received in baptism, but also useful

115. "Those words (*Illa*) 'I absolve you' manifest the effective remission of sins by the administration of this sacrament" (Roman Catechism, II, ch. 5, qu. 14; ed. note: Bavinck erroneously cites qu. 15, 2.15). The post–Vatican II edition titled *The Roman Catechism* (trans. Robert I. Bradley, SJ, and Eugene Kevane [Boston: Daughters of St. Paul, 1985] = Bradley and Kevane below) drops the enumeration of the introduction so that chapter 1 begins the section on baptism. In this annotation, the proper reference would be II, ch. 4, qu. 14.

116. J. H. Oswald, *Die dogmatische Lehre*, II, 102; cf. Council of Trent, XIV, c. 5: "If a sick person is ashamed to reveal his wound to the physician, the medicine does not heal it." C. Pesch, *Praelectiones dogmaticae,* 9 vols. (Freiburg: Herder, 1902–10), VII, 116–31; J. Pohle, *Lehrbuch der Dogmatik*, rev. M. Gierens, 10th ed., 3 vols. (Paderborn: Schöningh, 1931), III, 436.

and beneficial for those who have committed only venial sins and hence to be used at least once a year by every believer, according to the canon of the Fourth Lateran Council.[117] Penance, further, is distinguished from baptism especially in that in baptism the priest exclusively acts as priest who completely remits all sins and punishments in Christ's name. But in the sacrament of penance he also functions as judge. As such he first, by means of the confession, takes note of the sins committed; then, with the aid of penitential books, he assesses the degree of their culpability, subsequently determines the corresponding temporal penalties due, and finally, in the expectation that the penitent will bear these penalties willingly and completely, he pronounces a formally absolute pardon. Thus in Roman Catholicism the sacrament of penance is a spiritual court and the action of the priest is a judicial act.[118]

THE REFORMATION UNDERSTANDING: MORTIFICATION AND VIVIFICATION

[462] As we remarked earlier,[119] the Reformation had its origin in opposition to the Roman penitential system. Luther again discovered the scriptural meaning of μετανοια and could not believe his eyes when he compared to it the complicated system that Rome had made of penitence. In fact, there is hardly any article of faith where corruption and the consequent spiritual damage stands out so clearly as in the case of repentance and the forgiveness of sins. Of the simple invitation to a change of mind and amendment of life, Rome made a court of law in which the priest acts as judge, hears the guilty, determines the measure of

117. This council, held under Pope Innocent III in 1215, declared in canon 21: "All faithful persons of both sexes, after they have reached an age of discretion, ought faithfully to confess all of their own sins, at least once a year, to their own priest." Cf. Council of Trent, XIV, c. 5, can. 6; Roman Catechism, II, ch. 5, qu. 32ff. (ed. note: in Bradley and Kevane, II, ch. 4, qu. 32ff.); R. Bellarmine, "De poenit.," in *Controversiis*, bk. 3. The Greek church refers to penance four times a year: the Orthodox Confession, 164.

118. Of the wealth of literature on penance (penitence), see the book that probably dates from the eleventh century and is mistakenly credited to Augustine: *On True and False Penitence*. Cf. F. A. Loofs, *Dogmengeschichte*, 488ff.; P. Lombard, *Sent.*, IV, dist. 14–22; and commentaries on these sentences of Thomas: T. Aquinas, *Summa theol.*, III, qu. 84–90; suppl., qu. 1–28; idem, *Summa contra Gentiles*, IV, c. 70–72; Council of Trent, XIV; Roman Catechism, II, ch. 5 (ed. note: in Bradley and Kevane, II, ch. 4); R. Bellarmine, "De poenit.," in *Controversiis*, III, 376–482; cf. also idem, "De indulgentiis," in *Controversiis*, II, 436–81; G. Perrone, *Praelectiones theologicae*, 9 vols. (Louvain: Vanlinthout & Vandezande, 1838–43), VII, 365–479; idem, "De indulgentiis," ibid., VIII, 1–48; C. Pesch, *Prael. dogm.*, VII; J. Pohle, *Lehrbuch der Dogmatik*, III, 382–524; G. M. Jansen, *Praelectiones theologiae dogmaticae*, 3 vols. in 2 (Utrecht: Van Rossum, 1875–79), III, 597–743. On the history of penitential administration, see inter alia, D. Petau, "De poenitentiae vetere in ecclesia ratione diatribe," in *Op. theol.*, VIII, 407–673; M. Buchberger, *Die Wirkungen des Busssakramentes nach der Lehre des heiligen Thomas von Aquin* (Freiburg i.B.: Herd, 1901); J. Gartmeier, *Die Beichtpflicht* (Regensburg: G. J. Manz, 1905); P. Schmoll, *Die Busslehre der Frühscholastik* (Munich: J. J. Lentner, 1909); cf. the judgment of K. Müller, review of *Die Busslehre der Frühscholastik* (1909), by P. Schmoll, *Theologische Literaturzeitung* 35 (1910): 77–80. He defends himself against Loofs, who in his *Dogmengeschichte* (§§29, 45, 59) sets forth a different interpretation of the development of penance and therefore summarizes an altogether different set of sources concerning this subject.

119. H. Bavinck, *Reformed Dogmatics*, III, 517–19 (#417).

their temporal punishments, and at the same time, by a declaratory statement, grants them absolution.[120] One absolutely does not need to appeal to the immoral practices to which the confessional frequently gives rise[121] to condemn the Roman penitential system. Even apart from them there are sufficient internal reasons for condemning it.

It has led, after all, to the false distinction between a liability to guilt (*reatus culpae*) and a liability to punishment (*reatus poena*) and to a catalog of venial and mortal sins, the latter being forgiven by Christ, while the former have to be made good by believers themselves. It also denies the difference between punishment and chastisement and limits and degrades the merits of Christ and the grace of God. It leads to regarding as adequate the attrition that is born solely of fear; to the imposition of private confession on every believer; and to the elevation of penance to the level of a sacrament, for which there is no ground whatever in Scripture. In practice, the consequences are that laypersons are permanently—at least to their dying hour—kept dependent for their salvation on the priest. *Either*, like the priests, they resign themselves to a superficial and external assessment of their sins, cherish a false sense of security, in performing their religious duties put their trust in the word of absolution and in indulgences, *or*, on the other hand, spend day after day in dread and uncertainty over whether they have confessed all their sins, have suffered enough penalties for them, and whether at death they will go to heaven, or whether they will perhaps go to purgatory for an unknown number of years.

The Reformation was on firm ground when it directed its attack against this juridical system of penance and replaced it with the biblical idea of repentance or conversion. At an early stage, however, numerous questions arose in this connection, questions that gave rise to disagreements and divisions. If repentance, as generally stated in the early years [of the Reformation], consists in contrition and faith, by what factor(s) do they come about in the human person? Does God employ the law or the gospel or both in this connection? Does penitence precede faith, or does it follow it and flow from it? And if a distinction is to be made between the repentance that may precede faith and the genuine sorrow over sin that is born of faith, is it necessary in the case of those who are genuinely converted that penitence should always precede faith? May they pray in advance for their repentance? Must they endure a shorter or longer period of terror and fear, of dread and despair, in order later to be assured of their conversion, and must they know the manner and time, indeed the day and the hour, in which they truly turned to

---

120. The word μετανοια for that reason has little appeal to Roman Catholic theologians. After all, it expresses nothing more than a change of mind; J. H. Oswald, *Die dogmatische Lehre*, II, 23. They prefer to speak of *poenitentia* (penitence) and *poenitentiam agere* (doing penance), which suggests *poena* (punishment) and *punire* (to inflict punishment), and of "penance," which carries the same connotation.

121. Cf. C. P. T. Chiniquy, *Fifty Years in the Church of Rome* (reprinted, Grand Rapids: Baker Books, 1953); idem, *The Priest, the Woman, and the Confessional* (Chicago: A. Craig, 1880); K. Weiss, *Beichtegebot und Beichtmoral der römisch-katholischen Kirche* (St. Gallen: Wiser & Frey, 1901).

God and received Christ as their Savior? Or is such remorse and sorrow over sin actually not at all necessary, but superfluous and unprofitable? Can and may we even speak of conversion in the case of those who did not, as in the days of the New Testament or in response to missions, convert to Christianity out of Judaism or paganism, but were born and baptized in the church and from childhood onward brought up and nurtured in Christian truth? Is not their baptism a sign and seal of their conversion so that a later conversion is unnecessary?

Whatever the answer to these questions may be, in what does a true conversion consist? Is it a work of God or a work of human beings or of both? In this process, is a person active or passive? And where does it actually occur—in the intellect or the will? Is it exclusively religious or also ethical in character? And what are its parts—contrition, faith, as well as the new obedience, or a dying-away of the old self and the coming-to-life of the new? Is conversion completed in a single act, or is it a lifelong process? Can a person possibly be converted on one's deathbed and in the last moment of life, or must conversion always be manifested and confirmed in doing good works? Can those who have fallen [after conversion] be converted again, or is there no possibility of return? What, finally, is the fruit of conversion? Does conversion precede the forgiveness of sins or follow it? And if the former is true, how does it function—as means, as condition, or as a meritorious work? Why is it even necessary if Christ has made complete satisfaction and acquired salvation in its totality?

For us to answer all these questions, a clear definition of what we understand by "conversion" or "repentance" is indispensable. In Scripture the word sometimes has a broader meaning, at other times a more restricted sense. Sometimes it includes regeneration, faith, and the total renewal of a person, and sometimes faith is clearly distinguished from it. Conversion sometimes occurs at the beginning of the new life, in the transition especially from Judaism or paganism to Christianity, but also in the progression and restoration of the new life. Sometimes the internal change of mind and outlook is in the foreground (as in the word μετανοια); at other times, the accent lies on the external turnabout that is its outcome and manifestation (as in the word ἐπιστροφη).

At an early stage in the Christian church, three kinds of repentance or conversion were distinguished: that of the catechumens, that of the faithful, and that of the fallen (*lapsi*). For Luther, who had experienced a fearful version of it, the word made him think especially of the horrors of the conscience and the fear of judgment that is induced by the law and that precedes faith. But he himself understood and also repeatedly expressed the view that this repentance, which may also occur in people who never make it to conversion, is not the true and deep-seated sorrow that proceeds from faith and must continue throughout one's life. Consequently, especially the Reformed made a distinction between μεταμελεια (*metameleia*) and μετανοια (*metanoia*), between penitence and conversion, not only in degree but also in principle and essence. In that way, the concept of conversion was at least defined in one direction: it occurs not before and apart from but within the new life, proceeds from faith, and arises from regeneration (in the more restricted sense).

Gradually, however, conversion was also delimited in another direction. Initially, in Reformed theology as in Scripture, the word was very often still understood in a broad sense to refer to the overall change of a person from beginning to end. In that sense, conversion included rebirth, faith, and ongoing renewal or sanctification. But the conflict with Anabaptists raised the question whether also in the case of children, before they came to awareness, there could be faith and conversion. Furthermore, the controversy with the Remonstrants concerned the question whether God or man was the primary agent in the work of salvation and specifically in conversion. For these reasons the Reformed soon began to make a distinction between the disposition (*habitus*) of faith and the act (*actus*) of faith, and similarly between the disposition to conversion and actual conversion. "For the grace of conversion is twofold: habitual and actual. The former is that by which a human is regenerated by the power of the Holy Spirit or is given the powers of faith and love. The latter is that by which the already-regenerate person, with the aid of God's word and Spirit, exercises these powers in the activity of believing and loving."[122]

The Remonstrants, however, reversed this order. They started with actual conversion, which came about [synergistically] by a combination of God's sufficient grace and human free will. They then added that this actual conversion, by the repeated exercises of the acts of faith and repentance, became a habitual conversion (*conversio habitualis*). But the Reformed viewed habitual conversion as an infused (not an acquired) disposition, attributed it solely to the regenerating grace of God, and in this connection regarded the preaching of the gospel only as an antecedent means and customary adjunct. Among them, accordingly, actual conversion became the act of the regenerate person, endowed by God with the powers of faith and love, by virtue of which, aroused by God's Word and enabled by his Spirit, one also actually begins to exercise those powers.[123] Thus in the Reformed order of salvation, conversion gradually acquired a very definite place. On the one hand, it was essentially distinct from the law-driven repentance that also frequently occurs among unbelievers, as well as from faith and love or habitual conversion, that is, from what was later called regeneration in the restricted sense. On the other hand, as the "first actual conversion" (*conversio actualis prima*) it was also distinguished from the "continual conversion" (*conversio continua*) that goes on throughout the Christian life, as well as from the "second actual conversion" (*conversio actualis*

---

122. Ed. note: Bavinck fails to annotate this lengthy Latin citation. It is from the Leiden *Synopsis purioris theologiae*, disp. 32, 2. The author is Antonius Walaeus.

123. F. Gomarus, *Op.*, I, 104b, 107a; A. Walaeus, in *Synopsis purioris theologiae*, disp. 32, 2; P. van Mastricht, *Theologia*, VI, 4, 4, 5; H. Witsius, *The Oeconomy of the Covenants between God and Man*, III, 12, 128; F. Turretin, *Institutes of Elenctic Theology*, XV, 13; A. Kuyper, *Het werk van den Heiligen Geist*, 3 vols. in 1 (Amsterdam: Wormser, 1888–89), II, 197ff.; ed. note: ET: *The Work of the Holy Spirit*, trans. H. de Vries, 3 vols. (New York: Funk & Wagnalls, 1900).

secunda) that again is necessary in the case of believers after a period of aberrancy and a lapse from faith or following a slump in one's spiritual life.

Now, in what does this "first actual conversion" consist? Under the heading of penitence (repentance, conversion) the Lutherans usually list three components: contrition, faith, and good works (the new obedience). But these three do not, in their redemptive order, cohere organically. By "contrition" is meant the terrors of conscience that are induced by the law and precede faith. But these terrors of conscience do not with absolute certainty lead to faith and may, after a shorter or longer period of time, pass and disappear. By "faith," Lutherans understand the heart's reliance on the grace of God in Christ, but because in this connection they almost exclusively have in mind peace of conscience and the rest of soul that is the fruit of faith, it is not clear here how the new obedience proceeds from faith nor how it can arouse and spur on believers to practice it.[124] The Reformed, in contrast, following Calvin, gave to penitence (*poenitentia*) a place outside, and to full conversion (*resipiscentia*) a place inside the Christian life; they did not include faith in this full conversion but saw both as arising from the root of regeneration and recognized them in their relative independence. Consequently faith was especially related to justification and conversion to sanctification, and so conversion (*resipiscentia*) acquired, besides a religious sense, an eminently ethical meaning as well.[125]

This is especially evident from the fact that Calvin did not define conversion in terms of contrition and faith (with or without good works) but in terms of the putting-to-death of the old self and the bringing-to-life of the new self; he was followed in this by countless Reformed theologians—among others, by Ursinus in his catechism and commentary (*Explications*). A few, however, proposed another division. In Calvin's thought, regeneration did not yet have the restricted meaning later attributed to it but described a person's total renewal that proceeds from faith. Similarly, he did not yet distinguish conversion (*resipiscentia*) as actual conversion from habitual conversion (or regeneration in a restricted sense). For that reason, it was easy for him, following the example of Rom. 6, to ascribe to conversion the two parts of putting-to-death the old self (*mortificatio*) and bringing-to-life the new (*vivificatio*). But later, when all these terms became more refined, some commented that the putting-to-death of the old self and the bringing-to-life of the new—that is, the experience of being passively crucified and resurrected with Christ—were in fact aspects of regeneration. "The two terminal points of regeneration are two qualities: the formerly inherent corruption and the sanctity that is now being introduced." But "the terminal points of conversion (*resipiscentia*) are two acts: the sin committed and the good that must be done." It was consequently described as "hatred of sin and love of righteousness," as a turning away from evil and a turning to the good, or more extensively as "grief after having committed

---

124. H. Bavinck, *Reformed Dogmatics*, III, 520–22 (#418).
125. Ibid., III, 522–28 (#419).

the sin on account of its offense to God" and a "transformation of the whole spirit, out of grief, from evil to good.[126] But even if one continues to view the putting-to-death and the bringing-to-life as aspects of actual conversion, one always ascribes to them a different meaning than when they occur as aspects of regeneration. In the latter case they are exclusively acts of God in which a human is passive; but if the putting-to-death and the bringing-to-life are aspects of actual conversion (*resipiscentia*), they are activities of the person who has been regenerated by the Spirit of God and endowed with the virtues of faith and love.[127]

Accordingly, conversion as the "first actual conversion" (as it is considered here [in order] after regeneration in a restricted sense, alongside of and in connection with faith, and [in order] before justification) is the activity of the regenerate person by which one learns to know, hate, and flee sin in its true nature, returns with a humble confession of sin to God as Father in Christ, and proceeds with a joyful heart to walk in his ways. Hence there are several elements here: the illumination of the intellect by which a person learns to know sin in its true character, that is, as sin in the sight of God; grief, sorrow, regret, and shame over sin because we have displeased God with it; a humble confession made in secret before God or privately before another person, or in special cases in public before the council of the church or the whole congregation; hatred of sin and a conscious and firm decision to flee it; the act of standing up and returning to God as a gracious Father in Christ, hence in the confidence that he can and will forgive the sins; a heartfelt joy in God through Christ inasmuch as he has forgiven the sin and is a gracious Father; a sincere desire and love to live in keeping with the will of God, in all good works.

True conversion, therefore, does not consist in an incidental act of moral self-improvement, in breaking with some gross sin and adapting oneself to virtue. It is rather a complete reversal in one's way of life, a fundamental break with sin because it is sin. Conversion, however, can only be conversion when it bears a primarily religious character; that is, when we have learned to know sin—as God views it—in the light of his holy law, as it dishonors him and makes him angry. We then see its ethical nature as a natural implication of its religious character. For those who have thus learned to know sin as sin in the sight of God, cannot love it, but hate and flee it, separate themselves from it by a humble confession of guilt, and receive an inward desire and love for the good, that is, a life in harmony with God's will. True conversion, accordingly, encompasses the whole person, including one's intellect, heart, will, soul, and body. It makes one break with sin across the board and devote one's entire person and life to God's way and God's service. In conversion the focus is especially on the will. Faith and repentance both arise from regeneration. They are both rooted in the heart. But whereas faith tends to work from there to the side

126. W. Musculus, *Loci communes* (Basel: Heruagiana,1567), 312; F. Junius, *Opuscula theologica selecta*, ed. A. Kuyper (Amsterdam: F. Muller, 1882), I, 168, 209; W. Ames, *The Marrow of Theology*, I.26 (pp. 157–60); I.29 (pp. 167–71).

127. A. Polanus, *Syntagma theologiae christianae* (Hanover, 1609; Geneva, 1617), 469.

of consciousness and appropriates the forgiving grace of God in Christ, conversion exercises its activity more in the sphere of the will and turns it away from evil and toward the good. However, just as the intellect and the will share a common root in the heart of a person, are never separated, and continually impact each other, so also it is with faith and conversion. They are consistently interconnected and reciprocally support and promote each other.

VARIETIES OF CONVERSION

[463] Although true conversion is always the same in essence, yet, in the manner and the time when it occurs, there are all sorts of differences. When Christianity first made its appearance in the world, Jews and Gentiles who wanted to join the church had to break, each in their own fashion, from the religion in which they had been born and brought up. The Jew had to recognize that physical descent from Abraham, circumcision, the liturgy of temple and sacrifices, and so forth had lost their meaning; and the Gentile had to bid farewell to his idolatry, image-worship, sacrificial meals, superstitious and immoral practices, and begin to serve the living God. Since there was usually no honor or advantage connected with this transition, but on the contrary much opprobrium, disgrace, persecution, and oppression, there was little danger that people would have themselves baptized and incorporated in the church for their own secret reasons. Conversion (ἐπιστροφη) was generally a clear sign and proof of an inner change of mind (μετανοια). Yet from the beginning there was also chaff amid the wheat. There was a Judas in the circle of the apostles. In Samaria, Simon tried to obtain the gift of God in exchange for money (Acts 8:19–20), and both John and Paul complain about brothers who had left the church and again fallen in love with the present world (1 John 2:19; 1 Tim. 1:20; 2 Tim. 2:17–18, 20; 4:10).

Later, when the church had acquired power and honor, there were repeated instances of accession to the church that were prompted not by a true conversion but by an array of human calculations and considerations. One absolutely need not always think in this connection of conscious hypocrisy, intentional deception, carefully calculated ambition, and love of gain. But when a new religion appears on the scene, unmasks the vanity of the old religion, and makes many converts, there are always others who publicly climb aboard the bandwagon without inner conviction. That phenomenon occurred from the beginning, as Christianity expanded among the peoples of Europe, and recurs to this day on the mission fields.

When we take as our standard the way Paul, Augustine, and Luther came to conversion and apply it to the conversions of which our missions tell us, we are, aside from a few exceptions, sorely disappointed. The motives for the conversions that have come to our attention are frequently very different from what we would have expected or wished. One person accepts Christianity because in one way or another the powerlessness of the gods he has served up until now has become very obvious. Another, because it delivers him from the fear and dread in which belief in spirits and witchcraft has shackled him. A third feels attracted to the beauty of Holy Scripture, the simplicity of the Sermon on the Mount, the ethical content of the gospel, the sublime image of Christ. And a fourth follows because other persons whom he loves and trusts have preceded him. Sometimes it happens that entire groups or tribes suddenly burn their idols and accept the Christianity that had for years apparently with no effect been preached among them. In many Christian circles, there is still often much misunderstanding regarding the operation and success of missions—misunderstanding that has not infrequently been fostered by moving stories of conversions in mission reports, Christian novels, and tracts. One must bear in mind, however, that we cannot expect from those who have just recently come to know Christianity what we expect from those who have been brought up in it from childhood. In addition, as a rule the deepest motives for conversion remain unknown to others and often also to those driven by them. Finally, a deep sense of guilt is not a cause, but a fruit, of faith.

The situation is very different for those who as children were born, baptized, and brought up in the church of Christ. Unless they have strayed for a time and openly lived a life of sin, conversion in their case cannot, as in the case of pagans, consist in a change of religion and morality. Scripture's premise is that the children of believers belong to the covenant of grace, that theirs is the promise and the kingdom of heaven, and that they are "in the Lord." As is clear from its doctrine and the practice of pedobaptism, the Christian church in its totality adopted this scriptural position and proceeded from the reality of the covenant of grace. In this respect there is no difference between the Roman Catholic and the Eastern Orthodox churches, and between the Lutheran and the Reformed churches. The last-mentioned, however, have taken this covenant of grace much more seriously than the other churches, inasmuch as, over against them, they continue to hold to the inamissibility of grace and the unbroken continuity of the spiritual life. But when, since the middle of the seventeenth century, the Reformed churches in the Netherlands fell into decline, and the boundary of the covenant of grace was almost completely wiped out as a result of the neglect of discipline, the scriptural view gradually gave way to the pietistic and Methodist position. Although infant baptism was continued as a custom, faith in its sacramental power and value had vanished. Children were considered unregenerate and unconverted and therefore sinners and children of wrath. The preaching, catechetical instruction (insofar as it still existed), Sunday school, revival meetings, indeed even the regular instruction given at home and in the schools—it all had to be made subservient to the [goal of] conversion and deliverance.

This whole movement was in part fueled by a legitimate and healthy reaction to the indifference and lukewarmness of the established churches. But the moment it converted its protest into a system, it became seriously one-sided. It proceeded from distrust toward God's promise, denying the truth of the covenant of grace and weakening the meaning of baptism. It closed its eyes to the power of tradition, to the constant quiet work of the Christian family, to the mysterious inner working of God's Spirit in the heart. It robbed the school and education in general of their independence and gave to the upbringing of children an unnatural character, making them anxious, fearful, and nervously introspective. It focused completely on a sudden crisis, an intense wave of emotion, a conscious turnaround, and made it appear as if one were saved "by conversion rather than by Christ."[128] Against all these exaggerations and one-sidednesses, the Christian view of the children of believers—as it is expressed in the covenant of grace, in the practice of infant baptism, in catechetical instruction, and in admission to the Lord's Supper—retains its incontrovertible validity. The children of believers are to be regarded and treated as heirs of the promise until the contrary is clearly demonstrated by their "talk" and "walk."

This is not to make the conversion of the children of believers unnecessary, redundant, or useless. First of all, one should consider in general that during puberty every child goes through a crisis that is of the greatest importance for one's physical and mental development.[129] At that time, the child passes from a period of dependence into one of independence and freedom. In that weighty time of life, children form a personality and individuality of their own, proceed to lead their own lives, and attempt to capture in society the place that suits their character and talents. Now it certainly will not do to include conversion in that process as a natural and necessary component of it.[130] For in the first place, the years of puberty constitute a period when a boy or girl very often reacts to and loses the deep religious and moral impressions received in childhood, and plunges into a life of sin. In the second place, conversion (even according to a very defective and incomplete survey) definitely does not occur only in this period but also before and after, and also remains a distant deathbed possibility.[131] Still it is true that in the years of puberty and adolescence a person undergoes an enormous overall change. Whereas up until this time they were included in and represented by their parents, they now gradually have to answer for themselves. Now they have to appropriate for themselves and assimilate the cultural legacy they owe to their birth

---

128. C. L. Drawbridge, *Religious Education: How to Improve It* (London and New York: Longmans, Green, 1908), 106. The school controversy in England between Anglicans and Nonconformists is in large part based on this difference in viewing the children of believers. In addition to this work of Drawbridge, see also: T. Stephens, ed., *The Child and Religion* (New York: G. P. Putnam's Sons; London: Williams & Norgate, 1905); A. E. Garvie, *Religious Education Mainly from a Psychological Standpoint* (London: Sunday School Union, 1906).

129. H. Bavinck, *Reformed Dogmatics*, III, 556–64 (#427a).

130. E. D. Starbuck makes a pitch along these lines when in *The Psychology of Religion* (London: Walter Scott, 1901), 143, he states that the facts of conversion, though inexplicable, are manifestations of natural processes and (153) calls conversion "necessary."

131. Cf. H. Bavinck, *Reformed Dogmatics*, III, 556–64 (#427a), 584–88 (#431); Remonstrants attach little value to a deathbed conversion. When people have spent their whole lives "in sin" and have turned a deaf ear to all the invitations and warnings of the gospel, they consider such a last-minute conversion, which can no longer be proved by a new life, highly improbable, indeed impossible other than by an extraordinary act of divine mercy (Episcopius, *Op. theol.*, I, 2, 14ff.; P. van Limborch, *Theol. christ.*, 597). The Walloon preachers Jacques Bernard and Pierre Joncourt later expressed the same judgment. But on this subject, the Reformed generally held a more charitable opinion (C. Vitringa, *Doctr. christ.*, III, 100–104).

and upbringing. This is true in all kinds of ways, including the religious. When children who were born and baptized into the covenant of grace enter the years of discretion, they have to answer for their baptism and the new obedience to which it obliges and admonishes them. Even pagans recognized the significance of this critical period in human life when in this period they subjected boys and girls to a battery of tests and inducted them by means of solemn ceremonies into the next phase of life.[132] And Christian churches have generally fixed the first communion or confirmation, public confession, admission to the Lord's Supper, or the reception into full membership in this period.

It is certainly not desirable to rush this crisis in the religious life of the young by artificially starting Sunday school or youth meetings at an earlier age. What really counts is to follow and stimulate with great sensitivity and caution the religious development of children; to reckon with the nature of childhood and not demand from it what can only develop in later years—in a word, to leave much to the hidden and quiet guidance of the Holy Spirit. All that is alive requires time to grow and develop, and even the kingdom of heaven does not come with outward show but is like a seed that sprouts and grows, we know not how (Mark 4:27). Yet this period is usually the time in which the disposition turns into action, regeneration into faith and conversion. To that extent one can say that "conversion is a distinctively adolescent phenomenon."[133]

Still, also in the case of those who have been born in the Christian church and sooner or later experience conversion, there is much diversity in the way things happen. The empirical psychology of religion distinguishes between "healthy-minded" and "sick" souls, between "once-born" and "twice-born" persons.[134] If these terms are meant to imply that there are people who are so good and noble that they do not need conversion, then one would—on the authority of Scripture and in the name of experience—have to reject that distinction. For even if human observers could find neither stain nor wrinkle in the life of a given person, God judges by the heart. And out of the heart come all sorts of evil thoughts and lusts, of which all who know themselves somewhat, to their embarrassment become conscious time and again. Conversion, therefore, does not always entail any outward and visible change, but it always includes a heartfelt sorrow over sin and a sincere love for God and his commandments.

In addition there is potential for great diversity in the manner in which even those who are born of Christian parents later come to conversion. Some of them are led gently and cannot tell stories of powerful turnarounds. Quietly but steadily they grow from being children to young people, and from being young people to men and women, fathers and mothers in Christ. Others, by contrast, persons who for a time openly lived a life of sin or became inwardly estranged from the

132. G. S. Hall, *Adolescence*, 2 vols. (New York: D. Appleton, 1904), II, 232–80.
133. E. D. Starbuck, *The Psychology of Religion*, 28.
134. H. Bavinck, *Reformed Dogmatics*, III, 556–64 (#427a).

Christian upbringing of their youth, are sometimes suddenly—on a special occasion, being brought up short by a striking word or incident and with intense emotional turbulence—brought to conversion. They receive a vivid insight into the hideousness and culpability of sin, frequently spend lengthy periods in fear and dread, and only then, in an amazing way, reach the assurance of faith. All this concerns the time and manner of conversion. But there is also a wide range of differences in its character and nature.

In Luther's life, for example, it consisted in passing from a deep sense of guilt to a joyful sense of God's forgiving grace in Christ. Zwingli experienced conversion especially as a liberation from legalistic bondage to the glorious joy of the children of God. And Calvin experienced it above all as a deliverance from error to truth, from doubt to certainty.

Depending on upbringing and environment, nature and disposition, life and work, it is now one aspect of conversion and then another that stands out. All who attentively read the conversion stories in Scripture[135] and in the different churches[136] can find this out for themselves. Sin is so multiform that everyone has their pet sin of which they above all experience the power and from which they need deliverance. And the gospel is so full of riches that one moment it can enlighten and comfort a seeker-of-salvation with one truth and the next with another. This diversity in conversion is something we need to respect. We may not simply make one type the standard and apply it to all others. We must accept the varied hidden and amazing leadings of the Holy Spirit. We may no more demand from everyone a "penitential struggle" and "breakthrough," a period of dread and despair and a sudden subsequent surge of peace and joy, than we may at once infer the authenticity or inauthenticity of conversion from a variety of

---

135. J. Buchanan, *The Office and the Work of the Holy Spirit* (1842; repr., Edinburgh: Banner of Truth Trust, 1984), 239ff.

136. In the religious, devotional, homiletic, mystical, ascetic, and like literature of the Christian churches, there is a gold mine that has not yet been sufficiently appreciated by theology and has only in recent years become the object of intentional study. We cannot even begin to sum up that literature. Only by way of example do we wish to refer to J. von Görres, *Die christliche Mystik*, 4 vols. in 5 (Regensburg: G. J. Manz, 1836–42); F. I. Herbst, "Merkwürdige Bekehrungsgeschichten," in *Katholisches Exempelbuch*, 2 vols. in 1 (Regensburg: G. J. Manz, 1845); J. H. Reitz, *Historie der Wiedergeborenen*, 4 vols. (1698; repr., Tübingen: M. Niemeyer, 1982); J. Edwards, *A Faithful Narrative of the Surprising Work of God* (London: C. Whittingham for W. Button, 1737); ed. note: This treatise can be found in C. C. Goen, ed., *The Great Awakening*, vol. 4 of *The Works of Jonathan Edwards* (New Haven: Yale University Press, 1972) and in many other published formats. J. de la Combe, *Les nouveau-nés de l'Esprit* (Paris: Fischbacher, 1905). The conversion of famous people like Paul, Augustine, Francis, Loyola, Luther, Calvin, Zinzendorf, Wesley, Whitefield, and others has been repeatedly described and always again attracts new attention. Especially the conversion of Augustine has been carefully investigated and presented, as it concerns time and character, in different ways. Cf. the discussion of various works on this subject by O. Scheel, "Alte Kirchengeschichte," *Theologische Rundschau* 13 (June 1910): 220–40; E. M. ten Cate, "Augustinus' bekeering," *Teylers Theologische Tijdschrift* 7 (1909): 59–88; idem, "Augustinus' afdwalingen," *Teylers Theologische Tijdschrift* 8 (1910): 24–44; idem, "Augustinus' bekeerd," *De Gids* 74 (February 1910): 292–313; A. Bruining, "Naaraanleiding van de jongste Theorieën over Augustinus Bekeering," *Teylers Theologische Tijdschrift* 8 (1910): 399–419.

intense feelings and odd incidents. What matters more than anything else in the case of these most necessary and important changes in a person's life is not the form and the manner but the substance. And about that substance no human can judge but only God, who knows the hearts of people. All we can say is that true conversion always consists both in hating sin and fleeing from sin, and in a sincere love for God and his service.

FLEEING SIN AND LOVING GOD

[464] Of these two aspects of conversion, sometimes the one and then the other gets the lion's share of emphasis. There are Christians who reject the universal offer of grace and want nothing to do with preaching the gospel to the unconverted. They approach them with nothing but the law, confront them with its demands and penalties, and depict in a dramatic way the hellish torment and eternal damnation awaiting them in their unconverted state. In the Roman Catholic Church, such preaching used to occupy and still occupies a large place. When Protestant churches, by neglecting their confession and discipline, fell into decline, Pietism and Methodism seized on the proclamation of judgment to wake up the sleeping souls and to make them cry out in their misery for salvation and mercy. In this context, some posited the demand that their listeners had to spend a longer or shorter period in a state of dread and despair in order to attain to true conversion. Spener himself held broader views and fully recognized that God does not deal with all his children in the same manner. But his followers (A. H. Francke, J. Mishke, et al.), appealing to Matt. 11:12; Luke 13:24; Gal. 5:17; and other verses, preached that a fearful struggle of the soul was the only way to the state of grace. A long struggle originated, therefore, between the orthodox [Lutherans] and the Pietists over "the penitential struggle."[137] Under professor J. G. Joch at Wittenberg in 1730, a dissertation was defended by Strohbach on the subject of "salutary desperation."[138] The idea that a prolonged state of misery had to precede the state of grace reached numerous pious circles, and to this day one encounters in the church a great many Christians who year after year complain about their sins but almost never enjoy the heartfelt joy in God through Christ nor ever arrive at a peaceful and quiet life of gratitude.

When in reaction to this the desire awakens, in the manner of Methodism, to replace this chronic illness with an acute crisis and to pack the entire penitential struggle into a single point, this frequently arouses such intense feelings that the whole body is shocked by it. Convulsions and hysteria, loud screams and cries, wailing exclamations and unintelligible sounds, a flood of

---

137. For the literature, see J. G. Walch, *Bibliotheca theologica selecta*, 4 vols. (Jena: Croecker, 1757–65), II, 751ff.

138. J. G. Walch, *Bibliotheca theologica selecta*, II, 749ff.; M. Goebel, *Geschichte des christlichen Lebens*, 3 vols. (Coblenz: K. Bädeker, 1849–60), II, 632ff.; E. Ideler, "Joch," in *PRE*³, IX, 233. Ed. note: Bavinck erroneously cites *PRE*³, IV.

tears alternating with dancing and a leaping with joy—these give expression to what internally stirs the soul. Responses to these phenomena differed. Wesley and Whitefield, for example, were most pleased with them. But Jonathan Edwards, having learned from his experience, made careful distinctions between the affects that proceeded from spiritual workings on the heart and those that only arose as a result of impressions made on the imagination.[139] The ecstatic and visionary phenomena that occurred later, among the Camisards in the Cevennes[140] and in 1749 during the Nijkerk disturbances under G. Kuypers,[141] for example, similarly elicited a variety of verdicts. And when the revival in Wales under Evan Roberts produced the same psychological and physical abnormalities[142] and sparked them also in other countries (California, Norway, Denmark, Hesse, Silesia), opinions again strongly diverged. Pastor Paul viewed speaking in tongues and similar phenomena as a renewal of the gifts of Pentecost and powerful evidence of the working of the Holy Spirit, but others, like Rubanovitch, Dallmeyer, Urban, and Haarbeck (et al.), pronounced everything to be a work of the devil and a deception of the antichrist. In June 1909, at a meeting in Berlin, the leaders of the *Gemeinschaftsbewegung* (Fellowship movement) broke with the school of thought followed by [Pastor] Paul and his group.[143]

Frequently, however, the reaction to this one-sided form of Christian piety is even much stronger. Spinoza stated that grief, remorse, the knowledge of sin and meditation on death suppress life and must be overcome by the knowledge of God.[144] Frederik van Leenhof, a minister at Zwolle (from 1681 on), similarly taught that grief is an imperfection that must never be inculcated or recommended. Those who encourage grieving over one's sins, sin against love, which never permits grieving one's fellow humans. They are abandoning the gospel, which is the message of joy and gladness in God, and fail to do justice to God's grace and the perfect

139. In his *Treatise concerning Religious Affections* (1746), in *The Works of Jonathan Edwards*, vol. 2, *Religious Affections*, ed. J. E. Smith (New Haven: Yale University Press, 1959); cf. J. Ridderbos, *De Theologie van Jonathan Edwards* ('s Gravenhage: J. A. Nederbragt, 1907), 246ff.

140. Th. Schott, "Camisarden," in *PRE*[3], III, 693ff.

141. A. Ypey and I. J. Dermout, *Geschiedenis der Nederlandsche Hervormde Kerk*, 4 vols. (Breda: W. van Bergen and F. B. Hollingerus Pijpers, 1819–27), IV, 8ff.; A. Ritschl, *Geschichte des Pietismus in der reformierten Kirche* (Bonn: A. Marcus, 1880), I, 347ff.; J. C. Kromsigt, *Wilhelmus Schortinghuis* (Groningen: J. B. Wolters, 1904), 310ff.; A. Comrie and N. Holtius, *Examen van het ontwerp van tolerantie*, X, 32.

142. Vyrnwy Morgan, *The Welsh Religious Revival, 1904–1905: A Retrospect and a Criticism* (London: Chapman & Hall, 1909); Beukenhorst, "Evan Roberts en de Keswick-leer," *Stemmen vor Waarheid en Vrede* 44 (May 1907): 401–19; H. Bois, *Le réveil au pays de Galles* (Toulouse: Société des publications morales et religieuses, 1906); *idem, "Les dernières nouvelles du réveil gallois," *Foi et Vie* (1 November 1906); *E. Pensoye, "Les résultats du réveil gallois," *Foi et Vie* (16 November 1907).

143. Cf. H. Bavinck, *Reformed Dogmatics*, III, 499–503 (#412). *Joh. Urban, *Zur gegenwärtigen "Pfingstbewegung": Herzliche Warnung auf Grund persönlicher Erfahrung* (Striegau: Urban, 1910). *P. Th. Haarbeck, *Die "Pfingstbewegung" in geschichtliche, biblische, und psychologische Beleuchtung* (Barmen: Buchhandlung des Johanneums, 1910); M. Schian, *Die moderne Gemeinschaftsbewegung*.

144. Cf. H. Bavinck, *Reformed Dogmatics*, III, 540–45 (#423).

sacrifice of Christ.[145] Leenhof was fiercely opposed by many[146] and condemned in 1708 by the Synod of Overijsel, but his opinions were shared by others as well. Pontiaan van Hattem identified true conversion, not as grief and lament over sins committed, but as joy over the righteousness that God had granted in Christ. Verschorists[147] believed that after the perfect satisfaction of Christ, grief over past sins was no longer appropriate for New Testament believers. And some mystical and antinomian schools of earlier and later dates expressed themselves along the same lines.[148] But although many people did not go that far, they nevertheless felt repelled by a piety that consisted only in lamentation over sin and never rejoiced in the redemption accomplished by Christ. In particular, Zinzendorf opposed this kind of "miserable" Christianity. He had been reared in the pietistic view of the order of salvation, and when in 1727 he was told by members of this school that he was still unconverted inasmuch as he had not known the penitential struggle, he spent a long time in doubt and self-examination. But on June 19, 1729, he attained certainty concerning his own conversion and subsequently became increasingly convinced that the pietistic view was incorrect, and that believers may be incorporated into communion with Christ from their youth on. Typical Herrnhuter preaching, accordingly, pushed the penitential struggle ever farther into the background and replaced it with faith in the reconciliation accomplished in the blood of Christ, a quiet and childlike resting in the grace of the Lord, knowing oneself secure in the wounds of the Lamb, and a joyful and lively feeling of the love of the heavenly Bridegroom.[149]

Similarly, in America a reaction arose against the revivals that had already been started there in 1720 by Th. J. Frelinghuyzen and especially under the ministry of Jonathan Edwards beginning in 1735 and [George] Whitefield (who crossed the ocean in 1739) had become a national movement from Maine down to Georgia. But the "one-sidednesses" that marked the revivals repelled many. In 1741, when Gilbert Tennent preached a sermon before the synod at Philadelphia on "The Danger of an Unconverted Ministry," this even sparked a split in the Presbyterian church. The idea that unconverted ministers should not be allowed to preach and that people should not come to listen to them was too much for many church members. Against the theology of the revivalists there even arose a liberal theology that did not want to focus exclusively on conversion but, by contrast, valued

---

145. F. van Leenhof, *Den hemel* (Te Zwolle: Hakvoord, 1703). Cf. C. Vitringa, *Doctr. christ.*, III, 108ff.; Ypey and Dermout, *Geschiedenis der Nederlandsche Hervormde Kerk*, III, 240ff.

146. Especially by T. H. van den Honert, Fr. Burmannus, M. Leydekker, Bomble, Creyghton, d'Outrein, Sluiter, Tuinman, et al.; C. Vitringa, *Doctr. christ.*, III, 110ff.

147. Ed. note: The reference is likely to followers of Jacobus Verschoor (1648–1700), who, when refused candidacy in the Dutch Reformed Church, began meeting in conventicles. His theology apparently tended toward antinomianism. See "Verschoor (Jacobus)," in *Christelijke Encyclopaedie*, ed. F. Grosheide et al., 1st ed., 6 vols. (Kampen: Kok, 1929), V, 581.

148. B. de Moor, *Comm. theol.*, IV, 422.

149. H. Plitt, *Zinzendorf's Theologie*, 3 vols. in 1 (Gotha: F. A. Perthes, 1869–74), I, 157ff., 317ff.; II, 242ff.; J. T. Müller, "Zinzendorf," in *PRE*[3], XXI, 688.

religious nurture, gradual development, organic growth, and a holy life—that, in a word, sought to be more "cultural" than "experiential."[150]

Right up until the present, these two schools exist side by side in America, as they do in England. Yet Methodism also underwent a significant change in the nineteenth century. In the case of Edwards, preaching to the unconverted consisted especially in a graphic depiction of the wrath of God and the torments of hell, while conversion then assumed the character of a transition from dread and fear to comfort and peace, which, as a rule, was sparked by a sudden new understanding of a passage of Scripture. Charles Finney, on the other hand, proceeded from the assumption that human beings are sinners voluntarily, and that it is within their power not to be sinners. Accordingly, he urged the unconverted to make a decision, with the help of the Holy Spirit, to give their heart to God now, in this very moment. Moody also took this approach, but whereas Finney tended to be the preacher of duty, as Edwards was of fear, so Moody highlighted the love and gift of God in Christ and so tried to move people to faith.[151] By contrast, the new movement that is known by the name of Christian Science aligns itself with the pantheistic idea that grief and remorse over sins is unnecessary and useless. Sin is like sickness and death, and these are errors of the mind and can therefore be completely overcome by "mind cure": "thoughts are things, thoughts are forces, and therefore as a man thinks, so is he."[152]

Although these and similar reactions against a plaintive Christianity are understandable and to a degree warranted, they themselves are also marked by gross exaggeration. Since all of us have consciences that regularly accuse and judge us, we also have some sense that contrition and confession is the first step on the road to conversion.[153] Herbert of Cherbury even tried to argue that one of the five universally known truths that constitute the essence of religion consists in the duty to grieve over sins committed and to repent from them.[154] In any case, a Christian knows from experience that sin, to the degree it is understood in its true character, evokes a correspondingly stronger feeling of grief and regret. True

150. E. W. Miller, "The Great Awakening," *Princeton Theological Review* 2 (October 1904): 545–62.

151. The revivals conducted by Edwards, Finney, and Moody have been treated, in terms of their distinct character, by *J. Kaltenbach, *Foi et Vie* (16 February 1906): 102–7; (1 March 1906): 132–36; (16 May 1906): 237–304. Cf. C. Stowe, "Jonathan Edwards," in *PRE*³, V, 171–75; L. G. Brendel, "Charles Grandison Finney," in *PRE*³, VI, 63–66; idem, "Dwight L. Moody," in *PRE*³, XIII, 434–36.

152. Cf. H. Bavinck, *Reformed Dogmatics*, III, 569n212 (#427b). W. James, *The Varieties of Religious Experience* (New York: Modern Library, 1902), 96ff. Also the so-called Emmanuel Movement must be considered in this connection: see Elwood Worcester, Samuel McComb, and Isador H. Coriat, *Religion and Medicine* (New York: Moffat, Yard, 1908); E. Worcester, *The Living Word* (London: Hodder & Stoughton, 1909); Robert MacDonald, *Mind, Religion, and Health, with an Appreciation of the Emmanuel Movement* (New York and London: Funk & Wagnalls, 1908); Samuel McComb, "The Christian Religion as a Healing Power," *Hibbert Journal* 8 (October 1909): 10–27.

153. Cf. H. Bavinck, *Reformed Dogmatics*, III, 129–36 (#329).

154. Cf. G. V. Lechler, *Geschichte des englischen Deismus* (Stuttgart: J. G. Cotta, 1841), 42, 47. Others as well opposed him on this point: J. G. Walch, *Bibliotheca theologica selecta*, I, 782ff.; C. Vitringa, *Doctr. christ.*, III, 100.

inward confession of sin is heard not from the lips of the ungodly but from those of the devout. Psalmists (Pss. 6; 25; 32; 51; 130; 143), prophets (Ezra 9:6; Neh. 9:33; Isa. 53:4ff.; 59:12; Jer. 3:25; 14:20; Lam. 3:39; Dan. 9:5ff.), and apostles (Matt. 26:75; Rom. 7:14ff.; 1 John 1:8–9) offer clear proof of this. And although grief increases in depth along with the knowledge of sin and growth in grace, it is nevertheless from the start an integral part of conversion and constitutes the other side of the renewal of life (Luke 15:18; 18:13; Acts 2:37; 9:6ff.; 16:30; 2 Cor. 7:10). Nothing specific is said here, however, about the depth and duration of that grief, nor about the time in which it should appear. In pious circles there is frequently much misunderstanding on this matter, and too much is made of the idea that one should precisely know the time of one's conversion, spend a period of time in great dread and fear, and be saved from it in a special or miraculous manner.

But Scripture does not apply such a standard and only requires that there be uprightness and truth in the hearts of people. Grief over sin must be genuine. God knows the heart and tests the mind (Ps. 7:9; Prov. 17:3; 21:2; Jer. 11:20; 17:10; 20:12; Acts 1:24; Rev. 2:23); asks for the love of the whole person, mind, soul, and all strengths included (Deut. 6:5; 10:12; Prov. 3:5; Jer. 29:13; Matt. 22:37); and delights in integrity (Josh. 24:14; 1 Kings 9:4; 1 Chron. 29:17; Pss. 25:21; 139:23–24). Conversion is a matter of the heart (Jer. 3:10; Luke 1:17; Acts 16:14; Rom. 2:29; 10:10). The people that honor God with their lips keep their heart far from him (Isa. 29:13; Matt. 15:8), say "Lord, Lord" but do not do his will (Matt. 7:21), and arouse his wrath; yet he takes delight in those who are of a broken and humble spirit (Pss. 51:17; 138:6; Isa. 57:15; James 4:6; 1 Pet. 5:5).

This is the line consistently followed also by the theology of the church, as the doctrine of infant baptism and confirmation clearly demonstrates. One does not have to know precisely the time of one's conversion; what matters is not the time but the fact of it. In numerous cases it is not even possible to determine that time because conversion, arising as it does from the new life that has been implanted, occurs gradually.[155] It does not always have to be accompanied by "perceptible shakings and violent pullings" but can also occur slowly, little by little, and smoothly.[156] This is not only what professional theologians say; it is also the language of practical authors. However much they insist on a true conversion, there is not one of them who dares to claim that there is but one kind of conversion for all.[157] In connection with the misery of life, which was so much more extensive and more deeply felt in earlier centuries, vigils and fastings, prayers and vows, solitude and reflection, and a wide range of spiritual exercises occupied a much larger place in religion than they do today, and great

155. Cf. the literature published on this topic in Lutheran theology during the conflict between the orthodox and the Pietists in J. G. Walch, *Bibliotheca theologica selecta*, II, 572ff.

156. G. Voetius, *Select. disp.* II, 415, 460; also, H. Bavinck, *Reformed Dogmatics*, III, 579–84 (#430).

157. Cf. also F. A. Lampe, *De verborgentheit van het gnade-verbondt*, 4 vols. (Amsterdam: Antony Schoonenburg, 1726–39), 255, 362ff., 372; ed. note: Bavinck cites the date as 1718.

value was attached to "spiritual and salutary tears." Still also in this connection a man like Voetius urged moderation: "Such moderation must be maintained that vehemence and exaggeration do not harm either body or soul to such a degree that we are rendered unfit for the worship of God or the service of our neighbor in love."[158]

Such genuine and heartfelt grief over sin is neither unprofitable nor a waste of time, but the way God works with us to free us inwardly from sin. In later years Moberly, Frommel, and others, examining the psychological nature of repentance, brought out with some validity that repentance is proof that a person is still capable of righteousness. For in repentance a person condemns himself, dissociates himself from sin, sides with righteousness, and paves for himself the way to forgiveness.[159] In this connection, however, we must bear in mind three things: (1) not all repentance is the same. A lot of "repentance" does not have the character of repentance. There is a kind of repentance that is little more than regret, which, though it fears the consequences of sin, does not deplore the sin itself. True repentance, according to Scripture, does not arise from the natural "man" but from the new life that was planted in a person by regeneration; (2) this true repentance never bears—as Moberly, agreeing with Kant, seems to think—an expiatory character. Even though in repentance a person recognizes the justice of God and the culpability of sin, that person does not thereby take upon oneself the punishment of sin and, therefore, does not atone for sin. True repentance can neither objectively (as God views it) nor subjectively (psychologically, to the person's own mind) be considered a punishment for sin, but is exclusively the means God employs to free the sinner from sin; and (3) the fact that repentance (along with faith) serves and can serve to that end is exclusively due to Christ, who was obedient to God even to death on the cross and thereby gained in God's sight the right to redeem humans from the guilt as well as from the pollution and power of sin. In justification he does the former, and in regeneration (conversion, sanctification) he does the latter. True conversion, true grief over sin, and genuine restoration to God and his service, therefore, are brought about not just by the law but even to a much higher degree by the gospel. The knowledge of sin is most assuredly derived from the law inasmuch as all sin has its standard in the law and is therefore lawlessness (ἀνομια, *anomia*); but the fact that humans thus learn to see and acknowledge sin in its true nature is due to the gospel and is to be viewed as the fruit of faith. Law and gospel, accordingly, work together in human conversion. The law points pedagogically to Christ; but the gospel also sheds its light on the law.[160]

158. G. Voetius, *Exercitia pietatis* (Gorinchem: Paul Vink, 1664), 228; Roman Catechism, II, ch. 5, qu. 23, 27 (ed. note: in Bradley and Kevane, II, ch. 4, qu. 23, 27; Bavinck erroneously cites this as II, ch. 4, qu. 23, 27).

159. R. C. Moberly, *Atonement and Personality* (London: John Murray, 1901), 19ff.; cf. H. Bavinck, *Reformed Dogmatics*, III, 295–98 (#368), 370–73 (#384), 380–85 (#387), 399–402 (#390).

160. Cf. H. Bavinck, *Reformed Dogmatics*, III, 520–28 (##418–19); and additional literature in C. Vitringa, *Doctr. christ.*, III, 111ff.

CONFESSION OF SIN

[465] Since, then, conversion is a matter of the heart, the Reformers, and later also Jansen and Quesnel, rejected the Roman idea of "attrition" as being insufficient. There is no doubt, of course, that all sorts of terror and dread may precede the actual conversion, but this form of penitence is essentially different from true repentance (*resipiscentia*), is not even a part of it, and does not infallibly lead to it. It may also occur in those who never arrive at a genuine amendment of life.[161] But Rome makes a distinction between "contrition" and "attrition." Contrition is born of love for God that is complete, not in its degrees but in its parts (contrition perfected by love proceeding from love for God for his own sake, or the love of benevolence or friendship as distinct from the lesser love of desire, which loves God not as the supreme good in himself but as the supreme good for us). That contrition immediately and by itself restores to the state of grace a person guilty of a mortal sin and devoid of grace, even before that person has received the sacrament of penance. Of course, this sacrament still remains necessary as proof of obedience, as a sign of the genuineness of contrition. The intention (*votum*) of the sacrament is present in it. Accordingly, restoration to the state of grace, or reconciliation, can be attributed to contrition as inclusive of the intention of the sacrament. This does not alter the fact, however, that in the case of those who practice true contrition, the sacrament of penance does not effect reconciliation but already presupposes it. In this doctrine of contrition we note the lingering influence in Roman Catholicism of the old Scholastic view that contrition is the indispensable condition for the validity of the sacrament of penance, and absolution in this sacrament is merely declarative in nature, not effective.[162]

But the sacramental theory that developed in the Roman church during the Middle Ages and was consistently applied, especially by Duns Scotus, tended in another direction.[163] It cannot be denied that there was an antinomy between the view that perfect contrition already justified the penitent before the reception of the sacrament, and the view that without it the sacrament would lose its validity and power. Moreover, if contrition already acquired justification before

---

161. Cf. H. Bavinck, *Reformed Dogmatics*, III, 522–28 (#419).

162. Peter Lombard (*Sent.*, IV, 18, 4, 6), for example, explicitly says: "God alone cleanses human beings of the more intimate (*interius*) stain of sin and looses them from the debt of eternal punishment, who says: 'I alone blot out the sins of the people.'" The priests therefore have only the "power of showing human beings to be bound and loosed. Wherefore the Lord first restored the leper to health through himself (per se), and then sent him to the priests that their judgment might be manifest that he was clean." The priests "therefore dismiss and retain, but they only declare and manifest what has been loosed and retained by God." Bonaventure and others concur in this judgment. Cf. J. Kunze, "Schlüsselgewalt," in *PRE*³, XVII, 630ff.

163. That sacramental doctrine leads to this conclusion is clear from reasoning such as the following: "The sacrament of penance in and through itself (per se) is established for the transference [of the penitent] from the state of sin into the state of grace. But as a perfect act of contrition is required in order to the proper disposition for the reception of this sacrament, no one would ever be transferred in and through the sacrament of penance itself from a state of sin into a state of grace. Therefore, an act of perfect contrition is not required" (C. Pesch, *Prael. dogm.*, VII, 72).

the reception of the sacrament, it must itself, by virtue of the work-reward relationship, have exceptional value. Contrition, it must be granted, cannot justify
the penitent in the sense that it is the "formal cause of justification," but it does
prepare the penitent for the reception of grace and makes one fit for its reception
"to the extent that God deservedly gives sanctifying grace to a contrite person."[164]
Hence, to gain this grace prior to the sacrament, contrition must be "qualitatively
excellent," that is, the sinner must hate sin more than any other evil and at the same
time be "universal," that is, it must extend to all the grave sins one has committed,
whether one remembers them or not;[165] or, as the Roman Catechism puts it, the
grief over sins, which is implied in the word "contrition," must be "very great"
and "vigorous."[166]

But such vigorous, keen, and ardent contrition is only attainable by a few, and
if this were the only way to justification, only a small number would be able to
obtain it. God, accordingly, has provided for the salvation of humanity by an
easier method and in accordance with his marvelous counsel has opened another
means of access to salvation in the church's power of the keys.[167] And this consists
in so-called attrition or "imperfect contrition," which is to say that if a person is
sorry on account of one's sins, not out of love for God, but from "a consideration
of the ugliness of sin or from the fear of hell and of punishments," excludes from
it "the will to sin" and unites with it "the hope of pardon," then such an "imperfect
contrition" is still "a gift of God and an impulse of the Holy Spirit." And although
this attrition cannot by itself effect justification, it "disposes the sinner to obtain
the grace of God in the sacrament of penance."[168]

Despite this Tridentine pronouncement many [Roman Catholic scholars]
still more or less try to maintain their view on the basis of the old contritionist
position (Pallavicini, Lupus, Billuart, von Schäzler, and others) and plead for the
necessity of uniting with attrition at least an act of charity. But the attritionism
that considered fear of hellish, or even of temporal, punishments prior to the
reception of absolution in the sacrament to be sufficient gained the upper hand.
The famous decree of Pope Alexander VII, dated May 5, 1667, prohibited the
sharply contending parties from condemning each other as heretics but left the
issue itself unresolved, and this situation has continued to the present.[169] All of this
is remarkably significant for the theory and practice of Roman Catholic penance.
For what kind of fear is now sufficient, according to Rome, for the reception of

---

164. C. Pesch, *Prael. dogm.*, VII, 57; cf. 51: "Moreover, a complete turning from sin and turning to God is
the exact reason for which contrition justifies [a person]."

165. C. Pesch, *Prael. dogm.*, VII, 51.

166. Roman Catechism, II, ch. 5, qu. 26 (ed. note: in Bradley and Kevane, II, ch. 4, qu. 26).

167. Ed. note: Bavinck refers here to Roman Catechism, II, ch. 5, qu. 32, 2 (in Bradley and Kevane, II, ch.
4, qu. 32). However, this article makes no direct reference to the keys of the kingdom. The Roman Catechism
explicitly deals with the keys to the kingdom in part I, art. 10, par. 4 (Bradley and Kevane, p. 117).

168. The Council of Trent, sess. XIV, c. 4.

169. J. H. Oswald, *Die dogmatische Lehre*, II, 71ff.; C. Pesch, *Prael. dogm.*, VII, 61ff.; H. Th. Simar, *Lehrbuch
der Dogmatik*, 3rd ed., 2 vols. (Freiburg i.B.: Herder, 1893), 763ff.; J. Pohle, *Lehrbuch der Dogmatik*, III, 466ff.

the sacrament and the absolution granted in it? Is a doubly servile fear, the fear of punishment aside from guilt, sufficient, or is a simple servile fear required? Does the latter include—if not formally, then at least virtually—the love of benevolence or friendship or at least the love of desire? Theologians ponder these distinctions at great length while the Roman church leaves both confessors and penitents who think through such things in doubt about these serious questions. So one can imagine what happens in popular practice with such attrition! To prove its theory of attrition, Trent may appeal to the example of the Ninevites, and theologians may at this point add a few other scriptural references (Exod. 20:20; Ps. 119:120; Matt. 5:20; 10:28; Luke 3:7; 13:3; John 5:14; etc.), but casuistic inquiry into the question of how little can suffice for a person to obtain absolution is diametrically opposed to the spirit of the gospel.[170]

This is no less true of confession. According to the Fourth Lateran Council (1215), all believers of both genders are obliged to confess all their sins in secret at least once a year before their own priest as soon as they have reached the years of discretion (as a rule, their seventh year).[171] Actually, this confession is strictly necessary only for believers who have committed a mortal sin and have thereby lost God's sanctifying grace. The reason is that after baptism there is no other means by which to return to the state of grace than through the sacrament of penance. Furthermore, one is not obliged to confess one's daily sins, for they do not constitute an obstacle to salvation, and they can also be forgiven without confession before a priest. Yet for Roman Catholic believers, it would be highly imprudent, even if they were not conscious of having committed any mortal sin, never to make use of the sacrament of penance. For, in practice, it is often very difficult to distinguish the boundary line between mortal and venial sins. Apart from a few exceptions, all believers in fact commit mortal sins after baptism—not once but over and over. Repeatedly they fall from the state of grace back into the state of nature. And so confession is practically necessary for all believers, not just once a year but preferably as often as possible.[172] In that confession, believers must confess all the mortal sins of which, after diligent self-examination, they are conscious, no matter how secret they are and even if they consist only in their thoughts and desires. They must confess these sins one by one and also indicate the circumstances in which they were committed, for these factors may be of great importance for the determination of the gravity of the sin and for the satisfaction to be imposed. Confession must be both comprehensive and absolute.[173]

170. Protestant literature in which this Roman doctrine of attrition is refuted can be found in C. Vitringa, *Doctr. christ.*, III, 124–25.

171. Reiterated at the Council of Florence, 1439; Council of Trent, sess. XIV, cap. 5; Roman Catechism, II, ch. 5, qu. 38 (ed. note: in Bradley and Kevane, II, ch. 4, qu. 38).

172. Roman Catechism, II, ch. 5, qu. 39, 46 (ed. note: in Bradley and Kevane, II, ch. 4, qu. 39, 46).

173. Council of Trent, sess. XIV, c. 5; Roman Catechism, II, ch. 5, qu. 40–41 (ed. note: in Bradley and Kevane, II, ch. 4, qu. 40–41).

Of this private and secret auricular confession before a priest,[174] Catholic theologians themselves recognize that it does not directly and literally occur in Scripture.[175] In the Old and New Testaments there is repeated mention of the confession of sin: before the government (Lev. 5:5; Num. 5:7; Josh. 7:19), to one another (James 5:16), before God in public (Lev. 16:21; Ezra 10:11; Neh. 9:2–3; Matt. 3:6; Acts 19:18) or in secret (Ps. 32:5; Ezra 10:1; Neh. 1:6; Dan. 6:11; 9:4, 20; 1 John 1:9). Confession is inseparable from a true knowledge of sin and the way to God's mercy (Prov. 28:13). But Scripture nowhere mentions confession as Rome understands it. Accordingly, following the Council of Trent, theologians infer its warrant from reasoning based on the promise of Christ in Matt. 16:19 to Peter and in Matt. 18:18 to all the apostles, giving them the power of the keys, and from the fulfillment of that promise in John 20:22–23.

With these words, according to Rome, Christ appointed the apostles—and further the bishops and priests—to be rulers and judges "to whom all the mortal sins into which the faithful of Christ may have fallen should be brought in order that, by virtue of the power of the keys, they may pronounce the sentence of remission and retention of sins."[176] Granted, in baptism the church also dispenses grace, but there it does not do it "in the manner of a judgment" (*per modum judicii*) but "in the manner of a benefit" (*per modum beneficii*), for it has as yet no judicial power over those who have been baptized but only acquires this power through baptism. The baptized, however, are and remain under the jurisdiction of the church; can be compelled, if not physically then certainly ethically, to appear before its forum when they have committed mortal sins; and can be acquitted or condemned by the ecclesiastical court. For the judicial power that Christ granted to his church is twofold: the church can forgive (remit, dissolve) sins, but it can also retain them by refusing to forgive them or, along with forgiveness, to impose a punishment to compensate the justice of God (vindicative punishment, *poena vindicativa*) and to guard against a relapse into sin (medicinal punishment, *poena medicinalis*). In both cases, however, the judge (that is, the priest) is obligated to

---

174. For a long time in the church of Rome, lay confession (i.e., confession before laypersons), was also in use. We learn of it first from the chronicles of Bishop Thietmar of Merseburg in AD 1015. It was defended by a booklet (*Concerning True and False Penitence*) credited to Augustine, by Gratian, Lombard, et al. Peter Cantor even went so far as to recommend that, in cases of emergency, people confess before a woman, a heretic, or a Jew. The practice attained its broadest scope in the thirteenth century, the age of chivalry. But Thomas, Hales, and Bonaventure denied its sacramental character, although in some cases they still call it advisable and useful; cf. Council of Trent, sess. XIV, c. 5. Duns Scotus was firmly against it. The Council of Trent (sess. XIV, c. 6) restricted the power to forgive sins exclusively to bishops and priests. Cf. G. Gromer, *Die Laienbeicht im Mittelalter* (Munich: J. J. Lentner, 1909). C. Pesch, *Prael. dogm.*, VII, 180.

175. According to J. Pohle, *Lehrbuch der Dogmatik*, III, 484: "There are hardly any direct and explicit references to the sacrament of penance in the New Testament. Even though that is the case, this fact does not provide strong proof." For similar statements from Duns Scotus and others, see C. Pesch, *Prael. dogm.*, VII, 155ff., 161ff.

176. Council of Trent, sess. XIV, ch. 5.

carefully ascertain the number, nature, and circumstances of the sins; and he can only do that by hearing the confession, the honest and completed confession of the believing penitent. In Rome, accordingly, confession is a consequence of the judicial character of the church's remission of sins, just as this judicial character of the church's remission of sins is "to a certain extent the pivotal point of the entire Catholic view of the sacrament of penance."[177]

Considering the confession's occasional practical utility, one can understand that in some countries the Lutheran Church still for a time wanted to retain it,[178] and that some Protestants either want to restore it or at least want something to take its place.[179] But those who understand the link between confession and the falsification of the gospel, the grace of forgiveness, and the office and power of the church never want it back. Indeed, in Matt. 16:19; 18:18; and John 20:23 there is mention of the power Christ granted the apostles to open or close the kingdom of heaven by either forgiving or not forgiving people's sins. But this power is none other than that the apostles, now equipped with the word of Christ and the gift of the Holy Spirit, receive the right and authority, in their oral and written proclamation, to point out the way in which the benefit of the forgiveness of sins can be obtained and, in keeping with this, to determine the relation in which a person stands vis-à-vis the kingdom of heaven. Rome quite improperly made of it a judicial power granted to the bishops and by their authority to the priests. It is a power exercised by them, not in preaching or in baptism, but in the sacrament of penance; and it is extended over all believers and over all their sins and bears an absolute character. The advantage that can otherwise be associated with auricular confession has been much too dearly paid for with the price of numerous serious disadvantages. One should not forget that this same auricular confession carries with it the impermissible coercion of human souls, the torture of consciences on the one hand and the weakening of personal responsibility on the other. [It also leads to] an atomistic division and casuistic assessment of sins and their corresponding punishments, a rashness and shallowness of judgment that, produced by the routinization of practice in making confessions and dispensing absolution,

177. J. Wilhelm and T. B. Scannell, *A Manual of Catholic Theology*, 4th ed., 2 vols. (London: Kegan Paul, Trench, Trübner; New York: Benziger Brothers, 1909), IV, 3, 681. J. Pohle, *Lehrbuch der Dogmatik*, III, 416.

178. Joseph T. Müller, *Die symbolischen Bücher der evangelisch-lutherischen Kirche*, 8th ed. (Gütersloh: Bertelsmann, 1898), 41, 164, 321, 363, 773; ed. note: These specific references are to the following Lutheran documents: Augsburg Confession, arts. 11–12, in *The Book of Concord*, ed. Robert Kolb and Timothy J. Wengert (Minneapolis: Fortress, 2000), 45; Apology of the Augsburg Confession, art. 11 (Kolb and Wengert, 185ff.); Smalcald Articles, part III, art. 8 (Kolb and Wengert, 321–23); "The Sacrament of Holy Baptism," art. 4 of The Small Catechism (Kolb and Wengert, 360–62); "A Brief Exhortation to Confession" (Kolb and Wengert, 476–80); J. Gerhard, *Loci theologici*, ed. E. Preuss, 9 vols. (Berlin: G. Schlawitz, 1863–75), XV, 98ff.; J. A. Quenstedt, *Theologia*, III, 598ff.; W. Caspari, "Beichte," in *PRE*[3], II, 533–41. Ed. note: Bavinck erroneously cites pp. 336ff.

179. W. Caspari, "Beichte," in *PRE*[3], II, 540ff.; *cf. also, Prof. K. Lake, *Theologische Tijdschrift* 6 (1910): 528ff.

has to be a factor and undermines the moral consciousness. How can a finite and fallible human being possibly judge the deepest motives of the heart of his brother [or sister], and how can the latter ever put one's trust for all eternity in such a superficial and uncertain judgment? When the Roman Catholic Church authorizes its bishops and priests to be such judges, it is arrogating to itself a right and power that in the nature of the case can only belong to God as the infallible knower of human hearts. Who can forgive sins but God alone? (Isa. 43:25; Mark 2:7).[180]

PENANCE AND PUNISHMENT

[466] To this it must be added that the priest—since perfect contrition is usually lacking and only a kind of attrition is present—as a rule may only give absolution along with the imposition of a number of good works to be performed. For Rome asserts that the forgiveness of the guilt of sins and the remission of eternal punishment does not rule out that human persons here on earth still have to suffer a variety of temporal punishments. For this position it appeals to the examples of Adam and Eve (Gen. 3:16ff.), Miriam (Num. 12:14), Moses and Aaron (Num. 20:12; 27:13–14; Deut. 34:4), David (2 Sam. 12:13–14), and the believers in Corinth (1 Cor. 11:30), who, despite the forgiveness they received, were still subject to various kinds of punishment.[181] These facts are incontrovertible and can be increased with many others from Scripture and history, which show that believers, even though they shared in the benefits of the covenant of grace, continued to be subject to the suffering of the present time, had to bear the consequences of the sins committed earlier, and were often more severely afflicted on account of their trespasses than others (2 Sam. 7:14–15; Ps. 89:30–34; Isa. 48:9–11; Amos 3:2). The forgiveness of sins is a benefit of grace of which nature is ignorant, and the righteous must enter the kingdom of God through many tribulations (Acts 14:22).

But Scripture teaches that all the suffering that comes over believers on account of their own sins or those of others has lost for them the character of punishment and is for them a useful chastisement in order that they may share in God's holiness (Job 5:17; Prov. 3:11; 1 Cor. 11:32; Heb. 12:5–11; Rev. 3:19).[182] And they owe this to Christ, who has accomplished everything for them and completely redeemed them from all guilt and all punishment. Accordingly, in numerous cases, which Rome disregards, the forgiveness of sins is granted without any mention of any further punishment or chastisement (Matt. 9:2; Luke 18:14; 22:61; etc.).

But Rome reasons otherwise. For Christ indeed delivered believers from all the guilt of sin and also from eternal punishment in hell, but not from the temporal

---

180. J. Calvin, *Institutes*, III.iv.4–24; C. Vitringa, *Doctr. christ.*, III, 126ff.

181. Council of Trent, sess. XIV, c. 12–15; cf. VI, can. 30.

182. J. Calvin, *Institutes*, III.iv.31ff.

punishments on earth or in purgatory. Trent does say that the satisfaction we pay for our sins does not exclude the merits of Christ. On the contrary: "from him is all our sufficiency," "our satisfaction is through him," and "all our glorying is in him in whom we live, merit, and satisfy and without whom we can do nothing."[183] Still for Rome there is a serious difficulty here, for we must choose between one alternative or another. *Either* Christ paid only for the guilt of sin and delivered us from the punishment of hell but then did not bear the temporal punishments for sin and did not deliver us from them. We ourselves must then make satisfaction for them, albeit in his strength, and so add our own merits to the merits of Christ. Then the statement that our satisfaction is made "through Christ Jesus" only means that he gave us the power to make satisfaction for our sins by our own works. *Or* Christ also bore the temporal punishments due to sin for those who believe in him, and in that case the suffering that still comes over them in this life is no longer a punishment but only his fatherly chastisement. Moreover, the satisfactions that the confessor imposes "according to the quality of the crimes and the capacity of the penitents," while they also serve as "preservation of a new life" and a "medicine of infirmity," are especially meant "for the avenging and punishment of past sins."[184] They must therefore have the power to release penitents from temporal punishments, just as Christ by his satisfaction delivered his own from eternal punishments. But can they and do they really do this? There is not a Catholic who can say they do. For even the most saintly people in the Roman Catholic Church, with all their "satisfactions," indeed with all their "supererogatory works," have not been able to deliver themselves from the suffering of this present age or from death. Like all other humans, who may have far fewer "merits" than they, they are subject to this suffering and sometimes have even more than their share of it.[185] The "satisfactions of work"(*satisfactiones operis*), accordingly, have little or no significance for this life; their entire value, both theoretically and practically, consists in the diminution or mitigation of these punishments in purgatory.

Furthermore, there are many sins that God does not punish in this life at all. There are numerous believers who, according to Rome, are far behind others in holiness and yet experience a far more pleasant and easier life than they. In that case, they must atone all the longer and the more intensely in purgatory for the sins they committed on earth. Also for this reason, "these satisfactions especially pertain to the removal of the punishments of purgatory."[186] These satisfactions, moreover, are divided into three classifications: prayer, fasting, and alms. For humans possess three kinds of goods that they can offer to God in compensation

183. Council of Trent, sess. XIV, c. 8, 13.

184. Ibid., sess. XIV, c. 8.

185. According to C. Pesch, *Prael. dogm.*, VII, 107: "Notwithstanding, it is to be noted that a human being cannot ever by his own works avoid punishments in this life," nor indeed "the penalties of this life; for it belongs to all to suffer and to die."

186. C. Pesch, *Prael. dogm.*, VII, 104.

for the sins they have committed: goods of the spirit (*boni anima*), which they offer in prayer; goods of the body (*boni corporis*), which they surrender in fasting; goods of fortune (*boni fortunae*), which they offer up in the giving of alms.[187] Since they are performed by believers and in their case flow from a supernatural principle, they have a "satisfactory" value, or a meritorious value "of condignity." They can secure heavenly blessedness for believers, hence more easily deliver them from temporal punishments in purgatory.

But this is not all. In the early centuries of the church, the "satisfactions" that it imposed were very severe, but now they are greatly reduced.

> Since today such great severity would more likely be offensive and do harm rather than good, while the sacrament of penance was after all instituted only for the good of the soul, and while in any case the payment of the punishment of sin is assured in purgatory, the present leniency of the father-confessors in imposing the penalties connected with penance seems excusable in light of the second viewpoint, that of the capacity of the penitents.[188]

The Roman Catholic Church knows how to accommodate itself to circumstances. It weakens contrition, which can be attained only by the few, by adding attrition and augmenting the latter with the sacrament of penance, which works ex opere operato.[189] This sacrament instantly delivers the penitent from the guilt of sin and from hellish punishment but also immediately obligates him to "pay off" all temporal punishments either here or in purgatory. The punishments in purgatory, however, can be bought off by acts of penance performed on earth. These penances, depending on circumstances, can be either more severe or lighter, since "in any case the payment of the punishment of sin is assured in purgatory." These penances in turn can be replaced by indulgences, and the indulgences are in force not only for the living but "in the manner of suffrage" also for the poor souls in purgatory.

In this way, everything is made as easy as possible. Those who refrain from intentionally posing an obstacle and put their trust in priestly absolution can be certain of their ultimate salvation. In this system of give and take, after all, only the church's absolute power of the keys is certain. "A sin that the church on earth has retained (that is, bound) remains so with God in heaven until it

---

187. Council of Trent, sess. VI, c. 14 puts it this way: Penance for Christians after falling must include "satisfaction by fasting, almsgiving, prayers, and other devout exercises of the spiritual life, not indeed for the eternal punishment . . . but for temporal punishment." Ed. note: Bavinck cites only part of this passage and mistakenly places it in XIV, canon 13, rather than ch. 14 of sess. VI. The passage is in H. Denzinger, ed., *The Sources of Catholic Dogma*, trans. from 30th ed. by R. J. Deferrari (London and St. Louis: Herder, 1955), #806. Cf. T. Aquinas, *Summa theol.*, qu. 15, art. 3; C. Pesch, *Prael. dogm.*, VII, 109–10; J. Pohle, *Lehrbuch der Dogmatik*, III, 505.

188. J. Pohle, *Lehrbuch der Dogmatik*, III, 507.

189. Ed. note: This classic Latin term means "by the work performed" and refers to the belief that the sacrament itself has the power to communicate grace to the believer. Sacraments themselves have a gracious power.

has been forgiven (that is, loosed) by the church."[190] Only those are reconciled with God who are reconciled with the church. Yet, in the Roman system, everything remains uncertain for those who do not capitulate to a false security. For although contrition is not a prerequisite for the reception of the sacrament, the "simple servile fear" (*timor simpliciter servilis*) that is required in attrition cannot be readily distinguished, either by the penitent or the father-confessor, from the "doubly servile fear" (*timor serviliter servilis*) that is insufficient. The grace granted in the sacrament can at any moment be lost again by a mortal sin, and no one can precisely and with certainty indicate the boundary that separates it from a venial sin. The penances and the good works prescribed by indulgences do deliver from temporal punishment, but only when they meet the demand of God's righteousness and are performed with absolute precision. Inasmuch as the priest is not a "supreme master" but a "lower judge," he is never certain whether the punishment imposed is not perhaps less than God's justice requires, and therefore "only God knows how great a punishment is remitted by a given satisfaction."[191]

This entire penitential system was therefore rejected by the Reformation as absolutely incompatible with the spirit of the gospel. Luther admittedly still retained the term "sacrament of penance."[192] Even the Lutheran confessions explain that "absolution can properly be called the sacrament of penance."[193] For the sake of the individual application of absolution and the certainty of faith enhanced by it—"especially on account of absolution"—Lutherans in the early years even favored the retention of the practice of confession.[194] But everything now breathed a different spirit. The penitents did not have to recite all their sins, and the clergyman did not have to know them all. While confession of one's sins was necessary, it could also be done before one of the members of the church. The absolution (or forgiveness of sins) was not different from what everyone could obtain by believing the gospel and what every member of the church could say and promise to a penitent for that one's consolation. So, though the term "sacrament" was retained, materially the practice of penance was no longer a sacrament; it was nothing more than a particularization of the way the gospel is applied as a means of grace.[195]

190. J. Pohle, *Lehrbuch der Dogmatik*, III, 414.

191. C. Pesch, *Prael. dogm.*, VII, 109. "In the case of indulgences . . . prayer" (J. F. de Groot, *Handleiding bij het katholiek godsdienstonderwijs aan gymnasia, H. burgerscholen en kweekscholen* [Amsterdam: C. L. Van Langenhuysen, 1906], 194). On the uncertainty brought about by the Roman Catholic doctrine of penance, see J. Calvin, *Institutes*, III.iv.17, 22. Literature concerning the debate (pro and con) over the system of satisfaction and indulgences can be found in C. Vitringa, *Doctr. christ.*, III, 138–52.

192. F. A. Loofs, *Dogmengeschichte*, 731, 734.

193. Joseph T. Müller, *Die symbolischen Bücher*, 41, 173, 202; ed. note: These specific references are to the following Lutheran documents: Augsburg Confession, arts. 11–12 (Kolb and Wengert, 45); Apology of the Augsburg Confession, art. 12, pars. 41–45 (Kolb and Wengert, 193); ibid., art. 13 (Kolb and Wengert, 219).

194. See above, 167 (#465).

195. J. Gerhard, *Loci theol.*, XV, 19ff.; J. A. Quenstedt, *Theologia*, 587ff.

For the church's entire power of the keys consists in administering the Word of God. It is not a "power separate from the gospel,"[196] but coincides with it. When we look at the people who proclaim that gospel, such proclamation is not a power but a ministry, for Christ did not actually give that power to people but to his Word, "of which he made humans ministers."[197] That Word can be officially administered in public preaching, in the administration of the sacraments, in the exercise of discipline, in catechismal instruction and home visitation, by education and nurture, in public address and prayer. In all these ways God works upon the souls of people with a view toward conversion, instruction, admonition, consolation, and so forth. Conversion, accordingly, does not end with the "first actual conversion" but subsequently continues in "daily conversion." After the "repentance of the catechumens" comes the "repentance of believers," for, according to Luther in his Ninety-five Theses, Christ wants the whole life of a Christian to be penitential. Since believers remain imperfect to the end of their lives, and their redemption is only complete when they have been totally renewed after the image of Christ, they must continually fight against sin and train themselves in the faith. Their "restoration is not accomplished in a moment or in a day or a year; but through continual and sometimes even slow advances, God wipes out in his elect the corruptions of the flesh, consecrates them to himself as temples, renewing all their minds to true purity that they may practice repentance throughout their lives and know that this warfare will end only at death." The course of repentance that God assigns to them extends to the whole of life.[198]

In the Reformation, therefore, and particularly in Calvin,[199] conversion acquired profound ethical significance. In the case of Roman Catholic Christians, the stimulus to a holy life lies in the "satisfactions," or the merits of good works. But on the basis of Protestantism this cannot be the case, for Christ completed everything and atoned for all sins (Rom. 3:25; Heb. 10:14; 1 Pet. 2:24; 1 John 1:7; 2:1), and for his sake, hence out of grace, God did not count their trespasses against them (2 Cor. 5:19). The forgiveness of sins, of their guilt and punishment, accordingly, was a benefit of grace, a gift of God's great mercy that can never—neither at the beginning nor in the progression [of the Christian life]—be earned by good works done by humans. Like all the benefits of salvation, the forgiveness of sins, objectively speaking, is completely prepared and ready in Christ for his own. In that objective sense, it even precedes faith and repentance (conversion), while it remains true that it can only be accepted by faith and appropriated and enjoyed by way of repentance.[200] Good works, accordingly, are not the cause but the fruit of the forgiveness of sins,

196. J. Calvin, *Institutes*, III.iv.14.
197. Ibid., IV.xi.1.
198. Ibid., III.iii.9.
199. Cf. H. Bavinck, *Reformed Dogmatics*, III, 522–28 (#419).
200. C. Vitringa, *Doctr. christ.*, III, 100; cf. the following chapter (below) on "Justification."

and repentance is not "a second plank after shipwreck" but a return to one's baptism: an independent, personal and lifelong appropriation of the treasures of grace that are present in Christ, the progressive dying-away of the old self and the coming-to-life of the new.

Only in that way does Christ preserve his honor, but also in only that way can the human conscience obtain peace and rest.[201] For if we must gain God's favor by our contrition, confession, and satisfaction, we will be continually in fear and dread over whether in all these matters we have done what we ought and do not even arrive at doing good works out of childlike love and obedience. But if by faith in the forgiveness of our sins, we have been given assurance beforehand, we are also heartily willing to walk as children according to all God's commandments. Therein, then, we see the evidence of the genuineness of our faith and repentance. For "the fruits of true repentance are the duties of piety toward God, of charity toward men, and in the whole of life, holiness, and piety." And the more earnestly any persons measure their lives by the standard of God's law, the surer are the signs of true repentance they show.[202]

So then the first and continuing conversion does not consist exclusively, nor even primarily, in painful sensations of the heart but—though such feelings are not totally ruled out—in walking in God's commandments and doing everywhere and always what is pleasing to him.[203] The coming-to-life of the new self, the second part of true repentance, is not even limited to "the happiness that the mind receives after its disturbance and fear have been quieted," but rather means "the desire to live in a holy and devoted manner, a desire arising from rebirth; as if it were said that humans die to themselves that they may begin to live to God."[204] And if believers sometimes through weakness fall into sins, they must not for that reason despair of God's mercy, nor continue in sin, since baptism is a seal and indubitable testimony that they have an eternal covenant with God.[205] There is a repentance of the catechumens and a repentance of the faithful, but also, according to Scripture and contrary to Novatians and Anabaptists, a repentance of the fallen. Not only do the examples of David and Peter prove this, but also Christ himself admonished his churches in Asia Minor to "repent, and do the works you did at first" (Rev. 2:5, 16; 3:3, 18). This conversion then does not, like the first conversion, relate to the entire state of sin, but is especially focused on the specific grave sin into which the believer has fallen and from which, in the power of God, the believer now turns away.

201. J. Calvin, *Institutes*, III.iv.27; cf. III.iv.2.

202. Ibid., III.iii.16.

203. For the struggle between the orthodox [Lutherans] and Pietists over whether the intellect or the will is the actual locus of conversion, see B. de Moor, *Comm. theol.*, IV, 414; J. G. Walch, *Bibliotheca theologica selecta*, II, 750.

204. J. Calvin, *Institutes*, III.iii.3.

205. Bavinck here cites lines from the classic liturgy for infant baptism used in Reformed Churches for centuries. See *Psalter Hymnal* (Grand Rapids: CRC Publications, 1987), p. 957.

As a particular conversion, therefore, it is distinct from the former, which is an all-encompassing conversion.[206]

206. Walaeus, in *Synopsis purioris theologiae*, disp. 32, 48; P. van Mastricht, *Theologia*, VI, 4, 24; C. Vitringa, *Doctr. christ.*, III, 38–131; C. Boetticher, *Das Wesen des religiösen Glaubens im Neuen Testament* (Berlin: R. Gärtner, 1895); *J. E. Huther, "Die Bedeutung des Begriffes ζωη und πιστευειν in den Johanneischen Schriften," *Jahrbücher für deutsche Theologie* 17 (1872): 1–34; J. Haussleiter, "Was versteht Paulus unter christlichen Glauben?" in *Greifswalder Studien*, ed. Samuel Oettlie et al. (Gütersloh: Bertelsmann, 1895), 159–82; idem, *Der Glaube Jesu Christi und der christliche Glaube* (Erlangen and Leipzig: A. Deichert [G. Böhme], 1891); A. von Schlatter, *Der Glaube im Neuen Testament*, 3rd ed. (Stuttgart: Vereinsbuchhandlung, 1905); R. Seeberg, "Erleuchtung," in *PRE*[3], V, 457–59; idem, "Bekehrung," in *PRE*[3], II, 541–45; O. Kirn, "Glaube," in *PRE*[3], VI, 678; J. Köstlin, "Busse," in *PRE*[3], III, 584–91; B. B. Warfield, "Faith," in *DB*, I, 827–38; H. C. G. Moule, *Faith, Its Nature and Its Work* (London and New York: Cassell, 1909); K. Ziesché, *Verstand und Wille beim Glaubensakt* (Paderborn: Schöningh, 1909); ed. note: Bavinck incorrectly cites this as "Liesche." C. Pesch, "Glaubenspflicht und Glaubenschwierigkeiten," in *Theologische Zeitfragen*, 2 vols. in 1 (Freiburg i.B.: Herder, 1908); J. V. Bainvel, *La foi et l'acte de foi* (Paris: Lethielleux, 1908); C. Bos (= M. Boeuf), *Psychologie de la croyance*, 2nd ed. (Paris: F. Alcan, 1905); E. Murisier, *Les maladies du sentiment religieux*, 2nd ed. (Paris: F. Alcan, 1903; ed. note: Bavinck cites the publication date for the 2nd ed. as 1907). M. Hébert, *L'évolution de la foi catholique* (Paris: F. Alcan, 1905; ed. note: Bavinck cites the 1907 edition). J. de Lacombe, *Les nouveau-nés de l'Esprit* (Paris: Fischbacher, 1905); W. Schmidt, *Die verschiedenen Typen religiöser Erfahrung und die Psychologie* (Gütersloh: Bertelsmann, 1908; ed. note: Bavinck cites the 1910 edition). J. Herzog, *Der Begriff der Bekehrung* (Giessen: J. Ricker [Töpelmann], 1903); G. Jackson, *The Fact of Conversion* (New York and Chicago: Fleming H. Revell, 1908).

3

JUSTIFICATION

Of all God's benefits given in the covenant of grace, first place belongs to justification, to forgiveness of sins. All joy and peace, all certainty of communion with God, rests on this forgiveness, a benefit no mind can fully comprehend or believe. Forgiveness is not easy and often conflicts with our sense of justice. Here Christianity distinguishes itself by tying justice and love together at the cross. In traditional Eastern religions as well as in Western thought, the ironclad law of causal necessity reigns. Nature knows no forgiveness.

Scripture, using many varied metaphors, depicts God as gracious. Forgiveness is God's gift; it cannot be earned. The Old Testament, notably in the Psalms, portrays God's nature as merciful; the New Testament proclaims the One who came to seek and save the lost, to lift the burdens of the heavyhearted. Proclaimed throughout the New Testament in various ways, forgiveness is underscored in its forensic dimension as justification especially by the apostle Paul. Reflecting on his life experience as a Pharisee under the law, Paul accents the righteousness of Christ imputed to believers by faith alone. This justification produces liberty, frees believers for service, and assures them of eternal life.

Already in Paul's own day, this doctrine was misunderstood as antinomianism. In response, the church moved toward seeing the Christian life in terms of obeying God's commandments. Penance and good works became the preferred way of dealing with sins committed after baptism. Grace was seen as a divine infusion into the believer via the sacraments. Habitual grace then remains the ground of a believer's justification but, logically, God forgives people because he has made them holy. Rome fails clearly to distinguish between justification and sanctification.

Luther's great discovery about the "righteousness of God" was that it did not apply to God's righteousness in himself but rather to the righteousness applied to believers through faith in Christ. God's righteousness does not condemn us but justifies us. We are clothed in Christ's righteousness. We are not justified by good works, but for good works, by grace. Faith thus believes that we are sinners and that for Christ's sake we are justified. God's declaration of righteousness is not a mere sentence God pronounces to himself but brings with it the act of making us righteous in Christ. Believers are to take God at his word, recognizing nonetheless that their healing is a lifelong process. The Christian life is a life of faith; trusting in God's promises, we may neither despair nor be falsely secure.

From the start, the Reformation was both a religious and an ethical movement. Though time and polemics brought about changes in emphases as well as greater clarity, Luther's mature thought is true to what was germinally present in his early Lectures on Romans. Thanks especially to the polemics with Rome, Lutherans increasingly ascribed to justification an exclusively juridical meaning. In Lutheran circles there was a shift away from predestination, with the result that human achievement and good works began to have a role in faith. As a result, for Pietism and rationalism alike, justification increasingly became a subjective matter, an experience of forgiveness and renewal.

In the Reformed tradition, however, though neither the objectivity of Christ's satisfaction nor the benefit to believers was ever minimized, the emphasis was placed on righteousness as God's gift rather than as a benefit we accept by faith. The comfort of believers was important but even more so the glory of God. Calvin kept sanctification in the fore as much as justification; whom Christ justifies he also sanctifies, unto the glory of God. And that is also the believer's glory. Though Calvin kept justification closely connected to election and satisfaction on the one hand, and sanctification and glorification on the other, those who followed him did not. Rationalism, whether in Socinian, Remonstrant, Cartesian, or Amyraldian form, emphasized the human subject's faith and obedience, creating a new form of nomism or legalism. Pietism and Methodism, for all their differences with the preceding, also represented a turn toward human subjectivity and the experience of faith. In response, some Reformed theologians emphasized the objectivity of justification and placed it in the divine decree of love. This risked encouraging antinomianism by downplaying the importance of human response. Reformed theologians tried to avoid extremes and began to carefully distinguish active and passive justification. This distinction was intended as a logical distinction only, not a temporal one. To this day, the two different emphases—the objectivity of divine promise and the subjectivity of faith's response—both remain in the Reformed churches.

Justification is the doctrine on which the church stands or falls. Either we must do something to be saved, or our salvation is purely a gift of grace. God does not set aside the law that properly judges us; only because Christ bore the wrath of God are we reckoned righteous in him. Ethical consequences flow forth from justification, but they must not be imported into the very definition itself. To reverse the order would be to make justification dependent on sanctification—a hopeless measure since even our best works are imperfect and fail to measure up to God's standard. Though righteousness is through or from faith, faith is never the ground for our righteousness. Faith in itself does not save us; we are saved by faith in Christ. The faith that justifies is precisely the faith that has Christ as its *object and content. This affords great comfort to believers. If our weak faith is the ground for our justification, we will live in fear and anxiety. Instead of turning inward, we must turn toward Christ and his finished work, the sure ground of our hope.*

Against the objections raised against imputed righteousness (such as by Roman Catholic theology), it must be noted that the objection is really against the apostle Paul, who says in Rom. 4:5 and 5:16 that God justifies the ungodly. The best human analogy is adoption. Imputation is not a fiction; it is a real change of status with real benefits. The righteousness legally imputed to us must still become ethically effective in sanctification. Our being made righteous rests in God's decree and in the pactum salutis. *The covenant of grace precedes both our birth and our coming to believe. Our righteousness is "alien" in only a certain sense; it is the righteousness of the "head," which is therefore also that of the members.*

If our justification is grounded in the imputed righteousness of Christ, when exactly does this occur? In eternity or in time? The former view has been held by antinomians as well as antineonomians. For the former, eternal justification was the sum and substance of Christian truth—our faith only involves acknowledging what God has done in eternity. There is no justification in time. The latter, urgently seeking to keep the pure gospel of grace from being mixed with law, saw eternal justification as the beginning and foundation of justification in time. Though it is important to insist that God's decree of election is eternal, speaking of justification as taking place in eternity is not advisable. This usage is not scriptural and does not eliminate the problem of needing to explain its execution and outward realization in time. Reformed theology wisely distinguishes between the eternal decree and its execution in time.

We are on firm scriptural ground, however, when we tie justification to the death and resurrection of Christ. Our justification has been obtained by Christ; it is objectively accomplished. To clarify matters, Reformed theologians distinguished an active justification from a passive justification; justification is acquired and applied. Again, this is not a temporal distinction but a logical one; concretely, the two coincide and always go together. The distinction seeks to preserve the dual conviction that faith is both necessary for justification and that such a faith is itself the fruit of God's regenerating work through the Holy Spirit. This distinction helps us to avoid nomism, to strengthen believers' assurance by turning them away from introspective self-examination and toward Christ himself, and to recognize that faith is simultaneously a receptive organ and an active power. Faith is the very act of accepting Christ and all his benefits. This faith is active along with works and is brought to completion by works. Paul and James are not at odds.

Reformed theologians have not always agreed on the various elements of justification and how they are related to each other. It is best to define justification as the imputation of Christ's obedience as a whole to the believer and to consider its two parts to consist in forgiveness of sins and the right to eternal life. Forgiveness includes past, present, and future sins. The fear of antinomianism must not hinder us from making this claim but does call us to be vigilant in continuing to pray for forgiveness daily. This is necessary for believers to remain assured; confession and prayer are the means by which God the Holy Spirit arouses and reinforces our consciousness of forgiveness.

Although understanding of justification is sometimes limited to forgiveness, what must not be overlooked is our adoption as children and the right to eternal life. This adoption is both juridical (Paul) and ethical (John). We are God's children; our legal status is provided in Christ and guaranteed by the Holy Spirit as a pledge until the day of full redemption. This doctrine should provide the greatest comfort and assurance to believers, and it equips them for great works.

FORGIVENESS IS NOT NATURAL

[467] Rebirth, faith, and conversion are the conditions for the following benefits of the covenant of grace: they are the only way by which humans can receive and enjoy the forgiveness of sins and adoption as children of God, peace and joy, sanctification and glorification. Of all these benefits, first place is due to justification, for by it we understand that gracious judicial act of God by which he acquits humans of all the guilt and punishment of sin and confers on them the right to eternal life. Certainly there can be no peace of mind and conscience, no joy in one's heart, no buoyant moral activity, or a blessed life and death, before the guilt of sin is removed, all fear of punishment has been completely eradicated, and the certainty of eternal life in communion with God fills one's consciousness with its consolation and power. But this benefit—the complete forgiveness of sin—is so immense that the natural human intellect cannot grasp and believe it.

Pagans pictured the gods as human, endowing them with such passions as jealousy, spite, and vengeance, and therefore could not grasp the sublime idea of a free and gracious forgiveness. When the gods felt insulted and were angry, they had to be appeased by human gifts and prayers. Celsus[1] ridiculed that notion, considering it folly.[2] Yet this [pagan] notion witnesses to a greater seriousness and sense of truth than the shallow idea that forgiving is natural for God, just

1. Ed. note: Celsus was a Greek philosopher who flourished in the second half of the second century AD and was an important pagan critic of Christianity; see Origen, *Contra Celsum*, translated with an introduction and notes by Henry Chadwick (Cambridge and New York: Cambridge University Press, 1980).

2. Cf. H. Witsius, "De theol. gentilium circa justificationem," in *Miscellaneorum sacrorum*, 4 vols. (Utrecht: F. Halman, 1692), II, 668–721.

as sinning is normal for humans.[3] People who know themselves somewhat also know how terribly difficult true and complete forgiveness is, and how it can only be granted after a serious struggle with oneself.[4] Certainly an assortment of sinful attributes such as envy, hatred, and vindictiveness, which cannot be part of God's character, play a large role here. But there are also countless cases in which forgiveness is simply impossible and impermissible. When our honor and good name, our office and our dignity, have been publicly assaulted, no one is prepared to forgive without public redress, merely on the basis of a private apology and confession of wrongdoing.[5] And when actionable crimes have been committed, the civil government is called, not to forgive but to punish, since as God's servant it has to uphold justice and does not bear the sword in vain [cf. Rom. 13:4].

Opposition to the expiatory sacrifice of Christ, usually supported by an appeal to the parable of the prodigal son,[6] accordingly, arises from a total denial of the value of justice as well as of the very idea of forgiveness, for forgiveness in the true sense of the word precisely presupposes justice and stands or falls with it.[7] At the same time, the cross of Christ teaches us that forgiveness, however difficult and seemingly absurd, is nevertheless permitted and possible in accord with justice. In this respect, Christianity again distinguishes itself from other religions, especially from Buddhism. The ancient Southeast Asian Indians had such a strong sense of justice that they tried to explain all inequality among people in terms of thoughts, words, and deeds that they have entertained, uttered, and committed in a previous life and that had imprinted certain properties and habits on their souls. In that way their present lives determined their future destinies. Those who do good works are reborn in regions of blessedness; those who lead bad lives are degraded to a lower level and receive the form of an animal or other wretched being. Just as the law of gravity prevails in nature, so in the moral world the unbreakable law of karma prevails. There is no forgiveness, only retribution.[8] Under the influence of this (East) Indian worldview, joined to that of the law of causality that has been

---

3. According to Wernle, "If sin is fitting to humanity, then forgiveness is appropriate to God." Cited by W. Walther, *Rechtfertigung oder religiöses Erlebnis*, 2nd ed. (Leipzig: A. Deichert, 1917), 33.

4. Cf. Gaston Frommel, *La psychologie du pardon dans ses rapports avec la croix de Jésus-Christ* (Neuchatel: P. Atting, [1905]), 27ff.

5. Cf. the example of Paul in Acts 16:37; 22:25.

6. A. von Harnack, *What Is Christianity?* trans. Thomas Bailey Saunders, 2nd rev. ed. (New York and Evanston: Harper & Row, 1957), 142ff.; J. H. Scholten, *De leer der Hervormde Kerk in hare grondbeginselen*, 2nd ed., 2 vols. (Leyden: P. Engels, 1850–51), II, 47; cf. S. Hoekstra, *Het evangelie der genade door Jezus Christus selven verkondigd in de gelijkenis van den verloren zoon* (Sneek: Van Druten & Bleeker, 1855), 129ff. Hoekstra rightly observes that it is important to take note of the actual purpose of this parable. Jesus does not intend to teach *the means by which* we are reconciled to God, only how the Pharisees were in error when they accused him of receiving sinners and eating with them. *See also, Knoke, "Zum Verständnis des Gleichnisses vom verlornen Sohn," *Neue kirchliche Zeitschrift* 17 (1906): 407–18.

7. At the Assembly of Modern Theologians that took place on April 23–24, 1895, Mr. Chavannes even rejected the term "forgiving love" as a contradiction in terms (*contradictio in adjecto*) and as a meaningless expression. See the reports in *Bijblad van de Hervorming* (June 28, 1895): 69ff.

8. J. S. Speyer, *De Indische theosophie en hare beteekenis voor ons* (Leiden: Van Doesburgh, 1910), 83ff.

observed in operation everywhere by the natural sciences, many Westerners today reason in the same way. Operative everywhere is the law of cause and effect, not only in the physical but no less in the psychic and ethical world. One may later regret having committed some sinful act, but this in no way changes anything about its consequences. One simply has to bear them now and forever in all eternity. The idea of eternal punishment is not at all strange but completely natural. What has happened can never be undone. Nature knows no forgiveness and does not in the least take account of self-humiliation and confession of wrongdoing. Forgiveness is "physically impossible."[9]

In the Scriptures of the Old and New Testaments, however, we find a different circle of ideas. Immediately of great importance here is that the covenant of God is based not on nature or on a people's merit but on a gracious disposition of God and, by implication, on a historical act. Furthermore, in the sin offerings, the law, which presupposes the covenant of grace, while it opened a way of atoning for such sins as occurring "unwittingly" (Lev. 4:2ff.), also pronounced a sentence of destruction upon all sins that were committed "with a high hand" (Num. 15:30 RSV). Israel, however, did not adhere to the rule of the covenant. In later years, Israel repeatedly committed such sins as idolatry, image worship, Sabbath desecration, and so forth—sins that broke the covenant itself and that by implication could not be atoned for by covenant sacrifices. Then prophets, speaking in the name of the Lord, announced to a faithless and apostate people the coming day of judgment and the punishment of the exile. That punishment is necessary precisely because Israel is the people of the Lord (Amos 3:2), but it also paves the way for redemption. For God cannot abandon his people. He cannot forget his Israel (Hos. 11:8). He will be exalted in justice and show himself holy in righteousness (Isa. 5:16). Part of the people will be saved; a remnant will repent (Isa. 4:3; 6:13; 7:3ff.; etc.). The righteous will surely live (Ezek. 18:9), and they will live by faith (Hab. 2:4; cf. Isa. 7:9; 28:16; 30:15). Even if Israel is unable to repent and does not know how to blush (Jer. 6:15; 13:23), God remains true to his covenant and will, out of grace, grant to his people all those benefits that they have absolutely forfeited and cannot acquire by any merits of their own. He will make a new covenant with them, forgive them all their sins, give them a new heart and spirit, and cause them to walk in his statutes (Jer. 24:7; 31:31ff.; 32:37ff.; Ezek. 11:19ff.; 36:24ff.). According to the prophets, Isaiah in particular, God's righteousness consists above all in the fact that in the future he will not, on account of their sins, reject the people whom he chose out of grace but will lead them, through punishment and mercy, to complete redemption. He cannot abandon his people because he has bound his own name and honor to them in pledge. Through the Messiah, who will bring forth justice to the Gentiles (Isa. 42:1), he will prepare salvation for his people. His deliverance is not far off; his salvation will not tarry; he will give salvation to Zion and glory to Israel (46:13;

9. Rev. C. T. Ovenden, "The Forgiveness of Sin," *Hibbert Journal* 56 (April 1907): 589.

51:5; 54:17; 56:1; 60:1–2; 61:11). From him, accordingly, is their righteousness (54:17); only in him is righteousness and strength (45:24). He is the Lord, their righteousness (Jer. 23:6; 33:16).[10]

Now among all the spiritual and material benefits that God will give to his people in the future by virtue of this righteousness, the forgiveness of sins occupies a place of primary importance. Even in the days of the old covenant, it was already apportioned by God and enjoyed by the faithful (Exod. 34:7, 9; Num. 14:18–20; 1 Sam. 15:28; 1 Kings 8:30ff.; Pss. 25:11; 32:1–2, 5; 51:1ff.; 103:3; 130:4; 143:2; Isa. 6:7; Dan. 9:19; Mic. 7:18),[11] but occurs especially—like conversion, renewal of the heart, the communication of the Spirit, and the promise that they [believers] will be his people—as a benefit of the new covenant God will establish in the future.

Forgiveness in Scripture

The Old Testament depicts this benefit using different names and images. Examples are נָשָׂא (*nāśā'*, suspend, accept, pardon; 1 Sam. 15:25; Job 7:21; Pss. 32:1; 85:2; Isa. 33:24), סָלַח (*sālaḥ*, forgive; Exod. 34:9; Lev. 4:20; Pss. 25:11; 103:3), עָבַר (*'ābar*, pass over, through; hiph.: let pass by, put away; 2 Sam. 12:13; 24:10; Job 7:21), כָּבַשׁ (*kābaš*, tread underfoot, subdue, cast down; Mic. 7:19), כָּסָה (*kāsâ*, hide; pi.: cover; Pss. 32:1; 85:2; Prov. 10:12), כִּפֶּר (*kipper*; pi.: cover, make atonement [Lev. 16:17; etc.], and, hence, forgive; Pss. 65:3, 78:38; 79:9; Isa. 6:7; Jer. 18:23; Dan. 9:24), מָחָה (*māḥâ*, wipe, wipe out, eradicate; Ps. 51:1; Isa. 43:25; 44:22; Jer. 18:23), טָהֵר (*tāhēr*, be pure; pi.: cleanse, pronounce clean) and כָּבַס (*kābas*, wash, make clean; Ps. 51:2), סוּר (*sûr*, depart, cease; Isa. 6:7), and further expressions such as "not seeing" (Num. 23:21), "not imputing" (Ps. 32:2), "not entering into judgment" (143:2), "not remembering" (Isa. 43:25), "hiding one's face" (Ps. 51:9), "casting behind one's back" (Isa. 38:17), and "casting into the depths of the sea" (Mic. 7:19). In these connections, it is always God who grants forgiveness (Isa. 43:25; 45:21–25; 48:9–12). His divine nature shines out in forgiving the iniquity of his people (Mic. 7:18), for he forgives only for his name's sake (Pss. 25:11; 79:9; Isa. 43:25; Ezek. 36:11). He acts out of sheer

10. Cf. H. Bavinck, *Reformed Dogmatics*, II, 223–24 (#206); III, 491–95 (#410).

11. From the word παρεσις in Rom. 3:25 J. Coccejus ("More Nebochim," §18ff. [*Opera omnia theologica*, IX, 123, "De foedere," §339]) inferred that forgiveness of sins is a New Testament benefit, and his opinion was adopted by many (e.g., Burmannus, Allinga, Braun, Wittichius, et al.). But although the sins of Old Testament believers can be called "passed by" for the time when Christ had not yet made his appearance and was not yet put forward as an expiation, the forgiveness of their sins could nevertheless, with a view to that future expiatory sacrifice, be very well granted by God to Old Testament believers in advance. That this was indeed the case is equally evident (aside from the above-mentioned testimonies of the Old Testament) from what Paul himself says in Rom. 4 about Abraham and David, as well as Acts 10:43; 15:11; Rom. 3:21. Cf. H. Bavinck, *Reformed Dogmatics*, III, 206–12 (#345), 219–24 (#348); C. Vitringa, *Doctrina christiana religionis*, 8 vols. (Leiden: Joannis le Mair, 1761–86), VI, 218–31; B. de Moor, *Commentarius . . . theologiae*, 6 vols. (Leiden: Hasebroek, 1761–71), IV, 590ff.

compassion (Ps. 78:38), for the sake of his covenant with Abraham and David, for the sake of the oath he swore to them (Pss. 89:3ff.; 105:8–9; 111:5; Jer. 11:5; Ezek. 16:60; Mic. 7:20), for the sake of his fame and honor among the Gentiles (Exod. 32:12; Num. 14:13, 16; Deut. 9:28; 32:27; Ezek. 36:23).

[468] After the exile, however, instead of expecting their righteousness and salvation from God, the Jews increasingly took the path of nomism and sought to construct a righteousness of their own out of works.[12] John [the Baptist], accordingly, appears with the message that, despite their circumcision and descent from Abraham, the people of Israel need the baptism of repentance for the forgiveness of sins (Matt. 3:2–10). Jesus then proclaims the good news that another and better righteousness is needed than that of the Pharisees (5:20), that this righteousness is a good gift from God (6:33), and that God grants this benefit, not to the righteous, but to publicans and sinners, to the lost, to the burdened and heavy laden, to children who do not look for their salvation in themselves but expect all their well-being from God.

As proof of all this, he himself as the Messiah of the kingdom distributes the benefit of the forgiveness of sins (Matt. 9:2ff.; Luke 7:48ff.). Indeed, he gives his life as a ransom for many (Matt. 20:28), creates the new covenant in his blood, allows his body to be broken and his blood to be shed for the forgiveness of sins (26:26ff.), and promises eternal life to all who become his disciples (10:37ff.; 16:24ff.). All the apostles, consequently, unanimously and from the very beginning preach that in his name there is repentance and forgiveness of sins (Luke 24:47; Acts 2:38; 5:31; 10:36, 43; 13:38; 26:18).

In their preaching, to be sure, there is great diversity. John especially highlights the life (ζωη, zōē) that is obtained through faith in Christ (3:16, 36). James, for practical reasons, urgently warns people against a dead faith (2:14ff.). Peter exhorts believers to follow Christ's example (1 Pet. 2:21ff.), and the Letter to the Hebrews points above all else to the perfection (τελειωσις, teleiōsis) that has come with the single offering of Christ (10:14). But all of them regard the forgiveness of sins as the great benefit that Christ has won and that is received by faith (John 3:36; Heb. 8:12; 10:17, 22; James 2:1; 1 Pet. 1:2, 19; 2:24; 3:18; 1 John 1:9; 2:1–2, 12; 3:5).

It is especially Paul, however, who puts justification in the foreground and works out its richest and deepest implications. This is undoubtedly connected with his own life experience. Having been a Pharisee, he had in all seriousness and with passionate zeal striven for a righteousness of his own based on observing the law. But when it pleased God to reveal his Son in him, he saw the vanity of this attempt and sought his righteousness in God through Christ Jesus alone. Yet also as a Christian Paul remains faithful to the forensic scheme. He does not fight the idea that God is just and that salvation can be obtained only through righteousness. After coming to the faith, however, he differs from his earlier contemporaries about the

12. H. Bavinck, Reformed Dogmatics, III, 495–99 (#411).

way righteousness and salvation can become ours. He combats Jewish nomism, because, on account of sin, no flesh can be justified by the works of the law (Rom. 3:20; 8:3; Gal. 2:16); because then humans would always remain servants and be able to boast before God of their merits (Rom. 4:2, 5; Gal. 3:24–26; 4:1–7; cf. 1 Cor. 1:29; 4:7); in other words, humans would then live and labor for their own interest and make God subservient to it. Hence, Paul rejects the nomistic ethical principle and squarely bases himself on the religious position. But that does not alter the fact that the law as such is holy and just and good (Rom. 7:12, 14; 1 Tim. 1:8; cf. also Rom. 3:31; 8:4; 13:8, 10; Gal. 5:14). If there had not been sin, therefore, it [the law] would also have been able to grant life through works (Rom. 10:5; Gal. 3:12). But what the law by its very nature cannot do is grant *forgiveness*, which is precisely what we need. Paul, accordingly, while he does fight Jewish nomism, maintains the righteousness of God and proceeds from it in his soteriology. He takes a theocentric position, in which God does not exist for humankind but humankind for God, and communion with God is not the result of our exertion but God's free and unmerited gift.

It is wrong, therefore, to regard the so-called "juridical scheme" in Paul as a remnant or aftereffect of his earlier Pharisaism,[13] or to describe it as a temporary policy of transition that was very useful for as long as Christianity had to detach itself from Judaism but later lost all meaning and significance.[14]

Nor is it correct to regard the juridical component in Paul's theology as inferior to the mystical and to accord priority to the latter.[15] For although doctrine in the case of this apostle is most intimately tied in with his life experience, it nevertheless very clearly—especially in the letters to the Romans and the Galatians—highlights God's righteousness and revolves totally around the alternatives: our own righteousness or God's, law or gospel, work or faith, merit or grace. If communion with God, life, and salvation are to remain gifts of God, they must precede all our works and be their basis and starting point. In that case religion is the basis of morality. We love God because he first loved us (1 John 4:19).

On the basis of this religious position, the apostle now develops the following thoughts. Inasmuch as the law condemns humans on account of sin and can never lead them to salvation, it has pleased God to manifest his righteousness in another way, that is, apart from the law (Rom. 3:21). The term δικαιοσυνη (*dikaiosynē*), which Paul employs here and elsewhere, acquires a unique sense in his thinking

---

13. J. H. Scholten, *De leer der Hervormde Kerk*, II, 61ff.; idem, *De vrije will, kritisch onderzoek* (Leiden: P. Engels, 1859), 223ff.; O. Pfleiderer, *Der Paulinismus: Ein Beitrag zur Geschichte der urchristlichen Theologie*, 2nd ed. (Leipzig: O. R. Reisland, 1890), 6ff., 94ff.; H. J. Holtzmann, *Lehrbuch der neutestamentlichen Theologie*, 2 vols. (Freiburg i.B. and Leipzig: Mohr, 1897), II, 133; and many others such as Wendt, Titius, Wernle. Cf. G. Vos, "The Alleged Legalism in Paul's Doctrine of Justification," *Princeton Theological Review* 1 (April 1903): 161–79.

14. P. Wernle, *Die Anfänge unserer Religion* (Tübingen: J. C. B. Mohr [Paul Siebeck], 1901); ed. note: ET: *The Beginnings of Christianity*, trans. G. A. Bienemann, 2 vols. (London: Williams and Norgate; New York: Putnam, 1903–4). Cf. G. Vos, "Alleged Legalism in Paul."

15. Cf. J. A. Rust, "Paulus Mysticus," *Theologische Studien* 28 (1910): 349–84.

(Rom. 1:17; 3:5, 21–22, 25–26; 10:3; 2 Cor. 5:21; cf. Phil. 3:9; James 1:20; 2 Pet. 1:1). In the Old Testament, it generally refers to that virtue of God according to which he judges justly without respect of person, and hence does not declare the guilty to be innocent nor the innocent to be guilty, but rewards all according to their works. More specifically, however, it denotes the attribute and conduct of God according to which he helps, rescues, and recognizes the claims of the poor, the wretched, who though personally guilty have the right on their side.[16] But toward the end of the Old Testament economy, this righteousness of God seems to have totally vanished. For the whole world was now deserving of condemnation before God (Rom. 3:19). No one could be justified by the works of the law (3:20). In his divine forbearance God passed over the sins previously committed (3:25). Therefore, if salvation was still to be possible for humankind, God had to manifest his righteousness in a way other than he had done in the law. And this he did in Christ by offering a sacrifice of atonement for sins. This proved that God himself is righteous but also made it possible for him—while preserving his righteousness, indeed, in keeping with it—to justify those who have faith in Jesus (3:25–26). Accordingly, in considering the "righteousness of God" in Rom. 3:21–26 (cf. 1:17), we must not think of a human righteousness that, though existing outside of themselves in Christ, is by faith made their own and is now considered as such in the sight of God (Luther, Calvin, marginal notes in the Authorized Version, Philippi, Umbreit, and Fritzsche, with an appeal to Rom. 2:13; Gal. 3:11, "before God"; and Rom. 3:20, "in his sight"). Nor must we think of a righteousness of humans that derives from God, is infused into them by God, or is valid in his sight (Osiander, Schleiermacher, Rothe, Martensen, Nitzsch, Beck). Nor primarily of a righteousness that belongs to God, that he possesses, but that he by grace confers through faith on humans, so that elsewhere Paul can call it a "righteousness from God" (Phil. 3:9—as many modern exegetes claim, whether they describe the genitive as a subjective genitive [Haussleiter] or as a possessive genitive [Fricke] or as a genitive of efficient cause or authorship [Bengel, Rückert, van Hengel, Winer, et al.]).

But we must, in the first place, understand by that term that attribute or rather that conduct of God according to which he judges justly, and acquits those who have faith in Jesus. But for God to act thus it was necessary for him to put Christ forward as a sacrifice of atonement and to bring about in him a righteousness (1 Cor. 1:30; 2 Cor. 5:21; Phil. 3:9) that is the diametrical opposite of a righteousness of our own that comes from the law (Rom. 10:3; Phil. 3:9). The righteousness of God as virtue or mode of conduct has manifested itself most gloriously when in Christ he granted another righteousness apart from the law, on the basis of which he can justify—that is, absolutely and completely acquit—those who believe in Jesus.[17]

16. H. Bavinck, *Reformed Dogmatics*, II, 223–24 (#206).

17. There is in the Netherlands a major debate over the meaning of the genitive in the expression τον ἐκ πιστεως Ἰησου (Rom. 3:26), a debate with many participants but no clear conclusion. See J. H. Scholten, *De leer der Hervormde Kerk*, II, 77. J. Haussleiter (*Der Glaube Jesu Christi und der christliche Glaube* [Erlangen

Accordingly, those who believe in Christ are justified *through* faith (Rom. 3:22, 25, 30; Gal. 2:16; 3:26; Eph. 2:8; Phil. 3:9; 2 Tim. 3:15), *on the ground* of faith (Rom. 1:17; 3:30; 5:1; 9:30, 32; 10:6; Gal. 3:8, 24), *by faith* (Rom. 3:28). This faith does include the acceptance of the testimony of God (Rom. 4:18ff.; 10:9, 17; 1 Cor. 15:17; 1 Thess. 2:13) but consists further in heartfelt trust in God's grace in Christ, a personal relationship and personal communion with Christ (Rom. 10:9; 1 Cor. 6:17; 2 Cor. 13:5; Gal. 2:20; Eph. 3:17). It is a living, not a dead, faith that excludes all work, merit, and boasting (Rom. 3:28; 4:4; 11:6; Gal. 2:16; Phil. 3:9) but nevertheless proves its power in love (Gal. 5:6). This faith is reckoned to people as righteousness (Rom. 4:3, 5, 9, 11, 22; Gal. 3:6). The righteous person will live by faith (Rom. 1:17; Gal. 3:11; Heb. 10:38). This justification is one that carries life with it (Rom. 5:18). Given the justification that believers receive, they are immediately freed from all dread and fear. They have peace with God (Rom. 5:1). They are no longer under the law (Rom. 7:4; Gal. 2:19; 4:5, 21ff.) but under grace (Rom. 6:15), and they stand in freedom (Gal. 5:1). They are no longer servants but children, having the spirit of adoption and therefore also being heirs of God (Rom. 8:15–17; Gal. 4:5–7), awaiting with great assurance the completion of their adoption as children (Rom. 8:23) and the hope of righteousness (Gal. 5:5), for if God justifies, who is to condemn? (Rom. 8:31–39).[18]

THE PROBLEM OF NOMISM

[469] Even in Paul's time, the doctrine of justification by faith alone was already misunderstood and accused of being antinomian (Rom. 3:8, 31; 6:1, 15; etc.).

---

and Leipzig: A. Deichert (G. Böhme), 1891], 48–49) again takes the genitive as a subjective genitive and understands the expression in such a way that Christ was the end of the law through his faith. As Son he did not permit his relationship [with the Father] to be mediated by the law, but it was his meat and drink to do the Father's will. His faith consisted in this [desire] to which we too, as it were, must be born (48–49). This rendering is both exegetically and dogmatically unwarranted. Jesus, the Christ, or Jesus Christ, is according to Paul the object of faith (Rom. 3:22, 25; Gal. 2:16, 20; 3:26; Phil. 3:9). For Paul, faith is the technical term for the religious relation in which believers stand with respect to God. Paul never refers to the work of Christ as faith, but always as obedience, which is both passive and active. See above, 99–100 (#449), and also T. Zahn, *Der Briefe des Paulus an der Römer* (Leipzig: A. Deichert, 1910), 175, 197; W. Sanday and A. Headlam, *A Critical and Exegetical Commentary on the Epistle to the Romans*, 5th ed. (Edinburgh: T&T Clark, 1902), 83–84 (ed. note: Bavinck cites the 5th edition's publication date as 1908). In spite of this, G. Kittel ("Zur Erklärung von Röm. 3:21–26," *Theologische Studien und Kritiken* 80 [1907]: 217–33) took over Haussleiter's sentiments and defended them.

18. Ed. note: Bavinck makes reference here to the full page of references at the head of *Gereformeerde Dogmatiek*, §51, "Rechtvaardigmaking," adding the following: L. W. E. Rauwenhoff, *Disquisitio de loco Paulino, qui est de δικαιωσει* (Leiden: P. Engels, 1852). *Schultz, "Die Lehre von dem Gerechtigkeit aus dem Glauben im Alten und Neuen Bunde," *Jahrbücher für deutsche Theologie* 7 (1862): 510–72; H. Cremer, *Biblico-Theological Lexicon of New Testament Greek,* trans. D. W. Simon and W. Urwick (Edinburgh: T&T Clark; New York: Charles Scribner's Sons, 1895), s.v. δικαιοσυνη; C. Weizsäcker, *Das apostolische Zeitalter der christlichen Kirche*, 2nd ed. (Freiburg: Mohr, 1890), 143ff.; *H. Beck, "Die δικαιοσυνη θεου bei Paulus," *Neue Jahrbücher für deutsche Theologie* (1894): 249–61; E. Kühl, *Rechtfertigung auf Grund des Glaubens und Gericht nach den Werken bei Paulus* (Königsberg: Wilh. Koch, 1904).

There were those who engaged in libertinistic practices and needed James's warning that a dead, inactive faith is not sufficient for justification (James 2:14ff.). Others, acting out of reaction, began to cultivate a nomistic and ascetic lifestyle (Rom. 14:1ff.; Gal. 4:10; Col. 2:16; 1 Tim. 4:3–4). Later, when the Christian church had to take and maintain its own position in the face of numerous religious schools of thought and systems of philosophy, the dangers of swinging to one extreme or another were even considerably greater. Soon it became apparent that in this field of tension, it did not succeed in fully keeping itself free of pagan and Jewish influences. Increasingly, nomism penetrated the church, changing the gospel into a new law. Pauline terms indeed continued to be used. Grace remained primary, and faith was still considered indispensable for salvation. In certain ecclesiastical authors, such as Clement, Ignatius, Tertullian, Ambrose, and Augustine, and even more in the liturgical prayers, one encounters striking testimonies to the abundance of God's grace and the unmerited forgiveness of sins.[19] But these evangelical thoughts soon alternate with, or even completely give way to, the description of the Christian life as a life of fulfilling God's commandments. "The beginning is faith, the end is love."[20] Faith *and* works pave the way to heaven.

The common view of baptism had a powerful influence. Since baptism related only to the forgiveness of past sins and since many Christians committed various—even grave—sins also after baptism, therefore, unless the church was prepared to exclude them from its fellowship and from eternal salvation forever, it had to find a second remedy. And this remedy consisted in penances and good works that, especially under the influence of Tertullian, took on a "satisfactory" or "meritorious" character, and that led, after a long development, to the Roman Catholic sacrament of penance.[21] In this sacrament, after the contrition (or attrition) of the heart and the confession of the mouth, believers were absolved from the guilt of sin and eternal punishment, but remained obligated to bear the temporal punishments and to perform the good works imposed on them (the work of satisfaction). They are competent to fulfill this task, however, because in baptism or (if they had lost the grace of baptism by committing a mortal sin) in the sacrament of penance, they received not only the forgiveness of sin but also, by an infusion of grace, the eradication of the pollution and power of sin. In the thinking of Rome these two benefits are intimately connected. They are not identical, for the Council of Trent had expressly stated that justification is "not only the remission of sins but also the sanctification and renewal of the inward man through the voluntary reception of grace and the gifts."[22] But they do nevertheless always go together and are inseparable. In the abstract, one might perhaps

19. J. Buchanan, *The Doctrine of Justification* (Edinburgh: T&T Clark, 1867), 77ff.

20. Ignatius, *To the Ephesians* 14.1.

21. Cf. above, 142 (#460).

22. Council of Trent, sess. VI, c. 7. According to M. J. Scheeben and L. Atzberger, *Handbuch der Katholischen Dogmatik*, 4 vols. (orig. pub. 1874–98; Freiburg i.B.: Herder, 1933), IV, 60, there is a real difference between the two.

imagine that God forgave people their sins without incorporating them into the state of supernatural grace, inasmuch as the latter after all has the character of a superadded gift. But concretely there is no room for this split. In the order of redemption there is presently no forgiveness of sin apart from restoration to the state of grace. God cannot forgive sins without an infusion of grace. Even the view of Duns Scotus and his associates that the infusion of grace carries with it the forgiveness of sins, not by virtue of its own nature but only by virtue of a divine disposition, is almost universally rejected today, whereas Thomas's view, according to which habitual grace heals or justifies the soul and there can be no remission of guilt without the presence of infused grace, is recognized as correct.[23]

Although the Council of Trent did not make a formal decision on this issue, it did pronounce that "the only formal cause of our justification is the justice of God, not that by which he himself is just, but that by which he makes us just, that, to wit, with which *we* being endowed by him, are renewed in the spirit of our mind, and we are not only reputed but are truly called and are just, receiving justice within us."[24] Justification, in the thinking of Rome, is therefore that act of God by which he not only forgives the guilt of sin and absolves persons from eternal punishment, but also internally regenerates and renews them. The order of these two benefits is evidently construed in the sense that the latter results in the former. Habitual grace, after all, is the formal cause both of the remission of sins and of sanctification. God forgives people their sins because, logically speaking, he first makes them holy.[25] This sanctification is so complete that a person is cleansed of every sinful stain and keeps only the fountain of sin or concupiscence, which as such is no sin, and further receives in it the supernatural power to keep God's commandments, even to perform works of supererogation, and to merit thereby eternal life and a high degree of heavenly glory. In the thinking of Rome, the whole of Christianity (the person and work of Christ, the church and the sacraments) serves the end that in baptism or in penance God can restore to humans the superadded gift that has been lost and so enables them to do good works and to secure their heavenly reward. Justification, in fact, is the restoration of a human being to the state of integrity, elevation to the supernatural order. In this connection one must bear in mind, in all fairness, that Rome attributes this whole splendid benefit solely to the mercy of God, who purifies, sanctifies, and anoints people with the Holy Spirit of promise. Rome also recognizes as the sole meritorious cause the Lord Jesus Christ who, when we were still enemies, according to the greatness of the love with which he loved us, by his holy suffering on the tree of the cross, merited justification for us and made satisfaction for us to the Father. In this connection Rome also assigns a place to faith: faith is "the

23. T. Aquinas, *Summa theol.*, I, 2, qu. 111, art. 2; qu. 113, art. 2.

24. Council of Trent, sess. VI, c. 7.

25. This underevaluation of the benefit of sanctification is closely tied to the weakening of a sense of sin as guilt. Cf. H. Bavinck, *Reformed Dogmatics*, III, 93–97 (#321); F. Loofs, *Leitfaden zum Studium der Dogmengeschichte*, 4th ed. (Halle a.S.: M. Niemeyer, 1906), 570n7.

beginning of human salvation, the foundation and root of our justification," without which it is not possible to please God. Yet, inasmuch as that faith is no more than an assent to the truths that God has revealed and the church preserves, faith cannot truly unite us with Christ and make us into living members of his body unless hope and love are added to it.[26] In consequence, faith by itself cannot and may not give to Christians the certainty that they have received the forgiveness of sins and belong to the number of the elect.[27] Rome does not even oppose the idea that the righteousness of Christ is imputed to us in justification, but it denies that this exhausts the meaning of this benefit. It maintains that the righteousness of Christ is granted to us and infused into us not only juridically but also ethically. Although in the Old and New Testaments the term "to justify" sometimes has forensic import,[28] it is nevertheless the unquestionable teaching of Scripture, says Rome, that humans are internally justified and renewed by virtue of the merits of Christ (1 Cor. 1:30; 2 Cor. 5:21; Gal. 3:27; Eph. 4:24; etc.).[29]

THE REFORMATION RENEWAL: EXTRINSIC, FORENSIC JUSTIFICATION

The Reformation was triggered by Luther's opposition to the trade in indulgences and the entire Roman penitential system associated with it. But the ideas that led him to this opposition had for years already taken shape in his mind and sprang from the fresh insight he had gained into "the righteousness of God" (Rom. 1:17).[30] Whereas in the past he had always understood it to mean the avenging and punitive righteousness of God, a righteousness that filled him with dread and terror, he had gained a new understanding of it, probably as early as 1508 or 1509, and had discovered that it did not mean "the righteousness by which God is righteous *in* himself but the righteousness by which we are justified *from within* himself, which happens through faith in the gospel."[31] For Luther, this new insight was the turning point of his life. It gradually led him, especially under the influence of Paul and Augustine, to convictions that were very different from those current at the time. The seeds of all these convictions are already present in his lectures on the Letter to the Romans, which he gave in the years 1515 and 1516. It was not until 1899 that they were rediscovered and published, along with an extensive introduction by Johannes Ficker.[32] In these lectures Luther's convictions

---

26. Council of Trent, sess. VI, c. 7–8.

27. Ibid., c. 9, can. 13–16.

28. Scheeben-Atzberger, *Handbuch*, IV, 33.

29. C. Pesch, *Praelectiones dogmaticae,* 9 vols. (Freiburg: Herder, 1902–10), V, 186.

30. Cf. H. Bavinck, *Reformed Dogmatics*, III, 517–19 (#417).

31. This new understanding comes to expression in a marginal note on the *Sentences* of Peter Lombard, dating from 1509/1510; cf. H. Bavinck, *Reformed Dogmatics*, III, 517–19 (#417).

32. Johannes Ficker, ed., *Luthers Vorlesung über den Römerbrief 1515/1516*, 2 vols. (Leipzig: Dieterich, 1908). Ed. note: The preceding edition of Luther's lectures on Romans that Bavinck cites was a preliminary one; the definitive edition was published as vol. 56, *Die Brief an die Römer*, in the Weimar edition of *D. Martin*

were naturally still mixed with all sorts of ideas that he would later revise or abandon. At this point, for example, it did not even cross his mind to challenge the authority of the church. But he does already, with great decisiveness, turn against medieval Scholasticism and the philosophy of Aristotle. Moreover, he criticizes an assortment of church conditions and practices in regard to indulgences, fasting, the veneration of saints, and feast days and also has the courage to raise his voice against popes and bishops. He questions the correctness of the distinction between mortal and venial sins and does not regard original sin as merely the loss of the superadded gift but also considers it positively as the corruption of human nature, which is never completely eradicated in this life, and so forth. But the original material, which comes to light in this commentary on Romans and would later become the primary principle and driving force of the Reformation, is especially oriented to the contrast between sin and grace, law and gospel, works and faith, one's own righteousness and God's.

The core of the gospel, certainly, consists in the fact that God-in-Christ has manifested a righteousness other than what is required of us in the law. Now, in the time of grace without law, meaning "without the necessity of keeping the law, that is, without the aid of the law and the works that pertain to it," he has revealed a righteousness, "not one by which God is righteous but one with which he clothes humans when he justifies the ungodly, a righteousness by which God justifies us."[33] Righteousness and unrighteousness, accordingly, have a totally different meaning in Scripture than in the writings of philosophers and jurists. Such authors associate these terms with a quality of the soul, "but the 'righteousness' of Scripture depends on the imputation of God more than on the essence of a thing itself."[34] "To justify," in Scripture, means "to regard as just, to treat a person as accepted, not to impute sin, to remit impiety, to grant righteousness through reconsideration without works, to impute righteousness."[35] This act of God is so prominent in the work of salvation that Luther, in discussing the words "while we were enemies" (Rom. 5:10), also considers the following a possible explanation: "When, under the conditions of time, we were weak, we were nevertheless righteous before God in predestination, because in divine

Luthers Werke (Wiemar: Böhlau) in 1938. The initial two volumes containing Luther's "Glosses" on the text (vol. 1) and his "Scholia" (vol. 2) were joined together in the one Weimar volume. One year later (1939), Ficker also published extant student notebook manuscripts; these appeared as vol. 57 of the Weimar edition. English translation of the Romans commentary (glosses and scholia only) can be found in vol. 25 of *Luther's Works*, ed. H. C. Oswald (St. Louis: Concordia, 1972). Information concerning the manuscript history can also be found in the introduction to this volume. Though the translations of the Luther passages are our own, we will provide the corresponding reference in *Luther's Works* (English ed.). This will be followed by parenthetical references to *Luthers Werke* in the Weimarer Ausgabe edition (e.g., WA 56:35) as well as Bavinck's original reference to Ficker's preliminary two-volume text (e.g., Ficker, I, 32).

33. *Luther's Works*, 25:30–31 (WA 56:36; Ficker, I, 32).

34. *Luther's Works*, 25:274 (WA 56:287; Ficker, II, 121).

35. *Luther's Works*, 25:19n13 (WA 56:22n4; Ficker, I, 20); ibid., 25:35–36 (WA 56:40–41; Ficker, I, 38); ibid., 25:261–62, 277 (WA 56:274–75, 290; Ficker, II, 113, 119).

predestination all things have already been accomplished that in actual fact are still going to happen."[36]

This justification occurs completely apart from works, both those that precede and those that are done after one becomes a believer. "Indeed, neither preceding nor subsequent works justify—how much less the works of the law! Preceding works [do not justify] because they prepare for righteousness; subsequent works [do not justify] because they presuppose justification."[37] We are not justified on account of and by good works; we are justified for good works. It is only grace that makes us just. "We are not made just by doing right things but by being just do we do right things. Therefore only grace justifies us."[38] To be just and to become just are one and the same thing in the sight of God. "For the fact that a person is just is not the reason why God regards him as just, but he is just because he is so regarded by God."[39] The person, mind you, is antecedent to his works, just as the tree is there before the fruits. God does not accept the person on account of the works, but the works on account of the person: "first the person, then the works."[40] Accordingly, the way we receive justification can be no other than the way of faith. Luther understands by faith the act of taking God at his word. Luther distinguishes—we must note—a twofold justification of God, a passive and an active one. With reference to the passive one, he thinks of the fact that God is justified by us when we believe him at his word. In that word he tells us two things: first, that we are sinners, that there is no righteousness in us, and that we cannot obtain righteousness by works; and second, that we can nevertheless be justified and be righteous before God by the righteousness that he has revealed in the gospel apart from works.

FAITH AND JUSTIFICATION

Faith, therefore, includes two things: believing that we are sinners and believing that out of grace God justifies us for Christ's sake. We also have to accept the first [that we are sinners], not because we experience it ourselves, but because God says so.

> Even if we do not recognize any sin in ourselves, we must nevertheless believe that we are sinners. Hence the apostle says: "I am not aware of anything against myself, but I am not thereby justified" (1 Cor. 4:4). For just as the righteousness of God is alive in me by faith, so by the same faith sin is alive in me; i.e., by faith alone we must believe that we are sinners, because it is not obvious to us. If truth be told,

---

36. *Luther's Works*, 25:296 (WA 56:309; Ficker, II, 141); cf. *Luther's Works*, 25:278 (WA 56:290; Ficker, II, 124): "For just as God and his counsel are unknown to us, so also is our own righteousness which completely depends upon him and his counsel."

37. *Luther's Works*, 25:242 (WA 56:255; Ficker, II, 91).

38. Ibid.

39. *Luther's Works*, 25:19 (WA 56:22; Ficker, I, 20).

40. *Luther's Works*, 25:256 (WA 56:268; Ficker, II, 103–4).

most of the time we do not seem to be conscious of ourselves [as sinners]. Therefore we must stand by God's judgment and believe the words by which he tells us that we are unjust, because he cannot tell a falsehood.[41]

Usually, however, Luther distinguishes this belief that we are sinners from faith in a restricted sense and calls it contrition, confession, self-humiliation, and so forth. For the authentic belief that God grants us his righteousness is above all born from the knowledge and confession of our sins. "Those who know this cry to God and, humbled, seek to be raised up and to be cured of this (evil) will. Those who do not know [it], however, do not seek, and those who do not seek, do not receive; neither are they therefore justified, because they are ignorant of their own sin."[42] Contrition, accordingly, precedes the faith that embraces the righteousness of God in Christ. Now if people thus believe God at his word that there is no righteousness in themselves but only in Christ, they justify God, and that is passive justification. "To justify God in his words" is "for him to be made just and true in his speech, or, alternatively, for his speech to be made just and true. This happens, moreover, by believing and accepting [those works] and by holding them to be true and just."[43] But this passive justification by which we on our part justify God "coincides with God's justification of us actively, because he regards as righteousness the faith that justifies his words." The two coincide: "When he is justified he justifies, and when he justifies he is justified." Indeed: "God's passive and active justification and faith or belief in him are the same. The fact that we justify his speech is his own gift, and on account of that very gift he regards us as just, that is, justifies us."[44]

By virtue of the intimate connection that Luther posits here between justification and faith, he also refrains from reducing justification to a mere sentence that God pronounces to himself and that has no further consequences. Instead, the act of regarding as just immediately brings with it the act of making just. When we justify God by faith, he justifies us in his word (speech), that is, "he makes us to be like his Word, namely, righteous, true, wise, and so forth. And thus he transforms us into his Word, not, however, his Word into us. Moreover, he makes us such at the time when we believe his Word to be such, that is, righteous and true. For then the same formal character exists both in his Word and in the believer, that is, the character of truth and righteousness."[45] God is justified "when he justifies the ungodly and infuses grace, or when he is believed to be just in his own words." And thus God "is effectively justified in us and praiseworthy inasmuch as he makes

---

41. *Luther's Works*, 25:215 (WA 56:231; Ficker, I, 69); cf. *Luther's Works*, 25:239 (WA 56:252; Ficker, II, 89).

42. *Luther's Works*, 25:240 (WA 56:252–53; Ficker, II, 90): cf. also *Luther's Works*, 25:206, 247, 261–62, 271 (WA 56:221, 259–60, 274–75, 283; Ficker, II, 60, 95, 113, 119).

43. *Luther's Works*, 25:210 (WA 56:226; Ficker, II, 64).

44. *Luther's Works*, 25:211–12 (WA 56:226–27; Ficker, II, 65–66).

45. *Luther's Works*, 25:211 (WA 56:227; Ficker, II, 65).

us like himself."[46] The act of justifying is described as "regarding as righteous" (*justum reputare*) and so forth but sometimes—in the same sentence and for the sake of variety also—by "making, perfecting, and acquitting as righteous and as justice" (*justum facere, perficere ac absolvere justum ac justitiam*).[47] The death of Christ is the death of sin and his resurrection is the life of righteousness, because by his death he made satisfaction for sin and by his resurrection he brought about righteousness for us. His death, therefore, does not just signify, but also effects the forgiveness of sins. And his resurrection is not only "a sacrament of our righteousness but also effects it in us."[48] "All our good exists outside us in Christ, because that good is Christ," but all of this also exists in us by faith and hope in him.[49] In the same way Luther can say that our sin is covered by Christ's dwelling in us,[50] that God justifies believers because they confess their sins and seek their righteousness in him.[51]

Nevertheless, we would also err if we inferred from this that Luther located righteousness itself—the righteousness that is the basis for justification—in believers. His intent is clearly otherwise. The self-righteous person, that is, the person who wants to be justified by works, does not believe God at his word, does not justify God, but dishonors him and makes him a liar. Such a person does not humble himself nor acknowledge himself to be a sinner; he does not seek to be justified and yearn for righteousness but believes he already possesses it.

The situation is very different in the case of believers, not only at the start but also throughout their lives, and even in death. They do not say to God, "We can and will do what you command in your law," but rather confess, "We have not done, and cannot do, what you command, but give what you command; give us both the will and the ability to do what you ask! The self-righteous person trusts in a righteousness he achieved; the believer aspires to a righteousness to be acquired."[52] The believer is indeed in principle righteous, for although a person is only righteous because he is so regarded by God; still "no one is so regarded unless he fulfills the law by work. But no one fulfills the law except those who believe in Christ. And thus the Apostle argues that outside of Christ no one is just, no one fulfills the law."[53] In other words, while believers may in principle be righteous, the righteousness they possess is due solely to God's grace and is not the ground on which they put their trust. At the start of their lives as believers as well as in the course of their lives, they continue to take God at his word. They

46. *Luther's Works*, 25:205–7 (WA 56:220–22; Ficker, II, 59–61).
47. *Luther's Works*, 25:206–45 (WA 56:221–58; Ficker, II, 60–94).
48. *Luther's Works*, 25:284 (WA 56:296; Ficker, II, 129–30).
49. *Luther's Works*, 25:267 (WA 56:279; Ficker, II, 114–15).
50. *Luther's Works*, 25:265 (WA 56:278; Ficker, II, 113).
51. *Luther's Works*, 25:257 (WA 56:269; Ficker, II, 105); cf. *Luther's Works*, 25:265, 270, 274, 277 (WA 56:278, 282, 287, 290; Ficker, II, 113, 118, 121, 123).
52. *Luther's Works*, 25:251 (WA 56:264; Ficker, II, 99).
53. *Luther's Works*, 25:19 (WA 56:22; Ficker, I, 20).

continue to believe that they are sinners and that their righteousness is grounded solely in the righteousness of God.

Thus, while on earth, they are and remain sick as well as healthy, sinners as well as righteous, guilty and innocent. "Intrinsically the saints are always sinners; extrinsically, therefore, they are always justified. Hypocrites, on the other hand, are always intrinsically righteous; extrinsically, therefore, they are always sinners." To be extrinsically righteous signifies that we are not righteous in ourselves or on account of our works, "but only by virtue of God's imputation. For justification is neither in us nor in our power. Therefore our righteousness is neither in us nor in our power. Intrinsically and from within ourselves we are and will always remain impious."[54] Just as a sick person is sick within himself and may be called healthy if he believes the promise of improvement made by a competent physician and obeys his instructions, so believing sinners are "in actual fact sinners but righteous on account of the imputation and promise of God that they derive from him until they are perfectly healed."[55] Justification, accordingly, is always a work in progress. "People of faith spend their entire life in seeking justification."[56] In their case it is better to speak of "the justified" (*justificati*) than of "the just" (*justi*), for Christ alone "is just, and we are still always being justified and in the process of justification."[57]

Guided by this view of justification, Luther was led in the end to warn against both false security and despair. Our entire life on earth, he said, is "a time of desiring righteousness, yet in no way of fully attaining it; it is fully attained only in a future life." Even after our justification, God permits original sin to remain operative in us, in order that by it he might keep us in fear and humility and prompt us continually to resort to his grace. On the other hand, we need not give in to despair because we cannot radically remove internal sin from us, for that is not possible in this life, and God forgives those and does not impute sin to those who invoke his mercy. "Therefore the royal road and the road of peace in the Spirit is to know sin and to hate it and to walk in the fear of God in such a way that he does not impute sin and permit us to be controlled by it; and to pray for his mercy that we may be released from it and he does not impute it. Fear excludes the one: false security; and mercy [excludes] the other: despair. The former is a foolish complacency; the latter a lack of hope in God."[58]

Thus the life of Christians remains a life of faith. They do not experience and know that they are justified, for they are only righteous by imputation of God, but they call for it and hope it, believe and expect it,[59] and in that hope are gladdened

54. *Luther's Works*, 25:257 (WA 56:269; Ficker, II, 104–5).
55. *Luther's Works*, 25:260 (WA 56:272; Ficker, II, 108); cf. *Luther's Works*, 25:257, 258, 332, 335–36 (WA 56:269, 270, 343, 346–47; Ficker, II, 104–5, 176, 179–80).
56. *Luther's Works*, 25:252 (WA 56:265; Ficker, II, 100).
57. *Luther's Works*, 25:43n2 (WA 56:265n2; Ficker, I, 45).
58. *Luther's Works*, 25:270 (WA 56:282–83; Ficker, II, 116–18).
59. *Luther's Works*, 25:52 (WA 56:58; Ficker, I, 54); cf. *Luther's Works*, 25:209, 256, 278 (WA 56:224–25, 268, 290; Ficker, II, 89, 104, 124).

and assured.[60] God does not forsake the work of his hands but accomplishes what he has promised.[61] Christians exhibit that faith in their obedience to God's Word. For the best Christians are not those "who are very learned and read much and own many books. But they are the best who most freely do what they read in books and teach others. However, they are not able to act freely unless they possess love through the Holy Spirit." Therefore, in our age they are most to be feared who become very rich in book learning but remain unlearned as Christians.[62] Obedience, furthermore, does not consist in the accumulation of many good and great works with the idea that they are good because they are hard, but is frequently manifest in fidelity to what is small and of little significance.[63] In all that we do the main thing is that we let God work through us and do not assess his word by the standard of our works but our works by the standard of his word.[64]

[470] Germinally, the lectures on Romans already contain all the ideas that Luther would later develop at greater length, especially in his commentary on Galatians. From these lectures, it is utterly clear that, in the thinking of the Reformation, the doctrine of justification was certainly not born from the insight that original sin—which, according to Denifle, Luther further equated with sensual desire—was insurmountable in believers and that, therefore, a mere trust in God's mercy and an externally imputed righteousness of Christ was sufficient for salvation.[65] For Luther nowhere makes a sharp distinction, much less a separation between justification (in a forensic sense) and sanctification. Nowhere does he subordinate the latter to the former, but he always combines the two—declaring righteous and making righteous—under the single heading of justification. From the start, the Reformation was both a religious and an ethical movement. On the other hand, in the doctrine of justification, all that is of interest is concentrated in the thesis that salvation is totally, from beginning to end, the exclusive work of God, not that of man. Hence the contrast between law and gospel, the opposition to all the merits of congruity and condignity, the emphasis on justification apart from merits, the glorification of God's grace and the merits of Christ. God's grace and it alone is the object of a Christian's

60. *Luther's Works*, 25:465 (WA 56:465; Ficker, II, 287); cf. *Luther's Works*, 25:504 (WA 56:516; Ficker, II, 341).

61. *Luther's Works*, 25:41–42n27 (WA 56:48n2; Ficker, I, 44); cf. *Luther's Works*, 25:267 (WA 56:279; II, 128).

62. *Luther's Works*, 25:326 (WA 56:338; Ficker, II, 167).

63. *Luther's Works*, 25:420 (WA 56:427; Ficker, II, 253).

64. *Luther's Works*, 25:359 (WA 56:368–70; Ficker, II, 203); cf. *Luther's Works*, 25:407–10 (WA 56:415–18; Ficker, II, 242–43).

65. That the new ideas in Luther's thinking sprang not from a moral bankruptcy but, on the contrary, from a profound sense of sin has been documented with strong evidence by W. Braun, *Die Bedeutung der Concupiscenz in Luthers Leben und Lehre* (Berlin: Trowitzsch, 1908). Nor in Luther's thinking is concupiscence the same as sexual lust but refers to the root of a whole range—also of spiritual—sins. Cf. F. Loofs, *Dogmengeschichte*, 696; K. Holl, "Luthers Rechtfertigungslehre 1516," *Zeitschrift für Theologie und Kirche* 20 (1910): 265; H. Bavinck, *Reformed Dogmatics*, III, 98–100 (#322).

trust, at the beginning of a Christian's conversion and similarly to the end of one's life. For although they have in principle been renewed by a living faith, the ground of their confidence is certainly never their own righteousness but the righteousness that God has granted in Christ. What Luther was to say so often in later years ("You have and are as much as you believe") he also already affirms in his exposition of the Letter to the Romans: "For we are and have as much as we believe. Those therefore who believe and trust with a full faith that they are the children of God are the children of God."[66] In later years Luther indeed made a sharper distinction between faith and hope, gave greater prominence to "gratuitous imputation," laid more emphasis on the forgiveness of sins and adoption as children as these things are the possession of believers already on earth, and also does more justice to the assurance of salvation; yet all these things are not new elements but the development and expansion of what is germinally present already in the lectures on the Letter to the Romans.

This is not to say that Luther had ready-made answers to all the questions that might well occur in connection with this doctrine of justification. For justification, to him, was not a doctrine that he thought through scientifically and set forth systematically but the proclamation of a message that, guided by his own religious experience, he had found in others, especially in the writings of Paul. Hence, both in his earlier and later theology, there remains much uncertainty about the relationship between conversion (contrition, repentance) and faith, between faith and justification, between justification and sanctification. For example, in a section already cited earlier, he writes: "The fact that a person is just is not the reason why God regards him as just, but he is just because he is so regarded by God," but in the same breath he continues: "No one, however, is regarded as just unless he fulfills the law by work. But no one fulfills the law who does not believe in Christ. And thus the Apostle argues that outside of Christ no one is just, no one fulfills the law."[67] Reading this, one instinctively wonders how the one thing can be squared with the other. Does the act of "regarding" precede "being just" (by faith in Christ), or does the latter precede the former? Is justification a synthetic or an analytical judgment? Luther does not give a clear and firm answer. In his theology one can find statements supporting both positions. Also, the Augsburg Confession and its Apology do not express themselves clearly on this point. It is stated as forcefully as possible that justification cannot be obtained by our own powers, works, or merits but solely by grace, for Christ's sake, through faith. This confession is the "foremost head of Christian doctrine, the article by which the church stands or falls," as it was to be called later, for involved in it are the honor of Christ and the comfort of believers.[68]

---

66. *Luther's Works*, 25:71 (WA 56:79; Ficker, I, 73–74).

67. *Luther's Works*, 25:19 (WA 56:22; Ficker, I, 20).

68. Joseph T. Müller, *Die symbolischen Bücher der evangelisch-lutherischen Kirche*, 8th ed. (Gütersloh: Bertelsmann, 1898), 39, 87, 300; ed. note: These specific references are to the following Lutheran documents: Augsburg Confession, art. 4, in *The Book of Concord*, ed. Robert Kolb and Timothy J. Wengert (Minneapolis:

Nevertheless, at many points clarity is lacking. On the one hand, it is stated that the Holy Spirit is granted by the means of Word and Sacrament and works faith "where and when it seems good to him" in those who hear the gospel; and on the other hand, that faith itself brings the Holy Spirit with it and that we receive the Holy Spirit *after* we have been justified and born again by faith.[69] At one time we receive the impression that the promise of forgiveness, justification, and eternal life is included in the word of the gospel, and that we accept it by faith; then again it seems that, positing Christ as our mediator against the wrath of God by faith, we receive forgiveness and are justified.[70] "To be justified" is described in various ways. It "means that out of unrighteous people righteous people are made or regenerated," but "it also means that they are pronounced or regarded as righteous. [For Scripture speaks both ways.]"[71] At one point, regeneration is equated with "being made a righteous person out of an unrighteous one," and

Fortress, 2000), 38–41; Apology of the Augsburg Confession, art. 4, pars. 2–8 (Kolb and Wengert, 120–21); Smalcald Articles, part II, art. 2 (Kolb and Wengert, 300–301).

69. Joseph T. Müller, *Die symbolischen Bücher*, 39, 110–11; ed. note: These specific references are to the following Lutheran documents: Augsburg Confession, art. 4 (Kolb and Wengert, 38–41); Apology of the Augsburg Confession, art. 4, pars. 126–39 (Kolb and Wengert, 140–42).

70. Joseph T. Müller, *Die symbolischen Bücher*, 93–95, 98, 102, 107, 121, 123: "We receive through faith since we are reckoned righteous because of Christ." Ed. note: These specific references are to the following Lutheran document: Apology of the Augsburg Confession, art. 4, pars. 36–47, 61–67, 82–84, 106–10, 196–218 (Kolb and Wengert, 126–27, 130–31, 134, 138, 150–53).

71. Joseph T. Müller, *Die symbolischen Bücher*, 100–101, 103, 108; ed. note: These specific references are to the Apology of the Augsburg Confession, art. 4, pars. 79–120 (Kolb and Wengert, 133–40); the citation is from ibid., art. 4, par. 72 (Kolb and Wengert, 132). Attempts to reconcile these two definitions of justification have not been lacking in recent years. J. Kunze (*Die Rechtfertigungslehre in der Apologie* [Gütersloh: C. Bertelsmann, 1908]) even sought refuge in three corrections. However, O. Ritschl ("Der doppelte Rechtfertigungsbegriff in der Apologie der [Augsburg] Konfession," *Zeitschrift für Theologie und Kirche* 20 [1910]: 292–338) calls this a desperate tour de force and thinks that the words in the Apology—"It also means that they are pronounced or regarded as righteous. For Scripture speaks both ways"—need to be placed within parentheses so that the further explanation concerns only the meaning of *justificari* in the sense of "the making of a righteous person out of an unrighteous one, or as regeneration" (ed. note: Apology of the Augsburg Confession, art. 4, 78, in Kolb and Wengert, 133). Melanchthon originally understood *justificatio* not only to refer to forgiveness of sins but also to regeneration. Gradually, from 1529 to 1532, he came to realize that this word really included only the first benefit. In this transition period, he produced the Apology and strived to demonstrate that justification indeed was a matter of "making of a righteous person from an unrighteous one," whereas faith comforted a believer's heart and made it alive. At the same time, it is still a matter of being "reckoned righteousness," since even faith and the good works that flow from it are counted toward righteousness not for faith's own sake but only on account of Christ. The reason: faith is always incomplete and flawed. In fact, the intention is that faith, which in turn is a gift of God, makes one righteous in principle (and this is understood in two possible ways: that human beings who accept the promise of forgiveness in faith, are *consciously* comforted, lifted up, made alive, oriented to joy and gratitude; or that they through faith receive a desire and choose to do God's will and bring forth good works), but God also *declares* to the believer, at the beginning and throughout his life, that though he always remains imperfect, he is nonetheless righteous for Christ's sake. Justification in the sense of "being made a righteous person from an unrighteous one or as regeneration, accepting the forgiveness of sins," is called, "justification in consciousness" (later, passive justification). Justification in the sense of "being pronounced righteous or reckoned righteous" should be understood by what is later called "active justification," that is to say, the justification that takes place in God's judgment.

with the consolation and vivification that the faith that accepts the forgiveness of sins produces; then again it is viewed as the new life and the spiritual motions that the Holy Spirit—whom we receive by faith after being justified—plants in our hearts.[72]

But polemics with Rome, and later also in Lutheran circles with Osiander and Stancarus, Major and Amsdorf, forced theologians to refine their concepts and to arrange them in a more logical order. In this connection they followed Melanchthon, who from 1529 onward, increasingly ascribed to justification an exclusively juridical meaning. In the Apology it was already said that Scripture also uses this term in the sense of "pronouncing righteous or regarding as righteous." When James refers to "justification by works," he is not speaking of "the manner of justification" (*modus justificationis*) but describes "what sort of people the righteous are after they have been justified and born again." And "to be justified" (*justificari*) means here, "not to be made a righteous person from an unrighteous one, but to be pronounced just in a forensic sense." Similarly, in Rom. 5:1 to justify, in forensic language, has the meaning of "absolving the defendant and pronouncing him just," and that in keeping with an expression already used earlier by Luther,[73] "on account of another person's righteousness, namely Christ's, which other righteousness is communicated to us through faith." Since the righteousness of Christ is imputed or granted to us through faith, that faith is "imputative righteousness in us, that is, it is that by which we are rendered acceptable to God by his imputation and ordinance."[74] Proceeding on this track, the Formula of Concord rejected the view of Osiander and Stancarus, as well as that of Major and Amsdorf, and confessed: (1) Faith alone, which, however, "is not a mere knowledge of the stories about Christ," but "a gift of God and a true and living faith," is the means and instrument through which we lay hold of Christ as our Savior and thus, in Christ, lay hold of "this righteousness that avails before God." (2) God forgives us our sins by sheer grace, without any works, merit, or worthiness of our own in the past, at present, or in the future; that he gives us and reckons to us the righteousness of Christ's obedience; and that because of this righteousness, we are accepted by God into grace and regarded as righteous. (3) "Although the contrition that precedes justification and the good works that follow it do not belong in the article on justification before God, nevertheless a person should not concoct a kind of faith that can exist and remain with and alongside an evil intention to sin and

72. Joseph T. Müller, *Die symbolischen Bücher*, 98, 100, compared with 109–10, 146, etc.; ed. note: These specific references are to the Apology of the Augsburg Confession, art. 4, pars. 61–67, 72–78, 122–32, 346–57 (Kolb and Wengert, 130–31, 132–33, 140–41, 169–70).

73. *Luther's Works*, 25:136 (WA 56:157–58; Ficker, II, 2); cf. *Luther's Works*, 25:267–68 (WA 56:279–80; Ficker II, 114–15). Cf. O. Ritschl, "Der doppelte Rechtfertigungsbegriff," 325.

74. Joseph T. Müller, *Die symbolischen Bücher*, 100, 130–31, 139–40; ed. note: These specific references are to the Apology of the Augsburg Confession, art. 4, pars. 72–78, 226–46, 298–307 (Kolb and Wengert, 132–33, 154–58, 164–67). Cf. further, P. Melanchthon, *Corpus doctrinae christianae* (Leipzig: Ernesti Voegelini Constantiensis, 1560), 240ff., 414ff., 685ff.; ed. note: Bavinck cites the 1561 edition.

to act against conscience. . . . Good works always follow justifying faith and are certainly found with it, when it is a true and living faith. For faith is never alone but is always accompanied by love and hope."[75]

In this early period, Lutheran dogmatics brought about a change: while considerably expanding the loci of the order of salvation,[76] they nevertheless continued strictly to insist on the doctrine that we are justified apart from our own merits. In the seventeenth century, however, to the degree that the confession of predestination had been abandoned and faith was more or less considered a human achievement, the order of grace gave way to the order of reward, the gospel to the law, and faith to works. Pietism and rationalism tended—though for different reasons—in the same direction. Schleiermacher viewed justification as the reverse side of conversion and as part of regeneration, actually making it dependent on the new life in communion with Christ. The Mediating theologians indeed corrected him in that they maintained justification as an objective act of God, but they nevertheless had it take place on the basis of the infused righteousness of Christ, which guarantees the future perfection of believers. Even Hengstenberg distinguished a number of steps in justification and made its completion dependent on love and good works.[77] Ritschl, however, again fixed attention on the objective significance of justification and therefore viewed it as a synthetic judgment that preceded good works. But he saw it as implicit in Jesus's message of the love of God and as a good of the church in which the individual participated by joining the church, and thereby he cut its connection with the satisfaction of Christ on the one hand and the Christian's assurance of faith on the other. Actually, therefore, as in Schleiermacher, it was again reduced to a religious experience, a removal of the consciousness of guilt, and ceased to be an objective judgment that God by grace pronounces upon sinners and by which he frees them from guilt.[78] This view of justification not only found acceptance among Ritschl's followers but also exerted great influence outside of that circle. Dorner related justification most intimately to objective reconciliation in Christ and hence viewed faith as merely the organ by which one receives the forgiveness already granted on the part of God.[79] And others, like H. Cremer, E. Cremer, and Althaus, so construed justification that regeneration as a special concomitant benefit completely disappeared and was still maintained only as a renewal of life effected by faith.[80]

75. Ed note: Citations from Formula of Concord, "Epitome," art. 3, "Righteousness," in Kolb and Wengert, 495–96; Joseph T. Müller, *Die symbolischen Bücher*, 527–30, 611–24.

76. H. Bavinck, *Reformed Dogmatics*, III, 491–522 (##410–18, esp. #418).

77. Ibid., III, 554–55 (#426); F. A. Philippi, *Kirchliche Glaubenslehre*, 7 vols. (Gütersloh: Bertelsmann, 1883–1902), V, 1, 215ff., 298.

78. H. Bavinck, *Reformed Dogmatics*, III, 550–53 (#425).

79. I. A. Dorner, *A System of Christian Doctrine*, trans. A. Cave and J. S. Banks, 4 vols. (Edinburgh: T&T Clark, 1882), IV, 217ff.

80. See above, 83 (#445).

OBJECTIVE AND SUBJECTIVE; ACTIVE AND PASSIVE

[471] Although there is no material difference between Lutheran and Reformed theology with respect to the doctrine of justification, in the latter, nevertheless, it occupies a different place and acquires a different accent.[81] This is first of all evident in the fact that Luther ever-increasingly pushed predestination into the background. Calvin, on the other hand, increasingly made it the center of his theology and also viewed justification in its light. "When the Lord calls, justifies, and glorifies us, he declares nothing other than his eternal election."[82] It is the elect who are justified.[83] It is completely true that Calvin never for that reason weakens the objective satisfaction of Christ nor the benefit of justification,[84] but what does follow from this fact is that the righteousness of Christ is presented to us much more as a gift granted to us by God than as a benefit we accept by faith. The objective act of donation is prior to the subjective act of acceptance.[85] On the other hand, Calvin maintains our "being justified apart from our own merits" not only for the two reasons derived, respectively, from the sufficient merits of Christ and the comfort of believers, but no less firmly on account of the glory of God. Calvin feels that he is in the presence of God, placed before his judgment seat; and looking up at the holiness and majesty of God, he no longer dares to speak, with reference to puny sinful humans, of works of their own, of merits, or of reason for boasting in themselves. On the contrary, nothing befits such a person other than humility and confidence in God's mercy. The elect are justified by God so that they would glory in him and in nothing else.[86] In the third place, especially in his opposition to Osiander, Calvin makes a sharp distinction between justification and sanctification, for the former is a purely forensic act; but he never separates the two and consistently keeps them very closely connected. Christ, after all, cannot be divided anymore than the light and the warmth of the sun, though the two certainly produce distinct effects.[87] Christ does not justify anyone whom he does not also at the same time sanctify. We, accordingly, are not justified by works, but neither are we justified without works.[88] "Indeed, we do not contemplate Christ from afar in order that his righteousness might be imputed to us, but because we put on Christ and are ingrafted into his body—in short because he deigns to make us one with him. For this reason we glory that we have fellowship of righteousness with him."[89] Thus while in Calvin's thinking justification kept its place and value, it did not

---

81. E. F. K. Müller, *Symbolik* (Erlangen and Leipzig: A. Deichert, 1896), 472ff.
82. Cf. H. Bavinck, *Reformed Dogmatics*, III, 522–28 (#419).
83. J. Calvin, *Institutes*, III.xiii.2.
84. W. Lüttge, *Die Rechtfertigungslehre Calvins* (Berlin: Reuther & Reichard, 1909), 92–93.
85. J. Calvin, *Institutes*, III.xi.1, 7, 17–18; etc.
86. Ibid., III.xii. Cf. Lüttge, *Die Rechtfertigungslehre Calvins*, 76–82.
87. J. Calvin, *Institutes*, III.xi.6, 11, 24; III.xiv.9.
88. Ibid., III.xvi.1.
89. Ibid., III.xi.10; cf. H. Bavinck, *Reformed Dogmatics*, III, 522–28 (#419).

become the one thing that overshadowed everything else in the order of salvation. It was given a place between election and the gift of Christ on the one hand, and salvation and glorification on the other. It was "something in the middle of the transition from eternal predestination to future glory."[90]

Yet, although Calvin proved his independence also in the doctrine of justification, he did not solve all the problems that present themselves in the study of this article of faith. This applies especially to the relationship of justification to election and satisfaction, on one hand, and to sanctification and glorification, on the other. If justification has a place somewhere between the two, there is always a reason to connect it more with the preceding or more with the following group of benefits, depending on the choice made, and justification itself acquires a different meaning. If one's purpose is to maintain the objective forensic character of justification, it is natural to tie it closely with election and satisfaction. It then becomes the imputation of the righteousness of Christ, which took place long before, in the gospel, in the resurrection of Christ, or even from eternity, and is then appropriated much later by the subject in faith. Then that faith is no more than a vessel or instrument, a merely passive thing,[91] so that it becomes hard to derive from it the new life of sanctification. On the other hand, if a person is focused more on practical than on speculative interests, one naturally tries to forge a close connection between justification and faith. In that case, justification coincides with the benefit of the forgiveness of sins, which is received and enjoyed in faith, and faith becomes communion with Christ. It has Christ dwell in us through his Spirit, assures us of God's benevolence toward us, and pours out new life and new powers in our hearts.[92]

In Calvin, these two perspectives are still connected with each other,[93] but in Reformed theology they soon split apart, and both developed in a one-sided direction. Under the influence of Socinianism and Remonstrantism, Cartesianism and Amyraldism, there sprang up the neonomian view of the order of salvation, which made the forgiveness of sins and eternal life dependent on faith and obedience, which, in keeping with the new law of the gospel, had to be accomplished by the human agent. Parallel to this movement ran that of Pietism and Methodism, which, for all the difference between the two, nevertheless equally shifted the center of gravity to the side of the subject, and insisted either on a lengthy period of religious experience or on a sudden conversion as the condition for the acquisition of salvation. Out of reaction to this came antineonomianism, which had justification precede faith, and antinomianism, which traced justification to the eternal love of God and dissolved sin and satisfaction into "inadequate"

90. Lüttge, *Die Rechtfertigungslehre Calvins*, 102. Lüttge persuasively refutes the invalid ethical and eschatological interpretation of Calvin's doctrine of justification advocated by Schneckenburger and M. Schulze (36, 56, 70, 85, 89) and properly restores the correct role of Bucer on Calvin (83).

91. J. Calvin, *Institutes*, III.xi.7; III.xiii.5.

92. Ibid., III.i.1–2, 9, 12, 28–29; III.iii.10; etc.

93. Lüttge, *Die Rechtfertigungslehre Calvins*, 41–70.

concepts from which humans had to liberate themselves by the superior insight of faith.[94]

As a rule, Reformed theologians tried to avoid the two extremes and to that end soon began to employ the distinction between active and passive justification. This distinction does not yet occur in the works of the Reformers, who usually speak of justification in a concrete sense;[95] they do not deal with justification from eternity, in the resurrection of Christ, in the gospel, before and after the gift of faith, but sum up everything in a single concept. That is why in some of their pronouncements they offer support to those who place justification before faith,[96] but they can with equal warrant be cited as advocates of the belief that justification always occurs through and from within faith.[97] But with the rise of nomism and antinomianism, Reformed theologians were compelled to undertake [deeper] conceptual analysis and, to avoid both errors, differentiated between active and passive justification. On the one hand, they rejected the nomism that had the benefit of forgiveness come into being only upon faith, "experience," or conversion of the human agent. On the other hand, they were also on their guard against antinomianism and almost unanimously rejected the doctrine of

---

94. Cf. H. Bavinck, *Reformed Dogmatics*, I, 181–83 (#55); III, 535–40 (#422); P. J. Kromsigt, "Het Antinomianisme van Jacobus Verschoor," *Troffel en Zwaard* 9 (1906): 205–36, 272–89; 10 (1907): 1–21, 188–202; idem, "Het Antinomianisme van Pontiaan van Hattem," *Troffel en Zwaard* 13 (1910): 309–26, 371–81; 14 (1911): 31–45. The "New Lights" from Zwijndrecht also taught that God never exercises his wrath but only loves from eternity and that Christ has revealed this to us. What Christ delivers us from, therefore, is the despair and fear of God's wrath and punishment. In this way he reconciles us to God (not God to us). It is faith in Jesus's preaching, namely, that God is love, that justifies us and leads us to follow him. Ed. note: Zwijndrecht is a town in the Dutch province of South Holland, just across the Maas River from Dordrecht and southeast of Rotterdam. From the 1820s to the 1840s it was the home of a small mystical, pantheistic sect, referred to by its critics as "New Lights," thanks to their Quaker-like commitment to the inner light of revelation. Eschewing sacraments and civil laws of marriage, the group developed a bad reputation and disbanded in 1846 when a number of its members were attracted to Mormonism and emigrated to the United States. See A. B. M. W. Kok, "Zwijndrechtsche Nieuwlichten," in *Christelijke Encyclopaedie*, 2nd ed., 6 vols. (Kampen: Kok, 1961), VI, 720–21. G. P. Marang, *De zwijndrechtsche Nieuwlichters* (Dordrecht: H. De Graaf, 1909), 190.

95. Comrie also acknowledges this. See A. Comrie, *Brief over de regtvaardigmaking des zondaars* (Utrecht: A. Fisscher, 1899), 22.

96. For his views Comrie appeals to Luther, numerous church fathers, Roman Catholic theologians, Protestant confessions, and Reformed writers. See ibid., 1–67. Also see the references to Luther and Calvin above. On Melanchthon, see A. Ritschl, *Die christliche Lehre von der Rechtfertigung und Versöhnung*, 4th ed., 3 vols. (Bonn: A. Marcus, 1895–1903), II, 185–86. On Olevianus, see H. Heppe, *Dogmatik des deutschen Protestantismus im sechzehnten Jahrhundert*, 3 vols. (Gotha: F. A. Perthes, 1857), II, 315; and similar expressions can also be found in Ursinus, Hyperius, Pareus, Tossanus, et al.

97. See Petrus Boddaert, *Wolk van getuigen voor de leere der rechtvaardiginge door en uit het geloove* (1759; anonymously published against the views of Brahe); J. J. Schultens, *Uitvoerige Waarschuwing op verscheiden stukken der Catechismus verklaring van A. Comrie* (Leiden: A. Kallewier, 1761), 515ff., 741ff.; J. van den Honert, *Verhandeling van de rechtvaardiging des zondaars uit en door het geloof* (Leiden: Luchtmanns, 1755); and other works by Van der Sloot, Theoph. van Heber, Kennedy in B. de Moor, *Comm. theol.*, IV, 668; C. Vitringa, *Doctr. christ.*, III, 297, 298; A. Ypey, *Geschiedenis der Christliche kerk in de Achttiende Eeuw* (Utrecht: Van Ijzergorst, 1797–1811), VII, 313–27.

eternal justification.[98] Thus they commonly assumed that, even if one could with some warrant speak of a justification in the divine decree, in the resurrection of Christ, and in the gospel, active justification first occurred only in the internal calling before and until faith, but the intimation of it in human consciousness (in other words, passive justification) came into being only through and from within faith.[99] In this connection they did their utmost to keep the two parts as closely connected as possible and to assume only a logical, not a temporal, distinction between them.[100] Even at that, however, others continued to object to this distinction.[101] After all, the gospel mentions no names and it says to no one

98. Thus the Westminster Confession, XI, 4; in E. F. K. Müller, *Die Bekenntnisschriften der reformierten Kirche* (Leipzig: Deichert, 1903), 568; cf. A. F. Mitchell, *The Westminster Assembly, Its History and Standards* (London: J. Nisbet, 1883), 149–56; J. H. Alsted, *Encyclopaediae liber decimus quartus* (Herborn: C. Corvin, 1620), 1622; J. Maccovius, *Loci communes theologici* (Amsterdam: n.p., 1658), 676; G. Voetius, *Selectae disputationes theologicae*, 5 vols. (Utrecht, 1648–69), V, 281; J. H. Heidegger, *Corpus theologiae*, 2 vols. (Zurich: J. H. Bodmer, 1700), XXII, 79; P. van Mastricht, *Theoretico-practica theologia* (Utrecht: Appels, 1714), VI, 6, 18; F. Turretin, *Institutes of Elenctic Theology*, trans. G. M. Giger, ed. J. T. Dennison, 3 vols. (Phillipsburg, NJ: Presbyterian & Reformed, 1992), XVI, 9. It was also of utmost importance to Comrie, Holtius, and Brahe that justification be considered as eternal. They were correct in noting that the just judgment concerning the elect as an immanent act (*actus immanentus*) in God was eternal and indistinguishable from his essence. However, they judged it as indifferent whether one called this immanent act "justification" or not, as long as the substance remained firm (J. J. Brahe, *Godgeleerde stellingen over de leer der rechtvaardigmaking des zondaars voor God* [Amsterdam: J. H. den Ouden, 1833], 26, 28). Second, they accepted a notion of eternal justification since they regarded all of God's immanent acts as eternal, including, for example, creation. These, however, must never exclude God's acts in time. On the contrary, justification, which as a benefit is firmly fixed in God's decree, is nonetheless realized in time, for example, in the resurrection of Christ, in the gospel, in the application [of Christ's benefits] to all the elect in their proper time (A. Comrie, *Brief over de regtvaardigmaking des zondaars*, 91ff.). Third, they explained expressly that their chief concern was whether the application of Christ's righteousness was mediated or unmediated; whether it preceded or followed faith; and whether it is a free, sovereign act of God, or whether in some way it comes to pass through human cooperation, for example, by means of the condition of faith (J. J. Brahe, *Godgeleerde stellingen*, 20ff.; A. Comrie, *Brief over de regtvaardigmaking des zondaars*, 120ff.; A. Comrie and Nicolaus Holtius, *Examen van het ontwerp van tolerantie*, 10 vols. [Amsterdam: Nicolaas Byl, 1753], preface to the seventh address, 4ff.; preface to the tenth address, 44ff.).

99. Thus theologians mentioned above and many others, for example, Ursinus, Piscator, Bucanus, Owen, Trigland, Leydekker, Hoornbeek, Holtius; cf. B. de Moor, *Comm. theol.*, IV, 658ff.; H. Heppe, *Die Dogmatik der evangelisch-reformirten Kirche* (Elberseld: R. L. Friedrich, 1861), 402ff. In the Reformed Confessions, as is the case in Calvin, justification is described in such a way that we receive the righteousness, the benefits of Christ, even justification itself, by faith. E. F. K. Müller, *Die Bekenntnisschriften der reformierten Kirche*, 57, line 6; 128, 1–5; 192, 6; 225, 37–39; 281, 41–43; 568, 20–24; 620, 44. Ed. note: The Reformed Confessions cited here are Confessio Tetrapolitana (1530), art. 3; Genevan Catechism (1545), part I, "De fide"; Second Helvetic Confession (1562), ch. 15; Gallican Confession (1559), art. 17; Das Erlauthaler Bekenntnis von 1562, "De justificatione"; Westminster Confession (1647), ch. 11; Westminster Larger Catechism, Q71. Das Erlauthaler Bekenntnis von 1562 is an early confession of Hungarian Protestants under the sponsorship of Kaiser Ferdinand and King Maximilian of Bohemia. See E. F. K. Müller, *Die Bekenntnisschriften der reformierte Kirche*, XXXVI–XXXVII.

100. Thus, e.g., J. H. Heidegger, *Corpus theologiae*, XXII, 79; S. Maresius, *Syst. theol.*, XI, 58; F. Turretin, *Institutes of Elenctic Theology*, XVI, 9, 8–12.

101. For example, not only van den Honert, J. J. Schultens, van der Os, but also H. Witsius, *Irenaeus*, in *Miscellaneorum sacrorum*, c. 8; P. van Mastricht, *Theologia*, VI, 6, 13; T. van der Groe, J. Groenewegen, and A. van der Willigen, *Beschrijving van het oprecht en zielzaligend geloof* (Rotterdam: R. C. Huge, 1742), 36, 201;

personally: Your sins have been forgiven. Therefore no person can and may start with the belief that one's sins have been forgiven.

In the Reformed position, there seemed to be all the less warrant and freedom for such a personalized statement, inasmuch as on it the satisfaction of Christ is not universal but particular. The preacher of the gospel cannot give to anyone the assurance that one's sins are forgiven, since he does not know the elect; and the persons who hear that gospel can and may not believe this either, since before and without faith they cannot be conscious of their election. So it seemed that the practical conclusion was that they must first be cast down by a deep sense of guilt, then by faith seek refuge in Christ, surrender to him, become actively involved with him, and thus gradually, persuaded by self-examination of the genuineness of their refuge-taking faith, receive the boldness to consider themselves assured of the forgiveness of their sins and future salvation. The human agent, accordingly, must first believe, that is, become actively involved with Christ, so that then one could be justified by God. But in that way the ground of their justification had again been shifted from God to the human agent, from Christ's righteousness to the activities of faith, from the gospel to the law. Just as in Lutheran theology, so also in Reformed theology no agreement was achieved. Soon after the Reformation, two schools of thought emerged on the scene that have persisted and still today make themselves felt both in doctrine and in life.

JUSTIFICATION IS FORENSIC, NOT ETHICAL

[472] To correctly assess the benefit of justification, people must lift up their minds to the judgment seat of God and put themselves in his presence.[102] When they compare themselves with others or measure themselves by the standard that they apply to themselves or among each other, they have some reason perhaps to pride themselves in something and to put their trust in it. But when they put themselves before the face of God and examine themselves in the mirror of his holy law, all their conceit collapses, all self-confidence melts, and there is room left only for the prayer: "Enter not into judgment with your servant, for no one living is righteous before you" (Job 4:17–19; 9:2; 15:14–16; Ps. 143:2; cf. 130:3), and their only comfort is that "there is forgiveness before you, so that you may be revered" (Ps. 130:4). If for insignificant, guilty, and impure persons there is to be a possibility of true religion, that is, of genuine fellowship with God, of salvation and eternal life, then God on his part must reestablish the broken bond, again take them into fellowship with him and share his grace with them, regardless of their

---

F. A. Lampe, *De verborgentheit van het gnaade-verbondt*, 4 vols. (Amsterdam: Antony Schoonenburg, 1726–39), 409ff. (ed. note: Bavinck cites the 1718 edition). J. van Alphen, preacher at 's Bosch who repudiated a sermon of his ministerial colleague on Lord's Day 23; cf. A. Ypey, *Geschiedenis der Christliche kerk in de Achttiende Eeuw*, VII, 315; W. Meindertsma, "Het Bossche geschil in de achttiende eeuw over de rechtvaardigmaking," *Stemmen voor Waarheid en Vrede* 47 (November 1910): 1081–96.

102. J. Calvin, *Institutes*, III.xii.

guilt and corruption. He, then, must descend from the height of his majesty, seek us out and come to us, take away our guilt and again open the way to his fatherly heart. If God were to wait until we—by our faith, our virtues, and good works of congruity or condignity—had made ourselves worthy, in part or in whole, to receive his favor, the restoration of communion between him and ourselves would never happen, and salvation would forever be out of reach for us.

This is why so much depends on the benefit of justification, and it is rightly denominated the article on which the church either stands or falls. For the fundamental question that arises in this connection is this: What is the way that leads to communion with God, to true religion, to salvation and eternal life: God's grace or human merit, his forgiveness or our works, gospel or law, the covenant of grace or the covenant of works? If it is the latter, if our work, our virtue, our sanctification is primary, then the believers' consolation ends, and they remain in doubt and uncertainty to their last breath. Then Christ is violated in his unique, all-encompassing, and all-sufficient mediatorial office, and he himself is put on a level with other humans, with ourselves. Then God is robbed of his honor, for if humans are justified on the basis of their works, they have reason to boast of themselves and are, partly or totally, the craftsmen of their own salvation.

Driven by these three motives, the Reformation took up cudgels against Rome and confessed with great unanimity that the grace of God is the only impelling and efficient cause of our entire salvation. And by "grace" it meant not some metaphysical quality that was infused into humans who did "as much as they could" and elevated them to a supernatural state (*gratia elevans*), but rather the forgiving mercy and favor of God that precedes all human effort and again receives them, freely and without obligation, into his fellowship. The establishment of the covenant of grace proceeds from God and from him alone. It is he and he alone who for his own sake blots out our transgressions and no longer remembers our sins (Isa. 43:25). We are justified by his grace as a gift (Rom. 3:24; Gal. 3:18; Eph. 2:8; Titus 3:5–7). More specifically, it is the Father from whom this benefit proceeds, for he is the lawgiver and judge (James 4:12), but also the merciful God, who abounds in steadfast love, and blots out transgressions for his name's sake (Num. 14:18; Pss. 32:2; 103:3; 130:4; Isa. 43:25; Rom. 3:24; 4:6; 8:33; 2 Cor. 5:19). He himself paved a way in Christ to distribute this benefit, so that Christ, too, possessed the power to forgive sins (Matt. 9:2–6; John 5:22, 27), and himself sent the Holy Spirit to apply this benefit to the hearts of his children (John 14:26; Rom. 8:15–16; 1 Cor. 6:11). In the past, Reformed theologians put it as follows: The Father justifies effectively; the Son, meritoriously; the Holy Spirit, applicationally. And to complete the picture at once, let us add: faith apprehends, the sacraments seal, and works declare.[103]

But if the salvation of humans originates in a free and gracious act of God, it is certainly of the utmost importance to know of what this act consists, in other

103. B. de Moor, *Comm. theol.*, IV, 562.

words, what justification means. At this point it is already quite clear that in itself it cannot consist in anything other than a judgment, in our terms, a changed disposition and mood toward us. For when people are legitimately angry with another person, the former cannot begin a sincere and intimate relationship with the latter unless they start by putting aside their anger and again become favorably disposed toward the other. And so it is also with the Lord our God. In Christ he loved the world and reconciled it to himself, not counting their sins against them (John 3:16; 2 Cor. 5:19). Although his wrath was revealed from heaven against all ungodliness and wickedness of humans, yet in the gospel God brought to light a righteousness apart from the law (Rom. 1:17–18; 3:20ff.). This righteousness, therefore, is not opposed to his grace, but includes it as it were and paves the way for it. It brings out that God, though according to the law he had to condemn us, yet in Christ has had different thoughts about us, generously forgives all our sins without charging us with anything, and accords to us divine compassion and fatherly sympathy in place of wrath and punishment. Justification, therefore, is not an ethical but a juridical (forensic) act; nor can it be anything other than that because all evidence of favor presupposes favor, and every benefit of grace presupposes grace. Rome, indeed, asserts the contrary. But in doing so, it reverses the true order. It makes God's grace dependent on human conduct and, along with all other nomistic schools of thought, builds religion on a foundation of morality. To the degree that it nevertheless tries to explain good works in terms of a prevenient and infused grace, it contradicts itself and finds itself compelled to again trace the gift of grace to a free disposition of God that is in no way motivated by the human situation but has its basis solely in his good pleasure.

Furthermore, the ethical view of justification is directly contradicted by Scripture. The Hebrew הִצְדִּיק (hiṣdîq) denotes the act of a judge by which he declares a person innocent and is the antonym of הִרְשִׁיעַ (hiršîaʿ), to condemn (Deut. 25:1–2; Job 32:2; 33:32). It is so used of God (Exod. 23:7; 1 Kings 8:32; 2 Chron. 6:23; Isa. 50:8). In the Old Testament the word does not yet serve to express the forgiveness of sins. This is indicated by, or in any case implied in, the following words: to deliver (Pss. 39:8; 51:14), not to impute (Ps. 32:2), to forget and not remember (Isa. 43:25; Jer. 31:34), to cast behind one's back (Isa. 38:17), to blot out (Ps. 51:1, 9; Isa. 43:25), to forgive (Exod. 34:9; Ps. 32:1). In general the Greek word δικαιουν (dikaioun) means to deem right and fair; to judge what is right; it can therefore be used both in an unfavorable sense (to judge the wicked, that is, to punish) and a favorable sense (to do justice to the righteous, recognize the righteous as such). In the New Testament, under the influence of the Old, it acquired a consistently juridical and favorable sense. This is how it is used in general (Matt. 11:19), where Wisdom—in a juridical sense, of course, not in an ethical sense—is justified with respect to (ἀπο, apo) its children; similarly in Luke 7:29, where the tax collectors "justify" (acknowledge the justice of) God, and further Matt. 12:37; Luke 10:29; 16:15; 18:14. Also in the writings of Paul, the forensic meaning is certain. In Rom. 3:4 the word cannot have an ethical meaning because God is the subject, who is justified in his words. It alternates, moreover, with "to be reckoned as righteousness" (4:3, 5), and is opposed to the words "to judge" (κρινειν, *krinein*), "to bring a charge against" (ἐγκαλειν, *enkalein*), and "to condemn" (κατακρινειν, *katakrinein*; 8:33–34), just as δικαιωμα (*dikaiōma*, justification) is the opposite of κατακριμα (*katakrima*, condemnation, 5:16). It means, upon juridical examination, to acquit someone, to declare someone righteous (δικαιον καθισταναι, *dikaion kathistanai*; 5:19).[104]

The word הִצְדִּיק (*hiṣdîq*), δικαιουν (*dikaioun*), "to justify," can, to be sure, have an ethical meaning. The church fathers repeatedly employ it in that sense.[105] In Luther and Melanchthon and in the older symbols of the Lutheran Church, the word "to be justified" (*justificari*) is used in two ways as "to be pronounced or declared just" and "out of unrighteous people righteous people are made or regenerated."[106] Some scholars have mistakenly inferred from this that the Lutheran Reformation originally viewed justification not in a juridical but in an ethical sense and regarded faith as "righteousness itself" (*ipsa justitia*). On the other hand, neither is the assertion of the Formula of Concord[107] correct to the effect that "regeneration" in the Apology Confession is the same as "justification." In the early days, the opposition between Rome and the Reformation in the locus of justification was not formulated in terms of "ethical" versus "juridical," but in terms of justification by works (love) versus justification by faith, on the basis of our own works or on the basis of the righteousness of Christ accepted in faith. However, this justification on the basis of Christ's righteousness accepted by faith alone, which from the beginning was viewed also by Luther and Melanchthon and in the oldest Lutheran symbols as a declaration of righteousness, was not formally distinguished from but rather treated as synonymous with the regeneration of persons, meaning that they were comforted, lifted up, renewed, and made pleasing to God by that same faith. This is also what the Formula of Concord again recognizes when it says: "For when the human being is justified through faith (which the Holy Spirit alone bestows), it is truly a rebirth, because a child of wrath becomes a child of God and is therefore brought from death to life."[108]

104. See previous discussion above, 205 (#472). The manner in which Roman Catholic theology interprets these verses can be seen in Scheeben-Atzberger, *Handbuch*, IV, 1, 28ff.; B. Bartmann, *St. Paulus und St. Jakobus über die Rechtfertigung* (Freiburg i.B.: Herder, 1897), 67ff.

105. J. C. Suicerus, *Thesaurus ecclesiasticus* (Amsterdam: J. H. Wetsten, 1682), s.v. δικαιουν.

106. See above, 197 (#470).

107. Joseph T. Müller, *Die symbolischen Bücher*, 528, 613; ed. note: This claim is found in "Epitome," art. 3, par. 8 (Kolb and Wengert, 495–96) and Formula of Concord, art. 3, par. 18 (Kolb and Wengert, 565).

108. Joseph T. Müller, *Die symbolischen Bücher*, 614 (ed. note: Kolb and Wengert, 565); H. Heppe, *Dogmatik des deutschen Protestantismus im sechzehnten Jahrhundert*, II, 274ff.; J. Köstlin, *The Theology of Luther in Its Historical Development and Inner Harmony*, trans. Charles E. Hay, 2 vols. (Philadelphia: Lutheran Publication Society, 1897), II, 286; A. Ritschl, *The Christian Doctrine of Justification and Reconciliation*, trans. H. R. Mackintosh and A. B. Macaulay (Clifton, NJ: Reference Book Publishers, 1966), 590–91; F. A. B. Nitzsch, *Lehrbuch der evangelischen Dogmatik*, 3rd ed. prepared by H. Stephan (Tübingen: J. C. B. Mohr, 1912), 583; W. Walther, *Rechtfertigung oder religiöses Erlebnis* (Leipzig, 1904).

The Reformed also sometimes stated that the word "justification" could have a broader sense and should be understood in that sense in Isa. 53:11; Dan. 12:3; 1 Cor. 6:11; Titus 3:7; and Rev. 22:11.[109] Others, however, held to the more narrow meaning of justification in those same texts.[110] Indeed, the word as such allows us to understand by it the entire work of redemption. Just as the work of re-creation (*herschepping*) can in its totality be called a rebirth (*wedergeboorte*), so it is also from beginning to end a justification, a restoration of the *state* and the *condition* of the fallen world and humankind in relation to God and to itself.

But although this sense of the word is not impossible, and there is as such also no objection to the belief that Scripture sometimes uses the word in the sense of sanctification or at least includes this meaning, exegetically this is not probable. Isaiah 53:11 says that "through his knowledge" (i.e., the knowledge of himself or his knowledge) the servant of the Lord will make many righteous. The juridical meaning is not only possible here ["make many to be accounted righteous," RSV], but becomes probable by the addition: "and he shall bear their iniquities." Similarly, in Dan. 12:3 it is said of the leaders and teachers of the people of God that they will make many righteous; that is, by their righteousness, their fidelity to the law, they will be an example to many who will follow them and so be counted among the righteous. In 1 Cor. 6:11, the juridical meaning of δικαιουν (*dikaioun*) is almost universally recognized today. There Paul reminds the Corinthians that they, who were formerly unrighteous (ἀδικοι, *adikoi*), were washed, sanctified, and justified. As is evident from the first term, Paul is here thinking of baptism; although the three terms do not indicate that the Corinthians received these benefits successively, one after the other in time, it is evident from the thrice-repeated ἀλλα (*alla*, but) that they are arranged climactically. *Then*, in baptism, they were not only, negatively, washed from the sins of their earlier walk of life and, positively, sanctified, but they have also been transferred to an entirely different state, the state of the righteous, by a judicial judgment of God. All those benefits then become theirs in the name of the Lord Jesus "and in the Spirit of our God." Also these final words refer to justification, which has its objective basis in Christ and is realized, in the Spirit, in the life of believers.[111] In Titus 3:7 there is absolutely no reason to depart from the common juridical meaning of *dikaioun*. In Rev. 22:11, in light of the parallel forms, the reading δικαιωθητω (*dikaiōthētō*) deserves preference and means that those who are righteous, by acting righteous, will all the more be

109. A. Thysius, in *Synopsis purioris theologiae*, disp. 33, 3; Curaeus regarded sanctification as the other part of justification; see H. Heppe, *Dogmatik des deutschen Protestantismus im sechzehnten Jahrhundert*, II, 312.

110. H. Witsius, *The Oeconomy of the Covenants between God and Man*, 3 vols. (London, 1763; 2nd ed., rev. and corrected, 1775), III, 8, 6ff.; P. van Mastricht, *Theologia*, VI, 6, 19; B. de Moor, *Comm. theol.*, IV, 550; J. Owen, *De rechtvaardiging uit het geloof door de toerekening van Christus gerechtigheid*, trans. M. van Werkhoven (Amsterdam: Martinus de Bruyn, 1779), 140; ed. note: Owen's original 1677 work was reprinted as *Justification by Faith* (Grand Rapids: Sovereign Grace, 1959), 117ff.

111. J. Gloël, *Der Heilige Geist in der Heilsverkündigung des Paulus* (Halle: M. Niemeyer, 1888), 149ff.; P. Gennrich, "Studien zur paulinischen Heilsordnung," *Theologische Studien und Kritiken* 71 (1898): 402ff.

recognized as righteous. Thus any stringent evidence that the word δικαιουν is ever used in an ethical sense in Scripture is lacking. But even if this were the case at times, when the reference is to the justification of sinners before God, it always still has a juridical meaning. Nor is the meaning of the Latin word *justificare* and the English word *to justify* inconsistent with this, for the composition with *facere* (to make) no more confers an ethical meaning on the word than it does on the words *glorificare* (to make glorious) and *magnificare* (to make great).

FAITH IS NECESSARY BUT NO GROUND

[473] Now God says in his law (Deut. 25:1) that the righteous must be acquitted and the unrighteous condemned, and everyone's conscience and sense of justice agrees with this. Even God acts according to this rule: he by no means clears the guilty, nor does he condemn the innocent (Exod. 20:5ff., 34:7; Num. 14:18). "One who justifies the wicked and one who condemns the righteous are both alike an abomination to the Lord" (Prov. 17:15; cf. Exod. 23:7; Prov. 24:24; Isa. 5:23). Yet, seemingly in flat opposition to this and contrary to what he himself has said (Rom. 1:18; 2:13), Paul says that God justifies the ungodly (4:5). For humans have no righteousness in themselves on the basis of which they could be acquitted by God. Those who think in a Pelagian way and find the ground for acquittal in faith, that is, in the good disposition, virtues, and good works of humans, and mark them as perfect since they carry the warrant of perfection in themselves, or are counted as perfect by God for Christ's sake, are at all points in conflict with Scripture and the Christian confession. For Scripture testifies that by the works of the law no "flesh" can or will be justified (Isa. 64:6–7; Rom. 3:19–20; 8:7; Eph. 2:2; and so forth). The works accomplished after justification by faith cannot be considered for justification, because then the order of redemption would be reversed and justification would be made dependent on sanctification, and also because those good works are still always imperfect and polluted by sin, and not in keeping with the full requirement of the divine law (Matt. 22:37; Gal. 3:10; James 2:10). God, being faithful and true, cannot view as perfect that which is not perfect. As the righteous and holy One, God cannot give up the demands of the law nor content himself with a semirighteousness, which is basically no righteousness at all. Scripture, accordingly, sets the person's own righteousness and the righteousness of faith or the righteousness of God in contrast to each other (Rom. 10:3; Phil. 3:9); they are mutually exclusive as "works" and "faith" (Rom. 3:28; Gal. 2:16), as "reward" and "grace" (Rom. 4:4; 11:6). Hence, since according to the law God condemns, and has to condemn us on account of our sin, it has pleased him to disclose his righteousness, that is, his judiciary, and in this connection also his acquitting righteousness, in another way, that is, apart from the law and the works of the law, solely through the gospel. God, that is, put forward Christ as a means or sacrifice of atonement, thus showing himself to be righteous and at the same time able to justify or acquit those who have faith

in Jesus (3:21–26).[112] Christ's sacrifice, accordingly, provided the ground for his acquittal of those who, though of themselves ungodly, nevertheless have faith in Jesus. In this disclosure of acquitting righteousness, the person of Christ with his sacrifice and faith in his name occupy a pivotal place. The two are inseparably bound up with each other: the righteousness of God has been revealed in Christ by his being put forward as a sacrifice of atonement by his blood, but he is that δια πιστεως (*dia pisteōs*, through faith; 3:25), and people are justified freely, out of grace, through the redemption that is in Christ Jesus (3:24). In a word, the righteousness of God is the righteousness of God through faith in Jesus Christ (3:22). But what is the place occupied by each of these two in God's righteousness? Is Christ or is faith, or is a combination of these two, the ground, "the material or meritorious cause," for his act of acquittal? Aside from those who modernize Paul, view faith as a good disposition that is completely separate from Christ and his sacrifice, and have God accept the will for the deed, only two approaches are possible. The first is that of Roman Catholics, Remonstrants, rationalists, mystics, as well as numerous modern Protestants, who, though sharply diverging among themselves, have in common the fact that, while linking faith in some fashion with the person of Christ, they nevertheless locate the righteousness on the basis of which God acquits the sinner, in whole or in part, in the human subject. Granted that righteousness may be imperfect, but God nevertheless counts it as perfect, either for Christ's sake or because it is a form of obedience to God's will expressed in the gospel and makes the human agent acceptable to God, or because it is perfect in principle and carries within itself the warrant of future perfection.

But this view does not stand up in the face of the clear pronouncements of Scripture. For, in the first place, the righteousness of God in terms of which he acquits believers is objectively revealed in the gospel, apart from the works of the law and before faith (Rom. 1:17; 3:21), as is also the reconciliation that God brought about in Christ between himself and the world (2 Cor. 5:19). For God has put Christ forward as a propitiatory sacrifice (ἱλαστηριον, *hilastērion*; Rom. 3:25), and this Christ was handed over to death for our trespasses (4:25), died for us (5:6–11), became a curse for us (Gal. 3:13), was made to be sin (2 Cor. 5:21), and was thus raised for our justification (Rom. 4:25), because we were or had to be justified in him. He, therefore, is our righteousness (1 Cor. 1:30), and our righteousness is not based on works but is from God (Phil. 3:9), a gift of his grace (Rom. 3:24; 5:15–17). We are justified through the redemption that is in Christ Jesus (3:24), by his blood (5:9), in Christ (Gal. 2:16). In Rom. 5:12ff. Paul asserts that between Christ and Adam there is a kind of parallelism. On the basis of one trespass all humanity is condemned and subjected to death; similarly [but in the opposite direction], the gift of God, that is, righteousness in Christ, became a δικαιωμα, that is, a verdict of acquittal, for many (5:16). One δικαιωμα (*dikaiōma*, that is, the verdict of acquittal pronounced upon Christ in his resurrection; 4:25)

---

112. See above, 185 (#468).

leads for all to justification and life, that is, the act of justification that carries life with it (5:18). By the obedience of one person the many are treated as righteous (5:19). Alongside the righteousness that God granted in Christ and on the basis of which he justified Christ as mediator of the covenant for all his own in his resurrection, there is no room for a justification consisting in faith or love. If there were, the latter would nullify the former.

In the second place, faith is never presented as the ground for justification. Righteousness, or justification, is ἐκ πιστεως (*ek pisteōs*, through faith) or δια πιστεως (*dia pisteōs*, through faith) or πιστει (*pistei*, by faith; Rom. 1:17; 3:22, 26, 28, 30; Gal. 2:16; 3:8, 24; Phil. 3:9; and so forth) but never δια πιστιν (*dia pistin*, on account of faith). We do read in Phil. 3:9 that Paul possessed "a righteousness that is through faith in Christ, the righteousness from God that is based on faith," but this righteousness is clearly "through faith" and "from God." He only says that he possessed God's righteousness for himself on the basis of faith. Faith never occurs as righteousness itself or as a part of it; on the contrary, it is from faith precisely because it is according to grace. Grace and faith are not opposed to each other; but faith and works, the righteousness that is of faith and the righteousness that is of works, are [opposed to each other] (Rom. 3:20–28; 4:4–6, 13–14; 9:32; 10:5–6; Gal. 2:16; 3:11–12, 23, 25; 5:4–5; Eph. 2:8–9). Faith does not justify by its own essence or act because it itself is righteousness, but by its content, because it is faith in Christ, who is our righteousness. If faith justified on account of itself, the object of that faith (that is, Christ) would totally lose its value. But the faith that justifies is precisely the faith that has Christ as its object and content. Therefore, if righteousness came through the law, and if faith were a work that had merit and value as such and made a person acceptable to God, then Christ died for nothing (Gal. 2:21). In justification faith is so far from being regarded as a ground that Paul can say that God justifies the ungodly (Rom. 4:5). Even when his doctrine elicits the accusation that it leads to indifference and wickedness, he never defends himself by saying that faith is in whole or in part the ground of justification (3:5–8; 6:1). Instead, he affirms that there is no condemnation for those who are in Christ, inasmuch as Christ died and was raised for them (8:33–34).

In the third place, since faith is therefore not a work, but a relinquishment of all work, an unqualified trust in God who gives life to the dead (4:17), who raised Christ from the dead (4:24), who in Christ gave "a righteousness from God" (δικαιοσυνη ἐκ θεου: Phil. 3:9; Rom. 10:3–11; 1 Cor. 1:30), the expression that "faith was accounted as righteousness" cannot mean that faith itself was accepted by God as a work of righteousness in place of or alongside "the righteousness of God in Christ." The word λογιζεσθαι (*logizesthai*) can certainly mean "to hold or consider a person for what he or she is" (1 Cor. 4:1; 2 Cor. 12:6). However, it can also have the sense of "to credit to a person something one does not personally possess." Thus the sins of those who believe are not counted against them although they do have them (Rom. 4:8; 2 Cor. 5:19; cf. 2 Tim. 4:16); and thus they are counted against Christ, although he was without sin (Isa. 53:4–6; Matt. 20:28; Rom. 3:25; 8:3; 2 Cor. 5:21; Gal. 3:13; 1 Tim. 2:6). Similarly, to those who believe, a righteousness is imputed that they do not have (Rom. 4:5), and for that reason that act of imputation is a gift (κατα χαριν, *kata charin*, according to grace; 4:4), an act of crediting someone with righteousness apart from works (4:6). The phrase "to reckon faith as righteousness" is an abbreviated way of saying that God in faith imputes his righteousness—the righteousness granted in Christ—to persons and on that basis acquits them. This is confirmed by that other expression "the righteous will live by faith." Faith is not actually the principle and source of life, for Christ is life and grants life (Rom. 5:17–18; 6:4ff.; 2 Cor. 4:10–11; Gal. 2:20; Col. 3:3–4; 2 Tim. 1:10; cf. John 1:4; 6:33ff.; 11:25; 1 John 1:2; 5:11; etc.). Those who believe have life precisely because they receive it from Christ. Similarly, those who believe have the righteousness of God (δικαιοσυνη θεου, *dikaiosynē theou*), which God grants them in Christ.

Add to this, finally, that if faith itself is the ground of justification, God is contenting himself with a lesser righteousness than he demands in his law. In that case the gospel does not confirm the law, as Rom. 3:31 says, but nullifies it. God then relinquishes his own righteousness and denies himself. Or he accounts faith as something it is not, as a complete and sufficient righteousness, and so fails to do justice to his truthfulness. The charge lodged by the proponents of infused righteousness against imputed righteousness—that God regards certain people as something they are not—returns upon their own heads: they have God count something as righteousness which it is not. In addition, they deprive believers of consolation. If our faith—a faith that is often little and weak and hidden under an overlay of doubt and fear, and that according to the proponents of infused righteousness can be lost altogether—if that faith is the ground for our justification, the Christian life is a life of continual fear and uncertainty. Instead of being fixed on Christ, the eye of faith is then consistently turned inward to oneself. A truly Christian life lived in the service of God becomes impossible, for, before one can truly speak of good works, one's dread before God as Judge has to be transmuted into the consciousness of his fatherly love.

OBJECTIONS TO IMPUTATION

[474] Still, the objection that is raised against imputed righteousness has to be considered seriously. Bellarmine[113] developed this objection along the following lines: if the righteousness of Christ is only imputed to us and therefore remains outside of us, it cannot be the essential form in which we are justified before God. God's judgment, certainly, corresponds to truth. He cannot pronounce righteous a person who is not righteous. As long as the righteousness of Christ is only imputed and remains outside of a person, that person is not righteous and can therefore

---

113. R. Bellarmine, "De justif.," in *Controversiis*, II, c. 7.

not be declared righteous. People will say: but sinners are clothed by faith with the righteousness of Christ! Still, though that be the case, if someone appears in a dual form, an extrinsic and an intrinsic form, that person will be named not according to the first but according to the second form. Let an Ethiopian put on a white garment; he nevertheless remains a black man and is called thus, even if he is white in terms of his extrinsic form. Indeed, there is a stronger analogy. Christ, too, can be viewed in two ways (forms): according to his intrinsic form, he was holy; according to his extrinsic form, he was burdened with our sins. Yet he is not named after the latter form but after the former. Similarly, in justification the righteousness that is imputed cannot be our true form; we can only be justified on the basis of an indwelling righteousness. This objection of Bellarmine returns in the work of all the critics of Reformation doctrine. Everything that is charged against the doctrine of imputed righteousness can be materially summed up in this objection.

To begin with the last analogy: in Scripture Christ is very definitely named and treated according to his extrinsic form. It is even said that he was made to be sin for us and became a curse for us. In a legal or juridical sense Christ can be called a sinner, though to avoid the antinomian misunderstanding this practice is not to be recommended.[114] Thus it is said in Rom. 4:5 and 5:6 that God justifies the ungodly. It is impossible, in this connection, to use stronger language. The opponents of imputed righteousness should not lodge their objection against Luther and Calvin but against Paul. Furthermore, the simile of the Ethiopian is a most unfortunate choice. The two forms in which a human being appears in justification are related very differently than the black skin and the white garment in the case of the Ethiopian. A person is ungodly in an *ethical* sense, but on account of the righteousness of Christ that person becomes righteous in a *juridical* sense. The act of putting on a white garment in no way changes the legal state of the Ethiopian. A more correct image is that of a child who, having been graciously adopted by a wealthy man, can as a future heir be called rich even though at the moment he or she does not yet own a penny. God declares sinners righteous, adopts them as children, promises them Christ and all his benefits; for that reason they are called righteous and will one day gain possession of all the treasures of grace.

The imputation of Christ's righteousness, moreover, is totally misconstrued by Bellarmine and his associates. They picture it as a fiction that is opposed to reality. Imputed righteousness, according to them, is a righteousness that exists only in the imagination, whereas infused righteousness, according to them, is the only real and true righteousness. That picture, however, is completely mistaken. Justification is as real as sanctification, and imputation is no less real than infusion. The only difference is this: in justification righteousness is granted to us in a juridical sense, while in sanctification it becomes ours in an ethical sense. Both are very real and very necessary. The judge must first validate someone's claim

114. H. Bavinck, *Reformed Dogmatics*, III, 399–402 (#390).

to a piece of property before one can take possession of it. This first act is not a fiction or an illusion that cuts no ice and conflicts with reality. On the contrary: needed first is the imputation of righteousness, the recognition of a claim, and only then can the infusion of righteousness follow, the act of taking possession of that to which one is entitled. Now if all this is true in the case of an earthly judge, how much more in the case of the heavenly judge? If God justifies the ungodly, that is not a fiction, a putative imputation, but a present and future reality.[115] The way God administers justice is the way it is and remains forever, and that is also how one day, on the day of judgment, it will be recognized by everyone. For when God justifies the ungodly, he does it on the basis of a righteousness that he himself has effected in Christ. By Christ's sacrifice, against all hostile powers, he has acquired the right to acquit the ungodly, and when he issues a verdict he will also carry it out. After the ungodly have become righteous in a legal sense, they will certainly also become righteous in an ethical sense. For God is he who gives life to the dead and calls into existence the things that do not exist (Rom. 4:17). And a justifying faith consists above all in an unshakable trust in that God of miracles with whom all things are possible.

The righteousness on the basis of which the ungodly are justified, accordingly, is indeed not their own. It is "a righteousness of God" in contrast to their own. Still, it is not an alien and external righteousness in the sense that it does not concern the person so justified and is in no way connected with that person. On the contrary, already in the pact of salvation (*pactum salutis*) Christ positioned himself in relation to his own and assumed their place as mediator. In the state of humiliation he died for their sins and was raised for their justification. A covenant of grace, a mystical union between Christ and his church, existed long before believers were personally incorporated into it—or else Christ could not have made satisfaction for them either. The imputation and donation of Christ and all his benefits by God takes place before the particular persons come to believe. Specifically that imputation and donation takes place in the internal calling, and regeneration is the passive acceptance of this gift of grace. God also had to give that gift in order for us to be able to receive it. The very first gift of grace given us already presupposes the imputation of Christ, for Christ is the only source of grace, the acquisitor and distributor of the Spirit, who is his Spirit, the Spirit of Christ. Accordingly, the righteousness that is the basis for justification is only "alien" in a certain sense. It is the righteousness of the head, but for that reason also of all the members, of the Mediator but therefore also of all the members of the covenant.

JUSTIFICATION IN TIME OR ETERNITY?

[475] Now if it is not faith in its peculiar role and activity but the imputed righteousness of Christ that is the ground of our justification, one all the more

115. P. van Mastricht, *Theologia*, VI, 6, 12.

emphatically faces the question of precisely what role faith plays in justification. For there is no doubt that Scripture posits the closest possible connection between faith and justification. It is faith that is counted as righteousness (Gen. 15:6; Rom. 4:3; Gal. 3:6). The righteous live by faith (Hab. 2:4; Rom. 1:17; Gal. 3:11). The righteousness of God is manifested through faith (Rom. 3:22), and we are justified by faith (3:26; 5:1; 10:4, 10; Gal. 2:16). It is even written that we have believed in Christ Jesus *so that* we might be justified (Gal. 3:6–18, 22–24; also cf. Acts 10:43; 13:39; Heb. 10:38; and so forth). And by faith here Scripture always means saving faith, whose object is the person of Christ together with his benefits, whether promised in the days of the Old Testament as the seed of Abraham (Gal. 3:16), or whether in the fullness of time he appeared in the flesh, died, and was raised again (Rom. 8:34). Most closely and directly connected with this question concerning the role of faith in justification is that other question: whether justification occurs in eternity or in time and, if the latter, whether it occurs in the death or the resurrection of Christ, in the preaching of the gospel, or before or at the same time as, along with or after faith.

The first view was that of the true antinomians, such as Pontiaan van Hattem and his followers.[116] According to them, justification was nothing other than the love of God, which is not concerned about human sin, does not require satisfaction in Christ, and only needs to be made known so that humans may be able to believe it. And that faith consists in nothing other than putting aside the error that God is angry and achieving the insight that God is eternal love. To be sharply distinguished from this pantheistic school of thought is the view of the so-called antineonomians who, in England, Scotland, and the Netherlands, were up in arms against turning the gospel into a new law, against the construal of faith as a ground or cooperating factor in our justification, and, based on this position, sometimes arrived at the confession of an eternal justification. Between these two schools— aside from differences in many other loci (on election, the person and work of Christ, and so forth)—there is also a difference in the doctrine of justification. The former considered eternal justification the sum and substance of Christian doctrine and left no room for a justification in time. It was complete in itself, was fully realized in eternity, and only needed to be made known in time.[117] The latter, however, regarded eternal justification as only the beginning, the principle, and foundation of justification in time. They were led to make this acknowledgment only by the desire to keep the gospel of grace pure and to preserve it from being

116. Ed. note: Pontiaan van Hattem (1645–1706) was a Dutch Reformed minister who was deposed for alleged false teaching in 1683. His theology was highly christocentric, accenting divine love rather than wrath. The atonement in this view was for our benefit, to persuade us of God's love. Subsequently he and his followers were accused of antinomianism. His thought bears marks of a "Spirit philosophy," which serves as a prelude to the Idealism of the nineteenth century. See S. van der Linde, "Pontiaan van Hattem," *Christelijke Encyclopaedie*, 2nd ed., III, 378–79.

117. A. Comrie, *Brief over de regtvaardigmaking des zondaars*, 108ff.; idem, *Verhandeling van eenige eigenschappen des zaligmakenden geloofs*, 2nd ed. (Leiden: Johannes Haesbroek; Amsterdam: Nicolaas Byl, 1744), 64.

in any way mixed with law. The name to them, therefore, was merely a matter of secondary importance.

Thus presented, this doctrine of eternal justification contained a precious truth that can or may or will not be denied by any Reformed person.[118] For election is from eternity: the pact of redemption that includes the atonement of the Mediator for his own is from eternity.[119] All that happens in time, especially the work of salvation, is continually traced in Scripture to God's decree in eternity. Justification could not occur in time were it not securely established in eternity. But this does not yet make it advisable to speak of an eternal justification or of a justification from eternity. For Scripture nowhere models this usage.[120] Reformed theologians almost unanimously opposed it and distinguished between the eternal decree of justification and its execution in time.[121] If one says that justification, as an immanent act in God, necessarily has to be eternal, indeed identical with the God who justifies,[122] one must bear in mind that in that sense everything—including the creation, incarnation, satisfaction, calling, and regeneration—is eternal, and that one who for that reason began to speak of eternal creation, and so forth, would give rise to much misunderstanding.[123] For that matter, the proponents of this view themselves again retrace their steps when, from fear of antinomianism, they vigorously assert that eternal justification is not the only, full, and complete justification but rather tends, as a result of God's providence, to realize itself outwardly, so that then the elect are not "actually" justified but only in God's purpose and decree.[124] Now this interpretation in fact comes down completely to the common distinction between the decree and its execution. The counsel of God and all the decrees summed up in it are undoubtedly eternal "immanent acts," but the works of God *ad extra*—creation, providence, government, redemption, justification, and so forth—are in the nature of the case acts that pass from one condition to another (*actus transientes*). As works they do not belong to the order of reason (*ratio ordinis*) but to the order of execution (*executio ordinis*).[125]

---

118. A. Kuyper, *The Work of the Holy Spirit*, trans. Henri de Vries, 3 vols. (New York: Funk & Wagnalls, 1900), 304ff.; ed. note: Bavinck's reference is to *Het werk van den Heiligen Geest*, 3 vols. in 1 (Amsterdam: Wormser, 1888–89), II, 222ff.

119. Cf. H. Bavinck, *Reformed Dogmatics*, III, 212–16 (#346).

120. Those texts cited in support of this teaching (Rom. 8:30; Eph. 1:3, 5, 9; 2 Tim. 1:9; Rev. 13:8) are not persuasive.

121. Cf. above, 202 (#471).

122. A. Comrie, *Brief over de regtvaardigmaking des zondaars*, 94.

123. Ibid., 92.

124. Ibid., 108ff.; idem, *Verhandeling van eenige eigenschappen des zaligmakenden geloofs*, 64.

125. There are also, in addition, differences among the proponents of eternal justification concerning the order of God's decrees. Comrie places election first, then the covenant of grace, and then justification as one of its fruits (A. Comrie, *Brief over de regtvaardigmaking des zondaars*, 106ff.). However, according to Kuyper, justification also logically precedes the covenant of grace with its mediator (A. Kuyper, *The Work of the Holy Spirit*, 315ff.); ed. note: Bavinck's reference is to *Het werk van den Heiligen Geest*, II, 231ff.

Mention is also often made of a justification in connection with the death or the resurrection of Christ. For this view Scripture offers firmer ground when in 2 Cor. 5:19 it testifies that in Christ God reconciled the world to himself, not counting their trespasses against them, and in Rom. 4:25 that Christ died for our trespasses and was raised for our justification. This last expression can be understood in the sense that Christ was raised because we were justified in and through him, just as he died because we were sinners and he was made to be sin in our place. But it also permits the interpretation that Christ was raised because we, having been reconciled by his death, still had to be justified as well. In that case διά with the accusative is not intended retrospectively but prospectively. In connection with Paul's doctrine of the resurrection of Christ, this latter interpretation deserves preference. Christ was not raised because we were justified by his death, but conversely, Christ had to rise and did rise, because by his suffering and death he had completely atoned for our sins; in other words, he had totally completed the work assigned to him by the Father. For Christ, therefore, his resurrection constituted a divine endorsement of the work he had accomplished, a proof that he was the Son of God (Rom. 1:4), that our sins had been expiated by him (1 Cor. 15:17), and that we will be raised, spiritually and physically, in and by him (Rom. 6:7–10; 8:11; 1 Cor. 15:20–23; 2 Cor. 4:14; Col. 1:18).[126]

Nevertheless, according to 2 Cor. 5:19, there exists an intimate connection between reconciliation in Christ and the nonimputation of the sins of the world, a connection that has been consistently acknowledged in Reformed theology.[127] Even J. van den Honert, a sharp critic of Comrie, frankly admitted that the justification of the elect, given their juridical representation in their guarantor and covenant head, Christ, occurred at this resurrection and therefore long before their birth.[128] Comrie, on his part, conceded that in the resurrection of Christ the elect had not been completely, actually, and personally justified but only potentially, that is, by virtue of the power of Christ's resurrection.

Materially, therefore, there is no difference. Just as when Adam broke the commandment of God, all humankind, objectively speaking, fell and died, so, objectively speaking, in the death and resurrection of Christ, the whole body of his people died, was raised, reconciled, and justified in him. The gospel, accordingly, does not read: God will reconcile himself with you if you, humans, believe, repent, and fulfill his commandments. On the contrary it reads: Since in Christ God was reconciling the world to himself, he did not count their trespasses against them, but charged the apostles with the ministry and word of reconciliation. And the content of this word is this: God *is* reconciled; he *has* forgiven the world its trespasses. Now believe this gospel, people; enter into this reconciliation; on your

---

126. Sanday and Headlam, *A Critical and Exegetical Commentary on the Epistle to the Romans*, 116–18.

127. J. Calvin, *Institutes*, III.xi.11; Calvin often uses the words *regeneratio* and *justificatio* interchangeably.

128. A. Comrie, *Brief over de regtvaardigmaking des zondaars*, 75.

part, too, put aside your hostility; *be* reconciled to God.[129] To that extent justification comes to us objectively in the gospel of Christ as from the time of paradise onward it has been progressively proclaimed to us in ever clearer language. The forgiveness of sins does not come into being by faith and is not acquired by our activities, but it is completely stored up, so to speak, in Christ, precedes faith, and is received and apprehended by faith alone. As the Apostles' Creed has it: I believe in . . . the forgiveness of sins.[130]

Now to maintain this perfect righteousness of Christ and the full riches of the gospel, Reformed theologians, in speaking of actual justification, made a distinction between active and passive justification. Justification might in terms of principle have occurred in the decree and in terms of power in the resurrection of Christ; objectively it might be contained in the gospel and only be fully completed in the final judgment. Yet at each of these points active justification retained its own important place. The application of redemption by the Holy Spirit may in no respect be turned into the acquisition of redemption, for while the Holy Spirit takes everything from Christ, the application in its field of operation is as necessary and of equally great importance as the acquisition. In Scripture, therefore, entry into the kingdom of heaven is made dependent upon regeneration, faith, and repentance. And in this connection the acquisition and the application are so tightly connected that the former cannot be conceived or exist apart from the latter and vice versa. The acquisition necessarily entails the application. Christ, by his suffering and death, also acquired the astonishing blessing that all his benefits, hence also the forgiveness of sins, would be applied personally and individually to all his own. As Savior, Christ not only aims at objective satisfaction but also at the subjective redemption of his own from sin. Now this redemption is fully achieved, not by an objective justification in the divine decree or in the resurrection of Christ, but only when, both in terms of reality and of the consciousness of that reality, human beings are freed from sin and hence regenerated and justified. It is

---

129. Cf. H. Bavinck, *Reformed Dogmatics*, III, 447–52 (#402).

130. Others too—authors who otherwise in many respects oppose the confession of the Reformed churches—have recognized this rich meaning of the gospel of grace, cf. F. W. J. Schelling, *Ausgewählte Werke*, 4 vols. (Darmstadt: Wissenschaftliche Buchgesellschaft, 1968), II, 4, 217ff. Schopenhauer, *The World as Will and Representation*, trans. E. F. J. Payne, 2 vols. (New York: Dover Publications, 1966), I, 406; II, 605–7. According to Th. Erskine, J. M. Campbell, F. D. Maurice, C. Kingsley, and A. P. Stanley, the forgiveness of sins was once-for-all secured by Christ for humankind as a whole and was not first obtained by baptism and repentance but as benefit preceded these events (C. Clemen, "Der gegenwärtige Stand des religiösen Denkens in Großbrittannien," *Theologische Studien und Kritiken* 65 [1892]: 615; for bibliography, 603–715). When Ritschl calls justification a synthetic judgment, he is giving expression to the same idea, but he errs when he considers it to be only a good of the church and in no way relates it to the individual believer (A. Ritschl, *Justification and Reconciliation*, III, 105ff.). Scripture clearly teaches the contrary. See Rom. 3:26; 4:3, 24; 5:19; 8:1, 30; 10:4, 10; 1 Cor. 6:11; Gal. 2:16; Phil. 3:9; etc. Further on Ritschl's doctrine of justification, see G. Vellenga, "De leer der rechtvaardiging bij Ritschl," *Theologische Studiën* 20 (1902): 401–21; and A. S. E. Talma, "De Leer der Rechtvaardiging bij Ritschl," *Theologische Studiën* 21 (1903): 329–49; G. Vellenga, "Ritschl en de H. Schrift," *Theologische Studiën* 22 (1904): 162–73. The views of Dorner et al. have been considered above, 199 (#470).

of *this* justification that Scripture continually speaks, and it is *this* justification, as Comrie acknowledges, that is "the communication and actual impartation."[131]

However, under the influence of Remonstrantism and Saumurian theology, of Pietism and rationalism, there gradually arose a conception of this "actual justification" such that people first had to believe and repent, that in the court of heaven God subsequently sat in judgment and—on the basis of the believer's faith in Christ, one's unity with Christ, and one's "faithful" activities or good works—acquitted that believer; and that on earth, in the court of the individual self, God by his Spirit announced this verdict in the hearts of believers.

ACTIVE AND PASSIVE JUSTIFICATION

Now the distinction between active and passive justification served to escape this nomistic pattern. Active justification already in a sense occurred in the proclamation of the gospel, in the external calling, but it occurs especially in the internal calling when God by his word and Spirit effectually calls sinners, convicts them of sin, drives them out toward Christ, and prompts them to find forgiveness and life in him. Logically this active justification precedes faith. It is, as it were, the effectual proclamation of God's Spirit that one's sins are forgiven, so that persons are persuaded in their hearts, believingly accept—dare to accept and are able to accept—that word of God and receive Christ along with all his benefits. And when these persons, after first, as it were, going out to Christ (the direct act of faith), then (by a reflex act of faith) return to themselves and acknowledge with childlike gratitude that their sins too have been personally forgiven, then, in that moment, the passive justification occurs by which God acquits believers in their conscience and by his Spirit bears witness with their own spirits that they are children of God and heirs of eternal life [cf. Rom. 8:15–17].

Against this distinction nomists on their part advance the objection that in that scenario active justification is not a justification "from" or "by" faith, as Scripture regularly puts it, but "to" faith; and also that, given this view, this faith completely changes its character, inasmuch as it is then no longer an activity in relation to the person of Christ but an intellectual acceptance of the verdict that one's sins have been forgiven. But these objections can be readily refuted. Certainly one must take account of the fact that the above distinction, though it has logical import, has no temporal significance. While there is here a priority of order, it is coupled with simultaneity in time. Concretely the two coincide and always go together.[132] Active justification has a tendency, so to speak, to communicate itself in faith and by faith to bring about its own acceptance. How could a benefit of Christ be to our advantage if it did not enter into our possession? How could a prison inmate benefit from his acquittal if he was not informed of it and the prison doors were

---

131. A. Comrie, *Brief over de regtvaardigmaking des zondaars*, 154.
132. Not only in Heidegger but also in A. Comrie, *Brief over de regtvaardigmaking des zondaars*, 120, 153.

not opened for him? And what advantage would there be for us in a justification in the eternal decree, in the resurrection of Christ, and in the proclamation of the gospel, if God did not personally impart it to us in the internal call by faith? Further, just as the internal call (whose content is the gospel, Christ with all his benefits, hence also the benefit of forgiveness) directly and immediately, without any difference in time, results in regeneration with the gift of habitual faith, so from its very first moment onward, in terms of its principle and essence, this faith includes the assurance, that is, the consciousness that not only others but I too have been granted the forgiveness of sins. This assurance does not, as Rome claims, have to be added by a special revelation, at least if it ever comes at all, but is from the beginning an integral component in saving faith and arises organically from it.[133] Active and passive justification, accordingly, cannot be separated even for a second, and—in Scripture, in the writings of the Reformers, and in practical instruction—are combined in a single term.

Now when Scripture says of this justification in a concrete sense that it occurs *from* and *by* faith, it does not mean to say that it is produced and effected by that faith, for Christ after all is all our righteousness, and all the benefits of the covenant of grace are the fruits of his work and his work alone. They are completely given with his person and need in no way to be augmented by us. Hence the prepositions "from" and "by" only indicate that Christ, along with all his benefits, comes into our personal possession solely by faith. Thus, while the terms used in saying that active justification occurs *with a view to* faith and passive justification *from* and *by* faith may have some value against nomism, in fact the scriptural terms are perfectly adequate if only they are understood scripturally. Justification in the concrete sense is totally a justification *from* and *by* faith because, objectively included in Christ as it is, it can only be personally accepted, appropriated, and enjoyed by faith. But that faith, which thus accepts Christ with all his benefits, is a living faith—not a dead one; it is not a bare intellectual assent to the [judicial] sentence that God has forgiven [our] sins. On the contrary: it appropriates what is presented and offered to it in the Word by the external and internal call, hence also what that word says about our guilt and corruption, about the person and work of Christ, about the activity of the Holy Spirit. In a word, saving faith from the beginning directs our mind's eye and heart away from ourselves and toward God's grace in Christ.

The logical distinction between active and passive justification therefore offers an assortment of advantages that are not to be spurned either from the point of view of our confession or from that of practice.

In the first place, it enables us, against all forms of nomism, to maintain the rich and joyful content of the gospel that God is gracious and abounding in steadfast love and that in Christ he has brought about a complete righteousness in which we can rest both in life and in death and that in no way needs to be augmented or

---

133. A. Comrie, *Brief over de regtvaardigmaking des zondaars*, 170, 178.

increased by us. The forgiveness of all our sins is granted to us freely (for nothing). God on his part, freely and out of unconditional compassion, enters into a relationship with us, admits us by Christ into his fellowship despite all our trespasses, and assures us of his eternal and unchanging favor. Out of pure grace he establishes his covenant with us in order that we would afterward live in accordance with the demand of that covenant. Religion becomes the foundation of morality.

In the second place, this distinction explains that from which the believer derives the freedom and boldness to appropriate this benefit. Against special grace, as the Reformation understood it, Rome advanced the objection that the gospel refers to no one by name, and hence that a person who believed that one's sins were forgiven could not derive this belief from the gospel but only from oneself. And in later times, when the religious vitality of the Reformation declined, many people in fact chose the path of self-examination in order thus to be assured of the genuineness of their faith and salvation. In this way the focus of the believer shifted from the promise of God to the believer's own inner experience. But if we rightly understand the meaning of active justification, the whole subject appears to us in a different light. It is not we who upon self-examination come before the judgment seat of God with the genuineness of our faith in order to receive the forgiveness of sins there; God does not set up a tribunal in heaven for himself in order to listen to different parties and then to make a pronouncement—a conception that, according to Comrie, is all too anthropomorphic and unworthy of God.[134] But he himself comes to us in the gospel with the universal offer of grace and gives to every human the right to accept the forgiveness of sins with a believing heart. The particular appropriation is not added to that universal offer as an alien element from without but is implied in it and is only an individual application of it: the general promise of the gospel includes the particulars.[135] Thus the basis of faith exists outside of us in the promise of God. Those who build upon it will not be put to shame.

In the third place, the above distinction makes it possible for us to regard faith as simultaneously a receptive organ and an active power. If in every respect justification comes after faith, faith becomes a condition, an activity that has to be performed in advance and cannot be purely receptive. But if the righteousness on the basis of which we are justified exists completely outside of us in Christ Jesus, it can naturally be appropriated by us only because we accept it in childlike faith. "The forgiveness of sins is a thing promised for Christ's sake. Therefore it can be accepted only by faith, since a promise can be accepted only on faith."[136] Faith, therefore, is not the material or formal cause of justification; it is not even a condition or instrument (instrumental cause) of justification, for it does not relate to justification as, for example, the eye to seeing or the ear to hearing. Faith is not

---

134. Ibid., 158.
135. See above, 169–70 (#466); I. A. Dorner, *A System of Christian Doctrine*, IV, 211–12.
136. Apology of the Augsburg Confession, art. 4, pars. 40–47 (Kolb and Wengert, 126–27).

a condition on which, and not an instrument or organ by which, we receive this benefit, but the very act of accepting Christ and all his benefits as he by his Word and Spirit offers himself to us, and faith therefore includes the consciousness that he is my Lord and that I am his possession. Faith therefore is not an instrument in the true sense, one that serves as the means by which a person accepts Christ, but is a sure knowledge and firm confidence that the Holy Spirit works in one's heart and by which he [the Spirit] persuades and assures people that, despite all their sins, they share in Christ and all his benefits.[137]

But if this is saving faith, it cannot be a "knowledge of history" or a "bare assent" to certain truths; then it is by its very nature a living and active faith, and it is not in every respect antithetical to all work. It constitutes a contrast to the works of the law in a double sense, that is, in the fact that the latter can neither be the material nor the instrumental cause of justification. It is also antithetical to the works of faith (infused righteousness, obedience, love) the moment these are in even the slightest degree regarded as a ground for justification, as constituting in part or in whole the righteousness on the basis of which God justifies us. For that is Christ and Christ alone. Faith itself is not a ground for justification; neither, therefore, are the works that proceed from it. But faith is not opposed to work if by it one should mean that only a dead, inactive faith can justify us. For the dispute between Rome and the Reformation was not about whether we are justified by an active or an inactive faith, by a living or a dead faith. But the question was, as it was for Paul, whether faith with its works justifies us before God or in our conscience, or whether faith justifies apart from works. Nor is faith opposed to the works of faith insofar as these works, as the fruits of faith, are used by the Holy Spirit to assure believers of the genuineness of their faith and thus of their salvation.[138] In this sense faith itself is even a work (John 6:29), the best work and the principle of all good works. The Reformed therefore also said that, indeed, "it is faith alone that justifies; nevertheless the faith that justifies is not alone,"[139] and spoke, in addition to "the justification of the sinner," also of a "justification of the righteous." In this sense Paul and James are also in agreement. Granted, it is not correct to say that Paul speaks only of the "justification of the sinner" whereas James speaks of the "justification of the righteous." But both deny that the ground of our justification consists in the works of the law, and both acknowledge that faith, that is, living faith, the faith that includes and produces good works, is the means by which the Holy Spirit assures us of our

137. J. Calvin, *Institutes*, III.xi.5; Heidelberg Catechism, Q 61; Belgic Confession, art. 22; Westminster Confession, art. 14; H. Witsius, *Miscellaneorum sacrorum*, 4 vols. (Utrecht: F. Halman, 1692), II, 792, 797ff.; J. Trigland, *Antapologia* (Amsterdam: Joannam Janssonium et al., 1664), 515; P. van Mastricht, *Theologia*, VI, 6, 28; J. Owen, *Justification by Faith* (Grand Rapids: Sovereign Grace, 1959), ch. 3; B. de Moor, *Comm. theol.*, IV, 695; C. Vitringa, *Doctr. christ.*, III, 295.

138. Heidelberg Catechism, Q 86.

139. J. Calvin, "Acta Synodi Tridentinae cum Antidoto," in *Calvini opera*, VII (CR, XXXV), 477 (ed. note: Bavinck cites this as CR, VII, 477); idem, *Institutes*, III.xi.20.

righteousness in Christ. In this connection the only difference is that Paul fights against dead works while James wages a campaign against a dead faith. The faith that justifies is the certainty—produced in our hearts by the Holy Spirit—of our righteousness in Christ. Therefore, not the more passive but the more lively and forceful it is, the more it justifies us. Faith, accordingly, is active along with works and is "brought to completion by the works" (James 2:22).[140]

THE ELEMENTS OF JUSTIFICATION

[476] From the very beginning there was some disagreement in the churches of the Reformation over the elements of justification. The opinion of Osiander that the essential righteousness of Christ's divine nature constituted our righteousness, like that of Stancarus, according to which Christ was our righteousness only in his human nature, found little acceptance.[141] On the other hand, there were in fact several Lutheran and Reformed theologians who denied the active obedience of Christ, limited justification to the forgiveness of sins, and therefore sooner or later had to draw the conclusion that believers, after being delivered by Christ from the guilt and punishment of sin, themselves had to fulfill the law to gain eternal life.[142] Hence, this view too was fairly commonly rejected. Although the forgiveness of sins could be understood—as the part for the whole—for the whole of justification, justification does imply more than forgiveness alone. For Christ not only restored us to the state of Adam as it was before the fall but also fulfilled the law and acquired eternal life for us.[143] But even though it was widely recognized that justification encompassed more than the forgiveness of sins, there was still some disagreement over what that "more" was. As the second part of justification, earlier theologians frequently mention the imputation of the righteousness of Christ.[144] Although this is not exactly incorrect, if by the imputed

140. On Paul and James, see J. Calvin, *Institutes*, III.xvii.11; idem, *Commentary* on James 2; F. Turretin, *De concordia Pauli et Jacobi*, in *De satisfactione Christi disputationes* (Geneva: Tournes, 1666), 384ff.; J. Trigland, *Antapologia*, c. 21; H. Witsius, *The Oeconomy of the Covenants between God and Man*, III, 8, 21–26; C. Vitringa, *Doctr. christ.*, III, 317; J. Buchanan, *The Doctrine of Justification*, 491; J. M. Usteri, "Glaube, Werke, und Rechtfertigung," *Theologische Studien und Kritiken* 62 (1889): 211–56; G. Schwarz, "Jak. 2,14–26 erklärt," *Theologische Studien und Kritiken* 64 (1891): 704–37; *Böhmer, in *Neue kirchliche Zeitschrift* 9 (1898): 251–56; Sanday and Headlam, *A Critical and Exegetical Commentary on the Epistle to the Romans*, 102–6; E. Ménégoz, *Die Rechtfertigungslehre nach Paulus und Jakobus* (Giessen: J. Ricker, 1903; ed. note: Bavinck cites the date as 1902). For Roman Catholic interpretations, see H. Wilders, *De brief van den Apostel Jakobus* (Amsterdam: van Langenhuysen, 1906), 53ff.

141. Cf. H. Bavinck, *Reformed Dogmatics*, III, 345–51 (#378), 361–66 (#381).

142. Ibid., III, 345–51 (#378); A. Ritschl, *Rechtfertigung und Versöhnung*, I, 271; 63ff.; F. A. Loofs, *Dogmengeschichte*.

143. H. Bavinck, *Reformed Dogmatics*, III, 377–80 (#386), 393–98 (#389), 402–6 (#391); F. Gomarus, *Opera theologica omnia* (Amsterdam, 1644), I, 175ff. (on Luke 1:77); F. Turretin, *Institutes of Elenctic Theology*, XVI, 4; B. de Moor, *Comm. theol.*, IV, 681; C. Vitringa, *Doctr. christ.*, III, 284ff.

144. Thus Luther, Chemnitz, Gerhard, Quenstedt, Polanus, Wollebius, Junius, Trelactius, Rivetus, Belgic Confession, art. 23; cf. C. Vitringa, *Doctr. christ.*, III, 311; M. Schneckenburger and E. Güder, *Vergleichende*

righteousness of Christ we mean his active obedience, the two parts here are not accurately coordinated and also draw too sharp a distinction between Christ's passive and his active obedience.[145] It is therefore better to define justification as the imputation of Christ's obedience as a whole, just as in the writings of Paul the word δικαιουν (to justify) alternates with λογιζεσθαι εἰς δικαιοσυνην (*logizesthai eis dikaiosynēn*, to reckon as righteousness).[146] And it is still more accurate to have the two parts of justification consist in the forgiveness of sins and in the attribution of the right to eternal life, since these benefits are based on the imputation of Christ's obedience as a whole.[147] Sometimes the adoption as children[148] was mentioned as the second part of justification but others, such as Peter Martyr,[149] preferred to consider this a fruit of justification.

Now as it concerns the forgiveness of sins, this does not consist, as Rome asserts, in the removal of the pollution of sin, inasmuch as it has justification consist in the "infusion of grace" and has forgiveness depend on sanctification. Nor does it only consist in the removal of the liability to guilt (*reatus culpae*), that is, practically in the deliverance from eternal punishment, while the punishment for venial sins committed after the infusion of grace had to be expiated by believers themselves either here or in purgatory hereafter, since guilt and punishment are correlative concepts.[150] However, the forgiveness that is a part of justification is nothing less than the complete acquittal of all the guilt and punishment of sin, not only of past and present but also of future sins. Some, out of fear of antinomianism, objected to this rich and inclusive view of forgiveness and therefore confined it to acquittal from the guilt of past and repeatedly confessed sins,[151] with an appeal also to Matt. 6:12; 1 John 1:9; 2:1; and so forth. Against antinomianism they thus defended an important truth. It is a fact that believers, after receiving forgiveness, still make many mistakes, even fall into grave sins, and continue to experience numerous vicissitudes in life as punishment. Rome takes this to mean that believers still have to expiate for their venial sins themselves and thereby fails to do justice to the richness and grace of forgiveness. Antinomianism, wanting to

Darstellung des lutherischen und reformirten Lehrbegriffs, 2 vols. (Stuttgart: J. B. Metzler, 1855), I, 233ff., 285–439; A. Ritschl, *Justification and Reconciliation*, 63ff.

145. P. van Mastricht, *Theologia*, VI, 6, 17.

146. Cf. Heidelberg Catechism, Q 60; A. Thysius, in *Synopsis purioris theologiae*, disp. 33, 8.

147. G. Voetius, *Select. disp.*, V, 279ff.; F. Turretin, *Institutes of Elenctic Theology*, XVI, 4.

148. F. Turretin, *Institutes of Elenctic Theology*, XVI, 6; A. Ritschl, *Justification and Reconciliation*, 93; O. Pfleiderer, *Der Paulinismus*, 189; H. J. Holtzmann, *Lehrbuch der neutestamentlichen Theologie*, II, 124.

149. P. Martyr Vermigli, *Loci communes*, ed. R. Massonius (London, 1576), 354; C. Vitringa, *Doctr. christ.*, III, 324; cf. also, J. Orr, *Sidelights on Christian Doctrine* (London: Marshall Bros., 1909), 157; R. S. Candlish, "Adoption," in *DB*, I, 41.

150. Hengstenberg too relapsed to this Roman Catholic position and thus derived his ethical understanding of justification. See I. A. Dorner, *A System of Christian Doctrine*, IV, 202ff., 230, 232.

151. A. Rivetus, *Operum theologicorum*, 3 vols. (Rotterdam: Leers, 1651–60), III, 1099; B. Pictet, *De christelyke God-geleertheid*, 3 vols. ('s Gravenhage: Pieter van Thol, 1728–30), XI.xi.3; W. à Brakel, *The Christian's Reasonable Service*, trans. B. Elshout (Ligonier, PA: Soli Deo Publications, 1992–95), XXXIV, 53–62; LVI, 6, 62, etc.; C. Vitringa, *Doctr. christ.*, III, 313.

honor this grace, infers from it that the sins that believers commit are charged not to the new but to the old "person," and that believers no longer even have to pray for the forgiveness of their sins. Against this all Reformed theologians maintained that while forgiveness removes the "actual liability" of sin, it does not remove its "potential liability"; that is, forgiveness removes the punishment but not the fact that it deserves punishment. The latter remains as long as sin remains. Sin brings with it, especially in the case of believers, a sense of guilt, pain, regret, alienation from God, remorse, and so forth. It takes away one's tranquillity of conscience, the boldness and assurance of faith. That is unavoidable. The nature of sin is such that it necessarily brings with it a sense of guilt and liability to punishment. Even when believers, having long before received forgiveness, later take a deeper look at the corruption of their own heart, they feel a need even to confess the sins of their youth and to trace their guilt even to their conception and birth (Pss. 25:7; 51:4–5).

In that case, confession is not a condition for forgiveness, but those who truly know their sin naturally confess it and in the face of it feel all the greater need for the consolation of forgiveness. For believers, prayer for forgiveness remains a daily necessity. But in that case they do not pray in doubt and despair; they do not pray as though they are no longer children of God and again face eternal damnation; they pray from within the faith as children to the Father who is in heaven, and say Amen to their prayer. And this praying is not just a felt need but also an actual necessity, for justification does not consist in a transcendent acquittal of the sinner on the part of God in the court of heaven but is an act that passes from one sphere to another, is carried by the Holy Spirit into the consciousness of believers, and in this holistic sense bears the name "justification" in Scripture. Thus confession and prayer are the way by which God again arouses and reinforces this conscious- ness of forgiveness. Under the impact of the awareness of sin, this consciousness of forgiveness goes into hiding. Though faith as disposition (*habitus*) remains, it can no longer express itself in deeds. Needed, after our falling into sin, is self- humiliation, confession, the prayer for forgiveness, in order that this faith may again revive and the Spirit of God may again clearly and forcefully bear witness with our spirit that we are children of God.

If we were completely positioned in faith, we would never question the forgive- ness of our sins, our status as children of God, or our future inheritance in Christ, nor would we ever construe any disaster in this life as a punishment from the Lord, but only as fatherly chastisement. But to be perfectly positioned in faith would be possible only if we were also positioned above sin. Inasmuch as this is not the case, and sin always entails doubt, repentance and confession continue to be the means by which God restores us to his fellowship and assures us of his favor. From this, however, it must not be inferred, with Rivetus (et al.), that God over and over and in each case forgives only past sins and sins that have been confessed. The truth is, all the sins of the church have been transferred to Christ, and he has made full payment for them in his blood. In the imputation of Christ to the elect in the pact of redemption, in incarnation, and resurrection, in the external and internal call, he is granted to them with all his benefits. The moment they accept this gift of God, they are also on their part at once put in a new relation to God, one that is unchangeable and unbreakable. While for a time the activities of faith may be lacking, nevertheless the gift of faith by which they are incorporated into Christ and accept all his benefits cannot be lost (John 3:36; Rom. 8:30; Gal. 3:27; Heb. 9:12; 10:12, 14; etc.). Christ, moreover, is not given them for a moment at the beginning, but is and remains their mediator and with his righteousness continually covers all their iniquity.[152] He justifies not only their person but also their works, even though the best of them are still stained with sin.[153] Believers therefore also always have the right and the freedom, after every lapse, to go with confidence to the throne of grace and plead on the basis of the faithfulness of him whose gift of grace and calling are irrevocable (Rom. 11:29; Heb. 4:12; 1 John 1:9). As Luther put it: "Because Christ alone is righteous and possesses righteousness, we are to this very moment always in process of being justified."[154]

This benefit of the forgiveness of sins is so great and so prominent in Scripture that it sometimes seems to be all there is to justification. Linked with it, however, is another benefit that is equally rich and glorious and that, though it cannot be separated from forgiveness, is nevertheless distinct from it. It is the attribution of the right to eternal life, or adoption as children, which Paul mentions immediately after redemption from the law (Gal. 4:5; cf. Dan. 9:24; Acts 26:18; Rev. 1:5–6). Already in the Old Testament God is called the Father of his people and Israel his Son. But in the New Testament this fatherhood and sonship acquires a much deeper meaning. God is now the Father of believers, not in a theocratic but in an ethical sense; and believers are his children, born of him, and therefore by faith in Christ obtain the power to become his children (John 1:12) until one day, when they see him as he is, they will be perfected as his children (1 John 3:2). However, this ethical "sonship," especially as it occurs in John, does not belong in this chapter but must be discussed in connection with regeneration and sanctification.

Paul, on the other hand, speaks of υἱοθεσια (*huiothesia*, adoption) in a juridical sense. Just as on the basis of Christ's righteousness believers receive the forgiveness

152. "Christ does not stop being our mediator after we are reborn": Apology of the Augsburg Confession, art. 4 (Kolb and Wengert, 147). Ed. note: Bavinck's reference is to Joseph T. Müller, *Die symbolischen Bücher der evangelisch-lutherischen Kirche*, 141.

153. Some make this distinction in the doctrine of justification. See J. Vermeer, *De leer der waarheid, die naar de Godzaligheid is: Voorgesteld, bevestigd, en toegepast in 85 oefeningen over de Heidelbergse Catechismus*, 2 vols. (1749; repr., Rijssen: Stuut, 1982), I, 638; W. G. T. Shedd, *Dogmatic Theology*, 3rd ed., 3 vols. (New York: Scribner, 1888–94), II, 547.

154. *Luther's Works*, 25:43n2 (WA 56:265n2; Ficker, I, 45). Westminster Confession, ch. XI, 5. Ed. note: Bavinck cites E. F. K. Müller, *Die Bekenntnisschriften der reformierten Kirche*, 568; cf. further, J. Calvin, *Institutes*, III.xi.11; III.xiv.11–12; III.xx.19; G. Voetius, *Select. disp.*, V, 282; H. Alting, *Theologia problematica nova* (Amsterdam: J. Jansson, 1662), XVII, 10; H. Witsius, *Miscellaneorum sacrorum*, II, 806–10; C. Vitringa, *Doctr. christ.*, III, 313; A. Comrie, *Verhandeling van eenige eigenschappen des zaligmakenden geloofs*, 496; F. Kramer, *De vergeving der zonden* (Kampen: Kok, 1910), 69ff.

of sins, so they are also adopted as children (υἱοι θεου, *huioi theou*; not τεκνα θεου, *tekna theou*). This adoption, which therefore rests on a declaration of God, has been procured by Christ (Gal. 4:5) and becomes ours by faith (3:26). Those who have been pronounced free from the guilt and punishment of sin are thereby simultaneously adopted as children and counted as objects of God's fatherly love. Believers are thereby put in the same position as Christ, who is the firstborn among many brothers (Rom. 8:29). He was the Son of God by nature (8:32) and was so designated at his resurrection (1:3); believers become the "children of God" by adoption. And just as at his resurrection Christ was declared to be Son of God *according to the Spirit of holiness* (1:3), and believers are justified *in the Spirit of our God* (1 Cor. 6:11), so by *the Spirit of adoption* they are made the sons of God (Rom. 8:14–16) and are subsequently assured of their sonship by the same Spirit (Gal. 4:6). As children, then, they are also heirs according to promise (Gal. 3:29; 4:7; Rom. 8:17), and since this inheritance still awaits them in the future, also their adoption in its totality is still an object of hope (Rom. 8:23). Justification, which has its origin in eternity, is realized in the resurrection of Christ and the calling of believers, and is only fully completed when God in the last judgment repeats his sentence of acquittal in the hearing of the whole world and every tongue will have to confess that Christ is Lord, to the glory of God the Father. But though the "legal implications of adoption" are still awaiting them, believers have nevertheless already been adopted as children on earth. By the Spirit as pledge and guarantee, they are sealed for the day of their redemption (2 Cor. 1:22; 5:5; Eph. 1:13–14; 4:30) and kept for their heavenly inheritance as this is kept for them (1 Pet. 1:4–5). By that Spirit, they are continually led (ἀγονται, *agontai*, as in Rom. 8:14; not φερονται, *pherontai*, as in 2 Pet. 1:21), assured of the love that God has for them (Rom. 5:5; cf. 5:8) and of their adoption (8:15–16; Gal. 4:6), and are now already the beneficiaries of peace (Rom. 5:1; Phil. 4:7, 9; 1 Thess. 5:23), joy (Rom. 14:17; 15:13; 1 Thess. 1:6), and eternal life (John 3:16).[155]

Justification is able to produce all of these splendid fruits[156] because along with active justification it includes passive justification, and by the testimony of the Holy Spirit gives believers the consciousness and assurance that their sins are personally forgiven them (*fides specialis*). Those who oppose justification by faith and make it dependent on works cannot accept this assurance. Even Augustine did not feel comfortable accepting this doctrine and wrote: "God, however, has judged it better

155. On adoption, see, inter alia, P. van Mastricht, *Theologia*, VI, c. 7; J. Hoornbeek, *Disputatio theologica practica, de theologiae praxi* (Leiden: Elsevirium, 1659–61), I, 7, 5; H. Witsius, *The Oeconomy of the Covenants between God and Man*, III, 10; J. Gottschick, "Kindschaft Gottes," in *PRE*[3], X, 291–304; R. S. Candlish, "Adoption," in *DB*, I, 40–42.

156. Among the immediate fruits of adoption are reconciliation, the peace of God, a quiet conscience, spiritual joy (which in the early days of the Reformation, in Luther, and in the Augsburg Confession and its Apology were called "regeneration [of consciousness]"; cf. above, 197 [#470]), adoption, liberty, faith, expectation of inheritance, and certainty of salvation; see C. Vitringa, *Doctr. christ.*, III, 321–30; K. A. von Hase, *Hutterus redivivus* (Leipzig: Breitkopf & Härtel, 1855), 287.

to mingle some who will not persevere with the certain number of his saints, so that those for whom security in the temptations of this life is not helpful cannot be secure."[157] Rome, accordingly, established that no one can know with certainty that one has obtained God's grace except by special revelation,[158] and Catholic theologians therefore speak only of a "moral" or "conjectural" certainty.[159] In this connection Möhler said that it "would be extremely uncomfortable for him to be in the presence of a person who was always certain of his salvation," and that he could not resist the thought that "something diabolical was at work in such an attitude."[160] Also the Remonstrants[161] and in a later period the Lutherans[162] opposed the assurance of faith, at least with respect to the future. But the Reformed confessed the truth of election and ascribed to faith a firm assurance of salvation that could be obtained, not indeed from inquisitive inquiries into the secret counsel of God, but by the testimony of the Holy Spirit from the nature and fruits of faith.

For faith, by its very nature, is opposed to all doubt. Certainty is not added to it later from without, but is from the beginning implicit in faith and in due time produced by it, for it is a gift of God, a working of the Holy Spirit. In it he bears witness with our spirits that we are children of God (Rom. 8:16; Gal. 4:6), prompts believers to glory in the fact that nothing can separate them from the love of God in Christ (Rom. 8:38–39) and assures them of their future salvation (Rom. 8:23; 2 Cor. 1:22; Eph. 1:13–14; 4:30). And this assurance of faith gives buoyancy and strength to the Christian life. This is a point that Ritschl has made very clear: Among Catholics, justification is a process of equipping people for a moral purpose; among Protestants, it is the restoration of the religious relationship with God. The latter has to come first before there can even be a truly Christian life. As long as we still stand before God as judge, seek life by conformity to law, and are obsessed with the fear of death, that love is not in us that is the fruit of faith, the fulfillment of the law, the bond of perfection, which casts out all fear. But if in justification we have been granted peace with God, sonship, free and

---

157. Ed. note: Citation is from Augustine, *On the Gift of Perseverance*, in *Four Anti-Pelagian Writings*, trans. J. A. M. and W. J. Collinge, Fathers of the Church 86 (Washington, DC: Catholic University of America Press, 1992), 285. Bavinck cites A. Schweizer, *Die protestantischen Centraldogmen in ihrer Entwicklung innerhalb der reformirten Kirche*, 2 vols. (Zurich: Orell, Fuessli, 1854–56), I, 42; cf. also G. F. Wiggers, *Versuch einer pragmatischen Darstellung des Augustinismus und Pelagianismus* (Berlin: A. Rücker, 1821), 303ff.; J. Gottschick, "Augustins Anschauung von den Erlöserwirkungen Christi," *Zeitschrift für Theologie und Kirche* 11 (1901): 151ff.

158. Council of Trent, VI, c. 9 and can. 13–15; cf. C. Vitringa, *Doctr. christ.*, III, 89, 329.

159. T. Aquinas, *Summa theol.*, I, 2, qu. 112, art. 5; R. Bellarmine, "De justif.," in *Controversiis*, III, c. 2ff.; C. Pesch, *Prael. dogm.*, V, 200–203. P. Lombard, *Sent.*, III, 26, observes: "To hope for anything without merits is said to be not hope but presumption" (*sine meritis aliquid sperare, non spes sed praesuptio dici potest*).

160. J. A. Möhler, *Symbolik* (Regensburg: G. J. Manz, 1871), 197.

161. C. Vitringa, *Doctr. christ.*, III, 91, 330; S. Episcopius, *Opera theologica*, 2 vols. (Amsterdam, 1650–55), II, 194; P. van Limborch, *Theologia christiana* (Amsterdam: Arnhold, 1735), VI, c. 7.

162. J. Köstlin, *The Theology of Luther*, I, 79ff.; II, 507ff.; J. A. Quenstedt, *Theologia*, III, 567; F. A. Philippi, *Kirchliche Glaubenslehre*, IV, 1, 84ff.; M. Schneckenburger and E. Güder, *Vergleichende Darstellung*, I, 233, 258, 265; II, 71; F. J. Stahl, *Die lutherische Kirche und die Union* (Berlin: W. Hertz, 1859), 200ff., 231ff.

certain access to the throne of grace, freedom from the law, and independence from the world,[163] then from that faith will naturally flow a stream of good works. They do not serve to acquire eternal life but are the revelation, seal, and proof of the eternal life that every believer already possesses. Faith that includes the assurance that with God all things are possible, that he gives life to the dead, calls into existence the things that do not exist (Rom. 4:17), and always enables people to do great things. This faith says to a mountain: "Be lifted up and thrown into the sea," and it will be done (Matt. 21:21).[164]

163. On the freedom of the law, see discussion in ch. 8, "The Spirit's Means of Grace: Proclamation."

164. On the certainty of faith, see: J. Calvin, *Institutes*, III.ii.14ff.; idem, "Acta Synodi Tridentinae cum Antidoto," in *Calvini opera*, VII (CR, XXXV), 455; J. Zanchi, *De operum theologicorum*, 8 vols. (Geneva: Samuelis Crispini, 1617), VIII, 227; D. Chamier, *Panstratiae catholicae* (Geneva: Roverianis, 1626), III, 13, c. 8ff.; Canons of Dort, I, 12; V, 9–12; A. Rivetus, *Op. theol.*, III, 470–78; J. Trigland, *Antapologia*, c. 41; Keckermann et alia in H. Heppe, *Die Dogmatik der evangelisch-reformierten Kirche*, ed. E. Bizer (Neukirchen: K. Moers, 1935), 129–31; J. Hoornbeek, *Disputatio theologica practica*, II, 64ff.; C. Love, *Theologia practica*, 4th ed. (Amsterdam: J. H. Boom, 1669), 126ff.; E. Erskine, "De verzekering des geloofs," in *Levensgeschiedenis en werken van Ralph & Ebenezer Erskine* by R. Erskine and E. Erskine (Doesburgh: J. C. van Schenk Brill, 1904), VI; W. Marshall, *The Gospel-Mystery of Sanctification* (Grand Rapids: Zondervan, 1954), 195ff.; C. Vitringa, *Doctr. christ.*, III, 89ff.; 327ff.; L. Ihmels, "Rechtfertigung," in *PRE*³, XVI, 482–83.

4

Sanctification and Perseverance

From the beginning God's plan of redemption included sanctification and glorification. Israel was called to be a holy people; purity of heart and act was the goal, beyond mere proper cultic conformity. Having been forgiven, the disciple of Jesus is called to follow him, deny self, and take up a cross. Jesus uses the idea of reward as an incentive to spur us on to faithfulness; nonetheless, all rewards are a free gift of grace. God's children in Christ, for his sake, are holy; therefore they are commanded to become holy. We are God's workmanship.

The postapostolic church continued to insist on holiness of life but had to contend with the reality of postbaptismal sin, even grave sin. Distinctions began to be made among sins, with less serious ones addressed by legalistic works of penance as the way to forgiveness. A twofold morality—one for ordinary believers and the other for "saints"—contributed to the growth of the eremetic and monastic life. Regular precepts were supplemented by "counsels of perfection," namely, the three virtues of chastity, poverty, and obedience. The latter were deemed especially meritorious, and the church followed a semi-Pelagian line. The good works of the saints add to the "treasury of merit" that the church, through indulgences, can dispense to the faithful.

The Reformation repudiated this entire scheme and took its position on the doctrine of justification by faith alone. Better said, it is through faith that the believer receives Christ the Savior, who justifies the sinner. Though the theologians of the Reformation, especially the Reformed, understood this faith as a living faith rooted in the regenerating work of the Holy Spirit, Reformation sectarians and mystics wanted more. Among Pietists and Methodists, justification had to be followed by sanctification unto perfection, a constant communion with God in love and obedience. Though this emphasis can lead to eccentricities and to ascetic legalism, it has also, to its credit, produced great works of mission and philanthropy.

Christ is our holiness in the same sense in which he is our righteousness. Logically, justification, which clears our guilt, precedes sanctification, which cleanses us from our pollution. Furthermore, justification is a juridical act, completed in an instant, while sanctification is an ethical process that continues throughout our lives. Though justification and sanctification are distinct, they must never be separated. They are united in the power and work of the Holy Spirit. Sanctification as well as justification is a gift, purely of grace.

God's people are holy and called to be holy, set apart by God to be conformed to his Son and to live to his glory. The gift is also a call to active continued repentance on the part of the Christian. We are to die to sin and "present our members as instruments of righteousness." We are grafted into Christ the vine and also told that we must bear fruit. This duality has been misunderstood by nomists and antinomians alike. The former insist that good works are necessary conditions for salvation; the latter are indifferent to repentance, prayer for forgiveness, and good works, since Christ's perfect sacrifice made them superfluous. Lutherans had special difficulty with this tension and engaged in bitter debates over it. Reformed theologians had less difficulty, speaking of good works as necessary not in the sense of merit but in the sense of presence. The presence of good works is a sign of God's work of grace in a believer.

Good works in the strict sense are those done out of true faith, in conformity with God's law, and to his glory. The virtues of the pagans are not good works. It is out of faith working through love that believers seek to do God's will as expressed in the Ten Commandments. Both nomists and antinomians forget that the law of God is rich and full and cannot be reduced to "precept upon precept, line upon line." The commandments must be understood in their augmentation and application by the prophets and by our Lord. In addition, sanctification is both gift and task. The renewing power of the Holy Spirit puts us to work, and in our life of obedience there is also freedom for individual believers to apply the deeper life of love to their own circumstances and contexts. Both the adiaphora and the counsels of perfection must be seen within the unity and universality of the moral law. A legalistic double morality often leads to perfectionism and works righteousness.

Perfectionism is a heresy. It is important to maintain the Reformational understanding of Rom. 7 that sees the tension of sin and grace continuing in the life of the regenerate. We face a clear choice: If our works are imperfect and incomplete, all meritoriousness of our works disappears. This is the Reformation's answer to Rome. On the other hand, all notions of possible perfection in this life require a weakening of the law's demands and adaptation to existing practice. In both cases the organic unity of God's moral law is lost and therefore also the unity of the work of Christ. The Methodist separation of sanctification from justification as an isolated benefit obtained by a special act of faith (the "double cure") misconstrues the life of faith. Faith in Christ is a unitary act that actively appropriates the whole Christ and his benefits. In Christ, we are forgiven and holy; we grow more and more into Christ our head until we reach the fullness of our life in him and see him face to face. That is our reward, itself a gift of grace.

Preservation of the saints is also both gift and task. The New Testament repeatedly admonishes believers to remain faithful, to stay true to their Savior and Lord. At the same time Scripture clearly teaches that the covenant of grace does not depend on human obedience but on God's faithfulness. God has bound himself to the covenant with a solemn oath; he cannot and will not abandon his people. Faith will never disappoint us.

HOLINESS AS GIFT AND REWARD

[477] Since the redemption that God grants and works out in Christ is meant to accomplish complete deliverance from sin and all its consequences, it includes sanctification and glorification from the very beginning, along with justification. In Adam, God already made a covenant with humanity for the purpose of leading it to victory over the serpent's offspring. As soon as God had established his covenant with Abram, he commanded him to walk before him in all blamelessness (Gen. 17:1). He gave his people Israel a law that can be summed up by saying that Israel had to be a priestly kingdom and a holy nation (Exod. 19:6; Lev. 11:44; 19:2; 20:7, 26). This sanctification extended to the people as a whole and applied to all aspects of life—religious and moral, civil, and social—and under the Old Testament dispensation bore a specifically ceremonial character. For it implied that Israel, having been separated from the [heathen] nations and placed in a special relationship with YHWH, would live in this new state in keeping with the laws laid down for it. These laws were in part wholly moral but partly also civil and ceremonial in character.[1]

Soon, however, the people overstressed the value of this cultic purity and boasted of its external privileges. But prophecy opposed this tendency, deflated cultic worship, and highlighted the religious-ethical elements in the law. Obedience, the prophets said, is better than sacrifice (1 Sam. 15:22). The Lord delights in steadfast love and not sacrifice, in the knowledge of God rather than burnt offerings (Hos. 6:6). What does the Lord require of you but to do justice, and to love kindness, and to walk humbly with your God (Mic. 6:8)? And when, on account of its devious heart and moral impotence (Jer. 13:23; 17:9), Israel failed to meet this requirement of the covenant and was deserving of judgment, the prophets announced that God nevertheless would not forget his people and break his covenant with them, but in the last days would establish a new covenant in which he would forgive all their iniquities, form a new heart and a new spirit within them, and cause them to walk in his ways. Just as in the case of the forgiveness of sins, sanctification would be his work and his gift.[2]

1. H. Bavinck, *Reformed Dogmatics*, II, 218–21 (#205).
2. Ibid., III, 493–95 (#410).

But after the exile, Israel increasingly opted for the way of self-righteousness and regarded its relationship with God in such a consistently nomistic way that there was no longer any room for grace, and the whole of life, both that of the individual and that of humankind, was controlled by the scheme of work-and-reward.[3] Jesus, therefore, returned to the spiritual sense of the law as it had been explained by prophecy. The righteousness of the kingdom of heaven was different from that of the Pharisees (Matt. 5:20; Luke 18:10–14). God desires mercy, not sacrifice (Matt. 9:13). The tree must first be sound before it can bear good fruit (7:17). What matters before all else is the purification of the heart, from which flow all sorts of iniquities (5:8; 15:18–19; 23:25). The demand of the law is nothing less than perfection, just as our Father in heaven is perfect (5:48), a perfection that especially includes mercy (Luke 6:36; 10:37); a willingness to forgive (Matt. 6:14; 18:35); love for God with all one's heart, mind, soul, and strength; and love for one's neighbor as for oneself (Mark 12:33). But a person obtains such perfection only by conversion, faith, regeneration (Mark 1:15; John 3:3), leaving everything behind for Jesus's sake, taking up one's cross, and following him (Matt. 5:10ff.; 7:13; 10:32–39; 16:24–26). Jesus himself leads the way for his disciples. He left them his example (11:28–30). He is their Master and Lord (Matt. 10:24; 23:10–11; John 13:16). He laid down his life for his friends (John 15:10ff.). He gave up his soul for them in death (Matt. 20:28; 26:26, 28). By this act, he not only won for them the forgiveness of sins; his self-offering, his death, was also a total consecration to the Father, a perfect act of obedience to his will, a sanctification of himself that by his word they too might be sanctified in the truth (John 17:17, 19).

Although before long he will physically leave them, he nevertheless continues to live in their midst (Matt. 18:20; 28:20), represents himself to them by his Spirit, whom he will send from the Father and who will remain in them (John 14:16–17), and grafts them into himself as branches in the vine (15:1–10). In these ways they are enabled to bear fruits that glorify the name of the Father (15:8), to—by faith—do the works that he did (14:12), to keep his commandments and to remain in his love (14:15, 24; 15:5, 10). Among these good works that the disciples of Jesus have to accomplish, those of self-denial and crossbearing are undoubtedly foremost. With a view to the hatred and persecution that Jesus himself experienced and that would also be experienced by his disciples (15:18–19), things indeed could not be otherwise. Those who wanted to rally to Jesus's side and follow him had to be prepared to give up everything: marriage (Matt. 19:10–12), the love of family members (10:35–36), their wealth (19:21), indeed even their lives (10:39; 16:25).

But positive elements are not lacking either. Jesus himself was not an ascetic but took part in weddings and banquets (Matt. 11:19; John 2:2). Nor did he even condemn all wealth (Matt. 26:7–13). He did not impose on his disciples abstinence

---

3. Ibid., III, 495–99 (#411).

from marriage, food, or drink (6:16; 9:14) but viewed love as the fulfillment of the law (5:43–48; 22:37–40), was not content with the sloganeering of "Lord, Lord" but sought the fulfillment of the will of God (7:21; 12:50), called for conscientious stewardship of the talents entrusted to a person (25:15–30), insisted on faithfulness and caution (wisdom, prudence) in life (7:24; 10:16; 24:15–18), and said he would one day judge everyone according to their works.

He even repeatedly presents the kingdom of heaven and eternal life as a reward (Matt. 19:29; 25:34, 46) that is already stored up in heaven now (5:12; 6:20; 19:21; Luke 6:23) and will be distributed at the resurrection (14:14). And that reward will be paid for all sorts of works: for enduring persecution and disgrace (Matt. 5:10–12), loving one's enemies (5:46), giving alms (6:4), perseverance (10:22), confessing Jesus's name (10:32), service to his disciples (10:41–42), giving up everything and leaving it behind (19:21, 29), working in the vineyard (20:1–16), faithfulness in one's vocation (24:45–47), careful management of the goods entrusted to us (25:14–30), mercy toward the disciples of Jesus (25:32–46), and so forth. There is therefore no doubt whatever that Jesus uses the idea of reward as an incentive to spur his disciples toward faithfulness and perseverance in the pursuit of their calling. But he stated with equal forcefulness that those who do something to show off to others have already lost their reward from God (6:2, 5, 16); that the reward, which consists in the kingdom of God, far exceeds in magnitude all the labor and toil we have given it (5:46; 19:29; 20:1ff.; 25:21–23; Luke 12:33); that righteousness, forgiveness, and eternal life are benefits bestowed by God (Matt. 6:33; 26:28; Mark 10:30; Luke 1:77; 24:47), not to the righteous but to the poor in spirit (Matt. 5:1ff., 9:13; 18:3, 11; and so forth); that believers themselves view and receive these benefits as something that comes to them undeserved (25:37ff.); that they are unprofitable servants who only did what they were supposed to do (Luke 17:10); that the reward depends on God's free disposition (Matt. 20:14–15); that for all participants in the kingdom of heaven and its benefits this reward is the same (20:1–15); and finally that this kingdom is not purely a state of happiness consisting in external blessings but includes being a child of God and having purity of heart (5:8, 9, 45, 48, and so forth).

After Christ completed his work on earth, he was glorified at the right hand of God and by the Spirit communicated himself to his church on the day of Pentecost. Initially the Spirit was mainly the author of extraordinary gifts and powers, but from the beginning he also called into being in the church diverse virtues of faith and patience, comfort and joy. In later apostolic instruction he was increasingly presented as the One who establishes and maintains communion between Christ and his church, and who brings Christ himself to live and work in the church.[4] Believers are people who by the grace of God have not only received the forgiveness of sins but by their baptism have also been brought into fellowship with Christ, who died and rose again (Rom. 6:3–11), have been transferred out of darkness

4. Ibid., III, 499–506 (##412–13).

into the light (Col. 1:13), and now constitute an elect race, a royal priesthood, a holy nation (1 Pet. 2:9). They have received Christ not only as righteousness but also as ἁγιασμος (*hagiasmos*)—not holiness, as ἁγιοτης (*hagiotēs*) or ἁγιωσυνη (*hagiōsynē*), but sanctification—so that what is in view here is not the result but the progression of sanctification or consecration to God (cf. Rom. 6:22; 1 Thess. 4:4; 1 Tim. 2:15; Heb. 12:14). They have been transferred into a state of holiness (1 Thess. 4:4, 7; 2 Thess. 2:13; 1 Pet. 2:9) and were therefore washed and sanctified (1 Cor. 6:11), are temples of the Holy Spirit (1 Cor. 3:16; 6:19; 2 Cor. 6:16), with whom they were marked with a seal for the day of redemption (2 Cor. 1:22; 5:5; Eph. 1:13; 4:30), made new creatures (2 Cor. 5:17; Eph. 2:10), children of God not only by adoption but also by regeneration (John 1:12–13; 1 John 1:3), saints (Rom. 1:7; etc.) and sanctified (Acts 20:32; 26:18; 1 Cor. 1:2; Heb. 2:11; 10:10, 14). Sanctification, accordingly, is in the first place a work of God (John 17:17; 1 Thess. 5:23; Phil. 1:6), more specifically of Christ and his Spirit (Rom. 8:4, 9–11; 1 Cor. 1:30; 6:11; Eph. 5:27; Col. 1:22; 2 Thess. 2:13; Heb. 2:11; 9:14; 10:10, 14, 29; 13:12; 1 Pet. 1:2).

It is precisely for that reason, since God enables them both to will and to work, that believers must work out their own salvation with fear and trembling (Phil. 2:12–13; 2 Pet. 1:10). They must keep their entire spirit, soul, and body blameless in sanctification until the day of the Lord Jesus Christ (Eph. 1:4; Phil. 2:15; 1 Thess. 3:13; 5:23). Though they are in the flesh and continually have to battle against the flesh (1 Cor. 3:1; Gal. 5:17)—Paul himself in fact has not yet attained perfection (Phil. 3:12) and only expects it with the redemption of this "body of death" (Rom. 7:24; 8:23)—still they are called to purify themselves from all pollution of flesh and spirit, to present their bodies as a living sacrifice, holy and acceptable to God (Rom. 12:1; 2 Cor. 7:1), to crucify the flesh with all its passions and desires, to present their members as instruments of righteousness (Rom. 6:13; Gal. 5:24), not to sin but to overcome the world, to keep God's commandments, to purify themselves, and to walk in the light (1 John 1:7; 2:1; 3:6, 9; 5:4; etc.). They sum up all these commandments in the practice of love (Rom. 12:10; 13:8–10; 1 Cor. 13; Eph. 1:4; 5:2; Col. 3:14; 1 Thess. 4:9; 1 John 3:11ff.; 4:8; and so forth) and exclude all merely human precepts and self-willed religion (Matt. 15:9; Col. 2:18, 20–23; 1 Tim. 4:1; 2 Tim. 2:23; Heb. 13:9; Rev. 2:14–15). Though in some circumstances marriage may be inadvisable and undesirable (1 Cor. 7:8; 20ff.), the prohibition to marry and the injunction to abstain from foods is a teaching of those who have departed from the faith (1 Tim. 4:3). For nothing is unclean of itself (Matt. 15:11; Rom. 14:14); every creature of God is good, and nothing is to be rejected if it is received with thanksgiving (1 Tim. 4:4–5); grace does not suspend nature (1 Cor. 7:20–23), and no one ever hates his own body but nourishes and tenderly cares for it, just as Christ does for the church (Eph. 5:29).

Christians are indeed called to follow a simple lifestyle (1 Tim. 2:9; Titus 2:3; 1 Pet. 3:3) and to flee the desires of the world (1 John 2:15–17). While physical training is of some value, the main thing is godliness (1 Tim. 4:7–8) in conjunction with righteousness and self-control (Titus 2:12).

With many compelling reasons believers are urged to live this holy kind of life. They are obligated to this because God has first loved them, has had compassion on them, and has shown his love to them in Christ (Rom. 12:1; 2 Cor. 8:9; 1 John 4:19). They owe it to God because with Christ they have died to sin and been raised to a new life (Rom. 6:3–13; Col. 3:1–2); because they are not under the law but under grace and belong to Christ so as to bear fruit for God (Rom. 6:14; 7:4; Gal. 2:19); because they do not walk according to the flesh but according to the Spirit and are temples of the Holy Spirit (Rom. 8:5; 1 Cor. 6:15ff.); because they are children of light and must walk in the light (Rom. 13:12; Eph. 5:8; 1 John 1:6; etc.). A complete summary of these compelling reasons is impossible because there are so many. Among them, however, the reward of future glory occupies a significant place as well. All the benefits that believers enjoy or will obtain are gifts of the grace of God (Rom. 6:23; 2 Cor. 8:9; Eph. 2:8; etc.), yet everyone is rewarded according to his works (Rom. 2:6–11; 14:12; 1 Cor. 3:8; 2 Cor. 5:10; Gal. 6:5; Rev. 2:23; 20:12). Godliness holds promise for this life and also for the life to come (1 Tim. 4:8). The thought of future glory spurs them on to patience and perseverance (Rom. 8:18; 1 Cor. 15:19; 2 Cor. 4:10, 17; Rev. 2:7, 10–11, 17; etc.). For God rewards those who seek him (Heb. 11:6, 26). He distributes a just penalty for all transgression and disobedience (2:2), but also rewards generosity (1 Tim. 6:19), confidence of faith (Heb. 10:35), self-denial (Heb. 11:26), and the labor of his servants (1 Cor. 3:8, 14; 9:18; Col. 3:24; 2 Tim. 4:8; etc.).

In a few places, there is even mention of a special reward, because—according to 1 Cor. 3:12–15—those who on the foundation "Christ" build a work that endures will receive a reward, but if the work they build is burned up in the fire on the day of judgment, then though they themselves will be saved, they will suffer loss and lose their reward. And in 1 Cor. 9:16–17 Paul says that, because he preached the gospel not of his own free will but on account of a divine commission (necessity was laid on him!), he has not been paid a living. However, he also says that preaching the gospel free of charge and not using the right to accept an income has given him a claim to reward. To a couple of special cases, both passages apply the general idea that God will reward everyone according to one's works. Although salvation is granted to all believers, there will be differences in glory among them, depending on their works (Matt. 10:41; 18:4; 20:16; 25:14ff.). In Scripture, therefore, both in the New and in the Old Testament, there is a close connection between sanctification and glorification. What is sown here is harvested in eternity (Matt. 25:24, 26; 1 Cor. 15:42ff.; 2 Cor. 9:6; Gal. 6:7–8). Without sanctification no one will see God (Matt. 5:8; Heb. 12:14). This law of the kingdom is not nullified by grace but made serviceable to its structure. Believers are God's workmanship, created in Christ Jesus for good works, which God prepared beforehand to be our way of life (Eph. 2:10). As children we are also heirs of God and fellow heirs of Christ (Rom. 8:17). Precisely because, whatever their task, they work with enthusiasm, as serving the Lord and not humans, they also know that they will receive from the Lord the reward of their inheritance, for they serve the Lord Christ (Col. 3:23–24).

RIGORISM AND A DOUBLE MORALITY

[478] The high moral admonitions we encounter in the New Testament are repeated in the postapostolic era. All the Apostolic Fathers and apologists vie with one another in insisting on a holy way of living and a practical Christianity. They put no less stress on life than on doctrine. Any number of virtues are recommended and put into practice, which aroused even the admiration of pagans.[5] Prominent among them were faithfulness in confession, patience in time of oppression, purity in conduct, mercy toward the wretched, and truth and honesty in one's profession. Christians themselves were aware that by these virtues they were distinguishing themselves from the world and called themselves the people of God, the seed of Abraham, the true Israel, the Israel according to the Spirit, the elect, believers, brothers, and saints. But just as already in the time of the apostles all sorts of error and sin occurred in the church, so this evil continued to exist and later even worsened from the second half of the second century onward when the church expanded and was influenced by the surrounding world. At that juncture the church faced a difficult problem. Initially the idea prevailed that members of the church who had been admitted through baptism would not commit grave sins such as idolatry, murder, robbery, theft, fornication, and witchcraft. Since in baptism only sins committed in the past were forgiven, the church, it was believed, could no longer reckon with sins committed subsequently and forgiveness could no longer be obtained for them. Reality, however, soon taught otherwise: cases of a gravely offensive nature definitely did occur. The church then excommunicated members who had committed such sins, in some cases refused to readmit them to membership, and delivered them up to the mercy of God.

Gradually, however, a less rigorous practice emerged, which later led to the Roman Catholic sacrament of penance. Even so, the difficulty of less serious sins committed daily by believers remained. They could not be so grave that the church could take disciplinary measures against them. Still they were sins that required forgiveness. The problem became more and more serious, insofar as the grave sins that called for excommunication were limited in number (apostasy, murder, fornication), and it seemed impossible to solve, inasmuch as the grace of baptism pertained only to sins committed prior to the reception of this sacrament.

Thus, little by little, also under Jewish and Stoic influences, the idea arose that forgiveness for these lighter offenses could only be secured by doing good works, by repentance, confession (private or public), prayer, patience under the chastisements

---

5. Cf. A. von Harnack, *The Mission and Expansion of Christianity*, trans. J. Moffatt, 2 vols. (New York: Harper, 1908), I, 216ff.; II, 98ff.

of God, fasting, alms, and so forth.[6] It was believed that the gospel of grace actually had continuing effect only until baptism. Those who still sinned after receiving baptism fell under the law and had to work out their own salvation. Faith, ever increasingly viewed as "bare assent," led to baptism, but was later replaced by love or good works. Ethics, taking its cue from Cicero, became a theory of duties, like the one Ambrose, for example, wrote for pastors. This nomistic tendency, which construed the gospel as a new law, was significantly reinforced by the authoritarian and hierarchical development that the church experienced. To the degree that the authority of Scripture came to be shouldered by the church and the church could issue injunctions that bound people in their consciences, obedience to the church became the one all-inclusive virtue, and religion as well as morality began increasingly to consist in the observance of the duties imposed by it.

Naturally linking up with this nomism was the emergence of a twofold morality. We already find it in Stoicism in the distinction between "the things pertaining to duty and the things pertaining to virtuous conduct, the morally proper and the morally perfect,"[7] and in the apocryphal book Tobit (12:8), where prayer, fasting, and alms are praised as extraordinary virtues.[8] This distinction soon found its way into the Christian church, where it was favorably received. In the postapostolic period, as in the New Testament, the negative virtues became very prominent. In the Greco-Roman world, there was much from which Christians had to abstain—polytheism, emperor worship, theaters, and so forth—because as a matter of principle they could not participate in them. The situation was such that Christians were more intent on fleeing from the world than on winning it. All this could still have been coupled with principle-based opposition to asceticism, but the practice of life led in another direction. The rigorism that was observed in countless circles outside the Christian church—among Gnostics, Marcionites, Montanists, Jewish and pagan sects—was imitated in their own way by many Christians who envied them.

Men and women who had demonstrated greatness in self-denial and self-sacrifice—not only the apostles but also martyrs and confessors—became admired models. On their gravestones and in their chapels, people began gradually to venerate them with strong devotion. On them was bequeathed the name "saints," which in earlier times was a predicate of all believers. The observance of certain days of fasting and of set times for prayer, abstinence from luxury in food and drink and clothing, abstinence especially from marriage, and avoidance of the world in general, accordingly, from ancient times—in the writings of the Apostolic Fathers and apologists, such as *Shepherd of Hermas*, Ignatius, *Didache*, Justin

---

6. Cf. above, 142 (#460).

7. E. Zeller, *Die Philosophie der Griechen*, 3rd ed., 3 vols. in 5 (Leipzig: Fues's Verlag [L. W. Reisland, 1875]), IV, 264ff. Ed. note: ET: *Outlines of the History of Greek Philosophy* (London: Routledge & Kegan Paul; New York: Humanities Press, 1969).

8. Cf. F. W. Weber, *System der altsynagogalen palästinischen Theologie* (Leipzig: Dörffling & Franke, 1880), 318.

Martyr, Athenagoras, and so forth—were glorified as special Christian virtues.[9] And when in the second and third centuries the secularization of the church increased, many of its members fled and practiced their beliefs outside the church. This is how first the eremitic and later the monastic life began.

Now the distinction between two kinds of morality easily aligned itself with this practice. Hermas already taught that those who abstained from a second marriage gained abundant honor and great glory for themselves from the Lord,[10] and that those who do something good "beyond the Lord's commandment" enjoy greater honor with God than if they only adhered to the commandment.[11] Similarly, commenting on Rom. 3:3, Origen wrote that what Paul recommends in 1 Cor. 7:25 is "a work surpassing the precept." Tertullian translated 1 Cor. 7:25 into Latin with the words: "I do not have a precept [*praeceptum*] of the Lord, but I offer [this] advice [*consilium*]" and thereby introduced the fixed terminology for this distinction. This led to a doctrine that was further developed by Tertullian, as well as by Cyprian, Ambrose, Pelagius, and Augustine, and that, though never formally enacted by the church,[12] nevertheless constitutes an indispensable element and occupies a supremely important place in Catholic doctrine and practice. Gradually, the "counsels" (*consilia*), which surpass the "precepts" (*praecepta*), were construed (in line with the sins prohibited in 1 John 2:16) as the three virtues of chastity (abstention from marriage; Matt. 19:11–12; 1 Cor. 7:7ff.), poverty (Matt. 19:21; 1 Cor. 9:14), and obedience (Matt. 16:24; Luke 14:26ff.), but frequently this trio was expanded and augmented with counsels derived from the Sermon on the Mount (Matt. 5:16, 29–30, 34–37, 39–41, 44; 6:31; 7:1; etc.). The Catholic Church, therefore, besides upholding the duties that apply to everyone, keeps open a place for the free practice of virtue. Alongside the things that are commanded, it assumes the existence of an area for things that are desirable and praiseworthy. Over and above the practical life, it ascribes great value to the ascetic and contemplative life. The counsels furnished in the New Testament as "the law of liberty" have been added to the Old Testament "law of bondage." While the precepts are necessary for people to obtain eternal life, the counsels are free and optional but have the advantage that they enable people to reach this goal "better and more expeditiously."[13]

9. C. E. Hooykaas, *Oud-Christelijke ascese* (Leiden: A. W. Sijthoff, 1905).

10. Shepherd of Hermas, *Mandates* IV, 4.

11. Shepherd of Hermas, *Similitudes* V, 3.

12. The "counsels of perfection" received only incidental support at the Council of Trent (sess. XXIV, can. 10), where celibacy and virginity are pronounced better and more blessed than marriage. Ed. note: This canon is provided in H. Denzinger, ed., *The Sources of Catholic Dogma*, trans. from the 30th ed. by R. J. Deferrari (London and St. Louis: Herder, 1955), #980.

13. T. Aquinas, *Summa theol.*, II, 1, qu. 106–8; R. Bellarmine, "De monachis," in *Controversiis*, II, c. 7, 13; A. Lehmkuhl, *Theologia moralis*, 2 vols. (Freiburg i.B.: Herder, 1898), I, 295ff.; J. E. Pruner, *Lehrbuch der katholische Moraltheologie*, 2nd ed. (Freiburg i.B.: Herder, 1883), 71ff.; A. M. Weiss, *Apologie des Christentums*, 5 vols. in 7 (Freiburg i.B.: Herder, 1894–98). Ed. note: Bavinck erroneously cites this as Weisz. P. Höveler, *Professor A. Harnack und die katholische Ascese* (Düsseldorf: L. Schwann, 1902).

In addition, this nomistic trend, which characterized the thinking of the church, led automatically to the doctrine of the meritoriousness of good works. This doctrine too was already an element in Jewish theology, which casts the whole relationship between God and humanity in the scheme of *do ut des* (I give that you may give). Those who serve God and keep his commandments can claim a right to reward and all the more as these commandments are heavier and harder to keep.[14] This Jewish viewpoint exerted great influence in Christian circles, especially as a result of the apocryphal books included in the Septuagint. In the writings of the Apostolic Fathers, it is already said that the baptized, who received forgiveness for the sins committed earlier, must henceforth acquire eternal life by keeping the commandments of Christ.[15] Tertullian then gave this idea a rigorously juridical character by his theory of merit: if Christians do good works or offer "satisfactions" for sins still being committed, they make God into their debtor ("put God under obligation") and obligate him to reward them according to their merits on the day of judgment.[16] Augustine admittedly held a view that was theologically more sound and ascribed the genesis and progress of good works to divine grace, so that one could not really speak of merits in the case of humans, and God did not reward our merits but his own gifts.[17] The church, however, increasingly followed a semi-Pelagian line of thought and made the meritoriousness of good works an article of faith.

According to Rome, then, this doctrine implies the following propositions:

1. Since the will has indeed been weakened by sin but not deprived of all liberty, the natural human person can, under the guidance and with the help of God's providence, also still do naturally good works.[18]
2. Those who make good use of these natural powers and do what is within themselves to do, can, according to today's most prevalent view, in no way make themselves worthy of infused grace and can prepare themselves for that grace only in the negative sense that they pose no obstacle to its reception.[19]
3. Positive preparation is possible only with the aid of prevenient (actual) grace, which consists in the illumination of the mind and the immediate incitement of the will. But, if with the help of this grace people prepare themselves for infused grace, they make themselves worthy of a merit of congruity.[20]

---

14. H. Bavinck, *Reformed Dogmatics*, III, 496 (#411).

15. *2 Clement* 8; Shepherd of Hermas, *Vision* 1.3.

16. K. H. Wirth, *Der "Verdienst"-Begriff in der christlichen Kirche nach seiner geschichtlichen Entwicklung*, 2 vols. in 1 (Leipzig: Dörffling & Franke, 1892–1901); J. W. Kunze, "Verdienst," in *PRE*³, XX, 502.

17. Cf. J. Kunze, "Verdienst," in *PRE*³, XX, 502–3.

18. T. Aquinas, *Summa theol.*, II, 1, qu. 109, art. 2–5; Council of Trent, sess. VI, c. 1, can. 5–7.

19. Cf. H. Bavinck, *Reformed Dogmatics*, III, 514–17 (#416).

20. T. Aquinas, *Summa theol.*, II, 1 qu. 109, art. 6; Council of Trent, sess. VI, c. 5–6.

4. Those who following that preparation (or as children born in the church, immediately after birth) are baptized receive in this sacrament infused grace, that is, "a quality inhering in the soul" that delivers them from all the guilt and pollution of sin, renews them inwardly, and imparts the divine nature. It serves not only to heal persons but also to elevate them to the supernatural order and was therefore also granted to Adam in the form of the superadded gift.[21]

5. Added to this infused grace are the three theological virtues—faith, hope, and love[22]—which are not human but superhuman, or divine, virtues and therefore differ from human virtues. The latter are by nature present in human beings aptitudinally and inchoately but not according to perfection, and are differentiated as intellectual virtues (wisdom, science, understanding, prudence, art), as moral, or cardinal, virtues (prudence, justice, fortitude, temperance), and have as their object the final and supreme goal, a supernatural end.[23]

6. By this grace, with the theological virtues that follow it, humans are enabled to do supernaturally good works and by it to merit, according to a merit of condignity, an increase of grace, eternal life in the vision of God, and within that setting a lower or higher degree of glory (crown or nimbus). The Council of Trent, accordingly, states that the one justified "by the good works he performs truly merits an increase of grace, eternal life, and in case he dies in grace, the attainment of eternal life itself and also an increase in glory."[24] This merit, therefore, is a merit in the true sense, inasmuch as good works, proceeding from a supernatural principle, correspond to supernatural glory, and humans by their own free will accept and cooperate with the "habitual" and "actual" grace received. But it does not nullify grace since the entire juridical relationship between God and man rests on a free divine decree, and all human merit presupposes the merits of Christ and the gift of grace.[25]

---

21. H. Bavinck, *Reformed Dogmatics*, III, 515–17 (#416).

22. According to the catechism of the Council of Trent, "This grace is accompanied by a most splendid train of all the virtues, which are divinely infused into the soul along with grace" (Roman Catechism, II, ch. 2, qu. 50); ed. note: Bavinck erroneously cites this as qu. 39. The post–Vatican II edition titled *The Roman Catechism* (trans. Robert I. Bradley, SJ, and Eugene Kevane [Boston: Daughters of St. Paul, 1985]) drops the enumeration of the introduction so that chapter 1 begins the section on baptism. In this annotation, the proper reference would be II, ch. 1, qu. 51.

23. On the doctrine of the virtues in Roman Catholic theology, see T. Aquinas, *Summa theol.*, II, 2; *Theologia Wirceburgensis*, 3rd ed., 10 vols. in 5 (Paris: Berche & Tralin, 1880), VIII; P. G. Antoine, *Theologia moralis universa*, 6 vols. in 3 (Venice: Balleoniana, 1792), III; Cesare Manzoni, *Compendium theologiae dogmaticae*, 4 vols. (Turin: Berruti, 1909), III, 348ff.; A. Lehmkuhl, *Theologia moralis*, I, 173ff.; J. E. Pruner, *Lehrbuch der katholische Moraltheologie*, 96ff.

24. Council of Trent, sess. VI, can. 32.

25. Council of Trent, sess. VI, can. 16; T. Aquinas, *Summa theol.*, qu. 114; R. Bellarmine, "De justif.," in *Controversiis*, V, 1–22. In Roman Catholic theology, the doctrine of grace is usually discussed in three parts: actual grace (*gratia actuali*) is considered first; then habitual, or justifying, grace (*gratia habituali [justificante]*);

7. Belonging to the good works that merit such a great reward are especially those works that are not strictly commanded by the law but go beyond it, such as praying and fasting at set times, renouncing earthly possessions, abstaining from marriage, independence, and freedom, devoting oneself to works of mercy and mission, meditation, asceticism, contemplation, self-torture, martyrdom, and so forth. In the eyes of Rome, those who do these things are saints and "religious" par excellence.[26] They do far more than they are obligated to do. They belong to the class of the "perfect,"[27] store up a great treasure of merits in heaven, and by their works of supererogation[28] also acquire merits that, added to the superabundance of Christ's satisfaction, make up the "thesaurus" of the church. And the church, out of the fullness of this treasury, can distribute merits as it sees fit. It can, by means of indulgences, transfer the merits of those who had a surplus to those who are deficient, for all the members of the church are members of one body.[29]

JUSTIFICATION AND ITS DISCONTENTS

[479] The Reformation attacked this entire nomistic system at the roots when it took its position in the confession that sinners are justified by faith alone. By this act, after all, it all at once reversed the entire order of things. Communion with God came about not by human exertion, but solely on the part of God, by a gift of his grace, so that religion was again given its place before morality. If human beings received the forgiveness of sins, righteousness, adoption as children, and eternal life through faith alone, by grace, on account of the merits of Christ, then they did not need to exert themselves to earn all these benefits by good works. They already possessed them in advance as a gift they had accepted by faith. The

---

finally, the fruit of grace or concerning merits (*fructu gratiae seu de merito*): *Theologia Wirceburgensis*, VII, 467ff. M. J. Scheeben and L. Atzberger, *Handbuch der Katholischen Dogmatik*, 4 vols. (Freiburg i.B.: Herder, 1933 [orig. pub., 1874–98]), IV, 1, 92ff.; J. B. Heinrich and G. Konstantine, *Dogmatische Theologie*, 2nd ed., 10 vols. (Mainz: Kirchheim, 1881–1900), VIII, §§473ff.; J. Pohle, *Lehrbuch der Dogmatik*, rev. M. Gierens, 10th ed., 3 vols. (Paderborn: Schöningh, 1931), II, 556ff. (ed. note: Bavinck cites the 4th edition). C. Pesch, *Praelectiones dogmaticae*, 9 vols. (Freiburg i.B.: Herder, 1902–10), V, 209ff.

26. T. Aquinas, *Summa theol.*, II, 2 qu. 81, art. 1, ad 1; and, in addition, qu. 180ff., where Thomas discusses the contemplative life.

27. T. Aquinas, *Summa theol.*, II, 2 qu. 183, art. 4, distinguishes the states of beginning (*incipientes*), progressing (*proficientes*), and perfect (*perfecti*), judging that while absolute perfection is not possible, it is possible to achieve such a high level of perfection that someone "removes from the affections all that is contrary to charity" (see qu. 184, art. 2). According to the Council of Trent, VI, c. 11, can. 18, the righteous can fully keep the law. Cf. also, R. Bellarmine, among others, in C. Vitringa, *Doctrina christiana religionis*, 8 vols. (Leiden: Joannis le Mair, 1761–86), III, 397. Ed. note: To be more accurate to the sense of the main text, this note and the next one are in reverse order from Bavinck's original.

28. The term "supererogation" is derived from Luke 10:35, where the word προσδαπανησης has been translated into Latin by *supererogaveris*.

29. Cf. above, 143ff. (#461).

gratitude and joy that filled their hearts upon receiving all these benefits drove them to do good works before the thought that they had to do them even crossed their mind. For the faith by which they accepted these benefits was a living faith, not a dead one, not a bare agreement with a historical truth, but a personal heartfelt trust in the grace of God in Christ Jesus. In justification that faith of course manifested itself only from its receptive side because in this connection everything depended on the acceptance of the righteousness offered and bestowed in Christ. Yet, from its very inception, and at the same time as it justified, it was also a living, active, and forceful faith that renewed people and poured joy into their hearts. Actually, therefore, it was not faith that justified and sanctified, but it was the one undivided and indivisible Christ who through faith gave himself to believers for righteousness and sanctification, who was imputed and imparted to us on the part of God, and whom we therefore from the beginning possess in that faith as Christ for us and in us. From its very beginning, faith was two things at once: a receptive organ and an active force; a hand that accepts the gift offered but also works outwardly in the service of the will; a bond to invisible things and a victory over the visible world; at once religious and ethical.

In Reformed theology this was realized and upheld even better than in Lutheran theology, for faith, in Reformed theology, arose from regeneration and was accompanied by constant repentance. Accordingly, in doing those good works believers did not strive for extraordinary things in order thus to make their merits and reward greater. Basically, all asceticism is nothing other than self-willed religion. It consists in the accomplishment of a series of counsels that have not been enjoined by God but were instituted by human and ecclesiastical consent. True childlike obedience, the obedience of faith, consists in doing the will of our heavenly Father as it is concisely laid down for us in the Ten Commandments. These commandments confront us with our duties toward God and our neighbor. Alongside the commandments, prayer also occupies a prominent place in the Christian's life of gratitude. Religion and morality, accordingly, remain distinct. In Protestant theology, the discipline of ascetics emerged alongside ethics,[30] and as everywhere else, so also in the Lutheran and Reformed churches the hearts of some tended more in one direction and some in the other. Yet in the first period they were united and did not confront each other as adversaries.

However, when Melanchthon gradually returned to philosophy, he began to treat ethics and politics under the guidance of Aristotle and became the reason why philosophical ethics stood in the way of the emergence of a Christian and theological ethics, why the influence of Christianity was restricted to the interior life of the soul, and why the exterior life of the Christian came to be dualistically detached from it and continued to live out of a natural principle of its own. Calvin proceeded from another principle. In his description of the Christian life, he does

---

30. G. Voetius, *Exercitia pietatis* (Gorichem: Paul Vink, 1664); H. Heppe (*Geschichte des Pietismus und der Mystik in der reformirten Kirche* [Leiden: Brill, 1879], 23ff.) names other works as well.

not lose himself in a wide-ranging exposition of all sorts of virtues and duties but conceives all of life as a unity controlled by one universal rule.[31] Calvin derives this from Rom. 12:1, where the apostle indicates that it is the duty of believers to offer their bodies as living sacrifices, holy and pleasing to God. The entire life of the Christian is dedicated to the worship of God—we are not our own; we are God's. We belong to God completely and always, in life and in death.

Starting from this principle, Calvin then pictures the Christian life as expanding in three directions as he finds them described in Titus 2:12: Christians renouncing irreligion and worldly passions have to live sober, upright, and godly lives in this present world—soberly in relation to ourselves, justly in relation to others, and devoutly in relation to God. In Calvin's description of the Christian life, the negative virtues—self-denial, crossbearing, and meditation on the future life—are strongly emphasized,[32] but the positive virtues are not lacking either.[33] In Calvin's writings and later in the thinking of Reformed believers, these positive virtues were powerfully operative in church and state, in the life of the home and the workplace, but were less influential in science and art. Here humanism retained its hegemony.

From this humanism, accordingly, the Reformation experienced increasingly more vigorous opposition. Following a period of florescence, the history of humanism greatly resembles a process of fragmentation, in which reason emancipated itself from faith, and various areas of life were withdrawn from the dominion of the theology and the influence of Christianity. This process led to the shallow rationalism and moralism of the eighteenth century, in which, while Kant with his moral rigorism and succeeding philosophers with their idealistic systems indeed introduced some uplift, they did so in such a way that the direction of the movement was continued. Philosophical ethics to this day has pushed and still pushes aside theological morality; nowadays it is the former that poses the problems, examines numerous issues, gives guidance to human minds and direction to human life.

No less damage was done to the Reformation from another direction. From its very beginning there were those who accused it of halfhearted conservatism and

31. J. Calvin, *Institutes*, III.vi–x.

32. M. Schulze, *Meditatio futurae vitae* (Leipzig: Dieterich, 1901); idem, *Calvins Jenseits-Christentum in seinem Verhältnisse zu den religiösen Schriften des Erasmus untersucht* (Görlitz: Rudolf Dülfer, 1902). Ed. note: Bavinck incorrectly cites this as Schultze. Cf. H. Bavinck, *Reformed Dogmatics*, III, 522–28 (#419); and above, 201 (#471).

33. See H. Bavinck, "Calvin and Common Grace," *Princeton Theological Review* 7/3 (July 1909): 437–65. Important recent works include M. Weber, "Die protestantische Ethik und der 'Geist' des Kapitalismus," in *Archiv für Sozialwissenschaft und Sozialpolitik* (1905): 1–54; (1906): 1–10; ed. note: ET: *The Protestant Ethic and the Spirit of Capitalism*, trans. T. Parsons (New York: Scribner, 1958). E. Troeltsch, *The Social Teaching of the Christian Churches*, 2 vols. (1931; repr., Louisville: Westminster John Knox, 1992); cf. also, idem, *Protestantisches Christentum und Kirche in der Neuzeit* (Leipzig: B. G. Teubner, 1922); idem, *Die Bedeutung des Protestantismus für die Entstehung der modernen Welt* (Munich and Berlin: R. Oldenbourg, 1906); *idem, "Die Kulturbedeutung des Calvinismus," *Internationole Wochenschrift* 3 (1910): 449ff., 501ff.

were especially uncomfortable with the confession of justification by faith alone. These were the people who still lived from or returned to the mysticism of the Middle Ages, construed a sharp contrast between the internal and the external word, the spirit and the flesh, the church and the world, grace and nature. They viewed regeneration as the infusion of a new substance and described sanctification primarily in negative terms as avoidance of the world. When Protestant churches lapsed into doctrinalism, these mystical Anabaptist ideas resonated with many hearts.

All the sects that arose in Protestant churches more or less proceeded from the idea that the confession of justification by faith was, if not incorrect, at least defective and incomplete and had to be augmented with sanctification. Pietism prescribed a specific method of conversion and then gathered the devout in small sealed-off circles [conventicles] that were "extramundane" and marked by a rigorous but also in many respects narrowly defined moral life.[34] Methodism not only advanced a specific method of conversion but also gradually arrived at a special doctrine of sanctification. John Wesley not only distinguished justification from sanctification but separated the two. Although in a sense the latter is an immediate fruit of the former, in Wesley's opinion, it is nevertheless a special gift of God and of a very different character. Humans can no more do any good works after justification than before. But if God then tells us: "Be pure!" and regenerates and sanctifies us, the root of evil is removed from our hearts, and sin no longer exists. Hence this perfect sanctity is a second gift after justification by faith; it is a second change, but of a very different nature. It constitutes "a real change" whereas that of justification is only "a relative change."[35] It is true that Wesley sometimes also viewed sanctification as a process and that, especially when he became older, no longer saw it as removing all sin, but his deepest conviction nevertheless was that, after justification, complete holiness was at once obtainable by faith, for God wanted it and Christ was mighty and ready to grant it in an instant.[36]

This doctrine of Christian perfection, alongside of that of conversion, occupies such a prominent place in Methodism that it has frequently been called the formal principle, the great, all-controlling idea of Methodism, and the central idea of Christianity. It mainly comes down to the following:

1. The forgiveness of sins, which is received by faith, though an important benefit, is not the only one and has to be followed by a second. Christ, after all, is a complete Savior, who not only delivers us from the guilt and punishment of sin but also from its pollution and power. He accomplishes the first in justification, the second in the new birth, or sanctification.

---

34. H. Bavinck, *Reformed Dogmatics*, III, 535–40 (#422).

35. Ed. note: "Real change" and "relative change," in English, are Bavinck's own terms, though he provides no direct quotation or source.

36. H. Bavinck, *Reformed Dogmatics*, III, 536–40 (#422); R. Southey, *The Life of John Wesley* (London: Hutchinson, 1903), 234–64; F. Loofs, "Methodismus," in *PRE³*, XII, 799.

Among Methodists, there is disagreement over the connection between these two benefits. Some view sanctification as a continuation of the renewal that has already begun in justification. Others completely separate it from justification and regard it as a second benefit, a second change or blessing that has to follow the first and may occur much later. Still others drive this doctrine of sanctification to such extremes that they question, or even flatly deny, the salvation of those who, though they were regenerated and justified, have not yet attained Christian perfection.

2. This sanctification consists in complete deliverance from the pollution and power of sin. On this matter too there is some disagreement. Some assume a complete eradication of sinful corruption; others believe that in this sanctification Christians receive such spiritual power that they can control and suppress every thought of and desire for sin that still spontaneously arises in them. They may then still *have* sin, but they no longer *commit* it. Wesley initially viewed perfection in the strict sense, but later moderated it, saying that it did not include the power "never to think a useless thought nor speak a useless word," for such perfection would "be inconsistent with a corruptible body"; indeed it is compatible "with a thousand nervous disorders."[37] If people wanted to raise the perfection he preached to too great a height, they would in fact run the risk of driving it out of the world altogether.[38]

Nevertheless all of them viewed Christian perfection as "a constant communion with God, which fills the heart with humble love," as perfect love in doctrine and conduct, as a complete submission of our will to the will of God, as the impartation of the whole Savior, as a reception of the Holy Spirit in a special sense, or as the elevation to a higher level of faith.[39] While the preaching of Pearsall Smith in the so-called Oxford-Brighton-Keswick Convention movement was aimed at the conversion of the unconverted, it was aimed with at least the same sense of urgency at the conversion of the [already] justified and regenerate to complete sanctification. He augmented Luther's slogan "being righteous by faith alone" with the following: "as well as being completely holy by faith alone."[40]

---

37. Ed note: The words in quotation marks, in English, are Bavinck's own, though once again he provides no direct quotations or sources.

38. R. Southey, *Life of John Wesley*, 244.

39. Ed note: The words in quotation marks, in English, are Bavinck's own, though once again he provides no direct quotations or sources.

40. Ed. note: Bavinck refers to the so-called Oxford movement, which is a potentially confusing reference since the term is usually applied to the Tractarian renewal movement in nineteenth-century Anglicanism led by Newman, Keble, and Pusey. We have chosen the admittedly awkward term "Oxford-Brighton-Keswick Convention" to make the historical reference clear. Bavinck himself notes the two extended gatherings at Oxford and Brighton in 1874 but fails to note the continuation of the "higher life" tradition at Keswick still to this day. For a full treatment of the background and subsequent history of this movement, see Steven Barabas, *So Great Salvation: The History and Message of the Keswick Convention* (Westwood, NJ: Fleming H. Revell, 1952). The

3. This perfection can be obtained by faith but this faith is then given a special meaning. It is the conviction that God is mighty and willing to grant this complete holiness—which he consistently calls for in the law and brought about in Christ—*now* at this very moment and *here* at this very place, also to *me* personally. He can and will do this already in this life, at home as well as in the open air, now, in the body, as well as at the time of death. What counts is to believe this. The moment a person seizes this faith, the moment they bow completely before God and yield themselves totally and unconditionally to him, God says: "Let it be according to your faith!" and cleanses them from all iniquity. It is of the greatest importance, therefore, to believe in the immediacy and personal character of the gift of the Spirit, for those who are certain that the gift of the Holy Spirit lies ready for them, here and now, in Christ also receive it. Those who believe in me, says Jesus, rivers of living water will flow from their hearts. The Father gives the Spirit to everyone who asks him for it. The apostles imparted the Spirit during the laying on of hands. Whatever we ask for in prayer, believing that we have received it (in an alternate reading), will become ours (Mark 11:24). "Faith is not *only* expectation; there is a faith *that counts the thing that it asks as having been given*."[41]

4. The reception of the Spirit is often accompanied by deep emotions and strong physical tremblings. Sometimes it manifests itself in the distribution of those special charismata that were already bestowed on believers on and after the day of Pentecost and to which especially speaking in tongues (glossolalia) and the gift of healing belong.[42] Methodists sometimes speak of the bestowal of the Spirit observed in their circles as a second day of Pentecost in the church of Christ. The Johannine age of love has come. The great time of peace promised to Christ's church on earth has begun; tremendous events are at hand; the Pentecost of the nations is approaching; throughout the earth a movement toward Christ has begun; the Lord is near and is coming soon. This faith often leads to all sorts of eccentricities, to disdain for one's ordinary earthly occupation, to an elevation of the so-called direct works of the kingdom of God, to a devaluation of the church and confession,

---

Oxford Convention, led by Robert Piersall Smith, met from August 29 to September 7, 1874, and was followed by a gathering in Brighton on May 29, 1875, attended by many clergy and congregants from Germany, Norway, Sweden, Denmark, and the Netherlands. Attempts were made to carry these kinds of meetings into the Netherlands at such locations as Neerbosch, Amsterdam, Zwolle, and so on, though they did not catch on among the Dutch people. See R. P. Smith, *Account of the Union Meeting for the Promotion of Scriptural Holiness, Held at Oxford, Aug. 29 to Sept. 7, 1874* (London: Daldy, Isbitter, 1874); F. Lion Cachet, *Tien dagen te Brighton* (Utrecht: Kemink & Zoon, 1875). A balanced and fair critique is given by Johannes Jüngst, *Amerikanischer Methodismus in Deutschland und Robert Pearsall Smith* (Gotha: F. A. Perthes, 1875); and A. M. Bronsveld, *Uit het hoogd* (Utrecht, 1876).

41. R. A. Torrey, *The Holy Spirit: How to Obtain Him in Personal Experience, How to Retain Him* (Chicago: Bible Institute Colportage Association, 1900–1928), 23.

42. Cf. H. Bavinck, *Reformed Dogmatics*, III, 501–3 (#412).

the offices and sacraments. The fruits of the Spirit are frequently found in abstention from the use of tobacco, wine, beer—not to mention strong liquors—in the avoidance of all adornment and luxury and in wearing a simple, uniform dress. That same faith, however, also frequently enables people to do great works. All active Christianity, as it manifests itself today in the church and in society, in philanthropy and missions, is directly or indirectly due to Methodism.[43]

SANCTIFICATION IS ALSO *IN CHRIST*

[480] To understand the benefit of sanctification correctly, we must proceed from the idea that Christ is our holiness in the same sense in which he is our righteousness. He is a complete and all-sufficient Savior. He does not accomplish his work halfway but saves us really and completely. He does not rest until, after pronouncing his acquittal in our conscience, he has also imparted full holiness and glory to us. By his righteousness, accordingly, he does not just restore us to the state of the just who will go scot-free in the judgment of God, in order then to leave us to ourselves to reform ourselves after God's image and to merit eternal life. But Christ has accomplished everything. He bore for us the guilt and punishment of sin, placed himself under the law to secure eternal life for us, and then arose from the grave to communicate himself to us in all his fullness for both our righteousness and sanctification (1 Cor. 1:30). The holiness that must completely become ours therefore fully awaits us in Christ. Many people still acknowledge that we must be justified by the righteousness that Christ has acquired but believe or at least act in practice as if we must be sanctified by a holiness we bring about ourselves. If that were the case, we would not—contrary to the apostolic witness (Rom. 6:14; Gal. 4:31; 5:1, 13)—live under grace and stand in freedom but continue always to be under the law. Evangelical sanctification, however, is just as distinct from legalistic sanctification as the righteousness that is of faith differs from that which is obtained by works. For it consists in the reality that in Christ God grants us, along with righteousness, also complete holiness, and does not just impute it but also inwardly imparts it by the regenerating and renewing working of the Holy Spirit until we have been fully conformed to the image of his Son.

43. J. L. Nuelsen, "Methodismus in Amerika," in *PRE*³, XIII, 14; all these points on Methodism are based on J. Wesley, *A Plain Account of Christian Perfection* (New York: Methodist Book Concern, 1925). In Germany, this doctrine gained significant entry thanks to the work of Theodor Jellinhaus, *Das völlige gegenwärtigen Heil durch Christum*, 5th ed. (Berlin: Thormann & Goetsch, 1903). It was embraced by many representatives of the so-called *Gemeinshafts-* and *Pfingstbewegung*. See C. F. Arnold, *Gemeinschaft der Heiligen und Heiligungs-Gemeinschaften* (Gr. Lichterfelde, Berlin: E. Runge, 1909); P. Fleisch, *Die moderne Gemeinschaftsbewegung in Deutschland*, 2nd ed. (Leipzig: H. G. Wallmann, 1906); idem, *Die innere Entwicklung der deutschen Gemeinschaftsbewegungen in der Jahren 1906 en 1907* (Leipzig: H. G. Wallmann, 1908); idem, *Zur Geschichte der Heiligungsbewegung* (Leipzig: H. G. Wallmann, 1906); M. Schian, *Die moderne Gemeinschaftsbewegung* (Stuttgart: Greiner & Pfeiffer, 1909); idem, "Die moderne deutsche Erweckungspredigt," *Zeitschrift für Religionspsychologie* 10 (1908): 11.

Justification and sanctification, accordingly, while distinct from each other, are not for a moment separated. They are distinct; those who mix them undermine the religious life, take away the comfort of believers, and subordinate God to humanity. The distinction between the two consists in the fact that in justification the religious relationship of human beings with God is restored, and in sanctification their nature is renewed and cleansed of the impurity of sin. At bottom the distinction rests on the fact that God is both righteous and holy. As the Righteous One, he wants all his creatures to stand in the relation to him in which he put them originally—free from guilt and punishment. As the Holy One, he demands that they will all appear before him pure and unpolluted by sin. The first person, therefore, was created after God's image in righteousness and holiness and needed neither justification nor sanctification, though he had to be obedient to the law to be justified by the works of the law and to receive eternal life (legal justification). But sin has loaded us down with guilt and rendered us impure before God's face. In order, therefore, to be completely freed from sin, we must be freed from guilt and cleansed of its stains. And that is what happens in justification and sanctification. Hence, the two are equally necessary and are proclaimed in Scripture with equal emphasis. Logically justification comes first in this connection (Rom. 8:30; 1 Cor. 1:30), for it is an evangelical kind of justification, an acquittal on the basis of the righteousness of God granted in faith and not on the basis of the works of the law. It is a juridical act, completed in an instant. But sanctification is ethical: it is continued throughout the whole of life and, by the renewing activity of the Holy Spirit, gradually makes the righteousness of Christ our personal ethical possession. Rome's doctrine of grace or "infused righteousness" is not incorrect as such; wrong, only, is that it makes infused righteousness the ground for forgiveness and thus builds religion on the basis of morality. But believers do indeed obtain the righteousness of Christ by infusion. Justification and sanctification, accordingly, grant the same benefits, rather, the entire Christ; they only differ in the manner in which they grant him. In justification Christ is granted to us juridically, in sanctification, ethically; by the former we become the righteousness of God in him; by the latter he himself comes to dwell in us by his Spirit and renews us after his image.

So, though justification and sanctification are distinct in character, it is important that we continue to bear in mind the close connection between the two. Those who separate them undermine the moral life and make grace subservient to sin. In God righteousness and holiness cannot be separated. He totally hates sin, not only when it makes humans guilty but also when it renders them unclean. The acts of God performed in justification and sanctification are inseparably connected. Those whom he justified he also glorified (Rom. 8:30). Justification brings life in its train (5:18). Those who have been justified by God and adopted as his children at once share in his favor and begin immediately to live. Moreover, Christ has not only endured sin and fulfilled the law on behalf of his own, but was able to do this only because he had entered into a covenant relationship with them and was therefore their head and mediator. In him all his own were incorporated; with and in him they themselves died, were buried, raised up, and seated with him in heaven (Rom. 6:2–11; 2 Cor. 5:15; Gal. 2:20; Eph. 2:5–6; Col. 2:12; 3:1; and so forth). Christ is their righteousness (δικαιοσυνη, *dikaiosynē*) but in the same sense also their sanctification (ἁγιασμος, *hagiasmos*; 1 Cor. 1:30; that is, not their holiness [ἁγιοτης, *hagiotēs*; ἁγιωσυνη, *hagiōsynē*], but their sanctification). Christ, that is, by his suffering and death has not only accomplished the righteousness on the basis of which believers can be acquitted by God; he has similarly secured the holiness by which he can consecrate them to God and purify them from the stains of sin (John 17:19). His obedience to the point of death was aimed at redemption in its entire scope (ἀπολυτρωσις, *apolytrōsis*), not only as redemption from the legal power of sin (Rom. 3:24; Eph. 1:7; Col. 1:14) but also as deliverance from its moral domination (Rom. 8:23; 1 Cor. 1:30; Eph. 1:14; 4:30). To that end Christ gives himself to them, not only objectively in redemption, but also imparts himself subjectively in sanctification and unites himself with them in a spiritual and mystical manner.

Lutherans always viewed this mystical union from its anthropological aspect, and in that case it naturally comes into being only after justification and regeneration in an active faith.[44] But the theological approach of the Reformed led to another view. The mystical union starts already in the pact of redemption (*pactum salutis*). The incarnation and satisfaction presuppose that Christ is the head and mediator of the covenant. The covenant is not established after Christ's coming or after the convicting and regenerative activities of the Holy Spirit, but Christ was himself a member of the covenant, and all the activity of the Spirit as the Spirit of Christ occurs within and in terms of the covenant. There is after all no participation in the benefits of Christ apart from communion with his person. The imputation and granting of Christ to his own comes first, and our incorporation into Christ again precedes our acceptance of Christ and his benefits by faith. Heartfelt sorrow over sin, hungering and thirsting after righteousness, taking refuge in Christ, and so forth, are acts and activities that presuppose life and, hence, the mystical union and flow from it.

On the one hand this union of believers with Christ is not a pantheistic mingling of the two, not a "substantial union," as it has been viewed by the mysticism of earlier and later times, nor on the other hand is it mere agreement in disposition, will, and purpose, as rationalism understood it and Ritschl again explained it.[45]

44. M. Schneckenburger and E. Güder, *Vergleichende Darstellung des lutherischen und reformirten Lehrbegriffs*, 2 vols. (Stuttgart: J. B. Metzler, 1855), I, 185–225.

45. A. Ritschl, *Theologie und Metaphysik* (Bonn: A. Marcus, 1881); idem, *The Christian Doctrine of Justification and Reconciliation*, trans. H. R. Mackintosh and A. B. Macaulay (Clifton, NJ: Reference Book Publishers, 1966), III, 109, 584ff.; idem, *Geschichte des Pietismus in der reformierten Kirche,* 3 vols. (Bonn: A. Marcus, 1880), passim; W. Herrmann, *Der Verkehr des Christen mit Gott*, 6th ed. (Stuttgart: Cotta, 1908); J. Gottschick, "Luthers Lehre von der Lebensgemeinschaft des Gläubigen mit Christus," *Zeitschrift für Theologie und Kirche* 8 (1898): 406.

What Scripture tells us of this mystical union goes far beyond moral agreement in will and disposition. It expressly states that Christ lives and dwells in believers (John 14:23; 17:23, 26; Rom. 8:10; 2 Cor. 13:5; Gal. 2:20; Eph. 3:17), and that they exist in him (John 15:1–7; Rom. 8:1; 1 Cor. 1:30; 2 Cor. 5:17; Eph. 1:10ff.). The two are united as branch and vine (John 15), as are head and members (Rom. 12:4; 1 Cor. 12:12; Eph. 1:23; 4:15), husband and wife (1 Cor. 6:16–17; Eph. 5:32), cornerstone and building (1 Cor. 3:11, 16; 6:19; Eph. 2:21; 1 Pet. 2:4–5).[46] This mystical union, however, is not immediate but comes into being by the Holy Spirit. Furthermore, the connectedness between justification and sanctification is also firmly grounded in the Spirit. For the Spirit whom Jesus promised to his disciples and poured out in the church is not only a Spirit of adoption, who assures believers of their status as children, but also the Spirit of renewal and sanctification. This Spirit equipped Christ himself for his work, leading him from his conception to his ascension. By his humiliation Christ was exalted to the right hand of the Father, glorified into life-giving Spirit, the acquisitor and dispenser of the Spirit who is now his Spirit, the Spirit of Christ. By this Spirit he now also shapes and equips his church. The very first gift that believers receive is already communicated to them by the Spirit, who takes everything from Christ (John 16:14). It is he who regenerates them (John 3:5–6, 8; Titus 3:5); gives life to them (Rom. 8:10); incorporates them into fellowship with Christ (1 Cor. 6:15, 17, 19); brings them to faith (2:9ff.; 12:3); washes, sanctifies, and justifies them (6:11; 12:13; Titus 3:5); leads them (Rom. 8:14); pours out God's love into their hearts (5:5); prays in them (8:26); imparts to them an array of virtues (Gal. 5:22–23; Eph. 5:9) and gifts (Rom. 12:6; 1 Cor. 12:4), especially the gift of love (1 Cor. 13); prompts them to live by a new law, the law of the Spirit (Rom. 8:2, 4; 1 Cor. 7:9; Gal. 5:6; 6:2); and renews them in intellect and will, in soul and body (Rom. 6:19; 1 Cor. 2:10; 2 Cor. 5:17; 1 Thess. 5:23). In a word, the Holy Spirit dwells in them and

46. On the mystical union in Reformed thought, apart from Pierre de Bouquin (1510–82), see H. Heppe, *Dogmatik des deutschen Protestantismus im sechzehnten Jahrhundert*, 3 vols. (Gotha: F. A. Perthes, 1857), II, 372; J. Calvin, *Institutes*, III.xi.5; P. Martyr Vermigli, *Loci communes*, ed. R. Massonius (London, 1576), 259; A. Polanus, *Syntagma theologia christiana* (Hanover, 1609; Geneva, 1617), VI, 35; W. Ames, *The Marrow of Theology*, I.26 (pp. 157–60); G. Voetius, *Selectae disputationes theologicae*, 5 vols. (Utrecht, 1648–69), II, 459; P. van Mastricht, *Theoretico-practica theologia* (Utrecht: Appels, 1714), VI, c. 5; H. Witsius, *Miscellaneorum sacrorum*, 4 vols. (Utrecht: F. Halman, 1692), II, 788; C. Vitringa, *Doctr. christ.*, III, 78; A. Comrie, *Stellige en practikale verklaring van den Heidelbergschen catechismus* (Barneveld: Van Horssen, 1976), qu. 20–23; A. Kuyper, *The Work of the Holy Spirit*, trans. H. de Vries (New York: Funk & Wagnalls, 1900), 333ff.; O. Pfleiderer, *Der Paulinismus: Ein Beitrag zur Geschichte der urchristlichen Theologie*, 2nd ed. (Leipzig: O. R. Reisland, 1890), 214ff.; A. Krebs, *De unionis mysticae* (Marburg, 1871); H. Weiss, "Über das Wesen des persönlichen Christenstandes," *Studien und Kritiken* 54 (1881): 377–417; G. A. Deissmann, *Die neutestamentliche Formel "in Christo Jesu"* (Marburg: N. G. Elwert, 1892). Ed note: Pierre de Bouquin was born in France, trained in theology at Bourges, and a prior of a monastery before converting to Protestantism. He served as a professor of theology in Heidelberg from 1557 to 1578, when he moved to Lausanne. He is noted for his polemical writing against Jesuits and against the Lutheran understanding of the Lord's Supper.

they live and walk in the Holy Spirit (Rom. 8:1, 4, 9–11; 1 Cor. 6:19; Gal. 4:6; and so forth).[47]

PASSIVE AND ACTIVE SANCTIFICATION

[481] In this sense sanctification as much as justification is a gift and a work of God, attributed in turn to the Father (John 17:17; 1 Thess. 5:23; Heb. 13:20–21), to the Son as life-giving Spirit (1 Cor. 15:45; Eph. 5:26; Titus 2:14) and particularly also, as we saw a moment ago, to the Holy Spirit (Titus 3:5; 1 Pet. 1:2). In this connection believers are passive; they are sanctified (John 17:19; 1 Cor. 6:11), they died with Christ and were raised with him (Rom. 6:4ff.), they are sanctified in Christ Jesus (1 Cor. 1:2), God's workmanship (Eph. 2:10), creation (2 Cor. 5:17; Gal. 6:15), the work of God (Rom. 14:20); all this is from God (2 Cor. 5:18).

This sanctification consists first of all in the fact that believers are set apart from the world and placed in a special relationship with God. In the Old Testament, "holiness" marks that relationship of God with his people and of the people with God that is described and regulated in the various laws.[48] Also in the New Testament, the term "holy" has retained this sense of a relationship. One reads of a holy city (Matt. 4:5), a holy place (24:15), a holy covenant (Luke 1:72), holy prophets (Luke 1:70), holy ground (Acts 7:33), Holy Scripture (Rom. 1:2), holy sacrifice (Rom. 12:2), and a holy mountain (2 Pet. 1:18). Of Christ we read that, though he was without sin, he sanctified himself, that is, offered himself up in death to God as a holy sacrifice on behalf of his own (John 17:19). Similarly, believers are regularly described as "saints," because by being called (cf. Rom. 1:7; 1 Cor. 1:2: "called to be saints") they stand in a special relationship with God and, taking the place of the old Israel, they are "a chosen race, a royal priesthood, a holy nation, God's own people" (1 Pet. 2:9).

But this relationship is not merely an external one. It was not just external even under the Old Testament dispensation, for it was by virtue of that holiness that God undertook to give Israel his covenant and law, to save or to chastise it, and Israel was obligated "to walk in God's statutes." Now, in the New Testament, the law has been fulfilled in Christ. It therefore no longer regulates the holiness relationship that exists between God and his people. Now Christ has come in the place of the law; in and through him God regulates the relationship between him and his people. Believers are being "sanctified in Christ Jesus" (1 Cor. 1:2); and Jesus sanctifies his people by the Spirit (1 Cor. 6:11), who as such is now called the Holy Spirit and is the prime agent in sanctification. This sanctification

---

47. Cf. H. Bavinck, *Reformed Dogmatics*, III, 504–6 (#413); see above, 87–88 (#445); O. Pfleiderer, *Der Paulinismus*, 225ff.; H. J. Holtzmann, *Lehrbuch der neutestamentlichen Theologie*, 2 vols. (Freiburg i.B. and Leipzig: Mohr, 1897), II, 143ff.

48. H. Bavinck, *Reformed Dogmatics*, II, 216–21 (#205).

certainly does not only consist in the fact—as many people presently picture it[49]—
that Christians have been set apart from the world and appropriated for God in
an external cultic sense, but has profound ethical significance. For, as Scripture
testifies, the Holy Spirit regenerates, purifies, renews (John 3:3; 1 Cor. 6:11;
Titus 3:5). For believers "newness of life" (Rom. 6:4) begins with the indwelling
of the Holy Spirit. This newness of life forms a contrast to their early "walk" in
all sorts of sins and iniquities (1 Cor. 6:10; Eph. 2:1). Now they are new persons
(2 Cor. 5:17; Gal. 6:15; Eph. 2:10; 4:24; Col. 3:10) who live for God and present their members as instruments of righteousness for sanctification (Rom. 6).
The consequence of this relationship with God in Christ by the Holy Spirit is
that believers are freed from all the guilt of sin, but no less from all its pollution.
Consequently, sanctification in the New Testament consists fully in believers
being conformed to the image of the Son (Rom. 8:29; Gal. 4:19). To that extent
sanctification coincides with glorification. The latter does not just start in the
afterlife but is initiated immediately with the calling. "Those whom he called he
also justified, and those whom he justified he also glorified"—in that very same
moment (Rom. 8:30). And this glorification is continued throughout the Christian life (2 Cor. 3:18) until it is completed in Christ's return (1 Cor. 15:49, 51ff.;
Phil. 3:21; Col. 3:4).

Sanctification, however, is not exhausted by what is done for and in believers.
Granted, in the first place it is a work and gift of God (Phil. 1:5; 1 Thess. 5:23), a
process in which humans are passive just as they are in regeneration, of which it
is the continuation. But based on this work of God in humans, it acquires, in the
second place, an active meaning, and people themselves are called and equipped
to sanctify themselves and devote their whole life to God (Rom. 12:1; 2 Cor. 7:1;
1 Thess. 4:3; Heb. 12:14; and so forth). In fact, this active sanctification coincides
with what is called "continued repentance," which, according to the Heidelberg
Catechism, consists in the dying-away of the old self and the coming-to-life of
the new self. But while in repentance it is the negative side of the process that
stands out, in active sanctification it is the positive side that comes to the fore.
People themselves are active in both and can be active because, by regeneration
at the outset and by positive sanctification later on, believers receive the power
of the Holy Spirit to "present all their members as instruments of righteousness."
Scripture always holds on to both facets: God's all-encompassing activity and our
responsibility. Just as in the preaching of the gospel, faith is a gift of God and yet
people are responsible for their attitude toward God (e.g., Rom. 9:1–29 and
9:30–10:21), so here the possession of all the benefits of the covenant (forgiveness,
adoption, life, salvation) is secured before any kind of work, yet over and over and
with great urgency there is an insistence on good works as if those benefits can

---

49. Cf. P. Wernle, *Die Anfänge unserer Religion* (Leipzig: J. C. B. Mohr, 1901), 31, 39, 62; ed note: ET:
The Beginnings of Christianity, trans. G. A. Bienemann, 2 vols. (London: Williams & Norgate; New York:
Putnam, 1903–4).

only be obtained by these works. The kingdom of God is a gift granted by God according to his good pleasure (Matt. 11:26; 16:17; 22:14; 24:22; Luke 10:20; 12:32; 22:29), yet it is also a reward, a treasure in heaven, which has to be aggressively sought and gained by labor in the service of God (Matt. 5:12, 20; 6:20; 19:21; 20:1ff.; and so forth). Believers are branches in the vine who cannot do anything apart from Christ, yet at the same time they are admonished to remain in him, in his word, in his love (John 15). They are a chosen people, and still have to be zealous to confirm their call and election (2 Pet. 1:10). By a single offering of Christ they have been sanctified and perfected (Heb. 10:10, 14). God effects in them that which is good (13:21), yet they must still persevere to the end (3:6, 14; 4:14; 6:11–12). They have put on the new self and must continually clothe themselves with the new self (Eph. 4:24; Col. 3:10). They have crucified the flesh with its desires, and must kill its members who are on earth (Gal. 5:24; Col. 3:10). They are saints and sanctified in Christ Jesus, and must nevertheless become holy in all their conduct (1 Pet. 1:15; 2 Pet. 3:11), pursuing and perfecting their sanctification in the fear of God (2 Cor. 7:1; 1 Thess. 3:13; 4:3), for without it no one will see the Lord (Heb. 12:14).

Many authors have seen a conflict between this all-encompassing activity of God in grace and the self-agency of people maintained alongside of it. They have charged Scripture with self-contradiction and have for themselves sacrificed the one group of pronouncements to the other. On the one hand, it was stated that grace only serves to restore human willpower for good and to put humans themselves to work. Good works, in that case, were definitely necessary for salvation, whether by a necessity of merit (Rome) or by a necessity of causality and effectiveness (Remonstrants).[50] And from the antinomian side it was said objectively that the righteousness and holiness of Christ remained completely external to a person, not only in justification but also in sanctification, so that repentance, conversion, prayer for forgiveness, and good works were totally unnecessary, bore a legalistic character, and failed to do justice to the perfect sacrifice of Christ.[51]

Lutherans tried to avoid both extremes and conducted a long-lasting and vehement debate on the appropriateness or inappropriateness of the proposition "Good works are necessary to salvation." Some defended good works, but others considered them detrimental and went so far as to say that good works are

50. C. Vitringa, *Doctr. christ.*, III, 369–74.

51. Cf. H. Bavinck, *Reformed Dogmatics*, III, 528–31 (#420); and above, 201ff. (#471). To what extent Kohlbrugge himself embraced these antinomian sentiments is extensively and impartially examined by J. H. van Lonkhuijzen, *Hermann Friedrich Kohlbrügge en zijn prediking* (Wageningen: "Vada," 1905), 437–513. Since Kohlbrügge consistently understood sanctification as being placed in the sphere of grace, in the framework of God's glory (see H. Bavinck, *Reformed Dogmatics*, III, 351–56 [#379], 399–402 [#390]), he was unable clearly to distinguish justification and sanctification, change of status and condition. Even when he speaks of an inner sanctification, this always remains an external power outside of and over against the human "I." The human person was and remained ungodly. Here it is also appropriate to be reminded of those who follow Ritschl and consider justification as a "religious experience" (*religiöses Erlebnis*) and relate the joy and peace of this experience to regeneration. See above, 70ff. (#443), 199 (#470).

harmful to and pernicious for salvation. The Formula of Concord condemned both positions and stated only that good works are "signs of eternal salvation," inasmuch as it is God's will and express command that believers should do good works, which the Spirit works in their hearts and which God accepts and rewards for Christ's sake in this life and the life to come.[52]

The Reformed were more moderate in their judgment, regarded the Lutheran debate as a dispute over words, and could not see the big difference between the rejected formula "Good works are necessary to salvation" and another that some Lutherans (like Quenstedt and Buddeus) had approved: "It is impossible to be saved without good works." They had no objection to calling good works necessary to salvation provided this did not imply a "necessity of causality or merit or effectiveness" but implied a necessity of presence of the means and ways to obtain eternal salvation.[53] Voetius even believed that in a sense good works can be called "the cause of eternal life," that is, not a "meritorious" but a "preparatory" and "dispositional" cause.[54]

Speaking along these lines, they undoubtedly had Scripture on their side. For Scripture definitely insists on sanctification, both its passive and active aspects, and proclaims both the one and the other with equal emphasis. It sees no contradiction or conflict between them but rather knits them together as tightly as possible as when it says that, precisely because God works in them both to will and to do, believers must work out their own salvation in fear and trembling (Phil. 2:12–13). They are God's workmanship, created in Christ Jesus for good works, which God has prepared for them to walk in (Eph. 2:10). God and humanity, religion and morality, faith and love, the spiritual and the moral life, praying and working— these are not opposites. Dependence, here, coincides with freedom. Those who are born of God increasingly *become* the children of God and bear his image and likeness, because in principle they already *are* his children. The rule of organic life applies to them: Become what you are! Jesus and the apostles derive the most compelling reasons for spurring them on to a holy life from what believers now already *are* by grace through faith in Christ: Jesus is the vine, his disciples are the branches. Those who remain in him bear much fruit, for without him they can do nothing (John 15:5). Members of the church have died with Christ to sin but are alive to God in him (Rom. 6:11). They are not under the law but under grace, and sin therefore may not have dominion over them (6:14). By the law they have died to the law and belong to Christ in order that they may bear fruit for God (7:4; Gal. 2:19). They are not in the flesh but in the Spirit and must therefore walk according to the Spirit (Rom. 8:5). The night is far gone, the day is near;

---

52. Joseph T. Müller, *Die symbolischen Bücher der evangelisch-lutherischen Kirche*, 8th ed. (Gütersloh: Bertelsmann, 1898), 632ff.; ed. note: This specific reference is to the Formula of Concord, "Solid Declaration," art. 4, "Concerning Good Works," in *The Book of Concord*, ed. Robert Kolb and Timothy J. Wengert (Minneapolis: Fortress, 2000), 574ff.

53. C. Vitringa, *Doctr. christ.*, III, 359, 367ff.

54. G. Voetius, *Select. disp.*, V, 675ff.

the works of darkness must therefore be laid aside, and the armor of light must be put on (13:12). The bodies of believers are members of Christ and temples of the Holy Spirit; hence they must flee the sin of fornication (1 Cor. 6:15). They have been bought at a high price; so then they must glorify God in their bodies and spirits, which belong to God (1 Cor. 6:20). They stand in the freedom with which Christ has made them free; and in Christ, nothing has any power, except faith working through love (Gal. 5:1, 6). About Christ they have heard and through him they have learned that they must put away the old self and put on the new self, which is created according to the likeness of God in true righteousness and holiness (Eph. 4:21ff.). As beloved children, they must be imitators of God (5:1). They must live in love as Christ has loved them (5:2). They are light in the Lord and therefore they must walk as children of light (5:8). In a word: not law but gospel, the salvation granted and received in Christ, is the one mighty motive for a holy walk of life. Whether the apostles address men or women, parents or children, masters or slaves, wives or female servants, authorities or subjects—they admonish them all *in the Lord* (5:22ff.; 6:1ff.; Col. 3:18ff., 1 Pet. 2:13ff.; 3:1ff.). God's firm foundation stands, bearing this inscription: "Let everyone who calls on the name of the Lord turn away from wickedness" (2 Tim. 2:19).

GOOD WORKS

[482] Sanctification manifests itself in good works, which according to the Heidelberg Catechism arise from the principle of a true faith, conform to the law of God, and are done for his glory. They are therefore distinct from the virtues of the pagans and the virtues of all who do not have such saving faith. The Reformed have always fully acknowledged the existence and moral value of such virtues.[55] Since after the fall people have remained human and continue to share in the

55. The Pelagians obliterated the distinction between virtues and good works, between pagan religions and the Christian faith. They believed that the law of nature, the Mosaic law, and the law of Christ were essentially the same. The Romans distinguished natural good works and supernatural good works and judged even fallen humanity capable of the former. But Tertullian (*The Apology*, c. 45–46) and Augustine (*Against Julian*, trans. M. A. Schumacher, vol. 16 of *Writings of St. Augustine* [Washington, DC: Catholic University of America Press, 1984], IV, c. 3, §§17, 25, 33) judged otherwise. Reformed thinkers readily acknowledged the virtues of the pagans and considered them for the most part an example that should shame believers. However, they did not lose sight of the fundamental difference between these virtues and the good works of believers. See J. Calvin, *Institutes*, II.ii.12ff.; II.iii.3ff. (cf. H. Witsius, *Twist des Heeren met zijnen wijngaard* [1699], 5th ed. [Utrecht: Jacob van Poolsum, 1719], 214–50, esp. 234; M. Schneckenburger and E. Güder, *Vergleichende Darstellung*, I, 231; P. Lobstein, *Die Ethik Calvins in ihren Grundzügen entworfen* [Strassburg: C. F. Schmidt, 1877], 6ff.); H. Alting, *Theologia problematica nova* (Amsterdam: J. Jansson, 1662), VIII, 9–10; G. J. Vossius, *Historiae de controversiis, quas Pelagius eiusque reliquiae moverunt, libri septem*, 2nd ed. rev. (Amsterdam: L. & D. Elzevirii, 1655), III, 3; J. Trigland, *Antapologia* (Amsterdam: Joannam Janssonium et al., 1664), c. 17; P. Wittewrongel, *Oeconomia Christiana* (Amsterdam: Marten Jansz. Brant & Abraham van den Burgh, 1661), I, 288–99; F. Turretin, *Institutes of Elenctic Theology*, trans. G. M. Giger, ed. J. T. Dennison, 3 vols. (Phillipsburg, NJ: Presbyterian & Reformed, 1992), X, 5; B. de Moor, *Commentarius . . . theologiae*, 6 vols. (Leiden: J. Hasebroek, 1761–71), IV, 826–29; C. Vitringa, *Doctr. christ.*, III, 353.

blessings of God's common grace, they can inwardly possess many virtues and outwardly do many good deeds that, viewed through human eyes and measured by human standards, are greatly to be appreciated and of great value for human life. But this is not to say that they are good in the eyes of God and correspond to the full spiritual sense of his holy law. To the degree that human beings subject their own thoughts, attitudes, and actions to more precise scrutiny, they are all the more deeply convinced of their sinfulness. Not only Scripture teaches this, but the experience of all ages and the observations of all good judges of human character confirm this witness.[56] The truly spiritually good, the good in the highest sense as it can only exist in the eyes of God, can in the nature of the case be accomplished only by those who know and love God and, moved by that love, keep his commandments, that is, by those who truly believe. After all, for as long as we are on earth and cannot see God face-to-face, faith is the only means of accepting his revelation and of knowing him as he truly is. But, according to the Protestant confession, this faith is not intellectual assent to a historical truth but a practical knowledge of the grace that God has revealed in Christ, a heartfelt trust that he has forgiven all our sins and accepted us as his children. For that reason this faith is not only needed at the beginning in justification, but it must also accompany the Christian throughout one's entire life, and also play a permanent and irreplaceable role in sanctification. In sanctification, too, it is exclusively faith that saves us.

For if righteousness and holiness were through the law, we would have to bring about both by doing good works. But in the gospel they are a gift of God granted us in the person of Christ (John 1:17; 1 Cor. 1:30; Eph. 1:3; Col. 2:3, 9). As Christ with all his benefits can be given us on God's part only through and in the Spirit, so on our part he can only be received and enjoyed by faith. It is by faith that Christ dwells in our hearts (Eph. 3:17), that we live in Christ (Gal. 2:20), that we become children of God (3:26) and obtain the promise of the Spirit (3:14), and that we receive the forgiveness of sins and eternal life (John 3:16; Rom. 4:7). To live by faith is the flip side of the reality that Christ is in us (2 Cor. 13:5; Gal. 2:20). Faith, accordingly, is the one great work Christians have to do in sanctification according to the principles of the gospel (John 6:29); it is the means of sanctification par excellence. Faith is also competent to do this by virtue of its very nature. Having first received, it can now also give. It opens our heart to the grace of God, to communion with Christ, to the power of the Holy Spirit, and thereby enables us to do great things. Faith breaks all self-reliance and fastens on to God's promise. It allows the law to stand in all its grandeur and refuses to lower the moral ideal, but also refrains from any attempt, by observing it, to find life and peace; it seizes upon God's mercy and relies on the righteousness and holiness accomplished in Christ on behalf of humans. It fosters humility, dependence, and trust and grants comfort, peace, and joy through the Holy Spirit; it generates

56. Cf. H. Bavinck, *Reformed Dogmatics*, III, 123 (#327).

gratitude in our hearts for the benefits received and incites us to do good works. It prompts the believer to say with Paul: "I can do all things through Christ who strengthens me" (Phil. 4:13). In a word, the faith that receives the love of God that the Holy Spirit pours out in our hearts (Rom. 5:5) works through love (Gal. 5:6; 1 John 4:19). What is unknown remains unloved, but those who know the name of the Lord put their trust in him (Ps. 4:8).

By faith working through love, therefore, good works are born that have their standard in the will of God as it is concisely expressed in the Ten Commandments. But these Ten Commandments must then be well understood. What Israel, upon receiving the Decalogue, understood of it is one thing, and what God intended with it is another. Again, it makes a difference whether one takes the Ten Commandments in their literal meaning or whether one interprets them in the rich sense God gave to them in the course of his revelation by prophets and psalmists, by Christ and his apostles. It is in this latter sense that they have been understood in the Christian church and were made the foundation of its catechetical instruction and ethics.[57] However, by no means everyone followed the church in that direction. From the days of Paul already there existed an antinomian school of thought that, while considering the law of value for Old Testament believers, denied all validity to it for the life of Christians. According to this school, the law came from a lesser god and belonged to a lower level of functioning. Christians were above it and no longer had anything to do with it. They were no longer under the law but under grace; they walked in freedom and were led only by the impelling force of the Spirit.

This antinomianism occurs not only in the Christian church or in the sphere of religion but also frequently manifests itself in science and philosophy. In our time it achieved its greatest triumph in Friedrich Nietzsche, who advocated the transvaluation of all values, called good evil and evil good, and enthroned moral anarchism. This anarchism in morality, preceded by anarchy of thought and followed by anarchy of action, however, bore such pernicious fruit in practice that it could not be recommended as a universal rule of life.

Usually, therefore, antinomianism restrains and moderates itself: the law was not only of value in the past but remains so also in the present and the future for all those people who cannot elevate themselves to the supreme position of anarchism. Thus it remains in force for the common people who still need discipline and have to be governed by law and authority. But those who are really "in the know" (γνωστικοι, *gnōstikoi*), intellectuals and artists, geniuses and heroes, are above it and live freely and merrily as they see fit. Even Nietzsche himself really considered his morality to be fit only for "supermen." Hence there are two kinds of morality: one for inferior people and another for aristocrats of the intellect.

---

57. Paul Rentschka, *Die Dekalogkatechese des heiligen Augustinus: Ein Beitrag zur Geschichte des Dekalogs* (Kempten: Jos. Kösel'schen Buchhandlung, 1905); E. Chr. Achelis, *Der Dekalog als katechetisches Lehrstück* (Giessen: Alfred Töppelmann, 1905).

Although nomism is diametrically opposed to this antinomianism, it nevertheless—according to the rule that extremes meet—shows some kinship with it. As is evident from its development in Judaism and Romanism (and so forth), it has led to a similar, though differently elaborated, dualism in morality. According to Rome, the law that God gave in the Old Testament, though it is wise and holy and good and offers a rule of life for all Christians, is nevertheless capable of augmentation. Christ and his apostles, accordingly, have in fact augmented it. They are not only preachers of the gospel but also "new legislators": the gospel is a new law, not only in the sense that it counts faith (in contrast to the works of the law) as righteousness, but also in the sense that it has added to the "precepts" of the law "evangelical counsels," which are not binding for all Christians but may be followed by some who have been given the talents and strength for them, and which greatly increase their moral merits. We encounter a similar distinction in Pietism, Methodism, and related religious movements. Even though it is not theoretically elaborated, it does occur. For although these movements always start with the intention of bringing about the necessary reformation only within the church and not outside of it or against it, they soon proceed to form a "little church" (*ecclesiola*) in the church (*ecclesia*), look down on the official churches and ordinary Christians, and locate the hallmark of the Christian life in so-called "kingdom activities" and in arbitrary avoidance or abstinence.

In this double morality lies a truth that in Protestantism has not sufficiently come into its own. This is already evident from the mere fact that all of us, however many theoretical reservations we may have, practically and spontaneously deeply admire and look up to the men and women who with total self-denial and extraordinary dedication devote themselves to the cause of Christ. It is very easy to say that the renunciation of all earthly goods, abstention from marriage, avoidance of the world, and enduring all sorts of misery and pain all arise from a desire for merit and reward, but it is hard to prove it and even harder to follow this example, if not in form then in substance.

But there is something else as well: the moral law that confronts us in the Decalogue, in the Sermon on the Mount, and further throughout the Old and New Testaments is not a case of "precept upon precept, line upon line, here a little, there a little" [Isa. 28:10, 13] but comprises universal norms, great principles, that leave a lot of room for individual application and summon every believer to examine what in a given situation would for them be the good, acceptable, and perfect will of God (Rom. 12:2).[58] Since the moral law is not a code of articles we merely have to look up in order, from moment to moment, to know exactly what we must do, there is in its domain a freedom that may not be

---

58. Herein is the validity of casuistry, often misused, as ethicists seek to determine what obligations are faced by moral agents in a specific circumstance. This effort naturally leads to probabilism, equiprobabilism, probabiliorism, and tutiorism, and degenerates into the art of turning the conscience into an arbiter of possible moral obligation. Ed. note: For a helpful discussion of these terms, see the listings in *Hastings Encyclopedia of Religion and Ethics*. O. Zöckler, "Probabilismus," in *PRE*[3], XVI, 67.

curbed by human ordinances but must—precisely to safeguard the character of the moral life—be recognized and maintained. On the one hand that freedom includes the permissible, the adiaphora, and on the other what Rome calls the "counsels." Error begins in both schools of thought when the adiaphora and the counsels are located outside or alongside of, below or above, the moral law and are therefore detached from the moral life. There is no right or reason for this either in the one or in the other case. There are cases in which what is in itself permissible becomes impermissible (Rom. 14:21, 23; 1 Cor. 8:13; 10:23); and there also are circumstances in which abstention from marriage (Matt. 19:11; 1 Cor. 7:7), giving up remuneration (1 Cor. 9:14–19), the renunciation of all earthly goods (Matt. 19:21), or the like is a duty. But in "doing" these good works one is not accomplishing anything that is outside of the moral law or surpasses it. For there is a difference between a law that furnishes universally valid rules and a duty that is inferred from that law in a given case for everyone personally. Those who lose sight of this and assume the existence of a series of good works that really lie outside of and surpass the moral law fail to honor its unity and universality and degrade it.

THE PERFECTIONIST HERESY

[483] For that matter, this becomes evident in the case of all advocates of a double morality in that sooner or later they all arrive at the doctrine of the perfectibility of the saints, the meritoriousness of good works, and the transferability of merits. Perfectionism is a characteristic of almost all nomists[59] and in recent years, at least as far as the teaching of Scripture is concerned, received support from an unexpected quarter. Ritschl was the first to observe that Paul himself, after being converted, had no consciousness of being imperfect and also in no way reflects on that consciousness in believers in general.[60] Other scholars, working out this idea, even accused the apostle of an impractical idealism that, under the impression of Christ's imminent return, completely overlooked the presence of sin in the life of believers.[61]

---

59. Cf. above, 237–40 (##478–79); B. de Moor, *Comm. theol.*, IV, 805ff.; C. Vitringa, *Doctr. christ.*, III, 385–414; L. Lemme, "Vollkommenheit," in *PRE³*, XX, 733; O. Zöckler, "Perfectionisten of Oneida-Kommunisten in Amerika," in *PRE³*, XV, 130.

60. A. Ritschl, *Die christliche Lehre von der Rechtfertigung und Versöhnung*, 4th ed., 3 vols. (Bonn: A. Marcus, 1895–1903), II, 365.

61. H. Scholz, "Zur Lehre vom 'Armen Sünder,'" *Zeitschrift für Theologie und Kirche* (1896): 463ff. C. Clemen, *Die christliche Lehre von der Sünde* (Göttingen: Vandenhoeck & Ruprecht, 1897), I, 109ff. H. Holtzmann, *Lehrbuch der neutestamentlichen Theologie*, II, 150; and especially P. Wernle, *Der Christ und die Sünde bei Paulus* (Freiburg and Leipzig: J. C. B. Mohr, 1897); however, Wernle has changed his mind. When H. Windisch (*Die Entsündigung des Christen nach Paulus* [Leipzig: Hirschfeld, 1908]; and *Taufe und Sünde im ältesten Christentum bis auf Origenes* [Tübingen: J. C. B. Mohr, 1908]) adopted his theory and developed it further, Wernle himself wrote a critique, acknowledging that the theory was not true to life's experience and failed to take into account the practical character of early Christian writings. P. Wernle, "Windisch, *Taufe und Sünde im ältesten Christentum bis auf Origenes*," *Theologische Literaturzeitung* 34 (1909): 586–90; cf. also, L. Ihmels, *Die tägliche*

There is an element of truth in this assertion that may not be denied. Scripture can scarcely find words enough to describe the glory of the people of God. In the Old Testament, Israel is called a priestly kingdom, chosen by God, the object of his love, his very own possession and inheritance, his son and servant, made perfect in beauty by the glory of God (Exod. 19:5–6; Deut. 7:7ff.; 32:6, 8–9, 18; Isa. 41:8; Ezek. 16:14; etc.); and in the New Testament believers are called the salt of the earth (Matt. 5:13), the light of the world (v. 14), born of God and his children (John 1:12–13), his elect race and royal priesthood (1 Pet. 2:9–10), sharing in the divine nature (2 Pet. 1:4), anointed with the Holy Spirit (1 John 2:20), made kings and priests by Christ (Rev. 1:5), unable to sin (1 John 3:9; 5:18ff.), and so forth. Those who reject the teaching of Scripture about sin and grace can only see hyperbole in all these expressions. Given these descriptions, a radical change like regeneration and sanctification is neither necessary nor comprehensible. But Scripture judges otherwise. It assigns a high position to the church, calls it by the most splendid names, and ascribes to it a holiness and glory that render it godlike. However, this glorification of the church, which starts with regeneration, is as much an object of faith as justification. That in Christ the church stands free of guilt before the face of God is as hard to believe as the idea that by the Holy Spirit it has in principle been sanctified, glorified, and conformed to the image of the Son. Both are equally in conflict with the appearance of things; both belong to those things that one does not see and that are certain only to the eyes of faith. Also Scripture itself is aware of this. Despite its splendor-filled description of the state of believers, it nevertheless views them as sinners and does not conceal their transgressions and their confessions of sin. Examples are Abraham (Gen. 12:11ff.), Isaac (26:7), Jacob (26:35), Moses (Num. 20:7–12; Ps. 106:33), David (Ps. 51, etc.), Solomon (1 Kings 8:46; Prov. 20:9), Isaiah (Isa. 64:6), Daniel (Dan. 9:4), and so forth.

Also Paul knows that when he wants to do what is good, evil lies close at hand (Rom. 7:21). He is increasingly conscious, certainly, of the great transformation that has occurred in his life. With Christ he has been crucified to the world, and now it is no longer he that lives but Christ who lives in him. He is free from the law, righteous before God, assured of his sonship, glories in the grace by which he can do all things, offers himself as an example, praises the quality of his apostolic labor, and is conscious of his faithful conduct in office (see, e.g., Rom. 15:17; 1 Cor. 4:3; 9:15; 15:30–31; 2 Cor. 1:12; 6:3; 11:10; Phil. 2:16; 1 Thess. 2:10, 19). Still, he confesses that he lives in the flesh (Gal. 2:20), that what the flesh desires is opposed to the Spirit (Gal. 5:17), that nothing good dwells in his flesh (Rom. 7:18), and that he has not attained perfection (Phil. 3:12).

Romans 7:7–25 is especially important in this respect.[62] However much the Reformation exegesis of this text has largely been abandoned in modern times,

---

Vergebung der Sünden, 2nd ed. (Leipzig: Dörffling & Franke, 1916; ed. note: Bavinck cites the 1901 edition). M. Meyer, *Der Apostel Paulus als armer Sünder* (Gütersloh: Bertelsmann, 1903).

62. Cf. H. Bavinck, *Reformed Dogmatics*, III, 81–82 (#317).

the expositors who did so did not know what they were doing. Wernle, though he exaggerated, is not unreasonable when he says: "In fact the return to the ancient (Greek) tradition of Romans 7 means a much harder blow to our dogmatics than its practitioners usually sense. As a rule expositors concede that Romans 7 does not focus on the regenerate but they do not notice that by this concession Paulinism has been rendered useless to us."[63] Still this is not the strongest reason for maintaining the Reformation interpretation of Rom. 7. That reason lies in the text itself. The present tense Paul uses here can only be understood of the present. "In reality one turns the Apostle into a comedian if one believes he could only speak as he does here in the recollection of a state he left behind years before," says Clemen, who, however, sees no way to harmonize Rom. 7 with the other pronouncements of Paul and therefore writes: "It must spring from a particularly gloomy mood of the apostle, not from the predominant disposition he reveals elsewhere."

Added to this sin and this consciousness of sin in the lives of the saints of the Old as well as the New Testament is that Scripture everywhere proceeds from the assumption that sin remains a reality in believers to the very end of their lives. They are in permanent need of the prayer for forgiveness (Matt. 6:12–13) and confession of sins (1 John 1:9). All the admonitions and warnings in Scripture presuppose that believers only have a small beginning of perfect obedience. They all make many mistakes every day (James 3:2). If they say they have no sin, they deceive themselves (1 John 1:8). Paul's judgment of believers is no different. He esteems them very highly, calls them "elect," "called," "saints"; he notes with delight the Christian virtues that come to expression in them, and he readily and repeatedly speaks of them with high praise. In doing this the apostle is certainly not exaggerating. The transformation must have been tremendous if he could testify of Gentile Christians that in the past they lived in all sorts of horrible sins but were now washed, sanctified, and justified in the name of the Lord Jesus Christ and in the Spirit of God (1 Cor. 6:11). He nevertheless sees very clearly the sins that still cling to believers. The Corinthians are still carnal (3:1–4); the Galatians are disobedient (Gal. 5:7ff.); while the good work has been begun in the life of the Colossians, it is not complete (Col. 1:6); in fact their lives are still hidden with Christ in God (3:3). In Rom. 6, while Paul does not say that believers are sinless, he does say that faith in Christ is not compatible with a life in sin, and for that reason especially admonishes them to present their members as instruments of righteousness (6:13). Without harking back each time to the justification that at one time occurred in and through faith, he urges believers to reveal and demonstrate their new state in a life lived according to the Spirit.

In this connection we further need to note that Scripture, though always presupposing the imperfection of believers, nevertheless never weakens the demand of the law nor adapts it to existing practice. The proponents of perfectionism can

63. C. Clemen, *Die christliche Lehre von der Sünde*, I, 112, who also refers to W. C. van Manen, *De brief aan de Romeinen* (Leiden: Brill, 1891), 71.

never maintain it; they degrade the moral law and make a distinction between mortal and venial sins, or between committing and harboring sin, and similarly between earthly and heavenly, relative and absolute perfection. But Scripture does not take this line; it maintains the full and irreducible demand of the law: "Be holy as I am holy" (1 Pet. 1:16); "Be perfect as your heavenly Father is perfect" (Matt. 5:48; James 1:4). Believers must follow Christ, who committed no sin (1 Pet. 2:21ff.; Eph. 5:1–2), and in the day of Christ they must be blameless, pure, without blemish, irreproachable (1 Cor. 1:8; Phil. 1:10; 2:15; Col. 1:22; 1 Thess. 3:13; 5:23). They are, accordingly, unceasingly admonished in all seriousness to live a holy life. The admonitions that occur throughout Scripture and especially in the letters of the apostles to the churches are the strongest proof that they at no time hold to a theory of believers' sinlessness but always presuppose their deficiency and shortcomings. As long as they live in this life, they must fight against Satan, the world, and their own flesh; the desires of the flesh are opposed to the Spirit, and what the Spirit desires is opposed to the flesh, and these are opposed to each other so that they do not do what they want (Gal. 5:17).[64]

With this doctrine of the perfectibility of believers in this life also the doctrine of the meritoriousness of good works and of the transferability of merits in principle collapses. For if good works are all imperfect, if even the best work is still in some way deficient, and if the whole of the Christian life remains a striving after perfection, one can hardly speak of merit or reward and even less of a surplus of merits for others. In addition, however, this theory of the meritoriousness of good works is based on an atomistic view of the Christian life that is flatly contradicted by Scripture. In the first place, the moral law, which in its normative or didactic use (not as a law of the covenant of works) remains in force for believers,[65] is a single whole. While it comprises several commandments, it is nevertheless a single organism, which, when one of its parts is violated, is violated in its entirety (James 2:10–11). Corresponding to it in us is the one virtue, love, which, in whatever direction it develops and on whatever persons it is focused, always remains one and as such is the fulfillment of the whole law and the bond of perfection. In the second place, there is certainly an imputation, a transfer of Christ's merits to our account. But one must be careful to understand this transfer correctly. For Christ cannot be divided. One cannot possess a few of his merits without possessing all the others, nor all of them together without his person. Neither in justification nor in sanctification can one participate in his benefits without being in communion with his person. To whomever he is imputed and granted, he is imputed and granted totally. Those who believe in him are united with him, also possess righteousness and eternal life in him, and are at once children and heirs of God. When Methodism separates sanctification and sealing from justification and faith,

64. On this cf. H. Bavinck, *Our Reasonable Faith*, trans. H. Zylstra (Grand Rapids: Eerdmans, 1956), 492ff.; and also the literature cited by C. Vitringa, *Doctr. christ.*, III, 412.

65. Cf. below, ch. 8, "The Spirit's Means of Grace: Proclamation."

and considers the possession of the latter possible apart from that of the former, it overlooks this weighty truth of Christ's unity and indivisibility. Christ himself in his own person by faith and from the beginning is our wisdom, our righteousness and sanctification, our redemption.

In the third place, Methodism goes astray even farther when it considers this isolated benefit suddenly and fully communicable and obtainable by a special act of faith shortly or long after justification. For in so doing it misconstrues the nature of faith as well as that of sanctification. For from the very beginning, even where in justification it is considered from a passive perspective, faith is a living and active faith, which immediately appropriates the whole Christ. It can indeed increase and grow in that appropriation, but it nevertheless always has for its object the whole Christ and can never isolate him from his benefits nor can it isolate one benefit from the others. Sanctification, accordingly, both from the divine and the human side, is an organic process. The more Christ indwells us, the more we are strengthened in faith; and the more our faith increases, the more Christ communicates himself to us. In the church of Christ, therefore, there are lambs and sheep who nurse them (Isa. 40:11); those with little and those with great faith, first and last (Matt. 11:11; 20:16); those who are little and those who are great in faith (Matt. 6:30; 8:10, 26; 14:31; 15:28; 16:8); weak and strong (Rom. 14:1ff.; 15:1; 1 Cor. 8:7ff.; 9:22; 10:25); carnally minded and spiritually minded (1 Cor. 3:1, 3; Gal. 6:1); beginners and mature believers (1 Cor. 2:6; 3:2; 14:20; Phil. 3:15; Heb. 5:12, 14; 1 Pet. 2:7); young men and fathers (1 John 2:12–14). To each is given a personal measure of faith (Rom. 12:3); everyone has a place of their own in the body of Christ (Rom. 12:4–5; 1 Cor. 12:12ff.). All members must grow up together in the grace and knowledge of their Lord and Savior Jesus Christ (2 Pet. 3:18).

In the fourth place, therefore, the Christian life cannot be atomistically split up, neither can the works be separated from the person, nor one work from another. It is one organism, arising from one principle, regulated by one norm, and reaching out to one goal. This goal cannot be located on earth, in this life, in any particular creature, for if that were the case, all other creatures would be subordinated to that one creature and thus robbed of their relative independence. Philosophical ethics, which, as a consequence of its rejection of all revelation, cannot find any principle and norm for moral conduct, is also unable to indicate the final goal toward which all human conduct must be oriented. For such a goal it looks in turn to the state or society, the individual or the community, to material or ethical, to intellectual or aesthetic culture, and then sacrifices all the others to that one goal. But the final goal of moral conduct can be found only in God, who is the origin and hence also the final goal of all things, the supreme good that encompasses all goods, the Eternal One to whom all finite things return. Directed to that final goal, all things receive their own specific place in creation: prayer and commandment, religion and morality, an earthly and a heavenly calling, nature and culture. Each creature has its own relative independence, and all together they are subordinate and subservient to the glory of him from whom, through whom, and to whom all things exist. This is how Calvin in principle viewed the Christian life. In this matter he may have been somewhat too negative, puritanical, and rigoristic; but ascetic and dualistic he was not. Believers do not belong to themselves but to God, and they must therefore live moderately, justly, and piously in this present world.

Finally, and in the fifth place, this organic view sheds light on the connection that exists between this life and the future life, which is frequently presented in Scripture in the schematic image of work and wages. There is no room here for wages in the literal sense, wages such as are paid, and have to be paid, by a boss to his employees. Rome, too, acknowledges this when it bases the connection between work and wages in the domain of morality, not on the nature of things but on a free disposition of God. Even subject to this restriction, however, the wages here considered cannot be viewed in a literal sense but have to be regarded as figurative. Even in this earthly life, there are numerous relations between people that do not fit the category of work and wages but that do, on the one hand, include a service and, on the other, a reward. When a son helps his father in a given job, when a physician heals a seriously ill patient, when soldiers give their lives for their fatherland, when artists heighten the fame of their country and people, when inventors and discoverers make themselves useful to humankind, they receive honor and are frequently rewarded with expressions of thanks and praise, with badges of honor and statues. But no one thinks in this connection of work and wages in the economic sense. Hence when this category is transferred to the moral domain, it automatically gains a different meaning—and all the more when it is applied to the Creator-creature relationship. For God cannot and need not be served by human hands, since he himself gives to all humans life and breath and all things (Acts 17:25; cf. Job 42:1; Rom. 11:35; 1 Cor. 4:7). What pleasure would it give the Almighty if we were righteous? What would he gain if our ways were blameless (Job 22:3)? If we had done everything we were supposed to do, we would still be "unworthy slaves," slaves who gave the master more trouble than profit (Luke 17:10).

But now that not even this is the case, now that the most saintly people have only a small beginning of perfect obedience, now that even their best works are still defective and impure, and they owe everything they are, own, and do as believers to the grace of God, now all notions on their part of a reward, of merit, which would give them a right to reward in the true sense of the word, are out of the question. What child of God would have the nerve to let such an idea arise in one's mind and express it before the judgment seat of God? The situation is very different, however, if God on his part wants to picture the salvation and glory he desires to give to his children using the imagery of wages and reward. And that indeed is what he does throughout the Scriptures. He does that to spur on, to encourage, and to comfort his children, who being his children, are also already his heirs. He represents heavenly blessedness to them in the form of many images—of a city, a fatherland, eternal rest, a crown, an inheritance, an athletic prize, wages. But now who would dare to exploit this last image to their own advantage and boast of their own merit? The imperishable, undefiled, and unfading inheritance, which is kept for us in heaven, is not a wage paid out to employees in proportion to what they have earned but a reward that the Father in heaven grants to his children out of sheer grace. That reward is one of the many incentives for moral conduct, but by no means a rule or law, for it arises from God's will alone. It may, however, be an additional motive, because—according to the witness of the human conscience—there is a close inner connection between virtue and happiness, holiness and salvation, as also Kant admits. In salvation even holiness itself attains its most sublime and richest development.[66]

PERSEVERANCE OF THE SAINTS

[484] Scripture speaks of the perseverance of the saints in the same way it does about sanctification. It admonishes believers to persevere to the end (Matt. 24:13; Rom. 2:7–8); to remain in Christ, in his word, in his love (John 15:1–10; 1 John 2:6, 24, 27; 3:6, 24; 4:12ff.); to continue in the faith, not shifting (Col. 1:23; Heb. 2:1; 3:14; 6:11); to be faithful to death (Rev. 2:10, 26). Sometimes it speaks as if apostasy is a possibility: "If you think you are standing, watch out that you do not fall" (1 Cor. 10:12); it warns against superciliousness and threatens heavy punishment for unfaithfulness (Ezek. 18:24; Matt. 13:20–21; John 15:2; Rom. 11:20, 22; 2 Tim. 2:12; Heb. 4:1; 6:4–8; 10:26–31; 2 Pet. 2:18–22). It even seems to name various persons in whose lives there was a falling away: David in committing adultery, Solomon in his idolatry, Hymenaeus and Alexander (1 Tim. 1:19–20; 2 Tim. 2:17–18), Demas (2 Tim. 4:10), false prophets and teachers who deny the Lord who bought them (2 Pet. 2:1), believers who have fallen away from grace and the faith (Gal. 5:4; 1 Tim. 4:1). On the basis of these texts, Pelagians, Roman Catholics, Socinians, Remonstrants, Mennonites, Quakers, Methodists, and so forth, and even Lutherans have taught the possibility of a complete loss of the grace received.[67] Augustine, on the other hand, arrived at the confession of the perseverance of the saints. However, since he deemed uncertainty and fear with respect to salvation beneficial in the life of believers, he held that those who had been born again in baptism could lose the grace they had received, but if they belonged to the number of the predestined, they would in any case receive it back before their death. Hence while believers could totally lose the grace received,

66. C. Vitringa, *Doctr. christ.*, III, 373–84; Kirn, "Lohn," in *PRE*[3], XI, 605–14; V. Kirchner, *Der "Lohn" in der alten Philosophie, im bürgerlichen Recht, besonders im Neuen Testament* (Gütersloh: C. Bertelsmann, 1908); C. Stange, "Der eudämonistische Gedanke der christliche Ethik," *Neue kirchliche Zeitschrift* 18 (1907): 135–56; *Freytag, "Der Lohngedanke im Evang.," *Die Studierstube* (January–February 1909). Cf. for the Roman Catholic point of view also P. Kneib, *Die "Heteronomie" der christlichen Moral* (Vienna: Mayer, 1903); idem, *Die "Lohnsucht" der christlichen Moral* (Vienna: Mayer, 1904); idem, *Die "Jenseitsmoral" im Kampfe um ihre Grundlagen* (Freiburg i.B.: Herder, 1906).
67. C. Vitringa, *Doctr. christ.*, III, 415ff.

the elect could not finally lose it. In the Catholic and later Roman church, many theologians, in earlier and later times, agreed with him; still the Reformed, and the Reformed alone, maintained this doctrine and linked it with the assurance of faith.[68]

Now the question with respect to this doctrine of perseverance is not whether those who have obtained a true saving faith could not, if left to themselves, lose it again by their own fault and sins; nor whether sometimes all the activity, boldness, and comfort of faith actually ceases, and faith itself goes into hiding under the cares of life and the delights of the world. The question is whether God upholds, continues, and completes the work of grace he has begun, or whether he sometimes permits it to be totally ruined by the power of sin. Perseverance is not an activity of the human person but a gift from God. Augustine saw this very clearly. Only he made a distinction between two kinds of grace and considered possible a grace of regeneration and faith that by itself was amissible and that, for its continued existence, had to be augmented from without by a second grace, the grace of perseverance. That second grace, then, is a superadded gift, has no connection with the first, and has in fact no influence whatever outside the Christian life. Among the Reformed the doctrine of perseverance was very different. It is a gift of God. He watches over it and sees to it that the work of grace is continued and completed. He does not, however, do this apart from believers but through them. In regeneration and faith, he grants a grace that as such bears an inamissible character; he grants a life that is by nature eternal; he bestows the benefits of calling, justification, and glorification that are mutually and unbreakably interconnected. All of the above-mentioned admonitions and threats that Scripture addresses to believers, therefore, do not prove a thing against the doctrine of perseverance. They are rather the way in which God himself confirms his promise and gift through believers. They are the means by which perseverance in life is realized. After all, perseverance is also not coercive but, as a gift of God, impacts humans in a spiritual manner. It is precisely God's will, by admonition and warning, morally to lead believers to heavenly blessedness and by the grace of the Holy Spirit to prompt them willingly to persevere in faith and love. It is therefore completely mistaken to reason from the admonitions of Holy Scripture to the possibility of a total loss of grace. This conclusion is as illegitimate as when, in the case of Christ, people infer from his temptation and struggle that he was able to sin. The

---

68. U. Zwingli, *Opera*, 8 vols. in 7 (Turici: Schulthessiana, 1842), IV, 121; J. Calvin, *Institutes*, II.iii.11; II.v.3; III.xxiv.6–7; A. Polanus, *Synt. theol.*, VI, 43; Heidelberg Catechism, Q 1, 53–54; Canons of Dort, V; J. Trigland, *Antapologia*, c. 39–41; F. Gomarus, *Opera theologica omnia* (Amsterdam: J. Jansson, 1644), II, 280; D. Chamier, *Panstratiae catholica* (Geneva: Roverianis, 1626), III, 13, c. 20–22; B. de Moor, *Comm. theol.*, IV, 387; V, 158; C. Vitringa, *Doctr. christ.*, III, 415; F. Schleiermacher, *The Christian Faith*, ed. H. R. MacIntosh and J. S. Steward (Edinburgh: T&T Clark, 1928), §111; A. Schweizer, *Die christliche Glaubenslehre nach protestantischen Grundsätzen dargestellt*, 2 vols. in 3 (Leipzig: S. Hirzel, 1863–72), II, 368, 509; J. H. Scholten, *De leer der Hervormde Kerk in hare grondbeginselen*, 2nd ed., 2 vols. (Leiden: P. Engels, 1850–51), II, 505ff.; J. J. van Oosterzee, *Christian Dogmatics*, trans. J. Watson and M. Evans, 2 vols. (New York: Scribner, Armstrong, 1874), §121.

certainty of the outcome does not render the means superfluous but is inseparably connected with them in the decree of God. Paul knew with certainty that in the case of shipwreck no one would lose one's life, yet he declares, "Unless these men stay in the ship, you cannot be saved" (Acts 27:22, 31).

As for the examples Scripture is said to cite as instances of real apostasy, it is impossible to prove that all these persons (1) either had truly received the grace of regeneration (Hymeneus, Alexander, Demas, persons referred to in 1 Tim. 4:1; 2 Pet. 2:1); (2) or really lost it in their fall and later received it back again (David, Solomon); (3) or really did receive it but never got it back (Heb. 6:4–8; 10:26–31; 2 Pet. 2:18–22). These last texts seem to present the most formidable obstacle to the confession of the perseverance of the saints. Still this is an illusion. For, also those who hold to the possibility of falling away have to accept that the reference here is to a very particular sin. Even according to themselves, while grace is amissible, it can be regained after total loss. The opinion of Montanists and Novatians, who infer from these passages that the lapsed may never be readmitted to membership in the church, has been universally rejected by Christian churches. When Scripture expressly states that it is *impossible* to restore to repentance those who are in view in these texts (Heb. 6:4; 10:26; 2 Pet. 2:20; 1 John 5:16), it cannot be denied that the reference is to a sin that carries with it a judgment of hardening and that makes repentance impossible. And of such a sin—also according to the confession of those who hold to the impossibility of a falling away—there is only one, namely, the sin of blasphemy against the Holy Spirit.[69] Now if this is true, then the doctrine of the falling away of saints leads to the conclusion that either the sin of blaspheming the Holy Spirit can be committed also, or even perhaps only, by those who are born again,[70] or the above-mentioned texts lose all their evidential value against the doctrine of the perseverance of the saints. But this is not all. For those who consider total apostasy a possibility have to make a distinction between the sins by which the grace of regeneration is lost and other sins by which it is not lost. In other words, they are compelled to resort to the Roman Catholic distinction between mortal and venial sins, unless they would hold that that grace is lost by every—even the most minor—sin. But by adopting this view, they would falsify the whole of morality, misconstrue the nature of sin, and introduce an oppressive casuistry that would ensnare the believer's conscience. Furthermore, on this view one cannot arrive at the assurance of faith, achieve the ability to work in peace, and experience the quiet development and growth of the Christian life. Continuity can be lost at any moment. Hollaz tries to argue that regeneration can be lost three, four, or more times and still be recovered.[71] Finally, the doctrine of the possible apostasy of the saints is so far from escaping

---

69. Cf. H. Bavinck, *Reformed Dogmatics*, III, 155–57 (#334).

70. J. Quenstedt, *Theologia*, II, 157.

71. David Hollaz, *Examen theologicum acroamaticum* (Rostock and Leipzig: Russworm, 1718), 883 (ed. note: Bavinck erroneously cites this as Hollax). M. Schneckenburger and E. Güder, *Vergleichende Darstellung*, I, 233ff.

the difficulties it seeks to avoid that it rather magnifies and increases them. For if in this connection it holds on to the immutability of God's foreknowledge, then finally only those are saved whom God has eternally known would be, and the human will cannot undo the certainty of this outcome. Or it must proceed to deny predestination and foreknowledge in every sense of these terms, thus making everything uncertain and unstable, including the love of the Father, the grace of the Son, and the communion of the Holy Spirit. God may have manifested his love; Christ may have died for sinners; the Holy Spirit may have implanted rebirth and faith in the heart of people; the believer may be able to say with Paul: "I delight in the law of God in my inmost self" (Rom. 7:22). Yet ultimately, right up until the hour of one's death—indeed, why not also on the other side of the grave?—the human will remains the decisive and all-controlling power. Everything will be as that will determines it will be.

Scripture, however, teaches a very different doctrine. The Old Testament already clearly states that the covenant of grace does not depend on the obedience of human beings. It does indeed carry with it the obligation to walk in the way of the covenant but that covenant itself rests solely in God's compassion. If the Israelites nevertheless again and again become unfaithful and adulterous, the prophets do not conclude from this that God changes, that his covenant wavers and that his promises fail. On the contrary: God cannot and may not break his covenant. He has voluntarily—with a solemn oath—bound himself by it to Israel. His fame, his name, and his honor depend on it. He cannot abandon his people. His covenant is an everlasting covenant that cannot waver. He himself will give to his people a new heart and a new spirit, inscribe the law in their inmost self, and cause them to walk in his statutes. And later, when Paul confronts the same fact of Israel's unfaithfulness, his heart filled with grief, he does not conclude from this that the word of God has failed, but continues to believe that God has compassion on whom he will, that his gifts and calling are irrevocable, and that not all who are descended from Israel belong to Israel (Rom. 9–11).

Similarly, John testifies of those who fell away: they were not of us or else they would have continued with us (1 John 2:19). Whatever apostasy occurs in Christianity, it may never prompt us to question the unchanging faithfulness of God, the certainty of his counsel, the enduring character of his covenant, or the trustworthiness of his promises. One should sooner abandon all creatures than fail to trust his word. And that word in its totality is one immensely rich promise to the heirs of the kingdom. It is not just a handful of texts that teach the perseverance of the saints: the entire gospel sustains and confirms it. The Father has chosen them before the foundation of the world (Eph. 1:4), ordained them to eternal life (Acts 13:48), to be conformed to the image of his Son (Rom. 8:29). This election stands (Rom. 9:11; Heb. 6:17) and in due time carries with it the calling and justification and glorification (Rom. 8:30). Christ, in whom all the promises of God are Yes and Amen (2 Cor. 1:20), died for those who were given him by the Father (John 17:6, 12) in order that he might give them eternal life and not lose a single one of them (6:40; 17:2); he therefore gives them eternal life and they will never be lost in all eternity; no one will snatch them out of his hand (6:39; 10:28). The Holy Spirit who regenerates them remains eternally with them (14:16) and seals them for the day of redemption (Eph. 1:13; 4:30). The covenant of grace is firm and confirmed with an oath (Heb. 6:16–18; 13:20), unbreakable like a marriage (Eph. 5:31–32), like a testament (Heb. 9:17), and by virtue of that covenant, God calls his elect. He inscribes the law upon their inmost being, puts his fear in their heart (Heb. 8:10; 10:14ff.), will not let them be tempted beyond their strength (1 Cor. 10:13), confirms and completes the good work he has begun in them (1 Cor. 1:9; Phil. 1:6), and keeps them for the return of Christ to receive the heavenly inheritance (1 Thess. 5:23; 2 Thess. 3:3; 1 Pet. 1:4–5). In his intercession before the Father, Christ acts in such a way that their faith may not fail (Luke 22:32), that in the world they may be kept from the evil one (John 17:11, 20), that they may be saved for all times (Heb. 7:20), that their sins will be forgiven them (1 John 2:1), and that they may all be where he is to behold his glory (John 17:24). The benefits of Christ, which the Holy Spirit imparts to them, are all irrevocable (Rom. 11:29). Those who are called are also glorified (8:30). Those who are adopted as children are heirs of eternal life (8:17; Gal. 4:7). Those who believe have eternal life already here and now (John 3:16). That life itself, being eternal, cannot be lost. It cannot die since it cannot sin (1 John 3:9). Faith is a firm ground (Heb. 11:1), hope is an anchor (6:19) and does not disappoint us (Rom. 5:5), and love never ends (1 Cor. 13:8).

PART II

THE SPIRIT CREATES
NEW COMMUNITY

5

THE CHURCH'S SPIRITUAL ESSENCE

Though the term "church" should be restricted to Christianity, it must never be forgotten that the religious bond is the strongest form of all human community. Because we are all image bearers of God, our relationship with God flows out to other human beings. Religion cannot be purely individual and private. In the Old Testament, the covenant community of Israel was both a national and religious community, governed by a single divine law. However, after the exile, Judaism became a religious community only, gathered for worship in the temple and more importantly, especially in the Diaspora, in the synagogue.

The Christian church, initially often gathered in synagogues, soon became designated by the word ἐκκλησια (ekklēsia). After the ascension, the community of Christ-believers became the church, *an independent religious assembly acting in the place of Israel as the new people of God. Begun in Jerusalem, the church spread into Asia Minor, though the New Testament continues to speak of all the churches of Judea, Galilee, Samaria, and the missionary regions together, in the singular, as* ekklēsia. *The word underscores the basic organic unity of individual congregations and local gatherings of believers in the one universal body of Christ. The* ekklēsia *is the elect people of God.*

In the face of challenges to the apostolic faith, the unity and catholicity of the church was increasingly externalized and embodied in institutional form. The development of this "catholic" view of the church was fostered by opposition from heretical sects such as the Novatianists and Donatists. It was especially Augustine who articulated and defended this "high" view of the church. The climax of this doctrine of the church was reached in the medieval notion of the "teaching church" set over the "listening church," a vision of the church resisted by sectarian movements such as the Albigensians and Waldensians.

Not until the sixteenth-century Reformation was a fundamentally different view of the church posited as an alternative to Rome. A distinction was made between the visible and invisible church, the latter being an object of faith. The true visible church is marked by pure administration of the Word and sacraments; the church is the communion of saints, the congregation of the faithful. For Reformed theology the invisible church was characterized especially

273

as the elect, known only to God. In addition, the Reformed churches also placed
holy living and church discipline as a key mark. While election is the foundation
of the church, it only manifests itself in faith and good works.

The Reformation brought a multiformity into the church. In response,
mystical and pietist sectarian movements sought unity in religious experience
and separatism. In spite of attempts to impose unity through state power,
the church is increasingly losing its uniform character in the modern world.
Consequently, Protestantism is in danger of losing sight of the importance of the
church as a divine institution.

Scripture itself provides us with a rich language about the church. "Church,"
as the people of God, must not be confused or identified with the eschatological
notion of the kingdom of God. The kingdom is not organized on earth; the
church is. The characteristic essence of the church is that it is the people of God,
the realization of God's own electing love. Nonetheless, it is true that the benefits
of the kingdom, notably the gifts of the Holy Spirit, are given to the church on
earth for the mission of God's people. The gifts of the Holy Spirit are distributed
to believers to benefit others, to call men and women to faith in Christ. These
gifts include both supernatural and natural gifts, natural gifts that have been
heightened and sanctified by the Holy Spirit.

From the earliest times, the church has wrestled with the problem of
unbelievers in its midst. The fact is that the church is and remains an object of
faith. The internal state of a person's heart cannot be observed by the natural eye
and is known only to God. The word "church" thus is applied to the people of God
in terms of the believers who constitute its essential element and determine its
nature. The whole is called after the part. A church is and remains the gathered
company of true Christ-believers.

Another conceptual difficulty is that the church is both a living organism,
gathered by the Holy Spirit and charismatically led, and at the same time
an institution structured by a specific polity. Two errors can be noted here:
indifference to the earthly institution in favor of a purely spiritual membership in
the body of Christ, the error of enthusiasm; and an identification of the church
with its institutional, hierarchical structure, the error of Rome. These errors
are not addressed by identifying the visible church with the institution and the
invisible church with the organism. Institution and organism are aspects of the
visible church on earth, and both have an invisible spiritual background. The
only resolution is to acknowledge that the old Adam that continues to exist in
believers also does not belong to the church, and that the church is in a process of
becoming. The true and full measure of the church's identity is not achieved until
the consummation.

Though the church's true membership is known only to God, we are not
without guidance by which to discern the true church. Rome states more than

it can deliver when it asks for absolute certainty on this question. The church remains an article of faith, and the only standard by which the church can be judged is Scripture itself. The true church really has only one mark: the Word of God, which is variously administered and confessed in preaching, instruction, confession, sacrament, and life. The Word and the Word alone is truly the soul of the church.

The various objections raised against the Protestant understanding of the marks fail to hit the mark because they claim more for the marks than is warranted. For example, the criteria are not absolute or infallible; they do not set up completely false churches over against completely true churches, but give us criteria by which we can make informed judgments. Even though there are unbelievers within a body of believers and there remain impure elements in doctrine or practice, this does not disqualify a church body altogether. A true church in an absolute sense is impossible on earth. For that matter, neither can a wholly false church exist; to qualify for that description, it would no longer be a church at all.

The "real" church in history is not perfect but, rather, has an undeniably dark side to it. The church is rent asunder by schisms and divisions, some going back to the apostolic era. At the same time it is a mistake to reject all diversity in the church. In unity God loves diversity. From many races and languages and peoples, Christ gathers his church on earth. Breaking fellowship with the church is a serious matter; schism is sin. At the same time, we must be careful with the terms "heresy" and "schism." The former breaks the unity of the church on matters of doctrine, the latter in fellowship of communion. In practice, there is for us an inevitable elasticity thanks to the church's de facto pluriformity. We are obligated to first of all bind ourselves in spiritual bonds of unity rather than external, institutional ones. It is here, as we seek to understand the key church attributes of unity, holiness, catholicity, and apostolicity, that Protestantism finds itself with a different view than Rome. Protestants do not seek these attributes first of all, as Rome does, in a specific, hierarchically ordered institution. Like the attributes of indefectibility and infallibility, these are eschatological dimensions of the church; they are ours in Christ, true now but only fully realized in eternity. The attributes are thus callings to be pursued in the power of the Holy Spirit.

[485] The community of those who share in Christ and his benefits is called "the church." Strictly speaking, therefore, one can only speak of the church within the boundaries of Christianity. This does not, however, alter the fact that, just as there are analogies to the priesthood, sacrifices, altar, and an assortment of other elements in dogma and public worship in non-Christian religions, so there are also analogies to the church in these religions.

We are by nature social beings, "political animals" (ζῷον πολιτικον, *zōon politikon*);[1] we are born out of, in, and for community and cannot for a moment exist apart from it. The family, society, the state, associations of various kinds, and for various purposes, bind people together and cause us to live and act in concert with one another. Even stronger than all these institutions and corporations, however, is the bond that unites people in religion. There exists in religion a powerful social element.[2] The reason for this is not hard to find: religion is more deeply rooted in the human heart than anything else. It is the immediate result of our being created in God's image and therefore radically integral to our nature. In religion, we regulate our relationship to God, the relationship that is central and foundational. Our relationship to our fellow humans and to all other creatures is the outflow of our relationship to God. Foundational to all issues is that of religion. Those who agree with us in religion agree with us in our most basic, most sacred, and all-controlling convictions and sooner or later arrive at the same insights also in secondary matters. But differences in religious convictions, upon serious reflection, produce ever greater divergence between people also in all subordinate matters. That which unites people in religion is stronger than material interests, natural love, or enthusiasm for science and art. People are prepared to sacrifice everything, even their own lives, for religion. For if they lose it, they lose their own selves, their own identities. In religion, as everyone believes, a person's very soul and salvation is at stake. For that reason, too, every religion seeks to propagate itself and engages in mission. Religion is never merely a private matter, a subjective opinion, a matter of taste; it always implies the claim to being the true and saving religion and therefore seeks acceptance by others and expansion, if possible, throughout the human race. It is never a matter of the individual alone but always also a matter for the immediate and extended family, the people, and the state as a whole. Accordingly, it always produces a common dogma and a common form of worship, sustained as it were by the consciousness that not the individual but humanity as a whole is the completed image of God, his temple and body.

Apart from special revelation, however, the sense of the oneness of God and of humanity has been universally lost. The unity of religion is limited to the members of one's own tribe or people. The civil and religious community coincide. The state itself is also a cultic community. Religion, admittedly, manifests

---

1. Ed. note: Without attribution, Bavinck here directly cites Aristotle, "Man is a political animal" (from *The Politics*, 1253a2, 1253a3; ET: *The Politics*, trans. C. Lord [Chicago: University of Chicago Press, 1984], 37).

2. F. Schleiermacher, *The Christian Faith*, ed. H. R. MacIntosh and J. S. Steward (Edinburgh: T&T Clark, 1928), §6; A. J. Dorner, *Kirche und Reich Gottes* (Gotha: F. A. Perthes, 1883), 11–17; Th. Traub, "Die gemeinschaftbildende Kraft der Religion," in *Beiträge zur Weiterentwicklung der christlichen Religion*, ed. A. Deissmann (Munich: J. F. Lehmann, 1905), 305ff.; A. Sabatier, *Esquisse d'une philosophie de la religion d'après la psychologie et l'histoire*, 7th ed. (Paris: Fischbacher, 1903), 103ff.; C. P. Tiele, *Elements of the Science of Religion*, 2 vols. (Edinburgh and London: W. Blackwood & Sons, 1897–99), II, 155–81; H. Visscher, *Religie en gemeenschap bij de natuurvolken* (Utrecht: G. J. A. Ruys, 1907).

itself also in part in the independent organization of the priesthood, sacrifices, ceremonies, religious associations, and secret societies. The Buddhist religion in Tibet, for example, bears so much resemblance to that of Rome that when the Jesuit fathers first came to know it, they regarded it as a devil's game. Still none of the pagan religions managed to produce an independent organization like that which in Christianity is found in the church. Islam only founded a kind of theocratic state in which Arabs are the masters of subject peoples and the Qur'an serves as the statute book also for civil law. And Buddhism only formed societies of world-avoiding monks who exerted paralyzing pressure on civil society and never achieved independence from the state.[3]

THE JEWISH ROOTS OF THE CHRISTIAN CHURCH

The foundations of the Christian church were laid in the days of the Old Testament. In the patriarchal era the families of believers were religious communities with the fathers serving as priests. There was as yet no regulated common cult, although implied in Gen. 4:26 is that the Sethites as opposed to the Cainites began to call upon and proclaim the name of YHWH, and after the flood a split occurred among the Shemites, the Japhethites, and the Hamites. In the life of Abraham, this split was even given a permanent form lasting for centuries. From that time on, God allowed the nations to follow their own ways, and with Abraham and his offspring he established a covenant, which also externally separated the church from the world by the sign of circumcision and was confirmed at the foot of Mount Sinai and elevated into a national covenant. In Israel, the church and state were not identical. There was a difference between the priest and the king, the temple and the palace, religious and civil laws.[4] Still, the two were so closely united that citizens and believers, the nation and the people of God, coincided, and it was a single divine law that controlled the entire life of Israel. Israel as a people was an עֲדָה יהוה (*ʿēdâ YHWH*) or a קְהַל יהוה (*qāhāl YHWH*). Both words are used in the Old Testament for the assembly or congregation of Israel without any distinction in meaning. But after the exile Israel's national existence underwent a remarkable change. The Jews ceased to be a people like the other peoples of the earth and became a religious community. In every city within and outside of Palestine, assemblies of believers came together on the Sabbath (Ps. 74:8; Acts 15:21) to read the Torah and be instructed in it. The primary component of the worship service conducted there was teaching (Mark 1:21; 6:2).

---

3. P. D. Chantepie de la Saussaye, *Lehrbuch der Religionsgeschichte,* 2 vols. (Freiburg i.B.: Mohr [Siebeck], 1887–89), I, 132; O. Pfleiderer, *Religionsphilosophie auf geschichtlicher Grundlage* (Berlin: G. Reimer, 1896), 727ff.; L. W. E. Rauwenhoff, *Wijsbegeerte van den godsdienst* (Leiden: Brill & van Doesburgh, 1887), 835ff.; C. P. Tiele, *Elements of the Science of Religion*, II, 155–81; R. Falke, *Buddha, Mohammed, Christus,* 2nd ed., 2 vols. (Gütersloh: C. Bertelsmann, 1900), II, 155ff.

4. Ed. note: What Bavinck takes note of here is the basis for the modern democratic conviction that church and state must be *institutionally* separate. This is not to be confused with the *removal* of all religious commitment from the public square.

For the Jews, these meetings (συναγωγη, *synagōgē*) increasingly became the center of their religious life and in cities with a mixed or predominantly Greek population acquired an independent organization. The temple at Jerusalem indeed continued to exist and was still honored as the location of God's special presence, yet the Jews of the Diaspora gradually acquired a worship service that took shape apart from the temple and the altar, the priesthood and sacrifices, and consisted wholly in preaching and prayer. It was these assemblies which in the Old Testament era laid the groundwork for the Christian church community to come. Like the two Hebrew words cited above, so the Greek words συναγωγη (*synagōgē*) and ἐκκλησια (*ekklēsia*) were originally used interchangeably for these religious assemblies of the Jews. The LXX as a rule translated עֵדָה by συναγωγη and קָהָל by ἐκκλησια except in Exodus, Leviticus, Numbers, and Joshua, where קָהָל was also usually translated by συναγωγη. But among the Jews already there gradually arose a distinction such that συναγωγη tended to denote the actual empirical assembly (congregation, meeting), and ἐκκλησια became the word for the ideal community defined as those whom God had called to his salvation (convocation, community).[5]

[486] Against this background scholars explain the Christian usage, which continued to employ the word συναγωγη only with reference to the religious meetings of the Jews and the buildings in which they were held (Matt. 4:23; Acts 13:43; Rev. 2:9; 3:9) but otherwise began to use the word ἐκκλησια. In the New Testament this word indeed still occurs a few times with reference to popular assemblies (Acts 7:38; 19:32, 39, 41), but as a rule it is religious in nature and denotes the New Testament church. In patristic literature and especially in the writings of the Ebionites, the Christian church is occasionally still described by συναγωγη, but soon this word completely made way for ἐκκλησια.[6] For that matter it was Christ himself who first applied the word קָהָל, ἐκκλησια to the church community he gathered around himself (Matt. 16:18; 18:17). Many modern critics are of the opinion that this word was later put in Jesus's mouth.[7] But there is no ground for this conjecture, and there is nothing unusual in the fact that Jesus used the word in that sense. Jesus, admittedly, did go public with the message of the kingdom of heaven, but from the very beginning he presented a view of it that was very different from that of his contemporaries and certainly did not first entertain the

---

5. E. Schürer, *The History of the Jewish People in the Age of Jesus Christ* (*175 B.C.–A.D. 135*), rev. and ed. Géza Vermès and Fergus Millar (Edinburgh: T&T Clark, 1979), II, 423–53 (German reference: *Die Geschichte des jüdischen Volkes im zeitalter Jesu Christi*, 4th ed. [Leipzig: Hinrichs, 1907], II, 497ff.); H. L. Strack, "Synagogen," in *PRE*³, XIX, 223.

6. E. Schürer, *History of the Jewish People*, II, 429; R. Sohm, *Kirchenrecht*, 2 vols. (Leipzig and Munich: Duncker & Humblot, 1892–1923), I, 16ff.; H. Cremer, *Biblico-Theological Lexicon of New Testament Greek*, trans. D. W. Simon and W. Urwick (Edinburgh: T&T Clark; New York: Charles Scribner's Sons, 1895), s.v. ἐκκλησια.

7. H. J. Holtzmann, *Lehrbuch der neutestamentlichen Theologie*, 2 vols. (Freiburg i.B. and Leipzig: Mohr, 1897), I, 210; A. von Harnack, *The Constitution and Law of the Church in the First Two Centuries* (London: Williams & Norgate; New York: Putnam & Sons, 1910), 15.

expectation that the whole nation would repent and follow him. John already, by insisting on the baptism of repentance, separated the true Israelites from the mass of people. Not only was Jesus conscious from the beginning of his Sonship, messiahship and his future suffering,[8] but he also chose a number of disciples and gathered them around himself, sending them out to preach and win followers. To his followers he gave laws that were different from those in vogue in the circles of the Jewish people (Matt. 5–7; 18:15–35; 20; 28; etc.). Thus gradually a group of disciples positioned themselves around him, people who distinguished themselves and set themselves apart from the people of the Jewish nation. And to this group Jesus now applied the word קָהָל (ἐκκλησια). They were the true ἐκκλησια, the real people of God, the people the other Israelites should have been but now—in rejecting the Messiah—proved themselves not to be. For Jesus did not come to create something totally new but to bring about the fulfillment of the Law and the Prophets and to restore the real, the true קָהָל.[9]

Accordingly, when Jesus uses this word in Matt. 16:18 and 18:17 with reference to his "church," he is therefore still employing it in a very general sense. He does not say whether that קָהָל, ἐκκλησια, will be local or spread itself out over the whole earth. The later distinction between the local and the universal church cannot yet be found here. Instead, Jesus here states very generally that he will build *his* ἐκκλησια, in contrast to that of the Jews, not on the Torah, but on Peter's confession of his messiahship, and that he will therefore also organize and arrange it independently and cause it to live by its own laws. Present in the disciples whom Jesus gathered around himself are the beginnings of the New Testament community that will emerge later. But as long as Jesus was on earth, he himself remained the personal center, and the community of his disciples stood in the background. They were not yet able to stand on their own feet and daily had to be taught and guided by him. For as yet the Spirit had not been given, because Jesus was not yet glorified [John 7:39]. But after Jesus's departure, they immediately formed a close circle (Acts 1:14) and on the day of Pentecost received a life principle of their own in the Holy Spirit, which made them independent vis-à-vis the people of the Jews and united them most intimately among themselves. At that point, the church of Christ was in principle detached from Israel's national existence, from the priests and the law, the temple and the altar. It became an independent religious assembly in its own right. It now acts in the place of ancient Israel as the people, indeed the church, of God.

THE CHURCH IS ONE

Initially this ἐκκλησια existed only in Jerusalem. But before long there were believers also in Samaria, Antioch, and in many other locations among both Jews and Gentiles; their assemblies were also called ἐκκλησια. They, too, were

8. Cf. H. Bavinck, *Reformed Dogmatics*, III, 248–53 (#355).
9. Cf. T. Zahn, *Das Evangelium des Matthäus*, 4th ed. (Leipzig: A. Deichert, 1922), 540.

the people, the church, the church of God at that place. As a result, the word gradually acquired several different meanings. Jesus still uses the word in a general sense without thinking of the later distinctions. But after his departure, it was applied to the circle of believers in a certain specific location because there it *was* the people of God, and then it was applied to them whether or not they in fact came together in a certain gathering place. In Acts 5:11; 11:26; 1 Cor. 11:18; 14:19, 28, 35 the word ἐκκλησια clearly refers to the gathering or assembly of the congregation; but elsewhere it refers repeatedly to the church itself, even when it is not gathered, and one can therefore speak of ἐκκλησιαι (*ekklēsiai*) in the plural (Rom. 16:4; 1 Cor. 16:1; Gal. 1:2; 1 Thess. 2:14; etc.). The word acquires an even narrower meaning when it is applied to a group of believers meeting somewhere in a private dwelling. In cities where the number of Christians became very high, people simply had to form so-called house churches. In several cities, for example in Rome, the Jews possessed more than one synagogue; and Christians were all the more forced to split up for worship inasmuch as in that early period they had no church buildings but met in the home(s) of (one of) their church members. According to Acts 19:9, the Christians at Ephesus for a time came together in the lecture hall (perhaps rented for that purpose) of a certain Tyrannus, but as a rule they met in a private dwelling. As the church grew in numbers, they had to meet in several gathering places and form a kind of house church. This was the case in Jerusalem where the church soon numbered thousands of people (Acts 2:41, 46–47; 4:4; 5:14; 8:3; 11:21; 12:12, 17; 21:18, 20), and similarly in Rome (Rom. 16:23), Corinth (1 Cor. 16:19), Colossae (Philem. 2), and Laodicea (Col. 4:15). Each of these house churches was called an ἐκκλησια. But this does not mean the unity was in any way lost sight of, for though the believers in the same city sometimes—on account of their large numbers—met in different dwellings, they nevertheless together constituted one ἐκκλησια in that city (Acts 5:11; 8:1; etc.). If Tischendorf's reading in Acts 9:31 is correct, all the churches of Judea, Galilee, and Samaria are summed up under the one name (ἐκκλησια) in the singular. Similarly in Rom. 12:5; 1 Cor. 12:12–28; 15:9; Gal. 1:13; Eph. 1:22; 5:32; Phil. 3:6; and Col. 1:18, 24–25, all the churches are conceived of as one ἐκκλησια and described as the body, the bride, or the fullness (πληρωμα, *plērōma*) of Christ.

This oneness of all the churches does not just come into being a posteriori by the establishment of a creed, a church order, and a synodical system. Neither is the church an association of individual persons who first became believers apart from the church and subsequently united themselves. But it is an organism in which the whole exists prior to the parts; its unity precedes the plurality of local churches and rests in Christ. It is he who, continuing his mediatorial work in the state of exaltation, joins his churches together and builds them up from within himself as the head (Eph. 1:23; 4:16; 5:23; Col. 1:18; 2:19), gathers and governs it (John 10:16; 11:52; 17:20–21; Acts 2:33, 47; 9:3ff.), always remains with it (Matt. 18:20), is most intimately connected with it (John 15:1ff.; 17:21, 23; 1 Cor. 6:15; 12:12–27; Gal. 2:20), and dwells in it by his Spirit (Rom. 6:5;

8:9–11; 1 Cor. 6:15ff.; Eph. 3:17; etc.). The assertion that the universal ἐκκλησια precedes the local churches[10] is correct in the sense that while it is not historically prior it is logically so.[11] Every local church is the people of God, the body of Christ, built upon the foundation of Christ (1 Cor. 3:11, 16; 12:27), because in that location it is the same as what the church is in its entirety, and Christ is for that local church what he is for the universal church.[12]

In the various local gatherings of believers, it is the one church of Christ that comes to expression. Its essence, both as it concerns the church as a whole and each of its parts in particular, is grounded in that it is the people of God (Rom. 9:25; 2 Cor. 6:16, 18; Titus 2:14; Heb. 8:10; 13:12; 1 Pet. 2:9–10), consisting of people who have committed themselves to the Lord and have turned to him (Acts 5:14; 14:15), who bear the name of disciples, brothers and sisters, chosen ones, called ones, saints, believers (Acts 1:15; 6:1; 9:1, 32; Rom. 1:7; 1 Cor. 1:2; etc.). In its broadest sense the ἐκκλησια is the gathering of all the people of God, not only on earth but also in heaven (Heb. 12:23), not only in the past and present but also in the future (John 10:16; 17:20).

[487] This spiritual unity of the church of Christ still continually comes to the fore also in the postapostolic period. Christians are the saints, the elect; they have one God, one Christ, one Spirit of grace, one calling.[13] The church is a tower that, with the rock called Christ, forms one solid stone from which the stones that are unclean and black and do not fit are removed; it is the generation of the righteous from which the ungodly are separated.[14] Christians are the soul of the world,[15] the true Israel, the blessed people of God;[16] they are all priests[17] and have all received the Holy Spirit,[18] and their common unity is proved "by fellowship in communion, by the name of brother, and the mutual pledge of hospitality,"[19] and so forth. In this connection a distinction is usually made, as in Hermas, between true and false members of the church. With reference to the excommunicated, Origen stated: "Thus it happens that sometimes the person who is sent out is in and the person who seems to be kept in is out." Elsewhere he repeatedly asserts that many are called but few chosen, that there are spiritual and carnal members, that there are weeds among the wheat, and that the lifestyle of many conflicts with their confession.[20] Soon, however, a great change occurred in this view of the church as "the communion of the saints." When in the second century an

10. R. Sohm, *Kirchenrecht*, I, 20.
11. H. J. Holtzmann, *Lehrbuch der neutestamentlichen Theologie*, II, 177.
12. T. Zahn, *Introduction to the New Testament*, 3 vols. (Edinburgh: T&T Clark, 1909), I, 509.
13. *1 Clement* 46.
14. Shepherd of Hermas, *Similitudes* IX, 6–7, 13, 17–18.
15. *Epistle to Diognetus* 6.
16. Justin Martyr, *Dialogue with Trypho* 116, 123, 135.
17. Irenaeus, *Against Heresies* IV, 8.3; Tertullian, *On Exhortation to Chastity* 7.
18. Irenaeus, *Against Heresies* IV, 36.2.
19. Tertullian, *Prescription against Heretics* 20.
20. R. Seeberg, *Der Begriff der christlichen Kirche* (Erlangen: Deichert, 1885), 29.

assortment of sects and heresies arose, the question of course was, Which is the true church? And the reply given to it was, The church that remains with the body as a whole and maintains fellowship with the Catholic Church. The church was already called "catholic" by Ignatius,[21] because it embraces all believers on earth at all times and places, and outside of it there is no salvation.[22] This catholicity of the church, however, was no longer conceived in spiritual terms against heresy but externalized and embodied in a visible institution. The bishop, deemed to be in direct continuity with the apostles and in possession of the pure tradition, became the criterion of the true church. The universal church ceased to be logically prior and was considered to be historically prior to all local churches. Thus a total reversal came about in people's view of the church. It is not the local churches now that together form a unity; now the catholic church with its episcopate has priority. Local churches are parts of the whole and are true churches only for as long as they stick with that body as a whole and submit to it.

THE CHURCH IS CATHOLIC

The development of this "catholic" concept of the church was fostered by the opposition it experienced from heretics. Gnosticism turned the church into a school in which the "*pneumatikoi*" existed on a level far above the popular ideas of historical Christianity. Montanism wanted to ground the church in the alleged inspiration and prophecy [of their movement] and were averse to all church offices and authority. "The church is itself properly and principally the Spirit himself."[23] Novatianism and Donatism were zealously active on behalf of the holiness of the church at the expense of its catholicity. The church fathers took vigorous exception to all these errors and increasingly stressed the importance of the episcopal institution of the church. The church, which is led by the bishops, they said, is the sole custodian and proclaimer of the truth[24] and therefore the indispensable institute of salvation, the mother of all believers, the distributor of grace, the mediatrix of salvation, and the ladder of ascent to God. "For where the church is, there is the Spirit of God, and where the Spirit of God is, there is the church and every kind of grace, but the Spirit is truth."[25] Just as there is only one God and one Lord, so there is also but one church, one flock, one mother out of which all believers are born and outside of which there is no salvation. A ray of light cannot be separated from the sun, nor a branch from a tree, nor a stream from its spring.[26] Augustine, too, moves in this circle of ideas. Although the church by its

---

21. Ignatius, *To the Smyrnaeans* 8; cf. *Martyrdom of Polycarp* 5, 16, 19.

22. *1 Clement* 57; Ignatius, *To the Ephesians* 16; idem, *To the Trallians* 7; idem, *To the Philadelphians* 3; Shepherd of Hermas, *Similitudes* IX, 16.

23. Tertullian, *On Modesty* 21.

24. Irenaeus, *Against Heresies* I, 10, 2; Tertullian, *Prescription against Heretics* 28.

25. Irenaeus, *Against Heresies* III, 24, 1; Tertullian, *On Prayer* 2; Clement of Alexandria, *Paedagogus* I, 6; idem, *Stromateis* VIII, 17.

26. Cyprian, *De unitate ecclesiae* (New York and Toronto: Macmillan, 1928), 5, 7.

unity, catholicity, and majesty had already made a deep impression on him earlier, in his controversy with the Donatists (AD 393–411), he, for the first time, was forced to reflect more intentionally on its nature. But even then it was not the doctrine of the church that became the central focus of his thinking and his life, but the doctrine of grace that remained the focus, and the doctrine of the church to a certain extent took shape—independently and unreconciled—alongside of it. For if God is the only and absolute cause of grace, as Augustine teaches, then the church cannot be that cause. From the beginning, therefore, he distinguishes between the church as "the true body" and the church as "the mixed body" [of Christ].[27] There are members of the true church outside the visible church, such as the angels,[28] the murderer on the cross who only received the baptism of blood,[29] and all non-Israelites who were saved before Christ's coming,[30] for the Christian religion is as old as the world.[31]

Those also belong to the true church who presently still live an ungodly life or are snared in superstition and heresy, yet are known by God. "For in that unspeakable knowledge of God many who seem to be without are in reality within, and many who seem to be within yet really are without. Of all those, therefore, who—if I may say so—are inwardly and secretly within, is that enclosed garden composed, the foundation sealed, a well of living water, the orchard of pomegranates with pleasant fruits."[32] Conversely, there are many within the visible church who do not belong to the elect. "There is chaff among the wheat; there are bad fish among the good; there are many sheep outside and many wolves inside."[33] "Many who are in the fellowship of the sacraments *with* the church are nevertheless not *in* the church."[34]

On account of this distinction, the Donatists charged Augustine with teaching two churches. He replied that he did not separate the two any more than a person who in speaking of a human being distinguishes between the soul and the body, and that according to Christ weeds and wheat must grow up together. For Augustine, while the church is not the dispenser of grace, it is the circle within which God as a rule grants it. And in that way he defends the church against the Donatists. The church is the mediatrix of salvation because in it alone the Spirit, love, and perseverance are present. Outside of it there is no salvation. For while heretics and schismatics can take with them the Word and sacraments, they cannot take along regeneration and the love that are only given by the Holy Spirit within the church.

27. Augustine, *On Christian Teaching* III, 32.

28. Augustine, *Enchiridion* 29.

29. Augustine, *On Baptism* IV, 22.

30. Augustine, *City of God* XVIII, 23, 47.

31. Augustine, *Epistle* 102.

32. Augustine, *On Baptism* V, 27.

33. Chrysostom, *Homilie in Joannem* 45; Augustine, *Against the Letters of Petilianus* III, 3; idem, *On Baptism* I, 10.

34. Augustine, *De unitate ecclesiae liber* I, 74; ed. note: This work is also known as *Ad catholicos fratres* and is not available in English translation; Latin text is in PL, XLIII, 391–446; and in *Corpus scriptorum ecclesiasticorum latinorum* (Vienna: Tempsky, 1909), 52, 231–322.

"The apostle Jude openly declares (v. 19) that those who segregate themselves from the church do not have that Spirit." They may have the form but lack the substance, just as cutoff parts of the body may still be a hand, a finger, or an ear, but they do not have life. Those who do not have the church as their mother do not have God as their Father.[35] The church is the "devoted mother," "the bride without spot or wrinkle," "the precious dove," "the holy church." And the church remains holy even if the ungodly are in the majority, since to Augustine all its holiness, like its unity and catholicity, is to be found much more in the objective institution with its doctrine, means of grace, and cult than in its members. Separation from it, accordingly, is always impermissible, proof of pride and disobedience, for it exchanges the universal church for a particularistic or even a national church.[36] And precisely as a result of this powerful emphasis that Augustine in his polemic with the Donatists placed on the institutional church, he contributed in no small measure to the development of the Roman Catholic concept of the church.[37]

THE INSTITUTIONAL, TEACHING CHURCH

In the Middle Ages this concept of the church was practically fleshed out in the development of the hierarchy, the powerful organization of the church as institution, the struggle of the church with the state, and the elevation of itself above the state. It is all the more remarkable, therefore, that *theoretically* the concept was almost totally neglected.[38] In that period it was not theology but jurisprudence that guided the development.[39] It is only after it was challenged by Wycliffe, Hus, the Reformers, and others, that this view of the church was further developed and defended by Roman Catholic scholars.[40] In that view, then, the visible institution is in the foreground. For Christ founded a church whose visible and invisible aspects are inseparably bound up together. Just as in Christ there is the union of a divine and a human nature, and in humans the union of soul and body, and in the

---

35. Augustine, *On Baptism* VII, 44; idem, *De unitate ecclesiae liber* I; idem, *Answer to Letters of Petilian* III, 9 (*NPNF* [1], IV).

36. Augustine, *Contra Cresconium* II, 37 (PL, XLIII, 445–594); idem, *De unit. eccl.* I, 12, 14.

37. Cf. H. Schmidt, "Die Augustinische Lehre von der Kirche," *Jahrbücher für deutsche Theologie* 6 (1861): 197–250; H. Reuter, *Augustinische Studien* (1887; repr., Aalen: Scientia-Verlag, 1967), 4–105; A. J. Dorner, *Augustinus* (Berlin: W. Hertz, 1873), 276–95; T. Specht, *Die Lehre von dem Kirche nach dem heiligen Augustin* (Paderborn: Schöningh, 1892).

38. On the doctrine of the church, we find only a few items in Hugh of St. Victor, *De sacramentis christianae fidei*, II, 2; Alexander Hales, *Summa*, IV, qu. 4; T. Aquinas, *Summa contra gentiles*, IV, 76; idem, *Summa theol.*, I, 2, qu. 101, art. 2; II, 2, qu. 10, art. 10; II, 2, qu. 88, art. 12; III, qu. 8, arts. 3–4; III, qu. 68, art. 9.

39. A. von Harnack, *History of Dogma*, trans. N. Buchanan et al., ed. A. B. Bruce, 7 vols. (London: Williams & Norgate, 1896–99), VI, 127–28.

40. By Torquemada (1468), in the Roman Catechism, I, c. 10, and also by Canus, Bellarmine, and Becanus. Ed. note: Bavinck's reference is to Juan de Torquemada (1388–1468), of Spanish inquisition fame, and is likely to his major work *Summa de ecclesia contra impuggatores potestatis summi pontificis* (Rome: Eucharius Silber, 1489), which is partially translated as *The Antiquity of the Church*, trans. W. E. Maguire (Washington, DC: Catholic University of America Press, 1957). The actual date of publication of this work was 1448.

sacraments the union of the sign with the thing signified, so in the church there is a visible and an invisible side. The visibility of the church is grounded in the incarnation of the Word. Christ is the efficient as well as the exemplary and the final cause of the church. By the Holy Spirit he himself continues to live in it as prophet, priest, and king and pours out into it all the gifts of his grace. He imparts these gifts exclusively by means of the offices and sacraments. The institution, accordingly, has priority over the organism. The church is the mother of believers before it is a congregation of believers. The teaching church (*ecclesia docens*) with its hierarchical structures and grace-imparting sacraments is anterior to the listening church (*ecclesia audiens*) and highly elevated above it.

Applicable to this "teaching church," accordingly, are in the first place all those attributes that Roman Catholic Christians assign to their church. It is the one, only, exclusively Christian, Catholic, imperishable and infallible church that has come down by regular succession from the apostles. It denies to all other so-called churches the right to exist and is intolerant by virtue of its very nature. It neither tolerates nor recognizes any churches beside itself. To depart from it in doctrine or to separate from it in life is always a sin and never permitted. For since Christ imparts all grace only by means of the office and sacraments of the church, the teaching church, the Roman Catholic Church as institution, is the only mediatrix of salvation, the custodian and distributor of all grace to all people, the only ark of salvation for all of humankind. It alone leads people to the Scriptures, to the person of Christ, to communion with God. The true order of salvation is not that in which God by his Word leads people to the church; on the contrary, it proceeds from the church, then leads to the Scriptures and to Christ. The church, accordingly, must be knowable, identifiable, and even demonstrable for all people. By its attributes and distinguishing marks, it must be so conspicuous that no doubt is possible with respect to it and that only deliberate and culpable unbelief can deny and reject it. It is the primary and most important cognitive source of truth and for that reason many Catholic theologians treat the subject in the section of first principles.[41]

On this "teaching church" the so-called "listening church" is completely dependent. It only partakes passively in the glorious attributes of the church. Its only task is to accept supernatural grace from the hand of the priest in the sacrament. Its highest virtue—and necessary to salvation—is belief in what the church believes, obedience to the hierarchy, and submission to the pope. "Where the pope is, there is the church" (*ubi papa, ibi ecclesia*). The nature of the church therefore does not depend on the quality of this "listening church." It is indeed good and useful that the members of the church be believers. "The beauty of the church primarily consists in internal things."[42] But the "teaching church," the objective institution of salvation, would still remain the true church even if all its members were unbelievers and ungodly people.

---

41. Cf. H. Bavinck, *Reformed Dogmatics*, I, 511 (#133).
42. T. Aquinas, *Sent.*, IV, dist. 15, qu. 13, ad 1.

Nonmembers of the church are all those who are outside the Roman Catholic Church, such as the catechumens, the excommunicated, the schismatics, and the like. Their Christian faith and pious lifestyle are of no advantage to them: they are outside of the only salvific church. But members of the church are in fact all those who remain in fellowship with the church of Rome, even though they are acknowledged unbelievers and ungodly people. These are not actually but potentially the church.

They belong not to the soul but to the body of the church. They are not as perfectly the church as those who believe and live in the Roman Catholic Church; but they are nevertheless members of the church and integrally belong to it just as the body is integral to the essence of being human. Necessary to church membership in some fashion, more or less perfectly, is not the internal virtue of faith or love but only the "external profession of faith and participation in the sacraments." For the church is as "visible and palpable as the assembly of the people of Rome or the kingdom of Gaul or the republic of the Venetians. In a word, it is a gathering of humans bound together by profession of the same Christian faith and participation in the same sacraments under the control of legitimate pastors and particularly of Christ's vicar on earth, the pope of Rome."[43]

[488] To the extent that this Roman concept of the church was practically realized in the Middle Ages, it also encountered opposition and resistance from various directions. In the first centuries the catholization of the idea of the church took place under conditions of strong and persistent protest. Greek Christianity, though otherwise agreeing with Rome in its doctrine of the church, never acknowledged the primacy of the pope and thereby resisted the drive toward absolute unity and catholicity. Similarly in the Middle Ages a variety of sects rebelled against the development of the Roman idea of the church. Opposition sprang from different principles. In the case of Cathars, Albigensians, Bulgars, the followers of Almarik of Bena, the sects of the "new" and the "free" spirit, it was the fruit of dualistic-Manichaean or gnostic-pantheistic errors. Others such as the Waldensians, Bradwardine, Wycliffe, Hus, and the like were still being influenced by Augustine's view according to which the church was a gathering of the predestined. In their case the criterion for identifying the true church was not found in the objective ministry of Word and sacrament but in holy living, in life lived according to the law of Christ in love, poverty, and so forth. Hence the transition from the idea of the church to the reality of the world was lacking; attempts at reformation could not carry over into other areas or ended in disappointment.[44]

43. R. Bellarmine, "De eccl. mil.," in *Controversiis*, III, 1; ed. note: Bavinck also refers the reader to literature cited at the head of this chapter in the Dutch edition. Included are works from the Roman Catholic dogmatics of Becanus, Bossuet, Möhler, Perrone, Heinrich, Scheeben-Atzberger, and J. V. de Groot; for details, see the bibliography.

44. A. von Harnack, *History of Dogma*, VI, 118–49.

THE CHURCH AS "COMMUNION OF SAINTS"

Not until the sixteenth century was a fundamentally different concept of the church posited by the Reformation as an alternative to that of Rome. Luther found peace for his soul, not in the sacrament, which worked ex opere operato, nor in good works, but in the forgiveness of sins by faith alone. And on this basis he attacked the Roman Catholic Church: he rejected priesthood, sacrifices, the monastic system, the infallible church institute, and a magically working sacrament; proclaimed the freedom of the Christian; and viewed the church as a gathering of believers, a "communion of saints" as it is confessed as an object of faith in the Apostles' Creed. It was immensely painful and difficult for Luther to break with the Roman Catholic Church and its concept of the church. He had no program of reformation. Initially his only aim was to clean up abuses. But he found and kept his basic security in the justification of the sinner by faith alone and on that basis progressed much farther than he originally thought or intended. This principle also led him to another view of the church, to the view he found in Scripture.

The church was not simply a congregation of the predestined, nor of such people who conducted their lives in keeping with a few rules from the Sermon on the Mount. But it was a congregation of believers, of people who through faith had received the forgiveness of sins and hence were all children of God, prophets, and priests. For that reason it naturally had an invisible and a visible side. According to Seeberg[45] this distinction was first made not by Zwingli but by Luther. Yet by it he did not mean two churches but two sides of one and the same church. For Luther the church is not a platonic ideal, not an idea without a corresponding reality, but consists concretely in people who are alive and have by faith obtained the forgiveness of sins. On the one hand, it is invisible, an object of faith, for what one believes is not visible; on the other hand, it is visible, for it becomes manifest and can be known, not by the presence of a pope, bishops, vestments, and other external things, but by the pure administration of the Word and sacraments. Where this is present, one can be certain that there is a church there. There are true believers present, if only among the babies in the cradle. "God's Word cannot be without God's people." For though there are unbelievers in a church, just as alien constituents can enter a body, the essence of the church is determined by the presence of believers. The body as a whole is named after its most important component.[46] In the Lutheran symbols, accordingly, the church is described as a community or congregation of saints and true believers in which the gospel is rightly taught and the sacraments are rightly administered. It is indeed visible, has offices and institutions; yet "the church is

45. R. Seeberg, *Begriff*, 91.
46. Ibid., 84ff.; J. Köstlin, "Kirche," in *PRE*[3], X, 335ff.

not only a society of external things and rites but principally a society of faith and of the Holy Spirit in the hearts."[47]

The distinction between a visible and an invisible church, therefore, originally served only to assert against Rome that the essence of the church consists in that which is invisible, in faith, in communion with Christ and his benefits by the Holy Spirit, but absolutely not to detract in any way from the visibility or the reality of the church. Soon, however, it was used in another sense. People could not, after all, ignore the fact that "in this life many evil persons and hypocrites are mixed in with the church, who, though in the matter of the rites of the church they are members of the true church, nevertheless do not form the church and belong rather to the kingdom of the devil."[48] The church, accordingly, could be viewed more narrowly or more broadly as "the church strictly and broadly speaking."[49] Sometimes Luther spoke of two churches, and Melanchthon called this "a distinction between two bodies of the church,"[50] and later theologians such as Heerbrand, Chemnitz, Hutter, and Gerhard (et al.) applied to this situation the distinction between the visible and the invisible church. Here the church was called invisible, not because it has a spiritual side to it and is therefore an object of faith, but because we cannot know the precise circle of its true members; and "visible church" became the term, not for the manifestation of believers in their confession and conduct, but for the unbelievers who at an earlier time were counted by Luther and the confessions as belonging, not to the church, but to the kingdom of the devil. The idea and the reality, the essence and the appearance, are thereby detached from each other and put side by side. Now the believers constituted an invisible "*ecclesiola*" in a visible "*ecclesia*."[51]

THE REFORMED DOCTRINE OF THE CHURCH

The Reformed doctrine of the church, while largely agreeing with that of the Lutherans, nevertheless displays some peculiarities that are not insignificant. In

47. Apology of the Augsburg Confession, arts. 7–8; Smalcald Articles, art. 12, in *The Book of Concord*, ed. Robert Kolb and Timothy J. Wengert (Minneapolis: Fortress, 2000), 174–83; The Large Catechism (1529), part II, art. 3 (Kolb and Wengert, 435–39).

48. Joseph T. Müller, *Die symbolischen Bücher der evangelisch-lutherischen Kirche*, 8th ed. (Gütersloh: Bertelsmann, 1898), 153–55; ed. note: This specific reference is to the Apology of the Augsburg Confession, art. 7, pars. 9–16 (Kolb and Wengert, 174–77).

49. Ibid., 153; ed. note: This specific reference is to the Apology of the Augsburg Confession, art. 7, pars. 9–11 (Kolb and Wengert, 175).

50. P. Melanchthon, *Corpus doctrinae christianae* (Leipzig: Ernesti Voegelini Constantiensis, 1560), XXI, 507.

51. Cf. *Schultz, "Das protestantische Dogma von der unsichtbaren Kirche," *Jahrbücher für protestantische Theologie* 2 (1876): 673–90; A. Krauss, *Das protestantische Dogma von der unsichtbaren Kirche* (Gotha: F. A. Perthes, 1876), 80ff.; E. Rietschel, "Luthers Anschauung von der Unsichtbarkeit und Sichtbarkeit der Kirche," *Theologische Studien und Kritiken* 73 (1900): 404–56; W. Bleibtreu, *Die evangelische Lehre von der sichtbaren und unsichtbaren Kirche* (Tübingen: Mohr Siebeck, 1903). Ed. note: The preceding are additions to the works Bavinck cites at the head of this chapter in the Dutch edition, works that appear elsewhere in the notes to this chapter.

the first place, the institution of the church occupies a somewhat different place in it. Luther indeed viewed the church as the communion of saints, but nevertheless looked for its unity and holiness more in the objective institutions of office, Word, and sacrament than in the subjective fellowship of believers, which often leaves so much to be desired. Thus in his thinking the church increasingly became a divine institution whose task it was to realize the unity and holiness of believers. Melanchthon, thinking along the same lines, in the *Loci communes* of 1543 described the church as "the gathered company of those who are called" and said that "we should not dream of a chosen people anywhere but in this visible gathered company."[52] Later Lutheran dogmaticians observed a point of difference in the fact that according to their doctrine the elect are not to be found "outside of the gathered company of those who are called," and according to the Reformed they could also occur outside that circle. And it is really a Reformed doctrine that, though God ordinarily grants the benefits of Christ by means of Word and sacraments, he is not bound to this method and, be it very rarely, also grants salvation outside the institution of the church.[53]

In the second place, the Reformed linked the church most intimately with election and therefore frequently construed its invisibility differently from the Lutherans. Initially Zwingli indeed applied invisibility to the universal church, which is spread out over the whole earth and for that reason cannot be empirically observed by anyone, as opposed to the "particular" church, which is present and visible at a certain location. But in later years he took the invisible church to mean the body of elect people, an object of faith, as in the Apostles' Creed, which only becomes visible at Christ's parousia. In distinction from this position he called the universal and particular church a visible (*visibilis, sensibilis*) gathering of believers, in which there may also be hypocrites.[54] In his *Exposition of the Christian Faith* (1531), striking a somewhat different note, he says that the church of believers on earth is *invisible* insofar as it only includes true believers, and *visible* insofar as all belong to it who name the name of Christ the whole world over.[55]

Calvin aligns himself with this usage. When in the *Institutes* of 1543 he for the first time uses the term "invisible church," he means by it all the elect collectively who are known only to God; subsequently he characterizes the church as "the whole multitude of humans spread over the earth," a multitude that is visible and also includes hypocrites, yet is also invisible and an object of faith to the extent that

52. Ed. note: Bavinck cites no reference for Melanchthon here. The passage is found in *Loci communes* (1543), loci 12; ET: P. Melanchthon, *Loci communes: 1543*, trans. J. A. O. Preuss (St. Louis: Concordia, 1992), 131.

53. J. Calvin, *Institutes*, IV.xvi.19; Z. Ursinus, *The Commentary of Dr. Zacharius Ursinus on the Heidelberg Catechism*, trans. G. W. Williard (Grand Rapids: Eerdmans, 1954), qu. 21; G. Bucanus, *Institutiones theologicae*, 3rd ed. (Bern: Iohannes & Isaias le Preux, 1605), 400; F. Gomarus, *Theses theologicae de bonis hominum operibus* (Leiden: Franciscum Raphelengium, 1596), XXX, 29.

54. U. Zwingli, "Dei ratio," in *Opera*, 8 vols. in 6 (Zurich: F. Schulthessiana, 1842), IV, 8.

55. Zwingli, *Opera*, IV, 58.

we cannot know who in it are the true believers.[56] The church, accordingly, could up to this point already be called invisible in three senses: (1) as the universal church because a given individual cannot observe the church in other places and other times; (2) as the gathered company of the elect, which will not be completed and visible until Christ's return; (3) as the gathered company of the elect and called, because in the church on earth we cannot distinguish the true believers.

Later on still other viewpoints were added in terms of which the church could be called invisible: because it is not of this world; because Christ as its head, and hence also the church itself as his body, is invisible; because the major part of it is in heaven; because temporally and locally it may at times be deprived of the administration of the means of grace; because in times of persecution it goes into hiding in deserts and caves; because while it is observable in its external confession, it cannot be observed in the internal faith of the heart; finally, because the church is never just present at one place or time but spread out throughout the ages and nations.[57] And by contrast, the church was called "visible" because it manifests itself in its confession and conduct, or acts institutionally with its offices and ministries, or because it not only contains true believers but also hypocrites. Among the Reformed, the confessions and the study of dogmatics proceeded now from one view and then again from another.

Some highlighted the church as the communion of all the elect and called this "the invisible church."[58] However, since the elect who have not yet been born or called can only be called potential members of the church, others dropped this idea of the church and proceeded from the church as the gathered company of all those who are chosen and called.[59] In that case, however, theologians immediately had to make a further distinction between true believers and hypocrites and therefore proceeded to speak of the church in a strict and a broader sense, of being *of* the church and being *in* the church, or also occasionally of the invisible and the visible church.[60] In connection with the corruption that began to infect the church, this practice led to the distinction between two circles or groups of people in the one church,[61] and it prompted many theologians in the eighteenth century to posit the existence, side by side, of an external [covenant] and an

56. J. Calvin, *Institutes*, IV.i.1–9.

57. A. Polanus, *Syntagma theologiae christianae* (Hanover, 1609; Geneva, 1617), 531.

58. Genevan Catechism, in *Calvin: Theological Treatises*, ed. J. K. S. Reid, Library of Christian Classics (Philadephia: Westminster, 1954), 103; also in E. F. K. Müller, *Die Bekenntnisschriften der reformierten Kirche* (Leipzig: Deichert, 1903), 126; First Scotch Confession, art. 16; Westminster Confession, art. 25; J. H. Alsted, *Theologica didactica* (Hanau: C. Eifrid, 1618), 590, etc.

59. Basil, *Hexameron* I, 5; First Helvetic Confession, 15; Heidelberg Catechism, Q 54; Belgic Confession, art. 27; Second Helvetic Confession, art. 17; F. Gomarus, *Theses theologicae*, disp. 30; A. Polanus, *Synt. theol.*, 530; P. Martyr Vermigli, *Loci communes*, ed. R. Massonius (London, 1576), 390.

60. Z. Ursinus, *Explicationes catecheseos*, in *Opera*, I, 54; J. H. Alsted, *Theologica didactica*, 598; J. H. Heidegger, *Corpus theologiae*, 2 vols. (Zurich: J. H. Bodmer, 1700), XXVI, 29.

61. F. Turretin, *Institutes of Elenctic Theology*, trans. G. M. Giger, ed. J. T. Dennison, 3 vols. (Phillipsburg, NJ: Presbyterian & Reformed, 1992), XVIII, 3, 24.

internal covenant. This led to separating the external and the internal form of the church, and to preaching the doctrine that "ungraced" people, if they lived inoffensive lives, could also be true members of the church and make a legitimate claim to its goods and benefits.[62] Others, opposing this dichotomizing trend, tried in vain to maintain the unity of the church by saying that the invisible and the visible church were two sides of the same thing.[63] Doctrine and life increasingly went their own separate ways. And this was all the more serious for the Reformed view of the church since it identified the essence of the church much less with its institutional aspects than the Lutherans. For—and that is the third distinction, one which will later come out more clearly—the Reformed, while they also looked for the mark of the true church in the proper administration of Word and sacrament, usually added to it the exercise of church discipline and a Christian lifestyle. While election is the foundation of the church, it only manifests itself in faith and good works.[64]

REFORMATION TANGENTS

[489] The change that the Reformation made in the Roman Catholic view of the church also had practical consequences. Uniformity forever gave way to multiformity. Different creedal statements succeeded each other or appeared simultaneously and profoundly changed the form of religion and the church. The Reformation still attempted to hold the invisible and visible church together in a sound way, but history showed how difficult that was. And in the case of churches other than the Lutheran and the Reformed, the bond between them was often completely broken, and the invisible church was offered up to the visible or vice versa. Socinianism, though it still accepted the distinction, nevertheless spoke almost exclusively of the visible church, inasmuch as it viewed the Christian religion as acceptable to almost everyone.[65] The Remonstrants not only took the same tack but also deprived the church of its entire independent status, leaving it nothing but the right to preach and to admonish.[66] In the era of rationalism the church became a society of people interested in the practice of religion and

62. Cf. H. Bavinck, *Reformed Dogmatics*, III, 231–32 (#350).

63. A. Walaeus, in *Synopsis purioris theologiae*, disp. 40, 34; F. Turretin, *Institutes of Elenctic Theology*, XVIII, 7, 4; P. van Mastricht, *Theoretico-practica theologia* (Utrecht: Appels, 1714), VII, 1, 11, 13; *J. C. Appelius, *De Hervormde leer* (Groningen: Wed. J. Spandaw, 1769), 300ff.

64. On the Reformed doctrine of the church, see H. Heppe, *Die Dogmatik der evangelisch-reformirten Kirche* (Neukirchen: K. Moers, 1935), 479ff.; R. Seeberg, *Begriff*, 159ff. Ed. note: Bavinck also refers the reader to Reformed authors cited at the head of the chapter in the Dutch edition. Included are Calvin (*Institutes*), Peter Martyr Vermigli, Jerome Zanchi, Junius, Voetius, the Leiden *Synopsis*, de Moor, and Vitringa.

65. O. Fock, *Der Socinianismus* (Kiel: C. Schröder, 1847), 690ff.

66. Apology of the Remonstrants, 21–22; ed. note: This work is found in Simon Episcopius, *Apologia pro confessione sive declaratione sententiae eorum* (n.p., 1629); ET: *The Confession or Declaration of the Ministers or Pastors Which in the United Provinces Are Called Remonstrants, concerning the Chief Points of the Christian Religion*, trans. T. Taylor (London: Francis Smith, 1676). P. van Limborch, *Theologia christiana* (Amsterdam: Arnhold, 1735), VII.

the improvement of morals.[67] Employing the terms "invisible" and "visible," Kant described the church in terms of its normative idea and its empirical appearance. The latter, that is, the church with its statutory faith, is increasingly destined to turn into rational and moral religion, into the kingdom of God on earth.[68] In Hegel's thought the church similarly possessed merely a temporal and passing significance, for the state is the true realization of the moral idea, the rational-ethical substance that matters. The church only has a right to exist as long as the state does not yet fully answer to its idea.[69] On the basis of this rationalism, there remained no room for the church as instituted by Christ.

Though proceeding from a different principle, mysticism arrived at the same result. Anabaptism proceeded from the premise of an absolute antithesis between creation and re-creation, nature and grace, the world and the kingdom of God, and therefore viewed believers as persons who in being born again had become something totally different and therefore had to live in separation from the world. Its program was not reformation but separation: Anabaptism wanted a separated church. For centuries there had been no church but only Babel, and Babel had to be abandoned and shunned.[70] In Münster it was said that there had been no true Christian in 1,400 years.[71] The true church was a church of saints who, after making a personal profession of faith, were baptized, and who distinguished themselves from others by abstaining from oaths, war, government office, and a wide assortment of other worldly practices in food and drink, clothing, and social contact.[72]

The same dualistic principle underlies a range of sects that later emerged within the circle of Protestantism. At Middelburg in 1666, as earlier in Geneva and Amiens, Labadie called into existence conventicles to which he gave the name of "prophecies," and in 1669 he started an "evangelical church" that was to be composed solely of true believers. Later, at Herford, he distinguished himself by a domestic family life, a dubious marriage practice, and community of goods.[73] Pietism, both in the

---

67. J. A. L. Wegscheider, *Institutiones theologiae christianae dogmaticae*, 3rd ed. (Halle: Gebauer, 1819), §188; K. G. Bretschneider, *Systematische Entwicklung aller in der Dogmatik* (Leipzig: J. A. Barth, 1841), 760. J. C. Döderlein, *Institutio theologi christiani*, 2 vols. (Nuremberg: Monath, 1787), 716.

68. I. Kant, *Religion within the Limits of Reason Alone*, trans. T. M. Greene and H. H. Hudson (New York: Harper & Brothers, 1934), 92ff., 109ff.; *Cf. Katzer, "Kants Lehre von der Kirche," *Jahrbücher für deutsche Theologie* 12 (1886).

69. G. W. F. Hegel, *Philosophie der Religion*, in *Sämtliche Werke*, 26 vols. (Stuttgart: F. Fromman, 1949–59), XVI, 279 (*Werke*, XII, 279); cf. G. W. F. Hegel, *Lectures on the Philosophy of Religion*, vol. III, *The Consummate Religion*, ed. P. C. Hodgson (Berkeley: University of California Press, 1985), 322ff.

70. Menno Simons, *The Complete Writings of Menno Simons*, trans. L. Verduin, ed. Harold S. Bender (Scottdale, PA: Herald Press, 1956), 158–59, 175–89, 212–15; original Dutch reference: *Werken*, 262, 33ff., 289ff., 295, 409ff.

71. M. Goebel, *Geschichte des christlichen Lebens*, 3 vols. (Coblenz: K. Bädeker, 1849–60), I, 179.

72. *G. de Brès, *De wortel, den oorspronck, ende het fundament der Wederdooperen* (Amsterdam: Cloppenburgh, 1589), 39–45; J. Cloppenburg, *Theol. op.*, II, 233; M. Goebel, *Geschichte des christlichen Lebens*, 134ff.

73. M. Goebel, *Geschichte des christlichen Lebens*, II, 181–273; A. Ritschl, *Geschichte des Pietismus in der reformierten Kirche* (Bonn: A. Marcus, 1880), I, 194–268; M. Goebel, "Labadie," in *PRE*³, XI, 191–96; J. Herman Riemersma, "De Huiskerk der Labadisten," *Tijdspiegel* (November–December 1901).

Netherlands and in Germany, contracted the whole of life into the narrow circle of religion, became indifferent to the church and its offices, sacraments and formularies, gathered believers into segregated societies, and promoted separatism.[74] On August 12, 1729, Zinzendorf organized an apostolic congregation that in a variety of features resembled the church of Labadie.[75] In England, under the influence of Anabaptism, Robert Browne and John Robinson started the movement of Independentism, which sees the church arising totally out of the combination of individual believers.[76] Its enthusiasm having been tempered after Cromwell's revolution, it changed—like Anabaptism into Mennonitism—into the religion of the Quakers, who formed a church that was separated from the world and distinctive in all sorts of external features. Among them the church—separated from everything that is historical and objective—became the fellowship of those who participated in the illumination of the Spirit, and was, in addition, the name for those who met in one particular location, constituted one family, as it were, and by virtue of "the inner light" also agreed externally in their witness and conduct.[77]

Methodism as well was dominated by this contrast. Initially Wesley indeed tried to reform the church itself, but in 1784 he proceeded to separate his followers from the state church. He ordained preachers, putting them under the protection of the Act of Tolerance. He brought converts together into societies that met daily for prayer, from time to time held love feasts, days of fasting, nights of vigil, prayer meetings, and so forth, and whose principal task was to labor for the conversion of others.[78]

The Salvation Army of General William Booth flowed forth from this Methodism. Converts here no longer made up a church but formed a standing army of Christ, a corps of evangelists under the direction of an officer, and were separated from the world by a special mode of dress and manner of life. Given all these phenomena, it is no wonder that John Darby proceeded, openly and decisively, to reject every church and all ecclesiastical forms. In his opinion, the New Testament dispensation of the covenant of grace had initially indeed been blessed by God with a church and ecclesiastical offices, but these had already degenerated in the apostolic age as a result of human unfaithfulness and been rejected by God. Since then, accordingly, all churches were nothing but Babel, preparations for the antichrist, totally corrupt, and to be completely repudiated by believers. Now these believers' only task is to withdraw from the world, edify each other with their respective gifts at their meetings, and quietly await the return of Christ.[79]

74. A. Ritschl, *Geschichte des Pietismus in der reformierten Kirche*, II, 135ff.

75. M. Goebel, *Geschichte des christlichen Lebens*, II, 271.

76. H. Weingarten, *Die revolutionskirchen Englands* (Leipzig: Breitkopf & Hartel, 1868), 24ff.

77. *R. Barclay, *Verantwoording*, trans. J. H. Glazemaker (Amsterdam: A. Waldorp, 1757), 212ff.; H. Weingarten, *Die Revolutionskirchen Englands*, 185, 186.

78. M. Schneckenburger, *Vorlesungen über die Lehrbegriffe der kleineren protestantischen Kirchenparteien*, ed. K. B. Hundeshagen (Frankfurt a.M.: H. L. Brönner, 1863), 104ff.

79. *T. Kolde, *Die Heilsarmee* (Erlangen: Deichert, 1885), 49ff.; G. J. van der Flier, *Het Darbisme* ('s Gravenhage: W. A. Beschoor, 1879). Discussions of the above-named parties and sects, along with many others, can be found in the key handbooks of church history, history of dogma, and the relevant articles in dictionaries

Thus everything seems to point in the direction of the dissolution of the church and to a radical modification of the idea of the church. Over against these trends, however, we also witness a powerful reaction. The Russian church, whose supreme government rests with the Holy Synod and is bound to the emperor [czar] by way of a procurator, maintains its claim to being the only true orthodox church and strives, through the suppression of sects, for unity of belief throughout the empire. Pobedonoszew, the procurator who died in 1907, was an advocate of absolute monarchy and the state church, and he defended the doctrine that the masses find the standard of truth in power.[80] The Roman Catholic Church is still what it was earlier when it persecuted heretics and schismatics and had them executed. In principle it cannot recognize and tolerate churches beside itself. When Catholics speak up in favor of freedom of religion and the separation of church and state, they are to be viewed as friends of both out of calculating self-interest, and enemies of both on principle.[81] In England we first saw the rise of Irvingism, which sought to reform the church through the restoration of the apostolate,[82] and now, in the Anglican Church, the spread of ritualism, which increasingly distorts the offices, the sacraments, worship, and ceremonies along the lines of Roman Catholic theory and practice.[83] Even among the Lutherans many confessional conservatives returned to the objective institution of the church, the ecclesiastical offices and sacraments, and tied impartation of grace to them all.[84]

such as *PRE³*. Also see the series of brochures, *Kerk en Secte* (Church and Sects), edited by Prof. S. D. Van Veen and published by Hollandia (Baarn). Also see J. L. van Bueren, Chr. Hunningher, J. Th. de Visser, Ph. J. Hoedemaker, *Het Darbisme; De z. g. Apostolische kerk; De nieuwere theosophie; De kerk en de secten* (Amsterdam: Egeling's Boekhandel, 1906); J. van der Linden, *Waarheid of dwaling* (Den Haag: J. van der Burgh, 1910) (on Irvingites, Darbyites, Seventh-Day Baptists, Seventh-Day Adventists, and Sabbatarians); E. Kalb, *Kirchen und Sekten der Gegenwart*, 2nd ed. (Stuttgart: Evang. Gesellschaft, 1907; ed. note: Bavinck erroneously cites the author as Kolb). F. Kattenbusch, *Die Kirchen und Sekten des Christentums in der Gegenwart* (Tübingen: J. C. B. Mohr [Paul Siebeck], 1909).

80. See K. P. Pobedonoszew, *Streitfragen der Gegenwart* (Berlin: Deubner, 1897); ed. note: Bavinck cites an edition from 1907; *article in *Wetenschappelijke Bladen* (October 1901): 72–75; W. H. de Beaufort, "De staatkundige toekomst van Rusland," *De Gids* (November 1901/4).

81. A. Stöckl, *Lehrbuch der Philosophie* (Mainz: F. Kirchheim, 1868), III, 474; V. Cathrein, *Moralphilosophie*, 3rd ed., 2 vols. (Freiburg i.B.: Herder, 1899), II, 555ff.; F. Hettinger, *Apologie des Christenthums*, 2nd ed., 5 vols. (Freiburg i.B.: Herder, 1865), IV, 407ff.

82. Th. Kolde, "Irving," in *PRE³*, IX, 424–37; J. N. Köhler, *Het Irvingisme* ('s Gravenhage: Mensing & Visser, 1876).

83. R. Buddensieg, "Traktarianismus," in *PRE³*, XX, 18–53; W. Walsh, *The Secret History of the Oxford Movement*, 6th ed. (London: Church Association, 1899); M. C. Williams, "The Crisis in the Church of England," *Presbyterian and Reformed Review* 10 (July 1899): 389–412; R. F. Horton and J. Hocking, *Shall Rome Reconquer England?* (London: National Council of Evangelical Free Churches, 1910). J. Blötzer, "Der Anglikanismus auf dem Wege nach Rom?" *Stimmen aus Maria Laach* 73 (February–March 1904).

84. W. Löhe, *Drei Bücher von der Kirche* (Stuttgart: Sam. Gott. Liesching, 1845); T. F. D. Kliefoth, *Acht Bücher von der Kirche* (Schwerin: Stiller, 1854); A. F. O. Münchmeyer, *Das Dogma von der sichtbaren und unsichtbaren Kirche* (Göttingen: Vandenhoeck & Ruprecht, 1854); A. F. C. Vilmar, *Die Theologie der Thatsachen wider die Theologie der Rhetorik*, 4th ed. (Gütersloh: C. Bertelsmann, 1876), 48ff.; idem, *Handbuch der*

Despite all these attempts, however, the church is increasingly losing its uniform character. Not only in Protestant countries—and then especially in England and North America—but also in Russia the number of sects is expanding.[85] In the Roman Catholic Church, which loves to point out the divisions of Protestantism, unity is in many respects more appearance than reality. Within its walls believers and unbelievers are as equally far removed from each other as in many churches of the Reformation. The various orders of the Roman Catholic Church often relate to one another on anything but friendly terms. "The same motives of distinctive piety which lead in Catholicism to the creation of new orders tend in Protestantism to produce new sects."[86] And Reform Catholicism, the "Free-from-Rome" movement, and modernism[87] show how much unrest is hidden in many a heart under the glitter of outward unity. Belief in the one infallible, exclusively salvific church can no longer be maintained over against the existence and flourishing of so many other churches. Doctrine, here, is being contradicted with the utmost vigor by life and history.

Whereas Rome closes its eyes to this development of Christianity and the church, Protestant theology runs the danger of overlooking, for the sake of history, the divine institution of the church. According to Schleiermacher, "The Christian church takes shape through the coming together of regenerate individuals to form a system of mutual interaction and cooperation."[88] However, since regeneration does not constitute a magical change but ethical renewal, there always remain in regenerate individuals some parts of the world, and we must, therefore, distinguish in the church between that which is constant and that which changes and is evanescent.[89] To this distinction, Schleiermacher applies the terms of invisible and visible church. Previous usage of these terms, he says, was mistaken, for of the invisible church the major part is not invisible, inasmuch as regeneration is outwardly manifest in confession and conduct. Furthermore, of the visible church the major part is not church inasmuch as it belongs to the world. The term "invisible church" does not so much refer to persons as to the operation of the Spirit in persons, and the term "visible church" means that in all believers these operations of the Spirit are still accompanied by the aftereffects of sin.[90] Hence, the two are related to each other as essence and appearance, as idea and reality, and are so regarded also by numerous other theologians.[91] In discussing

---

evangelischen Dogmatik für studierende die Theologie (Gütersloh: C. Bertelsmann, 1895), II, 212; F. J. Stahl, Die Kirchenverfassung nach Lehre und Recht der Protestanten, 2nd ed. (Erlangen: T. Bläsing, 1862), 67ff.

85. Cf. H. Bavinck, Reformed Dogmatics, I, 133n49 (#41); G. Bonwetsch, "Raskolniken," in PRE³, XVI, 436–43; K. Grass, Die russischen Sekten, 2 vols. (Leipzig: J. C. Hinrichs, 1907–14).

86. A. Ritschl, Geschichte des Pietismus in der reformierten Kirche, III, 303.

87. Cf. J. Kübel, Geschichte des katholischen Modernismus (Tübingen: J. C. B. Mohr, 1909); G. Prezzolini, Wesen, Geschichte und Ziele des Modernismus (Jena: Diederichs, 1910).

88. F. Schleiermacher, The Christian Faith, §115.

89. Ibid., §§125–26.

90. Ibid., §148.

91. C. E. Nitzsch, System of Christian Doctrine (Edinburgh: T&T Clark, 1849), 186–88; J. P. Lange, Christliche Dogmatik, 3 vols. (Heidelberg: K. Winter, 1852), II, 1090ff.; H. Martensen, Christian Dogmatics,

these matters, some theologians abandon the old terms and speak instead of the kingdom of God and the church,[92] or of believing community and church.[93] One can certainly, with Stahl, still regard this visible church as a creation of Christ; but most view it as a form of existence the believing community has assumed for itself and can alter as circumstances change.[94] Some even judge that the institutional church has had its day and must become a confessing community[95] or even turn into the state.[96] Many theologians view the church as an institution that Christ neither wanted nor intended and which is in fact the reason for the corruption of Christianity.[97]

THE CHURCH AS THE "PEOPLE OF GOD"

[490] The word קָהָל (qāhāl), ἐκκλησια (ekklēsia), by virtue of its derivation from verbs that mean "to call together," already denotes a gathering of people who come together for some purpose, especially a political or religious purpose, or, even if at a given moment they have not come together, are nevertheless mutually united for such a purpose. Under the Old Testament dispensation Israel was the people that had been called together and convened for God's service. In the New Testament, the people of Israel have been replaced by the church of Christ, which is now the "holy nation, the chosen race, the royal priesthood" of God. The word "church" (kirk, kerk, kirche, chiesa), used to translate ἐκκλησια, does not express as clearly as the original this character of the church of Christ. It is probably derived from κυριακη (kyriakē; completed by οἰκια [oikia, house] being understood) or κυριακον (kyriakon; completed by οἰκον [oikon, house] being understood) and hence originally meant, not the congregation itself, but

---

trans. W. Urwick (Edinburgh: T&T Clark, 1871), §191; Julius Müller, *Dogmatische Abhandlungen* (Bremen: C. E. Müller, 1870), 332ff.; G. Thomasius, *Christi Person und Werk*, 3rd ed., 2 vols. (Erlangen: A. Deichert, 1886–88), II, 505; F. H. R. Frank, *System der christlichen Wahrheit*, 3rd rev. ed., 2 vols. (Erlangen and Leipzig: Deichert, 1894), II, 369; J. Kaftan, *Dogmatik* (Tübingen: Mohr, 1901), 573, 585.

92. A. J. Dorner, *Kirche und Reich Gottes*; A. Krauss, *Das protestantische Dogma von der unsichtbaren Kirche*.

93. F. J. Stahl, *Die Kirchenverfassung nach Lehre und Recht der Protestanten*, 67. H. Bavinck, *De theologie van Daniel Chantepie de la Saussaye* (Leiden: Donner, 1884), 66ff. J. J. van Oosterzee, *Christian Dogmatics*, trans. J. Watson and M. Evans, 2 vols. (New York: Scribner, Armstrong, 1874), §129.

94. R. A. Lipsius, *Lehrbuch der evangelisch-protestantischen Dogmatik* (Braunschweig: C. A. Schwetschke & Sohn, 1876), §859. C. P. Tiele, *Elements of the Science of Religion*, II, 165.

95. O. Pfleiderer, *Religionsphilosophie*, 745; R. Sohm, *Kirchenrecht*, passim; C. G. Chavannes, *Qu'est-ce qu'une église?* (Paris: Fischbacher, 1897); A. Sabatier, *Religions of Authority and Religions of the Spirit*, trans. L. S. Houghton (New York: McClure, Phillips, & Sons, 1904); L. W. E. Rauwenhoff, *Wijsbegeerte van den godsdienst*, 843.

96. D. F. Strauss, *Die christliche Glaubenslehre*, II, 618; ed. note: Bavinck erroneously cites this as *Dogmatik*. R. Rothe, *Theologische Ethik*, 2nd rev. ed., 5 vols. (Wittenberg: Zimmermann, 1867–71), §§124ff., 440ff., 1167ff.; cf. J. Happel, *Richard Rothes Lehre von der Kirche* (Leipzig: Heinsius, 1909); J. Thomä, "Richard Rothes Lehre von der Kirche," *Theologische Studien und Kritiken* (1910): 244–99.

97. H. Faber, *Das Christenthum der Zukunft* (Zurich: Schulthess, 1904).

its place of assembly, the church building.[98] Today we use the word in the sense of the building or of the worship service ("church starts at 10:00 a.m.") or of the organized group of congregations (the Roman Catholic or the Anglican Church). In the word "church" the meaning of the New Testament word ἐκκλησια has been obscured. In certain periods the sense that "church" is the name for "the people of God" has almost totally eroded.

Observations on translating ἐκκλησια:[99]

This is also the reason why ἐκκλησια is often translated in the Dutch (and German) language by *gemeente* (*Gemeinde*) instead of *kerk* (*Kirche*). As with the English word "community," this communicates more effectively the church as a *fellowship* of believers, a communion of saints. However, since *gemeente* also serves as a civic term to denote local government entities (*gemeentehuis* = city hall; *gemeenteraad* = city council; English language parallel: "community center"), the word *kerk* has become the preferred translation and standard usage. Dutch law, in a deliberate effort to disestablish the national Dutch Reformed Church in the nineteenth century, began to use the term *kerkgenoostschap* or "church society." This underscores the voluntary character of the church and its role as a social institution, but does so at the expense of its identity and its unity as the body of Christ created by the Holy Spirit.

Finally, it is not advisable to replace the word "church" in the sense of "the people of God" with the expression "kingdom of God." The difference between the two, after all, is not insignificant. In the first place, "the kingdom of God," with which Jesus's preaching begins, is an eschatological term for the messianic kingdom with all its benefits. Also, to the extent this kingdom is already present on earth in human hearts as a result of regeneration, forgiveness, and renewal, it consists rather in spiritual benefits than in a fellowship of persons. The kingdom of God is or becomes above all the possession of the poor in spirit, the pure in heart, the "children," and consists in peace, joy, and delight engendered by the Holy Spirit. For that reason it is not—at least on earth—organized. In principle it exists wherever the spiritual benefits of Christ have been granted and is nowhere completed on earth.[100] The church, however, is especially a this-worldly term,

98. J. C. Suicerus, *Thesaurus ecclesiasticus* (Amsterdam: J. H. Wetsten, 1682), s.v. ἐκκλησια; J. Köstlin, "Kirche," in *PRE*[3], X, 316. Some scholars still dispute this derivation and consider *circus* to be the source (ibid., 317). Also, according to E. Glaser (*Woher kommt das Wort "Kirche"?* [Munich: H. Lukaschik, 1901]), the word is derived from the root *krk* or *krkh* (from the Syriac *karkha* = a specific place) so that the word refers to the church building as a fortress or castle of God.

99. Ed. note: The following paragraph is a highly condensed adaptation of more than a page of text in the Dutch original where Bavinck provides a detailed discussion of the complications in translating ἐκκλησια into the Dutch language. His chief concern is to remind his Dutch readers not to forget that though the word *kerk* includes the building, the institution, and the civil/societal dimension of the fellowship of Christian believers in a specific time and place, the church is first and above all the body of Christ, the fellowship of the Holy Spirit, the communion of the saints, those who have been *called out*.

100. Cf. H. Bavinck, *Reformed Dogmatics*, III, 246–53 (##354–55).

a fellowship of persons equipped with offices and ministries that function in the visible world as the gathered people of God. The church, accordingly, is the means by which Christ distributes the benefits of the kingdom of God and lays the groundwork for its completion. And to advance the coming of that kingdom in the course of its journey through time, it absorbs all sorts of elements that are impure and actually do not belong to it (such as hypocrites and the "old" Adam in believers), whereas the kingdom of God, consisting in [spiritual] goods, is pure and uncontaminated and encompasses only what is regenerate. Christ has been given to be the head of the church precisely in order that in the end God might publicly appear as king of his people and be all things in all people.[101]

Now there is no doubt that according to Scripture the characteristic essence of the church lies in the fact that it is the people of God. For the church is a realization of election, and the latter is election in Christ to calling, justification, and glorification (Rom. 8:28), to being conformed to the image of God's Son (8:29), to holiness and blessedness (Eph. 1:4ff.). The blessings granted to the church are primarily internal and spiritual in character and consist in calling and regeneration, in faith and justification, in sanctification and glorification. They are the goods of the kingdom of heaven, benefits of the covenant of grace, promises for this life and, above all, for the life to come.

On these grounds, the church is the body of Christ (1 Cor. 12:27; Eph. 5:23; Col. 1:18), the bride of Christ (2 Cor. 11:2; Eph. 5:32; Rev. 19:7; 21:2), the sheepfold of Christ who gives his life for the sheep and is known by them (John 10), the building, the temple, the house of God (Matt. 16:18; Eph. 2:20; 1 Pet. 2:5), built up out of living stones (1 Pet. 2:5) on Christ as the cornerstone, and on the foundation of apostles and prophets (1 Cor. 3:17; 2 Cor. 6:16–17; Eph. 2:20–22; Rev. 21:2–4), the people, the possession, the Israel of God (Rom. 9:25; 2 Cor. 6:16; Heb. 8:10; 1 Pet. 2:9–10). The members of the church are called branches of the vine (John 15), living stones (1 Pet. 2:5), the elect, the called, believers, beloved, brothers and sisters, children of God and so forth. By contrast, those who are not really such are viewed in Scripture as chaff (Matt. 3:12), weeds among the wheat (13:25, 38), bad fish in the net (13:47), people without a wedding garment at the wedding (22:11), called but not chosen (22:14), bad branches in the vine (John 15:2), non-Israel though descended from Israel (Rom. 2:28; 9:6), evildoers who have to be put away (1 Cor. 5:2), vessels of dishonor (2 Tim. 2:20), such "who went out from us because they were not of us" (1 John 2:19), and so forth. All this makes it incontrovertible that in its essence the church is a gathering of true believers. Those who do not have an authentic faith may externally belong to the church; they do not make up its essential character. Though they are in the church, they are not the church.

---

101. F. A. Philippi, *Kirchliche Glaubenslehre*, 3rd ed., 7 vols. (Gütersloh: Bertelsmann, 1883–1902), V, 3, 203; F. H. R. Frank, *System der christlichen Wahrheit*, II, 375; J. Kaftan, *Dogmatik*, 584.

All this is further confirmed by the manner in which Scripture speaks of the communion of saints. Believers have one Lord, one baptism, one God and Father of all, and similarly they have one Spirit (Eph. 4:4–6), in whose fellowship they live, by whom they are regenerated, baptized into one body, and united with Christ (John 3:5; 14:17; Rom. 8:9, 14, 16; 1 Cor. 12:3, 13; 2 Cor. 1:22; 5:5; Eph. 1:13; 4:30; 1 John 2:20). And in this oneness the Spirit does not undo the diversity that exists among believers but rather maintains and confirms it. Just as in creation and providence the Spirit adorned and completed all things in their way[102] and in Israel granted an array of natural and spiritual gifts,[103] so on the day of Pentecost he communicated himself with all his charismata to the church of Christ. In a broad sense these charismata also include the benefits of grace imparted to all believers (Rom. 5:15–16; 6:23), but in a more restricted sense denote those special gifts that are granted to believers in a variable measure and degree for each other's benefit (Rom. 1:11; 1 Cor. 1:7; 2 Cor. 1:11; 1 Tim. 4:14; 2 Tim. 1:6; and particularly Rom. 12:6–9 and 1 Cor. 12:12ff.). Of all these gifts the Holy Spirit, who takes them all from Christ (John 16:13–14; Eph. 4:7), is the distributor. He apportions to each one individually as he wills, not arbitrarily but in connection with a person's measure of faith, with the position a person occupies in the church and the task to which that person is called (Rom. 12:3, 6; 2 Cor. 10:13; Eph. 4:7; 1 Pet. 4:10), so that every gift is "a manifestation of the Spirit" (1 Cor. 12:7).

These gifts are very numerous. Paul mentions several and intends by no means to list them all. Catholic scholars love to speak, with an appeal to Isa. 11:2–3, of seven gifts of the Holy Spirit,[104] as they do of seven deadly sins, seven virtues, and seven beatitudes. But these seven gifts of the Spirit do not include the actual charismata that are cited by Paul and discussed in Catholic theology under the heading of "the freely given graces" (*gratiae gratis datae*).[105] And these cannot be limited to a mere seven. To those enumerated by Paul, one can also add those of prayer and thanksgiving, admonition and consolation, communicativeness and hospitality, and so forth. It is therefore hard to classify them. Some clearly bear a supernatural character or are given only at the time of or after a person's conversion; others tend to be more like natural gifts that have been heightened and sanctified by the Holy Spirit. The former were more prominent in the early days of the church; the latter are more characteristic of the church in its normal historical development. But whatever these gifts may be, they all serve the good of the church. Whatever benefits God bestows on the community of saints, they in turn should share

---

102. Cf. H. Bavinck, *Reformed Dogmatics*, II, 261–64 (#213).

103. Ibid., II, 263–64 (#213).

104. P. Lombard, *Sent.*, III, dist. 34; T. Aquinas, *Summa theol.*, I, 2 qu. 68; II, 2 qu. 8; Bonaventure, *Brevilo-quium*, V, 5; M. Meschler, *Die Gabe des heiligen Pfingstfestes*, 3rd ed. (Freiburg i.B. and St. Louis: Herder, 1896), 233ff.; H. Th. Simar, *Lehrbuch der Dogmatik*, 2 vols. (Freiburg i.B.: Herder, 1879–80), 554; J. B. Heinrich and K. Gutberlet, *Dogmatische Theologie*, 2nd ed., 10 vols. (Mainz: Kirchheim, 1881–1900), VIII, 631.

105. H. Th. Simar, *Lehrbuch der Dogmatik*, 486.

with one another.[106] The Holy Spirit does not distribute the charismata to the members of the church for their own benefit but for the benefit of others. They must not be buried or neglected but used "readily and cheerfully for the benefit and enrichment of the other members";[107] they serve for the upbuilding of the church (1 Cor. 14:12; Eph. 4:12) and are subordinate to love, which is the most excellent gift. This love, after all, surpasses the universal love of one's neighbor; it is love for the brothers and sisters, the members of the household of faith. Jesus calls this love a new commandment (John 13:34–35; 15:12; 17:26). The reason is that love in Israel was not purely spiritual in character but intertwined with blood ties, and the love he now brings about among his disciples for the first time is completely pure, unmixed with other things, and free from earthly attachments. The members of Jesus's church are mutually brothers and sisters (Matt. 12:48; 18:15; 23:8; 25:40; 28:10; John 15:14–15; 20:17; Rom. 8:29; Heb. 2:11; and so forth). They are children of one family. God is their Father (Eph. 4:6). Christ is their eldest brother (Rom. 8:29). The Jerusalem that is above is their mother (Gal. 4:26). And in that light they must serve each other with all their spiritual and natural gifts. The church is a fellowship or communion of saints.[108]

[491] As long as we hold on to this as the church's essence, the idea of the church does not produce any unmanageable difficulties. In that case the church can always be defined in a broader or stricter sense as the gathered company of believers. In its broadest sense it embraces all who have been saved by faith in Christ or will be saved thus. When it is so defined, Adam and Eve before the fall do not yet belong to it, for at that time they did not yet need a Savior. Nor can the angels be counted as members of it, although this has been done by many theologians; for while Christ is indeed the Lord of angels and has by his cross reconciled all things, including angels and humans, to God and to each other, angels were not created in God's image, did not fall, and have not been redeemed by Christ, and so are not members of the church that Christ gathers to eternal life.[109] Believers, according to Heb. 12:22, do come to the community with its myriad angels, but these are clearly distinguished from "the festive assembly and church of the first-born" (v. 23). The members of the church are only people who have been saved

---

106. J. Calvin, *Institutes*, IV.i.3.

107. Heidelberg Catechism, A 55.

108. Cf. H. Bavinck, *Reformed Dogmatics*, III, 499–506 (##412–13); W. Ames, *The Marrow of Theology*, trans. J. D. Eusden (1968; repr., Grand Rapids: Baker Academic, 1997), I, 31–32 (pp. 175–81); ed. note: Bavinck's original reference is to *Medulla theologica* (Amsterdam: Ioannem Ianssonium, 1628), II, §§12–23; G. Voetius, *Selectae disputationes theologicae*, 5 vols. (Utrecht: 1648–69), II, 1086–1100; A. Neander, *Geschichte der Pflanzung und Leitung der christlichen Kirche durch die Apostel*, 5th ed., 2 vols. (Gotha: F. A. Perthes, 1862), 180ff.; ed. note: ET: *History of the Planting and Training of the Christian Church by the Apostles*, 2 vols. (London: Bell & Daly, 1864); O. Pfleiderer, *Der Paulinismus: Ein Beitrag zur Geschichte der urchristlichen Theologie* (Leipzig: O. R. Reisland, 1890), 242; H. J. Holtzmann, *Lehrbuch der neutestamentlichen Theologie*, II, 143, 175; Cremer, "Geistesgaben," in *PRE*[3], VI, 460. M. Lauterburg, *Der Begriff des Charisma und seine Bedeutung für die praktische Theologie* (Gütersloh: C. Bertelsmann, 1898).

109. Cf. H. Bavinck, *Reformed Dogmatics*, II, 461–63 (#265); III, 470–75 (##407–8).

by faith in Christ. Belonging to it, accordingly, are all the believers who lived on earth from the time of the paradisal promise to this very moment and were taken up, not into the limbus of the ancestors or purgatory, but into heaven (12:23). Belonging to it are all the believers who still live on earth now. And belonging to it, in a sense, are also those who will later, even to the end of the ages, believe in Christ. For the church, even taken in its broadest sense, is not a Platonic state that exists only in the imagination and never becomes a reality, but is a company of people that has the guarantee of its existence, now and in the future, in God's decree, in the firm security of the covenant of grace, the mediatorship of Christ, and the promise of the Holy Spirit.

At any given moment, then, the majority of its members are not on earth, for from the time of paradise [Eden] to the present, many thousands and millions have already been taken up into heaven and daily, from moment to moment, their number is increased (the church triumphant). There are also many who do not yet believe or have not even been born yet but who will nevertheless, with infallible certainty, come to believe. Hence the church as the gathering of believers who at a given time live on earth (the church militant) is only a small part of the church taken in its broadest sense. Still it is well, and also necessary, to hold on to the connectedness between the church on earth now and that of the past and the future. For it is one single gathering, one ἐκκλησια (ekklēsia), composed of those who are enrolled in heaven and who will one day stand before God as a bride without spot or wrinkle. And the maintenance of this unity of the whole church heightens the sense of community, steels one's nerve, and stirs a person to fight for it. If we further limit ourselves to the part of the church that is now on earth (the church militant), then it can again be taken more broadly or more narrowly. We can associate it with all the believers who are now present in all the churches, among all nations, and in all countries (the church universal), with the believers in one country or in a given province of that country (Acts 9:31; the national or provincial church), or with all the believers living in a certain place—city, town, or village (the particular or local church). In this connection it must be noted that the universal church is antecedent to the particular or local church. The church of Christ is an organism in which the whole is prior to the parts. It has its origin in paradise (Gen. 3:15), or, as it concerns the time of the New Testament, in Jerusalem (Acts 1:8). For as long as it alone was the church, the church of Jerusalem was the universal church of Christ on earth, and the churches that before long arose alongside of it were not autochthonous but came into being from action taken in Jerusalem through the preaching of the apostles and evangelists.

CHURCH DISTINCTIONS

Up to this point the meaning of the term "church" is plain and clear. But now we encounter two difficulties. The first consists in the fact that this scriptural concept of the church is applied to concrete, historically existing distinct groups of persons, in which there are always unbelievers as well. In the Old Testament, the entire nation was called the people of God, although far from everything that was called Israel was of Israel. In the churches of the New Testament, though to a much lesser extent, there was also chaff amid the grain and weeds among the wheat. And after the apostolic period, though the churches over and over became worldly, corrupt, and divided, we still call all of them churches. Theology, like Scripture, has at all times acknowledged this fact and, following Scripture, consistently stated that the basic nature of the church was determined by believers, not unbelievers.[110] Augustine illustrated the presence of unbelievers in the church with the scriptural image of chaff and grain, or with that of body and soul, the outer and the inner person, bad "humors" in the body: in the body of Christ unbelievers are a kind of "bad humors."[111] Scholastic and Roman Catholic theologians spoke in similar terms. Bellarmine, for example, though he attempted to show that unbelievers are also members of the church, did not get beyond asserting that they are members "in some fashion";[112] they only belong to the body, not to the soul of the church. The good are the interior part of the church, the bad are the exterior part; unbelievers are "dead" or "arid" members, who are bound to the church only "by an external connection"; they belong to the kingdom of Christ as far as their profession of faith is concerned, but to the realm of the devil so far as it concerns their perverse lifestyle. They are children of the family on account of the form of their piety, but strangers on account of their loss of virtues. While there may not be two churches, there are in fact two parties in the church.[113] And the Roman Catechism says that in the church militant there are two kinds of people, and that according to Scripture there are bad fish in the net and weeds on the field and chaff on the threshing floor, foolish virgins among the wise and unclean animals in the ark.[114] In theory, this is not very different from the doctrine of the Reformation, but practically, things in the church looked very different toward the end of the Middle Ages. And Rome also consistently fosters the idea that external membership, a historical faith, observance of the commandments of the church, and submission to the pope constitute the essence of the church.

Rising up against this view, the Reformation posited the distinction between the visible and invisible church. Of nominal Christians Augustine had already stated that though they seem to be inside, they are separated from it by an *invisible* bond of love.[115] Actually Rome cannot object to this distinction and does in fact itself accept it inasmuch as it distinguishes two kinds of people, two parties, in the church. Bellarmine speaks of "hidden unbelievers,"[116] and Mohler praises Luther

---

110. See above, 279–81 (#486).
111. R. Seeberg, *Der Begriff der christlichen Kirche*, 45.
112. R. Bellarmine, "De eccl. mil.," in *Controversiis*, III, 2.
113. Ibid., III, 9.
114. Roman Catechism, I, 10, qu. 6–7.
115. Augustine, *On Baptism* III, 19; R. Seeberg, *Der Begriff der christlichen Kirche*, 42.
116. R. Bellarmine, "De eccl. mil.," in *Controversiis*, III, 10.

when he conceives of the church as a communion of saints and says that believers, the invisible ones, are the bearers of the visible church.[117] But the distinction between the visible and the invisible church can be variously construed.[118] The majority of these views, however, are to be rejected or at least do not come up for discussion in dogmatics. The church cannot be called invisible because Christ, the church triumphant, and the church that will be completed at the end of the ages cannot now be observed; nor can the church be called invisible because the church on earth cannot be seen by us in many places and countries, or goes into hiding in times of persecution, or is sometimes deprived of the ministry of the Word and sacraments. The distinction between the visible and invisible church can only be applied to the church militant and then means that the church is invisible with respect to its spiritual dimension and its true members. In the case of Lutherans and the Reformed, these two meanings have fused and cannot be separated from each other. The church is an object of faith. The internal faith of the heart, regeneration, true conversion, hidden communion with Christ (and so forth) are spiritual goods that cannot be observed by the natural eye and nevertheless give to the church its true character (*forma*). No human being has received from God the infallible standard by which one can judge someone else's spiritual life. "The church makes no judgment concerning the most private things."[119] The Lord alone knows those who are his. Thus it is possible—and in the Christian church has always been a fact—that there was chaff amid the wheat and there were hypocrites hidden among true believers. The word "church," used with reference to the militant church, the gathering of believers on earth, therefore, always and among all Christians, both Catholic and Protestant, has a metaphorical sense. It is so called, not in terms of the unbelievers who exist in it, but in terms of the believers, who constitute the essential component of it and determine its nature. The whole is called after the part. A church is and remains the gathered company of true Christ-believers.

[492] So conceived, no one can take exception to the distinction between the visible and invisible church. Rather, it should be generally acknowledged. But there is still another difficulty associated with the idea of the church. The gathered company of believers on earth is not only structured charismatically but also institutionally. It is not only itself the possession of Christ but also serves to win others for Christ. It is a gathered company (*coetus*) but also the mother of believers (*mater fidelium*); an organism but also an institution; a goal but also the means to that goal. The relationship of the church as organism to the church as institution can only be discussed in the next section, which deals with the government of the church. For just as the idea of the *state* is hard to describe and only becomes clear when in it the people and the government are distinguished

---

117. J. A. Möhler, *Symbolik* (Regensburg: G. J. Manz, 1871), §49.
118. See above, 287ff. (#488).
119. *De intimis non judicat ecclesia* (F. L. Rutgers, *Die kerkrecht* [Amsterdam: Wormser, 1894], art. 61).

and treated separately, so one can only offer a good definition of the church if one guards against equating the gathering of believers with its organization as an institution.[120]

Many theologians, however, relate the distinction between the church as organism and the church as institution to that between the invisible and the visible church and imperceptibly accord to the latter a meaning that does not belong to it. On the one side are those who not only describe the church in terms of its [normative] idea, or its spiritual essence (the church triumphant), but also describe the church militant on earth as the gathering of the predestined or elect (Wycliffe), or of the perfected (thus Pelagius, according to Augustine;[121] and the Anabaptists, according to Calvin;[122] and numerous others). Others include those who have never fallen (Novatian), or those members of the church who participate in the Lord's Supper (communicants, as many people in North America mark the boundary of the church). On the other side are the Roman Catholics, who shift the church's center of gravity from the gathering of believers to the hierarchical institution, to "the external and supreme monarchy of the whole world," and look for its characteristic essence in the "teaching church" (*ecclesia docens*) rather than in the "listening church" (*ecclesia audiens*). And this is the direction taken by all those who, in order to hold on to unbelievers and hypocrites at least to some degree as true members, describe the church as the gathering of those who are called (Melanchthon, Löhe, Kliefoth, and so forth) or of the baptized (Münchmeyer, Delitzsch, Vilmar, and so forth).

Both of these views are one-sided and fail to do justice to the basic nature of the church. Given the first position, the church becomes totally invisible, remains an idea, and has no corresponding reality. Election by itself does not yet make a person a member of the church on earth. The elect who have not yet attained to faith do indeed belong to the church as it exists in the mind and decree of God. They can even be said to belong potentially to the church, but actually they are not yet members of it. Nor can the church be described as the gathering of the perfected, or of the nonfallen, or of communicants, for believers in this life do not reach perfection and are not safeguarded against every fall by the promises of God, and churches are not limited to the number of communicants.

The second of the two positions described above is equally out of alignment with the basic nature of the church. For external membership, calling, and baptism are no proof of genuine faith. Many are called who are not chosen. Many are baptized who do not believe. Not all are Israel who are of Israel. So, whereas the former group fails to arrive at a visible church, the latter neglects the invisible church. The two positions only come fully into their own when the church is conceived of as a gathering of believers. For it is genuine faith that saves persons and receives

---

120. F. Turretin, *Institutes of Elenctic Theology*, XVIII, 3, 10; F. J. Stahl, *Der Kirchenverfassung*, 46.
121. Augustine, *On Heresies* 88.
122. J. Calvin, *Institutes*, IV.i.8.

the forgiveness of sins and eternal life. While that faith is a matter of the heart, it does not remain within a person but manifests itself outwardly in a person's witness and walk (Rom. 10:10), and witness and walk are the signs of the internal faith of the heart (Matt. 7:17; 10:32; 1 John 4:2). Granted, a person's faith and witness are also often far from always in agreement. In the case of the children of believers, for example, there is faith that is not manifested in deeds, a confession that consists in saying "Lord, Lord" and is not born of true faith. Still, the advantage of defining the church as the gathering of believers over its description as the gathering of the called and the baptized is that it maintains precisely that on which everything depends, both for the individual and the whole church. Our being called and baptized is not decisive, for those who believe and are baptized will be saved, and, conversely, those who do not believe, even though they were called and baptized, will be condemned (Mark 16:16).

From this it follows that the distinction between the church as institution and the church as organism is very different from that between the visible and the invisible church and may not be equated with it. For both "institution" and "organism" describe the church in terms of its visible aspect. In this connection, one must also not forget that the institution and the organism of the church, when they assert themselves in the visible realm, have an invisible spiritual background. For office and gift, the administration of the Word and the sacraments, brotherly love and the communion of the saints, are all grounded in the operations of the glorified head of the church through the Holy Spirit. We must therefore repudiate the notion that the institution was mechanically added as something accidental and external to the church as the gathering of believers. Yet when thinking of the church as institution and as organism, we primarily have in mind the church in terms of its visible aspect; that is, in terms of the offices and ministries with which it is equipped and of the communion of saints as that is manifested in "brotherly" love. And in precisely these two ways the church becomes outwardly visible. Therefore the view that the church only becomes visible in the institution, the offices and ministries, the Word and the sacraments, and in some form of church government is correct. Even when all these things are removed from the screen of our mind, the church is still visible. For every believer manifests his or her faith in witness and walk in every sphere of life, and all believers together, with their faith and lives, distinguish themselves from the world. In heaven there will no longer be ecclesiastical offices and ministries, preaching of the Word and administration of the sacraments, yet the church will be fully visible. Visibility and invisibility therefore distinguish the church from a completely different perspective than institution and organism. The latter distinction tells us in what ways the church becomes visible and knowable to us; the former teaches us that this visible manifestation has an invisible spiritual aspect to it, which is known only to God.

This analysis automatically implies that the visible and the invisible church are not two distinct churches. The objection had already been lodged against

Augustine by the Donatists and was later repeated by Roman Catholics against Protestants. But this accusation is based on misunderstanding. Rome itself acknowledges, as we saw earlier, that there are two kinds of people in the church, that the church is composed of two groups. Though Rome attempts to demonstrate that unbelievers "in some fashion" belong to the church, it shrinks from saying that they constitute the essence of the church. In reality, therefore, Rome faces the same difficulty as the Reformation. For the idea that hypocrites "in some fashion" belong to the church is not a point in dispute. Protestants also acknowledge that they are in the church and belong to the church just as rotten branches belong to the vine and chaff to the wheat. Protestants deny, however, that these hypocrites define the true character of the church (its *forma*), for it is true faith alone that saves and incorporates us into Christ. Unbelievers, accordingly, are not the essence of the church; they are not the church. The invisible and the visible church, therefore, are definitely not terms collectively describing the unbelievers and believers who exist in the church. According to the Lord's command, discipline must be maintained in the church both with respect to doctrine and life, but every attempt to split believers from unbelievers and vice versa and to create a little church (*ecclesiola*) within the *ecclesia* is in conflict with the Lord's command. Matthew 13:30 does not contradict this, for the field intended there is not the church but the world (v. 38).

What follows from all this is that we are limited to noting people's witness and walk, and we neither can nor may judge their hearts. Unbelievers, therefore, no more constitute the essence of the visible church than of the invisible church. In neither of these respects do they belong to the church, even though we lack the right and the authority to separate them from believers and to cast them out. Even stronger: we can also say that the old Adam that still survives in believers does not belong to the church. This is not to agree with Schleiermacher when he locates the essence of the church in the operations of the Holy Spirit, for the church is not a gathering of operations but of persons. It is people who have been regenerated and brought to faith by the Holy Spirit, who as such, as new persons, constitute the essence of the church. Still, the church is a gathering of believers, and everything that does not arise out of true faith but from the old Adam does not belong to the church and will one day be cast out. For this reason the visible and the invisible church are two sides of one and the same church. The same believers are viewed in the one case from the perspective of the faith that dwells in their heart and is only known with certainty to God; and in the other case they are viewed from the perspective of their witness and life, the side that is turned toward us and can be observed by us. Because the church on earth is in process of becoming, these two sides are never—not even in the purest church—identical. There are always unbelievers within and believers outside the church. Many wolves are within and many sheep are outside the sheepfold. The latter occurred in the Old Testament, for example, in the case of Naaman the Syrian and is still true today of all who for one reason or another live outside the fellowship of organized ("instituted") churches and yet have true faith. But all this in no way detracts from the fact that the essence of the church consists in believers alone.

THE MARKS OF THE CHURCH

[493] If the church is in essence a gathering of true Christ-believers and these are known only to God, the important question arises by what marks we can know the church. Roman Catholic Christians especially object to the Reformation idea of the church because it undermines the certainty of the church and hence the salvation of their souls and opens the door to doubt, division, and indifference. Bellarmine states it with the utmost clarity: "It is necessary that we be agreed with infallible certainty as to which gathered company of humans is the true church of Christ, for since the traditions of Scripture and all dogmas clearly depend on the testimony of the church, unless we are very certain which is the true church, everything else will consequently also be uncertain as well." Now this is impossible if only genuine faith makes us truly a member of the church, for we can never know this with certainty. A conjectural knowledge is insufficient. At this point we need infallible certainty,[123] for "we are all bound, at the risk of eternal death, to join the true church and to persevere in it."[124] The true church must therefore be as clearly visible and palpable "as the assembly of the people of Rome, the kingdom of France, or the republic of the Venetians."[125] For that reason Bellarmine does his very best to prove the truth of the Roman Catholic Church, listing no fewer than fifteen marks:

1. The very name
2. The antiquity
3. The long duration
4. The multitude and variety of the believers of the Catholic Church
5. The succession of its bishops
6. Its agreement in doctrine with the ancient church
7. The unity of its members among themselves and with their head
8. The holiness of its doctrine
9. The efficacy of its doctrine
10. The holiness of life of the early fathers
11. The glory of its miracles
12. The light of prophecy
13. The confession of its adversaries
14. The unhappy fate of those who oppose the church
15. Temporal happiness[126]

123. R. Bellarmine, "De eccl. mil.," in *Controversiis*, III, 10.
124. Ibid., III, 12.
125. Ibid., III, 2.
126. Ibid., IV, c. 4–18.

Roman Catholic theologians, following this model, usually reduce the fifteen marks to four, which in the Nicene Creed are denominated the unity, sanctity, catholicity, and apostolicity of the church.[127]

It is noteworthy, furthermore, that in a real sense Rome has no marks or criteria by which the true church can be known. These, after all, presuppose a standard that is above the church and by which it may be judged by everyone. And Rome does not have such a standard, for Scripture depends on the church, and the church is itself the highest standard for doctrine and life. In the case of Rome, accordingly, the marks of the church are nothing but the indications or properties in which the church manifests itself. Proofs for the church are the same as those for Christianity itself, for to Rome the two are one. And these proofs, though they do not make the proposition that the Roman Catholic Church is the true church "evidently true," they make it "evidently credible."[128] Vatican I declares the same:

> God, through his only begotten Son, founded the church, and he endowed his institution with clear notes to the end that she might be recognized by all as the guardian and teacher of the revealed word. To the catholic church alone belong all those things, so many and so marvelous, which have been divinely ordained to make for the manifest credibility of the Christian faith. What is more, the church herself by reason of her astonishing propagation, her outstanding holiness and her inexhaustible fertility in every kind of goodness, by her catholic unity and her unconquerable stability, is a kind of great and perpetual motive of credibility and an incontrovertible evidence of her own divine mission.[129]

The truth of the church, accordingly, is not absolutely demonstrable to everyone. If it were, the church would not be an article of faith, and faith would not be free and meritorious. Added to the witness that proceeds from the church, according to the [First] Vatican Council, there has to be "the effective help of power from on high."[130] In saying this, Rome actually takes the same subjective position as the Reformation. The arguments, however strong, cannot actually move a person to faith. It is God's Spirit alone that can persuade a person inwardly and with full

---

127. G. Perrone, *Praelectiones theologicae*, 9 vols. (Louvain: Vanlinthout & Vandezande, 1838–43), I, 248; F. L. B. Liebermann, *Institutions théologiques*, 3rd ed., 5 vols. (Paris: Librairie de Gaume Frères, 1855), I, 255; M. Scheeben and L. Atzberger, *Handbuch der Katholischen Dogmatik*, 4 vols. (Freiburg i.B.: Herder, 1933; orig. pub. 1874–98), IV, 372; ed. note: See J. Wilhelm and T. B. Scannell, *A Manual of Catholic Theology*, 4th ed., 2 vols. (London: Kegan Paul, Trench, Trübner; New York: Benziger Brothers, 1909); G. M. Jansen, *Praelectiones theologiae dogmaticae*, 3 vols. in 2 (Utrecht: Van Rossum, 1875–79), I, 659; F. Hettinger, *Apologie des Christenthums*, IV, 411; V, 106.

128. R. Bellarmine, "De eccl. mil.," in *Controversiis*, IV, c. 3.

129. Vatican I, sess. III (April 24, 1870), ch. 3: "On Faith"; H. Denzinger, ed., *The Sources of Catholic Dogma*, trans. from the 30th ed. by R. J. Deferrari (London and St. Louis: Herder, 1955), ##1793–94; ed. note: English translation in text is from Norman P. Tanner, SJ, ed., *Decrees of the Ecumenical Councils*, 2 vols. (London: Sheed & Ward; Washington, DC: Georgetown University Press, 1990), II, 807–8.

130. *Efficax subsidium ex superna virtute.* Ed. note: Bavinck does not cite the source for this phrase; it is found in Denzinger, *Sources of Catholic Dogma*, #1794.

assurance of the truth of divine revelation. The deepest ground for faith, also in the case of Rome, is not Scripture or the church but the "interior light." Rome, with its infallible church and its infallible pope, fundamentally has no advantage over the churches of the Reformation, for the church and the pope, however visible, still remain "articles of faith."[131]

Accordingly, the marks that Rome cites for the true church are in no respect clearer and stronger than the pure administration of the Word, which is recognized as a mark of the true church by the Reformation. Some of the marks listed by Bellarmine are of very subordinate value. The gifts of miracles are absolutely inadequate proof for the truth of the doctrine someone proclaims (Deut. 13:1–2; Matt. 7:22–23; 24:24; etc.).[132] In most cases the unfortunate fate of the enemies and persecutors of the church is only legend, as also Roman Catholics acknowledge,[133] and the earthly prosperity of the church is always temporary, alternates with persecution and oppression, and can equally well be advanced against the truth of the church (Matt. 5:10; 16:24; John 16:33; Acts 14:22; 2 Tim. 3:12). With reference to other marks, everything depends on the sense in which they are understood. The qualification "catholic" has also been adopted by Protestant churches and as such no more constitutes an argument for the truth of the Roman Catholic Church than the name "Christ," which false Christs appropriate for themselves (Matt. 24:24), or the name "Israel" or "Abraham's seed," on which the Jews prided themselves (John 8:33; Rom. 9:6). Antiquity, historical continuity, and unbroken succession not only characterize Rome but also other churches, the Greek Orthodox, for example, and as such no more prove anything with respect to the truth of the Roman Catholic Church than they did with respect to that of the Jewish community in Jesus's day. Unity and catholicity are claims of Rome that cannot undo the fact that millions of Christians live outside of its communion. There is not just one church but many churches, not one of which embraces all believers. The other marks (agreement with the teaching of the apostles, the holiness of its doctrine, the transforming power which proceeds from it, the saintly lives of many of its confessors) absolutely do not apply only to Rome but also to many other churches and are subject to the same objections as those that Roman Catholics advance against the Protestant marks (to be discussed later).[134]

In this the Roman Catholic Church indeed boasts of its unity and points with self-satisfaction at the division present in Protestantism. But it pays a heavy price

131. Cf. H. Bavinck, *Reformed Dogmatics*, I, 510–12 (#133), 578–82 (#150).

132. Cf. ibid., I, 514–17 (#134).

133. N. Paulus, *Luthers Lebensende* (Freiburg i.B.: Herder, 1898).

134. Th. Beza, "De eccl. cath. notis," in *Tractationum theologicarum* (Geneva: Jean Crispin, 1570), III, 132; A. Polanus, *Synt. theol.*, 532ff.; W. Ames, *Bellarminus enervatus*, 3rd ed., 4 vols. (Oxford: G. Turner, 1629), II, 56–72; S. Maresius, *Syst. theol.*, XVI, 23ff.; F. Turretin, *Institutes of Elenctic Theology*, XVIII, qu. 13. P. van Mastricht, *Theologia*, VII, 1, 34; B. de Moor, *Commentarius . . . theologiae*, 6 vols. (Leiden: J. Hasebroek, 1761–71), VI, 50; C. Vitringa, *Doctrina christiana religionis*, 8 vols. (Leiden: Johannis le Mari, 1761–86), IX, 1, 98; J. Gerhard, *Loci theologici*, ed. E. Preuss, 9 vols. (Berlin: G. Schlawitz, 1863–75), XXII, c. 10, 11; J. A. Quenstedt, *Theologia* (1685), IV, 503.

for this self-congratulation. In the first place, it is increasingly forced to transfer its definition of the essence of the church from the gathering of believers to the institution of the hierarchy and ultimately to the pope. The pope has better grounds for declaring: "The church? That's me!" than Louis XIV had for saying "L'état c'est moi" (the state, that's me). "Where the pope is, there is the church" (*ubi papa, ibi ecclesia*). If in thinking of the church we bring to mind not just the institution but also and primarily the gathering of believers, as we should, then the divisions in the Roman Catholic Church are no fewer than those in Protestantism. The only difference is that Rome, banking on the strength of a celibate hierarchy, permits all kinds of schools of thought and opinions to flourish side by side, and deprives its members, even the most unbelieving, of the energy and love of freedom and truth to break with the church and their own untrue position.

In the second place, Rome pays for its self-congratulatory pleasure with the heavy price of the position that outside the church there is no salvation (*extra ecclesiam nulla salus*). The teaching of Scripture that salvation is bound up with faith in Christ was soon—in the struggle against schism and heresy—understood to mean that everyone who wanted to partake of salvation in Christ had to be connected with the bishop.[135] Those who want to be saved must seek refuge in the holy churches of God.[136] "It is the Catholic Church alone that maintains true worship. Here is the fount of truth, the domicile of faith, the temple of God in relation to which, if anyone does not enter it or departs from it, a person estranges himself from the hope of life and eternal salvation."[137] The church fathers often employed the image of the ark for the church, and especially Cyprian used it to leave no doubt that "apart from the church there is no salvation."[138] Augustine held the same view: "It is clear that one who is not among the members of Christ cannot possess Christian salvation."[139] Outside the church a person can participate in all things, "but he can never obtain salvation except in the catholic church."[140] Councils and popes have confirmed this doctrine. The Fourth Lateran Council (1215) declared in its opening chapter that there is one catholic church of believers "outside which no one at all is saved."[141] Trent testified in its fifth session [June 17, 1546] that without the catholic faith it is impossible to please God.[142] Boniface VIII declared that submission to the pope is "necessary to salvation."[143] Eugenius IV

135. Ignatius, *To the Ephesians* 4–5; idem, *To the Philadelphians* 3; idem, *To the Trallians* 7.

136. Theophilus, *Theophilus to Autolycus* II, 14.

137. Lactantius, *The Divine Institutes* IV, 30.

138. Cyprian, *On the Unity of the Church* 6; idem, *Epistles* 2, 11, 69, 74.

139. Augustine, *De unitate ecclesiae liber* 2.

140. Augustine, *Proceedings with Emeritus* (*Super gesta cum Emerito*); ed. note: This work does not exist in English translation; Latin text in PL, XLIII; *Corpus scriptorum ecclesiasticorum latinorum*, 53; cf. *C. Romeis, *Das Heil des Christen ausserhalb der wahren Kirche nach der Lehre des heiligen Augustin* (Paderborn: F. Schöningh, 1908).

141. Ed. note: Denzinger, *Sources of Catholic Dogma*, #430.

142. Ed. note: Ibid., #787.

143. Ed. note: Ibid., #469.

taught that apart from the catholic church no one could obtain eternal life.[144] And Pius IX, in his allocution of December 9, 1854, declared that "we must maintain on the basis of faith that outside of the apostolic Roman church no person can be saved."[145] By its very nature, therefore, Rome has to be intolerant. It cannot acknowledge any churches other than itself. It is itself the only church, the bride of Christ, the temple of the Holy Spirit.

Yet for Rome, too, the facts have proved to be too powerful. Thousands, in fact millions, of people have over the centuries broken fellowship with the church of Rome: Novatians, Donatists, Greek Christians, Arians, Monophysites, Mono-theletists, many medieval sects, and in the sixteenth century more than half of Christendom. And though, by its Counter-Reformation, Rome has won many people back, of the 500 million Christians now living it can barely claim a half and is declining rather than growing in numbers. In the face of these facts it cannot be maintained that outside the Roman church there is no salvation. Even for Roman Catholics themselves it is hard to remain true to this doctrine; many are inclined to make concessions. They distinguish between those who deliberately, intentionally, obstinately, and therefore culpably leave the church and those who, swept along and misled by others, are "in good faith" outside the church and still belong to the church, that is, to the soul of the church, in solemn intent, desire, and spirit. In the same spirit "the chair of St. Peter" rejected the thesis of Baius. "Purely negative unbelief even among those to whom Christ has not been preached is a sin," and in his allocution of December 9, 1854, Pius IX declared: "It must be considered certain that those who labor in ignorance of true religion, even if this ignorance is invincible, cannot be faulted on this account."[146]

[494] For Protestantism, the doctrine concerning the marks of the true church had a totally different meaning. As a result of the Reformation, the unity of Western Christianity had been broken once and for all, and different churches came on the scene either side by side or in opposition to each other. The Reformers had to argue that the church of Rome was not the true church and that the churches of the Reformation fit the scriptural description of the nature of the church. Their Reformational act presupposed that the church was not trustworthy in and of itself (αὐτοπιστος, *autopistos*), that it could stray and depart from the truth, and that there was a higher authority to which it too had to submit. And that authority could be nothing other than Scripture, the Word of God. All the Reformers, therefore, unanimously returned to Scripture, regarded it alone as the standard of the church, and in keeping with this standard determined the marks by which

---

144. Ed. note: Ibid., #715.

145. Ed. note: Ibid., #1647; the reference is to the Allocution, "Singulari quadem," December 9, 1854.

146. R. Bellarmine, "De eccl. mil.," in *Controversiis*, III, c. 3, 6; G. Perrone, *Prael. theol.*, I, 331; H. Klee, *Katholische Dogmatik*, 3 vols. (Mainz, bei Kirchheim: Schott & Thielmann, 1835), I, 141; G. M. Jansen, *Prael. theol.*, I, 344; P. Schanz, *A Christian Apology*, trans. M. F. Gancey and V. J. Schobel, 4th ed. (Ratisbon: F. Pustet, 1891), III, 188; E. Dublanchy, *De axiomate: Extra ecclesiam nulla salus; Dissertatio theologica* (Bar-le-Duc: Contant-Laguerre, 1895).

the true church was to be distinguished from the false church. In the specification of those marks there were indeed some differences. In his work *Of Councils and Churches*, Luther listed seven: the pure administration of the Word, of baptism, of the Lord's Supper, and of the keys of the kingdom; the lawful choice of ministers, public prayer and education, and the cross; but elsewhere he only mentioned two: the pure administration of the Word and sacraments. Melanchthon[147] and later Lutheran theologians[148] did the same. Only Melanchthon in his *Examen ordinandorum* added a third and rather hierarchical mark: "obedience owing to the ministerium with respect to the gospel." Among the Reformed, some, such as Beza, Sohn, Alsted, Ames, Heidanus, and Maresius, specified only one mark: the pure administration of the Word. Others, such as Calvin, Bullinger, Zanchius, Junius, Gomarus, Mastricht, and Marck (et al.), two marks: the pure administration of Word and sacraments. Many, such as the Gallic, Belgic, and First Scotch Confessions, as well as Hyperius, Martyr, Ursinus, Trelcatius, Walaeus, Amyraldus, Heidegger, and Wendelinus, added as a third mark: the proper exercise of discipline or holiness of life. However, Alsted, Alting, Maresius, Hottinger, Heidanus, Turretin, and Mastricht (et al.) rightly commented that this was more a difference in name than in substance and that actually there is only one mark, the one and the same Word, which is variously administered and confessed in preaching, instruction, confession, sacrament, life, and so forth.[149]

That the Reformation rightly sought the key mark of the church in the Word of God cannot be doubted on the basis of Scripture. Without the Word of God, after all, there would be no church (Prov. 29:18; Isa. 8:20; Jer. 8:9; Hos. 4:6). Christ gathers his church (Matt. 28:19), which is built on the teaching of the apostles and prophets, by Word and sacrament (Matt. 16:18; Eph. 2:20). By the Word he regenerates it (James 1:18; 1 Pet. 1:23), engenders faith (Rom. 10:14; 1 Cor. 4:15), and cleanses and sanctifies [the church] (John 15:3; Eph. 5:26). And those who have thus been regenerated and renewed by the Word of God are called to confess Christ (Matt. 10:32; Rom. 10:9), to hear his voice (John 10:27), to keep his Word (John 8:31, 32; 14:23), to test the spirits (1 John 4:1), and to shun those who do not bring this doctrine (Gal. 1:8; Titus 3:10; 2 John 9). The Word is truly the soul of the church.[150] All ministry in the church is a ministry of the Word. God gives his Word to the church, and the church accepts, preserves, administers, and teaches it; it confesses it before God, before one another, and before the world in word and deed. In the one mark of the Word the others are included as further applications. Where God's Word is rightly preached, there also the sacrament is purely administered, the truth of God is confessed in line with the intent of the Spirit, and people's conduct is shaped accordingly. Even Rome cannot deny that the Word of God is the mark of the church. Gerhard

---

147. P. Melanchthon, Augsburg Confession, art. 8; idem, *Loci communes* (Berlin: G. Schlawitz, 1856).
148. J. Gerhard, *Loci theol.*, XXII, 31; J. A. Quenstedt, *Theologia*, IV, 5.
149. C. Vitringa, *Doctr. christ.*, IX, 101–9.
150. J. Calvin, *Institutes*, IV.xii.1.

cites numerous church fathers who say this plainly and clearly.[151] Thus Tertullian states: "Those are the true churches that adhere to what they have received from the apostles." In earlier times, says Chrysostom, it could be shown in various ways which was the church of Christ, but since heresies have crept in, this can only be demonstrated by means of the Scriptures. In any case, those Scriptures are simple and true so that by using them it can easily be determined which doctrine is true. Augustine repeatedly speaks in this vein: "Between us and the Donatists the question is: Where in the world is the church? What are we going to do? Are we going to seek it in the words of Donatus or in the words of his head, the Lord Jesus Christ? I think that we ought to seek it in the words of him who is the truth and who knows his own body best, for he knows who are his own."

OBJECTIONS TO REFORMED MARKS

Bellarmine himself describes the church as "that gathered company of humans which is bound together by profession of the same Christian faith and by participation in the same sacraments." He includes the sanctity of doctrine among the marks of the church[152] and admits that, in some cases, if Scripture is accepted as the Word of God, Scripture is better known than the church and proves its truth.[153] In answering the question as to which are the distinguishing marks of the church, Rome too has to use Scripture as the basis of proof, if it does not want to end all discussion with the statement: "This is what I want; this is what I command; the will stands in the place of reason."[154]

Rome, nevertheless, rejects the marks that the Reformation listed for the true church. Bellarmine first of all advances against them that the pure administration of the Word at most indicates *where* the true church is but not *which* church is the true one; that is, who the true believers are who alone, according to Protestant tradition, constitute the essence of the church.[155] To some extent this objection is on target but actually also void. For it is absolutely unnecessary for us to know with infallible certainty who the true believers are. To search, with Julius Müller[156] for example, for infallible criteria in that regard leads to the false road taken by the Donatists. The pure administration of the Word is not a mark for determining the sincere faith of individual members but [a mark] of the church as the gathering of believers. The promise of God (as expressed in Isa. 55:11; 2 Cor. 2:15–16; and so forth) guarantees that the Word will have its effect wherever it is preached and not return empty. "God's word cannot be without God's people and similarly God's

151. J. Gerhard, *Loci theol.*, XXII, 138.

152. R. Bellarmine, "De eccl. mil.," in *Controversiis*, IV, 11.

153. Ibid., IV, 2.

154. Cf. additional similar statements in J. Gerhard, *Loci theol.*, XXII, 139; F. Turretin, *Institutes of Elenctic Theology*, XVIII, 12, 16. Scheeben-Atzberger, *Handbuch*, IV, 375.

155. R. Bellarmine, "De eccl. mil.," in *Controversiis*, IV, 2.

156. Julius Müller, *Dogmatische Abhandlungen*, 346ff.

people cannot be without God's word" (Luther). For that reason the Reformation did not mention as the first and foremost mark of the church the witness and walk of the believers but the administration of Word and sacrament. For the believers, who make up the essence of the church, are manifest in two ways: in the administration of Word and sacrament that takes place among them, and in the witness and walk by which they distinguish themselves from the world as well as from other churches, that is, in the church as institution as well as in the church as organism. Inherent in the nature of the case is that the mark derived from the administration of Word and sacrament, from the church as institution, bears a less deceptive, firmer, more constant and enduring character than that found in the witness and walk of believers. The latter can be very deficient without causing the former to cease to exist. This has to a high degree proved true of the Roman Catholic Church, but it also applies to Protestant churches. However important a pure confession and holy conduct may be in the case of believers, the main thing for everyone continues to be a pure administration of Word and sacrament. Hence this must be considered the foremost mark of the church. The Reformed, however, correctly emphasized that the church as gathering of believers is manifest not only in the institution but also in faith, the avoidance of sin, the pursuit of righteousness, love for God and neighbor, and the crucifixion of the flesh.[157] The pure administration of the Word also includes the application of ecclesiastical discipline.

Another of Bellarmine's objections is that the mark of the administration of the Word is much too general and vague for us to judge the true church by it. On the one hand, in true churches such as, say, the church at Corinth and the churches of Galatia, the ministry of the Word after all left much to be desired in purity; and on the other hand, in heretical and sectarian churches, it has not been completely lost. Socinians and Remonstrants, reasoning in the same vein, attacked the necessity and utility of marks by which the true church could be distinguished.[158] And although Lutherans and Reformed in that first period maintained very vigorously that they were the true church, the increasing impurity of their own churches and the appearance of other churches alongside their own made it increasingly more difficult to maintain this assertion in all its severity. Indeed, from the very beginning the attitude that Protestant churches adopted toward the Roman Catholic Church was very different from that which the Roman Catholic Church adopted toward them. Rome can recognize sects alongside itself but not churches.[159] The Protestants, though firmly rejecting the church hierarchy of Rome, continued to fully recognize the Christian elements in the church of Rome. However corrupted Rome might be, there were still left in it "vestiges of the church," "ruins of a disordered church"; there was still "some kind of church, be it half-demolished,"

157. Belgic Confession, art. 29.
158. Racovian Catechism, qu. 489; S. Episcopius, *Simon Episcopii disputationes theologicae [tres] partitae* (Amsterdam, 1646), III, 28; idem, *Opera theologica*, 2 vols. (Amsterdam, 1650–55), II, 2, 459.
159. F. Hettinger, *Apologie des Christenthums*, V, 118.

left in papacy.[160] The Reformation was a separation from the "Roman and papal church," not from "the true church."[161]

Furthermore, at least the Reformers soon were or became conscious that the pure administration of Word and sacrament cannot be considered an absolute mark. Calvin vigorously warns against all arbitrary separation. Even though something is lacking in the purity of doctrine or of the sacraments, even though the holiness of the life and the faithfulness of the ministers leaves much to be desired, one may not for that reason immediately leave the church. One has the duty to leave only when the "high points of necessary doctrine" or "the foremost doctrines of religion" have been exchanged for a lie.[162] When in later years degeneration increased in the state churches and many people felt pressure to leave, the majority of ministers were led to oppose separatism on the same grounds.[163] They all saw themselves compelled, with Calvin, to recognize that in the true church much that is unsound can occur in doctrine and life without this giving people the right to separate from it, and that in separated churches one may frequently find much that is good. In that way the concept "true and false church" underwent an important modification. On the one hand, one had to admit that a true church in an absolute sense is impossible here on earth; there is not a single church that completely and in all its parts, in doctrine and in life, in the ministry of the Word and sacrament, meets the demand of God. On the other hand, it also became clear that an absolutely false church cannot possibly exist, for in that case it would no longer be a church at all. Even though Rome was a false church insofar as it was

---

160. J. Calvin, *Institutes*, IV.ii.11; ed. note: Bavinck here cites a Dutch edition of Calvin's *Opera* by Schippers, *Op.*, VIII, 111, 309; IX, epist. 51, 57; the first reference is to a passage in Calvin's "Reply to Sadoleto": "But what arrogance, you will say, to boast that the church is with you alone, and to deny it to all the world besides! We, indeed, Sadoleto, deny not that those over whom you preside are Churches of Christ" (John Calvin and Jacopo Sadoleto, *A Reformation Debate*, ed. J. C. Olin [New York: Harper & Row, 1966], 75); epistles 51 and 57 can be found in John Calvin, *Selected Works of John Calvin*, ed. Henry Beveridge and Jules Bonnet, trans. David Constable, 7 vols. (1858; repr., Grand Rapids: Baker Academic, 1983), IV, 202–3, 220–21; T. Beza, *Tract. theol.*, III, 145, 192; H. Bullinger, *Decades,* IV, serm. 2; J. Zanchi, preface to "De natura dei," in *De operum theologicorum*, 8 vols. (Geneva: Samuelis Crispini, 1617), II; A. Polanus, *Synt. theol.*, 535, cf. 496; idem, *Partitiones theologiae christianae*, pars. I–II (Basel, 1590–96), 196; F. Junius, *Opuscula theologica selecta*, ed. A. Kuyper (Amsterdam: F. Muller, 1882), II, 1018–23; J. H. Alsted, *Theologia didactica*, 696; G. Voetius, *Desperata causa papatus* (Amsterdam: Joannis Jansson, 1635), 699–703; P. van Mastricht, *Theologia*, VII, 1, 25; F. Turretin, *Institutes of Elenctic Theology*, XVIII, 14, 24, 27.

161. F. Turretin, *Institutes of Elenctic Theology*, XVIII, 15, 8; idem, *De necessaria secessione nostra ab ecclesia Romana* (following his *Disputatio theologica . . . : De satisfactione Christi*); additional anti-Roman writings in C. Vitringa, *Doctr. christ.*, IX, 1, 116; B. de Moor, *Comm. theol.*, VI, 58.

162. J. Calvin, *Institutes*, IV.i.12–20; idem, *Commentary on Matthew*, on Matt. 13:40–41; idem, *Commentary on 2 Thess.*, on 2 Thess. 3:6.

163. G. Voetius, *Pol. eccl.*, IV, 488; W. à Brakel, *The Christian's Reasonable Service,* trans. B. Elshout, 4 vols. (Ligonier, PA: Soli Deo Gloria, 1992–95), II, ch. 25; *J. vander Waeyen and H. Witsius, *Ernstige betuiginge der Gereformeerde Kercke aan hare afdwalende kinderen* (Amsterdam: Joannes van Someren, 1670). *J. Koelman, *Historisch Verhaal nopens der Labadisten: Scheuring en veelerley dwalingen, met de wederlegginge derzelver,* 2 vols. (Amsterdam: Johannes Boeckholt, 1683–84); cf. also in our day, P. J. Hoedemaker, *Hoe oordeelt de Heilige Schrift en, hoe oordeelen de Gereformeerde vaderen over scheiding en doleantie,* 3rd ed. (Sneek: Campen, 1892).

papal, nevertheless there were many remnants of the true church left in it. There was a difference, therefore, between a true and a pure church.[164] "True church" became the term, not for one church to the exclusion of all others, but for an array of churches that still upheld the fundamental articles of Christian faith[165] but for the rest differed a great deal from each other in degrees of purity. And "false church" became the term for the hierarchical power of superstition or unbelief that set itself up in local churches and accorded itself and its ordinances more authority than the Word of God.[166]

THE REAL CHURCH IN HISTORY

[495] This development of the idea of the church that can be observed in history itself has an undeniable shadow side to it. The idea of a single, all-inclusive church institution is forever disturbed by it. Nor can it be denied that the endless divisions of the confessors of Christ offer the world an occasion for pleasure and scorn and give it a reason for its nonbelief in the One sent by the Father, inasmuch as it does not see the unity of believers in Christ (John 17:21). As Christians we cannot humble ourselves deeply enough over the schisms and discord that have existed all through the centuries in the church of Christ. It is a sin against God, in conflict with Christ's [high-priestly] prayer [for unity], and caused by the darkness of our minds and the lovelessness of our hearts.[167] And it is understandable that repeatedly many Christians have allowed themselves to be led astray by the attempt to bring about or to maintain this fervently desired unity of the church of Christ, either by violent means—especially by the strong arm of the state—or artificially by syncretism and fusion.[168] On the other hand, we must not forget either that the failure of all those attempts has something to teach us. History, like nature, is a work of God; it does not take shape apart from his providence. Christ,

164. A. Polanus, *Synt. theol.*, 532; J. H. Alsted, *Theologica didactica*, 601ff.; A. Walaeus, in *Synopsis purioris theologiae*, disp. 40, 37; S. Maresius, *Syst. theol.*, XVI, 20; C. Vitringa, *Doctr. christ.*, IX, 79.

165. Cf. H. Bavinck, *Reformed Dogmatics*, I, 612–13 (#158).

166. Belgic Confession, art. 29.

167. J. H. Gunning, *De eenheid der kerk* (Nijmegen: Ten Hoet, 1896); idem, *Hooger dan de kerk!* (Nijmegen: Ten Hoet, 1897); idem, *Rekenschap* (Nijmegen: Ten Hoet, 1898).

168. Cf. H. C. Rogge, "Hugo de Groots denkbeelden over de hereeniging der kerken," *Teylers Theologische Tijdschrift* 2 (1904): 1–52; F. X. Kiefl, *Der Friedensplan des Leibniz zur Wiedervereinigung der getrennten christlichen Kirchen* (Paderborn: Schöningh, 1903; ed. note: Bavinck cites a 1904 edition); K. Brauer, *Die Unionstätigkeit John Duries unter dem Protektorat Cromwells* (Marburg: Elwert, 1907); J. J. I. von Döllinger, *Ueber die Wiedervereinigung der christlichen Kirchen* (Nördlingen: C. H. Beck, 1888; ed. note: Bavinck cites an 1896 edition published in Leipzig); J. Moog, *Die Wiedervereinigung der christlichen Konfessionen* (Bonn: Alt-Katholischen Press- und Schriften-Vereins, 1909). In England, Scotland, America, and Australia there exists a powerful drive toward unity; the Edinburgh Missionary Conference strongly emphasized unity, and many strive for it in order to bring about what Principal Forsyth calls "the United States of the Church." And in Germany, home of confessional strife, there are repeated pleas for confessional peace; e.g., L. K. Goetz, *Ein Wort zum konfessionellen Frieden* (Bonn: Carl Georgi, 1906); P. Tschackert, *Modus vivendi* (Munich: Beck, 1908); R. Schmölder, *Zum Frieden unter den Konfessionen* (Bonn, 1910), 168.

by his resurrection and ascension, became king at the right hand of God and will remain king until he has put all his enemies under his feet [1 Cor. 15:25]. He reigns also over the divisions and schisms of his church on earth. And his prayer for unity was not born of unfamiliarity with its history nor from his inability to govern it. In and through the discord and dissension, that prayer is daily heard and is led to its complete fulfillment. The profound spiritual sense in which the unity of his disciples was understood by Jesus necessarily excludes all violent and artificial attempts to introduce it. Christ, who prayed for it, is also the One— and he alone—who can bring it about. His prayer is the guarantee that it already exists in him and that in due time, accomplished by him, it will also be manifest in all believers.

Accordingly, for a correct understanding of the divisions of the church of Christ, we must consider the following:

1. All the divisions and schisms that presently exist in the church of Christ basically already have their roots in the apostolic age. Despite the fact that at that time the churches for various reasons felt much more spiritually united than is the case today, even between churches having the same creedal background, those churches were in many respects distinct. The apostles in Jerusalem and Paul, Jewish-Christian and Gentile-Christian churches parted company over many and even important issues. A serious difference of opinion broke out between Peter and Paul (Gal. 2:11) and between Paul and Barnabas (Acts 15:39). Heresies and schisms of various kinds already occurred then as well (1 Cor. 1:10; 11:18–19; etc.). The church of Corinth was divided into parties, quietly ignored the scandalous life of one of the brothers, and in part did not even believe so significant a fact as the bodily resurrection of Christ and of believers. And a few decades after they were started by Paul, the churches in Asia Minor had sunk to a level far below the one they had initially adopted in doctrine and conduct.

2. The reason these divisions and schisms in the apostolic age do not leave such a deep impression is that in the New Testament we always have to deal primarily with local churches. At the time there was as yet nothing other than a spiritual bond that united all the churches. But when a hierarchy developed in the church of Christ and this hierarchy viewed itself as "the essence" of the church, it was this mistaken, unchristian idea of the church that throughout the centuries provoked schisms and heresies and alienated many true believers. Wherever and to the degree that the hierarchy developed, whether in the Roman Catholic, the Greek Orthodox, or the Anglican Church, there the sects sprang up again and again and, if they were not violently oppressed and rooted out, pushed the official church back and not infrequently overshadowed it. It is precisely the hierarchical idea of the church, an idea first of all intent upon the unity of Christianity, that throughout the centuries fostered discord and caused schism. Protestantism

denies its own first principle if it seeks to maintain the unity of Christianity by any form of hierarchical coercion.

3. Precisely because the Word [Scripture] is the mark of the church and there exists no infallible interpretation of that Word, Christ himself gave to everyone the freedom to understand that Word personally as he or she interprets it. Morally, of course, we are bound in this connection to Christ, and we will all have to give an account of how we have understood the word of Christ and put it into practice. But vis-à-vis our fellow humans and fellow Christians, we are completely free. Rome fears this freedom and charges Protestantism with individualism, subjectivism, and sectarianism. But that which is the weakness of Rome, inasmuch as it must maintain itself by hierarchical means, is the strength of Protestantism, since not a creature but Christ himself governs his church. It is perfectly true that, if the Word is the mark of the church and is put into everyone's hands, by that very token everyone has received the right to make judgments concerning the church and, if one sees fit, to separate from it. But we must completely respect this freedom, and no state or church must curb it. Even the horrendous misuse that can be made of it and has in fact been made of it may not even for a moment tempt us to abolish that freedom.

4. Undoubtedly the divisions of the church of Christ are caused by sin; in heaven there will no longer be any room for them. But this is far from being the whole story. In unity God loves the diversity. Among all creatures there was diversity even when as yet there was no sin. As a result of sin that diversity has been perverted and corrupted, but diversity as such is good and important also for the church. Difference in sex and age, in character and disposition, in mind and heart, in gifts and goods, in time and place is to the advantage also of the truth that is in Christ. He takes all these differences into his service and adorns his church with them. Indeed, though the division of humanity into peoples and languages was occasioned by sin, it has something good in it, which is brought into the church and thus preserved for eternity. From many races and languages and peoples and nations Christ gathers his church on earth.

5. If therefore we again understand by churches, according to New Testament usage, the local churches spread out over the globe wherever Christianity has gained a foothold, then there are no true and false churches in an absolute sense. A church is a gathering of true Christ-believers at a given place. If somewhere there is no longer a single believer, neither actually nor potentially, then at such a place the Word of God is unknown, and there is no longer a church. And conversely, if the Word of God is still somewhat known at a given place, it will certainly have its effect, and there will be a church of Christ there, however impure and adulterated. In saying this we are not intending to foster indifferentism and syncretism.

Nothing is indifferent, least of all in connection with "the truth which leads to godliness" [Titus 1:1]. The situation is not such that we can safely abandon and deny the so-called nonfundamental articles [of faith] if only we accept "the fundamental articles." While with respect to others we must apply the saying of Jesus that those who are not against us are for us [Matt. 9:40], with reference to ourselves we must adhere to that other saying: He that is not for me is against me [12:30]. There are great differences in the purity of confessions and churches, and we must aim and strive for the purest. Those, therefore, who have come to believe that the Protestant church is better than the Roman Catholic Church and that the Reformed church is purer than the Lutheran, the Remonstrant, or the Baptist, must, without condemning their own church as false, leave it and join the other. And to stay in one's own church despite much impurity in doctrine and life is our duty as long as it does not prevent us from being faithful to our own confession and does not force us, even indirectly, to obey humans more than God. For a church that pressured its members to do that would, at that very moment and to the extent it did that, reveal itself to the conscience of its members as a false church, which accorded itself and its ordinances more power and authority than the Word of God.

6. One must therefore be cautious with the terms "schism" and "heresy." Undoubtedly both of these are great sins. Guilty of schism are those who, though leaving the foundation of doctrine intact, nevertheless break with the church on subordinate points of worship or church government. Heretics are those who err in the substance of truth. The former break the communion of the church; the latter the communion of doctrine. Still, it is hard in practice to distinguish the boundary line that separates the legitimate and obligatory breaking of fellowship with a church or doctrine from an illegitimate one. For Rome this is rather easy, inasmuch as it recognizes only one church and one confession and anathematizes everything that lies outside it. But Protestantism can at most indicate some general rules and must in concrete cases leave the application of these rules to the conscience of believers. As a result the ideas of heresy and schism have acquired a certain elasticity that should make one cautious in using them. Since the [sixteenth-century] Reformation the church has entered the period of pluriformity; and this fact forces us to look for its unity in the spiritual bond of faith rather than in the external form of its government.[169]

---

169. W. E. Gladstone, "The Place of Heresy and Schism in the Modern Christian Church," *Nineteenth Century* 36 (August, 1894): 157–94; P. Hinschius, "Häresie," in *PRE*³, VII, 319–21; E. Sehling, "Schisma," in *PRE*³, XVII, 575–80. Concerning pluriformity in the church, see A. Kuyper, *Encyclopedia of Sacred Theology* (New York: C. Scribner's Sons, 1898), 658ff. Th. F. Bensdorp, *Pluriformiteit: Een fundamenteele misvatting van Dr. A. Kuyper of een hopeloos pleidooi* (Amsterdam: G. Borg, 1901).

THE ATTRIBUTES OF THE CHURCH

[496] In keeping with this reality, the so-called attributes (properties) of the church have, for the Protestant position, also acquired a meaning that is very different from Rome's. Rome has an absolute and exclusive conception of the church. It cannot recognize the ministry of the Word and sacraments as a mark of the church, since it occurs also outside the Roman Catholic Church, albeit in an impure form. Nor, therefore, can it make a distinction between the marks and the attributes of the church, for the attributes are precisely the indicators that point to the only true church. And finally it must view those attributes so sensibly, tangibly, and externally that they are applicable only to the Roman Catholic Church and make this church obvious to everyone as the exclusively salvific church.

The first attribute, the *unity* of the church, while it also suggests that the church has one Lord, one faith, and one baptism, this unity, according to Rome, is especially expressed in the fact that the church founded by Christ has one visible head in the person of the pope (a hierarchical unity or unity in government) and can never have another church alongside of itself (simultaneous unity) or succeeding it (successive unity). Actually the pope is the one sufficient mark of the true church.[170] As a result of this view of the unity of the church, Rome is obligated to now anathematize over half of the whole of Christendom. Even Pusey's idea, proposed in his *Eirenicon*, and that of W. Palmer in his *Christian Doctrine*,[171] that the Roman, the Eastern Orthodox, and the Anglican Church together constitute the one church cannot be acknowledged.[172] Apart from communion with the pope, there is no salvation.

---

170. Roman Catechism, I, 10, 10; cf. Vatican I's Dogmatic Constitution I on the Church of Christ (Denzinger, *The Sources of Catholic Dogma*, ##1821–40; ed. note: Bavinck also refers to an annotated version of this document in G. Schneemann, *Collectio lacensis*, 7 vols. (Freiburg i.B.: Herder, 1870–90), VII, 569, 586–88); Scheeben-Atzberger, *Handbuch*, IV, 340; P. Schanz, *A Christian Apology*, III, 6.

171. Ed. note: Edward B. Pusey, *An Eirenicon, in a Letter to the Author of "The Christian Year"* (New York: Appleton, 1866); William Palmer, *A Treatise on the Church of Christ: Designed Chiefly for the Use of Students in Theology*, 3rd ed., rev. and enl. (London: J. G. F. and J. Rivington, 1842).

172. Even stronger is the posture taken by the pope [Pius X] earlier this year [1910/11] to a similar proposal from Prince Max of Saxony. Ed. note: Bavinck refers to the papal letter "Ep. 'Ex quo, nono' ad Delegatos Ap. Byzantii, in Graecia, Aegypto, Mesopot., etc., 26 Dec. 1910" (Denzinger, *Enchiridion Symbolorum*, ## 3553–56, in *Sources of Catholic Dogma*, 550–52). In November 1910, Prince Max of Saxony (1870–1951), university professor of church polity and liturgy in Freiburg i.Ü., published "Pensées sur la question de l'union des Églises," *Roma e l'Oriente* (Grottaferrata) 1 (1910): 13–29; German translation: "Gedanke des Prinzen Max, Königliche Hoheit, Herzog zu Sachsen, über de Vereinigung des Kirchen," published by Baronin von Uxkull (Berlin: Rom und der Orient, 1912), 67–90. This essay, in German translation, is reprinted along with Pius X's letter and the editor's commentary in Iso Baumer, *Max von Sachsen: Primat des Andern, Text und Kommentare* (Freiburg, Switz.: Üniversitätsverlag, 1996), 83–106. The turn from the nineteenth to the twentieth century was filled with discussion about overcoming the ecclesiastical division between East and West, and in the first issue of a new journal dedicated to this topic, Prince Max of Saxony set forth a proposal that the only way forward was to repudiate all notions of subjugation by either party and for Rome to grant full and equal legitimacy to the polity and rites of the Orthodox Churches. This proposal was condemned by Pius X who called it a "grave error" to say that "St. Paul is held as a brother entirely equal to St. Peter" and to deny "that the primacy of the Catholic Church does not rest in valid arguments" (*Sources of Catholic Dogma*, 552).

Protestantism, on the other hand, associates the unity of the church first of all with the oneness of the head of the church (Eph. 1:10; 5:23), with the communion of all believers through one and the same Spirit (1 Cor. 6:17, 19; 12:13; 2 Cor. 12:18; Eph. 4:4), with Christ and with each other (John 10:16; 15:1; Rom. 12:5; 1 Cor. 12:12–13; Eph. 1:22), and further, with the unity of faith, hope, and love, and of baptism, and so forth (Eph. 4:3–5). This unity, though primarily spiritual in character, nevertheless exists objectively and really, and it does not remain completely invisible. It manifests itself outwardly—albeit in a very imperfect way—and at least to some degree comes to light in that which all Christian churches have in common. No Christianity exists above or beneath religious differences, but there is indeed a Christianity present amid religious differences. Because we tend to be most aware of the differences and schisms in Christianity, we constantly run the danger of disregarding this—nevertheless truly existing—unity. That which unites all true Christians is always more than that which separates them.

By the *holiness* of the church, Rome in the first place understands liturgical, ceremonial holiness, which consists in the fact that the church as an institution possesses the legitimate ministry of sacrifice and the salvific use of the sacraments, by which, as by the powerful means of divine grace, God works true holiness in believers; and in the second place, the personal holiness that, though it is not and does not need to be the possession of everyone or even of the majority in the church, is nevertheless found, and that again in varying degrees, in some of its members.[173] Inasmuch as the Reformation again made known the church as the communion of the saints, it looked for holiness not first of all in the supernatural character of the salvific institution, but in the spiritual renewal of the members of the church. The church is holy because it is a communion of saints. Still, in this connection the Reformation did not lapse into the error of Donatism and in practice all too often even neglected this attribute of the church. Yet this does not alter the fact that in accordance with the principle of the Reformation, the church is holy because it is a communion of saints. And believers are called saints, first of all, because they are objectively counted as saints in Christ by virtue of God's imputation to them of the righteousness of Christ. Second, believers are saints because, being born again of water and spirit in the inner self, they desire, with all seriousness of purpose, to live not only according to some but according to all the commandments of God[174] (John 17:19; Eph. 5:25–27; 1 Thess. 4:3;

173. Roman Catechism, I, art. 10, qu. 13; ed. note: Bavinck erroneously cites qu. 12; the post–Vatican II edition titled *The Roman Catechism* (trans. Robert I. Bradley, SJ, and Eugene Kevane [Boston: Daughters of St. Paul, 1985]) drops the enumeration of the introduction so that ch. 1 begins the first article of the creed. In this annotation, the proper reference would be II, ch. 9, qu. 15; R. Bellarmine, "De eccl. mil.," in *Controversiis*, c. 11–15; J. Wilhelm and T. Scannell, *A Manual of Catholic Theology*, IV, 347; P. Schanz, *A Christian Apology*, III, c. 10; G. M. Jansen, *Prael. theol.*, I, 452; cf. also F. Kattenbusch, "Der geschichtliche Sinn des apostolischen Symbols," *Zeitschrift für Theologie und Kirche* 11 (1901): 407–28; idem, *Das apostolische Symbol*, 2 vols. (Leipzig: J. C. Hinrichs, 1894–1900).

174. Ed. note: Bavinck here cites, without attribution, Heidelberg Catechism, Lord's Day 44, Q&A 114.

Titus 2:14; Heb. 12:14; 1 Pet. 2:9). This attribute of the church, too, is spiritual, but not totally invisible. Although even the holiest have only a small beginning of this perfect obedience in this life, they nevertheless conduct themselves according to the Spirit and not according to the flesh.

The third attribute is *catholicity*. In the case of Rome the church is said to have this attribute first of all because, though it constitutes a single whole and a complete unity, it is nevertheless spread out over the entire earth, whereas sects always remain restricted to one country or to one part of the world. It is catholic, in the second place, because, although in the past it existed in a less perfect form, it has nevertheless existed on earth from the beginning of the world, and from the days of Adam embraced all believers within itself, whereas sects always come and go. In the third place, it is called catholic because it completely possesses, preserves, and distributes all the truth and grace intended by God for communication to humans and is therefore for all people the sole and necessary salvific institution, whereas sects always possess only a part of the truth. Since for Rome catholicity must be a clearly visible mark of the church, it is especially to be understood in the sense that among all the peoples among whom it exists, it has a strikingly large number of members. In the early years of its existence, this was admittedly not yet the case, but soon the church experienced explosive expansion. And now the attribute of catholicity demands, not that the membership of the true church should exceed the number of all people not affiliated with it, but that it should be greater than the number of people affiliated with any individual sect and probably the number of all sects together.[175] In its external splendor and glory, in its spatial expansion and the numerical strength of its members, Roman Catholic Christians look for an essential mark of the true church.

Church fathers such as Tertullian, Origen, and Augustine already began the trend of exaggerating the expansion of Christianity among the peoples of the earth. And still to this day their example is being followed—especially in their mission statistics—by many Roman Catholics. Yet nowadays, unlike in years past, these Catholics cannot ignore the fact that there are almost a billion non-Christians in the world as against scarcely 500 million Christians, that the latter are again divided into approximately 110 million Greek Orthodox, 264 million Roman Catholic, and 166 million Protestant Christians, and that Roman Catholic Christians in this [the nineteenth] century are regularly declining in numerical strength everywhere and are outflanked by Protestant Christians. According to this mark of catholicity, which the Roman Catholic Church itself brandishes, therefore, the state of its truth is becoming progressively less promising. The Roman Catholic Church is progressively less entitled to the attribute of catholicity. Also mutually contradictory are the terms "Roman" and "catholic." Just as in the Old Testament,

175. Roman Catechism, I, art. 10, qu. 14 (ed. note: Bradley and Kevane, I, art. 9, qu. 16; Bavinck erroneously cites qu. 13); R. Bellarmine, "De notis eccl.," in *Controversiis*, c. 4, 7; Scheeben-Atzberger, *Handbuch*, IV, 351; P. Schanz, *A Christian Apology*, III, 7; R. Söder, *Der Begriff der Katholicität der Kirche und des Glaubens nach seiner geschichtliche Entwicklung* (Würzburg: Leo Wohrl, 1881).

the dispensation of grace was centered in Jerusalem and linked all believers to that city, so in the days of the New Testament the Roman Catholic Church makes the faith and salvation of humans dependent on a specific place and on a specific person and thereby fails to do justice to the catholicity of Christianity. The name "Roman" or "papal church" therefore expresses its nature much more accurately than "Catholic."

A "catholic church" is believed and confessed in the Apostles' Creed and sometimes also in their own confessions by all Protestants.[176] As a rule, people understand it to mean the universal church, which embraces all true believers and is manifest in varying degrees of purity in various churches, or the New Testament church, which, in distinction from the Old, is meant for all peoples and places on earth. The word "catholic" does not occur in Scripture. But the texts to which the church fathers appeal for the catholicity of the church (such as Gen. 12:3; Ps. 2:8; Isa. 2:2; Jer. 3:17; Mal. 1:11; Matt. 8:11; 28:19; John 10:16; Rom. 1:8; 10:18; Eph. 2:14; Col. 1:6; Rev. 7:9; and so forth) prove that its meaning consists especially in the fact that Christianity is a world religion suited and intended for every people and age, for every class and rank, for every time and place. That church is most catholic that most clearly expresses in its confession and applies in its practice this international and cosmopolitan character of the Christian religion. The Reformed had an eye for it when in various countries and churches they confessed the truth in an indigenous, free, and independent manner and at the Synod of Dort invited delegates from all over Reformed Christianity.[177]

The fourth attribute of the church is its *apostolicity*. According to Rome, it is entitled to claim this attribute because it was founded by the apostles and agrees in its doctrine, organization, and ministry with those of the apostles, but especially because its office-bearers [officeholders] are the successors, in an unbroken line, of the apostles and received their power and authority from those who themselves in turn received it in lawful succession from the apostles. In this connection the first meaning is totally subordinate to the second. It is not the word of the apostles, that is, Holy Scripture, that decides which church is apostolic, that is, agrees with the teaching of the apostles; but conversely, it is the church that descends by an unbroken line of succession from the apostles that decides what is apostolic, that is, what the doctrine of the apostles is. Indeed, following the proclamation of the dogma of infallibility, the apostolic succession of the office-bearers is totally determined by their fellowship with the pope. Even if a bishop is a participant in the apostolic succession, the connection is voided the moment he breaks fellowship with the pope. Conversely, the pope, "by virtue of his ecclesiastical authority, can remove any defect which perhaps attaches to the formal apostolicity of an ecclesiastical officebearer. Hence, union with the

176. Belgic Confession, art. 27; Apology of the Augsburg Confession, arts. 7–8.

177. H. Bavinck, "The Catholicity of Christianity and the Church," trans. John Bolt, *Calvin Theological Journal* 27 (1992): 220–51.

pope is necessary for an officebearer to become or be a legitimate successor of the apostles. This union is also immediately sufficient, however, for the recognition of the true apostolicity of the officebearer."[178] The pope makes everything right. Where the pope is, there is the true church, pure doctrine, and apostolic succession.

The truth is, there is not a word in Scripture about such an apostolic succession. Even as such it is no more a guarantee of purity of doctrine than the hereditary high-priestly office of Caiaphas validated the justice of his pronouncements and actions. For that reason Protestants were right in saying that not "the succession of places and persons" (*successio locorum et personarum*) but "the succession of doctrine" (*successio doctrinae*) is a distinguishing feature of the true church. If the latter is missing, the former can make no church into a true church; and if it is present, the former is of very minor significance.

Finally, belonging to the series of the attributes of the church are also the attributes of indefectibility and infallibility. Jesus promised the church that the gates of hell would not prevail against it, and that he would preserve it to the end of the world (Matt. 16:18; 28:20; Eph. 4:11–13; 1 Tim. 3:15). Roman Catholics infer from this promise that their church, the church of the papacy, will continue to the end of the world. In addition, they also infer that the papal church will always be the catholic church, which will be visible and knowable to everyone by the vast numbers of its members and its external splendor.[179] For this claim, however, adequate grounds are lacking. Not only has the church at different times—say, those of Noah, Abraham, Elijah, Christ, and so forth—been reduced to a few persons, but over and over certain churches in certain countries, in Asia Minor for example, have vanished. Indeed, the New Testament clearly states that in the last days corruption will increase and the church will be exposed to all sorts of temptation and persecution (Matt. 24:21–22; Luke 18:8; 2 Tim. 3:1).

Jesus's promise, therefore, is indeed a guarantee that there will always be a gathering of believers on earth—something Socinians and Remonstrants wrongly deny[180]—but it by no means implies that a specific church in a specific country will always continue to exist and be knowable by everyone on account of its size and glory. The same is true of the infallibility of the church. The Roman Catholic Church has long hesitated to answer the question with whom, finally, infallibility rests and has at last decided at the [First] Vatican Council in favor of the pope.[181] The pope guarantees that the teaching church cannot err in its teaching. But Holy Scripture nowhere links infallibility to a specific person or to a specific local church. Indeed, there exists an infallibility of the church that is also gladly recognized by Protestants, but this infallibility belongs to the church

178. J. Wilhelm and T. Scannell, *A Manual of Catholic Theology*, IV, 356.

179. R. Bellarmine, "De eccl. milit.," in *Controversiis*, c. 11, 13, 16; idem, "De notis eccl.," in *Controversiis*, c. 5–6; Scheeben-Atzberger, *Handbuch*, IV, 1, 359.

180. Cf. B. de Moor, *Comm. theol.*, IV, 122.

181. Cf. Denzinger, *The Sources of Catholic Dogma*, ##1832–40.

as the gathering of true believers, and it consists in the fact that Christ, as king of his church, will see to it that on earth there will always be a gathering of believers, however small and unimpressive it may be, which confesses his name and finds all its salvation in him.[182]

182. On the attributes of the church, see P. Martyr Vermigli, *Loci comm.*, 226; F. Turretin, *Institutes of Elenctic Theology*, XVIII, qu. 5ff.; J. H. Heidegger, *Corpus theologiae*, XXVI, 16ff. *S. Maresius, *Exeg. conf. Belg.*, art. 27; H. Witsius, *Exercitationes sacrae in symbolum quod apostolorum dicitur* (Amsterdam, 1697), 24; C. Vitringa, *Doctr. christ.*, IX, 81; P. van Mastricht, *Theologia*, VII, 1, 9; J. Quenstedt, *Theologia*, IV, 482, 497; Thomasius, *Christi Person und Werk*, II, 543; F. A. Philippi, *Kirchliche Glaubenslehre*, V, 3, 16ff.; K. von Hase, *Handbook to the Controversy with Rome*, trans. A. W. Streane, 2 vols. (London: Religious Tract Society, 1906), I, c. 1; J. J. van Oosterzee, *Christian Dogmatics*, §130.

6

THE CHURCH'S
SPIRITUAL GOVERNMENT

The church cannot do without government. Though all final authority rests in God, he appoints Christ as mediator, and is pleased to grant to human beings and their institutions an exercise of sovereignty for the benefit of the body. The church on earth is both passively a gathered community or organism, and actively the mother of all believers, an institution. Neither must be played against the other; both are the work of Christ.

The Reformation quarreled with Rome not on the importance of the institutional church but on the means of grace. Christ is not bound to the administration of sacramental grace by priests but graciously gathers his people through his proclaimed Word and his Spirit. In other words, Christ gathers his church through the church. In this way the Reformation avoided both the hierarchy of Rome and the enthusiasm of the Anabaptists and did justice to the truth in both. The distinguishing mark of the church is the pure administration of the Word and the confession and conduct of believers. Offices and gifts, governance and the people, institution and organism—all these belong together. They are inseparable.

The church is God's creation, from the beginning of human sinful history— Adam, Abram, Israel, the early church—all are religiously as well as civilly organized by tabernacle and altar, sacrifice, priesthood. John the Baptist's ministry and that of Jesus and his apostles called out a new people with a new rule of community. The role of Paul as an "apostle" and the broader sense of the term in the postapostolic period (as in the Didache*), which includes apostolic helpers called "evangelists" or "prophets," point to the reality of church offices as a continuing requirement. There is something distinct and unique about the original apostles, however; the church of all ages is bound to their witness; they shared the Holy Spirit in extraordinary measure; their witness was sealed by God the Holy Spirit with signs and wonders and rich spiritual blessings.*

Peter is foremost among the apostles, the first among equals; his bold confession of Jesus as Messiah (Matt. 16:13–20; par.) led to Jesus calling him and his confession a "rock." But the apostolic foundation of the church and its government does not mean a continuing apostolate. For us it survives, not as an institution but only in the apostolic word, which remains as the foundation of the church. When the apostles founded churches in various places, they instituted offices that differed essentially from their own, offices that came into being also through the cooperation of the churches themselves. There is a difference between the extraordinary apostolic office (as well as evangelists and prophets) and the ordinary offices of presbyters and deacons instituted within and by the churches themselves.

Christ himself appointed the apostles; those who followed them were appointed in and by the congregations that arose after the apostles' successful preaching. As the church spread and believers gathered in homes, arrangements for the community were made by designated people, perhaps on the model of the Jewish synagogue. While tasks and offices were initially quite fluid, over time the office of elder/overseer was differentiated between the tasks of ruling and teaching, and the distinct office of deacon was added (Acts 6). While the apostolate was an extraordinary and temporary office, even preceding the existence of the church as a gathering of believers, the offices of teacher, elder/overseer, and deacon presuppose the existence of the church, a church that as a local body has the right to designate and elect the bearers of these offices.

The organization described in the preceding paragraph, an organization that can be called aristocratic-presbyterial, soon developed into a monarchical-episcopal arrangement. This started early in the East; the West soon followed suit. Here the unity of the church came to be seen in the person and office of the bishop, who was no longer regarded as the first among equals but as one with definite priority and authority. The pattern in which the overseers and deacons were chosen by and with the consent of the community was reversed; the bishops came to be seen as the successors of the apostolate and thus vested with special authority as the bearers of the tradition. Central to this episcopal system is the distinction between the teaching church, or clergy, and the laity, or listening church.

In Roman Catholicism the episcopacy developed into a papal system, with the bishop of Rome having preeminent authority. Since the center of gravity had shifted from the church community to the person of the bishop, the prestige and eminence of the Roman church and its bishop seemed to make this a natural outcome. Increasingly, though the Eastern Church maintained its allegiance to the see of Constantinople, the Western Church centered its authority in Rome. The final, full statement of Petrine supremacy was declared by the First Vatican Council in 1870.

The Reformation set itself in full opposition to the very notion of a hierarchical church and the disjunction between clergy and laity. The New Testament knows nothing of a separate clerical class; the Holy Spirit is poured out on all believers and calls all to service (diakonia). *From a scriptural perspective, the presbyter and bishop/overseer are practically identical; there is no ground for hierarchical ordering of the offices. The Reformers categorically rejected the papal system as unscriptural. Aside from the lack of scriptural proof, the historical reasons usually adduced for Petrine and Roman primacy are also spurious.*

From the time of the Middle Ages, the Roman hierarchy provoked proportionally more resistance and opposition; sectarian groups rejected Rome as Babylon and the pope as the antichrist. But not all alternatives were equally valid. Lutheranism, for example, ceded much of the church's government to civil authorities. This is a mistake in that it fails to give to the church as an association of believers, formed by the Holy Spirit, the distinct, independent, and spiritual structure and government it requires. The Reformed tradition, understanding that Christ rules by his power over the world and by his Word and Spirit over his own body, sought a distinct, independent, and spiritual polity for the church. Every local church is thus regarded as an independent manifestation of the body of Christ and simultaneously *part of the universal church from which it arises and to which it is historically and spiritually connected. What is true of each local church is also applicable to each individual believer. Christ calls his own, distributes to them the gifts of the Holy Spirit for the body's well-being and growth, and guides his church by his Word and Spirit through the offices and office-bearers.*

Church office includes teaching and ruling but is always about service and never about power. Office-bearers are ministers of Christ who serve his church. The route by which Christ puts his servants into office runs through three stages: vocation, examination, and ordination. Internal calling, involving assessment of personal gifts and desire, must be confirmed by the external call of the church done on Christ's behalf. In the examination of teaching elders or ministers, though the church's own teaching doctors (professors of theology) may be deputized by the church and could certainly assist the church in its examination, yet the right and responsibility finally belongs to the church. The step of ordination, involving the laying on of hands, is not a sacrament and does not bestow but presupposes the charismata required for office. Ordination does not constitute the office; it is rather the solemn public declaration before God and his congregation that the person is indeed called by God and ought to be received, recognized, and honored as an office-bearer.

It is to Calvin that we owe the restoration of a biblically based presbyterial form of church government. By restoring the office of elder and deacon alongside that of the minister of the Word, the Reformed tradition most accurately grasped the idea of Scripture and most firmly recognized the rights of the local church. Christ alone is the king of the church. He continues his own threefold office of prophet, priest, and king, not exclusively, but also through the three offices he instituted for his church. By them he takes care of the spiritual and material interests of his church. In that care he uses people, all believers as well as office-bearers. All believers have a threefold obligation to join the church, use their gifts for the benefit of the body, and be active in the formation and reformation of the church. We follow the servant Lord in faithful, loving service.

THE CHURCH AS ORGANISM AND INSTITUTION

[497] Government is indispensable for the church as a gathering of believers. Just as a temple calls for an architect, a field a sower, a vineyard a keeper, a net a fisherman, a flock a shepherd, a body a head, a family a father, a kingdom a king, so also the church is unthinkable without an authority that sustains, guides, cares for, and protects it. In a sense even more special than is the case in the political realm, this authority rests with God, who is not only the Creator of all things but also the Savior of the church. As people of God, the church, under the new covenant as well as under the old, is a theocracy. The Lord is its judge, lawgiver, and king (Isa. 33:22). But just as in the civil realm God has granted sovereignty to the government, so in the church he has appointed Christ to be king. Already designated mediator from eternity, Christ carried out his prophetic, priestly, and kingly office from the time of paradise, continued it in the days of the Old Testament and during his sojourn on earth, and now fulfills it in heaven, where he is seated at the Father's right hand.[1] And this activity of Christ does not presuppose the existence of the church—except as conceived and willed in God's eternal counsel—but precedes and produces it. The church is built upon Christ like a temple upon a rock, and is born like a body from him as the head. Here the king exists prior to his people.

But in still another sense as well the church is not conceivable without a government. Granted, Christ could have exercised his office without any service from humans. If it had so pleased him, he could have dispensed his spiritual and heavenly blessings without the help of institutions and persons. But this was not his pleasure; it was his pleasure, without in any way transferring his sovereignty to people, to nevertheless use their services in the exercise of his sovereignty and to preach the gospel through them to all creatures. And also in that sense the church was never without a government. It was always organized and institutionally arranged in some fashion.

This is necessary—by hypothetical necessity,[2] inasmuch as on earth the church is a church in process of *becoming*. In heaven every ecclesiastical office and means

---

1. H. Bavinck, *Reformed Dogmatics*, III, 475–82 (#409).

2. Ed. note: Bavinck's term here is *necessitate hypothetica*. The following entry from Richard A. Muller, *Dictionary of Latin and Greek Theological Terms* (Grand Rapids: Baker Academic, 1985), s.v. *necessitas consequentiae*, is helpful: "necessitas consequentiae: *necessity of the consequences*; i.e., not an absolute necessity (*necessitas absoluta*, q.v.), but a necessity brought about or conditioned by a previous contingent act or event so that the necessity itself arises out of contingent circumstance; thus, conditional necessity. *Necessitas consequentiae* is also called

of grace will cease to function because the kingdom of God will be complete and God will be all in all. But on earth this is different. As the gathering of believers, the church is itself used by Christ as an instrument to bring others to his fold. By it Christ administers his mediatorial office in the midst of the world. Thus, from the very beginning, the church appears on the scene in a dual form. It is a gathering of the people of God in a passive as well as an active sense; it is simultaneously a gathered community and the mother of believers or, in other words, an organism and an institution. As stated earlier, this distinction is very different from that between the invisible and visible church. It is a distinction within the visible church and says that the church as gathering of believers is manifest to us in two ways: in the offices and means of grace (institution), and in a community of faith and life (organism). Now in this connection the question is always raised: Which of these has priority? Some theologians, highlighting the church as the mother of believers, assert that the institution of the church with its offices and ministries always precedes the church as gathering of believers. Others judge that the church as gathering of believers occupies first place and then, responding to the pressure of circumstances, in some fashion arranges itself institutionally. Some even claim that this constitutes the fundamental difference between Protestantism and Catholicism. Confusing the distinction between the church as institution and the church as organism with that between the visible and invisible church, Schleiermacher states that Protestantism makes the individual's relationship to the church dependent on his relationship to Christ, while Catholicism makes the individual's relationship to Christ dependent on his relationship to the church.[3] And according to Möhler, in the mind of Rome, the visible church is prior to the invisible church, while among Lutherans the reverse is true.[4]

But this entire representation, in my opinion, is far from complete or correct.

1. From the days of Tertullian onward[5] all Christians not only called the church a gathered community (*coetus*) but also the mother of believers

---

necessitas ex suppositione, necessity on account of supposition, or *necessitas ex hypothesi*, necessity on account of hypothesis, or hypothetical necessity, and sometimes *necessitas ex hypothesi dispositionis*, or necessity on account of a hypothesis of disposition. Each of these latter terms indicates a necessity that arises out of a set of circumstances or out of a disposition or capacity hypothetically rather than absolutely or necessarily conceived; i.e., the conditions that create the necessity are themselves a matter of contingency and are therefore only hypothetically or suppositionally the ground or reason for a necessity. The *necessitas consequentiae* occurs continually in the finite order and, unlike *necessitas absoluta*, is applicable to God in terms of his *potentia ordinata* (q.v.), or ordained power. There is no necessity that God decree what he decrees; but, granting the divine decree, God is bound to his own plan and promises. Therefore, the fulfillment of the divine plan and the divine promises is necessary, but by a *necessitas consequentiae*."

3. F. Schleiermacher, *The Christian Faith*, ed. H. R. MacIntosh and J. S. Steward (Edinburgh: T&T Clark, 1928), §24.

4. J. Möhler, *Symbolik* (Regensburg: G. J. Manz, 1871), §48.

5. Tertullian, *On Prayer* 2; idem, *On Monogamy* 7; idem, *Against Marcion* V, 4.

(*mater fidelium*). In this respect, Protestants agree with Catholics, and even Calvin himself very strongly emphasizes it.[6] And, in their opinion, this was true, not because the church freely and independently organized itself into an institution and gave itself a government of its own, but because Christ had so arranged it. The institution of the church, at least according to the Reformed confession, is absolutely not a product of the believing community but the work of Christ himself. That this conviction is based on good scriptural grounds will become clearly evident shortly.

2. The church as gathering of believers does not, as Schleiermacher claims, take shape "through the coming together of regenerate individuals."[7] In this picture the question: Whence are these regenerate individuals? remains unanswered. For certainly these regenerate individuals do not come into being because the Holy Spirit atomistically and without the use of means regenerates people and then joins them together. Certainly the Holy Spirit in all his operations, including that of regeneration, is bound to Christ, from whom he takes all things. And Christ is on earth only where his Word is. God's Word and God's people belong together. Granted, small children are frequently regenerated apart from having been able to hear the preaching of the Word personally. But these are children who have been born in the covenant of grace, live in the fellowship of the church, and have received the internal calling that proceeds from Christ through the Holy Spirit.

3. The difference between Rome and the Reformation on this point does not consist in the priority either of the visible or the invisible church, of the church as institution or the church as organism, of fellowship with the church or of fellowship with Christ—at least not without more precise definition. Rather, it lies in the fact that Rome binds salvation to priests and sacraments, and the Reformation [binds salvation] to the preaching of the Word. According to Rome, infused grace is only communicated through baptism, thus making this sacrament absolutely necessary. According to the Reformation, the Word is the first and principal means of grace, and hence faith is sufficient for salvation. And as a means of grace, that Word absolutely does not just work when it is officially administered in the gathering of believers, but also when it is brought to us in the family and at school, by our upbringing and education. God's people are where God's Word is, but that people and that Word can be there and also often are there where there is no priest or pope, no pastor or presbyter.

4. Also according to the Reformation it is the case that the church as the gathering of believers does not take shape without the use of means—from an operation of the Holy Spirit detached from the Word. Standing between Christ and the individual person is certainly not, as Rome teaches, the

6. J. Calvin, *Institutes*, IV.i.4.
7. F. Schleiermacher, *The Christian Faith*, §115.

priest and the sacrament, the teaching church; what does exist between them is the word of Christ, for, according to the testimony of Scripture, fellowship with Christ is bound to fellowship with the word of the apostles (John 17:3; 1 John 1:3). As it is in the natural world, so it is in the spiritual. Every human being is a product of communion, and the individual believer is born from the womb of the believing community. The universal church is anterior to the particular church and to individual believers just as in every organism the whole precedes the parts. The church of Christ is indeed a mother, but she is that not only as institution but also as organism. Believers are simultaneously producer and product. "The invisible church is gathered and formed in the visible church; the invisible church inheres and is contained in the visible church."[8] Through the church Christ gathers his church.

5. By adopting this position the Reformation avoided both the hierarchy of the Catholics and the enthusiasm of the Anabaptists and did justice to the truth present in both. On the one hand, it wanted no part in binding the operation of the Holy Spirit to priest and sacrament, and on the other, it wanted no part in welcoming an operation of the Holy Spirit apart from Christ and his Word! The church as gathering is manifest in both the institution and the organism. Its distinguishing mark is the pure administration of the Word and the confession and conduct of believers. It is arranged both institutionally and charismatically. The office does not suppress the gifts but organizes them and keeps them on track, and the gifts do not cancel out the office but vitalize it and make it fruitful. Both Irvingism and Darbyism contain a truth that must be recognized. Both offices and gifts—in conjunction—have been given by Christ to his church for the perfection of the saints and the upbuilding of his body (Rom. 12:5–8; 1 Cor. 12:25, 28; Eph. 4:11–12).

6. For that reason alone, already the question concerning the priority of the institution or of the organism betrays its own one-sidedness. The two are given in conjunction and continually interact with and impact each other. In the state, a people and its government are always most intimately bound up with each other. In the case of any people one can investigate the origin of some form of government. One can even demonstrate that political government was instituted on account of sin, but wherever there are people there is also a certain form of government. From the beginning Adam was created the head of humankind. Similarly, though its form of government is far from always having been the same, the church has never been without a government, either in the invisible realm in which Christ is its head, or in the visible in which it always possessed some form of organization.

8. A. Walaeus, in *Synopsis purioris theologiae*, disp. 40, 34.

CHURCH GOVERNMENT IN SCRIPTURE

[498] Holy Scripture makes this point very clear. When Adam fell and hid himself from God, God himself sought out and called him, proclaimed to him the promise of the gospel, and thus started his church. With Noah he established his covenant, imparting through it a wealth of blessings, and sealing it with a rainbow. He called Abram from Ur of the Chaldeans, made him his covenant partner, and gave him the sign of circumcision. In the patriarchal era, the families were the communities of believers, the fathers being the priests who passed on the promises to their children and offered sacrifices of worship and thanksgiving to God. At Sinai the people of Israel not only received a civil but also a religious organization and became manifest—in the priesthood and sacrifices, in the tabernacle and the altar, in a wide array of laws and ordinances—as the people of God. When, at the beginning of the New Testament, John the Baptist made his debut, he preached the baptism of repentance for the forgiveness of sins and thereby set apart the people of God from sinful Israel. Jesus took over this message and this baptism from John, later added the Lord's Supper, gathered around him an ἐκκλησια (*ekklēsia*),[9] directly governed it himself as long as he was on earth, and appointed twelve apostles, who would a short while later act as his witnesses. The institution of the apostolate is especially strong evidence for the institutional character that Christ gave to his church on earth. Christ himself is "the apostle" (Heb. 3:1) and continues this apostolate in the Twelve (John 20:21). This group of twelve men did not gradually form itself but was expressly called and appointed by Jesus himself. Although Jesus knew from the beginning whom he would choose as apostles and for that reason could say to them at the outset that he would make them "fishers of men" (Mark 1:17), there is nevertheless a clear distinction between their first calling to discipleship and their second calling to the apostolate (Matt. 4:18–22 and 10:1–2; Mark 1:16–20 and 3:14; Luke 6:1 and 13–16). Many theologians (Schleiermacher, Volkmar, Harnack, Seufert, Holtzmann, and so forth) have in fact denied this special calling to the apostolic office by Jesus, but the facts belie this denial. For long before Paul's public ministry in Christian churches, the entity known as "the twelve apostles" had been established (Matt. 26:33; 28:18–20; Luke 24:47; John 20:19, 21; 1 Cor. 15:5, 7; Rev. 21:14). Also the term "apostle" (שָׁלִוּחַ, *šālûaḥ*) had been assigned to them by Jesus[10] (Luke 6:13; cf. 11:49; Matt. 10:2; 23:34; Mark 6:30; Luke 9:10; 17:5; 22:14; 24:10) because they had been sent out to preach (Mark 3:14). For the implementation of his work Jesus, himself the one sent by the Father (John 3:34;

---

9. The manner in which Jesus speaks of his church (Matt. 16:18 and 18:17) already in principle includes its organization. Cf. P. A. E. Sillevis Smitt, *De organisatie van de Christelijke kerk in den apostolischen tijd* (Rotterdam: T. de Vries, 1910), 36.

10. It is not impossible that the term "apostles" had already been in vogue among the Jews for those men who were sent out by the Sanhedrin to carry out certain mandates with respect to Jewish customs outside of Judah. See A. von Harnack, *The Mission and Expansion of Christianity*, trans. J. Moffatt (New York: Harper, 1908), I, 458ff.; W. Staerk, *Neutestamentliche Zeitgeschichte*, 2 vols. (Berlin: G. J. Göschen, 1907), II, 43.

Heb. 3:1), needed witnesses to make known to the entire people of Israel (Matt. 10:6) the gospel that had appeared in him. The bestowal of this name by Jesus is confirmed by the fact that the word "apostle" was an office-related name from the beginning, even to the extent that the term "false apostle" (ψευδοαποστολος, *pseudoapostolos*) could be formed (2 Cor. 11:13). In any case, the word שָׁלוּחַ occurs only once in the LXX (1 Kings 14:6),[11] and the word ἀποστολος (*apostolos*) is very rare in secular Greek.

Still, these facts in Scripture concerning the apostolate seem to be contradicted by other data. In the first place, it is not exactly certain who must be counted as belonging to this group of twelve. Even though the variation between the four lists of apostles (Matt. 10:2–4; Mark 3:16–19; Luke 6:14–16; Acts 1:13) is resolved by the hypothesis that Lebbaeus called Thaddeus [Matt. 10:3] is the same as Judas the son of James [Luke 6:16; Acts 1:13], the problematic fact remains that Judas dropped out and was replaced by Matthias (Acts 1:15–26) and that Paul was later added to the Twelve. In this connection, the relationship of Paul to the Twelve is far from clear. Paul, admittedly, repeatedly makes the distinction that the apostles in Jerusalem would proclaim the gospel in Israel while he would do the same among the Gentiles (Acts 9:15; 13:47; 22:21; Rom. 11:13; Gal. 1:16; 2:7–9; Eph. 3:8; 1 Tim. 2:7; 2 Tim. 1:11). This distinction, however, is very relative, for Paul in his preaching of the gospel always turned first to the Jews (Acts 13:5, 14, 46; and so forth), and after the resurrection the twelve apostles received from Christ the express commission to preach the gospel to all peoples (Matt. 28:19; Acts 10:42) and also to a greater or lesser degree carried out this commission. Not just the Jewish-Christian church but also the entire New Testament church rests on the foundation of apostles and prophets (Eph. 2:20; Rev. 21:14) and shares in fellowship with Christ by the word of the apostles (John 17:20; 1 John 1:3). Paul's apostolate, however, is very different from that of the Twelve. He does indeed with the utmost vigor maintain the divine origin, the independence, and the authenticity of his apostolic office (Gal. 1–2; 1 Cor. 1:10–4:21; 2 Cor. 10:13). Yet he did not belong to the number of the disciples who were with Jesus during his sojourn on earth; instead, he persecuted the church of God. Paul was called by the ascended Christ in an extraordinary manner and at an unusual time, and he saw himself as the foremost of sinners and the least of the apostles (1 Cor. 15:9; Eph. 3:8; 1 Tim. 1:15). His apostolate, however independent and excellent, was a means of grounding the church in the apostolate of the Twelve. By his apostolate Paul, rather than limiting or undermining the apostolate of the Twelve, confirmed and expanded it. In the world of Gentiles he paved the way for the apostolate of the Twelve. On the one hand, he divested it of the Jewishness that still clung to the carriers of it, and on the other hand, he grafted the Gentiles as wild branches into the cultivated olive tree of Israel (Rom. 11:24). On Christ

---

11. Ed. note: Bavinck's claim here is imprecise; it is the word ἀποστολος, as the translation of שָׁלוּחַ, that occurs in the LXX of 1 Kings 14:6.

as the cornerstone, and the apostles as the foundation, Paul built the one church, the one people of God, spiritual Israel.

Having said this, we have in principle also answered a second objection advanced against the appointment and naming of the twelve apostles by Jesus. For it is a fact that the word "apostle" was used also in a broader sense, probably in Jerusalem already (Acts 14:4, 14; 2 Cor. 11:13; Rev. 2:2) but then especially by Paul, and applied also to people other than the Twelve. Paul had no choice but to do this, since he knew himself to be a called servant of Jesus Christ, equal in office and honor to the other apostles. He was an apostle in another sense than the apostles in Jerusalem, called as he was in another way and at a later time, and having been charged with a special task. But there was one thing he had in common with the apostles in Jerusalem. He was a called apostle of Jesus Christ who owed his calling, his gospel, specifically even the unique content of his gospel (that the Gentiles are fellow heirs) to a special revelation of Christ and not to humans (1 Cor. 9:1; 15:8; Gal. 1:1, 12, 15; 2:2; Eph. 3:3). But he needed help in the performance of his missionary labors. Besides the apostles, Jesus had also already *sent out* another seventy men to prepare for his coming in the cities and villages that he planned to visit (Luke 10).

When the Jerusalem church had been scattered by persecution, Philip, one of the seven men elected in Acts 6, started to preach the gospel among the Samaritans (8:5), to the eunuch of Candace, queen of Ethiopia (8:26; cf. 11:20), and beyond as far as Caesarea (8:40; 21:8). Thus in his missionary labors Paul used men like Barnabas, Mark, Luke, Silas, Tychicus, Aristarchus, Epaphras, Apollos, Timothy, and Titus, as well as others, who as his fellow workers assisted him (1 Thess. 3:2). Now these assistant missionaries of the apostles were also sometimes called "apostles" by Paul, because, though not directly sent by Jesus Christ, they were sent out under the guidance of the Holy Spirit by the church to preach the gospel also in other places (Acts 13:2–3; cf. 2 Cor. 8:23). Thus, in addition to a restricted sense, the word "apostle" also acquired a broader meaning (Acts 14:4, 14; Rom. 16:7; 1 Cor. 4:6, 9; 9:5; 15:7; 2 Cor. 11:5, 13; 12:11; Gal. 1:19; 1 Thess. 2:7; Rev. 2:2) and continued to be used in that sense also later, in the postapostolic period, in the *Didache*, for example.

Elsewhere these apostolic helpers are called "evangelists" (Acts 21:8; Eph. 4:11; 2 Tim. 4:5) inasmuch as, like Christ by the Father (Luke 4:18), and the apostles by Christ (Luke 9:1, 6), they in turn were set apart, under the guidance of the Spirit, by the church for the proclamation of the gospel (Acts 8:5, 12, 40; 11:19–20, 22; 13:2; 2 Cor. 8:18–19, 23; Phil. 2:25; 1 Tim. 4:14). In three respects, accordingly, they correspond to the apostles (in the restricted sense):

1. In the fact that they, too, are servants of God or of Christ (1 Thess. 3:2; 1 Tim. 4:6; 6:11; 2 Tim. 2:24) and have not just received a charisma (1 Tim. 4:14; 2 Tim. 1:6) but really—by virtue of a special calling and appointment—fulfilled an office under a specific name (Acts 21:8), with a rank and place of their own (Eph. 4:11), and a special task (2 Tim. 4:5).

2. In that their office is not restricted to a local church but extends to all the churches, the church universal (Acts 13:4ff.), so that, in the phrase of the ancient church, they "used to preach going around everywhere" and had power and authority over all the churches (Titus 1:5).

3. In that they took part in the basic church-planting labor of the apostles. These "evangelists" are their "fellow workers" (1 Thess. 3:2), "traveling companions" (Acts 19:29), "fellow soldiers" (Phil. 2:25), "fellow servants" (Col. 1:7; 4:7) who watered what the apostles had planted (1 Cor. 3:6) and, though relatively independent, were nevertheless subject to the apostles (Acts 19:22; 1 Cor. 4:17; 1 Tim. 1:3; Titus 1:5; and so forth) and worked partly alone and partly in the company of the apostles (ibid.; Acts 11:30; 12:25; 13:2; etc.). In the postapostolic period, the office disappears completely, and the name "evangelist" is used from the time of Tertullian, Origen, and Eusebius onward for the authors of the four Gospels, rendering, as it were, the persons of the evangelists superfluous.[12]

In the New Testament, alongside evangelists, we also encounter "prophets," who are even mentioned before them (Rom. 12:6; 1 Cor. 12:28–29; Eph. 4:11), sometimes without being linked to the apostles (Eph. 2:20; 3:5), and hence occupy a position that is higher than theirs in rank and honor. They were promised by Jesus (Matt. 23:34; Luke 11:49); raised up by the Holy Spirit, who was poured out on the day of Pentecost (Acts 2:17–18; 1 Cor. 12:11; Rev. 1:10); and occur in large numbers in almost all the churches: in Jerusalem (Acts 6:5, 8; 11:27), Antioch (11:27; 13:1), Caesarea (21:9–10), Corinth (1 Cor. 12), and all around, as is evident from their being mentioned in Rom. 12:6; 1 Cor. 12:28; Eph. 2:20; 3:5; 4:11; and 1 Thess. 5:20. The last of them is John the apostle (Rev. 1:1), and then as a class they totally disappear from the church. The Apostolic Fathers indeed still speak of prophets,[13] but in referring to them they have in mind men who traveled around and spoke in various churches about the Christian truth but had to be carefully examined in this connection and distinguished from false prophets. The time for prophecy was past. Montanism and other enthusiastic movements of earlier or later date indeed tried to revive prophecy. Rome in fact declares that the prophetic gift still continues.[14]

---

12. On the evangelists, see Suicerus, *Thesaurus ecclesiasticus* (Amsterdam: J. H. Wetsten, 1682), s.v. εὐαγγελιον; H. Witsius, *Miscellanea sacrorum*, 4 vols. (Utrecht, 1692), I, 315; II, 564; G. Voetius, *Tractatus selecti de politica ecclesiastica*, 2 vols. (Amsterdam: J. H. Kruyt, 1885–86); P. van Mastricht, *Theoretica-practica theologia* (Utrecht: Appels, 1714), VII, 2, 18; K. Lechler, *Die neutestamentliche Lehre vom heiligen Ambte* (Stuttgart: J. F. Steinkopf, 1857), 220ff.; F. A. Philippi, *Kirchliche Glaubenslehre*, 3rd ed., 7 vols. (Gütersloh: Bertelsmann, 1883–1902), V, 3, 277; R. Sohm, *Kirchenrecht*, 2 vols. (Leipzig and Munich: Duncker & Humblot, 1892–1923), 42; O. Zöckler, *Diakonen und Evangelisten* (Munich: C. H. Beck, 1893); V. H. Stanton, "Gospels," in *DB*, II, 234–49; N. J. D. White, "Gospels," in *DC*, I, 663–71.

13. Shepherd of Hermas, *Mandates* 11; *Visions* 3; *Didache* 11, 15.

14. R. Bellarmine, "De notis eccl.," in *Controversiis*, c. 15.

Zwingli and many after him introduced so-called prophecies that served to explain Scripture to the people.[15] But all that is essentially different from the prophecy that existed in the early Christian churches. The latter is distinguished by the following features:

1. While the New Testament prophets may be called office-bearers, their office is nevertheless much more charismatic than that of prophets and apostles. They are not immediately called and appointed by Christ or by his church but receive a special charisma from the Holy Spirit and are consequently called to fulfill a special task in the church of Christ.
2. With apostles and evangelists they have in common the fact that they fulfill an office that is valid for the whole church of Christ on earth, and thus also assist in the founding of the church (Eph. 2:20), but whereas the evangelists especially help the apostles in their missionizing and church-planting activity, the prophets assist them in the work of edification and instruction.
3. While New Testament prophecy is conscious and deliberate and hence to be rated higher than glossolalia (1 Cor. 14:5, 32), it is nevertheless momentary and extraordinary, the fruit of revelation (14:30). It expands the natural measure of knowledge, includes both the form and the content of speech (Matt. 10:19–20), and proves itself true by its own inherent persuasive power (2 Cor. 2:14–17). It served especially to win acceptance among believers and unbelievers, for the gospel preached by the apostles was an offense to the Jews and foolishness to the Greeks, and not yet accessible in written form to the church as a whole. Thus, by teaching, encouragement, and consolation (1 Cor. 14:3), it served to build up the church in the grace and knowledge of the Lord Jesus Christ.[16]

THE APOSTOLIC OFFICE: PETER

But, however closely related the prophets and evangelists are to the actual apostles, they are in fact essentially distinct from them. The apostles form a circle of their own. Their office is unique and marked by the following features:

15. Güder, "Prophezei," in *PRE*[3], XVI, 108–10; H. H. Kuyper, *De opleiding tot den Dienst des Woords bij de Gereformeerden* ('s Gravenhage: M. Nijhoff, 1891), 104ff.; J. C. Kromsigt, *Wilhelmus Schortinghuis* (Groningen: Wolters, 1904), 112ff.

16. On the New Testament prophets, see G. Voetius, *Politicae ecclesiasticae*, 3 vols. (Amsterdam: Joannis a Waesberge, 1763–76), III, 369; cf. idem, *Selectae disputationis theologicae*, 5 vols. (Utrecht, 1648–69), II, 1036ff.; G. Bonwetsch, "Die Prophetie im apostolischen und nachapostolischen Zeitalter," *Zeitschrift für kirchliche Wissenschaft und kirchliches Leben* 8 (1884): 408ff.; O. Zöckler, *Diakonen und Evangelisten*, 71ff.; C. Weizsäcker, *Das apostolische Zeitalter*, 2nd ed. (Freiburg: Mohr, 1890), 584ff; A. von Harnack, *The Mission and Expansion of Christianity*, I, 479; K. Burger, "Prophetentum im Neuen Testament," in *PRE*[3], XVI, 105–8.

1. The apostles have been given to Christ by the Father (John 17:6), chosen and called by himself (6:70; 13:18; 15:16, 19; 1 Cor. 1:17; 2 Cor. 5:20; Gal. 1:1) and chosen by God for their office (Acts 10:41).

2. They were trained and equipped for their task by Jesus himself, served as witnesses of his words and deeds, saw the Word of life with their eyes and touched him with their hands, and received their gospel not from any human being but from Christ himself (Luke 24:48; John 1:4; 15:27; Acts 1:21–22; 26:16; 1 Cor. 9:1; 15:8; 2 Cor. 12:1ff.; Gal. 1:12; Eph. 3:2–8; 1 Tim. 1:12; 1 John 1:1–3; and so forth).

3. They share, in an extraordinary measure, the Holy Spirit who taught and led them into all truth (Matt. 10:20; John 14:26; 15:26; 16:7, 13–14; 20:22; 1 Cor. 2:10–13; 7:40; 1 Pet. 1:12).

4. Equipped with that Spirit (John 20:22; Acts 1:8; Eph. 3:5), they acted publicly as witnesses of Jesus, specifically of his resurrection (Acts 1:8, 21–22; 2:14, 32; 3:15; 4:8–10; and so forth), were reliable witnesses (Luke 1:2; John 19:35; 21:24; 1 Cor. 7:25; Heb. 2:3; 1 Pet. 5:1; 2 Pet. 1:16; Rev. 1:3; 22:18–19), and preached the Word of God (John 1:14; 20:31; 1 Cor. 2:13; 2 Cor. 2:17; Gal. 1:7; 1 Thess. 2:13; 1 John 1:1–4; Rev. 22:18–19).

5. Their witness was sealed by God with signs and wonders and rich spiritual blessings (Matt. 10:1, 19–20; Mark 16:15ff.; Acts 2:43; 3:2ff.; 5:12–16; 6:8, and so forth; Rom. 12:4–8; 15:18–19; 1 Cor. 12:10, 28; 15:10; 2 Cor. 11:5, 23; Gal. 3:5; Heb. 2:4).

6. To this apostolic witness the church of all ages is bound. There is no fellowship with Christ except by fellowship with the word and the persons of the apostles (John 17:20; Gal. 1:7–9; 1 John 1:3). They are the church's foundation (Matt. 16:18; 1 Cor. 3:10; Eph. 2:20; Rev. 21:14). Their word, preserved for us in the Scriptures of the New Testament, is a means of grace (John 20:31; 1 Cor. 1:18ff.; 15:2; 1 John 1:1–4).

7. Their office, accordingly, is not for a time, nor limited to a local church, but continues and extends to the whole church. It is the only office that has been directly instituted by Christ and includes within itself all the powers and activities that are divided over the later offices: the pastoral, presbyterial, diaconal, even the activities of the evangelists and prophets. From the beginning, therefore, the apostles enjoyed universally recognized authority in the church of Christ. They are not only the overseers of the Jerusalem church, but also the founders, fathers (1 Cor. 4:15), and leaders of the whole church. They exercised oversight over the believers at Samaria (Acts 8:14), visited the churches (9:32; 11:22), instituted offices (6:2–6), made decisions in the Holy Spirit (15:22, 28), acted with apostolic authority (1 Cor. 4:21; 5:2ff.; 2 Cor. 2:9), issued binding orders (1 Cor. 7:40; 1 Thess. 4:2, 11; 2 Thess. 2:15; 3:6, 14; and so forth), and with their word are still authoritative for all of Christianity. Apostolicity

is undoubtedly an attribute and distinguishing mark of the church of Christ.[17]

Among the apostles, Peter is foremost. Simon (or Simeon) son of John (or Jonas), brother of Andrew, who, though originating from Bethsaida (John 1:44), was probably a resident of Capernaum from the time of his marriage (Mark 1:29). Already at his first encounter with Jesus, he received the commitment that he would later be called Κηφας (*Kēphas*, Cephas; the Greek form of the Hebrew כֵּף [*kēp*], with the Aramaic article [appended to the end of the word, כֵּיפָא]), the rock, ἡ πετρα (*hē petra*), as masculine proper name Πετρος (*Petros*; John 1:44). In giving him this name, Jesus undoubtedly alluded to his loyal character, which was his despite his sanguine impulsive nature, and which came out most clearly at Caesarea Philippi when, in contrast to the people who with their earthly minded expectations were disappointed in Jesus and left him, held on to and openly articulated the confession of Jesus's messiahship on behalf of his fellow disciples (Matt. 16:13–20; Mark 8:27–29; Luke 9:18–20; John 6:66–69). On this occasion, therefore, Jesus reminded him of the name he had already given him earlier (Matt. 16:18). By his bold and resolute confession of Jesus as the Christ, Peter showed he was the rock on which Christ would build his church so solidly that the gates of hades would not prevail against it. According to Launoy, seventeen church fathers identified the rock with Peter, eight with the apostles, forty-four with Peter's faith, and sixteen with Christ.[18]

Roman Catholics later equated the rock mostly with Peter and Protestants with his confession. But we do not have to make a choice here. The words "this rock" can only refer to the person of Peter, but he is and has proved himself to be a rock by his confession of Jesus as the Christ, a confession he owed, not to himself, but to the revelation of the Father. Precisely for that reason Jesus promised Peter that he would build his church on Peter as the confessor of Jesus's sonship and messiahship. Christ, accordingly, presented himself as the master builder of his church and Peter, the confessor, as the rock on which his church would rest. The same image occurs in Matt. 21:42; Acts 4:11; 1 Cor. 3:10; Eph. 2:20; and Rev. 21:14 (cf. 1 Pet. 2:4–6) but is applied differently. There the apostles are viewed as the master builders who by their preaching based the church on Christ as its foundation, but here in Matt. 16:18 Christ

17. Cf. H. Bavinck, *Reformed Dogmatics*, I, 397–402 (#108); G. Voetius, *Pol. eccl.*, III, 351–63; B. de Moor, *Commentarius . . . theologiae*, 6 vols. (Leiden: Hasebroek, 1761–71), VI, 250ff.; W. Seufert, *Die Ursprung und die Bedeutung des Apostolates in der christlichen Kirche der ersten zwei Jahrhunderte* (Leiden: Brill, 1887); W. Köppel, "Der Ursprung des Apostolates nach den heiligen Schriften Neuen Testaments," *Theologische Studien und Kritiken* 62 (1889): 257–331; E. Haupt, *Zum Verständnis des Apostolats* (Halle: Niemeyer, 1896); H. Monnier, *Le notion d'apostolat: Des origenes à Irénée* (Paris: Leroux, 1893); A. von Harnack, *The Mission and Expansion of Christianity*, I, 458ff.; W. Patrick, "Apostles," in *DC*, I, 101ff.

18. J. Wilhelm and T. B. Scannell, *A Manual of Catholic Theology*, 4th ed., 2 vols. (London: Kegan Paul, Trench, Trübner; New York: Benziger Brothers, 1909), II, 306ff.

is the master builder who builds his church on Peter, the confessor. Christ also kept this promise. Peter is the foremost of the apostles, the principal founder of the church, the example and leader of all the confessors of Christ throughout the centuries. For that reason he is always mentioned first in lists of the apostles (Matt. 10:2; Mark 3:16; Luke 6:14; Acts 1:13). With John and James he belonged to Jesus's intimate circle of friends who were permitted to come with him when the others had to stay behind (Matt. 17:1; Mark 5:37; 13:3; 14:33). He was the spokesman for and representative of the disciples (Matt. 16:16–17; 17:24; 18:21; 26:40). After Jesus's ascension as the first witness among the apostles, Peter occupied center stage (Acts 1:15; 2:14; 3:1ff.; 4:8ff.; 5:3ff., 29ff.; 8:14; 10:5ff.; 12:3ff.; 15:7ff.) and was also honored by Paul as the first among equals (Gal. 1:18; 2:7–9).[19]

[499] The church, accordingly, was never without a government; and it did not provide its own but received it from God. Over and over the institution and the organism were called into being by God at the same time and in conjunction with each other. Of the apostolate it can even be said that it preceded the existence of the New Testament church. The apostles were the founders of the church— the patriarchs of the people of God in the New Testament, as it were. But this apostolate was not continued. As the office for the founding of the church, it was in the nature of the case unsuited for continuation. For us it survives only in the apostolic word, which remains the foundation of the church and brings it into fellowship with the Father and with his Son Jesus Christ (1 John 1:3). The moment the apostles founded churches in various places, they instituted in those churches offices that differed essentially from their own and did not come about without the cooperation of the churches themselves. There is a great difference between the extraordinary offices of apostles, evangelists, and prophets, temporarily instituted for the founding of the church, and the ordinary offices of presbyters and deacons, which under apostolic leadership arose out of the churches themselves. These latter offices presuppose the existence of the churches in the same way a political government presupposes the existence of a people. Therefore they could not, like the apostolic office, be directly and immediately instituted by Christ, but could only arise when the congregations had been started and needed regular guidance. This happened very soon in the church at Jerusalem. As a result of the extraordinary Pentecost blessing, it experienced explosive growth and numbered thousands of members (Acts 2:41, 47; 4:4, 21, 32; 5:14; 6:1). Urgently needed here, naturally, was organization, which under apostolic leadership also became a reality.

19. F. A. E. Sieffert, "Petrus der Apostel," in *PRE*[3], XV, 186–212; C. A. Kneller, "Kritische Schwierigkeiten in der Apologetik," *Stimmen aus Maria Laach* 79 (1910): 486–98, mentions several Protestants (Schelling, Baur, Holtzmann, Grill) who acknowledge the accuracy of the Roman Catholic exegesis. But some of these then dispute the authenticity of the text; see, e.g., J. Grill, *Der Primat von Petrus* (Tübingen: Mohr, 1904). According to W. Köhler ("Die Schlüssel des Petrus: Erklärung von Matt. 16:18, 19," *Archiv für Religionswissenschaft* 8 [1905]: 214–43), there is no ground for rejecting the text's authenticity.

AFTER THE APOSTLES: ELDERS, BISHOPS, DEACONS

In the first place, this church with its thousands of members was—despite its unity—divided up in some fashion. It could not meet in a single building but had to gather in groups in private homes. Undoubtedly the first house churches, as we also encounter them elsewhere in the apostolic period,[20] originated in Jerusalem. We read that believers assembled not only in the temple courts but also κατ' οἶκον (*kat' oikon*, not "from house to house" but "at home" in different houses; Acts 2:46; 5:42), among others in the houses of Mary and of James (12:12, 17). In order that everything would be done "decently and in order" [1 Cor. 14:40], all sorts of arrangements had to be made for these gatherings; and in this connection the example of the Jewish synagogues, with their elders, officers, and attendants and their Scripture readings, preaching, prayer, and blessing perhaps exerted some—though certainly not a strong—influence.[21] Some such arrangement is suggested by the term "the young men," which occurs in Acts 5:6, 10. The definite article indicates that the younger [male] members of the church, like "the attendants" (Luke 4:20) in the synagogues, were automatically designated to perform a number of minor services. It is not improbable that as such they were the polar opposites of the older members of the church (οἱ πρεσβύτεροι, *hoi presbyteroi*). In Israel the senior members of a community were honored on account of their gray hairs and wisdom. From among them were appointed the rulers of the civil community and in a later period also the caretakers and overseers of the synagogues. So also, from the very start, there were "elders" in the Christian community: men and women who were not just senior in age but who also had known or met Jesus personally, heard him speak and witnessed his miracles, who even before the day of Pentecost confessed that he was the Messiah, and perhaps even belonged to the Seventy sent out by Jesus to the cities and villages of Palestine (Luke 10:1), and who, on account of all this, were very naturally held in high esteem among those who would later belong to the church. They held no office but nevertheless, by their knowledge and godliness, occupied a position of prominence in the church of Christ.

Elders and Overseers

A distinction must therefore be made between the "elders" (πρεσβύτεροι, *presbyteroi*) and the "overseers" (ἐπίσκοποι, *episkopoi*). Arguments for this distinction are as follows:

1. The term "elder" (πρεσβύτερος, *presbyteros*), used to describe the office of overseer, was later more precisely described and replaced by that of

---

20. See above, 278–81 (#486).

21. E. Schürer, *The History of the Jewish People in the Age of Jesus Christ (175 B.C.–A.D. 135)*, rev. and ed. Géza Vermès and Fergus Millar (Edinburgh: T&T Clark, 1979), II, 371ff., 423–84; III.1, 138–49; P. A. E. Sillevis Smitt, *De organisatie van de Christelijke kerk*, 68ff.

"overseer" (ἐπισκοπος, *episkopos*; Acts 20:28; Phil. 1:1; 1 Tim. 3:2; Titus 1:7; 1 Pet. 2:25).

2. Paul, after speaking about the offices in 1 Tim. 3, nevertheless describes in 1 Tim. 5 the attitude that Timothy must adopt toward various church members, both older and younger ones, both men and women (cf. 1 Pet. 5:5).

3. The Apostolic Fathers[22] speak clearly of a class of elders that continued alongside of the actual office-bearers in the church and deserved respect and obedience.

4. The familiar text "Let the elders who rule well be considered worthy of double honor" (1 Tim. 5:17) does not yield good sense—as will appear in a moment—unless we accept this distinction. It is probable, therefore, that we must picture the situation as follows. In the huge congregation of Jerusalem the twelve apostles were seriously understaffed and could by no means do all the work. So at a very early date, just as they employed "the young men" for the more menial services, so they began to use some of "the older men" (πρεσβυτεροι, *presbyteroi*) for higher ministries. We are not told in Acts when and how this occurred. The *presbyteroi* [of the church] are first mentioned in Acts 11:30; 14:23; 15:2, 4, 6, 22–23; 16:4; 20:17–28; 21:18; and James 5:14 without any explanation of their origin. It is not impossible that such use of the *presbyteroi* by the apostles already took shape before Acts 6, that is, before the institution of the diaconal office. The reference to "the young men" in Acts 5:6 (οἱ νεωτεροι, *hoi neōteroi*) and 10 [οἱ νεανίσκοι, *hoi neaniskoi*] implies a distinction from the older men (οἱ πρεσβυτεροι, *hoi presbyteroi*).

In any case, however, the book of Acts teaches us that at an early stage, under the guidance of the Holy Spirit, men were appointed in the churches whose task it was to exercise oversight over the congregation and, while they were first called "elders" because they were usually chosen from among the class of elders, were later, with a view to the work assigned to them, called "overseers" (οἱ ἐπισκοποι, *hoi episkopoi*). "Overseers," then, are elders who were designated for a specific ministry in the church. Hence all "overseers" were "elders" but far from all the "elders" were "overseers." The elders or presbyters constituted a class or group in the church, while overseers were office-bearers. However, when, as initially it happened often, the overseers were called elders, there was no difference in the name. In that case elders and overseers were the same persons and bearers of the same office (Acts 20:17, 28; 1 Tim. 3:1; 4:14; 5:17, 19; Titus 1:5, 7; 1 Pet. 5:1–2). This presbyterial or episcopal office was first instituted in Jerusalem and in other Jewish-Christian churches (Heb. 13:7, 17, 24; James 5:14) but later also in Gentile-Christian churches. According to Acts 14:23, Paul and Barnabas

22. *1 Clement* 1:3; 3:3; 21:6; 47:6; 57:1; 63:3–4; Shepherd of Hermas, *Visions* 2.4; 3.1.

appointed elders in every church. Now in Paul's letters to Rome and Corinth, there is no explicit mention of this office, but various texts (Acts 20:17, 28; Rom. 12:8; 16:5, 10, 11, 14, 15; 1 Cor. 14–16; 16:15–16; Phil. 1:1; 1 Thess. 5:12–14; 1 Tim. 3:1–7; Titus 1:5–9; 1 Pet. 5:1; Rev. 4:4, 10; 5:6, 8ff.) prove that the office of elder was a familiar, universally present apostolic institution. In addition, there is the further testimony of Clement of Rome[23] to the effect that the apostles, preaching in the countryside and in the cities, appointed their first converts as overseers and deacons over those who became believers later.

The task with which these elders were charged becomes clear from the description of their office. The name "presbyters" sheds no light on that office and for that reason made way for other names, especially that of "overseers" (Acts 20:28; Phil. 1:1; 1 Tim. 3:2; Titus 1:7), as also Christ himself bears that name (1 Pet. 2:25). In addition, they are called "those who are over you" (Rom. 12:8; 1 Thess. 5:12), "those with gifts of administration" (1 Cor. 12:28), "leaders" (Heb. 13:7, 17, 24), "pastors" (Eph. 4:11), who must care for the church, not for the sake of dishonest gain, not to lord it over others, but with eagerness to serve, ruling the church as the flock of God and therefore meeting a number of requirements, specifically also the requirement that they rule their own households well (Acts 20:28; 1 Tim. 3:1–7; Titus 1:5–9; 1 Pet. 5:1–3). From this description it is evident that the office of elder was charged primarily with the oversight, government, and guidance of the church. To this end it is of course necessary that they have some knowledge of the truth. At the council of Jerusalem, according to Acts 15:4, 22–23, the elders had to consider and decide, jointly with the apostles, the weighty issue posed by the conversion of the Gentiles in the matter of their relationship to the Mosaic law. Yet originally the office of overseer was not one of teaching but of ruling the church. Anyway, in that first period there was as yet no pressing need for a separate teaching office. Initially, the apostles, evangelists, and prophets served as teachers (Acts 13:1; 1 Cor. 14:3; 1 Tim. 1:11), and the gift of teaching was further given to many persons who held no office in the church of Christ (Rom. 12:7; 1 Cor. 12:8, 28–29; 14:26). The activity of teaching (διδασκαλια, *didaskalia*) was initially free, just as in the synagogue everyone was permitted to elucidate a part of Scripture (Luke 4:16).

Bishops or Elders?

But gradually teaching was more closely linked to the episcopal office. As churches expanded, the need for the administration of Word and sacrament could no longer be met by apostles, evangelists, and prophets. Needed was a local and permanent office charged with providing for it. Nor, in the long run, would it do to leave the task of teaching totally free, since this freedom occasioned all sorts of abuses. Thus everything combined to pressure the churches to charge the office of oversight with the task of teaching and thus to ensure a permanent place for it in the church. From

23. *1 Clement* 42.

Heb. 13:7 we learn that the "leaders" are also those who proclaim the Word of God. When Paul says in Eph. 4:11 that Christ has given some to be apostles, some to be evangelists, and further, some to be pastors and teachers, he is clearly saying that these last two functionaries do not carry out a clearly distinct office but perform activities in the church that are closely connected, yet different from each other. In the earliest period it is probable that more than one elder or even all the elders were authorized to administer the Word and sacraments. However, this situation, too, had to change soon. Indeed, the requirement that all overseers be "able to teach" remained (1 Tim. 3:2). But especially two circumstances were instrumental in bringing about a distinction that emerged among the overseers between those who were only charged with governing and others who also had to teach. In the first place, there was increasing pressure on those who had to preach the word of truth in the church. The apostles and evangelists passed away. The extraordinary gifts stopped. All sorts of errors and heresies surfaced inside and outside of the church. Competence in teaching not only consisted in instruction and admonition but also in refuting those who rejected the truth (1 Tim. 3:16; Titus 1:9). At this point training, preparation, and study became necessary for the exercise of this office in the church. For that matter, Jewish scribes already had their schools. Jesus himself had trained his disciples and prepared them for their ministry. Paul had instructed Timothy and charged him to entrust this doctrine, as a precious set of jewels, to reliable persons who would in turn be qualified to teach others (2 Tim. 2:2). In the second place, on top of this, there was Jesus's saying that the laborer in the ministry of the Word is worth his wages (Matt. 10:10; Luke 10:7), a rule that was universally recognized and observed in Christian churches (Rom. 15:27; 1 Cor. 9:6, 11, 14; 2 Cor. 11:7–9; Gal. 6:6; 1 Thess. 2:5; 1 Tim. 5:17–18; 2 Tim. 2:6). Originally this referred to apostles and evangelists, but it certainly applied as well to those who labored in the Word and in doctrine, and devoted their lives to that cause. The necessity of schooling and the provision of a living were the reasons that the ministry of the Word was assigned not to all the overseers but to only a few.

The well-known text, 1 Tim. 5:17–18, raises this issue beyond all doubt. The senior men there (οἱ πρεσβύτεροι, *hoi presbyteroi*; cf. v. 1) were not overseers, because in that case Paul would be making a distinction between the overseers who ruled badly and others who ruled well, and would consider the former worthy of some honor and the latter of double honor. But "the older ones" (*hoi presbyteroi*) are the older members of the congregation in general, who as such are entitled to honor. From them Paul distinguishes "the older men who rule well," the older men who at the same time hold the office of overseers (Rom. 12:8; 1 Thess. 5:12), and it is these—because they belong to the senior members of the church and are at the same time overseers—who are worthy of double honor. And distinguished from them again are the overseers who specifically labor in preaching and teaching and, according to Scripture, have a claim to an income. So according to this text, there is a clear distinction between overseers charged with governing and others charged with teaching and preaching and consequently with the administration of the sacraments. And still within the boundaries of the New Testament we encounter in the churches of Asia Minor a situation in which among the overseers only one person is charged with the ministry of the Word. He is the "angel" (ἄγγελος, *angelos*), the messenger, who in Christ's name must teach and lead the church and is responsible for its spiritual and moral state (Rev. 1:20ff.).

Deacons

Alongside this office of overseer and differentiated from that of ruling elder and teaching elder, a second office was soon instituted. In Jerusalem, Acts 6 tells us, there soon arose complaints among Christians who had been Greek proselytes that their widows were discriminated against and neglected in the—already functioning—practice of private charity by Christians from among the Jews. Responding to these complaints, the apostles called the whole community of disciples together and stated that it was not right for them to spend less time in the ministry of the Word of God in order to devote themselves to the care of the poor. The community, therefore, had to select from among themselves seven men whom the apostles would then appoint to this ministry of mercy and, after prayer, proceed to lay hands on them. From this it is clearly evident that the apostles, though they themselves designate the number and describe the qualifications of these διάκονοι (*diakonoi*, deacons), ascribe the right and authority to select these men to the community of believers. The apostles themselves were indeed expressly appointed by Christ. But Matthias was already chosen by lot as the twelfth apostle from a duo proposed by the 120 assembled believers. According to Acts 13:1–3, Paul and Barnabas were set apart for the work of evangelism by the prophets and teachers present in the church at Antioch. Timothy was chosen for the same ministry by prophetic designation in the presence of many witnesses and the laying on of hands by Paul and the combined elders (1 Tim. 1:18; 4:14; 6:12; 2 Tim. 1:6; 2:2). In 2 Cor. 8:19 (cf. v. 23) there is mention of an evangelist appointed by the churches. The prophets and teachers were of course not chosen by the congregations, since they arose and ministered freely and had a gift rather than an office, but in sharp contrast to the apostles, they were judged by the congregations and subject to them (1 Cor. 2:15; 12:10; 14:29; 1 Thess. 5:19–21; 1 John 2:20, 27; Rev. 2:2, 6, 14–15, 20; 3:1ff.). We may safely assume, therefore, that the election of overseers was something that did not occur—even less than that of the evangelists—outside the church's involvement. The words in Acts 14:23 ("And after they had appointed elders for them in each church . . .") say only that the apostles appointed some persons in each church as elders but do not indicate how they did this, and Titus 1:5 (cf. 2 Tim. 2:2) does not shed any light on this either. But we know from postapostolic writings that in the selection of overseers (ἐπίσκοποι, *episkopoi*) the congregation was either directly or indirectly involved.[24] And concerning the deacons the New Testament tells us very clearly in Acts 6 that they were designated by the congregation.

24. *Didache* 15; *1 Clement* 44; Polycarp, *To the Philippians* 11 (*ANF*, I, 135–46); cf. Ignatius, *To the Philadelphians* 10 (*ANF*, I, 113–17); *Apostolic Constitutions* VIII, 4.

What Are Deacons?

There is much disagreement, however, about the nature of the office that was instituted by the apostles here. Some exegetes believe that it was an extraordinary office that soon died out; others are of the opinion that it included within itself the offices of both elders and deacons, and still others think that in Acts 6 we are given the story of the institution of the office of presbyter. All these opinions are based on the fact that some of the men chosen in Acts 6, like Philip, also served as preachers of the gospel (8:5, 26ff.; 21:8), and that the presbyters in Jerusalem also received gifts from the church at Antioch for the relief of the believers in Judea (11:30). This last proof, however, is far from compelling. In 11:30 we are dealing with a very exceptional case, not of distributing the natural gifts that the church at Jerusalem put on tables for the poor, but of transferring monies that on a special occasion were collected in Antioch for the believers in Judea and were handed over by Barnabas and Paul to the presbyters. But according to Gal. 2:1 nothing came of this trip. We therefore do not know how and where these monies were transferred, nor by whom they were in fact received and distributed. And as far as Philip is concerned, in Jerusalem he was one of the Seven, but after the persecution broke out and the church was scattered, he served in Samaria and elsewhere as an evangelist and remained one afterward. He did not return to Jerusalem later but settled in Caesarea (Acts 21:8). On the other hand, all the evidence favors the idea that in Acts 6 we have before us the institution of what was later called the diaconate.

First to be considered is the name. Διακονια (*diakonia*) in the New Testament is the word for every office and gift that, having been given by the Lord, is used in the service of and for the benefit of the church community. Every member of the church is a δουλος (*doulos*, slave) of Christ and, along with all that one is and has, a διακονος (*diakonos*, servant) of fellow believers. Accordingly, there are diverse ministries (διακονιαι, *diakoniai*; 1 Cor. 12:5), particularly the ministry of the Word (Acts 6:4; 20:24; 1 Tim. 1:12) and the ministry of mercy to the poor, the sick, the stranger, and so forth (Rom. 12:7; 1 Cor. 12:28; 1 Pet. 4:11). There is no doubt that in Jerusalem there was such a service of mercy from the beginning; there was a "daily distribution of food" (Acts 6:1) that, though it may have been under apostolic supervision, was left to private individuals. The apostles, however, introduced some regularity into this ministry by the institution of an office. Now there has to be a reason why the later diaconate was especially described by the term διακονια (*diakonia*). That reason can be found nowhere other than in Acts 6. There we are told that the ministry of mercy in the special sense is a διακονια because it is "serving tables" (διακονειν τραπεζαις, *diakonein trapezais*). Second, the seven men are assigned precisely the task which elsewhere in the New Testament is more specifically designated with the term *diakonia*.

In considering the word *diakonia* in Acts 11:29; Rom. 12:7; 1 Cor. 12:5; 2 Cor. 8:4; 9:1, 12, 13; Rev. 2:19; and especially in all the places where the office of deacons and deaconesses are mentioned, we must above all think of the ministry of mercy. It is this ministry that is entrusted to the seven men (Acts 6). They have to see to it that the widows of the Hellenistic Christians are no longer neglected, and to that end they are generally charged with serving at tables. By those "tables" is meant not the tables in the homes of widows, nor the tables of the money changers (Matt. 21:12), but simply "the tables of the Lord." In every meeting place of the church, there was one table or there were several tables at which people sat, as members of the congregation, in order to enjoy the love feast (ἀγαπη, *agapē*) and the Lord's Supper. On those tables the wealthier members of the congregation laid their gifts, usually consisting in things they had grown themselves, so that the poorer members could enjoy them as well and later be sent off with them. Those tables were the tables of the Lord. What people consumed at those tables was the Lord's food and drink; and what was left of these provisions and distributed was the Lord's gift. Now the seven men in Jerusalem were appointed to serve at those tables, that is, to assist at the meals and, further, to distribute the Lord's gifts among the saints fairly and according to their needs. Third, the thesis that Acts 6 explains the origin of the diaconate is supported by the fact that the standards applied to it are so high and agree in this respect with those listed in 1 Tim. 3:8–10, 12. Why precisely seven men were chosen in Jerusalem is something we do not know—perhaps because this large congregation came together at seven different locations, each of which needed a deacon. In any case they had to be men known in the church as being "full of the Spirit and of wisdom." For that reason, the congregation first had to conduct a search and be discriminating in their selection. Similarly, Paul insists that the deacons be first tested and meet the many qualifications that largely coincide with those applied to the overseers. Hatch and Sohm go too far when they infer from this that the standards for presbyter and deacon are scarcely distinguishable. For, whereas in the case of the elders, teaching ability is highlighted, purity of conscience is required of the deacons with respect to the content of the faith (1 Tim. 3:9). But the rest of the religious and moral standards for elders and deacons are almost identical. As is evident from Acts 6 and 1 Tim. 3, the presbyterate and the diaconate are closely connected.

Fourth, there is little ground for the assertion that the diaconate did not arise till later, approximately at the same time as the episcopal office. While not too much can perhaps be inferred from the *diakonia* of Rom. 12:7 and the ἀντιληψεις (*antilēpseis*, those able to help others) of 1 Cor. 12:28, there is much to be said for the idea that along with the presbyterate the diaconate was also transplanted to other churches by the apostles of the Jerusalem church. One can hardly doubt that just as elders would be needed, so also there would soon arise a need elsewhere for deacons to serve at tables. In Phil. 1:1, accordingly, they are incidentally mentioned alongside of and after elders as something very common. In 1 Tim. 3 Paul sums up their qualifications, and in Rom. 16:1–2; 1 Tim. 3:11; 5:9–10, there is mention of deaconesses. Hence, while the apostolate as an extraordinary office may precede the existence of the church as the gathering of believers, the offices of teacher, elder, and deacon presuppose the existence of the church, a church that has the right to designate and elect the bearers of those offices.

FROM PRESBYTERIAN TO EPISCOPAL

[500] This aristocratic-presbyterial organization of the church did not last long; it soon turned into a monarchical-episcopal arrangement. How that happened we do not know; hence the field is wide open to conjectures and assumptions.[25] It is certain that various circumstances drove the church in this direction. In the first place, it was natural that in the beginning the churches could not yet make a sharp distinction between the extraordinary (apostles, evangelists, prophets) and the ordinary (overseers, deacons) offices. The charisma-based offices of apostle (in the sense of evangelist), prophet, and teacher continued to function in the churches even after the twelve apostles and Paul had passed away.[26] But when these ceased to function and progressively degenerated, so that it became increasingly more difficult to distinguish between true and false ones, the evangelistic, prophetic, and didactic activities of the church were attached to the office of the bishops: *they* became the true evangelists, prophets, and teachers.[27] As is always the case, so then too the broad stream of free life was gradually guided into the channel of a stable organization. Second, the conditions that, according to the New Testament and the Apostolic Fathers, existed in the churches clearly teach us that the early Christians were far from being able to absorb the truth of the gospel in all its richness and purity. Especially Paul's ideas were mixed with an assortment of alien, Jewish and Gentile components. Justification by faith was nowhere taught with precision. Faith in God's revelation in Christ merely continued to have meaning as the motive for a moral—often already ascetically flavored—life. The gospel became a new law by observing which people obtained eternal life, "incorruption" or "immortality" (ἀφθαρσια, *aphtharsia*). This entire moral and legalistic trend tended to favor the elevation of ecclesiastical office as an organ of divine revelation, stamped obedience and submission to the ecclesiastical authorities[28] as the primary Christian duty, and marked heresy and schism as the most horrendous of sins. Third, the rise of all sorts of heretical and sectarian tendencies made the organization and consolidation of Christian churches matters of urgent necessity. The question concerning the identity of the true church became important practically, and the answer to it was: The true church is the church that adheres to the body as a whole, the catholic church, and this church is where the bishop is.[29]

This change in government did not come about in all the churches at the same time. The *Didache* knows nothing of it. It does not mention presbyters

---

25. Cf. Karl Sell, "Forschungen der Gegenwart über Begriff und Entstehung der Kirche," *Zeitschrift für Theologie und Kirche* 4 (1894): 347–417; S. Dunin-Borkowski, *Die neueren Forschungen über die Anfänge des Episkopats* (Freiburg i.B.: Herder, 1900); R. Ruibing, *De jongste hypothesen over het ontstaan van het episcopaat* (Groningen: P. Noordhoff, 1900); A. Michiels, *L'origene de l'épiscopat* (Louvain: J. van Linthout, 1900); J. W. Falconer, *From Apostle to Priest: A Study of Early Church Organization* (Edinburgh: T&T Clark, 1900).

26. *Didache* 11ff.; Shepherd of Hermas, *Mandate* 11; Eusebius, *Ecclesiastical History* III, 37.

27. *Didache* 15.

28. Μαθετε ὑποτασσεσθαι [Learn to submit], *1 Clement* 57:2.

29. Ignatius, *To the Smyrnaeans* 8.

but speaks only of overseers (*episcopi*) and deacons (*diaconi*) who "must be an honor to the Lord" and "render the service of prophets and teachers."[30] Hermas mentions apostles, overseers, teachers, and deacons side by side without mentioning presbyters, but seems to assume, at the head of every congregation, a company of men composed of presbyters,[31] and therefore makes as yet no official distinction between presbyters and overseers. Accordingly, around the time when the Shepherd of Hermas was written, that is, in any case in the first half of the second century, the monarchical episcopate did not yet exist in Rome. It originated, for that matter, not in Rome, as Sohm asserts,[32] nor in the West, but in the East. *First Clement*, written in Rome at the end of the first century, does say that the apostles appointed the first converts as overseers and deacons, and that it is a sin to dismiss them when they fulfill their duties in an impeccable manner, but he is still unfamiliar with the distinction between overseers and presbyters and uses the two terms interchangeably.[33] By contrast, the monarchical episcopate developed very early in the East. Incontrovertible witnesses to this fact are the letters of Ignatius, bishop of Antioch, who died as a martyr at Rome under Trajan around the years AD 110–115, letters that would be such witnesses even if they were inauthentic, inasmuch as in that case they still could not be later than the years AD 130–140. Ignatius speaks repeatedly—as much as thirteen times—of overseers (*episcopi*), presbyters, and deacons as three distinct kinds of office-bearers. He regards the *episcopus* as a man sent from Christ, a gift of God (χαρις θεου, *charis theou*), a likeness of God or Christ,[34] and in the interest of the unity of the church, incessantly urges the members of the church to align themselves, in keeping with God's commandment, with the bishop, to do nothing ecclesiastical apart from him, and rigorously to avoid all heresy and schism.

Nevertheless, in the writings of Ignatius, the episcopal idea is still at the beginning of its development. The bishop, here, is not the bearer of the tradition, nor a New Testament priest, nor an apostolic successor. He is always surrounded by the council of presbyters and deacons, as Christ was by his apostles. He is an office-bearer in a local church and has no authority outside of it. In Paul's days (Acts 14:23; 20:17; Phil. 1:1; Titus 1:5) and even still later,[35] not one but several overseers (*episcopi*) were in charge in the churches of Asia Minor. According to 1 Tim. 4:14, they already jointly formed a body or council of elders. One of them, according to Rev. 1:20–3:22, played such a prominent role that he could be described as a messenger (ἀγγελος, *angelos*) and regarded as the representative

30. *Didache* 15.
31. Shepherd of Hermas, *Visions* 3.5; 2.4.
32. R. Sohm, *Kirchenrecht*, 157–79.
33. *1 Clement* 42, 44, 47.
34. Ignatius, *To the Ephesians* 6; idem, *To the Magnesians* 2, 7; idem, *To the Trallians* 2–3; idem, *To the Smyrnaeans* 8.
35. *1 Clement* 42:4; 44:2, 4, 6.

of the whole congregation.[36] It is likely that the development of the monarchical episcopate has its roots there. The presbyter charged with the leadership of the meetings and perhaps—in distinction from all his fellow office-bearers—with the ministry of the Word was gradually viewed as the bearer of a special office. He alone was the *episcopus*, while all the others were merely *presbyters*. This would also explain the fact that Ignatius presupposes the monarchical episcopate as having long existed [before him], that Clement of Alexandria speaks of John "as intending to appoint bishops in various places,"[37] and that soon, around the middle of the second century, this episcopacy had been introduced everywhere. If, in doing this, people had not believed they could base the practice on an apostolic tradition, the rapid expansion of it would be virtually inexplicable. The new features we encounter in Ignatius, then, consist in his use of the term *episcopus* exclusively for the person who initially was only the first among equals; that he indeed still consistently connects this *episcopus* to the presbyters and deacons, while at the same time already elevating him far above them in status; that he regularly compares him with God or with Christ; and that from the members of the church, he demands almost unlimited obedience to him. This is the direction in which the development of the episcopate continued. If in a given church community there could be only one bishop, it is natural that in a large community with numerous church buildings, the church with which the bishop was associated should acquire a certain priority. Similarly, country churches, having been started by emissaries from the cities, would naturally become affiliates of the mother church and constitute a "diocese" (διοικησις, *dioikēsis*—since the ninth century; before that time a παροικια, *paroikia*, ecclesiastical district) of the bishop. Finally, it helps explain how the bishop alone was authorized to conduct certain ecclesiastical rites such as the Eucharist, the ordination of office-bearers, and absolution.

In this development, we in principle witness a reversal of the entire earlier relationship. In the apostolic era there first were church communities, assemblies of believers, in which apostles appointed overseers (*episcopi*) and deacons (*diaconi*), who were chosen with the consent of these communities and subject to their judgment. But now this order is reversed; the true church, doctrine, baptism, Eucharist, and communion with God are where the bishop is—as Ignatius keeps saying and Irenaeus and Cyprian (et al.) work out after him. Moreover, the struggle against Gnosticism, which appealed to tradition and sought to demonstrate its own validity and truth by it, forced the church to rebut it with the true apostolic tradition. And this tradition was located in the bishops as the successors of the apostles and the bearers of the tradition. They had been appointed in the churches by the apostles, succeeded each other in regular succession, and were therefore the bearers of "the certain charisma of truth" (*charisma veritatis certum*).[38] This

36. Cf. the position of honor held by James, the Lord's brother, in the church of Jerusalem: Acts 12:17; 15:13; 21:18; Gal. 1:19; 2:9.

37. In Eusebius, *Ecclesiastical History* III, 23, 6.

38. Irenaeus, *Against Heresies* III, 2, 2; III, 3, 1–2; IV, 26, 2.

completely new view of the episcopate as the continuation of the apostolate and of its inviolable authority in the church found its completion in the fact that, beginning in the second half of the second century, the distinction between the clergy and the laity was introduced. The words κλῆρος (*klēros*), *clerus*, "lot," "inheritance," "possession" originally described the church of Christ as the inheritance or possession of God (Deut. 4:20; 9:29; 1 Pet. 2:5). Gradually, however, the use of this word was restricted. First it was applied only to the presbyters, then also to the deacons, and finally still to all the minor orders (acolytes, exorcists, lectors, janitors) which came up early in the third century. All these servants of the church became increasingly independent of the church and were made functionaries of the bishop, and then, along with them as "clergy," as "the teaching church," were contrasted with the laity, "the listening church," which no longer had anything to say and whose only role was to listen and obey.[39] Thus originated the episcopal system of church government that regarded the bishop as the legitimate successor of the apostles and the spiritual ruler of the believers. This is the system in accordance with which various Christian churches have been organized—the Greek Orthodox and many other Eastern churches and sects.[40] The Roman Catholic Church, however, moved on from the episcopal to the papal system and was therefore always criticized by the adherents of the pure episcopal system, such as the men of the reform councils, the Gallicans, the Jansenists, the Febronians, the Old Catholics.[41] And finally we have the Anglican Church, which in its early period via people like Cranmer, Parkington, Whitgift, and Ussher (et al.) defended the episcopal system only as a permissible and useful ecclesiastical order, but later, especially after the archbishops Bancroft and Laud, as a divine right.[42]

FROM EPISCOPAL TO PAPAL

[501] The Roman Catholic Church, however, did not stop with the episcopal system, as stated above, but developed it into the papal system. For centuries prior Rome had been a cosmopolis and from the beginning occupied an important place in the Christian church. Though Paul was not the founder of the Roman church, he yearned greatly to see it and addressed to it his longest and most important

39. H. Cremer, *Biblico-Theological Lexicon of New Testament Greek*, trans. D. W. Simon and W. Urwick (Edinburgh: T&T Clark; New York: Charles Scribner's Sons, 1895), s.v. κλῆρος; A. von Harnack, *History of Dogma*, trans. N. Buchanan et al., ed. A. B. Bruce, 7 vols. (London: Williams & Norgate, 1896–99), II, 87–88; idem, *Entstehung und Entwicklung der Kirchenverfassung und des Kirchenrechts in den zwei ersten Jahrhunderten* (Leipzig: Hinrichs, 1910), 51; R. Sohm, *Kirchenrecht*, I, 157–247; W. Caspari, "Geistliche," in *PRE*³, VI, 463; H. Achelis, "Laien," in *PRE*³, XI, 218.

40. R. H. Hofmann, *Symboliek of stelselmatige uiteenzetting van het onderscheidene Christelijke kerkgenootschappen en voornaamste sekten* (Utrecht: Kemink en Zoon, 1861), §§44, 55, 62ff.

41. Council of Trent, sess. 23; c. 4, 6; The Vatican Council, sess. 4, proem; R. Bellarmine, "De membris ecclesiae militantis," in *Controversiis*, II, 2; D. Petau, *De eccl. hierarchia*, in *Op. theol.*, VIII, 97–406; cf. E. Sehling, "Episcopalsystem in der römisch-katholischen Kirche," in *PRE*³, V, 427–30.

42. F. Kattenbusch, "Anglikanische Kirche," in *PRE*³, I, 525–47.

letter (Rom. 1:9ff.; 15:22ff.). Later, like Peter, he spent some time there, and the two of them suffered a martyr's death in Rome. On account of the church's generosity and helpfulness toward other weaker churches, it soon became famous. As evidenced by *1 Clement*, it felt a strong maternal concern for the church of Corinth. It was involved in all the great issues that came up in the second and third centuries as a result of the impact of Gnosticism and Montanism, carrying great weight in the debates. Around the middle of the second century, the first list of bishops was drawn up in Rome; it was there that the idea of episcopal succession and the bishops' apostolic dignity came up. The terms "Roman" and "Catholic" were linked from the start and evolved together.[43] The church of the cosmopolis became the center of the Christian church. The central significance that Rome had in the pagan empire was transferred to the church and made it the head of all Christendom.

In the early period, however, this primacy of the church at Rome did not yet bear a church-jurisdictional but only a moral-religious character. Rome was first among equals; all the other [Christian] church communities were on the same level; all the bishops were equal in rank with the bishop of Rome. Irenaeus, in a passage that has become famous,[44] indeed writes that every church and all believers should agree with the church of Rome "on account of its preeminent authority," since in it the apostolic tradition has been kept pure. However, he is here citing the church of Rome as an example, ascribes authority to all the churches founded by the apostles, and only says that Rome has a more eminent authority inasmuch as it is the largest, the most ancient, and the best-known church, the church founded by the apostles Paul and Peter. But he does not say a word about the primacy of Peter nor even about the bishop of Rome; all the emphasis is on the church of Rome. Later, accordingly, he opposed the excommunication that Victor I had pronounced over the Quartodecimans of Asia Minor, with the result that the latter had to revoke it. While this opposition may have been focused on a matter of discipline, it does prove the boldness and independence of Irenaeus and others vis-à-vis the bishop of Rome. Tertullian similarly puts all the churches founded by apostles—Ephesus, Corinth, Philippi (and so forth)—on the same level, even though he also says that authority over Carthage was located in Rome, and that in Rome the apostles "poured out all their teaching along with their own blood."[45] In his Montanist period he opposed the edict of Calixtus concerning the readmission of the lapsed, sarcastically called him the "Sovereign Pontiff indeed, the bishop of bishops," and viewed his action as high-handed and presumptuous.[46] Cyprian, too, still has the same view: all bishops are equal, share in the same episcopal dignity,

---

43. A. von Harnack, *History of Dogma*, II, 105.

44. Irenaeus, *Against Heresies* III, 3; cf. Roman Catholic exegesis defended by C. A. Kneller, "Der heilige Irenäus und die römische Kirche," *Stimmen aus Maria Laach* 78 (1909): 402–11.

45. Tertullian, *On the Prescription of Heretics* 36, cf. 20; idem, *On the Veiling of Virgins* 2.

46. Tertullian, *On Modesty* 1, 13, 21; cf. Karl Adam, *Der Kirchenbegriff Tertullians* (Paderborn: Schöningh, 1907), 70ff., 166ff., 204f.

are as it were one bishop, are jointly the head of the church, and must preserve "the love of [our] heart, the honor of [our] colleagues, the bond of faith and the concord of the priesthood."[47] In the controversy over baptisms administered by heretics, accordingly, he engaged in a polemic against the bishop of Rome, Stephen. Every bishop, while preserving the unity of the church, is nevertheless to some extent independent and responsible to God alone.[48]

The above-mentioned new view of the episcopate, however, in the nature of the case, had to be to the advantage of Rome. The center of gravity had been shifted from the church community to the person of the bishop. The latter was regarded as the successor of the apostles, the keeper of the treasury of truth, and the bearer of apostolic power. If this was indeed the case, which bishop could make more claims and assert more rights than the bishop of Rome? In power and status no church could match Rome. It outstripped them all—the churches of Palestine and Asia Minor but soon also those of Antioch and Alexandria. The bishops of Rome knew how to take advantage of their position and gradually began to claim as a right what had earlier been an advantage in moral influence. The recognition of this right, however, came about more slowly. Tertullian still denied that Matt. 16:18 gave the bishop of Rome any power over other churches, since it only amounts to a promise to Peter.[49] While Cyprian strongly emphasized the unity of the church and based it on the identity of the power of the bishops, he regarded the See of Peter at Rome as no more than a symbolic representation of the unity of that power.[50] The Council of Nicea in canon 6 still made the bishops of Rome, Alexandria, and Antioch equal, and in their respective provinces assigned to the latter two the same power (ἐξουσία, *exousia*) as the bishop of Rome already possessed in Italy ("since this is also the custom of the bishop of Rome"). With respect to these, as well as still other churches, the council held fast to the primacy (τα πρεσβεια [*ta presbeia*] or τα πρωτεια [*ta prōteia*]) due to them.

Following the development of episcopal power in the third century came that of the archepiscopal or metropolitan prerogatives in the fourth. Not just Rome but many other churches as well held a certain priority or primacy in their provinces.

47. Cyprian, *Epistles* 43.5; 49.2; 55.24; 73.26; idem, *On the Unity of the Church* 5.

48. Cyprian, *Epistles* 72.3; Roman Catholics, such as de la Rochelle, Ehrhard, Rauschen, Funk (et al.) also acknowledge the bishop of Rome. Cf. C. A. Kneller, "Der heilige Cyprian und die Idee der Kirche," *Stimmen aus Maria Laach* 72 (1903): 498–521; according to Hugo Koch, *Cyprian und der Römische Primat* (Leipzig: Hinrichs, 1910), the organization of the church does indeed come from one person, namely, Peter, but Peter himself is incidental to this. The emphasis is on the numerical unity of the church in its origin; this unity is the image of the church's moral/ethical unity, and the unity is not to be found in the primacy of Rome but in the entire episcopate. Cf. critique by C. A. Kneller, "Römisch-katholisch beim heiligen Cyprian," *Zeitschrift für katholische Theologie* 35 (1911): 253; idem, "Cyprian und der römisch Kirche," *Zeitschrift für katholische Theologie* 35 (1911): 639; ed. note: The two preceding references have been added by the editor. Bavinck himself refers to an untitled article by Kneller in *Stimmen aus Maria Laach* 79 (1910): 75–82; cf. also G. Kröger, "Koch, *Cyprian und der römische Primat*," (book review) *Theologische Literaturzeitung* 35 (1910): 486–89.

49. Tertullian, *On Modesty* 21.

50. Cyprian, *On the Unity of the Church* 4.

In the course of the fourth century, the bishops were all made subordinate to the archbishops. The East continued steadfastly to resist the aggressive dominance of the primacy of the bishop of Rome. From the middle of the fourth century, alongside that of Alexandria and Antioch, the ecclesiastical power of Constantinople steadily increased. The Council of Constantinople in 381, canon 2, stated that the bishop of Alexandria was to administer the affairs of Egypt only, that [the church of] Antioch would continue to assert the rights which according to [the canons of] Nicea belonged to it, and that the bishops of the East would only administer the affairs of the East. And after thus restricting the power of the bishop of Alexandria to Egypt, it added in canon 3 that "the bishop of Constantinople shall have the primacy of honor after the bishop of Rome, because the same is the new Rome." After the bishop of Rome, it is not the bishop of Alexandria (even though he has the oldest rights and credentials) but the bishop of Constantinople who will have precedence, not by virtue of any ecclesiastical or spiritual prerogative, but solely on the basis of the political consideration that Constantinople is the new Rome. The West was left to the bishop of Rome, but the East refused to bow to him and fell increasingly under the jurisdiction of Constantinople.

THE DEBATE OVER PETRINE PRIMACY

The Council of Chalcedon (451), canon 28, acknowledged the priority (τα πρεσβεια) of the older Rome because it was the imperial city ("because that city was imperial") but assigned equal priority (τα ἰσα πρεσβεια, *ta isa presbeia*) to "the most holy See of New Rome." Despite the protests of Rome, Constantinople maintained its rights. The papal power of the bishop of Rome was based in large part on the political prestige of the city; Constantinople, as the second Rome, could therefore assert the same claims. The bishop of Rome, accordingly, has never been the shepherd of all Christendom. He only became the head of Western (Latin) Christendom. And he first became this by right only in the fourth century. The Council of Sardica (AD 343—not recognized by the church later) already charged the bishop of Rome with making the decision of whether, in case a bishop had been deposed by a synod, a new synod had to be convened. In 380 Emperor Theodosius issued the famous edict in which he ordered: "It is Our will that all peoples ruled by the administration of Our Clemency shall practise that religion which the divine Peter the Apostle transmitted to the Romans and which he made clear from then until now."[51]

Among the church fathers of the fourth and fifth centuries, there is no longer any doubt that they considered communion with and submission to Rome necessary to the essence of the church. All the rights of the ecclesiastical community proceed from the church of Rome, "for the rights of the venerable community [Rome] spread from it to all people," says Ambrose. Jerome declares: "The well-

---

51. Ed. note: Translation is from Stephen Williams and Gerard Friell, *Theodosius—the Empire at Bay* (New Haven: Yale University Press, 1995), 53.

being of the church depends on the fitness and standing of the highest priest." With him rests the unadulterated tradition of the fathers. He is "the light of the world, the salt of the earth, the vessels of gold and silver." Rome is the standard of what is catholic. If Rufinus adheres to the faith of Rome, he is catholic. "If any of us responds à la Rome, we are catholics." When Innocent I confirmed the decisions of the Synods of Carthage and Mileve against Pelagianism and condemned Pelagius and Celestius, Augustine wrote: "This case is finished. If only error were finished at some future date as well!" Then, clearly and with all deliberateness, Leo I (440–461) in several letters developed this primacy of the Roman See and elevated it to the rank and value of a religious dogma, one which has its basis in Matthew 16:18.[52]

After developments had reached this point, the question naturally arose, To what does the pope owe his eminent position and high authority? In the Old-Catholic era, even after the introduction of the monarchical episcopate, the emphasis always fell on the local church. The church at Rome, having been founded by Peter and Paul, had the purest tradition. All other churches—in order to be Christian and catholic—had to agree in their beliefs with the church at Rome.[53] The bishop, accordingly, depended on his local congregation. He was chosen by it and in all important matters, especially in cases of excommunication, consulted it. Cyprian, in his letters to the Carthage presbyterium, expressly states that he does not want to do anything "without your counsel and without the consent of the common people."[54] In difficult cases, the counsel and assistance of representatives of neighboring churches was enlisted.[55] The most ancient church assemblies were gatherings of local churches, assisted at most by representatives of neighboring churches. But when the bishop was viewed as a successor of the apostles and distinguished from everyone by precisely this fact, he could no longer be chosen by the congregation nor be dependent on it. He had to receive his office from above, in the way of succession, and therefore had to be appointed and ordained by a council of bishops or a chapter. He no longer had to consult his congregation but was sovereign and decided everything alone, at most upon consultation with the chapter that had gradually evolved from the presbyterate.

And what had thus happened since the fourth century in local or diocesan churches was repeated on a larger scale in the universal church. In the course of time the episcopate produced the papal system, and the ancient gatherings of local churches expanded into synods and councils. Initially these councils were still composed of presbyters, deacons, and lectors, but subsequently only by bishops as representatives of local churches. These synods or councils did not regard themselves as infallible; in fact, in the fourth century a succeeding synod

52. J. B. Heinrich and K. Gutberlet, *Dogmatische Theologie*, 2nd ed., 10 vols. (Mainz: Kirchheim, 1881–1900), II, 325ff.

53. Irenaeus, *Against Heresies* III, 3.

54. Cyprian, *Epistles* 14.4; 17.1, 3; 19.2.

55. Acts 15:2; *Apostolic Constitutions* I; *1 Clement* 63; Cyprian, *Epistles* 17.3.

repeatedly nullified what a previous synod had decided. From that time to the ninth century, they also bore a political character; they were imperial synods, convened and officially or unofficially guided and validated by the emperor.

But the power of the pope expanded. As bishop of Rome and archbishop of Italy, he already had the power to convene and lead provincial and national synods, just as other bishops possessed this right elsewhere. Beginning in the twelfth century, the popes managed to expand this provincial and national synod into ecumenical synods of the entire Western church, just as the bishop of Constantinople had done this for the Greek church with his regional synods. The ecumenical councils of Western Christianity, accordingly, evolved from Roman synods and were therefore convened, led, and validated by the popes. Reform councils in the fifteenth century, under the influence of the humanistic theory of popular superiority, indeed tried, as assemblies of representatives from the entire church, to make themselves independent of the pope and to put themselves as infallible and above him in rank. But the popes managed to maintain themselves over against and above these ecumenical synods and therefore had to possess a prerogative that had been given to no other bishop. From the days of Irenaeus and for centuries afterward, agreement in belief with the church of Rome had been deemed essential to the nature of Christian churches, since "the certain charisma of truth" along with legitimate succession was based there; but now it was stated with increasing clarity that this indefectibility of the church of Rome had its basis in a special gift that had been granted by the Holy Spirit to the bishop of Rome as the successor of Peter. Initially, in this connection, the emphasis was still on the church at Rome. This church was indefectible inasmuch as it had been founded by the apostles Peter and Paul and continuously led by their lawful successors. Irenaeus, for example, says of the presbyters that "they received, along with the succession of the episcopate, the certain gift of truth according to the good pleasure of the Father."[56] But this was not a sufficient warrant, especially when many churches defected and completely disappeared despite their being founded by the apostles and their having had an unbroken line of legitimate bishops. For that reason the basis for the indefectibility of the church of Rome was increasingly found in the fact that at its head was a bishop who as successor of Peter—a person who among his fellow apostles similarly held a unique position—had a special gift from and the guidance of the Holy Spirit.

Augustine inferred the steadfast nature of Peter's faith from Jesus's prayer of intercession (Luke 22:32). Ephraem Syrus, in his eulogy on Peter, Paul, and Andrew, stated: "Christ is the lamp, Peter the candelabrum, but the Holy Spirit is the supplier of the oil." Leo the Great, in his letter to the bishops of the ecclesiastical province of Vienna, spoke of a "marvelous gift of grace" by which the building of the eternal temple on Peter's firmness is confirmed, and stated elsewhere that the Chair of Peter "has been built with such divine solidity that neither heretical

---

56. Irenaeus, *Against Heresies* IV, 26.

perversity nor pagan perfidy could ever prevail against it." Pope Hormisdas testified in his booklet (*libellus*) of the year 516 that the truth of Christ's promise to Peter is confirmed by the facts, "because in this unspotted apostolic See the Catholic religion has always been preserved." Pope Agatho, in a letter sent to the emperors of the year 680, similarly declared that, by the grace of God and the protection of Christ, the church of Rome had never departed from the way of truth, and by virtue of the Lord's promise never would depart from it. It was therefore nothing new when Gregory VII in his Papal Dictate declared that "the church of Rome has never erred; neither, as Scripture testifies, will it ever err." Boniface VIII in his bull Unam Sanctam of 1302 decreed: "We declare, we define, we proclaim, that it is absolutely necessary for salvation that every human creature be subject to the Roman Pontiff."[57]

The theologians agreed with this practice and theory of the popes. Some, like Bede, Alcuin, Paschasius Radbertus, Damiani, Anselm, and Lombard, still spoke only in passing and briefly about the authority of the pope.[58] The same is still true even in the case of Thomas and Bonaventure.[59] But the various attempts made from the fourteenth to the sixteenth century to reform the church brought Rome to self-awareness. The real papalism and curialism came out of hiding, clearly pronounced the fullness of the pope's power (*plenitudo potestatis*) as well as his infallibility, and frequently unpacked this position down to its ultimate implications.[60] On July 18, 1870, the dogmatic constitution concerning the church of Christ was adopted at the Vatican Council and declared: (1) a primacy of jurisdiction over the whole church was immediately and directly promised to Peter and conferred on him by Christ; (2) this primacy of Peter continues in the bishop of Rome as his successor; (3) this primacy of the pope consists in the "full and supreme power of jurisdiction over the whole church, and this not only in matters of faith and morals, but also in those which concern the discipline and government of the church dispersed throughout the whole world," so that he is "the supreme judge of the faithful," has the final decision in all matters pertaining to the churches, is above the judgment of all and subject to no council; (4) this primacy that the Roman pontiff possesses "includes also the supreme power of teaching," so that though the pope receives no new revelations and only, under the guidance of the

57. J. B. Heinrich and K. Gutberlet, *Dogmatische Theologie*, II, 357ff.

58. P. Lombard, *Sent.*, IV, dist. 24.

59. T. Aquinas, *Summa contra gentiles*, IV, 76; idem, *Summa theol.*, II, 2 qu. 1, art. 10; II, 2 qu. 11, art. 2; cf. F. Leitner, *Der hl. Thomas von Aquin über das unfehlbare Lehramt des Papstes* (Freiburg i.B.: Herder, 1872); Bonaventure, *Breviloquium*, VI, c. 12.

60. M. Canus, *Locorum theologicorum libri duodecim*, 6, in *Opera* (Bassani: Remanchi, 1746). Bellarmine, "De summon pontifice," in *Controversiis*, I, 188–255; M. Becanus, *Manuale controversiarium* (Patavii: Joannem Manfré, 1719), I, c. 4; *Theologia Wirceburgensis*, 3rd ed., 10 vols. in 5 (Paris: Berche & Tralin, 1880), I, 267ff.; J. M. Maistre, *Du Pape*, 2 vols. (Lyon: Rusand, 1819); G. Perrone, *Praelectiones theologicae*, 9 vols. (Louvain: Valinthout & Vandezande, 1838–43), VIII, 295–536; J. B. Heinrich and K. Gutberlet, *Dogmatische Theologie*, II, 163–476; J. Wilhelm and T. Scannell, *A Manual of Catholic Theology*, I, 94ff.; II, 328ff.; H. Ermann, *De paus* (Utrecht: Van Rossum, 1899).

Holy Spirit, guards and faithfully expounds the revelation transmitted by the apostles, he nevertheless does this in such a way that when he speaks ex cathedra and as Shepherd and Teacher of all Christians defines a doctrine concerning faith or morals, he by divine assistance possesses infallibility from himself and not in consequence of the consent of the church.[61]

THE REFORMATION REJECTION OF HIERARCHY

[502] Although this hierarchical church government is much older in origin than earlier Protestants were inclined to acknowledge and even goes back to the second century, and although by the logical course of its development and the splendor of its appearance it never ceases to make an impression, it is nevertheless, in principle and by its very nature, diametrically opposed to the government that Christ gave to his church.

In the first place, the distinction between "clergy" and "laity" that underlies this hierarchy is nowhere taught in the New Testament and is flatly contradicted by the organization of the first-century church. Aside from the argument of agreement (*convenientia*), Rome indeed appeals to the Old Testament priesthood, the offices that Christ instituted in his church, and the power that Christ entrusted to them. But this does not prove what needs to be proved. Scripture most certainly makes a distinction between shepherds and flock, builders and temple, planters and fieldwork, teachers and disciples, leaders and followers (and so forth). If the words "clergy" and "laity" only referred to this distinction, they could be used without doing any harm. But usage has attached a very different meaning to them. In the Roman Catholic Church "clergy" has become the word for a special class of ecclesiastical persons who by being tonsured and consecrated have been separated from all others, constitute a unique class of "clerics," are in a very special sense the Lord's possession, are equipped with absolutely sovereign power over the people, and serve the laity as necessary, even indispensable, mediators of salvation.[62] Now Scripture knows nothing of such a class of people. Even in the Old Testament the contrast between "clergy" and "laity" is not applicable. The people as a whole were the κλῆρος (*klēros*), the possession and inheritance of the Lord, a priestly kingdom, a holy nation (Exod. 19:5–6; Deut. 7:6; 14:2; 26:18–19; 32:9; 1 Kings 8:51, 53; Ps. 135:4; Isa. 19:25; 41:8; Jer. 12:7–8; Joel 2:17; etc.). The priesthood, which was not appointed but called to this ministry by virtue of Aaronic descent, was nevertheless most rigorously bound to the law of God (Lev. 10:11) and subject to the judgment of the prophets (Isa. 28:7; Jer. 1:18; 2:26; 6:13; Ezek. 22:26;

61. H. Denzinger, ed., *The Sources of Catholic Dogma*, trans. from the 30th ed. by R. J. Deferrari (London and St. Louis: Herder, 1955), ##1822–40.

62. Roman Catechism, II, ch. 7, qu. 13; ed. note: The post–Vatican II edition titled *The Roman Catechism* (trans. Robert I. Bradley, SJ, and Eugene Kevane [Boston: Daughters of St. Paul, 1985]) drops the enumeration of the introduction so that chapter 1 begins the section on baptism. In this annotation, the proper reference would be II, ch. 6, qu. 13.

Hos. 4:9; etc.). Though Israel was a theocracy, it was not a hierarchy. There is even much less reason to speak of a clerical class in the New Testament: the Holy Spirit was poured out upon all (Acts 2:17–18), and now all are led by the Spirit (Rom. 8:14; 1 Cor. 2:15; 3:1; Gal. 5:25; 6:1), share in his anointing (1 John 2:27), are a royal priesthood (1 Pet. 2:5, 9), a church of people called to be saints (Rom. 1:7), and a people and possession of God (2 Cor. 6:16; Heb. 12:22–24; 1 Pet. 2:10). The New Testament nowhere makes mention of a special priestly office to be carried out by the ministers of the church or of a special sacrifice to be offered up by them. Office in the church of Christ is not a magisterium but a ministerium, not a hierarchy but a hierodulia, a ministry (διακονια, *diakonia*) or stewardship (οἰκονομια, *oikonomia*), which utterly rules out any domination over the inheritance of the Lord (των κληρων, *tōn klērōn*; 1 Pet. 5:3; i.e., the churches entrusted to the care of the presbyters: Matt. 20:25–26; 1 Cor. 3:5; 4:1; 2 Cor. 4:1–2; Eph. 4:12).[63]

In the second place, Scripture nevertheless very clearly teaches that in his church Christ not only distributes gifts but also instituted certain offices, both extraordinary, such as those of apostle, prophet, and evangelist; and ordinary, such as those of elder and deacon. In this connection the greatest difference concerns the episcopate. The Greek Orthodox, Roman Catholics (also Gallicans and Old Catholics), and Anglicans consider this an office that is essentially and by divine law distinct from the presbyterate. By lawful and unbroken succession it stems from the apostolate and specifically possesses the power of teaching, jurisdiction, and ordination. Bishops actually have only the teaching office, the power to preach and to administer the sacraments. In carrying out this office they make use of the services of priests (pastors) as their vicars and have the exclusive right of mission and ordination. Patriarchs, metropolitans, and archbishops bear no other office but are only distinguished from bishops by an accidental power—by their jurisdiction over a larger area (and so forth).

Proofs from Scripture for this distinction can only be derived from the offices held by Timothy, Titus, and others, and from the ἀγγελος (*angelos*, messenger) in the seven churches of Asia Minor (Rev. 1:20). But in that early period Timothy and many others were called to the extraordinary office of evangelist by the apostles, and the "angels" of the churches were no more than the first among equals, like today's pastors, so that the singular in Rev. 2:10, 23–24 also alternates with the

---

63. Cf. Luther's doctrine of the universal priesthood of all believers, in J. Köstlin, *The Theology of Luther in Its Historical Development and Inner Harmony*, trans. Charles E. Hay, 2 vols. (Philadelphia: Lutheran Publication Society, 1897), I, 361, 371; II, 538ff.; J. Gerhard, *Loci theologici*, ed. E. Preuss, 9 vols. (Berlin: G. Schlawitz, 1863–75), loc. 23, §37; J. Calvin, *Institutes*, IV.iv.9; IV.xii.1; idem, *Commentary on 1 Peter*, on 1 Pet. 5:3; F. Junius, *Opuscula theologica selecta*, ed. Abraham Kuyper (Amsterdam: F. Muller, 1882), II, 1181; W. Ames, *Bellarminus enervatus*, 3rd ed., 4 vols. (Oxford: G. Turner, 1629), III, c. 1; G. Voetius, *Pol. eccl.*, III, 2; L. Cappel, M. Amyraut, and J. Placaeus, *Syntagma thesium theologicarum in academia salmuriensi* (Saumur: Johannes Lesner, 1664), III, 272–79; C. Vitringa, *Doctrina christiana religionis*, 8 vols. (Leiden: Joannis le Mair, 1761–86), IX, 423–37; W. Caspari, "Geistliche," in *PRE*[3], VI, 463.

plural. Bellarmine and Petavius (et al.), accordingly, do not advance arguments from Scripture but appeal to the tradition found in Irenaeus, Tertullian, Eusebius (and so forth), who say that the apostles appointed a bishop in a number of churches, and who furnish a list of bishops who served some of the churches. But though the monarchical episcopate was a very early development in the church, we must in any case view it as clearly a deviation from the ordinations of the apostles. The New Testament, after all, does not yet know of any official distinction between overseer (ἐπισκοπος, *episkopos*) and elder (πρεσβυτερος, *presbyteros*). Although in the beginning the term πρεσβυτεροι (*presbyteroi*) probably had a broader meaning and sometimes denoted the senior, venerable members of the congregation, as the term for an office it was nevertheless identical with that of the ἐπισκοποι (*episkopoi*). In the churches, we know that there were many ἐπισκοποι (Acts 20:17, 28; Phil. 1:1), and this work of overseeing was specifically charged to the πρεσβυτεροι (Acts 20:17, 28; 1 Tim. 3:1–7; 5:17; Titus 1:5, 7; 1 Pet. 5:1–3). In line with this, Peter also calls himself an elder (πρεσβυτερος, 1 Pet. 5:1). Of a special institution of the episcopate alongside the presbyterate, accordingly, the New Testament knows nothing. Aside from the extraordinary offices of apostle, prophet, and evangelist, there are only two ordinary offices, that of deacons and that of πρεσβυτεροι (Phil. 1:1; 1 Tim. 3:1, 8): pastors and teachers (Eph. 4:11; 1 Tim. 5:17), those with gifts of administration (1 Cor. 12:28), those in positions of authority (Rom. 12:8; 1 Thess. 5:12), and leaders (Heb. 13:7, 17).

These testimonies of Scripture are so strong that not just Arius in the fourth century, the Waldensians, Wycliffe, the Reformers, and so forth called the presbyterial and episcopal office identical, but also many church fathers such as Theodoret, Chrysostom, Epiphanius, and others saw themselves forced to acknowledge that in the New Testament the terms "presbyter" and "episcopus" are used interchangeably. Jerome even says that originally the presbyters and overseers were identical, but that later one of them was put over the others "as a remedy against schism."[64] Roman Catholics cannot come to terms with Scripture on this point. According to Acts 20:17, 28 and Phil. 1:1 there undoubtedly were several episcopi in one church. But Roman Catholics, unable to acknowledge this, say that sometimes the apostles simultaneously gave presbyters the episcopal consecration (Petavius), or that the episcopi of neighboring churches were simultaneously included under that consecration (Franzelin), or that the terms "presbyteri" and "episcopi" were not yet differentiated from each other.[65] In the last case the alleged difference between the presbyterial and episcopal office can obviously not be maintained. Added to this scriptural witness is the lesson of history that the Roman episcopate is the root of hierarchy, opens the door to papacy, carries with it the inequality of the local churches and makes believers slavishly dependent on the ecclesiastical offices.

---

64. D. Petau, *Dissert. eccles.*, I, c. 1–3; cf. also P. Lombard, *Sent.*, IV, 24, 9.
65. J. Wilhelm and T. Scannell, *A Manual of Catholic Theology*, II, 507; H. Ermann, *De paus*, 96.

Also these things are completely inconsistent with Scripture. There is no hierarchy in the church of Christ (Luke 22:25–26; 2 Cor. 1:24; 1 Pet. 5:3). There is no such thing as a diocesan, cathedral, patriarchal, or metropolitan church, for in the New Testament all churches are equal and all have their own ἐπίσκοποι; and believers are nowhere instructed to inquire into the legitimate succession of their ministers, but rather to examine the Scriptures and to remain in the teaching [handed down to them] (John 5:39; Acts 17:11; 1 Tim. 4:13–16; 2 Tim. 1:13–14; 3:14–17). Neither does legitimate succession guarantee purity of doctrine (John 8:39; Rom. 2:28; 9:6). [Such succession] would sooner make salvation dependent on certain specific persons and on impracticable, fallible, and often even impossible historical research.

For these reasons the episcopacy was unanimously rejected by the Reformers. The Lutherans were indeed prepared to recognize the right it had obtained in keeping with the [regnant] ecclesiastical polity, if only the essential feature in the episcopal office continued to be the ministry of Word and sacraments, since this was based on divine justice.[66] Also the term "bishop" was sometimes kept and transferred to the civil governor; and in some Reformed as well as Lutheran churches, one member of the circle of ministers was given the title "bishop" or "superintendent" and charged with the supervision of a group of local churches.[67] Calvin and many others, Knox, à Lasco, Saravia, Tilenus, Scultetus, Bochartus, and Spanheim, for example, had no serious objection to this practice.[68] But this certainly was something essentially different from the episcopal office in the Roman Catholic Church, which, according to the Council of Trent, differs essentially from the presbyterate, is based on divine right, and was also introduced and defended in the seventeenth century in the Anglican Church.[69]

In the third place, it is certain, according to Scripture, that the apostolate was an exceptional, temporary, and nonrenewable office in the New Testament church. Even if the episcopate was a different office from the presbyterate, this would by no means imply that it was identical with the apostolate and the continuation of it. Of course there can be good sense in saying that the episcopi or presbyteri are the successors of the apostles, for the latter appointed them in all the churches they founded and charged them with the care of those churches. But that fact does not remove the great and essential distinction between the two. Nor can theologians on the Roman Catholic side of this discussion wipe out this distinction.

66. Joseph T. Müller, *Die symbolischen Bücher der evangelisch-lutherischen Kirche*, 8th ed. (Gütersloh: Bertelsmann, 1898), 62, 205, 286, 340; ed. note: These specific references are to the following Lutheran documents: Augsburg Confession, art. 28, in *The Book of Concord*, ed. Robert Kolb and Timothy J. Wengert (Minneapolis: Fortress, 2000), 90ff.; Apology of the Augsburg Confession, art. 14 (Kolb and Wengert, 222–23); ibid., art. 28 (Kolb and Wengert, 289ff.); Treatise on the Power and Primacy of the Pope, "The Power and Jurisdiction of Bishops" (Kolb and Wengert, 340ff.).

67. E. Sehling, "Episkopalsystem in der evangelischer Kirche," in *PRE³*, V, 425.

68. C. Vitringa, *Doctr. christ.*, IX, 210ff.

69. J. Calvin, *Institutes*, IV.iii.8; IV.iv.2ff.; IV.v.1ff.; G. Voetius, *Pol. eccl.*, III, 832–69; C. Vitringa, *Doctr. christ.*, IX, 141–229.

The apostles, after all, enjoyed a very special guidance of the Holy Spirit and held an office that extended to the entire church, indeed, to the entire world (Matt. 28:20). But their successors, even if they are bishops in the Roman Catholic sense of the word, by no means hold such an office. Also, according to Rome, they are not infallible, and they oversee only a small part of the church, a diocese.[70] But the difference is even greater. The apostles had been the ear-and-eye witnesses of Jesus's words and deeds. They were directly called by Christ himself to their office, received a special measure of the Holy Spirit, and were called to a unique task, that is, to lay the foundation of the church and to offer in their message the permanent medium of fellowship between Christ and his church. In all these things they are distinguished from all others, are situated on a level far above all their successors, and hold an office that is nontransferable and nonrenewable. The extraordinary gifts in which they shared were given to no other ministers of the church. As apostles in the true sense, they have no successors, even though it is the case that the leadership of the church to which they were called has also been entrusted—in another mode and in a more limited circle—to others after them.

In the fourth place, there is no proof in Scripture that the primacy of Peter was again essentially different from the apostolate he had in common with the Eleven. Also Roman Catholic theologians recognize that nothing Scripture tells us about Peter's primacy over the other apostles proves his primacy of jurisdiction over the other apostles.[71] The fundamental proof texts for this teaching are only Matt. 16:18; Luke 22:32; and John 21:15–17. But even these do not contain what Rome infers from them. Matthew 16:18 teaches that Peter, by making his confession, is the rock on which Christ builds his church. This, of course, is metaphorical and, without the imagery, says no less but also no more than that Christ would use the person of Peter as the faithful confessor to gather his church. In the church as God's building, believers are the living stones that are built upon the apostles as the foundation stones. This is the place Peter occupies in God's edifice, and not he alone but all the apostles with him. For Peter made the confession of Jesus's messiahship on behalf of them all (Matt. 16:15–16). Even though he said it first and most clearly, he was nevertheless expressing what was more or less consciously present in everyone's heart. And not only Peter but also all the apostles, by making this confession—which they would soon proclaim in the midst of the world—laid the foundation of the church of Christ. Accordingly, figuratively speaking, along with Peter they were all of them the rock on which Christ built his church; or, in another application of the same image, Christ is the rock that the apostles by their preaching laid as the foundation of the church (Acts 4:11; Rom. 9:33; 1 Cor. 3:10–11; Eph. 2:20; 1 Pet. 2:5–6; Rev. 21:14). The power of the keys, which on account of his firm confession Peter already received

---

70. J. Schwane, *Dogmengeschichte,* 4 vols. (Freiburg i.B.: Herder, 1882–95), IV, 267, 285, 294; H. Th. Simar, *Lehrbuch der Dogmatik,* 2 vols. (Freiburg i.B.: Herder, 1879–80), 612; J. B. Heinrich and K. Gutberlet, *Dogmatische Theologie,* II, 247; H. Ermann, *De paus,* 89ff.

71. J. Wilhelm and T. Scannell, *A Manual of Catholic Theology,* II, 313ff.

in Matt. 16:19, was extended to all the apostles in 18:18 and John 20:23. The special enablement and guidance of the Holy Spirit was not only Peter's privilege but also the privilege equally of all the apostles (Matt. 10:20; John 14:26; 15:26; 16:13; 20:22; Acts 1:8; Eph. 3:5).

By its maintenance of the apostolate as an exceptional and nontransferable office, the Reformation did far more justice to all these texts and to Matt. 16:18 than did Rome. The apostles were and remain the founders of the church. Through their witness they are the foundation of the church. There is no communion with Christ except by communion with their witness! As far as the other text (Luke 22:31–32) is concerned, Jesus there tells his disciples that Satan would try to persuade all his disciples (ὑμας, *hymas*, you [plural]) to disown their Master, but that he would specifically pray for Peter (περι σου, *peri sou*, for you [singular]) that his own faith would not fail. Peter would need this *before* all the others because he would disown his Master first and in the strongest terms. That his faith did not cease is something he would owe to the very special intercession of Jesus. And if he would then be saved and rise again from his fall, then, having learned from this trial and being confirmed in his faith, he above all would be able to strengthen his brothers if they should perhaps stumble in their faith later on. Just as it is said of Paul with the same word (στηριζω, *stērizō*) that he strengthened the disciples (Acts 18:23; cf. Rom. 1:11; 16:25; 1 Thess. 3:2; 2 Thess. 3:3; 1 Pet. 5:10), so Peter here receives the promise that he would later serve his brothers as a source of encouragement, perseverance, and strength. Now a legalistic Rome converts this glorious spiritual support into a primacy of jurisdiction! Finally, in John 21:15–17 Peter was restored to the rank he formerly occupied with and among the apostles. He did not receive a new office, one that surpassed the office he held earlier. For his being addressed with the name of Simon, son of John, the threefold question, and the circumstances under which this incident took place—all show irrefutably that Peter was only restored to the rank that he had forfeited by his denial of Jesus, hence to the apostolate and primacy of honor that had already been granted him earlier. And so, when Jesus again entrusts to him the care and guidance of his flock in general and of the sheep in particular, he is charged with no other activity than that which was already implied in the apostolate as such and therefore also assigned to all the other apostles (Matt. 28:19; Mark 16:15; 2 Cor. 11:28). The priority that Peter enjoyed among the apostles, accordingly, did not in any way alter the fact that he was repulsed as a satan and an offense by Jesus, whom he sought to hold back from his forthcoming suffering (Matt. 16:23); humiliated on account of his self-elevation over the other apostles (John 21:15); rebuked by Paul in Antioch on account of his insincerity (Gal. 2:11); sent along with John to Samaria by the other apostles (Acts 8:14); had no jurisdiction whatever over Paul (Gal. 2:6, 9); is never mentioned individually in Scripture as head and prince of the apostles (1 Cor. 12:28; Eph. 2:20; 4:11; Rev. 21:14); and himself attributes the preservation of believers solely to the power of

God, calls himself a fellow elder, and warns against lording it over the churches (1 Pet. 1:5; 5:1, 3).

In the fifth place, even if Scripture had accorded to Peter a primacy in the Roman Catholic sense (which, however, is by no means the case), then still nothing would have been gained for the primacy of the bishop of Rome. For to that end a great many more things would have to be established: (1) that Peter was in Rome; (2) that he held the office of bishop and primate there; and (3) that he consciously and intentionally transferred these two offices to one specific successor. Now in recent years Baur and Lipsius (et al.)[72] wrongfully rejected the idea that Peter spent time in Rome. Should 1 Pet. 5:13, where according to many scholars "Babylon" stands for Rome, not be considered decisive, then the witness of the tradition from the earliest period on (in Clement of Rome, Ignatius, Marcion, Dionysius of Corinth, Irenaeus, Muratorian Canon, Caius, Tertullian, Hippolytus, Origen, Lactantius, and so forth) is so established and unanimous that its truth cannot reasonably be doubted. It may also be considered certain that Peter was martyred under Nero in the year 64, either in the same year as Paul or a couple of years earlier. Revelation 18:24 (cf. 17:6; 19:2) indicates that Rome shed the blood of the apostles; and the above-mentioned ancient Christian writers unanimously say, sometimes giving specific dates, that Peter and Paul were martyred in Rome under Nero.

But it is absolutely indemonstrable that Peter spent some twenty to twenty-five years in Rome, that he was bishop of the church there and the primate of the entire Christian church, and that Linus succeeded him as bishop and primate.

1. Acts 12:17 tells us that Peter left Jerusalem not long before the death of Herod (v. 23), who died in the year 44. That Peter at that time went to Rome is mere conjecture and without any evidence to support it. But even if this were true, the visit must have been short, like the visit he then perhaps made in Corinth (Harnack) (1 Cor. 1:13; 9:5). In any case, at the council in Acts 15, that is in the year 47, Peter was back in Jerusalem.

2. In the letter that Paul wrote from Corinth to the church in Rome in approximately the years 54–58, not a word is said about Peter's stay and ministry in Rome. The same is true in the letters to Philemon, Colossae, and Ephesus, which Paul probably wrote from Rome, and in that to the Philippians, which he certainly wrote from Rome in the years 57–58 or 61–63. Nor did Peter in his first letter, which he wrote from Babylon (1 Pet. 5:13), that is, perhaps Rome, say a word about Paul, so that Zahn suspects that Peter had been in Rome precisely between Paul's first and second imprisonment, when the latter was on his way to Spain, and suffered a martyr's death under

72. For example, by J. Rieks, "Das Papsthum eine göttliche Institution?" *Beweis des Glaubens* (1903): 2–21; cf. C. Erbes, "Petrus nicht in Rom, sondern in Jerusalem gestorben," *Zeitschrift für Kirchengeschichte* 22 (1901): 1–47, 161–231. Ed. note: Cf. also C. Erbes, *Die Todestage der Apostel Paulus und Petrus und ihre römischen Denkmäler: Kritische Untersuchungen* (Leipzig: J. C. Hinrichs, 1899).

Nero's administration in the year 64, a couple of years before Paul suffered the same fate. Peter, accordingly, spent no more than six months or a year in Rome.

3. In keeping with these data, the most ancient tradition consistently mentions Peter and Paul in the same breath and tells us that not Peter alone but Peter and Paul jointly started and built up the church at Rome. These ancient stories know nothing of a stay of many years and of an episcopacy of Peter at Rome. On the contrary, according to *1 Clement* (dating from the years 93 to 95), the Shepherd of Hermas (composed at Rome around 100 or 135–145), and Ignatius's letter *To the Romans*, the monarchical episcopate did not yet exist in Rome at the time (that is, in any case around the end of the first century), but the church was led by a college of presbyters or episcopi. It is clear from the bishops' lists in Hegesippus, Irenaeus, the Muratorian Fragment, Hippolytus, Tertullian, and Epiphanius that at the end of the second century and even in the beginning of the third, Peter was not yet considered a bishop of Rome. At the time the common view was still that Peter and Paul founded the church and charged Linus with the ministry of the episcopacy. And beginning with Linus as the first bishop, the following was then designated as the second, third, and so forth, so that the apostles Peter and Paul as "those who preached the gospel and laid the foundations of the church"[73] preceded them all, and that the bishops came after them and succeeded each other "from the time of the apostles."[74]

4. It was not until the time of Victor I or Zephyrinus (180–217) that this ancient tradition was modified so that Paul increasingly lost his share in the founding and establishment of the church at Rome, and Peter was exclusively pictured as the initiator of the episcopate and subsequently also as the first bishop of Rome. According to Tertullian,[75] Calixtus already called himself a bishop on the chair of Peter. Stephen asserted that he occupied the chair of Peter by right of succession.[76] And Cyprian continually described the chair of the bishop of Rome as the chair of Peter.[77] It was also about that time when the legend began to circulate that Peter had labored for twenty or twenty-five years in Rome and had been the bishop there for that length of time. Eusebius in his church history does not yet refer to Peter as bishop and still mentions Peter and Paul side by side, but elsewhere he refers to Peter alone and also states that Peter had already come to Rome during the reign of Claudius to oppose Simon Magus.[78] Here we simultaneously discover the origin of the legend. Already before the middle of the second

73. Irenaeus, *Against Heresies* III, 1, 1.
74. Ibid., I, 27, 1.
75. Tertullian, *On Modesty* 21.
76. Cyprian, *Epistles* 71.3; 75.17.
77. Ibid., 55.8; 59.14.
78. Eusebius, *Ecclesiastical History* III, 2; III, 4, 9; II, 14, 6.

century, it was assumed in Rome that Simon Magus had come to Rome during the reign of Claudius. The *Acts of Peter*, which originated around 160, taught with reference to Acts 8 that Peter and Simon Magus fought each other often over the years. These traditions were combined and so gave birth to the legend that Peter had come to Rome under Claudius and had lived there till his death in 64, hence for twenty years. Eusebius and Jerome then proceeded to make this legend a part of the Roman tradition.[79]

In the sixth place, Roman Catholics, though finding support in the tradition after Irenaeus, are in no small predicament when it comes to the most ancient witnesses (deriving from the first and second centuries). But even if these witnesses were more favorable and to their advantage, they still all have to admit that the primacy of the bishop of Rome is based on a historical assumption, namely, on the premise that Peter was in Rome, that he there held the office of bishop and primate, and that he transferred the office to his successor. Now this tradition, supposing it confirmed all these things, is no more than a historical witness that even according to Rome cannot claim infallible certainty but only a high degree of probability. The primacy of the bishop of Rome, the ecclesiastical dignity of the pope, and hence the truth of the Roman Catholic Church and the salvation of its members are all based on a historical probability that can at any moment be nullified by new witnesses. Eternity, here, hangs on a cobweb.

But in addition there is still another problem for Rome. The tradition in the writings of Julius Africanus, Origen, and Eusebius (et al.) tells us that, before his journey to Rome in the second year of Emperor Claudius, Peter had been in Antioch and instituted the episcopacy in that city.[80] Now while this tradition as such may be unreliable, for Roman Catholics it is nevertheless hard to deny its truth, inasmuch as then they create the appearance of measuring with two different standards. However, even apart from this tradition, it is very likely that, like the other apostles, so also Peter instituted the episcopacy in a variety of churches. Why then is specifically the bishop of Rome the successor of Peter and heir of the primacy? Certainly, according to Rome, Peter was also the primate when he spent time in Jerusalem, Antioch, and elsewhere. For him, accordingly, there was in any case no unbreakable link between his primacy and the episcopate of the church at Rome. He could therefore have just as well passed on that primacy to a bishop other than the one of Rome. If he—as is very likely—also appointed overseers (*episcopi*) in churches elsewhere, did he transmit the episcopacy but expressly reserve the primacy until he could pass it on to the bishop of Rome? And why

79. K. von Hase, *Handbook to the Controversy with Rome*, trans. A. W. Streane, 2 vols. (London: Religious Tract Society, 1906), I, 214ff.; F. Kattenbusch, *Lehrbuch der vergleichenden Confessionskunde* (Freiburg i.B.: J. C. B. Mohr [Paul Siebeck], 1892), 90ff.; A. von Harnack, *Die Chronologie der altchristlichen Literatur bis Eusebius*, 2 vols. (Leipzig: Hinrichs, 1897–1904), I, 171ff., 240ff., 703ff.; T. Zahn, *Introduction to the New Testament*, 3 vols. (Edinburgh: T&T Clark, 1909), II, 18ff.

80. A. von Harnack, *Die Chronologie der altchristlichen Literatur bis Eusebius*, I, 118, 705.

did he act in that fashion? On whose authority did he act? What evidence is there that Linus is Peter's successor, not only in the apostolate, but also in primacy? A historical, ecclesiastical, legal tradition that this is how it was always viewed is inadequate for this purpose, for it concerns precisely the foundation on which the entire Roman Catholic Church rests. There has to be a divine law underlying this episcopal papal structure. But this is where the shoe pinches: it does not exist. Christ never said a word about Peter's episcopacy at Rome nor about his successor. Neither according to Scripture nor according to tradition has Peter ever breathed a hint that the bishop at Rome would be his only true successor. The link between the primacy and the Roman episcopate is therefore only based on the fact that Peter did spend time in Rome and on the unhistorical assumption that he held the office of bishop and primate there.

But even if this latter point were historically correct, it still does not do what it is supposed to do. Lacking still, in that case, is the strictly necessary proof that Peter, consciously and intentionally, by virtue of his apostolic authority and divine mandate, wanted to and actually did transfer this episcopacy and this primacy to his successor at Rome. Conclusion: The primacy of the Roman bishop over the entire Christian church is totally unfounded. It cannot show the divine right on which it rests; it does not even have a reliable historical foundation. Roman Catholic theologians must therefore—despite themselves—acknowledge that the primacy of the Roman bishop possesses, along with a direct divine foundation, namely, the establishment of the primacy as a permanent institution [which, however, is also indemonstrable], a humanly mediated foundation of a historical nature.[81] For that reason, finally, Roman Catholic theologians are not of one mind either about the nature of the connection between "primacy" and Roman "episcopacy." Some of them, such as Dominicus Soto, Báñez, and Mendoza (et al.), are of the opinion that that connection is based only on ecclesiastical law and that the primacy of the episcopal See of Rome can be transferred to another. Ballerini and Veith (et al.) leave the question undecided and consider it perplexingly difficult to resolve. But Cajetan, Canus, and Suarez (and so forth) believe that Peter, after instituting the episcopacy in Antioch, received a special divine revelation and by virtue of this revelation united primacy inseparably with the episcopacy at Rome.[82] Although this dispute has not yet been formally settled, popes, councils, and theologians speak mostly in favor of this last sentiment. They instinctively and consistently proceed from the indissoluble connection between the two. It has been ruled by Pope Pius IX (*Syllabus of Errors*, proposition 35) that those eligible to vote

81. J. Wilhelm and T. Scannell, *A Manual of Catholic Theology*, II, 341ff.

82. J. Schwane, *Dogmengeschichte*, IV, 300, 311, 341; R. Bellarmine, "De rom. pontiff. lib.," in *Controversiis*, II; *Theologia Wirceburgensis*, I, 267–306; G. Perrone, *Prael. theol.*, VIII, 295–419; J. Wilhelm and T. Scannell, *A Manual of Catholic Theology*, II, 341ff.; G. M. Jansen, *Praelectiones theologiae dogmaticae*, 3 vols. in 2 (Utrecht: Van Rossum, 1875–79), I, 512–82; F. Hettinger, *Apologie des Christenthums*, ed. Eugen Müller, 7th ed., 5 vols. (Freiburg i.B.: Herder, 1895–98), IV, 499–618; W. Esser, *Das heiligen Petrus Aufenthalt* (Breslau: Coch, 1889); Joseph Hollweck, *Der apostolische Stuhl und Rom* (Mainz: Kirchheim, 1895).

may not transfer the supreme pontificate from the bishop and city of Rome to another bishop and another city. The only question that remains is whether the pope himself would have license to do this, and this, of course, is for that infallible one himself to decide. The Roman Catholic Christian, accordingly, is bound to believe that communion with the local church at Rome is necessary for salvation. The so-called Catholic Church is, in truth, the Roman church: that is its name and that is its essence.

POST-REFORMATION DEVELOPMENTS

[503] The Roman hierarchy, to the extent that it expanded, provoked proportionately more resistance and opposition. In the Middle Ages a number of sects came into being that rejected Rome as Babylon and the pope as antichrist. And in the century of the Reformation, this opposition spread out over all of Western Christianity. Out of understandable reaction, many people came to reject all ecclesiastical institutions, or to view them as merely a free and arbitrary creation of the believing community, or even tacitly to assign all church government to Christian civil authorities.[83] Even among the Lutherans, independent church government did not come into its own. Luther indeed originally proceeded from the universal priesthood of all believers and from the church as the communion of saints. But in this connection, too, his position was too anthropological for him to derive a special kind of government for his church from the confession of the kingship of Christ. To a certain extent he regarded the form of church government an external and indifferent matter. If necessary, he could accept a papal or episcopal form of government, provided it did not present an obstacle to the preaching of the gospel.[84] The church only becomes visible in Word and sacrament, but hardly at all in any mode of organization or form of government. Christ only governs his church by the ministry of preaching. This conviction, coupled with his view of civil government as "the foremost member of the church," led Luther as early as his *To the Christian Nobility of the German Nation* (1520) to call the government to the work of reformation. In 1526 he even requested the Elector of Saxony to undertake the work of visitation. On August 27, 1526, at Spires [Speyer], the Reformation was put under the protection of the princes and estates. And from 1527 onward, the government of the church was in the hands of the regional government. While the "ecclesiastical order" (the pastors) retained the ministry of the Word and sacraments, and the "economic order" (the congregation) received the right of consent and approbation, the "political order" (the civil government) was charged with everything that pertained to the "external government." This included the right to appoint, support, and dismiss pastors; to found churches and schools; to regulate the worship services; to reform doctrine; and so forth;

83. See above, 291–96 (#489).
84. Smalcald Articles, part II, art. 4 (Kolb and Wengert, 307–10).

the civil government exercised this power under Melanchthon's inspiration from 1529 onward by means of consistories.

The grounds on which the Lutherans accorded this extensive control over the church to the civil government differed. But whether the government was viewed as the substitute for bishops, or it was tacitly assumed that it had received this power from the church, or whether it was honored as "the foremost member of the church," it always came down to the fact that the church was almost completely deprived of any government of its own.

But all these systems of church government that emerged in many Protestant churches during and after the Reformation were not in keeping with what Scripture teaches on this score. The reasons are as follows:

1. However closely religious and civil life were intertwined in Israel, there was nevertheless a difference even then. Alongside the kings were the priests, who occupied an independent position and were called to a task of their own. In the days of the New Testament, the church as the people of God had become even much more independent. Not only was it disconnected from the national situation of Israel, on the day of Pentecost it also received an independent life principle in the Holy Spirit, which conferred on it a character of its own and an independent existence vis-à-vis the state and society.

2. The essence of the church consists in the fact that it is an association of Christ-believers. As such it is not and cannot be a creation of human beings. It originates, not from the will of the flesh, nor from the will of man, but by birth from God. It is not a product of human association, nor of the good pleasure of the state, but both in its origin and in its essence is a miracle, the fruit of a special gracious activity of God and therefore, by virtue of its nature, is self-reliant, independent, and free with respect to the good will or ill will of humans.

3. From this fact alone it follows that the church must have a government of its own. The church possesses a life of its own, is sustained in that life by a special law of life that God has created in it, and naturally demands for itself the right to give free and independent expression to that life. It is incorrect to say that the mode of its organization and the form of its government is an indifferent matter to the church of Christ. Being and form, the invisible and the visible, the internal and the external, are never so loosely and indifferently conjoined or opposed to each other. Granted, the nature of the church is primarily expressed in the ministry of Word and sacraments, in the purity of its doctrine and life, but its government, far from being unrelated to all these things, is directly connected to them. A good government is needed precisely in order that the Word and sacraments may be properly administered and that doctrine and life may be organized accordingly. The confession is primary, but church order is the means to

uphold it.[85] And just as an unsound confession falsifies the church's government, so a bad system of government exerts a corrupting influence on the church's confession.

4. Christ has, therefore, given his church a government of its own. He himself called, equipped, and ordained the apostles, who are the foundation of the church. And these apostles in turn, under his guidance, instituted the ordinary offices of overseers and deacons, in order that the churches of Christ would not be deprived of government in their absence and after their deaths. Also these ordinary offices have their origin in God (Acts 20:28; 1 Cor. 12:28; Eph. 4:11) and did not end in the apostolic era but were instituted so that they should remain to the end of this dispensation (Acts 14:23; 1 Tim. 3, Titus 1:5). Scripture itself is not a book of church order, but it does contain the principles of church government that cannot be disregarded without injury to the spiritual life.

5. Nor, therefore, is it correct to say that the church of Christ can form a government for itself as circumstances require or, either tacitly or deliberately, turn it over to a Christian government. For although it can be said in a sense that the church provides for its own government and establishes itself as a church institution, because the apostles in instituting the ordinary offices consulted the churches and the latter designated the persons for these offices, yet this is true only in a certain sense. It is always Christ who calls people to these offices and equips them for them. The churches can and may designate the persons, but in so doing they are not autonomous but bound to the ordinances of the Lord. In establishing the church as an institution, they may not go about it arbitrarily and according to their own insight but must also in this connection ask what the Lord wants them to do. The churches, therefore, are not at liberty to abolish the offices or to charge a Christian government with the task of governing them. For, although it is true that in a Christian society and under a Christian government, there will be increasing agreement and cooperation with the church in upholding the standards for, and the assessment and maintenance of, doctrine and life, even then the tasks of church and state are essentially distinct. The same sin will be differently punished in the church than in the state; the discipline that the former practices differs vastly from the punishment the latter imposes. The care of the poor, the oversight of the flock, the administration of Word and sacrament, the calling and election of ministers—these all remain the inalienable right and solemn duty of the local congregation.

The Reformed, thanks to their deep sense of the sovereignty of God, understood this. Those who proceed unilaterally from the goodness or the love or the

---

85. Over against Sohm, the connection between the church and its order has been maintained by F. L. Rutgers, *De kerkrecht* (Amsterdam: Wormser, 1894); A. von Harnack, *History of Dogma*, I, 126–27.

fatherhood of God do not come to this understanding. But those who do not just highlight one of God's attributes but bring all his attributes to the fore and proceed from God as [the living] God have no choice but to subordinate all creatures to him, in dependence and humility. God is sovereign always and everywhere, in nature and grace, in creation and re-creation, in the world and in the church. His statutes and laws are the rule of our lives, for humans are his creatures, subject to him, and obligated to respond in total obedience. In the church this view naturally led to the confession of the kingship of Christ. For just as in civil life God instituted the government on account of sin, so he anointed his Son to be king of Zion, the mountain of his holiness, and appointed him to be head over all things for the church (Ps. 2:6; Eph. 1:20; Phil. 2:9–11). Christ is not only a prophet who teaches by his word and example, not only a priest who atones by his sacrifice, but also the king who preserves and protects his own and to that end has been clothed with power in heaven and earth. He is king in a much more authentic sense than any secular ruler. He is that not only according to his divine nature but also according to his human nature. The human Christ Jesus has been exalted to sit at his Father's right hand. He was all this not just from eternity and in the days of the Old Testament and during his sojourn on earth, but is still all this today and will be to the end of the ages. He is the same yesterday, today, and forever. Indeed, he is this now in the state of exaltation in a much richer sense than he was in the state of humiliation and in the time that preceded it. Granted, he had from eternity been anointed king and exercised this office, along with that of prophet and priest, immediately after the fall and up until his death on the cross; but on account of his humiliation God highly exalted him and gave him a name above every name. By his resurrection he was declared with power to be the Son of God, became Lord, received all power in heaven and on earth, and now reigns until he has completed the kingdom and put all his enemies under his feet.[86]

This kingship of Christ is twofold. On the one hand, it is a kingship of power (Pss. 2:8–9; 72:8; 110:1–3; Matt. 28:18; 1 Cor. 15:27; Eph. 1:21–22; Phil. 2:9–11; Heb. 1:6; 1 Pet. 3:22; Rev. 17:14). In order that Christ may truly be king over his people, the king who redeems, protects, and preserves them, he must have power in heaven and on earth, over Satan and the world. It is a kingship of power, subordinate to, and a means for, his kingship of grace. It does not mean that the Father has ceased to govern the world and that now all authority in the creation comes down from Christ and is exercised in his name. But, based on Christ's perfect obedience, God has granted the Mediator the right and the power to gather his people together out of the world, to protect them against all their enemies, and to completely subdue those enemies themselves. God so rules the world that Christ may ask for the Gentile nations as his inheritance and the ends of the earth as his possession [Ps. 2:8]. In the event of Christ's exaltation, the Father recognized his Son and appointed him as the heir of all things (Heb. 1:2).

---

86. H. Bavinck, *Reformed Dogmatics*, III, 475–82 (#409).

On the other hand, the kingship of Christ is a kingship of grace (Ps. 2:6; Isa. 9:5–6; Jer. 30:9; Ezek. 37:24; Luke 1:33; John 18:33ff.; Eph. 1:22; 4:15; 5:23; Col. 1:18; 2:19). Inasmuch as this kingship is totally different from that of the kings of the earth, the New Testament much more frequently calls Christ "the head" than the king of the church. For it is a kingdom of grace in which Christ rules by his word and Spirit. His word comes to us from the past, binds us to the historical person of Christ and to the work he accomplished in time, and asks of us faith in the sense of assent and acknowledgment. But he who descended is the same as he who also ascended far above all the heavens [Eph. 4:10], is seated at God's right hand, and dwells in us "with his divinity, majesty, grace, and Spirit and never again departs from us" [Heidelberg Catechism, Q&A 47]. It is the living Christ exalted to sit at the right hand of God who consciously and endowed with all power gathers his church, defeats his enemies, and guides the history of the world to the day of his parousia. As our Mediator, he is still always active in heaven and present by his Spirit on earth in church and in the offices, in Word and sacrament.

Also the *application* of salvation is his work. He is the one who acts, and the offices and ministries are only the means in his omnipotent hand. It is absurd, therefore, to think that he would have transferred the government of his church to any human being, to a bishop or pope, to an institution or a sacrament. He is and remains the Lord from heaven, who was made the head of the church to the end that he would govern it himself and with his fullness fill all things [Eph. 1:23]. This kingship of Christ was the material principle of Reformed church government. It had already been announced by Zwingli and was developed and maintained by Calvin. It was included in almost all the confessions and, from the sixteenth century to the present, has been the driving force in combating all human dominance in the church of Christ and in regaining and preserving its freedom and independence.[87]

CHRIST IS KING OF THE CHURCH

[504] The kingship of Christ over his church consists in that by this word and Spirit he gathers and governs his own and protects and keeps them in the redemption acquired. The church has its foundation and unity in the counsel of God, in the covenant of grace, in the person of Christ, but consisting as it does of human beings, it must be gathered and added to by Christ's word and Spirit. This gathering activity proceeds from Christ and is accomplished by him. Even if in this

---

87. First Helvetic Confession, art. 18; Second Helvetic Confession, art. 17; Gallic Confession, art. 30; Belgic Confession, art. 31; Scots Confession, art. 16; Westminster Confession, arts. 25, 30; J. Calvin, *Institutes*, II.xv.3–5; P. Martyr Vermigli, *Loci communes*, ed. R. Massonius (London, 1576), 403; G. Bucanus, *Institutiones theologicae*, 3rd ed. (Bern: Johannes & Isaias le Preux, 1605), 464; *Synopsis purioris theologiae*, disp. 41; C. Vitringa, *Doctr. christ.*, IX, 125; K. Rieker, *Grundsätze reformierter Kirchenverfassung* (Leipzig: C. L. Hirschfeld, 1899), 105ff.

connection he uses the offices and the means of grace, it is nevertheless he who distributes the benefits of the covenant and by them builds his church. He himself builds the church on the rock of the confessing apostles (Matt. 16:18), and it is they who as instruments in his hand build the church on him as the foundation (1 Cor. 3:11). Christ is the vine, and believers are the branches who grow out of him, draw their nourishment from him, and so bear fruit (John 15). Christ is the head, and the church is the body, which is held by its ligaments and derives its growth from him (Eph. 4:16; Col. 2:19). Christ is the Shepherd, and the believers are his sheep, who are brought into the fold by him and joined together in a single flock (John 10:16). Christ is the Lord, who adds to the church those who are being saved (Acts 2:47). Inasmuch as the church is an organism, the head is antecedent to the members and the universal church antecedent to the particular [local] church. The church does not come into being by the atomistic conjunction of the various parts, but the universal church (*ecclesia catholica*) came first. It has its stability and permanence in Christ; in the days of the New Testament it was first made manifest in the church at Jerusalem and spread from there to other places. Every particular [local] church is a manifestation of the universal church, of the people of God, at the place where it manifests itself in action. Just by virtue of its origin, it is inseparably connected with the universal church. Not a single local church, after all, springs up autochthonically from the unconscious, but was planted by the seed of the Word that another church broadcast in that locality. It is indeed true, according to Scripture, that every local church, however small and unimpressive, is independent and complete. There are no mother churches in the sense that the one church might be free to lord it over other churches. Neither Jerusalem nor Rome has any title to such government. All churches are equal because they are all—even if one has been planted by another—dependent in the same way, that is, directly and absolutely, on Christ and bound to his word.

For that reason the Reformed not only broke their churches' connections with those of Rome but also abolished the diocese and the parish. A diocese, after all, is the ecclesiastical district of a bishop who, linked with the cathedral church, controls from there the entire circle of believers resident in that diocese. And a "parish" describes a given group of believers as the object of the activity of a parish priest who receives all his power from the bishop. While the word "parish" may originally not have implied dependence on a cathedral or mother church, it nevertheless gradually acquired this meaning in the mind of Rome.[88] In Scripture, however, every church is independent, completely equal in rights to all the other churches. But this does not yet make the interconnectedness of churches a matter of caprice. Sometimes, as is the case (for example) with the churches of the Huguenots in France, it may appear as though the connection between them arose in complete freedom by confederation. But that is not the Reformed view, which on this point is definitely the opposite of that of the Independentists. In

---

88. U. Stutz, "Pfarre, Pfarrer," in *PRE*[3], XV, 239ff.

their description of the essence of the church, all Reformed theologians proceeded from the universal church to the particular churches.[89] The latter are the local manifestations of the one mystical body of Christ. They are therefore spiritually one, connected with each other by virtue of their historical origin, and obligated by the Lord to maintain fellowship with all who share the same faith.

Every local church is therefore simultaneously an independent manifestation of the body of Christ *and* part of a larger whole. It is a particular church that arises from the universal church and is, spiritually as well as historically, connected with it.[90] And that which is true of every local church is applicable to each of its members in particular. No church and no living member of that church produced themselves by their own will and effort. Christ has called and gathered each one, be it by means of the ministry of the Word, and not only one but all who are members of the church. Accordingly, it is not we but Christ alone who determines who the members of the church are and with whom we have to live in fellowship. It is not simply up to us to decide whether we will join this or that church; it is rather the obligation of all believers to join the church that is the truest manifestation of the church of Christ (Belgic Confession, art. 28). On this matter, too, the Reformed take a position that is opposed to that of the Independentists. Believers do not arbitrarily split up into conventicles and congregations, nor decide on their own with whom they want to meet for worship and fellowship. But in a given city, town, or village all believers belong together and together constitute the people of God and the church of Christ. Just as it is God who determines allotted periods and the boundaries of everyone's habitation (Acts 17:26), so it is Christ who, in connection with this ordinance of the Father, gathers believers locally and causes them to act as an independent *ecclesia*. On this point, too, the Reformed do not tear nature and grace apart or relate them antithetically to each other, for grace restores nature, and the gospel is the fulfillment of the law.

The formation of so-called "parishes," however, is not inconsistent with the unit of the local church. Various churches in the New Testament (Jerusalem, Rome, Corinth, for example) were each of them a distinct unity. The church at Jerusalem was subject to the same college of apostles and as one local church in its entirety appointed seven deacons. The churches at Rome, Corinth, Colossae (and so forth) received letters from Paul in which all believers in a given city were collectively referred to by Paul as a single unit. But this did not alter the fact that those churches in their gatherings came together in separate buildings and so formed distinct house churches. And any church that reaches a membership of thousands of souls has to come to some such division. Just as it is then permissible and even obligatory to come together in different buildings, so in the interest of the spiritual well-being, government, and care of believers, it is also necessary to provide every group of believers meeting in a given building with a specific

89. C. Vitringa, *Doctr. christ.*, IX, 60.
90. K. Rieker, *Grundsätze reformierter Kirchenverfassung*, 80ff.

number of preachers, elders, and deacons. This need not undermine the unity of the church inasmuch as that unity can be expressed in a church council and a range of common ministries. Nor is there any objection to making churches whose areas cover widely separated city wards independent in the same way as those in villages that are sometimes less than a half hour's journey apart from each other. Given the current great expansion of many cities, the various sections of the city often differ more markedly from each other in character than villages and hamlets that all have their own civil government. In any case the theory that in large cities the local church has to be defined by civic boundaries is untenable and very harmful to the life of the church there.[91]

In these local churches Christ pours out a wide assortment of gifts, not only the saving gifts of rebirth, conversion, faith, and so forth but also the spiritual gifts known as charismata. In the time of the apostles there was a rich supply of them. But although they have partly changed in nature and operation, the Holy Spirit still imparts them to believers today so that by them they can serve each other and manifest themselves as a single body. The congregation is not voiceless; it is not a "listening church" or an "economic order" whose role is to listen and to be silent. But it has "an anointing from the Holy One" (1 John 2:20), consists of many members who all need one another, and may not neglect the gifts given them. Every local church is and has to be a salvation army that under Christ's leadership fights the devil, the world, and the flesh and knows no retired or de-activated soldiers. It is a communion of saints in which all suffer and rejoice with each other and use their special gifts "readily and cheerfully for the service and enrichment of the other members" [Heidelberg Catechism, Q&A 55]. And just as all believers have a gift, so also they all hold an office. Not only in the church as organism but also in the church as institution, they have a calling and a task laid on them by the Lord. The apostles indeed precede the existence of the church, are its founders, and bind it to their—that is, God's—word. Yet they do not, in advance and by their own authority alone, appoint office-bearers, but first they start churches and later let the churches themselves choose elders and deacons. Antecedent to the special office of overseer and caretaker of the poor, therefore, is the universal office of believers. After all, where two or three come together in his name, there Christ is in their midst (Matt. 18:19–20). He acquired for everyone the Holy Spirit, who dwells in all believers as his temple (Acts 22:17; 1 Cor. 6:19; Eph. 2:22; and so forth), so that they, being anointed with that Spirit, are [made] a holy, royal priesthood (1 Pet. 2:5, 9). They are prophets who declare the excellencies of God, confess his name, and know all things (Matt. 10:32; 1 John 2:20, 27);[92] priests who offer up their bodies as living sacrifices, holy and pleasing

91. J. R. Slotemaker de Bruine, "Nog een pleidooi voor het parochiestelsel," *Stemmen voor waarheid en vrede* 38 (May 1901): 489–98; idem, *Christelijke sociale studiën* (Utrecht: G. J. A. Ruys, 1908); H. H. Kuyper, "Onze stadskerken," *De Heraut* (May–June 1909); P. A. E. Sillevis Smitt, *De organisatie van de Christelijke kerk*, 113ff.

92. Ed. note: Bavinck also cites Matt. 8:38 here, which does not exist.

to God (Rom. 12:1; Heb. 13:16; 1 Pet. 2:5, 9; Rev. 1:6; 5:10); kings who fight the good fight, overcome sin, the world, and death, and will someday reign with Christ (Rom. 6:12–13; 1 Tim. 1:18–19; 2 Tim. 2:12; 4:7; 1 John 2:13–14; Rev. 1:6; 2:26; 3:21; 20:6); and therefore they bear the name Christians, "anointed ones" (Acts 11:26; 26:28; 1 Pet. 4:16).

This prophetic, priestly, and royal activity of believers may properly be called the exercise of an office. Even as a general reality we do not exist for ourselves but for the sake of God. He created us after his image in order that we might know, love, and glorify him and serve him as prophets, priests, and kings. Christ has been specifically appointed by the Father as mediator, servant of the Lord, prophet, priest, and king, in order again to bring about and to complete this work that humans neglected and disturbed. It is to this task that believers are called as well. As anointed people who share in fellowship with Christ, they are called to the same work, ministry, and struggle (John 12:26; 14:12). From the moment they are called, believers no longer belong to themselves but to Christ. They are his servants and must do his will and accomplish his work. They are the salt of the earth, the light of the world; and in and with respect to the church, they specifically have a threefold task.

In the first place, they are obligated to join the church. They are not isolates, but members of the body of Christ, and must therefore seek and maintain fellowship with it. Second, in that church they are called to all sorts of activity, to the use of their gifts for the benefit of others, to suffer and rejoice with their fellow church members, to attend the gathering of believers, to proclaim the Lord's death, to exercise oversight over each other, to engage in the ministry of mercy (and so forth). And finally they are also obligated, each in one's own way and extent, to be active in the formation and reformation of the church. If somewhere in the world there are believers, and there is no chance for ministers from elsewhere to lead them in electing people to the offices instituted by Christ and to lay hands on those chosen, they themselves have the right to jointly elect and ordain office-bearers in the name of the Lord. Thus it actually happened at Mainz and Paris in 1555;[93] thus judged the Reformed;[94] and thus Luther thought as well.[95] For the office does not depend on succession; it does not originate in an act of transmission. It is based on the gift and calling of Christ and designation by the congregation. That congregation itself has the right to speak and act, and it shares in the gifts of the Holy Spirit. The gifts needed for the exercise of office do not essentially differ from those granted to all believers. For that reason the congregation is able to point out from among its own members those who are endowed with gifts suited to the exercise of office, and call and elect them to office in Christ's name. But from this it also follows that, if necessary, believers themselves may proceed

93. G. V. Lechler, *Geschichte der Presbyterial- und Synodalverfassung seit der Reformation* (Leiden: Noothoven van Goor, 1854), 65, 67; É. Doumergue, *Jean Calvin,* 7 vols. (Lausanne: Bridel, 1899–1927), I, 232.

94. G. Voetius, *Desperata causa papatus* (Amsterdam: Joannis Jansson, 1635), 268ff.

95. J. Köstlin, *The Theology of Luther,* I, 406.

to reform the church. If a church in its offices and ministries shows that it assigns more authority to itself and its ordinances than to the Word of God and clearly reveals itself as a false church, then believers have the holy task and obligation to separate themselves from it and to proceed again to live ecclesiastically in accordance with the Word of the Lord.[96]

CHURCH OFFICE AS SERVICE

[505] On the basis of these gifts and this office of all believers, Christ has also instituted special offices in the church. The apostles indeed performed a ministerial service in this connection, but it is Christ nevertheless who gives these offices and equips and elects persons to them. However, in the Roman Catholic Church, Richer asserted that Christ had assigned all power, "primarily, properly, and essentially," to the church and then "instrumentally, ministerially, and with respect to its execution" to the pope and the bishops.[97] In his first period Luther inferred from the universal priesthood of believers that the ministry of the Word was actually given to all but, for the sake of order, was carried out by one of them.[98] Reformed authors sometimes voice the view that the power of the ministers actually belongs to the congregation but is exercised by them in its name.[99] Not infrequently the image is used that, just as persons see through their eyes and hear through their ears, so churches accomplish their institutional activities through the offices. In modern times there is the common view that the office is an organ of the church. All this is only partially correct. In Matt. 18:17–18 Jesus indeed grants the power of the keys to the entire church but still uses this word in a very general sense, without mentioning the organization that was to be introduced later. As soon as this organization exists, we note that the power of the keys rests with the apostles and then with the overseers. The power of the keys can in general be said to have been given to the church, since it conduces to its salvation and well-being and hence has been given to it, if not formally, then with a view to its purpose. It is "indeed intended for the edification of the whole church but must properly be handled by its ministers alone."[100] The offices in the church of Christ are not a ruling but a serving power. They exist for the sake of the church (1 Cor. 3:22; Eph. 4:12). Paul even calls himself and his fellow ministers "your servants for Jesus' sake" (2 Cor. 4:5). The purpose of the church as an institution consists in gathering the elect, in building up the body of Christ, in perfecting the saints, and thus in glorifying God (Eph. 4:11). God could certainly also have led his people

96. Belgic Confession, arts. 28–29.

97. E. Richer, *De ecclesiastica et politica potestate* (Paris, 1611); Cf. D. Petavius (Petau), "De eccl. hier.," in *Op. theol.*, III, c. 14–16; J. Wilhelm and T. Scannell, *A Manual of Catholic Theology*, II, 303ff.

98. J. Köstlin, *The Theology of Luther*, I, 406.

99. W. Ames, *Marrow of Theology*, trans. and ed. J. D. Eusden (1968; repr., Grand Rapids: Baker Academic, 1997), I, 35, 6; F. Turretin, *Institutes of Elenctic Theology*, trans. G. M. Giger, ed. J. T. Dennison, 3 vols. (Phillipsburg, NJ: Presbyterian & Reformed, 1992), XVIII, qu. 24, 7, 8, 19, 26.

100. S. Maresius, *Syst. theol.*, XVI, 70.

to salvation without the means of church or office, word or sacrament, but it was his pleasure to gather his elect by the ministry of human beings. The purpose of the church is the salvation of the elect; the offices of the church are necessary by virtue of that hypothesis (*necessitate hypothetica*).[101]

Still, even though in that sense the offices exist for the sake of the church, they are not its organ and do not derive their power from it. For in the Old Testament Moses and Aaron, priests and prophets, were called and appointed by the Lord; in the New Testament the apostles, including Paul, were directly chosen and equipped by Christ. False prophets and apostles are marked by the fact that they have not received their mission from God and come only in their own name (Jer. 23:21, 32; John 5:43). True servants, by contrast, base themselves on their mission from God and derive their power and authority from that mission (Isa. 6:8; Jer. 1:4–5; Hos. 1:1; Rom. 1:1; Gal. 1:1; and so forth). Accordingly, even though they exist to serve the church, they are nevertheless called "ministers of Christ" (διακονοι Χριστου, *diakonoi Christou*; Col. 1:7; Acts 20:24; 1 Tim. 1:12), "servants of Christ" (δουλοι Χριστου, *douloi Christou*; Rom. 1:1; Gal. 1:10; 2 Pet. 1:1; ὑπηρεται Χριστου, *hypēretai Christou*; Acts 26:16; 1 Cor. 4:1), "servants of God" (δουλοι θεου, *douloi theou*; Acts 16:17), and "fellow workers with God" (συνεργοι θεου, *synergoi theou*; 1 Cor. 3:9). All of these, being the mouthpieces of God and ambassadors on behalf of Christ, implore people on Christ's behalf to be reconciled with God (2 Cor. 5:20). Without seeking to please people, they preach the gospel entrusted to them (1 Thess. 2:4) and dispense the mysteries of Christ (1 Cor. 4:1).

For that reason they have been placed as overseers (ἐπισκοποι, *episkopoi*) and caretakers (προισταμενοι, *proistamenoi*) over the church. They are its overseers (*episkopoi*), those in charge (*proistamenoi*), its leaders (ἡγουμενοι, *hēgoumenoi*) responsible for its spiritual well-being, and can claim its esteem and obedience. And this is true not only of the extraordinary but also of the ordinary offices. These too are given by Christ (Matt. 9:38; 23:34; Acts 20:28; 1 Cor. 12:5, 28; Eph. 4:11). There is no preaching without mission (Rom. 10:15). No one may take that honor upon himself except those who are called by God (John 10:1–2; Heb. 5:4). Even though it is the case that all believers are called to proclaim the gospel (Acts 8:4; 13:15; 1 Cor. 14:26), yet to do this with power and authority in the Lord's name, "to one a fragrance from death to death, to the other a fragrance from life to life" [2 Cor. 2:16], demands a special mission and mandate.

The road by which Christ puts his servants in office runs through three stages: vocation, examination, and ordination. Since the vocation or calling no longer comes to a person in an extraordinary manner, as once it did to prophets and apostles, it can only be known by the correspondence between the internal and

---

101. Gallic Confession, art. 25; Belgic Confession, art. 30; Second Helvetic Confession, art. 18; G. Voetius, *Pol. eccl.*, I, 17; III, 213; C. Vitringa, *Doctr. christ.*, IX, 131ff.; F. Turretin, *Institutes of Elenctic Theology*, XVIII, qu. 22. Ed. note: For a clarification of *necessitate hypothetica*, see 329–30n2, above.

the external calling. The internal calling, which accordingly must be distinguished from the supernatural and extraordinary calling, consists (1) in the bestowal of gifts required for office; (2) in the pure, sincere, and steadfast desire that causes a person to strive for office; and (3) in the opening up of ways that lead to office.[102] This internal and subjective calling must be confirmed as genuine by the external calling of the church, inasmuch as here too error and deception cannot be ruled out.[103] For that reason this external calling is not at odds with the internal calling, but proceeds as much from Christ as the latter. He alone can call and does call a person in truth. This external call, however, is mediate and is issued by the church in Jesus's name. Scripture leaves no doubt about this (Acts 1:23–26; 6:2–6; 2 Cor. 8:19).[104]

In the early centuries the churches also actually exercised this right; even the bishop was chosen by the local church.[105] The election of the pope, the bishop of Rome, by the cardinals, that is, originally the presbytery of the local church there, is a vestige of the earlier custom. But gradually this right of the local congregation was curtailed and finally assigned in the Roman Catholic hierarchy to the pope and, under the influence of humanistic constitutional law, by Erastians and Remonstrants to the civil government. Even in the Reformed churches there was much disagreement over this issue. Even though it was maintained in theory that the right to call the ministers of the Word belonged to the local church, practically this right was often severely curtailed and surrendered to the church council or to patrons or to the government or to mixed bodies.[106] On the other hand, one must also avoid the error of Grotius and Pufendorf (et al.), who taught that the election of church ministers was a matter of natural law administered by believers, just as the right to elect a board rests with the members of a society.[107] For the church is not a society called into being by the will of human beings but a creation of Christ. All power belonging to the local church therefore has been granted by Christ; it is not a right but a gift. The church is not a democracy in which a people governs itself. Christ rules in it, and the choice of the local church has no other meaning than that it notes the gifts and designates the persons whom Christ has destined for office. This is why, though the congregation makes a choice, that choice is made under the leadership of those who are already in office, apostles, evangelists, and so forth (Acts 1:15; 6:2; 14:23; Titus 1:5), and later of neighboring bishops.

102. J. Gerhard, *Loci theol.*, XXIII, cap. 3; G. Voetius, *Pol. eccl.*, III, 529; H. Alting, *Theologia problematica nova* (Amsterdam: J. Jansson, 1662), I, 15; Wilhelmus à Brakel, *The Christian's Reasonable Service*, trans. Bartel Elshout (Ligonier, PA: Soli Deo Gloria Publications, 1992), XVII, 12; C. Vitringa, *Doctr. christ.*, IX, 298; B. de Moor, *Comm. theol.*, VI, 282.

103. Belgic Confession, art. 31.

104. Cf. above, 345–46 (#499).

105. R. Sohm, *Kirchenrecht*, 59, 229, 271, 275, 282, 285; E. Christian Achelis, *Lehrbuch der praktischen Theologie*, 2nd ed., 2 vols. (Leipzig: Hinrichs, 1898), I, 147; C. Vitringa, *Doctr. christ.*, IX, 308–10.

106. J. Calvin, *Institutes*, IV.iii.11–15; G. Voetius, *Pol. eccl.*, III, 557ff., 580ff.; F. Turretin, *Institutes of Elenctic Theology*, XVII, qu. 24; C. Vitringa, *Doctr. christ.*, IX, 311–21; B. de Moor, *Comm. theol.*, VI, 288–98.

107. C. Vitringa, *Doctr. christ.*, IV, 310.

That choice, moreover, is not absolutely free but bound to conditions and criteria that have been laid down by Christ for the office in question (Acts 1:21; 6:3; 1 Tim. 3). And finally, a person has not yet been ordained to office when he has been elected by the congregation but must await the laying on of hands (Acts 6:6; and so forth). Accordingly, a selection by the congregation and guidance by the church council must go hand in hand in calling a person to an office in the church of Christ, whether the church council in calling someone binds itself to a nomination made by the congregation or to a choice made by the congregation from a nomination made by the council.

But the choice of the congregation and the call issued by the church council (the calling strictly so called) does not exhaust the process of external calling. It is continued in a period of testing or in an examination. Of course, such a test or examination is not strictly necessary. If the congregation is certain that the person it is calling has the required gifts, further investigation is superfluous. But the congregation is not infallible; it may be mistaken. It does not itself bestow the gifts but can only discern to whom Christ has given gifts for ministry in his name. Now, in order to proceed as carefully as possible, it arranges a period of testing with a view to assuring the congregation that the person called possesses the required gifts. Paul therefore already demanded (1 Tim. 3:10) that the deacons—and the words καὶ οὗτοι δε prove that this was also the practice with presbyters—would, by some method unknown to us, be tested, and if they proved themselves blameless in doctrine and life, they would then serve. This was the basis for the right that the church would later use to institute a period of probation before the admission to office or to conduct an examination.[108] Here in the Netherlands, after the University of Leiden had been established, the Reformed churches relinquished the right to conduct the peremptory examination to the professors and contented themselves with their "academic testimonial."[109] But gradually they managed, everywhere (except

---

108. J. Bingham, *Origenes ecclesiasticae*, 9 vols. (London: W. Straker, 1843–45), II, 225.

109. Ed. note: Bavinck refers here to "Particular Question," #3, adopted by the Synod of Middelburg (1581) and to art. 18 of the church order drawn up by the Synod of 's Gravenhage (1586). The full text of the Middelburg question and answer is as follows:

> Whether the ministers who were called from the University of Leyden or any other (making profession of the Reformed religion) must be examined by the classis? Answer: It is sufficient that they prove by a lawful testimony that they have been examined and approved by the Professors of Theology. (De Ridder, 284)

The article from 's Gravenhage reads as follows:

> In churches where there are better qualified ministers, the use of exhorters shall be introduced in order that by such exercises to prepare persons for the ministry of the Word, (it being) clearly understood that no probationers shall teach the congregations publicly from the pulpit except those who have been examined and are known to be qualified by the university or classis. They shall not be permitted to administer the sacraments until such time as they are fully called and ordained. (Ibid., 353)

The preceding translations are taken from *The Church Orders of the Sixteenth Century Reformed Churches of the Netherlands*, trans. and collated by Richard R. De Ridder, with Peter H. Jonker and Leonard Verduin (Grand Rapids: Calvin Theological Seminary, 1987). This volume is not in print for sale, but copies are available

in Groningen) with great difficulty and not without much opposition even from Voetius and Maccovius, to take away from the professors the right to conduct both the peremptory and the preparatory examination and to keep it for themselves.

Leaving aside the question whether the churches would not do well to seek the help of professors in conducting these examinations in the various classes, we hold that, according to Scripture, the Reformed confession, and also in the nature of the case, the right to conduct such an investigation belongs to the churches. Let the school administer its own examinations, but the churches hold the right to call, to test, to send out its ministerial candidates, and to ordain them to the ministry of Word and sacrament. The real ecclesiastical examination, therefore, is the peremptory examination. The preparatory examination, though already mentioned in article 18 of the Synod of the Hague, is of secondary importance; it was only introduced gradually, especially as a result of the Remonstrant contentions, and, according to Voetius,[110] was not commonly in use until 1669. It served only to allow the provisionally examined candidates for a time to practice the defense of [theological] propositions under the guidance of a minister and a church council.

ORDINATION

Finally, in addition to the calling and examination, there is still the ordination, which takes place especially by the laying on of hands. In Israel, this ceremonial gesture was made on the occasion of a blessing (Gen. 48:14; Lev. 9:22), a sacrifice (Exod. 29:10; Lev. 1:4), an indictment (Lev. 24:14), the consecration of a Levite (Num. 8:10), the appointment to an office (27:18–23), and later also at the installation of judges and the promotion of teachers.[111] Jesus laid hands on people to heal them (Matt. 8:15; 9:18; Mark 5:23, cf. 2 Kings 4:34; 5:11) and to bless them (Matt. 19:15; Luke 24:50). Though people attached great value to this act (Matt. 9:18; Mark 5:23; 7:32), we nowhere read that Jesus also performed it in the ordination to office. He appointed his apostles only by uttering words, not by any ceremony (Matt. 10:1ff.; 28:19). In connection with the appointment of Matthias, Paul, Barnabas, Silas, and Luke (and so forth), there is nowhere any mention of the laying on of hands. It was certainly not a universal practice in inducting candidates into an ecclesiastical office. But the laying on of hands did take place on the occasion of a healing (Acts 9:12, 17), communicating the gift of the Spirit (8:17–19), and the appointing of deacons (1 Tim. 4:14; 2 Tim. 1:6). According to 1 Tim. 5:22, it was in common use at the ordination to an ecclesiastical office, and according to

---

for use at the Hekman Library of Calvin College and Seminary. De Ridder's translation was made primarily from the Dutch text of P. Biesterveld and H. H. Kuyper, *Kerkelijk handboekje* (Kampen: Bos, 1905) and C. Hooijer, *Oude kerkordeningen der Nederlandsche Hervormde gemeenten, 1563–1638* (Zalt-Bommel: Noman, 1865). Bavinck's subsequent references to the key synodical acts and documents will be given by referencing the specific synod and year, the article, and the location in the De Ridder volume.

110. G. Voetius, *Pol. eccl.*, III, 217; cf. B. de Moor, *Comm. theol.*, VI, 303–5.
111. E. Schürer, *The History of the Jewish People*, II, 164–65.

Heb. 6:2 it belongs to the elementary principles of the teaching of Christ. But it was not a realistic impartation of the spiritual gifts of office. For Acts 6:3 teaches that the deacons to be appointed had to be full of the Holy Spirit and of wisdom beforehand. In Acts 13:3 the laying on of hands occurs, not on the occasion of the ordination of Barnabas and Paul, but on that of their being sent forth as persons who had been in office beforehand. According to 1 Tim. 1:18 and 4:14, Timothy's appointment as evangelist was confirmed by prophetic testimonies and the laying on of hands by the body of elders (*presbyterium*). And while in 2 Tim. 1:6 the gift of office is indeed conceived as having taken place "through the laying on of hands," 1 Tim. 4:14 says that it was granted "through prophetic utterance" and "with the laying on of hands"—proof for the fact that prophecy and the laying on of hands were not the source of the gifts but the means by which they were introduced into the service of the church and designated for that ministry.

From the apostles, this custom of the laying on of hands passed into the Christian church, which applied it on the occasion of baptism, healings, the readmission of the fallen and heretics, marriage, penance, and ordination. In the last case, the right to administer this custom was in later years assigned only to the bishop and conceived as the bestowal of a special gift of office. Over against Gnosticism and Montanism, in any case, the truth of the church was demonstrated by the fact that in the churches founded by the apostles, the bishops were the custodians of the pure tradition. They had received this tradition from the apostles and handed it down unscathed to their successors. The "succession passed down from the beginning," argued on the basis of 2 Tim. 2:2, was the guarantee for this, for the office included the communication of a special "spirit" of office that saves the office-bearer, however ungodly he may be personally. In the ancient church the laying on of hands was certainly customary on the occasion of the ordination of presbyters, deacons, and the minor orders; it was always accompanied by prayer and viewed for a long time afterward as the symbolic sign of the communication of the gift of office. "The laying on of hands—what is it other than a prayer over a human being?"[112] But gradually it came to be viewed as a sacrament which ex opere operato effected an indelible mark.[113] The Lutherans first rejected it but later resumed it and sometimes assigned great value to it.[114] The Reformed unanimously judged that the laying on of hands was not an injunction of Christ and hence not strictly necessary. But while some considered it useful, venerable, and worth following,[115] others held it to be an indifferent matter and, out of fear of superstition, advised against its use.[116]

112. Augustine, *On Baptism* 3, 16.

113. Council of Trent, 23, c. 7; *De Ref.*, c. 3, 10; Roman Catechism, II, ch. 7, qu. 29 (ed. note: Bradley and Kevane, II, ch. 6, qu. 32); R. Bellarmine, "De clericis," in *Controversiis*, I, 14.

114. Apology of the Augsburg Confession, art. 13.

115. J. Calvin, *Institutes*, IV.iii.16; IV.xiv.20; IV.xix.31; see also Aretius, Spanheim, Koelman, et al.

116. Synod of Emden, art. 16: "The ministers of the Word shall be examined, that is questioned, by those who have chosen them. When their doctrine and life is acknowledged to be acceptable, they shall be installed

Laying on of hands is not an essential element in ordination, for neither in connection with Jesus himself, nor in connection with the apostles, nor even in connection with the elders (Acts 14:23; 20:28) is any mention made of it. Neither can it and may it be viewed as a mechanical impartation of a special "spirit" of office. For according to Scripture it does not bestow, but rather presupposes, the charismata required for office. Nor is it identical with the election or call to office, but follows these events and can therefore only be a public designation of the person called to a given office and a solemn introduction into and consecration to that office. Just as a marriage ceremony before a representative of the state does not constitute the essence of a marriage, and a coronation does not make a king, so also ordination, either with or without the laying on of hands, is not the impartation of an office or the spirit of an office. Rather, ordination is the solemn public declaration before God and his congregation that the person called has been sent by way of a lawful process and hence by God himself, that this person possesses the required gifts and as such ought to be received, recognized, and honored by the church in question.[117]

HOW MANY OFFICES?

[506] In the Christian church, there is little agreement concerning the number of offices that Christ has instituted in it. In the apostolic period, the boundaries between extraordinary and ordinary offices and hence between offices and gifts were, in the nature of the case, fluid. But the hierarchical development that began with the rise of the episcopacy deprived the local church of all freedom and independence and separated the offices from it by a huge gap. The members of the church became the laity who, excluded from the government of the church and absolutely dependent for their salvation on the priest and the sacraments, were left with nothing to do but to listen and obey. Separated from them by a special "character" and "spirit" of office and high above them are the clergy, who constitute a distinct class, propagate themselves by succession, and can belong to this clerical class even without having a specific ministry in the local church. These

---

with appropriate prayers and the laying on of hands (but without superstition and as a requirement)" (De Ridder, 116–17).

Synod of Dordrecht (1574), art. 24: "In view of the fact that the church is only in its beginning, the laying on of hands may lead to superstition and ridicule by some, the brothers have decided that the laying on of hands shall be left out and only the ministers shall be entrusted to God and the congregation as provided in the following articles" (De Ridder, 155).

Synod of Middelburg (1581), art. 5: "One who is already in the ministry of the Word and is called to another congregation shall be received with prayers and the giving of the right hand of fellowship. No one of the congregation shall be forced to attend against their will" (De Ridder, 175); G. Voetius, *Pol. eccl.*, III, 452, 579; B. de Moor, *Comm. theol.*, V, 352–56; VI, 327–31; C. Vitringa, *Doctr. christ.*, IX, 209, 353–57.

117. R. Sohm, *Kirchenrecht*, 56ff.; Th. Zahn, *Introduction to the New Testament*, II, 94; E. C. Achelis, *Lehrbuch der praktischen Theologie*, I, 139–73; E. C. Cremer, "Handauflegung," in *PRE*³, VII, 387–89; W. Caspari, "Geistliche," in *PRE*³, VI, 471.

clerics are divided in two ranks: the minor orders (unconsecrated) and the major orders (consecrated). The minor orders, to which the acolytes, exorcists, readers, and porters belong, were initially voluntary services rendered by members of the church but were organized in the first half of the third century in Rome into lesser orders, since they stood in relation to the holy and to some degree participated in it. Although frequently only in name, these orders are even today preparatory to the higher orders.[118] Even in the case of the minor orders, there is an evident tendency to separate them from the congregation and to incorporate them into the ecclesiastical hierarchy. But this is much more strongly the case with the major orders. These include the three offices of bishop, presbyter, and deacon; and of these three actually only the episcopal office is left. An assortment of distinctions of jurisdiction and dignity have indeed been introduced into the episcopacy, so that people speak of archbishops, patriarchs, metropolitans, and so forth, but these distinctions do not violate the unity and essence of the episcopal office itself. Even the papal office is essentially an episcopal office. Only this episcopal office has been extended to the entire church and endowed to that end with special gifts. It differs not hieratically but only hierarchically from the ordinary office of bishops.

In the Roman Catholic Church this episcopal office is actually the one true office. After it developed in the second century from the presbyterate, it took over the church's doctrine, tradition, and jurisdiction, separated itself from ordinary believers by succession, tonsure, and celibacy, and gradually made presbyters and deacons its agents. Still within the circle of the New Testament, we find at the head of the congregation a council of presbyters (a presbyterium, 1 Tim. 4:14), and even after one of them had made himself a bishop, this kind of council continued to exist around him for a long time. But this council increasingly lost all its ties with the congregation, became a chapter of the bishop, and was used under him, by virtue of authority conferred on it by him, as administrators of holy things, especially the sacraments.

Similarly, the diaconate soon totally changed in character. After the idea of priesthood and sacrifice had found acceptance, "the waiting on tables" (Acts 6:2) was no longer understood as the care of the poor but as auxiliary service rendered in connection with the celebration of the Eucharist. The bishop became the high priest, the presbyters became priests, and deacons became Levites who, leaving the care of the poor to private individuals and monastic orders, assisted the bishop in serving Mass. While presbyters and deacons were thus completely separated from the believing community and made into agents of the bishop, the bishop himself was and is distinguished from all other office-bearers especially by one power. The episcopal office is a priestly office, but it is connected with the power to reproduce it with "the generative power of the priesthood." It guarantees the

118. R. Sohm, *Kirchenrecht*, 128; B. Moeller, *Kirchengeschichte* (Frankfurt a.M.: Deutscher Klassiker Verlag, 1994), I, 370; F. Wieland, *Die genetische Entwicklung der sogenannte Ordines Minores in den drei ersten Jahrhunderten* (Freiburg i.B.: Herder, 1897); review of Wieland by R. Grützmacher in *Theologische Literaturzeitung* 23 (1898): 15.

continued existence of the priesthood and by implication the propagation of the church. The bishop is the "salient point" ["the point man"] in the church. Laypersons, deacons, and presbyters may be temporarily lacking, but the bishop cannot be. Where he is, there the church is, for he is the bearer of the doctrine, the propagator of the priesthood. Also presbyters are priests authorized to administer the sacraments, but they may not ordain anyone; they lack "the generative power of the priesthood"; their priesthood is infertile; they are the servants and helpers of the bishop because the latter cannot be everywhere and do everything. In the thinking of Rome the presbyterate and diaconate are extensions of the episcopate. They are three distinct degrees in the one priestly office, not coordinated but subordinated. The presbyter is also a deacon; the bishop is also a presbyter. Each time the gift of office goes one step higher until it culminates in the bishop or, as the next section will demonstrate, in the pope.[119]

In the face of this hierarchy Luther contented himself with the restoration of the original office of preacher. Admittedly, for the purpose of discipline, he acknowledged the need for a council of elders and, for the care of the poor, a council of deacons. But because the times were unfavorable, these offices were not restored. Nor were they as urgently necessary as the episcopal spiritual office of the preacher, the *Pfarramt*, which is the most important office and by which Christ governs his church in particular. In the Lutheran Church, therefore, the office of elders and the office of deacons was replaced by a consistory and a body of church wardens. The Roman Catholic orders made way for the "ecclesiastical," "political," and "economic" order.[120]

By contrast, we owe the presbyterial form of church government to Calvin. To be sure, even before him attempts were made, for example by Oecolampadius at Basel in 1530, to institute the office of elder in the interest of church discipline; still Calvin was the first to carry this out and make the office of elder a distinguishing mark of Reformed church government.[121] In so doing he proceeded on the basis of the Word of God. For though it is the case that personal character and historical circumstances opened Calvin's eyes to the significance of the offices in Scripture, yet the presbyterial system of church government was not derived by him from

---

119. T. Aquinas, *Summa theol.*, qu. 34–40; P. Lombard, *Sent.*, IV, dist. 24; Bonaventure, *Breviloquium*, VI, 12; Council of Trent, sess. 23; Roman Catechism, II, ch. 7 (ed. note: Bradley and Kevane, II, ch. 6); R. Bellarmine, "De clericis," in *Controversiis*, I, c. 11ff.; P. Dens, *Theologia moralis et dogmatica*, 8 vols. (Dublin: Richard Coyne, 1832), VII, 50ff.; J. H. Oswald, *Die dogmatische Lehre von den heiligen Sakramenten der katholischen Kirche*, 2nd ed., 2 vols. in 1 (Münster: Aschendorff, 1864), II, 315–35; J. N. Seidl, *Der Diakonat in der katholischen Kirche* (Regensburg, 1884); F. H. Vering, *Lehrbuch des katholischen, orientalischen, und protestantischen Kirchenrechts*, 3rd ed. (Freiburg i.B.: Herder, 1893), 558ff.

120. J. Köstlin, *The Theology of Luther*, II, 556ff.; Augsburg Confession and Apology, arts. 5, 14, 28 (Kolb and Wengert, 40, 46, 90–103, 222–23, 289–94); J. Gerhard, *Loci theol.*, XXIII, §§232–33; R. Sohm, *Kirchenrecht*, 460–542; E. C. Achelis, *Lehrbuch der praktischen Theologie*, I, 60ff.

121. G. V. Lechler, *Geschichte der Presbyterial- und Synodalverfassung seit der Reformation*; E. C. Achelis, "Presbyter in der alten Kirche," in *PRE*³, XVI, 5–9; E. F. K. Müller, "Presbyter, Presbyterialverfassung seit der Reformation," in *PRE*³, XVI, 9–16.

some abstract principle but from the Word of God and introduced into the church on its authority. In modern times theologians have indeed spoken of "the principle of the local congregation" (*Gemeindeprinzip*) and on that basis constructed sorts of presbyterial and diaconal offices. A congregation, it was said, had the right to govern itself, just as in the political realm the people increasingly acquire more influence on the government.[122] So also a congregation needed organs, that is, deacons and deaconesses, for the conduct of the work of "inner mission."[123]

But this is a very different idea from what one encounters in the thought of Calvin and the Reformed. Granted that they urge the necessity of church government by saying that the church can no more exist without its own government than can a people or a society,[124] yet they do not derive the offices from the congregation but from Christ's institution. The church as communion of saints is not autonomous; it is not free to decide whether or not it will organize itself at all or will organize itself this way or that, but is bound also in this regard to the Word of God and finds there the principles indicated and lines drawn that it has to follow in the government of its affairs. It was the general conviction that the government of the church must substantially rest on a divine law.[125] In this connection it was realized, however, that Scripture is not a book of statutes, does not deal in detail with a host of particulars, and leaves a great deal to the discretion of the churches.[126] There

---

122. Thus Stahl and many recent church orders, according to Rieker, *Grundsätze reformierter Kirchenverfassung*, 130ff.

123. Paul Wurster, *Die Lehre von der Inneren Mission* (Berlin: Reuther & Reichard, 1895), 128ff.

124. J. Calvin, *Institutes*, IV.xi.1; J. à Lasco, *Opera tam edita quam inedita,* ed. Abraham Kuyper, 2 vols. (Amsterdam: F. Muller, 1866), II, 45.

125. J. Calvin, *Institutes*, IV.xi.1; Gallic Confession, arts. 25, 29; Belgic Confession, art. 30; Helvetic Confession, II, 18; D. Neal, *Historie der rechtzinnige Puriteinen*, 3 vols. (Rotterdam: Kentlink, 1752–53), II, 182ff.; B. B. Warfield, "Westminster Synod," in *PRE*³, XXI, 176–85.

126. Synod of Wezel (1568), I, 9–10:

  9. It is our opinion, in harmony with the doctrine and the order of the apostles as well as with the irreproachable example of the ancient and purer church, that first of all and insofar as possible in all circumstances things which by [their] nature are indifferent and which have no firm foundation in the doctrine and example of the apostles and which also have no necessary and unavoidable reasons may not tie the freedom of the churches down by any prescribed form, so as to avoid all tyranny over the consciences and to cut off all cause for dispute. Instead, everyone shall be free to act according to what circumstances and experience teach is best. One may do so until the Provincial Synod shall have decided something specific concerning such matters.

  10. [Circumstances] of that nature appear to us to include the following with respect to the administration of baptism: the difference whether one sprinkles the person being baptized one, two, or three times; whether baptism must take place before or after the sermon; whether the [spiritual] nurture of the person baptized is entrusted to the witnesses as well as to the parents and the entire congregation. With respect to the Lord's Supper: whether one shall recline at the table or whether the bread and cup shall be offered while standing or sitting, whether at the administration of the Lord's Supper the Scriptures must be read or psalms be sung, or any similar matters which are proposed (concerning which free practice demands that the less knowledgeable persons shall be instructed whenever the situation requires this) which shall in no way take away from the free judgment of every church unless there are definite and very important reasons [for doing so] and then only after this has received approval by means of the concurring judgment of the entire province. (De Ridder, 77)

was no little disagreement even about the offices Christ instituted in his church. In the first place there were those who had no objection to an episcopate in the sense of a superintendency.[127] Then there was disagreement over the question of whether the office of "doctor," conceived as a professorate in theology, constituted a distinct ecclesiastical office or whether—since it does not derive from an apostolic institution—it can only be so called in a broad sense.[128] In addition, some preferred to speak, aside from the "doctorate," of three offices, that of pastor, of presbyter, and of deacon;[129] others listed two offices, that of presbyter and deacon and then split up the former into a teaching and a ruling eldership.[130] There were even those who, though they found a presbyterial church government useful, did not deem it necessary by virtue of a divine law and rejected the distinction between a teaching and a ruling elder.[131]

Synod of Emden (1571), 19–20:

> Whether to sprinkle with water once or three times in baptism is considered an indifferent and free matter. We therefore allow the churches to keep their custom in this until such time as this is otherwise ordered by a general synod.
>
> We consider it an indifferent matter whether to have witnesses at baptism. The churches shall therefore be allowed their previous custom, each one according to its freedom, until such time that this is otherwise decided by the general synod. (De Ridder, 117)

Westminster Assembly (1648), "Forms of Government," ch. 1, art. 6:

> That though the character, qualifications, and authority of church officers are laid down in the Holy Scriptures, as well as the proper method of their investiture and institution, yet the election of the persons to the exercise of this authority, in any particular society, is in that society. (*Constitution of the Presbyterian Church in the United States of America* [Philadelphia: Office of General Assembly, 1955], 240)

127. J. à Lasco, *Opera*, II, 51, 57; J. Knox, *First Book of Discipline*, in *History of the Reformation of Religion in Scotland* (Glasgow: Blackie, Fullarton, 1831); C. Vitringa, *Doctr. christ.*, IX, 210ff.; cf. above, 361 (#502).

128. H. Bavinck, *Het doctorenambt* (Kampen: Zalsman, 1899).

129. J. Calvin, *Ecclesiastical Ordinances*; Synod of Wezel (1568), chs. 2, 4–5 (De Ridder, 78–90); Synod of Emden (1571), 13–14:

> (13) The ministers of the Word shall be chosen by the consistory with the judgment and approbations of the classical meeting or of two or three ministers from the neighboring churches. Having been chosen, they shall be proposed to the congregation so that they, either through silent (approbation) of the congregation may be accepted, or should there be a reason why the congregation is not agreed with the election and so minded, it may without fear present its objection within 15 days. Nevertheless, if any churches, because the election has been delayed by the congregation, cannot proceed as usual, they shall not proceed until such a time as it is otherwise ordered by the general synod. (14) The same method shall also be followed in the election of elders and deacons, except that the opinion of the classis or of the ministers of the neighboring churches need not be solicited. (De Ridder, 116)

Church Order of Dort, 12: "Since a minister of the Word, once lawfully called as above, is bound to the service of the church for life, he shall not be allowed to enter a secular occupation except for great and weighty reasons of which the classis shall take note and judge" (De Ridder, 548). Synod of Middelburg, 2: "The offices are of four kinds: the ministers of the Word, Professors, Elders, and Deacons." Synod of 's Gravenhage (1586), 2: "The offices are of four kinds: the ministers of the Word, doctors [professors of theology], elders, and deacons." Canons of Dort, 2.

130. J. à Lasco, *Opera*, II, 51, along with many Scots and North American church orders, according to Rieker, *Grundsätze reformierter Kirchenverfassung*, 104.

131. L. Cappel, *Syntagma thesium theologicarum in academia Salmuriensi*, III, 330; F. Burman, *Synopsis theologiae*, 2 vols. in 1 (Amsterdam: Joannem Wolters, 1699), VIII, 7, 41ff.; C. Vitringa, *Doctr. christ.*, IX, 235ff.

Furthermore, the differentiation of deacons into those who served the poor and those who visited the sick, though introduced by Calvin,[132] was only rarely adopted,[133] while others restored the office of deaconesses.[134] Also, according to some, Acts 6 does not report the institution of the diaconate; this office, accordingly, is not of divine origin.[135] Finally, there was also disagreement over the manner of election; over bearing an office without carrying out a ministry in a local church;[136] over the usefulness of the laying on of hands in general but especially at the installation of elders and deacons;[137] over the repetition of ordination when elders and deacons were reappointed;[138] over the duration of the eldership;[139] and so forth. A treatment of all these topics belongs to the discipline of church order. But we can safely say this much: the Reformed, by restoring the office of elder and that of deacon alongside that of the minister of the Word, have most accurately grasped the idea of Scripture and most firmly recognized the rights of the local church. Christ alone is the king of the church.

From the standpoint of its invisible side, its government is strictly monarchical. And Christ was not only king in the past but he also is that still. From heaven he governs his church on earth by his Word and Spirit, by his prophetic as well as his priestly and royal activity. He continues the exercise of these three offices on earth, not exclusively yet also by means of the offices he has instituted. On the visible side of the church, his government is not democratic, nor monarchical, nor oligarchic, but aristocratic and presbyterial. These office-bearers are the ἄριστοι, the best, not in money and possessions but in spiritual gifts, whom he himself equips and allows the church to set apart for his service. By them he takes care of the spiritual and material interests of his church. By the teaching office he instructs, by the office of elder he leads, and by the diaconal office he takes care of his flock. And by all three of them in conjunction he proves himself to be our chief prophet, our eternal king, and our merciful high priest.

---

132. J. Calvin, *Institutes*, IV.iii.9.

133. J. Zanchi, *Op. theol.*, IV, 767; Synod of Wezel (1568), ch. 5, "Concerning the Deacons" (De Ridder, 87–90; ed. note: There are nineteen articles concerning deacons).

134. F. Junius, *Op. theol. select.*, I, 1567; A. Walaeus, *Opera omnia* (Leiden, 1643), I, 466; *G. Voetius, *Pol. eccl.*, II, 508ff., 529.

135. Cappel and many others, according to C. Vitringa, *Doctr. christ.*, IX, 235ff.

136. J. H. Heidegger, *Corpus theologiae* (Zurich, 1700), II, 571.

137. G. Voetius, *Pol. eccl.*, II, 466.

138. B. de Moor, *Comm. theol.*, VI, 329; C. Vitringa, *Doctr. christ.*, IX, 361.

139. F. L. Rutgers, "De bepaling van den diensttijd . . . ," *De Heraut* 944–46 (26 January–9 February 1896); 948 (23 February 1896).

7

THE CHURCH'S SPIRITUAL POWER

The family is the basic form of human community, combining civil and religious life under the leadership of a single patriarchal prophet, priest, and king. Sin split this unified life and created institutional social divisions, though in Israel all spheres were under God's theocratic rule. As Israel lost its political independence, especially after the exile, religious institutions became increasingly independent from the civil. Jesus organized his disciples into an ἐκκλησια with specific offices and endowed them with special spiritual power while at the same time recognizing the legitimacy of all other authority. The gospel is not a revolutionary force but a spiritual and reforming one; it acknowledges and honors all legitimate authority rooted in creation's institutions and opposes only the sin and deception found in all areas of life. The pervasive reform it seeks comes through the power of the proclaimed and lived gospel.

The power of the early church came through its testimony, proclamation, and the quiet, peaceable, godly, and respectful lives of believers. As the church gained prominence and cultural power, over time it also increasingly accented sacramental and juridical power in the episcopacy, in the teaching and ruling church. To its credit, in contrast to the Caesaropapist East, the Western church retained its independence from the power of the state. Nonetheless, the church's independence was severely compromised by the increasing secular power the church arrogated to itself, a power that eventually culminated in the full power of the infallible papacy as claimed by the First Vatican Council in 1870. Though the papal claim is politically and juridically impressive, it is exactly to that same degree that it is religiously and ethically weak. In the Roman Catholic Church, the pope, through his infallibility, is the only absolute sovereign, the source of all ecclesiastical authority and power. "Where the pope is, there the church is."

The Reformation rebelled against this degeneration of ecclesiastical power and sought to restore the understanding of spiritual power in the proclaimed Word. Church offices are restricted by their submission to Christ's authority as given in the word of the proclaimed gospel. This is the church's only proper power. For the Reformed churches this meant that private confessions, which assumed priestly sacramental power, were set aside for the exercise of Word-directed discipline in personal home visitation. What marks the Reformed tradition's polity is the conviction that, while church and state are distinct from each other, the church also distributes its spiritual goods for the benefit of the whole of humanity and for every aspect of human life. This is Christianity's true catholicity. The magistrate, appointed by God, is also bound to God's law and Word; the Bible that sheds light on the human condition as a whole is also accessible to governments. In practice, however, this theory was not sustained and, out of concern for freedom of conscience and religion, yielded to absolute separation of church and state.

The church cannot live without order, regulation, structure, and exercise of power. This is generally acknowledged; the debate concerns the exact form and nature of the church's polity. The power Christ gives to the offices and office-bearers in his church differs in kind from all political power with respect to its origin, operation, nature, purpose, and means. It is sinful to assign ecclesiastical power to the state as well as it is to change ecclesiastical power into political power. Both extremes are rooted in an excessive antithesis between nature and grace. Anabaptism tends to abolish nature by thinking of the church as a political entity; Rome suppresses nature by subordinating it to the realm of the sacerdotal church. The latter also robs ecclesiastical power of its spiritual character by turning it into something political. Traditionally, this meant an unwillingness to distinguish ecclesiastical power from civil power and punishment.

In its turn Reformation ecclesiology insisted on a purely spiritual power exercised in ministry of the Word and sacraments and through discipline. Three kinds of power were identified: power to teach (prophetic office), power to govern (kingly office), and the power or ministry of mercy (priestly office). The responsibility of teaching the truth of the gospel is given to all believers in their various places and callings but in an official way through the teaching of the minister of the Word. Official teaching is never to be taken as something primarily intellectual. Ministers require thorough training and supervision so that the church may maintain the truth of God's Word at all times, but ministers must preach appropriately to the various levels of their congregation. The minister is governed by the church's rule of faith, which is not a standard of coercion but of persuasion and voluntary submission.

Christ rules his church by the gift and power of governance. This too is the responsibility of all believers, but is especially entrusted to the office of elder/ presbyter. This governance is spiritual and characterized by loving service; earthly power and dominion are excluded. Discipling does involve discipline and chastisement, even excommunication in extreme cases. Scripture sets forth a clear pattern for church discipline, characterized by patience, love, and other spiritual means. The goal is always the restoration of the sinner.

The priestly office of Christ is characterized by the power of mercy. Our Lord healed people and calls his church to a robust diaconal ministry of mercy in his name. This ministry of mercy done by the church institution should never be absorbed in, fused with, or confused with state welfare. The church's diaconal ministry must remain independent.

*Christ rules his church through the offices of local congregations. However, believers do not stand apart in isolation from each other, and from the beginning local churches gathered together to address common concerns. An example already occurs in Acts 15, when the churches of Antioch and Jerusalem, along with others, gathered to address the circumcision of Gentiles. At the synods of the first three centuries, presbyters and deacons as well as bishops were in attendance. Increasingly, however, more hierarchical patterns were established, making the notion of an ecumenical council more difficult to determine. In Protestant churches, especially Reformed churches, synodical forms of church government began to take shape, and though their history is not always glorious, they are both necessary and useful. Synods or similar assemblies are not strictly necessary; they are permitted for the church's well-being (*bene esse*). The authority of all church assemblies comes from Christ, the Lord of the church.*

The church is a unique institution in the world, relating to others organically, spiritually, and morally. Its influence in the world is not political, and it seeks the reformation of society only through proclamation, persuasion, and witness.

RELIGIOUS AND CIVIL POWER IN ISRAEL

[507] The church no more belongs to the original institutions of the human race than the state. The most ancient form of life together in community was the family, in which civil and religious life were still intertwined and subject to the leadership of the father or patriarch, who was prophet, priest, and king in that family setting. It was sin that made the institution of church and state necessary for the preservation of the human race. God basically instituted government when he enjoined the death penalty for homicide (Gen. 9:6); consequently, after the building of the tower of Babel and under God's providence, government soon appeared in all the nations in which humanity was divided. The moment a government makes its appearance, a certain distinction and split between civilian and religious life automatically makes its appearance as well. Alongside the civil rulers we see priests in public life. Given this dual situation, the possibility of a clash is always there. The boundaries between the two are drawn differently in every nation, and the bonds between them are variously made. Whereas in the East, generally speaking, the power of rulers was subject to the priesthood, in the West, among Greeks and Romans, religion was a political matter and priests were functionaries of the state. A complete separation between the two was not to be found anywhere in antiquity: a neutral state was simply unknown. The state maintained and protected religion, if necessary by banishment and the death penalty (Socrates), for religion was the foundation and guarantee of its own existence.

Israel, too, was originally designed as a patriarchal society and divided into households, extended families, clans, and tribes. Under the monarchy the genealogical division continued to exist, which gave to the constitutional organization of the state a democratic cast. The result was that the heads of the tribes (etc.) had to settle important issues in tribal meetings. Even under the patriarchal form of religion, there was a difference between civil and religious interests, between Moses and Aaron, between scribes and judges, on the one hand, and priests and Levites, on the other. Only in the supreme court established at Jerusalem, where the most difficult cases were tried, were priests also members (Deut. 17:8–13; 19:17–18). It is therefore incorrect to say that in Israel church and state were identical. The two were clearly distinguished from each other in their respective laws, institutions, offices, and office-bearers and in part even in their membership.[1] The priests' role was to serve in the temple, draw near to God with the sacrifices of the people, distribute God's grace and blessing to the people, and instruct them in the Torah (Lev. 9:22; 10:11; 21:8; Num. 6:22ff.; 16:5; Ezek. 44:23), but they also had to offer sacrifices for themselves (Lev. 9:7; 16:6), were bound to the law (Deut. 33:10; Jer. 18:18), and were dependent for their livelihood on the people (Lev. 23:10; Num. 18:8–32; and so forth). They had no secret doctrine or art, no political or civil power, and no hierarchical control. Israel was never a hierocracy. In every way the freedom of the people was secured against the priestly class. The prophets were free to act in public, had to proclaim the Word of God, to be unsparing in making the people's sins known to Israel and announce God's judgments over both the people and its government but had no other power than their power of speech. Strangers could become citizens of Israel by the rite of circumcision (Exod. 12:48), and the impure and the leprous remained citizens even if they were temporarily segregated. Despite the division between Judah and the other tribes, the religious unity of the people as such might very well have continued to exist.

Now the peculiar nature of Israel's political system consisted in the fact that all these laws, offices, and institutions were given and upheld by God. Israel was a theocracy: God was its lawgiver, judge, and king (Isa. 33:22). In Israel, accordingly, there was no room in any area of life for autonomous sovereignty. Not even the king could be a despot, but he had to be chosen by God, taken from among his brothers, and bound by God's law (Deut. 17:14–20; 1 Sam. 10:25). The law of God was supreme over all offices, institutions, and persons, and it regulated Israel's entire life and had to be observed by everyone without distinction. Israel had to be a holy people and a priestly kingdom (Exod. 19:6; Deut. 7:6). From this it followed that, without erasing the difference between civil and religious life, the government nevertheless had to enforce the law of God in its own sphere. Idolatry, image worship, sorcery, blasphemy, Sabbath desecration, all of them violations of the first table of the law, were therefore often punished with death (Exod. 22:18, 20; Lev. 20:2, 6, 27; 24:11–16; Num. 25:5, 7; Deut. 13:1–5; 17:2–7; 18:9–12; and so forth). Religion was a national matter; sin was a crime; a violation of the first table of the law was a breach of the covenant.

---

1. Ph. J. Hoedemaker, "Kerk en staat in Israël," *Troffel en Zwaard* 1 (1898): 208–37.

In this connection it must be remembered, however, that the law furnished only a very few general rules and in many cases left the execution of punishment to God himself; that the destruction of the Canaanites, the execution of Agag and of Ahab's "house" are isolated cases; that Jehu's zeal went far beyond God's instructions; that the reformation undertaken by the kings was mostly restricted to the destruction of idol images and the restoration of the public worship of YHWH; that unbelief and heresy, though a frequent occurrence, were not tracked down by an inquisition; that coercion of conscience was entirely unknown; that strangers—on the condition of abstaining from the public violation of Israel's religion—were not only tolerated but treated with courtesy; that priests and prophets never aroused their audiences to persecute the ungodly but only warned them and called them to conversion (e.g., in Ps. 2:10) and expected the religious and political victory of Israel over all its enemies from God himself. That is also the reason why, when Israel increasingly lost its political independence, the religious community could continue to exist and organize itself in its own way. Although following the exile the power of priests and the high priest gradually increased, it soon had to contend with the dangerous competition of Pharisees and scribes. In the synagogue, religious life became independent, not only vis-à-vis the state but also vis-à-vis the temple and the priesthood. Life in its entirety was increasingly focused on the Torah, the teaching of which was the principal purpose of the synagogue (Matt. 4:23; Mark 1:21, etc.; Acts 15:21; 2 Tim. 3:15). Torah or, speaking more broadly the Old Testament Scripture, was the basis, center, and source of Israel's religious life; it had no power other than the power inherent in that Word. This explains why the synagogue clung to it with anxious and painstaking precision and banished from its midst all those who did not want to live by it, and either provisionally or permanently barred them—with or without anathemas—from its fellowship (Luke 6:22; John 9:22; 12:42; 16:2).[2]

NEW ECCLESIAL POWER

[508] When Jesus, coming to his own home, was not received by his own people, he organized his disciples into an ἐκκλησια (*ekklēsia*) that, hoping and suffering, had to await his second coming and the victory over all his enemies. In its organization and worship, this church community, while it does bear some resemblance to the synagogue, is nevertheless a much more free and independent organization of the new life that Christ introduced.[3] There can be no doubt that Christ founded such a church community and entrusted to it a certain power. After all, he himself speaks of it as having been so solidly based on a rock that the gates of hell will in no way prevail against it (Matt. 16:18), and further, he gives to those church communities offices, ministries, institutions, and gifts (Rom. 12:6ff.;

2. E. Schürer, *The History of the Jewish People in the Age of Jesus Christ (175 B.C.–A.D. 135)*, rev. and ed. Géza Vermès and Fergus Millar (Edinburgh: T&T Clark, 1973), I, 363ff.
    3. Cf. above, 340–47 (#499).

1 Cor. 12–14; Eph. 4:11), all of which indicate that they have their own free and independent existence and their own independent organization.

But this power that Christ furnishes his church has a special character. It consists in nothing other, but also in nothing less, than the power of the keys that was first accorded by Christ to Peter (Matt. 16:19). After first calling Peter a rock on account of his confession that Jesus was the Messiah, a rock, that is, on which Jesus would build his church, he then proceeds (v. 19) to appoint him a house steward (οἰκονομος, *oikonomos*) of the kingdom of heaven and entrust him with the keys of that kingdom. Keys are a sign of control or mastery (Isa. 22:22; Luke 11:52; Rev. 1:18; 3:7; 9:1; 20:1) and here denote the power of Peter to "open" and to "close" the kingdom of heaven, that is, to determine what will or will not be in effect. Zahn correctly makes the comment that in this text it is not persons but actions that are the object of "binding" and "loosing."[4] The Aramaic words, which in Matthew have been translated by δεειν (*deein*) and λυειν (*lyein*) and in English by "binding" and "loosing," signify "declaring something to be either permitted or prohibited," and as a rule refer not to past but to future matters. Peter, accordingly, here receives from Jesus the power to determine—on the basis of or in agreement with his confession of Jesus as the Christ—what will or will not be allowed in the kingdom of heaven that has been established here on earth and has its center in the church. And that ruling by Peter will have a weight of authority comparable to something said in heaven. Matthew 16:19, therefore, not only accords to Peter the right to exercise discipline but also the entire range of power that will soon also be entrusted to all the apostles (Matt. 18:18). To their word, the church of all ages will be bound (John 17:20; 1 John 1:3); there is no gospel other than that which was proclaimed by them (Gal. 1:8). Nevertheless, this power of the apostles does not merely extend to actions but does include the right to judge persons. This is clear from John 20:23, where on the basis of the gift of the Holy Spirit bestowed on them (v. 22), all the apostles receive the power to forgive or retain the sins of people in terms of whether they accept or reject the gospel. Now this power is, in the first place and in the full sense, given by Christ to his apostles, but it is not their possession to such a degree that the believing community is totally excluded from it. For in Matt. 18:17 the believing community in general also receives the right to regard an impenitent brother, after repeated and failed attempts at reconciliation, as "a Gentile and a tax collector." This community may and can act in this manner because the apostles, speaking with divine authority, have laid down this disciplinary measure (v. 18), and because Christ himself dwells in it (vv. 19–20).

The power that Christ here gave to Peter, to the apostles, and also to the church in its entirety, is further defined in many places in the New Testament. When we study them, it turns out that this power is not an authoritarian, independent, sovereign rule (Matt. 20:25–26; 23:8, 10; 2 Cor. 10:4–5; 1 Pet. 5:3), but a

---

4. T. Zahn, *Das Evangelium des Matthäus*, 2nd ed. (Leipzig: A. Deichert, 1905), 544ff.

ministry (διακονια, *diakonia*; λειτουργια, *leitourgia*; Acts 4:29; 20:24; Rom. 1:1; etc.), bound to Christ, to whom all power has been given in heaven and on earth (Matt. 28:18), who is the only head of the church (Eph. 1:22), and who as such distributes all the gifts and offices (Eph. 4:11). It is bound to his Word and Spirit, by which Christ himself governs his church (Rom. 10:14–15; Eph. 5:26), and exercised in his name and power (1 Cor. 5:4). Accordingly, it is indeed a power, a real and comprehensive power, consisting in the ministry of Word and sacrament (Matt. 28:19); in the determination of what will be the rule in the kingdom of heaven (16:19); in the forgiveness or retention of sins (John 20:23); in the exercise of discipline over the members of the church (Matt. 16:19; Rom. 16:17; 1 Cor. 5:4; 2 Thess. 3:6; Titus 3:10; Heb. 12:15–17; 2 John 10; 2 Tim. 2:17; Rev. 2:14); in the discernment of all things (1 Cor. 2:15); in teaching, consoling, and admonishing (and so forth) the members of the church (Col. 3:16); in the use of gifts for the benefit of others (Rom. 12:4–8; 1 Cor. 12:12ff.); and in performing miracles (Mark 16:17–18 and so forth).

But all this power is spiritual and moral in nature, essentially distinct from all other power that God has bestowed on persons over people or other creatures in the family, society, state, art, and science. For Jesus acted in no way other than as the Christ—as prophet, priest, and king. He had no other office nor performed any other function. He was not a father in the home, nor a scholar, nor an artist, nor a statesman. He respected all the Father's ordinances and works and only came to destroy the works of the devil (1 John 3:8). His kingdom did not originate from this world (John 18:36). For that reason, he recognizes all authority: that of the high priest, the Sanhedrin, Herod, Pilate, and so forth: he pays the tax (Matt. 17:24–27), refuses to be an arbitrator between two brothers who fought over an inheritance (Luke 12:14), tells his disciples to give Caesar his due (Matt. 22:21), rebukes John for wanting fire to come down from heaven (Luke 9:54–55) and Peter for cutting off Malchus's ear (John 18:10–11), and forbids his disciples to fight with the sword for his name and cause (Matt. 26:52).

The gospel of Christ never opposes nature as such. It did not come into the world to condemn but to save (John 3:16–17), and it leaves the family, marriage, and the relationships between parents and children, masters and servants, and government and people intact. The gospel, finding nothing reprehensible in itself and everything created by God as good if it is received with thanksgiving and consecrated by the word of God and by prayer (1 Tim. 4:4), allows everyone to remain in the calling in which one was called (1 Cor. 7:12–24; 1 Thess. 4:11). It also tells us to honor the civil government (Rom. 13:1; 1 Tim. 2:2; 1 Pet. 2:13), even allows slavery to exist (1 Cor. 7:22; Philem. 11), and when the gospel tells us to obey God rather than human beings, it preaches only passive resistance (Acts 4:19; 5:29). Still, while averse to all revolution, it is all the more committed to reformation. It never militates against nature as such but does join the battle—always and everywhere, in every area of life and into the most secret hiding places—against sin and deception. And thus it preaches principles that, by moral and spiritual but not by revolutionary channels, have their pervasive impact everywhere and reform and renew everything. While, in keeping with Jesus's command, the gospel must be preached to all creatures (Mark 16:15), it is "a power of God for salvation to everyone who believes" (Rom. 1:16), a two-edged sword that "pierces down to the division of soul and spirit" (Heb. 4:12), a leaven that leavens everything (Matt. 13:33), a principle that re-creates everything, and a power that overcomes the world (1 John 5:4).

THE DEVELOPMENT OF EPISCOPAL POWER

[509] For a long time this apostolic teaching concerning the power of the church continued to be recognized in the Christian church. In the early centuries it crossed no one's mind that this small community, which had few material resources at its disposal, would one day become a world church that prescribed laws for kings and nations. Its members only desired that under pagan governments they would be allowed to "lead a quiet and peaceable life, godly and respectful in every way" [1 Tim. 2:2 RSV]. But when the church gained prominence and cultural dominance, also its power was viewed very differently. The development of the episcopacy and tradition, the idea of priesthood and sacrifices, also implied that ordination was considered a sacramental act that, performed by the bishop, communicated the grace of office and conferred the right and authority to carry out ecclesiastical ceremonies. And although the power of the keys granted to Peter (Matt. 16:19 in combination with 18:18 and John 20:23) was initially understood to refer to the forgiveness of sins,[5] it gradually acquired—especially by way of the sacrament of penance—a juridical character. According to Rome, therefore, the power of the church is twofold: the power of ordination and the power of jurisdiction, the latter again being subdivided into the jurisdiction of the internal court (sacramental) and the jurisdiction of the external court (legislative, judicial, and coercive).[6] In order to gain a correct understanding of this power accorded by Rome to the church, we must note the following.

1. The power or right to teach (*potestas docendi*) is sometimes treated separately by theologians and, according to Rome, naturally also belongs to the

---

5. Cyprian, *On the Unity of the Church* 4; idem, *Epistle* 75.16.

6. T. Aquinas, *Summa theol.*, II, 2 qu. 39, art. 3; Roman Catechism, II, 7, 6; First Vatican Council, "Dogmatic Constitution I on the Church," in H. Denzinger, ed., *The Sources of Catholic Dogma*, trans. from 30th ed. by R. J. Deferrari (London and St. Louis: Herder, 1955); #1827; H. Klee, *Katholische Dogmatik*, 3 vols. (Mainz, bei Kirchheim: Schott & Thielmann, 1835), I, 162; F. X. Dieringer, *Lehrbuch der katholischen Dogmatik,* 4th ed. (Mainz: Kirchheim, 1858), 619, 715; F. L. B. Liebermann, *Institutions théologiques,* 3rd ed., 5 vols. (Paris: Gaume Frères, 1855), I, 290; H. Th. Simar, *Lehrbuch der Dogmatik,* (Freiburg i.B.: Herder, 1879–80), 593; J. Wilhelm and T. B. Scannell, *A Manual of Catholic Theology,* 4th ed., 2 vols. (London: Kegan Paul, Trench, Trübner; New York: Benziger Brothers, 1909), II, 335–40; H. Schell, *Katholische Dogmatik,* 3 vols. in 4 (Paderborn: F. Schöningh, 1889–93), III, 1, 396; G. M. Jansen, *Praelectiones theologiae dogmaticae,* 3 vols. in 2 (Utrecht: Van Rossum, 1875–1879), I, 380ff.

church. But actually it is a part of the power of jurisdiction. The Roman Catechism[7] might lead one to surmise that the power to teach belongs under the category of the power of orders because it says that it not only includes the power to administer the Eucharist but also the power "to prepare human souls to receive it and render them fit." But the [First] Vatican Council[8] expressly puts the magisterium under the power of jurisdiction. In the view of Rome, the ministry of the Word is part of the administration of justice, culminating in the infallible pronouncements of the pope. It is not preaching, but a proclamation of dogmata that as such bind the conscience, obligate people to believe them (i.e., give their assent to them) and can, if necessary, be imposed by force.[9]

2. The power of holy orders (*potestas ordinis*), which is the power to administer the sacraments, can only be obtained through the sacrament of orders, which is administered by the bishop. This sacrament communicates the grace of office, imprints an indelible character, and is therefore inamissible.[10] Even heretics and schismatics, who at one time were ordained in Rome by the bishop, retain this power. It therefore also exists by itself and is entirely independent of the administration of the Word. The priesthood, in the thought of Rome, can also exist apart from the preaching of the gospel. "If any one says that there is no . . . priesthood or . . . not any power of consecrating and offering the true body and blood of the Lord, and of forgiving and retaining sins, but only an office and bare ministry of preaching the gospel; or that those who do not preach are not priests at all—let him be anathema."[11]

3. In keeping with this view, according to Rome, the forgiveness of sins is not granted in the preaching of the Word, which has only preparatory significance, but in the sacrament, which contains within itself and infuses grace ex opere operato (by the act performed) in the recipient. It is specifically communicated in baptism, and for sins committed after baptism in the sacrament of penance. Gradually this latter sacrament became a judicial act, a court of law, in which the priests sit as presiding officers and judges, listen to the confessions of mortal offenses, casuistically determine the punishment in accordance with the standard of penitential books, and

---

7. Roman Catechism, II, ch. 7, qu. 7; ed. note: The post–Vatican II edition titled *The Roman Catechism* (trans. Robert I. Bradley, SJ, and Eugene Kevane [Boston, MA: Daughters of St. Paul, 1985]), drops the enumeration of the introduction so that ch. 1 begins the section on baptism. In this annotation, the proper reference would be II, ch. 6, qu. 7.

8. First Vatican Council, IV, ch. 3–4; in H. Denzinger, *Sources of Catholic Dogma*, ##1826–40.

9. A. L. Richter, R. W. Dove, and W. Kahl, *Lehrbuch des katholischen und evangelischen Kirchenrechts, mit besonderer Rücksicht auf deutsche Zustände,* 8th ed. (Leipzig: Tauchnitz, 1886), 305; E. C. Achelis, *Lehrbuch der praktische Theologie,* 2nd ed., 2 vols. (Leipzig: Hinrichs, 1898), I, 79.

10. T. Aquinas, *Summa theol.,* II, 2, qu. 39, art. 3.

11. Council of Trent, sess. 23, "Canons on the Sacrament of Order," canon 1, in H. Denzinger, *Sources of Catholic Dogma,* #961.

grant forgiveness (absolution) in the name of Christ, not conditionally and by a declaratory judgment, but absolutely, categorically, and peremptorily.[12] This juridical character of penance also comes to expression in the fact (a) that this sacrament may only be administered to those who are baptized, since the church has jurisdiction only over those who are subject to its power by baptism; (b) that the faithful may only receive this sacrament from the hands of the priest whose subjects they are according to decrees ecclesiastical, that is, papal; and (c) that higher clergy, such as bishops (et al.) and especially the pope, reserve for themselves certain very serious cases that they alone can adjudicate, such as, for example, the application by the popes of a ban or interdict to rulers or countries in the Middle Ages.[13]

4. In order to be able to exercise this jurisdiction "in the internal court," the Roman Catholic Church further asserts that it possesses the power of jurisdiction "in the external court" (the power of governing) differentiated in legislative, judicial, and coercive power. So that the church could be faithful to its calling, Christ first of all gave it legislative power. It has the power to bind and to loose, to prohibit or to permit, to impose or to cancel out moral obligations, and whatever it determines is in force in heaven. It is on the same level as a command of God. It therefore binds human consciences and calls for unconditional obedience (Matt. 16:19; 18:18; John 20:21, 23; Acts 15:27–29, 41; 1 Cor. 11:4–7; 14:26; 2 Cor. 8; 10:6, 8; 1 Tim. 3; Titus 1:5; Heb. 13:7, 17). This legislative power automatically includes judicial power, inasmuch as the former could not exist without the latter. Christ gave this power to the church in Matt. 18:15–17, and the apostles exercised it (Acts 5:1–10; 1 Cor. 5:3, 11–13; 1 Tim. 5:19–20). And, finally, the church also has executive and coercive power and can impose not only spiritual penalties—as Donatists, Waldensians, Albigensians, and so forth asserted—but also temporal and physical penalties, and that not only on the authority or by means of the state but also by virtue of its own authority and directly. Rome bases this power on Matt. 16:19; 18:18; 28:19; 1 Cor. 4:18–21; 5:4–5; 2 Cor. 10:6, 8; 13:2–3; 1 Tim. 1:20; Rome has repeatedly expressly taught it[14] and also frequently applied it.[15]

5. Finally, Rome teaches that this ecclesiastical power, essentially distinct from all earthly power, is fully independent and sovereign. It does say that with

---

12. Cf. above, 143–47 (#461).

13. Council of Trent, XIV, in H. Denzinger, *Sources of Catholic Dogma*, #893a ff.; Roman Catechism, II, ch. 5, qu. 32ff. (ed. note: Bradley and Kevane, II, ch. 4, qu. 32ff.).

14. H. Denzinger, *Sources of Catholic Dogma*, ##1367, 1546, 1572; First Vatican Council, "Dogmatic Constitution I on the Church," in H. Denzinger, *Sources of Catholic Dogma*, ##1827ff., 1847.

15. G. Perrone, *Praelectiones theologicae*, 9 vols. (Louvain: Vanlinthout & Vandezande, 1838–43), VII, 275; M. Scheeben and L. Atzberger, *Handbuch der katholischen Dogmatik*, 4 vols. (1874–98; repr., Freiburg i.B.: Herder, 1933), IV, 1/322; G. M. Jansen, *Prael. theol.*, I, 390.

respect to Christ this power is serving ministerial duties, but vis-à-vis all earthly authority and power it is completely independent.

With this doctrine of the independence of its ecclesiastical power, Rome chose a totally different direction from that of the church of the East. There, as a result of the policies of Constantine, Theodosius, and Justinian I, the church increasingly became an organ of the state. Although the emperor could not yet do with the church what he wanted—for he was bound to its dogma and, though not a high priest, the pious protector of orthodoxy—he nevertheless was as much the ruling head of the church as of the state. This view still prevails in the Russian church today. In 1721, Peter the Great put the supreme government of the church in the hands of a permanent Holy Synod that was bound to the czar by the intermediary role of a procurator. However severely the power of the czar has been restricted and weakened by comparison with that of the Byzantine emperors, it is still he who rules the church through the Synod, regulates the religious affairs of his people, and determines the degree of religious freedom to be accorded to his Roman Catholic and Protestant subjects. Orthodox dogma, in a formal sense, is still the law of the Russian constitution, and heresy is a crime against the state.[16]

Thus, whereas Caesaropapism developed in the East, the church in the West, its organization culminating in the pope, managed not merely to maintain its independence vis-à-vis the state but often even to expand its supremacy over the state. In the person of Charlemagne, imperial rule became a Christian, or Roman Catholic, institution and from that time on was frequently subordinate to the pope. This was the case not only in practice but increasingly also in theory. According to Rome, the state (the family, society, art, science, all that is earthly) and the church relate to each other as nature to grace, as flesh to the spirit, the natural good to supernatural good, the temporal to the eternal, the earthly to the heavenly. Just as the moon receives its light from the sun, so rulers owe their worldly power to the pope, who as the vicar of Christ naturally possesses all power in heaven and on earth (Alvarus Pelagius, et al.). In any case, the pope as head of Christendom also has the "supreme power of disposing the affairs of all Christians."[17] To him a secular domain is even strictly necessary for the exercise of his sovereign power. Even though the state is still free and independent within its own sphere, it is inferior to the church, bound to its pronouncements, and wherever the spiritual encroaches upon the natural, subject to the church. The state must be Christian, that is, Roman Catholic, may not recognize any church other than the Catholic, and is obligated to persecute and punish heretics if the church so desires and refrains from doing so itself.[18]

16. K. P. Pobedonoszew, *Streitfragen der Gegenwart* (Berlin: Deubner, 1907; ed. note: Bavinck cites the 1897 edition). F. Kattenbusch, *Lehrbuch der vergleichenden Confessionskunde* (Freiburg i.B.: J. C. B. Mohr [Paul Siebeck], 1892), I, 374–93.

17. R. Bellarmine, "De rom. pontif," in *Controversiis*, V, 6–7.

18. Cf. Augustine, "Letter to Vincentius against Donatus and Rogatus," *Letter* 83; idem, "Letter to Boniface (On the treatment of the Donatists)," *Letter* 185; idem, *Against the Letters of Petilianus* I, 16; esp. book II; idem,

DEGENERATION OF PAPAL POWER: INFALLIBILITY

[510] This power, accorded by Rome to the church, culminates and also finds the guarantee for its existence and permanence in the power of the pope. According to the [First] Vatican Council [1870],[19] this power is characterized by the following attributes:

1. It is not merely a primacy of honor, nor only an office of supervision and direction, but the full and supreme power of legislation, rule, and the administration of law, a power of jurisdiction independent of the bishops.
2. It is not an extraordinary and temporary authority, but an ordinary permanent power, which God has given him and which he can exercise always and not merely in extraordinary cases.
3. It is an immediate power, both as to origin, since Christ confers it, and as to its use, since the pope can exercise it not only through the bishops but also by himself or his legates without having to ask for permission or authorization from anyone, and can therefore communicate freely and immediately with all bishops and all the faithful.
4. It is not a limited but a full and supreme power, extensively covering the whole church, intensively containing all the power needed to direct and govern the church, and absolutely sovereign, subject to no laity, bishop, council, but only to God.
5. All the members of the church, whether individually or all together, and all bishops, whether individually or assembled in synods, owe absolute obedience to the pope, not only in matters of faith and morals, but also in matters of the discipline and government of the church. "This is the teaching of Catholic truth, from which no one can deviate without danger to faith and salvation."
6. One part of this power is the teaching office concerning which it is determined that when the pope speaks ex cathedra he is, by virtue of divine assistance, infallible.

After all that has been said earlier about the doctrine of Scripture and the most ancient ecclesiastical witnesses, we no longer need to argue that this papal system rests on an unscriptural foundation. Nor can the consensus of the fathers, that is, after Irenaeus, the teaching and practice of popes and councils, the concurrence

---

Against Gaudentius I, 20; II, 17; T. Aquinas, *On the Governance of Rulers,* trans. Gerald Bernard Phelan (London and New York: Sheed & Ward, 1938); R. Bellarmine, "De rom. pontif," in *Controversiis,* V; idem, "De membris eccl.," in *Controversiis,* III; J. Hergenröther, *Katholischer Kirche und christlicher Staat in ihrer geschichtlichen Entwicklung,* 2 vols. (Freiburg i.B.: Herder, 1872); L. von Hammerstein, *Kirche und Staat* (Freiburg i.B.: Herder, 1883); A. Stöckl, *Lehrbuch der Philosophie,* 3rd ed., 2 vols. (Mainz: Kirchheim, 1872), III, 451–80; V. Cathrein, *Moralphilosophie,* 3rd ed., 2 vols. (Freiburg i.B.: Herder, 1899), II, 529ff.; H. Hansjakob, *Die Toleranz und die Intoleranz der Katholischen Kirche,* 2nd ed. (Freiburg i.B.: Herder, 1899).

19. First Vatican Council, IV, c. 3–4; in H. Denzinger, *Sources of Catholic Dogma,* ##1826–40.

of later theologians as it has been set forth more extensively in Roman Catholic theology[20]—none can compensate for this deficiency. However powerfully this papal edifice, thanks to its rigorous unity, also often appeals to many Protestants, it is religiously and ethically weak to the degree that it is politically and juridically impressive. The reasons for this are as follows.

1. The nature and character of this infallibility are insufficiently defined. Up until now Rome has not gone so far as to ascribe to the pope the same infallibility it recognizes in the apostles. This step would be and is, of course, consistent with its position. One would expect that the apostles communicated full apostolic authority to the bishops they appointed and that especially Peter did so with respect to the bishop of Rome. But this is not the case. The pope is infallible, not by inspiration, but by the assistance of the Holy Spirit, by a special provision of God by which the church is kept from error and preserved in the truth. And his infallibility does not consist in his receiving new revelations and being able to propose a new doctrine, but only in the fact that he can faithfully preserve and explain the tradition handed down by the apostles. Nor must it be understood in the sense that the words spoken ex cathedra by the pope are literally God's Word, but only that they materially contain it.[21]

2. Although this infallibility is a special gift, it is not always a peculiar characteristic of the pope, not of his person nor of him as an author, a public speaker, a lawgiver, an administrator, nor as a secular ruler, as bishop of Rome, as metropolitan of the ecclesiastical province of Rome, or as patriarch of the West, but only as pope, as the head of the whole church. On this point, however, there is no unanimity. Especially considering the case of Pope Honorius, previous theologians and even Innocent III admitted[22] that privately a pope could fall into heresy and then *by divine right* and *on account of this very fact* be deposed as pope (Paludanus, Turrecremata, Alphonsus of Castro, Sylvester, et al.) or could be removed from a council by judicial ruling (Cajetan, Canus, et al.). This, however, had a questionable side and threatened the unlimited sovereignty and inviolability of the pope. For that reason others (like Pighius, Bellarmine, Suarez, et al.) found it easier to agree with the probable and pious opinion that divine providence will preserve the pope from heresy also personally.[23]

3. The [First] Vatican Council, using an expression perhaps first employed by Melchior Canus,[24] says that the pope is infallible when he speaks ex cathedra. This seems to draw a line but is practically very useless as a standard. For the system requires that no one can tell whether a pope has spoken ex cathedra except the

20. E.g., according to J. B. Heinrich and G. Konstantine, *Dogmatische Theologie*, 2nd ed., 10 vols. (Mainz: Kirchheim, 1881–1900), II, 323ff.

21. Ibid., II, 220–45; G. M. Jansen, *Prael. theol.*, I, 616.

22. J. Schwane, *Dogmengeschichte*, 4 vols. (Freiburg i.B.: Herder, 1882–95), III, 535.

23. J. B. Heinrich and G. Konstantine, *Dogmatische Theologie*, II, 257; J. Wilhelm and T. B. Scannell, *A Manual of Catholic Theology*, IV, 1, 450.

24. J. Schwane, *Dogmengeschichte*, IV, 302.

pope himself. And so a pope is always free to reject his own pronouncements or those of other popes by saying that they were not spoken ex cathedra, or to declare them binding by saying that they were. And later he can even say that he or one of his predecessors, thinking he spoke ex cathedra, actually did not do so.

4. The infallible teaching office is a part of the "full and supreme power of jurisdiction in the universal church." The [First] Vatican Council[25] indeed does not expressly declare that the pope is at all times infallible in the exercise of this "full and supreme power." But it does say that "this power obligates shepherds and faithful of every rite and dignity, both individually and collectively, to hierarchical subordination and true obedience, not only in matters pertaining to faith and morals, but also in those pertaining to the discipline and government of the Church throughout the world." Whether, therefore, the pope is fallible or infallible, all persons without distinction and any right of criticism ("nor may anyone examine judicially its decision") must unconditionally obey the pope, and that on peril of losing their soul's salvation.

5. In session IV, canon 4, of the [First] Vatican Council, infallibility is expressly assigned only to the pope when he speaks ex cathedra and, as shepherd and teacher of all Christians, defines a "doctrine concerning faith or morals which must be held by the whole church."[26] But from this statement we have absolutely no right to infer that at other times he is not infallible. How else could absolute and unconditional obedience to the pope be required in matters of discipline, governance, and jurisprudence? However this may be, in matters of "faith and morals" the pope is certainly infallible. And Roman Catholic theologians work out in detail the areas covered by this. The pope is infallible when he deals with the truths of revelation in Scripture, the truths of the divine institutions, the sacraments, the church, its organization and government, and the truths of natural revelation. But even with this we are far from having exhausted the scope of papal infallibility. For the pope to be infallible in all these things, say the theologians, he also has to be infallible in assessing the sources of the truths of the faith and in interpreting them. That is to say, [he is infallible] in establishing the authority of Scripture, of the tradition, the councils, the popes, the fathers, the theologians; in the use and application of natural truths, images, concepts, and expressions; in the assessment and rejection of errors and heresies, even in the establishment of dogmatic facts; in the prohibition of books; in matters of discipline; in the endorsement of orders; in the canonization of saints; and so forth. Faith and morals encompass almost everything, and everything the pope says about it is infallible. The term ex cathedra in fact draws no boundaries whatsoever. The truth is, this expression does not tell us that only those pronouncements are infallible in connection with which the ex cathedra is expressly mentioned, for in that case all the earlier papal regulations would be excluded from the category of papal infallibility. It

25. First Vatican Council, sess. IV, c. 3.
26. First Vatican Council, sess. IV, c. 4.

only refers, therefore, to something material and relevant. But then who can tell whether the pope is speaking ex cathedra? Practically, and by the common people, his pronouncements will always be viewed as infallible, if only from a fear of possibly rejecting an infallible pronouncement. Theoretically, only the pope can say with infallible certainty when he speaks ex cathedra, that is, infallibly.[27] Furthermore, *why* is the pope infallible? Because he himself says so? But that is a vicious circle. Because the council says so? But the council also is fallible in making this declaration. Accordingly, for the Roman Catholic Christian, where is this highly acclaimed certainty?

6. The [First] Vatican Council has put in place a result manufactured from a long historical process. In the early Christian period, all apostles, all churches, and all *episcopi* were equal in rank. At most there was a primacy of honor but in no sense a primacy of jurisdiction. But gradually the church and bishop of Rome managed to subordinate all other churches and bishops to themselves. Still, for a long time the independence of the latter within its own circles was to some extent maintained. Toward the end of the thirteenth century the controversy concerning the relationship between episcopal and papal power surfaced.[28] At that time some still tried to maintain the independence of the former in the sense that the bishop, though subordinate to the pope, nevertheless received the power due to him in his circle of authority from God (*ex jure divino*) and was only designated by the pope as the bearer of that power. Thus Henry of Ghent; Alphonsus of Castro, bishop of Bruges (Belgium; d. 1558); Vitoria (1480–1544), the father of neo-scholasticism at the University of Salamanca; Peter Guerrero, bishop of Grenada; and many other Spanish and French bishops at the Council of Trent who in canon 7 of session 23 sought to have certain [italicized] words included: "the bishops, *appointed by divine right*, are superior to the presbyters."[29] The most vehement debates that lasted throughout the winter of 1562 and past the middle of the following year were touched off by this issue at the council. On July 15, 1563, episcopal power was further defined in canons 6–8, but the question whether it originated from divine law or ecclesiastical law was intentionally left undecided. On the other side, accordingly, there was a strong party headed by Lainez, the general of the Jesuits, who asserted that, while bishops received the power of holy orders directly from God, they obtained the power of jurisdiction only by a free transfer on the part of the pope. The latter power, therefore, was to that extent derived from ecclesiastical law and could be limited, modified, or taken away by the pope at his pleasure, for the pope derived his full power over the whole church solely and immediately from God.

After [the Council of] Trent, as a result of Jesuit influence, this sentiment increasingly gained ground, triumphed over Gallicanism, and was made a dogma

27. J. B. Heinrich and G. Konstantine, *Dogmatische Theologie*, II, 554–654.
28. J. Schwane, *Dogmengeschichte*, III, 549.
29. Ibid., IV, 292ff.

at the [First] Vatican Council. In session IV, chapter 3, it is indeed stated that this power of the Supreme Pontiff is far from obstructing the ordinary and immediate power of episcopal jurisdiction and rather protects, strengthens, and upholds this power. The pope nevertheless has the full and supreme legislative, governing, and jurisprudential power over the whole church. He can, without anyone's mediation or intervention, freely communicate with all the shepherds and flocks of the entire church, and all without distinction are unconditionally subject to him. Bishops, councils, the entire church, and all believers are fallible in themselves and only infallible with and through him. The pope is the root, the firmness, and foundation of the unity, authority, and infallibility of bishops, councils, church fathers, theologians, and of all believers and the whole church. He alone receives all power and authority and infallibility directly from God. One single expression is still reminiscent of the old catholic view. Thus, for example, when in session IV, chapter 4, it is stated that the pope "possesses . . . that infallibility with which the divine Redeemer willed his church to be endowed in defining a doctrine concerning faith and morals," the Council then immediately and above all infers that "such definitions of the Roman Pontiff are infallible [irreformable] of themselves, but not from the consensus of the church."

7. The power of the pope, however, does not stop here. Although until the eighth century the popes were subjects of the Roman Empire and their spiritual office in no way included the possession of secular power, early in the history of the Roman Catholic Church the idea arose that the pope, in order to be independent in the spiritual sphere, also had to be sovereign in secular matters. And after the abolition of the ecclesiastical state in 1870, this idea gained increased prominence and was expressed with even stronger emphasis. Pius IX and Leo XIII have not neglected to repeat over and over that, as the universal bishop, the pope could not be the subject of any particular ruler nor bear a specific nationality,[30] and their pronouncements are binding for Catholic believers. This is true in spite of the following:

- The idea of an ecclesiastical or sacerdotal state is completely obsolete, and the existence of such a state would violate the unity of Italy.
- The pope cannot be the chief shepherd of the church and a worldly sovereign at the same time without thereby harming either the church or the state or both, and a spiritual power absolutely does not need political sovereignty.
- For centuries the pope had not governed any political territory, and following the illegitimate takeover of the ecclesiastical state in 1870, he did not lose any influence, any more than the German bishops after they ceased to be imperial electors.

30. G. M. Jansen, *Prael. theol.*, I, 657; K. von Hase, *Handbuch der protestantischen Polemik gegen die römisch-katholische Kirche*, 6th ed. (Leipzig: Breitkopf & Härtel, 1894), 254.

- The independence of the pope vis-à-vis the king of Italy had been more than adequately secured by the guarantee of May 13, 1871, and by the power of Catholic rulers and nations.

All this matters very little: Rome will not drop the demand that the pope again become a secular ruler. This, however, is still only a small part of the total demand. With an appeal to Matt. 28:18 and Luke 22:38, and following the teaching of Boniface VIII in the bull Unam Sanctam, many Roman Catholics have gone even much farther, asserting that the pope is the true sovereign over the whole world and can at his pleasure transfer secular power to rulers and kings as his ministers and vicars. For many Catholics, however, this notion was out of bounds. They oppose the view that the pope is sovereign over the unbelieving part of the world, for Christ only entrusted to Peter the care of the sheep, and those who are outside the sheepfold God will judge. Nor is the pope a secular ruler over Christian nations, for nowhere has such political power been assigned to the pope, and Christ gave Peter only the [spiritual] keys of the kingdom. The pope does not even possess temporal jurisdiction or secular power directly or by divine right, for Christ is a spiritual king and has a spiritual kingdom. Still, though these people thus rejected direct secular power, they continued to speak of an indirect power and not only assigned to the pope directive power in secular matters but also—in the interest of the kingdom of God—the supreme power of disposing over the temporal things of all Christians on the ground that pasturing sheep also requires power over the wolves. Secular power, after all, is subject to the church as the body is to the spirit. Unbelieving rulers who mislead their subjects into heresy may be resisted and deposed. Christian rulers, as Christians, are subject to Christ and must promote the faith and protect the church, as many kings did in the days of the Old Testament and in the history of the church.[31] But also where this theory of indirect power is held, the pope retains the right—in the interest of the kingdom of God—to require unqualified obedience from all rulers, to depose them in case of disobedience, to release their subjects from the oath of obedience, to assign non-Catholic nations and countries to Catholic rulers, and to invalidate laws and rights, and so forth. Even though many Catholics today convey the impression that all these rights only temporarily and incidentally belonged to the popes in the Middle Ages, the Syllabus of 1864 (no. 23) expressly states that Roman pontiffs and ecumenical councils have never wandered outside the limits of their powers, nor usurped the rights of princes, nor ever erred in deciding matters of faith and morals. Though as a result of circumstances the exercise of papal rights may have been suspended, there is no doubt that the rights themselves are inalienable. Rome does not change.[32]

31. R. Bellarmine, "De rom. pontif," in *Controversiis*, V.
32. Cf. J. F. von Schulte, *Die Macht der römischen Päpste über Fürsten, Länder, Völker und Individuen,* 3rd ed. (Giessen: E. Roth, 1896).

8. From all this one senses the all-determining place the pope has in the life of Catholic Christians. The Roman Catholic Church is a monarchy, a kingdom, a state headed by a spiritual ruler. From the days of Augustine onward, there has been a tendency to present the church as a state or a kingdom in which all the dogmas function as laws and rights that bind people on pain of losing their salvation. Boniface VIII, therefore, said of the pope that he is "considered to hold all the laws in the file of his mind."[33] The government in this state is absolutely monarchal. After the [Vatican] Council of 1870 it is no longer even tempered, as it used to be said, by the aristocracy of the bishops, for the bishops are fallible and derive their power from him. Indeed, according to the express statement of the [First] Vatican Council, the pope can directly communicate with all the shepherds and flocks and hence, completely bypassing the bishops, directly appoint or discharge any priest or chaplain, decide every trial, immediately discipline any layperson, and so forth. The bishops have fundamentally been robbed of their sphere of sovereignty.[34] Moreover, this monarchal papal government is no longer constitutional in principle, for Scripture and tradition are subject to his infallible interpretation. "I am the tradition," said Pius IX to Cardinal Guidi.[35] If necessary, the pope defines what the doctrine of Scripture and tradition is. In the Roman Catholic Church, the pope, through his infallibility, is the only absolute sovereign, the source of all ecclesiastical authority and, directly or indirectly, even of all secular power. Since the ninth century, therefore, he is called—in distinction from all other bishops—Papa,[36] not just the successor and vicar of Peter but the vicar of Christ, the vicar of God,[37] "the spiritual father of all fathers, indeed of all the faithful, the supreme hierarch, the unique bridegroom, the indivisible head, the supreme Pontiff, the fount and origin, the ruler of all ecclesiastical principalities."[38] The pope is the church, Christianity, the kingdom of God itself. "The pope and the church—it is all one," said Francis de Sales. "Where the pope is there the church is" (*ubi papa, ibi ecclesia*). The primacy of the pope is "the quintessence of the Christian religion" (*summa rei Christiane*).[39] Without the pope there is no church, no Christianity.[40] Submission to the pope is for all people a condition for salvation (Boniface VIII, Unam Sanctam). The pope is the mediator of salvation, the way, the truth, and the life. The only thing still lacking is that he is worshiped, but that too is only a matter of time.[41] Indeed, Scheeben and Atzberger are correct in saying that if the

---

33. According to ibid., 66.

34. Ed. note: Bavinck uses here the Neo-Calvinist technical term "sphere-sovereignty" (*souvereiniteit in eigen kring*).

35. Schulte, *Die Macht der römischen Päpste*, 80.

36. J. Schwane, *Dogmengeschichte*, I, 543.

37. Ibid., III, 536, 538.

38. Bonaventure, *Breviloquium*, VI, 12.

39. R. Bellarmine, "De rom. pontif," in *Controversiis*, in the foreword.

40. Veuillot, according to K. von Hase, *Handbuch der protestantischen Polemik* (1894), 187.

41. A. von Harnack, *History of Dogma*, trans. N. Buchanan et al., ed. A. B. Bruce, 7 vols. (London: Williams & Norgate, 1896–99), VII, 116–17.

primacy of the pope is not the work of God, it is "a blasphemous and diabolical usurpation."[42]

POWER RESTORED TO WORD AND SACRAMENT

[511] The Reformation rebelled against this degeneration of ecclesiastical power. It again confessed that the church is a communion of saints and that from Christ it had received a power that was essentially different from the power of the state. [In Luther's words:] "The kingdom of Christ is not a physical, worldly or earthly regime, like the way lords and kings govern on earth, but a spiritual and heavenly regime, in which one deals not with temporal goods, nor with the things that concern this life, but with hearts and consciences, how one must live before God and obtain his grace."[43] Calvin similarly differentiated between church and state as between soul and body, the future and the present life, and ascribed to the church its own offices, power, and jurisdiction.[44] The power of

42. Scheeben-Atzberger, *Handbuch*, IV, 427; cf. additional literature against the papacy: M. Luther, *Von dem Bapstum zu Rome: Widder den hochberumpten Romanisten zu Leiptzck* (Wittenberg: Melchior Lotter, 1520; ed. note: "Bapstum" is the original spelling), according to J. Köstlin, *The Theology of Luther in Its Historical Development and Inner Harmony*, trans. Charles E. Hay, 2 vols. (Philadelphia: Lutheran Publication Society, 1897), I, 363; ET: M. Luther, *On the Papacy in Rome: Against the Most Celebrated Romanist in Leipzig*, in *Luther's Works*, ed. Joel W. Lundeen (Philadelphia: Fortress, 1986), 39:49–104; The Smalcald Articles, art. 4, in *The Book of Concord*, ed. Robert Kolb and Timothy J. Wengert (Minneapolis: Fortress, 2000), 307–10; *Treatise on the Power and Primacy of the Pope* (1537; in Kolb and Wengert, 329–45); J. Calvin, *Institutes*, IV.iv–xi; W. Ames, *Bellarminus enervatus*, 3rd ed., 4 vols. (Oxford: G. Turner, 1629), I, lib. 3; D. Chamier, *Panstratiae catholicae* (Geneva: Roverianis, 1626), II, lib. 2; G. Voetius, *Politicae ecclesiasticae*, 3 vols. (Amsterdam: Joannis a Waesberge, 1663–76), III, 775ff.; idem, *Selectae disputationes theologicae*, 5 vols. (Utrecht: 1648–69), II, 684–882; idem, *Desperata causa papatus* (Amsterdam: Joannis Jansson, 1635); J. H. Heidegger, *Corpus theologiae* (Zurich, 1700), loc. 72, 2; F. Turretin, *Institutes of Elenctic Theology*, trans. G. M. Giger, ed. J. T. Dennison, 3 vols. (Phillipsburg, NJ: Presbyterian & Reformed, 1992), XVII, qu. 16–20; idem, *De necessaria secissiones nostra ab ecclesia romana*, in *Opera* (New York: Carter, 1848), IV, 1–203, disp. 5: "De tyrannide romana"; B. de Moor, *Commentarius . . . theologiae*, 6 vols. (Leiden: J. Hasebroek, 1761–71), VI, 195ff.; J. J. I. von Döllinger, J. Huber, and J. Friedrich, *Das Papstthum* (Munich: Beck, 1892; ed. note: Bavinck cites the publication date as 1894); idem, *The Pope and the Council* (Boston: Roberts, 1870); J. Langen, *Das vatikanische Dogma von dem Universal-Episcopat und der Unfehlbarkeit des Papstes*, 4 vols. (Bonn: E. Weber, 1871–76); W. Joos, *Die Bulle "Unam Sanctam" und das vatikanische Autoritätsprinzip*, 2nd ed. (Schaffhausen: Carl Schoch, 1897); P. K. Graf von Hoensbroech, *Das Papstthum in seiner sozial-kulturellen Wirksamkeit*, 2 vols. (Leipzig: Breitkopf & Härtel, 1901–2); L. L. F. Bungener, *Rome and the Council in the 19th Century* (Edinburgh: T&T Clark, 1870); W. E. Gladstone, *Rome and the Newest Fashion in Religion* (London: John Murray, 1875); K. von Hase, *Handbuch der protestantischen Polemik*, 5th ed. (Leipzig: Breitkopf & Härtel, 1890); P. Tschackert, *Evangelische Polemik gegen die römischen Kirche* (Gotha: F. A. Perthes, 1885); D. Snijder, *Rome's voornaamste leerstellingen en bedoelingen voor den Protestant* (Gorinchem: Knierum, 1890); idem, *Het Dogma van de onfeilbaarheid van den Paus vastgesteld op het Vaticaanische Concilie van 1870* (Rotterdam: Daamen, 1899).

43. Ed. note: The citation here is clearly from Luther, though Bavinck cites only secondary literature. [Cited by] R. Sohm, *Kirchenrecht*, 2 vols. (Leipzig and Munich: Duncker & Humblot, 1892–1923), 464, 488; cf. also, J. Köstlin, *Theology of Luther*, II, 521ff., 541ff.; P. Drews, *Entsprach das Staatskirchentum dem Ideale Luthers?* (Tübingen: J. C. B. Mohr [Paul Siebeck], 1908); K. Müller, *Kirche, Gemeinde und weltliche Obrigkeit nach Luther* (Tübingen: J. C. B. Mohr [Paul Siebeck], 1910).

44. J. Calvin, *Institutes*, IV.i–xi; cf. P. Lobstein, *Die Ethik Calvins* (Strassburg: C. F. Schmidt, 1877), 115ff.; E. Choisy, *La théocratie à Genève au temps de Calvin* (Geneva: Ch. Eggimann, 1897; ed. note: Bavinck cites the

the church, therefore, did not consist in the corpus of canon law that had been publicly burned by Luther at Wittenberg on December 10, 1520, but in the administration of God's Word. Since Christ is the only head of the church, only the Word of God can and may rule in the church, not by coercion, but only by love and free obedience.[45]

The administration of Word and sacrament is the only form of church government, the sum of all ecclesiastical power, the totality of the power of the keys. However, according to the Lutherans, this power of the keys includes a lawful call, obedience to the overseers, the evaluation of one's doctrine and life, the exercise of discipline, the exclusion of the ungodly from the church, and so forth.[46] Sohm clearly set forth the difference between the power assigned to the church by Rome and that assigned by Luther. In this connection, however, he goes too far when, assuming that all law and all coercion is merely human dominion and earthly power, he holds all church law to be in conflict with the essential nature of the church. Nonetheless, he clearly demonstrates that the enormous difference between Rome and Protestantism over the power of the church is linked with the political/juridical view of Christianity versus the spiritual/ethical view. He himself frequently recognizes that the church of Christ, though a communion of saints, nevertheless requires order and already possessed a certain kind of order in the beginning,[47] and also, according to Luther and the Lutherans, cannot exist without the offices, a lawful call, pastoral care, discipline, the ban, and governance.[48] Either directly or indirectly, all power in the church is administration of the Word. Every regulation it adopts or arrangement it makes is subject and serviceable to that end.

Reformed people also understood the church's power along these lines. All power in the church basically goes back to Christ, whom God anointed king over Zion, and hence has a spiritual character, since his kingdom is not of this world. To the extent that Christ, in the exercise of this power, employs instruments, these are not autonomous, independent, sovereign, but bound to him, that is, to his Word. Every office in the church of Christ is a ministry (διακονια, *diakonia*), without legislative, judiciary, and executive power of its own but able only to administer the things contained and implied in the word of Christ. In fact, therefore, there is in the church no other power than the power of the keys, the administration of the Word and the sacraments, which as a rule is again differentiated in the power to teach, the power to discipline, and the power to govern.[49]

1898 edition); G. von Schulthess-Rechberg, *Luther, Zwingli und Calvin in ihren Ansichten über das Verhältnis von Staat und Kirche* (Aarau: H. R. Sauerländer, 1909).

45. Luther, according to R. Sohm, *Kirchenrecht*, 464, 468.

46. Apology of the Augsburg Confession, arts. 14, 20; The Smalcald Articles, "De potestate et primatu papae" (Kolb and Wengert, 307–10).

47. R. Sohm, *Kirchenrecht*, 51ff.

48. Ibid., 471, 476, 486, 494, 519ff.

49. J. Calvin, *Institutes*, IV.viii–xii; P. Martyr Vermigli, *Loci communes*, ed. R. Massonius (London, 1576), 405ff.; A. Polanus, *Syntagma theologiae christianae*, 5th ed. (Hanover: Aubry, 1624), VII, 10ff.; F. Junius, *Theses theologicae*, 46; F. Turretin, *Institutes of Elenctic Theology*, XVIII, 29ff.

Though there was fundamental agreement between the Lutherans and the Reformed on the issue of the power of the church, nonetheless there soon emerged an important difference between them over its elaboration and application. In the first place, Luther took over from the Roman Catholic Church the official administration of the Word to the individual and therefore favored the maintenance of private confession. Although he regarded the preaching of the gospel as the forgiveness of sins (hence, "a Christian preacher can never open his mouth without pronouncing an absolution"),[50] this was not enough for him. The pastor must also apply the absolution individually in the confessional, which, though not strictly necessary, is highly useful.[51] But the institution of private confession encountered insurmountable difficulties (the insufficient number of pastors, the confessional fee, the uncertain meaning of absolution, and so forth) and gradually fell into disuse. Although the Reformed found the mutual confession of sins between church members useful, they had the official administration of the Word and hence also the proclamation of the forgiveness of sins, that is, the proclamation of pardon, take place only in the public gatherings of believers. For confession as an institution of the church, they only retained the regular or occasional confession of sins customary in preparing for the celebration of the Lord's Supper, and for the rest replaced private confession with the practice of personal home visitation.[52]

In the second place, the practice of discipline took another direction in the Lutheran Church than in the Reformed. Luther himself definitely desired the application of discipline in the church of Christ. Although he rejected the Roman Catholic ban and removed all civil penalties from ecclesiastical discipline, his ideal was a church that, after repeated admonition, removed the evildoer from its midst.[53] But the absence of the office of presbyter and the exercise of ecclesiastical discipline by the pastor alone led to such abuses that it soon disappeared altogether and, to the extent that it remained, was left to mixed consistories (consisting of both ecclesiastical and civil members).[54] Practically, this led to the same result as the

---

50. R. Sohm, *Kirchenrecht*, 488.

51. Cf. above, 160–75 (##465–66).

52. Thus Zwingli, according to E. Zeller, *Das theologische System Zwingli's* (Tübingen: L. F. Fues, 1853), 153; P. Martyr Vermigli, *Loci comm.*, 274; W. Ames, *Bellarminus enervatus*, III, 481; A. Rivetus, *Operum theologicorum*, 3 vols. (Rotterdam: Leers, 1651–60), III, 316; C. Vitringa, *Doctr. christ.*, III, 127ff.; P. Biesterveld, *Het huisbezoek* (Kampen: Bos, 1900).

53. J. Köstlin, *Theology of Luther*, II, 526ff., 533ff.; Th. Harnack, *Praktische Theologie*, 2 vols. (Erlangen: A. Deichert, 1877–78), II, 497ff.; A. W. Dieckhoff, *Luthers Lehre von der kirchlichen Gewalt* (Berlin: G. Schlawitz, 1865); the Lutheran Confessions in Joseph T. Müller, *Die symbolischen Bücher der evangelisch-lutherischen Kirche*, 8th ed. (Gütersloh: Bertelsmann, 1898), 75, 152, 165, 288, 329, 342; ed. note: These specific references are to the following Lutheran documents: Apology of the Augsburg Confession, "Preface" (Kolb and Wengert, 110); ibid., arts. 7–8 (Kolb and Wengert, 174ff.); ibid., art. 11, pars. 60–62 (Kolb and Wengert, 290–91); Treatise on the Power and Primacy of the Pope, pars. 7–11, 70–73 (Kolb and Wengert, 331, 341–42).

54. Ed. note: Bavinck's expression is simply "mixed consistories" [*gemengde consistoriën*]; from the context it is apparent that he is referring to a "mixture" of ecclesiastical and civil authorities.

doctrine of Zwingli, Erastus, the Remonstrants, the rationalists, and many modern theologians, in which the church relinquishes its power to exercise discipline to the civil authorities, since the civil government was now Christian. For Calvin, on the other hand, ecclesiastical discipline was a matter of life and death. For twenty years in Geneva he contended for the church's right to remove the evil person from its midst and only acquired it in the year 1555. Though discipline could not be the soul of the church, it nevertheless has to serve as its sinews. And this view of the obligatory nature, necessity, and usefulness of church discipline remained that of the Reformed and distinguished them on the one hand from Roman Catholics and Lutherans, and on the other from Anabaptists and Mennonites, who as a result of their nature-grace antithesis sometimes applied excommunication with excessive severity and deprived it of its spiritual character.[55]

In the third place, the relationship of Christianity to the natural life was defined differently by Luther than by Calvin. All the Reformers united in liberating the natural life from the pressure and power of the church, which in the view of Rome coincides with Christianity and constitutes a supernatural addition to nature, yet under that supernatural umbrella accords to the natural life a generous amount of latitude. Protestantism, on the other hand, posited the confession that the whole world, though it is under the control of the evil one [1 John 5:19], is in itself holy and good, a work of God the Almighty, Creator of heaven and earth. It traded the quantitative antithesis of the natural and the supernatural for the qualitative, ethical antithesis of sin and grace.

Yet for all that, there was also fundamental disagreement among the Reformers. Zwingli never quite transcended the medieval dualism between "flesh" and "spirit," between human and divine justice. Luther frequently so limited the work of Christ to the religious and ethical that the natural came to stand independently alongside that area. While the gospel only changed the internal, the mind, the heart, it had no transforming effect on the natural life as a whole. This explains the disdain with which Luther often spoke of reason, philosophy, and jurisprudence. This also explains the harsh judgment that the Formula of Concord pronounced over "the natural man" as a stone, a tree trunk, or slime. Hence also comes the Lutheran distinction and separation between the sensible and the spiritual as "two hemispheres one of which is inferior and the other superior."[56] This also explains the fact that the Lutheran Church, as long as it had the pure administration of

---

55. J. Calvin, *Institutes*, IV.xii; P. Martyr Vermigli, *Loci comm.*, 411; J. Zanchi, *De operum theologicorum*, 8 vols. (Geneva: Samuelis Crispini, 1617), IV, 736; F. Junius, *Theses theol.*, 47; G. Bucanus, *Institutiones theologicae*, 3rd ed. (Bern: Joannis & Isaias le Preux, 1605), 531; P. van Mastricht, *Theoretico-practica theologia* (Utrecht: Appels, 1714), VII, 6; *Synopsis purioris theologiae*, disp. 48; F. Turretin, *Institutes of Elenctic Theology*, XVIII, qu. 32; S. Maresius, *Syst. theol.*, XVI, 79–87; G. Voetius, *Politicae ecclesiasticae*, IV, 841ff.; Gallic Confession, art. 27; Belgic Confession, art. 29; Heidelberg Catechism, Q&A 83–85; Helvetic Confession, II, 18.

56. H. Bavinck, "The Catholicity of Christianity and the Church," trans. John Bolt, *Calvin Theological Journal* 27 (1992): 220–51; idem, "Common Grace," trans. Raymond C. Van Leeuwen, *Calvin Theological Journal* 24 (1989): 35–65.

Word and sacrament, was quite indifferent toward all other powers granted by Christ to the church. It did indeed know better and confessed that the church must have its own overseers and deacons, its own government and discipline, but in practice it ceded all this immediately and without a struggle to the government. If necessary, it could allow a monarchal (papal) and episcopal government, recognize many ceremonies as adiaphora, leave discipline to the consistories, and entrust the entire external government of the church to the civil government. The church kept for itself only the office of preaching, the administration of Word and sacrament, but for the rest it became a national or state church in which the government as the substitute for the Roman Catholic episcopate, or as the principal member of the church, or as the authorized agent of the church, had virtually unrestricted jurisdiction.[57] Materially and practically this distribution of power agreed completely with the power that Zwingli, Erastus, the Remonstrants, and so forth accorded to the government in relation to the church.

CHURCH POWER AND POLITICAL POWER

The Reformed churches, however, were principially opposed to this arrangement. Just as God had appointed the government as sovereign in the state, so he anointed Christ as king of his church. State and church, therefore, were essentially distinct from each other—in origin, nature, and government. To transfer the church's power to the state was a violation of the kingship of Christ. But the Reformed never meant the distinction to be a separation. On the contrary, just as the church distributes its spiritual goods for the benefit of all of natural life in family and society, in the arts and sciences, so the government in a Christian country has the awesome calling to protect the true church, to support its expansion and extension, to resist all idolatry and false religion, and to destroy the kingdom of the antichrist. They had no choice but to promote this teaching because they believed that the government had been appointed by God himself for the purpose of restraining sin; that as such it was bound to God's law and Word; that not only the second table of the law but also the first had to be maintained in its domain and its manner; that the content of the Bible was not exclusively religious and ethical and only valid for the church, but a word from God that goes out to the whole of humanity and sheds light on every creature and all of life; that under the Old Testament dispensation the government was specifically charged by God to carry out this task; and that Christian truth was universal and catholic, plain and clear, and therefore accessible also to the government.[58]

57. J. Köstlin, *Theology of Luther*, II, 560ff.; K. Lechler, *Die neutestamentliche Lehre vom heiligen Ambte* (Stuttgart: J. F. Steinkopf, 1857), 223ff., 230ff.; R. Sohm, *Kirchenrecht*, 542ff.; P. Melanchthon, "De magistr. civil," in *Loci comm.*; J. Gerhard, *Loci theol.*, XXIV; J. Quenstedt, *Theologia*, IV, 420–50; D. Hollaz, *Examen theologicum acroamaticum* (Rostock and Leipzig: Russworm, 1718); J. W. Baier, *Compendium theologiae positivae*, 3 vols. in 4 (St. Louis: Concordia, 1879), 639–49; J. F. Buddeus, *Institutiones theologiae dogmaticae* (Frankfurt and Leipzig, 1741), 1267–87.

58. Cf. H. A. Niemeyer, *Collectio confessionum in ecclesiis reformatis publicatarum*, 2 vols. (Leipzig: Iulii Klinkhardti, 1840), 9, 32, 54, 55, 82, 98, 114, 122, 326, 355, 387, 534, 610, 765, 810; ed. note: These specific

But life proved stronger than doctrine. Gradually this absolute position weakened. Already in the sixteenth century some Anabaptists and Socinians insisted that the government should abstain from all intervention in matters of religion and specifically from the punishment of heretics. Reformed teaching concerning the state, accordingly, encountered numerous practical difficulties. In theory church and state were indeed distinct, but in fact the state was frequently subject to the pronouncements of the church and bound to its confession. By virtue of its close connection with the church and the obligation it had assumed, the government engaged in acts of violence and coercion that were repugnant to the government itself, acts that gave the government a bad name among numerous noble-minded people, invited the appearance of Roman Catholic tyranny, and were inconsistent with Protestant demands for freedom of conscience and religion. As long as in a given country all citizens or at least the large majority of them were united by a single confession, the union of church and state could still be maintained; but when the Roman Catholic Church revived and in Protestantism a wide diversity of churches and creeds arose whose Christian character could not be denied, it became impossible even for the most rigorous Christians to maintain the confessional character of the state and to insist that heretics should be punished. In England this impossibility first became obvious in the seventeenth century. Not only Roman Catholics and Episcopalians vied with each other for priority; they were soon followed successively by Presbyterians, Independents, Quakers, Levellers, and Deists. Thus, guided by the facts, people gradually moved from a confessional to a generally Christian and from there to a deistic view of the state, and "tolerance" and "moderation" became the rallying cries of the eighteenth century. Roger Williams (c. 1603–83), the "archindividualist," was the first seventeenth-century person

references are to the following reformational documents: U. Zwingli, The Sixty-seven Articles (##29–41); idem, *An Account of the Faith of Huldreich Zwingli* (*Fidei ratio*, 1530), in *On Providence and Other Essays*, ed. S. M. Jackson and W. J. Hinke (1922; repr., Durham, NC: Labyrinth, 1983), 11th article on the magistrate; idem, Exposition of the Christian Faith, art. 87, "Magistratus"; First Confession of Basle (1534), art. 8; ibid., art. 8, disp. 221; Second Helvetic Confession, ch. XXX; Catechism of Geneva, art. 21; Gallican Confession, art. 24; First Scotch Confession, art. 24; Belgic Confession, art. 36; Thirty-nine Articles of the Church of England, art. 36 (art. 37); Tetrapolitan Confession (Strasburg Confession, 1530), art. 23; Bohemian Confession (1535), art. 16. J. Calvin, *Institutes*, IV.xx. Concerning the punishment of heretics, see John Calvin, *Defensio orthodoxae de sacra trinitate, contra prodigiosos errores Michaelis Serveti hispani* (1554), in *Calvini opera*, VIII (CR, XXXVI), 453–644; E. Blösch, *Geschichte der Schweizen-reformierten Kirchen*, 2 vols. (Bern: Schmid & Francke, 1898–99), I, 227ff.; T. Beza, "De haereticis a civili magistratu puniendis," in *Tractationum theologicarum* (Geneva: Jean Crispin, 1570), I, 85–169; J. Zanchi, *Op. theol.*, IV, 580–87; P. Martyr Vermigli, *Loci comm.*, 473; H. Bullinger, *Decades*, II, serm. 7; F. Junius, *Op. theol. select.*, I, 544; Bogerman, in H. E. van der Tuuk, *Johannes Bogerman* (Groningen: Wolters, 1868), 32ff.; J. Trigland, *Antapologia* (Amsterdam: Joannam Janssonium et al., 1664), c. 29; idem, *Kerckelycke geschiedenissen* (Leyden: Andriae Wyngaerden, 1650), 440ff.; S. Rutherford, *Examen arminianismi* (Utrecht: Smytegelt, 1668), c. 19 (ed. note: Bavinck cites the author as Rhetorford); Revius in E. J. W. Posthumus Meyjes, *Jacobus Revius, zijn leven en werken* (Amsterdam: Ten Brink & De Vries, 1895), 151–71; G. Voetius, *Pol. eccl.*, I, 124ff.; idem, *Desperata causa papatus*, II, 692–809; III, 206; *Synopsis purioris theologiae*, disp. 50; P. van Mastricht, *Theologia*, VII, 7, 14; F. Turretin, *Institutes of Elenctic Theology*, XVIII, qu. 34; B. de Moor, *Comm. theol.*, VI, 470–518.

to demand the separation of church and state. He called for absolute freedom of religion for everyone, including heretics and Jews, and applied these principles in the colony he founded in Rhode Island. This theory increasingly met with approval both among Christians and within the revolutionary camp. While some American states adopted it after 1776, the French Revolution made it mandatory in many countries. Nevertheless, it nowhere exists in a pure and consistent form, and in practice everyone shrinks from its consequences.

[512] That Christ has accorded a certain power to his church on earth can hardly be doubted. Generally speaking, it is an undeniable truth that nothing can exist without order and regulation, and that a true formless substance (ὕλη, *hylē*) is nothing more than a philosophical abstraction. A family cannot exist without a head, a people cannot function without a government, a society cannot do without a board, an army is helpless without a general, and so forth. Anarchy does not work. To say that Christ has founded a church without any organization, government, or power is a statement that arises from principles characteristic of philosophical mysticism but takes no account of the teaching of Scripture, nor of the realities of life. The question that divides people, accordingly, is not really whether the church of Christ needs a certain power and government for its continued existence, for everyone agrees with this position, whether they would have the church give this government to itself or charge the civil government with this task. Rather, disagreement is over the question whether Christ himself—not in massive detail, of course, but in terms of principles and key matters—assigned to his church a power and government that may therefore constitute an article of our faith and a part of our confession.[59] But this disagreement too is powerfully and with the utmost clarity settled by Scripture. Christ has indeed stated that his kingdom is not of this world, but he is not a spiritual king in the sense that he has absolutely no interest in external and earthly things. On the contrary, he assumed a fully human nature and came into the world not to condemn the world but to save it. Christ planted his kingdom in that world and made sure that it could exist in it and, like a leaven, have a transforming impact in all areas of life. It was his work to destroy the works of the devil everywhere and to spark the acknowledgment of the rights and honor of God. Intensively his reconciling and renewing activity extends as far as sin has destroyed and corrupted everything. For that reason he does not by his Spirit just bring some people individually to faith in him in order that they would then freely unite themselves and serve each other with the gifts given them by the Spirit. The truth is, he founded a community of believers, a church, and from the outset organized it in such a way that it can exist, propagate, expand, and fulfill its task on earth.

In the interest of clarity one may and must distinguish between the essence and the government of the church. But this distinction may never be understood to mean that originally believers were without any government and power. On

59. Belgic Confession, arts. 30–32.

the contrary, in the previous section we learned that from the first moment of its existence after the fall, the church had a certain organization, first in the families of the patriarchs, then in the nation of Israel, and since Christ's coming on earth, in the various ordinary and extraordinary offices that he instituted in his church (Mark 3:14; Luke 10:1; Acts 20:28; 1 Cor. 12:28; Eph. 4:11). Every office, however, implies power, rights, jurisdiction. Granted, there are many gifts in the church that, having been bestowed by the Holy Spirit, manifest themselves as ministries of Christ and as workings of God the Father and serve to edify the members of the church among themselves (1 Cor. 12:4ff.). Nevertheless, Christ linked to the offices he instituted in his church a special power (ἐξουσία, *exousia*), consisting in the proclamation of the gospel (Matt. 10:7; Mark 3:14; 16:15; Luke 9:2; and so forth), the administration of the sacraments (Matt. 28:19; Mark 16:15; Luke 22:19; 1 Cor. 11:24–26), performing different kinds of miracles (Matt. 10:1, 8; Mark 3:15; 16:18; Luke 9:1; 10:9, 19; and so forth), retaining or forgiving sins (Matt. 16:19; 18:18; John 20:23), feeding the flock (John 21:15–17; Acts 20:28), exercising discipline (Matt. 18:17; 1 Cor. 5:4), serving tables (Acts 6:2), and the right to earn a living from the gospel (Matt. 10:10; 1 Cor. 9:4ff.; 2 Thess. 3:9; 1 Tim. 5:18).

This description that Scripture gives of the power of the church points not only to its unquestionable existence but also to its complete independence from and uniqueness in comparison with all other powers in the world. There are all kinds of power and authority on earth: in the family, society, the state, art, science, and so forth. But the power of the church is essentially distinct and completely independent from all of these. For all this other power comes from God as the creator of heaven and earth (Rom. 13:1), but this ecclesiastical power comes directly from God as the Father of our Lord Jesus Christ (1 Cor. 12:28; Eph. 4:11; Acts 20:28) and is therefore completely free and independent from all other earthly powers. Those who, with the adherents of Caesaropapism or Erastianism, shrink this power of the church, limit it, and assign it to the civil government diminish the honor of Christ and fail to do justice to the rights and freedoms granted to the church. This power of the church must remain independent from all other earthly power, because it is altogether sui generis, can be taken over or exercised by no other power, and is therefore robbed of its nature and destroyed when transferred to another power. For all the powers that Christ has given to his church (the administration of Word and sacrament, the exercise of discipline, the service of the tables, and so forth), besides having their own origin, also have an organ, a nature, and a purpose of their own. It is bound to the offices that Christ alone has instituted in his church, to which he alone furnishes and can furnish the gifts, which he alone calls and sends. No one takes this honor upon himself except those who are called by God (cf. Rom. 10:15; Heb. 5:4). Moreover, this power is spiritual. That does not mean it is invisible and completely internal, for though Christ is a spiritual king, he rules over both body and soul. His Word and sacrament are directed toward the whole person. The ministry of mercy must even alleviate primarily the physical needs of humans. But when the power of the church is called spiritual, that signifies that it has been given by the Holy Spirit of God (Acts 20:28) and can only be exercised in the name of Christ and in the power of the Holy Spirit (John 20:22–23; 1 Cor. 5:4); only applies to humans as believers (1 Cor. 5:12); works and can only work in a spiritual and moral manner, not with coercion and penalties in money, goods, or life, but by conviction, faith, good will, freedom, and love, and hence only with spiritual weapons (2 Cor. 10:4; Mark 16:16; John 8:32; 2 Cor. 3:17; Eph. 6:7; and so forth). Finally, this power also has its own purpose. Even though for unbelievers it makes their judgment all the heavier, it is meant for salvation, for building up, not for destruction, for the perfection of the saints and the upbuilding of the body of Christ (Matt. 10:13; Mark 16:16; Luke 2:34; 2 Cor. 2:16; 10:4, 8; 13:10; Eph. 4:12; 6:11–18; and so forth).[60]

As a result of all this, ecclesiastical power differs in kind from all political power. Even under the Old Testament, state and church, though closely connected, were not identical. Christ much more clearly defined the difference, however, between his kingdom and the kingdoms of the world (Matt. 22:21; John 18:36). He himself refused all earthly power (Luke 12:13–14; John 6:15) and prohibited his disciples from undertaking anything that smacked of worldly rule (Matt. 20:25–26; 1 Pet. 5:3).

Accordingly, there are many differences between church and state and their respective powers. Not only in *origin*, as we noted above, but also in their respective *organs of operation*, for the offices in the church of Christ are all ministries (διακονίαι, *diakoniai*), but the political government is sovereign, and though God's servant it has the right and power to issue and enforce laws. There is a difference in *nature*, for the power of the church is spiritual, but the power of the political government is natural, earthly, secular. It extends to all subjects for no other reason than the fact that they are subjects and only regulates their earthly interests. They differ in *purpose*, for ecclesiastical power serves the upbuilding of the body of Christ, but political power is defined by its purpose in this life and strives for the natural and common good. They differ in the *means* employed, for the church only has spiritual weapons, but the government bears the sword, has power over life and death, and may exact obedience by coercion and violence.

CONFUSION OF POWERS

As impermissible as it is, therefore, on the one hand to assign ecclesiastical power to the civil government, so it is also sinful on the other hand to change ecclesiastical power into political power. Both Romanism and Anabaptism are guilty of the latter, because both think in terms of an antithesis between nature and grace. Only Anabaptism makes that contrast absolute and thereby destroys nature. Rome, viewing the contrast as relative, suppresses nature. In the Middle

---

60. G. Voetius, *Pol. eccl.*, IV, 783.

Ages when the Roman Catholic Church had absolute power, this striving was more obvious, but basically it has not changed and is still driven by the same desire to make the clergy as free as possible from political subordination, to draw all sorts of civil matters into its own sphere and to subject them to its judgment, to shine by external glitter and ostentation, to expand its holdings in capital and real estate, to exert political influence at the courts, to claim [authority] for the pope on the grounds of Matt. 28:18 and in accordance with the theory of the two swords—if not direct power then certainly indirect power over the whole world.[61] Not only is the Roman Catholic Church consistently minded to make all earthly and political power subservient to itself; what is worse is that it also robs ecclesiastical power of its spiritual character and transforms it into political domination. This is manifest in three ways.

1. The Roman Catholic Church ascribes to itself (i.e., to the pope) supreme legislative power. It used to be that this power was still limited by Scripture and tradition, by bishops and councils. The church's government was a monarchy tempered by aristocracy. But since the proclamation of the dogma of papal infallibility, this relationship has been reversed. The pope is formally an absolute monarch. By virtue of the alleged assistance of the Holy Spirit, he infallibly determines what has to be believed and done. There is no appeal to a higher authority. What he binds or looses is bound or loosed in heaven [cf. Matt. 16:19]. What he says has authority tantamount to that of Christ himself. The dogmas and laws he proclaims bind the human conscience and obligate people to faith and obedience on pain of forfeiting their eternal salvation. From the decrees of civil government one can appeal to God himself, but the sovereignty of the pope is supreme: God himself speaks through his mouth.

2. The Roman Catholic Church ascribes to itself (i.e., to the pope) supreme judicial power. Ecclesiastical power is twofold: the power of ordination [or holy orders] and the power of jurisdiction. The power to teach (*potestas docendi*), though mentioned separately, actually belongs to the power of jurisdiction. Implied here is that in the view of Rome the administration of Word and sacrament is not a proclamation of the gospel but a juridical transaction and pronouncement. All the baptized belong—not in a moral and spiritual sense but by right, in a juridical sense, by an immutable and inamissible right—to the pope. They are his sheep, which he may, if necessary by violent means, return to the sheepfold, though he may perhaps be prevented from so doing by circumstances prevailing at the time. "According to the laws of the Catholic Church all the baptized actually belong to the church, hence also to the parish, but in the absence of the means of coercion the enforceability of this claim is lacking with respect to those

61. Ibid., I, 115.

who believe otherwise."[62] And all the members of the Catholic Church listen to the preaching of their priest and come to the sacrament of penance to hear the church's judgment of them. The confessional is a court of law and the priest a judge. After hearing the accusations that the penitent makes against himself, he renders a verdict. He binds and looses, not by a prayer for pardon (*deprecari*) and conditionally, but by virtue of the "spirit of office" that is in him, peremptorily and absolutely. As he judges, so God judges in heaven.

3. The Roman Catholic Church (i.e., the pope) claims supreme executive and coercive power. The distinction between ecclesiastical and civil punishment is of no value to Rome. When the church deems it useful and is capable of it, it applies the latter equally well as the former. True, it did not itself execute the death penalty (for "the church is not bloodthirsty") but for the rest left no means untried to compel disobedient children to submit. And Rome was resourceful. Financial penalties, fines, imprisonment, inquisition, rack, assassination, ban, interdict, releasing subjects from obedience to their ruler, and so forth have all served its purpose. That was, and in principle still is, the view of ecclesiastical power held by Rome.[63]

Over against this position the Reformers again viewed ecclesiastical power in the scriptural sense as a spiritual power. As a result the power to teach (*potestas docendi*), the administration of Word and sacrament, naturally came to stand in the foreground. The Lutherans even—at least in practice—saw ecclesiastical power exclusively in terms of this administration of Word and sacrament; they had only pastors, no presbyters and deacons. But the Reformed churches also restored these offices and therefore accepted, besides the power to teach, also the power of jurisdiction. The word "jurisdiction," however, though Calvin adopted it,[64] was not generally accepted. Cocceius rejected it. Maresius said that, correctly and accurately speaking, there is no jurisdiction in the church, and that in the context of the church the term could be used only analogically.[65] All acknowledged that jurisdiction in the church was of a very different nature from that of the state and bore a spiritual character.[66] Many avoided the term and preferred to speak of "the power to govern, to ordain, or to discipline," and so forth. Furthermore,

---

62. F. H. Vering, *Lehrbuch des katholischen, orientalischen, und protestantischen Kirchenrechts*, 3rd ed. (Freiburg i.B.: Herder, 1893), 603.

63. In recent years, the right to apply the death penalty to heretics has again been openly stated and defended by various Roman Catholic scholars, such as M. de Luca, *Institutiones iuris ecclesiastici publici* (Regensburg: F. Pustet, 1901; ed. note: Bavinck cites the German edition: *Lehrbuch des öffentlichen Kirchenrechts* [1901]); A. M. Lépicier, *De stabilitate et progressu dogmatis* (Rome: Desclée, 1910); F. X. Brors, *Modernes ABC für das katholische Volk* (Kevelaer: Butzon, 1910); E. Pfenningsdorf, "Todesstrafe für die Ketzer," *Geisteskampf der Gegenwart* 46 (1910): 157–58. The respective statements of Lépicier are exactly quoted in *Foi et Vie* (1 July 1910): 393–96.

64. J. Calvin, *Institutes*, IV.xi.

65. S. Maresius, *Syst. theol.*, XV, 75ff.; XVI, 70.

66. G. Voetius, *Pol. eccl.*, IV, 798.

whereas some distinguished two kinds of power, others favored three. The power of the church, after all, is not exhausted by the administration of Word and sacrament and the exercise of discipline; it also possesses the right and authority, in the interest of order, to make laws and to take measures of various kinds. Thus, besides and often between the power to teach (*potestas docendi*) and the power to exercise discipline (*potestas disciplinae*) came the power to give direction (*potestas directionis*).[67] It is remarkable that under this heading of ecclesiastical power the diaconate is never mentioned. Yet also in this ministry God has given a power to his church that is of the greatest significance. Accordingly, in connection with the offices of pastor, presbyter, and deacon and further in connection with the threefold office of Christ—the prophetic, the royal, and the priestly office—we must distinguish three kinds of power in Christ's church: the power to teach, the power to govern (of which the power to discipline is a part), and the power or rather the ministry of mercy.

SPIRITUAL TEACHING POWER

[513] The power to teach has its roots in the prophetic office for which Christ has been anointed and which he himself continually still exercises by his Word and Spirit. Christ never transferred it to any human being and never appointed any pope or bishop, pastor or teacher, to be his special deputy and surrogate, but he is still continually our chief prophet, who from his place in heaven teaches his church by Word and Spirit. Still, in this connection he regularly employs people as his organs, not only office-bearers in the strict sense, but all believers, every one of them according to the grace given to them. The church itself is a prophetess, and all Christians share in Christ's anointing and are called to confess his name. The office does not suppress the gifts but, rather, only guides them. There are many charismata that belong to the church's teaching power: wisdom, knowledge, prophecy, and so forth (1 Cor. 12:8ff.). Christ is active in teaching through parents in the home, through the teacher at school, through the presbyter at the time of home visitation, and through all believers in their mutual contacts and association with others. But Christ does it particularly, in a distinct manner, officially, with an expressly given mandate and authority, in the public meetings of the people of God, by the minister of the Word. By the power to teach (*potestas docendi*) we must primarily mean this official administration of the Word. This ministry must be maintained in its independence in two directions. In the first place, in the direction of the Roman Catholic Church, which has made the Word subordinate to the sacrament, the homilete to the liturgist, preaching to worship, the power to teach to the power of jurisdiction. According to Scripture, in any case, the Word has precedence, and the sacrament is added as an appendage and seal. There is no sacrament without the Word, but there is a Word without the

---

67. J. Calvin, *Institutes*, IV.viii.1; G. Bucanus, *Inst. theol.*, 519; S. Maresius, *Syst. theol.*, 16, 70; G. Voetius, *Pol. eccl.*, I, 118; C. Vitringa, *Doctr. christ.*, IV, 1, 457.

sacrament. The sacrament follows the Word. Those who administer the Word do not therefore always have to administer the sacrament (1 Cor. 1:14–17) but can and may do so, and are ministers of the Word even then, that is, of the visible word that is added to the audible one.

In the second place, this official administration of the Word is independent in relation to all the teaching of the Word undertaken by believers among themselves or to "outsiders" and is even essentially distinct from the application that the presbyters have to make on the occasion of their visits to the members of the church. Certainly the official administration of the Word in the meetings of the congregation can and may also be viewed as a feeding of the flock. Scripture shows us the way here. The Lord is the shepherd of his people (Pss. 23:1; 80:1; Isa. 40:11; 49:10; Jer. 31:10; Ezek. 34:15). Christ is called the shepherd of the flock (Ezek. 34:23; John 10:11, 14; Heb. 13:20; 1 Pet. 2:25; 5:4; Rev. 7:17). And under his guidance as the chief shepherd (1 Pet. 5:4) his ministers also bear the name of shepherds or pastors (Isa. 44:28; Jer. 2:8; 3:15, 23:1ff.; Ezek. 34:2ff.; John 10:2; 21:15–17; Acts 20:28; 1 Cor. 9:7; Eph. 4:11; 1 Pet. 5:2).[68]

But since the two activities of pastoring and teaching, of ruling and laboring in the Word and in doctrine, have been separated, and each of them has obtained its own organ (Eph. 4:11; 1 Tim. 5:17), the name "teacher" has become the characteristic title of the minister of the Word. By his preparation and training, by his total devotion to laboring in the Word, by his right to live from the gospel, by his official administration of the Word and sacrament in the gathering of believers, he has been distinguished from the ruling elder, who is especially charged with feeding the flock (Acts 20:28; 1 Pet. 5:2).

This teaching, nevertheless, must not be understood in an intellectualist sense. With the formulary referred to above (note 68), it is rather to be explained in the sense that the ministers will thoroughly and sincerely present the Lord's Word to their people and apply it, both in general and in particular, for the benefit of the hearers of it. They do this by teaching, admonishing, comforting, and rebuking them according to everyone's need, proclaiming conversion to God and reconciliation with him through faith in Jesus Christ, and refuting by the Scriptures all errors and heresies that militate against this pure doctrine. Further implied in this power to teach is the right and duty of the church to do these things: (1) to provide for the training of its future ministers or to exercise careful supervision over that training; to call, examine, send, ordain, and support its ministers; to have the Word of God preached by their ministry both to believers and nonbelievers and thus to establish, expand, and propagate the church of God among humankind; (2) to administer the Word of God by means of the ministerial office in various ways according to everyone's need, specifically in the form of

---

68. Cf. *Formulier om te bevestingen de dienaren des Goddelicken Woorts* (Amsterdam and Haarlem: J. Brandt and Johannes Enschede, 1870); ed. note: ET: *Form of Ordination of the Ministers of God's Word,* in *The Psalter with the Doctrinal Standards and Liturgy of the Christian Reformed Church,* 2 vols. in 1 (Grand Rapids: Eerdmans-Sevensma, 1914), II, 70–72.

"milk" for the youthful members of the church and "solid food" for the adult members, but always in such a way that the full counsel of God, all the riches of his Word, are unfolded, developed, and applied according to the needs of every people and country, of every age and period, of every church and of all believers in particular (Isa. 3:10–11; 2 Cor. 5:20; 1 Tim. 4:13; 2 Tim. 2:15; 4:2); (3) to preserve, translate, and interpret the Word of God according to the rule of faith and to defend it against all deceptive opposition (1 Tim. 1:3–4; 2 Tim. 1:13; Titus 1:9–11, 13–14), and thus to build up the church on the foundation of apostles and prophets (Eph. 2:20) and make it a "pillar and foundation of the truth," that is, a pillar and foundation that undergirds the truth, displays it for everyone to see, and makes it known to all (1 Tim. 3:15).

Directly arising from these considerations is the authority of the church to confess the truth it believes and to maintain it as confession in its midst. The objection advanced against this on the part of Remonstrants in the preface to their Confession and Apology, of Baptists, Congregationalists, Quakers,[69] and many others is that the adoption of binding confessions is inconsistent with the all-sufficiency of Scripture, destroys Christian liberty, introduces intolerable tyranny, and cuts off further investigation and development. Scripture, however, clearly imposes on churches the duty to be a "pillar and foundation of the truth" and to confess it before all people, to avoid those who deviate from the doctrine of the truth, and to maintain the Word of God against all its adversaries. Almost from the outset (that is, from the beginning of the second century), the church has been a confessional church that found its unity in the rule of faith common to all, that is, in the baptismal confession, the original, later somewhat expanded, apostolic symbol, and over the centuries was further prompted repeatedly by heresy and slander to produce a more highly elaborated statement of the truth.[70] Also, in a world immersed in lies and deception, a church cannot exist without a rule of faith; it falls prey—as especially the history of the nineteenth century teaches—to all sorts of error and confusion without a fixed confession, and becomes subject to the tyranny of prevailing schools of thought and opinions. Moreover, with such a confession the church does not fail to do justice to the sufficiency of Scripture but only rearticulates what is contained in Scripture. The confession is not a statement alongside of, let alone above, but far below Scripture. Scripture alone is trustworthy in and of itself (αὐτοπιστος, *autopistos*), unconditionally binding us to

---

69. P. Schaff, *Creeds of Christendom*, 3 vols. (New York: Harper & Brothers, 1877), I, 834, 852, 864.

70. Th. Zahn, "Glaubensregel und Taufbekenntniss in der alten Kirche," in *Skizzen aus dem Leben der alten Kirche*, 2nd ed. (Erlangen: Deichert, 1898), 238–70; idem, *Das apostolische Symbolum* (Erlangen and Leipzig: Deichert, 1893); F. Kattenbusch, *Das apostolische Symbol*, 2 vols. (Leipzig: Hinrichs, 1894–1900); J. Kunze, *Glaubensregel, Heilige Schrift und Taufbekenntnis* (Leipzig: Dörffling & Franke, 1899); cf. also Alfred Seeberg, *Der Katechismus der Urchristenheit* (Leipzig: A. Deichert, 1903); idem, *Das Evangelium Christi* (Leipzig: A. Deichert, 1905); idem, *Die beiden Wege und das Aposteldekret* (Leipzig: A. Deichert, 1906); according to Seeberg a large section of the *Didache* (3–5), in fact even 1.2; 2.1–6; and 6.3, "already displays the similarity in form between the early Christian and Jewish patterns" (*Die beiden Wege*, 2).

faith and obedience, unchanging; a confession, on the other hand, always remains examinable and revisable by the standard of Scripture. It is not a standardizing norm (*norma normans*) but at most a standardized norm (*norma normata*), not a norm of truth (*norma veritatis*), but "a standard of doctrine received in a particular church," subordinate, fallible, the work of humans, an inadequate expression of what the church has absorbed from Scripture as divine truth and now confesses on the authority of God's Word against all error and deception. The church does not coerce anyone with this confession, nor does it fetter research, for it leaves everyone free to confess otherwise and to conceive the truth of God in some other sense. It listens attentively to the objections that may be advanced on the basis of God's Word against its confession and examines them as the confession itself requires. Only it refuses and has to refuse to degrade itself into a debating club or a philosophical society in which what was a lie yesterday passes for truth today. It is not like a wave of the sea but like a rock, a pillar and foundation of the truth.

SPIRITUAL RULING POWER; DISCIPLINE

[514] Christ is not only a prophet but also a king who still continually rules his church personally from heaven. While this is true, he nevertheless employs people in this process and therefore to that extent gave his church the power of government (*potestas gubernationis*). In a broad sense, we mean by this power all the leadership and care that believers exert and bestow on one another. In the church we are not governed by Cain's cry: "Am I my brother's keeper?" We are all members of one another; we suffer and rejoice with one another; we have the ability and calling also to teach, admonish, comfort, and edify one another (Rom. 15:14; Col. 3:16; 1 Thess. 5:11). There are gifts of guidance and government, which Christ by his Spirit distributes to the church and which he does not undo but keeps them on the right track by the offices (Rom. 12:8; 1 Cor. 12:28). And at the apex of those gifts is love, which makes one outdo the other in appreciation and esteem (Rom. 12:10; Phil. 2:3; 1 Pet. 5:5). Yet as king of his church Christ has also instituted a specific office, the office of the presbyter (elder), by which he governs his church. This government, however, has a spiritual character inasmuch as Christ is king in the realm of grace, and in Scripture it is called "taking care of the flock" (John 21:15–17; Acts 20:28; 1 Pet. 5:2). All that suggests earthly power and political dominion is excluded from it (2 Cor. 1:24; 1 Pet. 5:2–3).

While in a broad sense this "taking care of the flock" also includes the work of the minister of the Word, there is nevertheless a big distinction between the public proclamation of the Word and the personal and individual application of it, between shepherding the flock in general and caring for each of the sheep in particular. While believers are indeed called to consider how they may spur one another on toward love and good deeds (Heb. 10:24), yet in order to insure that no sheep is left uncared for, Christ has charged the feeding of the sheep to a particular office. That in so doing he met an essential need of his church is evident from the fact that when the presbyterate gradually vanished from the scene, a human surrogate for this official ministry was created in the form of the confessional. Undoubtedly, therefore, the confessional has something good in it (James 5:16),[71] but it cannot make up for the well-regulated ministry of the presbyterate. After all, it introduces the impermissible coercion of the human conscience and makes believers dependent on the absolution of the priest. Also, in demanding the confession of all special sins, specifically of all mortal sins, it imposes a duty that cannot possibly be complied with and makes grace and one's salvation at every moment uncertain and unsettled. Finally, it forces the church's ministers into a casuistic and quantitative treatment of sin and punishment, and occasions all sorts of immoral practices.[72]

Scripture, accordingly, nowhere speaks of such a compulsory confession. But what it tells us by example and precept is that Nathan went to David, and Elijah to Ahab, and Isaiah to Hezekiah, to remonstrate with them personally over their sins. It tells us that Christ passed through the land preaching and blessing; that he knows all his sheep by name and allows none of them to perish (John 10:3, 28); that he charges Peter and all the apostles not only to pasture the flock but also to feed the sheep (John 21:15–17); that he orders his disciples to preach the gospel in cities, villages, and houses (Matt. 10:11–12); that Paul visited the brothers in every town (Acts 15:36), strengthened the churches (15:41), and declared, both publicly and from house to house, to both Jews and Greeks that they must turn to God in repentance and have faith in Christ (20:20–21).[73]

In any case, the need for such ongoing spiritual care is automatically implied in the condition of the church of Christ in this dispensation. Even though the church has at one time been planted, it is not immediately perfect. On the contrary, it experiences conflict from within and without, is prey to all sorts of attacks by sin and deception, and at all times runs the danger of straying to the left or to the right. The church is a field that needs to be constantly weeded, a tree that must be pruned at the proper time, a flock that must also be led and pastured, a house that requires constant renovation, a bride who must be prepared to be presented as a pure virgin to her husband. There are the sick, the dying, the tested, the grieving; those who are under attack, conflicted, in doubt, fallen, imprisoned, and so forth, who need teaching and instruction, admonition and consolation. And even apart from these things, the church must increase in the knowledge and grace of the Lord Jesus Christ. The children must become young people, young people must become young women and young men, the young women and men must become mothers and fathers in Christ, and to that end they need guidance and care. Also, ministers are weak and sinful people and need supervision. If the council of elders and the gathering of neighboring churches do not assume this

71. J. Calvin, *Institutes*, III.i.13.
72. See above, 147–49 (#462).
73. J. Calvin, *Institutes*, IV.i.22.

role, the local church becomes a plaything of the pastor or else is in need of a superintendency or episcopate. In a word, the preachers sow the Word, the elders look for the fruit.[74]

[515] The work of church discipline (*potestas disciplinae*) belongs particularly to the task of the overseer. The Hebrew word for it is מוּסָר (*mûsār*), which really means "discipline by chastisement" and has been translated into Greek by νουθετημα (*nouthetēma*, admonition), διδασκαλια (*didaskalia*, instruction), νομος (*nomos*, custom, law), and σοφια (*sophia*, wisdom) and is rendered in the New Testament especially by παιδεια (*paideia*, training, education, mental culture). Both words indicate in general that something young, tender, small, and weak be brought up with care. However, since especially in the case of human beings this process of rearing always at the same time has to counter abnormal development, the word "discipline" has acquired the connotation of correction, chastisement, punishment. The words almost never refer to education or instruction alone (cf., however, Acts 7:20; 22:3), but always the kind of upbringing and education that is accompanied by correction and chastisement. Thus God disciplines his children (Heb. 12:5–11) and Christ his church (Rev. 3:19) by means of Scripture, which is "useful for teaching, rebuking, correcting, and training in righteousness" (2 Tim. 3:16). And this kind of discipline Christ has also instituted in his church.

In the Old Testament there was as yet no real church discipline, though Adam was in fact banished from paradise and though in Israel the uncircumcised, the lepers, and the impure were denied access to the sanctuary (Lev. 5ff.; Ezek. 44:9), inasmuch as for unintentional sins there was always atonement, for sins "with a high hand" there was the death penalty, and the ban (חֵרֶם, *ḥerem*) was simultaneously a civil penalty [1 Chron. 2:7]. Only when Israel became a synagogal community did the exclusively ecclesiastical penalty arise, the expulsion from the community of believers (Ezra 10:8), and in some cases this ban is still applied by the Jews today.[75] It is perhaps in line with this synagogal discipline that Christ instituted discipline in his church. In Matt.16:19 he gave the keys of the kingdom to Peter, in 18:18 to the church, in John 20:23 to the apostles, so that they might have the power, on the basis of their confession of Christ and under the illumination of the Spirit, to bind and to loose, to forgive or to retain the sins of a member. It is

---

74. Concerning the office of the presbytery: J. Calvin, *Institutes*, IV.i.22; IV.xii.2; P. Martyr Vermigli, *Loci comm.*, 392b.; J. Zanchi, *Op. theol.*, IV, 730; H. Bullinger, *Decades*, V, serm. 3; F. Junius, *Op. theol. select.*, I, 1563; G. Bucanus, *Inst. theol.*, 493; P. van Mastricht, *Theologia*, VII, 2, 22; G. Voetius, *Pol. eccl.*, III, 436–79; IV, 92–109; C. Vitringa, *Doctr. christ.*, IX, 229; L. van Renesse, *Van het regeer-ouderlinghschap* (Utrecht: M. van Dreunen, 1659); J. Koelman, *Het ambt en pligten der ouderlingen en diakenen* ('s Gravenhage: Van Velzen, 1837; ed. note: Bavinck cites the 1765 edition); Th. Harnack, *Praktische Theologie*, II, 281–350; Harnack in O. Zöckler, *Handbuch der theologischen Wissenschaft*, 3rd ed., 5 vols. (Nördlingen and Munich: C. H. Beck, 1889), III, 503–37; E. C. Achelis, *Lehrbuch der praktischen Theologie*, II, 177–323; H. A. Köstlin, *Die Lehre von der Seelsorge nach evangelischen Grundsätzen* (Berlin: Reuther & Reichard, 1895); A. Kuyper, *Encyclopaedie der heilige godgeleerdherd*, 2nd ed., 3 vols. (Kampen: Kok, 1908–9), III, 524; P. Biesterveld, *Het huisbezoek*.

75. J. H. Gunning III, *De Chasidim* (Groningen: Wolters, 1891), 55.

only because Christ has given this power to his church that it has the authority to exercise discipline.

Then in Matt. 18:15–17 he shows how this discipline must be exercised. God is not willing that any of these little ones who believe in him should be lost (18:1–14). Therefore, if anyone has been insulted or unjustly treated by his brother, he must first seek to win him over by rebuking him personally, then by rebuking him in the presence of two or three witnesses, finally by rebuking him on behalf of the entire church; and only if all this does not bring about the desired result, the insulted one (σοι, *soi*, you [sing.]; v. 17) may view him as he would a pagan or a tax collector; then he has tried every available remedy with him and is free of his blood. Such a judgment, then, has power in heaven. This is the ordinary way by which discipline in the church according to Jesus's command must be conducted.

To be distinguished from this process, however, is the discipline that God himself, Christ, and sometimes also the apostles practice in his name and power. God may visit sins in the church, such as the unworthy use of the Lord's Supper, with sickness and death (1 Cor. 11:30); Ananias and Sapphira fell down dead at Peter's feet because they lied against the Spirit of God (Acts 5:1–11); Paul struck Elymas with blindness (13:11). And in 1 Cor. 5, Paul, being present in spirit and having already pronounced judgment upon the incestuous person in the church (v. 3), tells the Corinthian church, when it is assembled and thus connected with the power of the Lord Jesus Christ, to hand such a person in Christ's name over to Satan "for the destruction of the flesh, so that his spirit may be saved in the day of Christ." In this connection, Paul reprimands the Corinthians (v. 2) for not already having removed this person from their midst and, hence, presupposes that they had the right and the obligation to do so. And precisely because they have not done this but have tolerated the sinner and thereby become complicit in his sin, he now considers a radical measure necessary. He himself as apostle has already passed judgment and now demands that the church, in full assembly, should immediately, without further admonition, judge the sinner in accordance with the plenary authority presently conferred on it by the apostle, indeed, according to the power of Christ himself and in his name. And it should not simply remove the person from its midst, as was desired of it in verse 2, but should specifically hand him over to Satan for physical discipline. Hence what we have here is not an ordinary act of excommunication, as for example in Matt. 18:17, but a special apostolic act of power.

This is also evident from 1 Tim. 1:20 and 2 Tim. 2:17, where Paul in his capacity as apostle, entirely by himself, apart from the congregation, similarly hands Hymenaeus and Alexander over to Satan that they may learn, through discipline, no longer to blaspheme. There is a great difference, accordingly, between these extraordinary punishments and the ordinary practice of discipline enjoined upon the congregation. It is of the latter that Paul speaks in 1 Cor. 5:2 and further in verses 9–13. There he writes that in an earlier letter, which therefore precedes the "first" one, he admonished them not to associate with sexually immoral people. But the

Corinthians, misunderstanding his words, inferred from them that they were to refrain completely from associating, also in civil affairs, with sexually immoral people, the covetous, swindlers, idolaters, or the like outside the church. But that was not the apostle's intent. That would have been an impossible demand, tantamount to asking them to leave this world. All he wanted was that they should not associate with a sexually immoral person if that person was called a brother and was a member of the congregation. Indeed, in that case they should not even eat with him, not in his home, nor invite him to theirs, that is, have no amicable and fraternal relations with him. Instead, while leaving others who are "outside" to the judgment of God, they should remove from their midst the evil person who is part of their own circle (2 Cor. 2:5–10). Elsewhere, Paul speaks along the same lines of the right and duty of the congregation to watch out for and keep away from those who cause divisions and put obstacles in their way (Rom. 16:17); to keep away, in Jesus's name, from every brother whose lifestyle is irregular (2 Thess. 3:6, 14); after a first and second warning, that is, after repeated admonition, to withdraw from, not to have anything to do with (παραιτεῖσθαι, *paraiteisthai*, ask for, decline, reject, avoid), a "heretical" person, who (as member of the church or perhaps someone who has crept in from the outside) destroys the unity of faith in the church (Titus 3:10). John says the same thing: if anyone comes to you and does not bring this teaching, do not let him into your house as a brother, do not have friendly or fraternal relations with him, and do not greet or welcome him as a brother (2 John 10). And finally, in Rev. 2:2 the church at Ephesus is commended because it cannot tolerate wicked people; in 2:14, 20, 24 the churches at Pergamum and Thyatira are reprimanded because they tolerate heretical teachings and pagan abominations.[76]

This teaching of Scripture has been most conscientiously applied in the discipline practiced by Reformed churches. [It is marked by the following seven features:]

1. According to these churches, the objects of this discipline are not impersonal things, writings, buildings, lands, but always persons; and not people in general, for God judges those who are outside (1 Cor. 5:10), not the deceased, not a group or class of people, but always specific individual persons who are members of the church, either by baptism or by profession of faith.

2. The reason for discipline is not an assortment of weaknesses into which believers fall, nor the appalling sins that a Christian government punishes (though the church then follows, its discipline being necessary as well),[77] but the sins that cause offense among the members of the congregation and are not, or only very mildly, punished by the government.[78]

---

76. *Meyer, "Die Lehre des Neuen Testaments von der Kirchenzucht," *Zeitschrift für kirchliche Wissenschaft und kirchliches Leben* 2 (1881).

77. J. Calvin, *Institutes*, IV.xi.3.

78. P. van Mastricht, *Theologia*, VII, 6, 8.

3. In the case of these sins, the sins that call for ecclesiastical discipline, a distinction has to be made between hidden or private sins and public sins. The former are dealt with according to the rule of Matt. 18 and only assume the character of public sins when private admonitions go unheeded, and hence the congregation as a whole, or its representation in the church council, becomes involved.

4. In the case of these sins, made public as a result of obstinacy, or inherently public sins by virtue of their character (murder, adultery, for example), the procedure is as follows: the moment the transgressor shows sincere repentance, all church discipline in the narrow sense stops. The Lord's Supper may still be denied in order that the scandal may be removed from the congregation and the sincerity of the confession may become more evident, but this is, strictly speaking, no longer discipline. Those who confess their sin find mercy with God and therefore also with his church. The discipline that leads to excommunication always starts only after impenitence and obstinacy have been evidenced. In order that the church may be fully convinced of this and does not lightly take the step of removing the sinner from its midst, the church council begins with admonitions. If the transgressor hardens himself against this, he is first of all barred from partaking of the Lord's Supper, and along with this the sin is announced to the congregation but not the name of the sinner; next follows the announcement of the sin along with the name of the sinner, though not before a well-founded advice from the classis has been received; then follows the announcement that, if he continues to persist in his sin, he will be cut off; and finally the expulsion itself, with the formulary of excommunication. The time that has to pass between all these admonition and disciplinary measures cannot be fixed since it is connected with the nature of the sin, the conduct of the transgressor, plus the offense present inside and outside of the congregation.

5. The punishments that the church applies in this connection are purely spiritual. They do not and may not consist in fines, corporal punishment, branding, torture, imprisonment, deprivation of honor, banishment, the death penalty, and so forth, as Rome claims; nor in the dissolution of family, civil, and political connections, as the Anabaptists taught; nor in the exclusion from the public worship services, a remedy applied by the Christian church in the early years. For the weapons of the church are not worldly but spiritual and therefore powerful before God (2 Cor. 10:4). But the discipline of the church is a serious test of whether a person who sinned and despite all admonition still hardens oneself can and may still be regarded as a brother or a sister. Excommunication, accordingly, is finally nothing other, but also nothing less, than a termination of communion; an act of self-withdrawal by the church; a final and painful release of those who acted as though they were brothers or sisters but proved themselves not

to be. It is not an act of delivering someone up to Satan, which in the New Testament occurs only as an apostolic act, neither an act of damnation or a malediction, nor an *anathema*, which is never used as church punishment in the New Testament, not even in Rom. 9:3.[79] It is only, but also nothing less than, a solemn declaration of the church in Jesus's name that the sinner in question has become manifest as not being a sincere brother or sister in Christ, and consequently it is an expulsion from the church and its fellowship in order that God alone may pronounce judgment.

6. Excommunication is an extreme remedy used in order that the person removed from fellowship may repent. Even the apostolic act of turning someone over to Satan still had this meaning (1 Cor. 5:5; 1 Tim. 1:20). Even though the church may view the outcast as though a "pagan" and a "tax collector" because it invested so much time and effort in the person's case without fruit; even though it had to cast someone out in order not to become partakers in the person's sins (1 Cor. 5:6–7; 11:30), still the hope remains that this one is a brother or sister who by admonition will be brought back from the error of their ways (2 Thess. 3:14).

7. For that reason readmission to the church always remains a possibility (Matt. 16:19; 18:18; John 20:23; 2 Cor. 2:5–10). Required then, however, is a preceding public confession that in all other cases may be demanded only with all appropriate caution and according to the judgment of the entire church council.[80]

THE POWER OF MERCY

[516] In the third place, Christ is also a priest who from heaven still consistently exercises this office in his church now. Just as he teaches his own as prophet and governs them as king, so as priest he demonstrates to them the riches of his mercy. When he was on earth, he went through all the towns and villages, not only teaching in their synagogues and preaching the good news of the kingdom, but also healing every disease and sickness among the people (Matt. 9:35). And this was no

---

79. Cf. H. Cremer, *Biblico-Theological Lexicon of New Testament Greek*, trans. D. W. Simon and William Urwick (Edinburgh: T&T Clark; New York: Charles Scribner's Sons, 1895), s.v. ἀνάθεμα.

80. J. Calvin, *Institutes*, IV.xii; Z. Ursinus, *The Commentary of Dr. Zacharius Ursinus on the Heidelberg Catechism*, trans. G. W. Williard (Grand Rapids: Eerdmans, 1954), qu. 83–85; J. Zanchi, *Op. theol.*, IV, 736; A. Polanus, *Synt. theol.*, 544; P. Martyr Vermigli, *Loci comm.*, 411; F. Junius, *Theses theol.*, 47; G. Bucanus, *Inst. theol.*, 531; J. H. Heidegger, *Corpus theologiae*, II, 600; *Synopsis purioris theologiae*, disp. 48; G. Voetius, *Pol. eccl.*, IV, 770–912; P. van Mastricht, *Theologia*, VII, c. 6; B. de Moor, *Comm. theol.*, VI, 400–425; C. Vitringa, *Doctr. christ.*, IX, 1, pp. 498–573. More recently: K. Scheele, *Die Kirchenzucht der evangelischen Kirche* (Halle: R. Mühlmann, 1852); G. K. C. Friedrich Fabri, *Über Kirchenzuch im Sinne und Geiste des Evangeliums* (Stuttgart: Steinkopft, 1854); E. A. Friedberg, "Bann, kirchlicher," in *PRE³*, II, 381–85; G. Uhlhorn, "Kirchenzucht in der ev.-lutherischen Kirche," in *PRE³*, X, 483–85; E. F. K. Müller, "Kirchenzucht in der reformierten Kirche," in *PRE³*, X, 485–92; J. W. Kunze, "Schlüsselgewalt," in *PRE³*, XVII, 621–40; P. Hinschius, "Gerichtsarbeit, kirchliche," in *PRE³*, VI, 585–602; Julius Müller, *Dogmatische Abhandlungen* (Bremen: C. E. Müller, 1870), 496ff.; A. F. C. Vilmar, *Von der christlichen Kirchenzucht* (Marburg: Elwert, 1872); *idem, Kirchenzucht und Lehrzucht* (1877).

secondary and incidental activity but a primary element in the work the Father had charged him to perform (8:17; John 5:36; 9:3–4; and so forth). Manifest in this activity were the fullness of his power and the riches of his mercy. The works of sin and Satan were broken as the result of it. The consequences of sin in the physical world were initially removed by it. They culminated and received their seal and completion in the resurrection, which was the victory over death and the principle of the renewal of all things. Accordingly, when he sent out his disciples, he not only charged them to preach the good news but, with equal firmness and emphasis, to cast out evil spirits and to heal every disease and sickness (Matt. 10:1, 8; Mark 3:15; Luke 9:1–2; 10:9, 17). The disciples not only performed this activity during Jesus's sojourn on earth but also after his ascension (Acts 5:16; 8:7; and so forth).

In that first period, in keeping with Jesus's own promise (Mark 16:17–18), many extraordinary gifts of healing and manifestations of power were granted to his disciples (Acts 2:44–45; 4:35; Rom. 12:7–8; 1 Cor. 12:28). As things went with the gifts of teaching and government, however, so they went with the works of mercy. The extraordinary state of the church gradually normalized, and although the gifts were not suppressed or destroyed, they were nevertheless increasingly linked with the offices: doctrine was assigned to the teacher (διδασκαλος, *didaskalos*), government to the presbyter, and similarly the ministry of mercy to the deacon (Acts 6). And the gifts themselves, though remaining the gifts of the Holy Spirit, became more simple and ordinary. While Rome claims that miracle-working power continues to operate in its midst, more beautiful than those miracles of which it boasts are the works of mercy that powerfully testify to its faith and love. For when the diaconate gradually but completely changed its character in the Christian church, the treasures of love and mercy that Christ poured out in his church richly manifested themselves in private benevolence. Even though the organization of the ministry of mercy in the Roman Catholic Church leaves much to be desired, among Christian churches the Roman Catholic Church still ranks first in the works of charity. For while the Reformed churches did restore the office of deacon, they did not properly define and regulate its role and ministry nor develop its outreach.

This development, which the distress of our times calls for, can in the main occur only along the following lines, [as I propose:]

1. That the diaconal office be honored more than it has been up until now as an independent organ of the priestly mercy of Christ.
2. That love and mercy be recognized and practiced as the most outstanding Christian virtues.
3. That deacons be instructed to persuade all the members of the church, particularly the wealthier ones, in the name of Christ, to practice mercy and to warn and guard them against the sin of covetousness, which is a root of all evil.
4. That the diaconate stimulate, regulate, and guide—not kill—the practice of private benevolence.

5. That in large churches the bearers of this office avail themselves, if necessary, of the assistance of deaconesses in the same way the two other offices employ catechists and pastoral visitors of the sick.

6. That they distribute their gifts, in Christ's name, as taken from the tables of the Lord on which they have been deposited by the congregation and given to Christ himself (Matt. 25:40).

7. That they extend their help to all the poor, the sick, the strangers, the prisoners, the mentally retarded, the mentally ill, the widows and orphans, in a word, to all the wretched and needy who exist in the church and are either completely or partly deprived of help from other sources, and that by word and deed they seek to relieve their suffering.

8. That the ministry of mercy be given a much larger place on the agenda of all ecclesiastical assemblies than has been the case up until now.

9. That, along with ministers and elders, deacons be delegated to the major assemblies of the churches and be given a vote in all matters pertaining to the ministry of mercy.

10. That at these assemblies the ministry of mercy be organized in terms of general principles, bearing in mind the difference in congregational circumstances; that for general needs it be undertaken communally and expanded by asking the local church to assist other churches and further by assisting poor and oppressed fellow believers abroad.

11. That this diaconal work be maintained as an independent ministry and not absorbed in or fused with the work of inner mission[81] or state welfare, which bear a very different character.[82]

CHURCH ASSEMBLIES

[517] This power, granted to his church by Christ, in the local church comes together in the church council. According to the New Testament, every local church is independent, a "complete church" (*ecclesia completa*), and therefore, like

81. Ed. note: Inner Mission: "The term and work of the Inner Mission are more comprehensive than Home Missions, and include, not only efforts to spread the gospel by preaching, but also various other agencies for the spiritual, as well as physical, welfare of the destitute" (Schaff-Herzog, eds., *Encyclopedia of Religious Knowledge*, II, 1089).

82. J. Calvin, *Institutes*, IV.iii.9; W. Musculus, *Loci communes theologiae sacrae* (Basel: Heruagiana, 1567), 425; H. Bullinger, *Decades*, V, serm. 3; J. Zanchi, *Op. theol.*, IV, 765; F. Junius, *Op. theol. select.*, I, 1566; G. Bucanus, *Inst. theol.*, 494; G. Voetius, *Pol. eccl.*, III, 496–513; C. Vitringa, *Doctr. christ.*, IX, 272–96; G. Uhlhorn, *Die christliche Liebesthätigkeit*, 3 vols. (Stuttgart: D. Gundert, 1882–90); *G. N. Bonwetsch, *Das Amt der Diakonie in der alten Kirche* (1890); H. Seesemann and N. Bonwetsch, *Das Amt der Diakonissen in der alten Kirche* (Mitau: Steffenhagen, 1891); Th. Schäfer, "Diakonik," in O. Zöckler, *Handbuch der theologischen Wissenschaften*, 3rd ed., 5 vols. (Nördlingen and Munich: C. H. Beck, 1889–90), III, 538–72; E. C. Achelis, *Lehrbuch der praktischen Theologie*, II, 324–451; P. Wurster, *Die Lehre von der Inneren Mission* (Berlin: Reuther & Reichard, 1895); Th. Schäfer, *Leitfaden der Inneren Mission*, 4th ed. (Hamburg: Agentur des Rauhen Hauses, 1903); H. Rahlenbeck, "Mission, innere," in *PRE*³, XIII, 90–100; A. Kuyper, *Encyclopaedie*, III, 535ff.; P. Biesterveld, J. van Lonkhuijzen, and R. J. W. Rudolph, *Het diaconaat* (Hilversum: J. H. Witzel, 1907).

the church in its entirety, bears the name "temple of God" (1 Cor. 3:16–17; 2 Cor. 6:16), "bride" (2 Cor. 11:2), or "body of Christ" (1 Cor. 12:27). Believers do not stand apart in isolation from each other but constitute a unity; in the same way the office-bearers in a local church do not remain detached from each other but join together to form a church council. Traces of this occur already in the New Testament. Believers in Jerusalem, after being incorporated by baptism into the church, came together from time to time, devoting themselves to the apostle's teaching and fellowship, to the breaking of bread and the prayers (Acts 1:14; 2:41ff.; 5:12; and so forth), and were subject to the leadership of the company of the apostles, who were soon assisted in this role by the presbyters (6:2; 15:2, 6, 22). All sorts of circumstances—the gifts of the Holy Spirit, particularly those of teaching, prophecy, and glossolalia; the assemblies of believers; the administration of Word and sacraments; the ingathering of the offerings; the care of the poor; and so forth—automatically made leadership and organization, consultation and deliberation, a necessity. Initially the apostles as much as possible provided for these needs, took measures, and made decisions (15:28ff.; 1 Cor. 11:4–6, 34; 14:27ff.; 16:1; 1 Tim. 3; and so forth). For in the church of Christ everything had to be done "decently and in order," peacefully and for edification (1 Cor. 14:26, 33, 40). But when the office of elder was instituted, they were charged with the leadership and government of the church, and soon they formed a body among themselves called a *presbyterium* (1 Tim. 4:14). Under such a body of elders, however, the churches in the early period enjoyed a large measure of independence and were regularly consulted in important matters. In Acts 1 the disciples come together for the election of an apostle. In Acts 6 the church chooses [the] deacons. In Acts 15 it attends the gathering of apostles and elders. In 1 Cor. 5 it exercises discipline. The first synods were meetings of the local church. But also the local churches together form a unity. Collectively they too are called an ἐκκλησια (*ekklēsia* [sing.]). They are all subject to the apostles, to whom has been given the task of leading and governing the whole church. All together they are one in Christ, hence one in doctrine, in faith, in baptism, in love; they greet one another (Rom. 16:16; 1 Cor. 16:20; 2 Cor. 13:12), serve each other with gifts of love (Rom. 15:26; 1 Cor. 16:1; 2 Cor. 8:1, 4; 9:1ff.; Gal. 2:10), and share with each other the letters they have received from the apostles (Col. 4:16). It was therefore completely natural that these churches, who were spiritually united, should consult with each other in matters of general interest.

The first example of this occurs in Acts 15, occasioned by the question of whether the Gentiles could be saved without being circumcised. The church of Antioch sent Paul and Barnabas and a handful of others to Jerusalem to exchange ideas on this important question with the apostles and elders there and so to arrive at unanimity. The apostles and elders, accordingly, held a meeting with these representatives from Antioch (15:6), a meeting that was perhaps attended also by the members of the Jerusalem church (15:12, 22; in v. 23 the words και οἱ [*kai hoi*] should probably be omitted before ἀδελφοι [*adelphoi*]). After much discussion and debate, those present not only formulated advice but also made a decision in the Holy Spirit, which was binding for the brothers in Antioch, Syria, and Cilicia, conveyed to them by a letter, and further also explained orally by Judas and Silas in a meeting of the congregation (15:22–31).

All these meetings reported in the New Testament were assemblies of the local church, attended only in Acts 15 by representatives from other places. This custom [of congregational involvement] was also followed later, as early as the second century. In important matters such as the appointment or deposition of a bishop, excommunication, the absolution of mortal sins, and so forth, not only did the presbyterium offer leadership, but the congregation also gave its consent. Cyprian still writes that from the beginning of his episcopate he did nothing without the advice of his presbyterium and the consent of the congregation.[83] Present at the synods of the second and third century, therefore, are not only the bishops but also the presbyters, deacons, and ordinary church members. Even the Council of Nicea was attended, aside from bishops, also by presbyters, deacons, and members who took part in the debates. And the delegates who were invited to congregational meetings of neighboring churches in that period were absolutely not only bishops but also included presbyters, deacons, or other members of the church. But the result of the development of the hierarchical idea was that the consent of the congregation was increasingly less frequently requested, the presbyters and deacons were detached from the congregation and changed into counselors and helpers of the bishop, and the synods were gradually held only by bishops.

In the second and third century, moreover, all congregational meetings, attended by delegates from neighboring churches, were equal in rank. There was as yet no hierarchy of ecclesiastical assemblies; there were as yet no provincial, metropolitan, or ecumenical councils. All assemblies took place in the name of Christ, made decisions in the Holy Spirit, and concerned the whole of Christianity (*concilium universale, catholicum*). But that too underwent change. Already in the third century there occurred specifically provincial synods, that is, assemblies of bishops held in a specific province. Additionally, in the fourth century, as a result of the huge controversies that divided the church, synods of bishops from various provinces were held. And the Council of Nicea, though absolutely not representative of Christianity as a whole (since it was attended only by a few bishops from the West), was nevertheless convened from all directions by the emperor. Thus gradually there emerged a ranking of provincial, national, patriarchal, and ecumenical councils.[84] But the characteristic feature of an ecumenical council is hard to designate. It cannot consist in the fact that it has been called together by the pope, for from the fourth to the tenth century it was convoked

83. Cyprian, *Epistles* 14.4.

84. R. Sohm, *Kirchenrecht*, 247–344; A. Hauck, "Synoden," in *PRE*³, XIX, 262ff.; von Harnack, *The Mission and Expansion of Christianity*, trans. J. Moffatt (New York: Harper, 1908), II, 172; O. Berzl, *Ursprung, Aufgabe, und Wesen der christlichen Synoden* (Würzburg: Stadenraus, 1908; ed. note: Bavinck erroneously cites the author as G. Osten).

by the emperor. Neither can it consist in the universal validity and momentous importance of its decisions, for the canons of ecumenical synods have frequently been rejected, while those of provincial synods were adopted. Nor can it consist in the fact that an ecumenical council represents the whole of Christianity, for this was far from being the case with the so-called ecumenical councils. Granted, toward the end of the Middle Ages the theory arose that a council was ecumenical and infallible only when it consisted of representatives from all the churches. But this theory was revolutionary in origin, led in practice to all sorts of difficulties, and was never accepted by Rome. To Rome a council is ecumenical only when its decrees have been endorsed by the pope and have thereby acquired an infallible, universally binding character.[85]

In Protestant churches, a synodical church government developed first on French soil. Synods did in fact occur in the Lutheran Church but consisted only in meetings of pastors. In 1528 at Zurich, Zwingli instituted synods convoked by the [city] council, consisting of preachers from the city and the country and a few members of the [city] council, that mainly had to weigh complaints against the teaching and conduct of the preachers.[86] Calvin similarly laid down in the *Ecclesiastical Ordinances* that the preachers had to assemble every three months to supervise each other's teaching and conduct and, additionally, introduced an annual visitation in 1546.[87] In 1526, Franz Lambert designed for Hesse a church order in which congregational meetings as well as synods, consisting of preachers and delegates appointed by the churches, were included, but this church order never took effect.[88] A synodical church order first came into being in France, where the churches were fast expanding and, out of a need for unity, first came together in synod at Paris on May 26, 1559, and united in adopting a common confession and church order.[89] Remarkable here is that the general synod originated first, that this synod introduced the provincial synods, and that later, in 1572, a classis was inserted between the provincial synods and local church councils.[90]

Later such a synodical form of church government was also introduced in other Reformed churches: in Poland, Bohemia, Hungary, Germany, the Netherlands, Scotland, England, America, and so forth. But soon opposition arose against it from two directions. The Remonstrants, taking their cue from Zwingli and

85. R. Bellarmine, "De conciliis et ecclesia lib.," in *Controversiis*, bks. I and II; J. B. Heinrich and K. Gutberlet, *Dogmatische Theologie*, II, 476ff.; J. Wilhelm and T. B. Scannell, *A Manual of Catholic Theology*, I, 230ff.; F. H. Vering, *Lehrbuch des katholischen, orientalischen, und protestantischen Kirchenrechts*, 613ff.

86. J. K. Mörikofer, *Ulrich Zwingli, nach den urkundlichen Quellen,* 2 vols. (Leipzig: Hirzel, 1867–69), II, 118ff.

87. F. W. Kampschulte and W. Goetz, *Johann Calvin: Seine Kirche und sein Staat in Genf,* 2 vols. (Leipzig: Duncker & Humblot, 1869–99), I, 408.

88. G. V. Lechler, *Geschichte der Presbyterial- und Synodalverfassung seit der Reformation* (Leiden: Noothoven van Goor, 1854), 14ff.

89. Ibid., 69.

90. Ibid., 81; cf. for Scotland, 97; H. E. von Hoffmann, *Das Kirchenverfassungsrecht der niederländischen Reformierten bis zum Beginne der Dordrechter Nationalsynode von 1618/19* (Leipzig: Hirschfeld, 1902).

Erastus, assigned ecclesiastical power to the government and deduced from this arrangement that, though synods were permissible, they were neither mandatory nor necessary to the being or well-being of the church, and that when they were held, the right to convocation, delegation, the establishment of an agenda, and determining the presidency belonged to the government.[91] The Independents, under the influence of the error of the Anabaptists, went even farther, considered every group of believers independent, and rejected every binding classical or synodical linkage.[92] And, indeed, the grounds that can be advanced against synodical church governments are weighty. For in the New Testament the local churches are all completely independent in relation to each other, and there is not a word in it about a legal, binding classical or synodical connection. Such a connection also seems completely at variance with the independence of local churches because it introduces assemblies that are above the local churches and act with authority over them, and thus again introduces an impermissible hierarchy and tyranny into the church of Christ. Additionally, the history of synods does not always speak well of their usefulness and frequently makes them appear to be the cause of all sorts of dissension and division, so that Gregory of Nazianzus could already say, "I saw the end of not even one synod as being useful," and there is some truth in the proverb that "every council gives birth to [further] battles."

Other considerations, however, clearly bring out the necessity and usefulness of synods.

1. In the New Testament there was as yet no classical or synodical connection among the churches, but neither was there as yet any need for them, since the apostles themselves were there. They assisted the churches with advice and also took care of them by evangelists as their substitutes.
2. Already then, the churches were connected in various ways by spiritual ties and obtained the right, not only to assemble by themselves, but also to send delegates to other churches and to request adjudication in certain disputes; Acts 1; 6; 15; and 21 show that in a very general sense "synods" are "permitted by divine law."
3. Though synods are not strictly necessary for the "being" of the church, and are not specifically mandated by the Word of God, they are permitted and necessary to the "well-being" of the church.
4. This necessity arises from the fact that the unity of doctrine, discipline, and worship to which the church is called, the order and peace and love it has to preserve, and the common interests assigned to it (such as the training,

91. J. Uytenbogaert, *Tractaet van t'ampt ende authoriteyt eener hoogher christelicker overheydt in kerckelicke saecken* ('s Gravenhage: Hillebrant Jacobsz., 1610), 107ff.; P. van Limborch, *Theologia christiana* (Amsterdam: Arnhold, 1735), VII, 19.

92. Robinson, according to Kist and Royaards, *Ned. Archief voor Kerk Geschiedenis* 8 (1848): 371ff.; D. Neal, *Historie der rechtzinnige Puriteinen*, 3 vols. (Rotterdam: Kentlink, 1752–53), II, 96; ed. note: ET: *The History of the Puritans or Protestant Non-conformists*, 2 vols. (London: J. Buckland, 1754).

calling, and sending out of ministers; evangelism; the support of needy churches; and so forth) can only come into their own by means of synods.

5. Synods are not a pedestal for hierarchy but the subversion of all hierarchy; they maintain the independence of local churches and protect them from confusion, division, pastoral hierarchy, and domination by a handful of members; and they confirm the freedom of ministries by giving them support in the connection with other churches and by permitting them to appeal to the major assemblies.

6. Neither are they a cause of divisions and dissensions but a means of settling the disputes that invariably arise in the church on earth over doctrine, discipline, and ministry. They do this in a peaceful manner, by careful investigation, and with ample discussion.

7. In order that they may serve their purpose, synods ought always to be assemblies of churches whose members (pastors, presbyters, deacons, or ordinary members) are the delegates of churches and bound to the credentialed letters of instruction from churches; to be convoked by the churches themselves and not by a government or pope, and so forth, and led by ecclesiastical persons chosen to serve in this capacity; and to freely and independently, without interference from the government, judge and decide ecclesiastical matters.

8. Ecclesiastical assemblies (local, classical, provincial, general, ecumenical) do not differ from each other in essence. One assembly is not per se higher, weightier, less exposed to error, or more assured of the leading of the Holy Spirit than another. For every church and each group of churches is independent vis-à-vis the others, and all are equally bound to the Word and share equally in the promise of the Spirit. Assembling in ecclesiastical gatherings are not the representatives of the people but the office-bearers of the church who are called, in Christ's name, to govern his church. Accordingly, they are distinguished, not by a different kind of power or a higher power, but only by more power—power that is brought together from and extends to a larger territory.

9. The authority of all ecclesiastical assemblies is none other than that of the churches themselves: it is subject to the word of Christ. Christ alone has authority in the churches and its various assemblies. His word alone is decisive. Only that which the Holy Spirit approves in and through the members is binding in the church of Christ. But even these decisions, decisions made according to the Word and under the guidance of the Spirit, the church can only maintain by moral means. It has no controlling or coercive but only ministerial power.[93]

93. J. Calvin, *Institutes*, IV.ix; A. Polanus, *Synt. theol.*, 541; H. Bullinger, *Von den Concilijs* (Zurich: Christoffel Froschower, 1561; ed. note: Bavinck cites a Dutch edition from 1611); P. Martyr Vermigli, *Loci comm.*, 407; F. Junius, *Op. theol. select.*, II, 1029; idem, *Theses Salmurienses*, III, 505; M. Amyraut, *Du gouvernement de l'Église, conte ceux qui veulent abolir l'usage de l'autorité des Synodes* (Saumur, 1653); J. H. Heidegger, *Corpus theologiae,*

THE CHURCH'S UNIQUE SPIRITUAL POWER

[518] Thus the church exists in the midst of the world with an origin, essence, activity, and purpose of its own. While in every respect it is distinct from that world, it never stands apart from or alongside the world. Various schools of thought in Christianity have indeed construed the church and the world as existing in an absolute ethical antithesis to each other, equating creation and re-creation with sin and grace. But these schools, however powerful they may have been now and then, have nonetheless never controlled the history of Christianity and could only lead a sectarian life alongside the churches. Apart from these schools, there are only two ways the relationship between the church and the world can be defined, the Roman Catholic and the Protestant way, the supernatural and the ethical way. Rome does not view the natural as sinful in the manner of Anabaptism and thus does not advocate avoidance and separation, but it does teach that the natural is of a lower order, easily becomes the cause of sin, and therefore needs the restraint of the supernatural. Just as the image of God as a supernatural image is added to "the natural man," so grace is mechanically added to nature from above, the church to the world, the higher to the lower morality. Those who want to live according to the ideal of Rome have to become ascetics, suppress the natural, and devote themselves totally to religion. Those unable to do this obtain the necessary space for the natural and find in the supernatural the boundary that marks the limits of this space.

The relationship between the church and the world that Protestantism adopted as true was very different. It replaced the quantitative, supernaturalist antithesis with an ethical one. The natural was not of a lower order but in its kind was as sound and pure as the supernatural, inasmuch as it had been created by the same God who revealed himself in the re-creation [of the world] as the Father of the Lord Jesus Christ. Only it had been corrupted by sin and therefore had to be reconciled and renewed by the grace of Christ. Grace, accordingly, serves here not to avoid, to suppress, or to kill the natural, but precisely to free it from its sinful corruption and to make it truly natural again. True, in applying these principles Luther stopped halfway, left the natural untouched, and restricted Christianity too severely to the domain of religion and ethics. But Calvin, the

---

II, 613; F. Turretin, *Institutes of Elenctic Theology*, XVIII, qu. 33; *Synopsis purioris theologiae*, disp. 49; G. Voetius, *Pol. eccl.*, IV, 114–272; lecture by C. Vitringa, *On Synods*, translated from the Latin by S. H. Van Idsinga (Haarlem, 1741); ed. note: This work is not found in the 8-volume *Doctrina christianae religionis*; Bavinck may be referring to *De synagoga vetere libri tres, quibus tum de nominibus, structura, origine, praefectis, ministris et sacris synagogarum agitur, tum praecipue, formam regiminis & ministerii earum in ecclesiam christianam* (1726); ET: *The Synagogue and the Church: Being an Attempt to Show That the Government, Ministers and Services of the Church Were Derived from Those of the Synagogue*, trans. Joshua L. Bernard (London: B. Fellowes, 1842); B. de Moor, *Comm. theol.*, VI, 439–61; C. Vitringa, *Doctr. christ.*, IX, 1, 574–653; Ch. Hodge, *Discussions on Church Polity* (New York: Charles Scribner's Sons, 1878), 364–456; K. Lechler, *Die neutestamentliche Lehre vom heiligen Ambte*, 254–75; F. J. Stahl, *Die Kirchenverfassung nach Lehre und Recht der Protestanten*, 2nd ed. (Erlangen: T. Bläsing, 1862), 332ff.; A. Hauck, "Synoden," in *PRE³*, XIX, 262–77.

man of action, who came after Luther and could therefore compare or contrast himself to Luther, continued the work of reformation and tried to reform all of life by Christianity. "Avoidance" is the cry of the Anabaptists; "ascesis" that of the Roman Catholics; "renewal" and "sanctification" that of the Protestant, especially of the Reformed, Christian.

This last view is, without doubt, the richest and most beautiful. There is only one God, after all, both in creation and in re-creation. The God of creation and of the Old Testament is not lower than the God of the re-creation, than the Father of Christ, than the God of the new covenant. Christ, the mediator of the new covenant, is also he by whom God created all things. And the Holy Spirit, who is the author of regeneration and sanctification, is the same as he who in the beginning hovered over the waters and adorned the heavens. Creation and re-creation, therefore, cannot be contrasted in terms of being lower and higher. They are both good and pure—splendid works of the one Triune God. Moreover, while it is true that the sin that entered the world has corrupted everything—not only the spiritual life, the ethical-religious life, but also the whole of the natural life, the body, the family, society, the whole world—yet that sin is not substantial or material but "formal" and hence not identical with the created world but dwelling in and attached to the created world and can, therefore, always be separated and removed from it by the grace of God. Substantially and materially the creation after the fall is the same as before the fall: it remains a work of God and is therefore to be honored and acclaimed. To regain that fallen world, God introduced the forces of grace into his creation. Neither is grace a substance or matter, enclosed in Word or sacrament and distributed by the priest, but a renewing and transforming force. It is not per se supernatural but only bears that character on account of sin and hence has it, in a sense incidentally and temporarily, for the purpose of restoring the creation.

This grace is distributed in a twofold form: as common grace with a view toward restraining [evil] and as special grace with a view to renewing [the world]. Both have their unity in Christ, the king of the realm of power and grace. Both are directed against sin; both ensure the connectedness between creation and re-creation. Neither has the world been left to itself after the fall, nor deprived of all grace, but it is sustained and spared by common grace, guided and preserved for special grace in Christ. Separation and suppression, accordingly, are impermissible and impossible. Humans and Christians are not two separate entities. The creation is incorporated and restored in [the process of] re-creation. Persons who are born again are substantially no different from what they were before regeneration. Incorporated in the church, they nevertheless remain in the world and must only be kept from the evil one. Just as Christ the Son of God took a full human nature from the womb of Mary and, having that nature, did not regard anything human and natural as strange, so the Christian is nothing other than a reborn, renewed, and hence, a truly human person. The same people who are Christians are and remain in the same calling with which they were called; they remain members of a family, members of a society, subjects of the government, practitioners of the arts and sciences, men or women, parents or children, masters or servants, and so forth.

Accordingly, the relationship that has to exist between the church and the world is in the first place organic, moral, and spiritual in character. Christ—even now—is prophet, priest, and king; and by his Word and Spirit he persuasively impacts the entire world. Because of him there radiates from everyone who believes in him a renewing and sanctifying influence upon the family, society, state, occupation, business, art, science, and so forth. The spiritual life is meant to refashion the natural and moral life in its full depth and scope according to the laws of God. Along this organic path Christian truth and the Christian life are introduced into all the circles of the natural life, so that life in the household and the extended family is restored to honor, the wife (woman) is again viewed as the equal of the husband (man), the sciences and arts are Christianized, the level of the moral life is elevated, society and state are reformed, laws and institutions, morals and customs are made Christian.

But there is still another way of regulating the relationship between church and state that is much more difficult and about which there is the greatest difference of opinion. Christ rules his church also by the offices and institutions. And the question is whether the church's relation to the various areas of the natural life can also be regulated officially and institutionally. The two opposites here are papalism and Caesaropapism. Caesaropapism regulates the relationship so that the church is subject to the Christian state and must conduct itself in accordance with its laws. There is some validity in this arrangement: the relationship of the church to the state has become very different, since the latter became Christian. Before the government became Christian, for example, many more sins fell under Christian discipline than afterward. Attendance at pagan festivals, idolatry, emperor worship, sabbath-breaking, perjury, blasphemy, marriages in forbidden degrees [of consanguinity], appalling sins of fornication and adultery, and so forth were in fact recognized and punished by the church but not by the state. Since the government was Christianized, however, there has been much greater agreement between them in moral outlook and judgment. In many cases, therefore, the church can appropriately wait for the treatment of serious offenses by the department of justice and needs no courts of its own. Still too much is inferred from this when people intellectually take away all power from the church and assign it to the Christian government. For the power of the church has essentially remained the same, however significantly its exercise has been modified. The ministry of Word and sacraments, after all, is the inalienable right of the church. In addition there are always many sins left—such as Sabbath-breaking, fornication, drunkenness, cursing, and so forth—that are either not at all punished by the government or, when the offenses are public and offensive, very mildly. Finally, even with respect to offenders whom the government punishes, the church does have a task of its own, for while the government is satisfied with the imposition of penalties, the church seeks to convict, convert, and save them.[94]

On the other side is the papal system, which indeed deserves praise insofar as it maintains the independence and freedom of the church, but for the rest seeks to subject, if not the whole world, then surely all of baptized Christianity in all of its spheres and relations, judicially and legally, to the pope. In the view of Rome, the family, society, the state, art, science, and so forth have to be ecclesiastical, for to be ecclesiastical is identical with being Christian, Roman Catholic, papal. This claim of Rome is not meant morally and spiritually, so that everyone who does not submit to the pope is by that token guilty before God. But it means that all who refuse to obey the pope are judicially and legally guilty before this vicar of Christ, can be punished by him if he deems it useful and he has the power to do it, and can be coerced into obedience, not only by spiritual and moral means but also by corporal and civil penalties. From this papal tyranny the religious courage and spiritual vitality of Luther and Calvin have delivered us. Their mighty act of reformation consisted in the fact that they restored the religious-ethical significance of Christianity as the religion of grace and delivered the realm of the natural, not from this Christianity but from the jurisdiction of the Roman Catholic Church.

From this position it naturally followed that the link between the church and the world could—aside from the above-mentioned organic mode—only be forged contractually. It is true that Calvin clung with might and main to the proposition that the government was subject to God's Word, that it had to maintain both tables of the law and listen to the church as interpreter of God's Word, and that it also had to punish with civil penalties the various offenses over which the church exercised discipline. He indeed sharply and clearly drew a boundary line between church and state but did so differently than we do. The area in which both church and state had authority was much larger than we today define it as being. Also in its domain and in its measure, the government as Christian government had to guard the honor of God, the vitality of his church, and the expansion of his kingdom. Nevertheless, the relationship between church and state, Calvin said, is contractual and free. The church has no choice but to preach the Word of God, to witness to his commandments in his name; but if the government or anyone else refused to listen, then the church, then Calvin himself, then any Christian whatever, no longer had any power or right to resort to coercion. All that is left, then, is passive resistance.[95] Such resistance, too, is a form of action, for as Doumergue so elegantly puts it, "It is the submission only of the body, not of the soul. Humbled before the God who chastises him, the Calvinist remains the relentless judge of the despot who oppresses him. There are submissions more deadly to tyranny than insurrections would be!"[96]

94. J. Calvin, *Institutes*, IV.xi.4.
95. J. Calvin, *Institutes*, IV.xx.29; B. de Moor, *Comm. theol.*, VI, 513.
96. É. Doumergue, *Calvin, la fondateur des libertés modernes* (Montauban: J. Granie, 1898), 14.

However, with respect to the government and every human being, all right to practice coercion and inflict punishment had been taken from the church, and Christianity was restored and respected as a purely spiritual power. The government, like every human being, remained responsible only to God for its unbelief, its rejection of the Word of God, for its violation of his commandments, and for the persecution and oppression of his church. If, however, the government freely and independently professed the Christian, that is, the Reformed, religion—which, it was constantly told from the pulpit, was in any case its duty and calling—then it followed that in its capacity as government and its sphere of jurisdiction, it had to promote this religion as well as oppose and root out heresy and idolatry. The error in this connection is not that the Christian government was charged with the promotion of God's honor and service, but that the boundary lines between state and church were mistakenly drawn, and unbelief and heresy and so forth were viewed as crimes against the state. In the age of the Reformation this was probably inevitable. But ever since the task of the government has been restricted in this respect, nations have become free and come of age, churches have increasingly split and divided, all sorts of movements in thought and conduct have made their appearance, and increasing numbers of people have more clearly discerned the difference between crime and sin and recognized all coercion as being definitely in conflict with the Christian confession.

In regulating the relationship between the church and the state, therefore, we must remember the following:

1. Though its witness has been weakened by its multiformity, the church cannot resist stating the demand that all creatures, arts, sciences, family, society, state, and so forth must submit to the Word of the Lord.
2. This demand is only a message, a moral witness, and may never be urged upon people, directly or indirectly, by means of coercion or punishment.
3. A Christian, or Reformed, government has the calling to promote the honor of God, to protect his church, and to destroy the realm of the antichrist.
4. However, it can and may do this only with means that are compatible with the nature of the gospel of Christ and only in the area that has been entrusted to its care.
5. Being itself responsible to God for its attitude toward his Word, it may neither interfere with the rights of the individual, nor with those of the family, society, arts and sciences, and is not responsible, accordingly, for what happens within these areas that is contrary to God's Word and law.
6. It must draw a boundary line between sin and crime according to the demand of the gospel and in keeping with the guidance of divine providence in the history of nations. These lines do not coincide with those between the first and second table of the law, for many sins against the second table fall outside the jurisdiction of the government, and many others against the

first table (perjury, Sabbath-breaking) are also punishable by a Christian government.

7. No one can designate fixed boundaries in the abstract, for they vary with different peoples and in different ages and can only be somewhat determined in their basic direction by the witness of the popular conscience.[97]

97. From the abundant literature on church and state, only the following will be cited here: E. Schall, *Die Staatsverfassung der Juden* (Leipzig: R. Werther, 1896); W. Köhler, *Die Entstehung des Problems Staat und Kirche* (Tübingen: Mohr, 1903); A. Pieper, *Christentum, römisches Kaisertum und heidnischer Staat* (Münster: Aschendorff, 1907); H. Weinel, *Die Stellung des Urchristenthums zum Staat* (Tübingen: Mohr, 1908); A. von Harnack, "Kirche und Staat bis zur Gründung der Staatskirche," in *Die christliche Religion,* ed. Paul Hinneberg (Berlin and Leipzig: Teubner, 1905), 129–60 (ed. note: Bavinck cites this from *Die Kultur der Gegenwart*); Th. Zahn, "Konstantin der Grosse und die Kirche," in *Skizzen aus dem Leben der alten Kirche*, 209–37; B. Seidel, *Die Lehre vom Staat beim heiligen Augustinus* (Breslau: G. P. Aderholz, 1909; ed. note: Bavinck erroneously cites this as *Die Lehre des heiligen Augustinus vom Staat*); J. Baumann, *Die Staatslehre des heiligen Thomas von Aquino* (Leipzig: S. Hirzel, 1873); G. von Schulthess-Rechberg, *Luther, Zwingli und Calvin in ihren Ansichten über das Verhältnis von Staat und Kirche* (Aarau: H. R. Sauerländer, 1909); K. Holl, *Luther und das landesherrliche Kirchenregiment* (Tübingen: Mohr, 1911). In addition, see the following general treatments: J. Hergenröther, *Katholische Kirche und christlicher Staat in ihrer geschichtlicher Entwicklung und in Beziehung auf die Fragen der Gegenwart,* 1st ed. (Freiburg i.B.: Herder, 1872); F. H. Geffcken, *Staat und Kirche, in ihrem Verhältniss geschichtlich entwickelt* (Berlin: Hertz, 1875); O. Mayer, "Staat und Kirche," in *PRE*[3], XVIII, 707–27.

8

THE SPIRIT'S MEANS OF GRACE:
PROCLAMATION

How does Christ communicate his benefits to his people, to the church? Does he use means? Mystics deny this; Rome insists that they are essential and tied to the sacramental power of the institutional church's priesthood. The Reformation adopted a position in between this mystical undervaluation and magical overvaluation of the means of grace.

According to the Reformation, Christ is the complete Savior, the only mediator between God and humanity, but he also instituted an official body of ministers (not priests!) to proclaim the Word of God. The Reformation changed the medieval Roman understanding of grace from a sacerdotal power to a spiritual power of the Word. Not the church but Scripture was regarded as the means of grace. Yet against mysticism, which denied the necessity of the means of grace in Word and sacraments, the Reformation understood the Word and sacraments to be God's ordinary means of imparting grace. The church is the mother of believers, and the offices are instituted for the administration of the Word and sacraments. Means of grace may never be detached from the person and work of Christ nor from the church he instituted on earth.

The most important means of grace is the word of God. Since the Word contains both the law and the gospel, the covenant of works and the covenant of grace, it has a universal significance even beyond its public proclamation in church as a means of grace. For this reason, we must distinguish between the "word of God" and Scripture. The "word of God" does not come only in the form of Scripture and its public proclamation; it also comes to us indirectly, secondarily, having been absorbed from Scripture into the consciousness of the church or a society of people. Above all, it is not merely a sound but also a power and the accomplishment of God's will (Isa. 55:11).

The Word is differentiated into law and gospel. The law finds its end in Christ, who sets believers free from the curse of the law (Gal. 3:13; 4:5) so that they may walk

Ed. note: The four chapters that follow (8–11) are treated as one chapter (chapter X: "Over de Middelen der Genade" [Concerning the Means of Grace]) in the original Dutch. Though we have divided them into four distinct chapters for this volume, the titles continue to reflect Bavinck's original intent.

according to the Spirit and delight in God's law in their inner selves. Antinomianism exacerbates the antithesis between law and gospel, while nomism weakens or cancels the antithesis. Rome equated the old and new covenants with law and gospel respectively, and denied the presence of the gospel in the Old Testament and that of the law in the New Testament, but by accepting its laws and threats turned the gospel into a new law, thereby erasing the Pauline antithesis of law and gospel.

The Reformation, however, held to the unity of the covenant of grace in its two dispensations while at the same time sharply contrasting law and gospel. According to the Reformed tradition, law and gospel describe two revelations of the divine will. The law is God's holy, wise, good, and spiritual will, which on account of sin has now been made powerless, fails to justify, and increases sin and condemnation. The gospel, as the fulfillment of the Old Testament promise, has Christ as its content and conveys grace, reconciliation, forgiveness, righteousness, peace, freedom, and life. The law proceeds from God's holiness, is known from nature, addresses all people, demands perfect righteousness, gives eternal life by works, and condemns. By contrast, the gospel proceeds from God's grace, is known only from special revelation, addresses only those who hear, grants perfect righteousness, produces good works in faith, and acquits. Faith and repentance are always components of gospel, not of law. The gospel, therefore, always presupposes the law and differs from it especially in content.

Since the law is an expression of God's being, humans are naturally subject to it. The law is everlasting; it was inscribed on Adam's heart, is again engraved on the heart of the believer by the Holy Spirit, and in heaven all believers will live according to it. While the law no longer makes demands upon the believer as a condition for salvation, it is still the believer's object of delight and meditation. Accordingly, the law must always be proclaimed in the church alongside the gospel.

Besides the relationship between law and gospel, there is often disagreement over the power and efficacy of the Word, as well as the relationship between Word and Spirit. Nomism (Judaism, Pelagianism, rationalism, Romanism) considers the special supernatural power of the Holy Spirit superfluous, while antinomianism (Anabaptism, mysticism) expects everything from the inner light of the Holy Spirit and finds in the Word only a sign and shadow.

By contrast, both Lutherans and Reformed, against nomism and antinomianism alike, taught that though the Holy Spirit can work apart from the Word, ordinarily Word and Spirit go together. Lutherans, however, prefer to speak of the Spirit working per verbum *(through the Word), while the Reformed prefer* cum verbo *(with the Word). We must never forget that the word of God, also through law, always comes with* power. *At the same time, it does not always produce the same effect, and the regenerating, renewing effect cannot be understood without acknowledging the work of the Holy Spirit as a distinct work. The Spirit who renews is always and only the Spirit of Christ, who works through the means appointed by Christ.*

BEYOND MYSTICISM AND SACRAMENTALISM

[519] All salvation and blessedness comes to fallen people via God's gracious character.[1] Objectively, that grace with all its benefits appeared in Christ, who acquired and distributes them in the way of the covenant. The fellowship of those who have received Christ with all his benefits is called "the church" or "the Christian community."

The question we now face is whether or not, in the communication of these benefits of his, Christ uses means. All mystics are disposed to answer this question in the negative. Altogether in keeping with their dualistic starting point, they cannot conceive of grace as being dependent on or bound to external signs and actions. According to this view, it is God himself alone, or the Christ in us, the Spirit, or the inner word or light that works grace in humans, and the Word and sacrament can do no more than point to or depict that internal grace. The written word, it is said, expresses what is written in the heart of every believer, and the sacraments only make externally visible to our eyes what Christ has granted internally by his Spirit.[2] Mysticism finally comes down to the same thing as rationalism, which, as interpreted by Socinians[3] and Remonstrants,[4] sees in the sacraments only ceremonial precepts, memorial signs, and acts of confession.

Directly opposed to this view is that of Romanism, which conceives of grace as absolutely bound to means. According to Rome, after all, the church, the visible church sustained by the invisible Spirit, is the actual, authentic, perfect means of grace, the sacrament par excellence. In it Christ continues his divine human life on earth; fulfills his prophetic, royal, and above all his priestly office; and communicates the fullness of his grace and truth. The church is Christ on earth, Christ who, following his completed work of redemption, entered into the development— bound by space and time—of the human race.[5] And the grace that Christ merited and communicated to his church serves above all to elevate humans from the natural to the supernatural order. It is elevating grace, a supernatural physical power that in the sacrament is infused ex opere operato[6] into "the natural man"

---

1. Ed. note: Bavinck speaks here of "grace as a virtue of God" (*als deugd Gods*). To translate this as "attribute" would be too strong and not consistent with Bavinck's own usage of *eigenschappen* for "attributes" in volume 2. Hence the translation "God's gracious character."

2. B. de Moor, *Commentarius . . . theologiae*, 6 vols. (Leiden: J. Hasebroek, 1761–71), I, 359ff.; R. H. Grützmacher, *Wort und Geist: Eine historische und dogmatische Untersuchung zum Gnadenmittel des Wortes* (Leipzig: Deichert, 1902), 153ff.

3. O. Fock, *Der Socinianismus* (Kiel: C. Schröder, 1847), 559ff.

4. Apologia pro confessione Remonstrantium (1629); Apology of the Augsburg Confession, c. 23; P. van Limborch, *Theologia christiana* (Amsterdam: Arnhold, 1735), V, c. 66.

5. J. H. Oswald, *Die dogmatische Lehre von den heiligen Sakramenten der katholischen Kirche*, 2nd ed., 2 vols. (Münster: Aschendorff, 1864), 8.

6. Ed. note: Ex opera operato, "by the work performed"; this refers to "the assumption of medieval scholasticism and Roman Catholicism that the correct and churchly performance of the rite conveys grace to the recipient, unless the recipient places a spiritual impediment (*obex*) in the way. Sacraments themselves, therefore,

by the priest.[7] Just as in Christ the divine and the human natures are inseparably united, and as in the church the invisible spirit is similarly united with the visible institution, so in the sacrament the spiritual grace and the visible sign are inseparably bound up together. Apart from Christ, apart from the church, apart from the priest, and apart from the sacrament, accordingly, there is no salvation. One must know that in the church Christ not only continues his priestly office but also his prophetic and royal office. The doctrine of Christ proclaimed in the church, however, serves only to arouse faith, that is, assent, and the discipline maintained in the church serves only to foster obedience to the moral law. Faith and obedience are not of themselves grace itself but only its preparation and its fruit.[8] The word of God, which according to Rome is contained in Scripture and tradition and viewed as law, therefore has only preparatory and pedagogical significance, and belief is only one of the seven preparations for grace.[9] The sacrament administered by the priest is the real means of grace through which "all true justice either begins, or being begun is increased, or being lost is repaired."[10]

The Reformation adopted a position in between this mystical undervaluation and magical overvaluation of the means of grace, introducing an immense change in the place and character of the church, the church's offices, and the means of grace. According to the Reformation, Christ is the complete Savior, the only Mediator between God and humanity, and the church is first of all the communion of saints, not the mediatrix of salvation but the assembly of believers who live in communion with Christ. Christ indeed instituted offices in that believing community, but all these offices do not constitute a priesthood (*sacerdotium*) but a body of ministers (*ministerium*), bound absolutely to Christ's word and having no other power than the power of that word.

Hence, the relationship between Scripture and the church is totally different in Protestantism than in Roman Catholicism.[11] In Rome's view the church is anterior to Scripture; the church is not built upon Scripture, but Scripture arose from the church; Scripture does indeed need the church, but the church does not need Scripture. The Reformation, however, again put the church on the foundation of Scripture and elevated Scripture high above the church. Not the church but Scripture, the Word of God, became the means of grace par excellence. Even the sacrament was subordinated to the Word and had neither meaning nor power apart from that Word. Now, in accordance with Christ's ordinance, that Word was indeed administered in the midst of the congregation of believers by the minister, but this did not alter the fact that that Word was [also] put into

---

have a *virtus operativa*, or operative power" (Richard A. Muller, *Dictionary of Latin and Greek Theological Terms* [Grand Rapids: Baker Academic, 1985], s.v. *ex opera operato*).

7. Cf. H. Bavinck, *Reformed Dogmatics*, III, 516–17 (#417).

8. J. H. Oswald, *Die dogmatische Lehre*, I, 10.

9. Cf. H. Bavinck, *Reformed Dogmatics*, III, 515 (#416); see above, 108–10 (#451), 188–89 (#469).

10. Council of Trent, sess. 7, "Foreword."

11. Cf. H. Bavinck, *Reformed Dogmatics*, I, 452–59 (##118–19).

everyone's hands, that it was plain to everyone who studied it with a desire for salvation, that it exerted its power not only when it was proclaimed in public but also when it was studied and read at home. In that way Christians, who accepted that Word with a believing heart, were liberated from sacerdotalism. No longer did any person or thing stand between them and Christ. By faith they appropriated the whole of salvation, and in the sacrament they received the sign and seal of that reality. Thus the Reformation changed the Roman Catholic doctrine of the means of grace.

On the other hand, however, there was the threat of mysticism, which totally rejected the means of grace and could advance a list of reasons for that rejection. God's omnipotence, after all, should not be bound by such external means. God, being sovereign and free, could, but did not have to, use such means to distribute the treasures of his grace. Neither was that grace something material or substantial, a physical force, a superadded gift, an elevation of human nature. It consisted primarily in being restored to God's favor, in the forgiveness of sins, in the spiritual renewal after his image. For that reason it could not be locked into a sign perceptible to the senses as in a physical container, nor distributed by the minister. Christ was and remained the only one who, having acquired it, could also distribute it. He did not designate anyone to be his deputy on earth, nor did he appoint a priest; instead he himself continued to exercise his prophetic, priestly, and royal office. True, he might entrust the sign to his servant, yet he himself remained the only distributor of the thing signified. Furthermore, was this truth not clearly evident in the world around us? Every day thousands of people receive the sign of the Word and the sacrament without participating in grace. Conversely, one daily witnesses the death of many covenant infants, who, though they could not hear the word of the gospel, nor actually repent, yet concerning whose salvation believing parents were not—according to God's Word—supposed to entertain any doubts.

Guided by these considerations and alarmed by the arguments of the Anabaptists, Lutherans partly retraced their steps and again bound grace entirely to the means, introduced lay baptism in case of emergencies, viewed baptism itself as the washing away of sins, and spoke of faith already [present] in the case of infants. And also in Reformed churches, specifically in the Anglican churches, this same Romanizing tendency has repeatedly surfaced and achieved dominance. But originally the Reformation adopted another position. One could not restrict the omnipotence and freedom of God. He could also glorify his grace in the hearts of sinners apart from external means. If in this connection he employed human agents and signs, that should be attributed only to his good pleasure, his great love and grace. Zwingli therefore said that God even elected, regenerated, and led to salvation in heaven pagans who had never heard of the gospel. And although the other Reformers did not go that far, they still had to admit, especially in the case of children of believers who died in infancy, that God could also regenerate and save people without the Word and the sacrament, that is, by the Holy Spirit alone.[12]

ORDINARY AND EXTRAORDINARY: AVOIDING ONE-SIDEDNESS

Nevertheless, they presented these cases as exceptions and maintained as the rule that for those who reached adulthood the Word and sacraments were the ordinary means by which God gave his Spirit and imparted his grace. The working of regeneration and faith by the preaching of the Word is "the only economy and system of dispensing the Lord is accustomed to apply among those he plans to call as his own."[13] "The Lord does not usually call human beings directly, that is, immediately."[14] This answer is not altogether satisfactory, since the number of children who are saved apart from the means of grace, at least apart from the means of the preached Word, is much higher than generally surmised and cannot be cited as an exception to the rule. In addition, in those who grow to adulthood, regeneration by the Holy Spirit certainly *can* precede, though it does not always precede, baptism, the hearing of the Word of God, and the exercise of faith. This is why among Lutherans grace was increasingly linked to the means, and specifically regeneration was linked to baptism, and why among the Reformed who viewed the sacraments as signs and seals of conferred grace, regeneration was conceived as preceding baptism, so that the means of grace did not serve to regenerate but to bring those regenerated to faith and repentance.

Still also this later development could not be exempted from the charge of one-sidedness. The Lutheran development led back to Rome, and the development among the Reformed ran the danger of leading people to regard the Word, the sacrament, church, and offices, indeed even the person and work of Christ, as superfluous for the acquisition and application of salvation and necessary only for the outward manifestation of life and truth in the world. In that manner, however, the significance of the means of grace was weakened and their comprehension all too much delimited. The means of grace, after all, do not stand by themselves but are closely connected with the church and the offices of the church, with Christ's person and work. One might as well ask whether God could not regenerate and save [sinners] apart from Christ and forgive sins aside from satisfaction. But such questions lead nowhere: we have to rest in God's good pleasure, which distributes salvation in no way other than in and through Christ. He is the Mediator between God and humanity, the only name given under heaven by which we must be saved [Acts 4:12]. Furthermore, it was equally God's good pleasure to distribute

12. Luther, according to R. H. Grützmacher, *Wort und Geist*, 9ff.; J. Calvin, *Institutes*, IV.xvi.17–18.

13. J. Calvin, *Institutes*, IV.i.5, 16, 19; Belgic Confession, art. 24; Heidelberg Catechism, Q 64; Second Helvetic Confession, II, 18; Westminster Confession, ch. 10, 14; Formula of Concord, "Solid Declaration," XI, §27.

14. J. Gerhard, *Loci theologici*, ed. E. Preuss, 9 vols. (Berlin: G. Schlawitz, 1863–75), XX, 121.

salvation in no other way than through and in the church of Christ. Whether God, as Zwingli taught, also caused his electing grace to work among the pagans can be left undiscussed here, since in any case, according to the confession of all Christian churches, this refers to an exception. The rule is that God freely binds the distribution of his grace to the church of Christ.

The church is the communion, and hence also the mother, of believers. God establishes his covenant with the parents and in them with their children. He distributes his benefits in the way of the covenant. In that sense it is true that the church as the communion of saints is the great means of grace that Christ in his good pleasure uses to gather his elect from the beginning to the end of the world. In that sense the church definitely aims at the salvation of the elect. That is not the only reason for its existence; it also serves to perfect the saints, to build up the body of Christ, to preach the gospel to all creatures, and to glorify God. In any case, then, it also exists on earth to be the holy circle within which Christ communicates all his benefits, also the benefit of regeneration. In order that it would be equipped to do this, he gave the church his Spirit, poured out in it a wide assortment of gifts, instituted in it the church's offices, and entrusted to it the administration of the Word and sacraments. And these, too, without exception, are the means that Christ employs to bring to the Father all those given him and to lead them to heavenly blessedness. Indeed, the comprehensive guidance of life with all its variations of prosperity and adversity in the hand of the Holy Spirit is very often a means to bring the elect to Christ or more closely into his fellowship. The term "means of grace" can even be stretched to include the things that are needed on our part to enjoy, for the first time or continually, the benefits of the covenant, such as faith, conversion, the struggle against sin, and prayer.[15]

Admittedly, it is not advisable to include all these things under the means of grace. For Christ is not a means but the mediator, acquisitor, and executor of salvation. The church is not a means of grace alongside of the Word and sacraments, for all the power entrusted to it consists in nothing other than the administration of these two. The church and its offices as such do not impart grace; this only occurs *through* the Word and the sacraments. Moreover, faith, conversion, and prayer are rather the fruits than the means of grace. They are not objective institutions but the subjective conditions for the possession and enjoyment of the remaining benefits of the covenant. Strictly speaking, the Word and the sacraments alone

15. J. Calvin, *Institutes*, IV; Second Helvetic Confession, #16; Westminster Confession, ch. 14.1; F. Schleiermacher, *The Christian Faith*, ed. H. R. MacIntosh and J. S. Steward (Edinburgh: T&T Clark, 1928), §127; D. Hollaz (*Examen theologicum acroamaticum* [Rostock and Leipzig, 1718], 991), distinguishes the strict means of salvation (*media salutis stricte*) and words broadly (*late dicta*). The former (*media*) are, from God's perspective, Word and sacrament, and from our perspective, faith. The latter are εἰσαγωγικα (introduced) and executed in the kingdom of glory and no doubt include death, resurrection of the dead, final judgment, and the consummation of the age. Ed. note: The terms *stricte* and *late* "are frequently used by Protestant scholastics as characterizations of definitions, *stricte* with reference to precise definition, *late* with reference to general or colloquial definition" (Richard A. Muller, *Dictionary of Latin and Greek Theological Terms* [Grand Rapids: Baker Academic, 1985], s.v. *stricte*).

can be viewed as means of grace, that is, as external, humanly perceptible actions and signs that Christ has given his church and with which he has linked the communication of his grace. Still they may not even for a second be detached from the person and work of Christ, nor from the church as organism and as institution. Christ brings his own to their destiny in many and varied ways and can do this since he alone is and remains the acquisitor as well as the distributor of grace. Accordingly, he does this either apart from or through the Word and the sacraments, but always through the internal calling of the Spirit, whom he bestowed on the church, in the fellowship of the church, which he instructed to preach the gospel to all creatures; in the way of the covenant that received the gospel as its content and the sacraments as sign and seal.[16]

[520] The first and most important means of grace is the word of God. On this point the Lutherans and Reformed are agreed. The latter, however, do not discuss the word of God under the heading of the means of grace inasmuch as they have usually treated it earlier in dogmatics, either in a separate chapter,[17] or on the law in connection with the covenant of works and on the gospel in connection with the covenant of grace.[18] This unique method of treating the subject does not warrant the assertion that the Reformed did not recognize the word of God as a means of grace, for they repeatedly say the opposite.[19] One may indeed properly infer from these statements that for the Reformed the word of God had a much richer meaning than one would gather from its use as a means of grace in the strict sense of the term. The word of God is also distinguished from the sacraments in that the latter only serve to strengthen faith and therefore only play a role in the midst of the believing community.

THE WORD AS LAW, GOSPEL, AND POWER

But the word of God, both as law and gospel, is the revelation of the will of God, the promulgation of the covenant of works and the covenant of grace. It concerns all human beings and all creatures and so has universal significance. The sacrament can only be administered by a lawfully called minister in the assembly of believers, but the word of God also has a place and life outside of it and also there exerts many and varied influences. As a means of grace in the true sense alongside the sacraments, the word of God only comes up for discussion insofar as it is publicly preached by the minister. The emphasis then falls on the Word as

16. Cf. Also, F. A. Philippi, *Kirchliche Glaubenslehre*, 3rd ed., 7 vols. (Gütersloh: Bertelsmann, 1883–1902), V, 2, 1ff.; F. H. R. Frank, *System der christlichen Wahrheit*, 3rd rev. ed., 2 vols. (Erlangen and Leipzig: Deichert, 1894), II, 298ff.; A. Kuyper, *E voto Dordraceno: Toelichting op den Heidelbergschen Catechismus*, 4 vols. (Amsterdam: Wormser, 1892–95), II, 400ff.

17. J. Calvin, *Institutes*, II.vii.7–9; W. Musculus, *Loci communes theologiae sacrae* (Basel: Heruagiana, 1567), §11.20; F. Junius, *Theses theologicae*, §§23–24; *Synopsis purioris theologiae*, disp. 18, 22–23.

18. J. Marck, *Christianae theologiae medulla didactico-elenctica* (Amsterdam: Wetstenios, 1716), ch. 11, 17.

19. Cf. Belgic Confession, art. 24; Heidelberg Catechism, Q 65.

proclaimed in God's name and by virtue of his mission.[20] But as a rule the people have for a long time already come into contact with that word—in the family, at school, by hearing speeches, and in their reading—before they hear it publicly proclaimed in church. Accordingly, the public administration of the Word falls far short of encompassing all the power that proceeds from that Word; it also serves to work faith in those who do not have it, but much more to strengthen faith in the hearts and minds of believers assembled in public worship.

In a Christian society, the word of God comes to people in all sorts of ways, in all kinds of forms, from all directions, and it comes to them from their earliest childhood onward. Indeed, in the internal calling, God frequently introduces that word, even before the consciousness has awakened, to the hearts of children to regenerate and to sanctify them, just as in every person from one's earliest existence God inscribes the work of the law in their hearts and plants in them the seed of religion.

For that reason, we must definitely distinguish between the word of God and Scripture. Not in the sense that the word of God could be found only *in* Scripture and was not Scripture itself; but in this other sense, that the word in most cases does not come to us at all as Scripture, that is, in the form of Scripture. In fact, it comes in such a way that, having been absorbed from Scripture into the consciousness of the church, it proceeds from there to the most diverse people in the form of admonition and speech, nurture and education, books, magazines, tracts, and speeches and exerts its effect. And always it is God who stands behind that word. It is he who causes that word to go forth to people in all those diverse forms and thereby calls them to repentance and life. In Scripture, accordingly, the expression "word of God" is never identical with Scripture, even though we may undoubtedly call Scripture "the Word of God." There may be the odd instance where the expression "Word of God" refers to a part of Scripture, say to the written law. But for the rest, the word of God in Scripture is never the same as Scripture, if for no other reason than that at the time, Scripture was not yet complete. The expression "word of God" in Scripture has a variety of meanings and can refer to the power of God by which he creates and upholds the world, or his revelation to the prophets, or the content of revelation, or the gospel that was preached by the apostles.[21] Yet it is always a word of *God*, that is, never just a sound but a power, not mere information but an accomplishment of his will (Isa. 55:11). By his word, God creates and maintains the world (Gen. 1:3; Pss. 33:6; 148:5; Isa. 48:13; Rom. 4:17; 2 Cor. 4:6; Heb. 1:3; 11:3), and Jesus stilled the sea (Mark 4:39), healed the sick (Matt. 8:16), cast out demons (9:6), and raised the dead (Luke 7:14; 8:54; John 5:25, 28; 11:43; etc.). By his word, he also works in the area of morality and spirituality.

20. Heidelberg Catechism, Q 65; cf. Luther, according to R. H. Grützmacher, *Wort und Geist*, 26: "For we are not so much harmed or advanced by a quantity of eloquent writings, but by a living voice."
21. Cf. H. Bavinck, *Reformed Dogmatics*, I, 401–2 (#108).

God uses his word to make his will known in the area of morality and spirituality, and it must be differentiated as law and gospel. When Jesus appeared on
earth to announce the coming of the kingdom promised in the Old Testament
(Mark 1:15), to bring the gospel of forgiveness and salvation to publicans and
sinners, the poor and the imprisoned (Matt. 5:1ff.; 11:5, 28–30; Luke 4:18–19;
19:10; and so forth), he automatically clashed with the Pharisaic and nomistic
view of religion, which prevailed in his day. Still, though he rejected the human
ordinances of past teachers of the law (Matt. 5:21ff.; 15:9), and though he has a
different view of murder (5:21–22), adultery (5:27–28), oaths (5:33–37), fasting
(6:16–18), divorce (19:9), and the Sabbath (Mark 2:27–28), he does uphold the
whole law, also its ceremonial elements (Matt. 5:23–24; 17:24–27; 23:2–3, 23;
Mark 1:44; 11:16). He also explains it in its spiritual sense (Matt. 5–7), stresses
its ethical content, considers love to God and one's neighbor its sum (7:12; 9:13;
12:7; Mark 7:15; 12:28–34), and desires a righteousness different from and more
abundant than the righteousness of the Pharisees (Matt. 5:20). Accordingly,
though he himself is greater than the temple (12:6), he positioned himself under
the law (3:15) and came to fulfill the law and the prophets (5:17). He therefore
knows that, though he never insists on the abolition of the law, his disciples are
inwardly free from it (17:26); that his church is not founded on the law but on
the confession of his messiahship (16:18); and that a new covenant has been
established in his blood (26:28). In a word, the new wine calls for new wineskins
(9:17), and the days of the temple and people and law have been numbered (Mark
13:2). Jesus's agenda is not a revolutionary overthrow of the legalistic dispensation
of the old covenant, but the reformation and renewal that is naturally born from
its complete fulfillment.[22]

And so, in fact, it happened. In the early period the church at Jerusalem still
stuck to the temple and the law (Acts 2:46; 3:1; 10:14; 21:26; 22:12). But a new
outlook began to take shape. With the conversion of the Gentiles, the question
arose about the meaning of the Mosaic law. And Paul was the first to understand
fully that in the death of Christ the written code of the law had been canceled
(Col. 2:14). By "law" (νομος, *nomos*) Paul always understands—unless a further
stipulation indicates otherwise (e.g., Rom. 3:27; Gal. 6:2)—the Mosaic law, the
entire Torah, including the ceremonial commandments (Rom. 9:4; Gal. 2:12;
4:10; 5:3; Phil. 3:5–6). And he does not, like the Letter to the Hebrews, view that
law as the imperfect, preparatory, Old Testament dispensation of the covenant of
grace, which vanishes after the high priest and mediator of a better covenant has
come, but as the revelation of God's will, as a religious/ethical requirement and
demand, as the God-willed regulation of the revelation between him and human
beings. And concerning this law, thus interpreted, Paul now teaches that, though it
is indeed holy and good and God-given (Rom. 2:18; 7:22, 25; 9:4; 2 Cor. 3:3, 7), it
cannot, as the Pharisees asserted, produce righteousness, but is made powerless by

22. Cf. ibid., III, 222 (#348).

the flesh (Rom. 8:3); stimulates covetousness (7:7–8); increases trespasses (5:20; Gal. 3:19); produces wrath, a curse, and death (Rom. 4:15; 2 Cor. 3:6; Gal. 3:10); and intervened only for a time for pedagogical reasons (Rom. 5:20; Gal. 3:19, 24; 4:2–3). In Christ, the offspring of the promise, therefore, that law has attained its end [τέλος, *telos*] (Rom. 10:4): believers are free from the law (Gal. 4:26–5:1), inasmuch as they have been delivered by Christ from the curse of the law (3:13; 4:5) and have received the spirit of adoption, the spirit of freedom (Rom. 8:15; 2 Cor. 3:16–17; Gal. 5:18). This freedom of faith, however, does not cancel out the law but confirms it (Rom. 3:31) since its just requirement is fulfilled precisely in the lives of those who walk according to the Spirit (8:4). The Spirit, after all, renews believers so that they delight in God's law in their inner selves and try to find out what God's holy will is (Rom. 7:22; 12:2; Eph. 5:10; Phil. 1:10). At the same time they are urged onward to do the will of God for all sorts of pressing reasons—the great mercy of God, the example of Christ, the high price with which they were purchased, the fellowship of the Holy Spirit, and so forth.[23]

MAINTAINING THE UNITY OF THE COVENANT OF GRACE

[521] In the Christian church this antithesis between law and gospel was even exacerbated and made irreconcilable, on the one hand, by antinomianism in its various forms: Gnosticism, Manichaeism, Paulicianism, Anabaptism, Hattemism, and so forth. The whole Old Testament, it was said, was derived from an inferior God, a wrathful, jealous, avenging God, and had now been replaced by the very different revelation of the God of love, the Father of Christ. On the other hand, this antithesis between law and gospel was weakened and canceled out by nomism in its various forms: Pelagianism, semi-Pelagianism, Romanism, Socinianism, rationalism, and so forth. By the church fathers already and later by Scholastic and Roman Catholic theologians, law and gospel were equated with the Old and the New Testaments, and then not construed antithetically but viewed as a lower and a higher revelation of the will of God. Law and gospel do not differ in the sense that the former only demands and the latter only promises, for both contain

23. Concerning the law in the New Testament, see among others, H. J. Holtzmann, *Lehrbuch der neutestamentlichen Theologie* (Freiburg i.B. and Leipzig: Mohr, 1897), I, 130ff., 22ff.; L. Jacob, *Jesu Stellung zum mosaischen Gesetz* (Göttingen: Vandenhoeck & Ruprecht, 1893); E. Grafe, *Die paulinische Lehre vom Gesetz nach vier Hauptbriefen*, 2nd ed. (Freiburg i.B.: Mohr, 1893; ed. note: Bavinck cites the publisher location as Leipzig); Rudolf Zehnpfund, "Das Gesetz in den paulinischen Briefen," *Neue kirchliche Zeitschrift* 8 (1897): 384–419; H. Cremer, *Biblico-Theological Lexicon of New Testament Greek,* trans. D. W. Simon and W. Urwick (Edinburgh: T&T Clark; New York: Charles Scribner's Sons, 1895), s.v. νομος; S. R. Driver, "Law (in Old Testament)," in *DB*, III, 64–73; J. Denney, "Law (in New Testament)," in *DB*, III, 73–83; A. S. Peake, "Law," in *DC*, II, 11–14; H. Currie, "Law of God," in *DC*, II, 15–17. Christian freedom is closely connected to the position that the New Testament takes over against the law; cf. J. Calvin, *Institutes*, III.xix; A. Rivetus, in *Synopsis purioris theologiae*, disp. 35; B. de Moor, *Comm. theol.*, V, 214–17; J. Weiss, *Die christliche Freiheit nach der Verkündigung des Apostels Paulus* (Göttingen: Vandenhoeck & Ruprecht, 1902); H. H. Kuyper, *De christelijke vrijheid* (Kampen: Bos, 1898).

commandments, threats, and promises; mysteries, promises, and precepts; things to be believed, things to be hoped for, and things to be done. Not just Moses but also Christ was a legislator.

But in all this the gospel of the New Testament, the new law, far surpasses the law of the Old Testament, the old law. The mysteries (Trinity, incarnation, atonement, and so forth) are much more clearly revealed in the New Testament; the promises are much richer in content and embrace especially spiritual and eternal goods; the laws are much more glorious and lighter since the ceremonial and civil laws have been abolished and replaced by only a handful of ceremonies. Furthermore, "the law . . . was given through Moses; grace and truth came through Jesus Christ" [John 1:17]. The law was temporary and designed for one people; the gospel is eternal and has to be carried to all peoples. The law was imperfect, a shadow and an example; the gospel is perfect and the substance of the good things themselves. The law fostered fear and servitude; the gospel generates love and freedom. The law could not fully justify, it conferred no riches of grace, it gave no eternal salvation. The gospel embodied in the sacrament, however, confers the power of grace that enables its recipients to keep God's commandments and to gain eternal life. In a word, the law is the incomplete gospel; the gospel the complete law. The gospel was contained in the law as a tree in a seed, a grain in an ear of corn.[24]

Now to the extent that the Old and the New Testament dispensations of the covenant of grace can be described—following Scripture and in terms of the most salient difference between them—with the terms "law" and "gospel," the distinction that Rome makes between the two can for the most part, but not completely, be endorsed. Rome, however, totally equated the old and the new covenants with law and gospel [respectively], denied the presence of the gospel in the Old Testament and that of the law in the New Testament, viewed the entire doctrine promulgated by Christ and the apostles as gospel, accepted in it the presence not just of promises but also of laws and threats, and thus made the gospel into a second law. The Pauline antithesis of law and gospel was erased. For though it is true that Paul understood by "law" the entire Old Testament dispensation, in so doing he views it above all in terms of its law-centered form and so contrasts it directly with the gospel. And even when he does this, he acknowledges that the law-centered dispensation by no means snuffed out the promise already made to Abraham (Gal. 3:17, 21), that the gospel was also preached in the days of the old covenant (Gal. 3:8), and that in those days, too, righteousness was obtained from and by faith (Rom. 4:11–12; 11:32; Gal. 3:6–7). Concerning the law as law, apart from the promises, to which in the Old Testament the law was made subservient,

---

24. Cf. H. Bavinck, *Reformed Dogmatics*, III, 206–12 (#345); J. C. Suicerus, *Thesaurus ecclesiasticus* (Amsterdam: J. H. Wetsten, 1682), s.v. νομος and εὐαγγελιον; Augustine, *City of God* VIII, 11; idem, *Sermon 30 on the Gospel of John*; idem, *On the Spirit and the Letter*, 19–20; P. Lombard, *Sent.*, III, dist. 25, 40; T. Aquinas, *Summa theol.*, III, qu. 106–8; Council of Trent, VI, can. 19–21; R. Bellarmine, "De justif.," in *Controversiis*, IV, c. 2ff.

Paul asserts that it cannot justify, that it increases sin, that it is a ministry of condemnation [2 Cor. 3:9], and precisely in that way prepares the fulfillment of the promise and necessitates another righteousness, that is, the righteousness of God in Christ by faith. And *this* antithesis between law and gospel was again understood by the Reformation. To be sure, some pronouncements made by the church fathers also testify to a better insight.[25] But no clarity was achieved because they consistently confuse the difference between law and gospel with that between the old covenant and the new.

While, on the one hand, the Reformers held on to the unity of the covenant of grace in its two dispensations against the Anabaptists, on the other hand, they also perceived the sharp contrast between law and gospel and thereby again restored the peculiar character of the Christian religion as a religion of grace. Although in a broad sense the terms "law" and "gospel" can indeed be used to denote the old and the new dispensation of the covenant of grace, in their actual significance they definitely describe two essentially different revelations of divine will. Also the law is the will of God (Rom. 2:18, 20); holy, wise, good, and spiritual (7:12, 14; 12:10); giving life to those who maintain it (2:13; 3:2); but because of sin it has been made powerless, it fails to justify, it only stimulates covetousness, increases sin, arouses wrath, kills, curses, and condemns (Rom. 3:20; 4:15; 5:20; 7:5, 8–9, 13; 2 Cor. 3:6ff.; Gal. 3:10, 13, 19). Over against it stands the gospel of Christ, the εὐαγγελιον, which contains nothing less than the fulfillment of the Old Testament promise (Mark 1:15; Acts 13:32; Eph. 3:6), which comes to us from God (Rom. 1:1–2; 2 Cor. 11:7); has Christ as its content (Rom. 1:3; Eph. 3:6); and conveys nothing other than grace (Acts 20:24), reconciliation (2 Cor. 5:18), forgiveness (Rom. 4:3–8), righteousness (3:21–22), peace (Eph. 6:15), freedom (Gal. 5:13), life (Rom. 1:17; Phil. 2:16), and so forth. In these texts law and gospel are contrasted as demand and gift, as command and promise, as sin and grace, as sickness and healing, as death and life.[26] Although they agree in that both have God as author, both speak of one and the same perfect righteousness, and both are addressed to human beings to bring them to eternal life, they nevertheless differ in that the law proceeds from God's holiness, the gospel from God's grace; the law is known from nature, the gospel only from special revelation; the law demands perfect righteousness, but the gospel grants it; the law leads people to eternal life by works, and the gospel produces good works from the riches of the eternal life granted in faith; the law presently condemns people, and the gospel acquits them; the law addresses itself to all people, and the gospel only to those who live within its hearing; and so forth.

25. See the references in J. C. Suicerus, *Thesaurus ecclesiasticus*, s.v. νομος and εὐαγγελιον; J. Gerhard, *Loci theol.*, XIV, 16.

26. The distinction between law and gospel was also weakened or eliminated by Protestants: for example, by C. Stange, *Die Heilsbedeutung des Gesetzes* (Leipzig: Dieterich, 1904); A. Bruining, "Godsdienst en verlossings-behoefte," *Teylers Theologisch Tijdschrift* 8 (1910): 399–419. Prior to that, even by Zwingli, according to F. A. Loofs, *Leitfaden zum Studium der Dogmengeschichte*, 4th ed. (Halle a.S.: M. Niemeyer, 1906), 799.

On account of this difference, there was even disagreement over whether the preaching of faith and repentance, which seemed after all to be a condition and a demand, really belonged to the gospel and should not rather (with Flacius, Gerhard, Quenstedt, Voetius, Witsius, Cocceius, de Moor, and others) be counted as law. And indeed, strictly speaking, there are no demands and conditions in the gospel but only promises and gifts. Faith and repentance are as much benefits of the covenant of grace as justification (and so forth). But, concretely, the gospel never comes in that form. In practice it is always united with law and is therefore always interwoven with the law throughout Scripture. The gospel always presupposes the law and also needs it in its administration. It is brought, after all, to rational, moral human beings, who are responsible for themselves before God and therefore have to be called to faith and repentance. The demanding and summoning form in which the gospel is cast is derived from the law. Every person is obligated not first of all by the gospel but by nature, the law, to believe God at his word and by implication to accept the gospel in which he speaks to us humans. The gospel therefore immediately takes possession of all human beings, binds it on their consciences, for the God who speaks in the gospel is none other than he who has made himself known to them in his law. Faith and repentance are therefore demanded of people in the name of God's law, by virtue of the relation in which humans stand to God as rational creatures; and that demand is addressed not only to the elect and regenerate but to all humans without distinction.

But faith and repentance themselves, nevertheless, are components of the gospel, not the workings or fruits of the law. For while the law demands faith in God in general, it does not demand the special faith that directs itself toward Christ, and while the law can produce penitence (μεταμελεια, *metameleia*), it cannot produce conversion (μετανοια, *metanoia*), which is rather the fruit of faith. And precisely because faith and repentance are components of the gospel—though humans are naturally obligated by law to display these attributes—one can speak of a law of faith, of a commandment of faith, of the obedience of faith (Rom. 1:5; 3:27; 1 John 3:23), of being disobedient to and judged according to the gospel (Rom. 2:16; 10:16; and so forth). Law and gospel, viewed concretely, do not so much differ in that the law always speaks with a commanding voice and the gospel with a promising voice, for also the law makes promises and the gospel utters admonitions and imposes obligations. But they differ especially in content: the law demands that humans work out their own righteousness, and the gospel invites them to renounce all self-righteousness and to accept the righteousness of Christ and even offers the gift of faith to that end. And law and gospel occur in that relation not only before and at the start of conversion, but also remain in it throughout the Christian life, right up until death. Lutherans almost exclusively have an eye for the accusing and condemning function of the law and therefore know no higher bliss than deliverance from the law. Law is necessary only because of sin. In the state of perfection, there is no law. God is free from the law; Christ was in no way subject to the law for himself; the believer is no longer subject to the law. Granted, Lutherans do speak of a threefold use of the law, not only of a political, that is, civil, use for the purpose of restraining sin, and of a pedagogical use to arouse the knowledge of sin, but also of a didactic use of the law to be a rule of life for believers. This last use, however, is solely necessary since and insofar as believers still continue to be sinners and have to be restrained by the law and led to a continuing knowledge of sin. By itself, when faith and grace come on the scene, the law expires and loses all its meaning.

THE SPIRIT, THE WORD, AND POWER

The Reformed held a very different view. The political use and the pedagogical use of the law have only become "accidentally" necessary because of sin. Even when these earlier uses cease, the most important one, the didactic or normative use, remains. The law, after all, is an expression of God's being. As a human being Christ was naturally subject to law for his own sake. Before the fall the law was inscribed on Adam's heart. In the case of the believer, it is again engraved on the tables of his heart by the Holy Spirit; and in heaven all its inhabitants will conduct themselves in accordance with the law of the Lord. The gospel is temporary; the law is everlasting and precisely that which is restored by the gospel. Freedom from the law, therefore, does not mean that Christians no longer have anything to do with that law, but that the law can no longer demand anything from them as a condition for salvation and can no longer judge and condemn them. For the rest they delight in the law in their inmost being [Rom. 7:22] and meditate on it day and night [Ps. 1:2]. For that reason that law must always be proclaimed in the church in the context of the gospel. Both law and gospel, the whole Word, the full counsel of God, are the content of preaching. Accordingly, among the Reformed the law occupies a much larger place in the doctrine of gratitude than in that of misery.[27]

[522] In Christian theology, aside from the relationship between law and gospel, there is also an important disagreement over the power or efficacy of the

---

27. Cf. Luther according to J. Köstlin, *The Theology of Luther in Its Historical Development and Inner Harmony*, trans. Charles E. Hay, 2 vols. (Philadelphia: Lutheran Publication Society, 1897), I, 183ff.; II, 230ff.; 495ff.; F. A. Loofs, *Dogmengeschichte*, 774ff.; Joseph T. Müller, *Die symbolischen Bücher der evangelisch-lutherischen Kirche*, 8th ed. (Gütersloh: Bertelsmann, 1898), 87, 181, 533, 633; ed. note: These specific references are to the following Lutheran documents: Apology of the Augsburg Confession, art. 4, par. 5, in *The Book of Concord*, ed. Robert Kolb and Timothy J. Wengert (Minneapolis: Fortress, 2000), 121; ibid., art. 12, par. 79 (Kolb and Wengert, 200); Formula of Concord, "Epitome," art. 5 (Kolb and Wengert, 500ff.); ibid., "Solid Declaration," art. 5 (Kolb and Wengert, 581ff.). J. Gerhard, *Loci theol.*, IV, 1–72; D. Hollaz, *Examen theologicum acroamaticum* (Rostock and Leipzig: Russworm, 1718), 996–1043; U. Zwingli in H. Bavinck, *De ethiek van Ulrich Zwingli* (Kampen: Zalsman, 1880), 47ff., 76ff.; J. Calvin, *Institutes*, II.vii–ix; J. Zanchi, *De operum theologicorum*, 8 vols. (Geneva: Samuelis Crispini, 1617), VIII, 509; H. Witsius, *Miscellaneorum sacrorum* (Utrecht, 1692), II, 840–48; B. de Moor, *Comm. theol.*, III, 377ff.; C. Vitringa, *Doctrina christiana religionis*, 8 vols. (Leiden: Joannis le Mair, 1761–86), VI, 253–92; M. Schneckenburger and Eduard Güder, *Vergleichende Darstellung des lutherischen und reformirten Lehrbegriffs*, 2 vols. (Stuttgart: J. B. Metzler, 1855), I, 127ff.; F. H. R. Frank, "Gesetz und Evangelium," in *Dogmatische Studien* (Erlangen: Deichert, 1892), 104–35; J. Gottschick, "Gesetz und Evangelium," in *PRE*[3], VI, 632–41.

word of God and, hence, over the relationship between word and Spirit. In this connection, too, the extremes are nomism, on the one hand, and antinomianism, on the other. The nomism that runs from Judaism through Pelagianism and as far as modern rationalism is content with an external call, an intellectual, moral, or aesthetic operation of the word, and in this connection considers a special supernatural power of the Holy Spirit to be superfluous.[28] Rome shows itself to be clearly akin to this school of thought insofar as it weakens prevenient grace, ascribes to faith merely the preparatory function and meaning of a historical assent, tends increasingly to favor the direction of Monism and Congruism, and only has real supernatural grace, plus the indwelling of the Holy Spirit, communicated by the sacrament.[29]

The opposite position is taken by the antinomianism that initially opposes only the law and the Old Testament, but soon moves on to dissent from every external word and the entire objective historical mediation of salvation, and expects everything from the operation of the Holy Spirit, from the Christ in us, from the internal word and inner light. In the Anabaptism of Schwenckfeld, Franck, Denck, and others, this school of thought expressed itself most clearly on this point. The external and internal word are related as body and soul, death and life, earth and heaven, flesh and Spirit, shell and core, foam and silver, image and truth, the sheath and the sword, a lantern and its light, the cradle and Christ, nature and God, creature and Creator. Knowledge of the word as such, accordingly, affords us nothing and leaves us cold and dead. Even to understand it one needs the inner light as a condition. Just as words can teach us something only when we know the things to which they refer, so Scripture teaches us something only when Christ already dwells in our hearts. The word is no more than a sign, a shadow, an image, and a symbol. It expresses, points out, and reminds us only of what is already internally written on our hearts. The internal word, therefore, precedes and is superior to Scripture, which is only a paper word and, additionally, obscure and full of contradictions. And that internal word is nothing other than God or Christ or the Holy Spirit himself, who is one and the same in all people from the moment of their rebirth or sometimes also dwells in them by nature as internal light and is the fullness of truth in its entirety. Accordingly, to find God and know the truth, we need not go outside of ourselves to Scripture or the historical Christ; but going down into ourselves, withdrawing from the world, killing the intellect and the will, and passively awaiting an internal and immediate revelation, we find God, live in communion with him, and are saved in contemplating him.[30] Actually this Anabaptism was a revival of the pantheistic

28. Cf. H. Bavinck, *Reformed Dogmatics*, III, 495–99 (#411), 508–9 (#414), 531–35 (#421).

29. Cf. ibid., III, 511–13 (#415).

30. J. Cloppenburg, *Theol. op.*, II, 200; J. Hoornbeek, *Summa contr.*, V; S. Episcopius, *Opera theologica*, 2 vols. (Amsterdam: Johan Blaeu, 1650–65), I, 527; J. Quenstedt, *Theologia*, I, 169; A. Hegler, *Geist und Schrift bei Sebastian Franck* (Freiburg i.B.: Mohr, 1892; ed. note: Bavinck erroneously cites this as *Geist und Wort*); J. H. Maronier, *Het inwendig word* (Amsterdam: Tj. van Holkema, 1890); R. H. Grützmacher, *Wort und Geist*.

mysticism that regards the finite as an eternally changing manifestation of the infinite and, hence, seeks communion with God in the intimate depths of feeling, where God and humans are one.

Over against both of these schools, nomism and antinomianism, the Reformers jointly maintained that the Word alone is insufficient to bring people to faith and repentance, that the Holy Spirit can but usually does not work without the Word, and that Word and Spirit, therefore, work in conjunction to apply the salvation of Christ to human beings. Initially there was little disagreement between the Lutherans and the Reformed on this point. Also the former taught that the Holy Spirit, though working through the Word and sacraments as his instruments, nevertheless effects and can effect faith only by a special power, and that he does this "where and when he pleases."[31] Yet from the very beginning there was already some difference as well. Whereas the Reformed usually say that the Holy Spirit unites with the Word (*cum verbo*), the Lutherans prefer to express themselves by saying and increasingly emphasizing that the Holy Spirit works through the Word (*per verbum*) as his instrument. And whereas the Reformed always made a distinction between the ordinary and the extraordinary manner in which God works his grace in the human heart, the Lutherans, out of fear of the Anabaptists, increasingly omitted the extraordinary manner and said, "God grants his Spirit or grace to no one except through or with the preceding outward word,"[32] or as Luther kept saying, "God does not give internal things except through external things." And when in 1621 the Danzig preacher Hermann Rahtmann (d. 1628) issued a work in which he taught that the Word alone did not possess the power to convert a person unless the Holy Spirit with his grace joined himself with it,[33] almost all Lutheran theologians rose up against him and articulated as the true Lutheran doctrine that the word of God has within it the power of the Holy Spirit to convert people, that that power has been put in it by divine providence and is so inseparably bound up with it that it is still present in the Word even "before and apart from its legitimate use," just as a human hand, even when it is not working, still retains the power to work.[34]

31. Joseph T. Müller, *Die symbolischen Bücher*, 39, 455, 456, 471, 524, 601, 712, 720; ed. note: These specific references are to the following Lutheran documents: Augsburg Confession, art. 5 (Kolb and Wengert, 40); The Large Catechism, part II, art. 3 (Kolb and Wengert, 435ff.); ibid., part III, "Second Petition" (Kolb and Wengert, 446ff.); Formula of Concord, "Epitome," art. 2 (Kolb and Wengert, 491ff.); ibid., "Solid Declaration," art. 2, pars. 52–55 (Kolb and Wengert, 554); ibid., "Solid Declaration," art. 11, pars. 36–40 (Kolb and Wengert, 646–47); ibid., "Solid Declaration," art. 11, pars. 74–77 (Kolb and Wengert, 652). J. Köstlin, *The Theology of Luther*, II, 493; R. Otto, *Geist und Wort nach Luther* (Göttingen: E. A. Huth, 1898); R. H. Grützmacher, *Wort und Geist*; other Lutheran theologians, according to Julius Müller, *Dogmatische Abhandlungen* (Bremen: C. E. Müller, 1870), 155ff.

32. Smalcald Articles, part III, art. 8 (Kolb and Wengert, 321–23).

33. On Rahtmann, cf. R. H. Grützmacher, *Wort und Geist*, 220ff.

34. J. Quenstedt, *Theologia*, I, 169; D. Hollaz, *Examen theologicum acroamaticum*, 992; J. F. Buddeus, *Institutiones theologiae dogmaticae* (Frankfurt and Leipzig, 1741), 110; H. F. F. Schmid, *The Doctrinal Theology of the Evangelical Lutheran Church*, trans. Charles A. Hay and Henry Jacobs, 5th ed. (Philadelphia: United Lutheran Publication House, 1899), §51; F. A. Philippi, *Kirchliche Glaubenslehre*, V, 2, 29ff.

Now the word that proceeds from the mouth of God is indeed always a power accomplishing that for which God sends it forth. It is such a power in the natural domain in creation and providence; it is also such a power in the work of re-creation in the domain of morality and spirituality. And this is even true not just of the gospel but also of the law. Paul, admittedly, says of the Old Testament dispensation of law that "the letter kills" (2 Cor. 3:6), but in making that point he is saying as powerfully as he can possibly say it that it is not a dead letter. Instead, it is so powerful that it produces sin, wrath, a curse, and death. "The law brings about wrath" (Rom. 4:15); it is "the power of sin" (1 Cor. 15:56), the "ministry of death," "the ministry of condemnation" (2 Cor. 3:7, 9). Over against it stands the gospel as the "power of God for salvation" (Rom. 1:16; 1 Cor. 1:18; 2:4–5; 15:2; Eph. 1:13). Since it is not a human word but God's (Acts 4:29; 1 Thess. 2:13), it is living and lasting (1 Pet. 1:25), living and active (Heb. 4:12), spirit and life (John 6:63), a lamp shining in a dark place (2 Pet. 1:19); it is a seed sown in the human heart (Matt. 13:3), growing and multiplying (Acts 12:24), of great value even if those who planted and watered it are nothing (1 Cor. 3:7); a sharp two-edged sword piercing the innermost being of a person and judging all the thoughts and intentions of the human heart (Heb. 4:12). For that reason it is not void and futile but works (ἐνεργεῖται, *energeitai*) in those who believe (1 Thess. 2:13); and the works it brings about are regeneration (John 1:18; 1 Cor. 4:15; 1 Pet. 1:23), faith (Rom. 10:17), illumination (2 Cor. 4:4–6; Eph. 3:9; 5:14; 1 Tim. 1:20), teaching, correction, consolation, and so forth (1 Cor. 14:3; 2 Tim. 3:15). The gospel exerts its effect even in those who are lost; to them it is a reason for their falling, an offense and foolishness, a stone over which they stumble, a fragrance from death to death (Luke 2:34; Rom. 9:32; 1 Cor. 1:23; 2 Cor. 2:16; 1 Pet. 2:8).

Over against spiritualism, this power of the word of God and specifically of the gospel must, with the Lutherans, be maintained in all its fullness and richness of meaning. The dualisms between the internal and external, the spiritual and the material, eternity and time, essence and form (and so forth) are products of a false philosophy and contrary to Scripture. God is the creator of heaven, yes, but also of the earth; of the soul, yes, but also of the body; of spirit, yes, but also of matter. Similarly, therefore, the word is not an empty set of vibrations in the air, nor an empty sign, or a cold symbol, but every word, also every human word, is a power greater and more durable than the power of the sword. Encapsulated within it is thought, mind, soul, and life. If this applies to words in general, how much more is it true of the word that proceeds from the mouth of God and is spoken by him? That is a word that creates and maintains, judges and kills, re-creates and renews, and always accomplishes what it is meant to accomplish and never returns empty. In the case of human words it makes a great difference whether it is written or printed, read or heard; and in the case of the spoken word the form and manner of presentation is again of the greatest importance.

The power of the human word also depends on the extent to which a person puts one's heart and soul into it, on the distance existing between the person and one's speech. But in the case of God that is different. It is always his word; he is always present in it; he consistently sustains it by his almighty and omnipresent power. It is always God himself who, in whatever form and by whatever means, brings it to people and calls them by it. Therefore, even though the word of God that is freely proclaimed by ministers or conveyed to people by way of personal admonition, public address, a book or other writing, is indeed taken from Scripture but not identical with Scripture, it is still a word from God, a word that comes to human beings but is originally from God, is spoken in the power of the Holy Spirit and therefore always effective. The word of God is never separate from God, from Christ, from the Holy Spirit; it has no permanence or existence in itself. It cannot be deistically separated from its creator and author. Just as Scripture was not just inspired at one time by the Holy Spirit, but is continually sustained, preserved, and made powerful by that Spirit, so it is with the word of God that, taken from Scripture, is preached in some fashion to people. Jesus spoke through the Spirit (John 6:63); the apostles who received the Spirit (Matt. 10:20; Luke 12:12; 21:15; John 14:26; 15:26) proclaimed the gospel not only in words but also "in power and in the Holy Spirit" (1 Thess. 1:5–6), with a "demonstration of the Spirit and of power" (1 Cor. 2:4), and handled it as "the sword of the Spirit" (Eph. 6:17). In that respect, the Lutherans are completely correct: always and everywhere the word of God is a power of God, a sword of the Spirit. "The Holy Spirit is always present with that word."

At the same time both Scripture and experience teach that the word does not always have the same effect. In a sense it is always efficacious; it is never powerless. If it does not raise people up, it strikes them down. If it is not "for the rising of many," it is for "the falling of many" [Luke 2:34]; if it is not "a fragrance from life to life," it is "a fragrance from death to death" [2 Cor. 2:16]. The question, then, is when that word of God is efficacious in the sense that it leads to faith and repentance. Now to render human beings inexcusable, Lutherans lock this divine and supernatural efficacy up in the word, but do not secure any advantage by it and, to explain the variable outcome of the word in people, have to resort to free will. The Reformed, however, taking into account that double outcome, did not view the efficacy as an impersonal magical power that had been put into that word, but always associated that word with its author, with Christ, who administers it by the Holy Spirit. And that Holy Spirit is not an unconscious power but a person who is always present with that word, always sustains it and makes it active, though not always in the same manner. In accordance with the unsearchable good pleasure of God, he uses that word for bringing people to repentance but also for hardening; for the rising but also for the falling of many. He always works through the word but not always in the same way. And when he wants to work through it so that it leads to faith and repentance, he does not objectively have to add anything to the word. That word is good and wise and holy, a word of God, a word of Christ, and the Holy Spirit takes everything from Christ.

Nonetheless, for the seed of the word to bear good fruit, it has to fall in soil that has been well prepared. Also the field has to be made ready for the reception of the seed. Hence the subjective activity of the Holy Spirit has to be added to the objective word. In the nature of the case, it cannot be enclosed in the word; it is another activity, an additional activity, a subjective activity, not through but along with the word, an opening of the heart (Acts 16:14), an internal revelation (Matt. 11:25; 16:17; Gal. 1:16), an act of drawing a person to Christ (John 6:44), an enlightenment of the mind (Eph. 1:18; Col. 1:9–11), a working both to will and to do (Phil. 2:13), and so forth.[35] In saying these things we are not detaching or separating the Spirit from the word, not even when, as in the case of infants, he effects regeneration without any means of grace. For the Spirit who regenerates is not the Spirit of God in general, but the Spirit of Christ, the Holy Spirit, the Spirit acquired by Christ, through whom Christ governs, who takes all things only from Christ, and whom Christ has poured out in the church and is therefore the Spirit of the believing community. Aside from whether the Holy Spirit sometimes also works and can work in pagans, something that is in any case exceptional, as a rule he effects regeneration only in those who live under the administration of the covenant. Also the infants he regenerates are children of the covenant, of the covenant that has the word of God as its content and received the sacrament as its sign and seal. The Holy Spirit, accordingly, follows Christ in his journey through history. He binds himself to the word of Christ and works only in the name, and in accordance with the command, of Christ. Individually and subjectively, for example when a child is considered in isolation from one's environment, the church in which the child was born, it may seem as if the Spirit worked without the word; objectively and materially the Holy Spirit only works in places where the covenant of grace, with the administration of Word and sacraments, has expanded itself. Therefore, in the case of infants, their regeneration is always known and proved to be genuine when they mature and it becomes manifest in acts of faith and repentance and links up with the word of God, which lies objectively before us in Scripture. The Holy Spirit, who in regeneration applies nothing other than the word, power, and merit of Christ, also automatically leads the conscious life of the person toward the word that he took from Christ and caused to be recorded by the prophets and apostles.

---

35. Cf. above, 41ff. (#435); Belgic Confession, art. 24; Heidelberg Catechism, Q 65, 67; Second Helvetic Confession, II, 18; Canons of Dordt, III, 6; V, 7, 14; J. Calvin, *Institutes*, III.ii.33; IV.xiv.11; idem, *Treatises against the Anabaptists and Libertines,* trans. and ed. Benjamin W. Farley (Grand Rapids: Baker Academic, 1982), ch. 9; F. Turretin, *Institutes of Elenctic Theology*, trans. G. M. Giger, ed. J. T. Dennison (Phillipsburg, NJ: Presbyterian & Reformed, 1992), XV, 4, 24; C. Hodge, *Systematic Theology*, 3 vols. (New York: Charles Scribner's Sons, 1888), III, 466–85.

9

THE SPIRIT'S MEANS OF GRACE:
THE SACRAMENTS

In addition to the Word, the sacraments are a second means of grace. In the apostolic era, after believers entered the church through baptism, they met on the Lord's Day. Initially, there were likely two gatherings, a ministry of the Word inclusive of nonmembers (1 Cor. 14:23) and a celebration of the Lord's Supper (11:33) particular to believers only. In the second century, however, these two ministries were united and the Lord's Supper was integrated into the regular worship service. Since the second part of the worship service, the Lord's Supper, was exclusively for baptized members, it gradually acquired a mysterious character. The New Testament word μυστηριον became understood by the church as synonymous with the incomprehensible and was translated by the Latin word sacramentum, *with the result that any content of revelation could be referred to as a "sacrament," and the exact number of sacraments remained indefinite. Augustine employed this broad sense of the term and was followed by Pseudo-Dionysius and Scholasticism.*

While the church fathers did not develop a clear doctrine of the sacraments, medieval Scholasticism elaborated on the sacraments in great detail. This medieval consensus established that Christ instituted seven sacraments in the new covenant, which supplied special grace, differed in value, were necessary for salvation, communicate grace "through the act performed" (ex opere operato), were lawfully administered only by ordained priests who acted according to the true intention of the church, and were truly received when the recipients intended to receive what the church bestowed. This development departed from Scripture in teaching that the sacraments imparted only sanctifying grace, almost severing the bond between sacrament and Word, and removing the requirement of faith in the recipient.

The Reformation modified the Roman Catholic doctrine according to Scripture. Zwingli, Luther, and Calvin all taught that the sacrament imparted forgiving grace, that it was valueless without the Word, and its operation presupposed faith in the recipient. Yet the Reformers also differed on the doctrine of the sacraments since the sacraments embodied in practice their theological

461

teaching. Luther emphasized their objective character against the Anabaptists, Zwingli taught that they were signs of faith, and Calvin taught that they were signs and seals of God's promises in the covenant of grace. Yet neither Calvin nor the later Reformed tradition were clear as to how God distributes grace in the sacraments. Zwingli's doctrine was increasingly accepted outside the Lutheran and Reformed churches, including among the Anabaptists, Socinians, Remonstrants, Rationalists, and Quakers.

Although the term "sacrament" does not occur in Scripture, it is useful for summarizing what the special ordinances in Scripture have in common. While Roman Catholic theology understands the sacrament as a "sacred, secret, and hidden thing," Scripture speaks of it as a sign and seal of the covenant (Gen. 9:12–13, 17; 17:11; Rom. 4:11). Accordingly, Reformed theology describes the sacraments as signs and seals that are instituted and distributed by God so that believers might understand more clearly and be reassured of God's promises and benefits in the covenant of grace.

The terms sign *and* seal *imply that the sacrament consists of two parts distinguished as "word" and "element." Signs may be either natural (e.g., smoke, footprints) or instituted (e.g., alphabet, slogans, flags). Instituted signs are further distinguished as either ordinary or extraordinary (e.g., miracles), regarding things past, present, or future. Sacraments are extraordinary signs taken, according to a preformed analogy, from visible things to designate invisible and eternal goods. They are seals since they confirm God's trustworthiness and strengthen for us the "element" of the covenant of grace that is summed up in Christ the Mediator, with all his benefits and blessings.*

In Lutheran dogmatics, the doctrine of consubstantiation led to the view that, in addition to the word, a "heavenly substance" or divine power was imparted through the sacrament. The Word and sacrament were thus viewed as imparting different benefits. Modern theology has repeatedly set forth this view as well. However, this view is an importation of Roman Catholicism and conflicts with Scripture. The sacrament does not impart one benefit that is not also received from the Word of God by faith alone; the content of both is identical. While differing in external form and manner, they nonetheless contain the same Mediator, covenant, benefits, salvation, and fellowship with God. The sacrament is nothing without the Word. It only strengthens the faith that is present.

The relationship between the sign and thing signified is not a physical, local, corporeal, or substantial connection. It is an ethical connection identical with that between Christ and the gospel. A special word from God was needed for us to see in the natural signs a depiction of the spiritual goods of salvation. The "form of the sacrament" therefore includes the relationship between sign and thing signified, and the divine institution that establishes the connection between sign and thing signified. In Roman Catholic and Lutheran theology, the words of institution either change or incorporate the sign into the thing signified, and consequently the words are directed more to the element than to the listeners. For the Reformed, by contrast, the public word does not change the sign but only sets it apart from common usage for the listeners. Accordingly, while the Reformed teach that God alone, rather than the minister, is the distributor of grace in the sacrament, Roman Catholics and Lutherans make the grace of the sacrament dependent on the minister.

Roman Catholics and Lutherans differ from the Reformed in their understanding of reality. While the Reformed hold to a spiritual communication since the essence of grace is spiritual, Roman Catholics view the visible sign as absorbing the invisible grace so that the sacrament works "by the act performed" (ex opere operato) and only requires negatively that the recipient does not pose an obstacle to its operation. For the Reformed, the sacraments are signs and seals of the covenant of grace, and therefore grace is only imparted where faith is present.

Despite the objections of Lutherans and Roman Catholics to the contrary, Reformed theology preserves the reality and objectivity of the sacrament. The connection between the sign and thing signified is the same as that between the word of the gospel and the person of Christ. The spiritual reality of the sacrament is no less real than physical reality. Even Lutherans require faith in adults for the reception of the sacrament. Roman Catholics and Lutherans no less than Reformed are equally faced with the difficulty of the question of when the sacraments impart grace to the recipients, since grace is not imparted always, everywhere, and in all cases.

To be sure, the sacraments are not absolutely necessary for salvation, since Scripture binds salvation only to faith (John 3:16). It is not deprivation of, but contempt for, the sacrament that makes a person guilty before God. However, the sacraments are valuable for reinforcing faith, joining believers together, and setting believers apart from the world as a witness.

The number of sacraments depends on whether the term "sacrament" is understood in a more restricted or a broader sense. Thus the Reformed counted a great many sacraments in Scripture both in the covenant of works (Sabbath, paradise, tree of knowledge, tree of life) and the various dispensations of the covenant of grace in the Old Testament (circumcision, Passover, expulsion from paradise, skin garments, Abel's sacrifice, Noah's rainbow, passage through the Red Sea, manna, water from the rock, bronze serpent, Aaron's rod, Gideon's fleece, Hezekiah's sundial, and so forth). When it came to the New Testament sacraments, however, the Reformed used a more restricted definition of "sacrament." Over against Rome, Protestants insist that scriptural evidence is lacking for the five sacraments added to baptism and the Lord's Supper. For Protestants, the two sacraments instituted by Christ and accepted in faith are enough to possess the whole Christ, with his perfect righteousness and holiness.

For it is not the number of sacraments that is decisive but Christ's institution and the fullness of grace he imparts in a sacrament.

DEFINING THE SACRAMENTS

[523] Alongside the Word, we must consider the sacraments as a second means of grace. Scripture does not have the word "sacrament," nor does it have a doctrine of the sacraments in general. It does indeed speak of circumcision and Passover, of baptism and the Lord's Supper, but does not sum up these ordinances under a single term. Nor did this as yet occur in the early Christian churches. Although we read in Acts 2:42 that the members of the church of Jerusalem "devoted themselves to the apostles' teaching and fellowship, to the breaking of bread and the prayers," and we can learn from Acts 6:4 that there was "a ministry of the Word," we know little about the way in which the gatherings of the Jerusalem church were arranged. From 1 Cor. 11:1–14:40 we know a little more about the worship services of believers from among the Gentiles. After believers, on the basis of a personal profession of faith, were admitted to the church ("into one body"— Rom. 6:3–5; 1 Cor. 12:13; Gal. 3:27) by baptism and in the name of Christ, they met regularly on the Lord's Day (Acts 20:7; 1 Cor. 16:2; Rev. 1:10). It is likely that on that day two gatherings were held, one for the ministry of the Word, to which also nonmembers were admitted (1 Cor. 14:23), at which a selection from the Old Testament Scripture and later also from the apostolic writings were read, every member of the church was free to speak up (14:26), and there was prayer and song (Acts 2:42; Rom. 12:12; 1 Cor. 14:14–15, 26). To this was added another for the celebration of the Lord's Supper ("for the purpose of eating," 1 Cor. 11:33), in which only believers were permitted to take part (10:16ff.; 11:20ff.).

Here there was first prayer and thanksgiving, then a common meal (ἀγαπη, *agapē*; Jude 12; 2 Pet. 2:13) composed of gifts presented by the believers themselves was held, again followed by prayers and thanksgiving (εὐχαριστια, *eucharistia*), and the Lord's Supper was celebrated. Jülicher, Spitta, Haupt, Hoffmann, and Drews (et al.) admittedly believe that in the apostolic era the Lord's Supper was not separated from the common meal but that the entire love feast (ἀγαπη) was a thanksgiving (εὐχαριστια), a "Lord's Supper," but this view is properly rejected by Harnack, Zahn, and Grafe (et al.). Jesus, after all, instituted the Lord's Supper after the common meal (Matt. 26:26; 1 Cor. 11:25). Paul makes a distinction between the two in 1 Cor. 11:20–21 and suggests that the two be totally separated by eating the regular meal at home beforehand (1 Cor. 11:22).[1]

---

1. C. H. von Weizsäcker, *Das apostolische Zeitalter der christlichen Kirche*, 2nd ed. (Freiburg: Mohr, 1890), 566ff.; B. Moeller and H. von Schubert, *Lehrbuch der Kirchengeschichte*, 3 vols. (Tübingen: Mohr, 1892–1907), I, 96ff.; T. Zahn, "Agapen," in *PRE*³, I, 234–37; P. Drews, "Eucharistie," in *PRE*³, V, 560–72; R. Knopf, *Das nachapostolische Zeitalter: Geschichte der christlichen Gemeinden vom Beginn der Flavierdynastie bis zum Ende Hadrians* (Tübingen: J. C. B. Mohr [P. Siebeck], 1905), 222ff.; P. A. E. Sillevis Smitt, *De organisatie van de Christelijke kerk in den apostolischen tijd* (Rotterdam: T. de Vries, 1910), 93ff.

In the second century, however, we witness a gradual but far-reaching change in this arrangement. For whatever reason,[2] the celebration of the Lord's Supper was separated from the love feasts, and the two gatherings, that for the ministry of the Word and that for the Lord's Supper, were united. From that time oward, the celebration of the Lord's Supper took place in the regular worship service after the ministry of the Word, and the service was distinguished in two parts. At the first part, the ministry of the Word, also pagans or at least the catechumens and penitents were allowed to be present; but the second part, the celebration of the Lord's Supper, was open only to baptized members of the church. As a result of the addition of the baptismal confession, the administration of baptism, the Lord's Prayer, and a wide range of ritual and symbolic actions, the Lord's Supper increasingly acquired a mysterious character.

The widespread system of Greek mystery religions began to exert influence on the Christian religion. In the New Testament, μυστηριον (*mystērion*) is the word for the mighty and marvelous acts of God that were formerly hidden but have now been revealed.[3] Soon, however, this word acquired a very different meaning in the Christian church and became the designation of everything that was mysterious and incomprehensible in the Christian religion. In the Latin, this word was translated by *sacramentum*, which carried the meaning of an oath, especially the oath a soldier had to swear before his country's standard, or of a sum of money that in a given trial had to be deposited in a sacred place and upon failure to win the trial fell to the gods, but that now absorbed the idea of a mysterious and holy act or matter. In this sense all that was in any way related to God and his revelation could be called a "sacrament"—the revelation itself and its content, a doctrine, the Trinity, the incarnation, and so forth, as well as an assortment of signs, such as the sign of the cross, the salt given to the catechumens, finally all sacred actions, the consecration of a priest, marriage, exorcism, the celebration of the Sabbath, circumcision, and all ceremonies.[4]

2. Cf. P. Drews, "Eucharistie," in *PRE*[3], V, 562.

3. Cf. H. Bavinck, *Reformed Dogmatics*, I, 619–21 (#160).

4. Edwin Hatch, *The Influence of Greek Ideas on Christianity* (1890; repr., New York: Harper, 1957); Gustav Anrich, *Das antike Mysterienwesen in seinem Einfluss auf das Christenthum* (Göttingen: Vandenhoeck & Ruprecht, 1894); Georg Wobbermin, *Religionsgeschichtliche Studien zur Frage nach der Beeinflussung des Urchristenthum durch das antike Mysterienwesen* (Berlin: E. Ebering, 1896). Ed. note: Bavinck refers here to the works of Edwin Hatch and others given in *Reformed Dogmatics*, I, 619–21nn47–55 (#160). He also adds the following, along with the history-of-dogma volumes of Schwane, Harnack, Loofs, and Seeberg: Bernd Moeller and Hans von Schubert, *Lehrbuch der Kirchengeschichte*, I, 32ff.; K. H. E. de Jong, *Das antike Mysterienwesen in religionsgeschichtlicher, ethnologischer, und psychologischer Beleuchtung* (Leiden: Brill, 1909); G. L. Hahn, *Die Lehre von den Sakramenten in ihrer geschichtlichen Entwicklung* (Breslau: E. Morganstern, 1864). The history-of-religions attempt to understand the Christian sacraments as coming completely or at least for the most part from the pagan mystery religions has not been at all successful. F. Kattenbusch ("Sakrament," in *PRE*[3], XVII, 349–81) says about this that although there is undoubtedly some influence, "the genre shows that there is little likelihood that such an influence had a major impact on Christianity." Also see Eduard Alexander von der Goltz, "Die Bedeutung der neueren religionsgeschichtlichen Forschungen für die Beurteilung der christlichen Sakramente," *Die Studierstube* 5 (1907): 609–22.

Now even though among the sacred actions denoted by the term "sacrament," baptism and the Lord's Supper were always clearly prominent, still the vagueness of the term was the reason the number of sacraments for a long time remained indefinite. Also Augustine still uses the term in a broad sense and in his definition of it assumes that meaning. Pseudo-Dionysius in the sixth century was the first to list six sacraments: baptism, confirmation, the Eucharist, holy orders, monastic consecration, and funeral customs. Scholasticism, however, in defining the term "sacrament," joined with Augustine and listed several holy matters and actions under this heading. Hugo of St. Victor mentions no fewer than thirty sacraments and divides them into three classes: (1) those necessary to salvation (baptism, confirmation, and so forth); (2) those that communicate a higher grace (use of holy water and so forth); and (3) those that serve in the preparation of the other sacraments (the consecration of holy instruments and so forth). Abelard lists five: baptism, confirmation, the Eucharist, extreme unction, and marriage, whereas Robert Pullus also has five but substitutes confession and holy orders for the last two. Bernard does not cite a number but in various places calls baptism, footwashing, confirmation, the Eucharist, confession, extreme unction, holy orders, investiture, and marriage by the name of sacraments. Lombard is the first to list the familiar seven,[5] but also after him theologians and synods (e.g., the [Third] Lateran Council of 1179) still speak of sacraments in a broad sense. And this continues until Lombard's *Sentences* became the general handbook for the study of theology and the Council of Florence (1439) established the number at seven.[6]

The definition of the term went hand in hand with this restriction of the number. Among the church fathers many holy actions, especially baptism and the Lord's Supper, were highly exalted and conceived as imparting supernatural power and grace, but a doctrine of the sacraments was still lacking. The relationship between the visible and the spiritual element was not clearly defined, and the sacramental mode of operation was not clearly described. In the sacraments Augustine distinguished between two components. "The reason these things [. . .] are called sacraments is that in them one thing is seen, another is to be understood. What can be seen has a bodily appearance, what is to be understood provides spiritual fruit."[7] "Take away the word, and the water is neither more nor less than water. The word is added to the element, and its result is the sacrament."[8] Sometimes he puts so much emphasis on the word and, for the efficacy of the sacrament, on the faith of the recipient, that the sign merely becomes an image of the thing signified. On the other hand, Augustine gave such a broad definition of the term "sacrament" that it could cover a wide range of ecclesiastical rites,

---

5. P. Lombard, *Sent.*, IV, dist. 2.

6. J. Schwane, *Dogmengeschichte*, 4 vols. (Freiburg i.B.: Herder, 1882–95), III, 584ff.; F. Loofs, *Leitfaden zum Studium der Dogmengeschichte*, 4th ed. (Halle a.S.: M. Niemeyer, 1906), 568ff.

7. Augustine, *Sermon* 272.

8. Augustine, *Homilies on the Gospel of John* 80, 3.

and against the Donatists he bound the sacraments so tightly to the church that, though they could be "abducted" by the heretics, they could still only impart grace within the church.[9]

The real doctrine of the sacraments is a product of medieval Scholasticism, which was the first to initiate careful and often very detailed research into the term, the institution, the administrator, the necessity, the functionality, the number, and the components of the sacraments. Also explored were the relationship between the sacrament and the thing signified by the sacrament; the difference between the sacraments in paradise, and in the Old and New Testaments; the mutual differences among the seven sacraments; the natural or moral effects of the sacraments; the distinct grace imparted by each; and the requirements of the distribution and reception of the sacraments.[10] The result of this Scholastic development was that, generally speaking, in part at earlier councils but especially at Trent, the following points were established in connection with the doctrine of the sacraments:

1. All the sacraments of the new covenant have been instituted by Christ and are seven in number: baptism, confirmation, the Eucharist, penance, extreme unction, holy orders, and marriage.
2. These are all true sacraments, essentially different from those of the old covenant, but differing among themselves in value.
3. Though not all of them are necessary for the salvation of every individual, they are necessary for salvation, so that without them or without the desire for them, by faith alone, that is, the grace of justification cannot be obtained.
4. They not only signify grace but also contain it and communicate it "through the act performed" (ex opere operato).
5. For the sacrament to be authentic, it is at least required of the administrators of the sacraments that they have the intention of doing what the church does, but for the rest it is immaterial whether or not they exist in a state of mortal sin.
6. The lawful administrators of the sacraments are only the ordained priests, but confirmation and holy orders are only performed by the bishop, and in case of emergency baptism may be administered also by laypersons.
7. Recipients are only required to have the intention to receive what the church bestows and not to put any obstacle in the way of grace.

9. A. von Harnack, *History of Dogma*, 7 vols., trans. N. Buchanan et al., ed. A. B. Bruce (London: Williams & Norgate, 1896–99), V, 156–57; F. Loofs, *Dogmengeschichte*, 373ff.; J. Hymmen, *Die Sakramentslehre Augustins in Zusammenhang dargestellt und beurteilt* (Bonn: C. Georgi, 1905).

10. Ed. note: Bavinck refers here to works he cites at the head of §57, "De sacramenten," in the Dutch edition. Most of these works have already been cited in this chapter, especially in note 4; others will be cited in subsequent notes. J. Schwane, *Dogmengeschichte*, III, 579–605; A. von Harnack, *History of Dogma*, VI, 204ff.; F. Loofs, *Dogmengeschichte*, 567ff.

8. Every sacrament supplies a special grace; and baptism, confirmation, and holy orders supply an "indelible character" (*character indelebilis*).[11]

SACRAMENTAL DOCTRINE

[524] The development of this doctrine of the sacraments shows that it progressively moved farther away from Scripture. This is true in especially three ways. In the first place, Rome views the grace imparted by the sacrament as being only sanctifying grace, that is, as a power that, being infused in persons, elevates them to the supernatural order and makes them partakers in the divine nature. Grace here has been almost completely separated from guilt and the forgiveness of sins and transformed into a supernatural gift coming down to people from without. In the second place, Rome almost completely severs the bond between the sacrament and the Word. Although the Word indeed has some meaning, it is only a provisional and preparatory meaning. The faith produced by the Word is nothing other than historical faith that is insufficient for salvation and has to be augmented with love, that is, by infused grace. And this grace is only imparted by the sacrament, which therefore occupies an independent place of its own next to the Word and far exceeds it in value. In the third place, faith is absolutely no longer a requirement in the recipient of the sacrament. Grace as sanctifying grace is enclosed within the sacrament as something material, is imparted by it ex opera operato, and therefore at most presupposes that the recipient will refrain from putting an insurmountable obstacle in its way. The sacrament, accordingly, works physically and magically by virtue of a power granted to the priest by God, as an instrument in his hand.

In all three ways, the Reformation revised and modified the Roman Catholic doctrine of the sacraments in accordance with Scripture. Zwingli, Luther, and Calvin were of one mind in this connection, and all stated that the grace imparted in the sacrament is in the first place forgiving grace and is directed, not to the lower nature, which is devoid of the superadded gift, but toward sin. They also insisted that the sacrament is a sign and a seal attached to the Word, did not impart any grace that was not also bestowed by the Word, and therefore is valueless without the Word. Finally, they said that not the sacrament itself but its operation and fruit depended on faith and hence always presupposed saving faith in the recipient.

In other ways, however, among the Reformers there soon appeared important differences in the construal of the doctrine of the sacraments. In fact, among Roman

---

11. Council of Trent, sess. VII; Roman Catechism, II, ch. 1. Ed. note: The post–Vatican II edition titled *The Roman Catechism* (trans. Robert I. Bradley, SJ, and Eugene Kevane [Boston: Daughters of St. Paul, 1985]) drops the enumeration of the introduction so that ch. 1 begins the section on baptism. In this annotation, the proper reference would be II, "Introduction." On sacramental theology in the Greek church, see F. Kattenbusch, *Lehrbuch der vergleichenden Confessionskunde* (Freiburg i.B.: J. C. B. Mohr [Paul Siebeck], 1892), I, 393ff. Ed. note: Bavinck here refers to the particular Roman Catholic works cited at the head of §57, "De sacramenten." Included are the following writers: Hugh of St. Victor, P. Lombard, Thomas Aquinas, Bonaventure, Bellarmine, P. Canisius, Möhler, Heinrich-Gutberlet, Scheeben-Atzberger, C. Pesch, Pohle, and Oswald.

Catholics, Lutherans, Zwinglians, the Reformed, the Anabaptists, and so forth the sacraments became the central focus of the struggle. They became the shibboleths of every dogmatic system. Practically and concretely they embodied the principles from which people proceeded in the church and in theology, in doctrine and in life. The relationship between God and the world, creation and re-creation, the divine and the human nature of Christ, sin and grace, spirit and matter—all found their practical application in the sacrament. The entire conflict revolved around the sacramental union, the union of the sign and the thing signified, the connection between the sacrament and the thing signified in the sacrament. Initially, in 1518 and 1519, Luther focused completely on the faith that alone makes the sacrament effective and thus makes us partakers in communion with Christ and his benefits. Then, from 1520 to 1524, he especially linked the sacrament to the Word, of which it is the sign and the seal. Finally, after 1524, out of fear of the Anabaptists, he increasingly came around to considering the sacraments indispensable, maintaining their objective character on the basis of Christ's institution, and viewing the connection between the sign and the thing signified as temporal, corporeal, and local. The result is that, according to the later Lutheran conception, the "heavenly substance" is concealed *in*, *with*, and *under* the elements, just as the power of the Holy Spirit entered the Word, and grace works through the sacraments as through its instruments, media, helps, vehicles, and organs.[12]

Zwingli, by contrast, taught that since the sacraments are administered only to those who have faith and through that faith share in Christ and all his benefits, they are in the first place signs and proofs of faith, acts of confession. Only in the second place are they also the means of strengthening faith, inasmuch as they remind us of the benefits toward which our faith is directed; they increasingly direct our faith away from ourselves to God's grace in Christ and so exercise and strengthen that faith.[13]

Calvin indeed also views the sacraments as acts of confession: "the mutual attestation of our piety toward God." But in Calvin they are only secondarily

12. J. Köstlin, *The Theology of Luther in Its Historical Development and Inner Harmony*, trans. Charles E. Hay, 2 vols. (Philadelphia: Lutheran Publication Society, 1897), II, 511; R. H. Grützmacher, *Wort und Geist: Eine historische und dogmatische Untersuchung zum Gnadenmittel des Wortes* (Leipzig: Deichert, 1902), 731ff.; H. Heppe, *Dogmatik des deutschen Protestantismus im sechzehnten Jahrhundert*, 3 vols. (Gotha: F. A. Perthes, 1857), III, 39ff.; Joseph T. Müller, *Die symbolischen Bücher der evangelisch-lutherischen Kirche*, 8th ed. (Gütersloh: Bertelsmann, 1898), 39, 41, 202, 264, 321; ed. note: These specific references are to the following Lutheran documents: Augsburg Confession, art. 5, in *The Book of Concord*, ed. R. Kolb and T. J. Wengert (Minneapolis: Fortress, 2000), 40; ibid., art. 13 (Kolb and Wengert, 46); Apology of the Augsburg Confession, art. 13, pars. 1–5 (Kolb and Wengert, 219–20); ibid., art. 24, pars. 69–70 (Kolb and Wengert, 270–71); Smalcald Articles, part III, art. 7 (Kolb and Wengert, 321). Bavinck also refers here to the Lutheran theologians cited at the head of §57, including Gerhard, Quenstedt, Hollaz, and Schmid.

13. U. Zwingli, *An Account of the Faith of Huldreich Zwingli* (*Fidei ratio*, 1530), in *On Providence and Other Essays*, ed. S. M. Jackson and W. J. Hinke (1922; repr., Durham, NC: Labyrinth, 1983), 7th article on the sacraments; idem, *Exposition of the Christian Faith*, "Sacraments"; E. Zeller, *Das theologische System Zwinglis* (Tübingen: L. F. Fues, 1853), 111ff.

such acts of confession. The sacraments are, first of all, "a testimony of divine grace toward us confirmed by an outward sign," signs and seals of the promises of God in his Word, mirrors in which we contemplate the riches of his grace. The invisible element, the matter and substance of the sacrament, accordingly, is the word, the promise, the covenant of grace, the person of Christ along with all his benefits. But the visible element does not keep these spiritual goods enclosed within itself, nor does it bestow them to us by some "intrinsic power of its own." God does not relinquish his work to the signs in the sacrament. He and he alone is the possessor and also remains the distributor of grace. The signs fulfill only an instrumental or ministerial function: God employs them to impart his grace. And he imparts this grace only to those who believe, and then he strengthens and nourishes their faith. Unbelievers only receive the sign, not the thing signified.

Just how God employs the sacraments to distribute his grace does not become clear either in Calvin or in the works of the later Reformed. So there is room left for a wide assortment of questions. Is grace always bound up with the sign so that the sacrament always remains the same objectively? Or does God unite grace with the sign only when the sacrament is received by believers? Or does God offer his grace in union with the sign also to unbelieving partakers so that it is their own fault if they only accept and receive the sign? In what way is sacramental grace distinguished from the grace that believers already received earlier? And in what way does it differ from the subjective working of the Holy Spirit, who opens the eyes of believers to the sacrament and their hearts to its substance? Does the distribution of grace accompany the administration or the reception of the sign? Does it occur simultaneously with the administration and reception of the sign, or can it also occur before or later? And can the sacrament's benefit therefore be received before, during, and after the reception of the sacrament?[14]

Outside of the Lutheran and Reformed churches, which, following Luther's and Calvin's example, maintained the objective character of the sacraments, Zwingli's doctrine found increasing acceptance. The Anabaptists still accepted foot washing, baptism, and the Lord's Supper as sacraments, to be sure, but only regarded them as signs and symbols, not as seals. True, the sacraments visibly represent the benefits that believers have received from God, but they do this as confessions of our faith and do not impart grace.[15] The Socinians, like Zwingli, disapproved of the

14. Cf. J. Calvin, *Institutes*, IV.xiv; Genevan Catechism, 5; Consensus tigurinus (1549), in *Selected Works of John Calvin: Tracts and Letters* (1849; repr., Grand Rapids: Eerdmans, 1958), II, 212–20; J. M. Usteri, "Calvins Sakraments- und Tauflehre," *Theologische Studien und Kritiken* 57 (1884): 417–56; Gallican Confession, arts. 34, 37; Belgic Confession, art. 33; Heidelberg Catechism, Q 66–67; J. à Lasco, *Opera tam edita quam inedita*, ed. Abraham Kuyper, 2 vols. (Amsterdam: F. Muller, 1866), I, 115–232, 511–14; H. Bullinger, *Decades*, V, serm. 6; G. Sohn, *Opera sacrae theologiae*, 2 vols. (Herborn: C. Corvin, 1598), I, 55; T. Beza, *Tractationum theologicarum* (Geneva: Jean Crispin, 1570), I, 206. Ed. note: Bavinck refers here to Reformed theologians cited at the head of §57, including Polanus, Maccovius, Mastricht, Turretin, de Moor, C. Vitringa, and J. H. Bachiene.

15. J. Cloppenburg, *Theol. op.*, II, 238; cf. Fr. W. Loetscher, "Schwenckfeld's Participation in the Eucharistic Controversy of the Sixteenth Century," *Princeton Theological Review* 4 (1906): 352–86, 454–500.

word "sacrament," regarded the Lord's Supper as a memorial meal, a statement of what we have in Christ, and denied that baptism was based on a command from Christ and was a permanent ordinance.[16] The Remonstrants in their confession still, to be sure, confessed that God displays his benefits in the sacraments ("in a certain manner exhibits and seals" them), but their Apology shows that by this they did not mean a sealing of God's promise, nor a communication of his grace. The sacraments are signs of the covenant between God and people in which the latter obligate themselves to live a holy life and God visibly represents his grace to them.[17] Among the Rationalists the sacraments became memorials and confessional signs whose purpose was the promotion of virtue and which could therefore easily be supplemented with other solemn ceremonies.[18] The Quakers rejected the sacraments as Jewish ceremonials, viewed baptism as Spirit-baptism that washes away our sins, and the Lord's Supper as a depiction of the feeding of our soul by Christ.[19]

This process of disintegration was arrested by Schleiermacher to the degree that he made an attempt to maintain the objective character of the sacraments and to combine all the various views into a higher unity. To that end he described them as "continued activities of Christ, enshrined in church actions and bound up therewith in the closest way. By their instrumentality he exerts his priestly activity on individuals, and sustains and propagates that living fellowship between him and us by virtue of which alone God sees individuals in Christ."[20] But this attempt at reconciliation failed. The [formulation] "activities of Christ, enshrined in church actions" left undecided what is primary and most important in the sacraments. Before long, theology again split into several different directions. Some theologians continued to hold a mediating position;[21] others reproduced Zwingli's views[22] or returned to the confessional position of the Lutheran and Reformed churches.[23]

16. O. Fock, *Der Socinianismus* (Kiel: C. Schröder, 1847), 559ff.

17. Apologia pro confessione Remonstrantium (1629), c. 23; P. van Limborch, *Theologia christiana* (Amsterdam: Arnhold, 1735), V, 66.

18. J. A. L. Wegscheider, *Institutiones theologiae christianae dogmaticae*, 3rd ed. (Halle: Gebauer, 1819), §165.

19. R. Barclay, *Verantwoording van de ware Christelyke Godgeleertheid*, trans. Jan Hendrik Glazemaker (Amsterdam: A. Waldorp, 1757), 325.

20. F. Schleiermacher, *The Christian Faith*, ed. H. R. MacIntosh and J. S. Steward (Edinburgh: T&T Clark, 1928), §143.

21. C. E. Nitzsch, *System of Christian Doctrines* (Edinburgh: T&T Clark, 1849), §191; J. J. van Oosterzee, *Christian Dogmatics*, trans. J. Watson and M. Evans, 2 vols. (New York: Scribner, Armstrong, 1874), II, 815.

22. R. A. Lipsius, *Lehrbuch der evangelisch-protestantischen Dogmatik* (Braunschweig: C. A. Schwetschke, 1893), §§807ff., 840ff.; A. Schweizer, *Die christliche Glaubenslehre nach protestantischen Grundsätzen dargestellt*, 2 vols. in 3 (Leipzig: S. Hirzel, 1863–72), II, 400ff.; A. E. Biedermann, *Christliche Dogmatik* (Zurich: Orell, Fussli, 1869), II, 632; A. Ritschl, *Unterricht in der christlichen Religion*, 3rd ed. (Bonn: A. Marcus, 1886), §83; J. H. Scholten, *De leer der Hervormde Kerk in hare grondbeginselen*, 2nd ed., 2 vols. (Leiden: P. Engels, 1850–51), II, 310.

23. F. A. Philippi, *Kirchliche Glaubenslehre*, 3rd ed., 7 vols. (Gütersloh: Bertelsmann, 1883–1902), V, 2; C. Hodge, *Systematic Theology*, 3 vols. (New York: Charles Scribner's Sons, 1888), III, 485.

And finally the Neo-Lutherans in Germany[24] and the Puseyites in England[25] set forth a theology of the sacraments that in many ways resembled that of Rome, saw grace as impacting—through the sacrament—not only the soul but also the psychophysical nature of man and the human body, and frequently expanded the number of the sacraments.

[525] Scripture does not know the word "sacrament," nor does it, in the abstract, contain a doctrine of the sacraments. It does speak of various religious actions in the Old and New Testaments but does not subsume these actions under a common term. And also in the Christian church the matter itself and not the concept was primary. A variety of church doctrines and usages began gradually to be described by the term "sacrament." It is understandable, therefore, that a great many people objected to this term and would rather replace it with those of signs, seals, code language, mysteries, and the like. Not only Carlstadt, Zwingli, Socinus, Schleiermacher, Doedes, and so forth disapproved of the term, but even Luther said in his "prelude to the Babylonian captivity" that Scripture does not know the word in the sense it has in theology. Calvin commented that the church fathers injected a new meaning into the Latin word.[26] In the first edition of his *Loci*, Melanchthon replaced "sacramenta" by "signa," and also Musculus, Hottinger, Burman, Cocceius, and others preferred the scriptural terminology of signs and seals. This objection to the term is even intensified by the fact that the Greek meaning of the word μυστηριον (*mystērion*), translated in Latin by *sacramentum*, exerted influence on the understanding of the church rites described by that term.

Still, all this is no reason to reject the word. Theology, we know, employs many terms that do not occur in Scripture and that have acquired technical meaning in their own sphere. If theology had to refrain from using such terms, it would have to cease all scientific labor and all preaching and exegesis of God's Word, and indeed even the translation of Scripture, would be impermissible. Nor, for the same reason, is it to be frowned on when we treat the [general] doctrine of the sacraments prior to that of baptism and the Lord's Supper. For though there is no separate doctrine on the sacraments to be found in Scripture, and this doctrine has to be constructed out of what Scripture teaches us about the special ordinances of circumcision and the Passover, baptism, and the Lord's Supper, a prior chapter

---

24. J. W. F. Höfling, *Das Sakrament der Taufe* (Erlangen: Deichert, 1859), I, 18–20; J. C. K. von Hofmann, *Der Schriftbeweis*, 3 vols. (Nördlingen: Beck, 1857–60), II, 2, 167ff.; G. Thomasius, *Christi Person und Werk*, 3rd ed., 2 vols. (Erlangen: A. Deichert, 1886–88), II, 355ff.; F. Delitzsch, *A System of Biblical Psychology*, trans. Robert E. Wallis, 2nd ed. (Edinburgh: T&T Clark, 1875), 400–401, 411–12, 416–17; H. Martensen, *Christian Dogmatics*, trans. W. Urwick (Edinburgh: T&T Clark, 1871), §§247–58; A. F. C. Vilmar, *Dogmatik*, 2 vols. (Gütersloh: C. Bertelsmann, 1874), II, 226ff.

25. Cf. R. Buddensieg, "Traktarianismus," in *PRE*³, XX, 26, 30, 32, 42, esp. 46ff.; E. Paget, "Sacraments," in *Lux Mundi*, ed. C. Gore, 13th ed. (London: Murray, 1892), 296–317; Charles Gore, *The Creed of the Christian*, 6th ed. [cf. 7th ed., London: Wells, Gardner, Darton, 1905], 76ff.; H. Rashdall, *Christus in ecclesia* (Edinburgh: T&T Clark, 1904). A refutation of this High Church doctrine can be found in J. C. Ryle, *Knots Untied*, 11th ed. (London: William Hunt, 1886).

26. J. Calvin, *Institutes*, IV.xiv.13.

on the sacraments in general specifically enables us to sum up what these special ordinances have in common in Scripture, and to posit this correct scriptural understanding against the unsound doctrine that has gradually penetrated the Christian church with respect to the sacraments.

In the definition of the sacraments, therefore, the Reformed aligned themselves as closely as possible with Scripture. Scholasticism argued over the question whether a definition could be given of the sacraments since, being composed by "things" (*res*) and "words" (*verba*), they were not a real being, not one thing by itself.[27] Still, Scholastics deduced from Augustine, who repeatedly distinguished a visible and an invisible component in the sacraments, the definition that they were "a sacred sign" or "the sign of a sacred thing,"[28] or also, "the visible form of an invisible grace."[29] Although not incorrect, this definition is definitely too broad. Hence later Roman Catholic theologians as a rule adopted the definition of the Roman Catechism and described the sacraments as "certain sensible signs which because of their institution by God have a power both of signifying and effecting holiness and righteousness."[30] Although this definition can be understood in the true sense, in Roman Catholic theology it acquired a meaning that is in conflict with Scripture and has therefore become unusable for the Reformation. Roman Catholic theology, after all, conceives the sacrament as a "sacred, secret, and hidden thing" and injects into it the sense not of the biblical but of the Greek μυστήριον. Furthermore, it emphasizes to the exclusion of all else that the sacraments contain grace within themselves, that they impart it "by the act performed" (ex opere operato), and that this grace especially consists in sanctifying grace. Scripture, however, speaks of the rainbow and circumcision as "signs of the covenant" (Gen. 9:12–13, 17; 17:11; cf. Exod. 12:13; Acts 7:8) and calls the latter a "sign of circumcision, a seal of the righteousness of faith" (Rom. 4:11); it similarly links baptism and the Lord's Supper as closely as possible with the covenant of grace, with the Mediator and the benefits of that covenant, and specifically with the forgiveness of sins (Mark 1:4; 14:22–24; and so forth).

SIGNS AND SEALS

In keeping with this, Reformed theology described the sacraments as visible, holy signs and seals instituted by God so that he might make believers understand more clearly and reassure them of the promises and benefits of the covenant of grace, and believers on their part might confess and confirm their faith and love before God, angels, and humankind.

Noteworthy in this connection is first of all that God is mentioned as the one who instituted the sacraments. Generally speaking, we can say that on this point

27. R. Bellarmine, "De sacr. in genere," in *Controversiis*, I, 10.
28. T. Aquinas, *Summa theol.*, III, qu. 60, art. 1–2.
29. P. Lombard, *Sent.*, IV, 1.
30. Roman Catechism, II, ch. 1, qu. 2, 6 (ed. note: Bradley and Kevane, II, Introduction, 2, 6).

there is no disagreement in the Christian churches. All believe that God alone can be the author, initiator, and "efficient cause" of the sacraments. He alone is the possessor and distributor of all grace. He alone can determine to what means he will bind himself in the distribution of his grace. Furthermore, also Christ has the right to institute sacraments, for as Mediator he is the acquisitor of all divine grace. "It is not for humans to institute and shape the worship of God; their task, rather, is to receive and preserve that which has been handed down by God."[31] But in this connection Rome finds itself in a peculiar difficulty. Since Christ did not institute any sacraments other than baptism and the Lord's Supper, it has to be said of the other sacraments either that they are not sacraments, or that also the apostles had the right to institute sacraments. Before the Council of Trent many theologians asserted that the sacraments—say, confirmation and confession— were not directly instituted by Christ but by the apostles.[32] The Council of Trent expressly declared,[33] however, that all seven sacraments were instituted by Jesus Christ our Lord himself, not mediately—for this was acknowledged by all; in that case no council decree would have been necessary—but immediately,[34] and in so declaring imposed on theology an obligation it could not fulfill. Yet the council was correct insofar as it recognized that the right to institute sacraments could not be transferred to creatures even by God. Human beings can make known the institution of a sacrament (Exod. 12:1ff.; Mark 1:4; 11:30; 1 Cor. 11:23), hand out the sign of it, and announce the grace of God; what they cannot do, in the nature of the case, is to actually grant this grace. Grace, certainly, is not a material something, but the favor and fellowship of God, something that is inseparable from God and therefore cannot be imparted by a creature, either a human or an angel. For that reason God in Christ, through the Holy Spirit, is the only "institutor" but also the only "distributor" of the sacrament. Only that sacrament is true that is administered by God himself. It is Christ himself who baptizes and celebrates the Lord's Supper in his church. He did not transfer his office to someone else and appointed no deputy on earth. He himself governs, and just as he alone administers the Word as prophet, so also he is the only administrator of the sacrament, even though it is true that in this connection he also employs humans as his instruments.[35]

Noteworthy in the Reformed definition of the sacraments, in the second place, is that they are described as signs. Although a few Reformed theologians occasion-

31. Second Helvetic Confession, 19.
32. P. Lombard, *Sent.*, IV, dist. 3; Hugh of St. Victor, *On the Sacraments of the Christian Faith*, trans. R. J. Deferrari (Cambridge, MA: Mediaeval Academy of America, 1951), II, 15, 2. See also Hales, Bonaventure; J. Schwane, *Dogmengeschichte*, III, 597.
33. Council of Trent, sess. VII, can. 1.
34. R. Bellarmine, "De sacr.," in *Controversiis*, I, c. 23.
35. Second Helvetic Confession, 19; A. Rivetus, in *Synopsis purioris theologiae*, disp. 43, 8; F. Turretin, *Institutes of Elenctic Theology*, trans. G. M. Giger, ed. J. T. Dennison (Phillipsburg, NJ: Presbyterian & Reformed, 1992), XIX, 1, 14; C. Vitringa, *Doctrina christiana religionis*, 8 vols. (Leiden: Joannis le Mair, 1761–86), VI, 338.

ally also assigned them—either as a rule or for a change—to the ceremonies, rites, or actions,[36] yet far and away the majority traced them to the generic concept of signs, seals, images, symbols, types, or antitypes.[37] In this regard they diverged, in part from the Roman Catholics but especially from the Lutherans, who were particularly fond of describing them as actions and saw here an important point of dispute with the Reformed.[38] This is surprising on the part of the Lutherans since in connection with the Word they teach that the power of the Holy Spirit is immanent in it even before or after its use. The analogy would require that the emphasis should fall, not on the action, but on the sign function of the sacrament. Yet this is not the case. Lutherans regard the sacrament first of all as an action consisting in the communication of grace in, with, and under the sign. Now the Reformed tradition absolutely did not deny that in the sacrament there occurs an action. But this is the hidden invisible action of Christ, who inwardly confers grace in the hearts of believers through the Holy Spirit. On the other hand, in the case of the sacrament the main thing is not the action of the minister, as if that action were so freighted with meaning as even to bring about a consubstantiation or transubstantiation, but in the sacrament's being a sign. It images and assures us of the action of Christ. Indeed, even the action of the administrator of the sacrament, though an action, is itself a significative action. And Scripture for that reason calls sacraments by the name of signs and seals and obligates Roman Catholics and Lutherans to endorse these names.[39]

The Reformed definition of the sacraments is special, in the third place, in that it unites the action of God with the confession of believers taking place in them. In that way Calvin reconciled Luther and Zwingli.[40] Calvin agreed with Luther in saying that God's action in the sacrament is primary, but Calvin with Zwingli judged that in the sacrament believers made confession of their faith and love before God, angels, and humans. In the sacrament God first comes to believers to signify and seal his benefits. He assures them with visible pledges that he is their God and the God of their children. He attaches seals to *his* Word to strengthen *their* faith in that Word (Gen. 9:11–15; 17:11; Exod. 12:13; Mark 1:4; 16:16; Luke 22:19; Rom. 4:11; and so forth). On the other hand, the sacraments are also acts of confession. In them believers confess their conversion, their faith, their obedience, their communion with Christ and with each other. While God assures them that he is their God, they solemnly testify that they are his children. Every

36. H. Bullinger, *Decades*, V, serm. 6; Lucas Trelcatius Jr., *Scholastica et methodica locorum communium institutio* (London: Orlers, 1604), 141; F. Junius, *Theses theologicae*, in vol. 1 of *Opuscula theologica selecta*, ed. Abraham Kuyper (Amsterdam: F. Muller, 1882), 50, 6.

37. B. de Moor, *Commentarius . . . theologiae*, 6 vols. (Leiden: J. Hasebroek, 1761–71), V, 231; C. Vitringa, *Doctr. christ.*, VI, 341.

38. J. Gerhard, *Loci theologici*, ed. E. Preuss, 9 vols. (Berlin: G. Schlawitz, 1863–75), XVIII, 22ff.

39. G. Bucanus, *Institutiones theologicae*, 3rd ed. (Bern: Johannes & Isaias le Preux, 1605), 559; S. Maresius, *Syst. theol.*, XVIII, 8; P. van Mastricht, *Theoretica-Practica theologia* (Utrecht: Appels, 1714), VII, 3, 14; F. Turretin, *Institutes of Elenctic Theology*, XIX, 3, 9.

40. J. Calvin, *Institutes*, IV.xiv.1.

observance of the sacrament is an act of covenant renewal, a vow of faithfulness, an oath that obligates those who take it to engage in the service of Christ (Mark 1:5; 16:16; Acts 2:41; 8:37; Rom. 6:3ff.; 1 Cor. 10:16ff.).[41]

[526] Implied in the terms "sign" and "seal" is that the sacrament consists in two parts distinguished as "word" and "element," the substance of the sacrament and the sacrament (in the restricted sense), the thing signified and the sign, the heavenly and the earthly substance, internal and external matter. Both the sign and the seal refer to something else of which they are the sign and the seal.

Signs are both numerous and diverse. As Augustine already remarked,[42] there are natural signs and positive, accepted, instituted signs. Belonging in the first category are things such as smoke, which prompts the association of fire; the dawn, which signals the advent of the sun; the footprint, which speaks of a walker; the fragrance, which suggests the presence of flowers; the laughter we associate with joy; the tear, which brings to mind sorrow. Positive signs are those that have been established by agreement, custom, or usage and are accepted and recognized in a more or less restricted circle. Belonging to this category are the letters of the alphabet, slogans, standards, flags, insignias, and so forth. All these are again distinguished as ordinary signs from extraordinary signs, in which category the miracles occupy primacy of place. In Scripture the latter are frequently described as σημεῖα, because they are proofs and signs of God's presence, of his grace or power, of his truth or righteousness. Signs are further subdivided in terms of whether, like memorial signs, they refer to something in the past (Josh. 4:6), or like predictive signs, to something in the future (Gen. 4:15), or also, like so many signs, to something present and permanent (Deut. 6:8). Now sacraments are among the instituted extraordinary signs that God has taken—not arbitrarily but according to an analogy preformed by him—from among visible things and uses for the designation and clarification of invisible and eternal goods.

Aside from being signs, the sacraments are also seals that serve to confirm and strengthen. Seals, after all, are distinguished from signs by the fact that they do not just bring the invisible matter to mind but also validate and confirm it. Inasmuch as there is so much deception and falsehood in the world, all sorts of means are used to distinguish the true from the false, the genuine from the spurious. Thus a trademark serves to authenticate and guarantee the genuineness of a manufactured product, a gauge to determine the precision of weights and measures, a mint to measure the true value of money, and a seal to mark the authenticity of documents.

In Scripture, too, there is frequent reference to seals when something has to be marked as genuine and protected from falsification. The letters of rulers (1 Kings 21:8; Neh. 9:38; Esther 3:12) or other persons (Jer. 32:10), as well as laws (Isa.

41. Cf. Belgic Confession, art. 36; C. Vitringa, *Doctr. christ.*, VI, 423ff.; H. Heppe, *Die Dogmatik der evangelisch-reformirten Kirche* (Elberfeld: R. L. Friderichs, 1861), 441. Ed. note: Bavinck also refers to the liturgical forms of the Dutch Reformed Church for baptism and the Lord's Supper.

42. Augustine, *On Christian Doctrine* II, 1.

8:16), books (Dan. 12:4; Rev. 22:10), Daniel's den of lions (Dan. 6:17), Jesus's tomb (Matt. 27:66), and so forth were sealed and thus protected from being violated or desecrated. God, too, has a seal (Rev. 7:2). He seals the stars when he conceals them and covers them with clouds (Job 9:7). He seals the book of judgment so that no one other than the Lamb can open and read it (Rev. 5:1). God seals the pit in which Satan has been confined so that he could no longer deceive the nations (20:3). He seals his servants in the final tribulation so that they can no longer be harmed (7:3; 9:4). God seals all believers with the Holy Spirit in order that, as heirs, they may be kept for future salvation (2 Cor. 1:22; Eph. 1:13; 4:30). He seals the Christ by all sorts of signs as the giver of the food that endures to eternal life (John 6:27). In blessing Paul's labors, God gave him a seal, a confirmation of his apostleship (1 Cor. 9:2). He presses his seal on the building of the church as a pledge that it is his possession (2 Tim. 2:19). Seals, accordingly, are always means for the purpose of guaranteeing the genuineness of persons and things or protecting them from violation. Similarly, in the sign of circumcision Abraham received a seal, that is, a confirmation, validation, and pledge of the righteousness that he possessed by faith (Rom. 4:11). Aside from being signs, therefore, sacraments are also seals that God attaches to his word in order to highlight its trustworthiness, not of course to the Word as such, for as the word of God it is reliable enough, but for our benefit and to our mind. Not only are the visible elements of water, bread, and wine signs and seals, but also the various ceremonial actions accompanying them have significative and sealing power. Sprinkling or immersion in baptism, the blessing, breaking, distribution, and reception of bread in the Lord's Supper—these are not arbitrary and indifferent customs, but combine to form the constituents of the sacraments, enable us to better understand the promises and benefits of the covenant, and together with the elements form the sacraments into signs and seals of the invisible benefits of redemption.[43]

THE "MATTER" OF THE SACRAMENTS

The "internal matter" in the sacrament, the invisible substance depicted and sealed in it, is the covenant of grace (Gen. 9:12–13; 17:11); the righteousness of faith (Rom. 4:11); the forgiveness of sins (Mark 1:4; Matt. 26:28); faith and repentance (Mark 1:4; 16:16); communion with Christ, with his death and resurrection (Rom. 6:3ff.), with his flesh and blood (1 Cor. 10:16); and so forth. Recapitulating this, one can therefore say that Christ—the full, rich, total Christ, both according to his divine and his human natures, with his person and work, in the state of his humiliation and in that of his exaltation—is the "internal matter," the "heavenly substance," the thing signified in the sacrament. For this Christ, with all his benefits and blessings, is the Mediator of the covenant of grace; the

---

43. C. Vitringa, *Doctr. christ.*, VI, 352.

head of the church; the Yes and Amen of all God's promises; the content of his word and witness; the wisdom, righteousness, sanctification, and redemption of believers; the prophet, priest, and king in whom alone God communicates all his grace; and the same yesterday, today, and forever. Jesus Christ is the truth of the sacraments, "without whom they would be nothing."[44] By the "internal matter of the sacraments," Roman Catholic theologians understand sanctifying grace, that is, the grace that is added to nature, enables believers to perform good works, and will someday enable them to see God. It is created grace, which does not essentially differ from uncreated grace, that is, from God himself, for in each created grace God actually gives himself.[45] And they teach that this grace has entered and is contained in the sign as something material, is therefore imparted with the sign "by the act performed" (ex opere operato), and can be obtained in no other way than by faith in God's Word alone.[46]

In the early period [of the Reformation] Lutheran dogmaticians called the two components of the sacrament "the word" and "the element," and so understood the sacrament to impart the same grace as that imparted by the Word. But as a result of their doctrine of consubstantiation, they gradually, especially since Gerhard, got to where they accepted, along with the word, a "heavenly substance" in the sacrament. As a result of the word of consecration, the element not only ceases to be, as the older dogmaticians said, an ordinary external element but also absorbs a special divine power that is distinct from the word, is described as a "heavenly substance," and works through the element as its medium and vehicle. Thus a difference emerged between the benefits of grace imparted through the Word and those imparted through the sacrament. In the Lord's Supper, remember, one received the very flesh and blood of Christ. However, since such a "heavenly substance," distinct from the benefits of salvation, could be shown to be present only in the Lord's Supper and not in baptism, Baier and others rose up to oppose the idea of speaking of a "heavenly substance" in connection with the sacraments in general.[47] Still modern theology repeatedly set forth such a view of the sacrament and so differentiated between the Word and the sacrament that the former exerted a person-centered effect and the latter a natural effect; that the former is a means of the "metanoetic" working of the Holy Spirit and the latter a means of the "anagennetic" working of the Holy Spirit; that the Word changes the consciousness, but the sacrament the mind, the self, the psychophysical nature of a person.[48]

44. Belgic Confession, arts. 33–35; Heidelberg Catechism, Q 67; Second Helvetic Confession, ch. XIX; Scotch Confession, art. 21; Westminster Confession, ch. 27.1; J. Calvin, *Institutes*, IV.xiv.16–17; A. Rivetus, in *Synopsis purioris theologiae*, disp. 43, 20–21; P. van Mastricht, *Theologia*, VII, 3, 7.

45. J. B. Heinrich and K. Gutberlet. *Dogmatische Theologie*, 2nd ed., 10 vols. (Mainz: Kirchheim, 1881–1900), VIII, 550ff.

46. Council of Trent, sess. VII, can. 4ff.

47. H. F. F. Schmid, *The Doctrinal Theology of the Evangelical Lutheran Church*, trans. Charles A. Hay and Henry Jacobs, 5th ed. (Philadelphia: United Lutheran Publication House, 1899), 532ff.

48. Cf. above, 62–63 (#441), 67–68 (#442), 73–75 (#443).

All this, however, is in conflict with Scripture and an importation of the erroneous doctrine of Roman Catholicism. The sacrament does not impart a single benefit that is not also received from the Word of God by faith alone. For those who believe are born again (John 1:12–13), have eternal life (John 3:36), are justified (Rom. 3:28; 5:1), sanctified (John 15:3; Acts 15:9), glorified (Rom. 8:30), have fellowship with Christ (Eph. 3:17), with his flesh and blood (John 6:47–51), with his Father (1 John 1:3), with the Holy Spirit (John 7:39; Gal. 3:2, 5), and so forth. The Word contains all the promises of God and faith appropriates them all. The content of the Word is Christ, the whole Christ, who is also the content of the sacrament. There is not a single benefit of grace that, withheld from us in the Word, is now imparted to believers in a special way by the sacrament. There is neither a separate baptismal grace nor a separate communion grace. The content of Word and sacrament is completely identical. The two contain the same Mediator, the same covenant, the same benefits, the same salvation, the same fellowship with God. They are even the same in mode and instrument of reception, for also in the sacrament Christ is enjoyed spiritually, not physically, by faith, not by the mouth. They only differ in the external form, in the *manner* in which they offer the *same* Christ to us. In a certain sense also the Word is a sign and a seal—a sign that makes us think of the matter it designates, a seal that confirms that which exists in reality. This is true of every word in general but especially of the word of God. Those who deny this make God a liar (1 John 5:10). But the Word signifies and seals Christ to us by the sense of hearing; the sacrament signifies and seals Christ to us by the sense of sight. Jointly they offer Christ and all his benefits to us by way of the two higher senses that God has given human beings, without thereby entirely excluding the sense of smell, taste, and touch.

From this difference in the *manner* in which they offer Christ and all his benefits to us, we may further infer that the sacrament is subordinate to the Word. It is a sign of the content of the Word; a seal that God has attached to his witness; a pillar, as Calvin puts it, which has been erected on the foundation of the Word; an appendix that comes with the Word and has been added to it. The Word, accordingly, is something, even much, without the sacrament, but the sacrament is nothing without the Word and in that case has neither value nor power. It is nothing less but also nothing more than the Word made visible. All the benefits of salvation can be obtained from the Word and by faith alone, while there is not a single benefit that could be obtained without the Word and without faith from the sacrament alone. The Word therefore effects and strengthens faith, directing itself to believers and unbelievers alike; but the sacrament says nothing to, nor contains anything for, unbelievers. It is destined exclusively for believers; it can only strengthen the faith that is present, for it is nothing but a sign and seal of the Word. In this function lies its only—though by God's intent also its sufficient— value and power to clarify and confirm the Word and thus to strengthen the faith of believers. In the struggle against Rome, the maintenance of this agreement and difference between Word and sacrament is of the greatest importance. Those who define the two differently and ascribe to the sacrament one operation of grace and another to the Word, separate Christ from his benefits; break the unity of the covenant of grace; materialize grace; make the sacrament something independent of, contrary to, and above the Word; reverse the relationship between Scripture and the church; and make the sacrament necessary for salvation and the people dependent on the priest. For that reason the Reformed, as well as the Lutherans in that early period, never tired of stating over and over again the correct, scriptural relationship between the Word and the sacrament and asserting ever anew that the sacrament is subordinate to the Word, and that they both serve to direct our faith toward Christ's sacrifice on the cross as the sole ground of our salvation.[49]

[527] The link that connects the sign with the thing signified was sometimes called the "form of the sacrament" and sometimes also "the sacramental union." Against the latter designation Gomarus took exception for good reason. He said: The relationship that exists between the sign and the thing signified and in a sense unites the two "is commonly, in imitation of the Ubiquitorians, called by a strange and obscure term, the sacramental union, which is not direct enough. Because the thing signified more truly unites with us than is denoted and confirmed by signs within signs."[50] Roman Catholics and Lutherans can to some extent speak in connection with the Lord's Supper of a union between "the external and the internal matter" in the sacrament, for they teach that the thing signified enters into and is contained in the sign: they assume the existence of a physical, corporeal, and local union. But even on their position there is a problem, for in the case of Roman Catholics the sign changes into the thing signified, and so no actual union is possible; and for the Lutherans the thing signified is, to be sure, present in, with, and under the sign and hence brought together with the sign in the same location and space, but such a juxtaposition is certainly something totally different from a union. Furthermore, in the case of the Word and baptism and the other sacraments accepted by Rome, this "sacramental union," is so different from that in the Lord's Supper that it will not do simply to speak in general of a "sacramental union."

From a Reformed position, however, the problem looms much larger. Scripture calls the sacraments "signs" and "seals" and with these terms describes the

49. Cf. J. Köstlin, *The Theology of Luther*, II, 511; Joseph T. Müller, *Die symbolischen Bücher*, 202, 320, 487, 500; ed. note: These specific references are to the following Lutheran documents: Apology of the Augsburg Confession, art. 13, pars. 1–5 (Kolb and Wengert, 219–20); Smalcald Articles, part III, arts. 5–6 (Kolb and Wengert, 319–21); The Large Catechism, part IV, "Concerning Baptism" (Kolb and Wengert, 458); ibid., part V, "The Sacrament of the Altar" (Kolb and Wengert, 467–68). H. Heppe, *Dogmatik des deutschen Protestantismus*, II, 36; J. Calvin, *Institutes*, IV.xiv.3, 5, 6, 14; Consensus Tigurinus (1549), in H. A. Niemeyer, *Collectio confessionum in ecclesiis reformatis publicatarum*, 2 vols. (Leipzig: Iulii Klinkhardti, 1840), 204, 206 (ed. note: English translation in J. Calvin, *Selected Works of John Calvin: Tracts and Letters*, II, 223–27); Gallican Confession, art. 34; Belgic Confession, art. 33; Heidelberg Catechism, Q 66; Second Helvetic Confession, ch. XIX; A. Polanus, *Syntagma theologia christianae*, 5th ed. (Hanover: Aubry, 1624), VI, 51; P. van Mastricht, *Theologia*, VII, 3, 11; F. Turretin, *Institutes of Elenctic Theology*, XIX, 3, 6.

50. F. Gomarus, "Theses theol.," in *Opera theologia omnia* (Amsterdam: J. Jansson, 1644), disp. 31, 36; cf. also J. H. Heidegger, *Corpus theologiae*, 2 vols. (Zurich: J. H. Bodmer, 1700), XI, 58.

connection between "the internal and the external matter." No one would call the connection existing between a word and the thing it signifies, between an image and the person it represents, between a pledge and that of which it is a pledge, a union. Yet the relationship that exists between the sign and the thing signified in the sacrament is of the same nature. It is not a physical, local, corporeal, or substantial connection. The signs of water, bread, and wine are not miracles, remedies, schemes, vehicles, channels, or physical causes of the thing signified. It is, rather, an ethical connection, a connection that is identical with that between Christ and the gospel, between the benefits of the covenant of grace and the Word of God that makes them known to us.[51] In the case of the Word, the connection with the things it describes is an automatic given. But in the case of the signs in the sacrament, this is not the case. Water, bread, and wine are not by nature signs and seals of Christ and his benefits. No one would be able or permitted to make that connection had not God specifically declared it to be there. This is not to say that God quite arbitrarily chose these signs from the world of visible things. On the contrary, now that God has informed us of it in his Word, we can see the most striking correspondence between the sign and the thing signified. For that matter, it is the same God and Father who rules both in the realm of nature and in that of grace. He so created the visible world that we can understand from it the things that are invisible. The natural is an image of the spiritual. Yet a special word from God was needed for us to see in the signs of baptism and the Lord's Supper a depiction of the spiritual benefits of salvation. And this was all the more necessary since water, bread, and wine not only depict grace but also seal it and so serve in God's hand to strengthen our faith. The "form of the sacrament," accordingly, consists in these two things: in the above-mentioned relationship between the sign and the thing signified ("the internal form"), and in the divine institution that by the word establishes such a connection between the two.[52]

In line with their doctrine of the sacramental union, Roman Catholic and Lutheran theologians ascribe to the words of institution a different force than the Reformed do. For them it has to serve (1) to change the sign into the thing signified or (2) to incorporate the thing signified in the sign. It therefore has a consecrative and operative force, is directed more to the element than to the listeners, and is for that reason articulated in the Roman Catholic Church by the priest in a mysterious whisper and the Latin language.[53] But in the Reformed tradition the words of institution spoken by the minister have no such hidden, mysterious, and magical power. They do not serve, nor do they have to serve, to incorporate the thing signified in the sign. It is rather a public or preached word that is spoken out

51. P. van Mastricht, *Theologia*, VII, 3, 8; F. Turretin, *Institutes of Elenctic Theology*, XIX, 4, 3.

52. G. Bucanus, *Inst. theol.*, 561; F. Junius, *Op. theol. select.*, 49, 8; S. Maresius, *Syst. theol.*, XVIII, 19; C. Vitringa, *Doctr. christ.*, VI, 400.

53. R. Bellarmine, "De sacr.," in *Controversiis*, I, 19. Ed. note: The "Constitution on the Sacred Liturgy" (Sacrosanctum Concilium), promulgated by the Second Vatican Council on December 4, 1963, changed the Tridentine Mass in a number of ways, including a shift from the use of Latin to the vernacular.

loud to the congregation, introduces absolutely no change in the sign, but only sets it apart from common usage to the consciousness of the listeners and gives it a special purpose in the here and now.[54] Without that word and aside from their use, water, bread, and wine are just ordinary daily fare. "Take away the word, and water is nothing more and nothing less than water; add the word to the element, and it becomes a sacrament" (Augustine). For that reason, even after the minister has spoken the words of institution, he has nothing in his hand but the sign and distributes nothing but the sign to the believers present. Only, God has obligated himself, where the sacrament has been administered according to his command, to grant the invisible grace by his Spirit. God and God alone remains the distributor of grace, and also in the sacrament, the Christian depends not on the minister but on God alone and must expect all things from him.

This dependence on God alone is altered by Roman Catholics and Lutherans into dependence on the minister, and in the case of Rome this dependence is further heightened by the fact that in the ministers, when they distribute the sacrament, there has to be at least the intention of doing what the church does.[55] In dogmatics this intention is reduced to a minimum. A general intention, not to hand out *this* sacrament but *a* sacrament, is sufficient, and this intention need not be "actualized" but is sufficient if it is "virtual." It is not even necessary to have the intention of doing what the Roman Catholic Church does. If only a minister in the church of Geneva has the intention of doing what the church does, that is, the church he considers to be the true one, then he meets the requirement and Rome recognizes the sacrament administered.[56] Nevertheless the requirement of intention, otherwise left unexplained, remains in the Tridentine canons as an infallible pronouncement and keeps the devout Roman Catholic Christian in perpetual uncertainty. And when Calvin points this out in his "Antidote," Bellarmine only replies that humans in this life do not need infallible certainty of their salvation, that a human and moral certainty is sufficient, and that this certainty can be adequately obtained even if one is dependent on the intention of the minister, "since it is not hard at all to have the intention."[57]

OBJECTIVITY OF THE SACRAMENTS

Even though the connection between the sign and the thing signified does not consist in a corporeal or local union of the two, it can nevertheless very well be objective, real, and essential. Roman Catholics and Lutherans, however, differ from the Reformed in their understanding of reality. When the thing signified is not physically united with the sign, they believe the connection between the two is not real or essential and that Christ along with his benefits is therefore

---

54. J. Calvin, *Institutes*, IV.xiv.4; F. Turretin, *Institutes of Elenctic Theology*, XIX, qu. 6.
55. Council of Trent, sess. VII, can. 11.
56. J. Schwane, *Dogmengeschichte*, III, 600; R. Bellarmine, "De sacr. in genere," in *Controversiis*, I, 27.
57. R. Bellarmine, "De sacr. in genere," in *Controversiis*, I, 28; cf. C. Vitringa, *Doctr. christ.*, VI, 458ff.

not imparted and enjoyed in the sacrament. The difference in the doctrine of the sacraments, however, does not concern the question whether God really imparts his grace but in what way he does this. In reply, the Reformed said: [God imparts grace] in a spiritual manner because in that way alone grace is, and can be, truly communicated. The physical communication of Christ and his benefits is inconsistent with the nature of the Christian religion, the essence of grace, and the nature of re-creation, and it would, even if possible, be of no avail (John 6:63). But the spiritual manner in which Christ with all his benefits is communicated in the sacrament is so far from being at variance with true reality that it rather brings it about and guarantees it in the full sense.

Things are no different with the sacrament than with the Word. In the Word, Christ is truly and essentially offered and granted to everyone who believes. And he is just as really communicated to believers in the sacrament. The sacrament grants the same full Christ as the Word and in the same manner, that is, a spiritual manner by faith, even though the means differ, one being audible and the other visible. For that reason, too, so-called "sacramental phraseology" comes fully as much into its own in Reformed theology as in Lutheran and Roman Catholic theology. For sometimes Scripture, to indicate the connection God established between the sign and the thing signified, refers to the thing signified by the name of the sign (Rom. 2:29), or the sign with the name of the thing signified (Matt. 26:26), or ascribes the character and operation of the thing signified to the sign (Acts 22:16; 1 Cor. 11:24). This use of terminology in no way detracts from the fact that, also according to Lutherans and Roman Catholics, God is the actual distributor and worker of grace in the hearts of humans. And with this view the Reformed are in full agreement. Whether God communicates that grace in, with, and under the sign, using the sign as a channel, or whether he does it in connection with the sign, does not affect the reality of that communication itself.

Also in Scholastic and Roman Catholic theology, there was at all times disagreement over the manner in which the sacraments work their grace. The Thomistic school attributed to the sacrament a physical operation, the Scotist a moral operation. According to Thomas and his followers, God so works through the sacrament that in a physical way the sacrament itself produces grace in the recipient. According to Scotus, however, God obligated himself to have grace follow the performance of the sacramental act, without for that reason channeling grace through the sign. He pictured the sacrament as an IOU on the basis of which the participant received grace from God. Rome, accordingly, does in fact teach that the sacrament works "through the act performed" (ex opere operato), but leaves undiscussed the manner in which God, the foremost efficient cause, communicates grace through the sacrament as the instrumental cause.[58] So, although the

---

58. J. Schwane, *Dogmengeschichte*, III, 595ff.; IV, 363ff.; G. M. Jansen, *Praelectiones theologicae dogmaticae*, 3 vols. in 2 (Utrecht: Van Rossum, 1875–79), III, 317; G. C. Reinhold, *Die Streitfrage über die physische oder moralische Wirksamkeit der Sakramente* (Stuttgart: J. Roth, 1899). Many medieval theologians, such as Durandus, Ockham, d'Ailly, Biel, with Scotus opposed Thomas's doctrine that the sacraments physically produced grace in

Reformed reject the doctrine that grace comes to us through the sign as its channel, in so doing they have in no way detracted from the authenticity of the sacrament. Indeed, by taking this position they have much more effectively maintained the spiritual nature of grace than Rome or Luther. For the rest, the manner in which God uses the Word and the sacraments in distributing his grace remains a mystery. Scripture also says of the word of God that it creates and re-creates, regenerates and renews, justifies and sanctifies. But who can describe the manner in which God uses the Word in this connection and, similarly, the sacraments?

[528] To the extent that the connection between the sign and the thing signified is conceived differently, to that extent also the power and effect attributed to the sacrament differs. Since in the view of Rome the visible sign has absorbed the invisible grace, the sacrament works "by the act performed" (ex opere operato) without requiring in the recipient anything more or different than not posing any obstacle to its operation, a purely negative requirement.[59] Augustine had already sought to explain the difference between the sacraments of the old and the new covenants by saying that while "the former promised the Savior, the latter provided salvation."[60] The Scholastics developed this position by saying that the sacraments of the Old Testament, inasmuch as they prefigured the future Christ, had no power in themselves to impart grace but worked only out of and through faith. In the Old Testament dispensation, therefore, everything depended on "performing the work," that is, on the believing subject, who looked forward to the future Christ. But all this changes with the sacraments of the New Testament: Christ's sacrifice has been brought, and therefore the sacraments now work through themselves (per se), by the energy proper to them (*propria virtute*), by the act performed (ex opere operato). This last expression, introduced into theology by William of Auxerre and Alexander Hales, initially did not yet imply a contrast to the idea that a certain disposition was required in the recipient of the sacrament. Thomas, for example, still says that "the power . . . inherent in the sacraments works chiefly through faith in Christ's passion."[61] The expression only meant that the New Testament sacraments received from Christ's completed passion the power "to confer justifying grace."[62] Nevertheless the maintenance of this objective, causative character of the sacraments was au-

---

the soul of the recipient, in the same manner as an ax in the hand of the woodcutter splits wood, the chisel in the hand of the sculptor produces the image, and so forth. In their judgment these images were inadequate because the sacrament does not operate physically in the soul of the recipient, but produces grace metaphysically. They understood the sacraments, therefore, not as causes and instruments of grace, but as conditions or opportunities by which God communicates his grace. Bonaventure, *Sent.*, IV, dist. 1, qu. 4, called this interpretation *satis probabilis* (sufficiently probable) and also said that the sacraments do not fully exhaust grace, but that grace is poured out into the soul by God through the reception of signs (cf. Gomarus, above). However, after Trent there is no longer any room in the Roman system for this sentiment.

59. Council of Trent, sess. VII, can. 6–8.

60. Augustine, *Expositions on the Psalms*, on Ps. 73:2.

61. T. Aquinas, *Summa theol.*, III, qu. 62, art. 5, ad. 2.

62. Ibid., III, qu. 62, art. 6.

tomatically and increasingly conducive to weakening the required disposition in the recipient and finally led to reducing it to the negative rule of "putting no obstacle in its way." This expression, which already occurs in Augustine,[63] was formerly associated with a positive disposition, "an inferior but good motive." But the sacraments of the New Testament worked "by the act performed" (ex opere operato) and excluded all power and merit on the part of the recipient. A "good motive," however, is meritorious, according to Rome, and therefore unnecessary for the reception of the sacrament. Indeed, even the seven preparations that in the case of adults precede baptism still have a merit of congruity and are therefore unnecessary for the reception of the sacrament. The sacrament, accordingly, works grace in everyone who does not deliberately harden oneself, who does not put a positive obstacle in the way, who simply undergoes the sacrament negatively and passively.[64]

The grace imparted by the sacraments is dispositional, infused, sanctifying grace, whether as in baptism it is bestowed for the first time, or as in the sacrament of penance it is renewed after being lost, or it is increased as in the other sacraments. Distinguished from it is the sacramental grace, which adds to sanctifying grace "a special kind of divine assistance to help in attaining the end of the sacrament," which is different in each of the sacraments and enables the recipient to attain the special goal that is inherent in each sacrament in particular.[65] Finally there are, additionally, three sacraments, namely, baptism, confirmation, and holy orders, which aside from this grace impress on the soul of the recipient an indelible mark (*character indelebilis*).[66] The church fathers already said that baptism is a spiritual sign and seal that is imprinted on the soul of the recipient, just as a brand that is burned into the hand of a soldier always marks him and continues to obligate him. So also baptism imprints a spiritual seal, a "mark, or character," which is never lost.[67] The Scholastics also further developed this point of doctrine. It described the "character" as a disposition or power that is imprinted on the soul and gives a person a right and power pertaining to divine worship. For there were three sacraments that incorporated persons into a different hierarchical class and irrevocably marked them as members of it before God, angels, and humankind. Baptism incorporates a person into the state of implanted faith, sets believers apart from unbelievers, and conforms them to Christ as their spiritual head. Confirmation incorporates us into the state of corroborated faith, sets the strong apart from the weak, and marks us as soldiers under Christ as king. Holy orders incorporates [persons] into the state of multiplied faith, sets the priests apart from the laity, and elevates them to conformity to Christ as high priest.

63. Augustine, *Epistles* 98, 10; F. A. Loofs, *Dogmengeschichte*, 599.

64. J. Schwane, *Dogmengeschichte*, III, 581; A. von Harnack, *History of Dogma*, VI, 221ff.; R. Bellarmine, "De sacr.," in *Controversiis*, II, 1ff.

65. T. Aquinas, *Summa theol.*, III, qu. 62, art. 2.

66. Council of Trent, sess. VII, can. 9.

67. J. Schwane, *Dogmengeschichte*, II, 734.

It is a sign that dedicates, sets apart, shapes, and obligates those marked by it; consecrates them to God to perform the service of Christ; and is never erased, not even in those who are lost.[68]

This teaching was unanimously rejected by the Reformation, inasmuch as Scripture clearly teaches that the sacraments are signs and seals of the covenant of grace, that they are meant only for believers and therefore always presuppose faith (Mark 16:16; Acts 8:37–38; 9:11, 17–18; 10:34–35; Rom. 4:11; and so forth). Only when faith is present are they means in God's hand of signifying and sealing the invisible goods of grace (Acts 2:38; 22:16; Eph. 5:26). Moreover, Scripture makes absolutely no distinction between the sanctifying grace granted in the sacrament and a special sacramental grace that differs from it, for the grace sealed in the sacrament is not inferior to and not even different from the grace granted in the Word and received in faith. The latter (faith) consists first of all in forgiving grace and subsequently also in sanctifying grace. Finally, not a word is said in Scripture about an "indelible mark" imprinted on the soul by baptism, confirmation, and holy orders. The texts (2 Cor. 1:22; Eph. 1:13; 4:30) to which Bellarmine appeals speak of a sealing of believers by the Holy Spirit with a view to future salvation but do not mention a sacrament to which that sealing is bound, nor of a distinct disposition or virtue in which that sealing would consist.

Although it is true that God holds all people responsible for, and judges them by, the measure of grace granted them, this does not imply that some kind of juridical membership in the church of Rome or any other church is imprinted by it. The Lutherans indeed later departed from their original position insofar as they had baptism effect regeneration in children and permitted unbelievers to physically consume the flesh and blood of Christ in the Lord's Supper. But in this connection they nevertheless at all times maintained that in the case of adults faith was a definite necessity for salvific reception of the sacrament.

With that as background, and despite the fact that according to them the working of the sacraments depends on faith, Protestants had to face the challenge of maintaining their objective and realistic character. In the Roman Catholic and Lutheran view, this character seems to be more secure because the operation of grace is incorporated in the Word and sacrament. Over against this position the Reformed seem to be in a double bind. In the first place, they say that the grace of God is distributed only *with* but not *through* the Word and sacrament. And in the second place, they maintain that an external call to salvation is insufficient, that the call by the Word has to be accompanied by a call from the Holy Spirit, and by consequence that the sacrament by itself, that is, without a special working of the Holy Spirit in the heart of believers, does not accomplish its purpose. This position, however, in no way destroys the reality and objectivity of the sacrament.

68. Ibid., III, 592; T. Aquinas, *Summa theol.*, III, qu. 63; Bonaventure, *Breviloquium*, VI, 6; R. Bellarmine, "De sacr.," in *Controversiis*, II, 18–22; O. Laake, *Über den sakramentalen Charakter* (Munich: Mainz, 1903); M. J. L. Farine, *Der sakramentale Charakter* (Freiburg i.B.: Herder, 1904); cf. F. Kattenbusch, "Sakrament," in *PRE*³, XVII, 366.

In the first place, the connection between the sign and the thing signified in the sacrament is neither different from nor less than that which exists between the word of the gospel and the person of Christ. Those who accept the word in faith truly, in accordance with God's promise, receive Christ himself; similarly those who accept the sacrament in faith receive Christ with all his benefits and goods in the same way and according to that same divine promise. On the other hand, those who reject the word out of unbelief thereby reject Christ himself, even though they have heard the word and have even accepted it as historically factual. In the same way, those who spurn the sacrament thereby spurn Christ himself. Even though they receive the sign they do not obtain the thing signified. One rule applies to both: objectively the bond between the word and Christ, the sacrament and Christ, continues to exist, for that bond was formed by God himself. God has said that whoever receives his word and sacrament in faith will never perish.

Second, Roman Catholics and Lutherans do not credit the sacrament with having a different and greater reality than what belongs to it according to the Reformed confession. For salvation, after all, nothing other, but also nothing less and nothing more, is needed than the whole Christ, who is presented in the Word and in the sacrament and received by faith. One cannot commit a more appalling act than to reject the same Christ in and with the Word and the sacrament. Whether unbelievers then consume the very flesh and blood of Christ physically and locally in the signs of bread and wine in no way detracts from the objectivity of the sacrament, is totally unprofitable, and does not aggravate the judgment, for the great sin here is the moral rejection, that is, unbelief. The grace of God in Christ is spiritual in nature and can therefore only be accepted spiritually.

Third, Lutherans too are afraid, in the case of adults, to drop the requirement of faith for the reception of the sacrament. In the case of children, they like the Roman Catholics believe in baptismal regeneration, but children form a category of their own that is in no respect less favorable according to the Reformed confession than according to the Roman Catholic and Lutheran confessions. In the case of adults, however, faith is required. And in that case even Roman Catholics demand that the recipient of the sacrament refrain from placing an obstacle in the way. According to both Lutherans and Roman Catholics, therefore, the sacrament does not absolutely work ex opere operato. Cases exist in which the sacrament does not work, that is, yields no grace, and nevertheless retains its objective character. Scholasticism was still unanimous in teaching "that those who come without faith or come feignedly receive the sacrament, not the thing [signified by the sacrament]."[69] And Roman Catholic theology still continues to debate the question whether the sacrament which has first been rejected by an obstacle (*obex*) can still have its effect later.[70] There is not a single confession according to which the operation of grace always coincides with the sacrament.

---

69. P. Lombard, *Sent.*, IV, dist. 4.

70. J. Schwane, *Dogmengeschichte*, IV, 371; G. M. Jansen, *Prael. theol.*, III, 330.

Yet the objectivity of the sacrament, the bond between the sign and the thing signified, is maintained.

Fourth, Roman Catholics and Lutherans finally face the same difficulty as the Reformed, that is, the question of when and in which case the sacraments are conducive to the salvation of the recipients and impart grace to them. The question is the same as that which came up earlier in connection with the gospel call. There it was answered by saying that the external call had to be augmented with an internal call. The case is no different with the sacraments. The "sacramental union" taught by Roman Catholics and Lutherans, however intimate, is still not capable as such of conferring grace, for in that case it would have to impart it always, everywhere, and in all cases. In the case of adults something has to be added on the part of the subject. The "obstacle" has to be removed, and faith must take its place. Objectively the sacrament is indeed sufficient. In it the whole Christ is communicated as truly and essentially as in the Word. But required on the part of the subjects is that their minds be illumined, their wills brought around, to truly understand and accept the sacrament. If one says that the subject is to blame for the unbelief, one is speaking the truth but fails to mention the final and deepest cause of the difference to be noted in connection with the observance of the sacrament as well as the hearing of the Word. For that reason the Reformed asserted that, though Christ is in fact objectively, truly, and seriously offered to all participants in the sacrament, as he is in the Word to all who hear it, still, subjectively, a working of the Holy Spirit is needed for them to enjoy the true power of the sacrament. "The signs are of benefit, not to all promiscuously but only to the elect of God to whom the inner and efficacious operation of the Spirit has already come."[71]

Fifth, to believers, those who receive and enjoy the sacraments in faith, they are signs and seals of the covenant of grace. With an eye to the many people who, though receiving the sacrament, do not believe, Gomarus and others already made a distinction between an internal [covenant] and an external covenant.[72] And when the condition of the church increasingly brought out a split and a contrast between the two, this distinction repeatedly occasioned controversy. On the one hand it was said that in the Old Testament there had existed an external covenant, but that now there was only an internal covenant (C. Vitringa, Labadie, and so forth). Many people on the other side of the issue asserted that even now there still exists an external covenant in which all who make profession of faith are participants and have a legitimate claim to the sacraments (Swarte, van Eerde, Janssonius). And between these two camps stood those who tried more or less felicitously to unite the external [covenant] and the internal covenant (Koelman, Appelius, Bachiene, Kessler).[73] In fact the older theologians and confessional

71. Consensus Tigurinus (1549), in Niemeyer, *Collectio confessionum*, 209. Ed. note: English translation in J. Calvin, *Selected Works of John Calvin: Tracts and Letters*, II, 231.

72. F. Gomarus, "Disp. de sacr.," in *Opera omnia*, disp. 31; A. Essenius, *Compendium theologiae dogmaticum* (Utrecht: Meinhard à Dreunen, 1669), VI, 6 (commentary on 1 Cor. 7:14).

73. Cf. H. Bavinck, *Reformed Dogmatics*, III, 228–32 (#350); C. Vitringa, *Doctr. christ.*, VI, 361–98.

writings know nothing of such a split. The internal and external covenant are two covenants no more than the invisible and visible church are two churches. And for that reason the sacraments cannot exclusively be signs and seals of an external covenant to which also the "ungraced but inoffensive ones" are entitled. They are not just a confirmation of the statement of the gospel that those who believe are saved, but to believers they are seals of the entire covenant of grace, all its promises, of the whole Christ and all his benefits. Therefore they do not just guarantee a general truth but are seals of the promise: "I am your God and the God of your children." They "present to our senses both that which he declares to us by his Word and that which he works inwardly in our hearts, thereby confirming in us the salvation he imparts to us." They are designed to help us understand more clearly and certify to us that, on account of Christ's one sacrifice finished on the cross, God grants to us, by grace alone, the forgiveness of sins and eternal life.[74] This is not to deny that those who receive the sacrament without faith may in fact enjoy some temporary benefit from it, for God is rich in mercy and even bestows many benefits on those who reject his Word and sacrament in unbelief. But the full and true benefit of the sacraments, like that of the Word, is only for believers. Believers are assured by them of their salvation.

From all these considerations follows the value of the sacraments. They are not inherently necessary, for God did not have to ordain them. His covenant and grace, his word and promise, being those of a true God, are firm and sure enough not to need the confirmation of the sacraments.[75] Nor are they absolutely necessary for salvation, for Scripture binds salvation only to faith (John 3:16; Mark 16:16). Roman Catholics and Lutherans, though they appear to teach their absolute necessity and therefore defend lay baptism in case of emergency, cannot in practice maintain this position. With Augustine, for example, they say that in the case of the murderer on the cross, a baptism by blood takes the place of water baptism. It is not the deprivation of but contempt for the sacrament that makes a person guilty before God.

Nevertheless, the sacraments have great value. Because we are not [disembodied] spirits but sensuous earthly creatures who can only understand spiritual things when they come to us in humanly perceptible forms, God instituted the sacraments in order that by seeing those signs we might gain a better insight into his benefits, receive a stronger confirmation of his promises, and thus be supported and strengthened in our faith. The sacraments do not work faith but reinforce it, as a wedding ring reinforces love. They do not infuse a physical grace but confer the whole Christ, whom believers already possess by the Word. They bestow on them that same Christ in another way and by another road and so strengthen the faith. Furthermore, they renew the believers' covenant with God, strengthen them in the communion of Christ, join them more closely to each other, set

74. Belgic Confession, art. 33; Heidelberg Catechism, Q 66ff.
75. J. Calvin, *Institutes*, IV.xiv.3, 6.

them apart from the world, and witness to angels and their fellow human beings, [showing] that they are the people of God, the church of Christ, the communion of the saints.[76]

HOW MANY SACRAMENTS?

[529] The number of the sacraments is most variously determined depending on whether the term "sacrament" is taken in a more restricted or a broad sense. If with Augustine we say, "Every sacred sign is a sacrament," the number becomes exceedingly large. And also when, with Calvin, we count as sacraments all those signs that God has ever given people to assure them of the truth of his promises, Scripture offers us a long list.[77] The Reformed, accordingly, tallied up a great many, especially when later the doctrine of covenants was elaborated, and every covenant plus every covenant dispensation had to have the requisite number of sacraments. Thus sometimes, in the covenant of works before the fall (when there really were no means of *grace*), they listed the Sabbath and paradise, the tree of knowledge and the tree of life, as sacraments. And in the Old Testament dispensation of the covenant of grace, not only circumcision and Passover, but frequently also the expulsion from paradise, the making of garments of skins, the sacrifice of Abel, the rainbow of Noah, the passage through the Red Sea, manna, the water from the rock, the bronze serpent, Aaron's rod, Gideon's fleece, Hezekiah's sundial, and so forth were counted as sacraments.[78]

Then, having come to the New Testament sacraments, they immediately shifted to a more restricted definition of the term "sacrament" and limited the number to two, even though Calvin still sometimes called the laying on of hands,[79] and Luther and Melanchthon[80] the practice of absolution, a sacrament. Rome, however, expanded the number of the sacraments to seven and in addition introduced a large number of so-called sacramentalia. The difference between the two consists in the fact that sacraments were instituted by God, the sacramentalia by the church. The former work by the power supplied by God, the latter by the intercession and blessing of the church. The former immediately effect the inner sanctification of people; the latter only contribute to that end by the provision of subordinate graces and preservation from temporal disasters. The sacraments are necessary by virtue of God's command; the sacramentalia are recommended by the church as useful and beneficial. Belonging to the category of sacramentalia

---

76. C. Vitringa, *Doctr. christ.*, VI, 422–37.

77. J. Calvin, *Institutes*, IV.xiv.18.

78. A. Polanus, *Synt. theol.*, VI, 50–54; H. Witsius, *The Oeconomy of the Covenants between God and Man: Comprehending a Complete Body of Divinity*, 3 vols. (London, 1763; 2nd ed., rev. and corrected, 1775), I, 6; IV, 7, 10; B. de Moor, *Comm. theol.*, V, 258–67.

79. J. Calvin, *Institutes*, IV.xiv.20.

80. Joseph T. Müller, *Die symbolischen Bücher*, 173, 202; ed. note: These specific references are to the following Lutheran documents: Apology of the Augsburg Confession, art. 12, par. 42 (Kolb and Wengert, 193); ibid., art. 13, pars. 1–5 (Kolb and Wengert, 219–20).

are objects such as churches, altars, priestly garments, chalices, clocks, water, oil, salt, bread, wine, palms, and so forth, which have been consecrated by the church and set apart for religious use. In addition, the actions of exorcism and blessing that the church undertakes to withdraw things and persons from the malevolent influence of the devil and to transfer them to the sacred domain of the church are also sacramentalia. To Rome, after all, the creation is of a much lower order than re-creation.[81] The creation is nature, re-creation is grace, that is, the elevation of nature. The world bears a profane character and is subject, moreover, to the influence of Satan. Accordingly, all that passes from the world into the service of the church must be withdrawn from the power of the devil and devoted to and blessed for the service of God.[82]

Whereas the sacramentalia thus constitute the enormous enclosure that separates the church from the world, the sacraments are the means by which God sanctifies the members of the church internally, imparts supernatural grace to them, and makes them partakers of his nature. They are the means for the redemption and elevation of the entire visible creation, which is represented in the four elements they use (water, oil, bread, and wine) and are seven in number because, linking the number of the Deity with the number of the world, they sanctify the entire creation and consecrate it to the service of God by supernatural grace. Baptism, instituted by Christ (Matt. 28:19), not only takes away all the guilt and punishment of sin but also frees believers from the pollution of sin, implants the principle of grace and holiness, the germ of the new life, in the soul by regeneration, and thus makes people living members of Christ's mystical body and incorporates them into the fellowship of the Triune God. Just as Adam entered into a higher world—the kingdom of grace—by means of the superadded gift, so the baptized are elevated to the status of supernatural sanctity. But just as Adam had to preserve the grace conferred by his free will, so also Christians must appropriate baptismal grace by their free will.

Serving to bring them to this point is the second sacrament, the sacrament of confirmation. Roman Catholics cannot prove that Christ instituted this sacrament and commanded the apostles to administer it, but they nevertheless have to believe it because the church says so and therefore appeal to Acts 8:15; 19:6; and Heb. 6:2, where there is mention only of the extraordinary gift of the Holy Spirit imparted by the apostles with the laying on of hands, as is clearly evident from Acts 8:18; 10:44–45; cf. 1 Cor. 14:1, 15, 37. Aside from the laying on of hands, confirmation further consists in anointing with oil and in the pronouncement of a formula by the bishop, which is totally unknown to Scripture and was only gradually introduced in the church. According to Rome, this sacrament imparts to baptized children, when they have reached the age at which they can use their

---

81. Ed. note: Bavinck's distinction between *schepping* (creation) and *herschepping* (re-creation) is central to his theological system. See below, ch. 17, note 5, for further clarification of the key terms Bavinck uses to make this point.

82. R. W. Dove, "Sakramentalien," in *PRE*³, XVII, 381–91.

reason, the power of the Holy Spirit so as to preserve the life of grace received in baptism and steadfastly to confess their faith by word and deed. This power of life is nurtured and strengthened by the third sacrament, which is called the sacrament of the altar, or the Eucharist. In this sacrament Christ himself is present with both his divine and human natures, sacrifices himself bloodlessly for sins, and gives his true body and blood to communicants for the nourishment of their souls. Since, given human weakness, the life of grace can be harmed by a wide variety of sins and even be lost, however, Christ has instituted a fourth sacrament, that of penance, in order to restore or renew his saving grace. For the institution of this sacrament by Christ, Rome appeals to the power that Christ conferred on his apostles to forgive sins (Matt. 16:19; 18:18; John 20:22–23). Now, though Christ's charge to the apostles is well established, there is not a word here saying that it has the character of a sacrament. There is no sign here, a circumstance Rome can only explain by saying that repentance, confession, and the disposition to make amends are the sign in this sacrament of penance.[83]

83. The Scotists contend that *contritio, confessio,* and *satisfactio* were indeed dispositions required before the reception of the sacrament of absolution but were not part of the sacrament, while the Thomists claimed that the *materia* of the sacrament of penance consisted not in substances but, just as in marriage, in acts, and indeed in the above-mentioned *actus poenitentis.* Trent did not decide this issue. Ed. note: Bavinck cites portions of Trent's session XIV, ch. 3, and canon 4. For greater clarity, they are given here in their entirety.

   Ch. 3. The Parts and Fruits of the Sacrament of Penance. Further, the holy Council teaches that the form of the sacrament of penance, in which its force chiefly consists, is set down in these words of the minister: "I absolve thee, etc."; to which indeed certain prayers are laudably added according to the custom of holy Church; yet in no way do they pertain to the essence of this form, nor are they necessary for the administration of the sacrament. The matter, as it were, of this sacrament, on the other hand, consists in the acts of the penitent himself, namely contrition, confession, and satisfaction [can. 4]. These, inasmuch as by the institution of God they are required in the penitent for the integrity of the sacrament for the full and perfect remission of sins, are for this reason called the parts of penance. The reality and *effectus* of this sacrament, however, so far as concerns its force and efficacy, is reconciliation with God, which at times in pious persons and in those who receive this sacrament with devotion is wont to be followed by peace of conscience and serenity with an exceedingly great consolation of spirit. The holy Council, while recording these matters regarding the parts and effect of this sacrament, condemns the opinions of those who maintain that the parts of penance are the terrors of conscience and faith [can. 4].

   Canon 4. If anyone says that after the completion of the consecration the body and blood of our Lord Jesus Christ is not in the marvelous sacrament of the Eucharist, but only in use, while it is taken, not however before or after, and that in the hosts or consecrated particles, which are reserved or remain after communion, the true body of the Lord does not remain: let him be anathema. (H. Denzinger, ed., *The Sources of Catholic Dogma,* trans. Roy. J. Deferrari [Fitzwilliam, NH: Loreto Publications, 2002], 270, 273–74)

   Bavinck calls attention to the expression *quasi materia* used by the Council of Trent and provides references to C. Pesch, *Praelectiones dogmaticae,* 9 vols. (Freiburg i.B.: Herder, 1902–10), III, 422; J. Pohle, *Lehrbuch der Dogmatik,* 4th ed., 3 vols. (Paderborn: Schöningh, 1908–10), III, 422; and to Roman Catechism, II, 5, qu. 12 (ed. note: Bradley and Kevane, II, ch. 4, qu. 13, "The Matter of the Sacrament [of Penance]"). This passage is cited here in full:

   Since nothing should be better known than the matter of this sacrament, the faithful must be taught that there is a major difference in this respect between it and the other sacraments. Whereas

In the Roman view, accordingly, the sacrament of penance became a court of law in which the priest judges on the basis of the penitential books the sins confessed, and though absolving penitents from guilt and eternal punishment, he nevertheless imposes a wide range of penalties on earth or in purgatory. These penalties, however, can then again be remitted by means of indulgences.[84] The sacrament of extreme unction serves, not to heal the sick as the proof text advanced (James 5:14) would lead one to expect, but to prepare the dying person for death. The anointing with holy olive oil denotes the anointing of the Holy Spirit, the communication of grace, which frees the soul from its defects and confers the strength needed for the final struggle.

Beyond these five sacraments there are still two more: the sacrament of holy orders, which distinguishes the priest from the layperson by an office-enhancing gift of the Holy Spirit and confers on him the power to change the bread and wine of the Mass into the body and blood of Christ and to forgive, in Christ's name, the sins of the penitent sinner; and the sacrament of marriage, which, according to the words of Eph. 5:25ff., makes the marital state into an image of the union between Christ and his church. To that end, it not only unites the spouses by natural ties but also by supernatural grace and gives them the strength to persevere in mutual love until death and to bring up their children in the fear of the Lord.[85]

From the side of Protestantism this set of seven sacraments was sometimes accorded superlatively high praise.[86] Over and over, in various places, there even surfaced a trend to expand the number of sacraments and ceremonies and so to enrich the Protestant churches with the symbolic rites of Rome. There is no reason, however, to be jealous of the concept and number of Rome's sacraments. For all the appreciation of beauty that comes to expression here, what settles the issue for Protestant Christians is that scriptural evidence is lacking for the five

---

in the other sacraments the matter consists of some material thing, either natural or fabricated, the matter of this sacrament is the very acts of the penitent himself. These acts, as stated in the Council of Trent, are contrition, confession and satisfaction. These three acts are required by divine institution for the integrity of the sacrament and for the full remission of sins; and for this reason they are called the "parts" of the sacrament of Penance.

The fact that the Council calls these three acts the "quasi-matter" of Penance is not because they are any less real as matter, but because they are not that kind of matter which is external to the recipient, such as water in Baptism or the chrism in Confirmation. As for the opinion of some authors, who say that the sins themselves constitute the matter of this sacrament, this is not really different from what we are saying, since the object of all three acts is the penitent's sins. Just as wood which is consumed by fire is the matter of fire, so too the sins which are destroyed by Penance may also be called quite properly the matter of Penance. (*The Roman Catechism* [Boston: Daughters of St. Paul, 1985], 261–62)

84. Cf. above, 143ff. (#461).

85. Council of Trent, sess. VII, XIII, XIV, XXI–XXIV; Roman Catechism, II, and previously mentioned Roman Catholic theologians.

86. G. W. von Leibniz, *System der Theologie nach dem Manuskripte von Hanover* (Mainz: Müller, 1825), 195ff.; F. W. von Goethe, *Aus meinem Leben* (Paderborn: Schöningh, 1895), II, 179; A. F. C. Vilmar, *Dogmatik*, II, 227; W. Bilderdijk, *Opstellen van godgeleerden en zedekundigen inhoud* (Amsterdam: J. Immerzeel Jr., 1833), I, 61; idem, *Brieven* (Amsterdam: W. Messchert, 1836–37), IV, 68, 174; V, 42.

sacraments Rome added to baptism and the Lord's Supper. Sometimes this fact is candidly acknowledged on the part of Roman Catholic theologians. Deharbe, for example, says that we nowhere read that Christ instituted the sacrament of confirmation, nor did Christ instruct his disciples to administer it.[87] This same applies to confession, extreme unction, marriage, and holy orders.

But apart from this objection, what does Rome actually achieve with all these sacraments? It seems the treasure and distribution of grace on the part of Rome is exceptionally rich, but actually it is so poor that over and over merely a small part of people's sins and penalties is and can be forgiven, and over and over a new sacrament is needed to impart grace and to release people from penalties. In fact, even if believers have enjoyed the benefits of baptism, the Lord's Supper, penance, and extreme unction, after this life they still need to make amends in purgatory. Rome tends so endlessly to divide and split up sins and penalties that all the sacraments, along with all the indulgences, cannot completely deliver believers from them. Counterbalancing this situation somewhat is that the saints can reach such a high level of achievement that they have merits to spare and enlarge the treasury of merits. But that is an exception. This is possible only for saints who aside from the precepts also fulfill the [evangelical] counsels and lead an exclusively religious life, and it still gives them neither certainty nor consolation. Ordinary Roman Catholic Christians who live in the midst of the world experience an even greater measure of uncertainty. Even after their death they continue to stand before God as before a Judge, a Judge whom they must satisfy and whom they must still reconcile by all sorts of penances. Their state of grace is never certain and firm; they are always in dread over whether they are indeed in a state of grace and will not fall from it the following moment. And this uncertainty, this lack of assurance, is not in the least removed by the teaching that the sacraments work ex opere operato. For although baptism, confirmation, and holy orders confer an indelible character, the sanctifying grace imparted by the sacraments can nevertheless always again be lost. Its reception, in the context of penance, communion, extreme unction, and marriage, is dependent on a penitential mood, and even when it has been granted, it does not release believers from all punishment. The work of satisfaction continues to be necessary, even in purgatory after this life.

And what sort of grace is it that the Roman Catholic Christian receives in the sacrament? Not a grace of forgiveness and of adoption as children, but a grace that as a superadded gift is added to nature, which never becomes one with believers, and therefore either drives them into a monastery or makes them live a dualistic life in the world. By contrast, for Protestant Christians it is enough to have the Word and the two sacraments instituted by Christ. In them, if they accept them in faith, they possess the whole Christ, the full treasure of his merits, perfect righteousness and holiness, and unbreakable fellowship with God. They are liberated

---

87. J. Deharbe, *Verklaring der katholieke geloofs- en zedeleer*, 3rd ed., 4 vols. (Utrecht: J. R. Van Rossum, 1880–88), IV, 174.

from all guilt, released from all punishment. Of this they are assured in baptism, and they are continually strengthened and confirmed in that faith by the Lord's Supper. They no longer need any special grace in confirmation, penance, and extreme unction, for by the Word, baptism, and the Lord's Supper they receive all the grace they need in life and in death, for time and eternity. Their only comfort is that they belong to Christ; they live in that comfort and die in that comfort. Christ, for them, has accomplished everything. From them no penance or penalty is demanded, either in this life or in the life to come. And all the grace that Christians receive is so little elevated above nature or opposed to nature that it rather renews and sanctifies all that is natural. When they marry, they therefore do not need a new sacramental grace, for by virtue of its origin, marriage is holy and does not therefore have to be elevated above its institution but needs only to be restored and renewed in its own natural order. Or when they desire the office of overseer, they are not incorporated by a sacramental grace into a special class but are called by God to a ministry in his church and are enabled by the same grace of Christ to perform that ministry. In baptism and the Lord's Supper, Protestant Christians possess infinitely more than Roman Catholic Christians do in their seven sacraments. For it is not the number of sacraments that is decisive, but the institution of Christ and the fullness of grace he imparts in it.[88]

88. About the Roman Catholic sacraments, cf. J. Calvin, *Institutes*, IV.xix; D. Chamier, *Panstratiae catholicae* (Geneva: Roverianis, 1626), IV, lib. 4; A. Rivetus, in *Synopsis purioris theologiae*, disp. 47; F. Turretin, *Institutes of Elenctic Theology*, XIX, qu. 31; B. de Moor, *Comm. theol.*, V, 330ff.; J. Gerhard, *Loci theol.*, XIX, 60ff.; K. von Hase, *Handbuch der protestantischen Polemik gegen die römisch-katholische Kirche*, 5th ed. (Leipzig: Breitkopf & Härtel, 1890), 414ff.; P. Tschackert, *Evangelische Polemik gegen die römischen Kirche* (Gotha: F. A. Perthes, 1885), 67.

10

THE SPIRIT'S MEANS OF GRACE: BAPTISM

In the New Testament baptism has its foundation in circumcision of the Old Testament (Gen. 17:10ff.). Circumcision was a sign and seal of the forgiveness of sins and sanctification in the covenant of grace. John the Baptist announced the coming kingdom and forgiveness of sins through baptism, which was proof that God had remembered his covenant. Despite objections to the contrary, John's baptism is identical to that of Jesus's disciples. Believers are baptized "into the name of Jesus" just as the Israelites were baptized "into Moses" (1 Cor. 10:2) and the disciples at Ephesus "into John's baptism" (Acts 19:3) because believers are adopted by Jesus and put their trust in him alone. Accordingly, Matt. 28:19 ("into the name of the Father and the Son and the Holy Spirit") does not prescribe what the apostles are to say but what they have to do. The name here indicates that the baptized person is placed in relationship with the Father, Son, and Holy Spirit. Throughout the New Testament baptism is thus described as salvation from sin, so that baptized people are new, spiritual people (πνευματικοι, pneumatikoi) who are simultaneously washed, sanctified, and justified (1 Cor. 6:11).

While the ancient Christian church did not have a universally practiced rite of baptism, beginning in the second century it acquired a more mysterious character, was surrounded by many rituals, and changed into a magically operative means of grace. Augustine contributed to this trend by teaching that baptism worked ex opere operato for infants, and was later followed by the Scholastics who deemphasized the importance of the subjective demands of baptism. This formed the basis for the Roman Catholic view, which understands baptism to be the entry into the church and strictly necessary for salvation.

While the Lutherans departed but little from Rome's teaching, the Reformed taught that baptism did not effect faith but strengthened it. This put the Reformed on the defensive with respect to infant baptism, on which issue they appealed to the covenant of grace. Even before baptism children were considered to be members of the covenant, so that baptism was not absolutely necessary for salvation. While many of the Reformed initially maintained the unity of

*election and covenant, on account of decay in the church baptism gradually was
totally separated from regeneration and deprived of its value. Remonstrants,
Rationalists, Quakers, and modernist Protestants likewise see in the sacrament a
human act of confession rather than a divine seal.*

*Apart from Baptist churches and mission fields, most now know baptism
almost exclusively as infant baptism. Yet Scripture nowhere speaks of infant
baptism and always assumes the baptism of adults. The whole world, both Jews
and Gentiles, were deserving of damnation, and therefore repentance and faith
were necessary prior to baptism. Accordingly, there is no disagreement among
Christian churches over the necessity of a confession of faith prior to the baptism
of adults.*

*The "form" of baptism is the deliberately chosen sign of the washing away
of pollution in the soul, just as dirt is washed away by water. In the first period
of the church, baptism consisted in immersion, as already indicated by the
Greek βαπτιζειν (baptizein) and the scriptural reports of baptism. Accordingly,
baptism by immersion was the standard practice in the West, while sprinkling
was less common. After the thirteenth century, however, sprinkling became more
common. Yet while immersion illustrates the meaning of baptism more clearly,
the issue itself is adiaphoron.*

*The water of baptism becomes a sacrament through the words of institution.
The trinitarian baptismal formula does not magically turn the water into the
blood of Christ. The work of the Holy Spirit in the sacrament, like that in the case
of the Word, is not physical but spiritual. Baptism then consists of the benefits of
justification, regeneration, and fellowship with the church.*

*Up until the present day infant baptism has been rejected for two chief
reasons: it does not occur in Scripture, and it presupposes faith and repentance,
which do not occur or are not recognized in small children. Due to the rapid
expansion and ordinary occurrence of adult baptism in the first and second
centuries of the church, direct witness to infant baptism is lacking until the time
of Tertullian. Tertullian mentions the practice of infant baptism in his day, while
Origen witnesses that infant baptism was in general use and of apostolic pedigree,
and Cyprian with the Council of Carthage in 256 defended the baptism of
infants on the second or third day following birth.*

*When infant baptism became the rule rather than the exception, it became
necessary to defend its legitimacy. In his defense of original sin, Augustine
appealed to the faith of parents to defend infant baptism. However, there are
many objections to this defense. Personal faith was still considered necessary,
and so children were considered recipients of grace, whether by disposition or act.
Also, the faith of another is superfluous since the operation of grace presupposes
only a "passive capacity" on the part of the child. Furthermore, when baptism
is detached from faith and the Word, it is robbed of its scriptural character and*

ceases to be a sign and seal of God's promises. Finally, the benefits of baptism are exaggerated and weakened since not all baptized children grow up to be believers. Hence, the Reformed instead based their defense on the scriptural teaching of the covenant of grace, which embraces both believers and their descendants.

While the Anabaptists argued against infant baptism, that children could not experience faith and repentance, the Reformed replied that although children did not possess the acts of faith, they still could possess the disposition (habitus) of faith. Since absolute certainty about the internal state of the recipient is never certain in the case of either adults or children, the question is whether we have the same certainty in either case. It is not surprising that the New Testament does not mention infant baptism since adult baptism was the rule, and infant baptism would have been the exception. Yet this does not exclude infant baptism since it may be derived from original baptism by legitimate inference. According to Col. 2:11–12, baptism replaced Old Testament circumcision. Baptism is therefore more than circumcision, not in essence but in degree. While circumcision pointed forward to Christ's death, baptism points back to it. Since as a poorer dispensation of grace circumcision was administered to children, it follows that as a richer dispensation of grace baptism ought to be administered to children as well. Also, the entire idea of the covenant as the historical and organic realization of election points toward the inclusion of infants through their connection with their parents in grace and blessing. Thus, despite the Jews' rejection of Jesus, he continues to regard their children as children of the covenant. The apostles likewise treat the covenant of grace as the same in essence and include the organism of the family as an institution of God in both its blessings and curses. Furthermore, while Anabaptism sets a limit to the operation of grace, in the New Testament all boundaries of people, country, sex, and age have been erased. Just as with adults, the hearts of infants should be judged according to charity.

In the administration of baptism Christ only employs ordained people, showing that the sacraments are subordinate to the preaching of the Word. Baptism is therefore not the cause but rather the sign and seal of regeneration, which is bestowed before and apart from the sacrament. This means that baptism is not strictly necessary for salvation. The sacrament must always be closely joined with the Word.

With respect to time of the administration of baptism, the Greek Orthodox, Roman Catholic, Lutheran, and Reformed all agree that it should be soon after birth. Baptismal sponsors have been considered by Lutheran and Reformed theologians to be adiaphoron, yet the Reformed insisted that parents should answer the baptismal questions. The Reformed, having closely aligned themselves with Scripture on the doctrine of baptism, have managed to avoid sectarianism and preserve the catholicity of Christian doctrine. Accordingly, they recognized the baptism of heretics and have consistently held to a broad policy in the recognition of baptism. Despite differences over baptism, all Christian churches continue to recognize one Lord, one faith, and one baptism.

THE BROADER RELIGIOUS CONTEXT OF BAPTISM

[530] The foundation for baptism in the New Testament was laid in the days of the old covenant by circumcision, a rite that God expressly enjoined upon Abraham (Gen. 17:10ff.). According to Herodotus, circumcision was also practiced among the Egyptians, Phoenicians, and Syrians. Reformed theologians sometimes tried to refute this witness or to demonstrate that these peoples had taken the practice over from Israel.[1] But this sentiment is untenable. Among the Egyptians the practice had been followed, at least in the case of priests, from ancient times. Modern ethnological studies have shown that circumcision is a ceremony that occurs among countless peoples in Asia, America, Africa, and even Australia.[2] Just as in the institution of the temple and the priesthood, of sacrifice and altar, of laws and ordinances in Israel, God utilized practices existing among other peoples, he also did so in the case of circumcision. He took it over, as it were, but gave it another, that is, a sacramental, meaning. For while among other nations physical circumcision did indeed occur, it by no means had the character of a sacrament there. There, too, as among the Egyptians, the rite was frequently administered to only a few persons, and usually not in the first few days of life, but at a later age.[3] When God initiated circumcision in the life of Abraham, however, he ordered that every male should be circumcised, the slave as well as the son of the house; that this circumcision must be administered on the eighth day; and that it should serve as a sign of the covenant, so that he who did not receive this sign was a covenant breaker and had to be "cut off" from his people. Hence, though circumcision may also have been a sanitary measure, that is not its purpose in Israel. Here it serves as a sign and confirmation of the covenant of grace, whose one great and all-embracing promise is: "I will be your God and the God of your descendants after you" (Gen. 17:7). Specifically it is a seal of two benefits of the covenant—of the righteousness of faith (Rom. 4:11) and the circumcision of the heart (Deut. 10:16; 30:6; Jer. 4:4; Rom. 2:28–29; Col. 2:11); that is, of righteousness or the forgiveness of sins, and of regeneration or sanctification. This does not mean that it confers these benefits mechanically, for external circumcision without the

---

1. Cf. H. Witsius, *Ægyptiaca et Dekaphylon* (Herborn: Nicolae Andreae, 1717), III, 6, 11–12; J. Marck, *Christianae theologiae medulla didactico-elenctica* (Amsterdam: Wetstenios, 1716), 29.8.

2. F. Delitzsch, *A New Commentary on Genesis,* trans. Sophia Taylor (Edinburgh: T&T Clark, 1899), Gen. 17; C. Orelli, "Beschneidung," in *PRE*³, II, 660–62; A. Glassberg, *Die Beschneidung in ihrer geschichtlichen, ethnographischen, religiösen und medicinischen Bedeutung* (Berlin: Boas, 1896).

3. E. Schürer, *The History of the Jewish People in the Age of Jesus Christ (175 B.C.–A.D. 135),* rev. and ed. G. Vermès and F. Millar (Edinburgh: T&T Clark, 1973), I, 537ff.; cf. *Theologische Literaturzeitung* (28 August 1903): 409–11 (ed. note: Bavinck is referring to a review of Schürer's first volume. However, he mistakenly cites the date as 13 Sept. 1902).

circumcision of the heart is of no value (Acts 7:51; Rom. 2:28–29; 3:21, 30; 1 Cor. 7:19). But being a seal of the righteousness of faith, it presupposes faith. When the Jews sought increasingly to establish their own righteousness on the basis of the law, they, like the Gentiles and despite their external circumcision, became similarly deserving of condemnation before God (Rom. 3:2).

For that reason God, through John [the Baptist], instituted water baptism even before Jesus started his public ministry. This baptism, too, was not something absolutely new, any more than circumcision was in former times. In religion, all of antiquity attributed a symbolic meaning to water. The water of the Euphrates, the Indus, and the Ganges had atoning and sanctifying power. Among Greeks and Romans, on all sorts of occasions, for example in the case of initiation into the mysteries, washings were prescribed.[4] Also in Israel, well before the divine institution of baptism, all kinds of washings were performed.[5] In the case of proselytes, along with circumcision and a sacrifice, baptism was a requirement for admission into the believing community.[6] This baptism, however, only becomes a sacrament, a sign and seal of grace, as a result of being instituted by God. The New Testament, accordingly, expressly teaches that "a word of God" came to John to baptize (Luke 3:2–3), that God sent him for this purpose (John 1:33), that his baptism was not "from men" but "from heaven" (Matt. 21:25), and that the publicans who had themselves baptized "justified God," while the Pharisees and scribes, having refused to be baptized by John, "rejected God's purpose for themselves" (Luke 7:29–30). With that baptism John proclaimed to the Jews of his day that, though they were circumcised and [some were] baptized proselytes, they were themselves culpable and impure and needed baptism to enter into the kingdom of heaven. John's baptism, therefore, was an indictment against and a condemnation of the Jews, a message of their "damn-worthiness," but—let us not forget this—also something more. It was incontrovertible proof that God remembered his covenant and fulfilled his promise. Despite the fact that the Jews were culpable and impure, there was forgiveness with God, and this forgiveness was going to be even more richly manifest than in the days of the Old Testament. John the Baptist, therefore, must not be viewed as the last of the Old Testament prophets, "for all the prophets and the law prophesied *until* John" (Matt. 11:13); he is to be regarded, rather, as the announcer of the coming kingdom (Matt. 3:2), as the messenger of the approaching good news (Luke 3:18), as the one who prepared the way for Christ (Mark 1:2), as the witness to the rising light (John 1:7, 29, 34, 36; cf. Matt. 3:11; Mark 1:7; Luke 3:16; Acts 19:4) who will soon make room for the One who is mightier than he [John], and who leads his disciples to Christ (John 1:35ff.; 3:27ff.).

4. T. Pfanner, *Systema theologiae gentilis purioris* (Basel: Joh. Hermann Widerhold, 1679), 346.

5. E. Schürer, *The History of the Jewish People*, II, 477ff.; W. Brandt, *Die jüdischen Baptismen* (Giessen: Alfred Töpelmann, 1910); J. Steinbeck, "Kultische Waschungen und Bäder im Heidentum und Judentum und ihr Verhältnis zur christlichen Taufe," *Neue kirchliche Zeitschrift* 21 (1910): 778–99.

6. E. Schürer, *The History of the Jewish People*, III, 165.

WATER BAPTISM AND SPIRIT BAPTISM

Conforming to the content of this message is John's baptism. His was a baptism of repentance for the forgiveness of sins (Mark 1:4). This does not mean that John's baptism merely served to prepare people for the forgiveness that Christ would bestow (Meyer), but very specifically that it conferred forgiveness in the way of repentance. In Acts 2:38 it is similarly said of Christian baptism, after all, that it took place "for the forgiveness of sins" because by baptism as sign and seal one obtains forgiveness. Furthermore, Jesus himself was baptized with John's baptism. He made absolutely no distinction between the baptism administered by his disciples and that of John (John 3:22–23; 4:1ff.) but simply adopted the disciples baptized by John without baptizing them again (John 1:37; Acts 18:25). Neither did Jesus (in Matt. 28:19) institute another or a new baptism but only expanded it to include all the nations. On these grounds both the Reformed[7] and the Lutherans,[8] though recognizing a difference in degree, firmly held on to the essential identity of the Johannine and Christian baptism. This identity was opposed, however, by Roman Catholics,[9] Anabaptists, Socinians, Arminians, and many modern theologians.[10]

And, indeed, weighty objections can be advanced against the assumption of identity. In the first place, from Matt. 3:11; Mark 1:8; and Luke 3:16 expositors derive the objection that John's baptism and Christian baptism are opposed to each other as water baptism is to Spirit baptism or baptism by fire. Acts 1:5, however, clearly teaches that John here does not contrast his baptism with Christian baptism but with the—figuratively so-called—"baptism" of the Holy Spirit on the day of Pentecost. True Christian baptism after all is also a baptism with water, signifying the washing away of sins; and John's baptism was similarly a baptism with water, but one that at the same time sealed repentance and forgiveness. The two baptisms, accordingly, completely agree both in the sign and in the thing signified. If that were not true, the absurd implication would be that not only John's baptism but also the baptism that Jesus himself had his disciples administer before the day of Pentecost had been no more than a baptism with water. And not even the opponents of the identity of John's baptism with that of Jesus dare draw that conclusion. They usually say that Christian baptism was instituted *either* when Jesus was baptized by John, *or* when Jesus had his disciples administer baptism.

7. J. Calvin, *Institutes*, IV.xv.7–8; P. van Mastricht, *Theoretico-practica theologia* (Utrecht: Appels, 1714), VII, 4, 17; F. Turretin, *Institutes of Elenctic Theology*, trans. G. M. Giger, ed. J. T. Dennison, 3 vols. (Phillipsburg, NJ: Presbyterian & Reformed, 1992), XIX, 16; C. Vitringa, *Doctrina christiana religionis*, 8 vols. (Leiden: Joannis le Mair, 1761–86), VII, 52.

8. J. Gerhard, *Loci theologici*, ed. E. Preuss, 9 vols. (Berlin: G. Schlawitz, 1863–75), XX, 15ff., 43ff.

9. T. Aquinas, *Summa theol.*, III, qu. 66, art. 4; Council of Trent, sess. VII, can. 1; R. Bellarmine, "De bapt.," in *Controversiis*, I, 5.

10. F. Schleiermacher, *The Christian Faith*, ed. H. R. MacIntosh and J. S. Steward (Edinburgh: T&T Clark, 1928), §136; J. W. F. Höfling, *Das Sakrament der Taufe* (Erlangen: Deichert, 1859), I, 26ff.; J. J. van Oosterzee, *Christian Dogmatics*, trans. J. Watson and M. Evans, 2 vols. (New York: Scribner, Armstrong, 1874), §87, 2.

But the two baptisms, both that of Jesus and that of John, were distinct from the Spirit baptism that was to take place on the day of Pentecost, even though both signified and sealed the same benefits of repentance and the forgiveness of sins.

But now—and this is the second objection to the above-mentioned identity—the Spirit baptism of the day of Pentecost is again being related to Christian baptism by water. According to Acts 19:1–7, Paul encountered in Ephesus a number of disciples who were baptized "into John's baptism" (v. 3), who were called "disciples" and "believers" and still had not received the Holy Spirit and did not even know "that there is a Holy Spirit" (v. 2). Having been better instructed by Paul on the subject of John's preaching, they had themselves baptized "in the name of the Lord Jesus," had Paul lay hands on them, and thus received the Holy Spirit and began to speak in tongues and prophesy. From this last statement, it is evident that, in considering the term "Holy Spirit" here, as in 8:15–18; 10:44; 11:15; and 15:8, we must think of the Spirit's gift of glossolalia and prophecy. The disciples in Ephesus had not received this gift nor even heard of it. Baptism did not always yield this gift, neither John's nor that of Jesus. For in Acts 8:15 we read that the believers in Samaria had indeed been baptized "in the name of the Lord Jesus," but none had as yet received the Holy Spirit and only obtained him through the laying on of hands by the apostles. Similarly Acts 19:6 views this gift, not as a consequence of baptism, but of the laying on of hands. The strange thing in Acts 19 is that *before* this laying on of hands the disciples in Ephesus were baptized in the name of the Lord Jesus. One therefore has to conclude that Paul did not regard the baptism they had received [earlier] as true and genuine. They had been baptized "into John's baptism" (v. 3). John's baptism was indeed good, for he administered the baptism of repentance unto faith in Christ. But all sorts of error, also regarding baptism, had crept into the circle of the disciples of John who had stayed with him and had not switched over to Jesus. Consequently, the disciples in Ephesus did not have to be baptized in Jesus's name again but *for the first time*, for their baptism into John's name was not a true baptism, not a truly Christian baptism, nor the true, original Johannine baptism.[11]

[531] The institution by God of baptism, accordingly, already occurs in the ministry of John, but Jesus, after undergoing it himself, adopted it from him and had it administered by his disciples (John 3:22; 4:1–2). In Matt. 28:19 he made it obligatory for all believers from all nations. Many expositors regard this last verse as inauthentic,[12] on the ground that in the apostolic era baptism still took

---

11. W. Baldensperger, *Das Prolog des vierten Evangeliums* (Freiburg i.B.: Mohr, 1898), believes that the entire prologue of John 1 is written to oppose these baptists or followers of John the Baptist. Cf. H. Oort, "Mattheüs XI en de Johannes-gemeenten," *Theologisch Tijdschrift* 42 (1908): 299–333.

12. A. von Harnack, *Entstehung und Entwicklung der Kirchenverfassung und des Kirchenrechts in den zwei ersten Jahrhunderten* (Leipzig: Hinrichs, 1910), 187–98, considers those who believe that the trinitarian formula is derived from pagan speculation (Usener, Dieterich) to be in error, and attempts to posit over against this that it derives from Judeo-Christian origins. In addition, there is no need to judge the text in Matt. 28:19 to be inauthentic or an interpolation, as Conybeare and Lake contend; cf. A. Plummer, *An Exegetical Commentary on*

place in the name of Jesus, and that the trinitarian formula is of a later date. Some scholars even say that Jesus did not institute baptism for his church at all.

This position, however, is open to a number of objections. It cannot be denied that Jesus himself had John's baptism administered to him and by that token recognized it. In a verse in which he expressly speaks of it, he deduces it from a command of God (Matt. 21:25). Nor is there any ground for denying that Jesus took over baptism and, if he did not administer it himself, had it administered by his disciples (John 3:22, 26; 4:1–2), for Jesus appeared in public with the same message as John, the message of the nearness of the kingdom of heaven, and laid down the same conditions for entering it (i.e., faith and repentance; Mark 1:15). It is therefore natural that, like John, he had the baptism of repentance administered to everyone who wanted to belong to the restricted circle of his disciples. In John 3:5, though there is no mention of baptism, there is evidence that the impartation of the Spirit in the church was viewed as having its symbol in water. To the degree that the opposition between the Jewish people and Jesus and his disciples became sharper, an act of separation on the one hand and an act of incorporation into the church of Jesus on the other increasingly became a necessity. Baptism as the rite of incorporation into the Christian church must also, to be sure, have been willed and intended by Jesus himself, or else there is no way we can explain that it was immediately, without any conflict, introduced and applied in all Christian churches, both in those of Jewish and those of Gentile origin (Acts 2:38, 41; 8:12–13, 16, 38; 9:18; and so forth; Rom. 6:3–5; 1 Cor. 1:13–17; Gal. 3:27; Eph. 5:26; and so forth). In 1 Cor. 1:17 Paul does say that Christ did not send him to baptize but to preach the gospel. But this does not in any way prove that Paul had a low opinion of baptism or considered it unnecessary. Romans 6 and other passages certainly teach otherwise. Jesus himself did not administer baptism either but had it done by others; also compare Peter (Acts 10:48). Similarly Paul occupied himself with the preaching of the gospel and left baptism and other activities involved in founding and building up churches to his fellow workers.

"IN THE NAME OF JESUS"

Now in that early period baptism is indeed described as occurring "in the name of Jesus" or "into the name of Jesus" (Acts 2:38; 8:16; 10:48; 19:5; Rom. 6:3; 1 Cor. 1:13; Gal. 3:27), but this is by no means to say that baptism was administered with that specific formula. In any case, Paul says in 1 Cor. 10:2 that the Israelites were baptized "into Moses," in 1:13 that believers in Corinth were not baptized "in the name of Paul," in 12:13 that they were all baptized "into one

the Gospel according to St. Matthew (London: E. Stock, 1909), 431ff. Furthermore, the evidence for a trinitarian formula undoubtedly goes back to the beginning of the second century, according to E. Riggenbach, Der trinitarische Taufbefehl: Matt. 28:19 nach seiner ursprünglichen Textgestalt und seiner Authentie (Gütersloh: C. Bertelsmann, 1903).

body," and in Acts 19:3 the disciples at Ephesus said they had been baptized "into John's baptism." In all of these cases no one thinks of a formula used in connection with the rite of baptism. The expression "in the name of Jesus" is not meant as a formula but is a description of the character of Christian baptism.[13] Upon their departure from Egypt, the Israelites let themselves be baptized—in the cloud and in the sea—"into Moses," in relation to Moses, so that they recognized him as their savior and redeemer, placed their trust in him, and let themselves be guided by him. The disciples at Ephesus were baptized "into John's baptism" and by it had joined the community of John the Baptist. So also Christian baptism is and is called a baptism in or into the name of Jesus because he adopts believers into his fellowship and directs them to put all their trust in him alone.

Now the same thing is meant when Jesus says in Matt. 28:19 that his disciples must be baptized "into the name of the Father and the Son and the Holy Spirit." It is not here prescribing to the apostles what they have to *say* during the administration of baptism but what they have to *do*. Christian baptism is and must be an incorporation into fellowship with the God who has revealed himself as Father, Son, and Spirit. The name denotes God in his self-revelation, and the supreme self-revelation of God consists in the fact that he makes himself known as, and has himself called, Father, Son, and Spirit. The reality of being baptized in that name, accordingly, does not simply make known the fact that one is baptized at God's command or with a view to confessing his name. After all, the expression "in the name" can be alternated with the person himself, just as Paul also speaks of being baptized "into Christ" (Rom. 6:3; Gal. 3:27). But it indicates that the person being baptized is placed in relationship and fellowship with the God who has revealed himself as Father, Son, and Spirit, and is now obligated on that basis to confess and glorify that name.[14] But although Jesus after his resurrection had described baptism as an incorporation into communion with the Father, Son, and Spirit, it was natural in that early period for baptism to be associated mostly with the person of Christ. Of primary importance in becoming a member of the church

---

13. T. Zahn, *Einleitung in das Neue Testament*, 3rd ed., 2 vols. (Leipzig: Deichert, 1906–7), 316.

14. The meaning of the formula "in the name of" is currently explained by history-of-religions scholars as a part of the Jewish and pagan superstitions concerning names. According to this view, the public declaration of a name gives to those present, when the name is voiced, a certain participation in the person's powers and thus exercises a magical influence. Cf. F. Giesebrecht, *Die alttestamentliche Schätzung des Gottesnamens und ihre religionsgeschichtliche Grundlage* (Königsberg: Thomas & Oppermann, 1901); W. Heitmüller, *Im Namen Jesu* (Göttingen: Vandenhoeck & Ruprecht, 1903); idem, *Taufe und Abendmahl bei Paulus* (Göttingen: Vandenhoeck & Ruprecht, 1903); J. Weiss, "Heitmüller: *Im Namen Jesu*," *Theologische Rundschau* 7 (1904): 185–96; J. Boehmer, *Die Studierstube* (1904): 388ff.; A. van der Flier, "Het gebruik van den israëlische Godsnaam," *Theologische Studiën* 21 (1903): 232–47; J. Boehmer, *Das biblische "im Namen"* (Giessen: Ricker, 1898); B. Jacob, *Im Namen Gottes* (Berlin: S. Calvary, 1903; ed. note: Bavinck cites the 1904 edition); W. Brandt, "Ὄνομα en het doopsformule in het Nieuwe Testament," *Theologisch Tijdschrift* 25 (1891): 565–610; idem, "Nog eens: Εἰς Ὄνομα," *Theologisch Tijdschrift* 36 (1902): 193–217; idem, "De tooverkracht van namen in Oud en Nieuw Testament," *Teyler's Theologisch Tijdschrift* 2 (1904): 335–88 (ed. note: Bavinck erroneously cites this as *Theologisch Tijdschrift* without the title). C. Orelli, "Name," in *PRE*[3], XIII, 625–31; G. B. Gray, "Name," in *DB*, III, 478–81; J. C. Lambert, "Name," in *DC*, II, 217–18.

were repentance and faith in Christ in order in that way to obtain forgiveness of sins, and of that forgiveness baptism is the sign and proof. For that reason baptism in the book of Acts is called—just as it was in connection with John—"a baptism of repentance . . . for the forgiveness of sins" (cf. Acts 2:38; 22:16).

But in that first period there was something else as well. John and also Jesus himself had contrasted this baptism of repentance with the Spirit baptism that was to take place on the day of Pentecost. This Spirit baptism was certainly not bound to water baptism, the baptism of repentance for the forgiveness of sins, for in Acts 2:33 all the disciples received that Spirit without [water] baptism. In Acts 9:17 and 10:44 the gifts of the Spirit are given to Paul, Cornelius, and others even before baptism (cf. 11:15–17). In Acts 8:15–17; 9:17; and 19:6 glossolalia and the gift of prophecy are not bestowed through baptism but through the laying on of hands. Still for those who were "outside," the baptism of repentance was the ordinary way by which they could also receive the gifts of the Spirit (Acts 2:38; 19:5–6). This connection, however, was temporary. Glossolalia and prophecy were not the true benefits of baptism. Christian baptism essentially remained a baptism of repentance and of faith in Christ for the forgiveness of sins.

This is also how it is understood and described throughout the New Testament. In 1 Pet. 3:20–21 Peter says that just as Noah and his family were saved from death by the water that bore up the ark, so believers are saved from perdition by baptism. But that baptism must then be viewed, not as σαρκος ἀποθεσις ῥυπου (*sarkos apothesis rhypou*, lit., putting away the filth of the flesh, i.e., not in the same way they externally remove the pollution of the flesh), but as συνειδησεως ἀγαθης ἐπερωτημα εἰς θεον, δι' ἀναστασεως Ἰησου Χριστου (*syneidēseōs agathēs eperōtēma eis theon, di' anastaseōs Iēsou Christou*, i.e., most likely, an appeal to God for a good conscience, free from guilt). Only baptism can be this through the resurrection of Jesus Christ, as a proof of our justification (Rom. 4:25). The same view returns in the Letter to the Hebrews. It indeed regards the "instruction about baptisms" (6:2), that is, not the doctrine of Christian baptism but of ceremonial washings in general—of which a correct view was urgently needed by Jewish Christians (cf. 9:10)—as belonging to the elementary principles of Christianity, and it distinguishes two elements in Christian baptism: the washing of the body with pure water, and the cleansing of our hearts from an evil, accusing conscience (10:22–23). Paul writes about baptism from another perspective, relating it not so much to justification as to sanctification. Baptism as a descent into and a rising out of the water depicts and is a pledge of our entering into fellowship with Christ, his death, and his resurrection (Rom. 6:3–6; Col. 2:12). For as many as were baptized into Christ, into fellowship with him, have put on Christ, appropriating Christ, so that now they are in Christ and belong to him (Gal. 3:27–29), walk in newness of life (Rom. 6:4, 6ff.; Eph. 5:26), live to God (Rom. 6:11, 13), and indeed carry the life of Christ within themselves (Gal. 2:20). And just as by baptism they entered into communion with Christ, so they also entered into fellowship with his church, which is his body. For by one Spirit they have all been baptized into one body (1 Cor. 12:13; Rom. 12:5). In Paul's view, water baptism is simultaneously a Spirit baptism, not a baptism with the spiritual gifts of glossolalia and prophecy, but with the Spirit as the principle of a new life. Baptized people are new, spiritual, people (πνευματικοι). But this renewal of human beings by the Holy Spirit in baptism is not something detached from and alongside of, nor an accidental addition to, justification by faith. Rather, the two coincide. The Corinthians are simultaneously washed, sanctified, and justified in the name of the Lord Jesus and by the Spirit of our God (1 Cor. 6:11). In baptism all these benefits are joined together and granted to believers, which does not alter the fact, however, that the Corinthians, despite their baptism, are still called "worldly," mere "infants in Christ," by Paul, and solemnly warned against the possibility of their falling away (1 Cor. 3:1, 3; 10:1–12).

THE RITE OF BAPTISM

[532] In the ancient Christian church we do not yet find a fixed doctrine and a universally practiced rite in connection with baptism. Yet the *Teaching of the Apostles* (*Didache*) already has the trinitarian formula, while Hermas still speaks of a baptism in the name of the Lord and calls it a seal of the Son of God, which gives life. Since baptism is the incorporation of a person into the church, it grants participation in all its redemptive benefits, especially in the forgiveness of past sins and in a new, supernatural, and eternal life by the Holy Spirit.[15] Although it is clearly stated that the water in baptism retains its ordinary nature, the linking of the sign and the thing signified is frequently expressed in a mystical manner: "If there is any grace in the water, it is not because of the nature of the water but because of the presence of the Spirit."[16] "Through that water divine grace bestows eternal life."[17] Baptism, accordingly, is described by various names derived from the mysteries: illumination, mystery, completion, fulfillment, initiation, induction into the mysteries, and regarded as "a vehicle toward heaven," "a vehicle toward God," or "a key of the kingdom of heaven."[18]

---

15. Justin Martyr, *First Apology* 61; Tertullian, *On Baptism* 4–5; Gregory Nazianzus, *Theological Orations* 40, 3ff.; ed. note: Bavinck refers here also to Cyprian, *De grat.* 3, 4. There appears to be no extant treatise of Cyprian's with this title, but Cyprian does refer to the renewing power of baptism in his treatise *Works and Almsgiving*, ch. 2, and in his *Exhortation to Martyrdom, to Fortunatus*, ch. 4.

16. Basil, *On the Holy Spirit*, c. 15.

17. Theodoret, *Questions on Genesis,* qu. 26 (ed. note: Patrologiae cursus completus: Series graeca, ed. J.-P. Migne [Paris: Migne], vol. 80; cf. also *Theodoreti cyrensis quaestiones in octateuchum*, ed. Natalio Fernández Marcos and Angel Sáenz-Badillos [Madrid: Biblia Poliglota Matritense, 1979]); J. C. Suicerus, *Thesaurus ecclesiasticus* (Amsterdam: J. H. Wetsten, 1682), s.v. βαπτισμα; cf. Tertullian, *On Baptism*, 4.

18. J. Schwane, *Dogmengeschichte*, 4 vols. (Freiburg i.B.: Herder, 1882–95), II, 735; E. Hatch, *Griechentum und Christentum* (Freiburg i.B.: Mohr, 1892), 219; J. C. Suicerus, *Thesaurus ecclesiasticus*, s.v. βαπτισμα; F. Kattenbusch ("Taufe, Kirchenlehre," in *PRE*³, XIX, 403) correctly observes: "Obviously this does not mean that the particular ideas by which people consider initiation rituals in the mystery religions as confirmation-seal or enlightenment were simply carried over into the ἐκκλησια by the action of name-giving in baptism." The term "seal," for example, was already used by the Jews with respect to circumcision (cf. Rom. 4:11).

And when from the second century onward worship services were split into a public and a private part, the administration of baptism and the Lord's Supper increasingly assumed a more mysterious character. Preceded by the catechumenate, baptism itself was fenced in by a wide range of symbolic actions, such as the presentation of the child or person receiving baptism by sponsors, making profession of faith, blowing on the face of the candidate for baptism and making the sign of the cross, putting consecrated salt into the mouth of the candidate for baptism, exorcism, the thrice-repeated immersion or sprinkling, the anointing with chrism, the giving of a new name, the putting on of a white garment, the handing over of a lighted candle, the admission to the church, the fraternal kiss, and sometimes the celebration of the Lord's Supper immediately afterward.[19] So, although in the apostolic era baptism immediately followed conversion and was administered in the simplest possible way (Acts 2:38, 41; 8:12, 36; 10:47; and so forth), from the second century onward it was clothed in an ever-expanding ritual and changed into a more or less magically operative means of grace. Even Augustine fostered the development of the doctrine of baptism along these lines, though in the case of adults he demanded prior faith and repentance for a beneficial effect. For, in the first place, he says that baptism only yields forgiveness of sins and regeneration within the church. The sacrament is a sacrament of Christ and given by him to the church. Heretics and schismatics can take it with them outside the church, but then it is stolen and illegitimate property and has no beneficial effect but tends rather to be destructive.[20] Second, in the case of infants, he seems to teach that baptism, working ex opere operato, has a beneficial effect. Unbaptized children who die in infancy are lost,[21] but in the case of those who are baptized, the baptism itself, or the intercession of the church, or the faith of the parents, takes the place of the faith that the children themselves cannot yet exercise.[22] And, third, Augustine in any case ascribes to baptism the effect of an "indelible character" by which the baptized by law belong to Christ and his church and may, if necessary, be returned to its care and protection by force.[23]

19. J. C. Suicerus, *Thesaurus ecclesiasticus*, s.v. βαπτισμα; B. Moeller and H. von Schubert, *Lehrbuch der Kirchengeschichte*, 3 vols. (Tübingen: Mohr, 1892–1907), I, 339; cf. Roman Catechism, II, ch. 2, qu. 45 (ed. note: The post–Vatican II edition titled *The Roman Catechism* [trans. Robert I. Bradley, SJ, and Eugene Kevane (Boston: Daughters of St. Paul, 1985)] drops the enumeration of the introduction so that ch. 1 begins the section on baptism. In this annotation, the proper reference would be II, ch. 1, qu. 46); R. Bellarmine, "De bapt." in *Controversiis*, c. 24–27; P. Drews, "Taufe, Liturg. Vollzug," in *PRE*³, XIX, 424–50.

20. Augustine, *The Unity of the Church* 68; idem, *On Baptism, against the Donatists* 3, 13, 5, 7ff.

21. Augustine, *The Soul and Its Origin* I, 9; III, 12; idem, *Merits and Remissions of Sins* I, 20; idem, *Nature and Grace* 8.

22. Augustine, *Merits and Remissions of Sins* I, 19, 34ff.

23. Augustine, *On Baptism* V, 21; VI, 1; idem, *Against the Letter of Parmenian* II, 16; cf. A. J. Dorner, *Augustinus* (Berlin: W. Hertz, 1873), 248; J. Schwane, *Dogmengeschichte*, II, 744ff.; A. von Harnack, *History of Dogma*, trans. N. Buchanan et al., ed. A. B. Bruce, 7 vols. (London: Williams & Norgate, 1896–99), V, 158ff.; F. Kattenbusch, "Taufe, Kirchenlehre," in *PRE*³, XIX, 408–11.

Scholasticism tended initially to confine itself to Augustine's teaching and recognized that in the case of adults baptism presupposed faith and was not strictly necessary for salvation. But it increasingly moved in the direction of saying that the sacrament worked ex opere operato and thereby increasingly caused the subjective demands to lose their importance.[24] In that way it laid the groundwork for Rome's doctrine of baptism, which in a nutshell comes down to the following: Baptism is the first sacrament, the door to the spiritual life, the entry into the church. It furnishes the first supernatural grace that is presupposed and augmented by the other sacraments and is therefore strictly necessary to salvation, except in a few cases where it can be replaced by "a baptism of blood" [martyrdom] or "a baptism of desire."[25] It must therefore be administered as soon as possible and in cases of emergency by laypersons or even non-Christians. Imparted by that baptism, in any case, are the following: (1) the *character indelebilis*, which brings a person under the jurisdiction of the church; (2) the forgiveness of all sins, both original and actual, which were committed before one's baptism, and the remission of all eternal and also all temporal sins insofar as they are "works of satisfaction" but not insofar as they are the natural penalties of sin; (3) the spiritual renewal and sanctification of a person by the infusion of sanctifying grace and the supernatural virtues of faith, hope, and love, so that the pollution of original sin is totally nullified and only the concupiscence that is integral to the nature of a human being as a physical creature remains. This concupiscence, however, is not itself sin but may become the occasion of sin; (4) the incorporation into the communion of saints and into the visible church of believers. Baptism exerts these effects by the fact that when the priest pronounces the familiar formula, the word of God or the power of the Holy Spirit mysteriously unites itself with the water, making it "living and efficacious water," a "maternal womb" of the new human being. Actually regenerated by the sacrament of baptism, therefore, are not only

---

24. P. Lombard, *Sent.*, IV, dist. 3–6; T. Aquinas, *Summa theol.*, III, qu. 66–71; Bonaventure, *Breviloquium*, VI, 7; cf. J. Schwane, *Dogmengeschichte*, III, 605–22; A. von Harnack, *History of Dogma*, VI, 220ff.

25. Ed. note: These two terms are defined by the new *Catechism of the Catholic Church* (San Francisco: Ignatius, 1992), ##1258–60, as follows:

1258. The Church has always held the firm conviction that those who suffer death for the sake of the faith without having received Baptism are baptized by their death for and with Christ. This *Baptism of blood*, like the desire for Baptism, brings about the fruits of Baptism without being a sacrament.

1259. For catechumens who die before their Baptism, their explicit desire to receive it, together with repentance for their sins, and charity, assures them the salvation that they were not able to receive through the sacrament.

1260. "Since Christ died for all, and since all men are in fact called to one and the same destiny, which is divine, we must hold that the Holy Spirit offers to all the possibility of being made partakers, in a way known to God, of the Paschal mystery." [62] Every man who is ignorant of the Gospel of Christ and of his Church, but seeks the truth and does the will of God in accordance with his understanding of it, can be saved. It may be supposed that such persons would have *desired Baptism explicitly if they had known its necessity*. (emphasis added)

all children but also all adults who have performed the seven preparations and placed no obstacle in the way of the sacrament.[26]

THE REFORMATION AND BAPTISM

[533] The battle that was waged by the Reformation against Rome's doctrine of the sacraments was concentrated, not around baptism, but around the Lord's Supper. The German Reformers even believed that baptism had been kept almost completely intact under papacy and therefore adopted it with only a few minor changes. Many ceremonies that had been gradually added to baptism—such as the giving of a name, the sign of the cross, exorcism, sponsorship, the laying on of hands, the white garment, the blessing, and so forth—also remained in use among the Lutherans. In addition, in the two catechisms and the Smalcald Articles, Luther taught that the words of institution turned the water into "divine, heavenly, holy and salvific water." Although he rejected the opinion of Thomas and the Dominicans, who misconstrued the words of institution and had God impart a "spiritual power" to the water, he nevertheless accepted an objective realistic union of the word with the water. Baptism is "a word of God joined with immersion in water included in the divine command and sealed with the word of God." The water in baptism, as Luther put it elsewhere in his *Sermon on Baptism*, "is permeated by the divine majesty and presence," as iron glows with the heat of fire. Later dogmaticians, working this out, held that by the words of institution "the heavenly matter, i.e., the entire Trinity, or the blood of Christ, or the Holy Spirit" so united itself with the earthly matter, that is, the water, that God, in, with, and through the water of baptism—not separately and by a particular action but in conjunction with the word of baptism and through it by a single and indivisible action—worked regeneration.

And finally, though in that early period Luther consistently made the beneficial effect of baptism depend on the faith with which the benefits of baptism were accepted, he later increasingly stressed the importance of the objective character of baptism and no longer asserted that infants are or can be believers, but based infant baptism only on God's command. Lutheran theologians therefore later taught that in the case of adults the beneficial effect of baptism indeed depends on faith, at least on a "latent capacity," and hence, if faith is present, consists in sealing and conformation. However, in the case of infants, baptism effects regeneration.

26. Council of Florence (1438–45), in H. Denzinger, ed., *The Sources of Catholic Dogma*, trans. from the 30th ed. by R. J. Deferrari (Fitzwilliam, NH: Loreto Publications, 2002), n. 696 (ed. note: Bavinck here erroneously cites n. 591); Council of Trent, sess. VI, can. 4; idem, sess. VII, "On Baptism" (ed. note: H. Denzinger, *Sources of Catholic Dogma*, ##857–70); idem, sess. XIV, "On Penance" (ed. note: H. Denzinger, *Sources of Catholic Dogma*, ##893–925); Roman Catechism, II, ch. 2 (ed. note: Bradley and Kevane, II, ch. 1); R. Bellarmine, "De sacr. bapt.," in *Controversiis*, ch. 1–27; J. H. Oswald, *Die dogmatische Lehre von den heiligen Sakramenten der katholischen Kirche*, 2nd ed., 2 vols. (Münster: Aschendorff, 1864), 141ff.; and for the teaching of the [Eastern] Orthodox Church, John of Damascus [d. 777], *The Orthodox Faith*, IV, 14; The Orthodox Confession, qu. 102–3; Confession of Dositheus (1672), decr. 16; F. Kattenbusch, *Lehrbuch der vergleichenden Confessionskunde* (Freiburg i.B.: J. C. B. Mohr [Paul Siebeck], 1892), I, 400ff.

It is "the ordinary means of regeneration and of cleansing from sins," yet always in such a way that, while the guilt and power of sin is removed, this is not true of all the pollution. The root of or fuel for sin remains.[27]

The Reformed tradition, however, rejected most of the ceremonies that had gradually become associated with baptism and returned to the simplicity of Scripture. They also proceeded from, and attempted to hold on to, the idea that baptism had been instituted for believers and therefore did not effect faith but strengthened it. Consequently they faced a twofold difficulty in connection with infant baptism. In the first place, they had to demonstrate—primarily against the Anabaptists but also against Roman Catholics and Lutherans—that the children of believers were to be regarded as believers even before baptism and as such ought to be baptized. And in the second place, they were obligated to answer the question in what the gracious operation of baptism consisted in the case of small children, since, if they had not yet reached the age of discretion and hence did not yet possess "actual faith," they could hardly be strengthened and confirmed in that faith. As a rule, however, little attention was paid to the latter issue. Theologians generally confined themselves to saying that baptism was proof to the parents that their offspring were included in the covenant of God; that it was a great source of consolation and blessing for the children later as they grew up; and that even before they were conscious of it, it gave them title to the benefits of the covenant of grace.[28] From the very beginning, however, the first question prompted a wide range of different answers. For the validity of infant baptism, they unanimously appealed to Scripture, specifically to its teaching concerning the covenant of grace. Children, but also adults, had to be judged in light of the rule of that covenant. A person is entitled to baptism not by faith and repentance but only because of the covenant. The children born of believing parents were not

27. J. Köstlin, *The Theology of Luther in Its Historical Development and Inner Harmony*, trans. Charles E. Hay, 2 vols. (Philadelphia: Lutheran Publication Society, 1897), II, 507ff.; A. von Harnack, *History of Dogma*, VII, 251; F. A. Loofs, *Leitfaden zum Studium der Dogmengeschichte*, 4th ed. (Halle a.S.: M. Niemeyer, 1906), 753ff.; F. Kattenbusch, "Taufe, Kirchenlehre," in *PRE*[3], XIX, 416ff.; Joseph T. Müller, *Die symbolischen Bücher der evangelisch-lutherischen Kirche*, 8th ed. (Gütersloh: Bertelsmann, 1898), 30, 40, 163, 320, 361, 384, 485, 768, 780; ed. note: These specific references are to the following Lutheran documents: Nicene Creed, in *The Book of Concord*, ed. Robert Kolb and Timothy J. Wengert (Minneapolis: Fortress, 2000), 23; Augsburg Confession, art. 9 (Kolb and Wengert, 42); Apology of the Augsburg Confession, art. 9, pars. 51–53 (Kolb and Wengert, 183–84); Smalcald Articles, part III, art. 5 (Kolb and Wengert, 319–20); The Small Catechism, "The Sacrament of Holy Baptism" (Kolb and Wengert, 359); The Large Catechism, "Preface" (Kolb and Wengert, 385); ibid., part IV, "Concerning Baptism" (Kolb and Wengert, 456ff.); M. Luther, *The Baptismal Booklet* (Kolb and Wengert, 371ff.). The Saxon Visitation Articles (1592), art. 3, in P. Schaff, *Creeds of Christendom*, 3 vols. (New York: Harper & Brothers, 1877), III, 183; P. Melanchthon, "De baptismo," in *Loci communes* (Berlin: G. Schlawitz, 1856); J. Gerhard, *Loci theol.*, XX; J. A. Quenstedt, *Theologia*, IV, 106–76; D. Hollaz, *Examen theologicum acroamaticum* (Rostock and Leipzig: Russworm, 1718), 1077–1103; H. F. F. Schmid, *The Doctrinal Theology of the Evangelical Lutheran Church*, trans. Charles A. Hay and Henry Jacobs, 5th ed. (Philadelphia: United Lutheran Publication House, 1899), §54; cf. also above, 55–56 (#440).

28. H. Witsius, *Miscellaneorum sacrorum*, 4 vols. (Utrecht: F. Halman, 1692), II, 648–67.

pagan children, not subject to the wrath of God, nor under the power of Satan, so that in their case an exorcism had to be conducted first. On the contrary: even before baptism they were children of the covenant. Baptism, accordingly, was not even absolutely necessary to salvation; neither was there any need for emergency baptisms administered by laypeople.

The moment people began to reflect on the implications of this inclusion of children in the covenant of grace, however, they parted company. There were those who sought as long and as closely as possible to maintain the unity of election and covenant. They asserted, accordingly, that all children born of believing parents had to be regarded—according to the judgment of charity—as regenerate until in their witness or walk they clearly manifested the contrary, or that at least the elect children were usually regenerated by the Spirit of God before baptism or even before birth (à Lasco, Ursinus, Acronius, Voetius, Witsius, et al.). But others, noting the problems of experience, which so often tells us that baptized children grow up without showing any sign of spiritual life, did not dare to construe this regeneration before baptism as being the rule. They all without exception acknowledged that God's grace is not bound to means and can also work regeneration in the heart of very young children, but they left open the question whether in the case of elect infants that regeneration occurred before, during, or also, sometimes even a great many years, after baptism (Calvin, Beza, Zanchius, Bucanus, Walaeus, Ames, Heidegger, Turretin, et al.). This view won the day when the church, by its neglect of discipline, fell into decay. Election and church, the internal and external side of the covenant, concepts formerly held together as much as possible but increasingly differentiated since the days of Gomarus, moved ever farther apart. In the church (*ecclesia*) one saw the formation of the conventicle (*ecclesiola*). Gradually, therefore, baptism was totally separated from regeneration, and, since people nevertheless wanted to continue this sacrament for their children, it was understood in one of the following ways: (1) conceived and justified as a sacrament of the church and a pledge of the children of believers in general; (2) as a confirmation of the objective conditional promise of the gospel; (3) as proof of participation in the external covenant of grace; (4) as a guarantee of an amissible rebirth—not one that was inseparable from salvation but one that was later to be confirmed by a personal faith; (5) as a pedagogical device that at a later age spurs the baptized on toward genuine repentance.[29]

Controversy repeatedly erupted in this connection over the wording of the [Reformed] liturgical form for the baptism of infants. In hearing the expression "sanctified in Christ" [in a first question put to the presenting parents] and associating it with internal renewal by the Holy Spirit, some people objected to having this question put to parents who, though they still presented their child for baptism, were otherwise religiously indifferent. Under pietistic influence they increasingly attached less value to the external act of baptism, insisted on personal

29. Cf. above, 55ff. (#440).

conversion, and withdrew into the narrow circle of the conventicles.[30] Others, interpreting the expression in an objective covenant sense, regarded baptism as nothing more than a sign of the external covenant, to which a historical faith and an inoffensive lifestyle sufficiently entitled them.[31]

Thus, in the Reformed churches themselves, baptism was almost completely deprived of its value. Introduced here, in fact, was the doctrine of baptism that in the age of Reformation was already held by Socinians and Anabaptists and later by Remonstrants and Rationalists. For all the differences among them, these groups agreed that baptism has its value, not as a seal of grace on God's part, but in the first place as an act of confession on man's part. Baptism does not effect or bestow anything. It is solely a symbol of the transition from Judaism and paganism to Christianity, a sign of faith and repentance, a promise of obedience, and therefore not instituted by Christ as a permanent sacrament at all, or in any case at most permitted and useful for children, but neither necessary nor required. Quakers even went so far as to reject water baptism altogether and to recognize only the baptism of the Spirit, while Rationalists debated the question whether baptism, which after all was no more than a solemn symbol, should not rather be abolished.[32] Modernist Protestantism still holds this position and makes baptism optional,[33] and in the case of many others disdain for the sacrament shows its influence in that the center of gravity is being shifted from baptism to an ever more solemnly arranged service of welcoming and confirming members.

In the face of this decline, an attempt is again being made by various persons and groups to maintain the objective character of baptism. Schleiermacher indeed first of all regarded baptism as an action of the church by which it receives the individual believer into its fellowship, but then, implied in this, is the simultaneous incorporation of that believer into full-life communion with Christ.[34] Other

30. Lodensteyn, Gentman, Koelman, Brakonier, Van de Putt, Kelderman, Vos; P. Proost, *Jodocus van Lodenstein* (Amsterdam: J. Brandt, 1880), 160, 229; A. Ypey and I. J. Dermout, *Geschiedenis der Nederlandsche Hervormde Kerk*, 4 vols. (Breda: W. van Bergen; F. B. Hollingerus Pijpers, 1819–27), III, 261–363; A. Ypey, *Geschiedenis der Christliche kerk in de achttiende eeuw* (Utrecht: Van Ijzergorst, 1797–1811), VI, 164; C. Vitringa, *Doctr. christ.*, VII, 108, 115ff.; B. de Moor, *Commentarius . . . theologiae*, 6 vols. (Leiden: J. Hasebroek, 1761–71), V, 489.

31. J. F. Ostervald, *A Compendium of Christian Theology*, trans. John McMains (Hartford: N. Patten, 1788), II, 6, 4, 4; *Vernet, *Christ. Onderw.*, 300; and above all Janssonius and van Eerde over against Appelius, cf. C. Vitringa, *Doctr. christ.*, VI, 426ff., 498ff.; VII, 125ff. On the origin and text of the Reformed baptismal liturgy, along with the objections raised against its required reading, see H. J. Olthuis, *De doopspraktijk der Gereformeerde Kerken in Nederland 1568–1816* (Utrecht: Ruys, 1908), 130–84.

32. Cf. C. Vitringa, *Doctr. christ.*, VII, 297–415; D. F. Strauss, *Speculative Betrachtungen über die Dogmatik* (Weilburg: Lanz, 1841), II, 549–58; J. A. L. Wegscheider, *Institutiones theologiae christianae dogmaticae*, 3rd ed. (Halle: Gebauer, 1819), §§171–72; I. Kant, *Religion within the Limits of Reason Alone*, trans. Theodore M. Greene and Hoyt H. Hudson (New York: Harper & Brothers, 1934), 187.

33. J. H. Scholten, *Dogmaticae christianae initia*, 2nd ed. (Lyons: P. Engels, 1856–58), 247; R. Ehlers, *Das Neue Testament und die Taufe* (Giessen: Ricker, 1890).

34. F. Schleiermacher, *The Christian Faith*, §§136–38; Cf. A. Schweizer, *Die christliche Glaubenslehre nach protestantischen Grundsätzen dargestellt*, 2 vols. in 3 (Leipzig: S. Hirzel, 1863–72), §171; R. A. Lipsius, *Lehrbuch der evangelisch-protestantischen Dogmatik* (Braunschweig: C. A. Schwetschke, 1893), §846.

theologians, highlighting the gracious act of God implicit in the sacrament, taught that, while baptism does not presuppose regeneration, it nevertheless imparts the power of regeneration or regeneration itself, is the point of initial contact established by Christ for the love bond between him and the believer, and lays a foundation for all later benefits, benefits that from then on can only be obtained in the way of faith.[35] Many Lutherans even returned to the old doctrine that the Holy Spirit effects regeneration in and through the water of baptism and further had it consist not only in spiritual renewal but also in the implantation of a heavenly corporeality.[36] In England tractarianism appeared on the scene with the doctrine of baptismal regeneration, consisting in the idea that children were so effectively renewed by baptism that they could later independently accept grace through faith.[37] In the Netherlands Dr. A. Kuyper attempted to maintain the objective character of baptism by ascribing a special grace to it. This grace consists, not in regeneration—which is presupposed in baptism and therefore no longer needs to be conferred—but in a special and otherwise unobtainable benefit, namely, in incorporation into the body of Christ, or rather, in the implantation in our faith of the disposition or tendency not to exist by oneself but in our feeling one with the entire body of Christ.[38]

35. F. A. Philippi, *Kirchliche Glaubenslehre*, 3rd ed., 7 vols. (Gütersloh: Bertelsmann, 1883–1902), V, 2, 83ff.; F. A. Kahnis, *Die lutherische Dogmatik, historisch-genetisch dargestellt* (Leipzig: Dörffling & Francke, 1861–68), II, 333; I. A. Dorner, *A System of Christian Doctrine*, trans. A. Cave and J. S. Banks, 4 vols. (Edinburgh: T&T Clark, 1882), IV, 290; F. H. R. Frank, *System der christlichen Wahrheit*, 3rd rev. ed., 2 vols. (Erlangen and Leipzig: Deichert, 1894), II, 266; A. von Oettingen, *Lutherische Dogmatik*, 2 vols. (Munich: C. H. Beck, 1897), II, 408ff.; P. Althaus, *Die Heilsbedeutung der Taufe im Neuen Testament* (Gütersloh: Bertelsmann, 1897); H. Cremer, *Wesen und Wirkung der Taufgnade* (Gütersloh: Bertelsmann, 1899); idem, *Taufe, Wiedergeburt, und Kindertaufe*, 2nd ed. (Gütersloh: Bertelsmann, 1901); E. Cremer, *Rechtfertigung und Wiedergeburt* (Gütersloh: Evangelischer Verlag der Rufer, 1907), 63ff. There is, however, significant difference among these. Von Oettingen, for example, considers baptism as an individual application of the word of grace that is offered to all in preaching and therefore sees in the means a personal reassurance of salvation. Frank considers baptism primarily as a sacrament of regeneration, since without regeneration there is no faith that accepts Christ and receives justification. Cremer and Althaus also regard baptism as the sacrament of regeneration but understand regeneration in a completely different way. Regeneration is not a theosophic-naturalistic nor even a spiritual renewal but is identical with justification (cf. above, 67–71 [##442–43], 190 [#470]).

36. A. F. C. Vilmar, *Dogmatik*, 2 vols. (Gütersloh: C. Bertelsmann, 1874), II, 233; H. Martensen, *Christian Dogmatics*, trans. W. Urwick (Edinburgh: T&T Clark, 1871), 308ff.; J. W. F. Höfling, *Das Sakrament der Taufe*, I, 17ff.; G. Thomasius, *Christi Person und Werk*, 3rd ed., 2 vols. (Erlangen: A. Deichert, 1886–88), II, 297ff.; J. H. A. Ebrard, *Christliche Dogmatik*, 2nd ed., 2 vols. (Königsberg: A. W. Unser, 1862–63), II, 308, 314; and others already mentioned above, 62–63 (#441), 67–69 (#442), 73–74 (#443). In addition, Grundtvig and his followers also belong here, including Hory, Lyng, Krogh-Tönning, according to O. Scheel, *Die dogmatische Behandlung der Tauflehre in der modernen positiven Theologie* (Tübingen: Mohr, 1906).

37. Cf. above, 56ff. (#440); C. Hodge, *Systematic Theology*, 3 vols. (New York: Charles Scribner's Sons, 1888), III, 591–604; W. Cunningham, *Historical Theology*, 2nd ed., 2 vols. (Edinburgh: T&T Clark, 1864), II, 133–42.

38. A. Kuyper, "Van degenademiddelen," *De Heraut*, 646ff. (11 May–July 1890).

THE MANNER OF BAPTISM

[534] Nowadays, most churches know baptism virtually exclusively as infant baptism. Aside from mission fields abroad and in Baptist churches, the baptism of adults is an exception. Yet in Scripture the reverse is true. Nowhere does it speak explicitly of infant baptism. It always assumes the baptism of adults. Also the Christian creeds and Christian theologians always followed the example of Scripture in this respect insofar as they took their point of departure in the baptism of adults and only then went on to infant baptism. Now this baptism was instituted at God's command by John and then by Jesus, because before God the entire world was deserving of damnation. That was true not only of the Gentiles but also of the Jews who, as we recall, strove to establish their own righteousness on the basis of the works of the law but did not succeed in fulfilling that law (Rom. 9:31). Even the prophets already proclaimed that God, who is faithful and remembers his covenant, would in the future grant to Israel repentance and life, a new heart and a new spirit, forgive all their sins, pour out his Spirit on them, sprinkle clean water upon them, and cleanse them from all their impurities (Hos. 6:2; Joel 2:28–29; Mic. 7:18–20; Isa. 1:16; chs. 40ff.; Jer. 31:31–34; 33:8; Ezek. 11:17–20; 36:25–28; 37:1–14; 39:29; Zech. 13:1; and so forth). Regeneration, repentance, and faith were necessary, for Israel as well as for the Gentiles, to enter into the kingdom of heaven and partake of its benefits. This was the message with which John and Jesus confronted Israel, and those who accepted it were baptized. Accordingly, the presentation and acceptance of the word of the gospel preceded baptism. Scripture tells us beyond any doubt that baptism has been exclusively instituted for believers. No other persons are baptized than those who confess their sins and evidence repentance and faith (Matt. 3:2, 6; Acts 2:37–38; 8:12, 37; 18:8). Baptism is called the baptism of repentance for no other reason than that people might in that way obtain the forgiveness of sins (Mark 1:4; Acts 13:24). In Matt. 28:19 the two participles "baptizing" and "teaching" indeed indicate the way in which the task of "discipling all the nations" has to be accomplished, but the act of baptizing them "in the name of the Father, the Son, and the Holy Spirit" presupposes precisely the preceding proclamation of that name and faith in that name, as this is also clearly expressed in Mark 16:15–16, and as in John 4:1 the making of disciples precedes the baptism. It is the children of God by faith in Christ Jesus who, through baptism, have put on Christ (Gal. 3:26–27).

As long as the reference is to the baptism of adults, there is no disagreement over baptism among Christian churches. There is not a single church that baptizes an adult without prior instruction in the truth and without a prior confession of faith. Even Rome recognizes that in the case of adults seven preparations have to precede baptism, and Rome makes not the objective validity of the sacrament but its subjective operation dependent on a "virtual intention" as a *conditio sine qua non* in the recipient of the sacrament.[39] Rome, however, has increasingly weakened these subjective conditions in the recipient and shifted the center of gravity from the Word and from faith to the sacrament. For this sacrament works ex opere operato (by the act performed) without demanding from the recipient anything other than a negative condition of "not putting up a barrier" to the working of the sacrament. Just as it did in the case of sins, so Rome endlessly split the benefits of grace and distributes them in bits and pieces in the "here" and the "hereafter." It is always the same notion of hierarchy that makes its influence felt here in the doctrines of grace as it does everywhere else. For that reason, too, Rome teaches that preaching and faith only have preparatory significance. Real, sanctifying, supernatural grace is only imparted by the sacrament of baptism, which for that reason—barring a few cases in which it is replaced by a "baptism of blood" (martyrdom) or a "baptism of desire"[40]—is strictly necessary for salvation for all people, adults as well as children. The Reformation, by contrast, posited the scriptural principle that the sacrament imparts no other benefit than that which believers already possess by trusting in the Word of God. Faith alone apart from any sacrament communicates, and causes believers to enjoy, all the benefits of salvation. Now if baptism presupposes this faith, there is no other remaining benefit that could be imparted to believers by baptism. Baptism can only signify and seal the benefits that are received by faith and thereby strengthen that faith.[41] Lutherans also assent to this view as it applies to the baptism of adults who were regenerated prior to baptism and made profession of their faith. Just as faith and the gift of the Holy Spirit are increased in the regenerate by the preaching of the Word, "so the same occurs through baptism in that baptism efficaciously seals the gift of regeneration in them."[42] Involved here is a Protestant principle: those who attribute to baptism a communication of grace that cannot be obtained through the Word and by faith open the door to the Roman Catholic doctrine of the sacrament.

The "form" of baptism consists in a divinely forged link between a visible sign and an invisible spiritual benefit. The sign in baptism is water (Matt. 3:6; Acts 8:36), a sign that was not chosen arbitrarily or accidentally but on account of its striking resemblance to the thing signified. What dirt—polluting, choking dirt—is to the body, that is what sin is to the soul. And just as water washes away the dirt from the body, so the blood of Christ cleanses us from all sins. Virtually among all peoples and in all religions, therefore, water has a richly symbolic meaning. It served in all sorts of ceremonial washings and foreshadowed the spiritual cleansing that all persons need to enter into communion with God. Water played a large role in Old Testament worship (Exod. 30:18–20; 40:30; Lev. 6:28; 8:6; 11:32; 15:12; Num. 8:7; 19:7ff.; etc.) and the prophets pictured the spiritual purification of the

---

39. Council of Trent, sess. VI, can. 5, 7; Roman Catechism, II, ch. 2, qu. 30, 44 (ed. note: Bradley and Kevane, II, ch. 2, qu. 31, 45; Bavinck erroneously cites ch. 3).

40. Ed. note: See note 25 above.

41. Belgic Confession, arts. 33–34; Heidelberg Catechism, Q 69.

42. J. Gerhard, *Loci theol.*, XX, 123; J. Quenstedt, *Theologia*, IV, 145; H. F. F. Schmid, *The Doctrinal Theology of the Evangelical Lutheran Church*, 542–43, 554–55.

people as a sprinkling with water (Ezek. 36:25; 37:23; Zech. 13:1). Of itself and by its very nature, that is, by virtue of the character God conferred on it at the time of creation, water is therefore extremely well adapted in baptism to depict and seal the washing away of sins and spiritual renewal. For that reason, too, it is not necessary, as Rome claims, for baptismal water to be consecrated the day before Easter or Pentecost Sunday and to be mixed with oil.[43] Much less may the church, with the Paulicians,[44] refrain from using water on the ground that Christ is the living water, or with other sects replace baptism by branding people with a mark of ownership or by flogging them to the point of drawing blood.[45] It is even needless to concede, with Beza and others, that if water is not available another fluid may be substituted, for such a case is virtually impossible.[46]

In the first period of the life of the church, the rite of baptism consisted in immersing candidates for baptism in water and after a moment lifting them out again. The Greek word βαπτιζειν (*baptizein*) [with related terms] already points in that direction, for it literally means "to dip" or "dip into" ([βαπτειν, *baptein*] John 13:26); and also, when it is used in a broader sense for washing ([νιπτειν, *niptein*] Matt. 15:2; [*baptizein*] Mark 7:4; Luke 11:38; [βαπτισμος, *baptismos*] Heb. 9:10) or figuratively ([*baptizein*] Matt. 3:11; 20:22; Acts 1:5; and so forth), it denotes an act in which the person who or thing which is "dipped" is completely immersed and cleansed. Furthermore, the cases that Scripture reports clearly show that in the apostolic era baptism occurred by way of immersion (Matt. 3:6; John 3:23; Acts 8:38). And, finally, "sacramental phraseology" is completely based on this mode of administering baptism (Rom. 6:4; Gal. 3:27; Col. 2:12). Accordingly, immersion remained in use in the Christian church for centuries. The Greek [Orthodox] church still adheres to it. Sprinkling or rather affusion only occurred in ancient times when there was not enough water[47] or when the sick had to be baptized on their bed (*baptismus clinicorum*). In this last case Cyprian[48] defended aspersion or perfusion with an appeal to Ezek. 36:25, but the rest of the church fathers speak of baptism as an immersion in water.[49] In AD 754 Pope Stephen II permitted baptism by affusion in cases of necessity involving infants or the sick, but a council of the year 816 still instructed priests "not to pour out water upon the heads of infants but always to immerse them in a bath." Thomas said: "It is safer to baptize by immersion because this is the more common usage."[50] The Council of Ravenna (1311) left the choice between immersion and affusion open. Until the

43. Roman Catechism, II, ch. 2, qu. 47 (ed. note: Bradley and Kevane, II, ch. 1, qu. 48).

44. Ed. note: The Paulicians were a dualistic sect, originating from Manichaeism, that repudiated the traditional sacramental teaching and practice of the church in favor of a "spiritual" understanding; true baptism and true Eucharist consists for them in hearing the word of Christ.

45. B. de Moor, *Comm. theol.*, V, 409–11.

46. C. Vitringa, *Doctr. christ.*, VII, 14.

47. *Didache* 7.

48. Cyprian, *Epistles* 69.12.

49. Suicerus, *Thesaurus ecclesiasticus*, s.v. ἀναδυνω.

50. T. Aquinas, *Summa theol.*, III, qu. 66, art. 7.

thirteenth century, therefore, immersion and sprinkling still occurred side by side in the West. After that, however, the latter became increasingly common. When in Christianized Europe adult baptism became the exception and infant baptism became the rule, there also occurred a change in the manner in which baptism was administered. This happened not for dogmatic but for hygienic reasons. In a sense all infants existed in "a state of infirmity." The Reformers also adopted this practice. Luther preferred immersion; Calvin considered the issue an adiaphoron; but the Anabaptists made it a matter of principle and returned to immersion.

And this alone is what needs to be combated. There is no doubt that in ancient times immersion was the general rule; it is still permitted today and also illustrates the rich meaning of baptism better than sprinkling. But one cannot make this a matter of principle for the following four reasons:

1. The water is not the blood of Christ itself and does not itself effect the washing away of sins but is the sign and seal of it. Therefore, what really matters in baptism is not the quantity of water that is poured out on the persons being baptized or in which they are immersed.
2. The spiritual benefit depicted in baptism is not only called a washing away of sins but also a sprinkling with clean water and with the blood of Christ (Ezek. 36:25; Heb. 12:24; 1 Pet. 1:2; cf. Exod. 24:6; 29:16, 20).
3. Although for centuries the practice of immersion remained in use, from the most ancient times onward sprinkling was also considered permissible in cases of necessity. The Christian church never even dreamed of regarding a baptism invalid only because it had been administered by way of sprinkling, and the proponents of immersion as a rule even themselves recoil in practice from drawing this conclusion.
4. Although, despite the threefold immersion that had been practiced from ancient times,[51] one must, with Gregory the Great, maintain that "whether it is performed by a single or a triple ablution, it does not matter";[52] yet sprinkling must not be reduced to such minute amounts that the whole idea of a "washing away" is lost. Just as the Lord's Supper, however shrunken, must remain a meal, so also the symbolism of "washing away" must be kept alive in the sprinkling [of infants or adults] with baptismal water.[53]

THE BENEFITS OF BAPTISM

[535] This water becomes a sacrament by the word[s] of institution. In Scripture baptism is sometimes called a baptism "in the name of Christ" (Acts 2:38;

---

51. *Didache* 7.
52. Roman Catechism, II, ch. 2, qu. 14 (ed. note: Bradley and Kevane, II, ch. 1, qu. 14).
53. J. Calvin, *Institutes*, IV.xv.19; G. Voetius, *Politicae ecclesiasticae*, 3 vols. (Amsterdam: Joannis a Westberge, 1663–76), I, 683–94; B. de Moor, *Comm. theol.*, V, 413–21; C. Vitringa, *Doctr. christ.*, VII, 16–30; J. W. F. Höfling, *Das Sakrament der Taufe*, I, 46–60; J. G. de Hoop Scheffer, *Overzicht der geschiedenis van den doop bij onderdompeling* (Amsterdam, 1882).

8:16; 10:48; 19:5; cf. Rom. 6:3; 1 Cor. 1:13–15; 6:11; Gal. 3:27) and at other times a baptism "in the name of the Father, the Son, and the Holy Spirit" (Matt. 28:19). These expressions are not intended to furnish a formula that has to be voiced in baptism but describe the essence of Christian baptism: this must be a baptism into the name of Christ and hence into the name of the Triune God. That these words are not intended to be a formula is evident from the fact that no such formula is mentioned on the occasion of circumcision and Passover or at John's baptism and the Lord's Supper. This is not in any way to deny that from the beginning during the administration and reception of baptism something or other was said: people confessed their sins (Matt. 3:6) or professed their faith in Christ (Acts 8:37; cf. 1 Tim. 6:12). Soon, by natural processes, there emerged for public use on this occasion a fixed formula that was derived from the words of institution in Matt. 28:19; the *Didache* speaks of Christians as "those who have been baptized into the name of the Lord," but it does already know the trinitarian formula.[54] Now, though in that early period baptism into the name of Christ or with the confession that Jesus is the Son of God (Acts 8:37) was perfectly adequate, later, when all kinds of heresies cropped up and especially to maintain the Christian character of baptism, the trinitarian formula must increasingly have been viewed as necessary.[55] But also this trinitarian formula is not couched in the same words in the different churches. The Greek church employs the words "This servant of God is baptized in the name of the Father—Amen! and of the Son—Amen! and that of the Holy Spirit—Amen! now and into all eternity." Although the Latin church recognizes the baptism thus performed, that church itself uses the formula "I baptize you in the name of the Father, and the Son, and the Holy Spirit,"[56] and this is the formula Protestant churches generally took over. The Syrian and Armenian churches again have a formula that diverges from both the Greek and the Latin versions.[57] Everything proves that the validity of baptism as such does not depend on the literal words used by the administrator. The trinitarian formula only became necessary to ward off heresy, to guarantee that the baptism administered was the true Christian baptism, and to introduce the desired consistency and stability into liturgical practice.

In this connection it is noteworthy that the trinitarian baptismal formula does not possess the magical power to change the water into the blood of Christ. It is not only the Reformed who deny that it has such power, but also the Greek [Orthodox], the Roman Catholic, and the Lutheran Church speak a different language in connection with baptism than they do in connection with the Lord's Supper. In the case of this latter sacrament, the emphasis falls on the recitation of the words of institution, on their power to consecrate, and on the trans- or

---

54. *Didache* 9.5; 7.1, 3; cf. Justin Martyr, *First Apology* 61.

55. Cyprian, *Epistles* 73.16–18; Suicerus, *Thesaurus ecclesiasticus*, s.v. βαπτισμος.

56. Roman Catechism, II, ch. 2, qu. 10–11 (ed. note: Bradley and Kevane, II, ch. 1, qu. 10–11).

57. J. W. F. Höfling, *Das Sakrament der Taufe*, I, 44.

consubstantiation thus effected. But even though people speak of a divine power (*divina virtus*) imparted to the water, of "living, holy, divine water," of regeneration through the water in the word, even the Roman Cathechism states that the words of institution must be pronounced plainly and clearly for the instruction of the people,[58] and it denies that in the case of baptism there occurs a transubstantiation, a change of the water into the blood of Christ.[59] The "sacramental union" in this case differs from that in the case of the Lord's Supper. But even aside from this matter, there certainly remains a difference. Roman Catholics and Lutherans, in considering the operation of the Holy Spirit, picture it in connection with baptism as going through the water. The Reformed reject the idea of a local and physical union and instead assume the presence of a union like that in the case of the Word. Just as the Holy Spirit indeed works with the Word but does not confine his power and operation within that Word, so it is also with the water of baptism. In Eph. 5:26 the words ἐν ῥήματι (*en rhēmati*, by the word) are not, as the Lutherans would have it, a further qualification of λουτρῳ (*loutrō*, washing) or ὕδατος (*hydatos*, water), for in that case they should have been preceded by the article (τῳ/του ἐν ῥήματι, *tō/tou en rhēmati*), but belong with ἁγιαση (*hagiasē*, making holy): Christ made his church holy by the word of the gospel, while he cleansed it by the washing of water. Paul here deliberately distinguishes the working of Christ by the Word from that by the water, as that is also done in Heb. 10:22 and 1 Pet. 3:21. It is not the minister nor the water but Christ who makes the church holy and gives the thing signified (Matt. 3:11; 1 Cor. 6:11; Heb. 9:14; 1 John 1:7). If the water of baptism effected regeneration, Paul would not have been able to say in 1 Cor. 1:14 that "Christ did not send me to baptize but to proclaim the gospel." But however much disagreement there may be over the manner in which the sign and the thing signified are connected in baptism, there is agreement about the reality of that connection. Reformed churches also confess that in baptism Christ promises and assures everyone who receives it that "as surely as water washes away the dirt from the body, so certainly his blood and his Spirit wash away the impurity of the soul."[60]

There is also substantial agreement with respect to the benefits that in baptism are granted to adult believers. These benefits are all included in the fellowship with the Triune God in which the believer is incorporated by baptism (Matt. 28:19). In baptism the Father witnesses to us that he makes an eternal covenant of grace with us and adopts us as his children and heirs (Gen. 17:7, 10; Acts 2:39). The Son assures us that he washes us in his blood and incorporates us into the fellowship of his death and resurrection (Rom. 6:3; Gal. 3:27). The Holy Spirit assures us that he lives in us and sanctifies us to be members of Christ (1 Cor. 6:11; 12:13; Titus 3:5).

---

58. Roman Catechism, II, ch. 2, qu. 2, 10 (ed. note: Bradley and Kevane, II, ch. 1, qu. 2, 10).
59. Ibid., II, ch. 2, qu. 4, 9 (ed. note: Bradley and Kevane, II, ch. 1, qu. 4, 9).
60. Heidelberg Catechism, Q 69.

Further elaborated, these benefits are the following:

1. *Justification or the forgiveness of sins* (Mark 1:4; Acts 2:38; 22:16; Heb. 10:22; 1 Pet. 3:21). Doedes is of the opinion that this benefit does not qualify for consideration at the time of baptism but only at the Lord's Supper, inasmuch as baptism is called the baptism of repentance *unto* the forgiveness of sins.[61] But this view is clearly contradicted by Acts 22:16; 1 Pet. 3:21; Heb. 10:22. While repentance is the way by which the forgiveness secured by Christ comes into our possession and is enjoyed by us, baptism is precisely the proof and pledge of the forgiveness obtained in the way of repentance. Confession of sins and justifying faith, after all, precede baptism. In baptism, therefore, all our sins along with all their guilt and punishment, not only past but also present and future sins, are forgiven, for justification is a juridical act. It implies a change of state and is therefore brought about at once, completely, and forever.

2. *Regeneration, repentance, the dying-away of the old self, and the coming-to-life of the new self through fellowship with the death and resurrection of Christ* (Mark 1:4; Rom. 6:2–10; 1 Cor. 6:11; Eph. 5:26; Col. 2:12). In baptism, according to Rome, the same grace is restored that Adam received as "superadded gift" but lost as a result of sin. Now, just as "concupiscence" existed before the fall in Adam as "a man of nature," a "concupiscence" that was restrained by "the superadded gift," the same is the case with the baptized. Concupiscence, though it remains in them, is not itself a sin, inasmuch as it is integral to a human consisting of flesh and spirit. It can easily become an occasion for sin, however, when people, instead of letting themselves be guided by the supernatural grace, listen and accede to it. Apart from this danger, which ever continues to threaten the baptized, they are freed not only from all guilt but also from all pollution of sin by the grace received in baptism. Over against this view, article 15 of the Belgic Confession states that original sin is not "altogether abolished or wholly eradicated even by baptism" (the original Walloon text of 1561 read: "et n'est pas aboli mesme par le baptesme," to which the synod of 1566 added the words: "ou desraciné du tout"). Although, with Doedes,[62] many theologians disapprove of these words, they are nevertheless correct and completely in harmony with Scripture. For in the passages cited above, Scripture clearly teaches that baptism, understood as sign and seal, regenerates and renews the baptized, breaks the power of original sin, and causes them to walk in newness of life, yet so that sin still continues to live in their flesh and takes them captive against their will under its own

61. J. I. Doedes, *De leer der zaligheid volgens het Evangelie in de Schriften des Nieuwen Verbonds voorgesteld* (Utrecht: Kemink, 1876), 326.

62. J. I. Doedes, *De Nederlandsche Geloofsbelijdenis en de Heidelbergsche Catechismus* (Utrecht: Kemink & Zoon, 1880–81), 173.

law. Original pollution, accordingly, is removed by baptism as sacrament in part and in principle, but not wholly. Although it no longer condemns believers, until death it remains in them a woeful source of all kinds of sin.

3. *Fellowship, not only with Christ himself but also with the church, which is his body.* The baptized person is saved from a corrupt generation, set apart from the world (Acts 2:40–41), made into a disciple of Jesus (Matt. 28:19; John 4:1), incorporated into his church (1 Cor. 12:13), and hence obligated to live a blameless life (Gen. 17:1), in newness of life (Rom. 6), to confess God's name and to keep his commandments (Matt. 28:19). All these benefits have already been bestowed on the baptized person before baptism in the word of the gospel. They were received on the part of the baptized by faith; but now these benefits are further signified and sealed to them in baptism. Hence the situation must not be pictured as one in which before baptism only a few and in any case not all of these benefits were granted in faith and that the one(s) still lacking are now bestowed in baptism. For the Word contains all the promises, and faith accepts them all. There is not a single grace that is not conveyed by the Word and only by the sacrament. Incorporation into the body of Christ also occurs through faith and receives its sign and seal in baptism. Baptismal grace exists and can, according to Scripture and the Reformed confession, exist in nothing other than in declaration and confirmation.[63]

INFANT BAPTISM

[536] Up to this point, there is substantial agreement among Christian churches on the doctrine of baptism. But all sorts of differences crop up the moment infant baptism comes up for discussion. From the beginning of its introduction until now, this baptism is rejected by a considerable part of Christianity. The grounds for this rejection are especially these two: (1) that it does not occur in Scripture, and (2) that according to its original purpose baptism always presupposes faith and repentance, things that do not occur in small children or in any case cannot be manifested and recognized.[64]

---

63. Heidelberg Catechism, Q 66, 69; cf. J. Calvin, *Institutes*, IV.xv; P. Martyr Vermigli, *Loci communes*, ed. R. Massonius (London, 1576), 435; A. Polanus, *Syntagma theologiae christianae* (Hanover: Aubry, 1624), 495; H. Bullinger, *Decades*, V, serm. 8 (ed. note: Bavinck cites here *Huijsboeck*, 1612, fol. 254); Z. Ursinus, *The Commentary of Dr. Zacharias Ursinus on the Heidelberg Catechism*, trans. G. W. Williard (Grand Rapids: Eerdmans, 1954), qu. 69.

64. W. Wall, *The History of Infant Baptism*, 4 vols. (Oxford: Oxford University Press, 1836); A. H. Newman, *A History of Anti-Paedobaptism from the Rise of Paedobaptism to A.D. 1609* (Philadelphia: American Baptist Publication Society, 1897); A. H. Strong, *Systematic Theology*, 3 vols. (Philadelphia: Griffith & Rowland, 1907–9), 534–38.

THE SPIRIT CREATES NEW COMMUNITY

Up until the time of Tertullian [c. 160–c. 220], all direct and firm witness to the fact that baptism was administered to the children of believers is, in fact, lacking.[65] Not too much should be made of this silence, however. It goes without saying that in the first and second centuries, when the Christian church was caught up in rapid expansion, the baptism of proselytes was much more a focus of attention than infant baptism. Initially the baptism of adults was the ordinary—regularly occurring—baptism; alongside of it infant baptism gradually sprang up as well. But finally, when the church was established, and one group of people after another had been baptized, infant baptism became the rule, and except for pagan countries, the baptism of proselytes became the exception. Accordingly, when Tertullian for the first time makes mention of infant baptism, he opposes it, to be sure, but not on the ground that it is an innovation and not customary in apostolic times, but because it is his general conviction that "deferment of baptism is more profitable. . . . All who understand what a burden baptism is will have more fear of obtaining it than of its postponement."[66]

Tertullian was not alone in holding this conviction. As long as Christianity could still expand among Gentiles in the villages, cities, and countries where it had been established, and hence conversions were still regularly taking place, many were of the opinion that it was best to postpone baptism for as long as possible, since one otherwise ran the danger of again falling into sin and of losing the grace received in baptism. But Tertullian was the only one who wanted to apply this view also in the case of the children of believers. The church in Africa also paid no attention to this opposition, however, and continued to practice infant baptism. Origen testifies that in his days infant baptism was in general use and of apostolic pedigree. Cyprian for his part, agreeing with the Council of Carthage held in 256, defended the view that infant baptism should not be delayed till the eighth day but already administered on the second or third day after the birth.[67]

The moment infant baptism became the rule and adult baptism the exception, it became necessary, of course, to further unfold its meaning and to defend its legitimacy against all sorts of critics. This was done in different ways:

1. When in his controversy with the Pelagians Augustine defended original sin and hence the necessity of the baptism of children, he had to give an account of the rightful claim children had on baptism. Confessing as he did that baptism had been instituted only for believers, yet recognizing that infants themselves were unable to believe, he appealed to the faith of the parents who presented the child for baptism and responded in the child's place. "About this there is a good pious belief that the child is benefited by

---

65. Ed. note: This judgment may be in error thanks to new historical evidence. See J. Jeremias, *Infant Baptism in the First Four Centuries*, trans. David Cairns (London: SCM, 1960).

66. Tertullian, *On Baptism* 18; cf. also, Irenaeus, *Against Heresies* II, 22, 4.

67. J. W. F. Höfling, *Das Sakrament der Taufe*, I, 104ff.

the faith of those who present it for baptism."[68] The children of believers must themselves be counted among the believers, for they believe "by reason of the faith of the parents." "He who sinned in the one puts his trust in the other."[69] And not only the faith of the parents but also the faith of the whole church is to their advantage: "Little ones are, of course, presented to receive spiritual grace, not so much from those in whose hands they are carried—though they do receive it from them if they are good believing people—as from the universal society of the saints and believers."[70] On this basis, says Augustine, the children of believers have a right to baptism, and in this baptism they themselves obtain the forgiveness of sins and regeneration, with the understanding, however, that "if baptized infants upon coming to the age of reason do not believe and do not refrain from illicit desires, they derive no benefit from what they received as children."[71]

2. Such dependence on the faith of another (*fides aliena*), however, cannot compensate for the lack of personal faith in the child and therefore leads imperceptibly to the doctrine of regeneration by baptism. While the faith of parents or of the church may give the child a right to be baptized, in the children themselves nothing is required other than at most a "passive capacity" inherent in them by nature, a negative act of refraining from placing an obstacle [in the path of the grace offered]. For that reason, the child who, so to speak, is consecrated to God with prayers by the whole church receives the grace it needs in baptism itself. But the grace that the child receives is then again described in very divergent terms. Some Scholastics said that in baptism no virtues were infused into children, neither the act nor the disposition nor the root, but that these were imparted to them later when they grew up, or were bestowed when they died and the soul was separated from the body. Others believed that the children received the virtues in baptism, either in terms of the root or in terms of the dispo-

68. Augustine, *On Free Will* III, 23.

69. Augustine, *On the Forgiveness of Sins, and Baptism*, ch. 41; ed. note: Bavinck cites this as *De verbis apost. sermo de bapt. parv. c. Pelag.*, c. 14.

70. Augustine, *Letter to Boniface (Letter 98)*, in *The Works of St. Augustine: A Translation for the 21st Century*, ed. John E. Rotelle, OSA., trans. Roland J. Teske, SJ, vol. II/1 (Hyde Park, NY: New City, 2001), 429.

71. Augustine, *The Punishment and Forgiveness of Sins and the Baptism of Little Ones*, I.xxv, in *The Works of St. Augustine*, vol. I/23 (1997), 47–48; cf. J. Crespin, *Bibliotheca studij theologici* (Geneva: Io. Crispinsum, 1565), 115–28; also the identical notion by theologians from a variety of confessions: P. Lombard, *Sent.*, IV, dist. 4; T. Aquinas, *Summa theol.*, III, qu. 68, art. 9; Bonaventure, *Breviloquium*, VI, 7; Roman Catechism, II, ch. 2, qu. 27, 30 (ed. note: Bradley and Kevane: II, ch. 1, qu. 28, 31); R. Bellarmine, "De bapt.," in *Controversiis*, I, 10–11; J. Köstlin, *The Theology of Luther*, I, 399; II, 45, 510; J. Calvin, *Defensio orthodoxae fidei* (1554), in *Calvini opera*, VIII (CR, XXXV), 483, 493; T. Beza, *Tractationum theologicarum* (Geneva: Jean Crispin, 1570), III, 345; and many others: Oecolampadius, Zanchius, Perkins, Bucanus, Marlorat, Rivetus, Venema, Hartmann. Cf. C. Vitringa, *Doctr. christ.*, VII, 136; J. Quenstedt, *Theologia*, IV, 148; C. Vitringa, *Observationum sacrarum* (Franeker: Wibii Bleck, 1712), II, c. 6; Kalchreuter. "Der stellvertretende Glaube und die Kindertaufe," *Jahrbücher für deutsche Theologie* 11 (1866): 523–44.

sition.[72] The Council of Trent decreed that the New Testament sacraments contain grace in themselves and impart it to all who place no obstacle in its path, so that in baptism also the children receive grace and the virtues *ex opere operato* (by the act performed) and though they are not believers beforehand, they become believers by baptism.[73] The Lutherans opposed the idea that children had faith before baptism and also that they were baptized "upon the faith of another" (*in aliena fide*); instead they taught that children received the faith in baptism and not just the disposition or power but even the act. "A true, saving, vivifying and *actual* faith arises in infants through baptism and in the baptism of the Holy Spirit, whence it is that baptized infants truly believe."[74] Also a number of Reformed theologians (Pareus, Baronius, Forbes à Corse, Davenant, Ward, de Brais in Saumur, et al.) taught that in baptism all children received a certain grace of forgiveness and regeneration that, if they died young, was sufficient for salvation, but which otherwise had to be accepted and confirmed on their part by a personal faith.[75] And corresponding to this is the doctrine of the High Churchmen [in the Anglican Church] who believe in baptismal regeneration.

3. This doctrine too is open to many objections.

    a. The "faith of another" (*fides aliena*), initially still maintained by Augustine and others as an allusion to the faith required for baptism in Scripture, becomes totally superfluous if baptism imparts grace ex opere operato and presupposes nothing other than a "passive capacity" in the child. When children can already receive the grace of baptism if only they place no obstacle in its path, it is advisable to baptize as many of them as possible, also pagan ones, for they are all passive and hence all capable of the reception of grace. The Scotist school, accordingly, defended this position over against the Thomist school and determined the practice of the Roman Catholic Church.[76]

    b. Baptism is robbed of its scriptural character when it is detached from faith and the Word, ceases to be a sign and seal of God's promises, becomes an independent self-operative means of grace, and even takes first place among the means of grace.

---

72. *Comm. on Sent.*, IV, dist. 4; Bonaventure, *Breviloquium*, par. 2, art. 2, qu. 2; T. Aquinas, *Summa theol.*, III, qu. 69, art. 6.

73. Council of Trent, sess. VII, can. 6–8; "De bapt.," chs. 13–14; R. Bellarmine, "De bapt.," in *Controversiis*, I, 10–11.

74. J. Quenstedt, *Theologia*, IV, 147.

75. Cf. H. Witsius, "De efficacia baptismi in infantibus," in *Miscellaneorum sacrorum*, II, 618; G. Voetius, *Selectae disputationes theologicae*, 5 vols. (Utrecht, 1648–69), II, 409; C. Vitringa, *Doctr. christ.*, VII, 72.

76. J. Schwane, *Dogmengeschichte*, III, 621.

c. The benefits imparted by baptism are exaggerated on one hand and weakened on the other. For in view of the facts to which both Scripture and experience testify, no one can maintain that all baptized children later prove to be believers and are saved. Hence, one must assume that the benefits bestowed in baptism are amissible and have to be accepted by a personal faith. They are sufficient for salvation in the case of children who die in infancy, but insufficient for growing children and put the latter in a dubious category between believers and unbelievers.[77]

The Reformed therefore returned to Scripture and in defending infant baptism unitedly took their position in the covenant of grace, which, according to God's promise, embraces not only believers but also their descendants. Not regeneration, faith, or repentance, much less our assumptions pertaining to them, but only the covenant of grace gave people, both adults and children, the right to baptism.[78] This covenant was the sure, scriptural, objective ground upon which all the Reformed, together and without distinction, based the right to infant baptism. They had no other, deeper, or more solid ground.

But the Anabaptists consistently advanced still another argument against infant baptism. They asserted not only that infant baptism is not mentioned in Scripture, but also that children could not experience or demonstrate faith and repentance and therefore were not permitted to be baptized. Over against this position the Reformed argued that though children could not—as the Lutherans held—possess the acts of faith, they could most certainly possess the disposition (*habitus*) of faith. They employed a wide variety of expressions—like the seed, the root, the inclination, the potency, the disposition, or the principle of faith, or the seed of regeneration, and so forth.[79] But on the issue itself there was complete agreement. On the basis of Scripture, Jer. 1:5 and Luke 1:35, and in keeping with the catholicity of the Christian religion, all the Reformed maintained against the Anabaptists that children as well as adults could be received by God through grace, regenerated by his Spirit, and gifted with the seed of faith. And over against the Anabaptists this was enough for them. Given this common conviction, the differences that arose among them the moment they began to work out and apply their principles receded into the background.

THE VALIDITY OF INFANT BAPTISM

[537] The validity of infant baptism depends exclusively on how Scripture regards the children of believers and hence wants us to regard them. If Scripture speaks about such children in the same way it does about adult believers, the right

---

77. A. Comrie and N. Holtius, *Examen van het ontwerp van tolerantie*, 10 vols. (Amsterdam: Nicolaas Byl, 1753), VI, 282–87; VII, 493–95; B. de Moor, *Comm. theol.*, V, 489; H. Witsius, *Miscellaneorum sacrorum*.

78. J. Calvin, *Institutes*, IV.xvi.23–24.

79. C. Vitringa, *Doctr. christ.*, VII, 134.

and hence the duty to practice infant baptism has been established. For we may not withhold from the children what we grant to adults. In the case of infant baptism, therefore, we are permitted to require neither less nor more than in the case of adult baptism. In the latter case we are and must, according to Scripture, be satisfied when someone confesses one's faith. We are never totally certain that a given person is not a hypocrite and hence receives the sacrament illegitimately, but we have no right to judge. "The church does not judge concerning intimate matters." This is also true in the case of the baptism of infants. Those who want absolute certainty can never dispense any sacrament. The question is only whether the certainty that in dealing with the children of believers we are dealing with believers is the same as the certainty we possess concerning those who confess their faith as adults. We do not need and may not demand another or stronger kind of certainty. Scripture offers a clear answer to the question thus framed.

1. First of all, we need to overcome our astonishment over the fact that the New Testament nowhere explicitly mentions infant baptism. This fact can be explained by saying that in the days of the New Testament, the baptism of adults was the rule, and the baptism of infants, if it occurred at all, was the exception. It was the period in which the Christian church had been founded and expanded by conversions from Judaism and paganism. It is precisely that transition that is clearly depicted in baptism. Adult baptism is therefore the original baptism; infant baptism is derivative; the former must not be conformed to the latter, but the latter must be conformed to the former. The validity of infant baptism does not lapse on that account, nor does it need tradition to sustain itself, as Roman Catholicism asserts. For also that which can be deduced from Scripture by legitimate inference is as binding as that which is expressly stated in it. This is how the church acts every minute of the day in the ministry of the Word, in the practice of life, in the development of its doctrine. It never stops with the letter but under the guidance of the Holy Spirit deduces from the data of Scripture the inferences and applications that make possible and foster its life and development. And this is also how it acts when it moves from adult baptism to infant baptism. Scripture indicates the general rule when baptism may and must be administered, and the church applies that rule concretely in the context of life. It does not have to say somewhere that children may be baptized. It says enough when it regards children in the same way as adults who have come to the point of professing their faith, and it never once mentions the administration of baptism to adults who were born of Christian parents.

2. In the Old Testament, circumcision was administered to male children on the eighth day after their birth. According to Col. 2:11–12 this circumcision was replaced by baptism. The Colossians, after all, though they were gentile Christians, were just as much circumcised as the Jews. But they were circumcised, not by a fleshly circumcision accomplished by human hands, but with a circumcision that consists in the putting off of the body of the flesh, of the entire fleshly sinful nature. And it took place in Christ by the means and power of the circumcision that Christ

himself underwent in his death with respect to sin, at the moment when they were buried and raised again with Christ in baptism. Through the death of Christ, which was a complete putting off of sin and victory over sin and hence fully realized the idea of circumcision, that circumcision has been rendered obsolete and came to its antitypical fulfillment in baptism. Baptism, therefore, is more than circumcision, not in essence but in degree. Circumcision pointed forward to the death of Christ; baptism points back to it. The former ends, the latter begins, with that death. If, however, that circumcision as the sign of the covenant could and must be administered to the children, the same applies a fortiori to baptism, which is not poorer but much richer in grace. This is made manifest in part by the fact that the sacrament of the old covenant was only administered to male persons, but the new covenant is also administered to female persons. Even opponents of infant baptism recognize in this respect the richer grace of baptism. In the case of human beings, we know sin bears the character of flesh (σαρξ, *sarx*). It reveals itself and works in the flesh, especially in the organs of procreation, and shows its power there. Circumcision calls attention to that fact, just as the impurity of a woman after childbirth does. But by his death, which is the true circumcision, Christ removed all sin, also the sin that clings to procreation. He has put the woman in an independent relation to himself. He causes her to share in his grace as fully as the man. In him there is neither male nor female, and in baptism both are therefore buried with Christ and raised to a new life. Finally, the more abundant grace of the sacrament of the new covenant is evident also from the fact that while circumcision could not be performed until the eighth day after the birth (for until then the children still shared in the impurity of the mother), now in the days of the New Testament the children have a right to baptism from the moment of their birth, since from the first moment of their existence they share in the grace of Christ.

3. Circumcision is far from being the only proof that the Old Testament regards the children as partakers of the covenant. The entire idea of the covenant carries this view with it. After all, the covenant is distinct from election in that it shows how election is realized in an organic and historical way. It is never established only with an individual person, but in that person also immediately with that person's descendants. It never encompasses the person of believers alone, in the abstract, but that person concretely as one exists and lives in history, hence together with all that is theirs. The covenant embraces them not just for the sake of their person but oneself also as father or as mother, with one's family, money, goods, influence and power, and so forth.[80]

Specifically the children are regarded in their connection with them. There is a kind of communion of parents and children in sin and misery. But over against this, God has also established a communion of parents and children in grace and blessing. Children are a blessing and heritage from the Lord (Ps. 127:3). They are always counted along with their parents and included with them. Together

---

80. Cf. H. Bavinck, *Reformed Dogmatics*, III, 231 (#350).

they prosper (Exod. 20:6; Deut. 1:36, 39; 4:40; 5:29; 12:25, 28). Together they serve the Lord (Deut. 6:2; 30:2; 31:12–13; Josh. 24:15; Jer. 32:39; Ezek. 37:25; Zech. 10:9). The parents must pass on to the children the acts and ordinances of God (Exod. 10:2; 12:24, 26; Deut. 4:9–10, 40; 6:7; 11:19; 29:29; Josh. 4:6, 21; 22:24–27). The covenant of God with its benefits and blessings perpetuates itself from child to child and from generation to generation (Gen. 9:12; 17:7, 9; Exod. 3:15; 12:17; 16:32; Deut. 7:9; Ps. 105:8; and so forth). While grace is not automatically inherited, as a rule it is bestowed along the line of generations. "For the infants of believers their first and foremost access of salvation is the very fact of their being born of believing parents."[81]

4. This view is continued in the New Testament. Like John, Jesus appears on the scene with the message: "Repent and believe the gospel!" He takes over John's baptism, thereby proclaiming that, despite their being circumcised, the Jews need repentance and forgiveness. The contrast gradually becomes so sharp that Jesus no longer expects anything from his people and they in turn reject him and hang him on a cross. Still, despite all this, he continues to regard their children as children of the covenant (Matt. 18:2ff.; 19:13ff.; 21:15–16.; Mark 10:13ff.; Luke 9:48; 18:15ff.). He calls them to himself, embraces them, lays hands on them, blesses them, tells them that theirs is the kingdom of heaven, marks them as an example to adults, warns the latter not to offend them, says that their angels watch over them, and reads their hosannas as a fulfillment of the prophecy that God has made the speech of children a power by which those who hate him are silenced, and he has ordained praise (αἰνον, *ainon*; LXX) from their lips.

5. The apostles proceed from the same idea. The covenant of grace established with Israel, though it changed in dispensation, remained the same in essence. The church (ἐκκλησια, *ekklēsia*) has replaced the Israel of the Old Testament. It is now the people of God, and God is its God and Father (Matt. 1:21; Luke 1:17; Acts 3:25; Rom. 9:25–26; 11:16–21; 2 Cor. 6:16–18; Gal. 3:14–29; Eph. 2:12–13; Titus 2:14; Heb. 8:8–10; 1 Pet. 2:9; Rev. 21:3). As was the case in the Old Testament, so now too the children of believers are included among the people of God. The church of the New Testament, after all, is not a collection of individuals, but an organism, a body, a temple, and as such, as a people, it took the place of Israel. As wild olive shoots—since some of the branches of the old olive tree have been broken off—they have been grafted onto the trunk of the same olive tree and so share in the nourishing sap from its root (Rom. 11:16–17). Hence at times entire households converted to Christianity. The household itself is an institution of God, an organic whole, which shares in a common blessing or a common curse. Jesus's disciples bring peace to the house they enter (Luke 10:5), and when Zacchaeus believes, Jesus himself says that salvation has come to his house (Luke 19:9). The apostles not only teach in the temple but also repeatedly proclaim the gospel of Christ in people's houses (Acts 5:42; 20:20). Along with the head of

81. T. Beza, *Resp. ad coll. Mompelg*, 103, according to J. Gerhard, *Loci theol.*, XX, 211.

the family, the entire family is saved (11:14; 16:31). Entire households believe and are baptized (16:15, 34; 18:8; 1 Cor. 1:16).

This is no proof, to be sure, that infant baptism was already administered by the apostles, but neither can the contrary be inferred from silence. From the early introduction of infant baptism, the general acknowledgment it was accorded from the start, and Origen's witness—from these follows the possibility and even the probability that it already was an apostolic practice. Peter, moreover, says that the promise of the old covenant that God would be the God of believers and of their children passed into the dispensation of the New Testament (Acts 2:39). This, admittedly, first of all applies to the Jews, and Gentiles are not mentioned until Peter says: "And all who are far away." But this does not alter the fact that the Jews who convert to Christ not only receive the promise of the covenant for themselves but also for their children. And the Gentiles who become believers share the same privileges and, according to the whole New Testament, are in no respect inferior to believers from the Jews. According to Paul (1 Cor. 7:14), even the children from a household of which only one of the parents has become a believer are holy. If such a case occurred, the believing partner must not think that oneself could not continue the marriage. On the contrary, as a result of the faith of the one spouse, the entire marriage, even the other spouse, is sanctified. And Paul proves this by arguing that otherwise the children of such a marriage would be unclean, but now they are holy. This point, then, was well established, generally accepted, and could therefore serve as an argument. The children of a household where either the father or the mother is a believer are counted according to the believing spouse, even if it is the woman of the house. In such a household it is the Christian confession that sets the tone. It is the standard by which the whole family must be judged. Faith is the higher condition, which overshadows the lower.

The holiness Paul mentions here must not be taken as subjective and internal holiness but as an objective, theocratic kind of holiness, for otherwise the children and the husband would not be holy on account of the believing mother and wife but on their own account. Nor is Paul in any way thinking here of infant baptism, nor of anything that might serve as a basis for it. His sole interest is to show that the Christian faith does not cancel out the natural ordinances of life, but rather confirms and sanctifies them (cf. 1 Cor. 7:18–24). This passage is of importance for infant baptism, however, because it teaches that the whole family is regarded in light of the confession of the believing spouse. The believer has the calling to serve the Lord not only for oneself but with all that belongs to oneself and with one's entire family. For that reason the children of believers are admonished by the apostles as Christian children in the Lord (Acts 26:22; Eph. 6:1; Col. 3:20; 2 Tim. 3:15; 1 John 2:13). Also the little ones know the Lord (Heb. 8:11; Rev. 11:18; 19:5), and have been given a place before his throne (Rev. 20:12). Scripture knows nothing of a neutral upbringing that seeks to have the children make a completely free and independent choice at a more advanced age.[82] The children

---

82. Council of Trent, sess. VII, "De bapt.," ch. 14.

of believers are not pagans or children of the devil who still—as Roman Catholics and Lutherans hold—have to be exorcized at their baptism,[83] but children of the covenant, for whom the promise is meant as much as for adults. They are included in the covenant and are holy, not by nature (Job 14:4; Ps. 51:5; John 3:6; Eph. 2:3) but by virtue of the covenant.[84]

6. All this is the more compelling because grace—especially in the New Testament dispensation—is much more abundant than sin (Rom. 5:12–21). If the rejection of infant baptism proceeded solely from the fact that it is not explicitly enjoined in Scripture, it would have to be judged with indulgence. But as a rule it is completely bound up with other considerations and flows from a restriction of grace and from a failure to appreciate the catholicity of Christianity. For Anabaptism (unless it denies original sin and considers regeneration unnecessary in the case of children) poses a limit to grace in the child's age, in the child's not yet having attained the age of discretion, that is, in law and ordinances that have been established by God at the time of creation in nature. Grace, however, knows no such boundaries. Under the Old Testament dispensation grace may in a sense have been limited to the people of Israel, but amid that people it was extended as widely as possible. And in the New Testament all boundaries of people and country, of sex and age, have been completely erased. In Christ there is neither male nor female, neither Jew nor Greek, neither child nor aged person, but only a new creation. The Father loved the world; Christ is an atoning sacrifice for the whole world and shed his blood also for children; and the Holy Spirit, who conceived Jesus in Mary's womb and was granted to Jeremiah and John from the very first moment of their existence (cf. also Ps. 22:9–10), has access to every heart and is not hindered in this by age or youth. Just as children are partakers of the condemnation in Adam without their knowledge, so they also are again received unto grace in Christ. Though they cannot *actually* believe in Christ, they can be regenerated and thereby also receive the capacity to believe.

7. All these considerations abundantly demonstrate the legitimacy and hence the duty of infant baptism. For if the children of believers are to be regarded as Scripture teaches us to regard them, then, according to the divine institution of baptism, they have a legitimate claim to this sacrament in the same measure as, and even in a greater measure than, adults who make profession of faith. Certainly, in neither of these cases can we obtain absolute certainty. We can no more judge the hearts of senior members of the church than we can the hearts of infants. The only possibility left for us who are bound to externals is a judgment of charity. According to that judgment, we consider those who make profession of faith to be believers and give them access to the sacraments. By that same judgment we count the children of believers as themselves believers because they are included with

83. Cf. G. Kawerau, "Exorcismus bei der Taufe," in *PRE*[3], V, 695–700; F. J. Dölger, *Der Exorcismus in der altchristlichen Taufritual* (Paderborn: Schöningh, 1909).

84. Heidelberg Catechism, Q 74; Canons of Dort, I, 17.

their parents in the covenant of grace. The likelihood that the baptized are true believers is even greater in the case of children than adults. For not only does the weakening of the meaning of baptism, the neglect of [church] discipline, and the deadening power of custom creep into a Baptist church as readily as into a church that practices infant baptism, but almost half of the population dies before they have reached the years of discretion. For all these children there is in Scripture, to the extent that they are included in the covenant of grace, a promise from the Lord that they cannot consciously and voluntarily reject. If they die before the time they are able to do so, "godly parents ought not to doubt the election and salvation of their children."[85] And even in the case of those children who come of age, we may and must—according to the judgment of charity that must prevail in the church of Christ—believe they are saved if the contrary is not patently evident. For it is out of the children of believers that the church, the gathering of true Christ-believers, is continually being built.

8. In this connection, however, we may never forget that this is no less a judgment of charity in the case of adults than in the case of children. It is not an infallible pronouncement that establishes the salvation of every baptized person, but only a rule according to which Scripture tells us to act in the practice of the life of the church. The basis for baptism is not the assumption that someone is regenerate, nor even that [there is] regeneration itself, but only the covenant of God. Things in no way depend on the subjective opinion of the minister in regard to the spiritual state of the candidate for baptism. Whether or not he is himself persuaded of the sincerity of the faith of the person being baptized, he must not go by that opinion but act in accordance with the revealed will of God and the rule of his Word. Furthermore, nothing is gained by closing one's eyes to the fact that baptism is frequently administered to those who later prove not to walk in the way of the covenant. Both Scripture and experience teach us that not all is Israel that is called Israel, that there is chaff among the wheat, that in the house of God there are not only vessels of gold and silver but also vessels of clay. Hence, far fewer than all these people were regenerate when they received baptism. It cannot even be proved that the elect are always regenerated by the Holy Spirit in their youth, before their baptism, or even before their birth. God is free in the distribution of his grace and can also let people enjoy the fruit of their baptism at a much later age. In the Christian church, therefore, there is always room for the preaching of the gospel, of regeneration, faith, and repentance. The prophets, John the Baptist, and Jesus all came to their people with that message, a people that after all was God's own possession. The apostles too administered the Word not only to bring to expression the hidden life of faith; they also preached it as the seed of regeneration and as a means of making that faith effective.[86]

85. Canons of Dort, I, 17; G. Voetius, *Select. disp.*, II, 408, 417; C. Vitringa, *Doctr. christ.*, II, 51.

86. Cf. above, 56 (#440); and also A. M. Diermanse, *De uitverkoren kinderen wedergeboren?* 2 vols. (Den Haag: A. van Zijl, 1906–7).

9. Still, the essence of baptism may not be made dependent on its effect in life. Just as a sincere faith is what it is according to the description of the Heidelberg Catechism [Lord's Day 7, Q&A 21], even though the reality of life shows deviations from and malformations of it, so also baptism is and may not be other than what Scripture teaches concerning it. True, essential Christian baptism is that which is administered to believers. Although baptism, like the external calling, still produces many a blessing even for unbelievers, its true fruit and full power can only be enjoyed by believers. Objectively baptism, like the Word, remains the same. Those who in faith receive the Word and hence also those who in faith receive baptism really obtain the promises that God has attached to it. God remains true to himself and bestows salvation on everyone who believes. But faith is not everyone's possession. Ultimately the fruit of baptism is only enjoyed by those who are elect and therefore come to faith in God's time. Everyone must acquiesce in that outcome, whether they are Catholic or Protestant, Lutheran or Reformed. "The sacraments effect what they depict only in the elect," said Augustine, and Scholasticism echoed this view.[87] The elect have laid hold of it; the rest were hardened. "It is the children of the promise who are regarded as Abraham's offspring" [Rom. 9:8 NIV].

10. The benefits of baptism are the same for children as for adults: the forgiveness of sins, regeneration, and incorporation into the church of Christ. And these benefits are not first granted only in baptism but are already enjoyed in faith by those who receive baptism according to the will of God. Baptism does not confer a single benefit that has not already been promised in the Word and accepted by faith, but conferring the same benefits as the Word, it confers them in a different manner and form so that faith is confirmed and strengthened by it in the measure that God has given to each. This rule also applies to children. For just as without their knowledge they can be regenerated by the Holy Spirit and endowed with the capacity to believe, so they can also without their knowledge be strengthened in that capacity by the same Spirit. At work here, as in so many areas, there is a mysterious reciprocal activity. Just as light and the human eye presuppose and support each other, so faith enjoys the sacrament more to the degree that it is stronger, and faith is sealed and reinforced by the sacrament to the same degree as well. For maturing believers, therefore, the sacraments do not gradually decrease in importance but continually gain in value. To the eye of faith they ever more beautifully and gloriously display the riches of God's grace. For every believer and for the whole church, they are proof of grace received, a sign of God's faithfulness, a basis for pleading one's case in prayer, a supporting pillar for one's faith, and an exhortation to new obedience.[88]

87. Also Lombard, Thomas, Bonaventure, *Sent.*, IV; J. Calvin, *Commentary on Ephesians*, on Eph. 5:26; J. Calvin, *Institutes*, IV.xiv.9–10; idem, in *Calvini opera*, VII (CR, XXXV), 694 (ed. note: This is a reference to the opening sections of Consensus Tigurinus [1549]); T. Beza, *Tract. theol.*, III, 124; G. Voetius, *Select. disp.*, II, 408; Westminster Confession, ch. 28.6; C. Vitringa, *Doctr. christ.*, VI, 90; VII, 378.

88. Concerning infant baptism, cf. J. Calvin, *Institutes*, IV.xvi; Z. Ursinus, *Volumen tractationum theologicarum* (Neustadt: M. Harnisch, 1584), 597–619; F. Junius, *Theses theologicae*, 52; G. J. Vossius, *De baptismo*

THE ADMINISTRATION OF BAPTISM

By Whom?

[538] The one who administers this baptism is Christ. And only when he baptizes a person and along with the sign also grants the thing signified is that person truly baptized. But in administering baptism Christ employs people whom he charges with the distribution of the mysteries of God. Under the dispensation of the Old Testament, circumcision was not bound to a special office. Any Israelite was permitted to perform the rite. As a rule, the father of the family performed it (Gen. 17:23); in a case of emergency the mother also did it (Exod. 4:25; 1 Macc. 1:60); later it was usually a physician, and nowadays it is commonly a specially designated *mōhēl* (circumciser). In the New Testament, however, baptism was only administered by those who held an office: John (Mark 1:4); Jesus's disciples (John 4:2); the apostles (Acts 2:38), who were specifically charged by Christ to do this (Matt. 28:19); Philip, who was a deacon in Jerusalem but later served as an evangelist (Acts 21:8) and as such administered baptism (8:38); Ananias, who laid hands on Paul and probably also baptized him (9:17–18); Paul, who sometimes baptized but for the rest left this rite to be administered by his fellow workers, since as apostle to the Gentiles he was first of all called to preach the gospel (1 Cor. 1:14–17; cf. Acts 10:48).

From this it is clearly evident that the administration of the sacraments, though subordinate to the preaching of the Word, was at all times bound up with it. The sacrament follows the Word, and so the right to administer it passed automatically from the apostles and evangelists to the ministers, those presbyters who labored in the Word and in teaching. When these ministers were later regarded as bishops, whose office was different from that of presbyters and who were superior to them, the administration of baptism was considered a prerogative of bishops.[89] But the numerical growth of the churches as well as the—increasingly accepted—view that baptism was strictly necessary to salvation led to the opinion that baptism could also be administered by presbyters, deacons, parishioners, and in case of emergency even by any human endowed with reason. The Roman Catholic Church recognizes a baptism when administered by a heretic, indeed even a baptism administered by an unbeliever, a Jew, or a pagan, even though the required "intention to do what the church does" is hard to demonstrate here. In so doing it reserves for itself the right to apply the rule "Compel them to enter" [cf. Luke 14:23] to all those who are baptized. There is only one exception: the Roman Catholic Church does not

---

disputationes XX, et una de sacramentorum vi, atque efficacia (Amsterdam: Elzevirium, 1648), 13; C. Vitringa, *Observationum sacrarum*, II, c. 16; F. Turretin, *Institutes of Elenctic Theology*, XIX, qu. 20; B. de Moor, *Comm. theol.*, V, 476; C. Vitringa, *Doctr. christ.*, VII, 99; H. Martensen, *De kinderdoop* (Utrecht: W. F. Dannenfelser, 1852); J. A. Wormser, *De kinderdoop* (Amsterdam: Hövecker, 1853); K. J. Pieters and J. R. Keulen, *De kinderdoop volgens de beginselen der Gereformeerde Kerk* (Franeker: T. Telenga, 1861); J. J. van Oosterzee, *Christian Dogmatics*, §138; A. Kuyper, "Van de genademiddelen," *De Heraut* 652–54 (11 May–6 July 1890).

89. Tertullian, *On Baptism*, ch. 17.

recognize a person's right to baptize himself. In cases where there is some doubt whether a person has been baptized at all or properly baptized, then to make sure, it has even introduced a conditional baptism at which the officiant says, "If you have not been baptized, I baptize you," and so forth.[90] Also other churches, such as the Greek Orthodox and the Lutheran Church, teach the necessity of baptism and therefore allow laypersons to perform it in case of emergency. But ultimately none of them dares accept the implication that a person would be lost solely because one totally without any fault of one's own died unbaptized. All of them allow for exceptions where a "baptism by blood" or "a baptism of desire" is sufficient.[91] "The conversion of the heart can be present when baptism has not been received but not when it has been despised."[92] In the Latin text of the Augsburg Confession, we do read that baptism "is necessary to salvation," but in the German text only "that it is necessary."[93] Lutheran theologians do not deny salvation to children who died unbaptized apart from any fault of their parents.[94] And all those who hold that baptism imparts a special grace acknowledge that such a grace can also be granted by God in some other way.

For that reason, the Reformed took a different position. Baptism, they asserted, was not the cause but the sign and the seal of regeneration, which God bestows before and apart from the sacrament. Not a single benefit is conferred by baptism that is not conferred by the Word and accepted by faith. Baptism, accordingly, cannot be strictly necessary for salvation. It is not the fact of being deprived of baptism, but contempt for baptism, that renders a person guilty before God. Mark 16:16, therefore, omits baptism in the second clause; and in John 3:5, a verse generally understood by the opposition to refer to baptism,[95] there is no reference to baptism, according to Calvin and his followers, but at best an allusion, for water occurs here as fire does in Matt. 3:11, as a symbol of the activity of the Holy Spirit, and is no longer mentioned at all in John 3:6 and 8. There is therefore no reason to depart from apostolic usage and in cases of emergency to permit people other than the ministers of the church to administer baptism.[96] In this connection the Reformed also favored having baptism consistently take place in the midst of the congregation. Although in the New Testament the administration of baptism took

90. J. C. Suicerus, *Thesaurus ecclesiasticus*, s.v. βαπτισμος; *Comm. on Sent.*, IV, dist. 5; T. Aquinas, *Summa theol.*, III, qu. 67; Council of Trent, sess. VII, "De bapt.," ch. 4; Roman Catechism, II, ch. 2, qu. 18, 23, 42 (ed. note: Bradley and Kevane, II, ch. 1, qu. 18, 23, 43); R. Bellarmine, "De bapt.," in *Controversiis*, ch. 7.

91. Ed. note: Cf. note 25 above.

92. P. Lombard, *Sent.*, IV, 4, 4.

93. Augsburg Confession, art. 9.

94. J. Quenstedt, *Theologia*, IV, 164.

95. Council of Trent, sess. VII, "De bapt.," ch. 2; Roman Catechism, II, ch. 2, qu. 31 (ed. note: Bradley and Kevane, II, ch. 1, qu. 32).

96. J. Calvin, *Institutes*, IV.xv.20; G. Bucanus, *Institutiones theologicae*, 3rd ed. (Bern: Johannes & Isaias le Preux, 1605), 613; W. Perkins, *The Workes of That Famous and Worthy Minister of Christ*, 3 vols. (London: John Legatt, 1612–18), I, 461; G. Voetius, *Pol. eccl.*, I, 631; C. Vitringa, *Doctr. christ.*, VII, 75, 163; B. de Moor, *Comm. theol.*, V, 435.

place wherever there was water (Matt. 3:6; John 3:23; Acts 8:36), it soon became a custom, when believers acquired their own meeting places, to have it take place there.[97] Yet in cases of emergency, in the wintertime, in the case of illness, for governors and distinguished persons, an exception was made and baptism was allowed to take place in private dwellings.

This is certainly in conflict with the general rule that has to be applied in the church. Although cases are conceivable in which the administration of baptism could be allowed to take place in private homes, they can and must be of a highly exceptional nature. Such cases are not to be judged by the minister of the Word alone but by the entire church council and even then require that the baptism take place only in the presence of the council. For what matters in the distribution of the sacrament is not the building but the gathering of the church. The sacrament is a constituent of a public worship service, a good that Christ granted to his church, and therefore it must be openly administered, together with the Word, in the midst of the congregation. The sacrament of baptism is connected with the Word. Christ himself joined the administration of baptism to that of the Word (Matt. 28:19). In situations where the church is being planted in a non-Christian population, baptism in the nature of the case cannot immediately take place in the midst of a gathering of believers. But the moment it exists, the administration of Word and sacrament must be transferred there, for they are constituents of a public worship service and goods of the church. Thus, in the apostolic era, the Lord's Supper was celebrated in the midst of the congregation (1 Cor. 11:20). And it should be so no less with baptism since this sacrament above all depicts our incorporation into Christ and his church (12:13) and is therefore most fittingly administered in the public gathering of believers.[98]

When?

About the time at which baptism should be administered there has been considerable disagreement in the church. Circumcision was performed on the eighth day. Baptism in the New Testament was usually administered immediately after

97. A. Drews, "Taufe: Liturgischer Vollzug," in *PRE*[3], XIX, 424–50.

98. J. Calvin, *Institutes*, IV.xv.16; G. Voetius, *Pol. eccl.*, I, 726–30; B. de Moor, *Comm. theol.*, V, 510–12; C. Vitringa, *Doctr. christ.*, VII, 171; Synod of Dort, sess. 163, 175; Church Order of the Synod of Dort (1618–19), art. 56: "God's covenant shall be sealed for the children of Christians by baptism as soon as its administration can take place, and that in a public meeting when God's Word is preached. But in places where few preaching services are held a certain day of the week shall be set aside to administer baptism extraordinarily. Nevertheless, this shall not take place without a sermon being preached" (De Ridder, 553). Ed. note: The preceding translation is taken from Richard R. De Ridder, Peter H. Jonker, and Leonard Verduin, eds., *The Church Orders of the Sixteenth Century Reformed Churches of the Netherlands* (Grand Rapids: Calvin Theological Seminary, 1987). This volume is not in print for sale, but copies are available for use at the Hekman Library of Calvin College and Seminary. De Ridder's translation was made primarily from the Dutch text of P. Biesterveld and H. H. Kuyper, *Kerkelijk handboekje* (Kampen: Bos, 1905), and C. Hooijer, *Oude kerkordeningen der Nederlandsche Hervormde gemeenten, 1563–1638* (Zalt-Bommel: Noman, 1865). Bavinck's subsequent references to the key synodical acts and documents will be given by referencing the specific synod and year, the article, and the location in the De Ridder volume.

someone believed and made profession of faith (Matt. 3:6; Acts 2:41; 8:12, 36; 9:18; 10:47; 16:15, 33; 18:8). But already in the second century, when all sorts of people wanted to join the church, people who were utterly unfamiliar with its doctrine and life, the catechumenate arose, an institution that gradually became increasingly regulated and according to the Synod of Elvira (c. 300) had to last two years. At the end of this period, preferably one of the great feast days, the catechumens were solemnly baptized and incorporated into the church. Guided by the idea that baptism forgave only past sins, many of them even postponed baptism for as long as possible, in some cases right up until their deathbeds. But infant baptism, a rite that was increasingly coming into vogue, and the doctrine of the absolute necessity of baptism nevertheless drove the church in another direction. It became a custom not to delay baptism for as long as possible but to administer it as soon as possible after the birth of a child. At first many people still argued in favor of having baptism administered in a person's third or thirtieth year. But others, with equal fervency, wanted it administered on the eighth or fortieth day after birth. The Synod of Carthage (AD 252), under the chairmanship of Cyprian, had already decreed that children should be baptized as soon as possible, on the second or third day after birth.[99] Soon this became the general practice and was regarded as an apostolic custom.[100]

The Greek Orthodox Church has no stipulation about the time, but as a rule it did not delay baptism beyond the eighth day and, in case of emergency, administers it even earlier, immediately after birth. The Roman Catholic Church insists that a child should be baptized as soon after the birth as possible.[101] With this general rule the Lutherans[102] and also the Reformed concur. The provincial Synod of Dort (1574), article 57, even declared that "the sentiment of parents who wish to postpone the baptism of their children until the mothers themselves can present their children or to wait a long time until the godparents can be present is not a legitimate reason for postponing it." But no other synod concurred with this pronouncement. Although all needless delay was frowned upon and synods repeatedly urged the speedy presentation of a child for baptism, it was never the intention of the church ordinances, when they speak only of fathers, to exclude the mothers, but rather to oppose the system of godparents and not let them take the place of the fathers.[103]

The system of "baptismal witnesses," "sureties," "sponsors," "guarantors," "receivers," "spiritual fathers and mothers," or "godparents" came up when infant

99. Cyprian, *Epistles* 59.

100. J. C. Suicerus, *Thesaurus ecclesiasticus*, s.v. βαπτισμος and κλινικος; J. Schwane, *Dogmengeschichte*, I, 378; II, 755; B. Moeller and H. von Schubert, *Lehrbuch der Kirchengeschichte*, I, 338.

101. Council of Trent, VII, "De bapt.," ch. 12; Roman Catechism, II, ch. 2, qu. 28 (ed. note: Bradley and Kevane, II, ch. 1, qu. 29).

102. J. Gerhard, *Loci theol.*, XX, 245.

103. G. Bucanus, *Inst. theol.*, 634; H. Bullinger, *Decades*, V, serm. 6 (ed. note: Bavinck cites here *Huijsboeck* [1612], p. 249). *Synopsis purioris theologiae*, disp. 44, 52; G. Voetius, *Pol. eccl.*, I, 724; B. de Moor, *Comm. theol.*, V, 512; C. Vitringa, *Doctr. christ.*, VII, 176.

baptism became the general custom and is already mentioned by Tertullian.[104] Needed at this time were persons who professed faith in the place of the child and answered the usual questions; who acted, as it were, as bondspersons and sponsors for the child and promised, on the basis of the child's baptism, to give the child a Christian upbringing. They were the representatives of the church, which, the reader will recall, itself in its entirety presents the child for baptism and sustains the child with its prayers. Now the obvious thing to do was to let the parents act as such sponsors at the child's baptism. And in the early years this is also what happened. But gradually fatherhood and godparenthood went hand in hand, like birth and rebirth, natural and spiritual kinship. Parents were already naturally obligated to give their child a Christian upbringing and seemed no longer able to make a special promise to that end. They were the natural parents of the child, and godparenthood was a very different spiritual relationship and therefore gradually became an "impediment to marriage" between the sponsors on the one hand and the baptized child and the child's parents on the other and also among themselves. The Council of Main (813), accordingly, already issued the following prohibition: No one receives from the baptismal font his own natural son or daughter.[105]

But this same catechism already had to complain that this ministry in the church was so neglected that "only the bare name of this function remains." Lutherans and Reformed theologians regarded this system of baptismal sponsors absolutely unnecessary, since it was neither prescribed nor even mentioned in Scripture, yet they usually considered it an "indifferent matter" (adiaphoron) that could at times be of some value.[106] The Reformed especially stressed that in the first place it was the *parents* who should answer the baptismal questions and act as receivers and sponsors for their child, and they demanded that if sponsors were invited to play a role, they should be sound in their confession and walk of life.[107] Add to this that in the Roman Catholic Church the godparents were obligated to instruct the child in the doctrine of the faith, since the pastors, as the Roman Catechism said,[108] had no time for it. But the Reformed churches, at the suggestion of Calvin,

---

104. A. Drews, "Taufe: Liturgischer Vollzug," in *PRE*³, XIX, 447ff.

105. Cf. Roman Catechism, II, ch. 2, qu. 20–24 (ed. note: Bradley and Kevane, II, ch. 1, qu. 20–24).

106. J. Gerhard, *Loci theol.*, XX, 267; J. F. Buddeus, *Institutiones theologiae dogmaticae* (Frankfurt and Leipzig, 1741), 1071; Church Order of the Synod of Dort (1618–19), art. 57: "Ministers shall do their best and strive to the end that the father present his child for baptism. In congregations where besides the fathers also godfathers or witnesses are taken to the baptism (which custom in itself is optional and should not be lightly changed) it is fitting that those be taken who hold to pure doctrine and are of pious behavior" (De Ridder, 553). A. Walaeus, in *Synopsis purioris theologiae*, disp. 44, 54; G. Bucanus, *Inst. theol.*, 640; G. Voetius, *Pol. eccl.*, I, 704; B. de Moor, *Comm. theol.*, V, 509; C. Vitringa, *Doctr. christ.*, VII, 159.

107. J. Calvin, "Letter to Caspar Olevianus, November 1560," in *Op. ed. Amsterdam* (Schippers), IX, 142. Ed. note: The letter concerns the polity of the church in Geneva and can be found in *Calvini opera*, XVIII (CR, XLVI), cols. 235–37. C. Hooijer, *Oude kerkenordeningen der Nederlandsche Hervormde gemeenten*, 7, 11, 17, 46, 69, 105, 153, 205, 265, 314, 344, 456.

108. Roman Catechism, II, ch. 2, qu. 20 (ed. note: Bradley and Kevane, II, ch. 1, qu. 20).

introduced the catechetical instruction of their baptized youth and assigned this task to their ministers. In a well-organized Reformed church, therefore, the system of baptismal witnesses, which had otherwise degenerated into "a bare name," except for a few special cases has become superfluous and unnecessary and has practically almost disappeared from the scene.[109]

The entire doctrine of baptism, as it has been developed by the Reformed, shows how closely they aligned themselves with Scripture. In light of this fact it is all the more noteworthy that despite this, or rather precisely because of this, they managed, in their recognition and administration of baptism, to avoid all sectarianism and to preserve a genuinely Christian magnanimity and breadth of vision. In accord with the Catholic Church in its struggle with the North-African churches, the Reformed unanimously taught that the baptism of heretics, provided it was administered in the name of the Triune God, had to be recognized. But since they did not have a magical view of the baptismal formula and did not detach baptism from the church and its offices, they added the further qualification that it had to be administered by a minister who was officially recognized as such in a Christian church.[110] And they indeed barred from baptism all things and objects, all dead fetuses or partially born babies, all monstrosities, all children

109. J. C. Suicerus, *Thesaurus ecclesiasticus*, s.v. ἀναδοκοι; J. W. F. Höfling, *Das Sakrament der Taufe*, II, 4–20; P. Drews, "Taufe: Liturgischer Vollzug," in *PRE*³, XIX, 447–50; *J. Boehmer, "Eine Reform des Patenamts," *Neue kirchliche Zeitschrift* 17 (1906); H. J. Olthuis, *De doopspraktijk der Gereformeerde Kerken in Nederland 1568–1816*, 191ff.

110. G. Voetius, *Pol. eccl.*, I, 631–45; F. Turretin, *Institutes of Elenctic Theology*, XIX, qu. 15; B. de Moor, *Comm. theol.*, V, 443–53.

Synod of Dort (1574), qu. 10: "The answer to the question of the brothers from den Briel whether a child baptized by a woman shall be baptized in the church is as follows: Yes, since baptism by a woman is not [a valid] baptism." (De Ridder, 166)

Synod of Dort (1578), qu. 29: "Whether baptism that has been administered by a private person or by an elder is valid. Answer: no. Meanwhile, if it happened that an elder administered baptism having been requested to do so by a church or a part of the same, the baptism shall not be repeated for the reason that he has some form of calling. He is, however, not to be praised or imitated." (De Ridder, 227–28)

Synod of Dort (1618), session 162: "In baptizing young children as well as older persons ministers shall use the respective forms of the institution and use of baptism which have been written for that purpose. Art. 58. Adults are incorporated into the Christian church by baptism and are therefore duty bound also to partake of the Lord's Supper, which they shall promise to do at [their] baptism. Art. 59."

2. Baptism by itinerant Papists and the Mennonites shall not be thoughtlessly repeated, but it should be clearly determined whether they retain the form and substantial things of baptism. If this is found to be so, the baptism may by no means be repeated. The baptism administered by an excommunicated minister shall be judged in the same way, if he has a regular call from any gathering. The churches shall thoroughly investigate and take note of all these things.

3. Marriages of those who are not yet incorporated into the Christian church by baptism may not be solemnized in the churches with the customary public and solemn blessing before they have been baptized. (De Ridder, 565)

Concerning the baptism of heretics, see G. N. Bonwetsch, "Ketzertaufe," in *PRE*³, X, 270–75; G. van Goor, *De strijd over den ketterdoop* (Utrecht: Kemmer, 1872).

of pagan parents who had been taken captive;[111] but they admitted to baptism all children who after the death of their parents, or as foundlings, had been adopted into Christian families, who were born from illegitimate unions or from excommunicate, schismatic, or heretical parents as long as there was some ground for the assumption that the lineage of the covenant was not completely broken.[112] The Reformed can more easily be accused of having too broad a policy of recognizing and administering baptism than too narrow a policy. But precisely for this reason they have maintained, in eminent fashion, the unity and catholicity of the church of Christ on earth. All Christian churches still recognize each other's baptisms and thereby in fact say that in all these churches there is still so much truth that the possibility of salvation is not ruled out. There is one confession on the foundation of which they have all been built, one faith in which they all share. Despite all the differences and controversy, all of them nevertheless recognize *one* Lord, *one* faith, and *one* baptism.

---

111. Synod of Dort, sess. 18–19.

112. G. Voetius, *Pol. eccl.*, I, 645–70; B. de Moor, *Comm. theol.*, V, 500–509; C. Vitringa, *Doctr. christ.*, VII, 95, 142–59; P. J. Kromsigt, "De doopspractijk in de oude Gereformeerde Kerk in Nederland," *Troffel en Zwaard* 3 (1905): 1–16; 65–83; H. H. Kuyper, *Hamabdil: Van de heiligheid van het genadeverbond* (Amsterdam: Bottenburg, 1907), 33ff.; H. J. Olthuis, *De doopspraktijk der Gereformeerde Kerken in Nederland 1568–1816.*

11

THE SPIRIT'S MEANS OF GRACE: THE LORD'S SUPPER

Like the Passover, the Lord's Supper is a meal where God meets his people in joyful celebration. God himself as the host shares the fruit of the supper with his people. Though first of all a sacrament, the Passover must also be seen as a meal. It is a sacrifice of atonement and a meal of communion with God, simultaneously a sacrament and a sacrifice.

As an Old Testament type, the Passover points to the Lord's Supper, which is, however, only a meal. Its sacrificial character is completely fulfilled once and for all by the sacrifice of Christ. Though modern scholars debate whether Jesus himself instituted the Lord's Supper, none of the arguments against it are very compelling. To doubt this is to doubt Jesus's own self-consciousness of his death and its saving significance. The variant Gospel readings of Jesus's Last Supper with his disciples confirm this and demonstrate that our Lord never prescribed an unchangeable formula for the meal. It is only commanded to his disciples that they "do this in remembrance of me." The Supper is to be enjoyed by the church of all ages until he returns and we drink with him the new wine of the new kingdom.

The Lord's Supper has played an important part in the church's life from its beginning. The simple service of confession and thanksgiving was followed by an agapē feast, which must be distinguished from the "Eucharist." Over time, the sacrament became more and more mysterious and was seen as a sacrifice. When this development was combined with a sacerdotal, clerical church structure, a "realistic" doctrine of the elements arose, eventually leading to the doctrine of transubstantiation, where the bread and wine are believed to be converted by a mysterious power of the ordained priest into the real body and blood of Christ. In time this led to such traditional Roman Catholic practices as the elevation, adoration, and [p]reservation of the host. With the minister as priest, the Eucharist is distinct, the most exalted of the sacraments. The Mass is the center of Roman Catholic worship.

The Reformation unanimously rejected the Roman Catholic doctrine of transubstantiation and the sacrifice of the Mass. Differences still remained,

540

however, among the followers of Luther, those who accepted Zwingli's notion of a memorial, and Calvin's doctrine of the presence through the Holy Spirit. Viewing sacraments as mere *signs led to the rationalism of the Socinians, the Remonstrants, and the Mennonites, who saw in the Supper only a memorial, a confession of believers, and not a means of grace. Some Protestant churches, notably the Church of England, even drifted back toward Rome, as in the Oxford movement.*

In Scripture and the Reformed tradition, the Lord's Supper is first of all a meal, food for the Christian pilgrimage. Christ is the host of the meal; it is Christ who instituted the Supper; he is its administrator. Presiding ministers do so in the name of Christ. As a meal, the bread and wine can be seen as something to be enjoyed, and enjoyed in fellowship with other Christians. The Lord's Supper is best served around a table, not an altar of sacrifice.

The "matter" of the sacrament, the thing signified in the meal, is the body and blood of Christ broken and shed for our sins, Christ and all his benefits. The Lord's Supper is above all a gift of God, not our memorial and confession. The Lord's Supper signifies the mystical union of the believer with Jesus Christ. On the point of this reality of communion with our Lord there is no disagreement between Roman Catholics, Lutheran, and Reformed Christians. However, practices such as Masses without communicants, the use of a single element (bread) alone, and withholding the cup diminish the significance of the Lord's Supper as a meal *of communion. The mystical union is always a union of persons, believers joined to Christ through the Holy Spirit. Faith is thus an indispensable requisite for the reception of the sacrament. Finally, the Lord's Supper is for believers only. To avoid all notions of magic concerning the sacrament, communicants must be properly prepared and required to examine themselves before they partake.*

A SHARED SACRIFICIAL MEAL

[539] As the second sacrament, after baptism, comes the Lord's Supper, whose Old Testament model is the Passover feast. Just as among the Gentiles (Num. 25:2), so also in Israel meals were frequently combined with sacrifices. Sometimes the sacrifices were totally consumed by fire on the altar of burnt offerings, but in the case of other offerings only a part was consumed by fire and the rest was kept for human consumption, either at the altar by the priests alone (Lev. 2:3, 10; 6:16, 25–30; 7:1–10; 10:12–13) as an act of atonement (10:17), or by the officiating priest with his family in a clean place as part of his maintenance (7:12–14, 31–34; 10:14), or by the sacrificer with his family and guests, provided they were levitically clean and outside the sanctuary (7:19–21; Deut. 12:7, 12; 1 Sam. 9:13ff.; 2 Sam. 6:19). The significance of these meals was that God met with his people and, on the basis of the sacrifice made and accepted, united himself

with his people in joy. In this sanctuary God comes to the children of Israel and dwells among them (Exod. 20:24; 29:42–46; 33:7; Num. 11:25; 12:5; 17:4; Deut. 31:15). He is the host who relinquishes a part of the sacrifice brought to him and invites his people to dine with him. Those who participated entered into a covenant with him. Participation in the sacrificial meals of the Gentiles, accordingly, was forbidden to Israel (Exod. 34:15); it was an act of attaching themselves to and joining themselves with false gods (Num. 25:3, 5; Ps. 106:28). The apostles later prohibited Christians from participation in them (Acts 15:29; 21:25) or warned against them for the sake of weak believers (1 Cor. 8:1ff.; 10:18ff.). As such unions of God with his people and also among themselves, these meals were characterized by good spirits and joy and, though frequently occasioning orgies and bouts of drunkenness (1 Sam. 1:13; Prov. 7:14ff.; Isa. 28:8), they also served on the other hand as signs and pledges of supreme joy in God (Deut. 27:7; Ps. 22:25ff.; Isa. 25:6; 62:8–9).[1]

Such a sacrificial meal occurred especially at the time of Passover. Many Protestants maintained against Rome that this was what Passover was all about.[2] But this is doubtlessly incorrect. Passover was first of all a sacrifice and then also a sacrament. In Exodus 12:27 and 34:25 it is called a sacrifice before the Lord. The act that accompanied it is called a "service" (Exod. 12:26), and the celebration of it (Num. 9:7ff.) is "the bringing of an offering to the Lord." Further, the father of a home, after selecting a one-year-old male lamb without blemish from the flock four days before the feast, on the tenth day of Abib or Nisan, had to slaughter it on the fourteenth day of that month at twilight, and with a brush of hyssop dab the blood on the sides and tops of the doorframes of the house (Exod. 12:3ff.). This blood served to make atonement. By itself Israel had deserved to die every bit as much as the Egyptians. Yet it is not treated as Egypt was, but graciously rescued from death and led out of the house of bondage by the Lord. Of this event the blood was the sign. When the Lord saw the blood on the doorframes of the house, he was reconciled, put aside his wrath, and passed over the doorway of that house, thus saving the people (פָּסַח, *pāsaḥ*, to pass or leap over [Isa. 31:5]; hence פֶּסַח, *pesaḥ*; πασχα, *pascha*; Exod. 12:13, 23, 27).

The sacrificial character of the Passover is even more clearly evident from the manner in which it was later celebrated in Canaan. There the lamb was no longer slaughtered by the father of a family but by the Levites (2 Chron. 30:16; 35:11; Ezra 6:19). The blood was sprinkled on the altar by the priests (2 Chron. 30:16; 35:11), the fat portions were burned on the altar (35:14), and the meal was held at the sanctuary (Deut. 16:2). So, although the Passover is first of all a sacrifice, it is not confined to being a sacrifice but later becomes a meal. After the lamb had

---

1. W. Robertson Smith, *Die Religion der Semiten* (Freiburg i.B.: Mohr, 1899), 206ff.; C. Orelli, "Opferkultus des Alten Testaments," in *PRE*³, XIV, 393.

2. B. de Moor, *Commentarius . . . theologiae*, 6 vols. (Leiden: J. Hasbroek, 1761–71), V, 322; H. Witsius, *The Oeconomy of the Covenants between God and Man*, 3 vols. (London, 1763; 2nd ed., rev. and corrected, 1775), IV, 9, 6.

been slaughtered at twilight on the fourteenth of Abib and its blood dabbed on the doorframes of the house, or in a later period sprinkled on the altar, it—without having a bone broken in its body—had to be roasted as a whole, head, legs and inner parts, over a fire. Then, in the same night of the fourteenth of Abib, it had to be eaten with unleavened bread and bitter herbs by everyone in the house. This included the women but not uncircumcised strangers, foreigners, or hirelings. It had to be eaten in haste, with loins girded, feet shod, and a staff in one's hand, in the house or later at the sanctuary, and what remained was to be burned with fire (Exod. 12:1–28, 43–49; 13:3–9; 23:15; Lev. 23:5–14; Num. 9:10–14; 28:16–25; Deut. 16:1ff.).

Consequently, the feast of Passover occupied an entirely unique place in the cultic life of Israel. It was indeed a sacrifice, but immediately afterward it became a meal. It did not belong to the category of sin offerings, for it was eaten, but neither to that of thank offerings, for the meal was always preceded by atonement. For that matter, it was instituted by God on a special occasion prior to all the other sacrifices and therefore has a nature of its own. It is a sacrifice of atonement and meal of communion with God and one another. It is simultaneously a sacrifice and a sacrament.[3]

The New Testament ascribes to this Passover a typological significance, so that it is not only an act of remembering the liberation from Egypt, but also a sign and pledge of liberation from the bondage of sin and of communion with God in the person of the promised Messiah. Jesus himself pointed this out when he deliberately associated the institution of the Lord's Supper with the celebration of the Passover.

About the manner in which he did this, however, there is much disagreement. Some exegetes, appealing to the Synoptics, say that on Thursday, the fourteenth of Nisan, Jesus along with his disciples celebrated the actual Passover and on that occasion instituted the Lord's Supper. Others, adhering to the Gospel of John (12:1; 13:1–2, 29; 18:28; 19:14, 31), assert that on Thursday, the thirteenth of Nisan, Jesus had an ordinary meal with his disciples and on that occasion washed their feet, and then on the fourteenth of Nisan, the actual day of the feast, died as the true Passover lamb. Now, whether one conforms the Synoptics to John or John to the Synoptics or lets the two stand side by side unreconciled or denies the authenticity of the Fourth Gospel on the basis of the testimony of the Quartodecimans in the second and third centuries, who, to undergird their practice of celebrating the Christian Passover on the evening of the fourteenth of Nisan, appealed to the apostle John[4]—in any case, there is always at least agreement in

---

3. C. Orelli, "Passah," in *PRE*[3], XIV, 750–57; W. J. Moulton, "Passover," in *DB*, III, 684–92.

4. The question is much too complicated to consider here. Recently it has been discussed inter alia by D. J. Veen, "In welk jaar en op welken dag en datum is Christus gestorven?" *Theologische Studiën* 23 (1905): 429–38, separately published as *Wanneer is Christus gestorven?* (Amersfoort: P. Dz. Veen, 1907); C. Mommert, *Zur Chronologie des Lebens Jesu* (Leipzig: E. Haberland, 1909); F. Westberg, *Die biblische Chronologie nach Flavius Josephus und das Todesjahr Jesu* (Leipzig: Deichert, 1910); G. H. Gwilliam, "Last Supper," in *DC*, II, 5–9.

saying that on Thursday night Jesus had a meal with his disciples, that he died on Friday, and that he rose again on Sunday. Now, even if this meal should not have been the regular Passover meal of the fourteenth of Nisan but was held the day before on Thursday the thirteenth, still there would be no objection to assuming that Jesus, who was to die the following day and hence could not eat the Passover with the Jews at the usual time, celebrated it the day before and in that way linked it to the Lord's Supper.

In any case, this latter event is not subject to any doubt. Both Paul (1 Cor. 10:16; 11:24–25) and the Synoptics have Jesus institute the Lord's Supper in the closest possible connection with Passover. From the Passover meal he derived the bread and wine, which had to serve as signs and seals in the Lord's Supper. Although he immediately took over baptism from John, he delayed the institution of the Lord's Supper to the time of [the] last Passover feast, and then he changed the covenant meal of the Old Testament into that of the New Testament. None of this is contradicted in John's Gospel, for the simple reason that John is completely silent about the institution of the Lord's Supper. Furthermore, the date of Jesus's death on either the fourteenth or the fifteenth of Nisan is totally immaterial to the fact that Jesus died as the true Passover lamb. For not only John's Gospel indicates this (19:33, 36), but also Paul expressly states in 1 Cor. 5:7 that our paschal lamb, Christ, has been slain, and that believers must therefore cleanse out the old leaven of sin and walk as "unleavened" persons, new creatures, unmixed with any unrighteousness. To this we may further add that the lamb led to the slaughter (Isa. 53:7) probably contains an allusion to the Passover lamb and is thus applied in the New Testament to Christ (John 1:29, 36; Acts 8:32; 1 Pet. 1:19; Rev. 5:6). Just as circumcision was a model for baptism and as a result of Christ's death passed into that baptism, so the Passover feast pointed forward to the Lord's Supper and was, in keeping with Christ's command, replaced by it. However, whereas Passover was still primarily a sacrifice, the Lord's Supper has entirely lost this character. The reason is that the sacrifice offered in the Passover found its complete fulfillment in the death of Christ. It is on the basis of that once-for-all, completed, and perfect sacrifice that Christ founded the new dispensation of the covenant of grace and invited his disciples to, and strengthened them at, his holy table.

INSTITUTED BY CHRIST?

[540] In the last few years, after a number of scholars had led the way in earlier times, Jülicher, Spitta, Mensinga, Brandt, and Grafe (et al.) mounted a serious attack on the idea that Jesus instituted the Lord's Supper. As grounds they adduced that the words "Do this in remembrance of me" are lacking in Matthew and Luke and only occur as a free addition by Paul in 1 Cor. 11:24–25 and Luke 22:19; that some manuscripts, especially Codex D, omit the words το ὑπερ . . . ἐκχυννομενον [to hyper . . . ekchynnomenon, "which is given for you, . . . poured for you"] in Luke 22:19–20, and therefore know nothing of the body of Christ

being given, of doing things in his remembrance, and of a cup of thanksgiving; that the Gospel of John makes no mention of it, and the other reports diverge strongly from each other. They especially argue that Jesus could not have linked bread and wine with his death, much less have given them to eat as signs of his body and blood, since these ideas could only arise when in the church a certain view about the person and death of Jesus had taken shape.

None of these arguments, however, is very compelling. It is a fact, after all, that in the period when the Gospel of John was written, the Lord's Supper was universally celebrated in the Christian church. The absence of any reference to the institution could, therefore, in no way arise from ignorance. The same is true for Luke. The absence of the words cited above in chapter 22:19–20 cannot mean that at the time people thought that all that happened at the Last Supper is contained in the words: "He took a loaf of bread, and when he had given thanks, he broke it and gave it to them, saying, 'This is my body.'" For in that case the action that then took place would be completely incomprehensible. The text in Codex D assumes that more things were done and said on that occasion, and it is either corrupt, therefore, or at best an incomplete report of what occurred at the Last Supper. From the time of John and Luke we can move to that of Paul, and then we learn that this apostle proceeds from the assumption that the Christian church in general knows and celebrates the Lord's Supper as an institution of Christ. Indeed, he even says that he has received from the Lord and passed on to the Corinthians the things pertaining to the institution of the Lord's Supper (1 Cor. 11:23). The time when Paul received this instruction (not παρα [*para*, with] but ἀπο του κυριου [*apo tou kyriou*, from the Lord]) undoubtedly coincides with the time of his conversion (Acts 9) and is therefore only a few years removed from the last night in which Christ instituted his Supper. From this it follows that even in the very first years after Jesus's death, the Christian church, along with all the apostles, knew the Lord's Supper as an institution of Christ. This conclusion is more than enough to raise the truth of that institution above all reasonable doubt.

Another question, however, is how Christ instituted this Supper and what he intended to accomplish by it. With a view to this question, we must first of all note that Jesus instituted his Supper on the occasion of the Passover meal. In Jesus's time the celebration of the Passover had been expanded to include a wide range of ceremonies and, in brief, took place as follows. At the approach of the feast, thousands upon thousands of Israelites traveled to Jerusalem, there they purchased lambs, and had them slaughtered in the temple court by the Levites the afternoon of the fourteenth of Nisan. In this context the priests stood ready to catch the blood in silver and gold basins, which they passed on from one to another and finally, in a single act, poured out over the altar. In the meantime, while the Levites sang the Hallel, the priests strung up the animals, removed their intestines, and brought them in a vessel to the altar. Then those who had brought the lamb to be slaughtered, who usually numbered somewhere between ten and twenty men, took the slaughtered lamb with them to a private dwelling and roasted it there without being permitted to break a single bone. The meal itself began with a cup of wine circulating around the room and with thanksgiving. Then the bitter herbs and a bowl of puree were brought to the table and eaten, whereupon the lamb was put with the unleavened cakes. Before it was eaten, however, the father, or later the official reader, related the story of the Exodus, the celebrants sang the first part (Pss. 113–14) of the Hallel (Pss. 113–18), and the second cup was passed around. At that point the actual meal began. When it was finished, the third cup was blessed by the father and emptied by him and all the participants. The whole event was then concluded with the pouring of the fourth cup, the singing of the second part of the Hallel (Pss. 115–18), the blessing of the fourth cup by the father with the words of Ps. 118:26, and the cup's emptying by the guests sitting around the table. These four cups were required for this meal, but sometimes a fifth went around while the celebrants sang Psalms 120–37.[5]

Jesus probably instituted the Supper after the Passover lamb had been eaten— "after the supper" (Luke 22:20)—in connection with the third cup, the cup of thanksgiving. He took the ordinary bread and the ordinary wine used at the Passover and, according to the witness of all four reports (Matt. 26:26–29; Mark 14:22–25; Luke 22:19–20; 1 Cor. 11:23–25), related them directly to his death. There is not a single reason for doubting this. Jesus knew of and anticipated his death and had already repeatedly explained its meaning to his disciples. He specifically construes his death as a sacrifice here: that way alone can we explain the words and actions that accompany the institution of the Supper. Just moments before, the Passover meal had been consumed, and that Passover had been the start and foundation of the covenant that God had established with Israel in the wilderness. For since the lamb had been slaughtered and its blood shed and sprinkled on the altar, the rite of Passover first served as an offering of atonement and was then used as a sacrificial meal to signify God's communion with his people. All this Christ transfers to himself. He is the true Passover lamb, who by his death, by the breaking of his body and the shedding of his blood, effects atonement with God and lays the foundation for a new covenant. Jesus clearly points this out by instituting the Supper on the occasion of the Passover; by administering the bread and wine of the Passover meal to that end; by taking the bread, blessing it, and also (according to all four reports; cf. Acts 2:42) by breaking it; and especially by the words he spoke in this connection. While breaking and distributing the bread, he said: "This is my body" (Matthew and Mark), "This is my body given for you" (Luke), or "This is my body which is for you" (Paul). ("Broken" [κλωμενον, *klōmenon*] is lacking in the most important manuscripts [of 1 Cor. 11:24] and alternates in others with "broken in pieces" [θρυπτομενον, *thryptomenon*] and "given" [διδομενον, *didomenon*].) And when he offered the

5. C. F. Keil, *Manual of Biblical Archaeology*, trans. P. Christie and A. Cusin, 2 vols. (Edinburgh: T&T Clark, 1887–88), §81; H. A. W. Meyer et al., *Critical and Exegetical Hand-Book to the New Testament*, 9 vols. (New York: Funk & Wagnalls, 1884), on Matt. 26:26; C. Orelli, "Passah," in *PRE*[3], XIV, 756.

cup, he said; "Drink from it, all of you. This is my blood of the covenant, which is poured out for many for the forgiveness of sins" (Matthew); "This is my blood of the covenant, which is poured out for many" (Mark); "This cup is the new covenant in my blood, which is poured out for you" (Luke); "This cup is the new covenant in my blood" (Paul).

The variant readings sufficiently demonstrate that Jesus no more prescribed a fixed unchangeable formula at the Supper than he did in connection with baptism. It is even impossible to determine the literal words employed by Jesus on this occasion. He did not define exactly what had to be said at the Supper, but he described what it was and had to be. And this is perfectly clear from the four reports. Jesus made the bread and wine of the Passover meal into signs of his body and blood, and indeed of the body and blood as they would before long be given up in death as a sacrifice of atonement. The objection that Jesus's body was not broken into pieces on the cross as the bread is, and that his blood was not shed there the way wine is poured out at the Supper, and that therefore these images do not fit—all this is of little weight. For Jesus proceeds here from the Passover meal and the Old Testament sacrifices, adopts the action and terminology customary in that connection, and applies them to his death. For that reason Luke and Paul add to the words "This is my body" the explanation "given for you" or just "for you." Whether or not Jesus literally used those words, that is the sense in which he meant them when he designated the bread as a sign of his body. It is a sign of the body of Jesus as it was offered up in death for the atonement of sins. This also explains why the meaning of the second sign is described so much more broadly in all four reports. In a sacrifice the shedding of blood is the main component (Heb. 9:22). The blood of Christ, of which the wine is the sign, is sacrificial blood, the blood of atonement that has been shed for many and is therefore the beginning and initiation of a new covenant. Just as Passover and the old covenant are connected, so also the Supper and the new covenant belong together. The cup, therefore, is "my blood of the covenant" or "the new covenant in my blood," that is, covenant blood (Exod. 24:8), which as sacrificial blood is necessary and serviceable for the fulfillment of the covenant with God; or the covenant itself that comes into being because this blood effects and carries with it the forgiveness of sins and is grounded in that reality. The disciples were sad, dreaded the death of Christ, and did not understand him. But here, at the institution of the Supper, Jesus explains to them that his death is to their advantage. It is by that death that the very forgiveness and the very covenant come about that were foreshadowed and foretold in the Old Testament. The time of promise is past; the time of fulfillment is dawning. The old is over; behold, all things are new.

But Jesus does not stop here. He not only offered an explanation of his death in the signs of bread and wine but also gave them to his disciples to be eaten and drunk. According to Matthew Jesus expressly used the words "Take, eat" and "Drink from it, all of you," and though Mark only reports the word "Take" and Luke and Paul do not mention any of these words at all, yet on the basis of all these statements it is certain that Jesus did not just change bread and wine into signs of his body and blood, but as such he also handed them to his disciples for their consumption. After the Passover meal had been eaten, Jesus instituted a new meal whose components were bread and wine, not of and by themselves, but as signs of his broken body and shed blood. It has been advanced against this by Spitta that the eating of Jesus's dead body and the drinking of his blood constitute "a thought as gruesome as it was intolerable to the Israelite mind." And people have therefore thought that, even if Jesus described bread and wine as signs of his body and blood, he nevertheless did not give them as such to his disciples for their consumption; that he only explained what before long would happen with him, not what his disciples would receive, eat, and drink; that eating Jesus's body and drinking his blood at that moment when Jesus himself sat at the table was an impossibility; that if this eating and drinking was the actual character of the Supper, that Supper had a different character later, after Jesus's death, than at the time of the institution; that the eating of bread and the drinking of wine matter so little as signs that up until the middle of the second century, at least in the churches of Rome and Ephesus, the Supper was celebrated with water, not with wine.

In these objections there is, of course, an element of truth. Even though the Passover in the Old Testament pointed toward Christ, the eating of the Passover lamb was not the same as eating Christ's broken body, as the eating of the bread in the Supper is now. And though in the sacrifices of the old covenant the blood was shed and sprinkled, it was never drunk. The idea that Jesus's flesh had to be eaten and his blood drunk, accordingly, was so alien to the Jews that they were offended by it and left Jesus (John 6:52, 60, 66). Although the institution of the Supper indeed occurred in connection with Old Testament ideas of sacrifice, it nevertheless far surpasses them. The Lord's Supper is akin to but not identical with Passover. As the new covenant is related to the old, as the sacrifice of Christ is related to that of the Old Testament, so the Lord's Supper is related to Passover. The Passover was a sacrament grounded in a sacrifice, but in both parts an adumbration and prophecy of the good things of the New Testament. Now, inasmuch as Christ has offered the true and complete sacrifice, the communion with God in the Lord's Supper, which is based on that sacrifice, is much richer and fuller than it could be in the days of the Old Testament. The Lord's Supper is a meal, the essential meal of God and his people; it is a sacrificial meal par excellence at which believers receive Christ himself as he gave his life for them. Jesus expresses this reality by the action of giving his disciples bread and wine as signs of his broken body and shed blood for them to "enjoy."[6] He not only gave himself *for* his own; he also gives himself *to* his own. The cup and the bread in the Lord's Supper is "a participation in the blood and in the body of Christ" (1 Cor. 10:16).

The objections mentioned above further carry weight in that they clearly show that a "Capernaitic" eating and drinking of the body of Christ [cf. John 6:51–59]

6. Ed. note: Here and below, "enjoy" is the translation of Bavinck's Dutch word *geniet, genieten.*

is definitely ruled out.[7] The Lord's Supper, which Christ himself instituted at the Passover table, is the same meal as that which since his death has been celebrated in the Christian church up until the present. Bread and wine do not relate to the person of Christ in general but specifically to Christ as crucified. In it he depicts his sacrifice before our eyes but also has us enjoy it. And that enjoyment is definitely what the Lord's Supper is about. Jesus *gave* us the signs of bread and wine. He did not keep them in his hands but distributed them and told his disciples to take and eat them, adding according to Luke (only with the distribution of the bread) and Paul (also in passing the cup) the words: "Do this in remembrance of me." The fact that these words are lacking in Matthew and Mark by no means proves that either they were not spoken by Jesus or were added by Luke and Paul against his wishes. For implied in the eating of the bread and the drinking of the wine as signs of Jesus's broken body and shed blood is doing these things "in remembrance of him." The former [eating and drinking] cannot be separated from the latter [remembering Christ]. These words, moreover, do not mean that the Lord's Supper is only a memorial meal but indicate that the entire Supper, which is in essence a sacrificial meal and an exercise of communion with Christ, must be done in remembrance of him. They do not describe the essence of the Lord's Supper but presuppose that before long Jesus will no longer be present among them and prescribe that the Supper must nevertheless be celebrated in remembrance of him as a continual proclamation of his death (1 Cor. 11:26). For that reason we find in Paul the additional words: "as often as you eat this bread and drink this cup" (1 Cor. 11:25–26).

Christ instituted the Supper as a permanent "good" for his church. It is a benefit added to all the other benefits to signify and seal the latter. And it will endure until the time of Christ's return. His death must be proclaimed until he comes. For in this dispensation the cross is and remains the source and cause of all blessings, the center of the church's remembrance. Jesus himself said that from then on, from the time of the institution and observance of the Supper, he would never again drink of the fruit of the vine until he would drink it anew with his disciples in his Father's kingdom (Matt. 26:29; Mark 14:25; cf. Luke 22:16, 18). He, we know, was going to heaven to prepare a place for his disciples. And only when he returns and has taken his disciples to himself will he sit down with them at the wedding supper of the Lamb and drink with them the new wine that his Father's kingdom will yield in the new heaven and on the new earth. For that intermediate period Christ instituted the Supper as an act of remembering his suffering, as a proclamation of his death, as a means of his abundant grace.[8]

7. Ed. note: The term "Capernaitic" derives from Capernaum. In John 6, those in the synagogue at Capernaum heard Jesus identify himself as the Bread of Life but thought only in terms of physical eating.

8. Ed. note: Bavinck cites here the literature at the head of §59, "Het Avondmaal," in the Dutch edition. Also see H. P. Rogaar, *Het Avondmaal en zijne oorspsrongelijke beteekenis* (Groningen: J. B. Huber, 1897); F. Schultzen, *Das Abendmahl im neuen Testament* (Göttingen: Vandenhoeck & Ruprecht, 1895); H. Josephson, *Das heiligen Abendmahl und das Neue Testament* (Gütersloh: Bertelsmann, 1895); Richard Adolf Hoffmann, *Die*

THE LORD'S SUPPER IN CHURCH HISTORY

[541] From the beginning the Lord's Supper occupied an important place in Christian worship. It was usually celebrated in a special gathering of the church in the evening of the Lord's day in combination with a regular meal. Little is known to us of the way it was celebrated. From the *Didache*,[9] we know only that the Supper opened with a confession of sins, and then a prayer of thanksgiving was pronounced separately over the cup and the bread. Next, the meal was held and the entire rite was concluded by a prayer of thanksgiving. In the second century, however, there gradually occurred throughout the church a separation between the love feasts (ἀγάπαι, *agapai*) and the eucharistic meal (εὐχαριστία, *eucharistia*). The former followed their own development and soon degenerated.[10] The latter was shifted to the morning service and linked with the administration of the Word. Several other changes accompanied this shift as well. The one worship service was soon split into two parts: the first, the administration of the Word, was also open to catechumens, penitents, and unbelievers: the second, the celebration of the Lord's Supper, was open only to those who had been baptized. The latter increasingly acquired a mysterious character. Both baptism and the Lord's Supper became a mystery (μυστήριον, *mystērion*), a sacrament,[11] and was thereby, as well as by various ceremonies, wrapped in secrecy and darkness. It is totally erroneous, therefore, to interpret the views of those early times in light of the opinions held later in the West and especially in the sixteenth century about the "sacramental union." Scripture says that the bread is the body of Christ, and the wine is the blood of Christ, terms that were taken over and understood and interpreted by everyone in one's own way. An official interpretation was nonexistent. No controversy sprang up over them, and the question concerning the nature of the union between the sign and the thing signified did not arise. A realistic idea of consubstantiation or transubstantiation was as far removed from the consciousness of that time as an exclusively symbolic or figurative meaning of the Lord's Supper. The symbol and the thing symbolized were much more intimately bound up with each other in the Eastern mind than in the Western. As Harnack rightly remarks, we understand by a symbol something that is not what it symbolizes, but at that time people tended to regard a symbol much more as something that in some sense is also what it symbolizes. From the beginning, in the Christian

---

Abendmahlsgedanken Jesu Christi (Königsberg: Thomas & Oppermann, 1896); O. Holtzheuer, *Das Abendmahl und die neuere Kritik* (Berlin: Wiegandi & Grieben, 1896); R. Schaefer, *Das Herrenmahl nach Ursprung und Bedeutung mit Rücksicht auf die neuesten Forschungen* (Gütersloh: Bertelsmann, 1897).

9. *Didache* 9–10, 14.

10. T. Zahn, "Agapen," in *PRE*[3], I, 234–37; J. F. Keating, *The Agapé and the Eucharist* (London: Methuen, 1901); E. Baumgartner, *Eucharistie und Agape im Urchristentum* (Solothurn: Buch und Kunstdruckerei Union, 1909); Baumgartner attempts to prove that the agape feasts in the primitive Christian church were definitely not connected with the Eucharist. This view has been correctly disputed in *Stimmen aus Maria Laach* 79 (1910): 323.

11. Tertullian, *Against Marcion* 4, 34.

church, it was established truth that the bread and wine were the body and blood of Christ, but the manner in which the union of the two was conceived is not clear and therefore open to various interpretations. This is true of Ignatius, Justin, Irenaeus, and many other writers.[12]

Sacrifice

The development of the doctrine of the Lord's Supper, however, was especially misdirected by the application of the idea of sacrifice. In the New Testament, to be sure, the sanctification of the body (Rom. 12:1), prayer (Heb. 13:15; cf. Rev. 5:8; 8:3), and doing good and sharing one's possessions (Phil. 4:18; Heb. 13:16) are called "sacrifices," but never the Lord's Supper. Now in that early period the Lord's Supper was connected with an ordinary meal.[13] For that meal it was the more affluent members who brought with them the necessary ingredients—bread, wine, oil, milk, honey, and so forth—which were probably received by the deacons, deposited on the main table as well as side tables (later the side altars) for the bishop, then served up at the meal and thereupon designated for the maintenance of the ministers and the support of the poor. These gifts were called "offerings" (oblations, sacrifices) and were blessed by the bishop with a prayer of thanksgiving. This view was then applied to the entire Supper. Named after the prayer of thanksgiving, soon even the Lord's Supper itself as well as the two elements were called "thanksgiving" (εὐχαριστια), and the Supper was before long also viewed as an offering brought to God by the congregation as a "pure sacrifice," as the *Didache*, appealing to Mal. 1:11, already calls it.[14] Now all this was rather innocent as long as the Lord's Supper was really regarded as a meal and a thanksgiving prayer was offered on behalf of the entire congregation. The content of the sacrifice was not the body and blood of Christ, but the gifts assembled by the congregation, so that in that early period people thought in this connection only of a thank offering and in no way of an expiatory offering.

Concealed in this idea of sacrifice, however, was a dangerous element that in due time would function adversely, especially when it was reinforced by the clerical interpretation of office. Clement already compared the *episcopi* and *diaconi* to the priests and Levites of the Old Testament, he describes their activity as "bringing forward the gifts of the *episcopus*," and links their thanksgiving with the sacrifices of the Old Testament.[15] And when the Lord's Supper and the love feasts, the presentation of bread and wine for the Lord's Supper, and the contributions

---

12. Cf. F. A. Loofs, "Abendmahl, Kirchenlehre," in *PRE³*, I, 38–44.

13. *Didache* 9–10; Ignatius, *To the Philadelphians* 4; idem, *To the Smyrnaeans* 7–8; Justin Martyr, *First Apology* 66.

14. *Didache* 14.3; cf. F. A. Loofs, "Abendmahl, Kirchenlehre," in *PRE³*, I, 44; P. Drews, "Eucharistie," in *PRE³*, V, 560ff.; F. Wieland in *Der vorirenaische Opferbegriff* (Munich: Lentner, 1909) acknowledges that the older understanding of sacrifice is directed toward thanksgiving but that modernist biases led to rethinking the relation.

15. *1 Clement* 40–44.

for the maintenance of the ministers and the support of the needy—when these went their separate ways, the Lord's Supper increasingly acquired the character of a sacrifice offered not by the congregation but by the bishop, consisting not in its presentation by the congregation but in its character of thanksgiving and consecration by the bishop, and relating not to the gifts for but to the elements of the Lord's Supper.[16] This view of the Lord's Supper as a sacrifice in turn influenced the idea people had of the sacramental union and vice versa. To the extent that the bishop was viewed as a priest, the thanksgiving as a consecration, and the Lord's Supper as a sacrifice, the realistic union of bread and wine with the body and blood of Christ also had to become more appealing. The symbolic and spiritualistic view of Origen, which is essentially found also in the thought of Eusebius of Caesarea, Basil, and Gregory of Nazianzus (et al.), made way, in close connection with Eastern Christology, in Cyril, Gregory of Nyssa, Chrysostom, and John of Damascus, for the realistic doctrine of transformation (μεταποιησις, *metapoiēsis*), which later passed over into the doctrine of transubstantiation (μετουσιωσις, *metousiōsis*).[17]

Augustine

The development in the West, though it unfolded much more slowly, later led to the same result. While Cyprian strongly highlighted the sacrificial character of the Lord's Supper, he merely saw in it an imitation of what Christ had in reality accomplished on Golgotha. And although Augustine, in using biblical terms, calls the bread "the body of Christ" and the wine "the blood of Christ," nothing of the future transubstantiation theory can yet be found with him.[18] On the contrary, Augustine emphatically distinguished between the "word" and the "element" ("add the word to the element and it becomes a sacrament"); bread and wine are called sacraments "because in them one thing is seen, another is understood." The sign is frequently called by the name of the thing signified, but this is because it bears some resemblance to it. "If the sacred rites had no resemblance to the things they represent, they would not be sacred rites; they generally take their names from the mysteries they represent. As, then, in a certain manner the sacrament of the Body of Christ is the Body of Christ, and the sacrament of the Blood of Christ is the Blood of Christ, so the sacrament of faith is faith."[19] Bread and wine, according to Augustine, are similitudes, signs, reminders of the body and blood of Christ. "The Lord did not hesitate to say: 'This is my body.' With the sign he

---

16. Justin Martyr, *Dialogue with Trypho* 41, 70; Irenaeus, *Against Heresies* IV, 18, 5.

17. John of Damascus, *Exposition of the Orthodox Faith* IV, 14; Orthodox Confession, qu. 107; The Confession of Dositheus, decr. 17; cf. G. E. Steitz, "Die Abendmahlslehre der gr. Kirche in ihrer geschichtlichen Entwicklung," *Jahrbücher für deutsche Theologie* 9 (1864): 409–81; 10 (1865): 64–152, 399–463; 11 (1866): 193–252; 12 (1867): 211–86; 13 (1868): 2–67, 649–700; F. Kattenbusch, *Lehrbuch der vergleichenden Confessionskunde* (Freiburg i.B.: J. C. B. Mohr [Paul Siebeck], 1892), I, 410ff.; F. A. Loofs, "Abendmahl, Kirchenlehre," in *PRE*³, I, 44–57.

18. Cyprian, *Epistles* 63.2, 14.

19. Augustine, *Epistle* 98.9 (to Boniface).

gives of his body."[20] Christ is no longer physically with us but has ascended to heaven. "We always have Christ in respect to the presence of his majesty, but in regard to the presence of his flesh he directly told his disciples: 'You will not always have me.'"[21]

So when Augustine frequently calls the Lord's Supper a sacrifice, he does not mean by this that Christ is again offered up in reality, be it in an unbloody manner, but that it is a memorial of Christ's sacrifice on the cross. "Before Christ's coming the flesh and blood of his sacrifice was promised under the likeness of sacrificial animals; it was rendered in very truth in Christ's passion; after Christ's ascension it is celebrated through the sacrament of remembrance."[22] "Christ offered himself as the supreme sacrifice for our sins and commanded that the resemblance of his sacrifice be celebrated in the remembrance of his passion."[23] At other times he identified the body of Christ that is being offered up in the Lord's Supper as the church. How, you ask, is bread the body of Christ? And he answers, "If you wish to understand the body of Christ, listen to the apostle speaking to the faithful, 'You are the body and members of Christ.' If, then, you are the body and members of Christ, your mystery has been put on the table, and you receive the mystery of God." And the bread is the sign of that mystery "because the bread has not been made from one grain but from many."[24] Augustine, accordingly, never tires of assuring us that the use of the Lord's Supper is not sufficient by itself; that it is only a blessing for believers, but for others it is to their ruin; that truly eating of Christ's body consists in believing: Believe and eat![25]

Transubstantiation

For a long time Augustine's teaching by its powerful influence held back the full development of the realistic theory and was still dominant under the Carolingian theologians. In Ratramnus's opposition to Paschasius Radbertus and later in Berengarius's opposition to Lanfranc, Augustine's views were increasingly suppressed and finally completely replaced by the metabolic theory.[26] The word "transubstantiation" occurred for the first time in the twelfth century,[27] but the

---

20. Augustine, *Against Adimantus*, ch. 12.

21. Augustine, *Homilies on the Gospel of John*, tract. 1.

22. Augustine, *Against Faustus the Manichee* 20–21.

23. Augustine, *Eighty-three Questions*, qu. 61; Augustine, *On Christian Doctrine* III, 16.

24. Augustine, *Sermon ad infantes*; idem, *City of God* X, 6; XX, 10.

25. Augustine, *Homilies on the Gospel of John*, tract. 25; *Bibl. studii theol.* (Geneva: J. Crispinum, 1565), 89–100; A. J. Dorner, *Augustinus* (Berlin: W. Hertz, 1873), 263–76; F. A. Loofs, "Abendmahl, Kirchenlehre," in *PRE³*, I, 61ff.; O. Blank, *Die Lehre des hl. Augustin vom Sakramente der Eucharistie* (Paderborn: Schöningh, 1906).

26. F. A. Loofs, *Leitfaden zum Studium der Dogmengeschichte*, 4th ed. (Halle a.S.: M. Niemeyer, 1906), §58; F. Pijper, *Middeleeuwsch Christendom*, 2 vols. ('s Gravenhage: M. Nijhoff, 1907–11), on pp. 1–25 especially discusses the doctrine of transubstantiation in Ratramnus, Berengarius, etc.

27. For a long time it was believed that the word [transubstantiation] was first used by Hildebert of Tours [1056–1133], but that has proved to be incorrect. Ed. note: Hildebert of Tours is also known as Hildebert of

thing expressed by it had already been established earlier. In 1079 Berengarius had to sign the formula that "the bread and wine are substantially converted by the mystery of sacred prayer and the words of our Redeemer into the true and proper, life-giving flesh and blood of our Lord Jesus. . . ." And the Fourth Lateran Council (1215) decreed that the body and blood of Christ "are truly contained in the sacrament of the altar under the appearance of bread and wine, the bread being transubstantiated into the body and the wine into blood by divine power."[28] This dogma confronted the dialectical spirit of Scholasticism with a series of problems about the nature, time, and duration of the change; about the relationship between the substance and the accidents; about the manner in which Christ is present in both elements and in every part of them; about the [p]reservation[29] and adoration of the host,[30] and so forth.

In the Roman Catholic Church and theology it was then conceptualized as follows. The signs in this sacrament are unleavened bread and wine mixed with a little water. These elements are changed by the word of consecration into Christ's very own body and blood. For when the Savior at the Last Supper spoke the words "This is my body, this is my blood," he did not just change bread and wine into his body and blood on that occasion alone, but in pronouncing these words simultaneously appointed his disciples as priests and injected into the words he spoke a power to change the substance of bread and wine. The administration of the Eucharist, therefore, is above all priestly work and may never be performed by anyone other than an ordained priest. When the priest pronounces the words of consecration, the substance of bread and wine changes into the substance of the body and blood of Christ. Certainly, the physical presence of Christ in the Eucharist cannot be effected by Christ's leaving heaven and indwelling in the sacrament, for Christ is and remains seated at the right hand of the Father, nor can it be effected by an act of creation, for then the bread would not be the true body of Christ, not the body with which he was born from Mary and died on the cross. Accordingly, this can take place only if the substance of bread and wine becomes the substance of Christ's body and blood, more or less in the way the

Lavardin. F. A. Loofs, *Leitfaden zum Studium der Dogmengeschichte*, 504; F. Kattenbusch, "Transsubstantiation," in *PRE*[3], XX, 56ff.

28. H. Denzinger, ed., *The Sources of Catholic Dogma*, trans. from the 30th ed. by R. J. Deferrari (London and St. Louis: Herder, 1955), 298, 357.

29. Ed. note: The ordinary word used to describe the Roman Catholic practice of perpetually keeping the host in a "tabernacle" is "reservation"; see A. A. King, *Eucharistic Reservation in the Western Church* (London: A. R. Mowbray, 1965). Bavinck uses the Dutch word *bewaring*, which signifies preservation and keeping. To capture this nuance we have chosen to use the term "[p]reservation" whenever Bavinck refers to this practice.

30. Lombard, T. Aquinas, Bonaventure, Duns Scotus, *Sent.*, IV, dist. 8–13; T. Aquinas, *Summa theol.*, III, qu. 73–83; idem, *Summa contra gentiles*, trans. the English Dominican Fathers (London: Burns, Oates & Washbourne, 1924), IV, 61–69; Bonaventure, *Breviloquium*, VI, 9; cf. J. Schwane, *Dogmengeschichte*, 4 vols. (Freiburg i.B.: Herder, 1882–95), 628–61; A. von Harnack, *History of Dogma*, trans. N. Buchanan et al., ed. A. B. Bruce, 7 vols. (London: Williams & Norgate, 1896–99), VI, 232–42; F. A. Loofs, *Leitfaden zum Studium der Dogmengeschichte*, 578ff.

food we eat is metabolized into a constituent of our body. The accidents of bread and wine, that is, the form, taste, smell, color, and even the nutritive power, while they remain after the consecration, no longer inhere in a subject. The substance of which they are the properties has been removed and replaced by a totally different substance of which they are not the properties, but which they only conceal from the eye by their appearance. Now, since Christ's body and blood cannot be separated from his human nature and his human nature cannot be separated from his deity, the whole Christ is fully present in each element and in every part of both elements. Therefore, though it is neither necessary nor prohibited, it is sometimes permissible to celebrate the Eucharist under one form, since in that one little piece of bread the whole Christ is present. And this Christ is present in the elements from the moment of consecration to the time they are consumed, hence also "before and apart from every use."

The Eucharist, accordingly, is distinct from all the other sacraments. For these others are all realized by their "use." Baptism, for example, is a sacrament only when a person is really cleansed by it. But this is not true in the case of the Eucharist. The formula uttered on this occasion is directed not to the recipient but to the element and serves to change this element into the body and blood of Christ. In the case of the Eucharist, therefore, its use—participation in it—is secondary; it belongs to the perfection, not to the necessity, of the sacrament. The sacrament of the Eucharist essentially consists in the consecration itself, in the transubstantiation effected by it, in the action of the priest, that is, in the sacrifice. In the thought of Rome the Eucharist is not only a sacrament; it is also primarily a sacrifice. When Christ spoke the words "This is my body," he at that very moment offered himself up to God. And when he said, "Do this in remembrance of me," he by that token ordained that his priests would repeat that sacrifice daily (Mal. 1:11). The sacrifice that the priest effects in the Mass is the same as that accomplished on the cross. It is not just an image, symbol, or reminder of it; it is completely identical with it. It is entirely the same sacrifice, the only difference being that the one on the cross was a bloody sacrifice, and the one that occurs in the Mass is unbloody. It is the same priest after all who sacrificed himself on the cross and who sacrifices himself here, for it is Christ himself who, through the priest, offers himself up to God and therefore through the priest's mouth speaks the words "This is *my* body." The sacrifice of the Mass therefore is not only an offering of praise and thanksgiving, but also a sacrifice of atonement, no less rich in its operation and fruit than the sacrifice on the cross. While the Eucharist as *sacrament* nourishes the spiritual life of people, preserves them from mortal sins, releases them from temporal punishments, unites believers, and guarantees future glory, as *sacrifice of the Mass* it effects the release from temporal punishments and the grace of penitence, not only for those who attend the Mass but also for those who are absent; not only for the living but also for the penitents in purgatory. The Mass is the center of Roman Catholic worship, the awe-inspiring mystery, the *mysterium tremendum*. And because the whole Christ is physically present in the elements of bread and wine, they must be carefully preserved, held out in a monstrance (receptacle) for the people to worship, to be carried around in solemn procession on the feast of Corpus Christi; and they can also be served to the sick in their homes and given to the dying as a *viaticum* [lit. "traveling provision"].[31]

THE REFORMATION DEBATES

[542] The Reformation unanimously rejected the Roman Catholic doctrines of transubstantiation and the sacrifice of the Mass, of the [p]reservation, adoration, and carrying about of the host, of refraining from the use of the cup, and of the use of Latin in worship, but in its concrete understanding of the Lord's Supper, it soon split apart.

Luther initially taught that bread and wine are signs and pledges of the forgiveness of sins secured by Christ's death and received by faith. But he soon reversed himself and maintained—especially from 1524 onward against Carlstadt and Zwingli, on the basis of a synecdochic interpretation of the words of institution—that the body of Christ, in keeping with the will and omnipotence of God and its own ubiquity, is realistically and substantially present in, with, and under the [elements of the] Lord's Supper. He saw this as being analogous to the presence of Christ's divine nature in his human nature and as heat is or can be present in iron. This opened up the possibility that Christ's body could be physically eaten also by those unworthy of it, albeit to their own destruction.[32] This doctrine passed into the Lutheran confessions[33] and was further elaborated

31. Council of Trent, sess. XIII, XXI–XXII; Roman Catechism, II, ch. 4 (ed. note: The post–Vatican II edition entitled *The Roman Catechism* [trans. Robert I. Bradley, SJ, and Eugene Kevane (Boston: Daughters of St. Paul, 1985)] drops the enumeration of the introduction so that ch. 1 begins the section on baptism. In this annotation, the proper reference would be II, ch. 3). R. Bellarmine, "De sacr. eucharistiae," in *Controversiis*, I, IV; idem, "De sacrificio missae," in *Controversiis* 1, II, 150–376; G. Perrone, *Praelectiones theologicae*, 9 vols. (Louvain: Vanlinthout & Vandezande, 1838–43), VI, 136–364; J. A. Möhler, *Symbolik* (Regensburg: G. J. Manz, 1871), §34; G. M. Jansen, *Praelectiones theologiae dogmaticae*, 3 vols. in 2 (Utrecht: Van Rossum, 1875–79), III, 408–596; J. H. Oswald, *Die dogmatische Lehre von den heiligen Sakramenten der katholischen Kirche*, 2nd ed., 2 vols. (Münster: Aschendorff, 1864), I, 301–584; C. Pesch, *Praelectiones dogmaticae*, 9 vols. (Freiburg: Herder, 1902–10), VI, 238–399.

32. J. Köstlin, *The Theology of Luther in Its Historical Development and Inner Harmony*, trans. Charles E. Hay, 2 vols. (Philadelphia: Lutheran Publication Society, 1897), I, 226ff., 390ff.; II, 344ff.; ed. note: Bavinck also refers here to pages 511ff. in the second volume of the German edition; we are unable to determine the passage to which Bavinck is referring. F. A. Loofs, *Leitfaden zum Studium der Dogmengeschichte*, 807ff.; F. Graebke, *Die Konstruktion der Abendmahlslehre Luthers in ihrer Entwicklung dargestellt* (Leipzig: Deichert, 1908; ed. note: Bavinck cites 1907 edition).

33. Joseph T. Müller, *Die symbolischen Bücher der evangelisch-lutherischen Kirche*, 8th ed. (Gütersloh: Bertelsmann, 1898), 41, 164, 248, 320, 365, 499, 538, 645, 779; ed. note: These specific references are to the following Lutheran documents: Augsburg Confession, art. 10, in *The Book of Concord*, ed. Robert Kolb and Timothy J. Wengert (Minneapolis: Fortress, 2000), 45; Apology of the Augsburg Confession, art. 10 (Kolb and Wengert, 184–85); ibid., art. 24, par. 1 (Kolb and Wengert, 258); Smalcald Articles, part III, art. 6 (Kolb and Wengert, 320–21); The Small Catechism, "The Sacrament of the Altar" (Kolb and Wengert, 362–63); The Large Catechism, part V, "The Sacrament of the Altar" (Kolb and Wengert, 467ff.); Formula of Concord,

by the dogmaticians.[34] But already early in the century of the Reformation, many folks held a very different opinion. At the suggestion of Honius,[35] Zwingli interpreted the words of institution figuratively and explained the vocable "is" by the word "means," a recurrent practice also elsewhere in Scripture: Gen. 41:26; John 10:9; 15:1, for example. The bread and wine in the Lord's Supper, therefore, are the signs and reminders of Christ's death, and believers, trusting in that reality, partake of the body and blood of Christ in these signs.

Zwingli definitely rejected the physical presence of Christ in the Lord's Supper, but in so doing he by no means denied that Christ is spiritually present in it to believers. On the contrary, Christ is very definitely received in the Lord's Supper, as John 6 clearly teaches, but Christ is present in the Supper and is received there in no other way than he is present in the Word and by faith, that is, spiritually. This reception of Christ consists in nothing other than in trusting in his death. "To eat the body of Christ spiritually is nothing other than to rest, in one's spirit and mind, in the compassion and goodness of God through Christ." And those who thus partake of Christ through faith and then come to the Lord's Supper also partake of him there sacramentally in the signs of bread and wine. In the Lord's Supper, accordingly, we confess our faith and express what Christ continually means to us by faith and what we enjoy of him. And we do this in remembrance of Christ, to proclaim and give thanks for his benefits.[36]

Between the German and Swiss Reformations it was not long, however, before schism and controversy broke out—a dispute that was settled neither by the Marburg conference on religion nor by the mediating attempts of Bucer on the Reformed side and Melanchthon on the Lutheran side. People just did not understand one another. On both sides they recognized that Christ was truly present in the Supper with both his divine as well as his human nature, with his own body and blood, and was received there, but they construed this "true" presence differently.

When Calvin appeared on the scene, there was no longer any hope of reconciliation, although with his doctrine of the Lord's Supper he took a position between and above the two parties. Calvin was absolutely on Zwingli's side insofar as he firmly rejected any kind of physical, local, and substantial presence of Christ in the signs of bread and wine. Such a presence, after all, is inconsistent with the

---

"Epitome," art. 7 (Kolb and Wengert, 503ff.); ibid., "Solid Declaration," art. 7 (Kolb and Wengert, 591ff.). The Saxon Visitation Articles (1592), art. 1, in P. Schaff, *Creeds of Christendom*, 3 vols. (New York: Harper & Brothers, 1877), III, 181.

34. J. Gerhard, *Loci theologici*, ed. E. Preuss, 9 vols. (Berlin: G. Schlawitz, 1863–75), XXI; J. Quenstedt, *Theologia*, IV, 176–255; D. Hollaz, *Examen theologicum acroamaticum* (Rostock and Leipzig: Russworm, 1718), 1103–41; H. F. F. Schmid, *The Doctrinal Theology of the Evangelical Lutheran Church*, trans. Charles A. Hay and Henry Jacobs, 5th ed. (Philadelphia: United Lutheran Publication House, 1899), §55.

35. J. G. de Hoop Scheffer, *Geschiedenis der kerkhervorming in Nederland van haar ontstaan tot 1531* (Amsterdam: G. L. Funke, 1873), I, 86ff.; O. Clemen, "Honius," in *PRE*[3], VIII, 312.

36. U. Zwingli, *Opera*, ed. Schuler and Schulthess, 8 vols. in 7 (Zurich: Schulthessiana, 1828–42), II, 1, 426; II, 2, 1ff.; III, 239–326, 459; IV, 51, 68; F. A. Loofs, *Leitfaden zum Studium der Dogmengeschichte*, 797ff.

nature of a body, with the true humanity of Christ, with Christ's ascension, with the nature of the communion that exists between Christ and his own, and is vastly different from an unprofitable eating with the mouth (*oralis manducatio*). But for the rest Calvin was not satisfied with Zwingli's interpretation. He had especially two objections against Zwingli's doctrine of the Lord's Supper. One was that Zwingli all too much allows the gift of God in the Lord's Supper to recede behind what believers do in it and hence one-sidedly views the Lord's Supper as an act of confession. And the other was that in the eating of Christ's body, Zwingli sees nothing other and higher than believing in his name, the act of trusting in his death. From that point on, therefore, Calvin put himself on Luther's side and said that Christ is present in the Supper and is received there—not physically and locally, to be sure, but certainly truly and essentially, with his whole person, including his body and blood. Between him and Luther there was disagreement not over the fact but only over the manner of that presence. And the eating of Christ's body in the Supper is not exhausted by believing in him, by relying on his death. Eating is not identical with believing, even though it always only comes about by believing, but is rather the fruit of it, just as in Eph. 3:17 Christ's indwelling in us, though it happens by faith, is nevertheless distinct from that faith. Calvin's concern evidently was the mystical union, the communion of believers with the whole person of Christ. While this communion does not come into being first of all by the Supper, for Christ is the bread of our soul already in the Word, it is nevertheless granted "more distinctly" in the Lord's Supper and sealed and confirmed in the signs of bread and wine. In the Supper there is not only a participation in the benefits but also communion with the person of Christ, and again not only with his divine but also with his human nature, his own body and blood, and this communion is called an "eating." This does not consist, therefore, in a physical descent of Christ from heaven, nor even in a mixture or transfusion of the flesh of Christ with our souls, but in the elevation of our hearts heavenward, in a union with Christ by the Holy Spirit, in communion with his body as a result of which "Christ, from the substance of his flesh, breathes life into our souls—indeed, pours forth his very life into us."[37] Calvin's representation is not clear in every respect, especially not as it concerns communion with the true flesh and blood of Christ and the life that flows from them. Utenhove therefore asked him with some justice to abstain from the use of more or less obscure expressions when he dealt with the Lord's Supper.[38]

So also in the confession and doctrine of Reformed churches and theologians there occasionally were different ways of expressing the truth about the Lord's Sup-

37. J. Calvin, *Institutes*, IV.xvii; idem, "Dilucida Explicatio sanae doctrinae de vera participatione carnis sanguinis Christi in sacra coena" (Geneva, 1561), in *Calvini opera*, IX (CR, XXXVII), 461–524; idem, "Breve et Clarum doctrinae de coena domini compendium" (Geneva), in *Calvini opera*, IX (CR, XXXVII), 681–88; cf. H. Bavinck, "Calvijns leer over het Avondmaal," *De Vrije Kerk* 13 (1887): 459–87; ed note: Also published in *Kennis en leven* (Kampen: Kok, 1922), 165–83.

38. F. Pijper, *Jan Utenhove* (Leiden: H. A. Adriani, 1883), 40.

per. Some, like Bucer, seeking to get closer to Luther's view, said that "substantially," that is, "with respect to its substance," Christ's body was present in the Supper.[39] But Calvin's main idea—that in the Lord's Supper, by the Holy Spirit, believers experience spiritual fellowship with the person of Christ and hence also with the body and blood of Christ and are thereby nourished and refreshed unto eternal life—has been taken over in the various Reformed confessions[40] and become the common property of Reformed theology.[41]

It was not long, however, before opposition to this Calvinistic doctrine of the Lord's Supper asserted itself. The statement in the French Confession of Faith, article 36, that Christ "feeds and nourishes us truly with his flesh and blood" drew considerable criticism in the Swiss churches. In 1572 they turned to the national Synod in France with the request that these words be changed, but this request fell on deaf ears. Consequently the criticism continued to smolder and even increased when [Jacques B.] Bossuet, in his *Exposition de la doctrine de l'église catholique sur les matières de controverse* (1671), drew strength from it for the Roman Catholic doctrine of the Lord's Supper.[42] Little by little the Zwinglian view again gained ground, according to which the eating is nothing other than believing, and fellowship with Christ no more than the acceptance of his benefits.[43]

Relaxation of discipline further contributed to this externalization of the Lord's Supper and prompted people to view the sacraments as being merely signs of an external covenant, to which everyone who lived a decent life was entitled.[44] Thus the door was opened to the rationalism that repeated the ideas of Socinians, Remonstrants, Mennonites, and so forth,[45] and saw in the Lord's Supper nothing

39. C. Vitringa, *Doctrina christiana religionis*, 8 vols. (Leiden: Joannis le Mair, 1761–86), VIII, 265–99; à Lasco must also be considered part of this mediating position, according to K. A. R. Kruske, *Johannes à Lasco und der Sacramentsstreit* (Leipzig: Deichert, 1901). In an earlier period, à Lasco was indeed more under the influence of Zwingli and Bucer, but he increasingly grew closer to Calvin. Kruske's unfavorable judgment of à Lasco is therefore markedly softened by K. Hein, *Die Sakramentslehre des Johannes à Lasco* (Berlin: C. A. Schwetschke & Sohn, 1904); as well as by H. Dalton, *Beiträge zur Geschichte der evangelischen Kirche in Russland*, 4 vols. in 3 (Berlin: Reuther & Reichard, 1887–1905); cf. P. Tschackert, "Daltons *Beiträge zur Geschichte der evangelischen Kirche in Russland*, IV. Band, und die Laski-Kontroverse der neuesten Zeit," *Theologisches Literaturblatt* (18 May 1906): 233–37.

40. Gallican Confession, art. 36; Belgic Confession, art. 35; Heidelberg Catechism, Q 75–80; Scots Confession, art. 21; Second Helvetic Confession, ch. XXI; Westminster Confession, ch. 29.

41. T. Beza, *Tractationum theologicarum* (Geneva: Jean Crispin, 1570), I, 30, 206, 211, 259; II, 121; III, 148; P. Martyr Vermigli, *Loci communes*, ed. R. Massonius (London, 1576), 445; J. Zanchi, *Opera theologicorum*, 8 vols. (Geneva: Samuelis Crispini, 1617), VII, 387; VIII, 517; F. Junius, *Theses theologicae*, disp. 52; Z. Ursinus, *Volumen tractationum theologicarum* (Neustadt: M. Harnisch, 1584), 359; A. Polanus, *Syntagma theologiae christianae*, 5th ed. (Hanover: Aubry, 1624), VI, 56; G. Bucanus, *Inst. theol.*, 649; cf. C. Vitringa, *Doctr. christ.*, VIII, 1, 266; H. Heppe, *Die Dogmatik der evangelisch-reformirten Kirche* (Elberfeld: R. L. Friderichs, 1861), 471.

42. C. Vitringa, *Doctr. christ.*, VIII, 1, 302ff.

43. *Cf. J. F. Ostervald, *Verhandeling van den geopenbaerden godsdienst of ontwerp der Kirstelyke godgeleerdheidt* (Leiden, 1742), 385.

44. Aldus Swarte, van Eerde, Janssonius; cf. A. Ypey and I. J. Dermout, *Geschiedenis der Nederlandsche Hervormde Kerk*, 4 vols. (Breda: W. van Bergen and F. B. Hollingerus Pijpers, 1819–27), III, 512.

45. Cf. C. Vitringa, *Doctr. christ.*, VIII, 2, 1014ff.

more than a memorial meal, an act of confession, and a means of moral education.[46] Through Schleiermacher, who not only rejected the doctrine of Roman Catholics but also that of Socinians and so forth, and recognized the teachings of Luther, Zwingli, and Calvin as all being orthodox, there sprang up a movement to maintain the Lord's Supper as an objective means of grace and to ascribe to it a strengthening of the believer's life-fellowship with Christ. This happened, however, in very different ways. Some, proceeding from the Lord's Supper as a symbolic rite and act of confession, added that believers by their participation in it testified that they accepted Christ as having died for them.[47] Others construed it as an action of the church, one that served by divine arrangement, along ethical and psychological pathways, to strengthen the faith of believers in the forgiveness of sins and their communion with God.[48] Many mediation theologians rejected the Lutheran doctrines of consubstantiation and *manducatio oralis* and approached Calvin's doctrine when they said that Christ was present in the Supper in a spiritual manner, just as he is in the Word, and imparts himself and his benefits (forgiveness, life, spiritual vigor, salvation) to believers.[49] The old Lutheran doctrine was again set forth by Scheibel, Rudelbach, and Philippi,[50] and was augmented by neo-Lutherans with the theosophical idea that Christ not only nourishes the soul by bread and wine, but also directly feeds the body by healing physical illnesses and strengthening the new resurrection being that was secretly implanted at the time of baptism.[51]

In the Church of England, finally, ever since the launching of the Oxford movement, the influence of Roman Catholic doctrine, worship, and ritual so dramatically increased that people frequently voiced the anxious question whether Rome would again capture England.[52] Many members of the High Church party specifically

---

46. J. A. L. Wegscheider, *Institutiones theologiae christianae dogmaticae*, 3rd ed. (Halle: Gebauer, 1819), 178–79.

47. J. I. Doedes, *De leer der zaligheid volgens het Evangelie in de Schriften des Nieuwen Verbonds voorgesteld* (Utrecht: Kemink, 1876), §§144ff.; ibid., p. 502, on the Belgic Confession; ibid., p. 352, on the Heidelberg Catechism.

48. R. A. Lipsius, *Lehrbuch der evangelisch-protestantischen Dogmatik* (Braunschweig: C. A. Schwetschke, 1893), §853; A. E. Biedermann, *Christliche Dogmatik* (Zurich: Orell, Fussli, 1869), §927; O. Pfleiderer, *Grundriss der christlichen Glaubens und Sittenlehre* (Berlin: G. Reimer, 1888), §156.

49. F. A. Kahnis, *Die lutherische Dogmatik, historisch-genetisch dargestellt* (Leipzig: Dörffling & Francke, 1861–68), II, 330; I. A. Dorner, *A System of Christian Doctrine*, trans. A. Cave and J. S. Banks, 4 vols. (Edinburgh: T&T Clark, 1882), IV, 305ff.; Julius Müller, *Dogmatische Abhandlungen* (Bremen: C. E. Müller, 1870), 467.

50. F. A. Philippi, *Kirchliche Glaubenslehre*, 3rd ed., 7 vols. (Gütersloh: Bertelsmann, 1883–1902), V, 2, 260ff.; A. von Oettingen, *Lutherische Dogmatik*, 2 vols. (Munich: C. H. Beck, 1897), II, 2, 445ff.

51. H. Martensen, *Christian Dogmatics*, trans. W. Urwick (Edinburgh: T&T Clark, 1871), §265; G. Thomasius, *Christi Person und Werk*, 3rd ed., 2 vols. (Erlangen: A. Deichert, 1886–88), II, 327, 341; J. C. K. von Hofmann, *Der Schriftbeweis*, 3 vols. (Nördlingen: Beck, 1857–60), II, 2, 220; A. F. C. Vilmar, *Dogmatik*, 2 vols. (Gütersloh: C. Bertelsmann, 1874), II, 245; Rudolf Rocholl, "Spiritualismus und Realismus," *Neue kirchliche Zeitschrift* 9 (1898). Cf. J. Köstlin, *The Theology of Luther*, II, 581ff.; ed. note: Bavinck also refers here to pages 516ff. in the second volume of the German edition; we are unable to determine the passage to which Bavinck is referring.

52. R. F. Horton and J. Hocking, *Shall Rome Reconquer England?* (London: National Council of Evangelical Free Churches, 1910); J. Blötzer, "Der Anglikanismus auf dem Wege nach Rom?" *Stimmen aus Maria Laach* 73 (February–March 1904).

hold that the consecrated elements in the Lord's Supper are truly (be it in a mystical manner) the body and blood of Christ. As a result of the weighty act of consecration, which Christ entrusted to his apostles and their lawful successors (*successio continua*), a "conversion of the whole substance" takes place so that the body of Christ is "really, truly, substantially and locally" present in the elements, however, without the elements themselves being changed. This view of the real presence of Christ in the holy Eucharist then of course leads further to the idea that the Lord's Supper is a commemorative sacrifice for the living and the dead for the forgiveness of sins, that also unbelievers receive the Christ present in the elements, and that this Christ, as present in the elements, may be the object of adoration.[53]

THE LORD'S SUPPER AS MEAL

[543] In Scripture the Lord's Supper is described by the terms "the Lord's supper" (1 Cor. 11:20), "the table of the Lord" (10:21), "the breaking of bread" (Acts 2:42; 20:7), "the cup of the Lord" (1 Cor. 11:27), and "the cup of blessing" (10:16). Later the church added many other terms to the list, such as love feast (ἀγαπη, *agapē*), because in that early period the Lord's Supper was bound up with a love feast; "the thanksgiving" (εὐχαριστια; already in *Didache* 9; Ignatius, *To the Smyrnaeans* 7–8; Justin Martyr, *First Apology* 66), because believers thanked God at the Lord's Supper for the gifts of his grace; "the blessing" (εὐλογια, *eulogia*), because by thanksgiving to God and praising God the blessing was pronounced over the bread and wine; the "coming together" (συναξις, *synaxis*) or "communion" (κοινωνια, *koinōnia*), inasmuch as believers, coming together at the Lord's Supper, exercise communion with each other; the "offerings" ("holy," "spiritual," "mystical"), because the believers brought the ingredients of the meal with them and offered them to God, or because the Supper was an image and reminder of Christ's sacrifice on the cross; and further also "the mystical supper," "food for the journey," "worship," "liturgy," "the awesome mystery," "the sacrament of the body and blood of the Lord," "the sacrament of the altar," the "missa" derived from the dismissal of the catechumens following the didactic part of the worship service, and so forth. Although Luther continued to speak of "the sacrament of the altar,"[54] Protestants in general favored the term "holy Supper" or "the Lord's Supper" and in so doing also held on to the principle that the Supper is a true meal. Some Roman Catholic theologians, for example Maldonatus in his exposition of Matt. 26:26, remarked against this principle that the expression "the Lord's supper" in 1 Cor. 11:20 applies not to the Supper but to the meal that was held after the

---

53. R. I. Wilberforce, *The Doctrine of the Holy Eucharist* (London: Mozley, 1854); E. B. Pusey, *The Doctrine of the Real Presence* (Oxford and London: John Henry Parker, 1855); cf. R. Buddensieg, "Traktarianismus," in *PRE*³, XX, 47ff.; J. C. Ryle, *Knots Untied*, 11th ed. (London: William Hunt, 1886), 205ff.; M. C. Williams, "The Crisis in the Church of England," *Presbyterian and Reformed Review* 10 (July 1899): 389–412.

54. Smalcald Articles, part III, art. 6 (Kolb and Wengert, 320–21); The Large Catechism, part V, "The Sacrament of the Altar" (Kolb and Wengert, 467ff.).

Supper and offered by the more affluent members of the church to the poorer members.[55] However, the Lord's Supper was not celebrated before but after the ordinary meal (11:21) and is therefore in any case included in the term if not the sole referent of it. But even if this were not the case, this would in no way prove the incorrectness of the term. For according to Scripture, the Lord's Supper is in any case a real meal. The linkage with the love feasts (ἀγάπαι, *agapai*), the institution on the occasion of the Passover meal, the constituents of bread and wine, the eating and drinking of the elements—they all point to the fact that we have to do with a true meal and may not deprive the Supper of this character.

But it is a meal of the Lord (δεῖπνον κυριακον, *deipnon kyriakon*). Jesus was the inaugurator of it and in this regard also fulfilled his Father's will, which it was his food to do [John 4:34]. The Lord's Supper, like baptism, is and has to be of divine origin to be a sacrament, for God alone is the distributor of grace, and he alone can bind its distribution to the means ordained by him. Jesus specifically instituted this Supper in his capacity as mediator. In it he acts as prophet, who proclaims and interprets his death; in it he acts as priest, who gave himself up to the cross on behalf of his own; in it he also acts as king, who freely makes available the grace secured and gives it to his disciples to enjoy under the signs of bread and wine. Besides being the inaugurator of the Supper, he is also its host and administrator. He himself takes the bread and wine, blesses them, and distributes them to his disciples. Nor was he only host and administrator when he physically sat at table with his disciples, but he also is and remains the host and administrator of it always and wherever *his* meal is celebrated. Every Supper, administered according to his institution, is a Supper of the Lord (δεῖπνον κυριακον). For Christ is not only its inaugurator as an example but also its inaugurator by precept. It is a meal in remembrance of him (1 Cor. 11:24), to proclaim his death (11:26), as a participation in his body and blood (10:16, 21; 11:27). In the Lord's Supper Christ comes together with his church, and the church comes together with Christ, thereby testifying to their spiritual communion (cf. Rev. 3:20).

The minister who blesses and distributes the bread and wine, accordingly, does this in the name of Christ and is only an instrument in his hand. In 1 Cor. 10:16 Paul speaks in the plural of those who bless the cup, and Tertullian says, "Where there is no hierarchy, you yourself offer sacrifice, you baptize, and you are your own priest. Obviously, where there are three gathered together, even though they are laypersons, there is a church."[56] Some, like Grotius, Salmasius, and Episcopius (et al.), assert that if a priest or regular minister is absent, the Lord's Supper may

---

55. C. Vitringa, *Doctr. christ.*, VIII, 10. Cf. on this point also the views of Jülicher, Spitta, Haupt, and P. Drews, "Eucharistie," in *PRE*³, V, 560–72. Ed. note: Bavinck does not list specific titles here but the likely references are to A. Jülicher, *Paulus und Jesus* (Tübingen: J. C. B. Mohr [Paul Siebeck], 1907); Fr. Spitta, *Die Kelchbewegung in Deutschland und die Reform der Abendmahlsfeier* (Göttingen: Vandenhoeck & Ruprecht, 1904); E. Haupt, *Die eschatologischen Aussagen Jesu in den synoptischen Evangelien* (Berlin: Reuther & Reichard, 1895).

56. Tertullian, *An Exhortation to Chastity* 7.

also be administered by an ordinary member of the church. But this opinion is not well grounded. In Matt. 28:19 the administration of baptism along with that of the Word has been entrusted to the apostles. They, along with the ministers, are the distributors of the mysteries of God, proclaimers of the "secrets" that God has revealed in the gospel of Christ (1 Cor. 4:1), stewards of God whose task is to distribute his grace (9:17; Titus 1:7–9). With reference to these mysteries, one must undoubtedly first of all think of the word of the gospel. But the sacrament follows the Word and is always connected with it. In Jerusalem the apostles devoted themselves to the ministry of prayer and the Word (Acts 6:4). At the breaking of bread (20:7, 11), Paul spoke. Voicing the thanksgiving at the Lord's Supper was a part of the ministry of the Word and therefore assigned to the minister, though like the breaking of bread in 1 Cor. 10:16, it is represented as an act of the congregation.[57] According to the *Didache*, therefore, the giving of thanks (εὐχαριστειν, *eucharistein*) is the proper task of the prophets; according to Ignatius, it is that of the bishop; according to Justin, it belongs to the presiding minister (προεστως, *proestōs*) while in this connection the deacons served and gave the bread and wine to the communicants.[58] This unique linkage of the administration of the Lord's Supper to that of the Word proves that the minister acts in the name of Christ and functions as the steward and distributor of his mysteries. The Lord's Supper is a meal whose host is Christ.

Second, the association of the Lord's Supper with a meal is strongly evidenced by the food and drink distributed and enjoyed in it. The signs of bread and wine in the Lord's Supper have no more been arbitrarily or accidentally chosen than the water in baptism. In the sacrifices of the Old Testament, flesh and blood were of primary importance, since they typologically pointed to the sacrifice of Christ on the cross. Yet the Lord's Supper itself is not a sacrifice, but a memorial of the sacrifice made on the cross, and expresses the communion of believers with that sacrifice. For that reason Christ did not choose flesh and blood but bread and wine as food and drink in the Lord's Supper, to indicate thereby that it is not a sacrifice but a meal—a meal on the basis of, in memory of, and as an exercise of communion with, the crucified Christ. To that end the signs of bread and wine are eminently suited. In the East they were the regular constituents of a meal. Everywhere and at all times even now they are easy to obtain. They are the chief means for strengthening and rejoicing the human heart (Ps. 104:15) and a graphic symbol of the communion of believers with Christ and one another.[59] In this connection it is immaterial whether the bread is made of wheat, rye, or barley and whether the wine is white or red; whether the bread is leavened

57. R. Sohm, *Kirchenrecht*, 2 vols. (Leipzig and Munich: Duncker & Humblot, 1892–1923).

58. *Didache* 10.7; Ignatius, *To the Smyrnaeans* 8; Justin Martyr, *First Apology* 65; cf. J. C. Suicerus, *Thesaurus ecclesiasticus* (Amsterdam: J. H. Wetsten, 1682), s.v. διακονος and συναξις; G. Voetius, *Politicae ecclesiasticae*, 3 vols. (Amsterdam: Joannis a Waesberge, 1663–76), I, 746–51; B. de Moor, *Comm. theol.*, V, 638–41; C. Vitringa, *Doctr. christ.*, VIII, 1, 327ff.

59. C. Vitringa, *Doctr. christ.*, VIII, 1, 43.

(the practice of the Greek Orthodox Church) or unleavened (the practice of the Roman Catholic Church); and whether the wine (in keeping with the doctrine of Armenian Christians) is unmixed, or mixed with water (in accord with the firm pronouncement of Trent).[60] In none of these points has Christ specifically laid down or prescribed anything. The Reformed did not even hesitate to say that in the event bread or wine were definitely lacking, another food and drink, say rice and bread, could be used as sign in the Lord's Supper.[61] This is not to say, however, that any arbitrary departure from the institution of Christ is permissible. Just as in our time, so in the early centuries there were some Christians (Tatians, Severians, Gnostics, Manichees, Aquarii) who, prompted by an ascetic principle, substituted water for wine at the Lord's Supper. But we must not be wiser than Christ, who expressly designated wine as the sign of his blood and whose command in this matter has at all times been followed by the Christian church.[62] For Zahn has sufficiently refuted Harnack's assertion that the custom of using water at the Lord's Supper was quite general in the first and second centuries and still had to be combated in the fifth century, and that even Paul himself, speaking of the cup, did not necessarily think of a cup with wine in it.[63] Similarly ill-advised is the practice by Roman Catholic and Lutheran Christians of serving the bread in the shape of a wafer (*oblie, oblata*, since in ancient times believers themselves offered the necessary ingredients of the Lord's Supper; *host, hostia*, since the bread is a sign of Christ's sacrifice). For, although the quantity of the bread is not defined any more than the quality, yet the character of a meal must be preserved, and this is almost completely lost when a small round wafer is used.[64]

Finally, also the place and the time at which the Supper was instituted and celebrated in ancient times clearly shows that it is a real meal. Jesus, after all, instituted the Supper on an occasion when he along with his disciples reclined at the Passover table. And in that early period the Lord's Supper was celebrated in conjunction with an ordinary meal (Acts 20:7, 11; 1 Cor. 11:21), in the congregation's public assembly (1 Cor. 10:17; 11:18, 20–21, 33), and daily or at least every Lord's Day (Acts 2:46; 20:7). Only gradually was the Lord's Supper detached from the love feasts (ἀγάπαι), shifted from the evening to the morning service, and administered also to the sick and dying in their homes totally outside of and apart from a meeting of the congregation; and the frequency of celebration was set for believers at three times or at least once a year as a minimum.[65] Although some of the Reformed were of the opinion that in very special cases the Lord's

---

60. Council of Trent, sess. XX, can. 7.

61. G. Voetius, *Pol. eccl.*, I, 732, 738; B. de Moor, *Comm. theol.*, V, 575; C. Vitringa, *Doctr. christ.*, VIII, 1, 46.

62. C. Vitringa, *Doctr. christ.*, VII, 1, 71–78.

63. T. Zahn, *Brot und Wein im Abendmahl der alten Kirche* (Erlangen: Deichert, 1892); cf. W. Schmidt, *Christliche Dogmatik*, 4 vols. (Bonn: E. Weber, 1895–98), II, 465.

64. G. Voetius, *Pol. eccl.*, I, 733; C. Vitringa, *Doctr. christ.*, 49.

65. Council of Trent, sess. XIII, can. 9.

Supper might be administered to the sick in their homes, but in any case in the presence of others,[66] they generally maintained that as part of public worship it belonged in the gathering of the congregation and should not be celebrated privately. And although practice proved stronger than theory and the celebration of the Lord's Supper was usually restricted to six or four times a year,[67] originally it was nevertheless Calvin's wish to celebrate it at least once a month.[68] If baptism as incorporation into the Christian church ought to take place in the public gathering of believers, this certainly applies even much more to the Lord's Supper, which is essentially a meal (δεῖπνον, *deipnon*), a coming together (συναξις, *synaxis*), a banquet (*convivium*), and includes not only an exercise of communion with Christ but also such an exercise with one's fellow believers.

TABLE OR ALTAR?

For that reason the determination of the character of the Lord's Supper finally revolves totally around the question whether it must be served around a table or from an altar. Jesus and his disciples sat at a table when they celebrated the Supper,

66. P. Henry, *The Life and Times of John Calvin, The Great Reformer*, 2 vols. (New York: R. Carter & Brothers, 1851–52), II, 210; G. Voetius, *Pol. eccl.*, I, 764.

67. Synod of Dort (1578), art. 73: "Since the Lord's Supper should not be celebrated in the places where no organized church is established, it shall be celebrated in the established churches every two months as much as possible. But the secret churches and those under the Cross shall be free to celebrate [the Lord's Supper] as often as is convenient" (De Ridder, 219).

Church Order of the Synod of Middelburg (1581), art. 45: "The Lord's Supper shall be celebrated, as much as possible, once every two months; however, in whatever place there is as yet no established order, elders and deacons must first be installed" (De Ridder, 280).

Church Order of the Synod of 's Gravenhage (1586), art. 56: "The Lord's Supper shall be administered once every two months, as much as possible, and in an edifying manner. Wherever the circumstances of the churches allow, the same shall be done on Easter, Pentecost and Christmas, but in places where as yet a church has not been established elders and deacons shall be provisionally installed" (De Ridder, 358).

Ed. note: The preceding translations are taken from Richard R. De Ridder, Peter H. Jonker, and Leonard Verduin, eds., *The Church Orders of the Sixteenth Century Reformed Churches of the Netherlands Together with Their Social, Political, and Ecclesiastical Context* (Grand Rapids: Calvin Theological Seminary, 1987). This volume is not in print for sale but copies are available for use at the Hekman Library of Calvin College and Seminary. De Ridder's translation was made primarily from the Dutch text of P. Biesterveld and H. H. Kuyper, *Kerkelijk handboekje* (Kampen: Bos, 1905) and C. Hooijer, *Oude kerkenordeningen der Nederlandsche Hervormde gemeenten, 1563–1638* (Zalt-Bommel: Noman, 1865). Bavinck's subsequent references to the key synodical acts and documents will be given by referencing the specific synod and year, the article, and the location in the De Ridder volume. "Formulier voor de heilige Doop," in *Biblia . . . ende volgens t' besluit van de Synode Nationael, gehouden tot Dordrecht, in de Jaren 1618 ende 1619* (Amsterdam: J. Brandt; Haarlem: Johannes Enschedé, 1870), art. 53; ed. note: ET: "Form for the Administration of Holy Baptism," in *The Psalter with the Doctrinal Standards and Liturgy of the Christian Reformed Church*, 2 vols. in 1 (Grand Rapids: Eerdmans-Sevensma, 1914), II, 57–61.

68. F. W. Kampschulte and W. Goetz, *Johann Calvin: Seine Kirche und sein Staat in Genf.*, 2 vols. (Leipzig: Duncker & Humblot, 1869–99), I, 460; Hermann Dalton, *Johannes à Lasco*, (Gotha: Perthes, 1881; Utrecht: Kemink, 1885), 383; G. Voetius, *Pol. eccl.*, I, 758–67, 801–2; B. de Moor, *Comm. theol.*, V, 660ff., 671ff.; C. Vitringa, *Doctr. christ.*, VIII, 1, 406–14.

and also the early Christians knew nothing of an altar. But gradually the difference between the Old and the New Testament dispensation was lost. The gathering place was changed into a temple, the minister became a priest, the Lord's Supper a sacrifice, and the table an altar. In the Roman Catholic and the Greek Orthodox Churches, worship was completely controlled by this view. The Anglican (Episcopal) Church largely took it over and presently tends increasingly in that direction. The Lutheran Church kept the altar, regarding the matter an adiaphoron [a matter of no spiritual consequence]. But the Reformed restored the scriptural idea of the Lord's meal, also in having a table for the Supper.

The difference between the worship of the Old and that of the New Testament consists, after all, in the fact that temple and altar, priest and sacrifice, are no longer on earth but in heaven. The Jerusalem that is above is the mother of us all (Gal. 4:26). This is where Christ, our eternal high priest, has entered on our behalf (Heb. 6:20), after having by one sacrifice accomplished an external redemption (9:12), to appear before the face of God for us (9:24). There Christians have their sanctuary, into which they enter with boldness through the blood of Jesus (4:16; 10:19; 12:22). Here on earth we merely meet among ourselves, a meeting in which there is no room for sacrifice (10:25). The only altar Christians have is the cross on which Christ brought his sacrifice (13:10; cf. 7:27; 10:10). From that altar, that is, from the sacrifice brought on it, they eat when by faith they have communion with Christ and his benefits. Believers have to bring no sacrifice other than the sacrifice of praise, the fruit of lips that praise his name (13:15). The Lord's Supper is a sacrificial meal, a meal of believers with Christ on the basis of his sacrifice and therefore one that must be served on a table, not an altar. "This is indeed very certain: that the cross of Christ is overthrown, as soon as the altar is set up."[69]

[544] So then, though the Lord's Supper is a real meal, as such it has a spiritual significance and purpose of its own. Christ did not institute it so that it would nourish us physically but rather spiritually. Before distributing the bread and wine, he blessed them both, saying that the bread was his body and the wine his blood. As such, as his broken body and shed blood, the bread and wine had to be taken and consumed by his disciples. The "matter" of the sacrament, the thing signified in the Lord's Supper, therefore, is the body and blood of Christ as in his sacrificial death it was broken and shed for the church for the forgiveness of sins; that is, the crucified, deceased Christ with all the benefits and blessings acquired by his death: "Christ himself with all his benefits."[70]

---

69. J. Calvin, *Institutes*, IV.xviii.3; G. Voetius, *Pol. eccl.*, I, 792; B. de Moor, *Comm. theol.*, V, 659; C. Vitringa, *Doctr. christ.*, VIII, 1, 414; N. Müller, "Altar," in *PRE³*, I, 391–404. F. Wieland (*Mensa und Confessio* [Munich: Lentner, 1906]), through his research, came to the conclusion that a table was original [in the celebration of the Lord's Supper], and that an altar was first placed in the Christian church under the influence of the link between sacrifice and the Lord's Supper. When this position was disputed, he defended it in *Die Schrift, Mensa und Confessio und P. Emil Dorsch in Innsbruck: Eine Antwort* (Munich: Lentner, 1908), and then again in *Der vorirenaische Opferbegriff* (Munich: Lentner, 1909).

70. H. Heppe, *Die Dogmatik der evangelisch-reformirten Kirche*, 466.

MEMORIAL OR SIGN OF UNION WITH CHRIST?

In a moral and rationalistic view of the Lord's Supper, this meaning does not come into its own. For in the first place, while the Lord's Supper is also a memorial meal, it is that only on the basis of the fact that Christ instituted bread and wine as signs of his body and blood. Of primary importance in the Lord's Supper is what God does, not what we do. The Lord's Supper is above all a gift of God, a benefit of Christ, a means of communicating his grace. If the Lord's Supper were only a memorial meal and an act of confession, it would cease to be a sacrament in the true sense. In that case, like prayer, it could only be obliquely and indirectly called a means of grace. The Lord's Supper, however, is on the same level as the Word and baptism and therefore must, like them, be regarded first of all as a message and assurance to us of divine grace.

Second, Christ does not make bread and wine in general the signs of his body and blood, but does this specifically with the bread and wine he has in his hands and distributes to his disciples. And he does not say that they must only view that bread and that wine as his body and blood but expressly states that they must take, eat, and drink them as such. He makes of these elements a meal in which the disciples consume his body and blood and thus enter into the most intimate communion with him. This communion does not merely consist in their sitting at one table, but they eat one and the same bread and drink one and the same wine. Indeed, the host here, in granting the signs of bread and wine, offers his own body and blood as nourishment and refreshment for their souls. That is a communion that far surpasses the communion inherent in a memorial meal and an act of confession. It is not merely a reminiscence of or a reflection on Christ's benefits but a most intimate bonding with Christ himself, just as food and drink are united with our body.

Third, in the Lord's Supper we indeed do not receive any other or any more benefits than we do in the Word, but also no fewer. Now in John 6:47–58 Jesus expressly states that, in the Word and by faith, we eat his flesh and drink his blood and so receive eternal life. Now, though in John 6 there is no direct reference to the Lord's Supper, this pericope may still serve to explain the second sacrament. By the Word and by faith we enter into an intimate communion with Christ, his body and blood, such as exists between the food a person eats and the person who eats it. This is not only the teaching of John 6 but also that of all the Scriptures. Neither the Word nor faith literally imparts that communion, but God has obligated himself to impart to those who believe his Word his fellowship in Christ and all the benefits associated with it.

Calvin, accordingly, correctly remarked against Zwingli that the meaning of eating Christ's body and drinking his blood is not exhausted by believing. Believing is a means, a means that is even temporary and destined to become seeing, but the communion with Christ engendered by it goes much deeper and endures forever. It is a mystical union that can only be made somewhat clear to us by the images of the vine and the branch, the head and the body, a bridegroom and his bride, the cornerstone and the building that rests on it. It is this mystical union that is signified and sealed in the Lord's Supper.

The Christian church almost unanimously upheld the teaching of this mystical union as the import of the Lord's Supper. Greek Orthodox and Roman Catholic, Lutheran as well as Reformed believers are agreed in affirming that in the Lord's Supper there occurs an objective and real communication of the person and benefits of Christ to everyone who believes. But among themselves they diverge widely over the *manner* in which this communication takes place. The first three groups cited above are not satisfied unless the body and blood of Christ are also physically and locally present in the signs and received and consumed orally. The Reformed, however, teach that, while Christ is truly and essentially communicated to believers, this occurs in a spiritual manner, and this in such a way that he can be received and enjoyed only by the mouth of faith. And for this position Scripture furnishes abundant evidence.

1. In the sentence "This is my body," the subject "this" can only mean the bread that Jesus holds in his hand. The predicate is "my body" and refers to Christ's very own body, the body he assumed from Mary and delivered up to death on behalf of his own. The copula is "is," which Jesus did not employ at all in the Aramaic, but in any case unites two disparate concepts, "bread" and "body," and hence *cannot* be a copula of true *being*. The word "is," therefore, must have significative, figurative meaning, for "a disparate thing cannot be predicated of another disparate thing, except figuratively." The sentence contains a trope, and it lies neither in the subject nor in the predicate but, as Zwingli correctly noted, in the copula "is" (ἐστι, *esti*), as this is so often the case in Scripture (e.g., Gen. 17:13; 41:26–27; Exod. 12:11; Ezek. 5:5; Luke 12:1; John 10:9; 15:1; etc.; 1 Cor. 10:4; Gal. 4:24; Heb. 10:20; Rev. 1:20; and so forth). And that such a trope has to be assumed in the words of institution is amply demonstrated further by the fact that, according to Luke and Paul, Jesus does not say "this wine" in reference to the second sign, but "This cup is the new covenant in my blood." Even Roman Catholics and Lutherans are forced at this point to assume a trope.

2. If the subject "this" does not refer to the natural bread and the natural wine but already to the substance of Jesus's body and blood concealed under the form or within the signs of bread and wine, then bread and wine have already been changed into Jesus's body and blood, or have already absorbed these components into themselves before the words "This is my body," "This is my blood" were even uttered, and they lose all the force and value Catholics and Lutherans have assigned to them. For then trans- or consubstantiation were not effected by those words but had already come into being prior to their utterance; and the words that are so heavily stressed then contain nothing but an explanation of what already exists and came into being earlier. It then becomes hard, indeed impossible, to say when and how the trans- or consubstantiation was effected. For, while there is indeed mention of a preceding blessing and thanksgiving,

not a word is said about their content. We absolutely do not know what Jesus communicated in them, nor do we know, therefore, what *we* have to say to bring about trans- and consubstantiation. Moreover, when Paul says in 1 Cor. 10:16, "The cup that we bless is a participation in the blood of Christ," he is assuming that the cup contains wine, not blood, for otherwise we could not bless it, and that as such, as containing wine, it is, by our blessing it, a participation in the blood of Christ.

3. The words Jesus uttered when he instituted the Supper are not intended as a fixed formula. This is evident from the fact that Matthew, Mark, Luke, and Paul reproduce them in different readings, and that the liturgical use of them by Christian churches displays all sorts of variation. According to the [Eastern] Orthodox Church, the so-called "epiklesis," the invocation of the Holy Spirit, belongs essentially to the words of consecration,[71] whereas, according to Rome, transubstantiation is effected by voicing the words "*Hoc enim est corpus meum*," where the word "*enim*" has been arbitrarily inserted and the words "which is broken for you" have been arbitrarily omitted. It is even less possible to prove that the words—assuming we knew which words specifically have to be used—possess a consecratory, operative, and conversive power. For Jesus does not say "This becomes" but "This is my body" and has therefore already set this bread apart from general use and consecrated it by words of blessing and thanksgiving for a higher purpose.

4. When Jesus instituted the Lord's Supper, he physically sat at table with his disciples. These disciples therefore could not even have formed the idea that with their physical mouth they could eat and drink Jesus's own body and blood, much less proceed to eat that body and drink that blood. It does not in any way help us to say with Philippi that "they were elevated far above the measure of their ordinary understanding by the illuminating Spirit,[72] or with Hollaz that Jesus sat at table "in the natural manner" but gave himself to eat "sacramentally."[73] Not only do we read nothing of this in Scripture, but also the question is precisely in what manner Jesus offered his body and blood at that first Supper, and this question may not be answered by dodging it. If the way Roman Catholics and Lutherans with their theories of trans- and consubstantiation picture this "enjoyment" of Jesus's body and blood is excluded by the first Supper, or can be maintained only by an appeal to miracle or a variety of evasions for which there is no basis in Scripture, then Christians who submit to the Word of God ought to abandon it. And if no trans- or consubstantiation and no literal eating with the mouth (*manducatio oralis*) took place at the first Supper, then neither may it be accepted at the Supper that the Christian church celebrates after Jesus's death at his command and according to his institution.

71. J. Schwane, *Dogmengeschichte*, II, 810; F. Kattenbusch, *Lehrbuch der vergleichenden Confessionskunde*, I, 413.

72. F. Philippi, *Kirchliche Glaubenslehre*, V, 2, 451.

73. D. Hollaz, *Examen theologicum acroamaticum*, 1119.

5. Just as trans- and consubstantiation are inconsistent with his physical sitting at table, so they are inconsistent with his physical ascension to and local sojourn in heaven. For if at the celebration of the Lord's Supper bread and wine are changed into Jesus's body and blood or absorb that body and blood, then that body has to come down from heaven or, as the Lutheran doctrine of ubiquity has it,[74] be everywhere present beforehand.

In any case, under the latter option, a further act is necessary by which the presence of Christ's body in the Supper is effected in a particular way, for in the nature of the case ubiquity by itself is not sufficient to that end. Luther and Brenz (et al.) therefore stated, "It is one thing for God to be present and another for God to be present *to you. To you* he is present, however, when he adds his word and obligates himself thereby and says: 'Here you will find me.'"[75] Hence in the thought of Rome and of Luther, the word effects a presence of Christ's body and blood in the Supper such that he is not only physically present in heaven but also on earth in the signs of bread and wine. Furthermore, this presence of Christ in the Supper is deemed to be such that Christ is totally present—not only according to his divine but also according to his human nature—in every Supper, wherever and whenever it is celebrated; that he is present with his entire divine and human nature in every sign of the Supper, indeed in every particle of the bread and in every drop of the wine—"completely in the entire offering and in all of its parts." Now this constitutes an endless multiplication of Christ, which is in direct conflict with the teaching of Scripture concerning his human nature, his ascension to heaven, and his sojourn in heaven. Certainly, that human nature was glorified at the resurrection and ascension but not thereby robbed of its essential attributes of finiteness and limitations. Jesus instituted the Supper in remembrance of himself precisely because he is departing and soon will no longer be physically present with his disciples, as he expressly states elsewhere (Matt. 26:11). And at his ascension he departed and was taken up (Acts 1:9–11) into heaven, which is a place (John 14:2, 4; 17:24; Acts 7:56; Eph. 4:10; Col. 3:1; Heb. 7:26), to remain there until his parousia (Acts 1:11; Phil. 3:20; 1 Thess. 1:10; 4:16).

6. However, even if Christ were physically and locally present in the Supper, one cannot see to what end this is necessary and useful. The utility of our oral eating (*manducatio oralis*) can in no way be demonstrated.[76] Suppose that with our physical mouth we literally ate Jesus's own body; how would that profit us? Is not the point of the Supper that our soul, that is, our spiritual life, be nurtured and strengthened? And this, in the nature of the case, cannot happen by our eating Christ's body with our physical mouth, for the things we eat with it in part become constituents of our body, and in part are expelled from the body. Some modern theologians have therefore come up with the idea that the literal eating

74. A. W. R. E. Hunzinger, "Ubiquität," in *PRE*[3], XX, 182–96.

75. Ibid., 188–89.

76. Ed. note: Bavinck refers here to pp. 516ff. in the second volume of the German edition of Köstlin, *Luthers Theologie*; we are unable to determine the passage to which Bavinck is referring.

of Christ's body plants within us a new body, that is, a resurrection body. But this notion is completely contrary to Scripture and the fruit of a false theosophy. Yet if this benefit cannot be connected with the eating of Christ's body, there is no other to be shown. This *manducatio oralis* is unprofitable, vain, and—however much people deny it—basically Capernaitic. The people of Capernaum were unable to imagine any other kind of eating Jesus's flesh than with the physical mouth (John 6:41, 52). And although Roman Catholics and Lutherans definitely accept a spiritual eating of Jesus's body, they still connect it with, and make it dependent on, a physical eating, without in any way making clear the manner of that connection or the nature of that dependence. In the entire address he delivered against the people of Capernaum, however, Jesus had in mind only a spiritual eating, an eating by faith, and does not so much as say a word about a physical eating.

TRANSUBSTANTIATION: THE MASS

[545] All the objections cited above concern both the Roman Catholic and Lutheran teaching on this point, but against the former we must further add the following.

7. The theory of transubstantiation is firmly contradicted by the testimony of our senses, by vision and touch, smell and taste. And our senses have a right to a voice here because bread and wine fall within their reach, and both may and can be judged by them. Here as well as elsewhere, they are to be trusted when they perceive things accurately, or else a skeptical nominalism lies in wait, and all certainty, both of faith and of science, vanishes. Also Rome, accordingly, has to yield to their witness, but Rome has come upon the idea that, while the substance changes, the accidents remain the same. The question of how this must be conceived remains unanswered. At Cana the water changed into wine but in such a way that both the substance and the accidents changed. Accidents, furthermore, cannot be separated from their substance and deemed to be self-sustaining, for then they cease to be accidents and themselves become substances. Moreover, in the bread and wine of the Lord's Supper, all the accidents remain unchanged, both those perceived by our sense of smell and taste and those perceived by sight and touch. Weight, consistency, color, perishability, nutritive power, and so forth all remain constant. But then what is left of the substance, which can change or has been changed?

8. The doctrine of transubstantiation is in conflict with the two signs ordained by Jesus in connection with the Lord's Supper. It is true that in earlier times in administering the Lord's Supper in private dwellings to the sick, prisoners and anchorites, newly consecrated virgins, and in Masses of the presanctified,[77] only the sign of bread was handed out, and conversely only the wine was served to minors,

---

77. Ed. note: Concerning the Masses for newly consecrated virgins, see A. A. King, *Eucharistic Reservation*, 15. On Masses of the presanctified, see ibid., 7, 11–13, 30, 54, 74.

as it is still even today in the Greek Orthodox Church. Since the twelfth century, however, the custom arose of withholding the cup from the laity, and not until the Council of Constance (1415) was this custom made the law of the church. Despite the criticism leveled against it by Hussites and other reform-minded people, the Council of Trent also gave its approval to the practice of withholding the cup, being induced to do so "for weighty and just reasons."[78] The Council does not list these reasons, but they are not hard to guess. Apart from the aversion of some to drink with others from the same cup,[79] dislike of wine, the danger of spilling it and of thereby desecrating the sacrament, and so forth, the Roman Catholic Church was especially moved to withholding the cup from the laity by a desire to elevate the priestly class above the laity, and by the conviction that each sign and every part of it was changed into the whole Christ.[80] Transubstantiation makes a second sign in the Lord's Supper completely superfluous. All of grace is already contained in the bread alone and even in the most minute part of it. Consequently the church of Rome comes into conflict with a direct command of Christ (Matt. 26:27, "Drink of it, all of you"), against which its appeal to the conjunction "or" in 1 Cor. 11:27 is of no avail; and at the same time, by its own confession, it comes into conflict with the custom of the Christian church in the early centuries. It can only defend itself with the assertion that it possesses the power, in dispensing the sacraments, to proceed as it deems expedient.[81]

Conversely, the institution of the Lord's Supper with two signs is strong proof that the doctrine of transubstantiation is not scriptural. Together, after all, they depict before our eyes the crucified Christ and impart him to believers in a spiritual, not a physical, manner, not *in* and *under* but simultaneously *with* the signs. Together they form one sacrament, as images and pledges of one spiritual good: communion with Christ and his benefits.

9. The doctrine of transubstantiation, finally, is further refuted by the idolatrous practices that followed its introduction. Although the groundwork for the Mass was laid by the ideas of "sacrifice" and "priest," which already at an early stage were associated with the Lord's Supper, it is nevertheless built upon the doctrine of transubstantiation first developed in the Middle Ages. And this is similarly presupposed by the [p]reservation, adoration, and carrying about of the host. By the introduction of the doctrine of transubstantiation, the Lord's Supper became

78. Council of Trent, sess. XXI.

79. In recent times, there has arisen in many churches a movement to replace the single chalice in the Lord's Supper by many cups. See, for example, Fr. Spitta, *Die Kelchbewegung in Deutschland*; H. Josephson, "Kelch oder Kelche?" *Die Studierstube* (1904): 222–46. Spitta contends that the individual cup (*Einzelkelch*) was originally used, and that Pope Gregory II (715–731) first instituted a communal cup. But this is certainly incorrect; cf. anonymous, *Ist der Einzelkelch bei der Feier des heiligen Abendmahl eine neutestamentliche Einrichtung?* (Hagen i.w.: Rippel, n.d.); O. Roepke and E. Huss, *Het onderzoek over de mogelijkheid van 't overbrengen van ziektekiemen door het gebruik van den gemeenschappelijken avondmaalsbeker* (Rotterdam: W. Nevens, 1905); H. H. Meulenbelt, *Kerkelijke opstelling* (Nijmegen: Ten Hoet, 1905), 1–17.

80. J. H. Oswald, *Die dogmatische Lehre von den heiligen Sakramenten*, I, 501.

81. Council of Trent, sess. XXI, can. 2.

the Mass and has thereby been completely deprived of its original character. Although, despite a variety of restrictions, the idea of communion has persisted, the Mass has nevertheless become the central focus of Roman Catholic worship. It is, accordingly, nothing less than the most complete elaboration of the Roman idea that the church with its priesthood is the mediatrix of salvation, the continually self-realizing God-man on earth. In the Mass, Christ continually and ever anew repeats his sacrifice on the cross. In it he essentially and truly continues to offer himself up—be it in an unbloody manner—and thereby brings it about with God that the fruits of his sacrifice on the cross, there obtained only in general and in the abstract, are now being applied[82] to all who live in fellowship with the church. This is so whether they are on earth or in purgatory, whether present at or absent from the Mass, whether they desire it for themselves or for others, out of spiritual or physical neediness, for the forgiveness of sins and the prevention or staving off of illness and accidents, drought and flooding, war and cattle plague, and so forth. *That* is what Rome has made of the Supper of our Lord Jesus Christ! Grounds, which in the case of so weighty a doctrine should be abundantly available and unfailingly solid, are totally lacking. In Gen. 14:18, where Melchizedek offers bread and wine to Abraham as refreshment, there is not a word about sacrifice, even though it is immediately followed by the statement, not because, but "and he [Melchizedek] was priest of God Most High." Malachi 1:11 perhaps does not even deal with the future, but even if that were the case, this passage states in Old Testament forms that the Lord's name will be great among the Gentiles, and that incense and a pure offering (מִנְחָה, *minḥâ*, offering in general) will be brought to him; and in the New Testament precisely these forms were replaced by prayer and spiritual sacrifice (Rom. 12:1). At the institution of the Lord's Supper, Jesus did say, "Do this in remembrance of me" (Luke 22:19), but in these words it is in no way implied that in so doing Jesus instituted the Lord's Supper as a sacrifice and made his disciples into priests. Neither, certainly, is this proved by saying that the Hebrew word עָשָׂה (*'āśâ*, do, make) and the Latin *facere* are occasionally used in the sense of "to sacrifice." In 1 Cor. 10:21 Paul contrasts the table of the Lord with the table of demons; but the fact that the table of demons was an altar by no means implies that also the table of the Lord is an altar on which sacrifices have to be offered. Now these are the most important and strongest arguments that Roman Catholics can draw from Scripture for their doctrine of the Mass. And their appeal to the church fathers is not much stronger, for in this connection they forget that these men, in applying the idea of sacrifice to the Lord's Supper, attached to this idea a very different meaning than Rome later associated with it.

Against all these pseudoarguments stands a series of proofs that in the clearest possible way demonstrate the unscriptural character of the Mass. All that resembles the Mass is absolutely foreign to the institution of the Lord's Supper and to the observance of it as it was usually celebrated in the apostolic church. The eternal

---

82. Council of Trent, sess. XXII, can. 1.

character of Christ's priesthood (Heb. 5:6; 7:17, 21–25) and the perfection of his sacrifice on the cross (7:27; 9:12, 28; 10:10, 12, 14) make a repetition of his self-offering—even an unbloody one—superfluous and impermissible. All the benefits of grace (forgiveness, sanctification, redemption, the whole of salvation) have been secured by Christ's sacrifice on the cross and cannot be, nor need to be, augmented. Indeed, since Christ has once for all offered himself up on the cross and surrendered himself to death, he cannot even do this again a second time. His sacrifice into death does not lend itself to repetition (9:26–28). His priestly activity, to be sure, continues in heaven, yet it consists not in any expiatory offering but in his intercession and appearance before the face of God on behalf of his people (7:25; 9:24); and in that intercession and appearance before God's face, the sacrifice completed on the cross continues to be effective—always—on behalf of his own. Because Christ himself dwells in heaven to pray for believers, and in that intercession lets his sacrifice have its ongoing effect, there is no longer any room on earth for a repetition of his sacrifice. His state of exaltation; his elevation above all suffering, sorrow, and death; his royal dominion as head of the church—these are directly contradictory to an expiatory and acquisitive sacrifice that, according to Rome, he would still have to make on earth and at thousands of places every day. Therefore, however many times Rome may say that the unbloody sacrifice does not weaken the bloody sacrifice on the cross but rather makes it operational, in fact it is a denial of the only sacrifice on the cross, for a sacrifice that does no more than cause people to enjoy the benefits of another sacrifice is a palpable absurdity. If the sacrifice on the cross is sufficient, other sacrifices are superfluous; if these other sacrifices are necessary, the former is inadequate and incomplete.

And this conclusion is confirmed by Roman Catholic practice. The attention of the believer is directed away from Christ and his cross and toward the priest and his Mass. Even for a minimum of grace the Roman Catholic Christian is dependent on one's priest and the church. One cannot for a moment do without them. In theory, the church maintains that Christ has acquired all grace, but in practice, grace is successively—bit by little bit—dispensed by the priest. In the hands of Rome, the Lord's Supper has become a fearful mystery (*mysterium tremendum*) that keeps believers in a state of perpetual immaturity, binds them for their whole life and well-being to a hierarchical priesthood, and causes them to kneel in idolatrous adoration before a god of its own making.[83]

83. Against the doctrine of transubstantiation and consubstantiation, see J. Calvin, *Institutes*, IV.xviii; T. Beza, *Tractationum theologicarum*, I, 211ff., 507ff.; III, 148ff.; P. Martyr Vermigli, *Loci comm.*, IV, c. 12; Z. Ursinus, *Heidelberg Catechism*, 78–80; idem, *Volumen tractationum theologicarum*, 359–596; D. Chamier, *Panstratiae catholicae* (Geneva: Roverianis, 1626), IV, 1, 6; W. Ames, *Bellarminus enervatus,* 3rd ed., 4 vols. (Oxford: G. Turner, 1629), 1, IV; A. Rivetus, *Operum theologicorum*, 3 vols. (Rotterdam: Leers, 1651–60), III, 339–76; F. Turretin, *Institutes of Elenctic Theology*, trans. G. M. Giger, ed. J. T. Dennison, 3 vols. (Phillipsburg, NJ: Presbyterian & Reformed, 1992), XIX, qu. 21; C. Vitringa, *Doctr. christ.*, VIII, 769; K. von Hase, *Handbuch der protestantischen Polemik gegen die römisch-katholische Kirche*, 5th ed. (Leipzig: Breitkopf & Härtel, 1890), 488–535. See F. Pijper, *Middeleeuwsch Christendom*, II, 26–60, concerning the adoration of the host; and ibid., III, 61–100, concerning the veneration of the host.

THE REFORMED DOCTRINE OF THE LORD'S SUPPER

[546] Even better than the Lutherans, the Reformed have cleansed the Lord's Supper of Roman admixtures and restored it in accordance with its original intent. According to Christ's institution, the Lord's Supper was a meal in which bread and wine were used as food and drink for strengthening the body, and served above all as signs and seals for the exercise of communion with the crucified Christ. It is both an ordinary natural meal and an extraordinary spiritual meal, in which the host, Christ, offers his own crucified body and shed blood as nourishment for our souls. Accordingly, in the meal that Christ has instituted, everything is important. Nothing in it is devoid of meaning. Everything about it is charged with deep meaning.

In the first place, the signs of bread and wine have not been selected arbitrarily but are eminently suited to give us an impression of the spiritual food and drink that Christ in his death has prepared for our souls. In the second place, all the actions that Christ performed at the institution of the Supper are significant. He does not—as he did earlier in the Passover meal—take the bread and wine from the hand of others ("having received" [δεξαμενος, *dexamenos*] the cup; Luke 22:17), he himself takes (λαβων, *labōn*; v. 19) it from the table in proof that he is the host and provides the food and the drink. He blesses (εὐλογησας, *eulogēsas*; Matt. 26:26; Mark 14:22; alternating with εὐχαριστησας [*eucharistēsas*, having given thanks] in connection with the cup; Matt. 26:27; Mark 14:23; whereas Luke 22:19–20 and Paul, in 1 Cor. 11:24–25, have only εὐχαριστησας) the bread and later also the cup. That act of benediction does not mean that Christ is asking God for his blessing upon the bread and wine; rather the alternation with εὐχαριστησας ("having given thanks") proves that Jesus blesses God, that is, praises and thanks God for the gifts he has bestowed. The actual content of that praise and thanksgiving is not reported, but it is certainly related to the gifts of creation represented in the bread and wine, and especially related to the gifts of grace that would be secured by the death of Christ and offered in his body and blood to the disciples. By that act of thanksgiving alone, the bread and wine were set aside from common use and designated for a higher purpose, and at the same time the disciples were prepared for a correct understanding of the meaningful words "This is my body" (and so forth), which Jesus would soon utter in explanation.

Second, Jesus broke the bread, which the Reformed correctly saw as an action that, though not belonging to the essence, definitely does belong to the integrity of the sacrament. Not only is this breaking of the bread mentioned in all four reports, but the entire Supper is named after it (Acts 2:42). Just as the breaking of the bread is necessary to make it fit for consumption, so Christ has to offer up his body into death in order that it may be food for our souls (John 6:51; 12:23–24). Finally Jesus himself distributes the bread and wine to his disciples in order that they would eat and drink of it. He does this with the emphatic words: "Take," "Eat," "Drink of it, all of you," words that strongly condemn the Roman

Catholic Mass without communicants. Communion belongs to the essence of the Lord's Supper.

Important, in the third place, are the words that Jesus uses in distributing the bread and wine. When he gave the bread to his disciples, he said, "This is my body, which is given for you" (Luke 22:19); and in handing over the cup he said, "This is my blood of the covenant, which is poured out for many for the forgiveness of sins" (Matt. 26:28). The idea that these words possess consecratory, operative power is absolutely not supported in the text of the reports. But after Jesus, by giving thanks, set aside the bread and wine from common use, designated them for a higher purpose, and had prepared his disciples, he spoke the words: "This is my body and blood." He does not say: "May this bread become my body." He does not order but simply explains and illustrates. After all, it is a symbolic action that he is performing, a spiritual meal that he is instituting. And of that meal his body and blood, as they are offered up in death, are the food and drink. All the signs, actions, and words in the Supper point our faith toward the sacrifice of Jesus Christ on the cross, to the only ground of our salvation.

This is not to say, however, that the Lord's Supper is no more than a meal of remembrance of Christ and his benefits. For with the signs of bread and wine, Jesus gives his own body and blood for our "enjoyment": the table of the Supper brings about true communion between Christ and believers, a communion not just with the benefits but above all with the person of Christ, both in his human nature and in his divine nature.

About the *reality* of that communion there is no disagreement between Roman Catholic, Lutheran, and Reformed Christians. In this respect they are all on the same side and opposed to that of Zwingli. They do, however, disagree among themselves about the *nature* of that communion and the *manner* in which it is enjoyed in the Supper. Roman Catholics and Lutherans believe that such communion cannot truly and fully come about unless Christ comes down physically from heaven to earth and they can eat his body and drink his blood, not just spiritually but physically, with their mouths. By contrast Calvin emphasized from the very beginning and ever anew that the communion of believers with Christ, also according to his human nature, is spiritual in nature, and this comes about, not because Christ comes down physically, but because we lift up our hearts spiritually to heaven, where Jesus Christ, our advocate, is at the right hand of his heavenly Father.

And this doctrine is based on Scripture and consistent with the nature of the New Testament dispensation:

1. The communion between Christ and believers, while it is so intimate and unbreakable that it can scarcely be expressed in words and can only be somewhat made clear by images (such as head and body, vine and branch, bridegroom and bride), it is still not a pantheistic mingling or identification, no transference of substance, no consubstantial oneness like that of

the three persons in the Trinity, nor a personal union like that of the two natures in Christ. Christ and believers remain distinct. Their personalities are maintained. The mystical union is a union of persons, not only in will and disposition but also in being and nature.

2. This communion is brought about by the Holy Spirit, who dwells in Christ as the head and in believers as his members. There is no other way to take part in it. A physical union—such as transubstantiation and consubstantiation, with the associated notion of a physical eating with the mouth, are designed to bring about—is totally groundless and useless. Only the Holy Spirit, who is the Spirit of God and the Spirit of Christ, can so unite people with Christ that they share in his person and benefits and cannot be separated from him by death or the grave, by the world or by Satan. For that reason this communion is always spiritual in nature. True, it also embraces the human nature of Christ and believers in their physical existence. For Christ cannot be conceived apart from his human nature, and he purchased not only believers' souls, but also their bodies. Yet the union between Christ and believers remains spiritual in nature, because it is brought about in no other way than by the Holy Spirit.

3. The communion with Christ, which is strengthened in the Supper, is nothing other than that which is brought about by the Word as a means of grace. The sacrament does not add any grace to that which is offered in the Word. It only strengthens and confirms that which has been received by faith from the Word. So when Catholics and Lutherans object that communion with Christ in the Supper, as the Reformed view it, is no true communion with Christ's own body and blood, we need only respond by saying that the communion confirmed in the Supper is not, nor can be, any other than that generated by the Word. In exactly the same manner in which a person is incorporated by faith into Christ, so that person is also strengthened and confirmed in that communion by the Lord's Supper. There simply is no other or higher communion. Those who believe become Christ's possession in body and soul; and those who receive the Lord's Supper in faith are confirmed in and reassured of that reality. The sacrament does not supply any other grace; it merely supplies the same grace for the strengthening of faith—only by another means.

4. So among the Reformed, too, Christ is truly and essentially present with his divine and human nature in the Supper, only in no way other than he is present in the gospel. Christ is no more enclosed physically in bread and wine than he is in the Word proclaimed, but those who believingly accept the sign also, according to the divine ordinance, receive true communion with the whole Christ. Along with the sign, not in and under the sign, Christ bestows the thing signified, that is, himself with all his benefits. For whereas, in the mind of Roman Catholics and Lutherans, grace is something material and passive that is received physically even by an unbeliever, so to

the Reformed it is the personal living Christ himself who imparts himself in the Supper as spiritual food to those who believe in him.[84] According to the Reformed, therefore, he is not less present, but more present, much more vigorously and authentically, than he is according to Rome and Luther, for he is not physically and locally present in the signs but spiritually, as the acting Christ himself, in the hearts of believers. "It is one thing for the present substance of Christ to be in the bread to make us alive; it is another for the flesh of Christ to be life-giving because from its substance life flows forth into our souls."[85]

5. Faith, accordingly, is the indispensable requisite for the reception of the sacrament. Granted, the truth of the sacrament does not depend on faith. For just as in the case of the Word, so in the case of the Supper, God has obligated himself truly to bestow Christ and all his benefits on everyone who believes. But the unbeliever, in the nature of the case, receives only the sign, just as in the case of the Word that one hears only the sound and does not receive the thing denoted by the Word. Needed—to receive the promises and benefits of Word and sacrament—therefore, is a working of the Holy Spirit in the heart of a person; and it is precisely this working of the Spirit that effects and maintains this communion with Christ, both apart from and in the Lord's Supper.

6. From this perspective it is not hard to infer the benefits enjoyed in the Lord's Supper. Foremost is the strengthening of the believer's communion with Christ. Believers already enjoy this communion by faith, and in the Supper they receive no other communion than that which they already enjoy by faith. But when Christ himself, acting through the minister, gives them, with the signs of bread and wine, his body to eat and his blood to drink, they are strengthened and confirmed in that communion by the Holy Spirit and ever more intimately united in soul and body with the whole Christ, both in his divine and in his human natures. For "the eating of the body of Christ is nothing other than the closest union with Christ."[86] In this connection, the Lord's Supper is distinguished from baptism by the fact that baptism is the sacrament of incorporation, while the Lord's Supper is the sacrament of maturation in communion with Christ. By baptism we are buried with Christ in his death and raised in his resurrection, and are therefore passive, but in the Lord's Supper we ourselves go into action, eating the body and drinking the blood of Christ, and are thus fed by communion with him unto eternal life.[87] But if we share in the person of Christ, we naturally also share in his benefits. Among these benefits the

84. Julius Müller, *Dogmatische Abhandlungen*, 458.

85. Ibid., 443; cf. Anglican Confession, art. 28; J. C. Ryle, *Knots Untied*, 235–54.

86. F. Junius, *Theses theol.*, in vol. 1 of *Opuscula*, 52, 7.

87. H. Weber, "Taufe und Abendmahl als Symbole unserer doppelten Stellung zum Heilsgut," *Zeitschrift für Theologie und Kirche* 19 (1909): 249–79.

forgiveness of sins is mentioned first of all and with the most emphasis in Scripture. In the Lord's Supper, Christ gives his body and blood as food for our souls, but that body and blood are not such food "because it is a bodily substance and as such food for the body but [it is such] to the degree that the body of Christ is given for the life of the world."[88] It is to that end that in the Supper the body and blood are depicted separately, each by a sign of its own. To that end Christ expressly states that his body was given and his blood shed for the forgiveness of sins. To that end the significance of the blood is even explained at greater length in the words of institution than that of the body, for it is the blood that makes atonement for sins on the altar. Even though Christ is worshiped, the communion that is realized through faith and is strengthened through the Lord's Supper is and remains a communion with his crucified body and with his shed blood.

On the position of transubstantiation and consubstantiation, this is impossible. There the deceased Christ recedes behind the glorified Christ. But if eating Christ's body and drinking his blood amounts to "our closest possible union with Christ,"[89] then this and every other benefit is exclusively a fruit of Christ's death, and we are only nourished by Christ because he was crucified for us.

And among the benefits Christ secured by his death, the forgiveness of sins is foremost. This benefit, too, is not granted to us for the first time in the Lord's Supper, because the Christian already possesses it by faith and has received the sign and seal of it in baptism. It is wrong, therefore, with Rome to distribute the different graces over the sacraments in such a way that in each sacrament a special group of sins is forgiven and a special grace granted, for the forgiveness that the Word, baptism, and the Lord's Supper offer to us is always the same. The forgiveness imparted in the Supper, therefore, absolutely does not relate only to our "daily faults" and "venial sins."[90] But it is the same full and abundant benefit of forgiveness that is offered in the Word, received by faith, and signed and sealed by the sacraments of baptism and the Lord's Supper. In this benefit it comes out clearly that the sacrament does not add a single new grace to the Word; with an eye to our weakness, it only bestows the same grace in another manner in order that we may firmly believe and be healed of all doubt.

Added to the benefit of forgiveness is that of eternal life. The Lord's Supper is a spiritual meal at which Christ feeds our souls with his crucified body and shed blood. Eating and drinking them serves to strengthen our spiritual, that is, our eternal life, for those who eat the flesh of the Son of man and drink his blood have eternal life and are raised up on the last day (John 6:54). From this

88. F. Junius, *Theses theol.*
89. G. Bucanus, *Inst. theol.*, 677.
90. Council of Trent, sess. XIII, can. 2; sess. XXII, can. 1.

it is clear that eternal life is a benefit granted to the whole person, not only spiritually but also physically. Some have mistakenly deduced from this that Christ's body, enjoyed in the Supper, exerts a direct influence on our body, so that it is healed of all sorts of illness and weakness and is in principle re-created into a new resurrection body. One can understand that people came to hold this sentiment especially from a Lutheran position, for if the literal eating of the body does not have *this* advantage, it has no value at all. Yet Scripture does not say a word about this. In 1 Cor. 11:30 Paul does say that on account of the appalling abuse of the Lord's Supper at Corinth, many people were ill and some even died. But this clearly refers to a judgment (v. 29), a punishment that God inflicted on the abuse of the Lord's Supper, and definitely does not prove that the use, or the believing use, of the Lord's Supper also serves to heal the ills of the body. Furthermore, though John 6 may be used to illustrate the Lord's Supper, it does not deal with it directly. This chapter further teaches only that those who by faith, also apart from the Lord's Supper, eat Christ's flesh and drink his blood have eternal life and will be raised on the last day (cf. John 6:40). It is therefore definitely not by a literal eating but by faith in general that humans become partakers of eternal life and receive the hope of the resurrection. The Holy Spirit, who dwells in believers, is the surest pledge of the resurrection of the body and the day of redemption (Rom. 8:11; Eph. 1:13–14; 4:30). But this Spirit of Christ does indeed use the Supper to strengthen believers in the hope of eternal life and of a blessed resurrection on the last day. "For where the soul is healed, the body is helped as well."[91] "Such is the presence of the body (I say) that the nature of the Sacrament requires a presence which we say manifests itself here with a power and effectiveness so great that it not only brings an undoubted assurance of eternal life to our minds, but also assures us of the immortality of our flesh. Indeed, it is now quickened by his immortal flesh, and in a sense partakes of his immortality."[92] In this sense the Lord's Supper may be called "the medicine of immortality."[93]

Finally, the Lord's Supper as a memorial celebration and the proclamation of Christ's death also serves as the confession of our faith before the world and conduces to the strengthening of the communion of believers among themselves. In 1 Cor. 10:17 the apostle argues that the bread must be a participation in the body of Christ, for how else could believers, who viewed by themselves are many, be one? The unity arises only because in the one loaf they have fellowship with the one body of Christ. Believers are one in Christ and therefore also one among themselves. "For as out of many grains one meal is ground and one bread baked, and out of many berries, pressed together, one wine flows and is mixed together,

---

91. Julius Müller, *Dogmatische Abhandlungen*, 419.

92. J. Calvin, *Institutes*, IV.xvii.32; cf. also, J. H. A. Ebrard, *Das Dogma vom heiligen Abendmahl und seine Geschichte*, 2 vols. (Frankfurt a.M.: Heinrich Zimmer, 1845–46), II, 460; F. A. Philippi, *Kirchliche Glaubenslehre*, V, 2, 282ff.; Julius Müller, *Dogmatische Abhandlungen*, 417.

93. Ignatius, *To the Ephesians* 20.

so shall we all who by true faith are incorporated in Christ be altogether one body."[94] And this they confess at the Lord's Supper in the face of a world that does not know their unity.

FOR BELIEVERS ONLY

[547] Like baptism, the Lord's Supper was instituted only for believers. Jesus observed it only with his disciples. Whether Judas was still present at that time or whether he left the room before the institution of the Lord's Supper cannot be said with certainty. Matthew 26:21–25; Mark 14:18–21; and John 13:21–35 all give the impression that Judas left before that time, but Luke 22:21–23 relates the discovery of Judas as the betrayer after the institution of the Supper in verses 19 and 20. It is possible, however, that in this connection Luke did not adhere to the chronological order. However this may be, the question has no dogmatic significance. If Judas participated in the Supper, he did so as a disciple of Jesus. That is what he was and that is what he pretended to be. What he inwardly considered doing against Jesus was his responsibility.[95] Later the Lord's Supper was exclusively celebrated by believers in the circle of the congregation (Acts 2:42; 20:7). Unbelievers did have access to the gathering of the congregation where the Word was administered (1 Cor. 14:22–24) but were excluded from gatherings in which the love feasts were held and the communion celebrated (11:18, 20, 33). This is how it remained also when in the second century the Lord's Supper was gradually separated from the love feasts and took place in the morning in the same gathering where the administration of the Word occurred. The first part of the service was accessible to all, but the second only started after unbelievers, catechumens, excommunicates, and so forth had been dismissed. In this second part of the service, the sacraments were administered, and it was an ancient and general custom that those who upon completion of their catechumenate were baptized received the Lord's Supper immediately thereafter. When infant baptism became a regular practice, this custom was also followed in the case of children and further insisted on by the prevailing exegesis of John 6:53, according to which this verse applied to the Lord's Supper and this sacrament therefore became as necessary to salvation as baptism.[96] In the West, however, this custom eroded especially after the beginning of the twelfth century, and was little by little declared unnecessary by a succession of synods.[97] But in the Greek and other Orthodox churches, the custom has been retained, and even today the Lord's Supper is administered to newborn infants in the form of a tiny piece of bread dipped in wine.[98]

---

94. Ed. note: These words are taken from the traditional Dutch Reformed Church's liturgy for the Lord's Supper.

95. C. Vitringa, *Doctr. christ.*, VIII, 347.

96. G. Rietschel, "Kinderkommunion," in *PRE*[3], X, 289–91.

97. Council of Trent, sess. XXI, can. 4.

98. C. Vitringa, *Doctr. christ.*, VIII, 368, 612.

But the magical construal of the Lord's Supper resulted in even more serious abuses. The original simplicity of the Supper was lost as a wide range of solemn ceremonies was added. Communicants had to prepare themselves for the Supper not only by self-examination, but also by fasting, the washing of their hands and clothing, and so forth. The bread was first received with one's bare hand, then in a piece of linen cloth or golden saucer, and still later, after the beginning of the eleventh century, from the priest with one's mouth and from a kneeling position near the altar. The consecrated bread was not only enjoyed by communicants in the church but also administered to the sick in their homes, given to the dying as "food for the journey" (*viaticum*), and deemed useful for averting disasters of every kind and obtaining a variety of blessings and benefits. The working of the sacrament not only extended to the living but also to the dead. From ancient times already there was the custom of bringing offerings for deceased relatives on the anniversary of their death and of praying for their souls. And when the doctrine of purgatory had been fixed by Gregory the Great, the Lord's Supper was viewed as an offering up of Christ's own body and blood, and the participation of the congregation increasingly diminished. It soon became a fixed doctrine that the Mass could bring about a lessening of penances and temporal punishments, not only for the living—whether present or absent—but also for the dead in purgatory.[99]

All these corruptions made necessary a return to Scripture, according to which the Lord's Supper is a meal that is inconceivable without guests in attendance and exclusively intended for believers. In order to run a true course and do full justice to Scripture in this matter, the Reformed as a rule posed two questions: (1) Who have a right as well as an obligation to come to the Supper? (2) Who must be admitted to or barred from the Supper by the church?[100] The first question deals with the duty of communicants, and the second with the duty of the church and its ministers. To the latter question the answer given was—and according to Scripture could not be other than—that the church had to bar all those who by their talk and walk presented themselves as unbelieving and ungodly people. The Lord's Supper is a good of the church given by Christ to his people and is therefore to be enjoyed only by the members of the household of faith. The unbaptized, unbelievers, heretics, schismatics, public sinners, and excommunicates are automatically excluded by that rule. But the number of those who were entitled to the Supper was even much more restricted. In the first place, by rejecting the Mass and purgatory, the church also had to abolish the administration of the Supper for the dead. Scripture, certainly, does not report a single instance of it. Paul does refer to people who had themselves baptized on behalf of the dead (1 Cor. 15:29). But even if this verse

99. Ibid., VIII, 733; P. Drews, "Messe, luturgisch," in *PRE*³, XII, 722ff.; H. A. Köstlin, "Requiem," in *PRE*³, XVI, 665–69.

100. Heidelberg Catechism, Q 81–82.

has to be understood as saying (which has definitely not been proved)[101] that at the time there were Christians who had themselves baptized on behalf of unbaptized deceased friends, still the apostle in fact refers to this practice only as proof for the resurrection and simply reports it without approval or disapproval. The church, at the [Third] Council of Carthage (397), firmly condemned baptism for the dead, a custom practiced by a number of sects, and therefore cannot derive from it an argument for the administration of the Supper on behalf of the dead.

In the second place, many Reformed leaders and churches objected to the idea of administering the Lord's Supper to the sick and the dying in their private dwellings, apart from the public gatherings of believers. So, for example, Musculus, Bullinger, Beza, Danaeus Aretius, and so forth, as well as the Reformed churches of France, Scotland, the Netherlands, and so forth. Others, like Calvin, Oecolampadius, Martyr, Zanchius, and the churches of England, Poland, Hungary, and so forth, sometimes permitted it, but even then they usually insisted that a small gathering of believers had to be present so that any occasion of superstition would be prevented or avoided.[102]

In the third place, also children were excluded from the Lord's Supper. Trent condemned only the necessity of serving the Supper to children, not the permissibility of it. And of the Reformed also Musculus, in his *Loci Communes*, adopted this position.[103] In support of it he advanced the following grounds: (1) Those who possess the thing signified also have a right to the sign. (2) Children who can receive the grace of regeneration (as is evident from baptism) can also be nurtured in their spiritual lives without their knowledge. (3) Christ is the Savior of the whole church, including the children, and feeds and refreshes all of its members with his body and blood. (4) The demand for self-examination (1 Cor. 11:26–29) is not intended by the apostle as a universal requirement.

But all these grounds lose their weight as a result of the following considerations: (1) In the Old Testament there was a great difference between circumcision and the Passover. Circumcision was prescribed for all children of the male sex, but the Passover feast was celebrated, not immediately at its institution but later in Palestine, near the temple at Jerusalem. Very young children were therefore automatically excluded. (2) Similarly there is a great difference between baptism and the Lord's Supper. Baptism is the sacrament of regeneration, a sacrament in which a human is passive; the Lord's Supper is the sacrament of maturation in communion with Christ, the formation of the spiritual life, and presupposes conscious and active conduct on the part of those who receive it. (3) Christ instituted the Lord's Supper in the midst of his disciples, saying to them all, "Take, eat and drink." It presupposes that they took the bread and wine from his hand. And Paul writes that the church

101. H. Cremer, *Biblisch-theologisches Wörterbuch der neutestamentlichen Gräcität* (Gotha: F. A. Perthes, 1880), 156; and many commentators on this text. Ed. note: ET: *Biblico-Theological Lexicon of New Testament Greek*, trans. D. W. Simon and W. Urwick (Edinburgh: T&T Clark; New York: Charles Scribner's Sons, 1895).

102. G. Voetius, *Pol. eccl.*, I, 758; C. Vitringa, *Doctr. christ.*, VIII, 356; B. de Moor, *Comm. theol.*, V, 660.

103. W. Musculus, *Loci communes theologiae sacrae* (Basel: Heruagiana, 1567), 471–73.

of Corinth came together to eat, and he leaves no other impression than that only self-conscious adult persons took part in the Supper. (4) In 1 Cor. 11:26–29 Paul specifically insists that people should examine themselves before celebrating the Lord's Supper in order to be able to discern the body of the Lord and not eat and drink unworthily. This demand is very general, addressed to all participants in the Lord's Supper, and therefore automatically excludes the children. (5) Withholding the Lord's Supper from the children does not deprive them of any benefit of the covenant of grace. This would be the case if they were excluded from baptism. For no one can do this except those who believe that children are outside the covenant of grace. But things are different with the Lord's Supper. Those who administer baptism to children but not the Lord's Supper acknowledge that they are in the covenant and share in all its benefits. They merely withhold from them a particular manner in which the same benefits are signed and sealed, since this manner is not suited to their age. The Lord's Supper, after all, does not confer a single benefit that is not by faith granted through the Word and through baptism.

Already at an early stage this distinction between baptism and the Lord's Supper made preparation for a worthy reception of the second sacrament necessary. In the apostolic period, when as a rule only adults were baptized, there was as yet no such preparation. Those who heard and accepted the word of the gospel were immediately baptized and admitted to the Lord's Supper. In the next century, however, when conversions to Christianity became more numerous and less reliable, the catechumenate gradually made its appearance. This was initially designed to prepare converts for baptism, and later, when infant baptism had become a general practice, for the Lord's Supper. In the Roman Catholic Church this preparation gradually found exhaustive expression in the sacrament of confirmation, which developed from the laying on of hands originally linked with baptism and was bound up with an anointing. The Reformation rejected this "sacrament," since it had no foundation in Scripture, and replaced it with catechesis and public profession of faith. By this process the transition was made from baptism to the Lord's Supper, at the same time preserving the church from corruption. It was Calvin's wish that, after a child had been sufficiently instructed in the catechism, the child would make public profession of one's own faith. John à Lasco's desire was that children who had reached the age of fourteen would make public profession of their faith before the congregation and partake of the Lord's Supper the following Sunday. But those who lived a bad life were admonished and finally, upon proved obduracy, cut off from the church at the age of eighteen or twenty.

The orders of the Dutch Reformed churches similarly prescribed a profession before the church council or in the midst of the congregation and sometimes still speak of a preceding examination before the church council.[104] This theory is sound

---

104. J. W. F. Höfling, *Das Sakrament der Taufe* (Erlangen: Deichert, 1859), II, 347ff.; J. F. Bachmann, *Die Geschichte der Einführung der Confirmation innerhalb der evangelischen Kirche* (Berlin: Wilhelm Schultze, 1852); W. Caspari, *Die evangelische Konfirmation, vornämlich in der lutherischen Kirche* (Erlangen: Deichert,

enough: the children of believers are baptized as believers, then instructed in the truth; upon sufficient instruction and after public profession of faith, they are admitted to the Lord's Supper, or, in case of unchristian views or irregular conduct, they are, after repeated admonition, removed from the church. Our church life should still be conducted along these doctrinal lines even though at every moment it runs into the problems of practice.[105] For Pietism and rationalism are ever prone to separate what God has joined together and either with disdain for the sacrament stress personal conversion or emphasize the practice of ecclesiastical confirmation. But the rule of the covenant is that the church must nurture its youthful members, who were born as children of the covenant and incorporated as members by baptism, to where they can make an independent personal profession of faith and on that basis admit them to the Lord's Supper. It does not and cannot judge the heart. Accordingly, while on the one hand it bars from the Lord's Supper all those who by their talk or walk manifest themselves as unbelieving and ungodly people, it never, on the other hand, desists from seriously preaching that the Lord's Supper is instituted only for those who are displeased with themselves because of their sins but who nevertheless trust that their sins have been forgiven for Christ's sake and who also desire more and more to strengthen their faith and lead a better life.[106]

1890); idem, "Konfirmation," in *PRE*³, X, 676–80; E. Sachsse, "Katechese, Katechetik," in *PRE*³, X, 121–29; F. Cohrs, "Katechismen und Katechismusunterricht," in *PRE*³, X, 135–64.

105. Nowadays, these problems are making themselves strongly felt in Germany. As a rule, the children there make profession of faith at the age of twelve, but their knowledge is usually still most inadequate. At that stage their profession is lacking in the requisite seriousness and sounds like the recital of a lesson. Their attendance at the Lord's Supper immediately following their confirmation becomes a routine that occurs apart from a heartfelt faith. In any number of cases, they are never seen again in church or at the Lord's Supper, and if they remain church-attending members, they are still not able to be fully active as voting members of the church, say, in connection with the calling of ministers. In reality, therefore, there develops an ever-growing gap between the members of a national church and the communicants. It is for that reason that a wide range of plans for reform have been proposed. Some want to keep the practice of examining the twelve-year-olds in a church-educational manner and postpone profession of faith and participation in the Lord's Supper to a later age (Stocker). Others want to move the whole confirmation process to a later age (Simons, Troeltsch) or insist on a simplification of the profession and promise (Teichmann, Ehlers, Kawerau) or accept the split between the baptized church and the church of communicants (Burger) or plead for the abolition of the practice of insisting on baptism and confirmation for everyone (Caspari, H. Cremer) and so forth. See inter alia E. Chr. Achelis, "Die Bestrebung zur Reform der Konfirmationspraxis und des Konfirmationsunterricht," *Theologische Rundschau* 4 (1901): 353ff.; 7 (1904): 212ff.; B. Dörries, "Zur Reform der Konfirmationsordnung," *Zeitschrift für Theologie und Kirche* 18 (1908): 81–106. In the Netherlands, H. H. Meulenbelt (*Kerkelijke opstelling*, 48–114) advocates a split between the "confirmed," who upon completing a course in catechetical instruction pass an examination of their knowledge, and "communicants," who upon professing their faith have been admitted to the Lord's Supper. On the other hand Pope Pius X decreed in *Quem singulari* (August 8, 1910) that a child's first communion should no longer take place at the age of twelve or thirteen but at the age of seven. Ed. note: This decree can be found in H. Denzinger, *Sources of Catholic Dogma*, ##2137–44.

106. Ed. note: This is a clear allusion to Heidelberg Catechism, Q 81, though Bavinck does not cite this specific reference.

PART III

THE SPIRIT MAKES ALL THINGS NEW

12

The Question of Immortality

The desire to know what happens to us after death is a universal human desire. The world's religions testify to the longing to overcome the finality of death. Classic philosophy developed sophisticated arguments for the immortality of the human soul though materialistic modern philosophy after Kant had abandoned such arguments. While Christian theology may find some of the traditional arguments for the immortality of the soul useful at points, Scripture itself is more restrained. In the face of death the immortality of the soul is no real comfort. While death is not the end, the shadowy afterlife of Sheol is seen as a diminished existence. The Bible affirms and celebrates God's gift of life as a blessing; death is punishment for sin. The victory of Christ over sin and death means that believers enjoy the firstfruits of Christ's kingly reign now and, immediately after death, a provisional bliss with Christ in heaven, while unbelievers enter a state of torment.

[548] The end of things, like their origin and essence, is unknown to us. To the question of their destiny science no more furnishes a satisfying answer than to that of their origin. Still, religion has an urgent need to know something of the destiny of the individual, of humanity, and of the world. All the peoples of the world, accordingly, have some idea of it, and all religions include some kind of eschatology. Admittedly, there are still some scholars who say that originally belief in the immortality of the soul was certainly not typical of all people and is to this day still lacking, for example, among the Weddas in Ceylon [Sri Lanka], the Seelongs in India, and others.[1]

True, from an evolutionary viewpoint, belief in God, the independent existence of the soul, and its immortality cannot have been an original part of

1. E. Haeckel, *The Riddle of the Universe at the Close of the Nineteenth Century*, trans. J. McCabe (New York: Harper & Brothers, 1900), 192; L. Büchner, *Kraft und Stoff* (Leipzig: T. Thomas, 1902), 156–77. Ed. note: Bavinck's own citation is clearly to a different edition since his reference is vol. 1, p. 423. A multivolume edition of *Kraft und Stoff* was not traceable. The section in the edition cited in this note is titled "Gehirn und Seele." An English edition of Büchner's much-printed volume is available as *Force and Matter; or Principles of the Natural Order of the Universe*, 4th ed., translated from the 15th German ed. (New York: P. Eckler, 1891).

human nature but must, as a consequence of a variety of circumstances, have arisen and evolved gradually and accidentally. Ancestor worship, affection for deceased relatives, the love of life and the desire for its continuation, a hope for better living conditions on the other side of the grave, the fear of punishment, and the hope of reward—these are then the factors that promoted the gradual rise of belief in immortality.

Over against this view, however, the most respected historians of religion tell us that belief in the immortality of the soul occurs among all peoples and is a component even of the most primitive religions. It is found everywhere and at every stage of human development, wherever it has not as yet been undermined by philosophical doubts or thrust into the background by other causes; and in every case it is bound up with religion.[2] One can even say that originally this belief was a very natural thing. Like the author of the Garden of Eden narrative in Genesis, says Tiele, all peoples take for granted that humans are by nature immortal and that it is death, not immortality, that requires explanation. It is death that seems an unnatural thing. Something must have happened to bring something so illogical into the world. The sagas of many different peoples, differing in origin and development, express the same idea: there was a time when neither sickness nor death was known on earth. Earlier humans in their natural state cannot even believe in death when they see it before their eyes. They call it "sleep," a state of unconsciousness; the spirit has taken leave of the body but may still return. And so they wait several days to see if this will happen. And if the dead man's spirit does not return, why, then he has only disappeared in order to enter into another body or to join the superterrestrial spirits.[3]

The forms in which the afterlife of the soul were presented were very diverse and often variously combined. Sometimes it was thought that souls after death lived on near their graves and for their continued existence needed the ongoing care of their blood relatives or led a gloomy shadelike existence in hades, far removed from the gods and living humans. Then again it was believed that the souls of the deceased, who before their indwelling in a human body had sometimes undergone a series of metamorphoses, after their departure from the human body still had to spend a period of time in other bodies, animal or human, to be purified or to attain perfection and be absorbed into the Deity or into an unconscious nirvana. There was also a doctrine saying that immediately after death the souls entered into divine judgment. If they had done good, they would pass over a dangerous bridge of the dead into the land of the blessed, where they lived in communion with the gods. If they had done evil, they were plunged into a place of everlasting darkness and torment.

2. C. P. Tiele, *Elements of the Science of Religion*, 2 vols. (Edinburgh and London: W. Blackwood & Sons, 1899), II, 113–14; O. Peschel, *Abhandlungen zur Erd und Völkerkunde* (Leipzig: Duncker & Humboldt, 1878), 257.

3. Ibid., 231f.

PHILOSOPHY

This teaching of personal immortality passed from religion into philosophy. Following the example of Pythagoras, Heraclitus, and Empedocles, especially Plato (in his *Phaedo*) sought to undergird his religious belief in immortality by philosophical argumentation. Essentially his proofs come down to the view that the soul, which draws its knowledge of ideas from memory, existed already before dwelling in a body and will therefore continue to exist after leaving it. Furthermore, by its contemplation of the eternal ideas, the soul is akin to the divine being and as an independent and simple entity, by its control over the body and its desires, is on a level far above that of the body. Above all, Plato argues that the soul—the principle of vitality and thus identical with life itself—cannot be conceived as nonliving and transient. With this theory of the immortality of the soul, Plato then combined a variety of notions about the soul's preexistence, fall, union with the body, judgment, and transmigration that in large part bear a mythical character and are certainly not all intended, even by Plato himself, in a purely scientific sense. Although other philosophers such as Democritus, Epicurus, and Lucretius opposed the doctrine of the immortality of the soul, or like Aristotle were not positive in their statements about it, Plato's doctrine exerted immense influence in both theology and philosophy. The mythical components of preexistence, metempsychosis, and the like, often found acceptance in sectarian circles. And under Plato's influence theology devoted much more attention to the immortality of the soul than Holy Scripture does. The doctrine of the natural immortality of the soul became an *articulus mixtus*, whose truth was argued more on the basis of reason than revelation.[4]

Still, some awareness of the difference between the two persisted. People never completely lost the sense that, aside from a physical meaning, Scripture also consistently attaches a religious-ethical meaning to life and death. In Scripture life is never merely ongoing existence, and death is never extinction; on the contrary, life includes communion with God, and death means the loss of his grace and blessing. That is the reason the church fathers keep saying that Christ came to *give* us immortality (ἀθανασια, *athanasia*), and sometimes it seems they deny the natural immortality of the soul. Also, on the grounds that God alone was in himself immortal and that the soul could only be immortal by his will, the fathers were bound to oppose Plato's theory of preexistence, that is, of the noncreatedness of the soul, and for that reason they sometimes objected to calling the soul by nature immortal.[5] This is something to be borne in mind in researching the question whether among the church fathers there were also advocates of conditional immortality. For although the odd theologian like Arnobius taught the annihilation of evil souls, and though Tatian believed that at death the soul died along with the

---

4. Tertullian, *A Treatise on the Soul* 22; Origen, *On First Principles* VI, 36; Irenaeus, *Against Heresies* II, 34.

5. Justin Martyr, *Dialogue with Trypho* 5; Theophilus, *To Autolycus* II, 27.

body in order to rise again on the last day, there was nevertheless a general belief that the soul was immortal by virtue of its God-given nature.[6]

In philosophy as well Plato's doctrine of immortality retained an important place. Descartes conceived spirit and matter, soul and body, as two separate substances, each with its own attribute, thought, and extension, each capable of existing by itself and therefore capable only of being united mechanically. Spinoza adopted the same two attributes but viewed them as manifestations of one eternal and infinite substance, as two sides of the same thing, which cannot exist separately but are always joined as subject and object, image and contrasting image, idea and thing. In his system there was no room for immortality, nor did he need it, for "even if we did not know that our mind is eternal, we should still consider as of primary importance piety and religion, and absolutely everything which in the Fourth Part we have shown to be related to strength of mind and generosity."[7] The philosophy of the eighteenth century, however, was not well disposed toward Spinoza; it bore a deistic character and was content with the trilogy of God, virtue, and immortality, and of the three it most esteemed the third. In the wake of Leibniz, Wolff, Mendelssohn and others, its truth was argued by means of a wide assortment of metaphysical, theological, cosmic, moral, and historical proofs, and it urged on readers by means of sentimental observations on the blissful recognition and reunions of souls on the other side of the grave.[8] According to Strauss, the statement by the poet of Ps. 73:25 ["There is nothing on earth that I desire other than you"] was converted into the sentiment "As long as I am sure of myself, God and the world are not important to me." Kant, however, put an end to this certainty of the self by demonstrating the inadequacy of all proofs advanced for the immortality of the soul and regarded this theory as acceptable only as a postulate of practical reason. Over against the self-centered wishes of rationalism, Schleiermacher made the statement "Whosoever has learned to be more than himself knows that he loses little when he loses himself" and knew no other and higher immortality than "in the midst of finitude to be one with the Infinite and in every moment to be eternal in the immortality of religion."[9]

Similarly, the idealistic philosophy of Fichte, Schelling, and Hegel left no room at all for the immortality of the soul, even though it was reluctant to express its convictions candidly on this issue. However, Richter's book on the doctrine of

6. A. von Harnack, *History of Dogma*, trans. N. Buchanan, vol. 2 (London: Williams & Norgate, 1897), 213; W. Münscher, *Lehrbuch des christlichen Dogmengeschichte*, ed. Daniel von Coelln, 3rd ed. (Cassel: J. C. Krieger, 1832–38), I, 333; A. J. Th. Jonker, "De leer der conditioneele onsterfelijkheid," *Theologische Studiën* 1 (1883): 167ff.; L. Atzberger, *Geschichte der christlichen Eschatologie* (Freiburg i.B. and St. Louis: Herder, 1896), 118f., 222f., 338f., 577f.

7. B. Spinoza, *Ethics*, V, 41.

8. See literature cited by K. G. Bretschneider, *Systematische Entwickelung aller in der Dogmatik* (Leipzig: J. A. Barth, 1841), 824.

9. F. Schleiermacher, *On Religion: Speeches to Its Cultured Despisers*, trans. John Oman (1893; 1958; repr., Louisville: Westminster/John Knox, 1994), 101. Cf. idem, *The Christian Faith*, ed. H. R. MacIntosh and J. S. Stewart (Edinburgh: T&T Clark, 1928), §158, 1.

the last things[10] brought to light the implications of Hegel's system and, despite much criticism, paved the way for the materialism that had already been loudly advocated by Feuerbach and was later supported by Vogt, Moleschott, Büchner, Haeckel, and others with arguments said to be derived from the natural sciences. These arguments so strongly impressed many people that they have totally abandoned the immortality of the soul[11] or at most assert its possibility and merely speak of a hope of immortality.[12] Theologians, too, often attach little or no value to the proofs for the immortality of the soul.[13] But in contrast to them there are still numerous persons of repute who regard all or some or at least one or two of the proofs strong enough for them to build on them a firm faith in the immortality of the soul.[14]

HISTORY AND REASON

[549] The arguments for the immortality of the soul derived from history and reason, though they fail to furnish adequate certainty, are nevertheless not without value. In the first place, it is significant that belief in immortality occurs among all peoples at every stage of their development. The consensus of the nations (*consensus gentium*) is as strong at this point as in the case of belief in God.[15] Though various considerations from which people have inferred belief in immortality (such as the fear of death and thirst for life, the experiences of dreams and ecstasy, the riddle of death and the impossibility of imagining an absolute annihilation of the cognitive essence of humans, the fear of punishment and the hope of reward)[16] may a posteriori support and confirm belief in immortality, they do not furnish a satisfying explanation of its origin. Even in places where such considerations are absent or are considered worthless, belief in immortality still occurs. Often, in the case of numerous people, the desire for continued existence is weaker than

10. F. Richter, *Die Lehre von der letzen Dingen* (Breslau: J. Hebenstreit, 1833–44).

11. D. F. Strauss, *Die christliche Glaubenslehre*, 2 vols. (Tübingen: Osiander, 1840–41), II, 738; idem, *Der alte und der neue Glaube*, 2nd ed. (Leipzig: Hirzel, 1872), 123f.; A. Schopenhauer, *The World as Will and Representation*, trans. E. F. J. Payne, 2 vols. (1958; repr., New York: Dover, 1966), I, 282; Eduard von Hartmann, *Religionsphilosophie* (Leipzig: Friedrich, 1888), II, 232.

12. S. Hoekstra, *De hoop der ontsterfelijkheid* (Amsterdam: P. N. van Kampen, 1867); L. Rauwenhoff, *Wijsbegeerte van de godsdienst* (Leiden: Brill & van Doesburgh, 1887), 811.

13. F. H. R. Frank, *System der christlichen Wahrheit*, 3rd ed. (Erlangen and Leipzig: Deichert, 1894), II, 427f.; A. F. C. Vilmar, *Handbuch der evangelischen Dogmatik* (Gütersloh: Bertelsmann, 1895), 295.

14. I. A. Dorner, *A System of Christian Doctrine*, trans. A. Cave and J. S. Banks (Edinburgh: T&T Clark, 1882), IV, 373ff.; J. I. Doedes, *Inleiding tot de leer van God* (Utrecht: Kemink, 1870), 248f.; J. J. van Oosterzee, *Christian Dogmatics*, trans. J. Watson and M. Evans, 2 vols. (New York: Scribner, Armstrong, 1874), §68; Chr. H. Weisse, *Philosophische Dogmatik*, 3 vols. (Leipzig: Hirzel, 1855–62), §§955–72; I. H. Fichte, *Die Idee der Persönlichkeit und der individuellen Fortdauer* (Leipzig: Dyk, 1855); C. F. Göschel, *Von den Beweisen für die Unsterblichkeit der menschliche Seele* (Berlin: Duncker & Humblot, 1835); F. A. Kahnis, *Die lutherische Dogmatik* (Leipzig: Dörffling & Francke, 1861–68), II, 485f.

15. Cicero, *Tusculan Disputations* I, 3.

16. G. Runze, "Unsterblichkeit," in *PRE*³, XX, 294f.

the desire that death might end their lives. The hope of reward does not explain the belief in the case of those who have died to all self-seeking and have found the highest bliss in communion with God. The notion of retribution is alien to representations of the afterlife as a shadowy existence in a spirit world. The riddle of death does not, except in rare instances, elicit conclusions about the immortality of animals and plants. And experiences of dreams and ecstasy do not extinguish the awareness of the real distinction existing between these phenomena and the phenomenon of death.

In the case of the belief in the immortality of the soul, as in that of the existence of God, we are dealing rather with a conviction that was not gained by reflection and reasoning but precedes all reflection and springs spontaneously from human nature as such. It is self-evident and natural, found wherever no philosophical doubts have undermined it. Along with the consciousness of having an independent, individual existence of one's own, there also arises an awareness of the continuation of the self after death. Genuine self-consciousness—not the abstract self-consciousness with which psychology occupies itself—the self-consciousness of humans as personal, independent, rational, moral, religious beings always and everywhere includes belief in immortality. Accordingly, it is not a mere wish or desire, nor an inference drawn from premises, but a mighty, ineradicable witness that arises from human nature itself and maintains itself in the face of all contrary argumentation and opposition. And the so-called arguments for immortality amount to nothing more than an assortment of rational attempts this belief undertakes to give some account of itself, without ever really depending on them. Therein lies their power and at the same time their weakness; they are witnesses *of*, not grounds *for*, the belief in immortality. The "knowing" lags far behind the "believing."

The *ontological* argument, which deduces the reality of immortality from the idea of it, no more succeeds in bridging the gap that separates thought from being than the ontological argument does for the existence of God. It only gives verbal form to the sense that belief in immortality is not arbitrary or accidental but a fact of human nature and morally necessary to human beings. A person does not derive the idea of immortality from the surrounding world—the message the world conveys to one is exclusively that of decay and death; rather, the idea is forced on a person by one's own nature. Just as God does not leave himself without a witness but speaks to us from all the works of his hands, so the conviction that a person does not perish like the beasts of the field is thrust upon a person from within one's own being. And this is what the ontological argument aims to show; it does not cross from the realm of thought to that of being but gives expression to the universality, the necessity, and the apriority of the belief in immortality.

The *metaphysical* argument, which deduces the soul's immortality from its very nature, goes a step further. It is able to do this and does this, however, in various ways. One can point to the idea that as vital principle and as identical with life itself, the soul is inviolable by death. Or that, by virtue of the unity of the consciousness of the self, the soul is a simple indivisible entity devoid of composition, and is therefore not capable of decomposition. Or that the soul, beneath all the material and physical changes that take place, consistently remains identical with itself—as appears again from the consciousness of the self—and therefore must possess a life and an existence independent of the body. And by these various routes one can then attempt to reach the conclusion that the soul is immortal.

But this argument is subject to certain very serious objections. Even though the soul is an active vital principle, it is nevertheless never identical with life itself. God alone is life itself; he alone is immortal (1 Tim. 6:16). If the soul continues to exist, this can only occur by virtue of God's omnipresent and omnipotent power. The soul is a created entity and therefore limited, finite, relative, never exempt from all passivity and composition, from change and variation. We can, for that matter, see before our own eyes that it changes, increases, or decreases in knowledge and vitality; is dependent on the body; and is subject to various influences. And the subjective unity and identity of the ego by no means proves the objective unity and simplicity of the soul; if this were the case, it would also prove the immortality of plants or at least of animals, as this has been consistently held by Leibniz, Bonnet, and Bilderdijk,[17] among others. Contradicting these objections again is the undeniable fact that life cannot be explained in terms of a mechanical metabolic process but points to a principle of its own. "Every living thing arises from something living" (*omne vivum ex vivo*) is to this day the last word of science. And something that is true of life in general is even more compelling when applied to conscious life: even the most primitive perception is unalterably separated from any neural vibration. By means of it we enter a totally new and higher world that differs essentially from that of sensible, tangible, and measurable things. The fact that life and by implication conscious life is most intimately bound up with the world of the senses has been known for a long time and can certainly not be called a recent scientific discovery. But the idea that it is generated by a cause in the world of the senses, though often asserted, has so far not been proved by anyone. The metaphysical argument retains its value to the degree that from sui generis psychic phenomena it arrives at an autonomous spiritual principle that is distinct from matter.

Still, this leaves untouched the objection that one can pursue the same line of reasoning in the case of plants or at least animals, and still not make their immortality plausible. For that reason we need to supplement the metaphysical argument with the *anthropological* argument, which, starting from the uniqueness of the psychic life of human beings, comes to the conclusion that there is a spiritual existence distinct from animals and plants. The soul of an animal, although simple and independent of the animal's metabolism, is oriented toward the sensible; it is restricted to the finite; it lives in the present; it is so restricted to

17. Ed. note: Willem Bilderdijk (1756–1831) was the great poet of Dutch nationalism who engaged in a titanic literary battle against the spirit of modernism.

the body that it cannot exist apart from it. Humans not only possess perception and observation but also intellect and reason. By the thinking process a person transcends the sensible, material, finite world. A person lifts oneself up toward the ideal, the logical, the true, the good, and the beautiful that eye has not seen and cannot be touched with hands. One seeks a lasting, an *ever*lasting, happiness, a highest good that this world cannot give, and as a result of all this, a person is a citizen and inhabitant of another, a higher kingdom than that of nature. The rational, moral, religious consciousness of humans points to a psychic existence that reaches beyond the visible world. That which by virtue of its nature seeks the eternal must be destined for eternity.

To this must be added the *moral* argument and the argument of *retribution*, which demonstrates the disharmony existing between morality (*ethos*) and nature (*physis*) and infers from it another kind of existence in which the two are reconciled. Let no one object to this by saying that this argument is based on human egoism, and that virtue is its own reward, just as sin brings with it its own punishment.[18] But this the devout of all ages knew very well; they were profoundly aware that God must be served for his own sake and not for the sake of any reward.[19] At the same time they maintained that if for this life only they had hoped in Christ, they would be of all people most to be pitied (1 Cor. 15:17, 19, 30, 32). At issue here is absolutely not the satisfaction of a selfish desire but nothing less than the rule and triumph of justice. The question underlying the moral argument is this: In the end, is it good or evil, God or Satan, Christ or the antichrist who will win? History itself fails to furnish an adequate answer.

From the viewpoint of the present world (*Diesseits*), no satisfying explanation of the world is possible; on this position there is all too much reason for the despair of pessimism. And our sense of justice, which a righteous God has himself implanted deep in the human heart, therefore demands that at the end of time the balance of justice be redressed. It demands harmony between virtue and happiness, between sin and punishment, and truth eternally overcoming the lie and lighting the darkness. Although it has been rightly said that "nothingness always was the horizon of bad consciences," even those who have no reason to expect any good from a life after this life are persuaded by their sense of justice that such restoration of justice is necessary. If justice does not prevail in the end, there is no justice. And if in the end God does not prove to be the conqueror of Satan, life is not worth living. What comes to expression in the moral argument is not an egoistic desire but a profound sense of justice, the thirst for harmony, a yearning for the total glorification of God in whom holiness and bliss are one. Even art, when it exhibits ideal reality visibly before our eyes, prophesies such a future. All these arguments or proofs—and especially those derived from human perfectibility, from the moral personality of humans, from the numerous uninhabited

18. B. Spinoza, *Ethics*, V, 41–42.
19. J. Calvin, *Institutes*, III.ii.26; III.xvi.2.

stars, from spiritistic experiences, and so on—are not proofs in the sense that they silence all contradiction. Rather, they are witnesses and indications that belief in immortality arises with complete naturalness and spontaneity from human nature itself. Whoever denies and combats it violates his own nature. "The idea of immortality is already the first act of immortality."[20]

[550] However valuable these indications may be that nature and history offer us in support of belief in the immortality of the soul, Scripture takes a position with respect to this doctrine that at first blush can only seem strange to us. While the immortality of the soul may seem to be of the greatest importance for religion and life, Scripture never explicitly mentions it. Scripture never announces it as a divine revelation, nor does it highlight it anywhere; still less does it ever make an attempt to argue its truth or to uphold it against those who oppose it. That is the reason why at various times many scholars have asserted that the doctrine of the immortality of the soul does not occur at all in the Old Testament, at least not in the oldest books, and was first imported into Israel from the outside.[21] But little by little they backed away from this position, and presently there is a general recognition that, like all other peoples, Israel in fact did believe in the soul's continued existence after death. In recent years many authors have even argued that in ancient times in Israel, as in other nations, the

20. Von Baer, cited by F. J. Splittgerber, *Tod, Fortleben und Auferstehung*, 3rd ed. (Halle: Fricke, 1879), 93. Further on immortality, see E. G. Steude, "Die Unsterblichkeitsbeweise," *Beweis des Glaubens* 39 (1903); 40 (1904): 73–82, 145–59, 172–83, 210–15; P. Kneib, *Die Beweise für die Unsterblichkeit der Seele als allgemeinen psychologischen Tatsachen* (Freiburg: Herder, 1903); O. Riemann, *Was wissen wir über die Unsterblichkeit der Seele* (Magdeburg: Frölich, 1900); H. Keyserling, *Unsterblichkeit, eine Kritik der Beziehungen zwischen Naturgeschehen und menschlichen Vorstellungswelt* (Munich: Lehmann, 1907); Th. Steinmann, *Der religiose Unsterblichkeitsglaube* (Göttingen: Vandenhoeck & Ruprecht, 1912); G. Heinzelmann, *Der Begriff der Seele und die Idee der Unsterblichkeit bei Wilhelm Wundt* (PhD diss., University of Göttingen, 1907; Tübingen: Mohr, 1910); Robert J. Thompson, *The Proof of Life after Death* (Boston: Small, Maynard, 1906); H. Frank, *Modern Light on Immortality* (Boston: Sherman, French, 1909); D. S. MacKay, "Personal Immortality in the Light of Recent Science," *North American Review* 185 (1907): 387–93; Josiah Royce, "Immortality," *Hibbert Journal* 5 (1907): 724–44; Oliver Lodge, "The Immortality of the Soul," *Hibbert Journal* 6 (1908): 291–304, 563–85; Rudolf Eucken, "The Problem of Immortality," *Hibbert Journal* 6 (1908): 836–51; *S. Jankélévitch, "La mort et l'immortalité de'après les donnees de la biologie," *Revue philosophique* (1910), no. 4; A. Bruining, *Het voortbestaan der menschelijke persoonlijkheid na den dood* (Assen: L. Hansma, 1904). Spiritualist proofs for immortality are advanced by Fred W. H. Myers in his *Human Personality and Its Survival of Bodily Death*, 2nd ed. (London: Longmans, Green, 1903); also see G. F. Stout, "Mr. F. W. Myers on *Human Personality and Its Survival of Bodily Death*," *Hibbert Journal* 2 (1903): 44–64; Oliver Lodge, *The Survival of Man* (London: Methuen, 1909), reviewed by Frank Padmore in *Hibbert Journal* 8 (1910): 669–72; F. Hesselink, *Staat de wetenschap het geloof aan de onsterfelijkheid in de weg?* (Middelburg: G. A. W. van Straaten, 1904); H. N. de Fremery, *Wat gebeurt er met ons als wij sterven* (Bussum: Van Dishoeck, 1910).

21. B. Stade, *Geschichte des Volkes Israel*, 2 vols. (Berlin: G. Grote, 1887–88), I, 387–427; idem, *Über die alttestamentische Vorstellungen vom Zustande nach dem Tode* (Leipzig: Vogel, 1877); F. Schwally, *Das Leben nach dem Tode: Nach den Vorstellungen des Alten Israel* (Giessen: J. Ricker, 1892); H. Oort, "De doodenvereering bij de Israelieten," *Theologisch Tijdschrift* 15 (1881): 358–63; J. C. Matthes, "Rouw en doodenvereering bij Israel," *Teylers Theologisch Tijdschrift* 3 (1905): 1–30; idem, "Twee Israelitische rouwbedrijven," *Teylers Theologisch Tijdschrift* 8 (1910): 145–69.

dead were venerated and were therefore undoubtedly assumed to exist. Arguments for this view were derived from the rituals followed in cases of bereavement, such as tearing one's garments and wearing mourning attire, covering one's face and head, removing ornaments, special hairstyles and self-mutilation, throwing up dust and ashes, refraining from washing and anointing oneself, fasting and eating, singing lament songs, and bringing sacrifices. All these customs are said to be explicable only from the veneration of the dead practiced earlier.[22] But Schwally himself has to admit that "at the time Israel emerged in history animistic nature religion had already been basically overcome."[23] And others have advanced such serious objections to his inferring bereavement practices from an original animism that the hypothesis of an original cult of the dead in Israel can only be made plausible by fresh evidence. Still it is clear that in Israel there was a great difference between the popular religion, which encompassed an assortment of superstitious and idolatrous components, and the service of YHWH championed by Moses and his followers. Yahwism on the one hand opposed, prohibited, and eradicated that popular religion but, on the other, quietly tolerated or adopted and sanctioned various religious notions and customs that in themselves were not wrong.[24]

THE OLD TESTAMENT

In revealing himself to Israel, God accommodated himself to the historical circumstances under which it lived; grace did not undo nature but renewed and consecrated it. This is also what happened with the popular belief in the afterlife. The custom of burial and the great importance attached to it was as such already proof for that belief. Cremation was not indigenous in Israel; it occurred only after an execution (Gen. 38:24; Lev. 20:14; 21:9; Josh. 7:15). From 1 Sam. 31:12 and Amos 6:10 we cannot draw any conclusions because the text is perhaps corrupt or else contains a report of isolated cases, while 2 Chron. 16:14; 21:19; and Jer. 34:5 only deal with burning aromatic spices at the time of burial. Burial, however, was highly valued and is therefore mentioned repeatedly in the Old Testament as something special. To remain unburied was a terrible disgrace (1 Sam. 17:44, 46; 1 Kings 14:11, 13; 16:4; 2 Kings 9:10; Ps. 79:3; Eccles. 6:3; Isa. 14:19–20; Jer. 7:33; 8:1–2; 9:22; 16:6; 25:33; Ezek. 29:5). A dead person no longer belongs in the land of the living; his unburied body arouses loathing. Shed blood calls for vengeance (Gen. 4:10; 37:26; Job 16:18; Isa. 26:21; Ezek. 24:7) because blood

22. J. Frey, *Tod, Seelenglaube und Seelenkult im alten Israel* (Leipzig: A. Deichert, 1898); C. Grüneisen, *Der Ahnenkultus und die Urreligon Israels* (Halle: Niemeyer, 1900); *Meusel, "War die vorjahwistische Religion Israels Ahnenkultus?" *Neue kirchliche Zeitschrift* 16 (1905): 484ff. S. Zandstra, "The Theory of Ancestor Worship among the Hebrews," *Princeton Theological Review* 5 (1907): 281–87. [Ed. note: This bibliographic essay is very useful for its summary of works cited by Bavinck in notes 20 and 21 above.]

23. Fr. Schwally, *Das Leben nach dem Tode*, 75.

24. G. Wildeboer, *Jahvedienst en volksreligie in Israel* (Groningen: Wolters, 1898).

is the basis of the soul (Lev. 17:11), and the deceased must therefore be covered, concealed, withdrawn from view.

Through death all souls enter the abode of the dead, Sheol (שְׁאוֹל, šĕʾōl). The etymology of the word is uncertain but, according to some, derives from שָׁאַל (šāʾal, to inquire, require, or to claim, bring to decision); according to others, it derives from שָׁעַל, שׁוּל (šʾl, šwl, to be feeble, hang down, sink).[25] Sheol is located in the depths of the earth so that one goes down into it (Num. 16:30; Pss. 30:3, 9; 55:15; Isa. 38:18); it belongs to the lowest places of the earth (Ps. 63:9; Ezek. 26:20; 31:14; 32:18), lying even below the waters and the foundations of the mountains (Deut. 32:22; Job 26:5; Isa. 14:15), and is therefore repeatedly reinforced by the adjective "lowest" (תַּחְתִּית, taḥtît) in such passages as Deut. 32:22 and Pss. 86:13; 88:6. For that reason Sheol is linked closely with the grave (קֶבֶר, qeber) or the pit (בּוֹר, bôr). However, the two are not identical, for the dead who have not been buried are nevertheless in Sheol (Gen. 37:35; Num. 16:32–33). Yet, just as soul and body together form one human and are thought to be in some kind of reciprocal relationship also after death, so also the grave and Sheol cannot be pictured in isolation from each other. The two belong to the lowest places of the earth, are both represented as the dwelling of the dead, and are repeatedly exchanged for each other. Sheol is the one great grave that encompasses all the graves of the dead; it is the realm of the dead, the underworld, and accordingly often mistakenly translated in the King James Version[26] by "hell." Sheol, after all, is the place where all the dead without exception congregate (1 Kings 2:2; Job 3:13ff.; 30:23; Ps. 89:48; Isa. 14:9ff.; Ezek. 32:18; Hab. 2:5), and from which no one returns except by a miracle (1 Kings 17:22; 2 Kings 4:34; 13:21). The realm of the dead is, as it were, a city, furnished with barred gates (Job 17:16: "Will it [my hope] go down to the bars of Sheol?"; 38:17; Pss. 9:13; 107:18; Isa. 38:10; Matt. 16:18), which by its power (Pss. 49:15; 89:48; Hos. 13:14) holds all people captive as in a prison (Isa. 24:22). Sheol is the eternal home (Eccles. 12:5). Israel's enemies who have been plunged into it will never rise up again (Isa. 26:14); those who go down to Sheol do not come up again (Job 7:9–10; 14:7–12; 16:22). This realm of the dead is therefore squarely opposed to the land of the living (Prov. 15:24; Ezek. 26:20; 32:23ff.).

True, the dead are thought of as existing and living: they are often pictured and described in the way they showed themselves here on earth, and are also recognized by each other and are moved by this encounter (1 Sam. 28:14; Isa. 14:9ff.; Ezek. 32:18ff.). There is also mention of the innermost chambers of Sheol (Prov. 7:27; Ezek. 32:23). Among the dead there is distinction inasmuch as each is gathered to one's fathers (Gen. 15:15; Judg. 2:10) or people (Gen. 25:8, 17; 35:29; 49:29), and the uncircumcised are all laid out together (Ezek. 32:19). But

25. F. Delitzsch, *A New Commentary on Genesis*, trans. Sophia Taylor (Edinburgh: T&T Clark, 1899), II, 264; L. Atzberger, *Die christliche Eschatologie* (Freiburg i.B.: Herder, 1890), 24.

26. Ed. note: For Bavinck, the Dutch *Statenvertaling*.

otherwise Sheol is always described in terms of its negative aspects, by contrast with the earth as the land of the living. It is the region of darkness and the shadow of death (Job 10:21–22; Pss. 88:11; 143:3), the place of corruption—indeed as corruption itself (אֲבַדּוֹן, *ăbaddôn*, Abaddon; Job 26:6; 28:22; 31:12; Ps. 88:11; Prov. 27:20)—without "ordinances" (i.e., firm contours and clear distinctions [Job 10:22]), a land of rest and silence and forgetfulness (Job 3:13, 17–18; Ps. 115:17), where neither God nor humans are visible anymore (Isa. 38:11), God is no longer praised or thanked (Pss. 6:5; 115:17), his virtues are no longer proclaimed (Ps. 88:5, 11–12; Isa. 38:18–19), and his wonders are no longer being witnessed (Ps. 88:10, 12). It is the place where the dead know nothing, no longer work, no longer calculate their chances, no longer possess wisdom and knowledge, and have no share whatever in all that happens under the sun (Eccles. 9:5–6, 10). The dead are רְפָאִים (*rĕpā'îm*), from the adjective רָפֶה (*rāpeh*, feeble; Job 26:5; Ps. 88:10; Prov. 2:18; 9:18; 21:6; Isa. 14:9), weak (Isa. 14:10), without strength (Ps. 88:4 KJV).

This entire representation of Sheol is formed from the perspective of this earthly existence and is valid only by contrast with the riches of life enjoyed by people on earth. In that framework death indeed means a breaking off of all ties, being dead to the rich life lived on earth, being at rest, being asleep, being silent, nonbeing in relation to things on this side of the grave. The state of Sheol, though not an annihilation of one's existence, is still a dreadful diminution of life, a deprivation of everything in this life that makes for its enjoyment.

In the Old Testament, there is no room for a view that permits only the body to die and comforts itself with the immortality of the soul. The whole person dies when at death the spirit, or "breath" (Ps. 146:4; Eccles. 12:7), or the soul (Gen. 35:18; 2 Sam. 1:9; 1 Kings 17:21; Jon. 4:3) departs from him. Not only his body but also his soul is in a state of death and belongs to the underworld; this is the reason there is mention of the death of the soul (Gen. 37:21; Num. 23:10; Deut. 22:20–21; Judg. 16:30; Job 36:14; Ps. 78:50) and of defilement by contact with the soul of a dead person (i.e., a corpse, Lev. 19:28; 21:11; 22:4; Num. 5:2; 6:6–7, 9–11; Deut. 14:1; Hag. 2:13). Just as the whole person was destined for life through obedience, so the whole person also by his transgression succumbs body-and-soul to death (Gen. 2:17). This idea had to be deeply impressed upon the consciousness of humankind; and in antiquity it was also realized by all peoples that death is a punishment, that it is something unnatural, something inimical to the essence and destiny of human beings. The revelation God gave to Israel is therefore bound up with this realization. In the same way that this revelation took over so many customs and ceremonies (sacrifice, priesthood, circumcision, and so forth) while purging them of impure accretions like self-mutilation (Lev. 19:28; 21:5; Deut. 14:1) or consulting the dead (Lev. 19:31; 20:6, 27; Deut. 18:10–11), so the idea of the unnaturalness of death was also allowed to continue and take over.

But revelation does something else and more as well. It not only maintains and reinforces the antithesis existing between life and death but also introduces into this life an even sharper contrast. This life, after all, is not the true life, inasmuch as it is a sinful, impure life plagued by suffering and destined for death. It only becomes real life and only achieves real content through the service of YHWH and in fellowship with God. Entirely in keeping with the then-prevailing dispensation of the covenant of grace and with the election of Israel as the people of God, the Old Testament conceives the connection between godliness and life in a way that regards godliness as receiving its benefits and reward in a long life on earth (Exod. 20:12; Deut. 5:16, 29; 6:2; 11:9; 22:7; 30:16; 32:47; etc.). Into the fabric of the universally known natural antithesis between life and death, there is also woven a moral and spiritual contrast—that between a life in the service of sin and a life in the fear of the Lord. Death is bound up with evil; life is bound up with good (Deut. 30:15). Those who are bent on finding the philosophical theory of the immortality of the soul in the Old Testament have not understood the revelation of God to Israel and have read Western ideas into the religion of an Eastern people. Pfleiderer, striking a much truer note, says: "What people have often considered a weakness of Israel's prophetic YHWH religion [namely, that the beyond has so little place in it] was in reality its characteristic strength. The living God who reveals himself in historical deeds has nothing in common with the shadows of Sheol."[27] The God of Israel is not a God of the dead but of the living.

For that reason the eschatological hope of Israel's pious was almost exclusively directed toward the earthly future of the nation, the realization of the kingdom of God. The question concerning the future of individuals in Sheol remained totally in the background. God, nation, and land were inseparably bound up with each other, and individuals were incorporated in that "covenant" and viewed accordingly. Only after the exile, when Israel became a religious community and religion was individualized, did the question of each person's future fate force itself into the foreground; the spiritual contrast that revelation had woven into the natural then made itself felt; increasingly the distinction between the righteous and the ungodly replaced that between Israel and the nations and extended itself on the other side of the grave as well.

The basic elements for this development were already present, for that matter, in the revelation of the past. The person who serves God continues to live (Gen. 2:17); life is bound up with the keeping of his commandments (Lev. 18:5; Deut. 30:20); his word is life (Deut. 8:3; 32:47). Though in Proverbs life is frequently understood as length of days (2:18–19; 3:16; 10:30), it is nevertheless remarkable that as a rule this book only associates death and Sheol with the wicked and, by contrast, attributes life almost exclusively to the righteous (2:18; 5:5; 7:27; 9:18). Wisdom, righteousness, and the fear of the Lord are the way to life (8:35–36; 11:19; 12:28; 13:14; 14:27; 19:23). The wicked person is thrust down when misfortune strikes, but the righteous one maintains confidence and consolation even in death (14:32 KJV). One is blessed whose God is YHWH (Deut. 33:29;

---

27. O. Pfleiderer, *Religionsphilosophie auf geschichtlicher Grundlage* (Berlin: G. Reimer, 1896), 616.

Pss. 1:1; 2:12; 32:1–2; 33:12; 34:8; etc.), even in the most dreadful adversities (Ps. 73:25–28; Hab. 3:17–19). The wicked, on the other hand, perish and come to an end no matter how much they prosper for a time (Ps. 73:18–20).

From within this perspective the pious not only expect deliverance from oppression and adversity in time, but also by looking at things through the eyes of faith frequently penetrate the world beyond the grave and anticipate a blessed life in fellowship with God as well. The passages usually adduced to support this viewpoint (Gen. 49:18; Job 14:13–15; 16:16–21; 19:25–27; Pss. 16:9–11; 17:15; 49:15; 73:23–26; 139:18) can be variously interpreted and, according to many commentators, apply only to a temporary salvation from death. But even if this were the case, the whole Old Testament still teaches that God is the Creator of heaven and earth, that there are no limits to his power, and that he is also absolutely sovereign over life and death. He is God, the Lord, who has given life to humanity (Gen. 1:26; 2:7) and still creates and upholds every human being and all that exists (Job 32:8; 33:4; 34:14; Ps. 104:29; Eccles. 12:7). He sovereignly binds life to [the keeping of] his law and decrees death upon its violation (Gen. 2:17; Lev. 18:5; Deut. 30:20, 32:47). Though heaven is his dwelling, he is also present by his Spirit in Sheol (Ps. 139:7–8). Sheol and Abaddon lie open before the Lord, as do the hearts of the children of humankind (Job 26:6; 38:17; Prov. 15:11). The Lord kills, keeps alive and makes alive, brings down to Sheol, and raises up from there again (Deut. 32:39; 1 Sam. 2:6; 2 Kings 5:7). He provides escape from death, can deliver when death threatens (Ps. 68:22; Isa. 38:5; Jer. 15:20–21; Dan. 3:26; etc.), take Enoch and Elijah to himself apart from death (Gen. 5:24; 2 Kings 2:11), and cause the dead to return to life (1 Kings 17:22; 2 Kings 4:34–35; 13:21). He can annihilate death and by raising the dead completely triumph over its power (Job 14:13–15; 19:25–27; Isa. 25:8; 26:19; Ezek. 37:11–12; Dan. 12:2; Hos. 6:2; 13:14).

INTERTESTAMENTAL JUDAISM

[551] This teaching of the Old Testament, though not entirely absent from later Jewish literature, was nevertheless modified and expanded by various nonindigenous elements. In general the writings of this period agree in that they have a more individualistic view of religion. Also, under the influence of the idea of retribution, they teach a provisional separation immediately at death between the righteous and the wicked, and offer a more elaborate account of the different places they inhabit. Still, they can be clearly divided into two groups, a Palestinian and an Alexandrian one. The first group—to which especially the apocryphal writings of the Maccabees, Baruch, *4 Ezra* [in the Vulgate Appendix; 2 Esdras in NRSV], *Enoch*, the *Testaments of the Twelve Patriarchs*, and so on belong—attributes only a provisional character to the intermediate state. Admittedly they too already include foreign elements and teach a certain division between the righteous and the wicked immediately at death. The *Apocalypse of*

Enoch, for example, locates Sheol in the west, describes it as being transected and surrounded by streams of water, and distinguishes four sections in it, two for the good and two for the wicked (*1 Enoch* 17:5–6; 22:2ff.). It further assumes the existence of a paradise that was situated high above and at the ends of the earth and became the abode of Enoch and Elijah at the moment of their death (12:1; 87:3; 89:52), and will be the abode for all who walk in their ways (71:16–17). But in the case of all the authors of this group, the point of emphasis lies in their universal eschatology, in the coming of the Messiah, and in the establishment of the kingdom of God at the end of time. Until then the souls of the dead are kept in hades—be it in different sections and a provisionally distinct state—as in a ταμιεία (*tamieia*, storehouse), *promptuaria animarum* (a repository of souls; 2 [*Apocalypse of*] *Baruch* 21:23; *4 Ezra* 4:35; 5:37). Resting and sleeping, they await the final judgment (*4 Ezra* 7:32–35; 2 [*Apocalypse of*] *Baruch* 21:23–24; 23:4; 30:2).

But the writings of the second group—such as Sirach, Wisdom of Solomon, Philo, Josephus, and so on—particularly stress individual eschatology, allowing the coming of the Messiah, the resurrection, final judgment, and the kingdom of God on earth either to recede totally into the background or to be kept completely out of the picture. The principal dogma is that of the immortality of the soul, which according to Philo was preexistent. On account of its fall it was temporarily locked up in the prison house of the body and, depending on its conduct, moves into other bodies after death, or in any case receives the definite settlement of its fate immediately after death (Sir. 1:13; 7:17; 18:24; 41:12; Wis. 1:8–9; 3:1–10). In the end it goes either to a holy heaven or to a dark hades.[28]

At the time of Christ, accordingly, a wide range of sometimes overlapping eschatological images whirled about the people of Israel. The Pharisees believed in a continued existence and a provisional retribution after death, but alongside of these held to the expectation of the Messiah, of the resurrection of the dead—if not of all people, then certainly of the righteous—and of the establishment of God's kingdom on earth. The Sadducees denied the resurrection (Matt. 22:23; Mark 12:18; Luke 20:27; Acts 23:8) and, according to Josephus,[29] retribution after death and immortality as well. The Essenes believed that the body was mortal but that the soul was immortal. Originally the souls dwelt in the finest ether but, being caught up in sensual lust, were placed in bodies, from which they are again liberated by death. Good souls are given a blessed life on the other side of the ocean in a place untouched by rain, snow, or heat, but the bad must suffer everlasting pains in a place of darkness and cold.[30]

28. Fl. Josephus, *Jewish War* III, 8, 5.

29. Fl. Josephus, *Jewish War* II, 8, 14; *Jewish Antiquities* XVIII, 1, 4.

30. Fl. Josephus, *Jewish War* II, 8, 11. On the eschatology of Judaism, see further also Fr. Schwally, *Das Leben nach dem Tode*, 131–92; P. Gröbler, "Die Ansichten über Unsterblichkeit und Auferstehung in der jüdischen Literatur der beiden letzten Jahrhunderte v. Chr.," *Theologische Studien und Kritiken* 52 (1879): 651–700; A. K.

THE NEW TESTAMENT

Consistent with the Law and the Prophets, the New Testament devotes much more attention to universal than to particular eschatology. Still it is incorrect to contend, as do Episcopius and others,[31] that Scripture says virtually nothing about the intermediate state or at least contains no teaching that is valid for us. Similarly, the opinion of Kliefoth[32] that the New Testament probably says everything that can be said about it is incorrect. Scripture is not lacking in statements that spread as much light as we need in and for this life. The New Testament brings out—even more forcefully than the Old—that death is a consequence of sin and punishment for sin (Rom. 5:12; 6:23; 8:10; 1 Cor. 15:21) and that death extends to all people (1 Cor. 15:22; Heb. 9:27). Only a rare individual, like Enoch, is taken so that he would not see death (Heb. 11:5). And also those who experience the parousia of Christ are changed in a twinkling of an eye without the intervention of death (1 Cor. 15:51–53; 1 Thess. 4:14–17; cf. John 21:22–23), so that Christ will not only judge the dead but also the living (Acts 10:42; 2 Tim. 4:1; 1 Pet. 4:5). But death is not the end of a person; the soul cannot be killed (Matt. 10:28), the body will one day be raised (John 5:28–29; Acts 23:6; Rev. 20:12–13), and believers even take part in an eternal life that cannot be destroyed (John 3:36; 11:25).

According to the New Testament, all the dead will be in hades, the realm of the dead, until the resurrection. In Matt. 11:23 and Luke 10:15 the expression "be brought down to hades" (καταβιβασθηση ἑως ᾁδου, *katabibasthēsē heōs hadou*) signifies that haughty Capernaum will be profoundly humbled. In Matt.16:18, Jesus promises his church that "the gates of hades" (πυλαι ᾁδου, *pylai hadou*) will have no power over it, that death will not triumph over it. According to Luke 16:23, the wretched Lazarus will be carried by angels to Abraham's bosom, and the rich man, upon his death and burial, immediately arrives in hades, where hades is not yet the same as a place of torment since this is indicated only by the addition "being in torment" (ὑπαρχων ἑν βασανοις, *hyparchōn en basanois*). Jesus, too, as long as he was in the state of death, dwelt in hades, even though it could not hold him there (Acts 2:27, 31). He, after all, descended to the "lower parts of the earth" (εἰς τα κατωτερα της γης, *eis ta katōtera tēs gēs*; Eph. 4:9). And so all the dead are "under the earth" (καταχθονιοι, *katachthonioi*; Phil. 2:10). Not only the wicked but also believers find themselves in hades after death. They are the dead in Christ (1 Thess. 4:16; cf. 1 Cor. 15:18, 23). At the time of the resurrection the sea, Death, and Hades give up all the dead who are in them, in order that they may be judged by their works (Rev. 20:13). Hades follows with and after Death, so

---

Wünsche, "Die Vorstellung von Zustande nach dem Tode nach Apokrypha, Talmud, und Kirchenvätern," *Jahrbuch für protestantische Theologie* 6 (1880): 355–83, 435–523; L. Atzberger, *Die christliche Eschatologie*, 96–156.

31. S. Episcopius, *Opera theologica*, 2 vols. (Amsterdam: Johan Blaeu, 1650–65), II, 2, 455; F. Schleiermacher, *The Christian Faith*, §159, 2; P. van Limborch, *Theologia christiana* (Amsterdam: Wetstein, 1735), VI, 10, 4; J. R. Oertel, *Hades* (Leipzig: E. Bredt, 1863), 4–6; J. C. K. von Hofmann, *Der Schriftbeweis* (Nördlingen: Beck, 1857–60), III, 462.

32. Th. Kliefoth, *Christliche Eschatologie* (Leipzig: Dörffling & Franke, 1886), 37.

that Death always brings about a relocation [of souls] into hades (Rev. 6:8). This view—from death until the resurrection believers too, according to Scripture, are in hades—is reinforced by the expression "resurrection from the dead" (ἀναστασις ἐκ [των] νεκρων, *anastasis ek [tōn] nekrōn*; Matt. 17:9; Mark 6:14; Luke 16:30; John 20:9; Eph. 5:14; etc.), which means not "from death" but "from the dead," that is, from the realm of the dead.

However, this common situatedness in the state of death does not exclude the fact that the lot of believers and unbelievers in it is very diverse. The Old Testament, too, already expressed this idea, but it is much more striking in the New Testament. According to the parable in Luke 16, the wretched Lazarus is carried by the angels to Abraham's bosom, which conveys the truth that in heaven, where the angels live, Lazarus enjoys blessedness in proximity to and in fellowship with Abraham (Matt. 8:11). Jesus promises one of the men crucified alongside him, "Today you will be with me in Paradise" (Luke 23:43). The word "paradise" is of Persian origin and in general refers to a garden (for pleasure) (Neh. 2:8; Eccles. 2:5; cf. Song of Songs 4:12). The Septuagint used it as the word for the Garden of Eden in Gen. 2:8–15, and the Jews used the word to describe the place where God grants his fellowship to the righteous after their death.[33]

Undoubtedly, according to the New Testament as well, paradise, like Abraham's bosom, is thought to be in heaven. Shortly after Jesus had promised the murderer that "today" he would be with him in paradise, Jesus commended his own spirit into the hands of his Father (Luke 23:46); in 2 Cor. 12:2, 4, "paradise" is used interchangeably with "the third heaven"; in Rev. 2:7 and 22:2 it refers to the place where in the future God will dwell among his people. In keeping with this, the Gospel of John teaches that believers who here on earth already possess the beginning of eternal life and have escaped the judgment of God (3:15–21; 5:24) share in a communion with Christ that is broken neither by his going away (12:32; 14:23) nor by death (11:25–26), and which will someday be completed in being together with him eternally (6:39; 14:3, 19; 16:16; 17:24). At the time of his death, Stephen prayed that the Lord Jesus would take his spirit to him in heaven (Acts 7:59). Paul knew that the believer shares in a life that is far superior to death (Rom. 8:10) and that nothing, not even death, could separate him from the love of God in Christ (8:38–39; 14:8; 1 Thess. 5:10). Although he must for a time still remain in the flesh for the sake of the churches, he nevertheless desires to depart and to be with Christ (2 Cor. 5:8; Phil. 1:23). According to Rev. 6:9 and 7:9, the souls of the martyrs are with Christ beneath the altar that stands before the throne of God in the temple of heaven (cf. 2:7, 10, 17, 26; 3:4–5, 12, 21; 8:3; 9:13; 14:13; 15:2; 16:17; see also Heb. 11:10, 16; 12:23).

And just as immediately after death believers enjoy a provisional state of bliss with Christ in heaven, so unbelievers from the moment of their death enter a

---

33. F. W. Weber, *System der altsynagogelen palästinischen Theologie* (Leipzig: Dörffling & Franke, 1880), 330; S. D. F. Salmond, "Paradise," in *DB*, III, 668–772.

place of torment. The rich man was in torment when he opened his eyes in hades (Luke 16:23). Unbelievers who reject Christ remain under the wrath of God and are condemned already on earth (John 3:18, 36) and must—along with all others—expect judgment immediately after death (Heb. 9:27). Still, this place of torment is not yet identical with Gehenna (γεεννα, *geenna*) or the lake of fire (λιμνη του πυρος, *limnē tou pyros*), for Gehenna is the place of inextinguishable and eternal fire prepared for the devil and his messengers (Matt. 18:8; 25:41, 46; Mark 9:43, 47–48), and the pool of fire is not the present but the future place of punishment for the kingdom of the world and the false prophet (Rev. 19:20), Satan (20:10), and all the wicked (21:8; cf. 2 Pet. 2:17; Jude 13). The case is rather that now they are all kept in a prison (φυλακη, *phylakē*; 1 Pet. 3:19) or in the abyss (ἀβυσσος, *abyssos*; Luke 8:31; cf. Matt. 8:29–32; Rom. 10:7; Rev. 9:1–2, 11; 11:7; 17:8; 20:1, 3). This difference in the intermediate state between the good and the evil does not conflict with the fact that they are all together in hades, for all the dead are as such καταχθονιοι (*katachthonioi*, inhabitants of the lower regions); before the resurrection they belong to the realm of the dead and only by that resurrection are completely liberated in soul and body from the rule of death (1 Cor. 15:52–55; Rev. 20:13).

13

AFTER DEATH, THEN WHAT?

Early Christian theology honored the scriptural reserve concerning the intermediate state. The delay of the parousia and challenges to Christian eschatology forced the church's theologians to seek greater clarity. The initial understanding of a more-or-less neutral abode of all the dead became increasingly differentiated into immediate bliss for believers and punishment for unbelievers. The notion of purification by fire and purgatory was developed to further discriminate among levels of merit and perfection in believers. The intercession of the church was believed to help hasten the process. The Reformation repudiated the idea of purgatory and again pictured entry into the intermediate state as entry into either immediate bliss or judgment. However, other ideas, including soul sleep, annihilation, reincarnation, and varieties of universalism also sprang up after the Reformation. This preoccupation with the intermediate state is not scriptural. The Bible gives the notion of the soul's immortality after death a decidedly subordinate value. Death breaks the varied and wonderful bonds of life relations in this world. In comparison with life on this side of the grave, death results in nonbeing, the disturbing negation of the rich and joyful experience of life on earth. Death is the fruit of sin; sin is death. Christ's death and resurrection is thus the restoration of life. For those who are in Christ, death is no longer the end but a passage into eternal life. This rich biblical perspective rules out other attempts to reduce the sting of death, such as belief in soul sleep, intermediate corporeality, and contact between the dead and the living, including veneration of saints.

[552] In the early period Christian theology limited itself to the simple givens of Holy Scripture. The Apostolic Fathers still had no doctrine concerning the intermediate state and in general believed that at death the devout immediately experience the blessedness of heaven and the wicked the punishment of hell. Burnet and others who followed him, such as Blondel, Ernesti, and Baumgarten-Crusius, attempted to show that the most ancient Christian writers had the real blessedness of believers begin only after the judgment of the world, but they have not been

able to advance adequate proofs for that position.[1] Only when the parousia of Christ did not come as soon as almost all believers initially expected, and various heretical thinkers distorted or opposed the doctrine of the last things, did the church's thinkers begin to reflect more intentionally on the intermediate state. Ebionitism tried to hold on to the national privileges of Israel at the expense of Christian universalism and was therefore generally disposed to millenarianism. Gnosticism, by virtue of its basic dualism, rejected Christian eschatology altogether and held to no other expectation than that of the liberation of the spirit from matter and its assumption into the divine *plērōma* immediately after death. As a result, Christian theology was compelled to seek a clearer understanding of the character of the intermediate state and of its connections both with this life and with the final state following the last judgment.

Justin already stated that after death the souls of the devout were in a better place and the souls of the unrighteous in a worse one as they awaited the time of judgment. He condemned as unchristian the teaching that there is no resurrection of the dead and that souls are taken up into heaven immediately at the time of death. According to Irenaeus, the souls of the devout at death do not immediately enter heaven, paradise, or the city of God—which following the last judgment will be three distinct dwelling places of the righteous—but an invisible place determined by God, where they await the resurrection and the subsequent vision of God. His reason was that Christ, too, first spent three days in the place of the dead, the lower places of the earth, to save the holy dead from it and, having thus fulfilled "the law of the dead" (*lex mortuorum*), was raised and taken up into heaven. There, in the shadow of death, in hades, every human receives a fitting habitation even before the judgment, the pious probably in Abraham's bosom, which is, accordingly, a division of hades.

We encounter the same view of the various "receptacles" in hades, where the dead await the last day, in Hippolytus, Tertullian, Novatian, Commodian, Victorinus, Hilary, Ambrose, Cyril, and also still in Augustine.[2] But to the degree that the parousia of Christ receded into the distance, it became increasingly harder to maintain the old representation of hades and to regard the stay in it as a brief, provisional, more or less neutral experience. Already at an early date an exception was made for the martyrs. These, said Irenaeus, Tertullian, and others, had entered heaven immediately after their death and were immediately admitted to the vision of God. In this connection Christ's descent into hades was interpreted to mean that by it believers who had died before Christ's sacrifice were released from the limbo of the fathers (*limbus patrum*) and transferred to heaven. And the teaching of the necessity and meritoriousness of good works, which made increasing inroads in the church,

---

1. See L. Atzberger, *Geschichte der christlichen Eschatologie* (Freiburg i.B. and St. Louis: Herder, 1896), 75–99.

2. Ibid., 275ff., 301ff.; J. Niederhuber, *Die Eschatologie des heiligen Ambrosius* (Paderborn: Schöningh, 1907), 58f.; J. Schwane, *Dogmengeschichte* (Freiburg i.B.: Herder, 1882–95), II, 585.

automatically led to the idea that those who had in a special way devoted their entire lives to God were now also, immediately at the time of their death, worthy of heavenly bliss. Thus hades was gradually depopulated. Admittedly unbelievers still remained, but this led precisely to the effect that hades was increasingly viewed as a place of punishment and equated with Tartarus or Gehenna. Only those Christians who up until then had not made enough progress in sanctification to be able, immediately at death, to enter the glory of heaven would have to spend time in hades.

THE MOVE TOWARD PURGATORY

Gradually linked with this development was the idea of purification by fire, first uttered by Origen. According to him, all punishments were medicines (φαρμακα, *pharmaka*), and all of hades, Gehenna included, was a place of purification.[3] Sins were specifically consumed and people cleansed by purifying fire (πυρ καθαρσιον, *pyr katharsion*), which at the end of this dispensation would set the world aflame.[4] Following Origen, Greek theologians later adopted the idea that the souls of many of the dead would have to suffer sorrows and could only be released from them by the intercessions and sacrifices of the living; they nevertheless objected to a special fire of purification, as the Western church taught it.[5] Not until the Council of Florence (1439) did the Greeks make any concessions on this point.[6] In the West, on the other hand, the fire of purification of which Origen spoke was moved from the last judgment to the intermediate state. Augustine occasionally said that following the general resurrection or at the last judgment certain additional purgatorial pains would be imposed.[7] Still, he usually has the development of the city of God end with the last judgment and therefore does not regard it as impossible that "some of the faithful are saved by a sort of purgatorial fire, and this sooner or later according as they have loved more or less the goods that perish."[8] Caesar of Arles and Gregory the Great, working this out, developed the idea that specifically venial sins could be expiated here or in the hereafter. And when this teaching was combined with the church practice, already reported by Tertullian,[9] of making intercessions and sacrifices for the dead, the dogma of purgatory was complete.

3. Origen, *Against Celsus* III, 75; VI, 25–26.

4. Ibid., VI, 12–13, 21, 64; V, 15–16. Cf. G. Anrich, "Clemens und Origenes als Begründer der Lehre vom Fegfeuer," in *Theologische Abhandlungen*, ed. W. Nowack et al. (Tübingen: Mohr, 1902), 97–120; R. Hofmann, "Fegfeuer," in *PRE³*, V, 788–92.

5. The Orthodox Confession of the Eastern Church, arts. 64–68, in *Creeds of Christendom*, ed. Philip Schaff (New York: Harper & Brothers, 1877), II, 342–48.

6. W. Münscher, *Lehrbuch des christlichen Dogmengeschichte*, ed. Daniel von Coelln, 3rd ed. (Cassel: J. C. Krieger, 1832–38), II, 313; J. Schwane, *Dogmengeschichte*, II, 587; III, 486; F. Kattenbusch, *Lehrbuch der vergleichenden Confessionskunde* (Freiburg i.B.: J. C. B. Mohr [Paul Siebeck], 1892), I, 327.

7. Augustine, *City of God* XX, 25; XXI, 24.

8. Augustine, *Enchiridion* 69.

9. Tertullian, *On Monogamy* 10, 11; *Exhortation to Chastity* 11.

The Scholastics[10] developed the doctrine of purgatory extensively; the Councils of Florence (1439) and Trent (1545–63)[11] made it a church doctrine; and later theology attached to it ever-increasing importance for the life of religion and the church. According to Catholic doctrine, the souls of the damned immediately enter hell (Gehenna, the abyss, the inferno), where they, along with the unclean spirits, are tormented in everlasting and inextinguishable fire. The souls of those who after receiving baptism are not again tainted by sin or are purified from it here or hereafter are immediately taken up into heaven. There they behold the face of God, be it in various degrees of perfection, depending on their merits.[12] By Christ's descent into hell also the souls of the saints who died before that time are transferred from the limbo of the fathers (Abraham's bosom) to heaven. Infants who die before being baptized—about whose lot the church fathers in some cases judged more gently, in others more severely—were consigned to the lower regions, where, however, the punishments are extremely unequal. According to the most common view, they go to a special division (*limbus infantum*) where they only suffer an "eternal punishment of condemnation" (*aeterna poena damni*) but no "physical punishment" (*poena sensa*).[13] But those who, after having received sanctifying grace in baptism or the sacrament of penance, commit venial sins and have not been able to "pay" the appropriate temporal punishments in this life, are not pure enough to be immediately admitted to the beatific vision of God in heaven. They go to a place between heaven and hell, not to acquire new virtues and merits, but to clear up the hindrances that stand in the way of their entry into heaven.

To that end, at the first moment after death, they are delivered from the guilt of venial sins by an act of repentance (payment made for a pardonable sin) and subsequently still have to bear the temporal punishments that remain the set penalty for those sins even after forgiveness. Purgatory,[14] accordingly, is not a place of repentance, of trial, or of sanctification, but of punishment, where fire—usually thought of as a material agent—serves, ideally, that is, by the representation of great pain, to have a purifying impact on "poor souls." In addition, by virtue of the communion of saints, the church can come to the aid of these suffering souls for the purpose of softening and shortening their punishment by intercessions, sacrifices of the Mass, good works, and indulgences. It is true that nobody knows for certain which souls have to go to purgatory, how long they must stay there, and under what conditions on their part the prayers and sacrifices of the living are to their benefit; but this uncertainty is in no way detrimental to the cult of the

10. P. Lombard, *Sent.*, IV, 21; T. Aquinas, *Summa theol.*, suppl., qu. 69, 74; Bonaventure, *Breviloquium*, VII, 2, 3; Bellarmine, "De purgatorio," in *Controversiis*, II, 228–69.

11. Canons and Decrees of the Council of Trent, VI, canon 30; XXII, c. 2, canon 3; XXV.

12. H. Denzinger, ed., *Sources of Catholic Dogma*, trans. from the 30th ed. by R. J. Deferrari (London and St. Louis: Herder, 1955), ##870, 875.

13. P. Lombard, *Sent.*, II, dist. 33; T. Aquinas, *Summa theol.*, suppl., qu. 69, art. 4.

14. Ed. note: Bavinck here in parentheses notes that the Dutch term for "purgatory," *vagevuur*, is etymologically derived from *vagen*, *vegen*, which means "purify" or "cleanse."

dead. For increasingly the rule is that, barring a few exceptions, such as martyrs or particular saints, the great majority of believers first go to purgatory. In any case they are far ahead of the living, who must go to heaven by way of purgatory as well. Though on the one hand they are "poor souls," viewed from another angle they are "blessed" souls who along with the angels and those in a state of beatitude are invoked for help by those living in distress.[15]

REFORMATION AND DEFORMATION

[553] The Reformation saw in this notion of purgatory a limitation on the merits of Christ and taught—by virtue of its principle of justification by faith alone—that a human, immediately after a particular judgment undergone in the death struggle, entered into the blessedness of heaven or the perdition of hell. Luther himself frequently pictured the intermediate state of the pious as a sleep in which they quietly and calmly awaited the future of the Lord.[16] Later Lutheran theologians, however, almost completely wiped out the distinction between the intermediate state and the final state: they said that immediately after death the souls of the faithful enjoyed a full and essential beatitude, and the ungodly immediately received a full and consummate condemnation.[17] In the main, we have to say, that was also the opinion of the Reformed.[18] But they usually showed more clearly than the Lutherans the difference that existed in the state of the dead before and after the last day. In his writing on "the sleep of the soul," Calvin states that "Abraham's bosom" only means that after death the souls of the faithful will enjoy full peace, but that up until the day of resurrection something will still be lacking, namely, the full and perfect glory of God to which they always aspire, and that therefore our salvation always remains in progress until the day that concludes and terminates all progress.[19] Others went even further,

15. Roman Catechism, I, c. 6, qu. 3. In addition to the works already cited, also see J. A. Möhler, *Symbolik* (Regensburg: G. J. Manz, 1871), §23; H. Faure, *De vertroostingen des vagevuurs*, trans. Br. Modestus (Amsterdam: Bekker, 1901); F. Schmid, *Der Fegfeuer nach katholischen Lehre* (Brixen: Pressvereins-Buchhandlung, 1904); M. Landau, *Hölle und Fegfeuer in Volksglaube, Dichtung und Kirchenlehre* (Heidelberg: Winter, 1910).

16. Julius Köstlin, *The Theology of Luther*, trans. Charles E. Hay (Philadelphia: Lutheran Publication Society, 1897), II, 577.

17. J. Gerhard, *Loci theologici*, ed. E. Preuss, 9 vols. (Berlin: G. Schlawitz, 1863–75), XXVI, 160, 191; J. Quenstedt, *Theologia*, IV, 540, 567; H. Schmid, *The Doctrinal Theology of the Evangelical Lutheran Church*, trans. Charles A. Hay and Henry E. Jacobs, 5th ed. (Philadelphia: United Lutheran Publication House, 1899), §63.

18. Heidelberg Catechism, Q 57–58; Belgic Confession, art. 37; Second Helvetic Confession, ch. XXVI; Westminster Confession, ch. 32; F. Junius, *Theses theologicae*, 55–56; G. Voetius, *Selectae disputationes theologicae*, 5 vols. (Utrecht: 1648–69), V, 533–39.

19. J. Calvin, *Institutes*, III.xxv.6: "The fact that the blessed gathering of saintly spirits is called 'Abraham's bosom' [Luke 16:22] is enough to assure us of being received after this pilgrimage by the common Father of the faithful, that he may share the fruit of his faith with us. Meanwhile, since Scripture everywhere bids us wait in expectation for Christ's coming, and defers until then the crown of glory, let us be content with the limits divinely set for us: namely, that the souls of the pious, having ended the toil of their warfare, enter into blessed rest, where in glad expectation they await the enjoyment of promised glory, and so all things are held in suspense until Christ the Redeemer appear." Cf. Calvin, "Psychopannychia"; A. Walaeus, in *Synopsis purioris theologiae*,

adopting a specific kind of intermediate state. L. Capellus said that after death the souls of the pious enter a state that, though it can be called blessed by comparison with what exists on earth, is very different from the blessedness that begins after the resurrection. The intermediate state, after all, consisted almost entirely "in the hope and expectation of a future glory, not indeed in the enjoyment of that glory." And in the same way the souls of the wicked arrived after death in a state in which they awaited in dread and fear the future punishment determined for them but did not yet suffer that punishment itself, for "the expectation of punishment is not the punishment itself." So in the main also William Sherlock, Thomas Burnet, and numerous other English theologians believed, and among the Lutherans similarly Calixtus, Horneius, Zeltner, and others.[20]

In Protestant theology, following the eighteenth century, all the ideas expressed earlier by pagans and Christians, philosophers and theologians returned. The Catholic doctrine of purgatory was again taken up by many mystics and pietists like Böhme, Antoinette Bourignon, Poiret, Dippel, Petersen, Arnold, and Schermer, and further by Leibniz, Lessing, J. F. von Meyer, and many others.[21] The Socinians, following certain ancient Christian writers, taught that just as bodies returned to earth, so souls returned to God and there, until the resurrection, led an existence without perception or thought, pleasure or discomfort.[22] Closely connected with this view was the doctrine of soul sleep, which had already earlier been advocated by certain heretics, later by the Anabaptists, and found acceptance again in the eighteenth century in the work of Artobe, Heyn, Sulzer,[23] and further in that of Fries, Ulrici, and the Irvingites. Others again modified this psychopannychism by saying that though the soul retained a kind of internal consciousness, it was cut off from contact with the external world.[24]

---

disp. 40, 17; H. Witsius, *The Oeconomy of the Covenants between God and Man*, 3 vols. (New York: Lee & Stokes, 1798), III, 14, 33; J. H. Heidegger, *Corpus theologiae*, 2 vols. (Zurich: J. H. Bodmer, 1700), 28, 38.

20. See C. Vitringa, *Doctrina christianae religionis*, 8 vols. (Leiden: Joannis le Mair, 1761–86), IV, 63–69. Hereafter cited as *Doctr. christ.* Ed. note: Bavinck consistently cites Vitringa as M. Vitringa.

21. Ibid., 81–82; G. W. von Leibniz, *System der Theologie* (Mainz: Müller, 1820), 345; G. E. Lessing, *Erziehung des Menschengeschlechts*, ed. Louis Ferdinand Helbig (Bern and Las Vegas: Peter Lang, 1980); J. F. von Meyer, *Blätter für höhere Wahrheit*, 11 vols. (Frankfurt a.M.: H. L. Brönner, 1818–32), VI, 233; J. H. Jung-Stilling, *Theorie der Geister-Kunde* (Leipzig: Dieter, ca. 1890), §211; J. P. Lange, *Christliche Dogmatik*, 3 vols. (Heidelberg: K. Winter, 1852), II, 1250f.; R. Rothe, *Theologische Ethik*, 2nd ed., 5 vols. (Wittenberg: Zimmermann, 1867–71), §§793–95; H. Martensen, *Christian Dogmatics*, trans. W. Urwick (Edinburgh: T&T Clark, 1871), §§276–77; I. A. Dorner, *A System of Christian Doctrine*, trans. A. Cave and J. S. Banks, 4 vols. (Edinburgh: T&T Clark, 1882), IV, §153; J. J. van Oosterzee, *Christian Dogmatics*, trans. J. Watson and M. Evans, 2 vols. (New York: Scribner, Armstrong, 1874), §142. Especially Anglican theologians had much sympathy for the doctrine of purgatory; cf. W. Walsh, *The Secret History of the Oxford Movement*, 6th ed. (London: Church Association, 1899), 281ff.

22. O. Fock, *Der Socinianismus* (Kiel: C. Schröder, 1847), 714ff.

23. Cf. K. G. Bretschneider, *Handbuch der Dogmatik der evangelisch-lutherischen Kirche*, 4th ed., 2 vols. (Leipzig: J. A. Barth, 1838), II, 395.

24. S. Episcopius, *Op. theol.*, II, 455; P. van Limborch, *Theologia christiana* (Amsterdam: Wetstein, 1735), VI, 10, 8; Julius Müller, *Die christliche Lehre von der Sünde*, 2 vols. (Bremen: C. E. Müller, 1889), II, 402–8;

Still others avoided this theory of the soul sleep by assuming that upon laying aside the material shell, the soul retained the basic organic form of the body, or that after death it received a new body made up of the finest, most delicate material, which enabled it to stay in contact with the external world.[25] Not a few thinkers have even returned to the ancient doctrine of the transmigration of souls or metempsychosis, commending a form of it that says that, by a process of repeated passages from one human body into another, souls may eventually arrive at perfection.[26] Nowadays, the idea of development is so strong that it is being applied even to the state after death. The doctrine of the limbo of the fathers (*limbus patrum*) has again been taken over by Martensen, Delitzsch, Vilmar, and the like,[27] and the view that in the intermediate state there will still be gospel preaching and the possibility of conversion is a favorite notion of the new theology.[28] Many even view the whole of the beyond (*Jenseits*) as an ongoing purgation. The result of this is that some may be lost forever (hypothetical universalism), or that those who persist in the wrong will be annihilated (conditional immortality), or that in the end all will be saved (ἀποκαταστασις, *apokatastasis*).[29]

H. Martensen, *Christian Dogmatics*, §276; J. H. A. Ebrard, *Christliche Dogmatik*, 2nd ed. (Königsberg: A. W. Unser, 1862–63), §570; I. A. Dorner, *Christian Doctrine*, IV, §153; F. H. R. Frank, *System der christlichen Wahrheit*, 3rd rev. ed. (Erlangen and Leipzig: Deichert, 1894), II, 460.

25. Including Paracelsus, Helmont, Böhme, Oetinger, Ph. M. Hahn, Swedenborg, Priestley, Schott, and Jean Paul. (Ed. note: Jean Paul Friedrich Richter [1763–1825], more commonly known simply as Jean Paul after his hero Jean-Jacques Rousseau, was a popular German novelist who significantly influenced the German Romantic movement as well as the Scottish historian and writer Thomas Carlyle [1795–1881]. His views tended toward nature pantheism.) See K. G. Bretschneider, *Handbuch der Dogmatik*, II, 396; Rothe, *Theologische Ethik*, §111f., 793f.; F. Delitzsch, *A System of Biblical Psychology*, trans. Robert E. Wallis, 2nd ed. (Edinburgh: T&T Clark, 1875), 499ff.; F. J. Splittgerber, *Tod, Fortleben, und Auferstehung*, 3rd ed. (Halle: Fricke, 1879), 45.

26. The doctrine of the transmigration of souls, reincarnation, or metempsychosis was traditionally one of the most fundamental tenets of Hinduism (J. S. Speyer, *De Indische theosophie en hare beteekenis voor ons* [Leiden: S. C. van Doesburgh, 1910], 86f.) and, according to Herodotus, was embraced also by the Egyptians and found acceptance later in the case of Pythagoras, Empedocles, Plato, the Stoics, Neoplatonists, Pharisees, Kabbalists, Gnostics, and Manichaeans; in later years again in Nolanus, Helmont, Dippel, Edelmann (on these, see C. Vitringa, *Doctr. christ.*, IV, 86–89); Lessing, Schlosser, Ungern-Sternberg, Schopenhauer (on these, see C. O. Flink, *Schopenhauers Seelenwanderungslehre und ihre Quellen* [PhD diss., University of Bern, 1906; Bern: Schleitin, Spring, 1906]; cf. D. Burger, *De zielsverhuizing* [Amersfoort: Slothouwer, 1877]; C. Andresen, *Die Lehre von der Wiedergeburt auf theistischen Grundlage*, 2nd ed. [Hamburg: Gräfe & Sillem, 1899]; A. Bertholet, *Seelenwanderung* [Tübingen: J. C. B. Mohr (Paul Siebeck), 1906]; J. Baumann, *Unsterblichkeit und Seelenwanderung* [Leipzig: S. Hirzel, 1909]).

27. H. Martensen, *Christian Dogmatics*, §277; F. Delitzsch, *Biblical Psychology*, 477ff.; A. F. C. Vilmar, *Handbuch der evangelischen Dogmatik* (Gütersloh: Bertelsmann, 1895), II, 290; F. J. Splittgerber, *Tod, Fortleben und Auferstehung*, 110f.; H. Cremer, *Über den Zustand nach dem Tode* (Gütersloh: Bertelsmann, 1883), 9f.

28. J. P. Lange, *Christliche Dogmatik*, II, 1250ff.; Rothe, *Theologische Ethik*, §786, 787; F. Delitzsch, *Biblical Psychology*, 483; Th. Kliefoth, *Christliche Eschatologie* (Leipzig: Dörffling & Franke, 1886), 97–113; J. I. Doedes, *De Nederlandsche geloofsbelijdenis* (Utrecht: Kemink & Koon, 1880–81), 521; J. J. van Oosterzee, *Christian Dogmatics*, §142.

29. For further discussion, see part 3 of this volume, section C, "The Consummation."

THE NEED FOR SCRIPTURAL RESERVE

[554] The history of the doctrine of the intermediate state shows that it is hard for theologians and people in general to stay within the limits of Scripture and not attempt to be wiser than they can be. The scriptural data about the intermediate state are sufficient for our needs in this life but leave unanswered many questions that may arise in the inquisitive mind. If one nevertheless insists on solving them, one can only take the course of conjecture and run the risk of negating the divine witness by the inventions of human wisdom. This becomes immediately evident when we speak about death and immortality. Philosophy deals with this subject in a way that is very different from Scripture. Philosophy views death as something natural and thinks that the idea of immortality, that is, the continued existence of the soul, is enough for it. But the judgment of Scripture is vastly different. Death is not natural but arises from the violation of the divine commandment (Gen. 2:17); from the devil insofar as he by his seduction caused humanity to fall and die (John 8:44); from sin itself inasmuch as it has a disintegrating impact on the whole of human life and, as it were, produces death from within itself (James 1:15); and from the judgment of God since he pays the wages of sin in the currency of death (Rom. 6:23). And in Scripture this death is never identical with annihilation, with nonbeing, but always consists in the destruction of harmony, in being cut off from the various life settings in which a creature has been placed in keeping with one's nature, in returning to the elementary chaotic existence that, at least logically, underlies the entire cosmos.

According to Herbert Spencer, life consists in continual adaptation to internal and external relations. Although this definition by no means explains the essence of life, it is nevertheless true that life is all the richer to the degree that the relations in which it stands to its surroundings are greater in number and healthier in nature. The highest creature, therefore, is the human being. By virtue of their creation, humans are linked with nature and the human world, visible and invisible things, heaven and earth, God and angels. And they live if, and to the degree that, they stand in the right, that is, in the God-willed relation to the whole of their surroundings. Accordingly, in its essence and entire scope, death is disturbance, the breakup of all these relations in which humans stood originally and still ought to stand now.[30] Death's cause, therefore, is and can be none other than the sin that disturbs the right relation to God and breaks up life-embracing fellowship with God. In this sense sin not only results in death but also coincides with it; sin is death, death in a spiritual sense. Those who sin, by that token and at the same moment, put themselves in an adversarial relationship toward God, are dead to God and the things of God, have no pleasure in the knowledge of his ways, and in hostility and hatred turn away from him. And since this relation to God, this being created in his image and likeness, is not something extraneous and additional, a *donum superadditum*, but belongs to the essence of being human

---

30. Henry Drummond, *Natural Law in the Spiritual World* (New York: J. Pott, 1887), 149ff.

and bears a central character, the disturbance of this relationship will inevitably have a devastating impact on all the other relationships in which human beings stand—to themselves, to their fellow humans, to nature, to the angels, to the whole creation. Actually, in terms of its nature, at the very moment it was committed, sin should have resulted in a full, across-the-board death (Gen. 2:17), a return of the entire cosmos to its primeval chaotic condition.

But God intervened: he broke the power of sin and death. True, as Schelling remarked, underlying all that exists there is an irrational remainder. Everything that is left to itself disintegrates. Nature, when it is not cultivated, becomes wild; persons who are not brought up properly degenerate; a people who fall outside the circle of civilization will become corrupt. By nature, all that is inside and outside humanity is torn up into mutually hostile segments, but God in his mercy has intervened. He intervened first with his common grace to curb the power of sin and death, then with his special grace to break down and conquer that power. Not only is physical death postponed, and not only did God by various measures make human existence and development possible; but also Christ by his cross fundamentally achieved a victory over sin and death and brought life and immortality to light (Rom. 5:12ff.; 1 Cor. 15:45; 2 Tim. 1:10; Heb. 2:14; Rev. 1:18; 20:14), so that everyone who believes in him has eternal life and will never die (John 3:36; 5:24; 8:51–52; 11:25). Now it is this life and this immortality that in Holy Scripture stands in the foreground.

Immortality in a philosophical sense—the continuation of the soul after death—is of subordinate value in the Bible; Scripture does not deny its reality but neither does it deliberately set out to teach it. Least of all has Scripture been given, as Deism thought, to make this immortality known to us as one of the weightiest truths of religion. This truth, after all, is sufficiently well known to humans. What Scripture had to teach us was that naked existence, mere unenhanced being, is not yet life as it befits and behooves human beings; this is the case on this side of the grave and even more on the other side. On earth human life, also the life of one who has no fellowship with God, still stands in a web of varied relationships and from it receives a measure of content and value. But when all this falls away and all these connections are broken, life sinks back into a poor, vacuous, and shadowy existence devoid of content. The Old Testament usually views the beyond from this side of the grave. Death, then, is an exit from this life, the breaking of *all* bonds with *this* world. By comparison with life on this side, death is nonbeing, a rest or sleep; in a word, it is being completely dead to the entire range of the rich and joyful experience of life on earth. Never again will the dead have any share in all that happens under the sun (Eccles. 9:6).

In the foreground, in the concept of Sheol, stands the negation of our earthly life and work, and if this negation is not its only component, it is certainly its most important one. The question of whether in Sheol this completely broken-down earthly life yields to another reality in which the deceased enter into new relations in another direction is touched on only a few times in the Old Testament, when the eyes of faith of the pious pierce the shadows of death and catch a glimpse of eternal life in fellowship with God. From the viewpoint of Old Testament revelation, it was enough to plant in the human consciousness the great idea that true life can be found only in fellowship with God. To the believers of the old dispensation, the horror of hell remained as nebulous as the joy of heaven. Only when Christ died and rose again did imperishable life come to light. Christ did not gain or disclose immortality in the philosophical sense, the sense of the continued existence of souls after death. On the contrary, both here and hereafter he again filled the life of humans, exhausted and emptied by sin, with the positive content of God's fellowship, with peace and joy and blessedness. For those who are in Christ Jesus, death is no longer death but a passage into eternal life, and the grave is a place of sanctified rest until the day of resurrection.

[555] Those who lose sight of this scriptural teaching on immortality fall into various errors. It is simply a fact that we cannot picture a pure [disembodied] spirit—its existence, life, and activity. About God, who is pure Spirit, we can only speak in an anthropomorphic manner, a procedure modeled to us by Scripture itself. Angels are spiritual beings but are presented in human form; when they appear on earth, they often assume human bodies. And though human persons are not merely physical beings, all their activities are bound to the body and dependent on it, not just the vegetative and animal functions but also the intellectual ones of thinking and willing. Although our brains are not the cause of our higher faculties of knowing and desiring, they are nevertheless the bearer and organ of these faculties. Every malfunction in the brain results in the abnormal functioning of the rational mind. Inasmuch as the body is not the prison house of the soul but belongs integrally to the essence of our humanity, we cannot form any mental picture of the life and activity of a soul that is separated from the body, and we are therefore readily inclined to conjectures and guessing. In the main, accordingly, three hypotheses have been conceived to make the existence of souls after death somewhat intelligible: soul sleep, intermediate corporeality, and some form of contact between the living and the dead.

SOUL SLEEP?

Many pagan thinkers and also some Christians have believed that souls, after being separated from the body, are capable only of leading a dormant life. The change that begins at death is indeed of extraordinary significance. The entire content of our psychic life is after all derived from the external world; all knowledge begins with sense perception; the entire form of our thought is material; we even speak of spiritual things in words that originally had a sensory meaning. If then, as Scripture teaches, death is a sudden, violent, total, and absolute break with the present world, there is ostensibly no other possibility than that the soul is completely closed to the external world, loses all its content, and sinks back as it were into itself. In sleep as well, the soul withdraws from the outside world and breaks off its interaction with it. But in sleep it does this only in a relative sense, since it continues to be united with the body and retains the rich life it has acquired from the world. In dreaming it even continues to occupy itself with that world, albeit in a confused fashion. Still, what enormous change mere sleep brings about in human life: the faculties of knowing and desiring cease their activity; the consciousness stands still; all perception and observation stop; only the vegetative life continues its regular rhythms. But if this is the case in sleep, how much more will all the activity of the soul come to a halt when death enters in and totally severs the ties that unite it with this world! Everything, therefore, seems to argue for the position that after death souls are in a dormant, unconscious state. And as would appear from a superficial reading, Scripture is so far removed from condemning the doctrine of soul sleep that it rather commends and favors it. After all, not only the Old but also the New Testament repeatedly refers to death as a sleep (Deut. 31:16 KJV; Jer. 51:39, 57; Dan. 12:2; Matt. 9:24; John 11:11; 1 Cor. 7:39, Greek; in KJV: 1 Cor. 11:30; 15:6, 18, 20, 51; 1 Thess. 4:13–15; 2 Pet. 3:4; etc.). Sheol is a land of silence, rest, and forgetfulness, where nothing ever shares in anything that happens under the sun. Jesus speaks of the night of death in which no one can work (John 9:4), and Scripture nowhere makes mention of anything that those who, like Lazarus and others, returned to life from the dead reported concerning what they saw or heard in the intermediate state.

Still, all these arguments are not sufficient to prove the theory of psychopannychism. For in the first place, it is clear that the soul's dependence on the body does not necessarily exclude its independence. The external world may prompt the awakening of our self-consciousness and be the initial source of our knowledge; thinking may be bound to our brains and have its seat and organ there; yet it has not been and cannot be proved that the psychic life of humanity has its source and origin in physical phenomena. Thinking and knowing are activities of the soul; it is not the ear that hears and the eye that sees but the psychic "I" of a human being that hears through the ear and sees through the eye. The body is the instrument of mind, or spirit. For that reason there is nothing preposterous in thinking that if necessary the soul can continue its activities without the body. Also, those who would deny conscious life to spirit as such would logically have to assume that consciousness and will are also impossible in the case of God and the angels. For though we speak of God in human fashion and often picture angels as corporeal, they are in themselves spirit and nevertheless possess consciousness and will.

In the second place, Scripture teaches with the greatest possible clarity that death is a total break with all of this earthly life, and to that extent it is a sleeping, resting, or being silent. The state of death is a sleep; the deceased person sleeps because interaction with the present world has ended. But Scripture nowhere says that the soul of the deceased sleeps. On the contrary, Scripture always represents the person after death as being more or less conscious. As revelation progresses, it becomes increasingly clear that, whereas in death all the soul's relationships with this world are cut off, they are immediately replaced by other relations with another world. The great scriptural idea that life is bound up with service to the Lord, and death with rejecting such service, also casts its light on the other side of the grave. Whereas immediately after his death the rich man is in torment, the wretched Lazarus is carried to Abraham's bosom (Luke 16:23). And all believers who on earth already participated in eternal life, so far from losing it by dying (John 11:25–26), after death enjoy it all the more intensely and blessedly in fellowship with Christ (Luke 23:43; Acts 7:59; 2 Cor. 5:8; Phil. 1:23; Rev. 6:9; 7:9–10). Being at home in the body is being away from the Lord; therefore, to die is the way to a closer, more intimate fellowship with Christ.

In the third place, it need not surprise us that those who rose again and returned to this life tell us nothing about what they saw and heard on the other side. For, aside from the possibility that they have reported some things not recorded in Scripture, it is most likely that they have not been permitted, or are unable, to convey their experiences on the other side of the grave. Moses and the prophets are enough for us (Luke 16:29). After being caught up into the third heaven, Paul could say only that he had heard things that are not to be told and that no mortal is permitted to repeat (2 Cor. 12:4).[31]

INTERMEDIATE CORPOREALITY?

[556] Others believe that after death, souls receive a new corporeality and are on that account able again to enter into contact with the external world. They base this opinion on the fact that we cannot visualize the life and activity of the soul aside from the body and, further, on those passages in Scripture that seem to accord a kind of corporeality to the souls of the dead. The denizens of the realm of the dead are described precisely as they appeared on earth. Samuel is pictured as an old man clothed with a mantle (1 Sam. 28:14); the kings of the nations sit on thrones and go out to meet the king of Babylon (Isa. 14:9); the Gentiles lie down to rest with the uncircumcised (Ezek. 31:18; 32:19ff.). In speaking of the dead, Jesus still refers to their eyes, fingers, and tongues (Luke 16:23–24). Paul expects that if the earthly tent is destroyed, he will have a building from God and not be unclothed but further clothed (2 Cor. 5:1–4). And John saw a great multitude, standing before the throne and the Lamb, robed in white, with palm branches in their hands (Rev. 6:11; 7:9).

But, in the first place, from this mode of speech in Scripture one cannot infer anything about the corporeality of souls after death. Scripture can speak of God

---

31. For opposition to the idea of soul sleep, see Tertullian, *A Treatise on the Soul* 58; J. Calvin, "Psycho-pannychia"; *H. Bullinger, *Huijsboeck*, Dec. 4, serm. 10; J. Cloppenburg, *Theol. op.*, II, 413–17; G. Voetius, *Select. disp.*, I, 832–34; H. Witsius, *Oeconomy of the Covenants*, III, 14, 18–22; B. de Moor, *Commentarius . . . theologiae*, 6 vols. (Leiden: J. Hasebroek, 1761–71), VI, 594–602; C. Vitringa, *Doctr. christ.*, IV, 82–86; J. Gerhard, *Loci theol.*, XXVI, 293; F. Delitzsch, *Biblical Psychology*, 490; F. J. Splittgerber, *Tod, Fortleben und Auferstehung*, 102; H. W. Rinck, *Vom Zustand nach dem Tode*, 2nd ed. (Ludwigsburg and Basel: Balmer & Riehm, 1866), 19; Th. Kliefoth, *Christliche Eschatologie*, 66; L. Atzberger, *Die christliche Eschatologie* (Freiburg i.B.: Herder, 1890), 212.

and angels, of the souls in Sheol, of joy in heaven and torment in hell only by using human language, with imagery derived from earthly conditions and relations. But alongside of this it states clearly and decisively that God is spirit and that the angels are spirits, and by saying this it gives us a standard by which all these anthropomorphic expressions need to be understood. And it does the same with respect to the dead. It can only speak of them as people of flesh and blood but states additionally that while their bodies rest in the grave, they are souls or spirits (Eccles. 12:7; Ezek. 37:5; Luke 23:46; Acts 7:59; Heb. 12:23; 1 Pet. 3:19; Rev. 6:9; 20:4). We have to hold to these clear pronouncements. Those who nevertheless attribute to souls a kind of body must, to be consistent, follow through and, along with theosophists, represent God and the angels as in some sense physical as well.

Second, the strongest passage speaking for a kind of "intermediate corporeality" (*Zwischenleiblichkeit*) of souls is 2 Cor. 5:1–4. But also this text, when properly exegeted, loses all its evidential value. There is no difference of opinion, after all, about the main point Paul is making here. The apostle knows that when his earthly body is "dissolved," he has "a building from God." Still he groans and feels burdened in this body, being anxious about death, and would therefore wish not to be "unclothed" from this body but to be clothed instantaneously, in both soul and body, with a heavenly dwelling, so that what is mortal is swallowed up by life. However, though this may be his dearest wish, he knows that after the destruction of this earthly body, even if it be that he has his body "taken off,"[32] he will still not be found naked but be at home with the Lord (vv. 1, 3, 8). But if this is the main idea, we cannot construe the dwelling from God as the resurrection body and, still less, as an intermediate body. For the thing Paul particularly longs for is to be clothed with that dwelling from God, without dying, while keeping his earthly body. Now the resurrection body is not one existing alongside the earthly body and is not put on over it, but under the impact of God's word of power, the new body arises from the earthly body or, in the case of those who are still alive, results from a transformation (1 Cor. 15:42, 51–52). And an intermediate body is all the more inconceivable because in that scenario Paul would know of no fewer than three bodies, each consecutively put on over the other. Holtzmann therefore correctly remarks that "it is best no longer to speak of any 'intermediate' body at all. Paul knows two, not three σώματα [*sōmata*, bodies],"[33] which, accordingly, cannot be put dualistically after and alongside of each other. For this reason the "building from God" cannot be anything other than a place and, simultaneously, the heavenly glory thought of as a garment, the eternal light that God himself inhabits (1 Tim. 6:16). It is something from God, not made with hands, from

32. The reading (2 Cor. 5:3) εἰ γε καὶ ἐκδυσάμενοι (*ei ge kai ekdysamenoi*, if indeed when we have taken it off) deserves preference, in my opinion, over εἰ γε καὶ ἐνδυσάμενοι (*ei ge kai endysamenoi*, if indeed when we have put it on).

33. H. J. Holtzmann, *Lehrbuch der neutestamentlichen Theologie*, 2 vols. (Freiburg i.B. and Leipzig: Mohr, 1897), II, 199.

and in heaven, into which at death or at the resurrection believers are transposed (cf. John 14:2; 17:24; Col. 1:12).

Finally, the corporeality ascribed to souls after death is a concept without any specifiable content; for this very reason, opinions on it tend to be very diverse. Franz Delitzsch, with his trichotomistic viewpoint, assumes that the soul performs the function of the intermediate body for the spirit. In his writings the soul stands between the spirit and matter; it is the principle of bodily life derived from the spirit, the external corporeal clothing of the spirit, and still at the same time the immaterial internal side of the body.[34] Güder teaches the theory that the power that organized our earthly body is preserved and, on the other side of the grave, forms a new body from the elements present there. Splittgerber says that the basic organic form of the body accompanies the soul and in the intermediate state gives it an imperfect provisional corporeality. Rinck believes that the "neural body" (*Nervenleib*), a fine and delicate internal body that is the bearer of the life of the soul, accompanies the soul after death and is clothed in the case of regenerates by the Spirit of God and formed into an intermediate body by the irradiation of the glorified body of Christ, while in the case of the ungodly it is increasingly pervaded by sin and darkness. But no matter how it is presented, it does not become any clearer. We know only of spirit and matter. An "immaterial corporeality" is a contradiction that was inauspiciously taken from theosophy into Christian theology and seeks in vain to reconcile the false dualism of spirit and matter, of thesis and antithesis.

CONTACT WITH THE LIVING?

[557] In the third place, there are many who believe that souls after death still maintain some kind of relationship with life on earth. Prevalent among many peoples is the idea that souls after death remain near the gravesite. The Jews, too, believed that for a time following death the soul hovered about the corpse, and used this circumstance to explain how the witch of Endor could still call up the spirit of Samuel.[35] There was the widespread practice of providing the deceased in their grave with food, weapons, possessions, and sometimes even wives and slaves. Usually this veneration of the dead was not restricted to the day of the burial or the time of mourning but continued afterward as well and was incorporated into ordinary private or public cultic practice. Not only the dead in general were venerated but also deceased blood relatives, parents and ancestors, the fathers and heads of the tribe, the heroes of the people, the princes and kings of the country, sometimes even when they were still living; in Buddhism and Islam the saints were venerated as well. This veneration consisted in maintaining their graves, taking care of their bodies (sometimes by embalming), from time to time placing flowers

---

34. Ed. note: Cf. F. Delitzsch, *Biblical Psychology*, esp. 503ff.
35. F. W. Weber, *System der altsynagogalen palästinischen Theologie* (Leipzig: Dörffling & Franke, 1880), 324.

and foods on their graves, paying respect to their images and relics, holding meals and conducting games in their honor, sending up prayers and making sacrifices to them. Though in this connection people frequently made a distinction—as they did in Persia, India, and Greece—between venerating these deceased persons and honoring the gods, still the cult of the dead was a prominent part of the religion. The purpose of this veneration by the people was in part to come to the aid of the dead but especially to avert the evil the dead could do and to ensure themselves, whether in ordinary or extraordinary ways, by oracles and miracles, of their blessing and assistance.[36]

From as early as the second century, all of these elements penetrated Christian worship as well. Just as monks in Buddhism and mystics in Islam, so the martyrs in the Christian church soon became the objects of religious veneration. Altars, chapels, and churches were built at sites where they had died or their relics were interred. Especially on the death dates of the martyrs, believers assembled at these sites to commemorate them by vigils and the singing of psalms, reading the acts of the martyrs, listening to sermons in their honor, and especially by celebrating the holy Eucharist. And after the fourth century this veneration of the virgin Mary, angels, patriarchs, prophets, and martyrs was extended to include bishops, monks, hermits, confessors, and virgins, as well as a variety of saints, their relics, and their images.[37] Despite resistance to this cult of the dead both inside and outside the Catholic Church, it is still, in an alarming way, consistently and increasingly forcing the worship of the one true God and of Jesus Christ into the background.

In this cult the Roman Catholic Church in a practical way celebrates the communion of the saints. The one Christian church has three divisions: the triumphant church (*ecclesia triumphans*) in heaven, the suffering church (*ecclesia patiens*) in purgatory, and the militant church (*ecclesia militans*) on earth. The share that the suffering church has in this communion consists in three things: (1) The blessed souls in heaven by their intercessions come to the aid of the poor souls in purgatory. (2) The church on earth, by its prayers, alms, good works, indulgences, and especially the offering of the Mass, seeks to soften and shorten the punishment of the souls in purgatory. (3) Finally, the souls in purgatory, who in any case are far ahead of the majority of the members of the militant church and may for that reason be invoked, by their intercessions help and strengthen believers on earth. This latter element, while it already plays a growing role in the communion with the suffering church, nevertheless forms the main constituent of the communion of the militant church with the triumphant church. The blessed in heaven, like the angels, share in perfect supernatural holiness and are for that reason the objects of adoration and veneration. In that holiness they do not all participate in the same degree; like the angels, they form a spiritual hierarchy—at the top stands

36. P. D. Chantepie de la Saussaye, *Lehrbuch der Religionsgeschichte*, 2 vols. (Freiburg i.B.: Mohr [Siebeck], 1887–89), I, 79–87.

37. J. Schwane, *Dogmengeschichte*, I, 389ff.; II, 620ff.

Mary, and after her follow the patriarchs, prophets, apostles, martyrs, confessors, and so on. It is a descending series, but in all of them something of the divine attributes shines forth. Participating in this sanctity, further, is everything that has in some way been connected with the saints—their body, parts of their body, clothes, dwellings, portraits, and the like. And in the measure by which a thing is closer to God and has a greater share in his holiness, to that extent it is the object of religious veneration.

In this veneration, therefore, there are also various differences. Adoration (*latria*) is due only to God. The human nature of Christ and all its parts (e.g., his holy heart) is in itself (*in se*), not by itself and on account of itself (*per se* and *propter se*), the object of *latria*. Mary is entitled to *hyperdulia*, the saints to *dulia* (veneration), their relics to relative religious devotion, and so on; there are as many kinds of adoration as there are kinds of excellence; adoration is varied according to the diversity of excellence.[38] In general, the veneration of saints consists in prayers, fastings, vigils, feast days, gifts, pilgrimages, processions, and the like; the purpose of it is, by their intercessions, to gain the favor of God and to obtain some kind of benefit from him.

This veneration and intercession, however, is not only general but also particular. There are specific saints for specific peoples, families, and persons; and there are special saints for distinct forms of distress and needs. St. George is the patron saint of England, St. James of Spain, St. Stephen of Hungary. Painters venerate St. Luke, carpenters St. Joseph, shoemakers St. Crispin. St. Sebastian is especially helpful in times of the plague; St. Othilia in case of eye trouble; St. Anthony for recovering lost objects. Even animals have their patron saints: geese receive protection especially from St. Gall, sheep from St. Wendelin, and so forth.[39]

Many of these notions returned from time to time in Protestant theology. Lutherans acknowledged that angels as well as the saints pray for the universal church generally.[40] Just as earlier Hugo Grotius in his *Votum pro pace* defended the invocation of saints, so Leibniz later gave his approval to this practice and even to the veneration of images and relics.[41] Ritualism in England moved in the same

---

38. See further H. Bavinck, *Reformed Dogmatics*, II, 468–72 (#267; *In the Beginning*, 88ff.); III, 281–82 (#364).

39. See Canons and Decrees of the Council of Trent, XXV; Roman Catechism, III, 2, qu. 4–14; P. Lombard, *Sent.*, IV, dist. 45; T. Aquinas, *Summa theol.*, II, 2, qu. 83, art. 11, suppl., qu. 71–72; Bellarmine, "De ecclesia triumphante," in *Controversiis*, II, 269–368. For the history of saint veneration, see Ernst Lucius, *Die Anfänge des Heiligenkults in der christliche Kirche* (Tübingen: Mohr, 1904); Charles R. Morey, "The Beginnings of Saint Worship," *Princeton Theological Review* 6 (April 1908): 278–90; F. Pfister, *Der Reliquienkult im Altertum*, vol. 1, *Das Objekt des Reliquienkultus* (Giessen: Alfred Töpelmann, 1909); M. von Wulf, *Über Heilige und Heiligenverehrung in den ersten christlichen Jahrhunderten* (Leipzig: Eckardt, 1910); G. Bonwetsch, "Heiligenverehrung," in *PRE*³, VII, 554–59; A. Hauck, "Reliquien," in *PRE*³, XVI, 630–34.

40. Apology of the Augsburg Confession, art. 21, in *The Book of Concord*, ed. Robert Kolb and Timothy J. Wengert (Minneapolis: Fortress, 2000), 237–45; Smalcald Articles, part II, art. 2 (Kolb and Wengert, 301–6).

41. G. W. von Leibniz, *System der Theologie*, 116–95.

direction.[42] Numerous theologians assumed that after death there continues to be a certain connection between the soul and the body, that souls maintain some kind of relationship with the earth, know about the most important events, pray for us, look down upon us, and bless us.[43] Many eighteenth-century thinkers like Swedenborg, Jung-Stilling, and Oberlin believed they were in direct contact with the spirits of the dead.[44] The possibility of such apparitions was acknowledged as well by men like Kant, Lessing, Jung-Stilling, J. H. Fichte, and others; and spiritism, which arose after 1848, seeks intentionally to put itself in touch with the spirit world and believes it can by this route receive all kinds of revelations.[45]

[558] To start with this latter issue, we need to note that superstitious practices occur among all peoples, also those with whom Israel came in contact, such as the Egyptians (Gen. 41:8; Exod. 7:11), the Canaanites (Deut. 18:9, 14), the Babylonians (Dan. 1:20; 2:2), and so on. These practices penetrated Israel as well and often flourished there (1 Sam. 28:9; 2 Kings 21:6; Isa. 2:6). Among these practices was that of consulting the dead; those who practiced it were called אֹבוֹת (ʾōbôt, mediums) or יִדְּעֹנִים (yiddōnîm, wizards). The word אֹב (ʾōb) refers first of all to the familiar spirit indwelling a person (Lev. 20:27), whom someone possesses (1 Sam. 28:7–8), who is consulted by someone (28:8), by whom someone can bring up a dead person (28:9), and who, as the dead were imagined doing, announces oracles in a mysterious, whispering tone (Isa. 8:19; 19:3; 29:4). In the second place, it refers to the person of the medium (1 Sam. 28:5, 9; 2 Kings 21:6; 2 Chron. 33:6; LXX: ἐγγαστρίμυθος, engastrimythos, ventriloquist). The other word יִדְּעֹנִים (yiddōnîm, the knowers or wizards) further describes the אֹבוֹת (ʾōbôt) and refers, first, to the mediums and, second, to the familiar spirit that was in them (Lev. 19:31; 20:6, 27; Isa. 19:3). Soothsaying might occur in many different ways, among others by consulting the dead (Deut. 18:11).[46] But the Law and the Prophets were firmly opposed to the practice and called the people back to the Lord, his revelation, and his testimony (Exod. 22:18; Lev. 19:26, 31; 20:6, 27; Deut. 18:11; 1 Sam. 28:9; Isa. 8:19; 47:9–15; Jer. 27:9; 29:8; Mic. 3:7; 5:12; Nah. 3:4; Mal. 3:5); the New Testament puts its seal on this witness (Luke 16:29; Acts 8:9ff.; 19:13–20; Gal. 5:20; Eph. 5:11; Rev. 9:21; 21:8; 22:15).

One cannot even prove that Holy Scripture accepts the possibility of calling up the dead and having them appear. Admittedly, by God's miraculous power the dead have sometimes been raised, and Scripture acknowledges the demonic

42. J. C. Ryle, Knots Untied, 11th ed. (London: William Hunt, 1896), 491f.

43. J. T. Beck, Umriss der biblischen Seelenlehre, 3rd ed. (Stuttgart: Steinkopf, 1871), 40ff. (ed. note: ET: Outlines of Biblical Psychology [Edinburgh: T&T Clark, 1877]); F. Delitzsch, Biblical Psychology, 444f.; F. J. Splittgerber, Tod, Fortleben und Auferstehung, 157ff.

44. See especially J. C. Wötzel, Meiner Gattin wirkliche Erscheinung nach ihrem Tode (Chemnitz: Jacobäer, 1804).

45. O. Zöckler, "Spiritismus," in PRE³, XVIII, 654–66.

46. B. Stade, Geschichte des Volkes Israel, 2 vols. (Berlin: G. Grote, 1887–88), I, 443f.; F. Schwally, Das Leben nach dem Tode: Nach den Vorstellungen des Alten Israel (Giessen: J. Ricker, 1892), 69f.

powers and workings that surpass the capacity of humans (Deut. 13:1–2; Matt. 24:24; 2 Thess. 2:9; Rev. 13:13–15). But nowhere does it teach the possibility or reality of the dead appearing. The only passage that can be cited for this view is 1 Sam. 28, where Saul seeks out the medium at Endor. (The appearance of Moses and Elijah with Christ on the Mount of Transfiguration [Matt. 17; Mark 9; Luke 9] was effected by God alone, without any human mediation.) But though we must reject the rationalistic explanation that only sees in this story the account of an intentional deception by the woman, neither can we accept the idea of a real, objective appearance of Samuel. The fact is that Saul does not actually see Samuel (v. 14); the woman does see him but is in a hypnotic state (v. 12), and she sees him as he looked during his lifetime, as an old man wrapped in a prophet's mantle (v. 14). The woman's horror (v. 12) is not inspired by the fact that, contrary to what she expected, she really saw Samuel, but by the fact that, being in a hypnotic state and seeing Samuel, she also immediately recognized King Saul and was in dread of him. After Saul has been given the impression that a subterranean spiritual being (אֱלֹהִים, ʾĕlōhîm; v. 13) has come up from the earth and that Samuel himself had appeared, the latter speaks to Saul from within and through the woman and announces his judgment. There is nothing in 1 Sam. 28 that goes beyond the familiar phenomena of hypnotism and somnambulism and cannot be explained in the same way.

There are many people, however, who believe that precisely from these phenomena of hypnotism, somnambulism, spiritism, and the like they must deduce the operation of spirits. But as yet this hypothesis seems completely unwarranted. Aside from the many hoaxes that have been perpetrated in this domain, the things that have been said of the appearance and operation of spirits are so puerile and insignificant that we certainly do not have to assume the involvement of the spirit world to explain them. This is not to deny that a wide range of phenomena occur that have not yet been explained; but these are all of such a nature (as, e.g., the sudden onset of the ability to understand and speak foreign languages, clairvoyance, hypnosis, suggestion, second sight, premonition, synchronic telecognition, telepathy, and so forth) that they are by no means made any clearer by the hypothesis of spirit apparitions. If, in addition, we consider that in their perceptions human beings are bound and restricted to a specific number of etheric vibrations so that any modification in that number would show them a totally different image of the world; and that they themselves possess a rich and profound psychic life that is only partially manifest in self-consciousness, then there is, even on this side of the "other" world (*Diesseits*), still so much room for occultism that for the time being we need not resort to the [hypothesis of] uncanny influences from the world of spirits.[47]

---

47. See Zöckler, "Spiritismus," in *PRE*[3], XVIII, 654–66; V. Kirchner, *Der Spiritismus: Die Narrheit unseres Zeitalters* (Berlin: Habel, 1883); Ed. von Hartmann, *Der Spiritismus* (Leipzig: Friedrich, 1885); idem, *Die Geisterhypothese des Spiritismus und seine Phantome* (Leipzig: Friedrich, 1891).

Further, the whole of Scripture proceeds from the idea that death is a total break with life on this side of the grave. True, the dead continue to remember the things that happened to them on earth. Both the rich man and Lazarus know who and what they were on earth and under what conditions they lived (Luke 16). In the final judgment, people know what they have done on earth (Matt. 7:22). Their deeds follow those who died in the Lord (Rev. 14:13). The things we have done on earth become our moral possession and accompany us in death. There is no doubt either that the dead recognize those whom they have known on earth. The denizens of the underworld mockingly salute the king of Babylon (Isa. 14). Out of the midst of Sheol the mighty chiefs address Egypt's king and people (Ezek. 32:21). The rich man knows Lazarus (Luke 16). The friends we make on earth by the good we do will one day receive us with joy in the eternal homes (Luke 16:9).

But for the rest, Scripture consistently tells us that at death all fellowship with this earth ends. The dead no longer have a share in anything that happens under the sun (Eccles. 9:5–6, 10). Whether their children come to honor or are brought low, the dead do not know of it (Job 14:21). Abraham does not know of the children of Israel, and Jacob does not recognize them either; therefore they call to the Lord since he is their Father (Isa. 63:16). Nowhere is there any sign that the dead are in contact with the living: they belong to another realm, one that is totally separate from the earth. Nor does Heb. 12:1 teach us that the great cloud of witnesses see and watch us in our struggles. For the μάρτυρες (*martyres*) are not eyewitnesses of our struggle but witnesses of faith who serve to encourage us.

For that reason there is no room for the invocation and veneration of saints. By itself there is nothing strange or improper in the idea that the angels and the blessed make intercession for people on earth. Indeed, Protestants frequently also accepted an interest [on their part] in the history of the militant church and a general intercession [on its behalf]. But for that reason it is all the more remarkable that while Scripture so often mentions the intercession of people on earth and specifically recommends and prescribes it (Matt. 6:9ff.; Rom. 15:30; Eph. 6:18–19; Col. 1:2–3; 1 Tim. 2:1–2) and further teaches that God frequently spares others for the sake of the elect and upon their intercession (Gen. 18:23ff.; Exod. 32:11ff.; Num. 14:13ff.; Ezek. 14:14, 20; Matt. 24:22; etc.), it never breathes a word about intercession by angels and the blessed in heaven for those who live on earth. With respect to the intercession of angels, we have already demonstrated this earlier,[48] and concerning the intercession of the blessed dead, Roman Catholics themselves admit that it does not occur in Scripture.[49] Only 2 Macc. 15:12–14 refers, in a vision of Judas, to the intercession of Onias and Jeremiah for their people, which proves only that at that time the Jews were convinced of the intercession of the blessed dead for people on earth.

48. H. Bavinck, *Reformed Dogmatics*, II, 468–72 (#267; *In the Beginning*, 88ff.).

49. For example, J. H. Oswald, *Eschatologie* (Paderborn: F. Schöningh, 1869), 132.

There is still less basis for the invocation and veneration of the saints. Holy Scripture does say that believers on earth may appeal to each other for intercession (Num. 21:7; Jer. 42:2; 1 Thess. 5:25), but never mentions asking the dead for their intercession; and both angels and human beings expressly refuse to accept the religious veneration that is due only to God (Deut. 6:13; 10:20; Matt. 4:10; Acts 14:10ff.; Col. 2:18–19; Rev. 19:10; 22:9). Nor is there any reference to the veneration of relics. Even though God sometimes performs miracles through them (2 Kings 13:21; Matt. 9:21; Luke 6:19; Acts 5:15; 19:12), they must not be the objects of veneration (Deut. 34:6; 2 Kings 18:4; 2 Cor. 5:16). Oswald, accordingly, counts the invocation and veneration of saints among the "dogmas of tradition." Even if one grants a general intercession of the saints for believers on earth, it by no means follows that they may be invoked and venerated for that purpose. Granted, a request for someone's intercession is absolutely not wrong as such and therefore occurs regularly among believers. But such a request always assumes a means of communication and must be conveyed either orally or in writing. And this is precisely what is lacking and diametrically opposed to what Scripture teaches concerning the state of the dead. Rome, therefore, does not dare to say that the invocation and veneration of saints is mandated and necessary, but only that "it is good and useful suppliantly to invoke them."[50]

Theology can in no way make clear how the saints come to know of our prayers, and hence it proposes a range of conjectures. Some believe that they are conveyed to them by angels who regularly visit the earth, or that the saints, like the angels, can travel at miraculous speeds and are in a sense ubiquitous. Others are of the opinion that the saints are informed by God himself concerning the content of our prayers or envision all the things they need to know in the consciousness of God. There are also theologians who say that it is not necessary for them to know everything, provided that they have a general idea of our needs; or that we need not be concerned about the way they learn of our prayers.[51] Further, Roman Catholics absolutely do not know with certainty which of the dead are in heaven and in the category of perfect saints. The faithful of the Old Testament were first in the limbo of the fathers and, though they were moved to heaven by Christ, they are too far removed from us to be invoked.[52] Concerning some of the New Testament faithful, such as Mary, the apostles, and some of the later martyrs, Rome does assume that they have been taken up into heaven, but this is the case with only a few, and even here we may be in error. In earlier times, it was the voice of the people that accorded the attribute of sanctity to one who had died; and in some cases it happened that men who possessed this attribute lost it again, as did Clement of Alexandria by the action of Pope Benedict XIV. To prevent these errors, the ecclesiastical act of declaring someone a saint, that is,

---

50. Canons and Decrees of the Council of Trent, session XXV (trans. J. Waterworth).
51. T. Aquinas, *Summa theol.*, II, qu. 83, art. 4; suppl., qu. 72, art. 1; J. H. Oswald, *Eschatologie*, 139.
52. J. H. Oswald, *Eschatologie*, 132, 167.

canonization, has since Alexander III and Innocent III become a prerogative of the apostolic See.[53] In this connection, however, it is a question again whether in this canonization the pope is infallible. And though this may in fact be the case, the pope of course makes rare use of his prerogative. By far the majority of saints are invoked and venerated without it being known precisely whether they are in heaven or are still in purgatory. One has to be content with a moral conviction, and consider in addition that a possible error need not have any bad consequences, and for safety's sake extend the invocation to the "poor souls" in purgatory, which is what is increasingly happening in practice.[54]

In the church of Rome, the invocation of saints is certainly no longer merely a request for their intercession (*ora pro nobis*) but changed gradually into a kind of adoration and veneration. The saints are the objects of religious veneration (*cultus religiosus*), even if it is not called worship (*latria*) but veneration (*dulia*). Now there is no doubt that if we should meet angels or the blessed dead, or if we had some kind of personal contact with them, we would owe them respectful homage. But precisely this circumstance does not occur. And consequently all invocation of angels and the blessed dead ends in a kind of religious veneration that is not made right by the name *dulia*. On the road on which Rome is going with this veneration of creatures, there is simply no stopping. Holiness is conceived by it as a superadded gift (*donum superadditum*), as something substantial that can be communicated in various measure to all creatures, and may then be religiously venerated in proportion. To the degree that a person or thing participates in the divine holiness, they may claim a kind of religious homage (*cultus religiosus*). First of all those possessing this prerogative, then, are Mary, the apostles, martyrs, and saints, but further all and everything that has been in contact with them or still exists in relation to them, hence relics, images, dwellings, and the like. By this principle all creatures can rightfully be religiously venerated "because and to the degree each has a relationship to God," including even the hands of the soldiers who arrested Jesus and the lips of Judas that kissed him.[55] In any case I see no reason why the saints who are on earth should not already be invoked and venerated by Catholic Christians, among them especially the pope, the saint par excellence. "As such there is no objection whatever to extending religious veneration to holiness as it occurs on earth. So then, if one were completely convinced of the godliness of a person, it could as such be venerated as this is done in the case of the saints in heaven. In individual cases it may have occurred privately and perhaps still does."[56] Whatever Oswald further advances against it is based on utility and shows that the veneration of living saints, specifically of the pope, is merely a matter of time in the Roman Catholic Church. The communion of saints degenerates into mutual veneration that crowds the Mediator of God and humanity into the background.

53. G. Bonwetsch, "Kanonization," in *PRE*[3], X, 17–18.
54. J. H. Oswald, *Eschatologie*, 148, 174.
55. G. Voetius, *Select. disp.*, III, 880, 896.
56. J. H. Oswald, *Eschatologie*, 157.

14

Between Death and Resurrection

*Scripture clearly teaches a distinction between the destiny of the righteous
and the unrighteous after death but not a great deal about their exact condition.
Over the years many have inquired about the possibility of a second chance to
respond to the gospel. This idea of a mission station in hades has no scriptural
ground, not even in 1 Pet. 3:18–22, which is frequently appealed to. Similarly,
the initially attractive notion of postdeath purification, including the Roman
Catholic doctrine of purgatory, also has no basis in Scripture. In fact, any and
all self-sanctification, in this life or the next, is wholly unnecessary since Christ's
perfect obedience fully entitles the believer to eternal life. In a juridical sense all
the benefits of Christ are possessed by believers now. Yet their earthly pilgrimage
ends only at death, when they enter their homeland. When we die, we die to sin.
The idea of purgatory is unnecessary as well as illogical; it is not at all clear how
purgatory's fires purify and cleanse. Since the doctrine of purgatory is untenable,
all offerings and intercessions for the dead are useless and weaken confidence
in the sufficiency of Christ's sacrifice and his effectual intercession. Nonetheless,
there still is and remains a communion between the church militant on earth
and the church triumphant in heaven that cannot be broken. Though the souls of
believers in heaven experience no change of status, they are confirmed and grow
in their knowledge and love of God.*

[559] Up until now we have discussed only whether the dead still have any
kind of contact with life on earth. Now the question arises whether Scripture
teaches us anything about the new relations and conditions in which the dead find
themselves on the other side of the grave. What Scripture reports on this subject
is not a lot. Still, already in the Old Testament the lines are present which, when
extended, lead to a difference in the state of the righteous and the unrighteous
after death. The fear of the Lord leads to life, but the ungodly perish and are
ruined. And according to the New Testament the rich man immediately enters a
place of torment, which, however, is not identical with Gehenna or the abyss. We
are not told in Scripture where we must look for it. It is true that Sheol, hades,

Gehenna, and the abyss are always represented as being below us. But this cannot and must not be understood topographically. The concepts "above" and "below," taken in a local sense, are very relative and in this context have only ethical significance. We locate the kingdom of darkness directly across from the kingdom of light, and in accordance with a natural symbolism we look for the first below us and for the second above us. All fixation of the place of punishment for the dead—in the earth, under the earth, in the sea, in the sun, in the air, or on one of the planets—is mere conjecture. What *can* be stated is that the beyond is not only a state but also a place, for though souls may not be circumscribed by time and space, they are certainly far from being eternal and omnipresent; they must be somewhere and pass through a succession of moments in time. For the rest it is more in keeping with the sparse data Scripture offers us to abstain from any attempt to determine the place of punishment for the dead. "Do not ask where it is but how you may escape it" (Chrysostom).

Nor do we know anything more about the state of unbelievers and the ungodly after death up until the last judgment. All we can say with certainty is that if here already the wrath of God continues to weigh on unbelievers, how much more intensely will it not weigh on them after death, when all the distractions of earthly life are absent and their naked existence is filled with nothing other than the consciousness and sense of that wrath?

A Second Opportunity?

The question has been raised, however, whether on the other side of the grave, for those who have not heard the gospel here on earth or only very dimly, there will not be another opportunity to repent and to believe in Christ. The first ones in the Christian church to give an affirmative answer to that question were Clement and Origen. They inferred from 1 Pet. 3:18–19 that Christ and also the apostles had proclaimed the gospel to the dead in hades who were susceptible to it. Although Augustine and others refuted this sentiment, and though Christ's descent into hell is usually interpreted differently, the idea kept coming back and, in the case of many people, found acceptance in the nineteenth century when the huge number and rapid increase of non-Christians began to dawn on them. It is indeed a fact of the greatest significance that there have been and still are millions of people who have never had any knowledge of the way of salvation in Christ and therefore never were in a position to embrace him with a believing heart or decisively to reject him. These people cannot be numbered among the unbelievers in a strict sense, and Scripture itself says that they must be judged by a different standard than Jews and Christians (Matt. 10:15; 11:20–24; Luke 10:12–24; 12:47–48; John 15:22; Rom. 2:12; 2 Pet. 2:20–22).

From this it does not follow, however, that there is or has to be preaching of the gospel on the other side of the grave. For Scripture never speaks a single word about it. Many passages that have at times been advanced for this view (such as

Matt. 12:40; John 20:17; Acts 2:24, 27, 31; 13:29–30, 34–37; 1 Tim. 3:16) have not the least evidential value and certainly do not deal with the preaching of Christ in hell. Nor does Ezek. 16:53–63 open up any perspective on this subject; the Lord there promises that despite the horrors perpetrated in Jerusalem, horrors worse than those in her sisters Sodom and Samaria, he will in the end restore it and accept it in mercy. Now in order to take away all false confidence in God's promise and all pride on the part of Israel, there is added that the Lord will not only restore the fortunes of Jerusalem but also those of Sodom and Samaria (v. 53), so that these too will return to their earlier state. From these data some have concluded that there is a possibility of conversion in the intermediate state. They reason that in Ezekiel's time Sodom and its sisters, that is, the other cities in the Valley of Siddim, had all long ago been destroyed and therefore could not be restored to their former state and be accepted by God in grace if their earlier inhabitants had not been converted by the preaching of the word of God in Sheol. But this notion is far removed from the text. The Lord here promises only that he will again, despite its harlotry, accept Jerusalem in grace; and besides, that Sodom and Samaria, which are evidently (cf. v. 61) types of all Gentile nations, will be restored to their former state; that is, in the future, Jerusalem will be restored, and the Gentile cities will be subject to it. But there is no question of preaching and conversion in Sheol, or of a resurrection and return of the earlier inhabitants of Sodom and Samaria.

The only texts to which one can appeal for a preaching of the gospel in hades with some semblance of justification are 1 Pet. 3:19–21 and 4:6. But these texts, also, do not contain what people wish to read in them. Even if it were true that they speak of a proclamation by Christ after his resurrection to the contemporaries of Noah in hades, this would only establish the fact that it occurred, but by no means would it warrant the teaching that there is ongoing preaching of the gospel in hades to all who have not heard it on earth. The truth, after all, is that Noah's contemporaries were precisely not the kind of people who had never during their lifetime heard the word of God on earth; on the contrary, they had willfully and maliciously despised the word of Noah, the preacher of righteousness, and had disobeyed the voice of the Lord while fully conscious that they were doing so (2 Pet. 2:5). Accordingly, they were a very special case that provides no warrant for any further conclusions. Also, the aorist ἐκήρυξεν (*ekēryxen*; 1 Pet. 3:19) indicates that this preaching by Christ occurred only once. This preaching, furthermore, cannot have been a proclamation of the gospel unto salvation. If one recalls how severely and consistently Scripture judges all the ungodly and how it always describes the generation of Noah's contemporaries as people who gave themselves up to all kinds of evil and unrighteousness, it becomes preposterous to think that Christ would have proclaimed the gospel of salvation to them above all others. At most, as the old Lutherans explained the text, the reference is to a solemn announcement of his triumph to the denizens of the underworld. In addition, all kinds of difficulties attend such ongoing preaching of the gospel in hades. According to 1 Pet. 3:18–19, Christ delivered that preaching specifically after he had been made alive and was risen. Did he at that time go physically to hades? When did he do that? How long did he stay there? And suppose all this were possible—however unlikely it is as such—who then is conducting this preaching in hades on an ongoing basis after this time? Is there a church in the underworld? Is there an ongoing mission, a calling and ordination to ministry? Are they humans or angels, apostles or other ministers of the Word, who after their death are proclaiming the gospel there? The theory of a mission center in hades is, in a variety of ways, in conflict with Scripture.

But, as demonstrated earlier,[1] it lacks all support in 1 Pet. 3:18–22 as well. All we are told there is that after his resurrection, Christ, made alive in the spirit, went to heaven and by his ascension preached to the spirits in prison and made angels, authorities, and powers subject to him. Nor does 1 Pet. 4:6 make any mention of such gospel preaching in hades. The aorist εὐηγγελίσθη (*euēngelisthē*) by its very form refers not to ongoing preaching but a specific event. That proclamation of the gospel occurred once, and with the intent that those who heard it would be judged like everyone else, "in the flesh," that is, they would die, but might live, as God does, "in the spirit." The preaching of the gospel, therefore, preceded their death; the νεκροί are those who are now dead but who heard the gospel during their lifetime. The reason why Peter calls these people νεκροί (*nekroi*, dead [ones]) can be found in the previous verse. There we read that Christ "stands ready to judge the living and the dead." Now then, just as the gospel is preached to the living today, so it was in the past preached to those who are now dead, so that, while they would indeed still die in the flesh [as everyone else does], they would nevertheless even now already live in the spirit in God's presence.

Given these objections, which are derived from Scripture, the entire theory of gospel preaching in the intermediate state collapses. For if it is not in Scripture, theology is not free to advocate it. But there are still many other objections as well. Assuming that the gospel is still being preached in hades, is that preaching addressed to everyone without distinction? Usually the answer given is no, restricting the audience to those who did not hear of it on earth. This is not only in conflict with their exegesis of 1 Pet. 3:18–22 (for if the reference in this passage is to gospel preaching by Christ in hades, it is addressed precisely to those who *did* hear the gospel through Noah), it also automatically raises the question whether life here on earth is totally immaterial to that preaching of the gospel in hades. To this question, too, people as a rule understandably do not dare to give a negative answer, for then this life would be completely without value or meaning. For that reason, along with Clement and Origen, they usually say that in the intermediate state the gospel is addressed only to those who are susceptible to conversion—

---

1. H. Bavinck, *Reformed Dogmatics*, III, 413–17 (#394), 480–82 (#409).

people who, on earth, by their attitude toward the real calling (*vocatio realis*),[2] have prepared themselves for an acceptance of the gospel by faith.[3] By saying this, one in fact again shifts the point of emphasis back to this life, and the preaching of the gospel in hades only brings to light what was already hidden in human hearts here on earth. That is to say, the decision with respect to salvation and perdition is made, not in response to the gospel, but in response to the real calling (*vocatio realis*), the law. And in essence this is the same opinion that was held also by the Pelagians, Socinians, Deists, and the like, namely, that there are three ways to salvation: the law of nature, the Mosaic law, and the law of Christ.

In addition, the theory of a kind of gospel preaching in hades is based on an array of incorrect assumptions. Basic to this theory is the assumption that it is God's intent to save all humans, that the preaching of the gospel has to be absolutely universal, that all humans must be personally and individually confronted by the choice for or against the gospel, that in making that choice the decision lies within human power, that original and actual sins are insufficient to condemn anyone, and that only deliberate unbelief toward the gospel makes a person worthy of eternal ruin. All these assumptions are in conflict with firm scriptural statements and make the theory of gospel preaching in the intermediate state unacceptable. And if, finally, the question is asked whether it is not hard to believe that all those who here on earth, quite aside from any responsibility of their own, failed to hear the gospel are lost, then the answer that has to be given is this: (a) In this most solemn matter, not our feeling but the Word of God decides. (b) The theory of a preaching of the gospel to the dead in no way relieves the problem, inasmuch as it only helps those who had already prepared themselves for the faith here on earth. (c) It even aggravates the problem because it pays no attention to the interest of the millions of children who die in infancy and in fact excludes them from the possibility of being saved. And (d) it takes no account of the sovereign freedom and omnipotence of God, which can save also without the external preaching of the Word, solely by the internal calling and regeneration of the Holy Spirit.

PURIFICATION?

[560] The state of deceased believers who have not yet attained full holiness here on earth is conceived by the church of Rome as a purification of souls by the punishment of fire. The idea of such a state of purification is of pagan origin and occurred especially in two forms. The theory of the transmigration of souls, found among the people of India, Egyptians, Greeks, Jews, and the like, holds that before

---

2. Ed. note: Cf. Richard A. Muller, *Dictionary of Latin and Greek Theological Terms* (Grand Rapids: Baker Academic, 1985), s.v. *vocatio*, 329: "General or universal calling is sometimes termed *vocatio realis*, or real calling, because it occurs in and through the things (*res*) of the world, whereas special, or evangelical, calling is sometimes termed a *vocatio verbalis*, since it comes only through the Word (*Verbum*)."

3. Cf., e.g., J. H. A. Ebrard, *Christliche Dogmatik*, 2nd ed. (Königsberg: A. W. Unser, 1862–63), §576.

entering the human body the soul has already lived in other bodies; after it has left the human body, it also enters new organisms—all with a view toward self-purification and ultimately reaching perfection. This theory is too contrary to Scripture for it ever to have found acceptance, aside from a few sects and individual persons, within the bounds of Christianity. It proceeds, after all, from the idea that souls are preexistent, that originally they did not possess a body and are indifferent to all bodies. It is, moreover, in conflict with the doctrine of redemption accomplished by Christ and views purification and perfection as the work of humans themselves. And, finally, it entirely fails to make clear how souls, by repeatedly passing into other bodies, could be freed from sins and trained toward holiness.[4]

Another idea, one that had greater influence on Christian theology, is that souls after death still need to be purified for a time by an assortment of punishments before they can attain the highest level of blessedness. In Parsism we encounter the belief that following the general resurrection there is a three-day period of purification in molten metal that feels gentle to the good but is very painful to the evil.[5] The Jews taught that only the perfectly righteous went immediately to heaven; the others were consigned to Gehinnom, which according to some was a purgatory for all people, but in any case it was so for the Jews.[6] Since Origen, this conception also spread among Christians, leading to the Catholic doctrine of purgatory, or a period of purification, which is accepted by many Protestants.

At first blush, this idea is quite appealing. Believers, after all, at the moment of their deaths are all still saddled with sin; even the most saintly still possess only a small beginning of perfect obedience. This sin that adheres to believers, furthermore, is not rooted in the body but in the soul, which for that reason cannot enter heaven unless it is freed in advance from the guilt of sin and completely purged of its pollution. It is hard to picture how this purification could suddenly take place at, or as a result of, death. Not only is sanctification in this life a slow process, but also in every domain of life sudden transitions are virtually unknown while gradual growth and development is everywhere. Hence everything favors the idea that after death the souls of believers need to undergo a purification before being taken up into heaven and admitted to the vision of God.

However, no matter what human argumentation would favor such a purgatory, the primary and conclusive objection is that Scripture nowhere speaks of it.

---

4. B. de Moor, *Commentarius . . . theologiae*, 6 vols. (Leiden: Hasebroek, 1761–71), II, 1081; C. Vitringa, *Doctrina christiana religionis*, 8 vols. (Arnheim, 1761–86), IV, 87–97; K. G. Bretschneider, *Systematische Entwicklung aller in der Dogmatik* (Leipzig: J. A. Barth, 1841), 846; E. Spiess, *Entwicklungsgeschichte der Vorstellungen vom Zustande nach dem Tode* (Jena: Herman Costenoble, 1877), 31, 558; J. F. von Meyer, *Blätter für höhere Wahrheit* (Frankfurt a.M.: H. L. Brönner, 1818–32), I, 244–99; P. Gennrich, *Die Lehre von der Wiedergeburt* (Leipzig: Deichert, 1907), 275–355; R. Falke, *Gibt es eine Seelenwanderung?* (Halle: S. E. Strein, 1904); Th. Traub, "Seelenwanderung," *Der Geisteskampf der Gegenwart* 45 (1909): 285–303.

5. P. D. Chantepie de la Saussaye, *Lehrbuch der Religionsgeschichte*, 2 vols. (Freiburg i.B.: Mohr [Siebeck], 1887–89), II, 51.

6. F. W. Weber, *System der altsynagogalen palästinischen Theologie* (Leipzig: Dörffling & Franke, 1880), 327.

Roman Catholic theologians admittedly advance a number of texts, but none of them really serves their purpose. Matthew 5:22 does not breathe a word about a purgatory but does refer to Gehenna. To take "prison" (φυλακη, *phylakē*) in 5:25 to mean purgatory is arbitrary; it is rather an image of Gehenna, for one who ends up in it has been previously condemned by a judge and will never have a chance to pay off the debt and to leave prison; the "until" (ἑως, *heōs*) in verse 26 indicates an unfulfillable period (cf. 18:30, 34). In Matt. 12:32 Jesus says that blaspheming against the Holy Spirit will not be forgiven in either this age or the age to come. The words "or in the age to come" only serve to underscore the unpardonableness of blaspheming against the Holy Spirit and hence by no means presuppose that some sins can still be forgiven even after this life is over. But even if this were the case, this text would still not prove anything to support the doctrine of purgatory, for the reference here is to the forgiveness of sin, whereas purgatory is not at all a place for forgiveness but only a place for "paying off" temporal punishments. The text speaks of forgiveness in the age to come, that is, the time after the parousia, while purgatory occurs before the parousia and ends with the last judgment.

According to 1 Cor. 3:12–15, the work of the ministers of the church must stand up under testing in the day of Christ's parousia. Those who have built on the foundation of Christ with gold, silver, and precious stones, that is, those who in their office and ministry have done solid work, though they will be tested in their work, will receive a reward since the work proves to stand up under the fire of judgment. On the other hand, those who have built on the foundation with wood, hay, and straw—which cannot withstand the fire—will suffer the loss of their reward, though they themselves will be saved through the fire of judgment. So, in fact, we read here of a revelatory fire (v. 13), a testing fire (v. 13), and a consuming fire (v. 15); but this is how Paul presents the fire of judgment in the future of Christ, and he therefore has no room for a purgatory that would purify believers now and end *before* the final judgment. Other texts on which the church of Rome could base its doctrine of purgatory—if only with some semblance of justification—are nonexistent. Only one passage in the Old Testament Apocrypha, 2 Macc. 12:41–45, shows that the Jews at that time considered offerings and prayers for the dead who had died in their sins to be a good and necessary thing—something we know from other sources as well. It is therefore all the more noteworthy that this folk belief existing among the Jews is never reported, much less sanctioned, in either the Old or the New Testament.

The doctrine of purgatory is most closely bound up with justification. By justification, the church of Rome understands the infusion of supernatural sanctifying grace that in turn enables humans to do good works and thereby earn eternal life. This grace, however, is subject to being increased and decreased; one who loses it as a result of mortal sin and then dies is lost; one who by keeping the precepts and counsels achieves perfection in the hour of death immediately enters heaven. However, one who still has to pay the debt and bear the temporal punishment due to a venial sin, or who in the sacrament of penance has received back the infused grace lost as a result of a mortal sin and is at his death still in arrears in "paying off" the temporal punishments—such a person is consigned to purgatory and remains there until he has paid the last penny. In the church of Rome, justification, sanctification, and glorification are the work of humans themselves, be it on the basis of the supernatural grace infused into them. After receiving it, they have to make themselves worthy of eternal life and the beatific vision of God in heaven by a condign or full merit;[7] if they fail to achieve this on earth, they must—just as the pagans pictured it—continue the work on earth in the hereafter until they have attained perfection.

But from Scripture the Reformation again learned to know the justification of sinners by faith and therefore had to come to a rejection of the fire of purification. Christ accomplished everything; not only did he bear the punishment, but he also won eternal life for us by his keeping of the law. And all the benefits that Christ gained by his suffering and death and that are present and available in him in perfection are immediately conferred on those who believe in truth. He who believes *has* eternal life. In justification not only the merit of Christ's passive obedience is imputed but also that of his active obedience. In that benefaction believers receive forgiveness, exemption from punishment, and are not returned to the prefall state of Adam, who with the power granted him had to keep the law and earn eternal life. On the contrary: on the basis of Christ's perfect obedience, they are immediately entitled to eternal life; the holy works accomplished by Christ are credited to them; they do not, by keeping the law, have to earn eternal life, but do good works based on the principle of eternal life already granted to them in faith. Accordingly, sanctification here is not self-preparation for heaven, or self-perfection, but solely the unfolding in believers of what they already possess in Christ, a walking in the good works that God in Christ prepared [for them] (Eph. 2:10). God therefore does not have to wait for any more good works before he can receive believers in heaven, inasmuch as in Christ that heaven is at once opened to everyone who believes. Those who believe have forgiveness and eternal life; they are ready and fit for heaven and need not go through a purgatory either here or hereafter. Even the suffering they often still—even as a result of sin—have to bear on earth is not a punishment, a penalty, a required late payment of the demands of the law, but a fatherly chastisement that serves their maturation.

THE END OF OUR PILGRIMAGE

On a Reformational basis, then, the only question is this: When do believers enter into full possession of the benefits that Christ has granted them? Those who believe receive them at once in a juridical sense; in Christ they are entitled to all the benefits of the covenant, the whole of salvation. But on earth they do not yet enter into full possession of them. When, then, does this occur? When

7. Ed. note: Cf. Richard Muller, *Dictionary of Latin and Greek Theological Terms*, s.v. *meritum de condigno* and *meritum de congruo*, 191f.

do believers cease to be pilgrims and arrive in their homeland? To this question Scripture has but one answer: at death. Nowhere does it represent the godly after death as still being tormented by punishment or suffering due to sin. The godly always express as their certain expectation that at death they will have reached the end of their pilgrimage and entrance into the eternal blessed life in heaven (Ps. 73:24–25; Luke 23:43; Acts 7:59; 2 Cor. 5:1; Phil. 1:23; 2 Tim. 4:7). After death there is no longer any sanctification; a state of sanctity begins in which the spirits of the righteous made perfect (Heb. 12:23) are clothed in long, white garments and stand before the throne and before the Lamb (Rev. 7:9, 14). The story is told of the modest de Sacy of Port Royal that he always lived in the fear of God and consequently never dared hope for immediate blessedness after death but at his death cried out: "O blessed purgatory!"[8] But such a state of mind is entirely foreign to the godly of the Old and New Testaments and can only be explained on the assumption that such a person, looking at himself, is blind to the finished work of Christ.

Of course, the manner in which the state of holiness commences immediately at the death of believers cannot be understood or clearly described. Regeneration and sanctification effected here on earth by the Holy Spirit is a mystery as well. But there is no doubt that death serves as a means. Not in the sense of Platonic dualism, as though the soul's mere liberation from the body would already constitute its sanctification, for sin is rooted precisely in the soul. Nor in the sense of sentimental rationalism, which has death, as a messenger of peace, turn people into angels, for death as such is a revelation of God's wrath and the wages of sin. But death does serve as such a means, according to Scripture, which portrays it for the believer as a dying to sin. For all discipline is for our good that we may share God's holiness (Heb. 12:10). Those who like Christ suffer in the flesh because of sin cease from sin (1 Pet. 4:1). This is especially true of death. The consequence of ethical death, that is, dying to sin in communion with Christ, is that a person is freed from and dead to sin and henceforth lives for God in Christ (Rom. 6:6–11; 8:10; 1 Pet. 2:24). And this ethical death culminates in physical death (Rom. 7:24; 2 Cor. 5:1; Phil. 1:21, 23). Death is an enormous change, a breaking of all ties with this earthly life and an entering into a new world with totally different conditions and relations. It is not at all strange that, as he does with all suffering, God should employ death as a means of sanctifying the soul of the believer and cleansing it from all the stains of sin.[9] Against this we cannot raise the objection that such a sanctification is mechanical and occurs in one leap, for death is the biggest leap a person can take, a sudden relocation of the believer into the presence of Christ and consequently a total destruction of the outer "human" and a total renewal of the inner "human."

8. Ed. note: Bavinck here refers to Isaac-Louis Le Maistre de Sacy (1613–84), spiritual director of the Jansenist order at Port-Royal, France, who completed a translation of the Bible into French that was begun by his brother Antoine.

9. Westminster Larger Catechism, qu. 85.

Add to this that the doctrine of purgatory in no way makes this sanctification of the believer any more understandable. In the first place, Catholic theology has to accord to death a similar critical significance. Purgatory, after all, is not a place where sins are still forgiven, but where still-remaining temporal punishments can be "paid off." So those who have committed venial sins and did not receive forgiveness for them in this life must receive it in death. Catholic theologians, accordingly, teach that the soul that dies in venial sin, in death immediately receives the forgiveness of sin in order subsequently to satisfy in purgatory the temporal punishments stipulated for those sins. It thus is not at all clear how purgatory brings about the sanctification of souls. Aside from the fact that Catholics usually describe purgatory as a material fire, which by that token cannot have an "ideal" impact on the soul, there is the question of how pain as such can sanctify a soul. That would indeed be possible if by means of the torment repentance, contrition, conversion, faith, love, and the like could be effected in the soul. But in the Catholic view, that may not be assumed. For purgatory is not a mission center, no institution for conversion, no school of sanctification, but a place where only temporal punishment can be "paid off." So on the one hand, the "poor souls" can no longer sin and take on new guilt, and on the other they cannot improve themselves either, for all improvement implies merit, and in purgatory the possibility of merit is excluded. Consequently, it is impossible for us to form any clear notion of the state of these "poor souls." If they are to be pictured as still more or less stained by sin, then in the Catholic view it is impossible to understand how they should not continue to sin and so again completely suffer loss of the grace received. If this possibility is excluded, then the souls are inherently pure and holy and only still have to bear certain temporal punishments they could not bear on earth; but then it is again incomprehensible that the perfectly righteous could still be temporarily excluded from heaven and subjected to the torments of purgatory. In both cases it remains puzzling how purgatory can be a "purifying fire" (*ignis purgatorius*); it is nothing but a fire of retribution (*ignis vindicativus*). Oswald correctly points out that the purifying character of purgatory belongs among the more difficult questions![10]

Finally, various questions remain that the doctrine of purgatory fails to answer. According to Catholic belief, the Old Testament devout went to the limbo of the fathers (*limbus patrum*). The question is: Is this limbo to be pictured as a purgatory, or did they not need a purgatory? And how are we to think of the purification of those who die shortly before the parousia and consequently can no longer enter purgatory, since it ceases to exist when this world comes to an end? The souls of those who died in earlier ages have much more to endure than those who enter purgatory later, inasmuch as the duration of torment in purgatory becomes increasingly shorter. How do Catholics square this fact with the justice of God and the soul's need for purification? If the answer is that to the extent that the end of the world approaches,

10. J. H. Oswald, *Eschatologie* (Paderborn: F. Schöningh, 1869), 116.

sanctification is shifted increasingly to the suffering of the present time and to the moment of death, then one seriously undermines the doctrine of purgatory and comes close to the view adopted by the Reformation against this doctrine.

INTERCESSION FOR THE DEAD?

If the doctrine of purgatory is untenable, all offerings and prayers for the dead automatically fall with it. Veneration of the dead by sacrifices and prayers was common among pagans. Intercession for the dead became a practice among the Jews later (2 Macc. 12:40–45) and remains to the present.[11] In the Christian church there soon arose the custom of wishing for the dead to receive peace, light, and refreshment (*refrigerium*) and remembering them in prayers and at the celebration of the Lord's Supper. In the early period, this was done with respect to all without distinction who died in the Lord, and these offerings and sacrifices were solely memorial in nature. But gradually a distinction was made between the souls who were immediately taken up into heaven and others who still had to spend time in purgatory. Communion with the first then gradually began to be practiced by invocation and veneration, and with the second by intercessions, good works, indulgences, and Masses for the soul.[12] In the ancient Catholic sense—as prayer to God that he would increase the blessedness of those who died in Christ and hear their prayers for the living, and simultaneously as commemoration of and communion with the dead—intercession for the dead was also approved by the Greeks, the Lutherans, Hugo Grotius, many Anglicans, and certain more-recent theologians.[13]

But the Reformed rejected this intercession for the dead on the ground that their lot was unalterably decided at death.[14] The fact is that neither the Old nor the New Testament breathes a word about such intercession. The only passage to which appeal can be made is 1 Cor. 15:29, where Paul mentions those who had themselves baptized ὑπὲρ νεκρῶν (*hyper nekrōn*). However, from this it cannot be inferred that such a baptism was received by the living for the benefit of the dead. There is no evidence whatever that such a practice existed in Paul's time or later. True, Tertullian and others report that this custom was found among the followers of Cerinthus and Marcion; but in the first place the correctness of this report is subject to doubt and, second, [if it is correct] the implication is that it was a heretical practice that never found acceptance in the Christian church. Those who would use the text to

11. F. Schwally, *Das Leben nach dem Tode: Nach den Vorstellungen des Alten Israel* (Giessen: J. Ricker, 1892), 188–90.

12. Canons and Decrees of the Council of Trent, XXII, 2, 3; XXV; Bellarmine, "De purgat.," in *Controversiis*, II, 15–18; G. Perrone, *Praelectiones theologicae*, 9 vols. (Louvain: Vanlinthout & Vandezande, 1838–43), VI, 289; VIII, 29; H. Th. Simar, *Lehrbuch der Dogmatik*, 2 vols. (Freiburg i.B.: Herder, 1879–80), 900.

13. C. Vitringa, *Doctr. christ.*, IV, 79, 80; VIII, 509, 515; A. Frantz, *Das Gebet für die Todten in seinem Zusammenhange mit Cultus und Lehre nach den Schriften des heiligen Augustinus* (Nordhausen: A. Büchting, 1857); K. M. Leibbrand, *Das Gebet für die Todten in der evangelischen Kirche* (Stuttgart: Schweizerbart, 1864).

14. J. C. Suicerus, *Thesaurus ecclesiasticus* (Amsterdam: H. H. Wetsten, 1682), s.v. ταφη; B. de Moor, *Comm. theol.*, V, 30–32.

support the right to pray for the dead should first of all begin by baptizing the living on behalf of the dead, so that that baptism could benefit them. Paul cites the dead as the reason why the living had themselves baptized. Because those who had died in Christ would rise again, because of what they stood for and on their behalf, the living who were believers had themselves baptized. The apostle here is only expressing the thought that baptism presupposes belief in the resurrection of Christ and of believers. Take away the resurrection, and baptism becomes an empty ceremony.

Intercession for the dead, therefore, has no basis whatever in Scripture, as Tertullian for that matter already recognized. For after he had discussed various church practices, including sacrifices for the dead (*De corona militis*, ch. 3), he added in chapter 4: "If, for these and other such rules, you insist on having positive scriptural injunction, you will find none. Tradition will be held forth to you as the originator of them, custom as their strengthener, and faith as their observer."[15] Because there is no prescription of [God] the Father, we have to content ourselves with the custom of the mother, that is, the church, which thus again receives a position alongside of and above the Word of God. Since, then, intercession for the dead cannot stand the test of Scripture, the question concerning its utility and comfort is no longer appropriate. All the same, these two things are hardly demonstrable. For though it seems a beautiful thing that the living can help the dead by their intercessions and make up for the wrong they have perhaps done to them during their lifetime, in fact this church practice takes Christian piety in a totally wrong direction. It gives the impression that—contrary to Matt. 8:22—caring for the dead is of greater value than love for the living; it credits one's own works and prayers with a meritorious, expiatory power that is effective even on the other side of the grave and benefits the dead; it is based on and conducive to the doctrine of purgatory, which, on the one hand, especially among the rich, fosters unconcern and, on the other hand, perpetuates the uncertainty of believers; and in the minds of Christians it weakens confidence in the sufficiency of the sacrifice and intercession of Christ.[16]

COMMUNION WITH THE CHURCH TRIUMPHANT

[561] Although there is no room for the veneration of saints and intercession for the dead, there still is and remains a communion between the church militant

15. Tertullian, *The Chaplet, or De Corona*, ch. 4 (translation from *The Ante-Nicene Fathers*, ed. A. Roberts and J. Donaldson [New York: Christian Literature, 1885], III, 95). Cf. Bellarmine, "De missa," in *Controversiis*, II, c. 7; J. H. Oswald, *Eschatologie*, 95.

16. For the repudiation of the doctrine of purgatory, see J. Calvin, *Institutes*, III.v; A. Polanus, *Syntagma theologia christianae* (Hanover: Aubry, 1624), VII, 25; D. Chamier, *Panstratiae catholicae* (Geneva: Roverianis, 1626), III, 26; W. Ames, *Bellarminus enervatus*, 3rd ed., 4 vols. (Oxford: G. Turner, 1629), II, 5; G. Voetius, *Selectae disputationes theologicae*, 5 vols. (Utrecht: 1648–69), II, 1240; John Forbes, *Instructiones historico-theologicae* (Amsterdam: Elzevirium, 1645), XIII; J. Gerhard, *Loci theologici*, ed. E. Preuss, 9 vols. (Berlin: G. Schlawitz, 1863–75), XXVI, 181f.; J. Quenstedt, *Theologia*, IV, 555; Th. Kliefoth, *Christliche Eschatologie* (Leipzig: Dörffling & Franke, 1886), 82f.; Charles H. H. Wright, *The Intermediate State and Prayers for the Dead* (London: Nisbet, 1900).

on earth and the church triumphant in heaven that cannot be broken. Believers on earth, when they became Christians, came to the heavenly Jerusalem above, which is the mother of us all; to the innumerable angels who serve and praise God there; to the assembly of the firstborn, that is, the devout of the Old Testament who are enrolled in heaven and have their citizenship there; to the spirits of the just, that is, the Christians who have already died and reached perfection, the consummation; to Christ the mediator of the New Testament and to God the judge of all (Heb. 12:22–24).

This communion does not imply that there has to be direct interaction between the members of the militant and triumphant segments of the church, for though this is lacking also between the different persons and peoples who lived at different times and places on earth, humankind is still an organism made up of one blood. The personal contacts that every believer has here on earth are limited to a few persons, but believers are nevertheless members of one, holy, catholic, Christian church. The unity that binds all believers together, the dead as well as the living, is anchored in Christ, and through him in fellowship with the same Father, in the possession of the same Spirit, and in joint participation in the same treasures of salvation. The love that remains even when faith and hope disappear permanently unites all believers with Christ and each other. And that love expresses itself on our part in the fact that we remember with deep respect the saints who have preceded us; speak of them worthily; imitate their faith and good works; and, spurred on by their example, run with patience the course that is set before us; and feel one with them and live in anticipation of going to them, that together with them and all created beings we may magnify the Lord.

Among the forms in which the communion of the church militant with the church triumphant manifests itself, the hope of reunion occupies a large place. Rationalism, indeed, has made appalling misuse of this fact. It seemed as if the blessedness of heaven consisted not in fellowship with Christ but in the sentimental enjoyment of one another's presence. But nevertheless there is here a good and true element. The hope of reunion on the other side of the grave is completely natural, genuinely human, and also in keeping with Scripture. For Scripture teaches us not a naked immortality of spectral souls but the eternal life of individual persons. Regeneration does not erase individuality, personality, or character, but sanctifies it and puts it at the service of God's name. The community of believers is the new humanity that bears within itself a wide range of variety and distinction and manifests the richest diversity in unity. The joy of heaven, to be sure, first of all consists in communion with Christ but, further, in the fellowship of the blessed among themselves as well. And just as this fellowship on earth, though it is always imperfect, does not infringe on the fellowship of believers with Christ but rather reinforces and enriches it, so it is in heaven. Paul's highest desire was to depart and to be with Christ (Phil. 1:23; 1 Thess. 4:17). But Jesus himself represents the joy of heaven by the image of a meal at which all the guests sit down with Abraham, Isaac, and Jacob (Matt. 8:11; cf. Luke 13:28). The hope of reunion is not bad in itself, therefore, as long as it remains subordinate to the desire for fellowship with Christ.

Nor is it absurd to think that the blessed in heaven yearn for the believers who are on earth. After all, they have a store of memories of the persons and conditions they knew on earth (Luke 16:27–31). The souls under the altar cry out for vengeance on account of the blood that had been shed (Rev. 6:10). The bride, that is, the entire community of believers both in heaven and on earth, pray for the coming of the Lord Jesus (22:17). Although Scripture gives us no warrant for believing that the blessed in heaven know everything that happens here on earth, still it is likely that they know as much about the church militant on earth as the latter does about them. And that small amount of knowledge, added to the knowledge that they possess from memory and that is perhaps regularly augmented by statements made by angels and the recently deceased, is sufficient to prompt them to think with ongoing warm interest about this earth and the mighty struggle taking place here. An added ingredient is that the state of the blessed in heaven, however glorious, still for various reasons bears a provisional character. After all, at this stage they are only in heaven and restricted to heaven and not yet in possession of the earth, the inheritance of which has been promised them along with that of heaven. Further, they are deprived of the body, and this incorporeal existence is not, as dualism must hold, a gain but a loss, not an increase but a diminution of being, inasmuch as the body is integral to our humanity.

Finally, the part cannot be complete without the whole; the fullness of Christ's love can only be known in communion with all the saints (Eph. 3:18–19); the one group of believers cannot be made perfect without the other (Heb. 11:40). For that reason, in the case of the blessed in heaven, there is still room for faith and hope, for longing and prayer (Rev. 6:10; 22:17). Like believers on earth, they eagerly await the return of Christ, the resurrection of the dead, and the restoration of all things. Only then has the end been reached (1 Cor. 15:24). This idea is so much in the foreground in Scripture that by comparison the intermediate state shrinks into a brief span of time of which no account whatever is taken at the final judgment. It also is nowhere stated that what has been accomplished by the dead in the intermediate state will be judged before the judgment seat of Christ on the last day. That judgment exclusively concerns what has been done in the body, whether good or evil (2 Cor. 5:10); to that extent the universal judgment is identical with the personal and particular judgment.

However, this still gives us no warrant to conclude with Kliefoth[17] that the souls after death live outside space and time and are denied all development or progress. For though there is certainly no progress like that on earth, and still less a possible change for good or ill, still genuinely existing living souls cannot possibly be without activity unless one thinks of them as being in a coma. The dead remain finite and limited and can exist in no way other than in space and time.

17. Th. Kliefoth, *Christliche Eschatologie*, 61–66.

Undoubtedly, on the other side of the grave the dimensions of space and the computations of time are very different from those on earth, where we measure by the mile and by the hour. Also, the souls who dwell there do not become eternal and omnipresent as God is; like the angels they must have a specific whereabouts (*ubi definitivum*), cannot be in two places at the same time, are always somewhere in a specific location, in paradise or heaven, and so on. Similarly, they are not elevated above all structured time, that is, above all succession of moments, inasmuch as they have a past they remember, a present in which they live, and a future toward which they are moving. The rich man knows that his brothers are still alive (Luke 16:28), the souls under the altar eagerly anticipate a day of vengeance (Rev. 6:10), the bride longs for the coming of Christ (22:17), those who come out of the great ordeal serve God night and day (7:15), and there is no rest day or night for those who have worshiped the beast (14:11).

If, then, the souls exist under some form of space and time, they cannot be conceived as being totally inactive. Jesus indeed says that in the night of death no one can work (John 9:4), and heavenly blessedness is often represented in Scripture as a state of being at rest (Heb. 4:9–10; Rev. 14:13). But just as it is not inconsistent to say that God rests from his work of creation (Gen. 2:2) and still always works (John 5:17), or that Christ had accomplished his work on earth (17:4) and nevertheless prepares a place in heaven for his own (14:3), so it is not contradictory to claim that believers rest from their labors and nevertheless serve God in his temple. Though their work on earth is finished, this does not alter the fact that they still have other works to do in heaven. Scripture teaches this plainly. Those who have died in the Lord are with Jesus (Phil. 1:23), stand before the throne of God and of the Lamb (Rev. 7:9, 15), cry out and pray, praise and serve him (6:10; 7:10, 15; 22:17). Anyway if they, being conscious, know God, Christ, the angels, and one another, they are by that very fact engaging in activities of intellect and will, increasing in knowledge, and being confirmed in love. If Paul can say that believers on earth, by seeing the glory of the Lord in the mirror of his Word, are being transformed into the same image from one degree of glory to another (2 Cor. 3:18), how much more will that be the case when they are admitted into his immediate presence and see him face to face? There is no change in their state, nor is there any development in an earthly sense, not even sanctification as in the church militant, for holiness itself is the possession of all. However, just as Adam before the fall and Christ himself in his humanity, though perfectly holy, could still increase in grace and wisdom, so in heaven there is an ongoing confirmation of one's state, an ever-increasing degree of conformity to the image of the Son, a never-ending growth in the knowledge and love of God.

Moreover, all have their own task and place. Roman Catholics assume that after death Old Testament believers waited in the limbo of the fathers and were not released until Christ freed them at his descent into hell; and they also believe that infants who were not yet baptized when they died will be received neither in hell nor in heaven but in a separate "receptacle," the limbo of infants. But Scripture presents no basis for either of these two "limbos." It is of course logical that those who lose sight of the unity of the covenant of grace, and view the benefits secured by Christ as a new substance that did not exist before—such are compelled to make the devout of the Old Testament wait in the limbo of the fathers for this acquisition and impartation of Christ's benefits. But those who acknowledge the unity of the covenant and view the benefits of Christ as the gracious benevolence of God that, with a view toward Christ, could be imparted already before his suffering and death—they have no need for a *limbus patrum*. Under the provisions of the Old Testament, the way to heavenly blessedness was the same as under the New Testament, even though there is indeed a difference in the light by which they walked then and now.

In the same way there is no room on the other side of the grave for a limbo of infants (*limbus infantum*); for the children of the covenant, whether baptized or unbaptized, go to heaven when they die; and so little has been disclosed to us about the fate of those outside the covenant that we had best abstain from any definite judgment.[18] Still, contained in the theory of the *limbus patrum* and the *limbus infantum* is the true idea that there are varying degrees both in the punishment of the ungodly and in the blessedness of the devout. There is distinction of rank and activity in the world of angels. There is diversity among all created beings and most abundantly among humans. There is distinction of place and task in the church of Christ; on earth every believer is given one's own gifts and charged with one's own task. And in death the works of each follow the person who dies in the Lord. Undoubtedly this diversity is not destroyed in heaven but, on the contrary, is purified of all that is sinful and multiplied abundantly (Luke 19:17–19). Still this difference in degree detracts nothing from the blessedness each enjoys in keeping with one's own capacity. For all will be at home with the same Lord (2 Cor. 5:8), are taken up into the same heaven (Rev. 7:9), enjoy the same rest (Heb. 4:9), and find joy in the same service of God (Rev. 7:15).

---

18. B. B. Warfield, "The Development of the Doctrine of Infant Salvation," in his *Two Studies in the History of Doctrine* (New York: Christian Literature, 1897).

15

Visions of the End

The universe is finite, and its history will come to an end. Those who live without God and without hope find this hard to accept and often turn to illusory dreams of progress or give up in despair. The Old Testament hope is based on an anticipated restoration of the earth as the kingdom of God. The expected day of the Lord brings judgment as well as salvation and is ushered in by the Messiah, David's Son. Prophetically prefigured in the return from Babylonian captivity, the conversion of Israel, and renewal of temple worship, the final expression of Israel's hope is cosmic—the Gentiles share in the full blessing of a cleansed and transformed earth. While the Old Testament regards the messianic kingdom as the full establishment of the kingdom of God, it also gives hints of a greater reality breaking through—the eternal, spiritual reign of God. The concrete, earthly character of Old Testament hope, politicized by intertestamental Judaism, gave rise to chiliasm, which posits a twofold return of Christ and a double resurrection. The first establishes an earthly millennial kingdom, the second the final consummation. The major objection to chiliasm is that it overlooks the New Testament's own spiritual application of Old Testament prophecy. It is the old rather than the new covenant that is the real intermezzo in salvation history.

[562] Just as it is appointed for humans to die once, so also there must come an end to the history of the world. Science as well as religion has always been convinced of this. Granted, a few people, such as Aristotle in antiquity and Heinrich Czolbe, Friedrich Mohr, and others in modern times, believed that this world was eternal and had neither beginning nor end. But today it is generally agreed that this opinion is untenable. There are many considerations that establish the finite duration of the world beyond all doubt. According to calculations, the rotational speed of the earth decreases by at least one second every 600,000 years. However small this decrease is, after billions of years it nevertheless brings about on earth a reversal in the relationship between day and night, which brings all life to an end. Further, the rotation of the earth is continually being slowed by the alternation of

high and low tides, the influence of which shifts parts of the earth and decreases the supply of kinetic energy. The earth therefore moves ever closer to the sun and must ultimately disappear in it. Furthermore, the space in which the planets move is not totally empty but is filled with ether or rarefied air, which, however weakly, holds back the planets' movement, decreases their rotational speed, causes their orbit to shrink, and thus brings them into ever closer proximity to the sun.

Neither can the sun last for ever. Whether its heat is produced by infalling meteorites or constant shrinkage or chemical processes, the sun gradually uses up that heat, contracts, and moves toward its end. According to [Robert] Thompson, the sun's diameter decreases thirty-five meters a year and, since it has been shining some twenty million years now, it has only some ten million years left. While kinetic energy, after all, can convert itself into heat, heat cannot be converted into kinetic energy unless it flows out upon a colder body. Therefore, once the temperature has become everywhere the same, the conversion of heat ceases, and the end of things has come. Consequently, the question is simply whether the sun or the earth will last longer. If it is the sun, the earth will ultimately be swallowed up by it, and everything will end in conflagration. If it is the earth, the heat supply will one day be exhausted, and life will expire in a death of extreme cold.[1]

Various other arguments for a finite world have been advanced as well. Because of its chemical affinity with minerals, the earth's supply of water has to grow increasingly smaller. Water and oxygen are increasingly bound up in solids. The earth's products—coal, wood, peat, nutriments—decrease. The earth, however rich in resources, will one day be exhausted, and this will occur all the sooner as the human race expands and the danger of overpopulation threatens. Accordingly, from the viewpoint of science, there is absolutely no room for an optimistic outlook on the future. Numerous people, nevertheless, have yielded to such an outlook and dreamed of steady progress and a future paradise of mankind in the present world (*Diesseits*). Humanists and materialists vie with each other in fostering such illusions. On the basis of the principle of cosmic evolution, they believe that their professional prophecies cannot go wrong. In their opinion, by the increase of ideal goods such as science, art, and morality, or by progress in material prosperity, that is, by an abundance of food, shelter, and clothing, the happiness of humanity will one day be fully realized. Kant, Lessing, Herder, Fichte, Schelling, and the like, envision a future in which the ethical kingdom of God will embrace all human

1. The law of entropy—according to which work can be completely converted into heat but heat can never be totally converted back to work, and which, applied to the universe by Clausius, leads to a state in which the temperature difference necessary for the conversion of heat into work has disappeared—has been used repeatedly as an argument for the end, hence also for the beginning of the world; and further, even as proof for the existence of God. *L. Dressel, "Der Gottesbeweis auf Grund des Entropiesatzes," *Stimmen aus Maria Laach* 78 (1909): 150–60; C. Isenkrahe, *Energie, Entropie, Weltanfang, Weltende* (Trier: Lintz, 1910). But B. Bavinck, "Das Entropiegesetz und die Endlichkeit der Welt," *Der Geisteskampf der Gegenwart* 45 (1909): 260–67, questions the validity of that argument. Cf. also the art. "Entropie" in *Meyers kleines Konversations-Lexikon*.

beings. All will participate in the Enlightenment, and full humanity will be the principle of the life of everyone.

Even Darwin, at the end of his book on *The Origin of Species* and in the final chapter of his *Descent of Man*, expresses the hope that humanity, which has already risen so far above its animal origins, is moving toward a still higher destiny in the distant future. In that future, says Pierson,[2] the most refined human beings will no longer crave marriage, but a man will live with his wife as with his sister, and sensuality will no longer be the death of the zest for living. Others claim that in the case of a highly civilized people, marriage will eventually assume the form of a double marriage, and two friends will jointly marry two women. Even more extravagant are the expectations of the Socialists, these millennialists of unbelief, who think that in the future state of their dreams all sin and struggle will have vanished, and a carefree life of contentment will be the privilege of everyone.

But, as we have already stated, there is not much ground on which to base these expectations. And even if a time of increased prosperity and greater happiness were to dawn, what would be the advantage if, as science teaches, all evolution would still finally end in death? At the end of his history of culture, Fr. von Hellwald[3] proves helpless to give even the slightest answer to the question for what purpose everything happened—to what end humanity, with all of its struggles and striving, its refinement and development, existed. And Otto Henne Am Rhyn ends his history of culture with the prediction that one day the whole of humankind along with its culture will disappear without a trace. "One day everything we have accomplished will be nowhere to be found." And in the face of that prospect, he can only console himself with the thought that it will be a long time before we will get there.[4] Those who live without God and without hope, and have to expect everything from the present world (*Diesseits*), from immanent cosmic forces, are without hope in the world as well.

Even culture cannot be conceived as endless. One may arbitrarily assume the passage of billions of years in the past or future of the world but cannot picture it concretely as being filled with history. If humanity were to last a billion years, a "textbook" on world history, which gave 10 pages to a century, would comprise no fewer than 200,000 volumes, each volume calculated at 500 pages; or 20,000 volumes if it devoted only one page to every century; or still 500 volumes if no more than one line was given to each century. And that is how it would be with everything that forms the content of our culture. Humanity is finite, and therefore human civilization cannot be conceived as endless either. Both for the earth and for our race, an infinite period of time is an absurdity, even more palpably so than the foolishness of the millions of years known to us from pagan mythologies. From

2. Allard Pierson, *Eene levensbeschouwing* (Haarlem: Kruseman, 1875), 269.

3. Ed. note: Bavinck may be referring to Friedrich von Hellwald (1842–92), *Die Erde und ihre Volker: Ein geographisches Hausbuch* (Stuttgart: Spemann, 1877–78).

4. Th. Ziegler, in his *Sittliches Sein und sittliches Werden* (Strassburg: K. J. Trübner, 1890), states: "What the final end, the goal of history itself is, I do not know, and none of us knows" (141).

the perspective of science, there is much more reason to accept the pessimism of Schopenhauer and Eduard von Hartmann, which stakes the salvation of the world on combating the alogical will by logical representation, on the absolute negation of will, that is, on the annihilation of the world itself. But even then there is not the slightest guarantee that the absolute will's negation will succeed and not pass over into another world process and ever and again start over ad infinitum. Many Greek philosophers believed that many other worlds preceded this one, and that many others would follow it. Even the Pythagoreans and Stoics were of the opinion that everything would return to precisely the same state in which it existed in this world and had existed in previous worlds. Also today many people have returned to such notions,[5] although Windelband rightly calls it a painful idea that "in the periodic return of all things the human personality, with all its activities and suffering, will return as well."[6]

A RELIGIOUS PERSPECTIVE ON THE END

[563] Religion has never been at peace with this idea of an endless development or the total ruination of the world. There are various reasons why it was kept from adopting these philosophical theories. It is obvious that all such theories fail to do justice to the value of personhood and tend to sacrifice it to the world as a whole. They further fail to appreciate the significance of the life of religion and morality and assign to it a position far below that of culture. And finally, for the present as well as for the future, they only build upon forces immanent in the cosmos and take no account whatever of a divine power that governs the world and ultimately, by direct intervention, causes the world to fulfill the purpose laid down for it. All religions, therefore, have another outlook on the future. All of them more or less clearly know of a struggle between good and evil; all of them cherish the hope of the victory of the good, in which the virtuous are rewarded and the wicked are punished; and as a rule they consider that future attainable in no other way than by a manifestation of supernatural forces.[7]

5. Cf. Ernst Haeckel, *The Riddle of the Universe*, trans. Joseph McCabe (New York: Harper & Brothers, 1900), 372; and esp. Nietzsche.

6. W. Windelband, *Geschichte und Wissenschaft*, 3rd ed. (Strassburg: Heitz, 1904), 22. For the end of the world, see further Friedrich Albert Lange, *Geschichte des Materialismus und Kritik seiner Bedeutung in der Gegenwart*, 8th ed. (Leipzig: Baedeker, 1908), 552; Tilmann Pesch, *Die grossen Welträthsel*, 2nd ed., 2 vols. (Freiburg: Herder, 1892), II, 352ff.; K. Mühlhäusser, *Die Zukunft der Menschheit* (Heilbronn: Henninger, 1881); F. Reiff, *Die Zukunft der Welt*, 2nd ed. (Basel: Bahnmaier's Verlag [C. Detloff], 1875); C. E. Fürer, *Weltende und Endgericht nach Mythologie, Naturwissenschaft und Bibel* (Gütersloh: Bertelsmann, 1896); H. Siebeck, *Lehrbuch der Religionsphilosophie* (Freiburg i.B.: J. C. B. Mohr, 1893), 399–427. See also H. Bavinck, *The Philosophy of Revelation* (New York: Longmans, Green, 1909), 242–315.

7. See H. Bavinck, *Reformed Dogmatics*, III, 238–40 (#351); and further T. Pfanner, *Systema theologiae gentilis purioris* (Basel: Joh. Hermann Widerhold, 1679), c. 18–20; R. Schneider, *Christliche Klänge aus den griechischen und römischen Klassikern* (Leipzig: Siegismund & Volkening, 1877), 250ff., 292f.; H. Lüken, *Die Traditionen der Menschengeschlechts*, 2nd, rev. ed. (Münster: Aschendorff, 1869), 407ff.; A. Kuyper, *Van de voleinding* (Kampen: Kok, 1929–31), I, 64–127.

Persian religion even expected the appearance, at the end of the third world period, of the third son of Zarathushtra, Saoshyant, who would introduce a thousand-year kingdom of peace and complete the redemptive work of his father.[8] Among the Muslims, along with belief in the return of Jesus, there gradually arose the expectation of a Mahdi who would take believers back to the golden age of the "four righteous Khalifs."[9] In Israel, future hopes were based on the foundation of the covenant God had established with Abraham and his seed. For this covenant is everlasting and is not nullified by human unfaithfulness. Even in the law God repeatedly testifies to the people of Israel that when they violate his covenant, he will visit them with the most severe punishments, but afterward will again have compassion on his own. When on account of its sins Israel is scattered among the nations and its land is devastated, in that day the Lord will arouse his people to jealousy by his acceptance of other peoples, bring his people to repentance, lead them back to their own country, bless them with innumerable spiritual and material blessings, and bring vengeance on all their enemies (Lev. 26; Deut. 4:23–31; 30:1–10; 32:15–43). Following the promise to the house of David that it will be made sure and that its throne will be established forever (2 Sam. 7:16; 23:5; 1 Chron. 17:14), what increasingly gains prominence in Israel's future hopes is that its conversion and restoration will be brought about by nothing other than the anointed king of the house of David. These ideas were further developed in prophecy and, despite the peculiar features they bear in each of the prophets, assume increasingly firmer forms.

In the expectation that the Old Testament fosters with respect to the future of the people of God, we can clearly discern the following components. All the prophets proclaim to Israel and Judah *a day of judgment and punishment*. The יְהוָה יוֹם (*yôm YHWH*), the time in which the Lord will have compassion on his people and inflict vengeance on their enemies, was viewed very differently by the prophets than by the people. The people misused this expectation and thought that—quite apart from their own spiritual state—YHWH would protect them from all danger (Jer. 28–29; Ezek. 33:23ff.; Amos 5:18; 6:13). But the prophets said that the day of the Lord would be a day of judgment for Israel as well. The people would be exiled and their land devastated (Isa. 2:11ff.; 5:5ff.; 7:18; Jer. 1:11–16; Hos. 1:6; 2:11; 3:4; 8:13; 9:3, 6; 10:6; 11:5; 13:12; 13:16; Joel 2:1ff.; Amos 2:4ff.; 5:16, 18, 27; 6:14; etc.; Mic. 3:12; 4:10; 7:13; Hab. 1:5–11; Zeph. 1:1–18; etc.).

Still, that punishment is *temporary*. After many days (Hos. 3:3), after a few days, that is, after a short while (6:2), after seventy years (Jer. 25:12; 29:10), after 390 years for Israel and forty years for Judah (Ezek. 4:4ff.), there will be an end to it. God's chastisement of his people is measured (Isa. 27:7ff.; Jer. 30:11). He leaves

8. E. Lehmann, in P. D. Chantepie de la Saussaye, *Lehrbuch der Religionsgeschichte*, 2 vols. (Freiburg i.B.: J. C. B. Mohr [Paul Siebeck], 1887–89), II, 225.

9. C. Snouck Hurgronje, *Der Mahdi* (Amsterdam, 1885; extract from the *Revue Coloniale Internationale*, 1 [1885]).

them only for a short while; his wrath is for a moment, but his loving-kindness is forever (Isa. 54:7–8). He loves his people with an everlasting love and therefore will again have compassion (Jer. 31:3, 20; Mic. 7:19). He cannot utterly destroy his people, though he shakes them as with a sieve (Amos 9:8–9). His heart recoils within him (Hos. 11:8). He remembers his covenant (Ezek. 16:60). He will redeem his people, not for the sake of Israel but for his name's sake, for his fame among the Gentiles (Deut. 32:27; Isa. 43:25; 48:9; Ezek. 36:22ff.).

At the end of the time of punishment, God sends the *Messiah* from the house of David. Obadiah still speaks in general of saviors who protect the community that has escaped to Mount Zion (vv. 17, 21; cf. Jer. 23:4; 33:17, 20–22, 26). Amos says that after Israel's judgment God will again raise up the fallen booth of David (9:11). Hosea expects that the children of Israel will repent and seek the Lord and David as king as well (1:11; 3:5; cf. Jer. 30:9; Ezek. 34:23–24; 37:22–24). Micah prophesies that Israel will not be saved from the power of its enemies until, at Bethlehem, the ruler from the royal house of David is born (5:1–2). The fact that, like David, he will come forth from Bethlehem, not from Jerusalem, is proof that the royal house of David has lost the throne and has relapsed into a state of lowliness. Isaiah, accordingly, says that a shoot will come out from the stump of Jesse (11:1–2); Ezekiel expresses the same idea by saying that the Lord will take a tender sprig from the topmost branch of the highest cedar (17:22). God will cause him to shoot forth from the house of David like a branch (Isa. 4:2; Jer. 23:5–6; 33:14–17), so that in token of this he will also bear the name "Branch" (Zech. 3:8; 6:12). Born in Israel's time of suffering, this son of David will grow up in poverty (Isa. 7:14–17). Though he is a king, he is just, gentle, humble, and therefore he will come riding on the foal of a donkey (Zech. 9:9). He will unite royal dignity with both prophetic dignity (Deut. 18:15; Isa. 11:2; chs. 40–66; Mal. 4:5) and priestly dignity (Ps. 110; Isa. 53; Jer. 30:21; Zech. 3; 6:13). The kingdom he comes to establish is one of righteousness and peace (Pss. 72; 100; Isa. 11; 40–66; Mic. 5:10). He himself is and wins righteousness and salvation for his people (Ps. 72; Isa. 11; 42; 53; Jer. 23:5–6; etc.). Therefore his appearance is not delayed until after the day of judgment but precedes it. Judah is not redeemed until God gives David a branch (Isa. 9:1–7; 11:1ff.; Jer. 23:5–6; 33:14–17).

Among the benefits to be conferred on his people by this Anointed One is, first of all, the *return from* the land of *exile*. The land, the people, the king, and God belong together. For that reason the restoration of Israel begins with its return from exile (Isa. 11:11; Jer. 3:18; Ezek. 11:17; Hos. 11:11; Joel 3:1; Amos 9:14; Mic. 4:6; etc.). That return, according to Isaiah's depiction of it, will be extraordinarily splendid. The wilderness will blossom like a rose. Mountains will be leveled and valleys filled up. There will be a paved road on which not even the blind can go astray (35:1–9; 41:17–20; 42:15–16; 43:19–20; etc.). Both Israel and Judah will take part in that return (Isa. 11:13; Jer. 3:6, 18; 31:27; 32:37–40; Ezek. 37:16–17; 47:13, 21; 48:1–7, 23–29; Hos. 1:11; 14:1–8; Amos 9:9–15). But the return from Babylonian captivity was only a very partial fulfillment of this expectation. For that reason the postexilic prophets view it as only a beginning of the realization of the promises. They detach their expectation from a return from exile and, except for Zechariah (8:13), no longer speak of the ten tribes. The returned exiles viewed themselves as representative of the whole of Israel (Ezra 6:17).

For that matter, all the prophets at the same time view Israel's return from exile as an ethical return, that is, as a *conversion*. Gathering together from among the nations and circumcision of the heart go together (Deut. 30:3–6). By no means all of them were to return and turn to the Lord. Many, the majority in fact, will perish in the judgment that the day of the Lord will bring on Israel. While the Lord will not completely destroy the house of Jacob, he will in fact shake it as in a sieve and bring about the death of sinners by the sword (Amos 9:8–10). When he brings Israel and Judah back, he will first lead them into the desert and purge out the ungodly (Ezek. 20:34ff.; Hos. 2:13). Then many men will fall so that seven women will take hold of one man (Isa. 3:25–4:1). The destruction is firmly resolved; only a mere remnant will return (Isa. 4:3; 6:13; 7:3–25; 10:21; 11:11). The Lord will thrash the children of Israel and then gather them up one by one (Isa. 27:12). He will destroy the proud but rescue a poor and wretched people (Zeph. 3:12), and keep alive his work (Hab. 3:2). One from a city and two from a family will be brought back (Jer. 3:14); two-thirds will be cut off, but one-third will be purified (Zech. 13:8–9). Those who remain, however, will be a holy people to the Lord, a people to whom he betrothes himself forever (Isa. 4:3–4; 11:9; Hos. 1:10–11; 2:15, 18, 22). The Lord forgives them all their iniquities, cleanses them from all their uncleanness, gives them new hearts, pours out his Spirit on them all, removes all idolatry and sorcery from their midst, and establishes a new covenant with them (Isa. 43:25; 44:21–23; Jer. 31:31; Ezek. 11:19; 36:25–28; 37:14; Joel 2:28; Mic. 5:11–14; Zech. 13:2; etc.). The unclean will no longer dwell among them (Isa. 52:1, 11–12); they will all be righteous (60:21); those who are taught by God will know him, trust in his name, and not do wrong or speak lies (54:13; Jer. 31:31; Zeph. 3:12–13). Everything will be holy, even the bells of the horses (Zech. 14:20–21). For the glory of the Lord has risen over them (Isa. 60:1; Zech. 2:5), and God himself dwells among them (Hos. 2:22; Joel 3:17; Obad. 21; Zech. 2:10; 8:8; etc.).

For Old Testament prophecy, these spiritual benefits include the expectation of the restoration of the *temple* and *the temple worship services*. According to Obadiah, there will be a place of refuge on Mount Zion; there will dwell the saviors who will protect Israel and judge its enemies (vv. 17, 21). Joel prophesies that the Lord will dwell on Zion, his holy mountain, and that Jerusalem will be holy—no longer accessible to strangers—and everlasting (3:17, 20). Amos expects that the cities of Palestine will be rebuilt and inhabited, and that Israel will never again be driven from it (9:14–15). Micah announces that, though Zion will be plowed as a field and Jerusalem reduced to a heap of ruins (3:12), still the mountain of the house of the Lord will be established as the highest of the mountains; out of Zion the law will go forth and the word of the Lord from Jerusalem, and the

Lord will dwell in Zion (4:1–2; 7:11). The same idea is expressed by Isaiah (2:2), who adds that Zion and Jerusalem, kingship and priesthood, temple and altar, sacrifices and feast days—these will be restored (28:16; 30:19; 33:5; 35:10; 52:1; 56:6–7; 60:7; 61:6; 66:20–23). In the same way Jeremiah expects that Jerusalem will be rebuilt, the Lord's throne reestablished there, and the temple services renewed (3:16–17; 30:18; 31:38; 33:18, 21). Haggai predicts that the splendor of the second temple will be greater than that of the first (2:6–10), and Zechariah announces that Jerusalem will be rebuilt and expanded, that the priesthood and temple will be renewed, and that God will dwell in Jerusalem in the midst of his people (1:17; 2:1–5; 3:1–8; 6:9–15; 8:3ff.).

But none of the prophets develops this vision of the future in such meticulous detail as Ezekiel. First, in chapters 34–37, he says that Israel and Judah will again be gathered together by the Lord, that they will be accepted as one people under the one shepherd from the house of David to be the Lord's possession, and will be given a new heart and a new spirit. After predicting in chapters 38 and 39 that Israel, now back in its own land, must still endure a final attack from Gog of Magog, in chapters 40–48 he presents an elaborate sketch of the Palestine of the future. The land west of the Jordan will be divided by parallel lines in almost equal strips. The top seven will be inhabited by the tribes Dan, Asher, Naphtali, Manasseh, Ephraim, Reuben, and Judah; the bottom five by Benjamin, Simeon, Issachar, Zebulun, and Gad. Between the upper and lower parts of the territory a strip of land will be reserved for the Lord. In the middle of this 25,000 by 25,000 cubit strip stands a high mountain; and on top of it is built the temple, which is filled with the glory of the Lord, measures 500 cubits square, and is surrounded by an area of 500 cubits on each side. Around this the priests, all of whom must be descendants of Zadok, will receive an allotment 25,000 cubits in length and 10,000 cubits in width to the south, and the Levites will get their equal-sized allotment to the north, while to the east and west a section of the holy strip is assigned to the prince. The city of Jerusalem is separate from the temple and situated south of the land allotted to the priests, on a plain that is 25,000 cubits in length and 5,000 cubits in width. In the wall, on each side of the city, are three gates, according to the number of the tribes of Israel. On the great feasts all of Israel comes to the temple to sacrifice, but Gentiles are forbidden access. If Israel thus lives in accordance with God's ordinances, it will enjoy immense blessing. From under the threshold of the temple door flows a stream that becomes ever deeper, makes the land fertile, and even makes fresh the stagnant waters of the Dead Sea. On its banks on both sides of the river are trees whose fruit is for food and whose leaves are for healing.[10]

Added to these spiritual benefits come a wide range of *material blessings*. Under the Prince of Peace of the house of David, Israel will live securely. There will no

---

10. For a correct understanding of this vision, see A. B. Davidson, *The Theology of the Old Testament* (New York: Charles Scribner's Sons, 1914), 343ff.

longer be war: bow and sword will be abolished (Hos. 2:18); horses will be cut off, chariots destroyed, strongholds thrown down (Mic. 5:10–11), and swords will be beaten into plowshares and spears into pruning hooks. All will sit down under their vine and their fig tree (Isa. 2:4; Mic. 4:3–4), for the kingdom is the Lord's and he is their stronghold (Joel 3:16–17; Obad. 21). The land will become extraordinarily fertile, so that the mountains will drip sweet wine and the hills will flow with milk. A fountain issuing from the house of the Lord will irrigate the dry land and turn the desert into a Garden of Eden. Wild beasts will be driven away, enemies will no longer rob the harvest, and all the trees, seasonably refreshed by gentle rains, will bear abundant fruit (Isa. 32:15–20; 51:3; 60:17–18; 62:8–9; 65:9, 22; Jer. 31:6, 12–14; Ezek. 34:14, 25–26, 29; 36:29; 47:1–12; Hos. 2:15, 18–19; 14:5–7; Joel 3:18; Amos 9:13–14; Zech. 8:12; 14:8, 10). An enormous reversal will occur, even in nature: animals will receive a different nature (Isa. 11:6–8; 65:25), heaven and earth will be renewed, and the former things will no longer be remembered (34:4; 51:6; 65:17; 66:22). Sun and moon will be altered: the light of the moon will be like the sun, and the light of the sun will be seven times its normal strength (30:26). Indeed, the sun and moon will be no more: there will be continuous day, for the Lord will be the people's everlasting light (60:19–20; Zech. 14:6–7).

In the human world as well the change will be enormous. Once Israel is gathered, Palestine will resound with people (Mic. 2:12–13). The descendants of the children of Israel will be like the sand of the sea, and especially the progeny of the house of David and of the Levites will be multiplied (Isa. 9:3; Jer. 3:16; 33:22; Hos. 1:10). On account of the multitude of people and animals, Jerusalem will become immeasurable and will have to be inhabited like villages (Zech. 2:1–4). Various causes underlie this marvelous increase. Many Israelites—after a number of them have been returned—will come to Jerusalem and share in the blessing of Israel (Jer. 3:14, 16, 18; Zech. 2:4–9; 8:7–8). Indeed, when the Lord's messengers will make this blessing known among the Gentiles, the latter will bring to Jerusalem the Israelites still residing among them in chariots, in litters, on horses, on mules, and on dromedaries (Isa. 66:19–20). Also the Israelites who have died will share in those blessings. All of Israel can then be said to have been brought back to life (Isa. 25:8; Ezek. 37:1–14; Hos. 6:2). Isaiah (26:19) and Daniel (12:2) specifically announce that the defeated Israelites will arise from the sleep of death and at least in part awaken to everlasting life. And finally, all the citizens of the kingdom will reach a very advanced age. And there will no longer be in it "an infant that lives but a few days, or an old person who does not live out a lifetime; for one who dies at a hundred years will be considered a youth, and one who falls short of a hundred will be considered accursed" (Isa. 65:20; cf. Zech. 8:4–5). There will no longer be sickness, nor mourning, nor crying (Isa. 25:8; 30:19; 65:19); the Lord will even destroy death, swallowing it up in victory (25:7).

Finally, the *Gentiles* will share in that blessing of the kingdom of God as well. Woven throughout Old Testament prophecy is the thought that God will avenge the blood of his servants on his enemies. The prophets of God, therefore, announce God's judgments over several peoples: Philistia, Tyre, Moab, Ammon, Edom, Asshur, and Babel. But the final effect of these judgments is not the destruction but the salvation of the Gentiles: in Abraham's seed all the nations of the earth will be blessed [Gen. 12:3]. Granted, in one prophet it is more the political side of this subjection of the Gentiles under Israel that comes to the fore, while in another it is the religious, spiritual side. All of them nevertheless expect that the rule of the Messiah will be extended to all peoples (cf. Pss. 2; 21; 24; 45; 46; 47; 48; 68; 72; 86; 89; 96; 98; etc.). Israel will, by hereditary right, possess the Gentiles (Amos 9:12; Rev. 17–21). While they will be judged (Joel 3:2–15), everyone who calls on the name of the Lord will be saved, for in Mount Zion is deliverance (Joel 2:32 KJV). The Ruler from Bethlehem will be great to the ends of the earth and protect Israel from its enemies (Mic. 5:3ff.).

Still, the Gentiles will go to Mount Zion to discover the ways of the Lord (Mic. 4:1–2). After the Lord has "shriveled" all the gods of the peoples (Zeph. 2:11; 3:8), the Gentile inhabitants of the islands will bow down to him, and he will give pure lips to all peoples, enabling them to call on his name (3:9). Ethiopia will bring gifts to the Lord in Zion (Isa. 18:7). Egyptians and Assyrians will serve him (19:18–25). Tyre will hand over its profits to the Lord (23:15–18), and on Mount Zion he will prepare for all peoples a feast of rich food (25:6–10). Indeed, the servant of the Lord will be a light also to the Gentiles. His messengers will make known the Lord among the nations of the earth, and he will be served by them. The Lord's house will be a house of prayer for all peoples. All will bring their sacrifices there, worship the Lord, and call themselves after his name. They will pasture Israel's flocks and cultivate its fields, so that the Israelites can completely devote themselves as priests to the service of the Lord (chs. 40–66, passim). When Israel has been restored and Jerusalem is the throne of the Lord, all the Gentiles will be gathered there around the name of the Lord, bless themselves, and boast in the Lord (Jer. 3:17; 4:2; 16:19–21; 33:9). In the end all peoples will acknowledge that the Lord is God (Ezek. 16:62; 17:24; 25:5ff.; 26:6; 28:22; 29:6; 30:8–26). All the Gentiles will bring their treasures to Jerusalem and fill the house of the Lord with splendor (Hag. 2:7–10). Peoples will come and say to one another, "Let us go to entreat the favor of the LORD." "Ten men . . . will take hold of a Jew, grasping his garment and saying, 'Let us go with you, for we have heard that God is with you'" (Zech. 8:21–23; cf. 2:11; 14:16–19). The people of the holy ones will receive dominion over all the nations of the earth (Dan. 7:14, 27).

THE UNIQUENESS OF OLD TESTAMENT ESCHATOLOGY

[564] These messianic expectations of the Old Testament, as any reader can see at once, are of a unique kind: they limit themselves to a future blessed state *on earth*. While in the Old Testament it may sometimes happen that a believer will express the hope that after death he will be taken up in eternal glory, this

expectation is individual and stands by itself. As a rule, the eye of prophecy is directed toward that future in which the people of Israel will live securely under a king of David's dynasty in Palestine and will rule over all the nations of the earth. An assumption of believers into the heaven of glory at the end of time is not part of the Old Testament outlook. Salvation is expected on earth, not in heaven. In this connection Old Testament prophecy knows only of one coming of the Messiah. It does know that the Anointed One will be born of the house of David when it has fallen into decline, that he will share in the suffering of his people, even that as servant of the Lord he will suffer for his people and bear their iniquities. He will be a totally different king from the rulers of the earth; he will be humble, gentle, doing justice, and protecting his people. He will be not only king but also prophet and priest. But in its view of the life of the Messiah, Old Testament prophecy never clearly separates the state of humiliation from the state of exaltation. It gathers up both in a single image. Nor does it make a distinction between a first and second coming and does not position the latter, which is for judgment, a long time after the former, which is for salvation. It is one single coming in which the Messiah bestows righteousness and blessedness on his people and brings it to dominion over all the peoples of the earth. The kingdom he is coming to establish, therefore, is the completed kingdom of God. He himself will in fact govern his people as king, but in that capacity he is still no more than a theocratic king who does not rule in accordance with his own powers but in an absolute sense realizes the rule of God.

Old Testament prophecy makes no temporal distinction between the rule of Christ and the rule of God. It does not expect that the Messiah of the house of David, after having temporarily exercised sovereignty, will turn his kingdom over to God. It does not view the future, which it depicts as being in the messianic kingdom, as an intermediate state that in the end must yield to a divine government in heaven. It regards the messianic kingdom as the final state and clearly views God's judgment over enemies, the repulsion of the final attack, the transformation of nature, and the resurrection from the dead as events that precede the initial and full establishment of this kingdom. And this kingdom is sketched by the prophets in hues and colors, under figures and forms, which have all been derived from the historical circumstances in which they lived. Palestine will be reconquered, Jerusalem rebuilt, and the temple with its sacrificial worship restored. Edom, Moab, Ammon, Assyria, and Babylon will be subdued. All citizens will be given a long life and a relaxed setting under vine and fig tree. The [projected] image of the future is Old Testament-like through and through; it is all described in terms of Israel's own history and nation.

But into those sensuous earthly forms prophecy puts everlasting content. In that shell is an imperishable core that, sometimes even in the Old Testament itself, breaks through. Return from exile and true conversion coincide. The religious and political sides of Israel's victory over its enemies are most intimately bound up with each other. The Messiah is an earthly ruler but also an everlasting king, a king of righteousness, an eternal father to his people, a prince of peace, a priest-king. The enemies of Israel are subjected to Israel but in the process acknowledge that the Lord is God and serve him in his temple. This temple with its priesthood and sacrificial worship are visible proof that all the citizens of the kingdom serve the Lord with a new heart and a new spirit and walk in his ways. And the extraordinary fertility of the land presupposes a total transformation of nature, the creation of a new heaven and a new earth, the home of righteousness.

Later Judaism introduced an assortment of changes in these Old Testament expectations. Robbed of political sovereignty and scattered among the nations, it began increasingly to take account of the future destiny of individuals and broadened its horizon to include humanity and the world as a whole. Someday—it was believed—on the basis of its own strictly law-abiding righteousness, Israel, led by the Messiah, would achieve political dominion over all nations. But this messianic kingdom was of a provisional and temporary kind. In the end it would make way for a kingdom of God, for a blessedness of the righteous in heaven, which would be introduced by the resurrection of all human beings and universal judgment. In that way the political and religious sides, which in the prophetic vision of the future were most intimately united, were torn apart. In Jesus's day Israel expected a tangible, earthly, messianic kingdom whose conditions were depicted in the forms and images of Old Testament prophecy. But now these forms and images were taken literally. The shell was mistaken for the core, the image of it for the thing itself, and the form for the essence. The messianic kingdom became the political rule of Israel over the nations—a period of external prosperity and growth. And at the end of it [in this scenario] universal judgment could only occur after the general resurrection, when people were judged according to their works and either received the reward of heavenly blessedness or the penalty of hellish pain.

THE RISE OF CHILIASM

This is how the doctrine of chiliasm arose. Admittedly, a large part of Jewish apocryphal literature continues to adhere to the future expectations of the Old Testament. But frequently, especially in the *Apocalypse of Baruch* and *4 Ezra*, we find the view that the glory of the messianic kingdom is not the last and the highest. On the contrary, after a specific period of time, often calculated—for example, in the Talmud—at four hundred or one thousand years, this kingdom has to make room for the heavenly blessedness of the kingdom of God. Accordingly, chiliasm is not of Christian but of Jewish and Persian origin.[11] It is always based on a compromise between the expectations of an earthly salvation and those of a heavenly state of blessedness. It attempts to do justice to Old Testament prophecy in the sense that it accepts the earthly messianic kingdom predicted

11. Cf. the literature cited above and, further, the history of chiliasm by K. G. Semisch (rev. and enl. by E. Bratke), "Chiliasmus," in *PRE*[3], III, 805–17; and G. E. Post, "Millennium," in *DB*, III, 370–73, and the literature cited there.

by it but claims that this kingdom will be replaced after a time by the kingdom of God. It would appear that chiliasm's strength lies in the Old Testament, but actually this is not the case. The Old Testament is decidedly not chiliastic. In its depiction of the messianic kingdom, it describes the completed kingdom of God that is without end and lasts forever (Dan. 2:44), preceded by judgment, resurrection, and world renewal.

Chiliasm, nevertheless, found credence among the Jews and also with many Christians. It surfaced over and over when the world developed its power in opposition to God and brought suffering on the church by persecution and oppression. In the earliest period we encounter it in Cerinthus, in the *Testaments of the Twelve Patriarchs*, in the thought of the Ebionites in the *Epistle of Barnabas*, and in Papias, Irenaeus, Hippolytus, Apollinaris, Commodian, Lactantius, and Victorinus. Montanism, on the other hand, urged caution. Gnostics, the theologians of Alexandria, and particularly Augustine resisted it most vigorously, while the changed situation of the church, which had overcome the world power of the day and increasingly viewed itself as the kingdom of God on earth, gradually prompted it to die out completely. It came up again before and during the Reformation, when many began to view Rome as the harlot of Revelation and the pope as the antichrist. It revived among the Anabaptists, the David-Jorists, and the Socinians and since then has not died out again although the official churches rejected it. Over and over political disturbances, the wars of religion, persecutions, and sectarian movements breathed new life into it. In Bohemia, it was preached by Paul Felgenhauer and Comenius; in Germany by Jacob Böhme, Ezekiel Meth, Gichtel, Petersen, Horche, Spener, J. Lange, and S. König; in England by John Archer, Newton, Joseph Mede, Jane Leade, and many Independents; in the Netherlands by Labadie, Antoinette Bourignon, Poiret, and so forth. Even some Reformed theologians tended toward a moderate form of chiliasm. Examples are Piscator, Alsted, Jurieu, Burnet, Whiston, Serarius, Cocceius, Groenewegen, Jac Alting, d'Outrein, Vitringa, Brakel, Jungius, Mommers, and others.[12]

In the eighteenth and nineteenth centuries, under the pressure of societal and political upheavals, it not only found acceptance among Swedenborgians, Darbyists, Irwingians, Mormons, Adventists, and others, but—after the turn toward realism taken by Bengel, Oetinger, Ph. M. Hahn, J. M. Hahn, Hasenkamp, Menken, Jung-Stilling, J. F. von Meyer, and so forth—was embraced by many theologians in the churches of the Reformation.[13]

---

12. Cf. H. Brink, *Toet-steen der waarheid en der dwalingen* (Amsterdam: G. Borstius, 1685), 656f.; G. Voetius, *Selectae disputationes theologicae*, 5 vols. (Utrecht, 1648–69), II, 1266–72; S. Maresius, *Syst. theol.*, VIII, 38; B. de Moor, *Commentarius . . . theologiae*, 6 vols. (Leiden: J. Hasebroek, 1761–71), VI, 155.

13. E.g., R. Rothe, *Theologische Ethik*, 2nd ed. (Wittenberg: Zimmermann, 1867–71), §586f.; J. C. K. von Hofmann, *Weissagung und Erfüllung im Alten und Neuen Testamente*, 2 vols. (Nördlingen: Beck, 1841), II, 372ff.; J. P. Lange, *Christliche Dogmatik*, 3 vols., Heidelberg: K. Winter, 1852), II, 1271ff.; H. Martensen, *Christian Dogmatics*, trans. W. Urwick (Edinburgh: T&T Clark, 1871), §280; J. J. van Oosterzee, *Christian Dogmatics*, trans. J. Watson and M. Evans, 2 vols. (New York: Scribner, Armstrong, 1874), §146. Of the many

The basic ideas of chiliasm are virtually the same in all its forms. They come down to the assertion that we must distinguish between a twofold return of Christ and a double resurrection. They go on to say that at his first return Christ will overcome the forces of the antichrist, bind Satan, raise the believers who have died, and gather the church around himself, in particular the community of Israel, now repentant and brought back to Palestine. From within that community he will rule over the world and usher in a period of spiritual florescence and material prosperity. At the end of that time he will return once more to raise all humans from the dead, judge them before his throne of judgment, and decide their eternal destiny. Still, these basic thoughts allow for an assortment of variations. The beginning of the thousand-year reign was variously determined. Following the example of the *Epistle of Barnabas*, many church fathers, and later the Cocceians as well, taught that it began with the seventh millennium of the world. The "Fifth-monarchmen" had it begin after the fall of the fourth world kingdom. Hippolytus fixed its beginning in the year 500, Groenewegen in 1700, Whiston in 1715 and later in 1766, Jurieu in 1785, Bengel in 1836, Jung-Stilling in 1816, and so on. Its duration was determined at 400 years (*4 Ezra*), or 500 (Joseph of Nicodemus), or 1,000 (Talmud, etc.), or 2,000 (Bengel), or only 7 (Darby) years. Sometimes it was assigned an indeterminate number of years, and the number given in Rev. 20:2–3 was consequently taken to be symbolic (Rothe, Martensen, Lange, et al.). A few people believed that before the establishment of a 1,000-year reign there will be no return of Christ (Kurtz), or at least no visible return (Darby), or a return that is visible only to believers (Irving), and that no resurrection of believers should be assumed before the millennium (Bengel).

Many are convinced that, upon his first return, Christ will remain on earth, but others are of the opinion that he will appear for only a short while—to establish his kingdom—and then again withdraw into heaven. According to Piscator, Alsted, and the like, Christ's rule in the millennium will be conducted from heaven. Participating in that rule, then, are the risen martyrs, who were either taken up into heaven (Piscator) or stayed behind on earth (Alsted), or all the risen believers who remain here on earth (Justin, Irenaeus, et al.), or those who upon his appearance in the clouds are brought out to meet Christ in the air (Irving), or the people of Israel in particular. The reason [for such participation] is that chiliasts

existing works on chiliasm, we will mention here only D. Bogue, *Discourses on the Millennium* (London: T. Hamilton, 1818); É. Guers, *Israel in the Last Days of the Present Economy*, trans. A. Price (London: Wertheim, MacIntosh, & Hunt, 1862); John Cumming, *The Great Consummation: The Millennial Rest, or, The World as It Shall Be* (New York: Carleton, 1864); idem, *The Great Tribulation* (New York: Rudd & Carleton, 1860); idem, *Great Preparation, or, Redemption Draweth Nigh* (New York: Rudd & Carleton, 1860); J. A. Seiss, *The Apocalypse* (New York: Charles C. Cook, 1909). Published in recent years are, among others, *F. von Beuningen, *Dein Reich komme* (Riga, 1901) (the author fixes the date of Christ's coming in 1933); and Charles T. Russell in America, *The Millennial Dawn* (Allegheny, PA: Watchtower Bible and Tract Society, 1898–1901). According to Russell, the history of mankind is divided into three ages: in the first, before the flood, it was subject to the rule of angels. In the second, from the flood to the millennium, it is under the rule of Satan, so that only a few people are saved. In the third period, which started in 1914, it will be ruled by Christ for a thousand years. Then follows the renewal of the earth.

usually expect a national conversion of Israel, and the majority imagine that Israel, upon its conversion, will be brought back to Palestine and be the most important citizens of the thousand-year kingdom there (Jurieu, Oetinger, Hofmann, Auberlen, et al.). Those who assume that after his first return Christ will stay on earth usually fix a rebuilt Jerusalem as his city of residence, although the Montanists at one time thought it would be Pepuza [in Phrygia] and Mormons today think of their Salt Lake valley. As a rule the ideas of the restoration of temple and altar, of priesthood and sacrifices, are rejected as being too obviously inconsistent with the New Testament but were nevertheless still defended by the Ebionites and in more modern times by Serarius, Oetinger, Hess, and others.

Concerning the character and conditions of the thousand-year kingdom, people entertain very different ideas. Sometimes it is depicted as a realm of sensual pleasures (Cerinthus, Ebionites, et al.). Then again it is viewed as more spiritual, and all enjoyment of food and drink, marriage, and procreation is removed from it (Burnet, Lavater, Rothe, Ebrard). Most often the millennium is viewed as a transitional state between this world (*Diesseits*) and the next (*Jenseits*). It is a realm in which believers are prepared for the vision of God (Irenaeus) or in which they enjoy tranquillity and peace, without being totally freed from sin and exempted from death. It is a realm in which nature (Irenaeus) as well as people (Lactantius) will be extraordinarily fertile, and in which, according to a popular notion held later, the church will especially fulfill its mission work to humanity (Lavater, Ebrard, Auberlen, et al.).

All of these variations constitute as many objections against chiliasm. It cannot even stand before the tribunal of Old Testament prophecy, a court to which it loves to appeal. Aside from the fact that, as stated earlier, the Old Testament does not view the messianic kingdom as provisional and temporary but as the end result of world history, chiliasm is guilty of the greatest arbitrariness in interpreting prophecy. It doubles the return of Christ and the resurrection of the dead, although the Old Testament does not give the slightest warrant for this. It is devoid of all rule and method and arbitrarily calls a halt, depending on the subjective opinion of the interpreter. With equal vigor and force, all the prophets announce not only the conversion of Israel and the nations but also the return to Palestine, the rebuilding of Jerusalem, the restoration of the temple, the priesthood, and sacrificial worship, and so on. And it is nothing but caprice to take one feature of this picture literally and another "spiritually." Prophecy pictures for us but one single image of the future. And either this image is to be taken literally as it presents itself—but then one breaks with Christianity and lapses back into Judaism—or this image calls for a very different interpretation than that attempted by chiliasm. Such an interpretation is furnished by Scripture itself, and we must take it from Scripture.

A SCRIPTURAL REPLY TO CHILIASM

[565] In the Old Testament already there are numerous pointers to a new and better interpretation of the prophetic expectations than chiliasm offers. Even the

modern view of the history of Israel recognizes that the Yahwism of the prophets distinguishes itself from the nature religions by its moral character and gradually gave a spiritual meaning to the religious laws and customs in use in Israel. True circumcision is that of the heart (Deut. 10:16; 30:6; Jer. 4:4). The sacrifices pleasing to God are a broken heart and a contrite spirit (1 Sam. 15:22; Pss. 40:6; 50:8ff.; 51:17; Isa. 1:11ff.; Jer. 6:20; 7:21ff.; Hos. 6:6; Amos 5:21ff.; Mic. 6:6ff.). The true fast is to loose the bonds of injustice (Isa. 58:3–6; Jer. 14:12). In large part the struggle of the prophets is directed against the external, self-righteous worship of the people. Accordingly, the essence of the future dispensation is that the Lord will make a new covenant with his people. He will give them a new heart and write his law on it. He will pour out his Spirit on all so that they will love him with their whole heart and walk in his ways (Deut. 30:6; Jer. 31:32–34; 32:38f.; Ezek. 11:19; 36:26; Joel 2:28; Zech. 12:10).

Now it is true that that future is depicted in images derived from the historical circumstances that then prevailed, so that Zion and Jerusalem, temple and altar, sacrifice and priesthood, continue to occupy a large place in it. But we must remember that we ourselves do the same thing and can only speak of God and divine things in sensuous, earthly forms. One reason God instituted Old Testament worship as he did was that we would be able to speak of heavenly things, not in self-made images but in the correct images given us by God himself. The New Testament, accordingly, takes over this language and in speaking about the future kingdom of God refers to Zion and Jerusalem, to temple and altar, to prophets and priests. The earthly is an image of the heavenly. All that is transitory is but an analogy ("Alles Vergängliche ist nur ein Gleichnis").

Nor must we forget that all prophecy is poetry that must be interpreted in terms of its own character. The error of the older exegesis was not spiritualization as such but the fact that it sought to assign a spiritual meaning to all the illustrative details, in the process, as in the case of Jesus's parables, often losing sight of the main thought. When it is stated, for example, that the Lord will cause a shoot to come forth from the stump of Jesse, that he will establish Mount Zion as the highest of the mountains, that of the exiles he will bring back one from a city and two from a family, that he will sprinkle clean water on all and cleanse them from their sins, that he will make the mountains drip sweet wine and the hills flow with milk, and so forth, everyone senses that in these lines one has to do with poetic descriptions that cannot and may not be taken literally. The realistic interpretation here becomes self-contradictory and misjudges the nature of prophecy.

It is also incorrect to say that the prophets themselves were totally unconscious of the distinction between the thing [they asserted] and the image [in which they clothed it]. Not only did the prophets undoubtedly view the above poetic descriptions as imagery, but also in the names for Sodom, Gomorrah, Edom, Moab, Philistia, Egypt, Asshur, and Babel they repeatedly refer to the power of the Gentile world that will someday be subject to Israel and share in its blessings (Isa. 34:5; Ezek. 16:46ff.; Dan. 2:17ff.; Obad. 16–17; Zech. 14:12–21). Zion often serves as the name for the people, the believing community of God (Isa. 49:14; 51:3; 52:1). And although it is true that Old Testament prophecy cannot conceive of the future kingdom of God without a temple and sacrifice, over and over it *transcends* all national and earthly conditions. It proclaims, for example, that there will no longer be an ark of the covenant, since all Jerusalem will be God's throne (Jer. 3:16–17); that the kingdom of the Messiah will be everlasting and encompass the whole world (Pss. 2:8; 72:8, 17; Dan. 2:44); that the inhabitants will be prophets and priests (Isa. 54:13; 61:6; Jer. 31:31); that all impurity and sin, all sickness and death, will be banished from it (Ps. 104:35; Isa. 25:8; 33:24; 52:1, 11; Zech. 14:20–21); and that it will be established in a new heaven and on a new earth and will no longer need the sun or the moon (Isa. 60:19–20; 65:17; 66:22). Even Ezekiel's realistic picture of the future contains elements that require a symbolic interpretation: the equal shares assigned to all the tribes, though in numbers [of tribal members] they vary widely; the precisely measured strips of land intended for priests, Levites, and the king; the separation of the temple from the city; the high location of the temple on a mountain and the brook that streams out from under the threshold of the east door of the temple toward the Dead Sea; and finally, the artificial way things are put together and the impossibility of implementing them practically—all these features resist a so-called realistic interpretation.

Finally, in Old Testament exegesis the question is not whether the prophets were totally or partially conscious of the symbolic nature of their predictions, for even in the words of classic authors there is more than they themselves thought or intended. It is a question, rather, what the Spirit of Christ who was in them wished to declare and reveal by them. And *that* is decided by the New Testament, which is the completion, fulfillment, and therefore interpretation of the Old. The nature of a tree is revealed by its fruit. Even modern criticism recognizes that not Judaism but Christianity is the full realization of the religion of the prophets.

The New Testament views itself—and there can certainly be no doubt about this—as the spiritual and therefore complete and authentic fulfillment of the Old Testament. The spiritualization of the Old Testament, rightly understood, is not an invention of Christian theology but has its beginning in the New Testament itself. The Old Testament in spiritualized form, that is, the Old Testament stripped of its temporal and sensuous form, is the New Testament. The peculiar nature of the old dispensation consisted precisely in the fact that the covenant of grace was presented in graphic images and clothed in national and sensuous forms. Sin was symbolized by levitical impurity. Atonement was effected by the sacrifice of a slain animal. Purification was adumbrated by physical washings. Communion with God was connected with the journey to Jerusalem. The desire for God's favor and closeness was expressed in the longing for his courts. Eternal life was conceived as a long life on earth, and so forth. In keeping with Israel's level of understanding, placed as Israel was under the tutelage of the law, all that is spiritual, heavenly, and eternal was veiled in earthly shadows. Even though the great majority of the people frequently fixated on the external forms—just as many Christians in participating in the sacraments continue to cling to the external signs—and while devout Israelites with their hearts indeed penetrated to the spiritual core that was hidden in the shell, they nevertheless saw that spiritual core in no other way than in shadows and images.

For that reason the New Testament says that the Old was "a shadow of the things to come, but the substance belongs to Christ" (σκια των μελλοντων, το δε σωμα του Χριστου, *skia tōn mellontōn, to de sōma tou Christou*; Col. 2:17), "a model and shadow of the heavenly sanctuary" (ὑποδειγμα και σκια των ἐπουρανιων, *hypodeigma kai skia tōn epouraniōn*; Heb. 8:5). The shadow, while not itself the body, does point to the body but vanishes when the body itself appears. The New Testament is the truth, the essence, the core, and the actual content of the Old Testament. The Old Testament is revealed in the New, while the New Testament is concealed in the Old (*Vetus Testamentum in Novo patet, Novum Testamentum in Vetere latet*). For that reason the New Testament frequently refers to "the truth." Over against the law given by Moses stands the truth that came through Jesus Christ (John 1:14, 17). Jesus Christ is the truth (14:6), and the Spirit sent out by him is the Spirit of truth (16:13; 1 John 5:6). The word of God he preached is the word of truth (John 17:17). The benefits of salvation promised and foreshadowed under the Old Testament have become manifest in Christ as eternal and authentic reality. All the promises of God are "yes" and "amen" in him (2 Cor. 1:20). The Old Testament was not abolished but fulfilled in the new dispensation, is still consistently being fulfilled, and will be fulfilled, until the parousia of Christ.

Christ, therefore, is the true prophet, priest, and king; the true servant of the Lord, the true atonement (Rom. 3:25), the true circumcision (Col. 2:11), the true Passover (1 Cor. 5:7), the true sacrifice (Eph. 5:2), and his body of believers the true offspring of Abraham, the true Israel, the true people of God (Matt. 1:21; Luke 1:17; Rom. 9:25–26; 2 Cor. 6:16–18; Gal. 3:29; Titus 2:14; Heb. 8:8–10; James 1:1, 18; 1 Pet. 2:9; Rev. 21:3, 12), the true temple of God (1 Cor. 3:16; 2 Cor. 6:16; Eph. 2:22; 2 Thess. 2:4; Heb. 8:2), the true Zion and Jerusalem (Gal. 4:26; Heb. 12:22; Rev. 3:12; 21:2, 10). Its spiritual sacrifice is the true religion (John 4:24; Rom. 12:1; Phil. 3:3; 4:18).[14] All Old Testament concepts shed their external, national-Israelitish meanings and become manifest in their spiritual and eternal sense. The Semitic no longer needs to be transposed into the Japhetic, as Bunsen wished,[15] for the New Testament itself has given to the particularistic ideas of the Old Testament a universal and cosmic meaning.

14. Cf. H. Bavinck, *Reformed Dogmatics*, III, 223–24 (#348).

15. Ed. note: Bavinck here refers to Christian Karl Josias Bunsen (1791–1860), Prussian diplomat, scholar, and theologian, who was chief librarian and professor of modern philology at the University of Göttingen.

Totally wrong, therefore, is the chiliastic view according to which the New Testament, along with the church composed of Gentiles, is an intermezzo, a detour taken by God because Israel rejected its Messiah, so that the actual continuation and fulfillment of the Old Testament can begin only with Christ's second coming. The opposite, rather, is true. Not the New Testament but the Old is an intermezzo. The covenant with Israel is temporary; the law has been inserted in between the promise to Abraham and its fulfillment in Christ, that it might increase the trespass and be a disciplinarian leading to Christ (Rom. 5:20; Gal. 3:24ff.). For that reason Paul always goes back to Abraham (Rom. 4:11ff.; Gal. 3:6ff.) and links his gospel to the promise made to him. Abraham is the father of believers, of *all* believers, not only believers from among the Jews, but also from among the Gentiles (Rom. 4:11). The children of the promise are his offspring (9:6–8). In Christ the blessing of Abraham comes to the Gentiles (Gal. 3:14). Those who belong to Christ are Abraham's offspring and heirs according to promise (3:29).

In the days of the Old Testament the people of Israel were chosen for a time that salvation might later, in the fullness of time, be a blessing for the whole world. Israel was chosen, not to the detriment of but for the benefit of the nations. From its earliest beginning the promise to Adam and Noah had a universal thrust and, after having put aside its temporary legalistic form under Israel, has in Christ fully revealed this before all the nations. The curtain has been torn, the dividing wall has fallen, the handwriting of the law has been nailed to the cross. Now Gentile believers, along with Jews, as fellow heirs, fellow citizens, fellow saints, fellow members of the household of God, have been brought near in Christ and are built upon the same foundation of apostles and prophets (Eph. 1:9–11; 2:11–22).

Therefore the New Testament is not an intermezzo or interlude, neither a detour nor a departure from the line of the old covenant, but the long-aimed-for goal, the direct continuation and the genuine fulfillment of the Old Testament. Chiliasm, judging otherwise, comes in conflict with Christianity itself. In principle it is one with Judaism and must get to where it attributes a temporary, passing value to Christianity, the historical person of Christ, and his suffering and death, and it only first expects real salvation from Christ's second coming, his appearance in glory. Like Judaism, it subordinates the spiritual to the material, the ethical to the physical, confirms the Jews in their carnal-mindedness, excuses their rejection of the Messiah, reinforces the veil that lies over their minds when they hear the reading of the Old Testament, and promotes the illusion that the physical descendants of Abraham will as such still enjoy an advantage in the kingdom of heaven. Scripture, on the other hand, tells us that the true reading and interpretation of the Old Testament is to be found with those who have turned in repentance to the Lord Christ (2 Cor. 3:14–16). It tells us that a person is a Jew who is one inwardly, and that circumcision is a matter of the heart (Rom. 2:29). It teaches that in Christ there is neither man nor woman, neither Jew nor Greek, but that they are all one in Christ Jesus (1 Cor. 12:13; Gal. 3:28; Col. 3:11). The Jewish person who becomes a Christian was not a child of Abraham but becomes such by faith (Gal. 3:29).[16]

16. Against chiliasm, cf. also Augustine, *City of God* XX, chs. 6–9; Luther in Julius Köstlin, *The Theology of Luther*, trans. Charles E. Hay, 2 vols. (Philadelphia: Lutheran Publication Society, 1897), II, 575; J. Gerhard, *Loci theologici*, ed. E. Preuss, 9 vols. (Berlin: G. Schlawitz, 1863–75), XXIX, ch. 7; J. Quenstedt, *Theologia*, IV, 649; J. Calvin, *Institutes*, III, 25, 5; A. Walaeus, *Opera omnia* (Leiden, 1643), I, 537–54; G. Voetius, *Select. disp.*, II, 1248–72; F. Turretin, *Institutes of Elenctic Theology*, trans. G. M. Giger, ed. J. T. Dennison, 3 vols. (Phillipsburg, NJ: Presbyterian & Reformed, 1992), XX, q. 3; B. de Moor, *Comm. theol.*, VI, 149–62; E. W. Hengstenberg, *Openbaring van Johannes* ('s Hertogenbosch: Muller, 1852); C. F. Keil, *Biblical Commentary on the Prophecies of Ezekiel*, trans. J. Martin (repr., Grand Rapids: Eerdmans, 1970), II, 382–434; Th. Kliefoth, *Christliche Eschatologie* (Leipzig: Dörffling & Franke, 1886), 147ff.; F. A. Philippi, *Kirchliche Glaubenslehre*, 3rd ed., 7 vols. (Gütersloh: Bertelsmann, 1883–1902), VI, 214ff.; C. Hodge, *Systematic Theology* (New York: Charles Scribner's Sons, 1888), III, 805; B. Warfield, "The Millennium and the Apocalypse," *Princeton Theological Review* 2 (October 1904): 599–617; G. Vos, "The Pauline Eschatology and Chiliasm," *Princeton Theological Review* 9 (January 1911): 26–60; H. Hoekstra, *Het chiliasme* (Kampen: Kok, 1903); A. Kuyper, *Van de voleinding*, 4 vols. (Kampen: Kok, 1928–31), IV, 254–62, 318–48.

16

Israel, the Millennium, and Christ's Return

The chiliast expectation that a converted nation of Israel, restored to the land of Palestine, under Christ will rule over the nations is without biblical foundation. Whatever the political future of Israel as a nation, the real ekklēsia, the people of God, transcends ethnic boundaries. The kingdom of God in the teaching of Jesus is not a political reality but a religious-ethical dominion born of water and the Spirit. The salvation rejected by Israel is shared by the Gentiles, and the community of Christ-believers has in all respects replaced national Israel. New Testament passages, such as Rom. 11, which initially seem to teach the contrary, in fact confirm the teaching that God's promises are fulfilled in the spiritual offspring of Abraham, even though they may be only a remnant. Furthermore, the New Testament nowhere suggests that the church of Christ will ever achieve earthly power and dominion such as that of Old Testament Israel. Instead, like its Master, the pilgrim church can expect a cross of persecution and suffering. The New Testament does not recommend virtues that lead believers to conquer the world but rather patiently to endure its enmity. John's Apocalypse assures the suffering church of all times that it shares the certainty of Christ's victory even in the face of terrible anti-Christian apostasy, lawlessness, and persecution. Revelation 20, when compared with the rest of Scripture, confirms this conclusion rather than lending support to chiliast dreams of world rule. Also, Rev. 20 does not teach the chiliast doctrine of a twofold resurrection; the "first" resurrection simply refers to those faithful who die and immediately live and reign with Christ in heaven. When human apostasy and wickedness reach the apex of power and the world is ripe for judgment, Christ the king will suddenly appear to bring about the end of world history. Jesus's disciples are to be watchful of the signs but they are also forbidden to calculate. All believers ought at all times to live as though the coming of Christ is at hand.

[566] Although in the previous chapter we generally established that the New Testament is antichiliastic,[1] we do need to demonstrate this in greater detail. Chiliasm includes the expectation that shortly before the return of Christ, a national conversion will occur in Israel, that the Jews will then return to Palestine and from there, under Christ, rule over the nations. In this connection there is some difference among chiliasts over whether the conversion will precede the return or vice versa.[2] Since it is hard to imagine that the dispersed Jews will first be converted successively and then jointly conceive the plan to go to Palestine, some believe that the Jews will first gradually return to Palestine and then later be jointly converted to Christ there. Others attempt to combine the two views in such a way that first a large part of the Jewish people will go to Palestine and that, after having first restored the city and the temple and the temple services and then converted to Christ, they will be gradually followed by their remaining fellow Jews. And they point out that this expectation is already in the process of being fulfilled. Thousands of Jews already live in Palestine. The question of the Near East is approaching solution, for Turkey owes its existence to the mutual jealousies of the great powers. Once Turkey is destroyed, there is every chance that Palestine will be assigned to the Jews to whom by rights it belongs. Furthermore, in the hearts of many Jews, as is evident from the Zionism that has emerged in recent years, there is a longing to return to Palestine and to form an independent state there. Finally, the greatly improved modes of transportation—which they read Nahum (2:3–4) and Isaiah (11:16; 66:20) as having predicted—make such a return simple and convenient.

However we may view these political combinations, the New Testament furnishes not the slightest support for such an expectation. When the fullness of time had come, the Jews, considered as a nation, were on the same level as the Gentiles. Together they were worthy of condemnation before God, because they sought to establish a righteousness of their own based on the law and rejected the righteousness that is through faith (Rom. 3:21). For that reason, God sent John to them with the baptism of repentance, thus telling them that, though they were circumcised and though they baptized proselytes, they were guilty and unclean before him and needed rebirth and conversion as much as the Gentiles to enter the kingdom of heaven. By baptism John already separated the true Israelites from the bulk of the people, and Jesus followed in his tracks. He took over John's baptism and had it administered by his disciples. Indeed, initially like John he publicly proclaimed that the kingdom was drawing near. But he understood that kingdom very differently from his contemporaries. He understood by it not a political but a religious-ethical dominion and taught that not physical descent from Abraham but only rebirth from water and Spirit gave a person access to the kingdom of

---

1. According to A. Kuenen, *The Prophets and Prophecy in Israel*, trans. Adam Milroy (London: Longmans, Green, 1877; repr., Amsterdam: Philo, 1969).

2. É. Guers, *Israel in the Last Days*, trans. Aubrey Price (London: Wertheim, MacIntosh, & Hunt, 1862), 155–57.

heaven. As a result he gradually gathered around him a group of disciples that distinguished and separated itself from the Jewish people. And these were the true ἐκκλησια (*ekklēsia*, church), the real people of God, as Israel should have been but now in its rejection of the Messiah proved itself not to be.

This separation between the Jews and the New Testament *ekklēsia* became increasingly sharper. Granted, there were many who believed in Christ but the people [as a whole], led by the Pharisees and scribes, rejected him. Though a rising for some, for many he was to be a falling and a sign that was opposed (Luke 2:34). He came to his own people, but they did not accept him (John 1:11). Jesus himself says that "prophets are not without honor except in their own country" (Matt. 13:57). Over and over he experienced that the Jews did not wish to come to him (John 5:37–47; 6:64); he testified that they would die in their sin (8:21), that they were children of their father the devil (8:44), plants not planted by the Father (Matt. 15:13–14); and he regarded their unbelief not as an accidental, unforeseen circumstance but as the fulfillment of prophecy (Matt. 13:13–15; John 12:37ff.). Not only did Jesus not expect anything *from* the Jews in the present; in the future also he expected nothing *for* them. On the contrary, he announced the total destruction of the city and the temple so that not one stone would be left upon another (Matt. 22:7; 23:37–39; 24:1ff.; Mark 13; Luke 21:6ff.; John 2:18–21). During his entry into Jerusalem he wept over the city (Luke 19:41–44). On the Monday before his death, on his way to Bethany, he cursed the fig tree, which, though it did not yet bear fruit but did already have leaves, was an image of pseudo-pious, self-righteous Israel, and said, "May no one ever eat fruit from you again" (Mark 11:12–14).

On the occasion of his going to the cross, he commanded the women not to weep over him but to weep over [the people of] Jerusalem (Luke 23:28). He even proclaimed that the salvation rejected by Israel would be shared by the Gentiles. The kingdom of God will be taken from Israel and given to a people who produce the fruits of that kingdom (Matt. 21:43). The vineyard will be rented out to other tenants (21:41). Invited to the wedding are the people from the main streets (22:9). The lost son takes precedence over the older son (Luke 15). Similarly, Jesus states that many will come from the east and the west and sit down in the kingdom of heaven with Abraham, Isaac, and Jacob (Matt. 8:10–12), and that he has other sheep not of this sheepfold (John 10:16). He rejoices that, as certain Greeks desire to see him, he will soon, like a grain of wheat, fall into the earth and die and so bear much fruit (John 12:24). Accordingly, after his resurrection he instructs his disciples to preach the gospel to all nations (Matt. 28:18–20).

In the case of the apostles we encounter the same judgment concerning Israel. As Jesus's witnesses they must indeed begin their work in Jerusalem but then continue to the ends of the earth (Acts 1:8). Peter therefore immediately brings the gospel to the Jews (2:14; 3:19; 5:31) but then learns in a vision that from then on no one is unclean but that anyone who fears God, no matter in what nation he has been born, is acceptable to him (10:35, 43). Paul always begins his preaching among the Jews, but when they reject it, he turns to the Gentiles (13:46; 18:6; 28:25–28). "First to the Jew but then also to the Greek" is the rule he observes on his missionary journeys (Rom. 1:16; 1 Cor. 1:21–24). For both Jews and Gentiles are worthy of condemnation before God and need the same gospel (Rom. 3:19ff.). There is but one way to salvation for all, faith—the faith as it was practiced by Abraham even before the law came, and was reckoned to him as righteousness (Rom. 4:22; Gal. 3). Those of the Jews who reject Christ are not really true Jews (Rom. 2:28–29). They are not the "circumcision" but the "mutilation" (Phil. 3:2). They are the irregulars, idle talkers, and deceivers, who must be silenced (Titus 1:10–11). They have killed the Lord Jesus and their own prophets as well. They persecute believers, do not please God, and oppose everyone. They hinder the apostles from speaking to the Gentiles. Thus they constantly fill up the measure of their sins, so that now God's wrath has reached its limit and is being discharged upon them (1 Thess. 2:14–16). The Jews who slander the church of Smyrna, though they say they are Jews, are not; rather they are a synagogue of Satan (Rev. 2:9; 3:9). Real Jews, the true children of Abraham, are those who believe in Christ (Rom. 9:8; Gal. 3:29; etc.). This is the New Testament's judgment concerning the Jews. The community of believers has in all respects replaced carnal, national Israel. The Old Testament is fulfilled in the New.[3]

DIFFICULT PASSAGES ON ISRAEL AND THE CHURCH

[567] Only a few passages seem to be at variance with this consistent teaching of Scripture and to mean something different. The first is Matt. 23:37–39 (Luke 13:34–35), where Jesus tells the inhabitants of Jerusalem that their house will be left to them desolate, and that they will not see him again until they say, "Blessed is the one who comes in the name of the Lord." Here Jesus in fact expresses the expectation that one day, namely, at his return, the Jews will recognize him as the Messiah. Now, if from another text we were certain of a millennium and a conversion coincident with it, then this passage could be explained in light of it. But since this is not the case, not even in Rev. 20, as will be made clear later, this passage can only refer to an acknowledgment of the Messiah by the Jews at Christ's coming again for judgment. And until then—Jesus expressly states—Jerusalem will be left desolate. Jesus therefore in no way expects a rebuilding of the city and the temple before his return.

A second passage to be considered is Luke 21:24, where Jesus says that Jerusalem will be trampled on by the Gentiles until the times of the Gentiles are fulfilled. The conjunction "until" (ἄχρι, *achri*) does not suggest or imply that, with the onset of the period described in the following clause, the opposite will occur (the Jews will rebuild and inhabit Jerusalem). But even if this were the case, Jesus is not saying that the trampling of Jerusalem will end before his parousia, for after having

3. Cf. A. Harnack, *The Mission and Expansion of Christianity*, trans. J. Moffatt (New York: Harper, 1908), 53ff.

pronounced judgment over Jerusalem, he immediately proceeds to discuss the signs that will occur before and at his return (Luke 21:25ff.). The times of the Gentiles continue until his return. Again, if the New Testament taught a twofold return of Christ, this passage could be interpreted in terms of it, but it will become evident in a moment that there is no ground in the New Testament for this position.

The third text that comes up in this connection is Acts 3:19–21. In this passage Peter calls the Jews to repentance that their sins may be wiped out, times of refreshing (καιροι ἀναψυξεως, *kairoi anapsyxeōs*) may come from the presence of the Lord, and he, that is, God, may send the Messiah appointed for the Jews, that is, Jesus, who must remain in heaven until the time of the restoration of all things. Some think that the "times of refreshing" referred to here will begin when the Jewish people are converted and all things are again restored in the millennium in keeping with their original destiny, and that these "times" will then last until the second return of Christ. But there are serious objections against this interpretation. The times of universal restoration (χρονοι ἀποκαταστασεως παντων, *chronoi apokatastaseōs pantōn*) can hardly be understood as the restoration of natural and moral relations expected by chiliasts in the millennium. We are clearly told that these times occur at the end of Jesus's stay in heaven. Until that time, then, Jesus will be at his Father's right hand and, since Scripture knows of only one return of Christ, the times of the restoration of all things will coincide with the consummation of the world. In addition, the expression "the restoration of all things" (ἀποκαταστασις παντων, *apokatastasis pantōn*) is much too strong for the restoration of the Jewish kingdom expected by chiliasm. Accordingly, the times of refreshing are not identical with but precede the times of the restoration of all things. Peter, after all, in speaking of the conversion of the Jews, refers to a twofold purpose: that times of refreshing may come for them and that God may send them the Christ appointed for them. The "times of refreshing" take place before the return of Christ and refer either to the spiritual peace that is the result of repentance and the forgiveness of sins, or to certain future times of divine blessing and favor. The latter is most probable because the times of refreshing are not immediately associated with the forgiveness of sins but with the mission of Christ. Then what Peter says here is this: "Repent, O Jews, that your sins may be wiped out, so that for you too, as a people who have handed over, rejected, and killed Christ (vv. 13–15), times of refreshing may come from the presence of the Lord, and God may afterward send the Christ who was appointed for you in the first place (v. 26) in order, also for your salvation, to restore all things." Whether such times will ever come for the Jews, Peter does not say. That depends on their conversion, a conversion of which nothing is said to suggest that it is to be expected.

"ALL ISRAEL" IN ROMANS 11

The final passage to be considered is Rom. 11:11–32. In Rom. 9–11 Paul deals with the awesome problem of how God's promise to Israel can be squared with the rejection of the gospel by the greater majority of the people of Israel. In response the apostle replies in the first place that the promise of God concerns not the carnal but the spiritual offspring of Abraham, and he works this out in great detail in chapters 9 and 10. In the second place he remarks that God still has his elect also in Israel and therefore has not rejected that people. Paul himself is proof of this, and many others with him. Though many have become hard and blind, the elect have received salvation: there has consistently been a remnant chosen by grace (11:1–10). But this hardening that has come over the great majority of the people of Israel is not God's final goal. In his hand it is rather a means to bring salvation to the Gentiles in order that they, accepting that salvation in faith, may in turn arouse Israel to jealousy (vv. 11–15). After admonishing believers from the Gentiles not to boast of their advantage (vv. 16–24), Paul further develops this thought, saying that a hardening has come over a part of Israel until the πληρωμα (*plērōma*) of the Gentiles, the full number of those from their midst who were destined for salvation, has come in (v. 25). And in that way, in keeping with God's promise, all Israel will be saved. Hence, though now the unbelieving Jews are enemies of God as regards the gospel in order that the salvation they have rejected should come to the Gentiles, as regards election they are beloved for the sake of their ancestors, for God's promises are irrevocable. Therefore, just as things were with the Gentiles, so will they go with the Jews who are hardened. First the Gentiles were disobedient and now receive mercy, so now the Jews too are disobedient that through the mercy shown to the Gentiles, they may receive mercy as well. For God has imprisoned all, Gentiles and Jews, in disobedience so that he may be merciful to all (vv. 25–32).

Most interpreters think that the question whether God has rejected his people (v. 1) has not been fully answered by the assertion that in Israel God always has his elect, the people who, in the course of centuries, are successively brought in (vv. 1–10). They judge, therefore, that everything that follows in chapter 11 is not just a further explication of, but an addition to, the answer given in verses 1–10, a new answer that only now fully disposes of the objection that God rejected his people. By "all Israel" (πας Ἰσραηλ, *pas Israēl*) they therefore understand that in the last days the whole of the people of Israel will repent and turn to the Lord.

But no matter how commonly held this explanation is, there are weighty objections to it. If in 11:25–32 it were the intent of the apostle to give a new, supplementary answer, he would render his reasoning at the end inconsistent with its beginning and starting point. In 9:6ff., after all, he stated that the promises of God have not failed because they concern the spiritual offspring of Abraham and will still consistently find their fulfillment in this spiritual offspring (11:1–10). It is a priori very unlikely that Paul later reconsidered this reasoning, supplementing and improving it in the sense that the promises of God are not fully realized in the salvation of spiritual Israel, but will be fully realized only when in the last days a national conversion of Israel takes place. In any case, in 9:1–11:10 Paul does not breathe a word about such an expectation for the people of Israel, nor is there any expression here that prepares or intimates it. Nor does even 11:11–24 as yet contain anything that points to it. Granted, 11:11–15 is understood by many in that sense. But even if these words were to be understood, not hypothetically as an element in an argument, but as the description of a fact, they convey no more than the idea that Israel's rejection of Christ was a great gain for the Gentiles, for by it the reconciliation effected by Christ's death fell to the Gentiles. God's *acceptance* of Israel will then be a much greater boon to the Gentiles, for when Israel has reached its πληρωμα (*plērōma*), the full number of its elect, and also the *plērōma* of the Gentiles has entered in, that will bring about life from the dead: the resurrection of the new humanity from the dead. The Gentile world owes its reconciliation, mediately speaking, to Israel's failure; to Israel's fullness (*plērōma*) it will someday owe its life from the dead.

If in 11:26 Paul is seeking to convey a new fact, the manner in which he does it is very odd indeed. For he does not say *and then*, or *thereupon*, that is, after the fullness of the Gentiles has come in, all Israel will, but "and in *that way* all Israel will be saved" (και ούτως πας Ἰσραηλ σωθησεται, *kai houtōs pas Israēl sōthēsetai*). That can only mean in the way described in the preceding verses. Just prior to this, in verse 25, Paul stated that a hardening has come over only a part (ἀπο μερους, *apo merous*) of Israel. Believers among the Gentiles might perhaps begin to think—as Israel used to think—that they alone were the elect people of God and that Israel was totally rejected. But Paul says that this is not so. No: Israel as such has not been rejected. Among them there has always been a remnant chosen by grace. True enough, some branches have been broken off, and in their place a wild olive shoot has been grafted in, but the stem of the tame olive tree has been preserved. When the *plērōma* (fullness) of the Gentiles comes in, also the *plērōma* of Israel is brought in, and *in that way* all Israel is saved.

This fact, that a hardening has come *upon a part* of Israel, Paul calls a mystery (μυστηριον, *mystērion*; 11:25). Elsewhere he frequently calls by that name the fact that now the Gentiles are fellow heirs and fellow citizens with the saints, fellow members of the household of God, and here he describes with the same word the fact that the Jews have only in part become hardened, and that God continually brings numerous elect from among them into his church. For that *partial* hardening will last until the *plērōma* of the Gentiles will have come in. Never, up until the end of the ages, will God totally reject his ancient people; alongside a part from the Gentile world, he will always bring to faith in Christ a part from Israel as well. The Gentiles, but also the Jews, had deserved a very different fate. But this is the great mystery: that God is rich in mercy; that he gathers his elect from every nation, also that of the Jews who rejected him; that he imprisoned all in disobedience that he might be merciful to all. That mystery sends the apostle into ecstasy and causes him to marvel at and adore the depth of God's wisdom and knowledge (11:33–36).

"All Israel" (πας Ἰσραηλ, *pas Israēl*) in 11:26 is not, therefore, the people of Israel that at the end of time will be converted en masse. Nor is it the church of the

Jews and the Gentiles together. But it is the *plērōma* that in the course of centuries will be brought in from Israel. Israel will continue to exist as a people alongside the Gentiles, predicts Paul. It will not expire or disappear from the earth. It will remain to the end of the ages, produce its *plērōma* for the kingdom of God as well as the Gentiles, and keep its special task and place for that kingdom. The church of God will be gathered out of all peoples and nations and tongues. Paul does not calculate how large that *plērōma* from Israel will be. It is very possible that in the last days the number of the elect from Israel will be much greater than it was in Paul's time or later in our time. There is not a single reason for denying this. The spread of the gospel among all peoples rather prompts us to expect that both from Israel and from the Gentiles an ever-increasing number will be saved. But that is not what Paul intends to say: he does not count, but weighs. A full *plērōma* will come from the Gentile world, as well as from Israel, and that *plērōma* will be all Israel (*pas Israēl*). In that *plērōma* all Israel is saved, just as in the church as a whole the whole of humanity is being saved.

It is also the case that a conversion of Israel other than the one indicated by Paul is hard to conceive. For that matter, just what is a national conversion, and how and when will it take place in the case of Israel? One cannot of course have the least objection—the continued existence of the people of Israel in the light of prophecy rather argues for it—to the fact that from Israel as well a very large number of people are still being brought to faith in Christ. But however large this number may be, it remains a remnant chosen by grace (Rom. 11:5). Certainly not even the most fervent chiliast thinks that at some point in the future all Jews without exception will be converted. And even if he did believe this, thinking that in that way alone Rom. 11:26 would be completely fulfilled, then such an end-time national conversion would still not help the millions of Jews who, throughout the ages and right up until the end, died in unbelief and hardness of heart. Were a person really to think that God's promise to Israel can only be fulfilled if—not a selection (ἐκλογή, *eklogē*) from the people but—the nation itself were brought into the fold, one would come into conflict with the history in question. Always, throughout all the ages, also in the days when Israel as a nation was the people of God, it was never more than a small segment of the people who truly served and feared God. And this is how it is, not only in the case of the Jews but also in the case of the Gentiles. It is always "a remnant chosen by grace" that, from within Christian nations, obtains salvation in Christ.

Further, there is no room left in Paul's sketch of the future for a national conversion of Israel such as chiliasts expect. For he expressly states that a hardening has come on part of Israel *until* the full number (*plērōma*) of the Gentiles has come in, and that *in that way* (not *after that*) all Israel will be saved (11:25–26). Therefore, the hardening on part of Israel will last until the *plērōma* from the Gentile world has come in and, after that, according to chiliasts, the national conversion of Israel has to occur. The question is: Is there, then, a lapse of time between the coming of the *plērōma* from the Gentile world and the end of the ages? If so, are there still Gentile nations in that period, and is there not a single person from among them that turns to the Lord? The truth is, the coming in of the *plērōma* of the Gentiles cannot be conceived as temporally antecedent to the salvation of all Israel. For Rom. 11:26 does not mention a new fact that takes place *after* the coming in of the full number of the Gentiles. But the coming in of the full number of the Gentiles and the salvation of all Israel run parallel because a hardening has come on only a part of Israel.

In conclusion, it should be noted that even if Paul expected a national conversion of Israel at the end, he does not say a word about the return of the Jews to Palestine, about a rebuilding of the city and a temple, about a visible rule of Christ: in his picture of the future there simply is no room for all of this.[4]

AN INTERIM MILLENNIAL AGE?

[568] In our discussion of the expectations that the New Testament fosters with regard to the future of the people of Israel, we left undecided the question whether the New Testament, in passages other than the ones cited in this connection so far, perhaps taught the existence of an interim state between this dispensation and the consummation of the ages. We acknowledged that if that were the case, Matt. 23:37–39; Luke 21:24; and Acts 3:19–21, although by themselves giving us no reason whatever for the acceptance of a transitional period, could nevertheless be understood and explained along those lines. We now face the question, therefore, whether according to Jesus and the apostles there still awaits the church a period of power and glory that precedes the general resurrection of the dead and the event of world judgment. If this were so, we would expect clear mention of it in the eschatological discourse that Jesus gave his disciples in the final days of his life (Matt. 24; Mark 13; Luke 21). But in this discourse not a word is said, not even an allusion is made, about such a kingdom. True, chiliasts try to insert their millennium into one part or another of the discourse, saying, for example, that Christ's first coming is mentioned in Matt. 24:27 and his second coming in verse 30, but this exegesis is certainly without any foundation.

In his eschatological discourse Jesus responds to two questions put to him by his disciples: (1) When will the things he has said concerning Jerusalem—namely, that not one stone of the temple will be left upon another—take place? And (2) what will be the sign of his coming and of the consummation of the world?

---

4. On the conversion of the Jews, in addition to commentaries on Rom. 11, compare also G. Voetius, *Selectae disputationes theologicae*, 5 vols. (Utrecht, 1648–69), II, 124ff.; H. Witsius, *The Oeconomy of the Covenants between God and Man*, 3 vols. (New York: Lee & Stokes, 1798), IV, 15, 20–32; B. de Moor, *Commentarius . . . theologiae*, 6 vols. (Leiden: J. Hasebroek, 1761–71), VI, 127–30; C. Hodge, *Systematic Theology* (New York: Charles Scribner's Sons, 1888), III, 805; Th. Kliefoth, *Christliche Eschatologie* (Leipzig: Dörffling & Franke, 1886), 147ff. For the rest, one must not underestimate the number of Jews converted to Christianity over the centuries and also in the nineteenth century. In terms of percentages, it is greater than the number of the Gentiles. Pastor Le Roi (*Der Geisteskampf der Gegenwart* 47 [1911]: 112) calculated the number of Jews who became Christians in the nineteenth century at more than 220,000.

Jesus replies to the question by first dealing with the early signs (Mark 13:1–8; cf. Matt. 24:1–8; Luke 21:5–11), then with the fate of the disciples (Mark 13:9–13; cf. Matt. 24:9–14; Luke 21:12–19), and finally with the catastrophe in Judea (Mark 13:14–23; cf. Matt. 24:15–28; Luke 21:20–24). The second question, the one concerning the parousia of Jesus and the consummation of the world, is answered in Mark 13:24–31 (cf. Matt. 24:29–35; Luke 21:25–33). And in this connection Jesus links his parousia immediately with the destruction of Jerusalem. In the fall of this city he sees the announcement and preparation of the consummation of the world (Matt. 24:29, "immediately," εὐθέως, *eutheōs*; Mark 13:24, "in those days," ἐν ἐκείναις ταῖς ἡμέραις, *en ekeinais tais hēmerais*). He even states that "this generation will certainly not pass away until all these things have taken place" (Matt. 24:34; Mark 13:30; Luke 21:32).

However this expectation on the part of Jesus of his early parousia—an event immediately following the destruction of Jerusalem—is to be understood (on which more later), in any case it is clearly evident that in this discourse there is no room for a thousand-year kingdom. Jesus first sums up (Mark 13:1–8) a number of general signs by which the disciples can tell that all things, specifically the destruction of Jerusalem and the end of the world, are approaching in tandem. These general signs (*signa communia*) are the rise of pseudo-christs; wars and rumors of wars; the disturbance and rebellion of nations against nations, along with earthquakes and famines and the like; then the preaching of the gospel in the entire world as a testimony to all the nations (Matt. 24:14; Mark 13:10). And finally, as a prelude to the drama of the end, the things that happen in Judea and Jerusalem (Matt. 24:15–28; Mark 13:14–23). Then follow the signs that immediately precede the parousia (the *signa propria*): the darkening of sun and moon, the falling down of the stars, and the shaking of the powers in the heavens (Mark 13:24–25).

Immediately linked with Christ's parousia, then, are the judgment, the separation of the good and evil, and the end of the world (Mark 13:26–27). Consonant with this is what Jesus says in Matt. 13:37–43, 47–50: the side-by-side growth of wheat and weeds, and the catching in a single net of all kinds of fish, events that continue to the end of the age, until the time of the harvest and the judgment of the world. Jesus only knows of two aeons: the present and the future aeons. In the present aeon [age] his disciples cannot expect anything other than oppression and persecution and must forsake all things for his sake. Jesus nowhere predicts a glorious future on earth before the end of the world. On the contrary, the things he experienced are the things his church will experience. A disciple is not above his teacher, nor a slave above the master. Only in the age to come will his disciples receive everything back along with eternal life (Matt. 19:27–30; cf. Matt. 5:3–12; 8:19–20; 10:16–42; 16:24–27; John 16:2, 33; 17:14–15; etc.). Accordingly, when the disciples in Acts 1:6 ask Jesus whether this is the time he will restore the kingdom to Israel, he does not deny it but tacitly admits that this will happen someday. But he says that the Father has set the times or seasons for this by his own authority, and that in this period the disciples have the calling to act as his witnesses from Jerusalem to the ends of the earth.

The whole New Testament, which was written from the viewpoint of the "church under the cross," speaks the same language. Believers, not many of whom are wise, powerful, or of noble birth (1 Cor. 1:26), should not expect anything on earth other than suffering and oppression (Rom. 8:36; Phil. 1:29). They are sojourners and foreigners (Heb. 11:13); their citizenship is in the heavens (Phil. 3:20); they do not look at the things that can be seen (2 Cor. 4:18), but mind the things that are above (Col. 3:2). Here they have no lasting city but are looking for the city that is to come (Heb. 13:14). They are saved in hope (Rom. 8:24) and know that if they suffer with Christ they will also be glorified with him (Rom. 6:8; 8:17; Col. 3:4). Therefore, along with the entire groaning creation, they wait with eager longing for the future of Christ and for the revelation of the glory of the children of God (Rom. 8:19, 21; 1 Cor. 15:48ff.), a glory with which the sufferings of the present time are not worth comparing (Rom. 8:18; 2 Cor. 4:17). Nowhere in the New Testament is there a ray of hope that the church of Christ will again come to power and dominion on earth. The most it may look for is that, under kings and all who are in high positions, it may lead a quiet and peaceable life in all godliness and dignity (Rom. 13:1; 1 Tim. 2:2). Therefore, the New Testament does not first of all recommend the virtues that enable believers to conquer the world but, while it bids them avoid all false asceticism (Rom. 14:14; 1 Tim. 4:4–5; Titus 1:15), lists as fruits of the Spirit the virtues of "love, joy, peace, patience, kindness, generosity, faithfulness, gentleness, and self-control" (Gal. 5:22–23; Eph. 4:32; 1 Thess. 5:14ff.; 1 Pet. 3:8ff.; 2 Pet. 1:5–7; 1 John 2:15; etc.).

It is a constant New Testament expectation that to the extent to which the gospel of the cross is spread abroad, to that extent the hostility of the world will be manifested as well. Christ is destined to be a rising for many but also to be a falling for many, and to bring out into the open the hostile thoughts of many. He has come into the world for judgment (κρίσις, *krisis*) so that those who do not see may see and that those who see may become blind (Matt. 21:44; Luke 2:34; John 3:19–21; 8:39; Rom. 9:32–33; 1 Cor. 1:23; 2 Cor. 2:16; Heb. 4:12; 1 Pet. 2:7–8). In the last days, the days that precede the return of Christ, the wickedness of human beings will rise to a fearful level. The days of Noah will return. Lust, sensual pleasures, lawlessness, greed, unbelief, pride, mockery, and slander will erupt in fearful ways (Matt. 24:37ff.; Luke 17:26ff.; 2 Tim. 3:1ff.; 2 Pet. 3:3; Jude 18). Among believers as well there will be extensive apostasy. Temptations will be so powerful that, if it were possible, even the elect would be caused to fall. The love of many will grow cold, and vigilance will diminish to the extent that the wise will fall asleep along with the foolish virgins. Apostasy will be so general that Jesus can ask whether at his coming the Son of Man will still find faith on earth (Matt. 24:24, 44ff.; 25:1ff.; Luke 18:8; 1 Tim. 4:1).

JOHN'S APOCALYPSE

The book of Revelation, which John wrote, is in agreement with this. The letters to the seven churches do indeed deal with concrete conditions prevailing in those churches at the time and are first of all addressed to those churches, to incite them to watchfulness and to prepare them for the coming persecutions and the return of Christ. Still their intent and import are clearly much broader. The number "seven," which in Revelation is consistently charged with symbolic meaning, already points in that direction. It is the number of completeness and makes the seven churches, which have here been selected from among the many churches in Asia Minor, appear as types of the Christian church as a whole. The letters addressed by John to the churches did not first have a separate existence and were not sent separately to the respective churches. Rather, they belong together, were composed together and joined to each other, and are addressed to the whole church: "Let anyone who has an ear listen to what the Spirit is saying to all the churches." But though the letters therefore undoubtedly have a significance that reaches far beyond the seven churches referred to by name and existing at the time in Asia Minor, this significance does not consist in that they describe successive periods in the history of Jesus's church and together make up a little compendium of the whole history of the church. Instead, they depict church conditions that were then present and are at the same time typical for the church of Christ as a whole, conditions that may recur over and over in the church and will recur especially at the end of history. For it is clear that they were all written under the impression of approaching persecution and the speedy return of Christ. They all contain a reference to the parousia, and with a view to it they exhort the churches to be watchful and faithful. They serve to call an increasingly worldly Christianity back to its first love, to arouse it from apathy, and with an eye toward the crown awaiting it, to equip it for battle and to prompt it to persevere, with unyielding loyalty, even unto death.

For the day of the Lord is drawing near. After describing the conditions that existed in the church of Christ of his time and would exist, especially toward the end of the world, John proceeds to report the things that are about to happen (4:1). The book of God's decrees concerning the end of all things is opened in heaven by the Lamb (chs. 4 and 5), and, in particular, that which relates to the very end of time (ch. 10) and concerns all the nations of the earth (10:11) is shown to John by an angel. John alternately positions the reader on earth and in heaven. In heaven, for there everything has already been settled and determined; there honor is already being brought to God and to the Lamb; there the battle has, as it were, already been fought and won (chs. 4 and 5). There the souls of the martyrs are already clothed in long white garments and await the fulfillment of their number (6:9–11). There John proleptically sees the whole multitude of the redeemed standing before the throne (7:9–17). There the prayers of the saints have already been heard by God (8:1–4). There, proleptically as well, the 144,000 who were sealed (7:1–8) have been taken up; as firstfruits they precede the rest (14:1–5), and have gained victory over the beast and his image (15:1–4). There the whole multitude of the redeemed are already bringing glory and honor to God since the marriage of the Lamb has come (19:1–8).

The church on earth therefore does not need to be afraid of the judgments with which God in the end visits the world. The 144,000 servants of God out of every tribe of the sons of Israel are sealed in advance (7:1–8). The temple and the altar and those who worship there are not abandoned to the heathen, and the two witnesses who prophesied there, though they were killed, are also raised up and taken up into heaven (11:1–12). The Christian church, though persecuted by Satan for Christ's sake, finds a place of refuge in the wilderness (12:1–14). In principle, the battle has been decided. For Christ has been taken up into heaven (12:5), and Satan has been defeated by Michael and his angels and thrown from heaven down to earth (12:7–11). Now he has but little time left on earth (12:12) and takes advantage of it. He effects the rise of the beast from the sea or from the bottomless pit (11:7; 13:1; 17:8) and gives it power and glory. This beast is the Roman Empire (13:1–10). It is supported by another beast, the beast of the earth, that is, the false prophet, false religion, the antichrist (13:11–18). This "beast" comes to full development in a single person, who can therefore himself be called "the beast" (13:3, 12, 18; 17:8, 10–11) and who has his center in the city of "Babylon," that is, Rome, the great harlot, who rules over all the nations (chs. 17–18). But this massive development of power is futile. By opening the seven seals, by blowing the seven trumpets, by emptying the seven bowls, God displays his wrath, visits nature and humanity with his judgments, and makes preparations for the final judgment. First "Babylon" falls (ch. 18). Then Christ appears (19:11–16) and conquers the beast from the sea and the beast of the earth (vv. 19–21), and soon Satan as well (20:1–3).

[569] Now it is very peculiar that this last victory over Satan occurs in two phases. First he is bound for a thousand years and thrown into the bottomless pit; then he again deceives the nations and makes war against the church. But finally he is overcome for good and thrown into the lake of fire and brimstone (20:1–10). Proponents of chiliasm find in this pericope—aside from the Old Testament—their most powerful support, while opponents are not a little perplexed at this passage and have tested all their exegetical skills on it. The idea that, following the conquest of the world empire, a final attack from the side of the nations still has to be repulsed is one that John undoubtedly borrowed from Ezekiel. The latter expects that Israel, having returned to its own land and living there in security, will once more be attacked by Gog of the land of Magog, the chief prince of Meshech and Tubal, that is, the nation of the Scythians allied with a variety of other nations from the north, east, and south. The attack ends, however, when God himself in his wrath destroys these nations on the mountains of Israel (Ezek. 38–39). In 38:17 the Lord says that, by the ministry of his prophets, he had already spoken of these nations earlier. And indeed these earlier prophets proclaimed that the

Lord in his day would judge not only those historic nations in the midst of whom Israel lived and with whom it came in contact, but also all the pagans living far off as well (Isa. 25:5–8; 26:21; Jer. 12:14–16; 30:23–24; Joel 2:32; 3:2, 11ff.; Mic. 4:5, 11–13; 5:7–9). A very similar prophecy clearly occurs in Zechariah, which in chapters 12–14 sketches how against the day of the Lord Jerusalem will be besieged by the nations, and how these will then be judged by the Lord. And Daniel not only regards Antiochus Epiphanes as the personified embodiment of the world empire that is hostile to God, but also expects that this hostile power will rise up once more and thus become ripe for judgment (11:40–45).

The expectation of prophecy was therefore twofold: it first envisioned a victory of the people of God over the nations in whose midst it lived, and then a victory over the nations that up until then had not yet appeared on the stage of world history. This double expectation passed into the apocryphal literature[5] and also into the New Testament. The first expectation is, of course, in the foreground. The appearance of Christ arouses and activates the anti-Christian principle. Jesus speaks of false prophets (ψευδοπροφηται, *pseudoprophētai*) and false Christs (ψευδοχριστοι, *pseudochristoi*), who position themselves against him and his kingdom (Matt. 7:15; 24:5, 24; Mark 13:21–22; Luke 17:23). In 2 Thess. 2, to moderate the impatience of the Thessalonians relative to their expectation of Jesus's speedy return, Paul points out that the day of Christ will not come unless the apostasy and the man of sin come first. The latter cannot yet come because there is something restraining him. Indeed, at work already is the mystery of lawlessness (το μυστηριον της ἀνομιας, *to mystērion tēs anomias*); only the man of sin cannot come until he who now restrains him is removed from their midst. Only then will the lawless one (ἀνομος, *anomos*) be revealed, but he will also immediately be slain by Jesus (2:6–8). The Apocalypse sees anti-Christian power embodied in the beast from the sea, the Roman Empire, whose center is the city of Rome and whose head is a specific emperor; and parallel to this, in the beast of the earth, false prophecy that seduces people into worshiping the world empire and its emperor. In his letters, John first calls this adversary of Christ by the name of antichrist (ἀντιχριστος, *antichristos*), in 1 John 2:18 probably even without the article; and he sees his essence realized in those who in principle deny the coming of Christ in the flesh (1 John 2:22; 4:2–3; 2 John 7).

In Scripture, the representations of antichrist are therefore diverse. Daniel sees his type in Antiochus Epiphanes. Jesus detaches the anti-Christian principle from the Old Testament antithesis between Israel and the nations and sees it embodied in many false Christs and many false prophets who will rise up after him and against him. Paul has the man of sin arise from a general apostasy and calls him the lawless one (ἀνομος, *anomos*) and the opponent (ἀντικειμενος, *antikeimenos*) of Christ but also depicts him with features derived from Daniel as the one "who exalts

---

5. Emil Schürer, *The History of the Jewish People in the Age of Jesus Christ (175 B.C.–A.D. 135)*, rev. and ed. G. Vermès and F. Millar (Edinburgh: T&T Clark, 1979), II, 525–26.

himself above every so-called god or object of worship, so that he takes his seat in the temple of God, declaring himself to be God" (2 Thess. 2:4). In his letters, John expresses the belief that antichrist has come in the heretics of his day. And the Apocalypse, in turn, sees his power emerge in the world empire supported by false prophecy. From this it is evident that in seeing the word "antichrist," we must not think exclusively of one person in particular, or of a group of persons, say, the heretics of the first centuries, the Roman Empire, Nero, the Jews, Muhammad, the pope, Napoleon, and the like. Scripture clearly teaches that the power of antichrist has its own history, manifests itself at different times and in different ways, and finally evolves into a general apostasy and the breakdown of all natural and moral ties that now still hold back such apostasy; then [this antichrist spirit] embodies itself in a world empire that utilizes the false church and apotheosizes itself by deifying the head of that empire. Christ himself, by his appearing, then destroys this anti-Christian power in its highest and latest manifestation.[6]

But with this, complete victory has not yet been achieved. In the nature of the case the anti-Christian principle can only become active in those nations that have known the gospel and have finally, in conscious and deliberate hostility, rejected it. But there have always been, still are today, and will be until the end of time nations that, like lopped-off branches of a tree, lie outside the history and culture of humankind. Jesus does say (Matt. 24:14) that the end will not come until the gospel has been preached throughout the entire inhabited world as a testimony to all nations. But certainly this prophecy does not imply that someday Christianity will be the dominant religion in all nations, or that it will be known to all people individually, for history teaches that millions of people and countless nations, also in the centuries following Christ's coming on earth, have died and disappeared without having had any knowledge of the gospel. But Jesus's saying only means that the preaching of the gospel will get through to all nations. It by no means defines the measure in which, or the limits to which, this will happen. Nor is this prophecy realized at one time, but successively in the course of centuries, so that many nations that once walked in the light of the gospel have later been deprived of it again. Although in the present century the gospel is spreading among pagans, in Christian nations apostasy is increasing at a rapid rate. It is therefore more than likely that toward the time of the parousia, many peoples on earth will be deprived of the knowledge of Christ.

THE MILLENNIUM IN REVELATION 20

It is this reality that is reflected in the twentieth chapter of John's Revelation. Because we read there of a thousand-year binding of Satan and of martyrs living and ruling with Christ in that time, many have believed that here, in clear, undeniable language, a thousand-year reign is being taught. In fact, however, this

6. Cf. F. A. E. Sieffert, "Antichrist," in *PRE*³, I, 577–84; M. R. James, "Man of Sin and Antichrist," in *DB*, III, 226–28, and the literature cited here.

interpretation of Rev. 20, though it is in accord with the analogy of apocryphal literature, is not in accord with the analogy of Scripture.[7] Revelation 20 as such contains nothing of all the things that belong to the essence of chiliastic belief.

The reasons for this latter statement are as follows. First, the chapter does not say a word about a conversion and return of the Jews, of the rebuilding of Jerusalem, of a restoration of the temple and temple worship, or of an initial renewal of the earth. These things, rather, are excluded. For even if the 144,000 in chapter 7 are to be understood as referring to the πληρωμα (*plērōma*, fullness) from Israel and are distinct from those mentioned in 14:1, what this would mean is nothing other and nothing more than that also many Christians from among the Jews will remain firm in the great tribulation and assume a place of their own among the multitude standing before the throne of God. But Rev. 20 in no way states that they will arise from the dead and live in Jerusalem. In this book Christians are the real Jews, and the Jews who harden themselves in unbelief are a synagogue of Satan (2:9). Although the earthly Jerusalem is occasionally called the holy city, and the temple in Jerusalem is called the temple of God (11:1–2), still that Jerusalem is allegorically called "Sodom" and "Egypt" (11:8). The true Jerusalem is above (3:12; 21:2, 10), and there too is the temple of God (3:12; 7:15; 11:19; etc.), the ark (11:19), and the altar (6:9; 8:3, 5; 9:13; 14:18; 16:7). And that Jerusalem does not come down from heaven in Rev. 20 but only in Rev. 21.

Second, the life and rule of the believers who remained faithful in the great tribulation take place in heaven, not on earth. Not a word is said about the earth. John saw the angel who binds Satan come down from heaven (20:1); the thrones he saw (20:4) are located in heaven (4:4; 11:16), and the souls of the martyrs are seen here (20:4), as in every other passage, in heaven (6:9; 7:9, 14–15; 11:12; 14:1–5; 18:20; 19:1–8). Christ already on earth made believers kings and priests to God (1:6). That is what they *are* in heaven (5:10), and they expect that one day they will be that on earth as well (5:10), but this expectation is only fulfilled in the new Jerusalem that comes down from above. Then they will be kings forever (22:5). But now, in heaven, this kingship is temporary: it lasts a thousand years.

Third, John also does not know of a physical resurrection that precedes the millennium and a second that follows it. Such a first resurrection is not taught anywhere in Scripture. There is indeed mention of a spiritual resurrection from sin (John 5:25–26; Rom. 6:4; etc.). There is also a resurrection from the dead (ἀναστασις ἐκ νεκρων, *anastasis ek nekrōn*) that refers to individual cases, like the resurrection of Christ (1 Pet. 1:3; cf. Acts 26:23; 1 Cor. 15:23), or only to believers (Luke 20:35–36; Acts 4:2), but in that case it is absolutely not distinguished temporally by a thousand-year reign from the universal resurrection from the dead (ἀναστασις νεκρων, *anastasis nekrōn*; Matt. 22:31; John 5:28–29; Acts 24:15;

7. Ed. note: Bavinck here refers to the hermeneutical principle of *analogia Scripturae*, the analogy of Scripture, in which unclear, difficult, or ambiguous passages are interpreted by comparing them with clear and unambiguous passages on the same topic. See Richard A. Muller, *Dictionary of Latin and Greek Theological Terms* (Grand Rapids: Baker Academic, 1985), s.v. "*analogia Scripturae*."

1 Cor. 15:13, 42). True, some writers have tried to find this distinction in 1 Cor. 15:20–28 and 1 Thess. 4:13–18, but they do so erroneously. In 1 Cor. 15:20–28 Paul is most certainly dealing only with the resurrection of believers, while he does not breathe a word, nor does he need to, about that of the ungodly. But of the resurrection of believers he clearly states that it will occur at the time of Christ's parousia, and *then* the end comes, when he delivers the kingdom to the Father (vv. 23–24). One could indeed infer from this passage that, according to Paul, there is no resurrection of the ungodly, but one could not possibly derive from it that the latter are separated by a thousand-year reign from that of believers. For the resurrection of believers is immediately followed by the end and the delivering up of the kingdom, because all [God's] enemies have been vanquished and the last enemy, death, has been destroyed.

Nor is there any hint of such a prior physical resurrection of believers in 1 Thess. 4:13–18. In Thessalonica, people were worried about the lot of those who died in Christ—we do not know why. Chiliasts think that, while the Thessalonians did not doubt the resurrection and eternal life of those who died in Christ, they believed in two resurrections, one before and one after the thousand-year reign, and were worried that the believers who had already died would rise again only in the second resurrection and would therefore have no part in the glory of the thousand-year reign. But this opinion is far-fetched and has no support whatever in the text. If in fact there was a first resurrection of believers, one would expect rather that the church in Thessalonica would not be worried about the lot of the dead, for these would of course be precisely the kind who would share in that first resurrection. And if someone were to respond by saying that the information that there is a prior resurrection of believers is precisely what the Thessalonians did not know, then the apostle could simply have informed them in a few words. But he does not do this at all. He does not speak of a first and second resurrection. He asserts only that the believers who will still be alive at Jesus's coming will have no advantage over those who earlier already died in Christ. We do not know in what respect the Thessalonians thought that the latter would be at a disadvantage by comparison with the former. But it does not matter. The fact is that this is what they thought in Thessalonica. And over against this idea Paul now says that this is not the case. In fact, through Jesus who will raise them from the dead, God will cause the now-dead believers to be immediately with him (with Jesus) in his future, so that he will, as it were, bring them along with him. And the believers who are left and alive will by no means have an advantage over them, inasmuch as the resurrection of the dead comes first and then all believers, both the resurrected and the transformed, will be caught up together in the clouds to meet the Lord. The text, therefore, does not say anything about a first and second resurrection.

If, then, such a twofold resurrection occurs nowhere else in Scripture, we will do well not to find it too quickly in Rev. 20. And in reality it does not occur there either. We only read in verses 4 and 5 that the souls of the believers who remained faithful in the great tribulation live and reign as kings with Christ a thousand years, and that this is the first resurrection. John clearly says that he saw the souls (τας ψυχας, *tas psychas*) of the martyrs (cf. 6:9) and makes no mention of the resurrection of their bodies. He further says that the souls lived and reigned immediately as kings with Christ a thousand years—not that they arose or were resurrected or entered into life. He speaks further of the rest of the dead (οἱ λοιποι των νεκρων, *hoi loipoi tōn nekrōn*) and therefore assumes that the believers whose souls he saw in heaven still in a sense belong to the dead but nevertheless lived and reigned. By contrast he does not say of the rest of the dead, as the Authorized Version [Dutch: *Statenvertaling*] has it, that they did not come to life again, but that they did *not* live (οὐκ ἐζησαν, *ouk ezēsan*). And finally he emphatically adds that this "living" and "ruling" of the souls of the believers who remained faithful, by contrast to the "not-living" of the rest of the dead, is the first resurrection.

One can, as it were, feel the contrast: the first resurrection [of which John speaks] is not the one accepted by some—even in John's time—as though a physical resurrection of believers would precede the thousand-year reign. Rather, the first resurrection consists in the "living" and "reigning" in heaven with Christ of the believers who remained faithful. The believers to whom John is writing and who are soon going to encounter the tribulation must not think that they will only experience salvation at the end of time. No: "Blessed are the dead who die in the Lord *from now on*" (ἀπ' ἀρτι, *ap' arti*; 14:13). They immediately gain rest from their labors. Upon their death they immediately receive a crown. They live and reign in heaven with Christ from the moment after their death, and they can therefore face the coming tribulation with confidence. The crown of life awaits them (2:10). Here, in 20:4–5, John is repeating, in brief, what he wrote earlier to the seven churches. The promises there given to believers if they would persevere to the end all come down to the assertion that he who conquers will be crowned: "To everyone who conquers, I will give permission to eat of the tree of life" (2:7), "I will give some of the hidden manna" (2:17), "I will give authority over the nations" (2:26), "I will also give the morning star" (2:28). "You will be clothed . . . in white robes" (3:5), "I will make you a pillar in the temple of my God" (3:12). You will "eat" the Last Supper "with" Jesus (3:20). In a word: "To the one who conquers I will give a place with me on my throne" (3:21). What John saw earlier in the form of a promise he now sees in the form of fulfillment in chapter 20: those who remain faithful until death immediately live and reign with Christ on his throne in heaven. And *that* is the *first* resurrection.

But John adds a further statement and by it confirms the above interpretation. For he says: "Blessed and holy are those who share in the first resurrection. Over these the second death has no power, but they will be priests of God and of Christ, and reign with him a thousand years" (20:6). According to 20:14, the second death is nothing other than the reality of being thrown into the lake of fire. Whatever may be the lot of the rest of the dead mentioned in verse 5, in any case the believers who have remained faithful, who live and reign with Christ, are secured against the second death. They already have the crown of life and already eat the manna of life and therefore need not fear the judgment to come. "Whoever conquers will not be harmed by the second death" (2:11), which goes into effect at the final judgment. If John had conceived the first resurrection in a chiliastic sense, namely, as a physical resurrection of believers before the thousand-year reign, he would not have had to furnish such consolation to believers. He could have confined himself to saying that they would rise again *before* the thousand-year reign. But no; in a sense the believers continue to belong to the category of the dead up until the final judgment. But this is no hardship: if they have persevered to the end, they will be immediately crowned, and though the *first* death still reigns over their bodies, they cannot be hurt by the *second* death.

[570] Against this interpretation it may be advanced that John nevertheless speaks clearly of a thousand-year reign of believers with Christ, even if it is in heaven, and that he situates it after the return of Christ (19:11–16) and the fall of the world empire and the false prophet (19:20). Still this objection is not as serious as it sounds.

The location of the vision in Rev. 20 following that of chapter 19 has no bearing whatever on the chronological sequence of events. Generally speaking, the art of writing, in distinction, say, from the art of painting, can only narrate consecutively events that are actually simultaneous. Scripture is no exception. It frequently relates successively things that in reality occurred side by side. In the prophets it often happens that they see and describe consecutively things that happen or will happen simultaneously or even in a totally different order. This is especially the case, as it is increasingly being recognized, in the book of Revelation. The letters to the seven churches do not furnish a description of ecclesiastical conditions succeeding each other in that same order. The seven seals, the seven trumpets, and the seven bowls do not constitute a chronological series but run parallel and in each case take us to the end, the final struggle of the anti-Christian power. And so in itself there is no objection to the assumption that what is narrated in Rev. 20 runs parallel to the events of the previous chapters.

It needs to be recognized that in reference to the world empire that he depicts, John is thinking of the Roman Empire. Prophecy in the Old as well as in the New Testament is not concerned with things high in the sky but has a historical basis and views the actual powers in the midst of which it exists as the embodiment of the struggle of world empires against the kingdom of God. The book of Daniel, for example, leads up to Antiochus Epiphanes and regards him as the personification of hostility against God and his people. John similarly derives from the Roman Empire of his day the features he needs for his world empire. Although everything that has been written beforehand has been written for our instruction, the Revelation of John is nevertheless primarily a book of consolation for "the church under the cross" of his own time, to urge it to persevere in the struggle and to encourage it by picturing the crown awaiting it. If John privately believed that in the Roman Empire he was seeing the very last development of world empire, and that Christ would come in just a few years to put an end to it, that would not in any way be unusual or something at variance with the spirit of prophecy. We are not bound by John's personal opinion but by the word of his prophecy. And the prophecy that throws its light on history is in turn interpreted and unveiled by history.

If privately John really believed that in a few years the Roman Empire would be destroyed by the appearing of Christ, it was in any case his opinion that this would not spell the end of world history, for in that case there would be no room for the reign of believers with Christ in heaven alongside it, and this reign could only begin after that time. But this "contemporary-historical" (*zeitgeschichtliche*)[8] view of things, however much truth there is in it, does not completely convey the thought of John's Revelation. For it is clearly evident that in chapter 19 the history of the world has reached its end. Babylon has fallen (ch. 18); God reigns as king (19:6); the marriage of the Lamb has come (19:7–9); Christ has appeared (19:11–16); the last battle of all the kings of the earth and their armies has been fought (19:17–19); the world empire and the false prophet have been destroyed and thrown into the lake of fire, which as the second death is not opened until after the judgment (19:20; cf. 20:14); and the rest were slain (19:21). The nineteenth chapter therefore clearly runs on to the same end of the world as that depicted in 20:10–15. There is no material left for a sequel to world history. The "contemporary-historical" (*zeitgeschichtliche*) exegesis leaves the origin of the nations that appear in 20:3, 8 unexplained or would otherwise come into conflict with 19:17–21. However, just as the letters to the seven churches and similarly the seven seals, trumpets, and bowls first of all relate to conditions and events in John's day but then have further implications for the church of all times and for the history of the world as a whole, so it is true of the world empire depicted in Revelation: It is modeled on the Roman Empire of the first centuries but does not achieve its full realization in that empire. It keeps rising again and again and must always again succumb to the appearance of Christ until it finally exerts its utmost powers, exhausts itself in a final gargantuan struggle, and is then forever annihilated by the coming of Christ.

If this view is correct, the vision of Rev. 20 is not intended to relate to us the things that will occur in chronological order after the events of Rev. 19, but has a place of its own and reports to us things that run parallel with the preceding. The ultimate ending of the history of the world to be narrated, it turns out, is twofold: one is the ending of the historic nations in which Christianity is openly active, and another is the ending of the barbaric nations that—as Rev. 20:8 clearly tells us—are "at the four corners of the earth," and have therefore lived away from the center of history and outside the circle of mankind's culture. The world empire and false prophecy could only arise and function among the former, for anti-Christianity presupposes familiarity with the gospel. The latter only succeed in making a fierce assault on the church of Christ. But it is the same Satan who

---

8. Ed. note: In English-speaking biblical scholarship, this view is usually referred to as "preterist."

works both over there and over here. Over and over, having been forced back and defeated among culture-producing nations, he forges a new instrument for the battle against Christ from among the barbaric peoples. First he is thrown from heaven; then he works on earth and raises up a world empire against Christ; and finally he summons up the barbaric nations from around the world to fight the final battle against Christ. But all this occurs, not in chronological sequence, but in a logical and spiritual sense.

The thousand years, as is generally recognized today, are symbolic. They contrast with the few days during which the believers who remain faithful are oppressed and persecuted here on earth (12:17), but also with the completed glory that is eternal (22:5). They denote the holy, blessed rest of believers who have died and are in heaven with Christ as well as the longing with which they look for the day when their blood will be avenged (6:10), while on earth the struggle of world empire and the international world against Christ continues. And after John in Rev. 20:1–9 has told the history of the barbaric nations up to the very same end with which the history of the culture-producing nations in 19:17–21 concluded as well, he picks up the thread of both visions and relates the ultimate end of world history as a whole. In 19:21 people are slain by the sword of Christ; in 20:9 they are consumed by fire from heaven. But after the world empire, the false prophet, and Satan have been condemned and thrown into the lake of fire (19:20; 20:10), all the dead arise and are judged according to their works (20:11–15).

THE RETURN OF CHRIST

The teaching of Scripture unfolded up to this point makes clear that the course and outcome of world history are very different from the way people usually imagine them. It is most certainly true of the end of things, if anywhere, that God's ways are higher than our ways and his thoughts higher than our thoughts. The kingdom of God, although analogous to a mustard seed and leaven and a seed that sprouts and grows aside from any knowledge and involvement of human beings (Matt. 13:31, 33; Mark 4:27), nevertheless does not reach its completion by way of gradual development or an ethical process. According to the incontrovertible testimony of Scripture, the history of humankind, both in the case of culture-producing and of uncultured nations, rather ends in a general apostasy and an appalling final struggle of a coalition of all satanic forces against God and his kingdom.

But then, in any case, the end is there. The world, in time and with the power given it by God, has done nothing, as in the days of Noah, other than make itself ripe for judgment; at the apex of its power, it suddenly collapses at the appearance of Christ. In the end a catastrophe, a divine act of intervention, terminates the rule of Satan here on earth and brings about the completion of the unshakable kingdom of heaven. Just as in the case of a believer, perfection is not the fruit of a slowly progressing process of sanctification but sets in immediately after death, so also the perfection of humanity and the world comes about, not gradually, but suddenly by the appearance of Christ.

It is specifically Christ who is appointed by the Father to bring about the end of the history of humankind and the world. And he is appointed to this role because he is the Savior, the perfect Savior. The work he completed on earth is only a part of the great work of redemption he has taken upon himself. And the time he spent here is only a small part of the centuries over which he is appointed as Lord and King. Anointed by the Father from all eternity, he began to engage in his prophetic, priestly, and royal activity immediately after sin came into the world. He continued that activity throughout all the revolving centuries since. And one day, at the end of the times, he will complete it. That which he acquired on earth by his suffering and death he applies from heaven by his word and the working of his Spirit; and that which he has thus applied, he maintains and defends against all the assaults of Satan, in order one day, at the end, to present it without spot or wrinkle, in total perfection, to his Father who is in heaven. Accordingly, the return of Christ unto judgment is not an arbitrary addition that can be isolated from his preceding work and viewed by itself. It is a necessary and indispensable component of that work. It brings that work to completion and crowns it. It is the last and highest step in the state of his exaltation.

Because Christ is the savior of the world, he will someday return as its judge. The crisis, or judgment (κρισις, *krisis*), that he precipitated by his first coming he consummates at his second coming. The Father gave him authority to execute judgment (κρισιν ποιειν, *krisin poiein*) because he is the Son of Man (John 5:27). Eschatology, therefore, is rooted in Christology and is itself Christology, the teaching of the final, complete triumph of Christ and his kingdom over all his enemies. In accord with Scripture, we can go back even further. The Son is not only the mediator of reconciliation (*mediator reconciliationis*) on account of sin, but even apart from sin he is the mediator of union (*mediator unionis*) between God and his creation. He is not only the exemplary cause (*causa exemplaris*) but also the final cause (*causa finalis*) of creation. In the Son the world has its foundation and example, and therefore it has in him its goal as well. It is created through him and for him as well (Col. 1:16). Because the creation is *his* work, it cannot and may not remain the booty of Satan. The Son is the head, Lord, and heir of all things. United in the Son, gathered under him as their head, all creatures return to the Father, the fountain of all good. The second coming is therefore required by his first coming. It is implied in the first; in time, by inner necessity, it will proceed from the first; the second coming brings the first coming to its full effect and completion and was therefore comprehended in a single image with the first coming by Old Testament prophecy.

Not only is the second coming ideally and logically linked with the first; there is between them a real bond as well. Just as the Old Testament was a continual coming of God to his people until in Christ he came to live bodily among them, so the dispensation of the New Testament is a continued coming of Christ to his inheritance in order in the end to take possession of it forever. Christ is not only he who was to come in the days of the Old Testament and actually came in the fullness of time. He is also the Coming One (ὁ ἐρχομενος, *ho erchomenos*) and the one who will come (ὁ ἐρχομενος ἥξει, *ho erchomenos hēxei*; Heb. 10:37; cf. Rev. 1:4, 8; etc.). Christ's second coming is the complement of the first.

[571] This ideal and real connection between the first and second comings of Christ also explains the manner in which the New Testament speaks of the time of his parousia. An entire series of texts posits this parousia as being very close at hand. Jesus links the prophecy of the consummation immediately to that concerning the destruction of Jerusalem (Matt. 24:29ff. and parallels). Paul considers it possible that he and his fellow believers will still experience the parousia of Christ (1 Cor. 15:51; 1 Thess. 4:15). And all the apostles assert that they are in the last days, that the future of the Lord is at hand, and derive from this expectation a motive for vigilance (Rom. 13:11; 1 Cor. 10:11; Heb. 3:14; 6:11; 10:25, 37; James 5:7–9; 1 Pet. 1:6, 20; 4:17; 5:10; 1 John 2:18; Rev. 1:3; 3:11, 20; 22:7, 10, 12, 20).

THE TIMING OF CHRIST'S RETURN

Errors have been made in both directions in the interpretation of this New Testament expectation of the early return of Christ. The New Testament absolutely contains no doctrine concerning the time of Christ's return. It by no means establishes as a fact that Christ's return will occur before or immediately after the destruction of Jerusalem. Many interpreters have indeed inferred this from Matt. 10:23; 16:28; 24:34; 26:64 and parallels, but mistakenly so. For it cannot be reasonably doubted that Jesus spoke of his coming in various senses. In John 14:18–24 (cf. 10:16–18) he speaks to his disciples of his coming in the Spirit after Pentecost or, according to other interpreters, of his coming after the resurrection, when he will again appear to his disciples for a little while. In Matt. 26:64, before the [Jewish] council, Jesus not only confirmed his messiahship under oath but also stated that he would convince them of it because they would from that time on (ἀπ' ἀρτι, *ap' arti*) see him sitting at the right hand of God's power and coming on the clouds of heaven.

Elsewhere also there is mention of such a coming in glory. Matthew 16:28 (cf. Mark 9:1; Luke 9:27) leaves no room for doubt about this. Jesus says here that some of his bystanders will not taste death before they see the Son of Man coming in his kingdom. A moment earlier he had admonished his listeners to be concerned above all about the salvation of their souls, underscoring this admonition by saying that the Son of Man would come in the glory of his Father and repay everyone for what they have done. And this coming would not even be very long ahead—he added in verse 28 by way of explanation—for even before all his bystanders had died, the Son of Man would come in his kingdom (ἐν τῃ βασιλειᾳ αὐτου, *en tē basileia autou*), that is, with the royal power and dignity the Father will give him. For by his resurrection and ascension Christ was appointed by the

Father to be head, king, and Lord (Acts 2:33; 5:31); and from that time onward, in the measure in which his kingdom is founded and extended on earth, he is continually coming in his royal dignity. In Mark 9:1 and Luke 9:27 the phrase is therefore explained by saying that many will not taste death before they have seen the kingdom of God, or have seen it come with power. Matthew 10:23 can be explained in the same way: the disciples are told they will not have gone through all the towns of Israel before the Son of Man comes. Although this coming is not in any way explained further, it cannot possibly refer to the parousia because in that case Jesus would be contradicting himself. In any case in Matt. 24 he has his parousia come after the destruction of Jerusalem. Jesus does not say how long after this appalling event his coming will occur. But in his prophecy he does indeed tie it to the fall of Jerusalem. The translation of εὐθεως (eutheōs) in Matt. 24:29 by "suddenly" instead of by "immediately" entails no change in this, for in the words following we are clearly told that the signs of the parousia will come immediately (eutheōs) after the tribulation of those days ("in those days, after that tribulation," Mark 13:24; cf. Luke 21:25–27).[9]

This is confirmed by Matt. 24:34 (cf. Mark 13:30; Luke 21:32), where Jesus says that "this generation will not pass away until all these things take place." The words "this generation" (ἡ γενεα αὑτη, hē genea hautē) cannot be understood to mean the Jewish people, but undoubtedly refer to the generation then living. On the other hand, it is clear that the words "all these things" (παντα ταυτα, panta tauta) do not include the parousia itself but only refer to the signs that precede and announce it. For after predicting the destruction of Jerusalem and the signs and his return and even the gathering of his elect by the angels, and therefore actually ending his eschatological discourse, Jesus proceeds in verse 32 to offer a practical application. Here he states that just as in the case of the fig tree the sprouting of leaves announces the summer, so "all these things" are signs that the end is near or that the Messiah is at the door. Here the expression *panta tauta* clearly refers to the signs of the coming parousia, not to the parousia itself, for else it would make no sense to say that when "these things" occur, the end is "near." In verse 34 the words "all these things" (*panta tauta*) have the same meaning. Jesus therefore does not say that his parousia will still occur within the time of the generation then living. What he says is that the signs and portents of it, as they would be visible in the destruction of Jerusalem and concomitant events, would begin to occur in the time of the generation then living. Of this Jesus is so sure that he says that while heaven and earth will pass away, his words will by no means pass away. For the rest, however, Jesus abstains from all attempts at further specifying the time. His intent is not to inform his disciples of the precise moment of his parousia, but to urge them to be watchful. And for that reason he does not say when he

9. Ed. note: Bavinck is suggesting that *eutheōs* is parallel to "after those days." Therefore, whether it is translated as "suddenly" or "immediately" does not affect the temporal dimension of what Jesus is saying. We do not solve the problem of the text by translating *eutheōs* as "suddenly" instead of "immediately."

will come, but what the signs of the times are that announce his coming. Taking notice of the signs of the times is a duty for Jesus's disciples; the calculation of the precise time of his coming is forbidden to them and also impossible. The former demands that Jesus shed his light on the events that will occur; and so he does, as did all the prophets before him, and as after him all his apostles have done.

For this reason, he also does not say that many centuries will still elapse between the destruction of Jerusalem and his parousia. That would immediately again have rendered powerless the admonition to be watchful. As prophecy has at all times done, so Jesus announces the approach of the end *in* the events of his time. And the apostles follow his example when, in heresy and deception, in ordeals and judgments, in Jerusalem's fall and Rome's empire, they depict for us the early messengers of Christ's return and the initial fulfillment of his prophecy. For all believers ought at all times to live as though the coming of Christ is at the door. "The proximity of the parousia is, so to speak, only another way of expressing its absolute certainty."[10] But for the same reason, the calculation of the precise moment of the parousia is also inappropriate for Christians. After all, Jesus deliberately left this completely uncertain. His coming will be sudden, unexpected, surprising, like that of a thief in the night (Matt. 24:43; Luke 12:39; cf. "like a trap," Luke 21:35).

Many things have to happen before the end comes (Matt. 24:6). The gospel must be preached throughout the whole world (24:14). The bridegroom is delayed, and the master of the servants stayed in a far country for a long time (25:5, 13, 19). Weeds and wheat must grow together until the harvest (13:30). The mustard seed must grow into a tree, and the yeast must leaven the whole batch of dough (13:32–33). In fact, once, when dealing with the topic of the parousia, Jesus expressly stated that the day and the hour of his coming are not known to anyone, neither to angels nor humans, indeed, not even to the Son of Man (Mark 13:32). Even after his resurrection Jesus still testifies that the Father has fixed the times and seasons for the establishment of his kingdom by his own authority (Acts 1:7). All the apostles echo this language. Christ comes like a thief in the night (1 Thess. 5:1–2; 2 Pet. 3:10; Rev. 3:3; 16:15). He will not appear until after antichrist has come (2 Thess. 2:2ff.). The resurrection is scheduled to occur in a fixed sequence, first that of Christ, then that of believers at his coming (1 Cor. 15:23). And that future is delayed inasmuch as the Lord uses another standard for measuring time than we and wishes in his patience that all should come to repentance (2 Pet. 3:8–9).

THE MANNER OF CHRIST'S RETURN

About the *manner* of Jesus's return Holy Scripture speaks as soberly as it does about its timing. In the New Testament, Christ's second coming is frequently

---

10. "Die Nähe der Parusie ist gewissermassen nur ein anderer Ausdruck für die absolute Gewissheit derselben." Baldensperger in H. J. Holtzmann, *Lehrbuch der neutestamentlichen Theologie* (Freiburg i.B. and Leipzig: Mohr, 1897), I, 312.

referred to with the name παρουσια (*parousia*, coming), either absolutely (Matt. 24:3) or further described as "the coming of the Son of Man" or as "the coming of our Lord Jesus Christ" (Matt. 24:27, 37, 39; 1 Thess. 3:13; 4:15; 5:23; etc.) or as "the coming of the day of God" (2 Pet. 3:12). The word *parousia* as such does not really include the idea of return but indicates that Jesus, after having been absent and hidden for a time (Acts 3:21; Col. 3:3–4) and having then come back (Matt. 16:27; 24:30; etc.; cf. Luke 19:12, 15), will again be and remain present. For that reason *parousia* alternates with ἐπιφανεια (*epiphaneia*, manifestation; 1 Tim. 6:14; Titus 2:13), ἀποκαλυψις (*apokalypsis*, revelation [or with the cognate verb]; Luke 17:30; 1 Cor. 1:7; 2 Thess. 1:7; 1 Pet. 1:7, 13), and φανερωσις (*phanerōsis*, appearance [or with the cognate verb]; Col. 3:4; 1 Pet. 5:4; 1 John 2:28); in 2 Thess. 2:8 we even read of "the manifestation of his coming" (ἡ ἐπιφανεια της παρουσιας αὐτου, *hē epiphaneia tēs parousias autou*).

This parousia is a work of God insofar as God will send his Anointed and to that end fixes the times and seasons (Acts 1:7; 3:20–21; 1 Tim. 6:14–16). But it is also an act of Christ himself as Son of Man, to whom the Father has given authority to execute judgment, and who must rule as king until all his enemies have been put under his feet (John 5:17; 1 Cor. 15:25). Since upon his departure from earth he was taken up into heaven, at his parousia he will return from heaven (Phil. 3:20; 1 Thess. 1:10; 2 Thess. 1:7; Rev. 19:11). And as at his ascension a cloud enclosed him and hid him from the eyes of his disciples (Acts 1:9), so, in the language of the Old Testament, he is also described as returning on the clouds of heaven, which like a triumphal chariot will carry him down to earth (Matt. 24:30; 26:64; Mark 13:26; 14:62; Luke 21:27; Rev. 1:7; 14:14). For he does not return in the form of a servant but with great power and with his own and the Father's glory (Matt. 16:27; 24:30; Mark 8:38; 13:26; Luke 21:27; Col. 3:3–4; 2 Thess. 1:9–10; Titus 2:13), as "King of kings and Lord of lords" (Rev. 17:14; 19:11–16), surrounded by his angels (Matt. 16:27; 25:31; Mark 8:38; Luke 9:26; 2 Thess. 1:7; Rev. 19:14), by his saints among whom the blessed in heaven are perhaps included (1 Thess. 3:13; 2 Thess. 1:10; Jude 14). Although on account of its unexpected character, his parousia is comparable with the breaking into a house of a thief in the night, it will nevertheless be visible for all human beings on earth, be like the lightning that flashes from one side of the sky to the other (Matt. 24:27; Luke 17:24; Rev. 1:7), and be announced by the voice of an archangel and the trumpet of angels (Matt. 24:31; 1 Cor. 15:52; 1 Thess. 4:16).

In connection with their doctrine of the ascension, Lutherans said that the return of Christ was not subject to a succession of moments but consisted solely in the sudden return to visibility of the body of Christ, which at his exaltation had once become invisible and ubiquitous. Although they generally recognized that the return of Christ was visible and local, they meant by this only that, by a special disposition of God (*singularis Dei dispositio*) and for the special purpose of judgment, Christ's human nature would become visible for a while at a specific place, without thereby relinquishing its presence elsewhere.[11] But Reformed theologians attributed to Christ's return a physical, local, and temporal character. They even recognized that this return, however sudden, was still subject to a succession of moments (*successiva*). Also at the highest step of his exaltation, at his return for judgment, Christ would maintain his true human nature.[12]

11. J. Gerhard, "De extr. jud.," in *Loci theologici*, ed. E. Preuss, 9 vols. (Berlin: G. Schlawitz, 1862–75), XXVIII, n. 35; J. Quenstedt, *Theologia*, IV, 614; D. Hollaz, *Examen theologicum acroamaticum* (Rostock and Leipzig, 1718), 1249.

12. On the return of Christ, aside from the works cited above, cf. also T. Aquinas, *Summa theol.*, III, qu. 59, art. 2, suppl., qu. 90, arts. 1, 2; J. H. Oswald, *Eschatologie* (Paderborn: F. Schöningh, 1869), 234f.; Jansen, *Praelectiones theologiae dogmaticae*, 3 vols. in 2 (Utrecht: Van Rossum, 1875–79), III, 1038; L. Atzberger, *Die Christliche Eschatologie* (Freiburg i.B.: Herder, 1890), 300f.; H. Simar, *Lehrbuch der Dogmatik*, 2 vols. (Freiburg i.B.: Herder, 1879–80), §166; J. Gerhard, "De extr. jud.," in *Loci theol.*, XVIII, c. 3; J. Quenstedt, *Theologia*, 649; A. Polanus, *Syntagma theologiae christianae* (Hanover: Aubry, 1624), VI, c. 65; G. Voetius, *Select. disp.*, II, 51, v; J. Marckius, *Exspectatio gloriae futurae Jesu Christi*, c. 1–24; C. Vitringa, *Doctrina christianae religionis*, 8 vols. (Arnheim: 1761–86), IV, 160; Th. Kliefoth, *Christliche Eschatologie*, 228f.; F. W. Grosheide, *De verwachting der toekomst van Jezus Christus* (Amsterdam: Bottenburg, 1907).

C. THE CONSUMMATION

17

THE DAY OF THE LORD

*The day of our Lord's return brings about the resurrection of believers, the
judgment of unbelievers, and the renewal of creation. The general resurrection
restores the temporary rupture of body and soul at the time of death and places all
human beings before God's judgment seat. Believers are comforted by [the hope
for] this bodily redemption, which represents Christ's final deliverance from sin
and its consequences and brings them into the full joy of communion with their
Lord. As our Lord's own resurrection shows, the final resurrection maintains
continuity between the earthly body and the glorified resurrection body. Persons
retain their individual identities. Precisely how this happens we do not know
and should not speculate; what is important is the substantial unity as well as
qualitative distinction between what the apostle calls the "natural body" and the
"spiritual body" (1 Cor. 15). Because the resurrection body is re-formed rather
than created wholly anew, burial rather than cremation is the preferred mode
of Christian care of the dead. After the resurrection comes the judgment. While
there is already an immanent judgment upon sin in our world and history,
it is a pantheistic error to reduce world judgment to world history. The final
judgment will be a global and public vindication of the gospel and Christ's rule.
The objections to eternal punishment of the wicked and the various alternatives
to it, such as hypothetical and unconditional universalism as well as conditional
immortality, appeal naturally to human sentiment but finally have no ground
in Scripture. The clear teaching of Scripture, along with firm conviction about
the integrity of God's justice, should be sufficient and deter us from undue
speculation. God will be God and will be glorified.*

[572] The day of the Lord (יוֹם יהוה, *yôm YHWH*) or the day of our Lord
Jesus Christ (ἡ ἡμερα του κυριου ἡμων Ἰησου Χριστου, *hē hēmera tou kyriou hēmōn
Iēsou Christou*; Matt. 24:36ff.; Luke 17:24ff.; 21:34; Acts 17:31; 1 Cor. 1:8; 5:5;
etc.) begins with the appearance of Christ on the clouds. By speaking of a "day"
Scripture does not by any means intend to convey that all the things that fall
under the heading of "the last things"—Christ's return, the resurrection of the

691

dead, the final judgment—will occur in a time frame of twelve or twenty-four hours. In Old Testament times the day of the Lord was the time in which God, in a marvelously glorious way, would come to his people as king to redeem them from all their enemies and to settle them with him in Jerusalem in peace and security. In that event of God's coming began the great turning point in which the old aeon passed into the new, and all conditions and connections in the natural and human world changed totally. In later Jewish thought, the idea was that in the day of the Lord the present world aeon would pass into the future world aeon, which would then frequently be still further differentiated in three generations or in the days of the Messiah—lasting 40 or 100 or 600 or 1,000 or 2,000 or 7,000 years—and the subsequently beginning eternity.[1]

According to the New Testament, the last part of the present aeon (αἰων οὗτος, *aiōn houtos*) began with the first coming of Christ, so that now we live in the last days or the last hour (1 Cor. 10:11; Heb. 1:2; 9:26; 1 John 2:18) and the aeon to come (αἰων μελλων, *aiōn mellōn*) starts with his second coming (Matt. 19:28–29; Mark 10:30; Luke 18:30; 20:35; 1 Cor. 15:23; Heb. 2:5; etc.). And this age to come (*aiōn mellōn*) begins with the day of the Lord (ἡμερα του κυριου, *hēmera tou kyriou*), that is, the time in which Christ appears, raises the dead, executes judgment, and renews the world. In the New Testament this period is never represented as lasting long. Paul says in 1 Cor. 15:52, for example, that the transformation of believers still living and the resurrection of believers who have died will occur in a moment, "in the twinkling of an eye" (cf. 1 Thess. 4:15–17). The resurrection and the last judgment are intimately associated as in a single act (Luke 14:14; 2 Cor. 4:14; Rev. 20:11–13). Judgment is fixed on a day (Matt. 10:15; 11:22; etc.) and even on an hour (Rev. 14:7). But this last term is proof that Scripture is in no way minded to fit all the events associated with Christ's parousia precisely into a time frame of twenty-four hours or sixty minutes: the word "hour" (ὡρα, *hōra*, originally "season") often refers to a much longer period of time than an hour of sixty minutes (Matt. 26:45; John 4:21; 5:25; 16:2, 32; Rom. 13:11; 1 John 2:18). The events that are destined to occur in the parousia of Christ are so comprehensive in scope that they are bound to take considerable time. The inventions of the past century—for the purpose of mutual contact, the exercise of community, hearing and seeing things at a great distance—have shrunk distances to a minimum; and it is likely that they are a mere beginning and prophecy of what will be discovered in the centuries ahead. The doctrine of the last things certainly has to reckon with all these things. Still, such events as the appearance of Christ so that all will see him, the resurrection of all the dead and the transformation of those still living, the rendering of judgment on all people according to their deeds, and the burning and renewal of the world—these are such immense occurrences that they can only take place over a certain period of time.

1. F. W. Weber, *System der altsynagogalen palästinischen Theologie* (Leipzig: Dörffling & Franke, 1880), 354.

THE RESURRECTION OF THE BODY

The first event that follows the appearance of Christ is the resurrection of the dead. This event is not the result of an evolution of bodies in general or of the resurrection body implanted in believers by regeneration and sacrament in particular but the effect of an omnipotent, creative act of God (Matt. 22:29; 1 Cor. 6:14; 15:38; 2 Cor. 1:9). The Father specifically carries out this work by the Son, whom he has "granted . . . to have life in himself" (John 5:26; 6:27, 39, 44; 1 Cor. 6:14; 2 Cor. 4:14; 1 Thess. 4:14). He is the resurrection and the life, the firstborn of the dead (John 11:25; Acts 26:23; 1 Cor. 15:20; Col. 1:18; Rev. 1:5), and must of necessity, therefore, bring about the resurrection of his own (John 6:39–40; 1 Cor. 15:20–23, 47–49). Undoubtedly Scripture teaches a general resurrection, a resurrection not only of believers but also of unbelievers and of all human beings (Dan. 12:2; Matt. 5:29–30; 10:28; John 5:29; Acts 24:15; Rev. 20:12–13), and attributes this resurrection to Christ as well (John 5:29). But it very rarely speaks of this general resurrection, the reason being that it is very differently related to Christ than the resurrection of believers. The resurrection of the dead in general is only obliquely a fruit of the work of Christ. It has become a necessity only because a temporal death has occurred; and this temporal death is separated from eternal death by God's gracious intervention. Originally the punishment of sin was death in its full scope and severity. But because, out of the fallen human race, God chose for himself a community for eternal life, he immediately delayed temporal death already in the case of Adam and Eve, allowed them to reproduce themselves from generation to generation, and only at the end of the ages consigns those who have disobeyed his law and his gospel to eternal perdition. The general resurrection, therefore, serves only to restore in all human beings the temporary rupture of the bond between soul and body—a rupture that occurred only with a view toward grace in Christ—to place them all before the judgment seat of God as *human beings*, in soul and body, and to let them hear the verdict from his mouth. The Father also brings about this general resurrection through Christ, because he gave not only life to the Son but also the authority to execute judgment, and this judgment must strike the whole person, in both soul and body (John 5:27–29).

The resurrection of the dead in general, therefore, is primarily a judicial act of God. But for believers this act is filled with abundant consolation. In Scripture, the resurrection of the believing community is everywhere in the foreground, so much so that sometimes the resurrection of all human beings is even left out of consideration or deliberately omitted (Job 19:25–27; Ps. 73:23–26; Isa. 26:19–20; Ezek. 37; Hos. 6:2; 13:14; Mark 12:25; 2 Cor. 5; Phil. 3:11; 1 Thess. 4:16). This is the real, the true resurrection won directly by Christ, for it is not just a reunion of soul and body, but also an act of vivification, a renewal. It is an event in which believers, united in soul and body, enter into communion with Christ and are being re-created after God's image (Rom. 8:11, 29; Phil. 3:21). For that reason Paul has the resurrection of believers coincide with the transformation of those who are left alive. The latter will have no advantage over the former, for the resurrection will take place prior to the transformation, and together they will go forth to meet the Lord in the air (1 Cor. 15:51–52; 2 Cor. 5:2, 4; 1 Thess. 4:15–17).

In this resurrection the identity of the resurrection body with the body that has died will be preserved. In the case of the resurrections that occur in the Old and New Testaments, the dead body is reanimated. Jesus arose with the same body in which he suffered on the cross and which was laid in the tomb of Joseph of Arimathea. At the time of Jesus's death many bodies of the saints were raised and came forth from their tombs (Matt. 27:52). In the resurrection of the last day, all who are in the tombs will hear Jesus's voice and come forth (John 5:28–29). According to Rev. 20:13, the dead will return to earth from the tombs, from the sea, from the realm of the dead and hades. And Paul teaches that the resurrection body proceeds from the body that has died, just as from the grain that has been sown God raises up new grain (1 Cor. 15:36ff.).

In the Christian religion this identity of the resurrection body with the body that was laid aside at death is of great significance. In this respect it is, in the first place, diametrically opposed to all dualistic theories according to which the body is merely an incidental dwelling place or prison of the soul. The essence of a human being consists above all in the most intimate union of soul and body in a single personality. The soul by nature belongs to the body, and the body by nature belongs to the soul. Although the soul does not itself create the body, it nevertheless has its own body. The continuity of an individual human being is maintained as much in the identity of the body as in the identity of the soul.

In the second place, Christ's redemption is not a second, new creation but a re-creation. Things would have been much simpler if God had destroyed the entire fallen world and replaced it with a completely new one. But it was his good pleasure to raise the fallen world up again and to free from sin the same humanity that sinned. This deliverance consists in the reality that Christ delivers his believing community from all sin and from all the consequences of sin,[2] and therefore causes it to completely triumph over death as well. Death is the last enemy to be annihilated. And the power of Christ is revealed in the fact that he not only gives eternal life to his own but in consequence also raises them on the last day. The rebirth by water and Spirit finds its completion in the rebirth of all things (Matt. 19:28). Spiritual redemption from sin is only fully completed in bodily redemption at the end of time. Christ is a complete Savior: just as he first appeared to establish the kingdom of heaven in the hearts of believers, so he will one day come again to give it visible shape and make his absolute power over sin and death incontrovertibly manifest before all creatures and bring about its acknowledgment. "Corporeality is the end of the ways of God" (Leiblichkeit ist das Ende der Wege Gottes).

---

2. Ed. note: Bavinck is speaking eschatologically here, that is, about the final judgment.

Directly connected with this truth is the care of the dead. Cremation is not to be rejected because it is assumed to limit the omnipotence of God and make the resurrection an impossibility. Nevertheless, it is of pagan origin; it was never a custom in Israel or in Christian nations, and it militates against Christian mores. Burial, on the other hand, is much more nearly in harmony with Scripture, creed, history, and liturgy; with the doctrine of the image of God that is also manifest in the body; with the doctrine of death as a punishment for sin; and with the respect that is due to the dead and the resurrection on the last day. Christians do not, like the Egyptians, artificially preserve corpses; nor do they mechanically destroy them, as many people desire today. But they entrust them to the earth's bosom and let them rest until the day of the resurrection.[3]

The Christian church and Christian theology, accordingly, vigorously maintained the identity of the resurrection body with the body that had died. It frequently swung over to another extreme and not only confessed the resurrection of the *flesh* but even at times taught that in the resurrection the totality of matter (*totalitas materiae*) that once belonged to a body was assembled by God from all corners of the earth and brought back, in the same manner and measure as was once there, to the various parts of the body.[4] But this notion is open to serious objections.

First, it leads to a variety of subtle and curious inquiries that are of no value for the doctrine of the resurrection. The question that is then pursued is whether the hair and the nails, the blood and the gall, the semen and the urine, the intestines and the genitals will all rise again and be composed of the same—in number and kind—atoms of which they were composed in this life. In the case of the physically handicapped, people who lacked one or more parts, and in the case of children who died in infancy and sometimes even before birth, this idea led to no little embarrassment. In all these and similar cases, whether they wanted to or not, people had to resort to the assumption that resurrection bodies would be augmented with components that did not belong to them earlier. Hence the resurrection cannot consist in a return to and the vivification of "the totality of matter."

Second, physiology teaches that the human body, like all organisms, is subject to a constant process of metabolism, so that after a period of seven years not a single particle would still be present of those that made up the substance of the body before that time. The chemicals of which our bodies consist, like oxygen, hydrogen, nitrogen, and so on, are the same as those that are found in other creatures around us, but they constantly change. This change is sufficient proof that the identity of human bodies cannot consist in that they are always

3. A. Kuyper, *Ons program*, 4th rev. ed. (Amsterdam and Pretoria: Höveker & Wormser, 1880), 274–75; K. Sartorius, *Die Leichenverbrennung innerhalb der christlichen Kirche* (Basel: C. Detloff, 1886); P. G. Groenen, *Lijkverbranding* ('s Hertogenbosch: Teulings, 1909).

4. Irenaeus, *Against Heresies* V, 12, 13; Augustine, *Enchiridion* 26; *City of God* XX, 4, 13f.; T. Aquinas, *Summa theol.*, III, qu. 75–86.

composed of the same chemicals in number. It is enough that they consist of the same chemicals in kind.

Third, this is reinforced by the many kinds of metamorphoses that nature exhibits in all its domains. As a result of the impact of air, water, heat, and the like, plants are transformed into peat and coal, carbons into diamond, clay into clay stone, and rock into fertile soil. In the plant and animal world, within the limits of the various species, there is endless variety. And during the time of its existence, every organism undergoes a series of changes. The maggot becomes a fly; every larva passes from an undeveloped into a more developed state; an embryo passes through various stages and then arrives at extrauterine existence; the caterpillar becomes a pupa and then a butterfly, and so on. We do not know what it is that remains the same under all these metamorphoses. Both matter and form change. In the whole organism there seems to be nothing stable. Still the identity is maintained, an identity that is therefore independent of the coarse mass of materials, its transformation, and its quantity.

[573] If we now relate these facts to what Scripture teaches us about the resurrection, we see a chance to maintain the substantial unity as well as the qualitative distinction between the present and the future body. For strictly speaking, Scripture does not teach the resurrection of the *flesh*, but of the *body*. From the resurrections Scripture reports and from the resurrection of Christ, we may indeed—not as far as the form and manner is concerned but as to the essence of it—draw conclusions about the resurrection of the dead in the last days. For in the case of all these resurrections, the body still existed as a whole, and Christ's body had not even been given over to corruption (Acts 2:31). But the bodies of those who rise in the parousia are totally decomposed and scattered in all sorts of ways and have passed into other creatures. In this case we can hardly speak of flesh in a literal sense, for flesh is always animated. That which is no longer alive and animated therefore also ceases to be flesh and returns to dust (Gen. 3:19). Job can indeed say—assuming now that this translation is correct—that from his flesh he will see God (19:26), and after his resurrection Jesus can testify that a spirit has no flesh and bones as he had (Luke 24:39).

However, this is still not sufficient to prove the resurrection of the *flesh* in the strict sense of this word. For though the flesh of which Job's body consisted was indeed the substratum for the resurrection body, it did not for that reason form the substance of it. And Jesus arose with the same body in which he died and which had not even seen corruption, and he remained moreover in a transitional state up until his ascension, so that he could still eat food as well. Paul certainly teaches very clearly that flesh and blood, being perishable, cannot inherit the kingdom of God, which is imperishable (1 Cor. 15:50). Holsten, Holtzmann, and others have altogether mistakenly inferred from this that, according to Paul, the deceased body does not rise at all, and that the actual resurrection occurs already at the time of a person's death. For the apostle expressly attests to his faith in the bodily resurrection and defends it against those in the church of Corinth who denied it, both in the case of Jesus and that of believers. And he is also thoroughly convinced that the very same body that is laid in the grave is raised again in the resurrection. At the same time he asserts that the resurrection is not a rehabilitation but a re-formation.[5] The body rises, not as a body of flesh and blood—weak, perishable, mortal—but as a body that is clothed in imperishability and glory. While the body composed of flesh and blood is the seed from which the resurrection body springs (1 Cor. 15:35–38), there is nevertheless a big difference between the two. Even on earth there is a lot of difference in kinds of "flesh," in the case of organic beings, and in "substance," in the case of inorganic creatures (vv. 39–41). Similarly, there is an important difference between the present body and the future body, as is evident from the contrast between Adam and Christ (vv. 42–49). The first is a natural body (σωμα ψυχικον, *sōma psychikon*) composed of flesh and blood, a body that is subject to change and animated by a soul (ψυχη, *psychē*), but the latter is a spiritual body (σωμα πνευματικον, *sōma pneumatikon*). Though it is a true body, it is no longer controlled by a soul but by the spirit (πνευμα, *pneuma*). It is no longer composed of flesh and blood; it is above the sex life (Matt. 22:30) and the need for food and drink (1 Cor. 6:13). In these respects it is distinguished even from the body that humans possessed before the fall; it is immortal, imperishable, spiritualized, and glorified (1 Cor. 15:42ff.; Phil. 3:21).

Therefore, according to Paul, the identity of the resurrection body with the body entrusted to the earth is independent of body mass and its constant change. All organisms, including human bodies, are composed of the same materials in kind, not in number. And therefore it is absolutely not necessary for the resur-rection body to consist of the same atoms in terms of number as those of which it consisted when it was laid in the grave. But for the resurrection body's identity with the flesh-and-blood body laid in the grave, it *is* required that it have the same organization and shape, the same basic configuration and type, which marked it here as the body of a specific person. In all the metamorphoses to which all crea-tures are subject, their identity and continuity are preserved. While after death the bodies of humans may disintegrate and, in terms of their material mass, pass into all sorts of other organisms, on earth something remains of them that constitutes the substratum of the resurrection body. Just what that is we do not know and will never be able to discover. But the oddness of this fact vanishes the moment we consider that the ultimate components of things are totally unknown to us. Even

5. Ed. note: Bavinck draws a distinction here between *restauratie* (translated "rehabilitation") and *reformatie*. This distinction, for which he more frequently uses the contrast between *restauratie* and *herstel* (re-creation), is used repeatedly by Bavinck to make the important point that the fullness of redemption in Christ is more than a mere repristination of the original created and prefallen status of Adam. Though grace restores rather than abolishes nature, the *status gloriae* is more excellent than the *status integritas*. Cf. H. Bavinck, *Our Reason-able Faith*, trans. H. Zylstra (Grand Rapids: Eerdmans, 1956), 218–20. For a helpful discussion of Bavinck's understanding of grace's relation to nature, see Jan Veenhof, *Revelatie en Inspiratie* (Amsterdam: Buijten & Schipperheijn, 1968), 345–65. This section of Veenhof's work has been translated into English by Albert Wolters and published by the Institute for Christian Studies, Toronto, and reprinted as *Nature and Grace in Herman Bavinck* (Sioux Center, IA: Dordt College Press, 2006).

the most minute atom is still amenable to analysis. Chemical analysis continues endlessly but never reaches the utterly simple. Still, in the case of all organisms and therefore also in the case of the human body, there has to be something that keeps its identity in the ever-ongoing process of metamorphosis. Then what is so absurd about believing that such an "organic mold" or "pattern of individuality" of the body remains even after death to serve as "seed" for the resurrection body? For, according to Scripture, it is a fact that the resurrection body does not, along with the blessed, come down from heaven, nor is it composed of nonmaterial (*geestelijke*) or celestial elements. The resurrection body does not come from heaven but from the earth. It is not a self-generated product of the spirit (*pneuma*) or the soul (*psychē*) but arises from the body that was laid in the grave at death. Accordingly, it is not spiritual in the sense that its substance is spirit (*pneuma*), but it is and remains material. That matter, however, is no longer organized into perishable flesh and blood but into a glorified body.[6]

THE JUDGMENT

[574] After the resurrection comes the judgment, an event pictured in the Old Testament as a victory of the Messiah over all Israel's enemies but described in the New Testament more spiritually as a judicial work of Christ in which he judges and sentences all people in accordance with the law God gave them. The first time, to be sure, Jesus came on earth, not to judge the world, but to save it (John 3:17; 12:47). Still, immediately at his appearance he produced a judgment (κρισις, *krisis*) whose purpose and result is that those who do not see can see, and that those who see may become blind (3:19–20; 9:39). As Son of Man Jesus continually exercises judgment when, to those who believe already, he grants eternal life here on earth and allows the wrath of God to continue to rest on those who do not believe (3:36; 5:32–38). Undoubtedly there is, therefore, an internal spiritual judgment at work, a crisis that is realized from generation to generation. It is an immanent judgment this side of the beyond that takes place in the consciences of human beings. Here on earth faith and unbelief already bear their fruit and bring their

6. Tertullian, *On the Resurrection of the Flesh*; Augustine, *City of God* XXII, ch. 12–20; *Enchiridion* 84–93; P. Lombard, *Sent.*, IV, dist. 43; T. Aquinas, *Summa theol.*, suppl., qu. 82–97; J. H. Oswald, *Eschatologie* (Paderborn: F. Schöningh, 1869), 262f.; J. Gerhard, *Loci theologici*, ed. E. Preuss, 9 vols. (Berlin: G. Schlawitz, 1863–75), XXVI, tract 2; J. Quenstedt, *Theologia*, IV, 576–605; A. Polanus, *Syntagma theologiae christianae* (Hanover: Aubry, 1624), VI, c. 66; *Synopsis purioris theologiae*, disp. 51; P. van Mastricht, *Theoretica-practica theologia* (Utrecht: Appels, 1714), VIII, 4, 6; F. Turretin, *Institutes of Elenctic Theology*, trans. G. M. Giger, ed. J. T. Dennison, 3 vols. (Phillipsburg, NJ: Presbyterian & Reformed, 1992), XX, qu. 1–3; J. Marckius, *Expectatio gloriae futurae Jesu Christi*, II, c. 1–18; C. Vitringa, *Doctrina christiana religionis*, 8 vols. (Leiden: Joannis le Mair, 1761–86), IV, 109–56; Th. Kliefoth, *Christliche Eschatologie* (Leipzig: Dörffling & Franke, 1886), 248f.; F. J. Splittgerber, *Tod, Fortleben und Auferstehung*, 3rd ed. (Halle: Fricke, 1879); F. A. B. Nitzsch, *Lehrbuch der evangelischen Dogmatik*, 3rd ed. prepared by H. Stephan (Tübingen: J. C. B. Mohr, 1912), 614f. (ed. note: Cf. C. E. Nitzsch, *System der christlichen Lehre*, 5th, rev. ed. [Bonn: Adolph Marcus, 1844], 319–40). E. Schaeder, "Auferstehung," in *PRE*[3], I, 219–24.

reward. Just as faith is followed by justification and peace with God, so unbelief leads to a progressive darkening of the mind and hardening of the heart and a yielding to all kinds of unrighteousness. Indeed, even apart from the antithesis between faith and unbelief, virtue and vice each bears its own fruit. Also in the natural life good and evil bring their own reward, not only in the excusing or accusing voice of conscience, but also in the external prosperity or adversity often associated with them. Scripture and history vie with each other in teaching that blessing and curse, compassion and anger, signs of favor and judgment alternate in the lives of people and nations. There is great truth in the poet Schiller's saying that "the history of the world is the judgment of the world" (die Weltgeschichte ist das Weltgericht).

Still, though in part this saying is true, it is also false. In origin it is pantheistic, not theistic, and undermines all judgment instead of confirming and honoring it. For *if* the history of the world is *the* judgment of the world, it totally ceases to be a judgment and becomes a natural process. This natural process is not at all concerned about the awesome contrast between good and evil and forces it back, and that only for a time, into the hidden recesses of the conscience. For then there is no longer a God who can make the natural order subservient to the moral order. All that remains is the power of nature, which controls the entire physical world and soon shrinks to a minimum and eliminates the restricted domain that had initially been reserved for the moral rule of the good. For the good is not a power that can withstand the power of nature if it lacks grounding in an omnipotent God, who is the Creator of both the natural and the moral orders. Against this, indeed, pantheism always objects that, after all, the good should be done for its own sake and not from a hope of reward or fear of punishment.

But the desire of the soul for the triumph of the good, the victory of justice, has nothing at all in common with the self-centered wish for earthly happiness and the satisfaction of the senses. On the contrary, though Scripture takes account of the reality that humans are sensuous beings and holds before their eyes a reward that is "great in heaven" [Matt. 5:12], that reward is always subordinate to the honor of God's name and is secured by Christ along with the good works in which believers walk [Eph. 2:10]. It is precisely the devout who with eager longing await the day in which God will glorify his name before the eyes of all creatures, and in their cause God brings about the triumph of his own over all opposition. And this desire becomes all the stronger as the blood that cries out for vengeance runs over the earth in wider and deeper streams, as injustice triumphs, as wickedness increases, as falsehood flourishes, and as Satan's domain expands and rises up against the realm of righteousness. All of history cries out for world judgment. The whole creation longs for it. All people witness to it. The martyrs in heaven cry out for it with a loud voice. The believing community prays for the coming of Christ. And Christ himself, the Alpha and the Omega, says: "See, I am coming soon; my reward is with me, to repay according to everyone's work" [Rev. 22:12]. So, however firmly Scripture—especially in the Gospel of John—recognizes spiritual judgment that is operative throughout history, it nevertheless speaks of a final judgment as well, the judgment that brings about the triumph of the kingdom of Christ over all unrighteousness. The history of the world may be *a* judgment of the world, but *the* judgment of the world will take place at the end of time, when Christ comes to judge the living and the dead.

In this connection, Scripture repeatedly attributes this judgment to the Father (Matt. 18:35; 2 Thess. 1:5; Heb. 11:6; James 4:12; 1 Pet. 1:17; 2:23; Rev. 20:11–12). Still he accomplishes this work through Christ, to whom all judgment has been given, whom he has appointed as judge (John 5:22, 27; Acts 10:42; 17:31; Rom. 14:9), and who will therefore summon all human beings before his judgment seat and judge them according to what they have done (Matt. 25:32; Rom. 14:9–13 KJV; 2 Cor. 5:10; 2 Tim. 4:1, 8; 1 Pet. 4:5; Rev. 19:11–21). For Christ is the Son of Man who already precipitated a crisis by his appearance, continues it in history, and completes it at the end of time. Their relationship to him decides the eternal weal or woe of human beings. In his judgment of the living and the dead, he celebrates his highest triumph and realizes the consummation of his kingdom and the total subjection of all his enemies. For that reason the main issue in the final judgment is that of faith or unbelief. For faith in Christ is the work of God par excellence (John 6:29; 1 John 3:23). Those who believe do not come into judgment (John 5:24); those who do not believe are already condemned and remain under God's wrath (John 3:18, 36).

Therefore, the standard in the final judgment will in the first place be the gospel (John 12:48); but that gospel is not opposed to, and cannot even be conceived apart from, the law. The requirement to believe, after all, is itself grounded in the law, and the gospel is the restoration and fulfillment of the law. In the final judgment, therefore, all the works performed by people and recorded in the books before God are considered as well (Eccles. 12:14; 2 Cor. 5:10; Eph. 6:8; 1 Pet. 1:17; Rev. 20:12; 22:12). Those works, after all, are expressions and products of the principle of life that lives in the heart (Matt. 7:17; 12:33; Luke 6:44) and encompass everything effected by humans, not in the intermediate state but in their bodies, not the deeds alone (Matt. 25:35ff.; Mark 9:41–42; Luke 6:35; 14:13–14; 1 Cor. 3:8; 1 Thess. 4:6; etc.) but also the words (Matt. 12:36) and the secret purposes of the heart (Rom. 2:16; 1 Cor. 4:5). For nothing remains hidden and everything will be revealed (Matt. 6:4, 6, 18; 10:26; Eph. 5:11–14; 1 Tim. 5:24–25). In the final judgment, therefore, the norm will be the entire Word of God in both its parts: law and gospel.

But in connection with this, Scripture nevertheless clearly states that consideration will be given to the measure of revelation that any given person has received. Those who knew the will of the Lord and did not do it will be given "a more severe beating" (Luke 12:47). It will be more tolerable for Tyre and Sidon in the day of judgment than for Jerusalem and Capernaum (Matt. 10:15; 11:22, 24; Mark 6:11; Luke 10:12, 14; Heb. 2:3). Those who did not hear the gospel are not judged by it but by the law. The Gentiles who did not know the Mosaic law but sinned against the law known to them by nature perish apart from the Mosaic law, whereas Jews are judged above all by this law (Rom. 2:12). Although Scripture views the judgment as extending to all humans without exception (Matt. 25:32; Acts 17:31; Rom. 2:6; 14:10; 2 Cor. 5:10; 2 Tim. 4:1; Rev. 20:12), it nevertheless makes a distinction between the nations that knew the gospel and finally produced anti-Christianity, and the other nations that never heard of Christ and therefore first learn of him at his parousia. It further speaks in particular of the judgment of evil angels, and of the role the good angels and believers play in the final judgment.

It is not at all easy to gain a clear picture of that judgment. There is certainly not exclusively an internal and spiritual event occurring solely in the human conscience. It is definitely a judgment that is realized externally as well and is visible to all creatures. However much the image and the reality may be intertwined, the appearance of Christ, the resurrection, and everything associated with the judgment are drawn too realistically to give us the freedom to spiritualize everything. That being the case, the execution of this judgment also requires a place and a space of time, for Scripture prompts us to think of it as occurring successively. The angels accompany Christ at his coming on the clouds, to be of service to him in the execution of the sentence. They gather the righteous, separate the evil from the righteous, and drive them away (Matt. 13:30, 49; 24:31). He is surrounded, moreover, by the blessed (1 Thess. 3:13; 4:16; 2 Thess. 1:6–10; Jude 14; Rev. 17:14; 19:14). Following the resurrection of the believers who died and the transformation of those who remain alive, they are together caught up in the clouds to meet the Lord in the air (1 Thess. 4:17). Just as Christ's resurrection and ascension were disjoined and even separated by a period of forty days, so it is not impossible that the resurrection and transformation of believers at the end of time will not yet, at one stroke, confer on them the full glory that they will receive after the renewal of the world in a new heaven and a new earth. However this be, the resurrection and transformation of believers includes, as it did for Christ, their justification.

Scripture does indeed say that all humans without distinction, hence also believers, must appear before the judgment seat of Christ. But it also attests that those who believe in him are not condemned and do not come into judgment, for they already have eternal life (John 3:18; 5:24); that the believers who have died are already with Christ in heaven and clothed in long white garments (2 Cor. 5:8; Phil. 1:23; Rev. 6:11; 7:9, 14); and that Christ is coming to be glorified in his saints and to be marveled at among all who believe (2 Thess. 1:10). Before pronouncing his verdict on the evil angels, on the anti-Christian world, and on barbaric peoples, Christ has already positioned the sheep at his right hand and is surrounded by his angels and his saints. This is also evident from 1 Cor. 6:2–3, where Paul expressly states that the saints will judge the world and the angels. This statement may not be watered down into an act of endorsement by believers of the judgment Christ pronounces over the world and the angels, but as the context shows, specifically indicates that the saints will participate in [Christ's] judgment of the world and the angels. For that matter, Jesus already promised his twelve disciples that they would sit with him on twelve thrones, judging the twelve tribes of Israel (Matt. 19:28; Luke 22:30). And around the throne of God, John saw thrones in heaven, on which were seated the elders of the church (Rev. 4:4; 11:16; 20:4, 6). For Christ and his church are one: that in which the world and the angels have wronged the believing community is counted as having been done against him (Matt. 25:40, 45; Mark 9:41–42). This judgment of Christ and his church is even extended to the good angels (1 Cor. 6:3), for the angels are ministering spirits sent forth to serve, for the sake of those who are to obtain salvation (Heb. 1:14). The angels will, therefore, receive a place in the future kingdom of God in accordance with the service they have rendered in relation to Christ and his church. Accordingly, in John's vision Christ, surrounded by his armies, goes out to meet the anti-Christian forces (Rev. 19:11–21). The church triumphant takes part in the royal reign of Christ (20:4–6). And Christ finally annihilates all opposition when he judges the nations who are at the four corners of the earth (20:7–10).[7]

THE PLACE OF PUNISHMENT

[575] In the New Testament the place to which the wicked are consigned is called Gehenna. The Hebrew גֵּי הִנֹּם (gê hinnōm) was originally the name for the valley of Hinnom, which was located southwest of Jerusalem and, according to Josh. 15:8 and 18:16, served as the boundary line between two tribes. Under Ahaz and Manasseh this valley became a site for the worship of Molech, in whose honor children were slain and burned (2 Kings 16:3; 21:6; 2 Chron. 28:3; 33:6; Jer. 32:34–35). Under Josiah this place was destroyed, therefore, and declared unclean by the priests (2 Kings 23:10). Jeremiah prophesied that here a terrible bloodbath would be inflicted on the Israelites, and the Topheth valley would be called the Valley of Slaughter (Jer. 7:32; 19:6). And the pseudepigraphic book of *1 Enoch* predicted that in this valley the wicked would be gathered up for judgment. For this reason the name "Gehinnom" was later transferred to the place of punishment for the wicked after death. According to others, however, the transfer had another reason. According to later Jews, after the valley of Hinnom had been destroyed by Josiah, it was used for dumping and burning all kinds of trash. Just as Gan [Hebrew for "garden"] Eden referred to the place where the righteous lived

7. On the final judgment, cf. P. Lombard, *Sent.*, IV, dist. 43f.; T. Aquinas, *Summa theol.*, suppl., qu. 88–90; J. H. Oswald, *Eschatologie*, 334f.; L. Atzberger, *Die christliche Eschatologie* (Freiburg i.B.: Herder, 1890), 356–70; J. Gerhard, *Loci. theol.*, XXVIII; J. Quenstedt, *Theologia*, IV, 605–34; A. Polanus, *Synt. theol.*, VI, c. 69; *Synopsis purioris theologiae*, disp. 51; P. van Mastricht, *Theologia*, VIII, 4, 7; F. Turretin, *Institutes of Elenctic Theology*, XX, qu. 6; J. Marckius, *Exspectatio*, III, c. 1–18; B. de Moor, *Commentarius . . . theologiae*, 6 vols. (Leiden: Hasebroek, 1761–71), VI, 706–18; Th. Kliefoth, *Christliche Eschatologie*, 236f., 275f.; B. Benzinger, "Gericht, göttliches," in *PRE*[3], VI, 568–85.

after death, Gehinnom became the name of the place to which the unclean and the ungodly were consigned to suffer punishment in the everlasting fire.

Fire, for that matter, was from ancient times the revelation and symbol of the anger and wrath of the Lord. Israel's God is a consuming fire, an eternal flame (Deut. 4:24; 9:3; Isa. 33:14). He spoke to the children of Israel from the midst of the fire (Deut. 4:12, 33; 5:4, 22–26; 9:10; 10:4; cf. Exod. 3:2, 4). His wrath is a red-hot fire flaming forth from his nostrils (Pss. 18:8; 79:5; 89:46; Jer. 4:4). Fire coming forth from the presence of the Lord consumes the offering (Lev. 9:24). By fire he destroyed Nadab and Abihu (10:2), complainers from among his people (Num. 11:1; Ps. 106:18), the descendants of Korah (Num. 16:35), and the regiments of fifty sent out against Elijah (2 Kings 1:10ff.). And one day he will come in a blaze of fire to do justice on earth and to punish the wicked (Deut. 32:22; Pss. 11:6; 83:14–15; 97:3; 140:10; Isa. 30:33; 31:9; 66:15–16, 24; Jer. 4:4; 15:14; 17:4; Joel 2:30; Amos 1:4ff.)—a fire burning to the depths of Sheol (Deut. 32:22), a fire that will never be quenched (Isa. 66:24) and that burns forever (Jer. 17:4).

This representation [of judgment] then passed into the New Testament. Gehenna, the place of punishment after the day of judgment, is distinct from hades (ἄδης, *hadēs*), the underworld (φυλακη, *phylakē*), and the pit (ἀβυσσος, *abyssos*) but identical with the furnace of fire (καμινος του πυρος, *kaminos tou pyros*; Matt. 13:42, 50) and the lake of fire (λιμνη του πυρος, *limnē tou pyros*; Rev. 19:20; 20:10, 14–15; 21:8). It is a place destined for the beast from the pit and for the false prophet (19:20), for Satan and his angels (20:10), for Death and Hades (20:14), and for all the wicked (20:15; 21:8). And these are all hurled into it *after* the resurrection (Matt. 5:29–30; 10:28), and *after* the final judgment (Rev. 19:20; 20:10, 14–15; 21:8). Before that time hades, the prison house (φυλακη, *phylakē*; 1 Pet. 3:19; Rev. 20:7), or the pit (ἀβυσσος, *abyssos*) were their abode, and the punishment of everlasting fire or the dimness of the outer darkness was still reserved for them (Matt. 8:29–32; 25:41, 46; 2 Pet. 2:17; Jude 13). Burning in that Gehenna is everlasting, unquenchable *fire* (Matt. 18:8; Mark 9:43–44, 48). This is where the *worm* that does not die keeps gnawing (Mark 9:44, 46, 48 KJV) and the *torment* never ends (Matt. 25:46; 2 Thess. 1:9; Rev. 14:11). It is a Gehenna or *furnace of fire* (Matt. 5:22; 13:42, 50; 18:9) and at the same time a place of extreme, outer *darkness* (Matt. 8:12; 22:13; 25:30; 2 Pet. 2:17; Jude 13; cf. Deut. 5:22; Ps. 97:2–3). It is located "outside" (Rev. 22:15), in the *depths*, so that one is thrown down into it (Matt. 5:29–30; Rev. 19:20; 20:10, 14–15).

This place is far from the marriage table of the Lamb (Matt. 8:11–12; 22:13), far from fellowship with God and with Christ (7:23; 25:41; Luke 13:27–28; 2 Thess. 1:9); it is rather in the company of Satan and his angels (Matt. 25:41; Rev. 20:10, 15). The *wrath of God* in all its terror is manifested there (Rom. 2:5–8; 9:22; 1 Thess. 1:10; Heb. 10:31; Rev. 6:16–17). Consequently, Gehenna is not only a place of privation but also of sorrow and pain, in both soul and body; a place of *punishment* (κολασις, *kolasis*; Matt. 25:46; Rev. 14:10–11), of *weeping* (κλαυθμος, *klauthmos*) and *gnashing of teeth* (βρυγμος των ὀδοντων, *brygmos tōn odontōn*; Matt. 8:12; 13:42; etc.), of *anguish* and *distress* (θλιψις, *thlipsis*; and στενοχωρια, *stenochōria*; Rom. 2:9; 2 Thess. 1:6), of *destruction* (ἀπωλεια, *apōleia*; Matt. 7:13; Rom. 9:22; Phil. 1:28; 3:19; 2 Pet. 3:7; Rev. 17:8, 11), of *corruption* (φθορα, *phthora*; Gal. 6:8), and of *ruin* (ὀλεθρος, *olethros*; 1 Thess. 5:3; 2 Thess. 1:9; 1 Tim. 6:9). Gehenna is the realm of the second death (Rev. 2:11; 20:6, 14–15; 21:8).

On this firm scriptural basis, the Christian church built a doctrine of the eternity of hellish punishment. Accordingly, in theology as well as in the pulpit, in poetry as well as in the graphic arts, people frequently vied with each other in offering graphic descriptions and realistic portrayals of the pains experienced in the eternal fire in both soul and body.

Alternatives to Eternal Punishment

Nevertheless, from time to time objections were raised against this doctrine. After the Enlightenment of the eighteenth century introduced a milder assessment of sin and crime, abolished instruments of torture, moderated punishments, and aroused a sense of humaneness everywhere, there also arose a very different view of the punishments of hell. Many people either altered their idea of them or rejected them altogether. The grounds on which people argue against the eternity of hellish punishment always remain the same:

    a. Eternal punishment is incompatible with the goodness, love, and compassion of God and makes him a tyrant who takes pleasure in inflicting pain and torment and who prepares praise for himself out of the everlasting moans of millions of unfortunate creatures.

    b. Eternal punishment is incompatible with the justice of God, since it is unrelated and in no way proportionate to the sin in question, which however appalling, is nevertheless limited and finite in character. It is inconceivable that God, who is perfect love and supreme justice, will punish human beings, even if they have sinned a thousand years, with everlasting torment.

    c. Such eternal punishment is also unimaginable and inconceivable. Scripture speaks of fire, a worm, and darkness, but these are all images. Taken literally, they are mutually exclusive. But aside from this, what is the value of an eternal punishment that has no purpose other than to torment the sinner for ever and ever? What is its utility for those who suffer it, since in the nature of the case it excludes the possibility of true repentance and only impels them to keep sinning? What glory does it bring to God's name if it does not overcome and destroy sin but only perpetuates it forever? And how is it possible that the unredeemed continually harden themselves under the burden of such an eternal punishment without ever coming to repentance and self-humiliation before God?

    d. Scripture, accordingly, does not teach an eternal and endless punishment in hell. It does indeed speak of eternal pain and the like, but here as elsewhere the word "eternal" does not mean "endless" but refers to a period of time the limit of which eludes our perception or calculation: a thing is eternal (αἰωνιος, *aiōnios*) if it exceeds a longer or shorter age (αἰων, *aiōn*). This is even reinforced by the fact that "eternal" (αἰωνιος, *aiōnios*), used in the positive sense of the benefits of salvation, say, of life, especially denotes an inner quality by which all these saving benefits are represented as being nonperishable. By contrast, the condition of the lost is described in terms of "destruction" (ἀπωλεια, *apōleia*), "corruption" (φθορα, *phthora*), "ruin" (ὀλεθρος, *olethros*), and "death" (θανατος, *thanatos*), which suggests that in this condition they cannot continue to exist forever but will either be utterly annihilated or at some point totally restored.

    e. For the latter [hint of restoration], Scripture offers hope when it teaches that Christ is the propitiation for the sins of the whole world (Col. 1:19–20; 1 John 2:2), and that God desires all humans to be saved that way (1 Tim. 2:4; 4:10). "For as all die in Adam, so all will be made alive in Christ" (Rom. 5:18; 1 Cor. 15:22). Now God gathers up all things under Christ as head (Eph. 1:10), so that someday every knee will bow before Christ (Phil. 2:10) and God may be all in all (1 Cor. 15:28). "God has imprisoned all in disobedience so that he may be merciful to all" (Rom. 11:32).

If for now we ignore pantheism and materialism, which deny all immortality and eternity, then on the basis of the above considerations, the following three hypotheses can be constructed with regard to the final end of the ungodly.

In the first place there are those who teach that a possibility of repentance remains open, not only in the intermediate state right up until the final judgment,[8] but also thereafter and for all eternity. Whether there is a hell and eternal punishment, therefore, depends totally on the persons involved and their free will. If they persist in opposing the call to conversion, they will dig themselves ever deeper and more firmly into sin and prolong their punishment. However, since the preaching of faith and repentance never stops and the human will continues to be free, an eternal punishment in hell becomes extremely improbable and people rather flatter themselves with the hope that in the end all will repent and enter into eternal life. Hence in Scripture eternal pain only means that those who wait so long before repenting always retain the memory of their stubborn recalcitrance and will eternally rank behind those who believed the gospel in this life. What this hypothetical universalism comes down to, therefore, is a theory of ongoing purgation and a renewal of the doctrine of the migration of the soul. In the main, the difference between them is only that metempsychosis has this purgation occur in the present world (*Diesseits*) whereas hypothetical universal-

8. Cf. above, 629–32 (#559).

ism situates it in the next (*Jenseits*). This doctrine found acceptance especially among eighteenth-century rationalists, but many contemporary theologians defend it as well.[9]

This sentiment of an ongoing repentance and purgation naturally leads to the theory of the so-called universalists, who think that in the end all creatures will participate in eternal salvation and glory. That which is desired and hoped for in the former is expected as certain and proclaimed as dogma by the latter. The doctrine of the return of all things into God already occurs in Indian and Greek philosophy; from there it passed into Gnosticism and Neoplatonism and was for the first time represented in Christian theology by Origen. While Origen indeed repeatedly mentions an eternal punishment in hell, he regards it only as a practical doctrine necessary for the ignorant but viewed very differently by the "knowers" (Gnostics). For, according to Origen, all spirits were originally created alike by God, but the acts of the free will produce unlikeness and bring about the transfer of human souls to a material world for the purpose of purgation and union with bodies. This process of purgation also continues after death and the final judgment until, from and through the greatest possible diversity, this likeness again emerges and all spirits return to God in the same condition in which they were originally with him. However, because the free will ever remains the same, it can equally well return from the evil to the good as from the good to the evil, and so there is a continual alternation between apostasy and the restoration of all things, an endless creation and annihilation of

---

9. J. Wegscheider, *Institutiones theologiae christianae dogmaticae*, 3rd ed. (Halle: Gebauer, 1819), §200; K. G. Bretschneider, *Handbuch der Dogmatik der evangelisch-lutherischen Kirche*, 4th ed., 2 vols. (Leipzig: J. A. Barth, 1838), II, 468f., 581f.; F. V. Reinhard, *Grundriss der Dogmatik* (Munich: Seidel, 1802), 706f.; J. P. Lange, *Positive Dogmatik* (Heidelberg: K. Winter, 1851), §131; I. A. Dorner, *A System of Christian Doctrine*, trans. A. Cave and J. S. Banks, 4 vols. (Edinburgh: T&T Clark, 1882), IV, 415–34; F. A. B. Nitzsch, *Lehrbuch der evangelischen Dogmatik*, 624 (ed. note: Cf. C. E. Nitzsch, *System der christlichen Lehre*, 319–40); W. Schmidt, *Christliche Dogmatik* (Bonn: E. Weber, 1895–98), II, 517; H. Bavinck, *De theologie van Daniel Chantepie de la Saussaye* (Leiden: Donner, 1884), 71–75; H. Ernst, "Twee pendant-leerstukken," *Geloof en Vrijheid* 20 (1886): 407–44; J. A. Cramer, "Het evangelie en de eeuwige straf," *Theologische Studiën* 20 (1902): 241–66. Cf. in England the advocates of the so-called future (or second) probation or of the wider hope, such as Robertson and F. D. Maurice ("The Word 'Eternal' and the Punishment of the Wicked," in *Theological Essays* [1853; repr., London: James Clarke, 1957], 302–25); T. de Quincey, "On the Supposed Scriptural Expression for Eternity," in *Theological Essays and Other Papers* (Boston: Ticknor, Reed, & Fields, 1854), 74–84; A. Tennyson, *In Memoriam: An Authoritative Text, Backgrounds and Sources, Criticism*, ed. Robert H. Ross (New York: Norton, 1973); F. W. Farrar, *Eternal Hope* (London: Macmillan, 1883); and idem, *Mercy and Judgment* (New York: E. P. Dutton, 1881); along with the literature produced in response to these two works: F. W. Farrar, J. Hogg, and T. de Quincey, *The Wider Hope: Essays and Strictures of the Doctrine and Literature of Future Punishment by Numerous Writers, Lay and Clerical* (London: Unwin, 1890). For America, we need to mention the defenders of the Andover position adopted by five professors of Andover College: Churchill, Harris, Hincks, Tucker, and Smyth, who deviated from several articles of the creed, also that concerning eternal punishment; cf. *Andover Review* (April 1890): 434–42. We may also add here the opinion of those who find the scriptural data too uncertain to warrant a firm conclusion and therefore abstain from making clear pronouncements in one direction or another: James Orr, *The Christian View of God and the World*, 7th ed. (New York: Charles Scribner's Sons, 1904), 397; K. Girgensohn, *Zwölf Reden über die christliche Religion*, 4th ed. (Munich: C. H. Beck, 1921), 319–37.

the material world.[10] In antiquity this notion of the restoration of all things found acceptance with Gregory of Nazianzus, Gregory of Nyssa, Didymus, Diodorus of Tarsus, Theodore of Mopsuestia, and others.[11] In the Middle Ages, Scotus Erigena, Amalric of Bena, and the Brothers and Sisters of the Free Spirit adhered to it. After the Reformation, it was held by Denck and numerous Anabaptists, Jane Leade, J. W. Petersen, Ludwig Gerhard, F. C. Oetinger, Michael Hahn, Jung-Stilling, Swedenborg, and so on; and in modern times by Schleiermacher and many others.[12]

A much better reception, however, was accorded a third opinion known as conditional immortality. Although an earlier theology very frequently spoke of immortality in a spiritual sense as a gift secured by Christ, still hardly a soul thought of denying the natural immortality of the soul. The Socinians, under the influence of their abstract supernaturalism, were the first to teach that souls were not by nature immortal but only became immortal by a gift of God in the case of obedience. From this it followed that, by virtue of a natural perishability, the wicked and the demons must one day cease to exist. Although Socinus did not yet say this clearly, his followers taught in plain terms that the second death consisted in annihilation. And according to Crell, Schmalz, and others, this event took place not at or shortly after death but only after the general resurrection and the judgment of the world.[13] This doctrine was taken over from the Socinians by Locke, Warburton, Whiston, Dodwell, Walter, and others, and in the nineteenth century by Rothe and Weisse.[14] It began to catch on and to gain adherents, however, particularly after it was advocated by Edward White in his *Life in Christ*.[15] This book produced numerous reactions, evoking not only serious dissent but also broad endorsement. Today conditionalism has a great many defenders in all countries.[16]

10. L. Atzberger, *Geschichte der christlichen Eschatologie* (Freiburg i.B. and St. Louis: Herder, 1896), 366–456.

11. D. Petavius (Petau), "De angelis," *Op. theol.*, III, 7–8.

12. Friedrich Schleiermacher, *The Christian Faith*, ed. H. R. MacIntosh and J. S. Stewart (Edinburgh: T&T Clark, 1928), §117–20, 163, 720–22, appendix on eternal damnation; A. Schweizer, *Die Glaubenslehre der evangelisch-reformirten Kirche*, 2 vols. (Zurich: Orell, Füssli, 1844–47), II, 577f., 591, 604; L. Schöberlein, *Prinzip und System der Dogmatik* (Heidelberg: C. Winter, 1881), 679; O. Riemann, *Die Lehre von den Apokatastasis*, 2nd ed. (Magdeburg: Frölich, 1897); O. Schrader, *Die Lehre von der Apokatastasis* (Berlin: R. Boll, 1901); W. Hastie, *The Theology of the Reformed Churches in Its Fundamental Principles* (Edinburgh: T&T Clark, 1904), 277ff.; J. H. Scholten, *Dogmaticae christianae initia*, 2nd ed., 2 vols. (London: P. Engels, 1856–58), 268f.; W. Francken, "Henricus Brouwer," *Geloof en Vrijheid* 20 (1886); J. C. Eykman, "Algemeene of conditioneele onsterfelijkheid," *Theologische Studiën* 26 (1909): 359–80. Cf. J. Köstlin, "Apokatastasis," in *PRE*³, I, 616–22.

13. O. Fock, *Der Socinianismus* (Kiel: C. Schröder, 1847), 714f.

14. R. Rothe, *Theologische Ethik*, 2nd ed. (Wittenberg: Zimmermann, 1867–71), §470–72; Chr. Weisse, "Über die philosophische Bedeutung der christliche Lehre von den letzten Dinge," *Theologische Studien und Kritiken* 9/2 (1836): 271–340; idem, *Philosophische Dogmatik oder Philosophie des Christentums*, 3 vols. (Leipzig: Hirzel, 1855–62), §970.

15. E. White, *Life in Christ: A Study of the Scripture Doctrine on the Nature of Man, the Object of the Divine Incarnation and the Conditions of Human Immortality*, 3rd, rev. and enlarged ed. (London: Elliot Stock, 1878).

16. See, e.g., C. A. Row, *Future Retribution* (New York: Whittaker, 1887); G. G. Stokes, *Conditional Immortality* (London: James Nisbet, 1897); S. D. McConnell, *The Evolution of Immortality* (New York and

THE ANSWER OF SCRIPTURE

[576] If human sentiment had the final say about the doctrine of eternal punishment, it would certainly be hard to maintain and even today find few defenders. First, it needs to be gratefully acknowledged that since the eighteenth century the idea of humaneness and the sense of human sympathy have had a powerful awakening and have put an end to the cruelty that used to prevail, especially in the field of criminal justice. No one, however, can be blind to the reality that this humanitarian viewpoint also brings its own imbalances and dangers. The mighty turnabout that has occurred can be described in a single sentence: whereas before the mentally ill were treated as criminals, now criminals are regarded as mentally ill. Before that time every abnormality was viewed in terms of sin and guilt; now all ideas of guilt, crime, responsibility, culpability, and the like are robbed of their reality.[17] The sense of right and justice, of the violation of law and of guilt, are seriously weakened to the extent that the norm of all these things is not found in God but shifted to the opinions of human beings and society. In the process all certainty and safety is gradually lost. For when the interest of society becomes the deciding factor, not only is every boundary between good and evil wiped out, but also justice runs the danger of being sacrificed to power. "It is better for you to have one man die for the people than to have the whole nation destroyed" (John 11:50) then becomes the language of the administration of justice. And the same human sentiment that first pleaded for the humane treatment of a criminal does not shrink, a moment later, from demanding death by torture of the innocent. Hosannas make way for a cross. The voice of the people (*vox populi*), which is often wrongly revered as the voice of God (*vox Dei*), recoils from no horrors whatever. And whereas the righteous person still takes account of the needs of his animals, even the soft interior of the wicked, their hearts and minds, is still cruel (Prov. 12:10). Human feeling is no foundation for anything important, therefore, and neither may nor can it be decisive in the determination of law and justice. All appearances notwithstanding, it is infinitely better to fall into the hands of the Lord than into human hands (1 Chron. 21:13). The same applies with respect to eternal punishment in hell.

London: Macmillan, 1901); H. Schultz, *Voraussetzungen der christliche Lehre von der Unsterblichkeit* (Göttingen: Vandenhoeck & Ruprecht, 1861); H. Plitt, *Evangelische Glaubenslehre*, 2 vols. (Gotha: Perthes, 1863–64), II, 413; L. Lemme, *Endlosigkeit der Verdammnis und allgemeine Wiederbringung* (Berlin: Runge, 1898); P. Paulsen, *Das Leben nach dem Tode*, 2nd ed. (Stuttgart: Chr. Belser, 1905); G. Wobbermin, *Theologie und Metaphysik, das Verhältnis der Theologie zur moderne Erkenntnistheorie und Psychologie* (Berlin: A. Duncker, 1901), 159, 201, 205; E. White, *L'immortalité conditionelle ou la vie en Christ*, French version of *Life of Christ* (1878), trans. Charles Byse (Paris: G. Fischbacher, 1880); E. Pétavel-Olliff, *Le problème de l'immortalité* (Paris: Fischbacher, 1891); A. Decoppet, *Les grands problèmes de l'au-delà*, 8th ed. (Paris: Fischbacher, 1906); P. Vallotton, *La vie après la mort* (Laussane: F. Rouge, 1906); P. Stapfer, *Questions esthétiques et religieuses* (Paris: F. Alcan, 1906), 178, 205; A. J. Th. Jonker, "De leer der conditioneele onsterfelijkheid," *Theologische Studiën* 1 (1883): 1–20, 155ff., 548ff.; 2 (1884): 1855ff.; *M. v. E., "De conditioneele onsterfelijkheid," *Stemmen voor Waarheid en Vrede* 44 (July 1907); *G. Posthumus Meyjes, *Lecture before Excelsior*, March 9, 1911.

17. See H. Bavinck, *Reformed Dogmatics*, III, 163–64 (#336).

It must be noted that this doctrine, though it is often depicted in too much realistic detail in the church and in theology, is nevertheless grounded in Scripture. And no one in Scripture speaks of it more often and at greater length than our Lord Jesus Christ, whose depth of human feeling and compassion no one can deny and who was the meekest and most humble of human beings. It is the greatest love that threatens the most severe punishments. Over against the blessedness of eternal life that he acquired for his own stands the disaster of eternal ruin that he announces to the wicked. In the Old Testament both were veiled in shadows and presented in imagery. But in the New Testament it is Christ who opens a vista both into the depths of outer darkness and into the dwellings of eternal light.

That the punishment in this place of outer darkness is eternal is not something one can doubt on the basis of Scripture. It is indeed true that the adjective αἰώνιος, *aiōnios* (from αἰών, *aiōn*; Heb. עוֹלָם, *'ōlām*, that is, duration of time; the course of a life; the length of a human life; a long, indefinite period of time in the past or future; the present world age, αἰὼν οὗτος, *aiōn houtos*; the age to come, αἰὼν μέλλων, *aiōn mellōn*), very often refers to a period of time that is beyond human calculation but certainly not endless or everlasting. In the New Testament it is also used frequently to describe the entire world dispensation that passed until the appearance of Christ, the period in which the counsel of God was announced by the prophets but not fully revealed (Luke 1:70; Acts 3:21; Rom. 16:25; Col. 1:26; 2 Tim. 1:9; Titus 1:2). But in the New Testament the word αἰώνιος (*aiōnios*) functions especially to describe the imperishable nature—a nature not subject to any corruption or decay—of the salvific benefits gained by Christ, and is very often linked with the word "life" (ζωη, *zōē*)—the eternal life that Christ imparts to everyone who believes. It has its beginning here on earth but will only be fully revealed in the future. It essentially belongs to the age to come (αἰὼν μέλλων, *aiōn mellōn*; Luke 18:30), is indestructible (John 11:25–26), and is called "eternal," like the building from God (οἰκοδομη ἐκ θεου, *oikodomē ek theou*; 2 Cor. 5:1), salvation (σωτηρια, *sōtēria*; Heb. 5:9), redemption (λυτρωσις, *lytrōsis*; 9:12), the inheritance (κληρονομια, *klēronomia*; 9:15), the glory (δοξα, *doxa*; 2 Tim. 2:10), and the kingdom (βασιλεια, *basileia*; 2 Pet. 1:11), just as God, Christ, and the Holy Spirit are also called "eternal" (Rom. 16:26; Heb. 9:14; 13:8; etc.). Over against this it is stated that the punishment of the wicked will consist in eternal fire (το πυρ το αἰωνιον, *to pyr to aiōnion*; Matt. 18:8; 25:41; Jude 7), eternal punishment (κολασις αἰωνιος, *kolasis aiōnios*; Matt. 25:46), eternal destruction (ὀλεθρος αἰωνιος, *olethros aiōnios*; 2 Thess. 1:9), and eternal judgment (κρισις αἰωνιος, *krisis aiōnios*; Mark 3:29 KJV). Like eternal life, so by this description also eternal punishment is presented as belonging to the coming age (αἰὼν μέλλων, *aiōn mellōn*) in which a change of state is no longer possible. Scripture nowhere with a single word indicates or even leaves open the possibility that the state that begins there can still come to an end. And positively it says that the fire there is unquenchable (Matt. 3:12), that the worm does not die (Mark 9:48), that the smoke of torment goes up forever (Rev. 14:11) and continues day and night for all eternity (20:10), and that as eternal pain it contrasts with the eternal life of the righteous (Matt. 25:46). Unbiased exegesis will not find anything here other than eternal, never-ending punishment.

The state of the lost is described as destruction (ἀπωλεια, *apōleia*; Matt. 7:13), corruption (φθορα, *phthora*; Gal. 6:8), ruin (ὀλεθρος, *olethros*; 2 Thess. 1:9), and death (θανατος, *thanatos*; Rev. 2:11; etc.), which agrees with the fact that, according to the Old and New Testaments, the wicked will be destroyed, eradicated, ruined, put away, cast out, cut off, burned as chaff, and so on. All these expressions are understood by the proponents of conditional immortality in terms of complete annihilation.[18] But this view is totally unfounded. Life, in Scripture, is never mere existence, and death is never the same as annihilation. Conditionalists cannot deny this fact with respect to the temporal physical death of humans. Like the Socinians they usually assume that the wicked will continue to exist also after death, either to be annihilated by God after the resurrection and the final judgment, or gradually to wither away and finally to perish physically as well. The latter idea is impossible, both philosophically and scripturally. For sin is not a substance, no material thing (*materia*), but a form (*forma*) that presupposes existence; sin does not destroy the existent but steers it in a wrong direction, a direction away from God. And physical death is not merely a natural consequence, but a positive— divinely threatened and executed—punishment of sin. In the event of that death, God does not annihilate human beings but temporarily separates soul and body in order to maintain both and to reunite them at the resurrection.

Scripture clearly and irrefutably teaches human immortality. When conditionalism views the destruction (ἀπωλεια, *apōleia*) that is the punishment of sin as an annihilation of the human substance, it is confusing the ethical with the physical. And just as God does not annihilate human beings in the first death, so neither does he annihilate them in the second. For in Scripture the latter, too, is described as punishment (Matt. 25:46), weeping and gnashing of teeth (8:12), anguish and distress (Rom. 2:9), never-ending fire (Matt. 18:8), the undying worm (Mark 9:44), and so on, expressions that all assume the existence of the lost. Still their state can be called destruction (ἀπωλεια, *apōleia*), corruption (φθορα, *phthora*), ruin (ὀλεθρος, *olethros*), and death (θανατος, *thanatos*) because in a moral and spiritual sense they have become total wrecks, and in an absolute sense they lack the fullness of life granted by Christ to believers. Thus the prodigal son is called "dead" (νεκρος, *nekros*) and "lost" (ἀπολωλως, *apolōlos*; Luke 15:24, 32); the Ephesians in their earlier state are described as "dead" (νεκροι, *nekroi*) through their trespasses and sins (Eph. 2:1; 4:18), and the people of the church of Sardis are called "dead" (νεκροι, *nekroi*; Rev. 3:1; etc.), but no one ever thinks of these three parties as being nonexistent.

The same failure to recognize the ethical character of sin marks the proponents of ἀποκαταστασις (*apokatastasis*, restoration of all things). The word derives from Acts 3:21, but there, as is universally acknowledged today, it does not at all mean

18. E. White, *Life in Christ*, 358–90.

what is now meant by it. Scripture nowhere teaches that one day all humans and even all devils will be saved. Often it indeed uses very universalistic language, but that is because, intensively, Christ's work is of infinite value and benefits the whole world and all of humanity in its organic form of existence. But it unambiguously excludes the idea that all human individuals or even the devils will at some time become citizens in the kingdom of God. The doctrine of the restoration of all things, accordingly, has at all times been taught by only a handful of persons. Even today the theory of conditional immortality has more support among theologians than that of the *apokatastasis*. Actually, and in any case, this doctrine is of pagan—not of Christian—origin; it is philosophical, not scriptural, in character. Underlying the theory is pantheism, which views all things as proceeding from God and, similarly, of successively returning to him. In this view God is not the lawgiver and judge who will one day judge the world with equity [Ps. 9:8] but an unconscious immanent force that propels all things to the end and will one day recapture all things into himself. Sin, in this view, is not lawlessness (ἀνομια, *anomia*) but a necessary moment in the evolution of the world. And redemption in Christ is not juridical restoration and ethical renewal but a physical process that controls everything.

In order to appreciate the fact of eternal punishment, it is above all necessary, therefore, to recognize along with Scripture the integrity of the justice of God and the deeply sinful character of sin. Sin is not a weakness, a lack, a temporary and gradually vanishing imperfection, but in origin and essence it is lawlessness (*anomia*), a violation of the law, rebellion and hostility against God, and the negation of his justice, his authority, even his existence. Granted, sin is finite in the sense that it is committed by a finite creature in a finite period of time, but as Augustine already correctly noted, not the duration of time over which the sin was committed but its own intrinsic nature is the standard for its punishment. "A momentary lapse into carelessness," as the saying goes, "can lead to a lifetime of weeping." The sins of a moment can result in a life of shame and punishment. A person who commits a crime is sometimes given the death penalty and thereby transferred into an irremediable state by an earthly government. God acts the same way: what the death penalty is on earth, the punishment of hell is in the final judgment. He judges and punishes sin in accordance with its intrinsic quality. And that sin is infinite in the sense that it is committed against the Highest Majesty, who is absolutely entitled to our love and worship. God is absolutely and infinitely worthy of our obedience and dedication. The law in which he requires this of us is therefore absolutely binding, and its binding nature is infinitely great. The violation of that law, viewed intensively, is therefore an absolute and infinite evil. Furthermore, the thing to be considered here is not so much the "duration of the sinning" as "the will of the sinner, which is such that it would always wish to sin if it could."[19] He who commits the sin is a slave to sin: he will not and cannot

---

19. Augustine, *City of God* XXI, 11: "[Not the] diuturnitas peccandi [but the] voluntas peccantis, quae huiusmodi est ut seper vellet peccare si posset."

do otherwise than sin. It is truly not his own doing when he is denied the opportunity to continue his sinful life. In terms of his interior desire, he would not want anything other than to live forever so that he could sin forever. Who then, looking at the sinful nature of sin, would have the nerve to say that God is unjust if he visits the sin not only with temporal but also with eternal punishments?

As a rule, this argument [against eternal punishment] derived from the justice of God is for that reason advanced somewhat tentatively and hesitantly but is all the more passionately regarded as inconsistent with the goodness and love of God. However, if it is not inconsistent with the justice of God, it is not and cannot be inconsistent with his goodness either. We have no choice at this point. If eternal punishment is unjust, then that condemns it, and one need no longer appeal to God's goodness. If, however, it is consistent with God's justice, then God's goodness remains unscathed: if a thing is just it is also good. The argument against eternal punishment derived from God's goodness therefore, in the manner of Marcion, secretly introduces a conflict between God's justice and his goodness and offers up the former to the latter. But goodness that nullifies justice is no longer true and real goodness. It is mere human weakness and wimpiness and, when projected onto God, an invention of the human brain, one that in no way corresponds to the true and living God who has revealed himself in Scripture as well as in nature. For if eternal punishment is inconsistent with God's goodness, then temporal punishment is inconsistent with it as well. But the latter is a fact no one can deny. Humankind is consumed by God's anger and terrified by his wrath [cf. Ps. 90:7]. Who can square this world's suffering with God's goodness and love? Still it must be possible, for it exists. Now if the existence of immense suffering in this world may not lead us to question God's goodness, then neither may eternal punishment prompt us to deny it. If this world is consistent with God's love, as it is and has to be, then hell is too. For aside from Scripture there is no stronger proof for the existence of hell than the existence of this world, the world from whose misery the features of the [biblical] picture of hell are derived.[20]

Furthermore, for the person who disputes [the reality of] eternal punishment, there is enormous danger of playing the hypocrite before God. Such a person presents himself as extremely loving, one who in goodness and compassion far outstrips our Lord Jesus Christ. This does not stop this same person, the moment one's own honor is violated, from erupting in fury and calling down on the violator every evil in this life and the life to come. Resentment, hatred, wrath, and vindictiveness arise in the hearts of all human beings against anyone standing in their way. We promote our own honor, but the honor of God is of no concern to us. We stand up for our own rights but let others trample the rights of God into the dirt. Surely this is sufficient evidence that we humans are not suitable judges

20. Cf. A. Strindberg, *The Dance of Death*, trans. A. Paulsen (New York: W. W. Norton, 1976), 41 (act 1, scene 1): "Don't you [believe in hell]—you who are living in one?" (German: Glaubst du nicht daran [an die Hölle], wo du mitten in ihr bist?).

of the words and actions of God. Nevertheless, in that act of standing up for our own rights and reputation, there is something good. However wrongly applied, there is implicit in it the fact that our rights and reputation are more precious than our goods and life. Slumbering even in the sinner, there is still a deep sense of justice and honor. And when that sense is violated, it is aroused and suppresses all pity. When, in a given conflict between two people or two nations, the issue is one of justice, each party passionately prays that God may bring about the triumph of the right and strike its violators with his judgment. All human beings still have an innate feeling for the saying "Let justice be done though the world perish" (*fiat justitia, pereat mundus*) and think it reasonable that justice should triumph at the expense of thousands of human lives. In the day of judgment, too, the issue is one of justice, not some private right or other, but *justice* par excellence, justice in its full import and scope, the justice of God—that God himself may be honored as God in all eternity.

There is, therefore, no doubt that in the day of judgment God will fully vindicate himself in the presence of all his creatures even when he pronounces eternal punishment upon sinners. Now we who know in part also know the horror of sin only in part. But if here already, upon hearing of certain horrors, we consider no punishment severe enough, what then will we think when at the end of time we gain insight into the depths of injustice? And on earth, furthermore, we are always one-sided. Over and over our sense of justice and our compassion clash. We are either too soft or much too severe in our judgment. But in the case of the Lord our God, this is not so and cannot be so. In Christ he has fully revealed his love, a love that is so great precisely because it saves us from the wrath to come and from eternal destruction. Critics of eternal punishment not only fail to do justice to the doom-worthiness of sin, the rigorousness of divine justice; they also infringe on the greatness of God's love and the salvation that is in Christ. If the object had not been salvation from eternal destruction, the price of the blood of God's own Son would have been much too high. The heaven that he won for us by his atoning death presupposes a hell from which he delivered us. The eternal life he imparted to us presupposes an eternal death from which he saved us. The grace and good pleasure of God in which he makes us participants forever presuppose a wrath into which we would otherwise have had to be plunged forever. And for that reason it is this Christ who will one day execute judgment and pronounce his sentence. A human being, a true and complete human being who knows what is in human beings, who is the meekest of human beings, will be the judge of human beings, a judge so just that all will acknowledge his justice, and every knee will bow before him, and every tongue confess that Christ is Lord to the glory of God the Father [Phil. 2:10–11]. In the end God will be recognized as God by all creatures, if not willingly then unwillingly.

This should be enough for us. Inquiries into the location and size of hell, the nature of the fire and the worm, the psychic and physical state of the lost—these lead nowhere because Scripture is silent on these topics. All we know besides the things we have discussed so far is that the punishment of hell does not begin until after the day of judgment; that such punishment is consistently threatened against those who stubbornly resist the truth of God—the cowardly, the faithless, the polluted, the murderers, the fornicators, the sorcerers, the idolaters, and the liars (Rev. 21:8); and that even so, this punishment differs in the measure of each person's unrighteousness. Scripture nowhere teaches that there will still be room in hell for repentance and forgiveness. The addition in Matt. 12:32 ("either in this age or in the age to come") is intended not to bring out the pardonability of the sin against the Son of Man in the age to come but to underline the absolute unpardonability of the sin against the Holy Spirit. In its essence punishment consists in the maintenance of justice and, after the judgment, serves specifically to requite all persons according to their work, not to purify them. Scripture nevertheless teaches very clearly that there are degrees of punishment. The penalty of damnation (*poena damni*) is the same, but the penalty of sensation (*poena sensus*) differs. All will receive according to their works (Matt. 10:15; 11:24; 23:14; 24:51; Luke 10:12, 14; 12:46–47; 2 Cor. 5:10; etc.). And this fact as such still demonstrates something of God's mercy.[21] All sin is absolutely opposed to the justice of God, but in punishing it God nevertheless takes account of the relative difference existing between sins. There is infinite diversity also on the other side of the grave.[22] For in eternal punishment God's justice always manifests itself in such a way that his goodness and love remain inviolate and can never be justly faulted. The saying that he does not willingly afflict or grieve anyone (Lam. 3:33) applies also in hell. The pain he inflicts is not an object of pleasure, either for him or for the blessed in heaven, but a means of glorifying his virtues, and hence [the punishment is] determined in severity and measure by this ultimate goal.[23]

21. Cf. H. Bavinck, *Reformed Dogmatics*, II, 386 (#244), 388–89 (#245).

22. Augustine says: "The penalties of the damned are to some extent mitigated at certain intervals" (poenas damnatorum certis temporum inter vallis aliquatenus mitigari; *Enchiridion* 110). Cf. Lombard, Thomas, Bonaventure on *Sent.*, IV, 46. Remarkable, further, is that Ambrose and Jerome make a distinction between the impious (unbelievers, non-Christians) and sinners (Christians who lived and died as sinners), and restrict eternal punishment in hell to the former. So, at least, says J. E. Niederhuber, *Die Eschatologie des heiligen Ambrosius* (Paderborn: Schöningh, 1907), 120, 248.

23. See further Augustine, *Enchiridion* 110–13; *City of God* XXI; P. Lombard, *Sent.*, IV, dist. 46–50; T. Aquinas, *Summa theol.*, suppl., qu. 97–99; A. Dante, "Inferno"; D. Petavius (Petau), "De angelis," III, c. 4–8, *Op. theol.*, IV; Josef Sachs, *Die ewige Dauer der Höllenstrafen* (Paderborn: Schöningh, 1900); J. Bautz, *Die Hölle in Anschluss an die Scholastiek dargestellt* (Mainz: Kirchheim, 1905); J. Stufler (*Die Heiligkeit Gottes und die ewige Tod* [Innsbruck: Rauch, 1903]) opposes H. Schell, who assumes the possibility of an *apokatastasis*. F. X. Kiefl undertook to defend him in "Herman Schell und die Ewigkeit der Hölle," *Theologisch-praktischen Monatsschrift* 14 (1904): 685–709, and received a reply from Stufler, *Die Verteidigung Schells durch Prof. Kiefl* (Innsbruck: Rauch, 1904); A. M. Weiss, *Die religiose Gefahr* (Freiburg i.B.: Herder, 1904), 277, 353. Protestantism was consistent in its view of eternal punishment; see, briefly, B. de Moor, *Comm. theol.*, III, 354–58; C. Vitringa, *Doct. christ.*, IV, 175; II, 305, 320. In modern times, the idea that the hereafter does not bring a state of bliss for everyone sometimes encounters greater appreciation on the basis of the absolute character of the moral law or on the basis of the law of retribution (karma) that makes the consequences of sin inevitable; cf. Bavinck, *Philosophy of Revelation* (New York: Longmans, Green, 1909), 295, 314. On the ideas of pagans relative to reward and punishment on the other side of the grave, cf. F. Hettinger, *Apologie du Christianisme*, 5 vols. (Bar-le-Duc: L. Guérin, 1869–70), IV, 320.

18

THE RENEWAL OF CREATION

The renewal of creation follows the final judgment. According to Scripture the present world will neither continue forever nor will it be destroyed and replaced by a totally new one. Instead it will be cleansed of sin and re-created, reborn, renewed, made whole. While the kingdom of God is first planted spiritually in human hearts, the future blessedness is not to be spiritualized. Biblical hope, rooted in incarnation and resurrection, is creational, this-worldly, visible, physical, bodily hope. The rebirth of human beings is completed in the glorious rebirth of all creation, the new Jerusalem, whose architect and builder is God himself. The salvation of the kingdom of God, including communion with God as well as the communion of the saints, is both a present blessing and a future, consummated, rich glory. The kingdom of God has come and is coming. The scope of God's mercy is wide. While we should abstain from a firm judgment concerning the salvation of pagans or children who die in infancy, the Reformed confessions are magnanimous in their outlook. Though many fall away, in Christ the human race, the world, is saved. The final rest of God's children is not to be conceived as inaction; his children remain his servants, who joyfully and in diverse ways serve him night and day. What we sow on earth is harvested in eternity; diversity is not destroyed in eternity but cleansed from sin and made serviceable to fellowship with God and others. Scripture even teaches degrees of glory in the future kingdom, commensurate with one's works. The blessedness of salvation is the same for all, but there are distinctions in glory. This distinction is not merited by good works but [comes through] a sovereign, free, and gracious covenantal disposition of God—a given right to believers merited by Christ. God thus crowns his own work in order that in such active diversity the glory of his own attributes shines out. All creatures will then live and move and have their being in God, who is all in all, who reflects all of his attributes in the mirror of his works and glorifies himself in them.

[577] Following the final judgment comes the renewal of the world. Some indeed, along with Thomas,[1] have put it before the final judgment, but the common

---

1. T. Aquinas, *Summa theol.*, suppl., qu. 74, art. 7.

view is that it will follow upon it and be inaugurated only after the wicked have been banished from the earth. This order undoubtedly best harmonizes with that in Holy Scripture. In the Old Testament the day of the Lord is indeed preceded by a range of fearful signs, and judgment on the nations takes place amid appalling events of different kinds. However, the new earth, with its extraordinary fruitfulness, only comes into being when victory over Israel's enemies has been achieved and the people have returned to their land and been restored in it. According to the New Testament as well, the day of judgment is preceded by many signs, like the darkening of sun and moon and stars, the shaking of the powers of heaven, and so on (Matt. 24:29). The burning of the earth, though, does not occur until the day of the Lord (2 Pet. 3:10), and then follows the coming of the new heaven and new earth in which righteousness dwells (3:13). Once judgment has been executed, John sees the new Jerusalem coming down out of heaven from God (Rev. 21:1f.).

In this expectation of world renewal, Scripture assumes a position between two extremes. On the one hand, many thinkers—Plato, Aristotle, Xenophanes, Philo, Maimonides, Averroes, Wolanus, La Peyrère, Edelmann, and Czolbe among them—have asserted that this world is destined to continue in its present form forever. On the other hand, Origen, the Lutherans, the Mennonites, the Socinians, Vorstius, the Remonstrants, and a number of Reformed theologians like Beza, Rivetus, Junius, Wollebius, and Prideaux believed that the world would not only be changed in form but also destroyed in substance and replaced by a totally new world.[2]

THE TRANSFORMATION OF CREATION

Neither of these two views, however, finds support in Scripture. Old Testament prophecy, while it looks for an extraordinary transformation in all of nature, refrains from teaching the destruction of the present world. The passages that are assumed to teach the latter (Ps. 102:26; Isa. 34:4; 51:6, 16; 65:17; 66:22) do indeed describe in very graphic terms the change that will set in after the day of the Lord, but they do not imply the destruction of the substance of the world. In the first place, the description given in these passages is much too rich in imagery for us to infer from them a reduction to nothing (*reductio ad nihilum*) of the entire world. Further, the perishing (אָבַד, *'ābad*) of heaven and earth (Ps. 102:26), which for one thing by itself never conveys an absolute destruction of substance, is explained by the fact that they will wear out like a garment, be changed like clothing, wither like a leaf on a vine, or vanish like smoke (Ps. 102:26; Isa. 34:4; 51:6). And finally, the Hebrew word "create" (בָּרָא, *bārā'*) used with reference to the new heaven and the new earth (Isa. 65:17) certainly does not always mean creating something out of nothing but frequently denotes a divine activity by which God brings forth something new from the old (Isa. 41:20; 43:7; 54:16; 57:18).

---

2. C. Vitringa, *Doctrina christiana religionis*, 8 vols. (Leiden: Joannis le Mair, 1761–86), IV, 194–200.

For that reason it also frequently alternates with planting, laying the foundations of, and making (Isa. 51:16; 66:22). The Lord can say (Isa. 51:16) that he begins the new creation by putting his word in Israel's mouth and hiding them in the shadow of his hand.

In the same way, the New Testament proclaims that heaven and earth will pass away (Matt. 5:18; 24:35; 2 Pet. 3:10; 1 John 2:17; Rev. 21:1), that they will perish and wear out like clothing (Heb. 1:11), dissolve (2 Pet. 3:10), be burned with fire (3:10), and be changed (Heb. 1:12). But none of these expressions implies a destruction of substance. Peter, for example, expressly teaches that the old earth, which originated as a result of the separation of waters, was deluged with water and so perished (2 Pet. 3:6), and that the present world would also perish, not—thanks to the divine promise—by water but by fire. Accordingly, with reference to the passing of the present world, we must no more think of a destruction of substance than [we would] with regard to the passing of the earlier world in the flood. Fire burns, cleanses, purifies, but does not destroy. The contrast in 1 John 2:17 ("the world and its desire are passing away, but those who do the will of God live forever") teaches us that the first statement does not imply a destruction of the substance of the world but a vanishing of the world in its present, sin-damaged form. Paul, accordingly, also states very clearly that the present form (το σχημα, *to schēma*) of this world passes away (1 Cor. 7:31). Only such a renewal of the world, for that matter, accords with what Scripture teaches about redemption. For the latter is never a second, brand-new creation but a re-creation of the existing world. God's honor consists precisely in the fact that he redeems and renews the same humanity, the same world, the same heaven, and the same earth that have been corrupted and polluted by sin. Just as anyone in Christ is a new creation in whom the old has passed away and everything has become new (2 Cor. 5:17), so also this world passes away in its present form as well, in order out of its womb, at God's word of power, to give birth and being to a new world. Just as in the case of an individual human being, so at the end of time a rebirth of the world will take place as well (Matt. 19:28). This constitutes a spiritual renewal, not a physical creation.[3]

This renewal of the visible world highlights the one-sidedness of the spiritualism that limits future blessedness to heaven. In the case of Old Testament prophecy one cannot doubt that it describes earthly blessedness. Its expectation is that following the great day, the people of God will live in security and peace in Palestine under the anointed king of the dynasty of David, surrounded and served by the Gentile nations. There is truth in Delitzsch's comments on Isaiah 66:24:

3. Cf. T. Aquinas, *Summa theol.*, suppl., qu. 74, art. 1, and qu. 91; L. Atzberger, *Die christliche Eschatologie* (Freiburg i.B.: Herder, 1890), 372f.; F. Gomarus, *Opera theologia omnia* (Amsterdam: J. Jansson, 1664), I, 131–33, 416; F. Spanheim, *Dubia evangelica* (Geneva: Petri Chovet, 1655–58), III, 670–712; F. Turretin, *Institutes of Elenctic Theology*, trans. G. M. Giger, ed. J. T. Dennison, 3 vols. (Phillipsburg, NJ: Presbyterian & Reformed, 1992), XX, qu. 5; B. de Moor, *Commentarius . . . theologiae*, 6 vols. (Leiden: J. Hasebroek, 1761–71), VI, 733–36; C. Vitringa, *Doctr. christ.*, IV, 186–215; Th. Kliefoth, *Christliche Eschatologie* (Leipzig: Dörffling & Franke, 1886), 297f.

This is just the distinction between the Old Testament and the New; that the Old Testament brings down the life to come to the level of this life, whilst the New Testament lifts up this life to the level of the life to come; that the Old Testament depicts both this life and the life to come as an endless extension of this life, whilst the New Testament depicts it as a continuous line in two halves, the last point in this finite state being the first point of the infinite state beyond; that the Old Testament preserves the continuity of this life and the life to come by transferring the outer side, the form, the appearance of this life to the life to come, the New Testament by making the inner side, the nature, the reality of the life to come, the δυνάμεις μέλλοντος αἰῶνος [dynameis mellontos aiōnos], immanent in this life.[4]

Still these comments do not do complete justice to the New Testament hope of future blessedness. Present in the New Testament there is undoubtedly some spiritualization of Old Testament prophecy. Since Jesus's advent breaks up into a first and a second coming, the kingdom of God is first planted in human hearts spiritually, and the benefits of that kingdom are all internal and invisible: forgiveness, peace, righteousness, and eternal life. The essence of future blessedness, accordingly, is also construed more spiritually, especially by Paul and John, as a being always with the Lord (John 12:26; 14:3; 17:24; 2 Cor. 5:8; Phil. 1:23; 1 Thess. 4:17; 5:10; 1 John 3:2). But this does not confine this blessedness to heaven.[5] This cannot be the case as is basically evident from the fact that the New Testament teaches the incarnation of the Word and the physical resurrection of Christ; it further expects his physical return at the end of time and immediately thereafter has in view the physical resurrection of all human beings, especially that of believers. All this spells the collapse of spiritualism, which if it remains true to its principle—as in Origen—has nothing left after the day of judgment other than spirits in an uncreated heaven.

But the teaching of Scripture is very different. The world, according to it, consists of heaven and earth; humans consist of soul and body; and the kingdom of God, accordingly, has a hidden spiritual dimension and an external, visible side. Whereas Jesus came the first time to establish that kingdom in a spiritual sense, he returns at the end of history to give visible shape to it. Reformation proceeds from the inside to the outside. The rebirth of humans is completed in the rebirth of creation. The kingdom of God is fully realized only when it is visibly extended over the earth as well. This is how also the disciples understood it when, after Jesus's resurrection, they asked him whether this was the time he would restore the

---

4. F. Delitzsch, *Biblical Commentary on the Prophecies of Isaiah*, trans. J. Martin, 2 vols. (Edinburgh: T&T Clark, 1869–80; repr., Grand Rapids: Eerdmans, 1954), II, 517. Ed. note: Bavinck cites only part of this passage from the German: "Das ist ja eben der Unterschied des A. und N.T., dass das A.T. das Jenseits verdiesseitigt, das N.T. das Diesseits verjenseitigt; dass das A.T. das Jenseits in den Gesichtskreis des Diesseits herabzieht, das N.T. das Diesseits in das Jenseits emporhebt."

5. As H. Bois thinks ("La terre et le ciel," *Foi et Vie* [15 August–1 October 1906]: 585) "the term 'heaven' runs less danger of materializing the future life" (le terme ciel fait moins courir le danger de matérialiser la vie future).

kingdom to Israel. In his reply Jesus does not deny that one day he will establish such a kingdom, but only says that the times for it have been set by the Father, and that now his disciples are called, in the power of the Holy Spirit, to be his witnesses to the ends of the earth (Acts 1:6–8). Elsewhere he expressly states that the meek will inherit the earth (Matt. 5:5). He pictures future blessedness as a meal at which the guests sit down with Abraham, Isaac, and Jacob (8:11), enjoy food and drink (Luke 22:30), eat of the new and perfect Passover (Luke 22:16), and drink of the fruit of the new vine (Matt. 26:29). True, in this dispensation and right up until the parousia, the eyes of believers are directed upward toward heaven. That is where their treasure is (6:20; 19:21); there Jesus, who is their life, sits at the right hand of God (John 14:3; 17:24; Col. 3:1–3); their citizenship is there while they are aliens here (Phil. 3:20; Heb. 11:13–16).

But this inheritance is destined to be revealed. Someday Christ will return visibly and then cause the whole believing community—indeed, the whole world—to participate in his glory. Not only are believers changed after his likeness (John 17:24; Rom. 8:17–18, 28; Phil. 3:21; Col. 3:4; 1 John 3:2), but also "the whole creation itself will be set free from its bondage to decay and obtain the freedom of the glory of the children of God" (Rom. 8:21). Earth and heaven will be renewed so that justice will be at home in them (2 Pet. 3:13; Rev. 21:1). The heavenly Jerusalem, which is now above and was the model for the earthly Jerusalem, then comes down to earth (Gal. 4:26; Heb. 11:10, 13–16; 12:22; 13:14; Rev. 3:12; 21:2ff.). This new Jerusalem is not identical with the believing community, even though it is figuratively called the bride of the Lamb (21:2, 9), for Hebrews 12:22–23 clearly distinguishes among the heavenly Jerusalem, the assembly of the firstborn (the Old Testament faithful), and the spirits of the righteous made perfect (deceased Christians). The heavenly Jerusalem is a city built by God himself (Heb. 11:10). It is the city of the living God, inasmuch as God is not just its architect but also makes it his home (Rev. 21:3). In it the angels are the servants and constitute the royal entourage of the great king (Heb. 12:22), while the blessed are its citizens (Rev. 21:27; 22:3–4).

The description John gives of that Jerusalem (Rev. 21–22) should certainly not be taken literally any more than his preceding visions. This option is excluded by the mere fact that John depicts it as a cube whose length, width, and height are equal, that is, 12,000 stadia or 1,500 miles; still the height of the wall is only 144 cubits, just under 75 yards (21:15–17). By this depiction John does not intend to give a sketch of the city; rather, since he cannot bring the glory of the divine kingdom home to us in any other way, he offers his ideas, interpreting them in images. And he derives these images from paradise, with its river and tree of life (21:6; 22:1–2); from the earthly Jerusalem with its gates and streets (21:12ff.); from the temple with its holy of holies, in which God himself dwelt (21:3, 22); and from the entire realm of nature, with all its treasures of gold and precious stones (21:11, 18–21). But although these are ideas interpreted thus by images, they are not illusions or fabrications, but this-worldly depictions of otherworldly realities. All that is true, honorable, just, pure, pleasing, and commendable in the whole of creation, in heaven and on earth, is gathered up in the future city of God—renewed, re-created, boosted to its highest glory.

The substance [of the city of God] is present in this creation. Just as the caterpillar becomes a butterfly, as carbon is converted into diamond, as the grain of wheat upon dying in the ground produces other grains of wheat, as all of nature revives in the spring and dresses up in celebrative clothing, as the believing community is formed out of Adam's fallen race, as the resurrection body is raised from the body that is dead and buried in the earth, so too, by the re-creating power of Christ, the new heaven and the new earth will one day emerge from the fire-purged elements of this world, radiant in enduring glory and forever set free from the "bondage to decay" (δουλειας της φθορας, *douleias tēs phthoras* [Rom. 8:21]). More glorious than this beautiful earth, more glorious than the earthly Jerusalem, more glorious even than paradise will be the glory of the new Jerusalem, whose architect and builder is God himself. The state of glory (*status gloriae*) will be no mere restoration (*restauratie*) of the state of nature (*status naturae*), but a re-formation[6] that, thanks to the power of Christ, transforms all matter (ὑλη, *hylē*) into form (εἰδος, *eidos*), all potency into actuality (*potentia, actus*), and presents the entire creation before the face of God, brilliant in unfading splendor and blossoming in a springtime of eternal youth. *Substantially* nothing is lost. Outside, indeed, are the dogs and sorcerers and fornicators and murderers and idolaters and everyone who loves and practices falsehood (Rev. 22:15). But in the new heaven and new earth, the world as such is restored; in the believing community the human race is saved. In that community, which Christ has purchased and gathered from all nations, languages, and tongues (Rev. 5:9; etc.), all the nations, Israel included, maintain their distinct place and calling (Matt. 8:11; Rom. 11:25; Rev. 21:24; 22:2). And all those nations—each in accordance with its own distinct national character—bring into the new Jerusalem all they have received from God in the way of glory and honor (Rev. 21:24, 26).

THE BLESSINGS OF THE REDEEMED

[578] The blessings in which the blessed participate are not only spiritual, therefore, but also material and physical in nature. As misguided as it is—along with pagan peoples and some chiliasts—to make the material into the chief component of future blessedness, so it is also one-sided and stoic to regard the physical indifferently or to exclude it totally from the state of blessedness. Scripture consistently maintains the intimate connectedness of the spiritual and the natural. Inasmuch as the world consists of heaven and earth and humans consist of soul and body, so also sanctity and glory, virtue and happiness, the moral and the natural world order ought finally to be harmoniously united. The blessed will therefore not only

---

6. Ed. note: See note 5 in the previous chapter.

be free from sin but also from all the consequences of sin, from ignorance and error (John 6:45), from death (Luke 20:36; 1 Cor. 15:26; Rev. 2:11; 20:6, 14), from poverty and disease, from pain and fear, hunger and thirst, cold and heat (Matt. 5:4; Luke 6:21; Rev. 7:16–17; 21:4), and from all weakness, dishonor, and corruption (1 Cor. 15:42; etc.).

Still the spiritual blessings are the more important and innumerably abundant: holiness (Rev. 3:4–5; 7:14; 19:8; 21:27); salvation (Rom. 13:11; 1 Thess. 5:9; Heb. 1:14; 5:9); glory (Luke 24:26; Rom. 2:10; 8:18, 21); adoption (Rom. 8:23); eternal life (Matt. 19:16–17, 29; etc.); the vision of, and conformity to, God and Christ (Matt. 5:18; John 17:24; Rom. 8:29; 1 Cor. 13:12; 2 Cor. 3:18; Phil. 3:21; 1 John 3:2; Rev. 22:4); and fellowship with, and the service and praise of, God and Christ (John 17:24; 2 Cor. 5:8; Phil. 1:23; Rev. 4:10; 5:9–13; 7:10, 15–17; 21:3; 22:3; etc.). Since in principle all these benefits have been given to believers on earth already—such as, for example, adoption (Rom. 8:15; 9:4; Gal. 4:5; Eph. 1:5) and eternal life (John 3:15–16, 36; etc.)—many people have construed Christian salvation exclusively as a present salvation that is increasingly realized solely in the way of an ethical process.[7] Ritschl and many of his followers also one-sidedly stressed the present-world orientation of people ("diesseitige Weltstellung des Menschen"). They consider the moral freedom relative to the world, which the Christian receives in faith, as the most significant benefit, and they say little or nothing about the eternal salvation that Christ prepares for his own in the future.[8]

Against the abstract supernaturalism of the Greek Orthodox and Roman Catholic Churches—which see salvation as exclusively transcendent and therefore, as it concerns the earth, consider the Christian life embodied ideally in monasticism—this [present-worldly] view stands for an important truth. The Reformation, going back to Scripture, in principle overcame this supernaturalistic and ascetic view of life. Those who believe, at the very moment of believing, receive the forgiveness of sins and eternal life. They are children of God, who serve the Father not as hired employees in hope of compensation, but as children who do the will of the Father out of love and gratitude. They carry out this will not by fleeing from the world, but by being faithful in the calling entrusted to them on earth. Living for heaven, therefore, does not compete with life in the midst of the world: it is precisely in that world that Christ keeps his disciples from the evil one.

The new heaven and earth, as we indicated earlier, is composed of the elements of the world that exists now, and the believing community is humanity restored under Christ as head. However much believers on earth in a sense already enjoy salvation, that is the case only in principle and not in full. For in hope we believers

7. O. Pfleiderer, *Grundriss der christlichen Glaubens und Sittenlehre*, 4th ed. (Berlin: G. Reimer, 1888), §177; A. E. Biedermann, *Christliche Dogmatik* (Zurich: Orell, Füssli, 1869), §974f.; J. Scholten, *Dogmaticae christianae initia*, 2nd ed., 2 vols. (London: P. Engels, 1856–58), c. 7.

8. A. Ritschl, *The Christian Doctrine of Justification and Reconciliation*, trans. H. R. Mackintosh and A. B. Macaulay (Edinburgh: T&T Clark, 1900), §§51, 53, 58, 65.

are saved (Rom. 8:24). Jesus pronounces his blessing on the poor in spirit (etc.), for theirs is the kingdom of heaven that in the future will be established on earth (Matt. 5:3–10). Believers are children of God but still await the full realization of their "sonship" (5:9; Rom. 8:23). They have eternal life but must still receive it at the resurrection—as even John points out (5:20–29; 6:40, 44–45). Both are therefore true: the kingdom of heaven has come and it is still coming. And this twofold truth conditions the entire character of the state of glory. As the new heaven and earth are formed out of the elements of this world, and the believing community is a re-creation of the human race that fell in Adam, so the life of the redeemed in the hereafter is to be conceived as analogous with the life of believers here on earth. On the one hand, it does not consist in the contemplation of God (*visio Dei*) in a Catholic sense, a contemplation to which human nature can only be elevated by a superadded gift (*donum superadditum*). On the other hand, neither is it a slow and gradual development of the Christian life as led by believers already on earth. It is a genuinely natural life but unfolded by grace to its highest splendor and its most bountiful beauty. The matter (*materia*) remains, but the form (*forma*) differs. In that life, religion—fellowship with God—is primary and central. But that fellowship will be richer, deeper, and more blessed than it ever was or could be on earth, since it will not be disturbed by any sin, or interrupted by any distance, or mediated by either Scripture or nature.

Now, as we look into the mirror of God's revelation, we only see his image; then we will see him face to face and know as we are known. Contemplation (*visio*), understanding (*comprehensio*), and enjoyment of God (*fruitio Dei*) make up the essence of our future blessedness. The redeemed see God, not—to be sure—with physical eyes, but still in a way that far outstrips all revelation in this dispensation via nature and Scripture. And thus they will all know him, each in the measure of his mental capacity, with a knowledge that has its image and likeness in God's knowledge—directly, immediately, unambiguously, and purely. Then they will receive and possess everything they expected here only in hope. Thus contemplating and possessing God, they enjoy him and are blessed in his fellowship: blessed in soul and body, in intellect and will. In theology, theologians have disputed whether this blessedness in the hereafter formally had its seat in the intellect or in the will and hence consisted in knowledge or love. Thomas claimed the former,[9] Duns Scotus the latter,[10] but Bonaventure combined the two, observing that the enjoyment of God (*fruitio Dei*) was the fruit not only of the knowledge of God (*cognitio Dei*) but also of the love of God (*amor Dei*) and resulted from the union and cooperation between the two.[11]

[579] The blessedness of communion with God is enjoyed in and heightened by the communion of saints. On earth already this communion is a wonderful benefit

---

9. T. Aquinas, *Summa theol.*, I, 2, qu. 3, art. 4.

10. Duns Scotus, *Sent.*, IV, dist. 49, qu. 4.

11. Bonaventure, *Sent.*, IV, dist. 49, p. 1, art. unic. qu. 4, 5. Cf. G. Voetius, *Selectae disputationes theologicae*, 5 vols. (Utrecht: 1648–69), II, 1217–39.

of faith. Those who for Jesus's sake have left behind house or brothers or sisters or father or mother or wife or children or fields already in this life receive houses, brothers, sisters, mothers, children, and fields—along with persecutions—(Mark 10:29–30), for all who do the will of the Father are Jesus's brother and sister and mother (Matt. 12:50). Through the mediator of the New Testament, believers enter into fellowship, not only with the militant church on earth, but also with the triumphant church in heaven, the assembly of the firstborn, the spirits of the righteous made perfect, even with innumerable angels (Heb. 12:22–24). But this fellowship, though in principle it already exists on earth, will nevertheless be incomparably richer and more glorious when all dividing walls of descent and language, of time and space, have been leveled, all sin and error have been banished, and all the elect have been assembled in the new Jerusalem. Then will be fully answered the prayer of Jesus that all his sheep may be one flock under one Shepherd (John 10:16; 17:21).

All the saints together will then fully comprehend the breadth and length and height and depth of the love of Christ (Eph. 3:18–19). They will together be filled with all the fullness of God (Eph. 3:19; Col. 2:2, 10), inasmuch as Christ, himself filled with the fullness of God (Col. 1:19), will in turn fill the believing community with himself and make it his fullness (πληρωμα, *plērōma*; Eph. 1:23; 4:10). And sitting down at one table with Abraham, Isaac, and Jacob (Matt. 8:11), they will unitedly lift up a song of praise to the glory of God and of the Lamb (Rev. 4:11; 5:12; etc.). Speaking of the believing community on earth, Scripture frequently says that it is a "little flock" (Matt. 7:14; 22:14; Luke 12:32; 13:23), a statement confirmed by history right up until the present. And even toward the end of history, when the gospel will have been preached among all nations, apostasy will increase and the faithful will be few. Old Testament prophecy already announced that only a remnant of Israel would repent and be saved. The New Testament likewise expects that those who persevere to the end will be few (Matt. 24:13; 25:1ff.; Luke 18:8).

On the other hand, however, Scripture often uses very universalistic language. In Adam the covenant of grace is made known to humanity as a whole (Gen. 3:15). The covenant of nature concluded after the flood embraces all creatures (9:9–10). In Abraham all generations of the earth are blessed (12:3). The salvation that will one day be granted to Israel profits all the Gentiles. Jesus says that he will give his life as a ransom for *many* (Matt. 20:28) and that *many* will come from east and west to sit down with Abraham, Isaac, and Jacob in the kingdom of heaven (8:11). The grace that appeared in Christ is much more abundant than the trespass of Adam: it comes to all people for justification and life (Rom. 5:12–20; 1 Cor. 15:22). In this dispensation all things in heaven and on earth will be gathered up under Christ (Eph. 1:10). And one day at the end every knee will bow before Christ and every tongue will confess him as Lord (Phil. 2:10–11). Then a great multitude that no one can number will stand before the throne and the Lamb (Rev. 7:9; 19:1, 6). *Nations* will be saved and walk in the light of the new Jerusalem (21:24, 26; 22:2). And God will then be all in all (1 Cor. 15:28).

THE WIDENESS OF GOD'S MERCY

Because of this last series of texts, many people have cherished the hope that in the end, if not all creatures, then surely all humans—or if this should fail, then far and away the majority of humans—will be saved. Hell will either be totally nonexistent or only a small and remote corner of the universe. They base this expectation either on the possibility of salvation by the works of the law (Pelagians, Socinians, Deists, et al.) or on the opportunity of hearing and accepting the gospel either after death in the intermediate state or even after the day of judgment (universalists). I have discussed these sentiments in the previous chapter[12] and therefore do not need to examine them in light of Scripture again here.

But even among those who adhere to the confession that no one comes to the Father except by Christ, and that only one name has been given under heaven for salvation (John 14:6; Acts 4:12), there have always been a few people who believed in the possibility of salvation in this life aside from the preaching of the gospel. They taught this view with respect to children of the covenant, to all children who die in infancy within or outside the bounds of Christianity, to the developmentally or emotionally handicapped, and to the hearing-and-speech-impaired who are practically shut off from the preaching of the gospel. The same applies to some or many pagans who in terms of their clear insights and virtuous life gave evidence of true piety. Some of the church fathers assumed that the Logos was active in the pagan world.[13] Augustine believed that from the beginning there have always been a few persons, in Israel but in other nations as well, who believed in the Logos and lived faithfully and righteously in accordance with his commandments.[14] Abelard asserted that pagans too could inherit salvation.[15] According to Strauss, Luther once expressed the wish that God would be gracious also to men like Cicero and Seneca, while Melanchthon left open the possibility that, in some cases and by a special method, God had communicated some knowledge of forgiveness in Christ to Solon, Themistocles, and others.[16] Zwingli was more definite and believed that God had his elect also among pagans.[17] But others left open only the possibility

---

12. Cf. above, 704–14 (##575–76).

13. Cf. H. Bavinck, *Reformed Dogmatics*, I, 229–30 (#68); II, 565–68 (#295); cf. above, 33–35 (#433), 51 (#438), 61 (#441).

14. Augustine, *Letters* 102; *City of God* XVIII, 47; and other places. Cf. H. Reuter, *Augustinische Studien* (Gotha: Perthes, 1887), 90ff.

15. In W. Münscher, *Lehrbuch des christlichen Dogmengeschichte*, ed. D. von Coelln (Cassel: J. C. Krieger, 1832–38), II, 147.

16. D. Strauss, *Die christliche Glaubenslehre* (Tübingen: Osiander, 1840–41), I, 271.

17. U. Zwingli, *Exposition of the Christian Faith*, ch. x, "Everlasting Life," in *On Providence and Other Essays*, ed. S. M. Jackson and W. J. Hinke (1922; repr., Durham, NC: Labyrinth, 1983), 272. In the eighteenth century the doctrine that also pagans could be saved had many advocates: e.g., Leibniz, in A. Pichler, *Die Theologie des Leibniz*

and did not venture to go beyond hoping and wishing.[18] This opinion, however, was never held by more than a handful.

In their confessions the churches made no pronouncements on this issue, and most theologians opposed the idea.[19] Somewhat more favorable were their views on the salvation of children who died in infancy. Catholics teach that all children of Christian parents who died, having been baptized through express intention (*voto*) or in reality (*re*), were saved, and that all other children who died young suffered a penalty of damnation but not of sensation (*poene damni*, not *sensus*) in the limbo of children (*limbus infantum*).[20] With respect to children of Christian parents, Lutherans hold the same view as Catholics and leave the others to the judgment of God.[21] The Reformed were inclined to believe that all children who were born in the covenant of grace and died before reaching the age of discretion attained to blessedness in heaven,[22] though in this connection as well many of them made a distinction between elect and reprobate children and did not dare to attribute salvation with certainty to each of these children individually.[23] As for children outside the covenant who died in infancy, the judgment of some was quite magnanimous. Junius, for example, would rather surmise out of love that they were saved than that they were lost.[24] Voetius said: As to whether they are lost or some among them are elect and were regenerated before they died, "I would not wish to deny, nor am I able to affirm" (*nolim negare, affirmare non possum*).[25]

(Munich: J. G. Cotta, 1869–70), I, 360ff.; J. A. Eberhard, *Neue Apologie des Sokrates, oder, Untersuchung der Lehre von der Seligheit der Heiden* (Berlin: F. Nicolai, 1772); cf. K. G. Bretschneider, *Systematische Entwicklung aller in der Dogmatik* (Leipzig: J. A. Barth, 1841), 679. In the Netherlands, the philosophical novel *Bélisaire* by Jean François Marmontel, published in 1766 [Paris: P. A. Le Prieur], occasioned a vehement dispute over whether the virtue practiced by Socrates, Titus, Antoninus, and others could bring them to blessedness in heaven. The Rev. P. Hofstede denied it, but the Remonstrant minister Nozeman defended the idea; cf. A. Ypey, *Geschiedenis van de kristlijke kerk in de achttiende eeuw* (Utrecht: Van Ijzerworst, 1797–1811), III, 166f.; A. Ypey and I. J. Dermout, *Geschiedenis der Nederlandsche Hervormde Kerk*, 4 vols. (Breda: Van Bergen; F. B. Hollingerus Pijpers, 1819–27), III, 539; J. P. de Bie, *Het leven en werken van Petrus Hofstede* (Rotterdam: Daamen, 1899).

18. So, for example, J. à Lasco, in A. Kuyper, "Van de gemeene gratie," *De Heraut* 1047 (16 January 1898); Jerome Zanchius, in W. G. T. Shedd, *Dogmatic Theology*, 2 vols. (New York: Charles Scribner's Sons, 1888), I, 436; II, 704; W. Bilderdijk, *Brieven* (Amsterdam: W. Messchert, 1836–37), V, 81; A. Kuyper, "Over het graf," *De Heraut* 594 (12 May 1894); 1047 (16 January 1898); J. H. A. Ebrard, *Das Dogma vom heiligen Abendmahl und seine Geschichte*, 2 vols. (Frankfurt a.M.: Heinrich Zimmer, 1845–46), II, 77. For Roman Catholic views, see J. Pohle, *Lehrbuch der Dogmatik*, 4th ed. (Paderborn: F. Schöningh, 1908–10), II, 414–33.

19. Cf. the literature in C. Vitringa, *Doctr. christ.*, I, 29.

20. P. Lombard, *Sent.*, II, dist. 33.

21. J. Gerhard, *Loci theologici*, ed. E. Preuss, 9 vols. (Berlin: G. Schlawitz, 1863–75), XVI, §169; J. F. Buddeus, *Institutiones theologiae dogmaticae* (Frankfurt and Leipzig, 1741), V, 1, 6.

22. Canons of Dort, I, 7; G. Voetius, *Select. disp.*, II, 417.

23. P. Martyr Vermigli, *Loci communes*, ed. R. Massonius (London, 1576), 76, 436; and similarly Beza, Pareus, Zanchius, Perkins, and others.

24. F. Junius, *Opuscula theologica selecta*, ed. A. Kuyper (Amsterdam: F. Muller, 1882), II, 333.

25. G. Voetius, *Select. disp.*, II, 413; further: C. Vitringa, *Doctr. christ.*, II, 51–52. Cf. esp. B. B. Warfield, "The Development of the Doctrine of Infant Salvation," in *Two Studies in the History of Doctrine* (New York: Christian Literature, 1897), 143–299.

In light of Scripture, both with regard to the salvation of pagans and that of children who die in infancy, we cannot get beyond abstaining from a firm judgment, in either a positive or a negative sense. Deserving of note, however, is that in the face of these serious questions Reformed theology is in a much more favorable position than any other. For in this connection, all other churches can entertain a more temperate judgment only if they reconsider their doctrine of the absolute necessity of the means of grace or infringe upon that of the accursedness of sin. But the Reformed refused to establish the measure of grace needed for a human being still to be united with God, though subject to many errors and sins, or to determine the extent of the knowledge indispensably necessary to salvation.[26] Furthermore, they maintained that the means of grace are not absolutely necessary for salvation and that also apart from the Word and sacraments God can regenerate persons for eternal life.[27]

Thus, in the Second Helvetic Confession, article 1, we read: "At the same time we recognize that God can illuminate whom and when he will, even without the external ministry, for that is in his power" (*agnoscimus Deum illuminare posse homines, etiam sine externo ministerio, quos et quando velit; id quod ejus potentiae est*). And the Westminster Confession states (in ch. X, §3) that "elect infants, dying in infancy, are regenerated and saved by Christ through the Spirit, who works when, and where, and how he pleases" (*Christus, qui quando et ubi et quo sibi placuerit modo operatur*), and that this applies also to "all other elect persons who are incapable of being outwardly called by the ministry of the Word" (*quotquot externae vocationis per ministerium verbi sunt incapaces*). Reuter, accordingly, after explaining Augustine's teaching on this point, correctly states: "One could in fact defend the paradox that it is precisely the *particularistic* doctrine of predestination that makes possible those *universalistic*-sounding phrases."[28] In fact, even the universalistic passages of Scripture cited above come most nearly and most beautifully into their own in Reformed theology. For these texts are certainly not intended universalistically in the sense that all humans or even all creatures are saved, nor are they so understood by any Christian church. All churches without exception confess that there is not only a heaven but also a hell. At most, therefore, there is a difference of opinion about the number of those who are saved and of those who are lost. But that is not something one can argue about inasmuch as that number is known only to God. When Jesus was asked: "Lord, will only a few be saved?" he only replied: "Strive to enter through the narrow door; for many . . . will try to enter but will not be able" (Luke 13:24).

26. G. Voetius, *Select. disp.*, II, 537–38, 781; F. Spanheim, *Dubia evang.*, III, 1291; Witsius, *Apost. Geloof*, II, 2, 15; ed. note: Bavinck is likely referring to H. Witsius's *Exercitationes sacra in symbolum quod apostolorum dicitur* (Amsterdam: 1697) or the Dutch translation, *Oeffeningen over de grondstukken van het Algemeyne Christelijke gelloove* (Rotterdam: Jan Daniel Beman, 1743).

27. Calvin, *Institutes*, IV.xvi.19.

28. "In der That es lässt sich das Paradoxon rechtfertigen, gerade die partikularistische Prädestinationslehre habe jene universalistisch klingenden Phrasen ermöglicht" (H. Reuter, *Augustinische Studien*, 92).

Directly important to us is only that we have no need to know the number of the elect. In any case, it is a fact that in Reformed theology the number of the elect need not, for any reason or in any respect, be deemed smaller than in any other theology. In fact, at bottom the Reformed confessions are more magnanimous and broader in outlook than any other Christian confession. It locates the ultimate and most profound source of salvation solely in God's good pleasure, in his eternal compassion, in his unfathomable mercy, in the unsearchable riches of his grace, grace that is both omnipotent and free. Aside from it, where could we find a firmer and broader foundation for the salvation of a sinful and lost human race? However troubling it may be that many fall away, still in Christ the believing community, the human race, the world, is saved. The organism of creation is restored. The wicked perish from the earth (Ps. 104:35); they are cast out (John 12:31; 15:6; Rev. 22:15). Still, all things in heaven and earth are gathered up in Christ (Eph. 1:10). All things are created through him and for him (Col. 1:16).

SERVICE IN THE ETERNAL SABBATH

[580] The communion with God that is enjoyed in the communion of saints no more excludes all action and activity in the age to come than it does in the present dispensation. As a rule Christian theology indeed paid little attention to this fact and primarily spoke of heavenly blessedness as a matter of knowing and enjoying God. And this, undoubtedly, is the core and center, the source and power, of eternal life. Also, Scripture offers but little information enabling us to form a clear picture of the activity of the blessed. It describes this blessedness more in terms of resting from our earthly labors than of engaging in new activities (Heb. 4:9; Rev. 14:13). Still, the rest enjoyed in the new Jerusalem is not to be conceived, either in the case of God (John 5:17) or in the case of his children, as blessed inaction. Scripture itself tells us that eternal life consists in knowing and serving God, in glorifying and praising him (John 17:3; Rev. 4:11; 5:8–10; etc.). His children remain his servants, who serve him night and day (Rev. 22:3). They are prophets, priests, and kings who reign on earth forever (1:6; 5:10; 22:5). Inasmuch as they have been faithful over little on earth, they will be put in charge of many things in the kingdom of God (Matt. 24:47; 25:21, 23). All will retain their own personalities, for the names of all who enter the new Jerusalem have been written in the Lamb's book of life (Rev. 20:15; 21:27), and all will receive a new name of their own (Isa. 62:2; 65:15; Rev. 2:17; 3:12; cf. 21:12, 14). The dead who die in the Lord rest from their labors but each is followed by one's own works (Rev. 14:13). Tribes, peoples, and nations all make their own particular contribution to the enrichment of life in the new Jerusalem (5:9; 7:9; 21:24, 26). What we have sown here is harvested in eternity (Matt. 25:24, 26; 1 Cor. 15:42ff.; 2 Cor. 9:6; Gal. 6:7–9). The great diversity that exists among people in all sorts of ways is not destroyed in eternity but is cleansed from all that is sinful and made serviceable to fellowship with God and each other. And just as the natural diversity

present in the believing community on earth is augmented with spiritual diversity (1 Cor. 12:7ff.), so also this natural and spiritual diversity is in turn augmented in heaven by the diversity of degrees of glory present there.

Moved by their opposition to the meritoriousness of good works, some Reformed scholars[29] have denied—as did Jovian in the fourth century, and later certain Socinians, and Gerlach even today—that there is any distinction in glory. And it is in fact true that all believers have been promised the same benefits in Christ's future: they all receive the same eternal life, the same abode in the new Jerusalem, the same fellowship with God, the same blessedness, and so on. Nevertheless, Scripture leaves no doubt whatever that in all that oneness and sameness there is enormous variation and diversity. Even the parable frequently cited to prove the opposite (Matt. 20:1–16) argues for such distinction. By this parable, Jesus makes the point that many who in their own opinion and that of others have worked long and hard will certainly not be behind in the messianic kingdom of the future by comparison with those who worked in the vineyard a much shorter period. The latter catch up with the former for, though many have been called and labor in the service of the kingdom of God, in the hereafter few will on that account enjoy special status and receive a position of distinction.

Such degrees of distinction in glory are taught much more clearly in other passages in Scripture, especially in those stating that all will receive a reward commensurate with their works. That reward is now kept in heaven (Matt. 5:12; 6:1ff.; Luke 6:23; 1 Tim. 6:19; Heb. 10:34–37) and will be publicly distributed only at the parousia (Matt. 6:4, 6, 18; 24:47; 2 Thess. 1:7; 1 Pet. 4:13). It is then given as compensation for that which the disciples of Jesus have given up and suffered on his account on earth (Matt. 5:10ff.; 19:29; Luke 6:21ff.; Rom. 8:17–18; 2 Cor. 4:17; 2 Thess. 1:7; Heb. 10:34; 1 Pet. 4:13) and also as a reward for the good works they have done; for example, the good use they made of their talents (Matt. 25:14ff.; Luke 19:13ff.), the love of one's enemies and the practice of selfless generosity (Luke 6:35), the care of the poor (Matt. 6:1), prayer and fasting (6:6, 18), ministering to the saints (10:40–42), and faithful service in the kingdom of God (24:44–47; 1 Cor. 3:8; etc.). That reward will be linked with and proportionate to the works performed (Matt. 16:27; 19:29; 25:21, 23; Luke 6:38; 19:17, 19; Rom. 2:6; 1 Cor. 3:8; 2 Cor. 4:17; 5:10; 9:6; Gal. 6:8–9; Heb. 11:26; Rev. 2:23; 11:18; 20:12; 22:12). Blessedness is indeed the same for all, but there are distinctions in "brightness" and glory (Dan. 12:3; 1 Cor. 15:41). In the Father's house, in which all God's children are welcomed, there are many dwelling places (John 14:2); the churches all receive from the King of the church a precious token and crown of their own in accordance with their faithfulness and dedication (Rev. 1–3).

On these statements of Scripture, Roman Catholic theologians have built the doctrine of the meritoriousness of good works and ascribed especially to martyrs,

---

29. Examples: P. Martyr Vermigli, *Loci comm.*, III, 17, 8; similarly Cameron, Tilenus, Spanheim, and others.

celibates, and teachers the right to special rewards in heaven. These (following Exod. 25:25 Vulgate) are called aureoles (*aureolae*) and are added to the crown of gold (*corona aurea*) everyone receives.[30] This misuse, however, does not alter the truth that there is disparity in glory depending on the works done by believers on earth. There is no reward to which humans are by nature entitled, inasmuch as the law of God is absolutely binding and does not let the demand of fulfillment depend on the free choice of people. Therefore, even if they have fulfilled the whole law, it only behooves them to say: "We are worthless slaves; we have done only what we ought to have done!" (Luke 17:10). All claims to reward can therefore flow only from a covenant, a sovereignly free and gracious disposition of God, and hence [reward] is a *given* right. That is how it was in the covenant of works and is even much more so in the covenant of grace.[31] For Christ has fulfilled all the requirements; he not only suffered the penalty but also, by fulfilling the law, won eternal life. The eternal blessedness and glory he received was, for him, the reward for his perfect obedience. But when he confers this righteousness of his on his own people through faith and unites eternal life with it, then the two, both the righteousness conferred and future blessedness, are the gifts of his grace, a reality that utterly excludes all merit on the part of believers. For believers are what God has made them, created in Christ Jesus for good works, which God prepared beforehand to be their way of life (Eph. 2:10). In the cause of Christ it is graciously given them not only to believe in him, but also to suffer for him (Acts 5:41; Phil. 1:29). God crowns his own work, not only in conferring eternal life on everyone who believes but also in distributing different degrees of glory to those who, motivated by that faith, have produced good works.

His purpose in doing this, however, is that, on earth as in heaven, there would be profuse diversity in the believing community, and that in such diversity the glory of his attributes would be manifest. Indeed, as a result of this diversity, the life of fellowship with God and with the angels, and of the blessed among themselves, gains in depth and intimacy. In that fellowship everyone has a place and task of one's own, based on personality and character, just as this is the case in the believing community on earth (Rom. 12:4–8; 1 Cor. 12). While we may not be able to form a clear picture of the activity of the blessed, Scripture does teach that the prophetic, priestly, and royal office, which was humanity's original possession, is fully restored in them by Christ. The service of God, mutual communion, and inhabiting the new heaven and the new earth undoubtedly offer abundant opportunity for the exercise of these offices, even though the form and manner of this exercise are unknown to us. That activity, however, coincides with resting and enjoying. The difference between day and night, between the Sabbath and the workdays, has been suspended. Time is charged with the eternity of God. Space is full of his presence. Eternal becoming is wedded to immutable being. Even the

---

30. T. Aquinas, *Summa theol.*, III, qu. 96; Bonaventure, *Breviloquium*, VII, 7.
31. Cf. H. Bavinck, *Reformed Dogmatics*, II, 569–70 (#296); and above, 265 (#483).

contrast between heaven and earth is gone. For all the things that are in heaven and on earth have been gathered up in Christ as head (Eph. 1:10). All creatures will then live and move and have their being in God [Acts 17:28], who is all in all [1 Cor. 15:28], who reflects all his attributes in the mirror of his works and glorifies himself in them.[32]

32. On the topic of heavenly blessedness, cf. Augustine, *City of God* XXII, chs. 29–30; P. Lombard, *Sent.*, IV, dist. 49; T. Aquinas, *Summa theol.*, suppl., qu. 92–96; Bonaventure, *Breviloquium*, VII, c. 7; J. H. Oswald, *Eschatologie* (Paderborn: F. Schöningh, 1869), 38–57; L. Atzberger, *Die Christliche Eschatologie*, 238f.; O. Ritschl, "Luthers Seligkeitsvorstellung in ihrer Entstehung und Bedeutung," *Die christliche Welt* 3 (1889): 874–80; J. Gerhard, *Loci theol.*, XXXI; J. Quenstedt, *Theologia*, I, 550–60; A. Polanus, *Syntagma theologiae christianae*, 5th ed. (Hanover: Aubry, 1624), VI, c. 72–75; A. Walaeus, in *Synopsis purioris theologiae*, disp. 52; P. van Mastricht, *Theoretico-practica theologia* (Utrecht: Appels, 1714), VIII, 4, 10; F. Turretin, *Institutes of Elenctic Theology*, XX, qu. 8–13; J. Marckius, *Exspectatio gloriae futurae Jesu Christi*, III, c. 8, 10, 11; B. de Moor, *Comm. theol.*, VI, 718–33; C. Vitringa, *Doctr. christ.*, IV, 179; Th. Kliefoth, *Christliche Eschatologie*, 311f.; M. Kähler, "Ewiges Leben," in *PRE³*, XI, 330–34; idem, "Seligkeit," in *PRE³*, XVIII, 179–84.

BIBLIOGRAPHY

This bibliography includes the items Bavinck listed at the head of sections 49–62 in the *Gereformeerde Dogmatiek* as well as the additional works cited in his footnotes. Particularly with respect to the footnote references, where Bavinck's own citations were quite incomplete by contemporary standards, with titles often significantly abbreviated, this bibliography provides fuller information. In some cases full bibliographic information was available only for an edition other than the one Bavinck cited. Where English translations of Dutch or German works are available they have been cited rather than the original. In a few instances where Bavinck cited Dutch translations of English originals, the original work is listed. In cases where multiple versions or editions are available in English (e.g., Calvin's *Institutes*), the most recent, most frequently cited, or most accessible edition was chosen. Not included here is the literature Bavinck refers to at the beginning of his bibliography heading section 62 of the *Gereformeerde Dogmatiek*, literature dealing with Old Testament and Jewish messianic expectation and listed in the *Gereformeerde Dogmatiek*, III, 214–24. These items were included in the bibliography of *Reformed Dogmatics*, vol. 3. In spite of best efforts to track down each

The improvement of this bibliography over Bavinck's own citations in the *Gereformeerde Dogmatiek* is largely thanks to a valuable tool he did not have available to him—the Internet—and its diligent perusal by a number of Calvin Theological Seminary students who labored as the editor's student assistants. Graduate students Raymond Blacketer and Claudette Grinnell worked on the eschatology section in *GD* IV, which was published separately as *The Last Things* (Baker Academic, 1996). Colin Vander Ploeg, Steven Baarda, and Marcia De Haan-Van Drunen worked on the creation section of *GD* II, which was published as *In the Beginning* (Baker Academic, 1999). The PhD students Steven J. Grabill and Rev. J. Mark Beach worked on volume 1 of *Reformed Dogmatics*, and Courtney Hoekstra worked full-time during the summer of 2002 to complete the bibliography of volume 1. She was also the major contributor to the completed bibliography of volumes 2–4. Joel Vande Werken worked diligently with Courtney Hoekstra in tracking down information for items in the bibliography of the present volume as well as that of volume 3. Dr. Roger Nicole carefully checked the eschatology and creation bibliographies and helped reduce the number of errors and asterisks. The assistance of all is gratefully acknowledged here.

reference to confirm or complete bibliographic information, some of Bavinck's abbreviated and cryptic notations remain unconfirmed or incomplete. Where information is unconfirmed, incomplete, and/or titles have been reconstructed, the work is marked with an asterisk.

ABBREVIATIONS

ANF	*The Ante-Nicene Fathers*. Edited by Alexander Roberts and James Donaldson. 10 vols. New York: Christian Literature Co., 1885–96. Reprinted, Grand Rapids: Eerdmans, 1950–51.
CR	Corpus reformatorum. Edited by C. G. Bretschneider, H. E. Bindseil, et al. 101 vols. Halle a. Salle and Brunsvigae: Schwetschke, 1834–1959.
DB	*Dictionary of the Bible*. Edited by James Hastings. 5 vols. New York: C. Scribner Sons, 1898–1904.
DC	*A Dictionary of Christ and the Gospels*. Edited by James Hastings. 2 vols. New York: C. Scribner Sons, 1906–8.
ET	English translation
NPNF (1)	*A Select Library of Nicene and Post-Nicene Fathers of the Christian Church*. Edited by Philip Schaff. 1st series. 14 vols. New York: Christian Literature Co., 1887–1900. Reprinted, Grand Rapids: Eerdmans, 1956.
NPNF (2)	*A Select Library of Nicene and Post-Nicene Fathers of the Christian Church*. Edited by Philip Schaff and Henry Wace. 2nd series. 14 vols. New York: Christian Literature Co., 1890–1900. Reprinted, Grand Rapids: Eerdmans, 1952.
PL	Patrologiae cursus completus: Series latina. Edited by J.-P. Migne. 221 vols. Paris: Migne, 1844–65.
PRE[3]	*Realencyklopädie für protestantische Theologie und Kirche*. Edited by Albert Hauck. 3rd rev. ed. 24 vols. Leipzig: J. C. Hinrichs, 1896–1913.

BOOKS

Aalst, Gerardus van. *Geestelyke mengelstoffen: Ofte godvrugtige bedenkingen over eenige gewigtige waarheden*. Amsterdam: Hendrik Vieroot, 1754. Reprinted, Ermelo: Snoek, 2000.

Achelis, Ernst Christian. *Der Dekalog als katechetisches Lehrstück*. Giessen: Alfred Töppelmann, 1905.

———. *Lehrbuch der praktischen Theologie*. 2nd ed. 2 vols. Leipzig: Hinrichs, 1898.

Acta Synodi nationalis: In nomine Domini nostri Jesu Christi. Authoritate illustr. et praepotentum DD. Ordinum generalium Foederati Belgii provinciarum, Dordrechti habitae anno 1618 et 1619; accedunt plenissima, de quinque articulis, theologorum judicia. Dortrechti: Isaaci Joannidis Canini, 1620.

Adam, Karl. *Der Kirchenbegriff Tertullians*. Paderborn: Schöningh, 1907.

Alexander of Hales. *Summa theologica*. 4 vols. in 5. Florence: Typographia Colegii S. Bonaventurae, 1924–48.

Alighieri, Dante. *The Divine Comedy*. Translated by L. G. White. New York: Pantheon Books, 1948.

Alsted, Johann Heinrich. *Encyclopaedia*. Stuttgart and Bad Cannstatt: Frommann-Holzboog, 1630.

———. *Theologica didactica, exhibens locos communes theologicos methodo scholastica*. Hanau: C. Eifrid, 1618.

Althaus, Paul. *Die Heilsbedeutung der Taufe im Neuen Testament*. Gütersloh: Bertelsmann, 1897.

Alting, Heinrich. *Theologia problematica nova.* Amsterdam: J. Jansson, 1662.

Ames, William. *Bellarminus enervatus, sive disputationes anti-Bellarminianae.* 3rd ed. 4 vols. Oxford: G. Turner, 1629.

———. *Conscience with the Power and Cases Thereof.* London: Rothwell, Slater & Blacklock, 1643.

———. *Guiliel Amesii medulla theologica.* Amsterdam: Ioannem Ianssonium, 1628.

———. *The Marrow of Theology.* Translated and edited by John Dykstra Eusden. Boston: Pilgrim, 1968. Reprinted, Grand Rapids: Baker Academic, 1997.

Amyraut, Moise. *Du gouvernement de l'Église, conte ceux qui veulent abolir l'usage de l'autorité des Synodes.* Saumur, 1653.

———. *Verhandeling van den Staet der Gelooven na de Doodt.* Utrecht: F. Halma, 1680.

Andresen, Carl. *Die Lehre von der Wiedegeburt auf theistischen Grundlage.* 2nd ed. Hamburg: Gräfe & Sillem, 1899.

Anrich, Gustav. *Das antike Mysterienwesen in seinem Einfluss auf das Christenthum.* Göttingen: Vandenhoeck & Ruprecht, 1894.

Antoine, Paul Gabriel. *Theologia moralis universa.* 6 vols. in 3. Venice: Balleoniana, 1792.

Apostolic Constitutions. ANF, VII, 385–508.

Appelius, Johannes Conrad. *De Hervormde leer van den geestelyken staat der mensen.* Groningen: Wed. J. Spandaw, 1769.

Aquinas, Thomas. *See* Thomas Aquinas.

Aristotle. *The Politics.* Translated by Carnes Lord. Chicago: University of Chicago Press, 1984.

Arminius, Jacob. *Opera theologica.* Leiden: Godefridum Basson, 1629.

———. *The Writings of James Arminius.* Translated by James Nichols and W. R. Begnall. 3 vols. Grand Rapids: Baker Academic, 1952.

Arnold, Carl Franklin. *Gemeinschaft der Heiligen und Heiligungs-Gemeinschaften.* Gr. Lichterfelde, Berlin: E. Runge, 1909.

Atzberger, Leonhard. *Die christliche Eschatologie in den Stadien ihrer Offenbarung im Alten und Neuen Testamente: Mit besonderer Berücksichtigung der jüdischen Eschatologie im Zeitalter Christi.* Freiburg i.B.: Herder, 1890.

———. *Geschichte der christlichen Eschatologie innerhalb der vornicänischen Zeit mit theilweiser Einbeziehung der Lehre vom christlichen Heile uberhaupt.* Freiburg i.B. and St. Louis: Herder, 1896.

Augustine, Aurelius. *Against Adimantus.* PL, XLII: 129–72.

———. *Against Cresconius the Grammarian.* PL, XLIII, 445–594.

———. *Against Faustus the Manichee.* NPNF (1), IV, 155–345.

———. *Against Gaudentium a Donatist Bishop.* PL, XLIII, 707–58.

———. *Against Julian.* Translated by M. A. Schumacher. Vol. 16 of *Writings of Saint Augustine.* Fathers of the Church 35. Washington, DC: Catholic University of America Press, 1984.

———. *Against the Letter of Parmenian.* PL, XLIII, 33–108.

———. *Answer to Letters of Petilian.* NPNF (1), IV, 519–628.

———. *The City of God.* NPNF (1), II, 1–511.

———. *Eighty-three Different Questions.* Translated by David L. Mosher. Fathers of the Church 70. Washington, DC: Catholic University of America Press, 1982.

———. *The Enchiridion.* NPNF (1), III, 229–76.

———. *Expositions on the Psalms.* NPNF (1), VIII, 1–683.

———. *Homilies on the Gospel of John.* NPNF (1), VII, 7–452.

———. *Letters.* NPNF (1), I, 209–593.

———. *Merits and Remission of Sins.* NPNF (1), V, 15–78.

———. *Nature and Grace.* NPNF (1), V, 121–53.

———. *On Admonition and Grace.* NPNF (1), V, 468–92.

———. *On Baptism, against the Donatists.* NPNF (1), IV, 411–514.

———. *On Christian Teaching.* NPNF (1), II, 519–97.

————. *On Free Will. NPNF* (1), V, 436–43.

————. *On the Gift of Perseverance.* In *Four Anti-Pelagian Writings.* Translated by John A. Mourant and William J. Collinge. Fathers of the Church 86. Washington, DC: Catholic University of America Press, 1992.

————. *On Heresies.* PL, XLII, 21–50.

————. *On the Predestination of the Saints. NPNF* (1), V, 493–520.

————. *On the Spirit and the Letter. NPNF* (1), V, 80–114.

————. *Proceedings with Emeritus.* PL, XLIII, 697–706.

————. *Sermons. NPNF* (1), VI, 237–545.

————. *The Soul and Its Origin. NPNF* (1), V, 311–72.

————. *The Unity of the Church.* PL, XLIII, 391–446.

Bach, Ludwig. *Der Glaube nach der Anschauung des Alten Testaments: Eine Untersuchung über die Bedeutung im alttestamentlichen Sprachgebrauch.* Gütersloh: Bertelsmann, 1900.

*Bachiene, Jan Hendrik. *De leer van de sakramenten na den aart van de Goddelijke verbonden verklaard.* Utrecht, 1771.

Bachmann, Johann Friedrich. *Die Geschichte der Einführung der Confirmation innerhalb der evangelischen Kirche.* Berlin: Wilhelm Schultze, 1852.

Baier, Johann Wilhelm. *Compendium theologiae positivae.* 3 vols. in 4. St. Louis: Concordia, 1879.

Bainvel, Jean Vincent. *Faith and the Act of Faith.* Translated by Leo C. Sterk. St. Louis: Herder, 1926.

Baldensperger, Wilhelm. *Das Prolog des vierten Evangeliums.* Freiburg i.B.: Mohr, 1898.

Barclay, Robert. *Verantwoording van de ware Christelyke Godgeleertheid.* Translated by Jan Hendrik Glazemaker. Amsterdam: A. Waldorp, 1757.

Barnabas, Epistle of. ANF, I, 133–50.

Bartlett, Robert Edward. *The Letter and the Spirit.* London and New York: Rivingtons and E. & J. B. Young, 1888.

Bartmann, Bernhard. *St. Paulus und St. Jakobus über die Rechtfertigung.* Freiburg i.B.: Herder, 1897.

Basil of Caesarea. *Exegetic Homilies.* Translated by Agnes Clare Way. Fathers of the Church 46. Washington, DC: Catholic University of America Press, 1963.

————. *On the Holy Spirit. NPNF* (2), VIII, 1–50.

Baumann, Julius. *Die Staatslehre des heiligen Thomas von Aquino.* Leipzig: S. Hirzel, 1873.

————. *Unsterblichkeit und Seelenwanderung: Ein Vereinigungspunkt morgenlandischen und abendlandischen Weltansicht.* Leipzig: S. Hirzel, 1909.

Baumer, Iso, ed. *Max von Sachsen: Primat des Andern; Texte und Kommentare.* Freiburg, Switz.: Universitätsverlag, 1996.

Baumgartner, Ephrem. *Eucharistie und Agape im Urchristentum.* Solothurn: Buch und Kunstdruckerei Union, 1909.

Bautz, Joseph. *Die Hölle in Anschluss an die Scholastiek dargestellt.* Mainz: Kirchheim, 1905.

Bavinck, Herman. *De algemeene genade.* Kampen: Zalsman, 1894.

————. *The Certainty of Faith.* Translated by H. der Nederlanden. St. Catharines, ON: Paideia, 1980.

————. *Het doctorenambt.* Kampen: Zalsman, 1899.

————. *De ethiek van Ulrich Zwingli.* Kampen: Zalsman, 1880.

————. *De katholiciteit van Christendom en kerk.* Kampen: Zalsman, 1888.

————. *Magnalia Dei.* Kampen: Kok, 1909.

————. *Our Reasonable Faith.* Translated by H. Zylstra. Grand Rapids: Eerdmans, 1956.

————. *Paedagogische beginselen.* Kampen: Kok, 1904.

————. *The Philosophy of Revelation.* New York: Longmans, Green, 1909.

————. *Roeping en wedergeboorte.* Kampen: Zalsman, 1903.

————. *De theologie van Daniel Chantepie de la Saussaye.* Leiden: Donner, 1884.

Becanus, Martin. *De ecclesia Christi, itemque de ecclesia Romana, quae est catholicorum, et de Reformata, quae est Luthernorum & Calvinistarum.* Mainz: Johannes Albinus, 1615.

———. *Manuale controversiarum huius temporis.* Wurzburg: Johannes Volmar, 1626.

Beck, Johann Tobias. *Outlines of Biblical Psychology.* Edinburgh: T&T Clark, 1877.

———. *Umriss der biblischen Seelenlehre.* 3rd ed. Stuttgart: Steinkopf, 1871.

———. *Vorlesungen über christliche Glaubenslehre.* 2 vols. Gütersloh: Bertelsmann, 1896–97.

Bellarmine, Robert. *De controversiis christianae fidei adversus huius temporis haereticos.* Cologne: G. Gualtheri, 1617–20.

Bengel, Johann Albrecht et al. *Gnomon of the New Testament.* 5 vols. Edinburgh: T&T Clark, 1877.

Bensdorp, Th. F. *Pluriformiteit: Een fundamenteele misvatting van Dr. A. Kuyper of een hooeloos pleidooi.* Amsterdam: G. Borg, 1901.

Beringer, Franz. *Die Ablässe, ihr Wesen und Gebrauch: Handbuch für Geistlichen und Laien.* Paderborn: Schöningh, 1900.

Bertholet, Alfred. *Die israelitischen Vorstellungen vom Zustand nach dem Tode, ein offentlicher Vortrag.* Freiburg i.B.: J. C. B. Mohr (Paul Siebeck), 1899.

———. *Seelenwanderung.* Tübingen: J. C. B. Mohr (Paul Siebeck), 1906.

Berzl, Otto. *Ursprung, Aufgabe, und Wesen der christlichen Synoden.* Würzburg: Stadenraus, 1908.

*Beuningen, Friedrich von. *Dein Reich komme.* Riga, 1901.

Beyschlag, Willibald. *Neutestamentliche Theologie, oder geschichtliche Darstellung der Lehren Jesu und des Urchristenthums nach den neutestamentlichen Quellen.* 2nd ed. Halle: E. Strien, 1896.

Beza, Theodore. *Ad acta colloquii Montisbelgardensis Tubingae edita, Theodori Bezae responsio.* Geneva: Joannes le Preux, 1588.

———. *Tractationum theologicarum.* Geneva: Jean Crispin, 1570.

Bie, Jan Pieter de. *Het leven en werken van Petrus Hofstede.* Rotterdam: D. A. Daamen, 1899.

Biedermann, Aloys Emmanuel. *Christliche Dogmatik.* Zurich: Orell, Fussli, 1869.

Biesterveld, Petrus. *Het huisbezoek.* Kampen: Bos, 1900.

Biesterveld, Petrus, and H. H. Kuyper. *Kerkelijk handboekje.* Kampen: Bos, 1905.

Biesterveld, Petrus, Jan van Lonkhuijzen, and Roelof Jan Willem Rudolph. *Het diaconaat.* Hilversum: J. H. Witzel, 1907.

Bilderdijk, W. *Brieven.* Vol. 5. Amsterdam: W. Messchert, 1836–37.

Bingham, Joseph. *Origenes ecclesiasticae, or, the Antiquities of the Christian Church.* 9 vols. London: W. Straker, 1843–45.

Blank, Oskar. *Die Lehre des hl. Augustin vom Sakramente der Eucharistie.* Paderborn: Schöningh, 1906.

Bleibtreu, Walther. *Die evangelische Lehre von der sichtbaren und unsichtbaren Kirche.* Tübingen: Mohr Siebeck, 1903.

Blösch, Emil. *Geschichte der schweizerisch-reformierten Kirchen.* 2 vols. Bern: Schmid & Francke, 1898–99.

*Boddaert, Petrus. *Wolk van getuigen voor de leere der rechtvaardiginge door en uit het geloove.* 1759.

Boehmer, Heinrich. *Luther im Lichte der neuren Forschung.* 2nd ed. Leipzig: Teubner, 1910.

———. *Luther in Light of Recent Research.* Translated by Carl Frederick Huth. New York: Christian Herald, 1916.

Boehmer, Julius. *Das biblische "Im Namen."* Giessen: Ricker, 1898.

Boeles, J. *De mysteriis in relig. Christ.* Groningen: C. M. van B. Hoitsema, 1843.

Boetticher, Carl. *Das Wesen des religiösen Glaubens im Neuen Testament.* Berlin: R. Gärtner, 1895.

Boeuf, Marie [pseudonym: Camille Bos]. *Psychologie de la croyance.* 2nd ed. Paris: Alcan, 1905.

Bogue, David. *Discourses on the Millennium.* London: T. Hamilton, 1818.

Bois, Henri. *Le réveil au pays de Galles.* Tolouse: Société des publications morales et religieuses, 1906.

Bonaventure. *The Breviloquium.* Vol. 2 of *The Works of Bonaventure.* Translated by Jose DeVinck. Paterson, NJ: St. Anthony Guild Press, 1963.

*Bonwetsch, G. Nathanael. *Das Amt der Diakonie in der alten Kirche.* 1890.

Bos, Camille. *See* Boeuf, Marie

Bossuet, Jacques Bénigne. *An Exposition of the Doctrine of the Catholique Church in the Points of Controversie with Those of the Pretended Reformation.* Translated by [Walter Montagu]. 1672. Reprinted, Paris: Vincent du Moutier, 1983.

Boston, Thomas. *Human Nature in Its Fourfold State.* 1720. Reprinted, London: Banner of Truth Trust, 1964.

Brahe, Jan Jacob. *Godgeleerde stellingen over de leer der rechtvaardigmaking des zondaars voor God.* Amsterdam: Den Ouden, 1833.

Brakel, Wilhelmus à. *The Christian's Reasonable Service.* Translated by Bartel Elshout. 4 vols. Ligonier, PA: Soli Deo Gloria Publications, 1992–95.

———. *Redelijke godsdienst.* Leiden: D. Donner, 1893.

Brandt, Wilhelm. *Die jüdischen Baptismen.* Giessen: Alfred Töpelmann, 1910.

Brauer, Karl. *Die Unionstätigkeit John Duries unter dem Protektorat Cromwells.* Marburg: Elwert, 1907.

Braun, Wilhelm. *Die Bedeutung des Concupiscenz in Luthers Leben und Lehre.* Berlin: Trowitzsch, 1908.

Brès, Guy [Guido] de. *De wortel, den oorspronck, ende het fundament der Wederdooperen.* Amsterdam: Cloppenburgh, 1589.

Bretschneider, Karl Gottlieb. *Handbuch der Dogmatik der evangelisch-lutherischen Kirche, oder, Versuch einer beurtheilenden Darstellung der Grundsätze, welche diese Kirche in ihren symbolischen Schriften bei die christliche Glaubenslehre ausgesprochen hat, mit Vergleichung der Glaubenslehre in den Bekenntnisschriften der reformirten Kirche.* 4th ed. 2 vols. Leipzig: J. A. Barth, 1838.

———. *Systematische Entwicklung aller in der Dogmatik verkommenden Begriffe: Nach den symbolischen Schriften der evangelisch-lutherischen und reformierten Kirche und den wichtigsten dogmatischen Lehrbüchern ihrer Theologen.* Leipzig: J. A. Barth, 1841.

Briet, J. P. *De eschatologie of leer der toekomende dingen.* 2 vols. Tiel: H. C. A. Campagne, 1857–58.

Brink, Henricus. *Toet-steen der waarheid en der dwalingen.* Amsterdam: G. Borstius, 1685.

*Bronsveld, A. W. *Uit het hoogd.* Utrecht, 1876.

Brors, Franz Xaver. *Modernes ABC für das katholische Volk.* Kevelaer: Butzon, 1910.

Bruining, Albert. *Het voortbestaan der menschelijke persoonlijkheid na den dood.* Assen: L. Hansma, 1904.

Bucanus, Guillaume. *Institutiones theologicae, seu locorum communium christianae religionis, ex dei verbo, et praestantissimorum theologorum orthodoxo consensu expositorum.* 3rd ed. Bern: Johannes & Isaias le Preux, 1605.

Buchanan, James. *The Doctrine of Justification: An Outline of Its History in the Church and of Its Exposition from Scripture.* Edinburgh: T&T Clark, 1867.

———. *The Office and Work of the Holy Spirit.* 1842. Reprinted, Edinburgh: Banner of Truth Trust, 1984.

Buchberger, Michael. *Kirchliches Handlexikon: Ein Nachschlagbuch über das Gesamtgebiet der Theologie und ihrer Hilfswissenschaften.* 2 vols. Freiburg i.B.: Herder, 1907–12.

———. *Die Wirkungen des Busssakraments nach der Lehre des heiligen Thomas von Aquin.* Freiburg i.B.: Herder, 1901.

Büchner, Ludwig. *Force and Matter; or Principles of the Natural Order of the Universe.* 4th ed. Translated from the 15th German ed. New York: P. Eckler, 1891.

———. *Kraft und Stoff, oder, Grundzüge der natürlichen Weltordnung.* Leipzig: T. Thomas, 1902.

Buddeus, Joannes Franciscus [Franz]. *Institutiones theologiae dogmaticae variis observationibus illustratae*. Frankfurt and Leipzig, 1741.

Bueren, J. Lammerts van, Chr. Hunningher, J. Th. de Visser, and Philippus Jacobus Hoedemaker. *Het Darbisme; De z. g. Apostolische kerk; De nieuwere theosophie; De kerk en de sekten*. Amsterdam: Egeling's Boekhandel, 1906.

Bullinger, Heinrich. *The Decades of Henry Bullinger*. 4 vols. in 2. Grand Rapids: Reformation Heritage Books, 2004.

———. *Huijsboeck*. Amsterdam: Hendrick Laurensz, 1612. *Huys-boeck*. Amsterdam: Barentsz, 1612.

———. *Von den Concilijs*. Zurich: Christoffel Froschower, 1561.

Bungener, Laurence Louis Felix. *Pape et concile au XIXe siècle*. Paris: M. Lévy, 1870.

———. *Rome and the Council in the 19th Century*. Edinburgh: T&T Clark, 1870.

Burger, Dionys. *De zielsverhuizing*. Amersfoort: Slothouwer, 1877.

Burmann, Frans. *Synopsis theologiae & speciatim oeconomiae foederum dei: Ab initio saeculorum usque ad consummationem eorum*. 2 vols. in 1. Amsterdam: Joannem Wolters, 1699.

Burnet, Thomas. *De statu mortuorum et resurgentium*. London, 1726.

Bussy, Izaak Jan le Cosquino de. *Ethische Idealisme*. Amsterdam: J. H. de Bussy, 1875.

Calvin, John. *Canons and Decrees of the Council of Trent, with the Antidote*. Vol. 3, pp. 17–188 in *Selected Works of John Calvin*. Edited by Henry Beveridge and Jules Bonnet. Translated by David Constable. 1851. Reprinted, Grand Rapids: Baker Academic, 1983.

———. *Commentaries*. 22 vols. Translated by John King et al. Grand Rapids: Baker Academic, 1999.

———. *Consensus tigurinus*. Vol. 2, pp. 199–244 in *Selected Works of John Calvin*. Edited by Henry Beveridge and Jules Bonnet. Translated by David Constable. 1851. Reprinted, Grand Rapids: Baker Academic, 1983.

———. "Ecclesiastical Ordinances." Pp. 58–72 in *Calvin: Theological Treatises*.

Library of Christian Classics, vol. 22. Translated by J. K. S. Reid. Philadelphia: Westminster Press, 1954.

———. *Institutes of the Christian Religion* (1559). Edited by John T. McNeill. Translated by F. L. Battles. 2 vols. Philadelphia: Westminster, 1960.

———. *Ioannis Calvini opera quae supersunt omnia*. Edited by W. Baum, E. Cunitz, and E. Reuss. 59 vols. Braunschweig: C. A. Schwetscke et Filium, 1864–97.

———. "Psychopannychia; or, the Soul's Imaginary Sleep between Death and Judgment." Vol. 3, pp. 413–90 in *Selected Works of John Calvin*. Edited by Henry Beveridge and Jules Bonnet. 1851. Reprinted, Grand Rapids: Baker Academic, 1983.

———. "Reply by John Calvin to Letter by Cardinal Sadolet to the Senate and People of Geneva." Vol. 1, pp. 23–68 in *Selected Works of John Calvin*. Edited by Henry Beveridge and Jules Bonnet. 1851. Reprinted, Grand Rapids: Baker Academic, 1983.

———. *Treatises against the Anabaptists and Libertines*. Translated and edited by Benjamin W. Farley. Grand Rapids: Baker Academic, 1982.

Candlish, Robert Smith. *The Atonement: Its Reality, Completeness, and Extent*. London: T. Nelson & Sons, 1861.

Canisius, Petrus. *Summa doctrinae christianae*. Antwerp: J. Withagus, 1558.

Canons and Decrees of the Sacred and Oecumenical Council of Trent. Translated by J. Waterforth. Chicago: Christian Symbolic Publication Society, 1848.

Canus, Melchior. *De locis theologicis*. Salamanca: Gastius, 1563.

———. *Opera, clare divisa*. Venice: Remondini, 1776.

Cappel, Louis, Moïse Amyraut, and Josué de la Place. *Syntagma thesium theologicarum in academia salmuriensi*. Saumur: Johannes Lesner, 1664.

Carrière, Moriz. *De zedelijke wereldorde*. Translated by P. C. van Oosterzee. Utrecht: Kemink, 1880.

Caspari, Walter. *Die evangelische Konfirmation, vornämlich in der lutherischen Kirche.* Erlangen: Deichert, 1890.

Cathrein, Victor. *Moralphilosophie.* 3rd ed. 2 vols. Freiburg i.B.: Herder, 1899.

Chamier, Daniel. *Panstratiae catholicae, sive controversiarum de religione adversus pontificios corpus.* Geneva: Roverianis, 1626.

Chantepie de la Saussaye, Pierre Daniel. *Lehrbuch der Religionsgeschichte.* 2 vols. Freiburg i.B.: Mohr (Siebeck), 1887–89.

Chavannes, C. G. *Qu'est-ce qu'une église?* Paris: Fischbacher, 1897.

Cheetham, Samuel. *The Mysteries: Pagan and Christian.* London and New York: MacMillan, 1897.

Chiniquy, Charles Pascal Telesphore. *Fifty Years in the Church of Rome.* Montreal: Drysdale, 1886. Reprinted, Grand Rapids: Baker Books, 1953.

———. *The Priest, the Woman, and the Confessional.* Chicago: A. Craig, 1880.

Choisy, Eugène. *La théocratie à Genève au temps du Calvin.* Geneva: Eggimann, 1897.

Chrysostom, John. *The Homilies.* Oxford: J. H. Parker, 1843.

Cicero, Marcus Tullius. *The Speeches.* Translated by John Henry Freese. London: W. Heineman; New York: G. P. Putnam's Sons, 1930.

———. *Tusculan disputations.* London: W. Heineman; New York: G. P. Putnam's Sons, 1927.

Clemen, Carl. *Die christliche Lehre von der Sünde.* Göttingen: Vandenhoeck & Ruprecht, 1897.

Clement of Alexandria. *The Instructor. ANF,* II, 207–98.

———. *Stromata. ANF,* II, 299–568.

Clement of Rome. *First Epistle of Clement to the Corinthians. ANF,* I, 1–22.

———. *Second Clement. ANF,* VII, 517–23.

Cloppenburg, Johannes. *Theologica opera omnia.* 2 vols. Amsterdam: Borstius, 1684.

Coccejus, Johannes. *Opera omnia theologica, exegetica, didactica, polemica, philologica: Divisa in decem volumina.* Amsterdam: Nicolaas Byl, 1753.

Coe, George Albert. *The Spiritual Life: Studies in the Science of Religion.* Chicago: F. H. Revell, 1903.

Comrie, Alexander. *The ABC of Faith.* Translated by J. Marcus Banfield. Ossett: Zoar, 1978.

———. *Brief over de regtvaardigmaking des zondaars, door de onmiddelijke toerekening der borg-geregtigheid van Christus.* Utrecht: Fisscher, 1889. Reprinted, Ermelo: Snoek, 2003.

———. *Stellige en practikale verklaring van den Heidelbergschen catechismus.* Barneveld: Van Horssen, 1976.

———. *Verhandeling van eenige eigenschappen des zaligmakenden geloofs.* Leiden: Johannes Hasebroek; Amsterdam: Nicolaas Byl, 1744.

Comrie, Alexander, and Nicolaus Holtius. *Examen van het ontwerp van tolerantie.* 10 vols. Amsterdam: Nicolaas Byl, 1753.

Cremer, Ernst. *Rechtfertigung und Wiedergeburt.* Gütersloh: Evangelischer Verlag der Rufer, 1907.

Cremer, Hermann. *Biblico-Theological Lexicon of New Testament Greek.* Translated by D. W. Simon and William Urwick. Edinburgh: T&T Clark; New York: Charles Scribner's Sons, 1895.

———. *Biblisch-theologisches Wörterbuch der neutestamentlichen Gräcität.* Gotha: F. A. Perthes, 1880.

———. *Die paulinische Rechtfertigungslehre im Zusammenhange ihrer geschichtlichen Voraussetzung.* Gütersloh: Bertelsmann, 1899. 2nd ed., 1900.

———. *Taufe, Wiedergeburt, und Kindertaufe.* 2nd ed. Gütersloh: Bertelsmann, 1901.

———. *Über den Zustand nach dem Tode: Nebst einigen Andeutungen über das Kindersterben und über den Spiritismus.* Gütersloh: Bertelsmann, 1883. 4th ed., 1893.

Crespin, Jean. *Bibliotheca studij theologici.* Geneva: Io. Crispinum, 1565.

Cumming, John. *Beschouwingen over het dui-zendjarige rijk*. 1866.

———. *The Great Consummation: The Millennial Rest, or, the World as It Will Be*. New York: Carleton, 1864. (Dutch translation titled *De duizendjarige rust*. Translated by G. Jasperus. Amsterdam: H. de Hoogh, 1863.)

———. *Great Preparation, or, Redemption Draweth Nigh*. New York: Rudd & Carleton, 1860. (Dutch translation titled *De verlossing nabij*. Amsterdam: H. de Hoogh, 1862.)

———. *The Great Tribulation*. New York: Rudd & Carleton, 1860. (Dutch translation titled *De groote verdrukking*. Amsterdam, 1861.)

Cumont, Franz Valery Marie. *Die orientalischen Religionen im römischen Heidentum*. Translated by Georg Gehrich. Leipzig: Teubner, 1910.

Cunningham, William. *Historical Theology*. 2nd ed. 2 vols. Edinburgh: T&T Clark, 1864.

Cyprian. *Epistles*. ANF, V, 275–420.

———. *On the Unity of the Church*. ANF, V, 421–29.

Dähne, August Ferdinand. *Geschichtliche Darstellung der jüdisch-alexandrinischen Religions-Philosophie*. 2 vols. Halle: Waisenhauses, 1834.

Dalton, Hermann. *Beiträge zur Geschichte der evangelischen Kirche in Russland*. 4 vols. in 3. Berlin: Reuther & Reichard, 1887–1905.

———. *Johannes à Lasco*. Gotha: Perthes, 1881.

———. *John à Lasco*. Translated by Maurice J. Evans. London: Hodder & Stoughton, 1886.

Davidson, Andrew Bruce. *The Theology of the Old Testament*. Edited from the author's manuscripts by S. D. F. Salmond. New York: Charles Scribner's Sons, 1904.

Decoppet, Auguste. *Les grands problèmes de l'au delà*. 8th ed. Paris: Fischbacher, 1906.

Deharbe, Joseph. *Verklaring der katholieke geloofs- en zedeleer*. 4 vols. 3rd ed. Utrecht: J. R. Van Rossum, 1880–88.

Deissmann, Adolf. *Die neutestamentliche Formel "in Cristo Jesu."* Marburg: Elwert, 1892.

Delitzsch, Franz. *Biblical Commentary on the Prophecies of Isaiah*. Translated by James Martin. 2 vols. Edinburgh: T&T Clark, 1869–80. Reprinted, Grand Rapids: Eerdmans, 1954.

———. *Das Land ohne Heimkehr, die Gedanken der Babylonier-Assyrer über Tod und Jenseits: Nebst Schlussfolgerungen*. Stuttgart: Deutsche Verlags-Anstalt, 1911.

———. *A New Commentary on Genesis*. Translated by Sophia Taylor. Edinburgh: T&T Clark, 1899.

———. *A System of Biblical Psychology*. Translated by Robert E. Wallis. 2nd ed. Edinburgh: T&T Clark, 1875.

Denifle, Heinrich, and Albert Maria Weiss. *Luther und Luthertum in der ersten Entwicklung, quellenmässig dargestellt*. 2 vols. Mainz: Kirchheim, 1904–9.

Dens, Pierre. *Theologia ad usum seminariorum et sacrae theologiae alumnorum*. Mechliniae: P. J. Hanicq, 1828–30.

———. *Theologia moralis et dogmatica*. 8 vols. Dublin: Richard Coyne, 1832.

Denzinger, Heinrich, ed.. *The Sources of Catholic Dogma (Enchiridion symbolorum)*. Translated from the 30th edition by Roy J. Deferrari. London and St. Louis: Herder, 1955. Reprinted, Fitzwilliam, NH: Loreto Publications, 2002.

———. *Vier Bücher von der religiösen Erkentniss*. 2 vols. 1856. Reprinted, Frankfurt/M.: Minerva-Verlag; Würzburg: Stahel, 1967.

De Ridder, Richard, Peter H. Jonker, and Leonard Verduin, eds. *The Church Orders of the Sixteenth Century Reformed Churches of the Netherlands: Together with Their Social, Political, and Ecclesiastical Context*. Grand Rapids: Calvin Theological Seminary, 1987.

Didache (The Lord's Teaching through the Twelve Apostles to the Nations). ANF, VII, 369–83.

Dieckhoff, August Wilhelm. *Luthers Lehre von der kirchlichen Gewalt*. Berlin: G. Schlawitz, 1865.

Dieringer, Franz Xavier. *Lehrbuch der katholischen Dogmatik*. 4th ed. Mainz: Kirchheim, 1858.

Diermanse, A. M. *De uitverkoren kinderen wedergeboren, eisch des Verbonds?* 2 vols. Den Haag: A. van Zijl, 1906–7.

Diognetus, Epistle to. ANF, I, 23–30.

Döderlein, Johann Christoph. *Institutio theologi christiani*. 2 vols. Nuremberg: Monath, 1787.

Doedes, Jacobus Izaak. *Inleiding tot de leer van God*. Utrecht: Kemink, 1870.

———. *De leer der zaligheid volgens het Evangelie in de Schriften des Nieuwen Verbonds voorgesteld*. Utrecht: Kemink, 1876.

———. *De Nederlandsche geloofsbelijdenis en de Heidelbergsche Catechismus*. Utrecht: Kemink & Zoon, 1880–81.

Dölger, Franz Joseph. *Der Exorcismus in der altchristlichen Taufritual*. Paderborn: Schöningh, 1909.

Döllinger, Johann Joseph Ignaz von. *Ueber die Wiedervereinigung der christlichen Kirchen*. Nördlingen: C. H. Beck, 1888.

Döllinger, Johann Joseph Ignaz von, and Johanes Huber. *Der Papst und das Concil*. Leipzig: E. F. Steinacker, 1869.

———. *The Pope and the Council*. Boston: Roberts, 1870.

Döllinger, Johann Joseph Ignaz von, Johannes Huber, and Johann Friedrich. *Das Papstthum*. Munich: Beck, 1892.

Dorner, August Johannes. *Augustinus*. Berlin: W. Hertz, 1873.

———. *Kirche und Reich Gottes*. Gotha: F. A. Perthes, 1883.

Dorner, I. A. *A System of Christian Doctrine*. Translated by A. Cave and J. S. Banks. 4 vols. Edinburgh: T&T Clark, 1882.

Doumergue, Émile. *Calvin, la fondateur des libertés modernes*. Montauban: J. Granie, 1898.

———. *Jean Calvin*. 7 vols. Lausanne: Bridel, 1899–1927.

Drawbridge, Cyprian Leycester. *Religious Education: How to Improve It*. New York and London: Longmans, Green, 1908.

Drews, Paul. *Entsprach das Staatskirchentum dem Ideale Luthers?* Tübingen: Mohr, 1908.

Driessen, Anton. *Oude en nieuwe mensch*. Groningen: Laurens Groenewout en Harmannus Spoormaker, 1738.

Drummond, Henry. *Natural Law in the Spiritual World*. London: Hodder & Stoughton, 1890.

———. *Das Naturgesetz in der Geisteswelt*. Bielefeld: Velhagen & Klasing, 1910.

Dublanchy, Edmund. *De axiomate: Extra ecclesiam nulla salus*; *Disseratatio theologica*. Bar-le-Duc: Contant-Laguerre, 1895.

Dunin-Borkowski, Stanislaus. *Die neueren Forschungen über die Anfänge des Episkopats*. Freiburg i.B.: Herder, 1900.

Duns Scotus, John. *Quaestiones in libros sententiarum*. Frankfurt: Minerva, 1967.

Eberhard, Johann August. *Neue Apologie des Sokrates, oder, Untersuchung der Lehre von der Seligkeit der Heiden*. Berlin: F. Nicolai, 1772.

Ebrard, Johannes Heinrich August. *Christliche Dogmatik*. 2nd ed. 2 vols. Königsberg: A. W. Unser, 1862–63.

———. *Das Dogma vom heiligen Abendmahl und seine Geschichte*. 2 vols. Frankfurt a.M.: Heinrich Zimmer, 1845–46.

Edwards, Jonathan. *A Narrative of Many Surprising Conversions in Northampton and Vicinity*. Worcester: Moses W. Grout, 1832.

———. *Religious Affections*. Edited by J. E. Smith. [1746]. New Haven: Yale University Press, 1959.

Eenhorn, Wilhelmus van. *Euzoia, ofte, welleven*. Amsterdam: Adriaan Wor, 1746–53.

Ehlers, Rudolph. *Das Neue Testament und die Taufe*. Giessen: Ricker, 1890.

Episcopius, Simon. *Apologia pro confessione sive declaratione sententiae eorum. . . .* n.p., 1629.

———. *The Confession or Declaration of the Ministers or Pastors Which in the United Provinces Are Called Remonstrants, concerning the Chief Points of the Christian Religion.* Translated by Thomas Taylor. London: Francis Smith, 1676.

———. *Disputationes theologicae tripartitae.* Amsterdam: Ioannem Blaev, 1646.

———. *Opera theologica.* 2 vols. Amsterdam: Johan Blaeu, 1650–55.

Ermann, Herman. *De paus.* Utrecht: Van Rossum, 1899.

Erskine, Ebenezer. *The Assurance of Faith, Opened and Applied.* Boston: Fowle & Draper, 1759.

Essenius, Andreas. *Compendium theologiae dogmaticum.* Utrecht: Meinhard à Dreunen, 1669.

Esser, Wilhelm. *Das heiligen Petrus Aufenthalt, Episkopat und Tod zu Rom.* Breslau: Coch, 1889.

Eswijler, Jan. *Ziels-eenzame meditatiën over de voornaemste waerheden des evangeliums.* Rotterdam: Hoefhout, 1739 [1685].

Eucken, Rudolf. *Hauptprobleme der Religionsphilosophie der Gegenwart.* 2nd ed. Berlin: Reuther & Reichard, 1907.

———. *The Truth of Religion.* Translated by W. Tudor Jones. New York: G. P. Putnam's Sons, 1911.

———. *Der Wahrheitsgehalt der Religion.* 2nd ed. Leipzig: Veit, 1905.

Eusebius of Caesarea. *Church History. NPNF* (2), I, 73–403.

Faber, Hans. *Das Christentum der Zukunft.* Zurich: Schulthess, 1904.

Fabri, G. K. C. Friedrich. *Über Kirchenzuch im Sinne und Geiste des Evangeliums.* Stuttgart: Steinkopft, 1854.

Fabricius, Johann Albert. *Bibliographia antiquaria.* Hamburg and Leipzig: Christian Liebezeit, 1713.

Falconer, James W. *From Apostle to Priest: A Study of Early Church Organization.* Edinburgh: T&T Clark, 1900.

Falke, Robert. *Buddha, Mohammed, Christus.* 2nd ed. 2 vols. Gütersloh: Bertelsmann, 1900.

———. *Gibt es eine Seelenwanderung?* Halle: S. E. Strein, 1904.

Farine, M. J. Lucian. *Der sakramentale Charakter.* Freiburg i.B.: Herder, 1904.

Farrar, Frederick W. *Eternal Hope.* London: MacMillan, 1883.

———. *Mercy and Judgment: A Few Last Words on Christian Eschatology, with Reference to Dr. Pusey's "What Is of Faith?"* New York: E. P. Dutton, 1881.

Farrar, Frederick W., James Hogg, and Thomas de Quincey. *The Wider Hope: Essays and Strictures on the Doctrine and Literature of Eternal Punishment.* London: T. Fisher Unwin, 1890.

Faure, H. *De vertroostingen des vagevuurs, volgens de leeraren der kerk en de openbaringen der heiligen.* Translated by Br. Modestus. Amsterdam: Bekker, 1901.

Feine, Paul. *Einleitung in das Neue Testament.* Leipzig: Quelle & Meyer, 1913.

Felten, Joseph. *Neutestamentliche Zeitgeschichte: Oder, Judentum und Heidentum zur Zeit Christi und der Apostel.* 2 vols. Regensburg: Manz, 1910.

Fichte, Immanuel Hermann. *Die Idee der Personlichkeit und der individuellen Fortdauer.* Leipzig: Dyk, 1855.

Ficker, Johannes, ed. *Luthers Vorlesung über den Römerbrief.* 2 vols. Leipzig: Dieterich, 1908.

Fischer, Ernst Friedrich. *Melanchthons Lehre von der Bekehrung.* Tübingen: Mohr, 1905.

Fischer, Friedrich Franz Karl. *De deo Aeschyleo.* Amsterdam: J. A. Worsmer, 1892.

Fleisch, Paul. *Zur Geschichte der Heiligungsbewegung.* Leipzig: H. G. Wallmann, 1906.

———. *Die innere Entwicklung der deutschen Gemeinschaftsbewegung in den Jahren 1906 und 1907.* Leipzig: H. G. Wallmann, 1908.

———. *Die moderne Gemeinschaftsbewegung in Deutschland.* 2nd ed. Leipzig: H. G. Wallmann, 1906.

Flier, Gerrit Jacobus Van der. *Het Darbisme: Geoordeeld door de H. Schrift en de geschiedenis.* 's Gravenhage: W. A. Beschoor, 1879.

Flink, Carl Otto. *Schopenhauers Seelenwan-derungslehre und ihre Quellen*. PhD diss., University of Bern, 1906; Bern: Schleitin, Spring, 1906.

Fock, Otto. *Der Socinianismus nach seiner Stellung in der Gesammtentwicklung des christlichen Geistes, nach seinem histo-rischen Verlauf und nach seinem Lehrbe-griff*. Kiel: C. Schröder, 1847.

Forbes, John. *Instructiones historico-theologi-cae*. Amsterdam: Elzevirium, 1645.

Formulier om te bevestingen de dienaren des Goddelicken Woorts. In *Biblia ... ende volgens t' besluit van de Synode Nationael, gehouden tot Dordrecht, in de Jaren 1618 ende 1619*. Amsterdam: J. Brandt; Haar-lem: Johannes Enschedé, 1870. ET: Form of Ordination of the Ministers of God's Word. Vol. II, pp. 70–72 in *The Psalter with the Doctrinal Standards and Liturgy of the Christian Reformed Church*. 2 vols. in 1. Grand Rapids: Eerdmans-Sevensma, 1914.

Formulier voor de heilige Doop. In *Biblia ... ende volgens t' besluit van de Synode Nationael, gehouden tot Dordrecht, in de Jaren 1618 ende 1619*. Amsterdam: J. Brandt; Haarlem: Johannes Enschedé, 1870. ET: Form for the Administration of Holy Baptism. Vol. II, pp. 57–61 in *The Psalter with the Doctrinal Standards and Liturgy of the Christian Reformed Church*. 2 vols. in 1. Grand Rapids: Eerdmans-Sevensma, 1914.

Formulier voor de viering van het heilig Avondmaal. In *Biblia ... ende volgens t' besluit van de Synode Nationael, gehouden tot Dordrecht, in de Jaren 1618 ende 1619*. Amsterdam: J. Brandt; Haarlem: Johannes Enschedé, 1870. ET: Form for the Cel-ebration of the Lord's Supper. Vol. II, pp. 62–66 in *The Psalter with the Doctrinal Standards and Liturgy of the Christian Re-formed Church*. 2 vols. in 1. Grand Rapids: Eerdmans-Sevensma, 1914.

Frank, Franz Herman Reinhold. *Dogmatische Studien*. Erlangen: Deichert, 1892.

———. *System der christlichen Wahrheit*. 3rd rev. ed. 2 vols. Erlangen and Leipzig: Deichert, 1894.

Frank, Henry. *Modern Light on Immortality*. Boston: Sherman, French, 1909.

Frantz, Alexander. *Das Gebet für die Todten in seinem Zusammenhange mit Cultus und Lehre nach den Schriften des heiligen Au-gustinus*. Nordhausen: A. Büchting, 1857.

Fremery, H. N. de. *Wat gebeurt er met ons als wij sterven?* Bussum: Van Dishoeck, 1910.

Frey, Johannes. *Tod, Seelenglaube und Seelenkult im alten Israel*. Leipzig: A. Deichert, 1898.

Fricke, Gustav Adolf. *Der paulinische Grund-begriff der δικαιοσυνη θεου erörtert auf Grund von Röm. 3,21–26*. Leipzig: Georg Böhme, 1888.

Frommel, Gaston. *La psychologie du pardon dans ses rapports avec la croix de Jésus-Christ*. Neuchatel: P. Atting, [1905].

Fürer, C. E. *Weltende und Endgericht nach Mythologie, Naturwissenschaft und Bibel: Vortrag gehalten im Altrathaus-saal zu Braunschweig am 29. November 1895 zum Besten des Marienstiftes*. Gütersloh: Ber-telsmann, 1896.

Gartmeier, Joseph. *Die Beichtpflicht*. Regens-burg: Manz, 1905.

Garvie, Alfred Ernest. *Religious Education: Mainly from a Psychological Standpoint*. London: Sunday School Union, 1906.

Geelkerken, Johannes Gerardus. *De empirische godsdienstpsychologie*. Amsterdam: Schel-tema & Holkema, 1909.

Geffcken, Friedrich Heinrich. *Staat und Kirche, in ihrem Verhältniss geschichtlich entwickelt*. Berlin: Hertz, 1875.

Gennrich, Paul. *Die Lehre von der Wiederge-burt: Die christliche Zentrallehre in dog-mengeschichtlicher und religionsgeschichtli-cher Beleuchtung*. Leipzig: Deichert, 1907.

Gerhard, Johann. *Loci theologici*. Edited by E. Preuss. 9 vols. Berlin: G. Schlawitz, 1863–75.

Gerretsen, Jan Hendrik. *Rechtvaardigmaking bij Paulus in verband met de prediking van Christus in de synopticien de beginselen der Reformatie*. Nijmegen: Ten Hoet, 1905.

Giesebrecht, Friedrich. *Die alttestamentliche Schätzung des Gottesnamens und ihre reli-*

gionsgeschichtliche Grundlage. Königsberg: Thomas & Oppermann, 1901.

Gihr, Nikolaus. *Das heilige Messopfer, dogmatisch, liturgisch und aszetisch erklärt*. 9th ed. Freiburg i.B.: Herder, 1907.

———. *The Holy Sacrifice of the Mass*. St. Louis: Herder, 1914.

Girgensohn, Karl. *Zwölf Reden über die christliche Religion*. 4th ed. Munich: C. H. Beck, 1921.

Gladstone, W. E. *Rome and the Newest Fashion in Religion*. London: John Murray, 1875.

Glaser, Eduard. *Woher kommt das Wort "Kirche"?* Munich: H. Lukaschik, 1901.

Glassberg, Abraham. *Die Beschneidung in ihrer geschichtlichen, ethnographischen, religiösen und medicinischen Bedeutung*. Berlin: Boas, 1896.

Gloël, Johannes. *Der heiligen Geist in der Heilsverkündigung des Paulus*. Halle: M. Niemeyer, 1888.

Goebel, Max. *Geschichte des christlichen Lebens in der rheinisch-westphälischen evangelischen Kirche*. 3 vols. Coblenz: K. Bädeker, 1849–60.

Goethe, Johann Wolfgang von. *Aus meinem Leben*. 4 vols. in 2. Berlin: G. Grote, 1871.

———. *The Autobiography of Johann Wolfgang von Goethe*. Translated by John Oxenford. 2 vols. New York: Horizon, 1969.

———. *Goethe: A Critical Introduction*. Translated by Henry Hatfield. Cambridge, MA: Harvard University Press, 1963.

Goetz, Karl Gerold. *Die Abendmahlsfrage in ihrer geschichtlichen Entwicklung*. Leipzig: Hinrichs, 1907.

Goetz, Leopold Karl. *Ein Wort zum konfessionellen Frieden*. Bonn: Carl Georgi, 1906.

Goguel, Maurice. *L'eucharistie des origines à Justin Martyr*. Paris: Fischbacher, 1910.

Gomarus, Franciscus. *Disputationum theologicarum quarto repetitarum quadragesimatertia de paedobaptismo*. Leiden: Ioannis Patii, 1606.

———. *Opera theologica omnia*. Amsterdam: J. Jansson, 1644.

Goor, Gerrit van. *De strijd over den ketterdoop*. Utrecht: Kemmer, 1872.

Gore, Charles. *The Body of Christ*. London: Murray, 1901.

———. *The Creed of the Christian*. 6th ed. London: Wells Gardner, Darton, 1905.

———. *The Incarnation of the Son of God*. London: Murray, 1891.

Görres, Joseph von. *Die christliche Mystik*. 4 vols. in 5. Regensburg: G. J. Manz, 1836.

Göschel, Carl Friedrich. *Von den Beweisen für die Unsterblichkeit der menschliche Seele*. Berlin: Duncker & Humblot, 1835.

Gottlob, Adolf. *Kreuzablass und Almosenablass*. Stuttgart: Enke, 1906.

Gottschick, Johannes. *Die Kirchlichkeit der sogenannte kirchliche Theologie*. Freiburg i.B.: J. C. B. Mohr, 1890.

Graebke, Friedrich. *Die Konstruktion der Abendmahlslehre Luthers in ihrer Entwicklung dargestellt*. Leipzig: Deichert, 1908.

Grafe, Eduard. *Die paulinische Lehre vom Gesetz nach vier Hauptbriefen*. 2nd ed. Freiburg i.B.: Mohr, 1893.

Grass, Konrad. *Die russische Sekten*. 2 vols. Leipzig: Hinrichs, 1907–14.

Gregory Nazianzus. *Theological Orations*. *NPNF* (2), VII, 309–18.

Grétillat, Augustin. *Exposé de théologie systématique*. 4 vols. Paris: Fischbacher, 1885–92.

Grill, Julius. *Der Primat von Petrus*. Tübingen: Mohr, 1904.

Groe, Theodorus van der. *Beschrijving van het oprecht en zielzaligend geloof*. Veenendaal: Kool, 1974.

———. *Toetssteen der waare en valsche genade*. 8th ed. 2 vols. Rotterdam: H. van Pelt & A. Douci Pietersz., 1752–53.

Groe, Theodorus van der, Jacob Groenewegen, and Adriaan van der Willigen. *Beschrijving van het oprecht en zielzaligend geloof*. Rotterdam: R. C. Huge, 1742.

Groe, Theodorus van der, and H. P. Scholte. *Het zaligmakende geloof*. New ed. Amsterdam: H. Hövecker, 1838.

Groenen, Petrus Gerardus. *Lijkverbranding*. 's Hertogenbosch: Teulings, 1909.

Gromer, Georg. *Die Laienbeicht im Mittelalter: Ein Beitrag zu ihrer Geschichte.* Munich: J. J. Lentner, 1909.

Groot, Johannes Frederik de. *Handleiding bij het katholiek godsdienstonderwijs aan gymnasia, h. burgerscholen en kweekscholen.* Amsterdam: C. L. Van Langenhuysen, 1906.

Groot, Johannes Vincentius de. *Summa apologetica de ecclesia catholicae.* 3rd ed. Regensburg: Manz, 1906.

Grosheide, F. W. *De verwachting der toekomst van Jezus Christus.* Amsterdam: Bottenburg, 1907.

Grüneisen, Carl. *Der Ahnenkultus und die Urreligion Israels.* Halle: Niemeyer, 1900.

Grützmacher, Richard Heinrich. *Modern-Positive Vorträge.* Leipzig: A. Deichert, 1906.

———. *Wort und Geist: Eine historische und dogmatische Untersuchung zum Gnadenmittel des Wortes.* Leipzig: Deichert, 1902.

Guers, Émile. *Israel in the Last Days of the Present Economy.* Translated by Aubrey Price. London: Wertheim, MacIntosh, & Hunt, 1862.

Gunning, Johannes Hermanus, III. *De Chasidim: Eene bladzijde uit de geschiedenis van het hedendaagsche jodendom.* Groningen: J. B. Wolters, 1891.

———. *De eenheid der kerk.* Nijmegen: Ten Hoet, 1896.

———. *Hooger dan de kerk!* Nijmegen: Ten Hoet, 1897.

———. *Rekenschap.* Nijmegen: Ten Hoet, 1898.

Haarbeck, Theodor. *Die "Pfingstbewegung" in geschichtlicher, biblischer, und psychologischer Beleuchtung.* Barmen: Buchhandlung des Johanneums, 1910.

Haeckel, Ernst. *The Riddle of the Universe at the Close of the Nineteenth Century.* Translated by Joseph McCabe. New York: Harper & Brothers, 1900.

Hahn, G. Ludwig. *Die Lehre von den Sakramenten in ihrer geschichtlichen Entwicklung.* Breslau: E. Morganstern, 1864.

Haldimann, Hector. *Le Fidéisme.* Paris: Fischbacher, 1907.

Hall, Granville Stanley. *Adolescence: Its Psychology and Its Relations to Physiology, Anthropology, Sociology, Sex, Crime, Religion and Education.* 2 vols. New York: D. Appleton, 1904.

Hammerstein, Ludwig. *Kirche und Staat.* Freiburg i.B.: Herder, 1883.

Hansjakob, Heinrich. *Die Toleranz und die Intoleranz der katholischen Kirche.* 2nd ed. Freiburg i.B.: Herder, 1899.

Happel, Julius. *Richard Rothes Lehre von der Kirche.* Leipzig: Heinsius, 1909.

Häring, Theodor. *The Christian Faith.* Translated by John Dickie and George Ferries. 2 vols. London: Hodder & Stoughton, 1913.

———. Δικαιοσυνη θεου *bei Paulus.* Tübingen: J. J. Heckenhauer, 1896.

Harless, Gottlieb Christoph Adolf von, and Theodosius Harnack. *Die kirchlich-religiöse Bedeutung der reinen Lehre von den Gnadenmittel.* Erlangen: Deichert, 1869.

Harnack, Adolf von. *Die Chronologie der altchristlichen Literatur bis Eusebius.* 2 vols. Leipzig: Hinrichs, 1897–1904.

———. *The Constitution and Law of the Church in the First Two Centuries.* Translated by Frank Lubecki Pogson. London: Williams & Norgate; New York: Putnam & Sons, 1910.

———. *Entstehung und Entwicklung der Kirchenverfassung und des Kirchenrechts in den zwei ersten Jahrhunderten.* Leipzig: Hinrichs, 1910.

———. *History of Dogma.* Translated by N. Buchanan, J. Millar, E. B. Speirs, and W. McGilchrist. Edited by A. B. Bruce. 7 vols. London: Williams & Norgate, 1896–99.

———. *Die Mission und Ausbreitung des Christentums in den ersten drei Jahrhunderten.* 2 vols. Leipzig: J. C. Hinrichs, 1905.

———. *The Mission and Expansion of Christianity.* Translated by James Moffatt. New York: Harper, 1908.

———. *Das Wesen des Christentums*. Leipzig: Hinrichs, 1902.

———. *What Is Christianity? Lectures Delivered in the University of Berlin during the Winter-Term 1899–1900*. Translated by Thomas Bailey Saunders. 2nd, rev. ed. New York and Evanston: Harper, 1957.

Harnack, Theodosius. *Praktische Theologie*. 2 vols. Erlangen: Deichert, 1877–78.

Hartmann, Eduard von. *Die Geisterhypothese des Spiritismus und seine Phantome*. Leipzig: Friedrich, 1891.

———. *Religionsphilosophie*. Leipzig: Friedrich, 1888.

———. *Der Spiritismus*. Leipzig: Friedrich, 1885.

Hase, Karl von. *Handbook to the Controversy with Rome*. Translated by A. W. Streane. 2 vols. London: Religious Tract Society, 1906.

———. *Handbuch der protestantischen Polemik gegen die römisch-katholische Kirche*. 5th ed. Leipzig: Breitkopf & Härtel, 1890. 6th ed., 1894.

———. *Hutterus redivivus, oder, Dogmatik der evangelisch-lutherischen Kirche*. 8th ed. Leipzig: Breithof & Härtel, 1855.

Hastie, William. *The Theology of the Reformed Churches in Its Fundamental Principles*. Edinburgh: T&T Clark, 1904.

Hatch, Edwin. *The Influence of Greek Ideas on Christianity*. 1890. Reprinted, New York: Harper, 1957.

Haupt, Erich. *Die eschatologischen Aussagen Jesu in den synoptischen Evangelien*. Berlin: Reuther & Reichard, 1895.

———. *Zum Verständnis des Apostolats*. Halle: Niemeyer, 1896.

Haussleiter, Johannes. *Der Glaube Jesu Christi und der christliche Glaube: Ein Beitrag zur Erklärung des Römerbriefs*. Erlangen and Leipzig: Deichert (G. Böhme), 1891.

*Hébert, Marcel. *L'evolution de la foi*. Paris: F. Alcan, 1907 [1905].

Hefner, Josef. *Die Entstehungsgeschichte des Trienter Rechtfertigungsgeschichte*. Paderborn: Schöningh, 1909.

Hegel, Georg Wilhelm Friedrich. *Lectures on the Philosophy of Religion*. Edited by Peter C. Hodgson. 3 vols. Berkeley: University of California Press, 1984–87.

———. *Sämtliche Werke*. 26 vols. Stuttgart: F. Frommann, 1949–59.

Hegler, Alfred. *Geist und Schrift bei Sebastian Franck*. Freiburg i.B.: Mohr, 1892.

Heidegger, Johann Heinrich. *Corpus theologiae*. 2 vols. Zurich: J. H. Bodmer, 1700.

Hein, Karl. *Die Sakramentslehre des Johannes à Lasco*. Berlin: C. A. Schwetschke & Sohn, 1904.

Heinrich, Johann Baptist, and Konstantine Gutberlet. *Dogmatische Theologie*. 2nd ed. 10 vols. Mainz: Kirchheim, 1881–1900.

Heinzelmann, Gerhard. *Der Begriff der Seele und die Idee der Unsterblichkeit bei Wilhelm Wundt*. Tübingen: Mohr, 1910.

Heitmüller, Wilhelm. *Im Namen Jesu*. Göttingen: Vandenhoeck & Ruprecht, 1903.

———. *Taufe und Abendmahl bei Paulus*. Göttingen: Vandenhoeck & Ruprecht, 1903.

Hellwald, Friedrich von. *Die Erde und ihre Volker: Ein geographisches Hausbuch*. Stuttgart: W. Spemann, 1877–78.

Hengstenberg, E. W. *Openbaring van Johannes*. 's Hertogenbosch: Muller, 1852.

Henry, Paul. *The Life and Times of John Calvin, the Great Reformer*. 2 vols. New York: R. Carter & Brothers, 1851–52.

Heppe, Heinrich. *Dogmatik des deutschen Protestantismus im sechzehnten Jahrhundert*. 3 vols. Gotha: F. A. Perthes, 1857.

———. *Die Dogmatik der evangelisch-reformirten Kirche*. Elberfeld: R. L. Friderichs, 1861.

———. *Geschichte des Pietismus und der Mystik in der reformirten Kirche*. Leiden: Brill, 1879.

Hergenröther, Joseph. *Katholische Kirche und christlicher Staat in ihrer geschichtlicher Entwicklung und in Beziehung auf die Fragen der Gegenwart*. 2 vols. Freiburg i.B.: Herder, 1872.

———. *Katholische Kirche und christlicher Staat in ihrer geschichtlicher Entwicklung und in Beziehung auf die Fragen der Gegenwart.* 2nd ed. Freiburg i.B.: Herder, 1874.

Hermas, Shepherd of. ANF, II, 1–58.

Herrmann, Wilhelm. *Der Verkehr des Christen mit Gott.* 6th ed. Stuttgart: Cotta, 1908.

Herzog, Johannes. *Der Begriff der Bekehrung im Lichte der heiligen Schrift, der Kirchengeschichte, und der Forderung des heutigen Lebens.* Giessen: J. Ricker (Töpelmann), 1903.

Hesselink, F. *Staat de wetenschap het geloof aan de onsterfelijkheid in de weg?* Middelburg: G. A. W. van Straaten, 1904.

Hettinger, Franz. *Apologie des Christenthums.* 2nd ed. 5 vols. Freiburg i.B.: Herder, 1865.

Hodge, Charles. *Discussions on Church Polity.* New York: Charles Scribner's Sons, 1878.

———. *Systematic Theology.* 3 vols. New York: Charles Scribner's Sons, 1888.

Hoedemaker, Philippus Jacobus. *Hoe oordeelt de Heilige Schrift en hoe oordeelen de Gereformeerde vaderen over scheiding en doleantie?* 3rd ed. Sneek: Campen, 1892.

Hoekstra, Hendrik. *Bijdrage tot de Kennis en de Beoordeling van het Chiliasme.* Kampen: Kok, 1903.

Hoekstra, Sytze. *De hoop der onsterfelijkheid.* Amsterdam: P. N. van Kampen, 1867.

———. *Het evangelie der genade door Jezus Christus zelven verkondigd in de gelijkenis van den verloren zoon.* Sneek: Van Druten & Bleeker, 1855.

Hoensbroech, Paul K. Graf von. *Das Papstthum in seiner sozial-kulturellen Wirksamkeit.* 2 vols. Leipzig: Breitkopf & Härtel, 1901–2.

Hoffmann, Hermann Edler von. *Das Kirchenverfassungsrecht der niederländischen Reformierten bis zum Beginne der Dordrechter Nationalsynode von 1618/19.* Leipzig: C. L. Hirschfeld, 1902.

Hoffmann, Richard Adolf. *Die Abendmahlsgedanken Jesu Christi: Ein biblisch-theologischer Versuch.* Königsberg: Thomas & Oppermann, 1896.

Höfling, Johann Wilhelm Friedrich. *Das Sakrament der Taufe.* Erlangen: Deichert, 1859.

Hofmann, Johann Christian Konrad von. *Der Schriftbeweis.* 3 vols. Nördlingen: Beck, 1857–60.

———. *Weissagung und Erfüllung im Alten und Neuen Testamente.* 2 vols. Nördlingen: Beck, 1841.

Hofmann, Rudolf Hugo. *Symboliek of stelselmatige uiteenzetting van het onderscheidene Christelijke kerkgenootschappen en voornaamste sekten.* Utrecht: Kemink en Zoon, 1861.

Holl, Karl. *Luther und das landesherrliche Kirchenregiment.* Tübingen: Mohr, 1911.

———. *Die Rechtfertigungslehre im Lichte der Geschichte des Protestantismus.* Tübingen: Mohr, 1906.

Hollaz, David. *Examen theologicum acroamaticum.* Rostock and Leipzig: Russworm, 1718.

Hollweck, Joseph. *Der apostolische Stuhl und Rom.* Mainz: Kirchheim, 1895.

Holmes, E. E. *Immortality.* London: Longman, Green, 1908.

Holtius, Nicolaus. *Godgeleerde verhandeling over het oprecht geloof.* Leiden, 1747.

Holtzheuer, Otto. *Das Abendmahl und die neuere Kritik.* Berlin: Wiegandi & Grieben, 1896.

Holtzmann, Heinrich Julius. *Lehrbuch der neutestamentlichen Theologie.* 2 vols. Freiburg i.B. and Leipzig: Mohr, 1897.

Honert, Johannes van den. *Verhandeling van de rechtvaardiging des zondaars uit en door het geloof.* Leiden: Luchtmans, 1755.

Honig, Anthonie Gerrit. *Alexander Comrie.* Utrecht: H. Honig, 1892.

Hooijer, Cornelis. *Oude kerkenordeningen der Nederlandsche Hervormde gemeenten, 1563–1638, en het concept-reglement op de organisatie van het Hervormd Kerkgenootschap in het Koningrijk Holland 1809.* Zalt-Bommel: Noman, 1865.

Hoop Scheffer, Jacob Gijsbert de. *Geschiedenis der kerkhervorming in Nederland van haar ontstaan tot 1531.* Amsterdam: G. L. Funke, 1873.

———. *Overzicht der geschiedenis van den doop bij onderdompeling.* Amsterdam, 1882.

Hoornbeek, Johannes. *Disputatio theologica practica, de theologiae praxi.* Leiden: Elsevirium, 1659–61.

———. *Summa controversiarum religionis, cum infidelibus, haereticis et schismaticis.* Utrecht: J. à Waersberge, 1658.

Hooykaas, Cornelis Elias. *Oud-Christelijke ascese.* Leiden: A. W. Sijthoff, 1905.

Horton, Robert F., and Joseph Hocking. *Shall Rome Reconquer England?* London: National Council of Evangelical Free Churches, 1910.

Höveler, P. *Professor A. Harnack und die katholische Ascese.* Düsseldorf: L. Schwann, 1902.

Hugh of St. Victor. *On the Sacraments of the Christian Faith.* Translated by Roy J. Deferrari. Cambridge, MA: Mediaeval Academy of America, 1951.

Hurgronje, C. Snouck. *Der Mahdi.* Amsterdam, 1885. Extract from the *Revue Coloniale Internationale* 1 (1885).

Hymmen, Johannes. *Die Sakramentslehre Augustins in Zusammenhang dargestellt und beurteilt.* Bonn: C. Georgi, 1905.

Ignatius of Antioch. *Epistle to the Ephesians. ANF,* I, 45–58.

———. *Epistle to the Magnesians. ANF,* I, 59–65.

———. *Epistle to the Philadelphians. ANF,* I, 79–85.

———. *Epistle to the Smyrnaeans. ANF,* I, 86–92.

———. *Epistle to the Trallians. ANF,* I, 66–72.

Ihmels, Ludwig. *Die tägliche Vergebung der Sünden.* 2nd ed. Leipzig: Dörffling & Franke, 1916.

Irenaeus. *Against Heresies. ANF,* I, 309–567.

Isenkrahe, Caspar. *Energie, Entropie, Weltanfang, Weltende.* Trier: Lintz, 1910.

Ist der Einzelkelch bei der Feier des heiligen Abendmahl eine neutestamentliche Einrichtung? Hagen i.W.: Rippel, n.d.

Jackson, George. *The Fact of Conversion.* New York: Fleming H. Revell, 1908.

Jacob, Benno. *Im Namen Gottes.* Berlin: S. Calvary, 1903.

Jacob, Leonhard. *Jesu Stellung zum mosaischen Gesetz.* Göttingen: Vandenhoeck & Ruprecht, 1893.

James, William. *The Varieties of Religious Experience: A Study in Human Nature.* New York: Modern Library, 1902.

Jansen, Gerardus Martinus. *Praelectiones theologiae dogmaticae.* 3 vols. in 2. Utrecht: Van Rossum, 1875–79.

Jeremias, Alfred. *Hölle und Paradies bei den Babyloniern.* Leipzig: J. C. Hinrichs, 1900.

John of Damascus. *Exposition of the Orthodox Faith. NPNF* (2), IX, 259–360.

Jong, Karl Hendrik Eduard de. *Das antike Mysterienwesen in religionsgeschichtlicher, ethnologischer und psychologischer Beleuchtung.* Leiden: Brill, 1909.

Joos, Wilhelm. *Die Bulle "Unam Sanctam" und das vatikanische Autoritätsprinzip.* 2nd ed. Schaffhausen: Carl Schoch, 1897.

Josephson, Hermann. *Das heiligen Abendmahl und das Neue Testament.* Gütersloh: Bertelsmann, 1895.

Josephus, Flavius. *The Works of Josephus.* Translated by William Whiston. New updated ed. Peabody, MA: Hendrickson, 1987.

Jülicher, Adolf. *Paulus und Jesus.* Tübingen: J. C. B. Mohr (Paul Siebeck), 1907.

Jüngst, Johannes. *Amerikanischer Methodismus in Deutschland und Robert Pearsall Smith.* Gotha: F. A. Perthes, 1875.

Jung-Stilling, Johann Heinrich. *Theorie der Geister-Kunde: In einer natur-, vernunft- und bibelmüssigen Beantwortung der Frage was von Ahnungen, Geschichten und Geisterscheinungen geglaubt und nicht geglaubt werden müsste.* Nuremberg: Raw, 1808; Leipzig: Dieter, ca. 1890.

Junius, Franciscus. *Opuscula theologica selecta.* Edited by Abraham Kuyper. Amsterdam: F. Muller, 1882.

———. *Theses theologicae.* In vol. 1 of *Opuscula.*

Justin Martyr. *First Apology. ANF,* I, 159–87.

———. *Dialogue with Trypho. ANF*, I, 194–270.

Kabisch, Richard. *Die Eschatologie des Paulus in ihrem Zusammenhang mit dem Gesammtbegriff des Paulinismus*. Göttingen: Vandenhoek & Ruprecht, 1893.

Kaftan, Julius. *Dogmatik*. Tübingen: Mohr, 1901.

Kähler, Martin. *Dogmatische Zeitfragen: Alte und neue Ausführungen zur Wissenschaft der christlichen Lehre*. 2nd ed. 3 vols. Leipzig: Deichert, 1907–13.

———. *Die Sakramente als Gnadensmittel*. Leipzig: Deichert, 1902.

———. *Die Wissenschaft der christlichen Lehre*. 3rd ed. Leipzig: A. Deichert, 1905.

Kahnis, Friedrich August. *Die lutherische Dogmatik, historisch-genetisch dargestellt*. Leipzig: Dörffling & Franke, 1861–68.

Kahnis, Karl Friedrich. *Die Lehre vom Abendmahle*. Leipzig: Dörffling & Franke, 1851.

Kalb, Ernst. *Kirchen und Sekten der Gegenwart*. 2nd ed. Stuttgart: Evang. Gesellschaft, 1907.

Kampschulte, Franz Wilhelm, and Walter Goetz. *Johann Calvin: Seine Kirche und sein Staat in Genf*. 2 vols. Leipzig: Duncker & Humblot, 1869–99.

Kant, Immanuel. *Religion innerhalb der Grenzen der blossen Vernunft*. Berlin: Heimann, 1869.

———. *Religion within the Limits of Reason Alone*. Translated by Theodore M. Greene and Hoyt H. Hudson. New York: Harper & Brothers, 1934.

Kattenbusch, Ferdinand. *Das apostolische Symbol*. 2 vols. Leipzig: Hinrichs, 1894–1900.

———. *Die Kirchen und Sekten des Christentums in der Gegenwart*. Tübingen: Mohr, 1909.

———. *Lehrbuch der vergleichenden Confessionskunde*. Freiburg i.B.: J. C. B. Mohr (Paul Siebeck), 1892.

Kayser, August. *Theologie des Alten Testaments*. Prepared by Karl Marti. 2nd ed. Strassburg: Friedrich Bull, 1894.

Keating, John Fitzstephen. *The Agape and the Eucharist in the Early Church*. London: Methuen, 1901.

Keckermann, Bartholomäus. *Systema s. s. theologiae*. Hanover: Guilielmum Antonium, 1602.

Keil, Carl Friedrich. *Biblical Commentary on the Prophecies of Ezekiel*. Translated by James Martin. Reprinted, Grand Rapids: Eerdmans, 1970.

———. *Manual of Biblical Archaeology*. Translated by P. Christie and A. Cusin. 2 vols. Edinburgh: T&T Clark, 1887–88.

Keyserling, Hermann. *Unsterblichkeit, eine Kritik der Beziehungen zwischen Naturgeschehen und menschlichen Vorstellungswelt*. Munich: Lehmann, 1907.

Kiefl, Franz Xaver. *Der Friedensplan des Leibniz zur Wiedervereinigung der getrennten christlichen Kirchen*. Paderborn: Schöningh, 1903.

———. *Herman Schell und die Ewigkeit der Höllenstrafen*. Mainz: Kirchheim, 1907.

Kirchner, Viktor. *Der "Lohn" in der alten Philosophie, im bürgerlichen Recht, besonders im Neuen Testament*. Gütersloh: Bertelsmann, 1908.

———. *Der Spiritismus: Die Narrheit unseres Zeitalters*. Berlin: Habel, 1883.

Kirn, Otto. *Grundriss der evangelischen Dogmatik*. Leipzig: Deichert, 1905.

Klee, Heinrich. *Katholische Dogmatik*. 4th ed. Mainz: Kirchheim, 1861.

Kleutgen, Joseph. *Die Theologie der Vorzeit*. 2nd ed. 5 vols. Münster: Theissing, 1867–74.

Kleyn, Hendrik Gerrit. *De zoon Gods onder de wet en het leven van Christus onder de wet*. Sneek: Campen, 1901.

Kliefoth, Theodor F. D. *Acht Bücher von der Kirche*. Schwerin: Stiller, 1854.

———. *Christliche Eschatologie*. Leipzig: Dörffling & Franke, 1886.

Knapp, Georg Christian. *Vorlesungen über die christliche Glaubenslehre nach dem Lehrbegriff der evangelischen Kirche*. Edited by Carl Thilo. 2 vols. Halle: Waisenhauses, 1827.

Kneib, Philipp. *Die Beweise für die Unsterblichkeit der Seele als allgemeinen psychologischen Tatsachen*. Freiburg i.B.: Herder, 1903.

———. *Die "Heteronomie" der christlichen Moral*. Vienna: Mayer, 1903.

———. *Die "Jenseitsmoral" im Kampfe um ihre Grundlagen*. Freiburg i.B.: Herder, 1906.

———. *Die "Lohnsucht" der christlichen Moral*. Vienna: Mayer, 1904.

———. *Die Unsterblichkeit der Seele*. Vienna: Mayer, 1900.

Knopf, Rudolf. *Das nachapostolische Zeitalter: Geschichte der christlichen Gemeinden vom Beginn der Flavierdynastie bis zum Ende Hadrians*. Tübingen: J. C. B. Mohr (P. Siebeck), 1905.

Knox, John. *The First Book of Discipline*. In *History of the Reformation of Religion in Scotland*. Glasgow: Blackie, Fullarton, 1831.

Köberle, Justus. *Sünde und Gnade im religiösen Leben des Volkes Israel bis auf Christum: Eine Geschichte des vorchristlichen Heilsbewusstseins*. Munich: Beck, 1905.

Koch, Hugo. *Cyprian und der römische Primat*. Leipzig: Hinrichs, 1910.

Koelman, Jacobus. *Het ambt en pligten der ouderlingen en diakenen*. 's Gravenhage: Van Velzen, 1837.

———. *Historisch verhaal nopens der Labadisten*. 2 vols. Amsterdam: Johannes Boeckholt, 1683–84.

———. *De natuur en gronden des geloofs*. Ede: Hardeman, 1988.

Köhler, Johan Nicolaas. *Het Irvingisme*. 's Gravenhage: Mensing en Visser, 1876.

Köhler, Walter. *Die Entstehung des Problems Staat und Kirche*. Tübingen: Mohr, 1903.

Kolb, Robert, and Timothy J. Wengert, eds. *The Book of Concord*. Minneapolis: Fortress, 2000.

Kolde, Theodor. *Die Heilsarmee: Ihre Geschichte und ihr Wesen*. Erlangen: Deichert, 1885.

König, Eduard. *Geschichte des Reiches Gottes*. Berlin: M. Warneck, 1908.

———. *Der Glaubensact des Christen nach Begriff und Fundament*. Erlangen: Deichert, 1891.

Köstlin, Heinrich Adolf. *Die Lehre von der Seelsorge nach evangelischen Grundsätzen*. Berlin: Reuther & Reichard, 1895.

Köstlin, Julius. *Luthers Lehre von der Kirche*. Stuttgart: Liesching, 1853.

———. *The Theology of Luther in Its Historical Development and Inner Harmony*. Translated by Charles E. Hay. 2 vols. Philadelphia: Lutheran Publication Society, 1897.

———. *Das Wesen der Kirche nach Lehre und Geschichte des Neuen Testaments*. 2nd ed. Stuttgart: Schloessman, 1872.

Kramer, F. *De vergeving der zonden*. Kampen: Kok, 1910.

Kramer, Geerhard. *Het verband van doop en wedergeboorte*. Breukelen: De Vecht, 1897.

Krauss, Alfred. *Das protestantische Dogma von der unsichtbare Kirche*. Gotha: F. A. Perthes, 1876.

Krebs, Albertus. *De unionis mysticae quam vocant doctrinae lutheranae origine et progressu saeculo XVII*. Marburg, 1871.

Kromsigt, Johannes Christiaan. *Wilhelmus Schortinghuis*. Groningen: J. B. Wolters, 1904.

Kruske, Karl Adolph Richard. *Johannes à Lasco und der Sacramentsstreit: Ein Beitrag zur Geschichte der Reformationzeit*. Leipzig: Deichert, 1901.

Kübel, Johannes. *Geschichte des katholischen Modernismus*. Tübingen: Mohr, 1909.

Kübel, Robert Benjamin. *Ueber der Unterschied zwischen dem positiven und der liberalen Richtung in der modernen Theologie*. 2nd ed. Munich: Beck, 1893.

Kuenen, Abraham. *The Prophets and Prophecy in Israel*. Translated by Adam Milroy. London: Longmans, Green, 1877. Reprinted, Amsterdam: Philo, 1969.

Kühl, Ernst. *Rechtfertigung auf Grund des Glaubens und Gericht nach den Werken bei Paulus*. Königsberg: Wilh. Koch, 1904.

Kunze, Johannes. *Glaubensregel, Heilige Schrift und Taufbekenntnis*. Leipzig: Dörffling & Franke, 1899.

———. *Die Rechtfertigungslehre in der Apologie*. Gütersloh: Bertelsmann, 1908.

Kurz, Anton. *Die katholische Lehre vom Ablass vor und nach dem Auftreten Luthers*. Paderborn: Schöningh, 1900.

Kuyper, Abraham. *Encyclopaedie der heilige godgeleerdherd*. 2d ed. 3 vols. Kampen: Kok, 1908–9.

———. *E voto Dordraceno: Toelichting op den Heidelbergschen Catechismus*. 4 vols. Amsterdam: Wormser, 1892–95.

———. *Ons program*. 4th ed. Amsterdam and Pretoria: Höveker & Wormser, 1880. 5th ed. Hilversum: Hoveker & Wormser, 1907.

———. *Principles of Sacred Theology*. New York: C. Scribner's Sons, 1898.

———. *Van de voleinding*. 4 vols. Kampen: Kok, 1928–31.

———. *Het werk van den Heiligen Geist*. 3 vols. in 1. Amsterdam: Wormser, 1888–89.

———. *The Work of the Holy Spirit*. Translated by Henri de Vries. 3 vols. New York: Funk & Wagnalls, 1900.

Kuyper, Abraham, Jr. *De band des verbonds*. Amsterdam: Kirchner, 1906.

———. *Johannes Maccovius*. Leiden: D. Donner, 1899.

Kuyper, Herman Huber. *De christelijke vrijheid*. Kampen: Bos, 1898.

———. *Hamabdil: Van de heiligheid van het genadeverbond*. Amsterdam: Bottenburg, 1907.

———. *De opleiding tot den Dienst des Woords bij de Gereformeerden*. 's Gravenhage: M. Nijhoff, 1891.

Laake, Otto. *Über den sakramentalen Charakter*. Munich: Manz, 1903.

Lacombe, Jacques de. *Les nouveau-nés de l'Esprit: Étude de psychologie religieuse*. Paris: Fischbacher, 1905.

Lactantius. *The Divine Institutes*. ANF, VII, 9–223.

Laidlaw, John. *The Bible Doctrine of Man*. Edinburgh: T&T Clark, 1895.

Lambert, John C. *The Sacraments in the New Testament*. Edinburgh: T&T Clark, 1903.

Lampe, Friedrich Adolph. *De verborgentheit van het genaade-verbondt: Ter eeren van den grooten Verbonds-Godt, en tot stichtinge van alle heylbegeerige zielen geopent*. Amsterdam, 1718.

———. *Einleitung zu dem Geheimnis des Gnaden-Bunds*. Elberfeld: Lueas, 1837.

Landau, Marcus. *Hölle und Fegfeuer in Volksglaube, Dichtung, und Kirchenlehre*. Heidelberg: Winter, 1910.

Lange, Friedrich Albert. *Geschichte des Materialismus und Kritik seiner Bedeutung in der Gegenwart*. 8th ed. Leipzig: Baedekker, 1908.

Lange, Johann Peter. *Christliche Dogmatik*. 3 vols. Heidelberg: K. Winter, 1852.

———. *Positive Dogmatik*. Heidelberg: K. Winter, 1851.

Langen, Joseph. *Das vatickanische Dogma von dem Universal-Episcopat und der Unfehlbarkeit des Papstes in seinem Verhältniss zum Neuen Testament und der patristischen Exegese*. 4 vols. Bonn: Eduard Weber, 1871–76.

Lasco, John à. *Opera tam edita quam inedita*. Edited by Abraham Kuyper. 2 vols. Amsterdam: F. Muller, 1866.

Lauterburg, Moritz. *Der Begriff des Charisma und seine Bedeutung für praktische Theologie*. Gütersloh: C. Bertelsmann, 1898.

Lechler, Gotthard Victor. *Geschichte des englischen Deismus*. Stuttgart: J. G. Cotta, 1841.

———. *Geschichte der Presbyterial- und Synodalverfassung seit der Reformation*. Leiden: Noothoven van Goor, 1854.

Lechler, Karl. *Die biblische Lehre vom heiligen Geiste*. 3 vols. Gütersloh: Bertelsmann, 1899–1904.

———. *Die neutestamentliche Lehre vom heiligen Ambte*. Stuttgart: J. F. Steinkopf, 1857.

Leenhof, Frederik van. *Den hemel op aarden of een korte beschrijvinge van de waare en stantvastige blydshap.* Zwolle: Hakvoord, 1703.

Lehmkuhl, Augustin. *Theologia moralis.* 2 vols. Freiburg i.B.: Herder, 1898.

Leibbrand, Karl M. *Das Gebet für die Todten in der evangelischen Kirche.* Stuttgart: Schweizerbart, 1864.

Leibniz, Gottfried Wilhelm von. *System der Theologie nach dem Manuskripte von Hanover.* Mainz: Müller, 1825.

Leitner, Franz. *Der hl. Thomas von Aquin über das unfehlbare Lehramt des Papstes.* Freiburg i.B.: Herder, 1872.

Lemme, Ludwig. *Endlosigkeit der Verdammnis und allgemeine Wiederbringung.* Berlin: Runge, 1898.

Lépicier, Alexius Maria. *De stabilitate et progressu dogmatis.* Rome: Desclée, 1910.

Le Roi, Johannes Friedrich Alexander de. *Judentaufen im 19 Jahrhundert: Ein statistischer Versuch.* Leipzig: J. C. Hinrichs, 1899.

Lessing, G. E. *Erziehung des Menschengeschlechts.* Edited by Louis Ferdinand Helbig. Bern and Las Vegas: Peter Lang, 1980.

Liebermann, Franz B. *Institutiones theologicae.* 8th ed. 2 vols. Mainz: Kirchheim, 1857.

Limborch, Philippus van. *Theologia christiana ad praxin pietatis ac promotionem pacis christianae unice directa.* Amsterdam: Arnhold, 1735.

Linden, J. van der. *Waarheid of dwaling.* Den Haag: J. van der Burgh, 1910.

Lion Cachet, Frans. *Tien dagen te Brighton: Brieven aan een vriend.* Utrecht: Keminck & Zoon, 1875.

Lipsius, Richard Adelbert. *Lehrbuch der evangelisch-protestantischen Dogmatik.* Braunschweig: C. A. Schwetschke & Sohn, 1893.

―――. *Die paulinische Rechtfertigungslehre.* Leipzig: Hinrichs, 1853.

Lobstein, Paul. *La doctrine de la sainte Cène.* Lausanne: Bridel, 1889.

―――. *Die Ethik Calvins in ihren Grundzügen entworfen.* Strassburg: C. F. Schmidt, 1877.

Lodensteyn, Jodocus van. *Beschouwinge van Zion.* Utrecht: Willem Clerck, 1674.

Lodge, Oliver. *The Survival of Man: A Study in an Unrecognized Human Faculty.* London: Methuen; New York: Moffat, Yard, 1909.

Löhe, Wilhelm. *Drei Bücher von der Kirche.* Stuttgart: Liesching, 1845.

―――. *Three Books concerning the Church.* Translated by Edward T. Horn. Reading, PA: Pilger, 1908.

Lombard, Peter. *Sententiae in IV libris distinctae.* 3rd ed. 2 vols. Grottaferrata: Colleggi S. Bonaventurae ad Claras Aquas, 1971–81.

Lonkhuijzen, Jan van. *Hermann Friedrich Kohlbrügge en zijn prediking.* Wageningen: "Vada," 1905.

Loofs, Friedrich. *Leitfaden zum Studium der Dogmengeschichte.* 4th ed. Halle a.S.: M. Niemeyer, 1906.

Lotze, Hermann. *Mircrocosmus.* Translated by Elizabeth Hamilton and E. E. Constance Jones. Edinburgh: T&T Clark, 1885. New York: Scribner & Welford, 1886.

―――. *Mikrokosmus.* 3 vols. Leipzig: S. Hirzel, 1872–78.

Love, Christopher. *Theologica practica: Dat is, Alle de theologische Werken.* 4th ed. Amsterdam: J. H. Boom, 1669.

Luca, Mariano de. *Institutiones iuris ecclesiastici publici.* Regensburg: F. Pustet, 1901.

Lucius, Ernst. *Die Anfänge des Heiligenkults in der christlichen Kirche.* Tübingen: Mohr, 1904.

Lüken, Heinrich. *Die Traditionen des Menschengeschlechts oder die Uroffenbarung Gottes unter den Heiden.* 2nd, rev. ed. Münster: Aschendorff, 1869.

Lütgert, Wilhelm. *Gottes Sohn und Gottes Geist: Vorträge zur Christologie und zur Lehre vom Geiste Gottes.* Leipzig: A. Deichert (G. Böhme), 1905.

Luthardt, Christoph Ernst. *Compendium der Dogmatik.* Leipzig: Dörffling & Franke, 1865.

―――. *Die Lehre von den letzten Dingen.* 3rd ed. Leipzig: Dörffling & Franke, 1885.

Luther, Martin. *Luther's Large Catechism.*
Translated by J. N. Lenker. Minneapolis:
Augsburg, 1967.

———. *Luther's Works.* Edited by J. Pelikan
and H. T. Lehman. 55 vols. St. Louis:
Concordia; Philadelphia: Fortress,
1955–86. Vol. 25. Edited by Hilton C.
Oswald. 1972. Vol. 39. Edited by Joel W.
Lundeen. 1986.

———. *On the Papacy in Rome: Against the
Most Celebrated Romanist in Leipzig.*
Vol. 39, pp. 49–104 in *Luther's Works,*
edited by Joel W. Lundeen. Philadelphia:
Fortress, 1986.

———. *Von dem Bapstum zu Rome: Widder
den hochberumpten Romanisten zu Leiptzck.* Wittenberg: Melchior Lotter, 1520.

Lüttge, Willy. *Die Rechtfertigungslehre Calvins
und ihre Bedeutung für seine Frömmigkeit.*
Berlin: Reuther & Reichard, 1909.

Maccovius, Johannes. *Collegia theologica.*
3rd ed. Franeker: Joannis Fabiani Deuring,
1641.

———. *Loci communes theologici.*
Amsterdam: n.p., 1658.

MacDonald, Robert. *Mind, Religion, and
Health, with an Appreciation of the
Emmanuel Movement.* New York and
London: Funk & Wagnalls, 1908.

Maistre, Joseph Marie. *Du pape.* 2 vols. Lyon:
Rusand, 1819.

———. *The Pope, Considered in His Relations
with the Church, Temporal Sovereignties,
Separated Churches, and the Cause of Civilization.* Translated by Aeneas McD.
Dawson. New York: H. Fertig, 1975
[1850].

Mandel, Hermann. *Die scholastische Rechtfertigungslehre: Ihre Bedeutung für Luthers
Entwicklung, ihr Grundproblem, und des-
sen Lösung durch Luther.* Leipzig:
Dieterich, 1906.

Manen, Willem Christiaan van. *De brief aan
de Romeinen.* Leiden: Brill, 1891.

Mannens, Paulus. *Theologiae dogmaticae
institutiones.* 3 vols. Roermand: Romen,
1910–15.

Manzoni, Cesare. *Compendium theologiae dogmaticae e praecipuis scholasticis antiquis et*
modernis redactum. 4 vols. Turin: Berruti,
1909.

Marang, G. P. *De zwijndrechtsche Nieuwlichters.* Dordrecht: De Graaf, 1909.

Marck [Marckius], Johannes. *Christianae
theologiae medulla didactico-elenctica.*
Amsterdam: Wetstenios, 1716.

———. *Compendium theologiae christianae
didactico-elencticum.* Groningen: Fossema,
1686.

———. *Exspectatio gloriae futurae Jesu
Christi.* Leiden: Abraham Kallewier, 1730.

Maresius, Samuel. *Collegium theologicum sive
systema breve universae theologiae compre-
hensum octodecim disputationibus.* Groningen, 1645, 1659.

———. *Foederatum belgium orthodoxum sive
confessionis ecclesiarum belgicarum exegesis.*
Groningen: Nicolaus, 1653.

———. *Systema theologicum.* Groningen:
Aemilium Spinneker, 1673.

Marmontel, Jean François. *Belisarius* [1767].
New York: Garland, 1975.

Maronier, Jan Hendrik. *Het inwendig word.*
Amsterdam: Tj. van Holkema, 1890.

Marshall, W. *The Gospel-Mystery of Sanctification.* Grand Rapids: Zondervan, 1954.

Martensen, Hans. *Christian Dogmatics.* Translated by William Urwick. Edinburgh:
T&T Clark, 1871.

———. *De Kinderdoop.* Utrecht:
W. F. Dannenfelser, 1852.

Marti, Karl. *Die Religion des Alten Testaments
unter den Religionen des vorderen Orient.*
Tübingen: J. C. B. Mohr, 1906.

Martyrdom of Polycarp. ANF, I, 37–44.

Mastricht, Peter van. *Theoretico-practica
theologia.* Utrecht: Appels, 1714.

McConnell, Samuel David. *The Evolution of
Immortality.* New York and London:
MacMillan, 1901.

Melanchthon, Philipp. *Confessyon of the fayth
of the Germaynes. The apologie.* Amsterdam: Theatrum Orbis Terrarum, 1576.
Reprinted, Norwood, NJ: W. J. Johnson,
1976.

————. *Corpus doctrinae christianae*. Leipzig: Ernesti Voegelini [Ernst Vögelin] Constantientis, 1560.

————. *Loci communes*. Berlin: G. Schlawitz, 1856.

————. *Treatise on the Power and Primacy of the Pope* (1537). Pp. 329–45 in *The Book of Concord: The Confessions of the Evangelical Lutheran Church*, edited by Robert Kolb and Timothy J. Wengert; translated by Charles P. Arand. Minneapolis: Fortress, 2000.

Ménégoz, Eugène. *Publications diverses sur le Fidéisme et son application à l'enseignement chrétien traditionnel*. Paris: Fischbacher, 1900.

————. *Die Rechtfertigungslehre nach Paulus und nach Jakobus*. Giessen: Ricker, 1903.

Meschler, Maurice. *Die Gabe des heiligen Pfingstfestes*. 3rd ed. Freiburg i.B.: Herder, 1896.

————. *The Gift of Pentecost*. Translated by Amabel Kerr. St. Louis: Herder, 1903.

Meulenbelt, Hendrik Huibrecht. *Kerkelijke opstelling*. Nijmegen: Ten Hoet, 1905.

Meyer, Heinrich August Wilhelm, et al. *Critical and Exegetical Hand-Book to the New Testament*. 9 vols. New York: Funk & Wagnalls, 1884.

Meyer, Johann Friedrich von. *Blätter für höhere Wahrheit*. 11 vols. Frankfurt a.M.: H. L. Brönner, 1818–32.

Meyer, Max. *Der Apostel Paulus als armer Sünder*. Gütersloh: Bertelsmann, 1903.

Meyers kleines Konversations-Lexikon. 5th ed. Leipzig and Vienna: Bibliographische Institute, 1892–93.

Meyjes, Egbert Johannes Wernhard Posthumus. *Jacobus Revius, zijn leven en werken*. Amsterdam: Ten Brink & De Vries, 1895.

Michiels, Andreas. *L'origene de l'épiscopat*. Louvain: J. van Linthout, 1900.

Mitchell, Alexander Ferrier. *The Westminster Assembly: Its History and Standards*. London: J. Nisbet, 1883.

Moberly, Robert Campbell. *Atonement and Personality*. 6th ed. London: Murray, 1907.

Moeller, Bernd, and Hans von Schubert. *Lehrbuch der Kirchengeschichte*. 3 vols. Tübingen: Mohr, 1892–1907.

Möhler, Johann Adam. *Symbolik*. Regensburg: G. J. Manz, 1871.

Mommert, Carl. *Zur Chronologie des Lebens Jesu*. Leipzig: E. Haberland, 1909.

Monnier, Henri. *Le notion d'apostolat: Des origenes à Irénée*. Paris: Leroux, 1893.

Moog, Joseph. *Die Wiedervereinigung der christlichen Konfessionen*. Bonn: Alt-Katholischen Press- und Schriften-Vereins, 1909.

Moor, Bernhard de. *Commentarius perpetuus in Joh. Marckii Compendium theologiae christianae didactico-elencticum*. 6 vols. Leiden: J. Hasebroek, 1761–71.

Moor, Johannes Cornelis de. *De rechtvaardigmaking van eeuwigheid*. Kampen: Kok, 1905.

Morgan, John Vyrnwy. *The Welsh Religious Revival, 1904–1905: A Retrospect and a Criticism*. London: Chapman & Hall, 1909.

Mörikofer, Johann Kaspar. *Ulrich Zwingli, nach den urkundlichen Quellen*. 2 vols. Leipzig: Hirzel, 1867–69.

Moule, Handley Carr Glyn. *Faith: Its Nature and Its Work*. London and New York: Cassell, 1909.

Mühlhäusser, Karl. *Die Zukunft der Menschheit*. Heilbronn: Henninger, 1881.

Mulder, Roelof. *De conscientiae notione, quae et qualis fuerit romanis*. Leiden: Brill, 1908.

Müller, Ernst Friedrich Karl. *Die Bekenntnisschriften der reformierten Kirche*. Leipzig: Deichert, 1903.

————. *Symbolik*. Erlangen: Deichert, 1896.

Müller, Joseph T. *Die symbolischen Bücher der evangelisch-lutherischen Kirche*. 8th ed. Gütersloh: Bertelsmann, 1898.

Müller, Julius. *Die christliche Lehre von der Sünde*. 2 vols. Bremen: C. E. Müller, 1889.

————. *Dogmatische Abhandlungen*. Bremen: C. E. Müller, 1870.

Müller, Karl. *Kirche, Gemeinde, und weltliche Obrigkeit nach Luther.* Tübingen: Mohr, 1910.

Münchmeyer, August Friedrich Otto. *Das Dogma von der sichtbaren und unsichtbaren Kirche.* Göttingen: Vandenhoeck & Ruprecht, 1854.

Münscher, Wilhelm. *Lehrbuch des christlichen Dogmengeschichte.* Edited by Daniel von Coelln. 3rd ed. Cassel: J. C. Krieger, 1832–38.

Muratorian Canon. ANF, V, 603–4.

Murisier, Ernest. *Les maladies du sentiment religieux.* 2nd ed. Paris: Alcan, 1903.

Musculus, Wolfgang. *Loci communes theologiae sacrae.* Basel: Heruagiana, 1567.

Myers, Frederick William Henry. *Human Personality and Its Survival of Bodily Death.* 2nd ed. London: Longmans, Green, 1903.

Neal, Daniel. *Historie der rechtzinnige Puriteinen.* 3 vols. Rotterdam: Kentlink, 1752–53.

———. *The History of the Puritans or Protestant Non-conformists.* London: J. Buckland, 1754.

Neander, August. *Geschichte der Pflanzung und Leitung der christlichen Kirche durch die Apostel.* 5th ed. 2 vols. Gotha: F. A. Perthes, 1890.

———. *History of the Planting and the Training of the Christian Church by the Apostles.* Translated by J. E. Ryland. 2 vols. London: Bell & Daly, 1864.

Newman, Albert Henry. *A History of Anti-Pedobaptism from the Rise of Pedobaptism to A.D. 1609.* Philadelphia: American Baptist Publication Society, 1897.

Niederhuber, Johann Evangelist. *Die Eschatologie des heiligen Ambrosius: Eine patristische Studie.* Paderborn: Schöningh, 1907.

Niemeyer, H. A. *Collectio confessionum in ecclesiis reformatis publicatarum.* 2 vols. Leipzig: Iulii Klinkhardti, 1840.

Nitzsch, Carl [Karl] Emmanuel. *System of Christian Doctrines.* Edinburgh: T&T Clark, 1849.

———. *System der christlichen Lehre.* 5th ed. Bonn: Adolph Marcus, 1844.

Nitzsch, Friedrich August Berthold. *Lehrbuch der evangelischen Dogmatik.* Freiburg i.B.: J. C. B. Mohr, 3rd ed. prepared by Horst Stephan. Tübingen: J. C. B. Mohr, 1912.

Nösgen, Karl Friedrich. *Das Wesen und Wirken des Heiligen Geistes.* 2 vols. Berlin: Trowitzsch, 1905–7.

Nowack, W., et al. *Theologische Abhandlung: Eine Festgabe für Heinrich Julius Holtzmann.* Tübingen: J. C. B. Mohr, 1902.

Oehler, Gustav Friedrich. *Theologie des Alten Testament.* 2nd ed. Stuttgart: J. F. Steinkopf, 1882.

Oertel, J. R. *Hades: Exegetisch-dogmatische Abhandlung über den Zustand der abgeschiedenen Seelen.* Leipzig: E. Bredt, 1863.

Oetinger, Friedrich Christoph. *Die Theologie aus der Idee des Lebens abgeleitet und auf sechs Hauptstücke zurückgeführt.* Stuttgart: J. F. Steinkopf, 1852.

Oettingen, Alexander von. *Lutherische Dogmatik.* 2 vols. Munich: C. H. Beck, 1897.

Olthuis, Hendrik Jan. *De doopspraktijk der Gereformeerde Kerken in Nederland 1568–1816.* Utrecht: Ruys, 1908.

Oosterzee, J. J. van. *Christian Dogmatics.* Translated by J. Watson and M. Evans. 2 vols. New York: Scribner, Armstrong, 1874.

Origen. *Against Celsus. ANF,* IV, 395–669.

———. *On First Principles. ANF,* IV, 239–384.

Orr, James. *The Christian View of God and the World as Centering in the Incarnation.* New York: Randolph, 1893. 7th ed. New York: Charles Scribner's Sons, 1904.

———. *Sidelights on Christian Doctrine.* London: Marshall Bros., 1909.

Ostervald, Jean Frédéric. *A Compendium of Christian Theology.* Translated by John McMains. Hartford: N. Patten, 1788.

Oswald, Johann Heinrich. *Die dogmatische Lehre von den heiligen Sakramenten der katholischen Kirche.* 2nd ed. 2 vols. in 1. Münster: Aschendorff, 1864.

———. *Die dogmatische Lehre von den heiligen Sakramenten der katholischen Kirche.*

5th ed. 2 vols. Münster: Aschendorff, 1894.

———. *Eschatologie, das ist die letzten Dinge, dargestellt nach der Lehre der katholischen Kirche.* Paderborn: F. Schöningh, 1869.

———. *Eschatologie, das ist die letzten Dinge, dargestellt nach der Lehre der katholischen Kirche.* 5th ed. Paderborn: F. Schöningh, 1893.

Otto, Rudolf. *Geist und Wort nach Luther.* Göttingen: E. A. Huth, 1898.

Owen, John. *The Doctrine of Justification by Faith through the Imputation of the Righteousness of Christ.* London: R. Boulter, 1677.

———. *Justification by Faith.* Originally published in 1677 under the title *The Doctrine of Justification by Faith through the Imputation of the Righteousness of Christ, Explained, Confirmed, and Vindicated.* Issued with the author's *Gospel Grounds and Evidences of the Faith of God's Elect,* originally published in 1709. Grand Rapids: Sovereign Grace, 1959.

———. *Pneumatologia, or, A Discourse concerning the Holy Spirit.* London: J. Darby, 1674.

———. *De rechtvaardiging uit het geloof door de toerekening van Christus gerechtigheid.* Translated by Marinus van Werkhoven. Amsterdam: Martinus de Bruyn, 1779.

Palmer, William. *A Treatise on the Church of Christ: Designed Chiefly for the Use of Students in Theology.* 3rd ed., rev. and enl. London: J. G. F. and J. Rivington, 1842.

Paulsen, Peter. *Das Leben nach dem Tode.* 2nd ed. Stuttgart: Chr. Belser, 1905.

Paulus, Nikolaus. *Johann Tetzel, der Ablassprediger.* Mainz: Kirchheim, 1899.

———. *Luthers Lebensende.* Freiburg i.B.: Herder, 1898.

Perkins, William. *The Workes of That Famous and Worthy Minister of Christ.* 3 vols. London: John Legatt, 1612–18.

Perrone, Giovanni. *Praelectiones theologicae.* 9 vols. Louvain: Vanlinthout & Vandezande, 1838–43.

Pesch, Christian. *Praelectiones dogmaticae.* 9 vols. Freiburg: Herder, 1902–10.

———. *Theologische Zeitfragen.* Freiburg i.B.: Herder, 1908.

Pesch, Tilmann. *Die grossen Welträthsel.* 2nd ed. 2 vols. Freiburg i.B.: Herder, 1892.

Peschel, Oscar. *Abhandlungen zur Erd und Völkerkunde.* Leipzig: Duncker & Humboldt, 1878.

Petau, Denis (Dionysius Petavius). *De ecclesiastica hierarchica.* Paris: Sebastian Cramoisy, 1643.

———. *Opus de theologicus dogmatibus.* Antwerp: Gallet, 1700.

Pétavel-Oliff, Emmanuel. *Le problème de l'immortalité.* Paris: Fischbacher, 1891.

Pfanner, Tobias. *Systema theologiae gentilis purioris.* Basel: Joh. Hermann Widerhold, 1679.

Pfister, Friedrich. *Der Reliquienkult im Altertum.* Vol. I, *Das Objekt des Reliquienkultus.* Giessen: Alfred Töpelmann, 1909.

Pfleiderer, Otto. *Grundriss der christlichen Glaubens und Sittenlehre.* 4th ed. Berlin: G. Reimer, 1888.

———. *Der Paulinismus: Ein Beitrag zur Geschichte der urchristlichen Theologie.* 2nd ed. Leipzig: O. R. Reisland, 1890.

———. *Religionsphilosophie auf geschichtlicher Grundlage.* Berlin: G. Reimer, 1896.

Philippi, Adolph. *Commentary on St. Paul's Epistle to the Romans.* Translated by John S. Banks. Edinburgh: T&T Clark, 1878–79.

Philippi, Friedrich A. *Kirchliche Glaubenslehre.* 3rd ed. 7 vols. Gütersloh: Bertelsmann, 1883–1902.

Pichler, Aloys. *Die Theologie des Leibniz.* Munich: J. G. Cotta, 1869–70.

Pictet, Benedictus. *De christelyjke God-geleertheid en kennis der zaligheid.* Translated by Johannes Wesselius. 's Gravenhage: Pieter van Thol, 1728–30.

———. *Christian Theology.* Translated by Frederick Reyroux. Philadelphia: Presbyterian Board of Publication, 1845.

Pieper, Anton. *Christentum, römisches Kaisertum und heidnischer Staat.* Münster: Aschendorff, 1907.

Pierson, Allard. *Eene levensbeschouwing.* Haarlem: Kruseman, 1875.

Pieters, K. J., and J. R. Keulen. *De kinderdoop volgens de beginselen der Gereformeerde Kerk.* Franeker: T. Telenga, 1861.

Pijper, Fredrik. *Jan Utenhove.* Leiden: H. A. Adriani, 1883.

——. *Middeleeuwsch Christendom.* 2 vols. 's Gravenhage: M. Nijhoff, 1907–11.

Piscator, Johannes. *Aphorismi doctrinae Christianae, maximam partem ex Institutione Calvini excerpti.* 3rd ed. London: Richard Field, 1595.

Plitt, Hermann. *Evangelische Glaubenslehre.* 2 vols. Gotha: Perthes, 1863–64.

——. *Zinzendorf's Theologie.* 3 vols. in 1. Gotha: F. A. Perthes, 1869–74.

Plummer, Alfred. *An Exegetical Commentary on the Gospel according to St. Matthew.* London: E. Stock, 1909.

Pobedonoszew, Konstantin Petrovich. *Streitfragen der Gegenwart.* Berlin: Deubner, 1907.

Pohle, Joseph. *Lehrbuch der Dogmatik.* 3rd ed. 3 vols. Paderborn: Schöningh, 1907–8. 4th ed. 1908–10. Revised by M. Gierens. 10th ed. 3 vols. 1931.

Polanus, Amandus. *Partitiones theologicae.* Basel, 1590–96.

——. *The Substance of the Christian Faith, Set Forth in Two Books, by Definitions and Partitions.* London: John Oxenbridge, 1597.

——. *Syntagma theologiae christianae.* Hanover, 1609. Geneva, 1617. 5th ed. Hanover: Aubry, 1624.

Polycarp. *Letter to the Philippians.* ANF, I, 31–36.

Pont, J. W. *De Luthersche kerken in Nederland.* Baarn: Hollandia, 1908. Reprinted, Amsterdam: Swets & Zeitlinger, 1929.

Prezzolini, Giuseppe. *Wesen, Geschichte und Ziele des Modernismus.* Jena: Diederichs, 1910.

Proost, Pieter. *Jodocus van Lodenstein.* Amsterdam: J. Brandt, 1880.

Pruner, Johann Evangelist. *Lehrbuch der katholischen Moraltheologie.* 2nd ed. Freiburg i.B.: Herder, 1883.

Pusey, Edward Bouverie. *The Doctrine of the Real Presence.* Oxford and London: John Henry Parker, 1855.

——. *An Eirenicon, in a Letter to the Author of "The Christian Year."* New York: Appleton, 1866.

Quenstedt, Johann Andreas. *Theologia didactico-polemica sive systema theologicum.* 1685.

The Racovian Catechism. Translated by Thomas Rees. London, 1609. Reprinted, London, 1818.

Rashdall, Hastings. *Christus in ecclesia.* Edinburgh: T&T Clark, 1904.

Rauwenhoff, Lodewijk W. E. *Disquisitio de loco Paulino, qui est de δικαιωσει.* Leiden: Engels, 1852.

——. *Wijsbegeerte van den godsdienst.* Leiden: Brill & van Doesburgh, 1887.

Reiff, Franz. *Die Zukunft der Welt.* 2nd ed. Basel: Bahnmaier's Verlag (C. Detloff), 1875.

Reinhard, Franz Volkmar. *Grundriss der Dogmatik.* Munich: Seidel, 1802.

Reinhold, George Christopher. *Die Streitfrage über die physische oder moralische Wirksamkeit der Sakramente.* Stuttgart: J. Roth, 1899.

Reischle, Max Wilhelm Theodor. *Leitsätze für eine akademische Vorlesung über die christliche Glaubenslehre.* Halle a.S.: Niemeyer, 1899.

——. *Der Streit über die Begründung des Glaubens auf den geschichtlichen Jesus Christus.* Freiburg i.B.: Mohr, 1897.

Reitz, Johann Heinrich. *Historie der Wiedergeborenen.* 4 vols. Tübingen: M. Niemeyer, 1982 [1698].

Rendtorff, Franz Martin. *Die Taufe im Urchristentum im Lichte der neueren Forschungen.* Leipzig: Hinrichs, 1905.

Renesse, Lodewijk Gerard van. *Van het regeer-ouderlinghschap.* Utrecht: Meinardus van Druenen, 1659.

Rentschka, Paul. *Die Dekalogkatechese des heiligen Augustinus: Ein Beitrag zur*

Geschichte des Dekalogs. Kempten: Jos. Kölel'schen Buchhandlung, 1905.

Reuter, Hermann. *Augustinische Studien.* Gotha: Perthes, 1887. Reprinted, Aalen: Scientia-Verlag, 1967.

Richer, Edmond. *De ecclesiastica et politica potestate.* Paris, 1611.

Richter, Aemelius Ludwig, Richard Wilhelm Dove, and Wilhelm Kahl. *Lehrbuch des katholischen und evangelischen Kirchenrechts, mit besonderer Rücksicht auf deutsche Zustände.* 8th ed. Leipzig: Tauchnitz, 1886.

Richter, Friedrich. *Die Lehre von der letzten Dingen.* Breslau: J. Hebenstreit, 1833–44.

Ridderbos, Jan. *De Theologie van Jonathan Edwards.* 's Gravenhage: J. A. Nederbragt, 1907.

Ridderus, Franciscus. *De mensche Godts verthoont in de staet.* Hoorn: Gerbrant en Ian Martensz., 1658.

Rieker, Karl. *Grundsätze reformierter Kirchenverfassung.* Leipzig: Hirschfeld, 1899.

Riemann, Otto. *Die Lehre von den Apokatastasis.* 2nd ed. Magdeburg: Frölich, 1897.

———. *Was wissen wir über die Unsterblichkeit der Seele?* Magdeburg: Frölich, 1900.

Riggenbach, Eduard. *Die Rechtfertigungslehre des Apostel Paulus.* Stuttgart: D. Gundert, 1897.

———. *Der trinitarische Taufbefehl: Matt. 28:19 nach seiner ursprünglichen Textgestalt und seiner Authentie.* Gütersloh: C. Bertelsmann, 1903.

Rinck, Heinrich Wilhelm. *Vom Zustand nach dem Tode.* 2nd ed. Ludwigsburg and Basel: Balmer & Riehm, 1885.

Ritschl, Albrecht. *The Christian Doctrine of Justification and Reconciliation.* Translated by H. R. Mackintosh and A. B. Macaulay. Edinburgh: T&T Clark, 1900. Reprinted, Clifton, NJ: Reference Book Publishers, 1966.

———. *Die christliche Lehre von der Rechtfertigung und Versöhnung.* 4th ed. 3 vols. Bonn: A. Marcus, 1895–1903.

———. *Geschichte des Pietismus in der reformierten Kirche.* 3 vols. Bonn: A. Marcus, 1880.

———. *Theologie und Metaphysik.* Bonn: A. Marcus, 1881.

———. *Unterricht in der christlichen Religion.* 3rd ed. Bonn: A. Marcus, 1886.

Rivetus, Andreas. *Operum theologicorum.* 3 vols. Rotterdam: Leers, 1651–60.

Robertson, Andrew. *History of the Atonement Controversy: In Connexion with the Secession Church, from Its Origin to the Present Time.* Edinburgh: Oliphant, 1846.

Roepke, O., and E. Huss. *Het onderzoek over de mogelijkheid van 't overbrengen van ziektekiemen door het gebruik van den gemeenschappelijken avondmaalsbeker.* Rotterdam: W. Nevens, 1905.

Rogaar, Herman Philippus. *Het Avondmaal en zijne oorspsrongelijke beteekenis.* Groningen: J. B. Huber, 1897.

Rogers, J. Guinness. *The Church Systems of England in the Nineteenth Century.* 2nd ed. London: Congregational Union of England and Wales, 1891.

Rohde, Erwin. *Psyche: Seelenkult und Unsterblichkeitsglaube der Griechen.* 2nd ed. 2 vols. in 1. Freiburg i.B.: J. C. B. Mohr, 1898.

Rohnert, Wilhelm. *Die Lehre von den Gnadenmitteln.* Leipzig: G. Böhme, 1886.

Romeis, Capistran. *Das Heil des Christen ausserhalb der wahren Kirche nach der Lehre des heiligen Augustin.* Paderborn: F. Schöningh, 1908.

Rothe, Richard. *Theologische Ethik.* 2nd rev. ed. 5 vols. Wittenberg: Zimmermann, 1867–71.

Row, Charles Adolphus. *Future Retribution Viewed in the Light of Reason and Revelation.* New York: Whittaker, 1887.

Ruibing, Roelof. *De jongste hypothesen over het ontstaan van het episcopaat.* Groningen: P. Noordhoff, 1900.

Runze, Georg. *Katechismus der Dogmatik.* Leipzig: J. J. Weber, 1898.

Russell, Charles. *The Millennial Dawn*. Allegheny, PA: Watchtower Bible and Tract Society, 1898–1901.

Rutgers, Frederik Lodewijk. *De kerkrecht: In zoover het de kerk met het recht in verband brengt*. Amsterdam: Wormser, 1894.

Rutherford, Samuel. *Examen Arminianismi*. Utrecht: Smytegelt, 1668.

Ryle, John Charles. *Knots Untied: Being Plain Statements on Disputed Points of Religion from the Standpoint of an Evangelical Churchman*. 11th ed. London: William Hunt, 1886.

Sabatier, Auguste. *Esquisse d'une philosophie de la religion d'après la psychologie et l'historie*. 7th ed. Paris: Fischbacher, 1903.

———. *Les religions d'authorité et la religion de l'esprit*. Paris: Fischbacher, 1904.

———. *Religions of Authority and the Religion of the Spirit*. Translated by Louise Seymour Houghton. New York: McClure, Phillips, 1904.

Sachs, Josef. *Die ewige Dauer der Höllenstrafen*. Paderborn: Schöningh, 1900.

Salmond, S. D. F. *The Christian Doctrine of Immortality*. 4th ed. Edinburgh: T&T Clark, 1901.

Sanday, William, and Arthur C. Headlam. *A Critical and Exegetical Commentary on the Epistle to the Romans*. 5th ed. Edinburgh: T&T Clark, 1902.

Sartorius, Karl. *Die Leichenverbrennung innerhalb der christlichen Kirche*. Basel: C. Detloff, 1886.

Schaefer, Rudolf. *Das Herrenmahl nach Ursprung und Bedeutung mit Rücksicht auf die neuesten Forschungen*. Gütersloh: Bertelsmann, 1897.

Schäfer, Theodor. *Leitfaden der Inneren Mission*. 4th ed. Hamburg: Agentur des Rauhen Hauses, 1903.

Schaff, Philip. *Creeds of Christendom*. 3 vols. New York: Harper & Brothers, 1877.

Schall, Eduard. *Die Staatsverfassung der Juden auf Grund des alten Testaments und namentlich der fünf Bücher Moses mit fortlaufender Beziehung auf die Gegenwart*. Leipzig: R. Werther, 1896.

Schanz, Paul. *Apologie des Christentums*. 3 vols. Freiburg i.B.: Herder, 1903.

———. *A Christian Apology*. Translated by Michael F. Glancey and Victor J. Schobel. 4th rev. ed. Ratisbon: F. Pustet, 1891.

Scheeben, Matthias Joseph, and Leonhard Atzberger (for vol. 4). *Handbuch der katholischen Dogmatik*. 4 vols. 1874–98. Reprinted, Freiburg i.B.: Herder, 1933.

Scheel, Otto. *Die dogmatische Behandlung der Tauflehre in der modernen positiven Theologie*. Tübingen: Mohr, 1906.

Scheele, Karl. *Die Kirchenzucht der evangelischen Kirche*. Halle: R. Mühlmann, 1852.

Schell, Herman. *Katholische Dogmatik*. 3 vols. in 4. Paderborn: F. Schöningh, 1889–93.

Schelling, F. W. J. *Ausgewählte Werke*. 4 vols. Darmstadt: Wissenschaftliche Buchgesellschaft, 1968.

Schian, Martin. *Die moderne Gemeinschaftsbewegung*. Stuttgart: Greiner & Pfeiffer, 1909.

Schlatter, Adolph von. *Erläuterung zum Neuen Testament*. 3 vols. Stuttgart: Calwer Verlag, 1908–10.

———. *Der Glaube im Neuen Testament*. 3rd ed. Stuttgart: Vereinsbuchhandlung, 1905.

Schleiermacher, Friedrich. *The Christian Faith*. Edited by H. R. MacIntosh and J. S. Steward. Edinburgh: T&T Clark, 1928.

———. *Gelegentliche Gedanken über Universitäten in deutschen Sinn, nebst einem Anhang über eine neu zu errichtende*. Berlin: Realschulbuchhandlung, 1808.

———. *On Religion: Speeches to Its Cultured Despisers*. Translated by John Oman. 1958. Reprinted, Louisville: Westminster/John Knox, 1994.

Schmid, Franz. *Der Fegfeuer nach katholischen Lehre*. Brixen: Pressvereins-Buchhandlung, 1904.

Schmid, Heinrich Friedrich Ferdinand. *The Doctrinal Theology of the Evangelical Lutheran Church*. Translated by Charles A. Hay and Henry Jacobs. 5th ed. Philadelphia: United Lutheran Publication House, 1899.

——. *Die Dogmatik der evangelisch-lutherischen Kirche.* 7th ed. Gütersloh: Bertelsmann, 1893.

Schmidt, Wilhelm. *Christliche Dogmatik.* 4 vols. Bonn: E. Weber, 1895–98.

——. *Die verschiedenen Type religiöser Erfahrung und die Psychologie.* Gütersloh: Bertelsmann, 1910 [1908].

Schmölder, Robert. *Zum Frieden unter den Konfessionen.* Bonn, 1910.

Schmoll, Polykarp. *Die Busslehre der Frühscholastik.* Munich: Lentner, 1909.

Schneckenburger, Matthias. *Vorlesungen über die Lehrbegriffe der kleineren protestantischen Kirchenparteien.* Edited by K. B. Hundeshagen. Frankfurt: H. L. Brönner, 1863.

Schneckenburger, Matthias, and Eduard Güder. *Vergleichende Darstellung des lutherischen und reformirten Lehrbegriffs.* 2 vols. Stuttgart: J. B. Metzler, 1855.

Schneider, Leonhard. *Die Unsterblichkeitsidee im Glauben und in der Philosophie der Volker.* Regensburg: Alfred Coppenrath, 1870.

Schneider, Richard. *Christliche Klänge aus den griechischen und römischen Klassikern.* Leipzig: Siegismund & Volkening, 1877.

Schöberlein, Ludwig. *Prinzip und System der Dogmatik.* Heidelberg: C. Winter, 1881.

Scholten, Johannes Henricus. *Dogmaticae christianae initia.* 2nd ed. 2 vols. London: P. Engels, 1856–58.

——. *Het Evangelie naar Johannes.* Leiden: P. Engels, 1864.

——. *De Leer der Hervormde Kerk in hare grondbeginselen.* 2nd ed. 2 vols. Leiden: P. Engels, 1850–51.

——. *De vrije wil, kritisch onderzoek.* Leiden: Engels, 1859.

Schopenhauer, Arthur. *Die Welt als Wille und Vorstellung.* Vols. 2 and 3 of *Sammtliche Werke.* Leipzig: F. M. Brodhaus, 1919.

——. *The World as Will and Representation.* Translated by E. F. J. Payne. New York: Dover, 1966.

Schortinghuis, Wilhelmus. *Historisch verhaal aangedande de akademische approbatie van de hoog eerw. theol. faculteit van de Universiteit van Stad en Lande over een zeker boek … genaamt Innige Christendom.* Groningen: Spandaw, 1740.

——. *Het innige Christendom to overtuiginge van onbeganadigde, bestieringe en opwekkinge beganadigde zielen, in desselfs allerinigste en wesentlikste deelen gestaltelik en bevindelik voorgestelt in t'Zamenspraken.* Groningen: Spandaw, 1740.

Schrader, Otto. *Die Lehre von der Apokatastasis.* Berlin: R. Boll, 1901.

Schulte, Johann Friedrich von. *Die Macht der römischen Päpste über Fürsten, Länder, Völker und Individuen.* 3rd ed. Giessen: E. Roth, 1896.

Schultens, J. J. *Uitvoerige Waarschuwing op den Catechismus van den Heer Comrie.* Leiden: A. Kallewier, 1761.

Schulthess-Rechberg, Gustav von. *Luther, Zwingli und Calvin in ihren Ansichten über das Verhältnis von Staat und Kirche.* Aurau: H. R. Sauerländer, 1909.

Schultz, Hermann. *Alttestamentliche Theologie: Die Offenbarungsreligion auf ihrer vorchristliche Entwickelungsstufe.* 5th ed. Göttingen: Vandenhoeck & Ruprecht, 1896.

——. *Grundriss der evangelischen Dogmatik zum Gebrauche bei akademischen Vorlesungen.* Göttingen: Vandenhoeck & Ruprecht, 1892.

——. *Voraussetzungen der christlichen Lehre von der Unsterblichkeit.* Göttingen: Vandenhoeck & Ruprecht, 1861.

Schultzen, Friedrich. *Das Abendmahl im neuen Testament.* Göttingen: Vandenhoeck & Ruprecht, 1895.

Schulze, Martin. *Calvins Jenseits-Christentum in seinem Verhältnisse zu den religiösen Schriften des Erasmus.* Görlitz: Rudolf Dülfer, 1902.

——. *Meditatio futurae vitae.* Leipzig: Dieterich, 1901.

Schürer, Emil. *Die Geschichte des jüdischen Volkes im Zeitalter Jesu Christi.* 3rd ed. 3 vols. Leipzig: Hinrichs, 1901.

——. *The History of the Jewish People in the Age of Jesus Christ (175 B.C.–A.D. 135).*

Original edition, 1885. Revised and edited by Géza Vermès and Fergus Millar. 3 vols. Edinburgh: T&T Clark, 1973–87.

Schuts, Jacobus. *Het nodigst middel der saligheyd ofte beschrijvinge des salig-makende geloofs.* Rotterdam: R. van Doesburgh, 1692.

Schwally, Friedrich. *Das Leben nach dem Tode: Nach den Vorstellungen des Alten Israel und des Judentums einschließlich des Volksglaubens im Zeitalter Christi; Eine biblisch-theologische Untersuchung.* Giessen: J. Ricker, 1892.

Schwane, Joseph. *Dogmengeschichte.* 4 vols. Freiburg i.B.: Herder, 1882–95.

Schweizer, Alexander. *Die christliche Glaubenslehre nach protestantischen Grundsätzen dargestellt.* 2 vols. in 3. Leipzig: S. Hirzel, 1863–72.

———. *Die Glaubenslehre der evangelisch-reformirten Kirche.* 2 vols. Zurich: Orell, Füssli, 1844–47.

———. *Die protestantischen Centraldogmen in ihrer Entwicklung innerhalb der reformirten Kirche.* 2 vols. Zurich: Orell, Füssli, 1854–56.

Seeberg, Reinhold. *Der Begriff der christlichen Kirche.* Erlangen: Deichert, 1885.

———. *Die beiden Wege und das Aposteldekret.* Leipzig: Deichert, 1906.

———. *Das Evangelium Christi.* Leipzig: Deichert, 1905.

———. *Der Katechismus der Urchristenheit.* Leipzig: Deichert, 1903.

———. *Textbook of the History of Doctrine.* Translated by Charles A. Hay. 2 vols. in 1. Philadelphia: Lutheran Publication Society, 1905.

Seesemann, Heinrich, and Nikolaus Bonwetsch. *Das Amt der Diakonissen in der alten Kirche.* Mitau: Steffenhagen, 1891.

Seidel, Bruno. *Die Lehre vom Staat beim heiligen Augustinus.* Breslau: G. P. Aderholz, 1909.

Seidl, J. N. *Der Diakonat in der katholischen Kirche.* Regensburg, 1884.

Seiss, Joseph Augustus. *The Apocalypse: Lectures on the Book of Revelation.* New York: Charles C. Cook, 1909.

Seufert, Wilhelm. *Die Ursprung und die Bedeutung des Apostolates in der christlichen Kirche der ersten zwei Jahrhunderte.* Leiden: Brill, 1887.

Shedd, William Greenough Thayer. *Dogmatic Theology.* 3rd ed. 3 vols. New York: Scribner, 1888–94.

Siebeck, Herman. *Lehrbuch der Religionsphilosophie.* Freiburg i.B.: J. C. B. Mohr, 1893.

Sillevis Smitt, P. A. E. *De organisatie van de Christelijke kerk in den apostolischen tijd.* Rotterdam: T. de Vries, 1910.

Simar, H. Th. *Lehrbuch der Dogmatik.* 2 vols. Freiburg i.B.: Herder, 1879–80. 3rd ed. 1893.

Simons, Menno. *The Complete Works of Menno Simons.* Elkhart: John F. Funk and Brother, 1871.

Smend, Rudolf. *Lehrbuch der alttestamentlichen Religionsgeschichte.* Freiburg i.B.: J. C. B. Mohr, 1893.

Smith, Robert Pearsall. *An Account of the Union Meeting for the Promotion of Scriptural Holiness, held at Oxford, Aug. 29 to Sept. 7, 1874.* London: Dalby, Isbitter, 1874.

Smith, William Robertson. *Die Religion der Semiten.* Freiburg i.B.: Mohr, 1899.

Smyth, John Paterson. *The Gospel of the Hereafter.* London: Hodder & Stoughton, 1910.

Snijder, D. *Het dogma van de onfeilbaarkeit van den Paus vastgesteld op het Vatikaansche Concilie van 1870, in zijn ontstaan en zijne beteekenis geschetst.* Rotterdam: Daamen, 1899.

———. *Rome's vornaamste leerstelling en bedoelingen voor den Protestant.* Gorinchem: Knierum, 1890.

Söder, Rudolf. *Der Begriff der Katholicität der Kirche und des Glaubens nach seiner geschichtlichen Entwicklung.* Würzburg: Leo Woerl, 1881.

Sohm, Rudolf. *Kirchenrecht*. 2 vols. Leipzig and Munich: Duncker & Humblot, 1892–1923.

———. *Wesen und Ursprung des Katholizmus*. Leipzig: Teubner, 1912.

Sohn, Georg. *Opera sacrae theologiae*. 2 vols. Herborn: C. Corvin, 1598.

Southey, Robert. *The Life of John Wesley*. London: Hutchinson, 1903.

Spanheim, Friedrich. *Dubia evangelica in tres partes distributa*. Geneva: Petri Chovet, 1655–58.

———. *Opera*. 3 vols. Lyon: Cornelium Boutestein [etc.], 1701–3.

Specht, Thomas. *Die Lehre von der Kirche nach dem heiligen Augustin*. Paderborn: Schöningh, 1892.

Speyer, Jacobus Samuel. *De Indische theosophie en hare beteekenis voor ons*. Leiden: S. C. van Doesburgh, 1910.

Spiess, Edmund. *Entwicklungsgeschichte der Vorstellungen vom Zustande nach dem Tode: Auf Grund vergleichender Religionsforschung*. Jena: Hermann Costenoble, 1877.

Spinoza, Baruch (Benedictus de). *The Ethics*. Malibu, CA: J. Simon, 1981.

Spitta, Friedrich. *Die Kelchbewegung in Deutschland und die Reform der Abendmahlsfeier*. Göttingen: Vandenhoeck & Ruprecht, 1904.

Spitta, Friedrich, and Richard Bürkner. *Abendmahls-Feiern mit Einzelkelch: Ihre Notwendigkeit und Gestaltung*. Göttingen, 1904.

Splittgerber, Franz Joseph. *Tod, Fortleben und Auferstehung*. 3rd ed. Halle: Fricke, 1879.

Stade, Bernhard. *Geschichte des Volkes Israel*. 2 vols. Berlin: G. Grote, 1887–88.

———. *Über die alttestamentliche Vorstellung vom Zustande nach dem Tode*. Leipzig: Vogel, 1877.

Staerk, Willy. *Neutestamentliche Zeitgeschichte*. 2 vols. Berlin: G. J. Göschen, 1907.

Stahl, Friedrich Julius. *Die Kirchenverfassung nach Lehre und Recht der Protestanten*. 2nd ed. Erlangen: T. Bläsing, 1862.

———. *Die lutherische Kirche und die Union*. Berlin: W. Hertz, 1859.

Stange, Carl. *Die Heilsbedeutung des Gesetzes*. Leipzig: Dieterich, 1904.

Stapfer, Paul. *Questions esthétiques et religieuses*. Paris: F. Alcan, 1906.

Starbuck, Edwin Diller. *The Psychology of Religion*. London and New York: Charles Scribner's Sons, 1901.

Steinmann, Theophil. *Der religiose Unsterblichkeitsglaube*. Göttingen: Vandenhoeck & Ruprecht, 1912.

Stephens, Thomas, ed. *The Child and Religion*. New York: G. P. Putnam's Sons; London: Williams & Norgate, 1905.

Stern, Alexander. *Das Jenseits: Der Zustand der Verstorbenen bis zur Auferstehung nach der Lehre der Bible und der Ergebnissen der Erfahrung*. 3rd ed. Gotha, 1907.

Stevens, George Barker. *The Theology of the New Testament*. New York: C. Scribner's Sons, 1899.

Stöckl, Albert. *Lehrbuch der Philosophie*. 6th ed. 2 vols. Mainz: Kirchheim, 1887.

Stokes, George Gabriel. *Conditional Immortality: A Help to Sceptics*. London: James Nisbet, 1897.

Strauss, David Friedrich. *Der alte und der neue Glaube*. 2nd ed. Leipzig: Hirzel, 1872.

———. *Die christliche Glaubenslehre in ihrer geschichtlichen Entwicklung und im Kampfe mit der moderne Wissenschaft*. 2 vols. Tübingen: Osiander, 1840–41.

———. *Speculative Betrachtungen über die Dogmatik*. Weilburg: Lanz, 1841.

Strindberg, August. *The Dance of Death*. Translated by Arvid Paulsen. New York: Norton, 1976.

Strong, Augustus Hopkins. *Systematic Theology*. 3 vols. Philadelphia: Griffith & Rowland, 1907–9.

Stuckert, Carl. *Die katholische Lehre von der Reue*. Freiburg i.B. and Leipzig: Mohr, 1896.

Stufler, Johann. *Die Heiligkeit Gottes und die ewige Tod*. Innsbruck: Rauch, 1903.

———. *Die Verteidigung Schells durch Prof. Kiefl*. Innsbruck: Rauch, 1904.

Suicerus, Johann Caspar. *Thesaurus ecclesiasticus, e patribus graecis ordine alphabetico.* Amsterdam: J. H. Wetsten, 1682.

Synopsis purioris theologiae, disputationibus quinquaginta duabus comprehensa ac conscripta per Johannem Polyandrum, Andream Rivetum, Antonium Walaeum, Antonius Thysium. Leiden, 1625. 4th ed. Leiden: Elzeviriana, 1652. 6th ed. Curavit et praefatus est Dr. H. Bavinck. Leiden: Donner, 1881.

Teellinck, Willem. *Noodwendigh vertoogh, aengaende den tegen woordigen bedroef den staet van Gods volck.* Middelburg: Hans vander Hellen, 1627. Rotterdam: Pieter van Waesberghe, 1647. Reprinted, Urk: Willem Teellinck Fonds, 1978.

————. *De Toetssteen des geloofs, waer in de gelegentheyt des waren salighmakende geloofs nader ontdeckt wordt, soo dat een yder sich selven daer aen kan toetsen of hy ook het salighmakende geloove heeft.* Amsterdam: Joannes van Someren, 1662.

Teichmann, Ernst. *Die paulinischen Vorstellung von Auferstehung und Gericht und ihre Beziehung zur jüdischen Apokalyptic.* Freiburg i.B.: J. C. B. Mohr, 1896.

Tennyson, Alfred. *In Memoriam: An Authoritative Text, Backgrounds and Sources, Criticism.* Edited by Robert H. Ross. New York: Norton, 1973.

Tertullian. *Against Marcion. ANF,* III, 269–475.

————. *The Apology. ANF,* III, 17–60.

————. *The Chaplet, or, De Corona. ANF,* III, 93–104.

————. *On Baptism. ANF,* III, 669–80.

————. *On Exhortation to Chastity. ANF,* IV, 50–58.

————. *On the Flesh of Christ. ANF,* III, 521–42.

————. *On Modesty. ANF,* IV, 74–101.

————. *On Monogamy. ANF,* IV, 59–73.

————. *On Prayer. ANF,* III, 681–91.

————. *On the Prescription of Heretics. ANF,* III, 243–65.

————. *On the Resurrection of the Flesh. ANF,* III, 545–95.

————. *On the Veiling of Virgins. ANF,* IV, 27–38.

————. *A Treatise on the Soul. ANF,* III, 181–235.

Theologia Wirceburgensis. 3rd ed. 10 vols. in 5. Paris: Berche & Tralin, 1880.

Theophilus. *To Autolycus. ANF,* II, 85–121.

Thomas Aquinas. *On the Governance of Rulers.* Translated by Gerald Bernard Phelan. London and New York: Sheed & Ward, 1938.

————. *Scriptum super libros sententiarum magistri Petri Lombardi episcopi parisiensis.* 4 vols. Paris: P. Lethielleux, 1929–47.

————. *Summa contra gentiles.* Translated by the English Dominican Fathers. London: Burns, Oates & Washbourne, 1924.

————. *Summa theologiae.* Translated by Thomas Gilby et al. 61 vols. New York: McGraw-Hill, 1964–81.

Thomasius, Gottfried. *Christi Person und Werk.* 3rd ed. 2 vols. Erlangen: A. Deichert, 1886–88.

Thompson, Robert J., ed. *The Proofs of Life after Death: A Collection of Opinions as to a Future Life by Some of the World's Most Eminent Scientists and Thinkers.* Boston: Small, Maynard, 1906.

Thuynen, Theodorus van. *Korte uitlegginge van het gereformeerde geloof.* Te Leeuwarden: Henrik Halma, 1722.

Tiele, Cornelis Petrus. *Elements of the Science of Religion.* 2 vols. Edinburgh and London: W. Blackwood & Sons, 1897–99.

————. *Inleiding tot het godsdienstwetenschap.* 2 vols. Amsterdam: P. N. van Kampen, 1897–99.

Tillmann, Fritz. *Die Wiederkunft Christi nach den paulinischen Breifen.* Freiburg i.B.: Herder, 1909.

Titius, Arthur. *Die neutestamentliche Lehre von der Seligkeit und ihre Bedeutung für die Gegenwart.* Freiburg i.B.: J. C. B. Mohr (Paul Siebeck), 1895–1900.

Torge, Paul. *Seelenglaube and Unsterblichkeitshoffnung im alten Testament.* Leipzig: J. C. Hinrichs, 1909.

Torquemada, Juan de. *Summa de ecclesia contra impuggatores potestatis summi pontificis.* Rome: Eucharius Silber, 1489 [1448]. Partially translated as *The Antiquity of the Church.* Translated by William Edward Maguire. Washington, DC: Catholic University of America Press, 1957.

Torrey, Reuben Archer. *The Holy Spirit: How to Obtain Him in Personal Experience, How to Restrain Him.* Chicago: Bible Institute Colportage Association, 1900–1928.

Trelcatius, Lucas, Jr. *Scholastica et methodica locorum communium institutio.* London: Orlers, 1604.

Trigland, Jacobus. *Antapologia.* Amsterdam: Joannam Janssonium et al., 1664.

———. *Kerckelycke geschiedenissen.* Leiden: Andriae Wyngaerden, 1650.

———. *Opuscula.* Amsterdam: Marten Jansz. Brandt, 1639–40.

Troeltsch, Ernst. *Die Bedeutung des Protestantismus für die Entstehung der modernen Welt.* Munich and Berlin: R. Oldenbourg, 1906.

———. *Protestantisches Christentum und Kirche in der Neuzeit.* Leipzig: Teubner, 1922.

———. *The Social Teaching of the Christian Churches.* Translated by Olive Wyon. 2 vols. 1931. Reprinted, Louisville: Westminster John Knox, 1992.

———. *Soziallehren der christlichen Kirchen und Gruppen.* 2 vols. Tübingen: Mohr, 1912.

Tschackert, Paul. *Evangelische Polemik gegen die römischen Kirche.* Gotha: F. A. Perthes, 1885.

———. *Modus vivendi.* Munich: Beck, 1908.

Turretin, Francis. *Institutes of Elenctic Theology.* Translated by George Musgrove Giger. Edited by James T. Dennison. 3 vols. Phillipsburg, NJ: Presbyterian & Reformed, 1992.

———. *De necessaria secissiones nostra ab ecclesia Romana.* Vol. IV, pp. 1–203 in *Opera.* New York: Carter, 1848.

Tuuk, H. Edema van der. *Johannes Bogerman.* Groningen: Wolters, 1868.

Twisse, William. *Guilielmi Twissi opera theologica polemico anti-arminiana.* Amsterdam, 1699.

Uhlhorn, Gerhard. *Die christliche Liebesthätigkeit.* 3 vols. Stuttgart: D. Gundert, 1882–90.

Urban, Johannes. *Zur gegenwärtigen "Pfingstbewegung": Herzliche Warnung auf Grund persönlicher Erfahrung.* Striegau: Urban, 1910.

Ursinus, Zacharias. *The Commentary of Dr. Zacharias Ursinus on the Heidelberg Catechism.* Translated by G. W. Willard. Grand Rapids: Eerdmans, 1954.

———. *Volumen tractationum theologicarum.* Neustadt: Mathes Harnisch, 1584.

Uytenbogaert, Johannes. *Tractaet van t'ampt ende authoriteyt eener hoogher christelicker overheydt in kerckelicke saecken.* 's Gravenhage: Hillebrant Jacobsz., 1610.

Vallotton, Paul. *La vie après la mort.* Laussane: F. Rouge, 1906.

Veen, D. J. *Wanneer is Christus gestorven?* Amersfoort: P. Dz. Veen, 1907.

Vering, Friedrich H. *Lehrbuch des katholischen, orientalischen, und protestantischen Kirchenrechts.* 3rd ed. Freiburg i.B.: Herder, 1893.

Vermeer, Justus. *De leer der waarheid, die naar de Godzaligheid is: Voorgesteld, bevestigd, en toegepast in 85 oefeningen over de Heidelbergse Catechismus.* 2 vols. 1749. Reprinted, Rijssen: Stuut, 1982.

Vermigli, Peter Martyr. *The Common Places of Peter Martyr.* Translated by Antony Marten. London, 1583.

———. *Loci communes.* Edited by R. Massonius. London, 1576.

Verschuir, Johannes. *Waarheid in het binnenste.* Appingedam: H. C. Mekel, 1862.

Vilmar, August Friedrich Christian. *Dogmatik.* 2 vols. Gütersloh: C. Bertelsmann, 1874.

———. *Handbuch der evangelischen Dogmatik für studierende die Theologie.* Gütersloh: C. Bertelsmann, 1895.

*———. *Kirchenzucht und Lehrzucht.* 1877.

———. *Die Theologie der Thatsachen wider die Theologie der Rhetorik.* 4th ed. Gütersloh: C. Bertelsmann, 1876.

———. *Von der christlichen Kirchenzucht.* Marburg: Elwert, 1872.

Visscher, Hugo. *Guilielmus Amesius: Zijn leven en werken.* Haarlem: J. M. Stap, 1894.

———. *Religie en Gemeenschap bij de Natuurvolken.* Utrecht: G. J. A. Ruys, 1907.

Vitringa, Campegius. *Doctrina christianae religionis, per aphorismos summatim descripta.* 6th ed. 8 vols. Leiden: Joannis le Mair; Arnheim: J. H. Möelemanni, 1761–86.

———. *Korte schets van de christelyke zeden-leere, ofte van het geestelyk leven ende deselfs eigenschappen.* Amsterdam: Antoni Schoo-nenburg, 1724.

———. *Observationum sacrarum libri sex, in quibus de rebus varii argumenti, & utilissimae investigationis, critice ac theologice, disseritur: Scarorum imprimis librorum loca multa obscuriora nova val clariore luce perfunduntur.* Franeker: Wibii Bleck, 1712.

Voetius, Gisbert. *Ta askètika, sive, Exercitia pietatis in usum juventutis academiae nunc edita.* Gorichem: Paul Vink, 1664.

———. *Desperata causa papatus.* Amsterdam: Joannis Jansson, 1635.

———. *Politicae ecclesiasticae.* 3 vols. Amsterdam: Joannis a Waesberge, 1663–76.

———. *Selectae disputationes theologicae.* 5 vols. Utrecht, 1648–69.

Vossius, Gerardus Johannes. *De baptismo disputationes XX, et una de sacramentorum vi, atque efficacia.* Amsterdam: Elzevirium, 1648.

———. *Historiae de controversiis, quas Pelagius eiusque reliquiae moverunt, libri septem.* 2nd ed. rev. Amsterdam: Ludovicus & Daniel Elzevirii, 1655.

Vrolikhert, Cornelis. *Twee godgeleerde verhandelingen.* Dordrecht: Braam, 1732.

Wacker, Emil. *Wiedergeburt und Bekehrung in ihrem gegenseitigen Verhältnis nach der Heiligen Schrift.* Gütersloh: Bertelsmann, 1893.

Waeyen, Johannes van der, and Herman Witsius. *Ernstige betuiginge der Gereformeerde Kercke aan hare afdwalende kinderen.* Amsterdam: Joannes van Someren, 1670.

Walaeus, Antonius. *Opera omnia.* Leiden, 1643.

Walch, Johann Georg. *Bibliotheca theologica selecta, litterariis adnotationibus instructa.* 4 vols. Jena: Croecker, 1757–65.

———. *[Io. George Walchii] Miscellanea sacra, sive, Commentationum ad historiam ecclesiasticam sanctioresque disciplinas pertinentium collectio.* Amsterdam: Romberg, 1744.

Wall, William. *The History of Infant Baptism.* 4 vols. Oxford: Oxford University Press, 1836.

Walsh, Walter. *The Secret History of the Oxford Movement.* 6th ed. London: Church Association, 1899.

Walther, Wilhelm. *Das Erbe der Reformation im Kampfe der Gegenwart.* 4 vols. in 3. Leipzig: Deichert, 1903–17.

———. *Rechtfertigung oder religiöses Erlebnis.* Leipzig: Deichert, 1917.

Watts, Isaac. *The World to Come.* 1739 and 1745. Reprinted, Chicago: Moody, 1954.

Weber, Ferdinand Wilhelm. *System der altsynagogalen palästinischen Theologie aus Targum, Midrasch und Talmud.* Leipzig: Dörffling & Franke, 1880.

Weber, Max. *The Protestant Ethic and the Spirit of Capitalism.* Translated by Talcott Parsons. New York: Scribner, 1958.

Wegscheider, Julius August Ludwig. *Institutiones theologiae christianae dogmaticae.* 3rd ed. Halle: Gebauer, 1819.

Weinel, Heinrich. *Die Stellung des Urchristentums zum Staat.* Tübingen: Mohr, 1908.

Weingarten, Hermann. *Die revolutionskirchen Englands.* Leipzig: Breitkopf & Hartel, 1868.

Weiss, Albert Maria. *Apologie des Christentums.* 4th ed. 5 vols. in 7. Freiburg i.B.: Herder, 1904–8.

———. *Die religiose Gefahr.* Freiburg i.B.: Herder, 1904.

Weiss, Bernhard. *Die Religion des Neuen Testaments*. Stuttgart: Cotta, 1908.

Weiss, Johannes. *Die christliche Freiheit nach der Verkündigung des Apostels Paulus*. Göttingen: Vandenhoeck & Ruprecht, 1902.

Weiss, Karl. *Beichtgebot und Beichtmoral der römisch-katholischen Kirche*. St. Gallen: Wiser & Frey, 1901.

Weisse, Christian Herman. *Philosophische Dogmatik oder Philosophie des Christentums*. 3 vols. Leipzig: Hirzel, 1855–62.

Weizsäcker, Carl Heinrich von. *Das apostolische Zeitalter der christlichen Kirche*. 2nd ed. Freiburg i.B.: Mohr, 1890.

Wernle, Paul. *Die Anfänge unserer Religion*. Tübingen: Mohr, 1901.

———. *The Beginnings of Christianity*. Translated by G. A. Bienemann. 2 vols. London: Williams & Norgate; New York: Putnam, 1903–4.

———. *Der Christ und die Sünde bei Paulus*. Freiburg i.B.: Mohr, 1897.

Wesley, John. *A Plain Account of Christian Perfection*. New York: Methodist Book Concern, 1925.

Westberg, Friedrich. *Die biblische Chronologie nach Flavius Josephus und das Todesjahr Jesu*. Leipzig: Deichert, 1910.

White, Edward. *L'immortalité conditionelle ou la vie en Christ*. Translated by Charles Byse. Paris: G. Fischbacher, 1880.

———. *Life in Christ: A Study of the Scripture Doctrine on the Nature of Man, the Object of the Divine Incarnation and the Conditions of Human Immortality*. 3rd, rev. and enlarged ed. London: Elliott, Stock, 1878.

Wiedemann, Alfred. *Die Toten und ihre Reiche im Glauben der alten Ägypter*. 2nd ed. Leipzig: J. C. Hinrichs, 1902.

Wieland, Franz. *Die genetische Entwicklung der sogenannte Ordines Minores in den drei ersten Jahrhunderten*. Freiburg i.B.: Herder, 1897.

———. *Mensa und Confessio*. Munich: Lentner, 1906.

———. *Die Schrift, Mensa und Confessio und P. Emil Dorsch in Innsbruck: Eine Antwort*. Munich: Lentner, 1908.

———. *Der vorirenaische Opferbegriff*. Munich: Lentner, 1909.

Wiggers, Gustav Friedrich. *Versuch einer pragmatischen Darstellung des Augustinismus und Pelagianismus*. 2 vols. Hamburg: F. A. Perthes, 1830–31.

Wilberforce, Robert Isaac. *The Doctrine of the Holy Eucharist*. London: Mozley, 1854.

Wildeboer, Gerrit. *Jahvedienst en volksreligie in Israel*. Groningen: Wolters, 1898.

Wilders, H. *De brief van den Apostel Jacobus*. Amsterdam: van Langenhuysen, 1906.

Wilhelm, Joseph, and Thomas Bartholomew Scannell. *A Manual of Catholic Theology: Based on Scheeben's "Dogmatik."* 4th ed. 2 vols. London: Kegan Paul, Trench, Trübner; New York: Benziger Brothers, 1909.

Windelband, Wilhelm. *Geschichte und Naturwissenschaft*. 2nd ed. Strassburg: Heitz, 1900. 3rd ed. 1904.

Windisch, Hans. *Die Entsündigung des Christen nach Paulus*. Leipzig: Hirschfeld, 1908.

———. *Taufe und Sünde im ältesten Christentum bis auf Origenes: Ein Beitrag zur altchristlichen Dogmengeschichte*. Tübingen: Mohr, 1908.

Wirth, Karl Hermann. *Der "Verdienst"-Begriff in der christlichen Kirche nach seiner geschichtlichen Entwicklung*. 2 vols. in 1. Leipzig: Dörffling & Franke, 1892–1901.

Witsius, Herman. *Ægyptiaca et Dekaphylon*. Herborn: Nicolae Andreae, 1717.

———. *Conciliatory or Irenical Animadversions on the Controversies Agitated in Britain under the Unhappy Names of Antinomians and Neonomians*. Translated by Thomas Bell. Glasgow: W. Lang, 1807.

———. *Exercitationes sacrae in symbolum quod apostolorum dicitur*. Amsterdam, 1697.

———. *Miscellaneorum sacrorum*. 4 vols. Utrecht: F. Halman, 1692.

———. *The Oeconomy of the Covenants between God and Man: Comprehending a Complete Body of Divinity*. 3 vols. London: E. Dilly, 1763. 2nd ed., rev. and corrected, 1775. New York: Lee & Stokes, 1798.

————. *Oeffeningen over de grondstukken van het Algemeyne Christelijke gelloove*. Rotterdam: Jan Daniel Beman, 1743.

————. *Twist des Heeren met zijn wijngaart*. Utrecht: Balthasar Lobe, 1692.

Wittewrongel, Petrus. *Oeconomia christiana*. Amsterdam: Marten Jansz. Brant & Abraham van den Burgh, 1661.

Wobbermin, Georg. *Religionsgeschichtliche Studien zur Frage nach der Beeinflussung des Urchristenthum durch das antike Mysterienwesen*. Berlin: E. Ebering, 1896.

————. *Theologie und Metaphysik, das Verhältnis der Theologie zur moderne Erkenntnistheorie und Psychologie*. Berlin: A. Duncker, 1901.

Worcester, Elwood. *The Living Word*. London: Hodder & Stoughton, 1909.

Worcester, Elwood, Samuel McComb, and Isador H. Coriat. *Religion and Medicine: The Moral Control of Nervous Disorders*. New York: Moffat, Yard, 1908.

Wormser, J. A. *De kinderdoop*. Amsterdam: Hövecker, 1853.

Wötzel, Johann Carl. *Meiner Gattin wirkliche Erscheinung nach ihrem Tode: Eine wahre unlängst erfolgte Geschichte für jedermann zur Beherzigung und vorzüglich für Psychologen zur unpartheiischen und sorgfältigen Prüfung*. Chemnitz: Jacobäer, 1804.

Wright, Charles H. H. *The Intermediate State and Prayers for the Dead Examined in the Light of Scripture and Ancient Jewish and Christian Literature*. London: Nisbet, 1900.

Wulf, Max von. *Über Heilige und Heiligenverehrung in den ersten christlichen Jahrhunderten*. Leipzig: F. Eckardt, 1910.

Wurster, Paul. *Die Lehre von der Inneren Mission*. Berlin: Reuther & Reichard, 1895.

Ypey, Annaeus. *Geschiedenis van de kristlijke kerk in de achttiende eeuw*. Utrecht: W. van Ijzerworst, 1797–1811.

Ypey, A., and I. J. Dermout. *Geschiedenis der Nederlandsche Hervormde Kerk*. 4 vols. Breda: W. van Bergen and F. B. Hollingerus Pijpers, 1819–27.

Zahn, Theodor. *Das apostolische Symbolum: Eine Skizze seiner Geschichte und eine Prüfung seines Inhalts*. Erlangen and Leipzig: Deichert, 1893.

————. *Der Brief des Paulus an die Römer*. Leipzig: Deichert, 1910.

————. *Brot und Wein im Abendmahl der alten Kirche*. Erlangen: Deichert, 1892.

————. *Einleitung in das Neue Testament*. 3rd ed. 2 vols. Leipzig: Deichert, 1906–7.

————. *Das Evangelium des Matthäus*. 2nd ed. Leipzig: Deichert, 1905.

————. *Introduction to the New Testament*. 3 vols. Edinburgh: T&T Clark, 1909.

————. *Skizzen aus dem Leben der alten Kirche*. 2nd ed. Erlangen: Deichert, 1898.

Zanchi, Jerome. *De operum theologicorum*. 8 vols. [Geneva]: Samuelis Crispini, 1617.

Zeller, Eduard. *Outlines of the History of Greek Philosophy*. Translated by L. R. Palmer. 13th ed. New York: Humanities Press, 1969.

————. *Die Philosophie der Griechen*. 4th ed. 3 vols. Leipzig: O. R. Reisland, 1879.

————. *Das theologische System Zwingli's*. Tübingen: L. F. Fues, 1853.

Ziegler, Theobald. *Sittliches Sein und sittliches Werden*. Strassburg: K. J. Trübner, 1890.

Ziesché, Kurt. *Verstand und Wille beim Glaubensakt: Eine spekulativ-historische Studie aus der Scholastik im Anschluss an Bonaventura*. Paderborn: Schöningh, 1909.

Zöckler, Otto. *Diakonen und Evangelisten*. Munich: C. H. Beck, 1893.

————. *Handbuch der theologischen Wissenschaften*. 3rd ed. 5 vols. Nördlingen and Munich: C. H. Beck, 1889–90.

Zwingli, Ulrich. *Commentary on True and False Religion*. Edited by Samuel Macauley Jackson and Clarence Nevin Heller. Philadelphia, 1929. Reprinted, Durham, NC: Labyrinth Press, 1981.

————. *Opera*. Edited by Schuler and Schulthess. 8 vols. in 7. Zurich: Schulthessiana, 1828–42.

ARTICLES AND ESSAYS

Achelis, E . Chr. "Die Bestrebung zur Reform der Konfirmationspraxis und des Konfirmationsunterricht." *Theologische Rundschau* 4 (1901): 353–94.

———. "Ein neues evangelisches Kirchenbuch." *Theologische Rundschau* 7 (1904): 491–507.

Achelis, Hans. "Laien." *PRE*[3], XI, 218–19.

———. "Presbyter in der alten Kirche." *PRE*[3], XVI, 5–9.

Anrich, G. "Clemens und Origenes als Begründer der Lehre vom Fegfeuer." Pp. 97–120 in *Theologische Abhandlungen: Eine Festgabe zum 17. Mai 1902 für Heinrich Julius Holtzmann*, edited by W. Nowack et al. Tübingen: Mohr, 1902.

Bartlett, J. V. "Regeneration." *DB*, IV, 214–21.

Bavinck, B. "Das Entropiegesetz und die Endlichkeit der Welt." *Der Geisteskampf der Gegenwart* 45 (1909): 260–67.

Bavinck, Herman. "Calvijns leer over het Avondmaal." *De Vrije Kerk* 13 (1887): 459–87.

———. "Calvin and Common Grace." *Princeton Theological Review* 7 (July 1909): 437–65.

———. "The Catholicity of Christianity and the Church." Translated by John Bolt. *Calvin Theological Journal* 27 (1992): 220–51.

Beaton, D. "Broad Churchism and the Christian Life." *Princeton Theological Review* 4 (1906): 306–38.

Beaufort, W. H. de. "De staatkundige toekomst van Rusland." *De Gids* 19 (1901): 270–83.

*Beck, H. de. "Die Δικαιοσυνη Θεου bei Paulus." *Neue Jahrbücher für deutsche Theologie* (1894): 249–61.

Beer, G. "Der biblische Hades." Pp. 3–29 in *Theologische Abhandlung: Eine Festgabe für H. J. Holtzmann*. Tübingen, 1902.

Benzinger, B. "Gericht, göttliches." *PRE*[3], VI, 568–85.

Beukenhorst. "Evan Roberts en de Keswickleer." *Stemmen voor Waarheid en Vrede* 44 (1907): 401–19.

*Blötzer, J. "Der Anglikanismus auf dem Wege nach Rom?" *Stimmen aus Maria Laach* 73 (February–March 1904).

*Bois, Henri. "Les dernières nouvelles du réveil gallois." *Foi et Vie* (1 November 1906).

———. "La terre et le ciel." *Foi et Vie* (15 August–1 October 1906).

Bonwetsch, G. Nathanael. "Arkandisziplin." *PRE*[3], II, 51–55.

———. "Heiligenverehrung." *PRE*[3], VII, 554–59.

———. "Kanonization." *PRE*[3], X, 17–18.

———. "Ketzertaufe." *PRE*[3], X, 270–75.

———. "Die Prophetie im apostolischen und nachapostolischen Zeitalter." *Zeitschrift für kirchliche Wissenschaft und kirchliches Leben* 8 (1884): 408–24; 9 (1885): 460–77.

———. "Raskolniken." *PRE*[3], XVI, 436–43.

Brandt, W. "Nog eens: Εἰς Ὄνομα." *Theologisch Tijdschrift* 36 (1902): 193–217.

———. "Ὄνομα en het doopsformule in het Nieuwe Testament." *Theologisch Tijdschrift* 25 (1891): 565–610.

Brendel, Ludwig G. "Charles Grandison Finney." *PRE*[3], VI, 63–66.

———. "Dwight L. Moody." *PRE*[3], XIII, 434–36.

Brieger, Theodor. "Indulgenzen." *PRE*[3], IX, 76–94.

Bruining, Albertus. "Godsdienst en verlossingsbehoefte." *Teylers Theologisch Tijdschrift* 8 (1910): 399–419.

Buddensieg, Rudolf. "Traktarianismus." *PRE*[3], XX, 18–53.

Burger, Karl. "Prophetentum im Neuen Testament." *PRE*[3], XVI, 105–8.

Candlish, Robert Smith. "Adoption." *DB*, I, 40–42.

Caspari, Walter. "Beichte." *PRE*[3], II, 533–41.

———. "Geistliche." *PRE*[3], VI, 463–73.

———. "Konfirmation." *PRE*[3], X, 676–80.

Cate, E. M. ten. "Augustinus' afdwalingen." *Teylers Theologische Tijdschrift* 8 (1910): 24–44.

———. "Augustinus' bekeerd." *De Gids* 74 (February 1910): 292–313.

768   BIBLIOGRAPHY

———. "Augustinus' bekeering." *Teylers Theologische Tijdschrift* 7 (1909): 59–88.

Charles, R. H., A. B. Davidson, and S. D. F. Salmond. "Eschatology." *DB*, I, 734–57.

Clemen, Carl Christian. "Der gegenwärtige Stand des religiösen Denkens in Großbrittannien." *Theologische Studien und Kritiken* 65 (1892): 603–715.

Clemen, Otto. "Honius." *PRE*[3], VIII, 312–13.

Cohrs, Ferdinand. "Katechismen und Katechismusunterricht." *PRE*[3], X, 135–64.

Conrad, P. "Begriff und Bedeutung der Gemeinde in Ritschls Theologie." *Theologische Studien und Kritiken* 84 (1911): 230–92.

Cramer, J. A. "Het evangelie en de eeuwige straf." *Theologische Studiën* 20 (1902): 241–66.

Cremer, Hermann. "Abendmahl, Schriftlehre." *PRE*[3], I, 32–38.

———. "Geistesgaben." *PRE*[3], VI, 460–63.

———. "Handauflegung." *PRE*[3], VII, 387–89.

Currie, Hugh. "Law of God." *DC*, II, 15–17.

Dalman, Gustaf. "Hades." *PRE*[3], VII, 295–99.

Darling, T. G. "The Apostle Paul and the Second Advent." *Princeton Theological Review* 2 (April 1904): 197–214.

Davis, John D. "The Future Life in Hebrew Thought during the Pre-Persian Period." *Princeton Theological Review* 6 (October 1907): 246–68.

Denney, James. "Law (in New Testament)." *DB*, III, 73–83.

De Quincey, Thomas. "On the Supposed Scriptural Expression for Eternity." Pp. 74–84 in *Theological Essays and Other Papers.* Boston: Ticknor, Reed, & Fields, 1854.

Dobschütz, Ernst. "Zur Eschatologie der Evangelien." *Theologische Studien und Kritiken* 84 (1911): 1–20.

Dörries, Bernhard. "Zur Reform der Konfirmationsordnung." *Zeitschrift für Theologie und Kirche* 18 (1908): 81–106.

Dove, Richard Wilhelm. "Sakramentalien." *PRE*[3], XVII, 381–91.

*Dressel, L. "Der Gottesbeweis auf Grund des Entropiesatzes." *Stimmen aus Maria Laach* 78 (1909): 150–60.

Drews, Paul. "Eucharistie." *PRE*[3], V, 560–72.

———. "Messe, luturgisch." *PRE*[3], XII, 697–723.

———. "Taufe: Liturgischer Vollzug." *PRE*[3], XIX, 424–50.

Driver, Samuel Rolles. "Law (in Old Testament)." *DB*, III, 64–73.

Erbes, Carl. "Petrus nicht in Rom, sondern in Jerusalem gestorben." *Zeitschrift für Kirchengeschichte* 22 (1901): 1–47, 161–231.

Ernst, H. "Twee pendant-leerstukken." *Geloof en Vrijheid* 20 (1886): 407–44.

Erskine, Ebenezer. "De verzekering des geloofs." In *Levensgeschiedenis en Werken van Ralph en Ebenezer Erskine,* by R. Erskine and E. Erskine, with an introduction and foreword by Herman Bavinck. Doesburgh: J. C. van Schenk Brill, 1904.

Eucken, Rudolf. "The Problem of Immortality." *Hibbert Journal* 6 (1908): 836–51.

Eyckman, J. C. "Algemeene of conditioneele onsterfelijkheid." *Theologische Studiën* 26 (1908): 359–80.

Feine, Paul. "Taufe, Schriftlehre." *PRE*[3], XIX, 396–403.

Flier, A. van der. "Het gebruik van den Israëlische Godsnaam." *Theologische Studiën* 21 (1903): 232–47.

Francken, W. "Henricus Brouwer." *Geloof en Vrijheid* 20 (1886).

Friedberg, Emil Albert. "Bann, kirchlicher." *PRE*[3], II, 381–85.

Gayford, Sydney. "Church." *DB*, I, 425–39.

Gennrich, Paul. "Studien zur paulinischen Heilsordnung." *Theologische Studien und Kritiken* 71 (1898): 377–431.

Gladstone, W. E. "The Place of Heresy and Schism in the Christian Church." *Nineteenth Century* 36 (1894): 157–94.

Goebel, Max. "Labadie." *PRE*[3], XI, 191–96.

Goltz, Eduard Alexander von der. "Die Bedeutung der neueren religionsgeschichtlichen Forschungen für die Beurteilung der christlichen Sakramente." *Die Studierstube* 5 (1907): 609–22.

Gooszen, M. A. "Jubeljaar en Jubelaflaat." *Theologisch Tijdschrift* 37 (1903): 97–110.

Gottschick, Johannes. "Augustins Anschauung von den Erlöserwirkungen Christi." *Zeitschrift für Theologie und Kirche* 11 (1901): 97–213.

———. "Gesetz und Evangelium." *PRE*³, VI, 632–41.

———. "Hus', Luther's, und Zwingli's Lehre von der Kirche." *Zeitschrift für Kirchengeschichte* 8 (1886): 345–94.

———. "Kindschaft Gottes." *PRE*³, X, 291–304.

———. "Luthers Lehre von der Lebensgemeinschaft des Gläubigen mit Christus." *Zeitschrift für Theologie und Kirche* 8 (1898): 406–34.

Grafe, Eduard. "Die neuesten Forschungen über die urchistliche Abendsmahlfeier." *Zeitschrift für Theologie und Kirche* 5 (1895): 101–38.

Gray, G. Buchanan. "Name." *DB*, III, 478–81.

Gröbler, Paul. "Die Ansichten über Unsterblichkeit und Auferstehung in der jüdischen Literatur der beiden letzten Jahrhunderte v. Chr." *Theologische Studien und Kritiken* 52 (1879): 651–700.

Güder, Eduard. "Prophezei." *PRE*³, XVI, 108–10.

Gwilliam, G. H. "Last Supper." *DC*, II, 5–9.

Harnack, Adolf von. "Kirche und Staat bis zur Gründung der Staatskirche." Pp. 129–60 in *Die christliche Religion*, edited by Paul Hinneberg. Berlin and Leipzig: Teubner, 1905.

Hauck, Albert. "Reliquien." *PRE*³, XVI, 630–34.

———. "Synoden." *PRE*³, XIX, 262–77.

Haussleiter, Johannes. "Was versteht Paulus unter christlichen Glauben?" Pp. 159–82 in *Greifswalder Studien*, edited by Samuel Oettli et al. Gütersloh: Bertelsmann, 1895.

Herbst, F. I. "Merkwürdige Bekehrungsgeschichten." In *Katholisches Exempelbuch*. 2 vols. in 1. Regensburg: G. J. Manz, 1845.

Herrmann, Wilhelm. "Der geschichtliche Christus, der Grund unseres Glaubens."

Zeitschrift für Theologie und Kirche 2 (1892): 232–73.

———. "Die Lage und Aufgabe der evangelischen Dogmatik in der Gegenwart." *Zeitschrift für Theologie und Kirche* 17 (1907): 1–33, 172–201, 315–51.

Hinschius, Paul. "Gerichtsarbeit, kirchliche." *PRE*³, VI, 585–602.

———. "Häresie." *PRE*³, VII, 319–21.

Hoedemaker, Philippus Jacobus. "Kerk en staat in Israël." *Troffel en Zwaard* 1 (1898): 208–37.

Hofmann, Rudolf. "Fegfeuer." *PRE*³, V, 788–92.

Holl, Karl. "Noch einmal: Zur Rechtfertigungslehre." *Zeitschrift für Theologie und Kirche* 18 (1908): 67–71.

———. "Die Rechtfertigungslehre in Luthers Vorlesung über den Römerbrief." *Zeitschrift für Theologie und Kirche* 20 (1910): 245–91.

Hunzinger, August Wilhelm Reinhold Emil. "Ubiquität." *PRE*³, XX, 182–96.

Hurgonje, Christian Snouck. "Der Mahdi." *Revue Coloniale Internationale* (1885).

Huther, Johann Eduard. "Die Bedeutung des Begriffes ζωη und πιστευειν in den Johanneischen Schriften." *Jahrbücher für deutsche Theologie* 17 (1872): 1–34.

Ideler, Ernst. "Joch, Johann Georg." *PRE*³, IX, 233–34.

Ihmels, Ludwig. "Rechtfertigung." *PRE*³, XIV, 482–515.

James, M. R. "Man of Sin and Antichrist." *DB*, III, 226–28.

*Jankélévitch, S. "La mort et l'immortalité d'après les donnees de la biologie." *Revue philosophique* (1910): no. 4.

Jonker, A. J. Th. "De leer der conditioneele onsterfelijkheid." *Theologische Studiën* 1 (1883): 1–20, 155ff., 548ff.; 2 (1884): 185ff.

Josephson, Hermann. "Kelch oder Kelche?" *Die Studierstube* (1904): 222–46.

Kähler, Martin. "Ewiges Leben." *PRE*³, XI, 330–34.

———. "Seligkeit." *PRE*³, XVIII, 179–84.

*Kalchreuter. "Der stellvertretende Glaube und die Kindertaufe." *Jahrbücher für deutsche Theologie* 11 (1866): 523–44.

Kattenbusch, Ferdinand. "Anglikanische Kirche." *PRE³*, I, 525–47.

———. "Der geschichtliche Sinn des apostolischen Symbols." *Zeitschrift für Theologie und Kirche* 11 (1901): 407–28.

———. "Messe, dogmengeschichtlich." *PRE³*, XII, 664–97.

———. "Sakrament." *PRE³*, XVII, 349–81.

———. "Taufe, Kirchenlehre." *PRE³*, XIX, 403–24.

———. "Transsubstantiation." *PRE³*, XX, 55–79.

Katzer, Ernst. "Kants Lehre von der Kirche." *Jahrbücher für protestantische Theologie* 12 (1886).

Kawerau, Gustav. "Exorcismus bei der Taufe." *PRE³*, V, 695–700.

———. "Flacius." *PRE³*, VI, 82–92.

Kirchner, Viktor. "Subjekt, Objekt und Zustandekommen der Sündenvergebung auf der prophetischen und levitischen Religionsstufe des Alten Testaments." *Theologische Studien und Kritiken* 80 (1907): 1–44.

———. "Subjekt und Wesen der Sündenvergebung, besonders aus der frühesten Religionsstufe Israels." *Theologische Studien und Kritiken* 78 (1905): 163–88.

Kirn, Otto. "Glaube." *PRE³*, VI, 674–82.

———. "Lohn." *PRE³*, XI, 605–14.

———. "Wiedergeburt." *PRE³*, XXI, 246–56.

Kittel, Rudolf. "Πιστις Ἰησου Χριστου bei Paulus." *Theologische Studien und Kritiken* 79 (1906): 419–36.

———. "Zur Erklärung von Röm. 3:21–26." *Theologische Studien und Kritiken* 80 (1907): 217–33.

*Knabenhauer, Joseph. "Jesus und die Erwartung des Weltendes." *Stimmen aus Maria Laach* 77 (1908): 487–97.

Knappers, L. "De Theologie van Petrus Bloccius." *Theologisch Tijdschrift* 38 (1904): 307–48.

Kneller, C. A. "Der heilige Cyprian und die Idee der Kirche." *Stimmen aus Maria Laach* 72 (1903): 498–521.

———. "Der heilige Irenäus und die römische Kirche." *Stimmen aus Maria Laach* 78 (1909): 402–11.

———. "Kritische Schwierigkeiten in der Apologetik." *Stimmen aus Maria Laach* 79 (1910): 486–98.

———. "Review of *Cyprian und der römische Primat* by Hugo Koch." *Stimmen aus Maria Laach* 79 (1910): 75–82.

*Knoke. "Zum Verständnis des Gleichnisses vom verlornen Sohn." *Neue kirchliche Zeitschrift* 17 (1906): 407–18.

Köberle, Justus. "Die Bedeutung der Sündenvergebung in der altt. Frömmigkeit." *Neue kirchliche Zeitschrift* 16 (1905): 20–50.

Köhler, W. "Die Schlüssel des Petrus: Erklärung von Matt. 16:18, 19." *Archiv für Religionswissenschaft* 8 (1905): 214–43.

Kok, A. B. M. W. "Zwijndrechtsche Nieuwlichten." Vol. 6, pp. 720–21 in *Christelijke Encyclopaedie*. 2nd ed. 6 vols. Kampen: Kok, 1961.

Kolde, Theodor. "Irving." *PRE³*, IX, 424–37.

König, Eduard. "Der biblisch-reformatorische Glaubensbegriff und seine neueste Bekämpfung." *Neue kirchliche Zeitschrift* 19 (1908): 628–60.

———. "Glaubensgewissheit und Schriftzeugniss." *Neue kirchliche Zeitschrift* 1 (1890): 439–63, 515–30.

Köppel, W. "Der Ursprung des Apostolates nach den heiligen Schriften Neuen Testaments." *Theologische Studien und Kritiken* 62 (1889): 257–331.

Köstlin, Heinrich Adolf. "Requiem." *PRE³*, XVI, 665–69.

Köstlin, Julius. "Apokatastasis." *PRE³*, I, 616–22.

———. "Ein Beitrag zur Eschatologie der Reformatoren." *Theologische Studien und Kritiken* 51 (1878): 125–35.

———. "Busse." *PRE³*, III, 584–91.

———. "Kirche." *PRE³*, X, 315–44.

Kromsigt, Pieter Johannes. "Het Antinomianisme van Jacobus Verschoor." *Troffel en Zwaard* 4 (1906): 205–36, 272–89; 5 (1907): 1–21, 188–202.

———. "Het Antinomianisme van Pontiaan van Hattem." *Troffel en Zwaard* 8 (1910): 309–26, 371–81; 9 (1911): 31–45.

———. "De doopspractijk in de oude Gereformeerde Kerk in Nederland." *Troffel en Zwaard* 3 (1905): 1–16, 65–83.

———. "Iets over Calvijns doopsbeschouwing." *Troffel en Zwaard* 3 (1905): 102–6.

Krüger, Gustav. "Gnosis, Gnosticismus." *PRE*³, VI, 728–38.

Kunze, Johannes W. "Schlüsselgewalt." *PRE*³, XVII, 621–40.

———. "Verdienst." *PRE*³, XX, 500–508.

———. "Windisch: *Taufe und Sünde im ältesten Christentum bis auf Origenes*." *Theologisches Literaturblatt* 30/20 (1909): 244–50.

Kuyper, Abraham. "Over het graf." *De Heraut* 594 (12 May 1894).

———. "Van de gemeene gratie." *De Heraut* 981–1003, 1047 (11 October 1896–17 March 1897; 16 January 1898).

———. "Van de genademiddelen." *De Heraut* 646–47, 649–54 (11 May–6 July 1890).

———. "Van de volleinding." *De Heraut* 1732ff. (12 March 1911ff.).

Kuyper, Herman Huber. "Onze Stadskerken." *De Heraut* 1637–44 (16 May–4 July 1909).

Lake, Kirsopp. "Zonde en doop." *Theologisch Tijdschrift* 43 (1909): 538–54.

Lambert, J. C. "Name." *DC*, II, 217–18.

Lelièvre, Ch. "La doctrine de la justification par la foi dan la théologie de Calvin." *Revue chrétienne* 56 (1909): 699–710, 767–86.

Lemme, Ludwig. "Volkommenheit." *PRE*³, XX, 733–37.

Linden, S. van der. "Pontiaan van Hattem." Vol. III, pp. 378–79 in *Christelijke encyclopaedie*. 2nd ed. 6 vols. Kampen: Kok, 1961.

Lodge, Oliver. "The Immortality of the Soul." *Hibbert Journal* 6 (1908): 291–304, 563–85.

Loetscher, Fr. W. "Schwenckfeld's Participation in the Eucharistic Controversy of the Sixteenth Century." *Princeton Theological Review* 4 (1906): 352–86, 454–500.

Loofs, Friedrich Armin. "Abendmahl, Kirchenlehre." *PRE*³, I, 38–68.

———. "Methodismus." *PRE*³, XII, 747–801.

MacKay, D. S. "Personal Immortality in the Light of Recent Science." *North American Review* 185 (1907): 387–93.

Massie, John. "Evangelist." *DB*, I, 793–97.

Matthes, J. C. "Rouw en doodenvereering bij Israel." *Teylers Theologisch Tijdschrift* 3 (1905): 1–30.

———. "Twee Israelitische rouwbedrijven." *Teylers Theologisch Tijdschrift* 8 (1910): 145–69.

Maude, J. H. "Church." *DC*, I, 324–30.

Maurice, F. D. "The Word 'Eternal' and the Punishment of the Wicked." In *Theological Essays*. 1857. Reprinted, London: James Clarke, 1957.

Mayer, Otto. "Staat und Kirche." *PRE*³, XVIII, 707–27.

McComb, Samuel. "The Christian Religion as a Healing Movement." *Hibbert Journal* 8 (October 1909): 10–27.

Meindertsma, W. "Het Bossche geschil in de achttiende eeuw over de rechtvaardigmaking." *Stemmen voor Waarheid en Vrede* 47 (November 1910): 1081–96.

Methorst, H. W. "Eenige cijfers betreffende de sterfte van kinderen beneden hat jaar in Nederland." *Economist* 58 (September 1909): 665.

*Meusel. "War die vorjahwistische Religion Israels Ahnenkultus?" *Neue kirchliche Zeitschrift* 16 (1905): 484ff.

*Meyer. "Die Lehre des Neuen Testaments von der Kirchenzucht." *Zeitschrift für kirchliche Wissenschaft und kirchliches Leben* 2 (1881).

Miller, Edward Waite. "The Great Awakening." *Princeton Theological Review* 2 (October 1904): 545–65.

Morey, Charles A. "The Beginnings of Saint Worship." *Princeton Theological Review* 6 (April 1908): 278–90.

Moulton, Warren Joseph. "Passover." *DB*, III, 684–92.

Müller, Ernst Friedrich Karl. "Kirchenzucht in der reformierten Kirche." *PRE*³, X, 485–92.

———. "Presbyter, Presbyterialverfassung seit der Reformation." *PRE*³, XVI, 9–16.

Müller, Joseph T. "Zinzendorf." *PRE*³, XXI, 679–703.

Müller, Karl. "Beobachtungen zur Paul." Pp. 87–110 in *Theologische Studien: Martin Kähler zum 6. Januar 1905*, edited by Friedrich Giesebrecht and Martin Kähler. Leipzig: Deichert, 1905.

———. "Schmoll: *Busslehre der Frühscholastik.*" *Theologische Literaturzeitung* 35 (1910): 77–80.

Müller, Nikolaus. "Altar." *PRE*³, I, 391–404.

Muirhead, Lewis. "Eschatology." *DC*, I, 525–38.

Nuelsen, J. L. "Methodismus in Amerika." *PRE*³, XIII, 1–25.

Oort, H. "De doodenvereering bij de Israelieten." *Theologisch Tijdschrift* 15 (1881): 358–63.

———. "Mattheüs XI en de Johannesgemeenten." *Theologisch Tijdschrift* 42 (1908): 299–333.

Oorthuys, G. "Het gebed vóór den doop in ons doopsformulier." *Troffel en Zwaard* 10 (1907): 351–74.

Orelli, Conrad. "Beschneidung." *PRE*³, II, 660–62.

———. "Name." *PRE*³, XIII, 625–31.

———. "Passah." *PRE*³, XIV, 750–57.

Ovenden, Charles T. "The Forgiveness of Sin." *Hibbert Journal* 5/2 (1907): 587–99.

Paget, F. "Sacraments." Pp. 296–317 in *Lux Mundi*, edited by Charles Gore. 13th ed. London: Murray, 1892.

Patrick, William. "Apostles." *DC*, I, 101–11.

———. "Evangelist." *DC*, I, 549–50.

Peake, Arthur S. "Law" *DC*, II, 11–14.

Pfenningsdorf, Emil. "Todesstrafe für die 'Ketzer.'" *Geisteskampf der Gegenwart* 46 (1910): 157–58.

Podmore, Frank. "Sir Oliver Lodge: *The Survival of Man.*" *Hibbert Journal* 8 (1910): 669–72.

Post, G. E. "Millennium." *DB*, III, 370–73.

Rahlenbeck, Hermann. "Mission, innere." *PRE*³, XIII, 90–100.

Reischle, Max Wilhelm Theodor. "Der Streit über die Begründung des Glaubens auf den geschichtlichen Jesus Christus." *Zeitschrift für Theologie und Kirche* 7 (1897): 171–264.

Rieks, J. "Das Papsthum eine göttliche Institution?" *Beweis des Glaubens* (1903): 3–21.

Rietschel, Ernst. "Luthers Anschauung von der Unsichtbarkeit und Sichtbarkeit der Kirche." *Theologische Studien und Kritiken* (1900): 404–56.

Rietschel, Georg. "Abendmahlsfeier in der Kirchen der Reformation." *PRE*³, I, 68–76.

———. "Kinderkommunion." *PRE*³, X, 289–91.

Ritschl, Otto. "Der doppelte Rechtfertigungsbegriff in der Apologie der augsburgischen Konfession." *Zeitschrift für Theologie und Kirche* 20 (1910): 292–338.

———. "Luthers Seligkeitsvorstellung in ihrer Entstehung und Bedeutung." *Die christliche Welt* 3 (1889): 874–80.

*Rocholl. "Spiritualismus und Realismus." *Neue kirchliche Zeitschrift* 9 (1898).

*———. "Umkehr zum Idealismus." *Neue kirchliche Zeitschrift* 15 (1904): 622.

Rogge, H. C. "Hugo de Groots denkbeelden over de hereeniging der kerken." *Teylers theologische Tijdschrift* 2 (1904): 1–52.

Royce, Josiah. "Immortality." *Hibbert Journal* 5 (1907): 724–44.

Runze, Georg. "Unsterblichkeit." *PRE*³, XX, 294–301.

Rust, J. A. "Paulus Mysticus." *Theologische Studiën* 28 (1910): 349–84.

Rutgers, Frederik Lodewijk. "De bepaling van den diensttijd der ouderlingen historisch eengezins toegelicht." *De Heraut* 944–46

(26 January–9 February 1896); 948 (23 February 1896).

Rutz, Paul. "Taufe und Wiedergeburt mit besonderer Berücksichtigung der Kindertaufe." *Neue kirchliche Zeitschrift* 12 (1901): 585–620.

Sachsse, Eugen. "Katechese, Katechetik." *PRE³*, X, 121–29.

Salmond, S. D. F. "Paradise." *DB*, III, 668–72.

Schaeder, Erich. "Auferstehung der Todten." *PRE³*, I, 219–24.

Schaefer, Rudolf. "Das Herrenmahl nach Ursprung und Bedeutung." *Neue kirchliche Zeitschrift* 14 (1903): 472–85.

Scheel, Otto. "Alte Kirchengeschichte." *Theologische Rundschau* 13 (June 1910): 220–40.

*Schian, Martin. "Die moderne deustche Erweckungspredigt." *Zeitschrift für Religionspsychologie* 10 (1908).

*Schmidt, H. "Die Augustinische Lehre von der Kirche." *Jahrbücher für deutsche Theologie* 6 (1861): 197–255.

Schmidt, Wilhelm. "Die Universalität des göttlichen Heilswillens und die Particularität der Berufung." *Theologische Studien und Kritiken* 60 (1887): 1–44.

Scholz, H. "Zur Lehre vom 'Armen Sünder.'" *Zeitschrift für Theologie und Kirche* 6 (1896): 463–91.

Schott, Theodor Friedrich. "Camisarden." *PRE³*, III, 693–96.

*Schultz. "Die Lehre von der Gerechtigkeit aus dem Glauben im Alten und Neuen Bunde." *Jahrbücher für deutsche Theologie* 7 (1862): 510–72.

*———. "Das protestantische Dogma von der unsichtbaren Kirche." *Jahrbücher für protestantische Theologie* 2 (1876): 673–90.

Schwarz, G. "Jak. 2,14–26 erklärt." *Theologische Studien und Kritiken* 64 (1891): 704–37.

Seeberg, Reinhold. "Bekehrung." *PRE³*, II, 541–45.

———. "Berufung." *PRE³*, II, 657–59.

———. "Erleuchtung." *PRE³*, V, 457–59.

———. "Gnadenmittel." *PRE³*, VI, 723–27.

———. "Wort Gottes." *PRE³*, XXI, 496–505.

Sehling, Emil. "Episcopalsystem in der römisch-katholische Kirche." *PRE³*, V, 427–30.

———. "Schisma." *PRE³*, XVII, 575–80.

Sell, Karl. "Forschungen der Gegenwart über Begriff und Entstehung der Kirche." *Zeitschrift für Theologie und Kirche* 4 (1894): 347–417.

Semisch, Karl Gottlob (rev. and enl. by Eduard Bratke). "Chiliasmus." *PRE³*, III, 805–17.

Sieffert, Friedrich Anton Emil. "Antichrist." *PRE³*, I, 577–84.

———. "Petrus, der Apostel." *PRE³*, XV, 186–212.

Slotemaker de Bruine, J. R. "Nog een pleidooi voor het parochiestelsel." *Stemmen voor waarheid en vrede* 38 (May 1901): 487–98.

Spitta, Friedrich. "Die grosse eschatologische Rede Jesu." *Theologische Studien und Kritiken* 82 (1909): 348–401.

Stange, Carl. "Die eudämonistische Gedanke der christliche Ethik." *Neue kirchliche Zeitschrift* 18 (1907): 135–56.

*Steinbeck, Joh. "Kultische Waschungen und Bäder im Heidentum und Judentum und ihr Verhältnis zur Christlichen Taufe." *Neue kirchliche Zeitschrift* 21 (1910): 778–99.

*Steinmetz, R. "Zusammenhang von Taufe und Wiedergeburt." *Neue kirchliche Zeitschrift* 13 (1902).

Steitz, Georg Eduard. "Die Abendmahlslehre der gr. Kirche in ihrer geschichtlichen Entwicklung." *Jahrbücher für deutsche Theologie* 9 (1864): 409–81; 10 (1865): 64–152, 399–463; 11 (1866): 193–252; 12 (1867): 211–86; 13 (1868): 2–67, 649–700.

Steude, Ernst Gustav. "Die Unsterblichkeitsbeweise." *Beweis des Glaubens* 39 (1903); 40 (1904): 73–82, 145–59, 172–83, 201–15.

Stout, G. F. "Mr. F. W. Myers on Human Personality and Its Survival of Bodily Death." *Hibbert Journal* 2 (1903): 44–64.

Stowe, C. "Jonathan Edwards." *PRE*³, V, 171–75.

Strack, Herman L. "Synagogen." *PRE*³, XIX, 223.

Stutz, Ulrich. "Pfarre, Pfarrer." *PRE*³, XV, 239–52.

Talma, A. S. E. "De leer der rechtvaardiging bij Ritschl." *Theologische Studiën* 21 (1903): 329–49.

Thomä, J. "Richard Rothes Lehre von der Kirche." *Theologische Studien und Kritiken* 83 (1910): 244–99.

*Traub, Th. "Die gemeinschaftbildende Kraft der Religion." In *Beiträge zur Weiterentwicklung der christlichen Religion*, edited by A. Deissmann. Munich: J. F. Lehmann, 1905.

———. "Seelenwanderung." *Der Geisteskampf der Gegenwart* 45 (1909): 285–303.

*Troeltsch, Ernst. "Die Kulturbedeutung des Calvinismus." *Internationale Wochenschrift für Wissenschaft Kunst und Technik* 3 (1910): 449ff., 510ff.

Tschackert, Paul. "Daltons *Beiträge zur Geschichte der evangelischen Kirche in Russland*, IV. Band, und die Laski-Kontroverse der neuesten Zeit." *Theologisches Literaturblatt* (18 May 1906): 233–37.

Uhlhorn, Gerhard. "Kirchenzucht in der ev.-lutherischen Kirche." *PRE*³, X, 483–85.

Usteri, J. Martin. "Calvins Sakraments- und Tauflehre." *Theologische Studien und Kritiken* 57 (1884): 417–56.

———. "Glaube, Werke, und Rechtfertigung." *Theologische Studien und Kritiken* 62 (1889): 211–56.

Veen, D. J. "In welk jaar en op welken dag en datum is Christus gestorven?" *Theologische Studiën* 23 (1905): 429–38.

Vellenga, G. "De leer der rechtvaardigheid bij Ritschl." *Theologische Studiën* 20 (1902): 401–21.

———. "Ritschl en de H. Schrift." *Theologische Studiën* 22 (1904): 162–73.

Vos, Geerhardus. "The Alleged Legalism in Paul's Doctrine of Justification." *Princeton Theological Review* 1 (April 1903): 161–79.

———. "The Pauline Eschatology and Chiliasm." *Princeton Theological Review* 9 (January 1911): 26–60.

*Wahlenberg. "Die biblische Abendmahlberichte und ihre neuere Kritik." *Neue kirchliche Zeitschrift* 17 (1906).

Warfield, Benjamin. "The Development of the Doctrine of Infant Salvation." In *Two Studies in the History of Doctrine*. New York: Christian Literature, 1897.

———. "Faith." *DB*, I, 827–38.

———. "The Millennium and the Apocalypse." *Princeton Theological Review* 2 (October 1904): 599–617.

———. "Westminster Synod." *PRE*³, XXI, 176–85.

Weber, Heinrich. "Taufe und Abendmahl als Symbole unserer doppelten Stellung zum Heilsgut." *Zeitschrift für Theologie und Kirche* 19 (1909): 249–79.

Weber, Max. "Die protestantische Ethik und der 'Geist' des Kapitalismus." *Archiv für Sozialwissenschaft und Politik* (1905): 1–54; (1906): 1–10.

*Weerts. "Schleiermachers Lehre von der Wiedergeburt in ihrem Verhältnis zu Kants Begriff des intelligibelen Charakters." *Neue kirchliche Zeitschrift* 20 (1909): 400–415.

Weiss, Herman. "Über das Wesen des persönlichen Christenstandes." *Theologische Studien und Kritiken* 54 (1881): 377–417.

Weiss, Johannes. "Heitmüller: *Im Namen Jesu*." *Theologische Rundschau* 7 (1904): 185–96.

Weisse, Chr. H. "Über die philosophische Bedeutung der christliche Lehre von der letzten Dinge." *Theologische Studien und Kritiken* 9 (1836): 271–340.

Wernle, Paul. "Windisch: *Taufe und Sünde im ältesten Christentum bis auf Origenes*." *Theologische Literaturzeitung* 34 (1909): 586–90.

Williams, Meade C. "The Crisis in the Church of England." *Presbyterian and Reformed Review* 10 (July 1899): 389–412.

Wünsche, August Karl. "Die Vorstellung von Zustande nach dem Tode nach Apokrypha, Talmud und Kirchenvätern." *Jahrbücher für protestantische Theologie* 6 (1880): 355–83, 435–523.

Zahn, Theodor. "Agapen." *PRE*³, I, 234–37.

Zandstra, Sidney. "The Theory of Ancestor Worship among the Hebrews." *Princeton Theological Review* 5 (1907): 281–87.

———. "Sheol and Pit in the Old Testament." *Princeton Theological Review* 5 (October 1907): 631–41.

Zehnpfund, Rudolf. "Das Gesetz in den paulinischen Briefen." *Neue kirchliche Zeitschrift* 8 (1897): 384–419.

Zöckler, Otto. "Perfectionisten of Oneida-Kommunisten in Amerika." *PRE*³, XV, 130–31.

———. "Probabilismus." *PRE*³, XVI, 66–70.

———. "Spiritismus." *PRE*³, XVIII, 654–66.

COMBINED SCRIPTURE INDEX

Jeremiah

OLD TESTAMENT APOCRYPHA

NEW TESTAMENT

Combined Name Index

COMBINED SUBJECT INDEX